▶ To delete a document you n[...] right-click on it and choose [...]

▶ To recover an accidentally de[...] you can see the Recycle Bin. Double-click on the bin to open it, find the document, higlight it, and choose File ➤ Restore.

▶ To move a document between folders, between the Desktop and a folder, or to another drive, first save the document and close it, then drag it to the destination location.

▶ To quickly copy a document to a floppy disk, right-click on the document and choose Send To ➤ Floppy Disk.

Folders

1996 Reports

▶ To see the folders in your computer, double-click on My Computer, then double-click on the drive containing the folders.

▶ To see a specific folder's contents, double-click on it.

▶ To display a larger number of documents in a folder's window, enlarge the window and/or choose View ➤ List.

▶ To create a new folder, right-click where you want the new folder to go (such as inside another folder or on the Desktop). Choose New ➤ Folder, name the folder, and press Enter.

▶ To move a folder, drag it to its new location.

System

My Computer

▶ To set the colors of the screen, Desktop background, or screen saver, right-click on the Desktop and choose Properties.

▶ To empty the Recycle Bin, right-click on the bin and choose Empty Recycle Bin.

▶ To make other system settings, choose Start ➤ Settings ➤ Control Panel and double-click on the related icon.

▶ To see the Desktop, right-click on the clock in the Taskbar and choose Minimize All Windows.

Mastering
Windows® 95

Robert Cowart

SYBEX®

San Francisco • Paris • Düsseldorf • Soest

Acquisitions Manager: Kristine Plachy

Developmental Editor: Gary Masters

Editor: Laura Arendal

Technical Editor: Arthur Knowles

Book Designer: Helen Bruno; Adapted by Jan Haseman

Technical Artist: Cuong Le

Desktop Publishers: Alissa Feinberg, Deborah Maizels, Thomas Goudie Bonasera, Debi Bevilacqua, and Lynell Decker

Production Assistants: Taris Duffié and Ron Jost

Indexer: Matthew Spence

Cover Designer: Design Site

Cover Photographer: Mark Johann

Screen reproductions produced with Collage Plus.

Collage Plus is a trademark of Inner Media Inc.

SYBEX is a registered trademark of SYBEX Inc.

Library of Congress Card Number: 95-67727

ISBN: 0-7821-1413-X

Manufactured in the United States of America

20 19 18 17 16 15 14 13 12 11

To my mother, who still *doesn't do windows*

To Rudolph Langer:

This book is dedicated by the publisher and staff at Sybex to the memory of Dr. Rudolph Langer, Editor-in-Chief at Sybex for nearly 15 years. His talent, dedication, and constant search for excellence were well-known by all who met him, worked with him, or read our titles.

Acknowledgments

I am indebted to the talented people at Sybex for their invaluable assistance in the production of this book. Special thanks indeed go to Dr. R.S. Langer for his support in acquisitional, developmental, financial, and contractual matters; Managing Editor Barbara Gordon for her central role in coordinating everything; Production Manager Jim Curran for his support; my developmental editor, Gary Masters, for assistance in fine-tuning the book's contents; to my editor, Laura Arendal, for her patience and ability to excise superfluous material and improve readability; Arthur Knowles for his technical editing; Taris Duffié, production assistant; Thomas Goudie Bonasera and Alissa Feinberg, lead desktop publishers; and everybody else who worked behind the scenes to ship the book.

Not to be overlooked are the people responsible for the distribution and sales of Sybex books, including the one you're holding. Sybex has its own independent sales and marketing force working to get these books onto shelves around the world—from small independent bookstores to the national chains. Thanks to Kip Triplett, Vice President of Sales; Julie Simmons, academic coordinator; and the rest of the crew in Alameda and around the country. I can pay my rent!

A project as ambitious and time-pressured as this book required a team effort in the writing department, too. I am indebted to several people for their research, writing, and editorial contributions. For his technical sidebars and condensation of the networking section, I greatly thank Arthur Knowles. For his elucidation of Windows 95 communications aspects, my appreciation goes to John Ross. For his extensive coverage of Windows 95 networking, heartfelt thanks to Jim Blaney. And special thanks to my multitalented friend and writing colleague Dr. Steve Cummings, whose assistance was responsible for the Accessories section.

Finally, warm thanks to my friends (especially Elizabeth and Eric) who put up with my kvetching and hair-pulling during the year of research, writing, upgrades (there were more than 490 versions of Windows 95 as it was being developed), and even traveling with laptop, that went into compiling this volume.

Contents at a Glance

Table of Contents

Part 5: Networking with Windows 95   933

Chapter 24: An Overview of Windows 95 Networking   934

Chapter 25: Planning Your Windows 95 Network   954

Introduction

Thank you for purchasing (or considering the purchase of) this book! *Mastering Windows 95* is designed to help you get the most out of Windows 95 with the least amount of effort. You may be wondering if this is the right book for you. I've written this book with both the novice and the experienced PC user in mind. The intention was to produce a volume that would prove both accessible and highly instructive to all Windows users.

Based on the best-selling *Mastering Windows 3.0* and *Mastering Windows 3.1*, this Third Edition uses the same time-tested approach for teaching Windows that has helped hundreds of thousands of beginners in many countries become Windows-literate.

From the outset, this book doesn't require that you have a working knowledge of Windows. All I assume is that you have a modicum of familiarity with an IBM PC. So, if you are new to Windows, a bit PC-literate, and ready to learn, this book is a good choice. I think you'll find it easy to read and not over your head. There are a lot of everyday examples to explain the concepts, and all the accessory programs free with Windows 95 are explained in detail so you can get up and running right away.

What About Power Users?

If you're a *power user*, familiar with earlier versions of Windows and the intricacies of DOS, the explanations and procedures here will quickly bring you up to speed with Windows 95 and how it's different from its predecessors. For example, the first chapter (which can be skipped by novices), is a thorough analysis of what's new in Windows 95 and how it compares to the competition and to the other members of the Windows family of operating systems. By quickly skimming the next several chapters, you'll learn how to use the new folder system, property sheets, right-click menus, the Explorer, the new OLE 2.0, and other basics.

The advanced discussions in Parts 2, 3, 4, and 6 will be extremely useful whether you're an MIS professional, an executive, an instructor, or a home user. There's significant coverage of the increasingly important area of electronic communications from the Windows workstation, be it through the Internet, over a LAN, via services such as CompuServe, or with computerized faxing. A multimedia chapter explores the possibilities for adding audio, video, CD-ROM, and MIDI elements to your Windows setup. If you want to optimize your Windows setup for high performance, that's covered as well, with discussions of hardware and software modifications, hard-disk management, video accelerator cards, and so forth.

A major section (Part 5) on networking—something you're not likely to find in the other books of this type on the market—tackles the most salient aspects of Windows 95 networking; from the initial planning stages of choosing and routing cabling, through internetworking with Windows NT, Novell, and TCP/IP, and using remote access services (RAS). Of course, simple peer-to-peer networking—which Windows 95 can do right out of the box—is covered, as is how to best manage your network.

Because laptops have become so prevalent (some say as much as 33 percent of personal computing is done on laptops as of this writing), we've given special attention to Windows 95's mobile-computing abilities. Topics such as advanced power management (APM) support, file synchronization, hot-docking stations, PCMCIA card support, and remote access—along with some tips for road warriors—are explained in Part 6.

Although for many users Windows 95 will be factory installed on the computer, this isn't always the case. So, if you haven't installed Windows yet, procedures and considerations are included in the Appendix.

This is just a sample of the topics you'll find between the covers of this book. I've addressed the topics that Windows users are likely to need, carefully chosen notable and savory value-added information, and supplied it all in one place. Please consult the table of contents for the exact topics covered.

Why This Book?

As you know, there is a manual supplied with Windows 95 and there is online Help built into Windows 95 as well. So why do you need a book? Because the Windows 95 manual is very sketchy, and often the Help system doesn't tell you what you want to know. True, great efforts have been made on Microsoft's part to simplify Windows 95 and make it more intuitive and friendly in hopes that reference tomes like this one will no longer be necessary. But until a computer can talk to you in everyday language, you will still need a good book, especially with a computer program or operating system as all-inclusive as Windows 95. If you happen to find some technical manuals from the manufacturer, explanations are often written in computerese, assuming too much knowledge. This is often true of other books as well. Either they are too technical or they speak only to the *newbie* (novice user), with nothing left for intermediate or advanced users and nothing for the novice to grow into.

Here I've done the legwork for you: I've boiled down the manuals, had discussions with many Windows 95 testers, experimented on various machines from laptops to Pentiums, and then written a book explaining Windows 95 in normal, everyday English.

The authors of this book have a wide diversity of experience with both Windows 95 and other PC software and hardware. Pooling their knowledge and working with Windows 95 since its first incarnation in alpha form more than a year before its release, I have come up with a thorough cross-section of useful information about this landmark operating system and condensed it into the book you see before you.

In researching this book, I have tried to focus on not just How To's but also on the Whys and Wherefores. Too many computer books tell you only how to perform a sample task without explaining how to apply it to your own work. In this book, step-by-step sections explain how to perform specific procedures, and descriptive sections explain general considerations about what you've learned. As you read along and follow the examples, you should not only become adept at using Windows, but you should also learn the most efficient ways to accomplish your own work.

What You Need in Order to Use This Book

There are a few things about your level of knowledge and your computer setup that this book assumes.

What You Should Know

If you are new to computers, you should at least have some understanding of PC terminology. Though Windows 95 takes much of the effort out of using your computer, it's still a good idea for you to understand the difference between things such as RAM and hard-disk memory, for example. And although I'll be covering techniques for performing typical tasks in Windows—such as copying files, formatting disks, and moving between directories—I'm assuming that you already understand why you'd want to do these things in the first place. Of particular importance is a basic understanding of the differences between data files and program files. I'll describe these things within the book, but you may also want to take some time out to bone up on these topics if your knowledge is a little shaky.

What You Should Have

For this book to make sense, and for Windows to work, it is assumed that you have the following:

▶ an IBM or compatible computer with an Intel 80386, 80486, or Pentium (or compatible CPU), with at least 4 MB of RAM and a floppy drive

▶ a hard disk with about 50 MB of free space on it (you can get away with less if you do a Compact install)

▶ optionally, a CD-ROM drive

▶ a Windows-compatible video card and monitor

▶ a printer if you want to use Windows to print out your work on paper. Some of the exercises in this book cover printing, and a whole chapter is devoted exclusively to it. Though not necessary for most of the book, it will be to your advantage if you have a printer.

▶ a mouse. Though you can operate Windows without a mouse (from the keyboard), it's quite a bit more cumbersome to do so. The mouse makes almost all Windows operations so much easier that you really should get hold of one. Most instructions will assume you have a mouse.

How This Book Is Organized

There are essentially six parts to this book. Here's the quick rundown:

Part 1   ...consists of six chapters. The first chapter is an in-depth look at what's so great about Windows 95. If you are a newcomer to Windows, you might opt to skim or skip this chapter—or you may find it interesting. Next is a discussion of some issues facing people upgrading from Windows 3.x to Windows 95. The book gets rolling with Chapter 3, where you'll find step-by-step coverage of the parts of the screen—stuff like what a window is, how to use menus and dialog boxes, that sort of thing. Then, starting with Chapter 4, you'll get started running your programs so you can get your work done rather than having to read this whole book just to write a simple letter. Following that, you'll get some lessons in organizing your work (an important issue on a computer) so you won't be searching all over the place for your projects. Finally, you'll learn how to share information between different documents with simple cut, copy, and paste techniques or with the fancier DDE and OLE methods. After reading this part and following along on your computer, you'll know how to control the Windows graphical environment, run programs, copy data between programs, and manage your files. You should definitely read these chapters if you've never used Windows before.

Part 2   ...takes you the next step in discovering, exploring, and adjusting Windows 95. The section on printing is a must for virtually all users, as everyone wants to print things out, and printers are for one reason or another (it's mostly Murphy's Law) a pain. The section on the Control Panel is great if you like to personalize the way your computer works—colors, mouse pointers, screen savers, fonts, and so on. You'll find stuff here about upgrading your computer to multimedia to use CD-ROMs and sound, the new Properties sheets, using the

right mouse button, and the new version of the Windows 3.x File Manager—the Explorer.

Part 3 ...is about *communications* (the buzzword these days): e-mail, faxing, working on the Internet, the Microsoft Network, CompuServe, and so forth. Windows 95 has a lot of communications features built right into it, and this section tells you how to use them to best advantage: how to set up your Inbox, your Outbox, and how use what is essentially Windows 95's central switching station—called Microsoft Exchange—to compose, organize, send, and receive e-mail, faxes, and other forms of electronic communications.

Part 4 ...covers the supplied programs—the Windows accessories. There you'll learn all the ins and outs of the many helpful programs and utilities supplied with Windows 95. The list has grown considerably since Windows 3.0. The list now includes WordPad, MS Paint, HyperTerminal, Notepad, Phone Dialer, Calculator, Character Map, CD Player, Media Player, Sound Recorder, Backup, ScanDisk, and DriveSpace, among others. Though not the most sophisticated programs in their respective classes, these programs are well thought out, handy, and thrown in for free with Windows. Like me, you'll probably end up using them more than you might think at first, which is why I've included a sizable section on them. Some of the utilities such as the DriveSpace disk-compression program and ScanDisk hard-disk–checking program are extremely useful for getting the most out of your computer system.

Part 5 ...is required reading if you're interested in local- or wide-area networking with Windows 95. Even home users have taken to setting up "living room networks" these days, especially as used or hand-me-down computers pile up around the house. And of course, everyone seems to have gotten networked at the office in the past few years. Windows 95 has networking built right in, so these chapters take you from the basics of what networking is through how to install, use, and manage your networking environment. Whether you are new to networks or are an MIS professional, you'll find useful information in this part.

Part 6   ...covers several diverse subjects. The first is how to best take advantage of Windows 95 on a laptop computer, including the use of plug-in cards, docking stations, external monitors, and so on. Various general tips on laptop usage and toting can be found here as well (I am a serious laptop junkie). Next, you'll see that I've come up with some tips for serious Windows 95 hackers who desire to make radical adjustments to the Windows 95 environment. Coverage of some of the more arcane areas of Windows 95 such as multiple-user arrangements, passwords, multiple language support, regional settings, use of the System applet for poking around inside and altering device-driver settings, optimizing the Recycle Bin and virtual memory settings, and an analysis of various performance determinants are discussed here.

Capping off the book, you'll find a chapter on the Windows 95 add-on product Microsoft Plus. Because many Windows 95 users are likely to purchase this product, I decided to cover this add-on package's many attractions and features even though this book is about Windows 95, not about add-ons. But Microsoft Plus dovetails so smoothly with Windows 95 (as they are both from Microsoft) that I decided a discussion of improved disk compression, Internet access, video display enhancements, and automated program control were topics worthy of a few additional pages.

Appendix   ...tells you how to install Windows 95 on your computer.

Conventions Used in This Book

There are a few conventions used throughout this book that you should know about before beginning. First, there are commands that you enter from the keyboard and messages you receive from Windows that appear on your screen. When you have to type something in, the text will be boldface: Enter **a:setup**. When referring to files and folders, the text may be on its own line like this:

```
My thesis on arthropods.doc
```

or it might be included right in a line like this: Now enter the folder name `Letters to the Editor`.

More often than not, responses from Windows will be shown in figures so you can see just what the screens look like. Sometimes, though, I'll skip the picture and just display the message like this:

```
Cannot read from drive A
```

Second, you'll see sections that look like this:

1. Do this...

2. Do this...

3. Do this...

   These are step-by-step instructions (obviously). Although such steps are sometimes example tutorials that are a onetime deal to show you how to use, say, the word processor, more often they're the exact procedures you'll use to perform an everyday task such as formatting a disk. You might want to bookmark such a page for easy future reference.

   Finally, there are many notes in this book. They are positioned below the material to which they refer. There are four kinds of margin notes: Note, Tip, Tech Tip, and Caution.

NOTE   Notes give you information pertinent to the procedure or topic being discussed.

TIP   Tips indicate practical hints that might make your work easier.

TECH TIP   Tech Tips are tips that are more technical in nature; they may be skipped by the nontechnical reader.

CAUTION   Cautions alert you to something very important. Generally, they inform you of potential problems you might encounter if you were to follow a procedure incorrectly or without careful forethought.

Before You Begin...

Before you can begin working with Windows, make sure you have correctly installed Windows 95 on your computer's hard disk. A large percentage of what appears to be software problems is often the result of incorrect installation. If your copy of Windows is already installed and operating correctly, you have no need to worry about this and can move ahead to Chapter 1. However, if you haven't installed Windows, you should do so by turning to the Appendix, which covers the Windows Setup program. If your copy of Windows is installed but appears to be operating significantly differently than what is discussed in this book, you might want to seek help from a computer professional or friend who can determine whether your Windows 95 system was installed correctly. For the purposes of this book I installed all the options in my machine, so my setup might look a little different from yours. The chapters about the Control Panel explain how you can install options you may have omitted when initially installing Windows 95 on your computer.

Happy reading. I hope this book helps you on your way to success in whatever line of work (or play) you use your computer for.

Up and Running with Windows 95

1

Chapter 1

Introducing Windows 95

FEATURING

As of this writing, there were an estimated 60 million users of Windows 3.x (3.x includes 3.0, 3.1, and 3.11). That's a lot by any standards, certainly by the standards of PC software sales. Nothing tops that number except for the users of DOS, the operating system running on virtually every IBM PC in the world.

It's likely you're upgrading to Windows 95 from one of its earlier incarnations, so this book will discuss right up front just what's so new and great about Windows 95. Please bear in mind that some terms or concepts may not make sense to you just yet. Don't worry, you'll understand them later as you work through the various chapters in the book. With that said, let's dive into the world of the latest and greatest graphical operating system for IBM PCs.

What Are Windows and Windows 95?

Windows 95 is Microsoft Corporation's latest upgrade to its phenomenally successful and ubiquitous software, which has been generically dubbed *Windows.*

Windows is a class of software called a GUI (graphical user interface). How you interact with your computer to do things like entering data or running programs like the spelling checker is determined by the *interface.* On most computers, the hardware part of the interface consists of your screen and the keyboard. But the software part of the interface determines what things look like on the screen, how you give commands such as "check the spelling" or "print this report" to the computer, how you flip between pages of text, and so forth.

In days of old, before Windows, all this was done with keyboard commands, and often very cryptic ones at that. With the advent of Windows, many everyday computer tasks—such as running programs, opening files, choosing commands, changing a word to italic, and so forth—can be done using a graphical approach that is much more intuitively obvious to people who are new to computers (Figure 1.1). Also, because all Windows programs (even ones from different software manufacturers) use essentially the same commands and graphical items on the screen, once you've mastered your first Windows program, learning others is much easier.

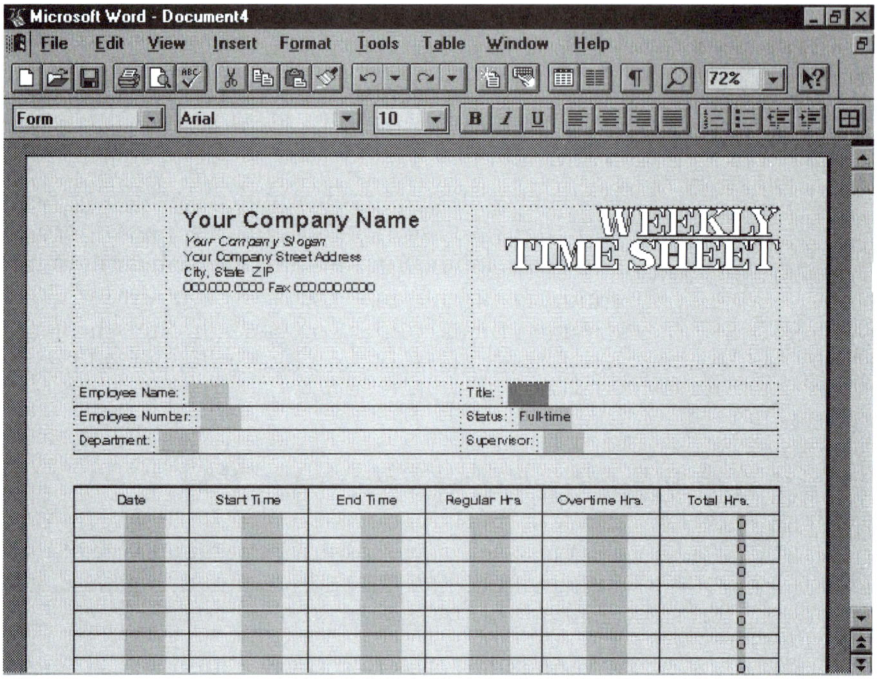

Figure 1.1   Word for Windows 6.0 displays text as it will print. Commands are found on
menus and are fairly consistent between different Windows programs.

If you've used a Mac, you know all its programs work the same way
and look much alike. Non–computer people gravitated to the Mac
over the years primarily because it is easy to use and isn't intimidating.
The problem is that up until recently the Mac's GUI could be used
only on computers made by Apple Corporation, and there weren't
any inexpensive Mac clones, either; Apple saw to that by making it
legally impossible for computer manufacturers to copy the internal
design of the Mac. So if you wanted a computer that was easy for novices to master, you had to pay top dollar for an Apple computer.

Windows changed all that by bringing the essentials of the Macintosh
interface (the mouse, the pointer arrow on the screen, the little icons
on the screen, and so forth) to the IBM PC and the thousands of super-
cheap PC-compatible brands readily available today. Really, Windows
is very much the PC's version of the Mac.

The microcomputer business is software driven. More programs are being written for the Windows platform than all other microcomputer GUIs combined (e.g., NeXTSTEP, OS/2, and variants of Unix). Windows is here to stay.

This being the case, Windows detractors have slowly had to face facts: Windows is the only big game in town, and besides, it really isn't so bad after all. Most Windows applications look and feel identical to their Mac counterparts, and because most users are running programs just to get work done, not critiquing the finer points of the operating system, the issue of Mac vs. PC is technically almost moot at this point.

About Windows 95

Targeting the needs and demands of home and small business users and hoping to keep Windows users from being wooed away by the frills of IBM's OS/2 or various Unix alternatives to DOS and Windows 3.x, Microsoft has spent the last several years developing a robust and feature-rich operating system intended to replace the somewhat glitchy Windows 3.1 and make us all (even Mac users) happy.

And of course, Microsoft thought it wise to address the needs of the burgeoning portable-computer community. Upper management, sales personnel, and technical users who have shifted from desktop systems to heavy reliance on portable computers have developed a new set of computing needs that Windows 95 caters to.

In technical terms, here are some of the features of Windows 95. I'll explain many of these later in this chapter. Windows 95:

▶ Is a graphical operating system much like Windows 3.1, with a facelift and reliability improvements.

▶ Will run DOS, Windows 3.0 and 3.1, and some Windows NT 32-bit applications. It will be running powerful 32-bit Windows 95 programs as they appear on the market. Microsoft promises that existing Windows 3.x applications will run as fast as—if not faster than—under Windows 3.1 with 4 MB of RAM and even faster with more than 4 MB.

▶ Is not planted on top of an old version of MS-DOS, but rather on a modern DOS designed to work hand-in-hand with Windows 95. The new DOS/Windows 95 combination is finally a full-fledged graphical operating system in its own right, not a GUI tacked on top of a dinosaur. This renders it quite a bit more reliable than its predecessors and also does away with many evils, such as the large DOS "footprint" that impinged on MS-DOS programs running under Windows or the overall lack of stability of the operating system that caused erratic behavior.

▶ Is a multithreaded and preemptive multitasking operating system, which means it can run multiple applications simultaneously more smoothly than did Windows 3.1, especially if those programs are of the new breed of 32-bit applications written for Windows 95 or Windows NT. If the programs are of the older 16-bit variety designed for Windows 3.x, they will take less advantage of Windows 95's preemptive features, but overall system performance will still be smoother than in Windows 3.x.

▶ Has major portions of the operating system written in 32-bit code, taking better advantage of the Intel 80386, 80486, and Pentium processors. The memory manager, scheduler, and process manager are all 32-bit. Some sections of the operating system are still written in 16-bit code to ensure compatibility with existing 16-bit applications, however.

▶ Has a more Mac-like interface, doing away with the confusing Program Manager/File Manager design and incorporating a single integrated arrangement that allows you to place document icons and folders right on the Windows Desktop and work with them from there. A *Taskbar*, always easily accessible on screen, has buttons listing the currently running applications, letting you easily switch between them.

▶ Supports long file names rather than the severely limited eight-letter (8.3) file names used by DOS. In Windows 95, files can have names up to 255 characters long. This applies even to files used and created in DOS boxes.

▶ Stores the bulk of important hardware settings, system settings, applications settings, and user-rights settings in a central location called the Registry. These settings were previously stored in a number of different files such as `autoexec.bat`, `config.sys`, `win.ini`, and `system.ini` files. This arrangement allows for a more easily managed PC. These settings can be accessed from a remote PC on a network, allowing a network administrator to more easily maintain a network of corporate PCs.

> **NOTE** For backward compatibility with older device drivers and systems, the `autoexec.bat` and `config.sys` files are still used by Windows 95, so the implementation of the Registry is not as complete as it is in Windows NT. However, reliance on the older files is greatly lessened, with Windows 95 doing more system housekeeping than before and using 32-bit device drivers when possible.

▶ Lets you set up the computer for use by different people, each with their own Desktop, shared resources, user rights, and other settings.

▶ Supports installable 32-bit file systems, allowing easier future expansion of Windows 95 to incorporate other file-system schemes. It also ensures faster disk performance than the 16-bit file system used by Windows 3.1 and DOS.

▶ Is more proficient at cleaning up after a faulty application crash, thus preventing Windows from crashing altogether (i.e., you'll see fewer General Protection Fault error messages). If a program crashes, you can eliminate it from the task list without affecting other running applications. Memory and other resources the application was using are freed for use by the system.

▶ Automatically adapts more fully to the hardware it is running on and thus requires less fine-tuning to take full advantage of your particular computer setup, available disk space, amount of RAM, and so forth.

▶ Provides much more *conventional memory* space for DOS applications by implementing device drivers such as SmartDrive, mouse drivers, `share.exe`, CD-ROM, and SCSI device drivers as 32-bit VxDs handled by Windows 95. This means that with Windows 95 there's less chance of running out of memory space for your DOS applications.

▶ Includes built-in peer-to-peer networking, much like Windows for Workgroups, only with more-efficient 32-bit network drivers as well as support for the increasingly popular TCP/IP protocol for accessing Unix-based systems such as the Internet. It also supports NDIS 2.x, 3.x, and ODI drivers and will provide 32-bit NetBEUI and IPX/SPX as well. Redirectors for SMB and NCP-based networks will be included. (Sorry about all the acronyms!) The upshot is that a Windows 95 workstation will interface easily with most existing local- and wide-area networks such as NetWare, Banyan, LANtastic, Windows NT, LAN Manager, Windows for Workgroups, and many others. These network connections can be mixed and matched, and you'll work on these networks using the same commands and interface regardless of which one you're connected to.

▶ Incorporates Object Linking and Embedding version 2.0. This allows you to easily create fancy compound documents combining information from several different application programs, especially when using applications that support OLE 2.0 (Figure 1.2). This makes it a cinch to incorporate graphs, charts, music, video, clip art, and so forth right into your word-processing documents.

▶ Is more document-centric than Windows 3.1. This means that the new Windows user interface lets you organize your work on the computer by organizing your documents on the Desktop or in folders, then clicking on them to open them (Figure 1.3). You don't have to think about finding and running a specific application, then finding and

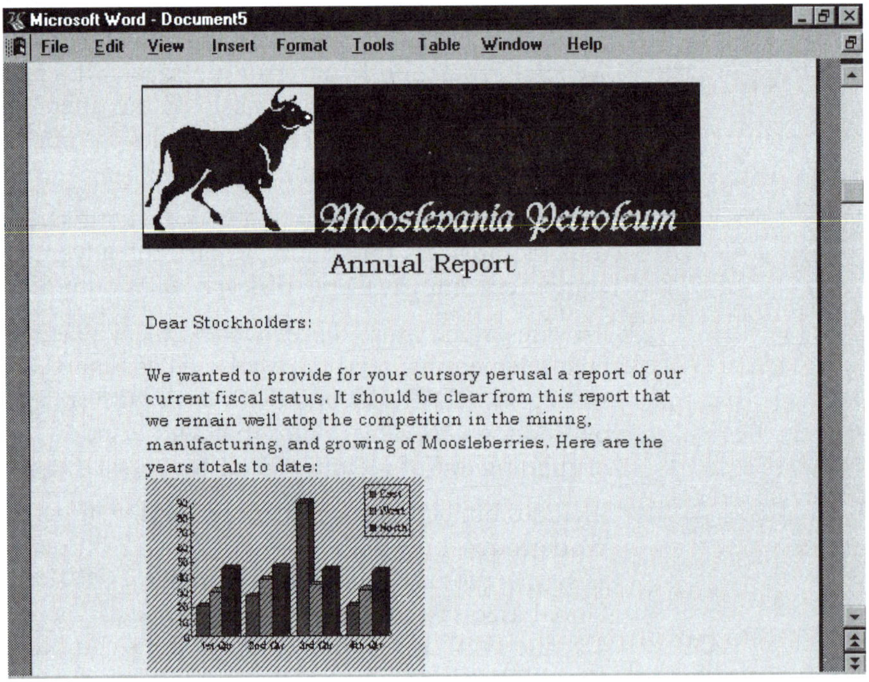

Figure 1.2   Windows 95's OLE 2.0 makes creating complex documents a simple process.

opening a given document. You just organize your documents into folders named things like My PhD Thesis and click on each one to open it. You can create a new document simply by clicking on the Desktop and choosing New from a pop-up menu.

▶ Offers workstation security (within limits), some useful administration tools, and system tools (such as disk doublers) and comes with more than a handful of useful (though limited) accessory applications.

▶ Has Remote-Access Services, which allow Windows 95 users on the road to call into a Windows 95 network, log on, and connect just as they do from their desktop machine, sharing data and resources supplied by network servers, printers, fax modems, and other workstations.

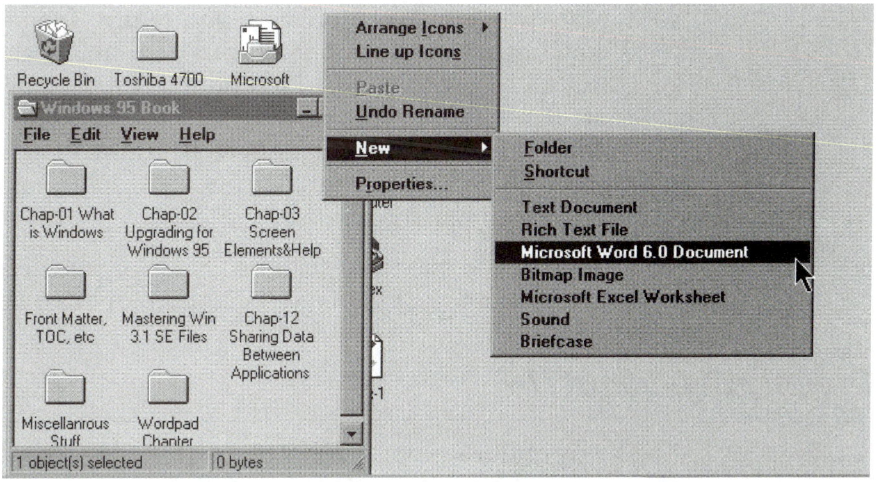

Figure 1.3   *Document-centricity means you organize and work with your computer the same way you organize and work at your desk. You simply put your documents on the Desktop or in a folder. You open the folder or find the document on the Desktop and open it. You create a new item by clicking the right mouse button and choosing New.*

▶ Supports the new Plug-and-Play standard being developed by PC makers that allows you to simply plug a new board (such as a video or network card) into your computer without having to set switches or make other settings. Windows 95 will figure out what you plugged in and make it work. No more configuration headaches!

▶ Supports PCMCIA cards for laptop computers and the use of laptop docking stations. Without rebooting the operating system, it will acknowledge what you plugged in and automatically reconfigure the system accordingly.

▶ Supports a new mail system called Microsoft Exchange for managing all the types of messages computer users typically have to deal with, such as e-mail, Internet communications, faxes, and documents. No need for separate communications programs (such as Microsoft Mail, WinCIM, or Eudora) or fax programs (such as WinFAX). Once set up, clicking a single button gets and sends e-mail from CompuServe, Internet, The Microsoft Network, or a network e-mail post office, and also sends queued-up faxes.

▶ Comes with a disk-compression program you can easily run right in Windows, essentially doubling your hard-disk space without having to purchase a new hard disk. Disk doubling can be used on floppies, too, making a 1.44-MB disk store up to 2.88 MB. The compression/decompression tool is much more facile to use than in previous incarnations of DOS or Windows, letting you *easily* change the size of compressed partitions.

These are the main new features. Now for some explanation and discussion on a few of the more salient topics listed here.

Preemptive What??

Many of the adjectives listed above probably sound like marketing hype, so let me break down the terminology a bit. Let's start with *preemptive multitasking*. Operating systems that can run a number of programs at once, such as Windows 3.1, OS/2, and Windows NT (not just software *switchers* like the DOS-based Software Carousel or Multiple Choice, which basically put one application to sleep while resuming another), need some means of servicing each of the running programs. For example, you might be typing a letter in Word for Windows while Excel is calculating a spreadsheet and you're printing a brochure you just set up in PageMaker. As you know, all these activities can occur in a typical Windows 3.1 session (though not always smoothly, of course). How can Windows do that?

Well, it's the miracle of *multitasking*, and it works much the same way you do when you're driving a car, listening to the radio, and having a conversation with a friend. The computer's "attention" switches very rapidly among the jobs it's doing. In the computer, attention to a job occurs when the CPU chip (e.g., the brains of the computer—the 486 chip, for example) turns its sights on that job and begins processing away on it. This is called giving the task "CPU time."

Now here's the catch. In Windows 3.1, this attention-switching process doesn't always behave properly. This is because of the way Windows 3.1 assigns CPU time to tasks. Ideally, no job should hog the CPU's time because this will bring other tasks to a halt. Windows 3.1 programs are supposed to be written in such a way that they use only small slices of CPU time, allowing other running applications to have the CPU, too. However, if the application was written poorly, this didn't always happen. Some programs, such as File Manager, for example, could effectively sabotage time-sensitive programs such as fax or communications programs by hogging the CPU's attention while copying files.

Windows 3.1's multitasking style is referred to as *cooperative multitasking*. On the other hand, Windows 95's *preemptive* multitasking doesn't leave control of the CPU up to the applications, but rather gives this responsibility to the operating system itself. Thus, Windows 95 can *preempt* one program's CPU time and democratically allot it to another whenever Windows 95 deems necessary. Because the operating system itself also needs attention from the CPU to keep the basics of the computer going, it can also demand CPU time as it sees fit. The overall effect of preemptive multitasking is to ensure that you can keep working with a minimum of instances of the old hourglass cursor telling you to wait. Also, application mixes that might have previously caused problems in Windows 3.1 shouldn't cause even a hiccup in Windows 95. Background communications sessions, for example, shouldn't drop data while other CPU-intensive tasks are running.

Another advantage is that in Windows 95, you'll not only find that single tasks are prevented from bringing others to a crawl, but the scheduler—the part of the operating system responsible for doling out the CPU time—can see to it that some applications are given a higher priority than others.

Multithreading?

If you've followed the reviews of Windows 95 (and NT for that matter) over the last year or two, you've probably heard the term *threading* bandied about rather glibly. Here's the scoop on threading, in everyday language.

Every task that Windows 95 performs, whether it's copying a file, calculating a statistical average, accessing the system's clock, or fetching some data from RAM, can be referred to as a *process*. During any given time period, Windows is busily performing and switching between these processes, as discussed above in the section about tasking. Thus, processes are for all intents and purposes identical to tasks.

In Windows 95 (as well as in NT), processes are further divisible into *threads*. Although most processes contain only a single thread, this isn't always the case. A single process can consist of multiple threads if the programmer writes it that way. Lost yet?

Here's an example. A typical thread would be the recalculation part of a spreadsheet program. Another thread might be the part of the program that charts a graph for you. Another two might be file saving and printing. Breaking the program down this way lets you, in Windows 95, perform these functions concurrently. By contrast, if the whole program were written as a single thread, you wouldn't be able to do the chart until the recalculation was complete or save a file until printing was finished.

The salient point is that smartly written applications can now run very smoothly—in fact much more smoothly than under Windows 3.1.

Although Windows 95 is being touted as all new and improved, what it offers the user isn't really all that new. Many of Windows 95's features have been around in other forms for some time. For example, OS/2 and the Macintosh operating system have both offered a nice object-oriented interface, one much more intuitive than Windows 3.1's. Windows NT and various forms of Unix (such as NeXTSTEP) offer sophisticated application protection and smooth preemptive multitasking. And connectivity experts such as Novell have been meeting the needs of serious corporate MIS departments with state-of-the-art networking and remote-access capabilities for years.

What *is* new is that Microsoft has done its research, fine-tuned its product, and wrapped it up neatly in one package—a package that works right out of the box. With just a little work, you can be up and running Windows 95 on a single station or set up a workgroup on a number of PCs with very little hassle. If you're upgrading a machine from Windows 3.x, all your application groups in Program Manager and the pertinent Windows settings—such as installed fonts, Desktop settings, application settings, and so forth—from the system.ini and win.ini files will automatically migrate over from Windows 3.1. All your Windows 3.x and DOS applications will run as fast, if not faster. Next, throw into the mix the ability to run the efficient 32-bit applications that'll soon appear, the support of long file names, and a more intuitive interface. Finally, mix in the facts that Windows 95 promises to work with all your existing Windows 3.1 hardware drivers (such as those for fax modems, scanners, mice, video cards, sound cards, and so on), that it has remote-access communications ability, supports Plug and Play, and allows an MIS professional to manage a Windows 95 PC from across the network, and all this adds up to a pretty spiffy package.

The Importance of Application Software

Even though the first iterations of Windows had shortcomings, the sheer number of software programs available for them ensured their success. If the demand were only for a serious operating system with most or even all of the features Windows provided, Windows 3.1 wouldn't have really caught on. Corporations heavily invested in PC-based information systems could have adopted Unix or OS/2 en masse by now, but they haven't bothered. These alternatives have been feature-rich, and each has had an advantage over Windows, but the success of an operating system, particularly in business settings, has more to do with application availability and compatibility than any other variable.

Actually, to be fair, applications aren't the only thing that matters when choosing an operating system. MIS professionals need to not only think about what's available for the platform, but whether their current hardware, software, and training investments will be jeopardized or enhanced by a specific operating-system decision.

First and foremost, Windows 95 is simply supposed to make single-user PCs and laptops easier to learn and use and easier to fully exploit. Studies have shown that the majority of PC users are confused by their computers and feel that they are not taking full advantage of the power they paid dearly for when purchasing their PC. For example, most Windows 3.1 users do not know they can run multiple programs simultaneously, don't know what happens to one program when another program's window overlaps it, and are afraid to use the File Manager.

Secondly, Windows 95 was designed to make networking easier. Workgroups that don't need serious data protection and/or security shouldn't be a hassle to set up, configure, and maintain. With Windows 95, networking is much easier both to set up and to use. It also offers remote management of the workstation. For example, a manager can connect to and alter the security settings on a Windows 95-equipped PC from anywhere on its network, even via remote access from home or another city.

Finally, Windows 95 implements some of the newest technology available (such as Plug and Play), pushing PC manufacturers into finalizing design and development of those emerging technologies in hopes of maintaining a competitive edge against other lines of computers. All three of these strategies, of course, are geared towards making PCs friendlier and thus spurring on the sales of computers and software.

This appears to be fairly true of Windows 95. As a result, if you are using MS-DOS, Windows 3.x, or Windows for Workgroups, migration to Windows 95 will be relatively easy. Most applications will work fine under Windows 95, and sometimes faster than in Windows 3.x. Windows 3.x settings will be imported into Windows 95 so your Windows 95 Program Manager, Control Panel, and applications settings will be automatically preconfigured for you.

NOTE   Actually a File Manager and Program Manager à la Windows 3.x are supplied with Windows 95, just to help veteran users get over the hump. However, the idea is that once you get used to the new interface, you won't find yourself using them much anymore. Instead, you'll use the Taskbar to launch and switch applications and the Desktop to manage your documents. To dig into the file system, you'll use the new turbocharged File Manager replacement called the Explorer.

Unlike NT, which boasts the ability to escape crashed hard drives and power outages on huge networks with nary a hiccup, Windows 95 is no Houdini. However, Windows 95 has other key features. For example, it's the first Microsoft product since Windows 3.0 to offer a significantly improved interface (one that will be incorporated into NT's Cairo version, incidentally). It was also designed to run very well without users having to do much of anything to their systems, particularly adding RAM or upgrading to a faster processor. (By contrast, Windows NT Workstation requires 8 MB *minimum* and a fast 486.) Windows 95 should run reasonably well on a 386DX 33 or better, with as little as 4 MB of RAM (though I'd suggest 8).

Windows 95 is aimed at the mass-market, non-power users, who may or may not be networked. Most new computers will be shipped with Windows 95, just as they have been with Windows 3.x. For many demanding networking needs Windows 95 will also suffice, allowing connection to other Windows 95 workstations, to NT Workstation and NT Server, to Novell, and to LAN Manager, Banyan Vines, and the Internet, among others. Support for additional networks can be easily added by the network supplier.

Which Operating System for the Desktop or Laptop?

In our opinion, Windows 95 is currently the ideal solution for the bulk of Windows users. Even OS/2 users will probably want to come back to the fold, because Windows 95 now has everything that OS/2 does (except, of course, the ability to run OS/2-specific software). In my opinion, certainly everyone currently running Windows 3.1 should upgrade, assuming they have a 386DX-based PC or higher. Judging just from my use of the Windows 95 beta software, I can say that Windows 95 runs much more smoothly and crashes less often than Windows 3.1, recovers more gracefully from an application crash, and once you get used to doing things a bit differently in Windows 95, manages your documents more efficiently.

Which Client Operating System to Choose—NT Workstation or Windows 95?

Because there are two Windows workstation operating systems (NT Workstation and Windows 95), which should you choose? And is Microsoft shooting itself in the foot by offering both?

Actually, Microsoft's strategy makes sense. There are two options because there are two markets for network workstations—high performance and low performance. If your applications require the utmost in performance or if your application mix is highly network oriented, you are using large networks, and you need top-notch workstation and network management, you should be using NT (or possibly Novell NetWare).

Windows NT provides US Government "C-2"-rated security features. For most intents and purposes, NT has essentially bulletproof security that can prevent an unauthorized user from entering the system or in other ways gaining access to files on the hard disk. Without a proper password, NT can totally protect sensitive files from being reached. Tools for assigning permission levels for various tasks are supplied, providing great flexibility in security arrangements.

If the application mix is heavy on the Windows side, I'd especially recommend NT (over NetWare) because NetWare tacked on top of DOS with Windows tacked on top of that can lead to some headaches. For one thing, it decreases the available conventional memory for DOS applications. NT removes at least one software level and has IPX/SPX drivers to connect with NetWare networks if you need to. Figure 1.4 demonstrates this. Connection to a NetWare network with Windows 3.1 and DOS requires three levels (four modules) of software. Connection with Windows 95 requires just one, with the inherent security and connectivity advantages of Windows 95. If you're running only DOS applications, stick with NetWare.

Consider that if you need to run Unix applications, NT may be able to run them because it can handle any Unix applications written to the POSIX specification.

> **NOTE**   To be specific, NT can only run POSIX applications written in compliance with the POSIX 1003.1 specification.

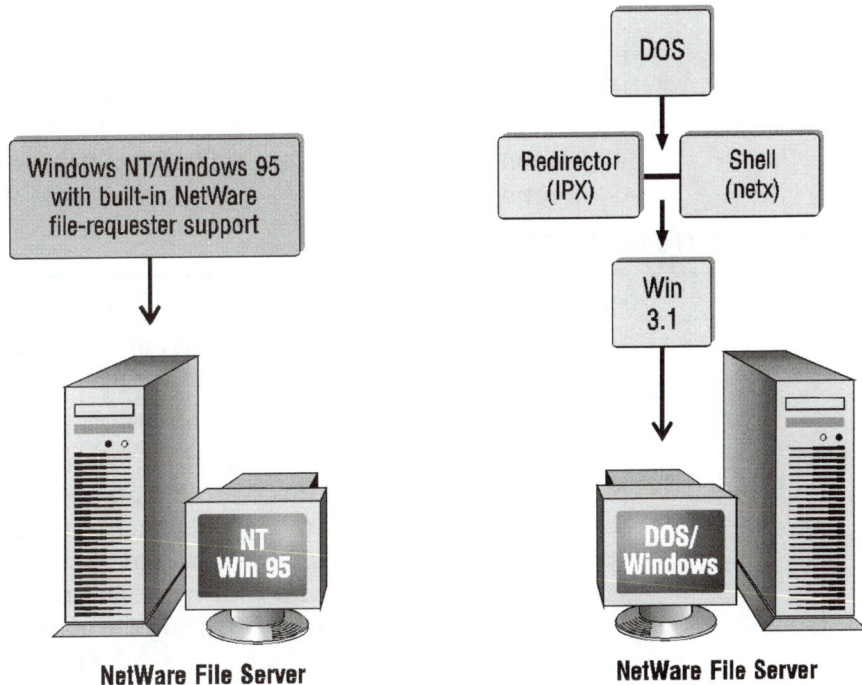

Figure 1.4 *32-bit NetWare drivers are incorporated into both Windows 95 and Windows NT, improving performance and eliminating hassles caused by loading NetWare drivers into DOS.*

It can also run many OS/2 applications. Finally, if your machines are speedy 486s or Pentiums well-endowed with RAM (and thus you wouldn't have to upgrade your hardware), why not go for NT? Just make sure that all your add-in boards and devices have NT device drivers available before you begin. Remember, NT can't use your old Windows 3.1 16-bit device drivers for your printers, video boards, mice, SCSI drives, CD-ROM drives, sound cards, and the like. It needs special 32-bit drivers written for NT.

Now for the Windows 95 argument. If the computers you are considering upgrading aren't top of the line, if having a fully 32-bit operating system with C2-level system security is nothing more than academic to you, and if you'd like to have Chicago's new object-oriented user interface as soon as possible, then Windows 95 is a sensible choice.

You can start with all Windows 95 workstations connected to one another in a peer-to-peer fashion (see Part V on networking for more about peer-to-peer networks) and then add an NT Server station later if you want more network security and performance. And remember that if you have been using or are still using a NetWare network, 32-bit NetWare client support is built in. Getting a Windows workstation up and running on a NetWare network is finally a no-brainer.

About Remote-Access Services

I've mentioned the term "remote access" (or RAS for Remote-Access Services) several times in this chapter, usually touting it as a considerable bonus to the Windows 95 user. But what exactly is RAS?

RAS allows you to dial into a network or even a single computer from a remote computer (such as a laptop) over phone lines. Each computer has a modem to connect it to the phone lines. You simply call the host machine's modem (typically back at the office) from your computer out in the field. After the host machine's modem answers, and you log onto the system with your name and password, interaction is just as if you were at the host site using the computer. For example, you could call up from home, log in, send a print job to the laser printer, use some data on a mainframe (if the network is attached to one), run applications, leave e-mail for other users, and so on. Figure 1.5 illustrates the RAS connection. Though the illustration depicts a network as the recipient of the call, you could use RAS to connect to a standalone computer as well, such as a desktop machine in your office.

You can think of a RAS connection as nothing more than a network connection made over a modem instead of through the direct cable connection that other workstations on the network use. Such a connection isn't the same as running a *remote-control* program such as PC-Anywhere with which you "take over" a remote computer. You're simply logging on as a network client.

The Windows 95 workstation that receives the call can act as a RAS server to the rest of the network, whether that network is a Windows NT, NetWare, or Windows 95-based network. RAS can also be used, incidentally, for cabled connections (through a serial port à la LapLink), infrared connections, or wireless links between two local PCs.

Setting up RAS can be a hassle. Microsoft has added a Wizard that helps the uninitiated user do this. Figure 1.6 shows the dialog box for setting up RAS for a Windows 95 PC.

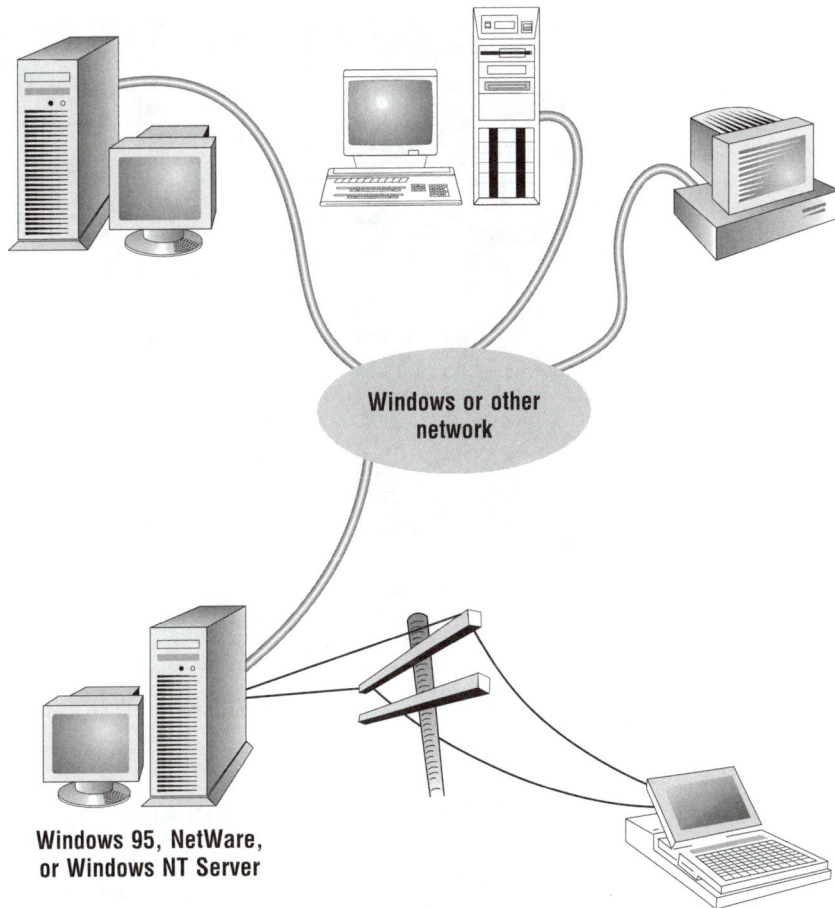

Figure 1.5   *Remote-Access Services in Windows 95 lets you connect to a network or an office computer as though you were there.*

User Interface Problems

When you run Windows 95 for the first time, its new look and feel are evident. Windows has been given a face-lift that is as obvious as the one that marked the introduction of Windows 3.0. Previous versions looked nothing like it. Figures 1.7 and 1.8 illustrate the difference between the Windows 3.1 and Windows 95 start-up screens.

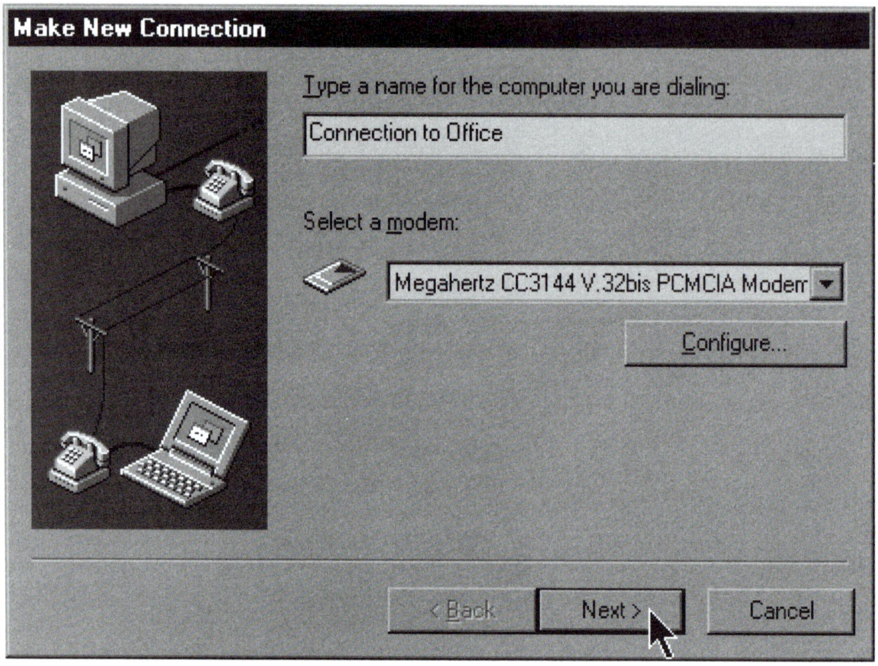

Figure 1.6   Setting up a RAS connection is fairly straightforward.

USABILITY STUDIES AND THE NEW INTERFACE

Much of the retooling of Windows for the Windows 95 release has centered on the need for a more sophisticated, robust, and powerful operating system that could keep up with the competition and could take full advantage of the hefty hardware many computer users were purchasing. From a software architectural design perspective, the internals of the 16-bit DOS/Windows combination were way more than ready for a serious upgrade.

Programmers have been chomping at the bit for a true 32-bit operating system with a "flat" memory model—an arrangement that renders programming infinitely simpler. Programmers tired years ago of writing 16-bit code simply to be backward-compatible with the ancient 8086 and 80286 microprocessors. Those chips' memory-offset requirements are a major headache.

If the success of a computer operating system or GUI is dependent on application availability, then it can also be said that application availability is tied to ease of writing for that platform. Microsoft is certainly well aware of this and is supplying programmers with Windows-related tool- and software-development kits.

The major difference, you will note, is that there is no Program Manager window evident. Though Windows 95 sports many subtle aesthetic improvements such as more attractive menus, sunken dialog box buttons, and so forth, probably the resolution of what I call the "Program Manager/File Manager dichotomy" is the most striking advance.

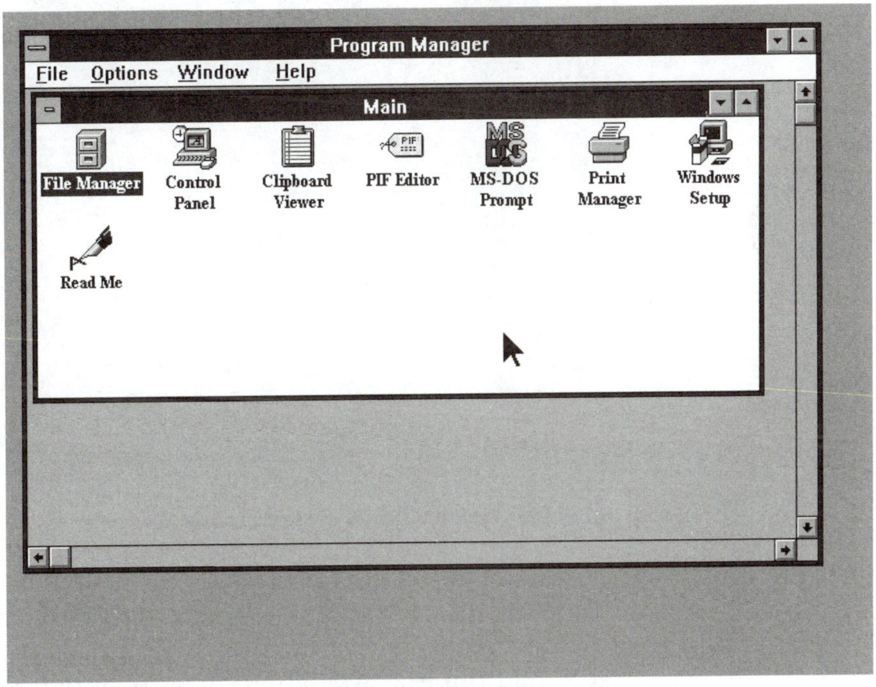

Figure 1.7   *Typical Windows 3.1 start-up screen*

Shells

Detractors of Windows have made a hobby of pointing out the shortcomings of the Windows *shell*. The shell refers to the control program that you use to interact with an operating system. With MS-DOS, for example, the shell is provided by command.com—the command-line interface. You simply type in commands at the C:> prompt and press Enter. With Windows, the big attraction is that you could point and click on icons to essentially issue commands to the command-line interpreter. Some think this is easier than typing in commands. Others think it is more abstract even than typing commands.

Figure 1.8   Typical Windows 95 start-up screen

Since Windows 3.0, the shell (when the MS-DOS Executive of earlier Windows versions was removed) has consisted primarily of Program Manager and File Manager. (Technically, the Control Panel, Task Manager, and Print Manager also form portions of the shell.) Program Manager allowed you to organize your favorite documents and applications into groups by adding representative icons to the group window. Then, by opening the correct group window and clicking on the desired icon, the associated document or program would open.

This was a nifty idea, but problems arose because users didn't grasp a fundamental concept: These icons were really *aliases*, not documents or programs themselves. Dragging the icons around within the shell didn't actually manipulate the object they were pointed to by the icon. And likewise, deleting one of these icons didn't actually remove the item from the hard disk—only from the group window in Program Manager. Even more challenging to figure out was how to add new icons to your program groups. Without a fairly thorough understanding of DOS's directory structure, this was next to impossible.

The only time most users saw new icons appear in groups was when they installed a new application. Application-installation programs would often mysteriously create new groups and add icons to groups, but most users didn't know how this happened.

An obvious void was created by Program Manager's lack of skills. If Program Manager couldn't perform real file operations such as copying, deleting, moving, and creating documents, how were these chores to be done? File Manager was the solution, but research at the Microsoft usability lab determined that people did not easily grasp File Manager's use of a hierarchical tree structure in the left pane and a matching "contents" pane on the right side, as Figure 1.9 illustrates.

In addition to the conceptual problems people have with File Manager, its power to wreak havoc on the operating system when put in the wrong hands is considerable! One slip of the mouse, and the unsuspecting novice can unwittingly produce such glorious effects as relegating the Windows directory to the status of a subdirectory of, say, the WordPerfect directory. After a slick move like this, Windows

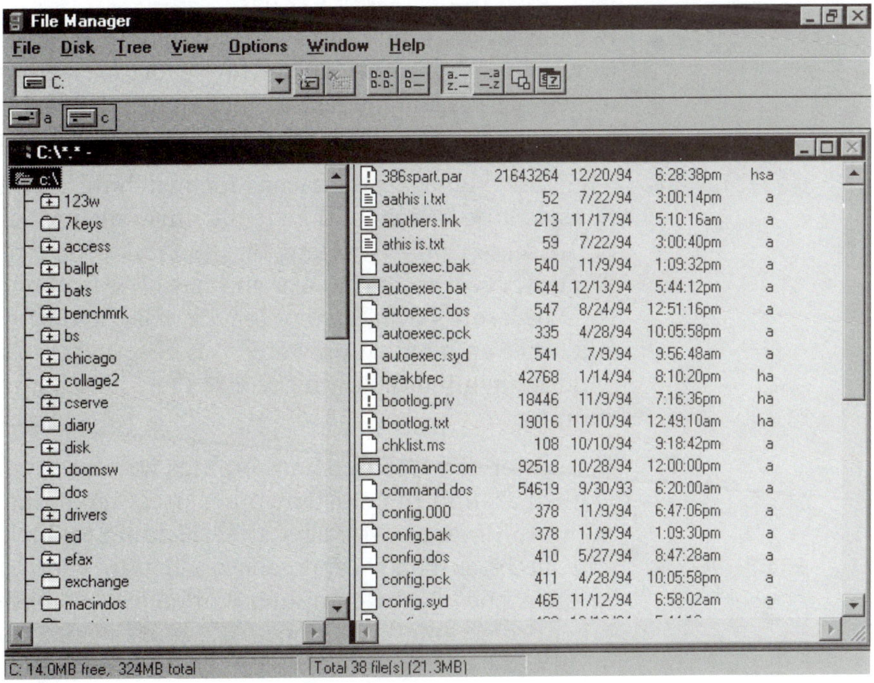

Figure 1.9 *Typical two-pane File Manager screen*

won't even boot. Because no simple utilities are provided for helping users easily and safely copy files from drive to drive (such as to make backups of critical documents on a floppy), catastrophes such as this have happened far too frequently in Windows.

Finally, consider a few other problems inherent in the Windows 3.1 interface:

▶ When Windows first boots, users are faced with numerous strange icons and no intuitively easy way to begin working.

▶ Users don't understand that icons only appear on the Desktop when applications are running and their windows are minimized.

▶ It isn't possible to leave icons representing documents on the Desktop for use the next time the users boot up.

▶ Unless there is an association set up in File Manager for a specific document type (as identified by its three-letter DOS file extension), double-clicking on the document in File Manager results in an error message. The procedure for setting up associations is too complex for most users.

▶ File names are limited to the MS-DOS "8.3" naming convention, which doesn't cut the mustard for most users. Trying to create and remember cryptic file names such as RPT4DAVE.DOC is a royal headache for everyone. This was simply a carryover from DOS days.

▶ The Task Manager, the means for switching between running applications, is little known and generally misunderstood. Pressing Alt-Tab, Ctrl-Esc, or double-clicking on the Desktop are tricks the average Windows user is ignorant of and has little likelihood of discovering. (In Microsoft's own terminology, it was "undiscoverable.") As a result, once an application window is obscured from view by another window, many users didn't realize the covered application was still running.

For power users, these shortcomings weren't tragic. People simply worked around them. Many other users scouted around for an alternative to Program Manager after deciding to ditch it. The dilemma with all the alternative approaches is that they introduce user-interface inconsistency in the computer workplace—something corporate computer professionals had hoped Windows would help eliminate!

In researching ways to improve the Windows user interface, Microsoft relied on several sources. In fact, it's quite likely that the interface of Windows 95 is the most thoroughly researched piece of software ever developed. Several phases of study were conducted in a variety of settings:

➤ *Usability Lab test groups.* Users were watched from behind mirrors and taped with video cameras as they performed tasks such as launching programs, creating new files, and printing. Their interaction at the keyboard and mouse as well as their reactions were all recorded and later analyzed by experts in learning theory and cognition.

➤ *Long-Term Testing.* Longer-term testing, also know as *summative* testing, was conducted both at Microsoft and in the field at various customer locations.

➤ *Expert consultants.* Experts in user interfaces were hired to perform a professional critique of the Windows 95 interface.

Reactions to the product design were then tabulated, digested, and fed back to the design, development, and programming staff.

Document Centrality

In addition to control issues, Microsoft claims its research findings indicated that a new interface would have to be made more *document-centric*. Recall that this means that rather than thinking about running applications and then opening documents from the application, you'll simply locate the desired document and open it.

As things stand today, Windows 3.1 and NT are primarily application-centric: Users typically first run the desired application, such as Excel, then use the File ➤ Open command and resulting dialog box to dredge through the DOS directory tree to find the document.

In a document-centric world, the computer's operating system assumes the job of appropriately linking the document and the application that created it. All the user needs do is find the document (just like in the physical world) and double-click on it. Once clicked on, the document launches the associated application and opens the document in it. Windows 95 determines the appropriate application by checking information stored in the system Registry.

There are some important features that make Windows 95 significantly more document-centric:

▶ As mentioned earlier, you can create new documents right from the Desktop by clicking the right mouse button and choosing New, or you can wander through your document folders (without using File Manager or Program Manager) and pull any existing documents onto the Desktop in icon form for super-easy access. This is done from the *My Computer* icon, which I'll discuss below. Figures 1.10 and 1.11 illustrate these two approaches.

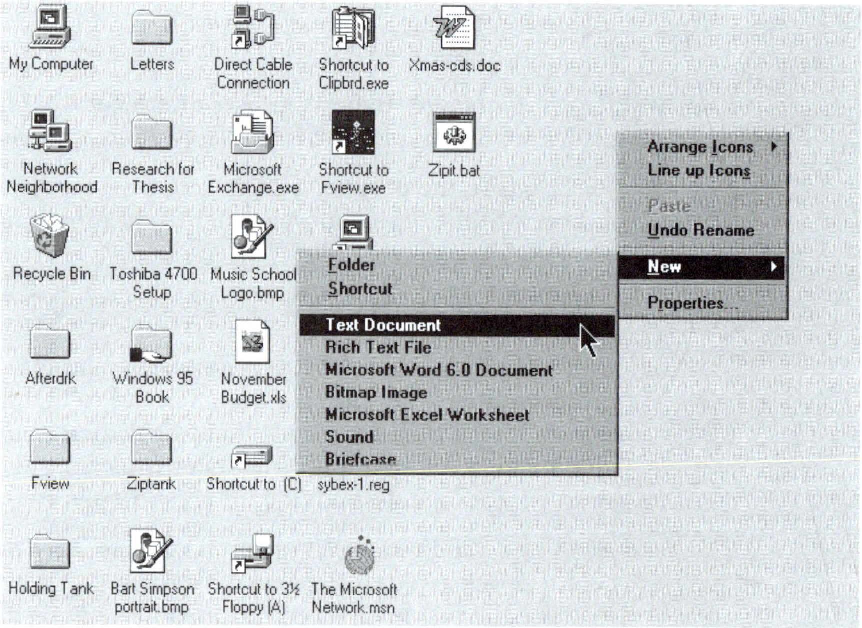

Figure 1.10   *Clicking the right mouse button on the Desktop lets you create a new document in any application that will install itself appropriately in the Registry.*

▶ Another document-centric tool is supplied as part of the Taskbar's Start button. The Start button, which is always visible on the screen and in easy reach (unless you choose to hide the Taskbar), provides a number of handy shortcuts I'll describe in detail below. Among other things, it remembers and lists the last fifteen or so documents you've been working on, regardless of application. Simply clicking on the Start button and choosing *Documents* displays the list. Then you just

Figure 1.11   *Opening documents from the My Computer window*

select the document you want to work with. Windows 95 launches the application and loads the document (Figure 1.12).

▶ Windows 95's OLE 2 brings you a more document-centric feeling because you can edit embedded objects in place.

▶ Finally, Windows 95 gives a document window the same name as the document that was double-clicked on. Clicking on a document named *Fred's Thesis* opens a window called *Fred's Thesis* in the appropriate application. (This assumes the application was written to take advantage of long file names, which means that the application is a Windows 95 application.)

The Desktop

I've described a few of the Desktop's features above (see Chapter 3 for more detail). Take a look again at how the Desktop first appears when you boot Windows 95 (Figure 1.13).

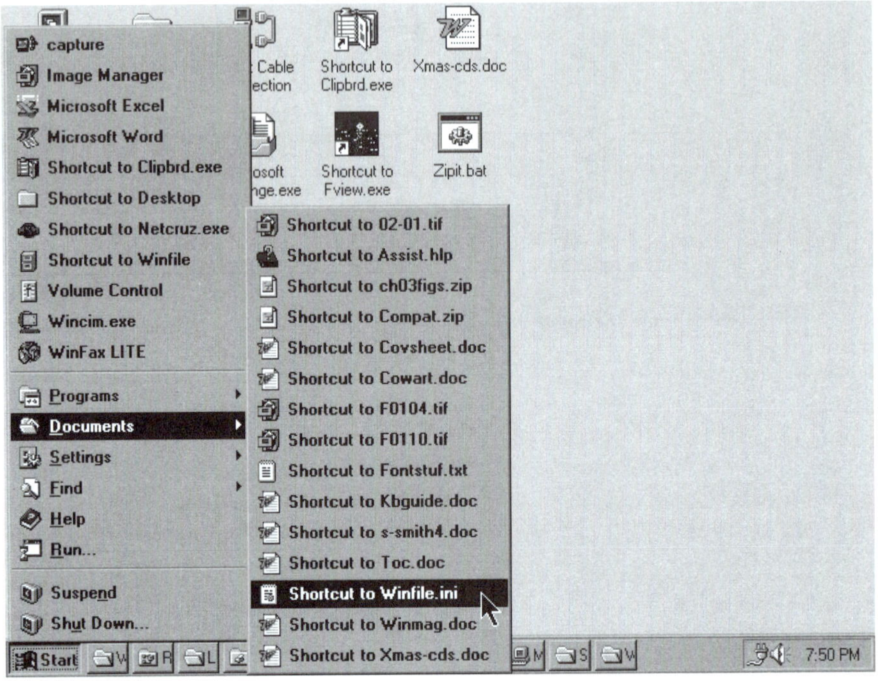

Figure 1.12   *Using the Start button to open a document*

Microsoft's simplifications here render access to system and network components such as disk directories (now called folders) and workstations much more graphical. Let's take a look at each of these new elements and discuss how they affect the way you'll work with Windows 95.

The Taskbar

The Taskbar (Chapter 3) can be placed at any of the four edges of your screen, and it can be set to get lost (disappear) when you don't want it and to reappear when you move the pointer to the far edge of the screen or press Ctrl-Esc. Figure 1.14 illustrates.

The Taskbar has two primary functions: it's a program launcher and a task switcher. It's also a bit of a status bar, containing a clock and little icons to indicate such things as waiting e-mail, that you're printing a document, volume settings for sound, and the battery condition

Easy access to all folders, disk drives, fonts, printers, and dial-up networking

Easy access to all networked computers and printers

My Computer

Network Neighborhood

Recycle Bin

The Microsoft Network.msn

Microsoft Exchange.exe

Start   2:39 PM

Microsoft Exchange In Box (optional) for working with e-mail, modem, and fax documents

Taskbar

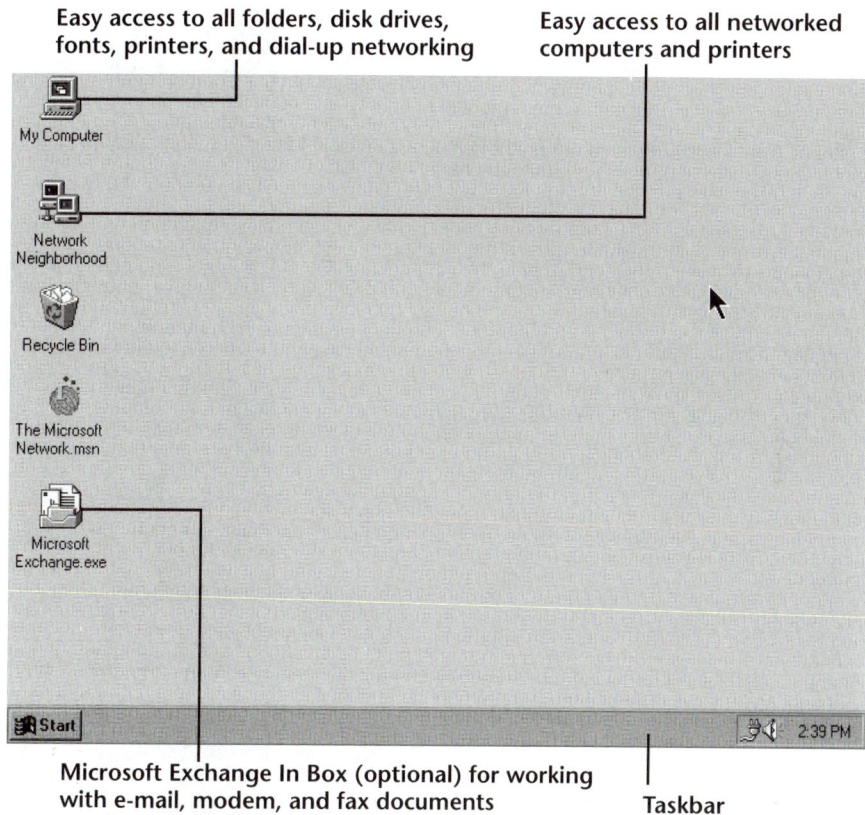

Figure 1.13 *The basic Desktop*

for laptops. Clicking on one of the icons typically brings up a related settings box.

The Start button at the far left end of the bar (or top, when the bar is located on the side of the screen) is responsible for launching applications, opening documents, and making settings (see Figure 1.15).

Any buttons to the right of the Start button represent currently running programs or open folders and are for task switching.

The figure shows what happens when you click on the Start button—a menu appears. Notice that four of these menu choices—Programs, Documents, Settings, and Find—are *cascading* menus: choosing any one of these opens a submenu. In the case of the Programs choice, the submenu lists what amount to Program Manager groups. If you

Figure 1.14   The Taskbar can be relocated.

upgraded to Windows 95 from Windows 3.1, your existing Program Manager groups are ported into this new format, which is quicker and easier to use than the old Program Manager was.

If you're dual-booting Windows 3.x and Windows 95 (which is possible should you feel the need to keep Windows 3.11 around for a while), each time you boot Windows 95, a Program Group converter ensures this list of groups is up to date. This also happens when you use the supplied Program Manager to adjust the contents of your

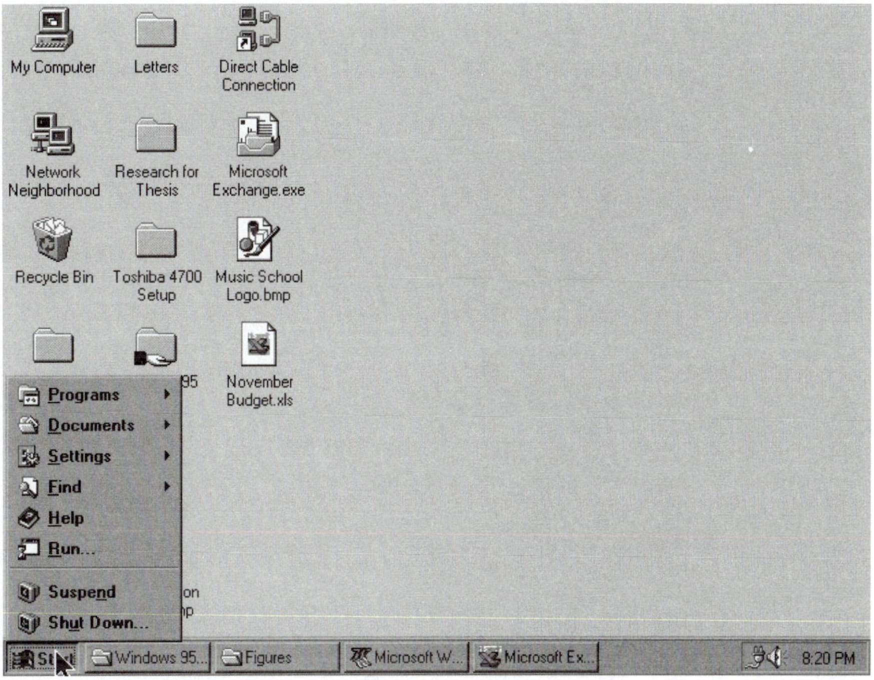

Figure 1.15   *The Start button*

groups. However, there's another more intuitive and more direct way to alter the contents of groups. That option is available through the Start button's *Start Menu* option. I'll get into that a little later in this section.

The Start button's Program option lets you set up groups within groups within groups, and everything is alphabetized. Figure 1.16 illustrates nesting with the Games group (we'll start calling groups *folders* soon, incidentally, so get ready), which is a subgroup of the Accessories group.

NOTE   Though the Program button is intended to help you launch your programs, actually it will display whatever *is* in existing group folders. Thus, documents such as Readme files that come with applications that are dumped into a program's folder will also display in the list. Such documents when double-clicked on will open in an appropriate window. You can also organize any of your own documents in this way. Thus, the Start button provides a neat, clean, and organized way for users to hierarchically arrange their documents as well as their programs.

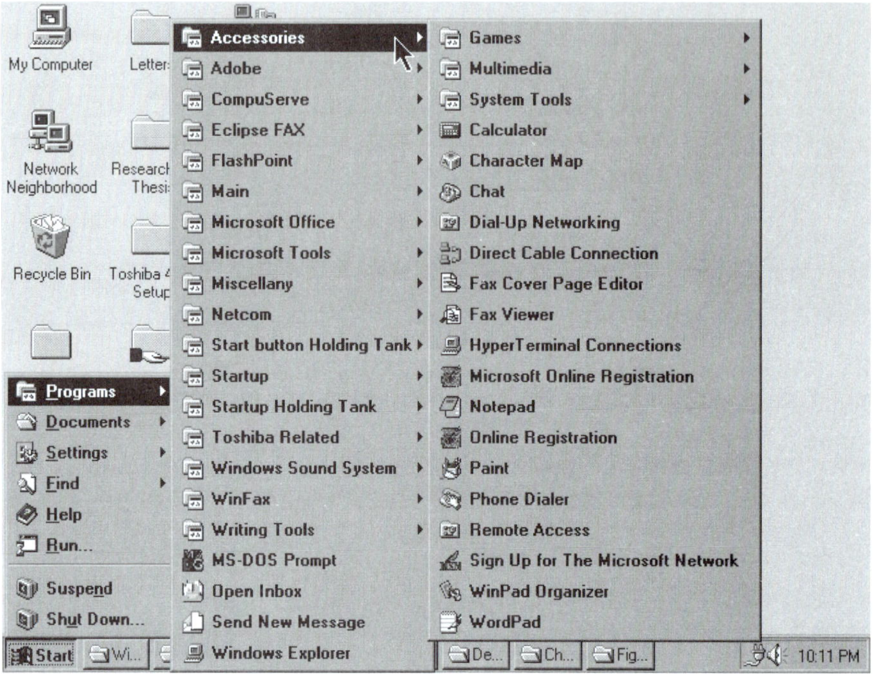

Figure 1.16   *Notice that the Games group is a subgroup of the Accessories group. Nesting of groups is possible in Windows 95, whereas it wasn't in Windows 3.x.*

One last feature of the Start button is that instead of walking through the cascading menus to reach one of your favorite applications, you can just add it to the first-level menu. For example, say you wanted Word for Windows available for launching right from the Start button. You just use the Settings option, which I'll explain in a minute. The result would look something like this:

The Latest Document List

Moving along down the Start button's options, consider the next one, Documents (Chapter 4). Choose this option, and a list of the last fifteen documents you've worked with are revealed. Figure 1.17 displays an example.

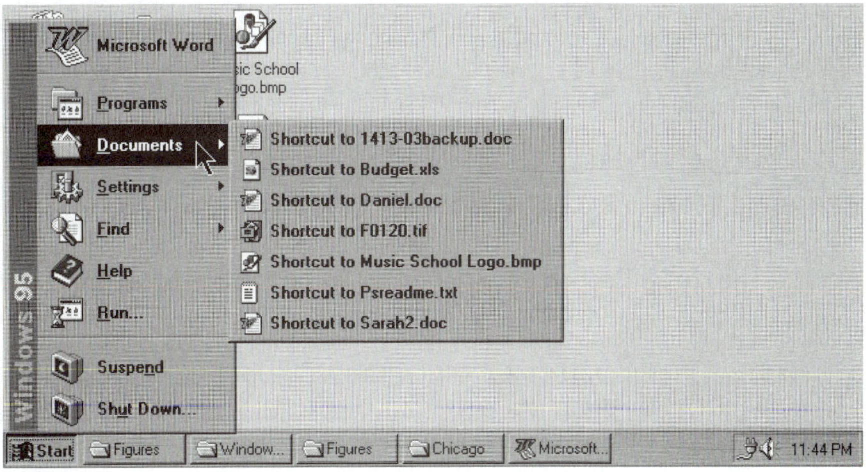

Figure 1.17   *The Document option on the Start button makes getting to the last fifteen documents you've been editing much easier.*

Just click on the document you want. The document appears in the appropriate application window. One caveat is that only selected applications know how to update this Documents list. Thus, not all of your most recently edited documents will appear there.

The Settings Option

By building a Settings option (Chapter 7) right into the Start button, the path to system customization is much more discoverable.

When you click on Settings, you'll see the menu shown here:

The options are Control Panel, Start Menu, Printers, and Taskbar.

Control Panel   This option simply runs the Control Panel, which operates much the same way the old one did. The only changes are a few new *applets* (icons for specific kinds of settings) and a new style of dialog boxes for each applet.

Start Menu   This displays a window somewhat similar to the old Program Manager, only with groups shown as folder icons rather than the traditional boxy-shaped Program Manager icons. Figure 1.18 shows you what I mean.

These folders are *live*, meaning you can run applications and open documents here. You can also create new folders, move applications and documents around between folders, and so on. Figure 1.19 shows an example of a folder open in a new window.

Printers   Simply click on Printers (see Chapter 8), and you'll see an icon for each installed printer and an additional icon called Add Printer, used for installing a new printer.

Double-clicking on one of the printers will give you something you wouldn't expect: a Print Manager-like window for each printer, showing print jobs currently queued up for the printer. You can make configuration changes to the printer here as well as rearrange the print queue or delete print jobs.

Now for the coup de grâce. Want to install a new printer? Microsoft's little helpful taskmasters, the Wizards, have been built into Windows 95

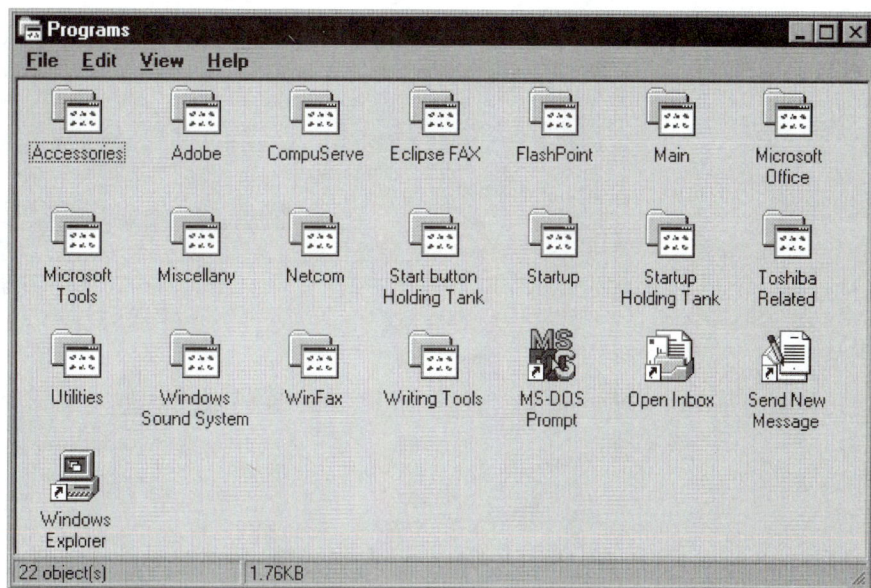

Figure 1.18   *Choosing Programs from the Start button lets you adjust the contents of folders (groups), including which applications will appear on the first level of the Start menu. You can also run applications and open documents from here.*

to make life easier for novices. Wizards walk you through complex tasks and even in some cases do the whole task for you.

When you click on the Add New Printers icon, up comes a series of Wizard dialog boxes, asking some simple questions about the printer.

Taskbar   The final option on the Settings menu is Taskbar (Chapter 7). This lets you set up some nifty aspects of the Taskbar. Notice the new *tabular* design of the dialog box. Clicking on a tab brings its page of settings to the front.

The first page lets you add your most-used programs to the top of the Start menu. The second page is for setting some useful Taskbar options, such as when it will disappear and whether the time and various other indicators will appear on the bar.

Figure 1.19   *Double-clicking on a folder displays its contents in a new window.*

The Find Button

The next item on the Start menu is the Find button (Chapter 4). Find is a standalone program. It will search for either files, folders, or computers:

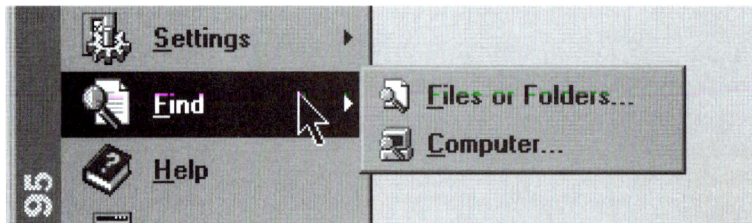

Yes, computers—that is, computers on a network. In keeping with the new Windows 95 document-centric metaphor, the Find command lets you search for document folders, too.

In the third tab sheet, Advanced, the *Of type* option lets you choose from the list of all registered document types. For example, on my machine, opening this list results in the following:

You can even search an entire hard disk for all files containing specific text. The results of a search are displayed in an extension to the bottom of the Find box.

Improved Help

Next, the Start button lets you get Help about Windows. The new interface draws on the book paradigm we're all used to: the Table of Contents and Index. Take a look at the Help system for Windows 95:

Some other points about the new Help:

▶ Help topics have been shortened whenever possible. Material has been broken down into subtopics. When you choose a topic, you're not going to be overwhelmed by too much to read. Subtopics open up like a directory when clicked on.

▶ Tips and tricks sections are supplied by Microsoft for Windows 95 and are encouraged by other software makers for their own Help systems.

▶ You've probably seen the ?-arrow tool: rather than just the normal question-mark–tool button, this button (called the "What's this?" button), when clicked on, changes the pointer's shape. When an object on the screen is then clicked on, an explanation appears. Developers are being encouraged to exploit this Help function in their own applications.

► A new type of button, called a *shortcut* button, can jump a user to the procedure he or she is reading about. For example, the Help screen for changing the system clock looks like this:

To change your computer's time

1 Click here [ ] to view Date/Time properties.
2 In the area below the clock, double-click the hours, minutes, seconds, or AM/PM indicator.

Clicking on the shortcut button will take you right to the Control Panel rather than having to read and follow any directions.

Running Applications

The Start button also lets you run a program from a Run box (Chapter 4). One improvement is that the last several commands you issued are available from the drop-down list.

Also, you can enter not only executables (application names such as wp.exe) but also the name of any document (e.g., letter.doc). If Windows 95 recognizes the extension of the file, it will be opened in a window for you.

One last nicety is that the Run box will not only run DOS applications, but like its big brother Windows NT, it will also run Windows applications. Enter **calc**, for example, and the calculator runs.

Application Switching with the Taskbar

Alt-Tab (Chapter 4) is still a part of Windows 95, but the good news is that it's been improved. Now it looks like this:

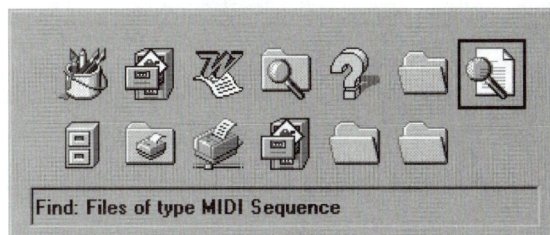

Find: Files of type MIDI Sequence

Each press of Alt-Tab advances the little box along the tasks so you can target the one you're headed for a little better. In fact, with just a press of Alt-Tab you can get a sense of how many tasks are running, even if you've decided to hide the Taskbar from view.

The even better news about task switching is that each time you run an application or open a folder, a button for it is added to the Taskbar. Simply click on the button, and the associated window jumps to the foreground ready for you to work with it.

If the task's window was minimized (iconized), it is restored to original size from the icon.

My Computer

There's one very important addition to the interface that's so obvious that nobody ever thought of it. It's called My Computer (Chapter 4). Every Windows 95 computer screen has an icon by this name in the upper-left corner. Double-click on it, and you can poke around at literally everything in your computer, hardware and software alike. Though all these services can be reached through other means, making them available in a window called My Computer makes perfect sense and is easily discoverable by even novice users. Figure 1.20 shows My Computer open and drive C, Printers, and Fonts displayed.

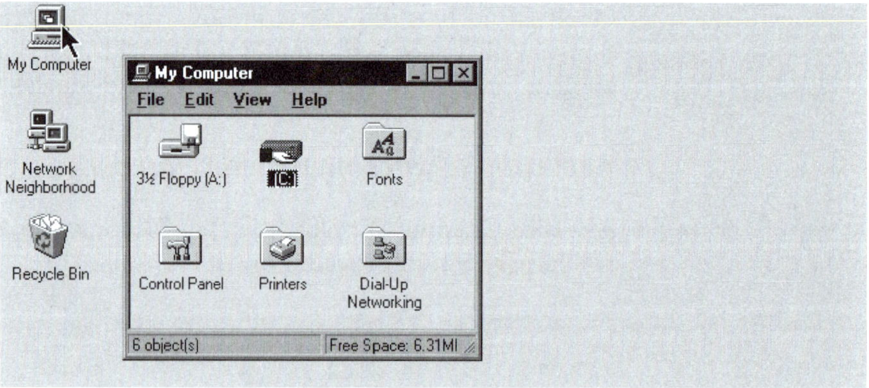

Figure 1.20 *For most users, My Computer will be the central hub of Windows 95. Through this icon you can get to any aspect of your computer from opening a document to adding a device driver or establishing remote-access dial-in connections.*

Properties and Property Sheets

Interesting and extremely powerful additions to the user interface
are supplied by something called *Property Sheets* (Chapters 8 and 11).
Almost every object (folders, files, Desktop, Taskbar, networked computer, etc.) has properties associated with it that can be easily examined
and altered. It takes a *right* mouse click to bring up the menu from
which Properties are selected.

When the Properties option is selected from this menu, the associated
property sheet appears. Figure 1.21 shows the property sheet for the
folder above.

Just some of the many settings you can make using Properties are

▶ Share a folder on the network

▶ Change the name of your hard disk and check its free space

▶ Change a program's icon

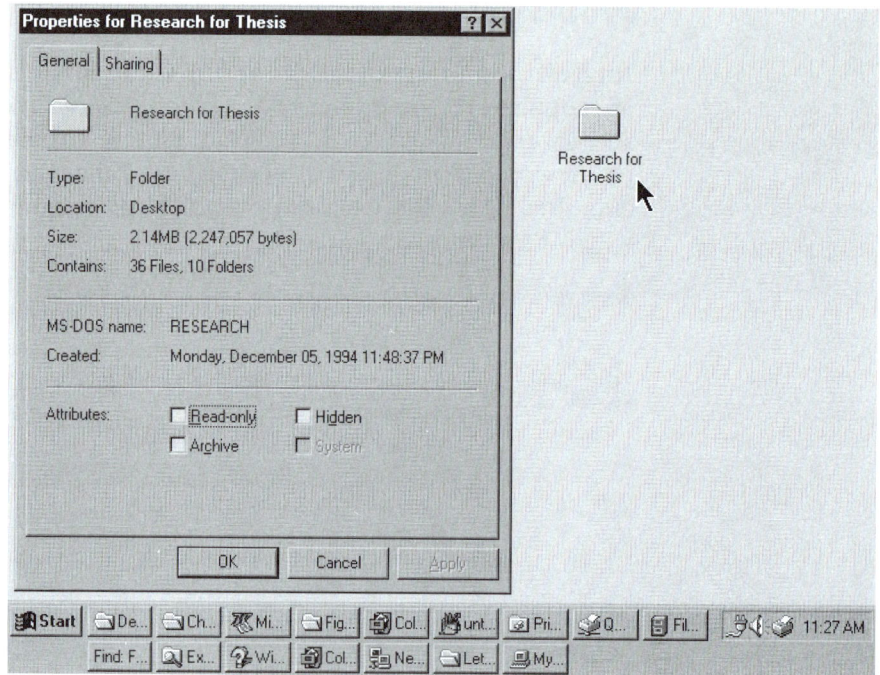

Figure 1.21   The Properties sheet for the Research for Thesis folder

▶ Set the Desktop's colors, background, screen saver, etc.

▶ Display a font's technical details

Right-Clicking

The right mouse button (Chapters 4 and 11) has been deemed a sort of power-user mouse button, and its application has been implemented throughout the Windows 95 user interface. In general, the right mouse button (actually the *secondary* button, which would mean the left button if you're using a left-handed mouse) implements activities that can be done using commands elsewhere in the interface, but using the mouse button provides a number of time-saving shortcuts.

Shortcuts

Shortcuts (Chapter 4) are icons that can represent almost anything in Windows 95. You can create a shortcut for almost anything, then you can drop that icon almost anywhere. Clicking on the icon then runs the application, opens the document, presents the folder window to you, and so on, depending on the type of shortcut it is.

Here's an example shortcut icon on the Desktop. Notice that it looks just like a regular icon, only with a little arrow in the lower-left corner.

Shortcut to
WinCIM

What's so great about shortcuts is that they are only pointers to objects, so deleting the shortcut above doesn't actually delete WinCIM. Nor does making a copy of a shortcut (to place elsewhere) copy the file, application, drive, or whatnot to which it points.

The New Look of Windows Elements

All your existing applications will benefit from the new, more refined look of Windows 95. Take a look at Figures 1.22 and 1.23, which are both of the same application, one shown in Windows 3.1 and the other under Windows 95.

Tab Buttons

I've already mentioned the new dialog-box design that relies on tabs (Chapter 3). A good example of this new dialog-box design is shown in Figure 1.24, from which you make screen display attributes. Notice that you can now alter the resolution of your display (e.g., from 640×480 to $1,024 \times 768$) more easily, and in many cases without rebooting Windows.

Title Bar Changes

The entire Title Bar (Chapter 3) of every document or application window incorporates a new design: the Minimize, Maximize, and

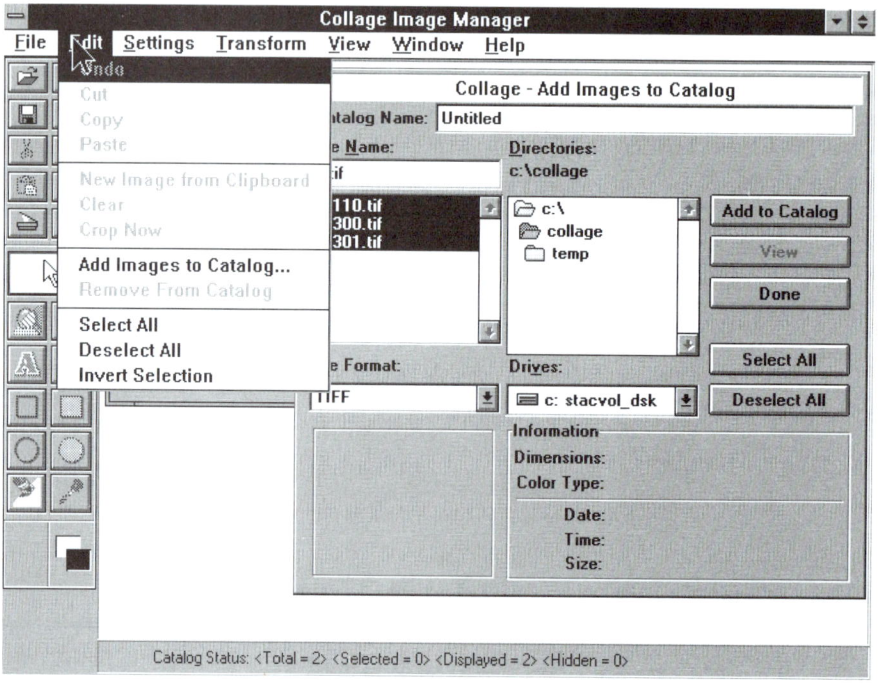

Figure 1.22   *A Windows 3.x application running in Windows 3.1*

Close buttons as well as the window's title have all been given a face-lift. Compare these two Title Bars, old and new:

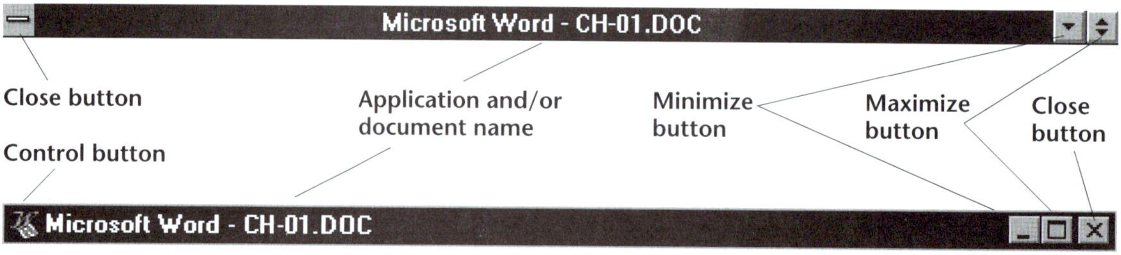

The Minimize, Maximize, and Close buttons now have more intuitive icons, and the Close button is now in the far-right corner. An X is now the universal designator for *close*. Any window can now be closed with a single click on the X.

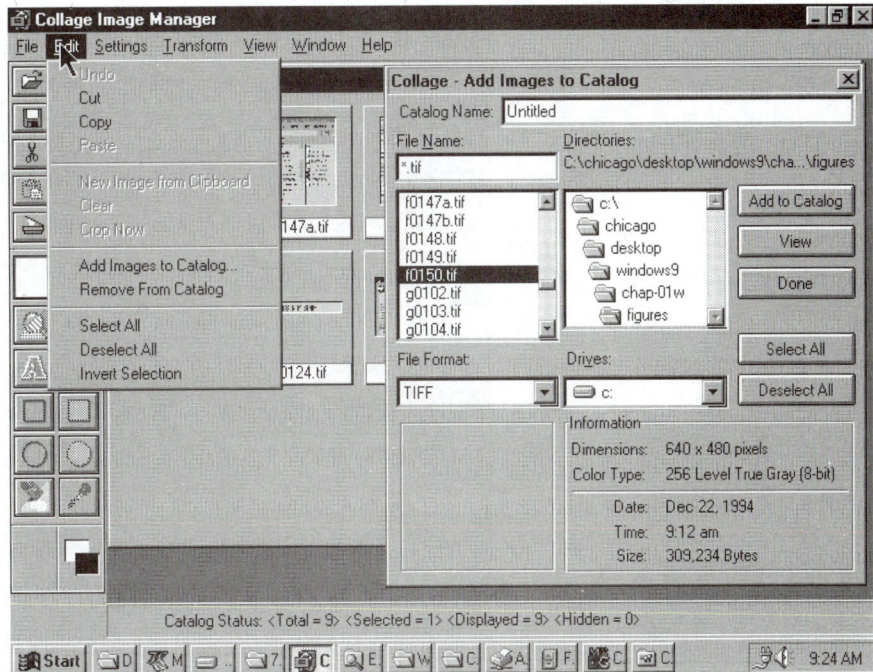

Figure 1.23 *A Windows 3.x application running in Windows 95*

The Minimize button is the shape of a button that will appear on the Taskbar or in a window when a document is iconized within an application window. The Maximize button will change to a Restore button when the window is maximized:

Restore button

This button returns the window to an intermediate size between full and iconized.

Notice, finally, that the old Control Box that was in the upper-left corner of the window is now replaced with a miniature icon. The icon that appears here is the application's personalized icon.

Shading

Shading details around buttons, menu items, borders, and so forth have been refined and standardized to produce a more coherent and

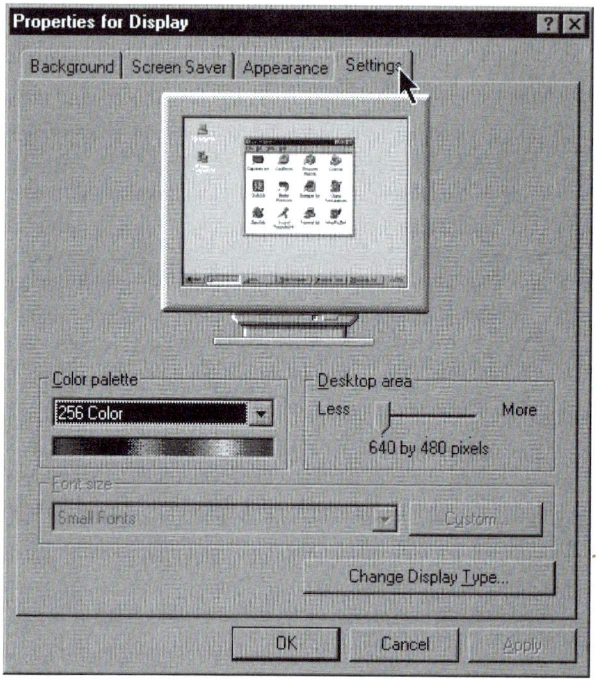

Figure 1.24   *Typical dialog box with tabs. Clicking on a tab brings up the related settings.*

integrated feel in the Windows 95 environment. Grayed-out text (options not available for some reason or other) are now displayed as sunken rather than just gray, and the new borders have a highlighted effect. Finally, the standard light source is from the upper left, and all boxes, buttons, frames, and other elements use this format, resulting in a more visually pleasing and consistent look throughout.

Easier-to-Grab Sliders

Scroll buttons (Chapter 3) are now proportionally sized to indicate the size of the document. If the document is fully displayed in the window, the button's length is the same as the whole scroll bar; if only one half of the document can fit in the window, the button will be half the scroll-bar size. More often than not, you'll have much larger scroll buttons to aim at, grab, and drag, as you see in Figure 1.25.

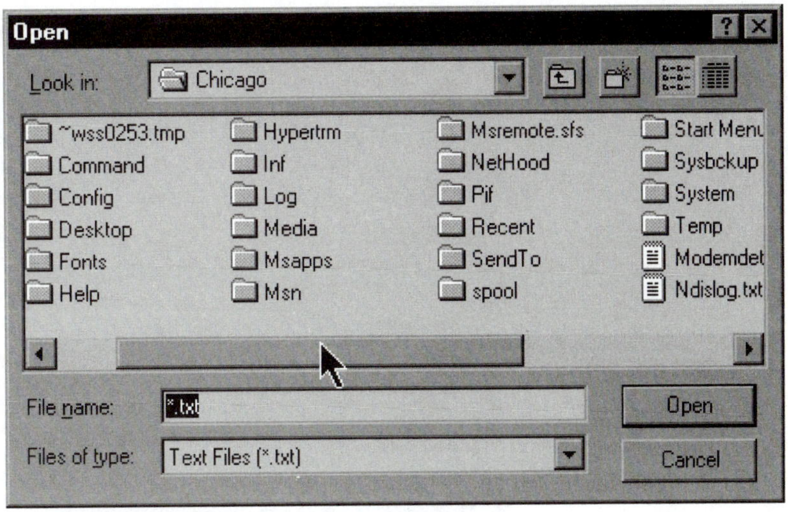

Figure 1.25   *Scroll buttons tend to be larger in Windows 95.*

Column-Heading Control

This control will likely be used whenever columns of information are displayed, allowing you to change the column width and optionally sort the data in the columns. By positioning the pointer on the division between the column heads, clicking, and dragging, the column resizes. Clicking on any column head sorts the data under the columns. Figure 1.26 illustrates this. Note that I've just sorted the listing by clicking on the Size column heading.

Video Enhancements

Microsoft has built some rather nice video stuff into Windows 95. "Live" resolution switching is one case in point; another nicety runs along the same lines, capitalizing on fancy video boards' meteoric *bit blitting* capability. (Bit blitting is short for *bit block transferring*, the kind of data juggling necessary to move a block of graphics around on the screen.) Windows 95's Control Panel offers an option that keeps the insides of your windows alive while you move them around the screen. If you purchase an add-on package called Microsoft Plus (see Chapter 32), a so-called full window drag/size option moves the guts of the window around along with its border. This works even if the

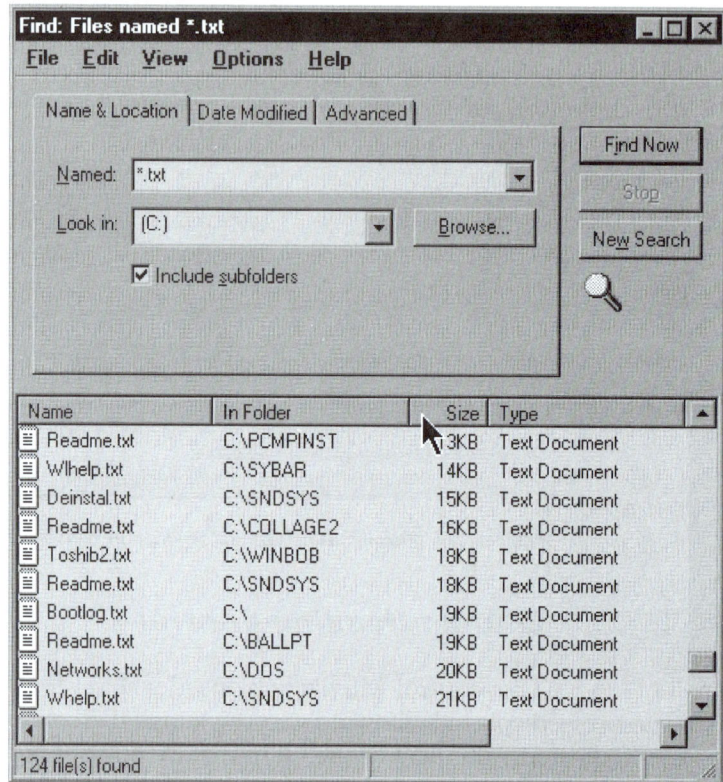

Figure 1.26 Column heads will appear in dialog boxes and applications in Windows 95.
Easy column resizing and sorting are possible with a few mouse clicks.

contents of the window is being modified at the time, such as when a chart is being redrawn or numbers are recalculating in a spreadsheet.

Changeable System Text Sizes

Right off the bat, everyone loves to futz with their system's color scheme (Chapter 7). The color-scheme settings in Windows 95 are far juicier than in Windows 3.x. There's support for 256-color schemes, for starters, which means that the color schemes can be more subtle and pleasing to the eye.

But wait. There's more.

In addition to some really nice canned settings, you can also use True-Type fonts for system-related doodads such as the Title Bar and dialog boxes. Figure 1.27 shows an example scheme chosen from the Display dialog box.

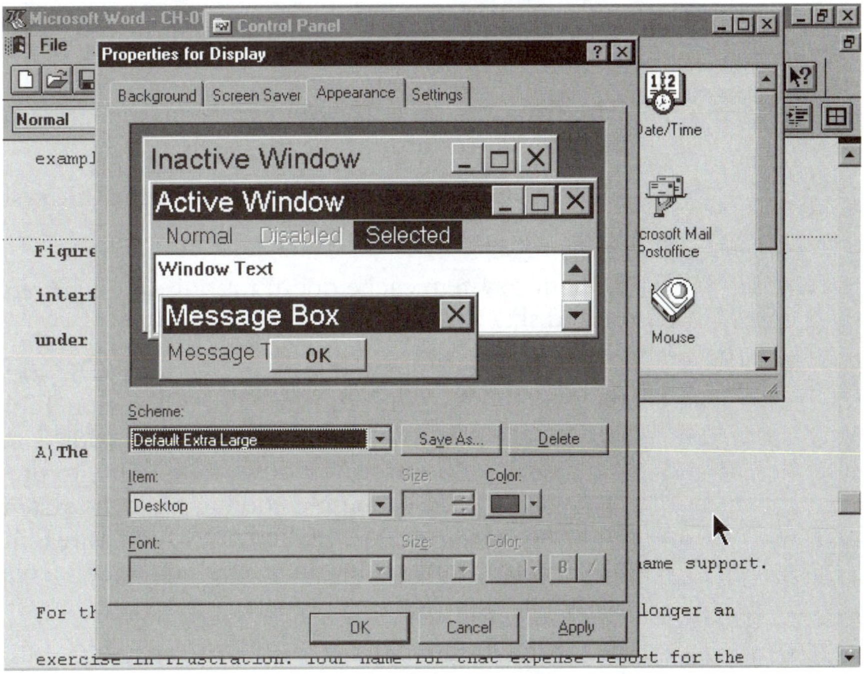

Figure 1.27   *A greater degree of color and font variation for overall interface appearance are supported in Windows 95 than are available under Windows 3.x and NT. Notice the large fonts shown in this example, which could be useful for the visually impaired or for instructional purposes.*

The New File System

Windows 95 now finally gives you long file-name support (Chapters 5 and 12). A file name can be as many as 255 characters long (including spaces). But there's more to the file-system improvement in Windows 95 than long file names:

▶ The entire file system is now multithreaded protected-mode 32-bit code for improved performance and reliability.

▶ It incorporates what is essentially an enhanced MS-DOS file system called VFAT.

▶ There is a 255-character file-name limit, yet it is still compatible with MS-DOS and Windows 3.1 applications.

▶ Users don't have to see extensions in their file names unless they want to.

▶ The Explorer (an enhanced File Manager) indicates the type of file, meaning the creator of the file, such as Paint.

▶ Open architecture allows support for other file systems in the future.

▶ It has a 32-bit CD-ROM file system.

▶ Dynamic system cache doesn't require a dedicated swap file on your hard disk.

From the user's point of view, the Windows 95 file system is essentially MS-DOS. The old FAT (File Allocation Table) system continues on, albeit written in 32-bit code. The code is multithreaded as well, so, in addition to Windows 95's ability to preemptively multitask, you'll do less thumb twiddling while the system is copying files or performs other disk-related activities such as reading the CD-ROM drive, auto-saving a file you're working on, or serving a file to a workstation across the network.

In MS-DOS (and Windows 3.0), whenever the disk was accessed, the operating system had to transition into what's called *real-mode* operations. Real mode is a CPU chip operating mode that emulates the old 8086 and 80286 chips and was included for backward-compatibility with those chips. Real-mode operations are problematic, firstly because they require today's 386, 486, and Pentium CPUs to switch into real mode before they can read or write to the disk. This takes a little time, slowing down throughput.

After Windows 3.1 was around for some time, Microsoft released 32-bit protected-mode disk drivers, which, if opted for, pepped up disk performance and eliminated mode switching on supported disk drives. Still, SCSI devices often were left running on manufacturer-supplied 16-bit real-mode drivers.

Secondly, and more importantly, real-mode operations bring other operations the CPU might be handling to a halt, sort of like an adult regressing into infantile behavior where he or she can't multitask. The

and drives you've assigned for use by networked colleagues. Finally, VCACHE uses intelligent dynamic algorithms to allocate or reduce RAM from the cache as suits the situation.

Virtual Memory

As you may know, Windows 3.x uses a portion of the hard drive to simulate RAM, acting as though your computer has more RAM than it physically does, letting it run more applications and open more documents at once than would otherwise be the case. This technique is called *virtual memory management.*

The new virtual memory manager takes the onus off the user on a number of counts. It uses more-intelligent algorithms and more-efficient 32-bit access methods (via the new file-system drivers), and determines for the user the optimal maximum and minimum file sizes. Because of the increased efficiency of the hard-disk access methods the new VMM employs, even a highly fragmented hard disk (a disk with a considerable number of noncontiguous sectors) won't result in a serious performance penalty.

Long File Names

As Windows NT, Mac, and OS/2 users (among others) will attest, the "8.3" file-name restriction (eight characters, a period, and a three-letter extension) of DOS is ridiculous.

Windows 95, now free of many DOS limitations (even though technically it's running on top of DOS 7—you can even prevent Windows 95 from loading and be dumped into the old [well, new] C> prompt), supports long file names, up to 255 characters: a terrific improvement. The 255 characters can be letters, numbers, spaces, and certain punctuation marks, but Windows 95 doesn't differentiate between upper- and lowercase letters, so Letter to Fred and LETTER TO FRED, though displayed differently on screen listing, are considered to be the same file name.

NOTE   In Windows NT, long file names are also supported in two varieties: the FAT version (like Windows 95's) and on specially formatted disk volumes called NTFS partitions. The NTFS arrangement is somewhat bothersome because it requires setting aside and reformatting part of your hard disk for use by the NTFS partition. What's more of a headache, NTFS partitions can't be seen by DOS, Windows 3.1, or Windows 95. You have to boot up Windows NT to gain access to them. The pros of that design are that NTFS partitions have numerous data-protection schemes built in, such as bulletproof security, the ability to gang multiple hard disks into a group to work faster, and the ability to recover data even if one of the drives in the group crashes. The other variety, VFAT, has been supported by NT since the release of Windows NT 3.5 Workstation and Server, allowing Windows 95 and Windows NT machines to recognize, display, and share each other's long file names on any VFAT partitions.

Unfortunately, you can't create files with long names using just any application. New 32-bit applications written for Windows 95 will eventually support this feature, but in the meantime, when you open and save files from within your old 16-bit Windows or DOS applications, you'll see the same old-style File/Save box:

If you try to enter a long name, you'll get an error message stating that such a file name isn't valid. Only programs designed for Windows 95 will allow the actual use of long file names, so relief from DOS's naming limitation isn't going to be instantaneous.

Windows 95 will translate long names into short names for use by your old applications, so it's not as if there are any incompatibilities to worry about. When you save a file using a long name, or rename an existing file to a long name, two names are actually generated—the long one, and a short 8.3 name derived from the long one. For example, a Word document renamed to

```
My thesis on the mating behavior of arthropods
```

would show up as

```
mythesis.doc
```

under the old File Manager or in a File/Open box of a 16-bit Windows or DOS application.

As a workaround to the file-name limitation of older programs, Windows 95 allows you to do the following: You can create a document file in a 16-bit program, as usual, and save it. Then you use Windows 95's interface to rename the file to the long name of your choice. You can then open and edit the file by double-clicking on its long name or selecting the truncated name in the 16-bit program's File Open dialog boxes. After editing in the 16-bit program, when you save the file its long file name isn't truncated. Looking at it with the Explorer or in a folder also lists its full name.

NOTE   Even for long file names, Windows 95 assigns an extension. Therefore the file name above is actually `My thesis on the mating behavior of anthropods.doc`. The extension is normally hidden when displayed as a long name in the Windows 95 interface, but it reappears in 16-bit applications. (This is an option that can be defeated.) The extension is still important, however. If you have removed the extension, Windows won't know what application to associate it with.

File-Compatibility Issues: DOS, NTFS, HPFS

Windows 95 uses a superset of the old tried and true FAT file system pioneered by DOS and living on more hard disks around the world than any other. Understand that hard drives can be formatted to conform to many different specifications, depending on the needs of a particular *disk operating system* (what DOS stands for, by the way, and is a generic acronym Microsoft can't lay claim to). Thus, installing some variant of Unix on your system, such as SCO Unix or NeXTSTEP, may chop up your hard disk into sectors, directories, boot tracks, and so forth according to quite a different scheme than MS-DOS or Windows 95 will.

Who cares, you may be asking? I'm going to run Windows 95, so what difference does it make? Well, in that case, you're right—it doesn't make any difference. You will still have access to all your old DOS and Windows 3.x drives and directories just as if nothing had happened. But for those who have been running OS/2 and using that operating system's advanced disk file scheme, or NT's operating system, which is quite similar though more secure, you should sit up and listen.

Windows 95 supports only FAT- and VFAT-formatted drives. If you have formatted a drive or partition to NTFS, HPFS, or another specification, until an installable file system driver supporting that format is available for Windows 95, you'll have to use a multi-boot method to gain access to those partitions.

Luckily, a variety of installation options are built into Windows 95's setup program, so it's possible to keep two operating systems on your computer and choose from a menu the one you want at boot time. Operating-system components can be spread out across additional drives if you have them, but the boot information has to be on drive C.

Security

Windows 95 has the same level of security as Windows for Workgroups. You can sign in when booting up, or not. If you cancel the password box, you simply don't get special treatment. If you do enter the correct password, personalized Desktop arrangements, shared printers, drives, and directories can be set to automatically go into effect. This isn't much in the way of security.

What Windows 95 has to offer in the area of security comes in two flavors:

▶ Share-level security. When the user shares a disk, a directory, a printer, or other shareable resource, they have the option of requiring a password before access will be granted to a network user attempting to log onto the resource.

▶ User-level security. An administrator can give a user the right to access all shared resources on the network. As a convenience, such rights can be assigned to a group of users, which will take less time than assigning rights individually. In any case, when the user or group member logs on and supplies the correct password, the shared resources become available to him or her.

In the final analysis, the true amount of security against prying eyes and ill-intended hackers is minimal. The design of the VFAT disk system itself simply doesn't allow the kind of bulletproof security an operating system like Windows NT can muster and that government agencies' security policies mandate. However, because most businesses really don't have to concern themselves with the possibility of sophisticated hackers entering their systems, Windows 95 is the operating-system solution for the bulk of PCs in the workplace today. The lessened security of the system decreases the amount of RAM needed to run Windows 95, as well as increasing its overall speed.

Windows 95 v. the Competition

It is fairly certain among PC industry pundits that Windows 95 will take the market by storm. Market analysts are even beginning to prophesy that IBM might as well be rearranging the furniture on the Titanic as it prepares its next OS/2 release. Similarly, even though Apple has finally woken up and smelled the coffee, consenting to license its technology to wannabe Mac cloners, its days may be numbered.

So, in some very real sense, those in a position to make operating-system purchasing decisions for their business, corporation, school, or government agency shouldn't have any serious head scratching to do. Still, for anyone who's still pondering the alternatives, let's take a look at how Windows 95 stacks up against some of the competition.

Windows 95 v. DOS and Windows 3.x

Though some Windows 95 users will be making a lateral (some would say downward) move from Unix or OS/2, most newcomers to Windows 95 will be migrating upward from the DOS/Windows platform. When I say DOS/Windows, I mean typically DOS 6.x and Windows 3.11 or DOS and Windows for Workgroups 3.11.

The Importance of the DOS

Despite the enormous popularity of Windows 3.1 (some estimates put the user base as high as 60 million), this GUI is really only a shell placed on top of DOS. This is also true of other PC-based graphical user interfaces such as the now-defunct TopView from IBM, Digital Research's GEM, and VisiCorp's VisiOn.

The seed of many problems in the DOS/Windows combo is DOS itself. It truly was never designed to form the basis of a multitasking operating system, much less the underpinnings of a graphical user interface. In other words, all previous versions of Windows (with the exception of Windows NT) have been *kludge jobs*—held together with good intentions and Scotch tape. And as any veteran Windows user knows, the result of this unlikely marriage is that kinky and unpredictable anomalies arise all too frequently.

The most insidious problem is that of a single crashing program bringing your whole Windows session to its knees, including any other applications that were running quite happily. Having to reboot at this point usually meant loss of work. Windows 3.0 was particularly prone to this malady, and the state of affairs was somewhat improved in Windows 3.1. Even still, it was the limitations in the architecture of DOS itself that prevented Microsoft from building a crashproof shell.

For years it's been acknowledged that DOS as it was (single-user, nonnetworking, real-mode, nonmultitasking) needed to be jettisoned before a sturdy workhorse could be made of Windows. Otherwise, trying to make Windows behave was like trying to make a silk purse out of a sow's ear: thus the incentive for architecting OS/2, begun as a joint project between Microsoft and IBM, later taken over solely by IBM. It was also the seed of Windows NT.

In a nutshell, DOS was intended to run a single application at a time. That means only one program—the hard or floppy disk, the communications ports, the parallel ports, the keyboard, screen, and so on— was to have access to the computer at a time. This is called *device contention*. Once you get into running two or more programs at once, negotiation with DOS gets tricky. Windows 3.x certainly had its hands full trying to arbitrate all this, and because DOS runs in real mode, memory space was limited (real mode can only address 640K of RAM—or 1,024K if you include so-called upper memory and areas of memory where hardware devices such as video cards sometimes reside), and programs weren't protected from accidentally walking on top of each other. Because portions of Windows 3.x were written in protected mode, mode switching took up time as well.

Windows 95 and DOS Compatibility

Certainly the reason for sticking with DOS (and for many other apparently retrograde decisions at Microsoft, such as offering a real mode for Windows 3.0) was to provide backward-compatibility—the ability to run older software on newer machines—for as long as possible.

Though DOS is for all intents and purposes not available to the user at boot up, DOS applications are supported by Windows 95 in a DOS "box" just like the ones in Windows 3.x and Windows NT. In fact, the DOS in Windows 95 is, as IBM says about OS/2, a better DOS than DOS.

When Windows 95 boots up, it actually boots a fancy version of DOS that we can call DOS 7 for want of a better name. You can control the booting of Windows 95 in the following ways:

▶ Pressing F4 during bootup reloads your previous operating system (typically DOS 6.x). This is a potential way to have an older version of Windows, such as 3.1 or OS/2, still alive on your system.

▶ You can press F5 for a *fail-safe* boot into Windows 95. Fail-safe mode is a minimal system load that eliminates any unnecessary drivers that might be preventing the system from loading.

▶ Pressing F8 lets you make choices from a menu about how you want to start up, including getting to the DOS 7 prompt, stepping through the lines of your `autoexec.bat` and `config.sys` files line by line, or booting your previous version of DOS.

In any case, Windows 95's support of DOS apps is superior to Windows 3.x's. For one thing, graphics programs are better supported. Microsoft says even squirrely game programs known not to run under Windows 3.x because they attempt to directly address video hardware will run fine. These programs can even be run in a window. The intention was to make all graphics programs and games at least run under Windows and to make as many as possible run in a window.

> **NOTE** Note however, that not all graphics programs will run in a window. Some programs—for example, DOOM (DOS version)—must be run full-screen. For super-demanding DOS programs, you can set a flag that tells Windows to switch into DOS Mode when such a program is launched. Windows 95 then automatically closes all Windows programs, temporarily giving control of the computer over to the DOS program. When you end the DOS program, Windows is reloaded automatically. This may be a solution to applications and systems developers who want to prevent users from accidentally altering files on a network server while they are concurrently running a DOS-based application such as a corporate database front end. By setting up the user's front-end program as a DOS-mode application, all Windows facilities on the user's workstation will be shut down while they are accessing the corporate database.

In addition to hard-to-run graphics programs, Windows 95 was designed to run other "ill-behaved" DOS applications that attempt to write to other pieces of hardware such as the keyboard or ports.

The Windows 95 DOS box supports all DOS commands included in the latest version of non-Windows DOS. When you launch a DOS program under Windows 95, the system creates what's called a VDM (Virtual DOS Machine). The DOS VDM fools an MS-DOS program into thinking it's running on a regular PC that it has all to itself. By default, all the settings in the `autoexec.bat` and `config.sys` files used to start up your computer are loaded into this VDM, so any device drivers such as scanner drivers, TSRs, pop-up programs, network drivers, and the like are all available to whatever DOS program you load into the box. However, custom start-up files can be assigned to a given program. In addition, a whole catalog of session-specific settings to the DOS environment can be made from the DOS window's toolbar or menu once it's running. Figure 1.28 shows one of the five tabs in this dialog box. Suffice it to say there are many options here, including all the ones you may have used in the PIF Editor in Windows 3.x.

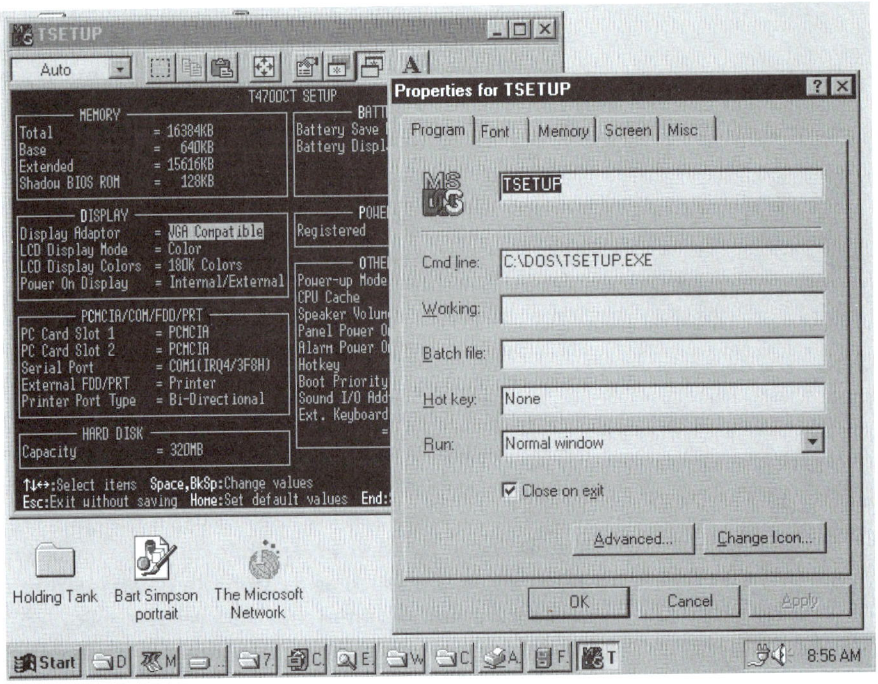

Figure 1.28   *The DOS settings dialog box lets you alter the DOS environment for each DOS session individually.*

Changes you make to one DOS VDM (say, for a running copy of WordPerfect 6) don't affect settings for other running DOS applications. What's more, such settings are automatically saved as PIF files (just like those in Windows 3.x) without the confusion of running the PIF editor and figuring out where to store the PIF file. The settings are reinstated the next time you run the specific program you've set them for. All PIF files are consolidated into one directory, the \Windows\PIF directory, which eliminates some confusion for users as well.

Though you might not think it possible, the new DOS window supports long file names. Though few DOS applications at this point will display them, developers may decide to rewrite some applications to support this feature. The replacement for the DOS editor (EDIT.COM) supplied in Windows 95 does support long names.

Unruly DOS programs that attempt to write directly to sound cards, play with the system timer, or futz with the keyboard are promised to work under Windows 95. This is possible by virtue of how the DOS VDM is set up.

Another nice feature of Windows 95's DOS support lets you display a toolbar at the top of the window (Figure 1.29). The toolbar certainly eases use of DOS under Windows, bringing a modicum of Windows ease of use to DOS. The toolbar by default is turned off, but turning it on gives you easy access to these functions:

▶ Mark, cut, copy, and paste for easy data sharing between DOS applications and between DOS and Windows applications.

▶ Change the font and resulting window size of the DOS box.

▶ Set the tasking of the box to "exclusive" for applications that need to assume control of the whole machine.

▶ Quickly set the Properties for the box (i.e., PIF settings).

▶ Quickly turn on or off background tasking for the box.

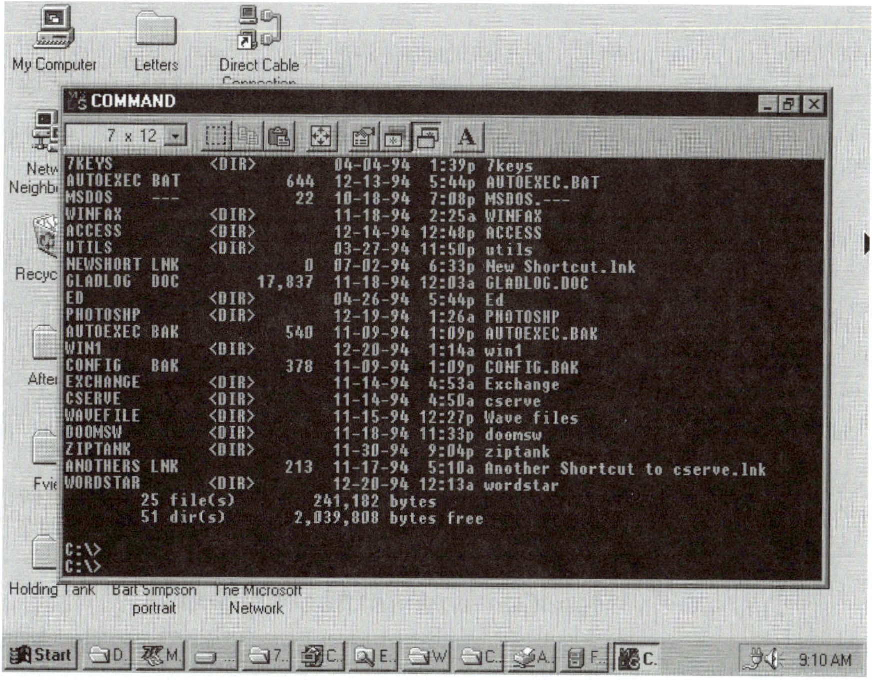

Figure 1.29   *The DOS box sports a useful toolbar.*

Significant thought on Microsoft's part went into determining the default settings for a DOS session. In Windows 3.x, background tasking was set off as a default, suspending a DOS application when it was switched away from. Now it's set on. Also, the new defaults have DOS applications come up windowed rather than full-screen.

One other little nicety is that you can now close a DOS application using the same "X" button (the one in the upper-right corner of the window) you use to close Windows applications. If you declare on its property sheet that a DOS application can be closed without having to terminate it, you'll be able to kill the DOS application with a single click. You'll want to use this option carefully because any unsaved data at the time of closure will be lost. As an option, a warning box will alert you that the application is running, warn you about possible loss of data, and ask for confirmation. Windows 95 will carefully clean up memory resources the application was using and free them for use by other programs. This is something Windows 3.x was not terribly good at doing. Figure 1.30 illustrates this.

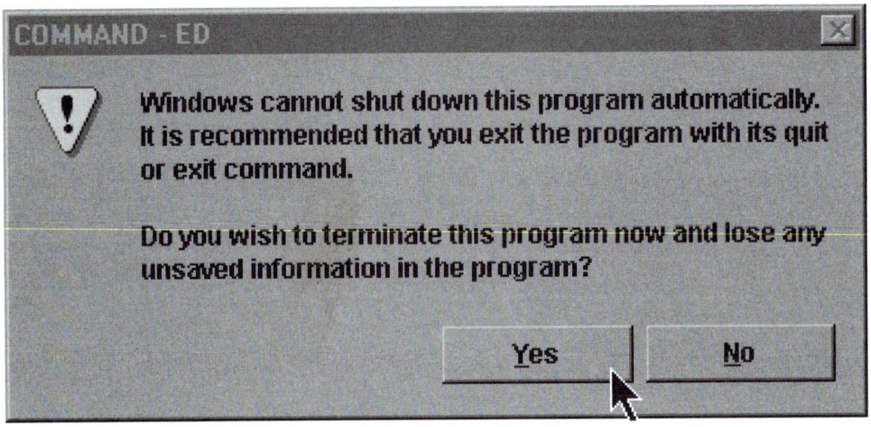

COMMAND - ED

Windows cannot shut down this program automatically. It is recommended that you exit the program with its quit or exit command.

Do you wish to terminate this program now and lose any unsaved information in the program?

Yes   No

Figure 1.30   Close a DOS application by clicking on the Close button. A warning box lets you know the application is still active but you can close it anyway.

More Conventional Memory Space!

Finally, and this is a big finally, Windows 95 ups the conventional memory space available for your DOS applications.

How? Windows 95 simply uses 32-bit protected-mode driver replacements for the most popular 16-bit memory-hogging drivers used in DOS environments. These drivers provide the same functionality, but suck up zero bytes from your conventional memory map because they're supplied by the Windows 95 internals rather than the DOS VDM. Table 1.1 shows you the overall memory savings these drivers will supply you.

Description	File(s)	Conventional Memory Saved (in K)
Microsoft Network client software	net.exe (full)	95
	protman	3
	netbrui	35
	exp16.dos (MAC)	8
Novell NetWare client software	lsl	5
	exp16odi	9
	ipxodi.com	16
	netbios.exe	30
	netx.exe	48
	vlm.exe	47
MS-DOS extended file sharing and locking support	share.exe	17
Adaptec SCSI driver	asp14dos.sys	5
Adaptec CD-ROM driver	aspicd.sys	11
Microsoft/Adaptec CD-ROM extensions	mscdex.exe	39
SmartDrive disk-caching software	smartdrv.exe	28
Microsoft Mouse driver	mouse.com	17

Table 1.1   *Conventional memory saved by use of 32-bit protected-mode drivers supplied with Windows 95 (table courtesy of Microsoft)*

These savings can easily be enough to make the difference between being able to run a program and not. In severe cases, users have had to use a boot manager to load different `autoexec.bat` and `config.sys` settings for each of their major applications, loading a subset of their TSRs and drivers. Windows 95 may eliminate this need.

Windows 95 v. OS/2

Released in the fall of 1994, OS/2 version 3.0—trade-named Warp— has a 32-bit operating system that multitasks Windows and DOS programs, runs on 4 MB of memory, and costs less than $100. As Figure 1.31 shows, Warp's user interface, called *Presentation Manager*, looks much like Windows on the screen. You can run Windows 3.1,

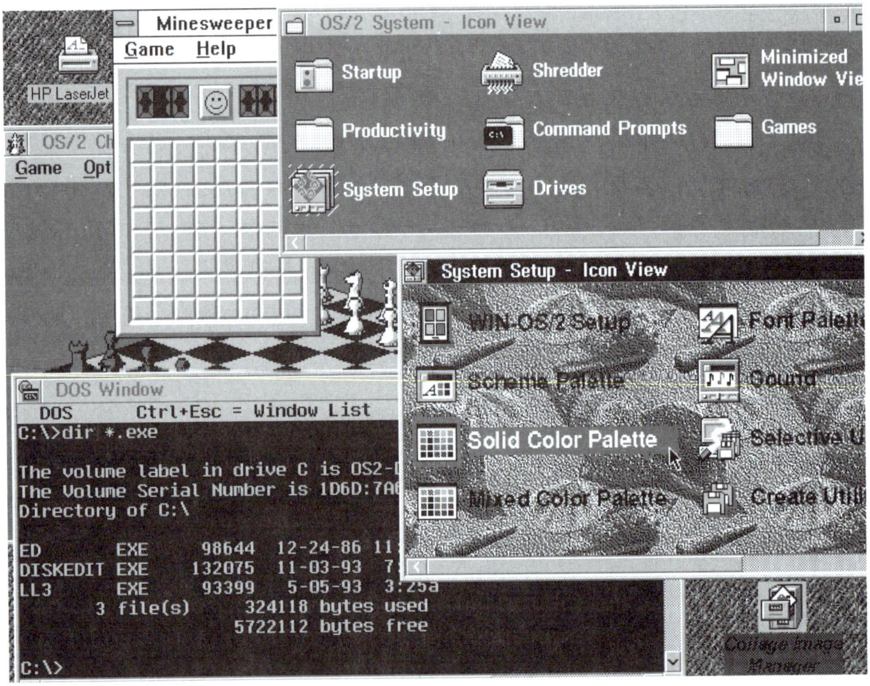

Figure 1.31   *Here's a view of the OS/2 Warp desktop. As shown here, Warp lets you choose a different appearance (background color or pattern as well as font) for each folder and for the desktop itself. In addition, you can see how Warp lets you mix OS/2, Windows 3.1, and DOS windows at will (Minesweeper is a Windows 3.1 program, while the 3-D chess game comes with Warp). The icon at the lower right is that of another running Windows program. You can print files by dragging and dropping them onto the printer icon at the upper left.*

DOS, and OS/2 programs in separate windows on the Warp desktop (at this writing, Warp can't run programs written for Windows 95, but IBM says they will add this capability if enough users request it).

For choosing system options, Warp relies heavily on tabbed dialog boxes, as shown in Figure 1.32. There's even a slick LaunchPad (Figure 1.33) that works much like the Windows 95 Taskbar.

In fact, IBM accomplished more than beating Microsoft to market— Warp actually has quite a few technical advantages over Windows 95. But whether or not these will matter to you is another story.

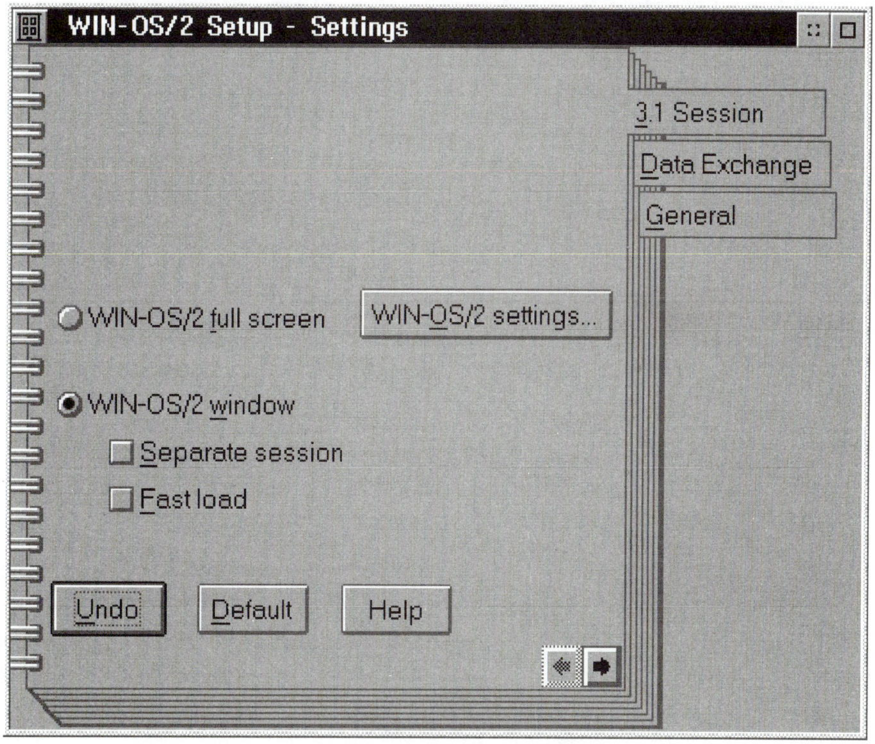

Figure 1.32 *A typical tabbed dialog box in Warp. As you can see, the Warp look is different from Windows 95's. You use the page shown here to set options for running Windows 3.1 programs. Your main choices are to run them on a separate full-screen Windows desktop or within individual windows on the Warp desktop. The Fast load check box preloads key components of Windows when you first start your computer, so individual Windows programs start up faster (often faster than in Windows 3.1).*

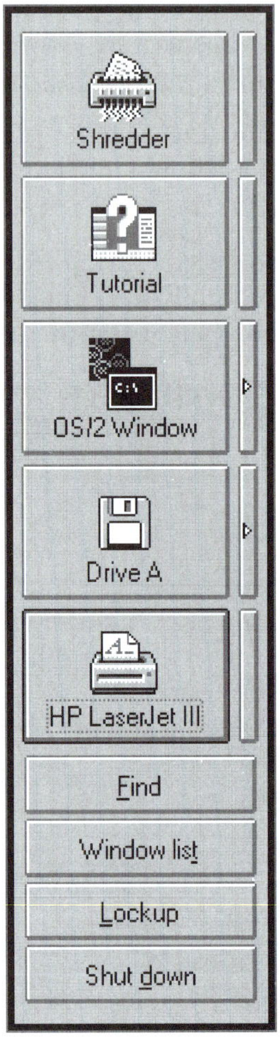

Figure 1.33   *The OS/2 LaunchPad. Along the right side, the buttons that have small arrowheads let you access documents or functions related to the corresponding main button.*

IBM touts Warp as having several important advantages over Windows 95:

▶ Better crash protection. IBM claims that Warp is much more reliable—less vulnerable to failures caused by malfunctioning programs—than is Windows 95. Like earlier versions of Windows, Windows 95 provides a single address space that must be shared by all 16-bit Windows applications as well as by some key elements of the Windows core. If a program goes haywire, it may improperly modify the memory areas used by other programs or by Windows itself. As a result, other programs may stop working, or the entire system may come to a sudden halt. In Warp, on the other hand, each 16-bit program has its own separate "virtual machine." In other words, it is completely isolated from other programs and from the operating system, so if it malfunctions, nothing else is affected.

▶ True preemptive multitasking for all supported applications. Although Windows 95 can run multiple DOS and Windows applications at the same time, it often falls back on "cooperative" multitasking, a less efficient system. Preemptive multitasking is available only if *all* the programs you're running are 32-bit applications specifically developed for Windows 95. By contrast, Warp can preemptively multitask with a mix of DOS programs, older (16-bit) Windows applications, and 32-bit OS/2 programs.

▶ A more intelligent user interface. Windows 95's new system of shortcuts makes it easier to start applications or open documents. But there's a potential problem: If you move the files to which the shortcuts refer to another location on the disk, Windows will have to look around to find them. Warp keeps track of the links between shortcuts and their files, updating the shortcuts when the files are moved. Warp also provides more extensive drag-and-drop control of the user interface. For example, to change the fonts used in the interface (say in the menu bars), you can just drag the new font from the font window to the item you want to change.

▶ Better included applications. The programs in the BonusPak that comes with Warp cover more ground and have more features than the Windows 95 accessories. The core of the BonusPak is IBM Works, which includes a word processor, a spreadsheet, a charting program, a simple database manager, and a personal information manager. Figure 1.34 shows several of these components, while Figure 1.35 gives you an idea of the word processor's advanced features (read the text shown in the screen image for details). All these components share the same basic commands, and you can drag information from one component to another. Other programs in the BonusPak include: a quick-and-easy system for accessing the full range of information and services available on the Internet, a utility for streamlining access to the CompuServe information service, a communications program similar to HyperTerminal, and a faxing utility superior to the one that comes with Windows 95.

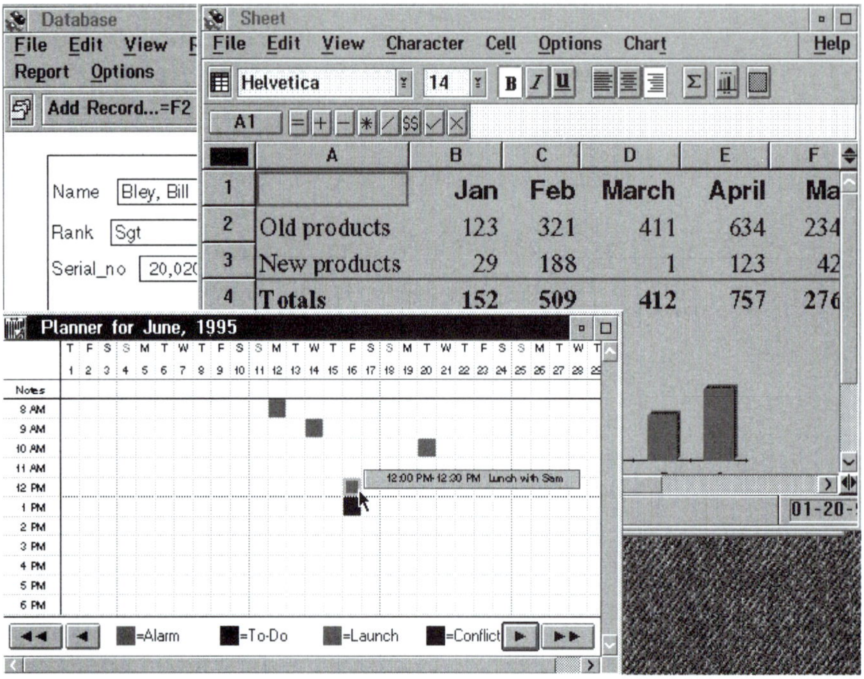

Figure 1.34   *This screen shows the spreadsheet, schedule planner, and database components of IBM Works, part of the BonusPak that comes with Warp.*

Warp's advantages will appeal to people who drive their PCs to the limit. But while these advantages are real, less-demanding users may not find them compelling. Most individual users won't notice the performance boost resulting from preemptive multitasking. Similarly, system crashes are a pain, but they usually aren't so frequent as to cause major problems. And for most people, DOS programs are fading from memory.

The bottom line is this: While Warp is arguably a slightly better product in technical terms, Windows makes the better choice for most people just because it is so popular. So many people use Windows that you'll find it easier to get help with problems and to share tips and tricks with other users. Support for new hardware products like modems and CD-ROM drives appears first for Windows—just because the market is so large—and only later for OS/2. Besides, to my eyes at least, Windows 95 looks snazzier.

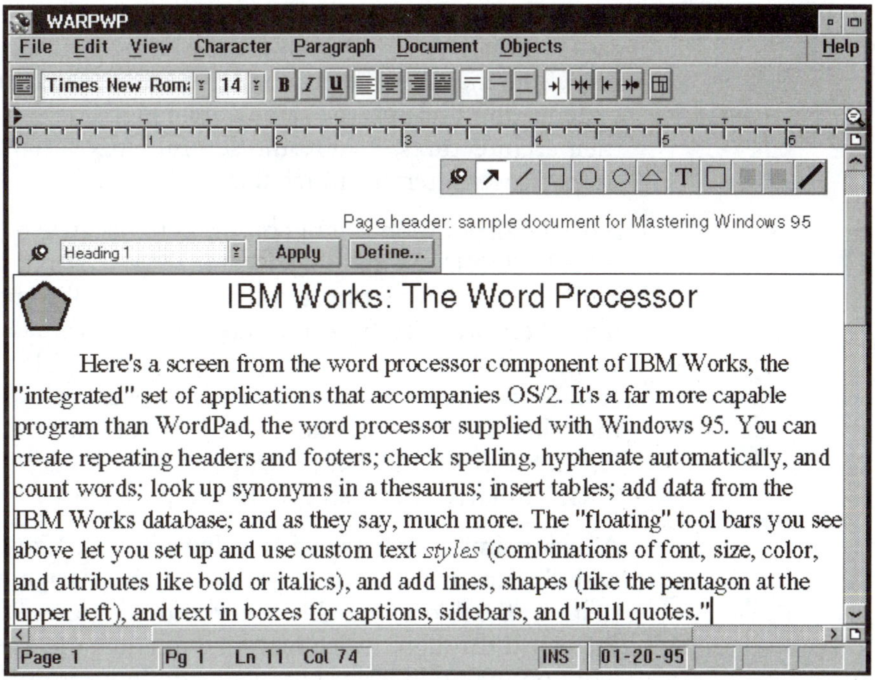

Figure 1.35 *The IBM Works word processor*

Windows 95 v. Unix

Unix is losing its stronghold as the champion of inscrutable operating systems usable only by academics and rocket scientists on mainframe computers. Unix popularity is rising for a number of reasons, not the least of which is the sudden fashionability of Internet. The abundance of Unix workalikes for PCs, sort of bridging the gap between the mainframe and Windows, has furthered Unix's cause as well.

NOTE   Actually, as odd as it sounds, much of Windows 95 has its origins in Unix, as filtered down through Microsoft from NT. Windows NT is more than partially based on a variant of Unix called Mach, which was developed at Carnegie-Mellon University. In a sense, though NT is a far richer operating system, much of the homework for Windows 95 was done in the NT development labs at Microsoft.

During the last few years, Unix vendors have cooperated in standardization initiatives in hopes of Unix gaining a stronger marketplace foothold. The main problem to be solved has been that the differing Unix systems don't all run the same applications because of differences in their architectures. As a result, several Unix variants now have a friendly user interface much like Windows.

Novell Corporation is a big player here because of its acquisition of AT&T's UNIX Systems Laboratory (these are the people that made Unix). Some have suspected that with Novell's upcoming Unix product, which will also be a multitasking, multithreaded, client/server network operating system, Novell might just be able to give Microsoft a run for its money. In case you haven't been following the Unix game, the other primary contenders for PC marketshare are SCO, IBM, DEC, SunSoft, and NeXT, with their products SCO Unix, AIX, ULTRIX, Solaris, and NeXTSTEP, respectively.

A major similarity between Windows 95 and Unix is how they interact with devices attached to the computer. To design an operating system that's as flexible as possible, Unix and Windows 95 both connect to the world through device drivers that allow the operating system to work on many different hardware configurations.

Another major likeness is the way Windows 95 and Unix use memory. Both can access a large, "flat" memory space of many megabytes, which makes programming easy. As mentioned above, Windows 95 offers a memory space of 2 gigabytes per application. Many Unix systems offer closer to 4 gigabytes. Both systems (assuming you're running 32-bit applications in Windows 95) prevent applications from creaming each other because memory areas are strictly separated. However, unlike Windows 95 which will run okay on 4 MB and fly on 8, Unix systems tend to require much more memory than even the older version of NT (NT 3.1). That's to say, more than 16 MB.

> **NOTE** Also worth considering is that a full-blown version V of Unix takes up a huge amount of disk space (almost 100 MB) and comes on close to 100 disks. It also requires significant upkeep.

Contrary to popular belief, you're not relegated to using cryptic command-line interfaces with Unix anymore. Interacting with a Unix computer used to be like using DOS on a PC. But now graphical user interfaces for Unix have appeared. However, because of the open design philosophy of Unix, standardization has proved problematic. Competing graphical interfaces such as OPEN LOOK and Motif operate differently for users and programmers alike. One of the key advantages of Windows 95 over Unix is simply that a large industry has adopted the standardized Windows interface, building thousands of applications around it.

Should You Consider Unix?

Unix competitors like NeXTSTEP and Solaris certainly have their advantages. Unix is an old, mature operating system, not something just cooked up—as, let's be honest, Windows 95 is.

However, the disparity between Unix and the PC world as we know it today is too great. Few Unixes offer the kind of DOS- or Windows-applications support that Windows 95 does, and if your company or group is well entrenched in a DOS/Windows applications mix, Unix won't cut the mustard.

Although there is a huge collection of Unix gurus the world over who have been developing Unix utilities, applications, and extensions to the operating system for many years, Unix suffers mostly from being too huge and not being fully standardized. In the final analysis, if you're looking for the kind of advanced features that Unix can brag about, you'll probably do as well, if not better, with NT, and you'll have greater Windows/DOS compatibility to boot.

Obviously, if you're already previously invested in Unix applications and networked hardware but feeling constricted when it comes to running Windows and DOS apps, it makes perfect sense to install a few Windows 95 workstations and interconnect them via Windows 95's supplied TCP/IP client drivers.

Conclusion

In this chapter, you've gotten a quick introduction to Windows 95. We've covered the most prominent new features Windows 95 brings to your desktop and laptop computer screens and contrasted Windows 95

MORE CPUS INSTEAD OF MORE RAM?

Windows 95 is designed to take intelligent advantage of additional RAM and hard-disk space you might plug into your system. But what about CPUs? If the bottleneck in computing is often because of the CPU not having enough oomph to churn through all those bits and bytes fast enough, why not add more, you may wonder?

Unfortunately, Windows 95 isn't internally designed in such a way that can take advantage of multi-CPU machines. However, both versions of Windows NT (Windows NT Workstation and Windows NT Server) can. While the standard Workstation version supports only one or two CPUs, the Server version can take advantage of up to four. (Actually, with proprietary drivers from a manufacturer, NT can work with even more CPUs.)

Why add CPUs? Adding CPUs is the perfect solution to sluggish performance, which can develop as your network grows, as the applications load becomes heavier, or as your need for increased productivity and throughput increases. Of course, the traditional fix of adding RAM to any Windows system helps, too. But if processing power is what's suffering, only adding CPUs or increasing the speed of the existing CPU will help.

But there's a catch. Only applications that are multithreaded will benefit from multiple CPUs under NT. Without an application being divvied up into multiple threads, NT has no way of dishing out separate tasks to the individual CPU chips. But, considering the lowering cost of CPUs and the fact that now Windows 95 is multithreaded, too, we're likely to see more and more multithreaded applications. These applications will run well under Windows 95 and *will* be able to take advantage of extra CPUs under NT. You can expect to see more multiple-CPU machines, typically with 486DX 2's and 4's or Pentiums available in the near future.

with some of the other comparable PC operating systems available today. In the next chapter, I'll discuss what you may want to know about upgrading your computer system and your software applications for use with Windows 95. Then, in Chapter 3, we'll get down to the business of running Windows 95 (assuming you've installed it as described in the Appendix) so you can begin to understand what the parts of the screen are, how you work with them, and so forth.

Chapter 2

Getting Your Hardware and Software Ready for Windows 95

FEATURING

What software to kiss good-bye and why

What software to keep and what to upgrade

Assuming you made it through the last chapter unscathed, you should have a pretty good idea now of what Windows 95 is all about. Because this book is slated for publication at the same time Windows 95 is released in the market, part of our mission here is not only to teach you how to use Windows 95, but also what it has to offer you, how you're probably going to benefit from it, and how you can get ready for this new darling when it's finally available (most likely in the fall of 1995). But that's sort of a tall order. First let's step back for a minute and consider the landscape.

Windows Extravaganza!

Windows has had a terrific influence in spurring the computer market, both in hardware and software development. Eight years after Windows 3.0, we now have many thousands of Windows applications to choose from, many on CD-ROM (a standard enthusiastically promoted by Microsoft) and hundreds if not thousands of Windows-specific hardware devices such as mice, video accelerators, tape-backup systems, video capture and editing boards, voice-recognition systems, and so forth. With the help of price competition and the free market, an entry-level Pentium machine with CD-ROM drive and monitor can be had now for about $2,000. With an audience of an estimated 60 million Windows users/consumers, you'd expect no less.

Are We Confused Yet?

But the downside of all this Windows R&D that's making the world a better place for us is that users can't follow the technology curve without having a master's degree in science. If they're shopping, they simply don't know what to buy. How do you choose? It's not exactly like looking at a telephone, comparing a few features, and saying "I'll take the green one." There are too many decisions to make. Too many numbers, bytes, RAMs, mega this and mega that, screen sizes, CD players, and then that ever-present mouse. What's worse, people who already have computers often don't even know how best to use what they have.

Hey, sometimes even *I'm* confused, and I write computer books for a living. I've written six books on Windows and have a degree in electronics. Does it help? To be honest, not much. The technology simply changes too fast.

It's tough shooting at moving ducks. If the stuff you needed to run (applications, that is) just stayed the same, and if the operating system would hold still long enough, we could all figure out the perfect computer system, sort of like which size TV or frying pan you like best. But no such luck. On the eve of Windows 95's debut you can rest assured we'll all be barraged by a bevy of magazine articles and advertisements commanding you to run out and upgrade this or that hardware and software.

So, in this chapter, let's look at the story as best we know it at this point. What's the minimum base system you'll need to run Windows 95, really? And then how can you upgrade your system to capitalize on Windows 95's new 32-bit operating-system underpinnings, advanced processing features, display, networking, and communications options? Also, what new software will you have to (or want to) buy? What will you have to jettison or pass on to Uncle George? These considerations may affect your timing when moving up to Windows 95 and may also ease the transition.

What Software to Kiss Good-Bye and Why

First, let's look at software compatibility. As I discussed in Chapter 1, one of the cornerstones of the Windows 95 mandate was to design in backward-compatibility with existing 16-bit DOS and Windows applications. In fact, it was to provide even greater compatibility with DOS applications than Windows 3.x did. As it turns out, this seems to have been achieved; there are going to be a few bugs to work out, but that's to be expected.

The good news is that compatibility with your existing software is likely to be high. Not only that, all your Windows software will benefit from having a face-lift—nicer borders, dialog boxes, menus, and so forth. But there is some bad news, which is there will be classes of programs that Windows 95 won't be able to run, at least not in their current incarnations. Also, there will be some programs that, even though they run OK, you'll probably want to upgrade.

Applications v. Utilities

As you probably know, there are two basic categories of PC applications for the mass market: applications and utilities. Applications are programs such as dBASE, PhotoStyler, PageMaker, or Works. These programs, often called *productivity-enhancement software,* assist you in doing a certain class of work, such as generating textual documents, managing graphical images, or organizing huge amounts of data. By contrast, programs called *utilities* perform computer housecleaning of various types. For example, the Norton Utilities can help you by undeleting files you accidentally erased, defragmenting your hard disk, combing through your hard disk to find files, or determining your system's speed by putting it through its paces.

> **NOTE**   In common parlance, the word "applications" usually includes utilities and simply means any program short of the operating system itself.

Applications programs work at the highest level of the operating system, a bit like a ship on the sea. They "ride" on top of the operating system and GUI software and don't have to interfere with the lower *primitives* of the operating system to get things done. Let me explain.

About APIs

When an application needs the operating system to do something, such as display a dialog box on the screen, accept your key press, or display letters you've typed, it does this by asking the operating system for help. This type of request is called an *API call.* (API stands for applications programming interface.) APIs are little tricks, if you will, that the operating system can do for the programmer. Sort of like saying to your dog, "Spot, roll over," the application can say: "display the Save As dialog box and ask for a file name." Then the application can say "OK, now store this file on the disk somewhere." The operating system then finds some room on the disk and saves the file.

The operating system can do these things because it is directly in touch with the operating-system *primitives,* such as writing to the hard disk, reading the keyboard, putting graphics on the screen, reading data from the COM port, and so on. Because of this, applications don't have to handle the drudgery of system housekeeping on their own. The existence of an API makes writing Windows programs much easier because the programmer doesn't have to write code to perform myriad common tasks that every program needs, such as having a window, having a menu bar, opening and closing files, and printing. The fact that Windows has a pretty good library of API calls has made life easier for Windows programmers because a lot of their work is already done for them. (Even still, 16-bit applications writing is a pain, and 16-bit DOS is a pain, which is why programmers are really going to like writing for Windows 95 and NT.)

But there's another reason why operating-system primitives are handled by API calls—it helps protect the operating-system software from failure. If every program running in the computer were allowed to have access to resources such as the screen, keyboard, hard disk, and ports, your computer could be in big trouble. For starters, your hard-disk directory could get trashed pretty quickly, and you'd in essence lose all your files. Or if you printed from two programs at the same time, both files would go to the printer at the same time (normally, in Windows, Print Manager sees to it that files are sent sequentially rather than simultaneously). The result would be a combination of, say, your 3rd Quarter Income and Expense Report with that Print Shop birthday card for Harriet, three cubicles down the hall. It wouldn't be pretty.

Here's another example. You may have used a defragmenting program such as the one in Norton Utilities or PC-Tools. There's also one supplied with DOS called `defrag.exe`. (It's in your DOS directory.) Though useful, these programs are in a sense dangerous because they fiddle directly with your hard disk. This is one reason you're not supposed to run them while other programs are also running on the same computer. Because they twiddle with the hard disk's directory, as well as moving your disk's files all over the place one block at a time, the whole process can be bollixed up if another program asks the operating system for disk access simultaneously.

NOTE   When a file becomes too large for your computer to store in a single location on a disk, it becomes fragmented. The operating system splits it up and puts it into different sections of the hard disk. Fragmented files can still be used, but it takes the computer longer to find them because the hard-disk heads have to jump around on the disk, like the arm of a record player jumping from cut to cut. This slows down overall throughput in the computer. Defragmenting rearranges the files and free space on your computer and speeds up disk access. After defragmenting, free space is consolidated in one contiguous block and files are stored contiguously on the rest of the disk.

When programs use the prescribed Windows API calls, everything is cool. Applications that do obey the rules go sailing along minding their manners, receiving the proper help from Windows, and other programs that are running are happy too. Perhaps they will have to wait in line to gain access to the hard disk or printer, but that's OK. Spot knows how to roll over and does his job when asked.

When all the programs you're running are Windows programs, there usually isn't a problem. If a communications program needs access to a COM port, for example, it is supplied by Windows. If the particular COM port is already in use, Windows says, in effect: sorry, that port isn't available.

But things get tricky when you're running DOS programs and Windows programs simultaneously or two DOS programs at once. This is because DOS programs were written to think they are the only program running on the computer and they have the whole computer to themselves, including the hard disk, ports, screen, keyboard, printer, and any other resources. They don't know about other programs that might be running at the same time, and they might try to access the computer's hardware directly.

When programs try to bypass the API and directly access hardware that is normally controlled by the operating-system primitives, trouble can ensue. In Windows 3.x, such breaches of system security were often not perceived and prevented (especially by DOS programs), and this is one reason it wasn't a "secure" operating system. DOS-based viruses are a good case in point. Viruses make a hobby of fiddling with the innards of your operating system (typically by altering data on the hard disk), with insidious effects. Windows 3.x couldn't prevent such security breaches because it had no way of knowing they were occurring.

TROJAN HORSE VIRUSES AND WINDOWS NT

Speaking of viruses, here's a little tidbit. If you've used NT, recall that you can't even log on until you press Ctrl-Alt-Delete. Then you see the log-on box where you enter your password. You might have found this curious because these are the three keys you normally use to reboot your computer after it hangs up, not something you'd use to log on. NT uses this log-on command because what it really does is flush out any "Trojan Horse" viruses that might have loaded while NT was booting. A Trojan Horse is a program that masquerades as another in an attempt to capture information and violate either system security (capturing your password) or system integrity (wiping out your hard disk).

Protecting the System from Programs That Circumnavigate the API

Although NT is really the flagship Microsoft product when security is the issue, Windows 95's designers hoped to make it at least more secure (*robust* is the popular adjective) than Windows 3.x. There are several means to this end, but the primary approach is to disallow any program direct access to the computer's hardware. Thus, any program that tries to perform an action that the operating system thinks would jeopardize its security will be stopped from doing so.

In the case of Windows 95, the designers have achieved this kind of hardware isolation by "virtualizing" all the hardware. (This is the same approach used in Windows NT, incidentally.) Every physical piece of hardware in the computer is accessed only by virtual device drivers (called VxDs in Windows lingo). When an application wants the use of a device, it asks the operating system for it via the API call. Then the operating system validates the request and passes it along to the device driver, which in turn handles the actual communication with the device.

The 386's Device-Protection Capabilities

When a DOS program is running, all standard DOS calls (similar to Windows API calls, but invented for DOS applications way back before Windows was invented) are translated into Windows API calls and sent to the correct device. This works great until a DOS application tries to access hardware directly. Because of a nifty little feature called the *I/O permission bitmap* that is built into the Intel 386 and subsequent chips, Windows 95 can detect any illegal attempt to directly access the computer's hardware.

Each time an application is run, Windows 95 knows whether it's a DOS or Windows application. If it's a DOS application, a *virtual DOS machine* (VDM) is created. A virtual DOS machine is a software replica of an IBM PC, providing all the services that a real PC running DOS would supply to a program. Such services would include means for hardware access to the screen, keyboard, memory, and disk drives, for example. Along with this VDM, Windows 95 creates an I/O permission bitmap for the application. The bitmap is essentially a table with entries for each of the computer's internal ports (there are many, used for different things, such as the system clock, network boards, and so on), and shows which, if any, of the ports allow direct access. If the DOS application tries any funny business, it will probably generate an error message indicating your program has done something naughty and Windows will terminate it. Not only that, instead of the program crashing Windows (as in Windows 3.x's General Protection Fault error message and resultant system lockups), Windows will terminate the errant program and keep on going.

Because the designers wanted to retain as much older-DOS-program compatibility as possible, they didn't want to go overboard on this protection thing, so some direct hardware calls will be allowed. For example, if a DOS communications program wants to access COM1 and COM1 isn't currently in use by another application, Windows 95 will allow it. However, some ports, such as the hard or floppy disk's, are off limits.

So What Does This Mean to Me?

Any well-behaved Windows application or utility program is likely to run under Windows 95, no problem. However, some DOS programs, especially hard-disk utilities, may have trouble running in a Windows session. Windows 95's new "DOS Mode" (as explained in Chapter 1) lets you run particularly demanding DOS programs by temporarily exiting Windows. However, just because you can run many of your older disk utilities by forcing the issue doesn't mean that it's advisable. The new VFAT disk directory structure and support of long file names is rather magical by design, and pre-Windows 95 utility programs may indeed stomp on new long file names you create with Windows 95. Even Microsoft-supplied DOS 6.x utilities such as DEFRAG don't know about long file names and will shorten them rather crudely. Running such programs is not recommended, and I suggest you jettison them.

But don't despair. There will be new programs that do what yours did, and they'll run in Windows 95. For example, there will be multitasking and multithreading disk defragmenters with an attractive interface that will run in Windows 95. There are also some workarounds that let you use squirrely DOS programs. The numerous DOS box Property settings often provide workarounds to limitations imposed by Windows 95's DOS application defaults. But even these won't allow ambitious DOS programs access to your hard disk. Finally, realize that limitations imposed on DOS applications serve to protect your system and data against any errant programs, so in the long run it means happier computing.

The other good news is that because Microsoft has built many tricks into Windows 95 that allow far more DOS applications to run than did under Windows 3.x yet still protect the system, you should try each program first before concluding that it's history.

Which programs can and can't you run? Well, providing such a list here wouldn't be meaningful because Windows 95 is in flux. When you purchase Windows 95, you can check the software-compatibility list supplied with it.

USING UTILITY PROGRAMS UNDER WINDOWS 95

Do you have a MS-DOS utility that you just can't live without? Does it access hardware directly? Does it check to see if you are trying to run the program under Windows and fail to run if it detects that? If so, don't despair: there may be hope for the application. Just try the following steps:

1. Launch an MS-DOS box. You can use the Start ➤ Programs ➤ MS-DOS Prompt or any other method you desire.

2. Click on the system control box in the upper-left corner of the MS-DOS Prompt window.

3. Select Properties.

4. Click on the Advanced button.

5. Enable (check) the *Prevent MS-DOS-based programs from detecting Windows* check box. Now the MS-DOS application will think it is running under MS-DOS rather than under Windows.

6. Click on the OK button of the Advanced Programs Settings dialog box.

7. Click on the OK button of the MS-DOS Prompt Properties Settings dialog box.

8. In the MS-DOS box, run the **lock** command. This will give the MS-DOS Prompt exclusive access and allow direct access to the hard disk.

9. In the MS-DOS box, run the utility program.

10. When finished with the utility program, run the **unlock** command. This will remove the ability to directly access the hard disk within the MS-DOS Prompt and restore hard-disk access to other applications.

CAUTION   If you run an MS-DOS disk utility under Windows 95 that is unaware of long file names, you run the risk of losing all of your long file names (directories and actual files with names greater than the 8.3 limitation) and of possible disk corruption. Before attempting to run an application like this for the first time, back up all your important data.

What Software to Keep and What to Upgrade

As you might have figured out by now, there will be at least three, possibly four, criteria on which to decide whether to keep or upgrade your software:

▶ Does it still run?

▶ Is it safe to use?

▶ Is it a Windows 3.x program that does something that Windows 95 now has built in?

▶ Do I want a faster 32-bit version of the program?

The last section discussed why programs might not run. Consider now why you might not *want* to run a particular program. Consider programs such as Norton Desktop for Windows, WinTools, or another such "shell" replacement for Windows 3.x. These are programs that improve on what was a relatively useless, annoying, and confusing shell. They also tend to include a number of useful utility programs for organizing your hard disk, finding files, recovering files, and so on.

Because Windows 95 is backward-compatible with Windows 3.x applications, you'll still be able to run your favorite shell replacements. For that matter, you'll be able to run Program Manager (`progman.exe`) and File Manager (`winfile.exe`) if you're a glutton for punishment. If you've become so accustomed to organizing your work according to the Norton view of the world that going cold turkey would be a hardship, you can stick with it. Of course, you might find that using the Windows 95 Taskbar and the Desktop arrangement is enough like Norton Desktop for Windows that you can live with it. And because the Windows 95 Desktop gives you integrated drag-and-drop capabilities, property sheets, shortcuts, and other such goodies, I'll bet my two cents on people ditching their add-on shell programs. As usual, Microsoft has learned from the competition.

Of course, better mousetraps will hit the market soon enough. And of course, Norton and all the other shell makers will be recompiling their utilities in 32-bit code so they will run faster. There will be new Norton something or other, sporting bells and whistles Microsoft opted not to include or didn't think of: stuff like password protection for all objects or a workaround for the fact that moving files to the Desktop literally means they get moved into the \Windows\Desktop directory. (This can be confusing because getting to these files in File Manager or other applications takes a little searching. Also, if you drag a program (such as excel.exe) to the Desktop and try to run it, it's likely not to work. This is because the application's support files will still be in the old directory (e.g., \Msoffice\Excel), while excel.exe is now in the Windows\Desktop directory.

NOTE I'm still using PC-Kwik's Toolbox (application and document organizer) on one of my systems, just to see which interface I gravitate towards. I'm still using it for some things, and it does seem to work just fine even though it was designed for Windows 3.x. However, I'm quickly getting addicted to dropping folders and documents right on the Desktop, dragging files to a floppy drive on the Desktop, and so forth. After my first full month of heavy Windows 95 use, I noticed that I had unintentionally weaned myself from my trusty home base, File Manager. The Taskbar and Desktop have their problems, but they are well integrated and convenient.

NOTE Microsoft hasn't been totally remiss on this point. Once you understand what's going on when programs and documents are dragged onto the Desktop, you can easily prevent accidental screwups through the use of shortcuts. See Chapter 5 for shortcut instructions.

Other Extinct and Unnecessary Utilities

Shells are only one class of popular Windows utilities. And we've already discussed disk managers that might be thwarted when attempting microsurgery on your hard disk. But there are scads of other utility programs for Windows, some of which you may rely on daily. For example, I have one called PowerScope that scans my hard disks and generates about five different views of where all my precious disk space went. I have others that test the speed of my Windows system, quit Windows really fast, speed up the floppy disk duplication, scour the disk for a particular file, and so on. Will you still be able to run these, and will they work?

Again, because most Windows 3.x applications were written according to Microsoft's standard Windows 3.x API, execution of these utilities shouldn't be a problem. Theoretically, only a program that goes outside the API will bomb. I've been experimenting with a lot of Windows 3.x utilities and have found that most still perform as expected. However, I've begun to rely on some utilities less. For example, the Start button's Find option is worth its weight in gold. It gives you a box like that in Figure 2.1.

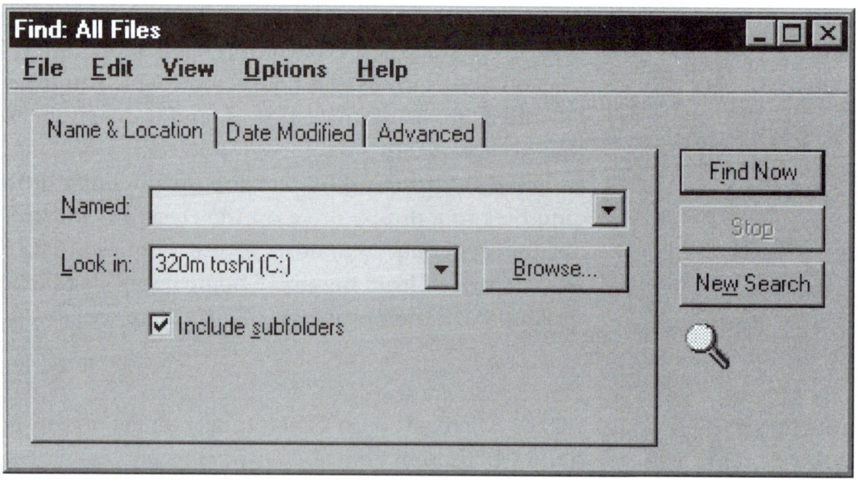

Figure 2.1   *The built-in Find utility*

It's not only always at your fingertips, but once a file, folder, or computer is found, you can manipulate the found object in a manner consistent with other objects in the Windows 95 interface. That is, with a right-mouse click you can run it, view it, cut it, copy it, rename it, create a shortcut to place on the Desktop, or alter its properties (see Figure 2.2).

This is a pretty comprehensive Find utility. It will, for example, scrutinize every file on your hard disk while prospecting for a particular string of text, or list out only files of a certain size. Windows 95's Find isn't the last word in such utilities, though, and future programs from third parties will certainly incorporate the right-mouse-button features. In fact, Microsoft is pushing developers to do just that.

```
┌─────────────────────────────────────────────────────────────┐
│ Find: Files named *.wk3                          _ □ ×        │
├─────────────────────────────────────────────────────────────┤
│  File   Edit   View   Options   Help                          │
│                                                               │
│  ┌ Name & Location │ Date Modified │ Advanced ┐               │
│                                                               │
│                                              ┌ Find Now ┐     │
│    Named:  *.wk3                        ▼                      │
│                                                Stop           │
│    Look in: 320m toshi (C:)      ▼    Browse...               │
│                                               New Search      │
│              ☑ Include subfolders                             │
│                                                 🔍            │
│                                                               │
│  Name            In Folder         Size   Type           ▲    │
│  Books.wk3   Open With...          2KB    WK3 File            │
│  File0001.wk Quick View            1KB    WK3 File            │
│  Invoice.wk3                       4KB    WK3 File        ▼    │
│              Send To          ▶                               │
│  6 file(s) found                                              │
│              Cut                                              │
│              Copy                                             │
│                                                               │
│              Create Shortcut                                  │
│              Delete                                           │
│              Rename                                           │
│                                                               │
│              Properties...                                    │
└─────────────────────────────────────────────────────────────┘
```

Figure 2.2   *A found object with the right-mouse-click menu open*

Many other classes of Windows 3.x utilities exist, of course, and many will not only be operable but will still supply added value to your system because their functions will not be provided by Windows 95. These include:

▶ advanced font management and translation

▶ virtual screen panning and zooming

▶ cursor shape alteration

▶ macro recording and playback

▶ mouse button assigners

▶ interesting screen savers

▶ floppy- and tape-backup programs

▶ virus checkers

▶ benchmarking programs

Again, it's difficult to prophesy just which older Windows utilities will and won't work, partially because Windows 95 is in flux and partially because compatibility will pivot on how strictly a program adheres to the Windows API. One class of utility that will certainly run into trouble, if not bomb, on Windows 95 are Windows 3.x system optimization (tune-up) programs. Tune-up utilities (e.g., WinSleuth and System Engineer, among others) are popular among power users who want to squeeze every last drop of performance from their Windows systems.

By examining computer's hardware and then thoroughly checking out its Windows configuration settings, these programs either recommend changes or actually go ahead and make them. They churn through the `config.sys`, `autoexec.bat`, `win.ini`, and `system.ini` files, examining their contents, rearranging entries when necessary, possibly deleting items, and so forth. They also typically optimize disk caching and virtual memory settings.

The problem with running these programs under Windows 95 is as follows: The configuration files that these programs fiddle with are either not actually used by Windows 95 or are used very differently by Windows 95 than by DOS and Windows 3.x. Thus, many changes such a utility makes won't be appropriate or won't make a difference in Windows 95's operation.

As mentioned in Chapter 1, Microsoft developed the Configuration Registry to provide a centralized, easily managed repository of system and applications settings. The Registry replaces or augments these Windows 3.x files:

▶ `autoexec.bat`, which stores start-up information for the DOS operating system pertaining to some device drivers and TSR programs, declares the system search path, and executes any start-up programs

▶ `config.sys`, which also loads device drivers, memory managers, and sets up system variables

NOTE   For backward-compatibility reasons, `autoexec.bat` and `config.sys` files have not been completely replaced. The operating system will boot up without them, using its own 32-bit Windows 95–supplied drivers for such things as disk-caching, CD-ROMs, drive doubling, and so forth. However, these two files will likely still be in your start-up drive's root directory and *will* be used by Windows 95 when booting. However, when you run Setup to install Windows 95, Setup will do its best to pare down the `autoexec.bat` and `config.sys` files, removing commands that are no longer valid or are not necessary, so the effect is a definite decrease in reliance on them.

▶ `win.ini`, which stores information about the appearance and configuration of the Windows environment

▶ `system.ini`, which stores software and hardware information that pertains directly to the operation of the operating system, its device drivers, and other system-specific information

▶ `*.ini`, which comprises various initialization files that store user preferences and start-up information about specific applications (e.g., `winfile.ini` for File Manager, `clock.ini` for the `clock.exe` program, and `control.ini` for Control Panel).

Compatibility with 16-bit Windows 3.x applications that expect to find and modify the `win.ini` or `system.ini` files is still present under Windows 95. Any applications that use the Windows 3.x API for making `ini` settings will still be supported under Windows 95. However, that doesn't mean Windows 95 will actually use all those settings. Application-specific `ini` files will still be used by the source application (e.g., when you run a 16-bit version of MS-Works, it'll read `msworks.ini` to load in user preferences), but `win.ini` settings and most `system.ini` settings won't have any effect on Windows 95. The only exception to this is the [enh 386] section of `system.ini`, which *will* be read. If there are any virtual device drivers in this section not already recorded in the Registry, they'll be noticed as Windows 95 boots and will be loaded.

Notwithstanding the ineffectuality of some `ini` files, utility programs conceived to fine-tune Windows 3.x do so by futzing with the Smart-Drive, virtual memory, drivers, and other base system settings. Windows 95 not only incorporates new 32-bit drivers for disk caching and virtual memory management that would likely not be affected by these alterations, but Windows 95 also dynamically and intelligently scales many resources to best take advantage of the hardware and software mix on which Windows 95 is running. Therefore, for example, a utility that adjusts the permanent swap file size will have no effect because the swap file in Windows 95 is temporary and changeable in size.

The upshot of all this discussion is that system utilities for Windows 3.x optimization will need at least a face-lift, and more likely a serious overhaul, before you use them on Windows 95. No doubt their manufacturers are busying themselves doing just that even as you read this.

NOTE When you upgrade an existing Windows 3.x system to Windows 95, some application-specific `win.ini` settings *are* migrated into the Windows 95 Registry (for example, associations and OLE-related information). Any preexisting installed application packages—such as 1-2-3, Excel, WordPerfect for Windows, and so on—are noted by the Windows 95 Setup program and incorporated into the Registry so you don't have to install them again. (If you opt to install Windows 95 into its own directory rather than on top of the old Windows 3.x so that you can run either Windows version, then you *will* have to install those applications again from within Windows 95.) After this initial installation, 16-bit applications will still have their `ini` files and will use them to store their settings. 32-bit applications developers are being encouraged to use the Registry to stow applications settings in hopes that one day a preponderance of system and applications settings for each workstation will live in a central repository that can be managed from anywhere on a network.

Faster 32-Bit Applications

Obviously, as Windows 95 takes hold in the market, it will behoove software developers to recompile their applications into 32-bit versions. This will give them a performance edge over their competition and satisfy the needs of users for faster, more reliable, and more efficient programs. Windows 95's compatibility with older 16-bit applications is really only a stopgap measure on Microsoft's part, allowing users to gracefully upgrade to Windows 95 while still using their existing applications.

As a user, some of the decisions about what programs you can and cannot use with Windows 95 will become moot because the attraction to new features and faster performance of 32-bit applications will spur you to upgrade. No doubt many manufacturers will offer a variety of upgrade incentives just as they have in the past.

In the long run, though DOS and Windows 3.x applications support will probably be built into successive iterations of Windows for a long, long time, the impetus really is toward the Windows 32-bit design model. Without 32-bit applications, Windows 95 offers not much more than a face-lift for Windows 3.x. Sure, the new interface offers several key improvements, the colors and screen presentation looks snappier, and long file names are great. But until we're running 32-bit multithreaded applications that have built-in OLE 2.0 support, we're still kind of in the Dark Ages. It's going to get pretty groovy once a critical mass of OLE 2.0 network-aware multimedia applications starts running over the Internet, across your company, or even between bedrooms in your house. In the coming year or two we'll begin to see such spectacles as video teleconferencing for the average home, more very far-out multimedia CDs, interactive groupware, fancy computer-based video-editing systems, virtual-reality games, and who knows what else. Software is a sort of virtual reality in and of itself, and developers' ideas seem limited only by the box with which they have to work.

These developments will affect not only the way we work (and play) but our buying decisions and purchasing patterns. The desire for more functionality in software will lead more software writers to market their software on CD-ROMs because it's cost-inefficient (and even embarrassing) to supply a product on as many as ten or twenty floppies. All of this probably leads to your purchase of 32-bit software just as you bagged your WordPerfect 5.1 in favor of a Windows word processor.

But what does 32-bit software mean? There is a great deal of confusion about 32-bit Windows applications and what will be compatible with what. This is because of the different versions of the 32-bit API and competing versions of the 32-bit operating systems reputed to be capable of running the programs. With terms such as Win32, Win32s, Windows NT, Daytona, Cairo, and Chicago all being bandied about as 32-bit operating systems, it's no wonder.

WHAT THE TERMS MEAN

Win32s: The Win32 Subset API, generally used as the base 32-bit API for Windows 3.x. This is the minimalistic approach to writing 32-bit applications. A Win32s application will run on any 32-bit Microsoft platform (i.e., Windows 3.x, Windows 95, and Windows NT), but does not contain support for multiple threads, security APIs, or a few more APIs that are NT specific.

Win32c: Another Win32 Subset API. This approach includes support for multiple threads and will run on Windows NT and Windows 95 but not Windows 3.x. It also does not include support for security and a few other APIs that are NT specific.

Win32: The full-blown 32-bit API that is based on Windows NT. Some applications that use this API set will not run on Windows 3.x or Windows 95 if those use APIs that are not supported by the other subset versions (Win32s/Win32c).

Windows NT: Windows NT 3.5

Daytona: Windows NT 3.5

Cairo: Windows NT? Will this be Windows NT 95 or Windows NT 4.0? It's not clear. But its primary feature is that it will include an object-oriented file system. OLE 2.0–compliant applications will run unmodified on this version and be able to take advantage of some features of this object-oriented file system. This version of NT will really take the document-centric approach to the extreme.

Chicago: Has been replaced by Windows 95.

So here's the simple lowdown. There is only one 32-bit API, but it's somewhat in flux. Think of the API as a list of ingredients. Depending on which subset of the ingredients from the API a program uses, it'll be able to run higher or lower on the Windows food chain. So if a program uses all the ingredients, it can only run on NT. A slightly lesser use of the API will allow it to run on Windows 95. Even less, and it'll run in Windows 3.x.

However, according to Microsoft, by following simple guidelines, third-party developers have written 32-bit programs (not 16-bit, mind you) that will run on Windows 3.x, Windows 95, and Windows NT platforms with no modification. If this is so, these are programs with the least amount of 32-bit goodies built in, unless they have conditional code (such as multithreading) that kicks in only once they sense they're running in Windows 95 or NT. To keep the size of programs down, software makers are more likely to recompile their software into several versions, one for each platform. You'll be reading the labels on boxes much the way you read the ingredients on the back of food jars in the grocery store, I'd imagine. "Windows 95-compatible" will not mean the same thing as "Fully Windows 95 Aware" or "Multithreaded Version." Keep your eyes peeled.

What Hardware to Keep and What to Upgrade

In the context of this chapter's discussion about "getting ready for Windows 95," next I'll provide an overview of the hardware requirements and considerations pertinent to running Windows 95 successfully.

The Box

Let's start with the basic box, the computer itself, if you will. Windows 95 is going to run its fastest, of course, on fast 486 and Pentium machines. Actual performance of Windows 95 is impossible to judge at this point because optimization of the Windows 95 code (called *performance tuning*) is the last stage of software development just before a product ships. However, Microsoft's advance documentation claims Windows 95 will run reasonably speedily on typical 386 DX machines.

If you can lay your hands on a real Plug-and-Play machine (it needs a Plug-and-Play BIOS built in) *and* a fast processor such as a 486 DX/100 or Pentium, this is the formula for a Windows 95 powerhouse that'll prove effortless to upgrade when it comes time to stuff in a new card or two.

For low-to-medium performance using productivity applications such as word processors, 33-MHz 386 DX machines will likely prove adequate under Windows 95. For slightly slower—but still workable—performance, you may use an SX machine. For more demanding application mixes, such as graphics, computer-aided design, heavy database use, and particularly for networked machines that will serve as printer and communication servers, you'll want to be running Windows 95 on 486 50s, 66s, DX4/100s, and Pentiums. With the price of systems dropping like lead balls off the Tower of Pisa, it doesn't make sense to buy anything short of a DX2/66 at this point. For only a tad more you'll get a Pentium. You should purchase a system with a *local bus*, either VLB or PCI.

The jury is out as to which is better. Add-on cards for VLB are more abundant and a bit cheaper at this point. A new version of VLB (VLB 2.0) is about to hit the streets, so if you decide on VLB, you might look for a machine with this spec.

Suffice it to say that older 286-based machines are now out of the picture. They simply won't run the 32-bit code on which Windows 95 is built. If you want Windows or Windows networking compatibility on these machines, your only options are to run Windows 3.0 or Windows 3.1 in Standard mode or to run the DOS program *Workgroup Connection* (included with Windows for Workgroups) to connect to a Windows network.

RAM

Microsoft has a big-time incentive to make Windows 95 run well with 4 MB of RAM. This is simply because of the number of 4-MB machines out there and the cost of RAM chips. Just as auto manufacturers had a huge incentive (not to mention federal mandates) to make autos with higher gas mileage during the mid-seventies oil crisis, Windows 95 is going to have to do well with relatively little RAM. For the last couple of years RAM prices have hit the roof. This was particularly true in 1993, supposedly because of the accidental decimation of a major plastic fabrication plant in Japan. Prices hit as much as $100 per megabyte. Whether the fire was legitimate or trumped up is another question. Still, the vast majority of existing and new systems are endowed with no more than 4 MB of RAM. Upgrades at the time of this writing are about $40 per megabyte.

Just as with NT, even the beta version of Windows 95 scales automatically and intelligently to avail itself of any extra RAM you throw its way. I'm writing this on a Toshiba T4700 with 16 MB of RAM, and things are flying right along. Two of the other machines I've been testing the beta on have 4 MB and 8 MB respectively. The 4-MB machine does a lot more disk swapping (slowing operations as Windows 95 temporarily writes out RAM data to the hard disk or restores it from disk back into RAM). However, this impact will probably be minimized once Windows 95 is tuned. The 8-MB machine works just dandy. If there is advice to be given, it's that 4 MB is going to be acceptable, but you're really going to really appreciate 8 MB if you can find it in your budget.

Hard Disk

You'll need about 50 MB of free space to install Windows 95, so you'll want a hard disk with plenty of space. Add to this the advantage you'll get from having free disk space for the dynamically sized virtual-memory cache, and you can see why free disk space will be important when installation time comes rolling around. Whether Windows 95's Setup program will be forgiving in this regard when upgrading (many Windows 3.x files will be erased and/or replaced as part of the setup process) remains to be seen. The good news is that drives are *cheap* now. You can buy a 500-MB drive for about $300 these days if you shop. Also, the Windows 95 support files (basically everything you see in the directories) do not have to be on the boot drive. If you have a two-drive system, drive D can hold everything except the boot tracks. The Setup program sleuths around for a drive with enough space to handle the install process and suggests a drive and directory.

You'll want to use a fast hard disk. So what else is new. Well, not every-one knows that the hard disk and video card are the two most likely bottlenecks in a system. Your hard-disk system should preferably be a SCSI II system, but if not, it should at least be a SCSI or IDE type us-ing a local bus controller. You'll want a drive with a fast access time, too, 'round about 12 ms (milliseconds) average access time. (Average access time is a specification that will likely be advertised along with the drive's price.)

Monitor/Video-Card Support

You can bet Windows 95 will be packaged with 32-bit driver support for many devices, including a wide variety of video cards. Even in the beta, support for all generic VGA cards and the more popular cards based on chip sets such as the Mach, S3, ET-4000, Western Digital, and Weitech were all on board. In fact, Setup will run around and look at your hardware, investigating the video card's identity and do-ing its best to load the appropriate drivers. In all four of my systems, this has worked reliably.

However, if drivers for your board(s) are not supplied with Windows 95, you won't have to fret. Unlike the situation with Windows NT, Mi-crosoft says your old Windows 3.x 16-bit drivers happily glom right on to Windows 95. I tested this promise on a very freaky monitor, the

19-inch monochrome WYSE 1790 whose controller card is built around the Tseng Labs ET-3000 chip set. After installation, Windows 95 was running just fine using the old WYSE proprietary Windows 3.x driver I've been relying on for years.

Because slowpoke video cards can bring even the zippiest of systems to a seeming crawl, and because Microsoft has gone video happy with Windows 95, you'll want to lay your hands on a fast video card before upgrading, if possible. The full-window drag (Plus Pack option), for example, is so boss, you'll definitely want to set this option *on*. But if your video card is slow (i.e., it's on the ISA bus and/or doesn't have a coprocessor), windows will then leave trails as you move them around on screen. The only solution then is to turn off full-window drag, which only shows the outline of a window as you drag it.

Of course more and more programs and games are getting bit-blit intensive, meaning they rely on heavy-duty graphics and the ability to rapidly move images around the screen. Because some of the color schemes in such programs, and even in the Windows interface itself, call on a palette of 256 colors or more, it'll serve you to shop for a card with at least 1 MB of VRAM (not DRAM—see an explanation of the distinction in Chapter 31), resolution equal to or above that of your monitor, and a refresh rate of at least 72 Hz, noninterlaced, at the desired resolution. For really great color, you'll want the card to display at least 64 thousand colors at your desired resolution.

If your computer has a local bus, the video card should be one that plugs into one of the edge connectors attached to this bus (e.g., VLB or PCI bus) rather than into the normal, slower system-bus slots. If your system doesn't have a local bus, it's not a big deal. As far as operating Windows 95 goes, even the most prehistoric, simple VGA cards will run fine. I've been using a very old, generic VGA card on one of my systems. It's not flashy, but it works.

Plug-and-Play Items

Just plug in a board, reboot your computer, and you're off and running. All existing peripherals, sound boards, video boards, network cards, and so forth are automatically configured for you as the operating system boots up. No DIP switches to set, no IRQ conflicts, no hassles. Sounds impossible, right? Well, yes, it's currently a pipe dream,

but this is the scenario which, when Plug and Play (PnP) is fully implemented, we'll all become quickly accustomed to.

NOTE   For more about what Plug and Play is and how it works, turn to
Chapter 31.

For PnP to work, three areas of technology must coordinate: the system BIOS, the operating system, and the applications. That leaves out
all existing 16-bit applications, the huge majority of existing plug-in
cards (with the exception of credit-card PCMCIA), and all "legacy"
systems (any computer without PnP specifically built into the BIOS).

NOTE   To gain the "Windows-95 compatible" logo, hardware and software
must be PnP capable. Look for this logo when buying.

With the number of older computers around that do not have PnP-
aware BIOS chips in them, such as traditional ISA and EISA machines, we've got major sticking point number one. Windows 95 itself,
of course, will be PnP-aware, so the operating-system angle is covered.
Then there's the applications. Well, we'll have to wait for the next generation of PnP-aware 32-bit Windows 95 applications for that.

So, in preparation for Windows 95's release, should you be considering buying PnP boards? Whole PnP computers? Definitely. Estimates
are that by the end of 1995 the preponderance of new systems will be
PnP-ready. Ditto for add-in cards. Purchasing systems and boards now
that comply with the spec will save you precious time and Excedrin
headaches later.

In addition, even though legacy systems will always be somewhat
handicapped in supporting PnP, Plug-and-Play cards will still work in
them and can provide you at least half the advantage of a fully PnP-
aware system. How? A product called the Plug-and-Play toolkit from
Microsoft can help bridge the gap. It works on ISA machines with
both DOS and Windows 3.x (and eventually Windows 95) to simulate
a sort of first-generation PnP. The kit helps your computer keep track
of hardware in the system, using an internal database that you generate by entering various existing card settings into the database yourself. Thereafter, however, this utility manages negotiations with the

operating system when you add new PnP cards. These database configuration settings will then be imported into Windows 95 when you later upgrade to it.

There's no doubt that PnP is going to become an industry standard. If implemented correctly, it will eliminate the most common headache in PC support—system-expansion incompatibilities. When shopping for new hardware at this point, you will want to look for as much PnP-awareness as possible, both for your add-on cards and complete systems. Be aware that equipment must bear the full Plug-and-Play moniker (with capital letters) to be truly compliant. And like other evolving industry standards (SCSI, PCMCIA, VLB, PCI, just to name a few) the spec for PnP is likely to fluctuate as bugs or oversights become evident over time. We're all held hostage on that account. A first-generation PnP anything may have a short half-life, but it beats shelling out good money for a system or card that's totally PnP brain-dead. Be aware also, that not all peripherals benefit from PnP awareness.

Other Upgrades

What else is there to consider? Sound cards, SCSI cards, CD-ROM drives, network boards. Don't worry about any of these. If these hardware items work with Windows 3.x, they'll operate correctly within Windows 95. If drivers for your cards aren't supplied initially by Windows 95, you can use your old ones. Eventually, every board manufacturer will supply 32-bit drivers for their hardware.

As mentioned above, if you're replacing or upgrading a board, consider a PnP-compliant one. As of this writing, finding such boards isn't easy, but this state of affairs should change in the second half of 1995.

Chapter 3
What Is Windows?

FEATURING

n this chapter, I'll begin explaining Windows so you can start using your computer to get your work done. If you're an experienced Windows user, you can skim this chapter just to get the gist of the new features of Windows 95. If, on the other hand, you're new to Windows, you should read this chapter thoroughly because it will introduce you to essential Windows concepts and skills that you'll need to have no matter what your line of work is or what you intend to do with your computer. A solid grasp of these concepts will also help you understand and make best use of the rest of this book.

A Brief Windows Recap

Windows owes its name to the fact that it runs each application or document in its own separate *window*. A window is a box or frame on the screen. Figure 3.1 shows several such windows.

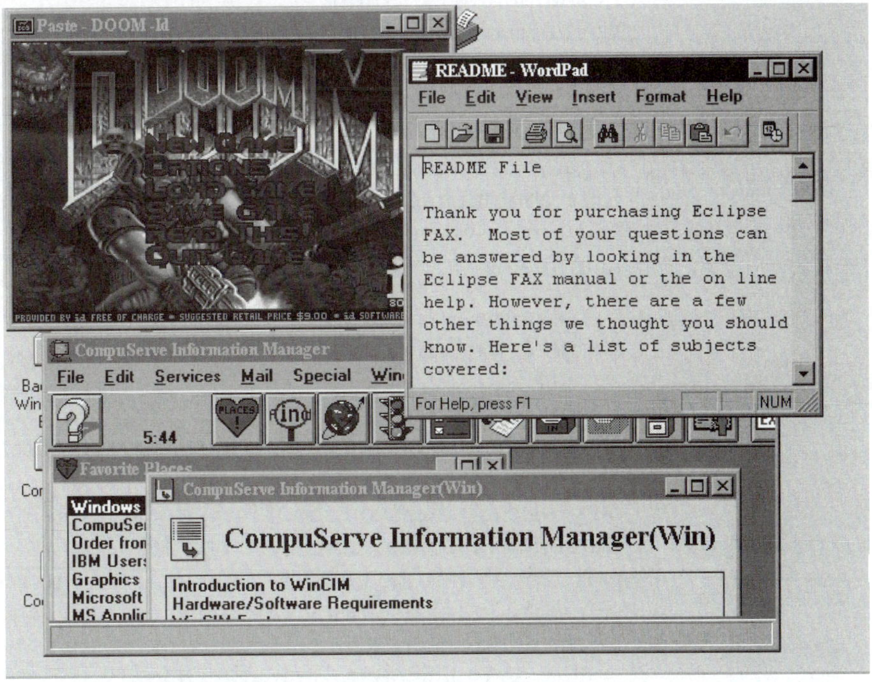

Figure 3.1   *Windows are frames that hold information of some sort on the screen.*

You can have numerous windows on the screen at a time, each containing its own program and/or document. You can then easily switch between programs without having to close one down and open the next.

Another feature that Windows has is a facility—called the Clipboard—that lets you copy material between dissimilar document types, making it easy to *cut* and *paste* information from, say, a spreadsheet into a company report or a scanned photograph of a house into a real-estate brochure. In essence, Windows provides the means for seamlessly joining the capabilities of very different application programs. Not only can you paste portions of one document into another, but by using an advanced document-linking feature—called Object Linking and Embedding (OLE) —those pasted elements remain *live*. That is, if the source document (such as some spreadsheet data) changes, the results will also be reflected in the secondary document (such as a word-processing document) containing the pasted data.

In addition to expediting the way you use your existing applications, Windows comes with quite a handful of its own little programs. For example, there's a word-processing program called WordPad; a drawing program called Paint; a communications program called HyperTerminal for connecting to outside information services with a modem; a couple of games; utilities for keeping your hard disk in good working order (or even doubling the amount of space on it); a data-backup program; and a mail system for communicating with the outside world—just to name a few.

Before Moving Ahead

Before going on in this book, make sure you've read the introduction and installed Windows correctly on your computer (installation is explained in the Appendix). Then, while experimenting with Windows on your computer, you should feel free to experiment (if with some caution) as I explain things you can do, offer tips, and so forth. Experimentation is the best way to learn. I'll try to warn against things you shouldn't do, so don't worry. Experience really is the best teacher—especially with computers. Contrary to popular belief, they really won't blow up if you make a mistake!

Part
1

Up and Running
with Windows 95

If at any time while reading this chapter you have to quit Windows to do other work or to turn off your computer, just jump to the end of this chapter and read the section called *Exiting Windows*. Also, if at any time you don't understand how to use a Windows command or perform some procedure, read the section near the end of this chapter that covers Windows' built-in Help facility.

If you truly get stuck and don't know how to escape from some procedure you're in the middle of, the last resort is to reboot your computer and start up Windows again. Though this isn't a great idea, and you may lose part of any documents you're working on, it won't actually kill Windows or your computer. You reboot your computer by pressing the Ctrl, Alt, and Del keys simultaneously (in other words, press Ctrl and hold, press Alt and hold both, then tap Del. Don't try to hit all three at once!) and then clicking on the Shut Down button. Sometimes you might have to press Ctrl, Alt, and Del again (that is, twice in a row). Other surefire ways to reboot the computer are by pressing the reset switch on your computer or turning your computer off, waiting about five seconds, and then turning it on again.

> **NOTE**   These are last resorts to exiting Windows and can result in losing some of your work! It's better to follow the instructions at the end of this chapter.

Starting Windows

To start up Windows and get to work, follow these steps:

1. Remove any floppy disk from the computer's floppy disk drives.

2. Turn on your computer, screen, and any other stuff you're likely to use (for example an external CD-ROM drive or external modem).

3. Wait. Unlike in the old days of Windows 3.1, the DOS prompt (C:>) will not appear. Instead, after a few seconds you'll see the Windows 95 start-up logo, which may seem to sit there a long time. You'll see some action on the screen, such as some little arrows moving across the bottom or little windows flitting about. This means don't worry, your computer is still alive. Windows takes quite a while to load from your hard disk into RAM, so just wait.

TECH TIP   If you have 16-bit device drivers included in your `autoexec.bat` file, you may see a command prompt instead of the Windows 95 logo while Windows 95 loads. Also, if you press Esc while the Windows 95 logo is displayed, the logo will disappear and you'll see a listing of your `config.sys` lines as they load.

4. After about 15 seconds or so, the Windows sign-on dialog box appears and asks you to type in your user name and password.

Enter your password. If this is the first time you've run Windows, then you can think up and enter your password at this point. If you upgraded from Windows for Workgroups, your old user name and password should work just as it did before. Then click on OK (or press Enter).

NOTE   *Clicking* means positioning the mouse pointer on the item in question and then clicking the left button once. Double-clicking means clicking on an item twice in quick succession.

5. If you are hooked up to a network and Windows 95 detected the network and installed itself for network activities, you'll be prompted to enter your network password, like this:

This might seem redundant, as you entered a password already. No, it's not Fort Knox. It's just that there are two possible password requirements—one that gets you into your own computer and into a workgroup, and another one for signing you onto a network domain. A typical peer-to-peer network of Windows 95 machines is considered a workgroup. If your workgroup machine is interconnected with a Windows NT Server, then the second password will be used by Windows 95 to authenticate you on the Microsoft Network domain. If you don't already have a network user name and password, enter it now. You'll be prompted to confirm it.

> **NOTE** The sequence of boxes that prompt you for your user name and password the first time you run Windows 95 will likely be different from subsequent sessions. You'll have fewer steps after signing in the first time because you won't be asked to confirm your password.

6. Click on OK (or press Enter).

Now the Windows 95 starting screen—the Desktop—appears, looking approximately like that in Figure 3.2. Take a look at your screen and compare it to the figure. Your screen may look a bit different, but the general landscape will be the same. You may see a Welcome box asking if you want to take a tour of Windows or get some help about Windows. Just click on the Close button. We'll discuss the Help system and the Windows Tour later.

> **NOTE** If you or someone else has used your Windows 95 setup already, it's possible that some open windows will come up when Windows 95 boots. It's also possible that you'll see more icons on the Desktop than what's shown in Figure 3.2, depending on what options you installed when you set up Windows 95.

Parts of the Windows Screen

Now let's take a quick look at the three basic parts of the Windows start-up screen: the Desktop, icons, and the Taskbar. Once you understand these three essential building blocks (and one other—a *window*—which you'll see in a few minutes) you'll begin to get a feel for how Windows works.

Figure 3.2   *The initial Windows 95 screen. This starting screen is called the Desktop—the place where you can organize your work and interact with your computer a bit like the way you use your real desk.*

The Desktop

The *Desktop* is your overall work area while in Windows. It's called the Desktop because Windows uses your whole screen in a way that's analogous to the way you'd use the surface of a desk. As you work in Windows, you move items around on the Desktop, retrieve and put away items (as if in a drawer), and perform your other day-to-day tasks. You do all of this using graphical representations of your work projects.

The analogy of the Desktop falls a bit short sometimes, but it's useful for understanding how the program helps you organize your activities.

You can put your favorite (e.g., most oft-used) items on the Desktop so getting to them requires less hunting around. Each time you run Windows, those items will be right there where you left them. This is a great feature of Windows 95.

In Figure 3.2, which displays a "virgin" system where nobody has added anything new to the Desktop, there are four items ready to go. (You may have slightly different items, depending on options you chose when installing Windows 95.) We'll get to what those items actually do later, but you get the picture. When you add your own items, such as your thesis, your recipe list, or your latest version of Doom, they'll be represented by little graphics just like these four items are.

Icons

Icons are the second basic element of the Windows screen. Along the left side of your Desktop, you'll see a few icons. Icons are small symbols with names under them. Windows 95 uses icons to represent folders, documents, and programs when they are not currently opened up and running. Below are a couple of icons.

My Computer   Research for Thesis

Icons that look like file folders are just that—folders. Folders, just like on the Mac, are used to keep related documents or programs together. You can even have folders within folders, a useful feature for really organizing your work from the top down.

NOTE Folders, in DOS and Windows 3.x terminology, were called *directories,* or when used to group collections of programs and documents in Program Manager, *groups.* As of Windows 95, groups and directories are now called folders.

There's another kind of icon-ish sort of thing you'll need to know about. Technically, it's called a *minimized window.* When you want to get a window off the screen temporarily but within easy reach, you minimize it. This lets you do work with a document that's in another window without any extra clutter on the screen. When a window is *minimized* in this way, it's as if its program or document is shoved

untitled - Paint

to the edge of your desk for a moment and put in a little box.

There are several variations on these boxes, but the upshot is the same: the program or document's window will pop up again if you simply click or double-click on it (more about double-clicking later). Sometimes a minimized window is referred to as being *iconized*.

NOTE   Incidentally, while minimized, the program or document will actually be running. It's just that because it's shrunken, you can't interact with it. This means a spreadsheet could still be calculating, a database could be sorting, or a communications program could still be sending in your e-mail while it's minimized.

What Is a Window, Anyway?

Just in case this whole "windows" thing is eluding you, here's the scoop on what a window is and the various types of windows. Because there are different types, people can get somewhat confused when looking at a bunch of windows on the screen.

When you want to do some work, you open up a program or document with the mouse or keyboard, and a window containing it appears on the Desktop. This is similar to pulling a file folder or notebook off the shelf, placing it on the desk, and opening it up. In Windows, you do this for each task you want to work on.

Just as with a real desktop, you can have a number of project windows scattered about, all of which can be in progress. You can then easily switch between your projects, be they letters, address lists, spreadsheets, games, or whatever. This is unlike old-style PC computing under DOS where you have to "put away" one project before opening the next.

Of course, if you happen to be a neatnik, you can opt to have only one document or program open at a time and keep the Desktop clutter free, so to speak. But there are advantages to the messy-desk approach. For example, you can view two documents (such as a spreadsheet and a report you are writing about) simultaneously by placing each document side by side in separate windows that you size to fit on the screen, as you see in Figure 3.3. This approach also allows you to copy material from one document to another more easily by cutting and pasting between them.

Another feature designed into Windows is that it can be instructed to remember certain aspects of your work setup each time you quit. For example, if you use a certain group of programs regularly, you can set up Windows to come up with those programs already running—or ready to run with just a click of the mouse. Programs you use less frequently will be stored away within easy reach without cluttering your Desktop.

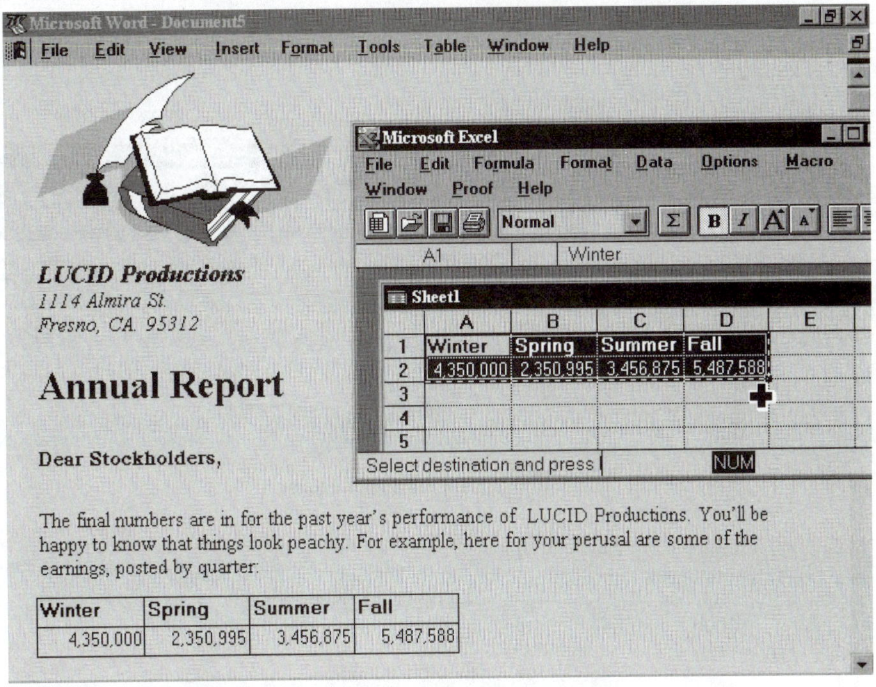

Figure 3.3 *Windows let you see several documents simultaneously.*

Types of Windows

Now let's look a little more closely at the various parts of the Desktop. There are three types of windows that you'll encounter while working: *application windows, document windows,* and *folder windows.*

NOTE   If you want to place a window on the screen that you can play with a bit as you read the next section about window sizing, double-click on the My Computer icon.

Application Windows

Application windows are those that contain a program that you are running and working with, such as Microsoft Word, Excel, PC Paint-brush, WordPerfect, and so on. Most of the work that you do will be in application windows. Figure 3.4 shows a typical application window, sometimes called a *parent window*.

Figure 3.4   An application window is a window that a program is running in.

Document Windows

Some programs let you have more than one document open within them at a time. What does this mean? Well, take the spreadsheet program

Microsoft Excel, for example. It allows you to have several spread-sheets open at once, each in its own document window. Instead of running Excel several times in separate application windows, (which would use up too much precious RAM) you just run it once and open several document windows within Excel's main window. Figure 3.5 shows Excel with two document windows open inside it.

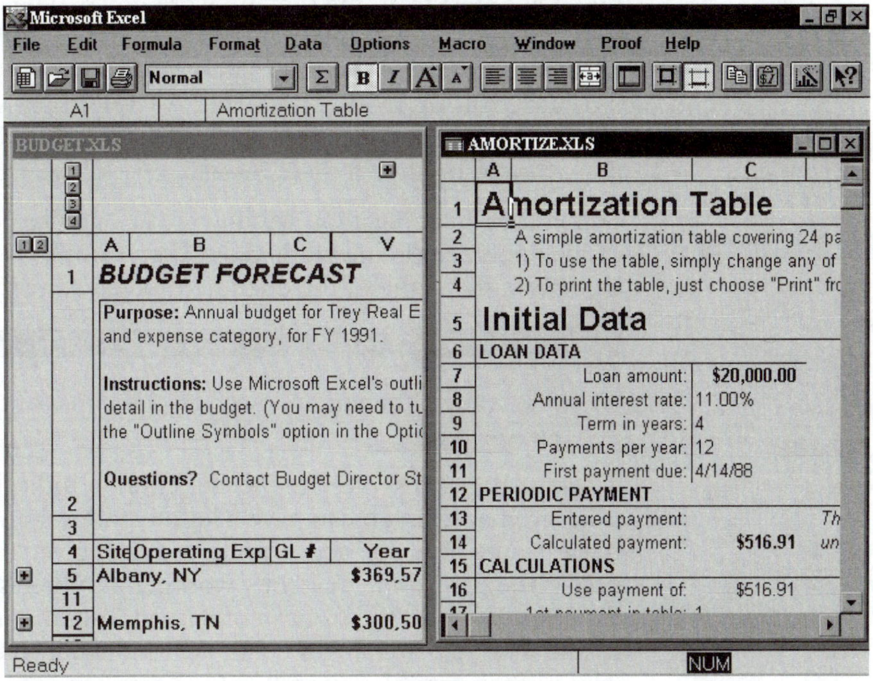

Figure 3.5   *Two document (child) windows within an application (parent) window*

> **NOTE**   Incidentally, document windows are sometimes called *child windows*.

Anatomy of a Window

Now let's consider the parts of a typical window. All windows have the same elements in them, so once you understand one of them, the rest will make sense to you. Of course, some programs have extra stuff like fancy toolbars built in, but you learn about those things as you experiment with the particular program. Here we're talking about the elements common to any kind of window.

The Title Bar

OK. Let's start from the top and work down. The name of the program or document appears at the top of its respective window, in what's called the *title bar*. In Figure 3.5, notice the title bars read Microsoft Excel, BUDGET.XLS, and AMORTIZE.XLS. If you were running another application, such as Ventura Publisher or Paint, its name would be shown there instead.

Sometimes an application window's title bar also contains the name of the document being worked on. For example, here Notepad's title bar shows the name of the document being edited:

The title reads Notepad, followed by the name of the file being edited, `networks.txt`.

The title bar also serves another function: it indicates which window is *active*. Though you can have a lot of windows on the screen at once, there can be only one active window at any given time. The active window is the one you're currently working in. When a window is made active, it jumps to the front of other windows that might be obscuring it, and its title bar changes color. (On monochrome—black and white—monitors, the intensity of the title bar changes.) You make a window active by clicking anywhere within its border.

Minimize, Maximize, and Close

There are three small buttons at the right end of the title bar with small graphics in them—the Minimize, Maximize, and Close buttons.

Referring to Figure 3.6, the button with the skinny line in it is the *Minimize* button. The one to its right is the *Maximize* button. The third one is called the *Close* button. These are little control buttons with which you quickly change the size of a window, as I'll explain in a moment.

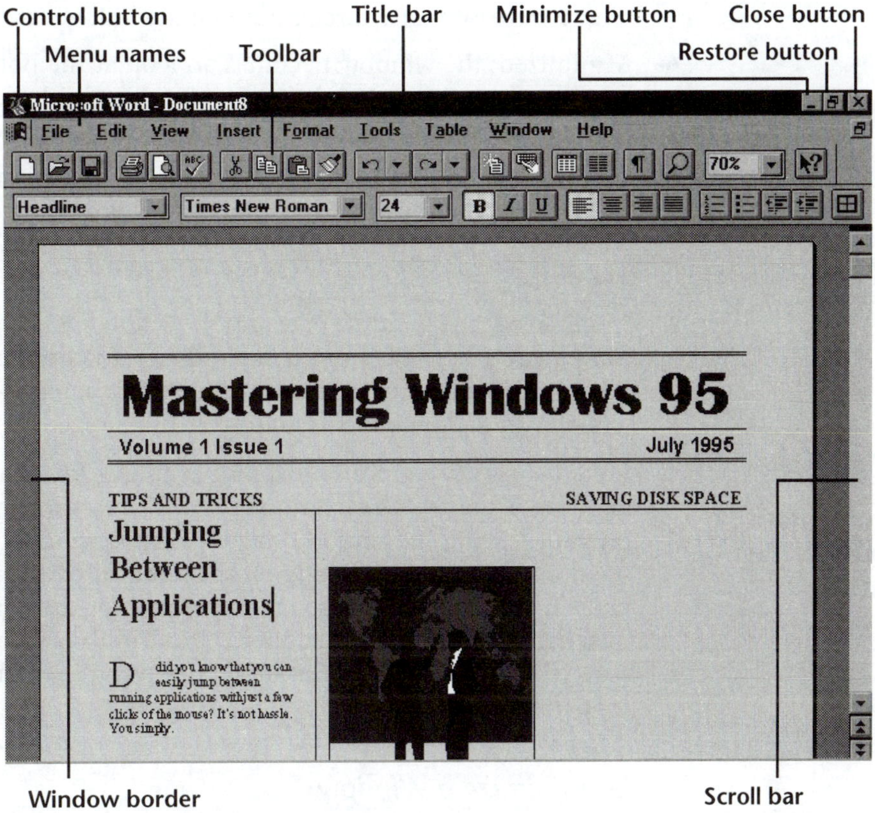

Control button   Title bar   Minimize button   Close button
Menu names   Toolbar   Restore button

Figure 3.6   *Parts of a typical window*

NOTE   In Windows 3.x there were only two buttons at the right side of title bars, and they had small arrows in them. Now there are three buttons, and the graphics have changed a bit. Minimize and Maximize are still there, but a single-click Close button has been added. This new button eliminates the need for double-clicking the Control Box or choosing File/Close to close an application (these techniques varied too much between applications, confusing users). Now you can close any application (including a DOS box) with a single click on the "X" button.

After a window has been maximized, the Maximize button changes to the *Restore* button. Restore buttons have two little boxes in them. (Restored size is neither full screen nor minimized. It's anything in between.)

There are essentially three sizes that a window can have:

▶ Minimized: the window becomes an icon at the bottom of the Desktop (or of the application's window if it's a child window), where it's ready to be opened again but takes up a minimum of screen space.

▶ Normal: the window is open and takes up a portion of the Desktop, the amount of which is determined by how you manually size the window, as explained in the next section. This is also called the *restored* size.

▶ Maximized: the window takes up the whole Desktop. When you maximize a document window, it expands to take up the entire application window. This may or may not be the entire screen, depending on whether the application's window is maximized.

Here are the basic mouse techniques to quickly change the size of a window. To try these techniques, you'll first want to open a window on your screen. If you don't already have a window open, you can open one by double-clicking on the icon called My Computer. I'll explain this icon's purpose later. But just for discussion, try double-clicking on it. If nothing happens, you didn't click fast enough. Make sure you're clicking the left mouse button (on a standard right-handed mouse or trackball).

To Minimize a Window

1. First, if you have a number of windows open, click inside the perimeter of one you want to work with. This will activate it.

2. Position the mouse pointer (the arrow that moves around on the screen when you move the mouse) on the Minimize button (the one with the short line in it) and click.

The window reduces to the size of an icon and "goes" down to the bottom of the screen in the Taskbar. The window's name is shown beside the icon so you know what it is.

To Restore a Window from an Icon

OK. Now suppose you want to get the window back again. It's simple. The window is waiting for you, iconized down on the Taskbar.

1. Move the mouse to position the pointer just over the little My Computer button down at the bottom of your screen, in the Taskbar. (Unless for some reason your Taskbar has been moved to one of the other edges of the screen, in which case use that. Changing the Taskbar's location is covered in Chapter 4.)

2. Click on the button. The window is now restored to its previous size.

To Maximize a Window

You maximize a window when you want it to be as large as possible. When maximized, a window will take up the whole screen. Unless you have a very large screen, or need to be able to see two application windows at the same time, this is the best way to work on typical documents. For example, in a word-processing program, you'll see the maximum amount of text at one time with the window maximized.

1. Activate the window by clicking within its perimeter.

2. Click on its Maximize button:

The window expands to fill the entire screen. If you're maximizing a child window (remember, that means a window within a window), the window can only be as big as its parent. So it might not be able to get as large as the screen; you'd have to maximize the parent window first. You have to look carefully to find the location of maximize and minimize buttons for child windows. Don't confuse them with the buttons for the parent application window. As an example, look at Figure 3.7.

After you maximize a window, its Maximize button changes to a Restore button.

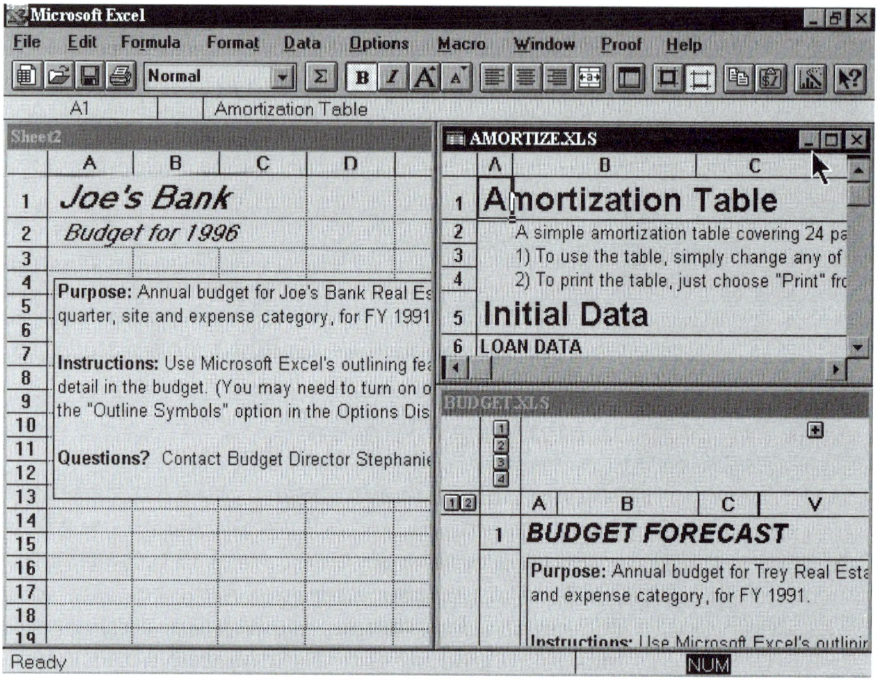

Figure 3.7   *Document windows have their own Minimize, Maximize, Close, and Restore buttons. Don't confuse them with the buttons for the application they're running in.*

Clicking on this button will restore the window to its "restored" size, which is neither full nor iconized; it's the intermediate size that you either manually adjusted it to (see below) or the size that it originally had when you opened the window.

To Manually Adjust the Size of a Window

Sometimes you'll want to adjust the size of a window manually to a very specific size. You might want to arrange several windows side by side, for example, so you can easily see them both, copy and paste material between them, and so forth.

TIP Clicking on and dragging a corner allows you to change both the width and height of the window at one time.

You manually resize a window using these steps: Carefully position the cursor on any edge or corner of the window that you want to resize. The lower-right corner is easiest on windows that have a little triangular tab there, designed just for resizing. (You'll only see this feature in newer programs, though, or those supplied with Windows 95.) When you are in the right position, the cursor shape changes to a two-headed arrow, as you can see in Figure 3.8. Press the left mouse button and hold it down. A "ghost" of the window's outline moves with the arrow to indicate that you are resizing the window. Drag the window edge or corner to the desired position and then release the mouse button.

> **NOTE** Dragging simply means keeping the mouse button depressed while moving the mouse.

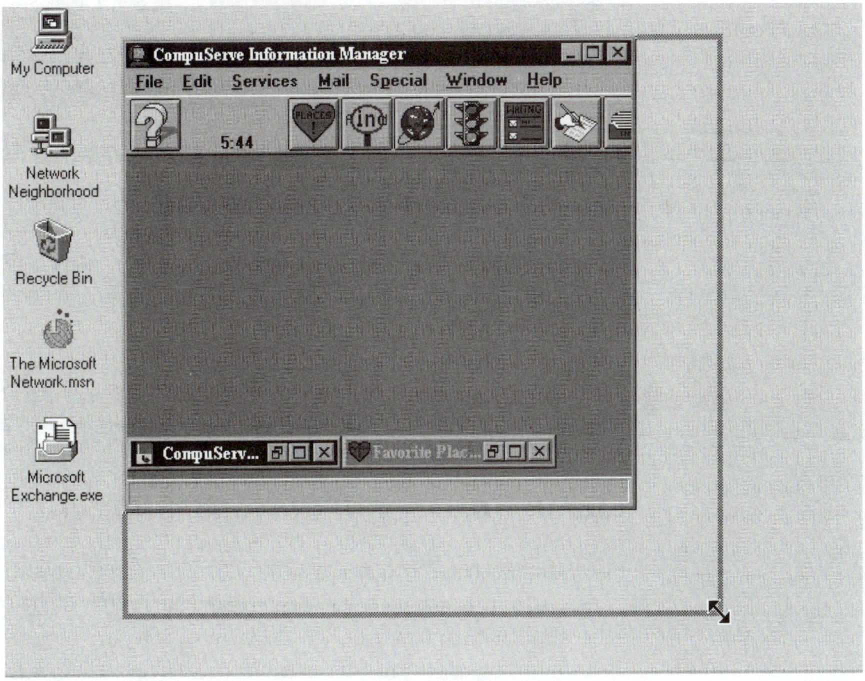

Figure 3.8 *Change a window's size by dragging its corner.*

The Control Box

Every title bar has a little icon at its far left side. This is the Control box. It has two functions. First, it opens a menu, called the Control menu. Figure 3.9 shows a Control box with its Control menu open. This is the same menu you get when you single-click on an iconized window. This menu only comes up from the Control box when you single-click. Most of the commands on this menu let you control the size of the window. (Menus are covered in detail later in this chapter.)

Figure 3.9   Single-clicking on the Control box brings up the Control menu.

Second, the Control box for a program or document will close the window (terminate the program or close the document) when you double-click on it.

NOTE   Pressing Alt-Hyphen opens the Control box of the active child window; Alt-Spacebar opens the Control box of the active parent window.

Scroll Bars, Scroll Buttons, and Scroll Boxes

On the bottom and right edges of many windows, you'll find *scroll bars*, *scroll buttons*, and *scroll boxes*. These are used to "pan across" the information in a window: up, down, left, and right. This is necessary when there is too much information (text or graphics) to fit into the window at one time. For example, you might be writing a letter that is two pages long. Using the scroll bars lets you move around, or scroll, within your document to see the section you're interested in, as two full pages of text won't be displayed in a window at one time. Scrolling lets you look at a large amount of data through what amounts to a small window—your screen. Figure 3.10 illustrates this concept. Many Windows operations—such as listing files on your disks, reading Help screens, or displaying a lot of icons within a window—require the use of scroll bars and boxes.

Figure 3.10 *Scrolling lets you work with more information than will fit on your screen at one time.*

Scroll bars have a little box in them called the *scroll box*, sometimes called an *elevator*. Just as an elevator can take you from one floor of a building to the next, the scroll bar takes you from one section of a window or document to the next. The elevator moves within the scroll bar to indicate which portion of the window you are viewing at any given time. By moving the elevator with your mouse, you cause the document to scroll.

Try these exercises to see how scroll bars and boxes work:

1. If you haven't already double-clicked on the My Computer icon, do so now. A window will open. (We'll discuss the purpose of the My Computer windows later. For now just use one as an example.) Using the technique explained above, size the window so that it shows

only a few icons, as shown below. A horizontal or vertical scroll bar (or possibly both) appears on the bottom edge of the window. This indicates that there are more icons in the window than are visible because the window is now so small. What has happened is that several icons are now out of view.

2. Click on the elevator with the left mouse button, keep the button held down, and slide the elevator in its little shaft. Notice that as you do this, the elevator moves along with the pointer, and the window's contents are repositioned. (Incidentally, this mouse technique is called *dragging*.)

3. Now try another approach to scrolling. Click on the scroll buttons (the little arrows at the ends of the scroll bar). With each click, the elevator moves a bit in the direction of the button you're clicking on. If you click and hold, the elevator continues to move.

4. One more approach is to click within the scroll bar on either side of the elevator. Each click scrolls the window up or down a bit. With many programs, the screen will scroll one full screenful with each click.

This example used only a short window with relatively little information in it. In this case, maximizing the window or resizing it just a bit would eliminate the need for scrolling and is probably a better solution. However, with large documents or windows containing many icons, scrolling becomes a necessity, as you'll see later.

All About Menus

The *menu bar* is a row of words that appears just below the title bar. (It appears only on application windows. Document windows do not have menu bars.) If you click on one of the words in the menu bar (called a menu *name*), a menu opens up, displaying a series of options that you can choose from. It is through menus that you tell all Windows programs what actions you want carried out.

Try this as an example:

1. With the My Computer window open and active, click on the word *File* in the menu bar. A menu opens, as you see in Figure 3.11, listing seven options. You can see why it's called a menu; it's a bit like a restaurant menu listing things you can order.

> **TECH TIP**   You could also have pressed Alt-F to open the File menu. If there is an underlined letter in any menu's name, holding down the Alt key and pressing that letter opens the menu.

Figure 3.11   *Open a menu by clicking on its name in the menu bar.*

2. Slide the mouse pointer to the right to open the other menus (Edit, View, or Help) and examine their choices.

As you might surmise, each menu contains choices somewhat relevant to the menu's name. The names on menus vary from program to program, but there are usually a few common ones, such as File, Edit, and Help. It may take a while for you to become familiar with the commands and which menus they're located on, but it will become more automatic with time. In any case, it's easy enough to look around through the menus to find the one you want.

Selecting Menu Commands

Once a menu is open, you can select any of the commands in the menu that aren't dimmed (dimmed choices are explained below).

NOTE   At this point, don't select any of the commands just yet. We'll begin using the commands in a bit.

When a menu is open, you can select a menu command in any of these ways:

▶ By typing the underlined letter in the command name

▶ By sliding the mouse down and clicking on a command's name

▶ By pressing the down-arrow or up-arrow keys on your keyboard to highlight the desired command name and then pressing Enter

You can cancel a menu (that is, make the menu disappear without selecting any commands) by simply pressing the Esc key or by clicking anywhere outside of the menu.

Special Indicators in Menus

Menus often have special symbols that tell you a little more about the menu commands. For example, examine the menus in Figure 3.12. Notice that many of these commands have additional words or symbols next to the command name. For example, the Options command has ellipses (three dots) after it. Other commands may have check marks, triangles, or key combinations listed beside them. Here are the meanings of these words or symbols:

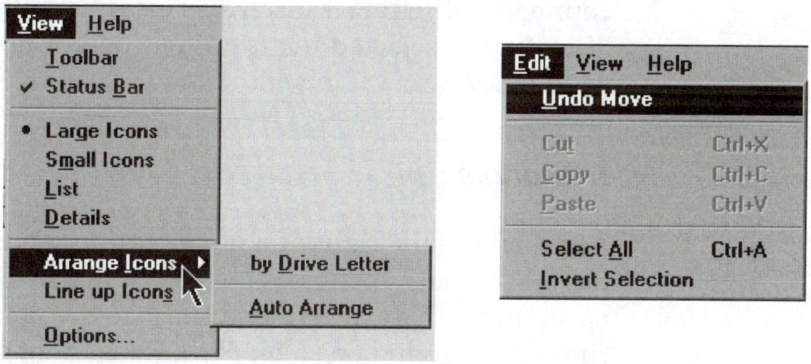

Figure 3.12   *Typical menus*

A Grayed (Dimmed) Command Name

When a command is shown as *grayed*, or *dimmed*, it means that this choice is not currently available to you. A command can be dimmed for a number of reasons. For example, a command for changing the typestyle of text will be grayed if you haven't selected any text. Other times, commands will be grayed because you are in the wrong program mode. For example, if a window is already maximized, the Maximize command on the Control menu will be dimmed because this choice doesn't make sense.

Ellipses (…)

Ellipses next to a command means that you will be asked for additional information before Windows or the Windows application executes the command. When you select such a command, a dialog box will appear on the screen, asking you to fill in the needed information. (I'll discuss dialog boxes in the next section of this chapter.)

A Check Mark (✓)

A check mark preceding a command means the command is a *toggle* that is activated (turned on). A toggle is a command that is alternately turned off and on each time you select it. It's like those old high-beam switches on the car floor that you step on to change between high beams and low beams. Each time you select one of these commands, it switches from *active* to *inactive*. If there is no check mark, then the command or setting is inactive. This is typically used to indicate things like whether selected text is underlined or not, which font is selected, what mode you are in within a program, and so on.

A Triangle (▶)

A triangle to the right of a menu command means that the command has additional subchoices for you to make. This is called a *cascading menu* (because the next menu starts to the right of the previous one and runs down from there, a bit like a waterfall of menus). You make selections from a cascaded menu the same way you would from a normal menu. The lower-left example in Figure 3.12 shows a cascaded menu. The Taskbar also uses cascading menus, but we'll get to that in a moment.

A Dot

A dot to the left of the command means that the option is currently selected and is an exclusive option among several related options. For example, in Figure 3.12, the center section of one of the menus contains the options Large icons, Small icons, List, and Details. Only one of these options can be selected at a time. The dot indicates the current setting. By simply opening the menu again and clicking on one of the other options, you set that option on.

A Key Combination

Some menu commands list keystrokes that can be used instead of opening the menu and choosing that command. For example, in the My Computer's Edit menu, shown below, notice that the Cut command could be executed by Ctrl-X, the Copy command could be executed by pressing Ctrl-C, and the Paste command with Ctrl-V. These alternative time-saving keystrokes are called *shortcut keys*. (Don't worry if you don't understand these commands yet. They will be explained later.)

Edit	View	Help	
Undo Move			
Cut			Ctrl+X
Copy			Ctrl+C
Paste			Ctrl+V
Select **A**ll			Ctrl+A
Invert Selection			

NOTE   A keystroke abbreviation such as Ctrl-C means to hold down the Ctrl key (typically found in the lower-left corner of your keyboard) while pressing the C key.

All About Dialog Boxes

As I said above, a dialog box will always appear when you select a command with ellipses (…) after it. Dialog boxes pop up on your screen when Windows or the Windows application program you're using needs more information before continuing. Some dialog boxes ask you to enter information (such as file names), while others simply require you to check off options or make choices from a list. The list may be in the form of additional sub-dialog boxes or submenus. In any case, after you enter the requested information, you click on OK, and Windows or the application program continues on its merry way, executing the command.

Though most dialog boxes ask you for information, other boxes are only informative, alerting you to a problem with your system or an error you've made. Such a box might also request confirmation on a command that could have dire consequences or explain why the command you've chosen can't be executed. These alert boxes sometimes have a big letter *i* (for "information") in them, or an exclamation mark (!). A few examples are shown in Figure 3.13.

More often than not, these boxes only ask you to read them and then click on OK (or cancel them if you decide not to proceed). Some boxes only have an OK button. Let's look at some typical dialog boxes and see how they work.

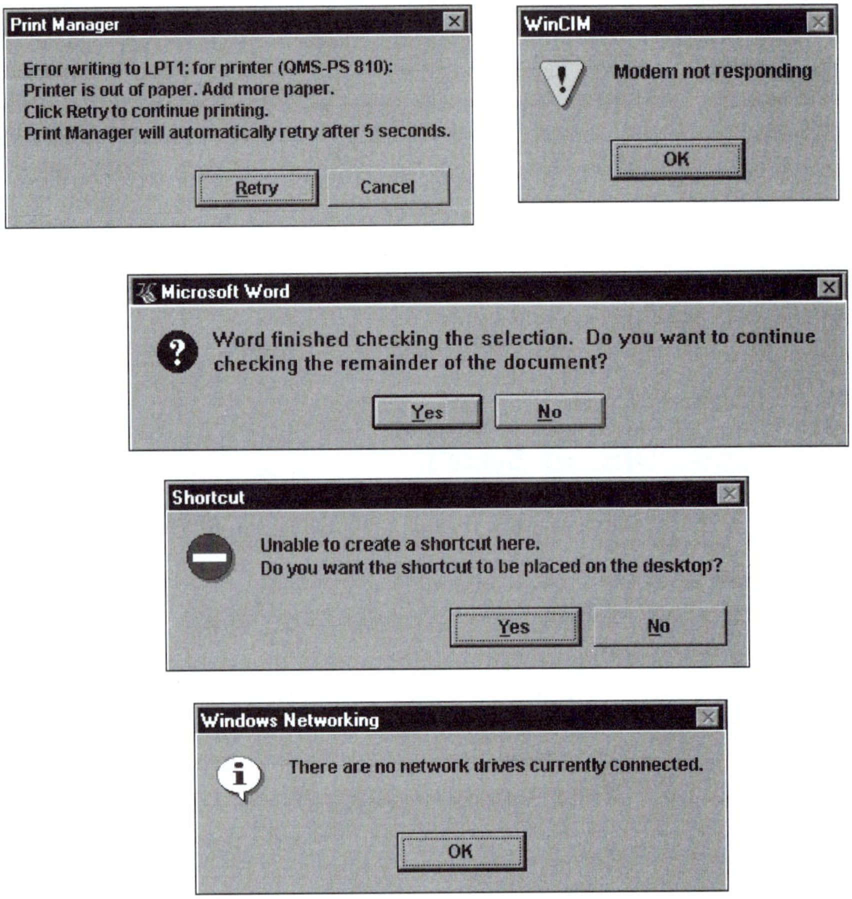

Figure 3.13   *Dialog boxes are used for a wide variety of purposes. Here are some examples of dialog boxes that are informative only and do not ask you to make settings or adjust options.*

Moving between Sections of a Dialog Box

As you can see in Figure 3.14, dialog boxes often have several sections to them. You can move between the sections in three ways:

▶ The easiest way is by clicking on the section you want to alter.

▶ If you are using the keyboard, you can press the Tab key to move between sections and press the Spacebar to select them.

▶ You can also use the Alt key with the underlined letter of the section name you want to jump to or activate. Even when you are using a mouse, the Alt-key combinations are sometimes the fastest way to jump between sections or choose an option within a box.

Notice that one of the dialog boxes here has a Preview section. This is a feature that more and more dialog boxes will be sporting as applications become more *user friendly*. Rather than having to choose a formatting change, for example, and then okaying the dialog box to see the effect on your document, a Preview section lets you see the effect in advance. This lets you "shop" for the effect you want before committing to it.

Many newer Windows programs have dialog boxes with *tab pages*, a new item introduced around the time of Windows 95. I discussed this feature somewhat in Chapter 1 but will mention it here in the context of dialog boxes. Tab pages keep a dialog box to a reasonable size while still letting you adjust a lot of settings from it. To get to the page of settings you want, just click on the tab with the correct name. Figure 3.15 illustrates this concept. I've clicked on the View menu of Word's Options dialog box.

Entering Information in a Dialog Box

Now let's consider how you enter information into dialog boxes. There are seven basic types of sections in dialog boxes:

▶ text boxes

▶ check boxes

▶ option buttons

▶ command buttons

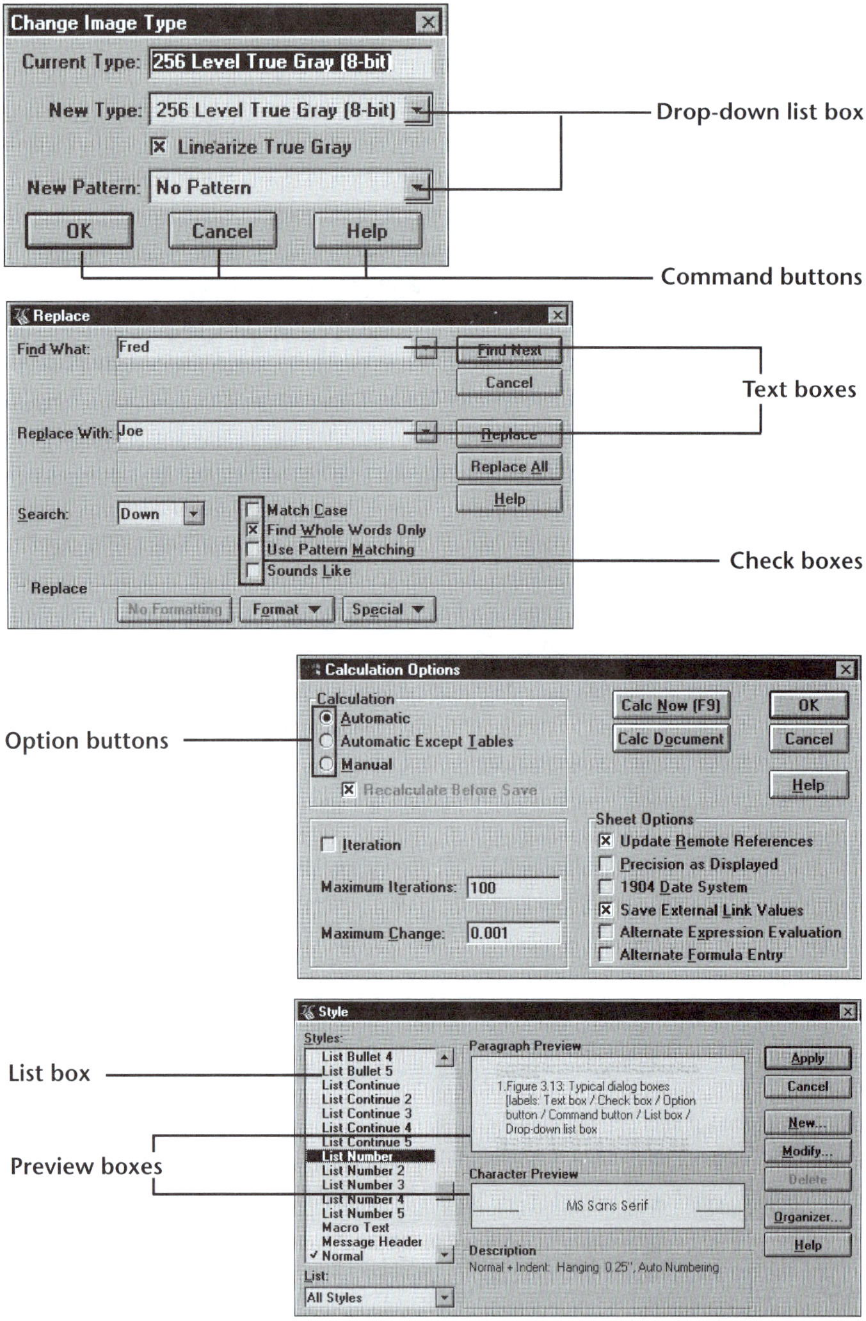

Figure 3.14   *Typical dialog boxes*

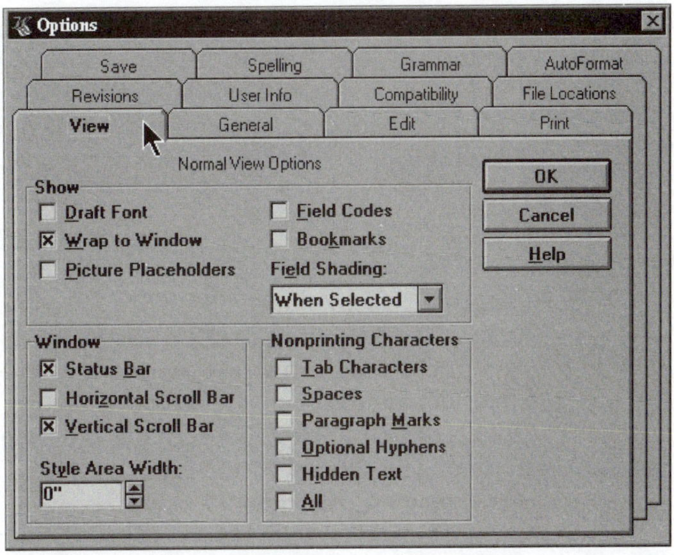

Figure 3.15   *Newer dialog boxes have multiple tabs that make the boxes easier to understand and appear less cluttered. Click on a tab, and a new set of options appears.*

▶ list boxes

▶ drop-down list boxes

▶ file dialog boxes

Once you've jumped to the correct section, you'll need to know how to make choices from it. The next several sections explain how to use each kind. (Please refer to Figure 3.14 during the next discussions.)

Text Boxes

In this sort of section, you are asked to type in text from the keyboard. Sometimes there will be text already typed in for you. If you want to keep it as is, just leave it alone. To alter the text, simply type in new text. If the existing text is already highlighted, then the first key you press will delete the existing entry. If it is not highlighted, you can backspace over it to erase it. You can also edit existing text. Clicking once on highlighted text will *deselect* it and cause the *text cursor* (a vertical blinking bar) to appear when you put the pointer inside the text area. You can then move the text cursor around using the arrow keys or the mouse and insert text (by typing) or delete text (by pressing the Del key). Text is inserted at the position of the text cursor. Text boxes are most often used for specifying file names when you are saving or loading documents and applications or specifying text to search for in a word-processing document.

Check Boxes

Check boxes are the small square (or sometimes diamond-shaped) boxes. They are used to indicate nonexclusive options. For example, you might want some text to appear as bold *and* underlined. Or, as another example, consider the Calculation Options dialog box from Excel shown in Figure 3.14. In this box, you can have any of the settings in the Sheet Options section set on or off. These are toggle settings (as explained previously) that you activate or deactivate by clicking on the box. When the box is empty, the option is off; when you see an ×, the option is on.

Option Buttons

Unlike check boxes, which are nonexclusive, option buttons are exclusive settings. Sometimes called *radio buttons*, these are also round rather than square or diamond shaped, and only one option can be set on at a time. For example, using the same Calculation Options dialog box referred to above, you may select Automatic, Automatic Except Tables, *or* Manual in the Calculation section of the dialog box—not a combination of the three. Clicking on the desired button turns it on (the circle will be filled) and turns any previous selection off. From the keyboard, you first jump to the section, then use the arrow keys to select the option.

Command Buttons

Command buttons are like option buttons except that they are used to execute a command immediately. They are also rectangular rather than square or circular. An example of a command button is the OK button found on almost every dialog box. Once you've filled in a dialog box to your liking, click on the OK button, and Windows or the application executes the settings you've selected. If you change your mind and don't want the new commands on the dialog box executed, click on the Cancel button.

There is always a command button that has a thicker border; this is the command that will execute if you press Enter. Likewise, pressing the Esc key always has the same effect as clicking on the Cancel button (that's why there's no underlined letter on the Cancel button).

Some command buttons are followed by ellipses (...). As you might expect, these commands will open additional dialog boxes for adjusting more settings. Other command buttons include two >> symbols in them. Choosing this type of button causes the particular section of the dialog box to expand so you can make more selections.

List Boxes

List boxes are like menus. They show you a list of options or items from which you can choose. For example, when choosing fonts to display or print text in, WordPad shows you a list box. You make a selection from a list box the same way you do from a menu: by just clicking on it. From the keyboard, highlight the desired option with the arrow keys and then press Enter to choose it. Some list boxes are too small to show all the possible selections. In this case, there will be a scroll bar on the right side of the box. Use the scroll bar to see all the selections. Some list boxes let you make more than one selection, but most only allow one. To make more than one selection from the keyboard, press the Spacebar to select or deselect any item.

TECH TIP   You can quickly jump to an option in a list box by typing the first letter of its name. If there are two choices with the same first letter and you want the second one, press the letter again, or press the down-arrow key.

Drop-Down List Boxes

Drop-down list boxes are indicated by a small arrow in a box to the right of the option. The current setting is displayed to the left of the little arrow. Clicking on the arrow opens a list that works just like a normal list box and has scroll bars if there are a lot of options. Drop-down list boxes are used when a dialog box is too crowded to accommodate regular list boxes.

File Dialog Boxes

A dialog box like one of the three shown in Figure 3.16 often appears when you're working in Windows programs. This type of box is called a *file dialog box* or simply *file box*. Though used in a variety of situations, you're most likely to run into file boxes when you want to open a file or when you save a document for the first time. For example, choosing File ➤ Open from almost any Windows program will bring up such a box asking which document file you want to open.

> **NOTE**　If you're new to Windows, you may want to mark this section with a paper clip and refer back to it when you have to save or open a file for the first time.

File dialog boxes vary somewhat from program to program, even though they perform the same job. Some boxes, as you will note in the figure, allow you to open a file as Read Only, for example, or help you search for a file with a Find button or a Network button (if you're connected to a network). The file box went through a major redesign by Microsoft after they finally figured out that novices were thoroughly confused by it. Now the new design is much more intuitively obvious and is very similar to the file boxes used on the Mac. Because the older two boxes and new type are pretty different from one another, I'll explain the steps for each separately, starting with the two older-style files boxes.

The two older-style boxes (which 16-bit Windows 3.x applications will use) are divided into two main sections, listing files on the left and directories on the right. In most applications, directories are represented by a folder. In really old programs you only see the directory's name enclosed in brackets, like this:

    [cserve]

Using Older-Style File Boxes　Here are the steps you can take to use these older boxes. If you know how to run a program (we'll cover that in the next chapter), you might try running a 16-bit program, opening its File menu, and choosing Open to experiment a bit.

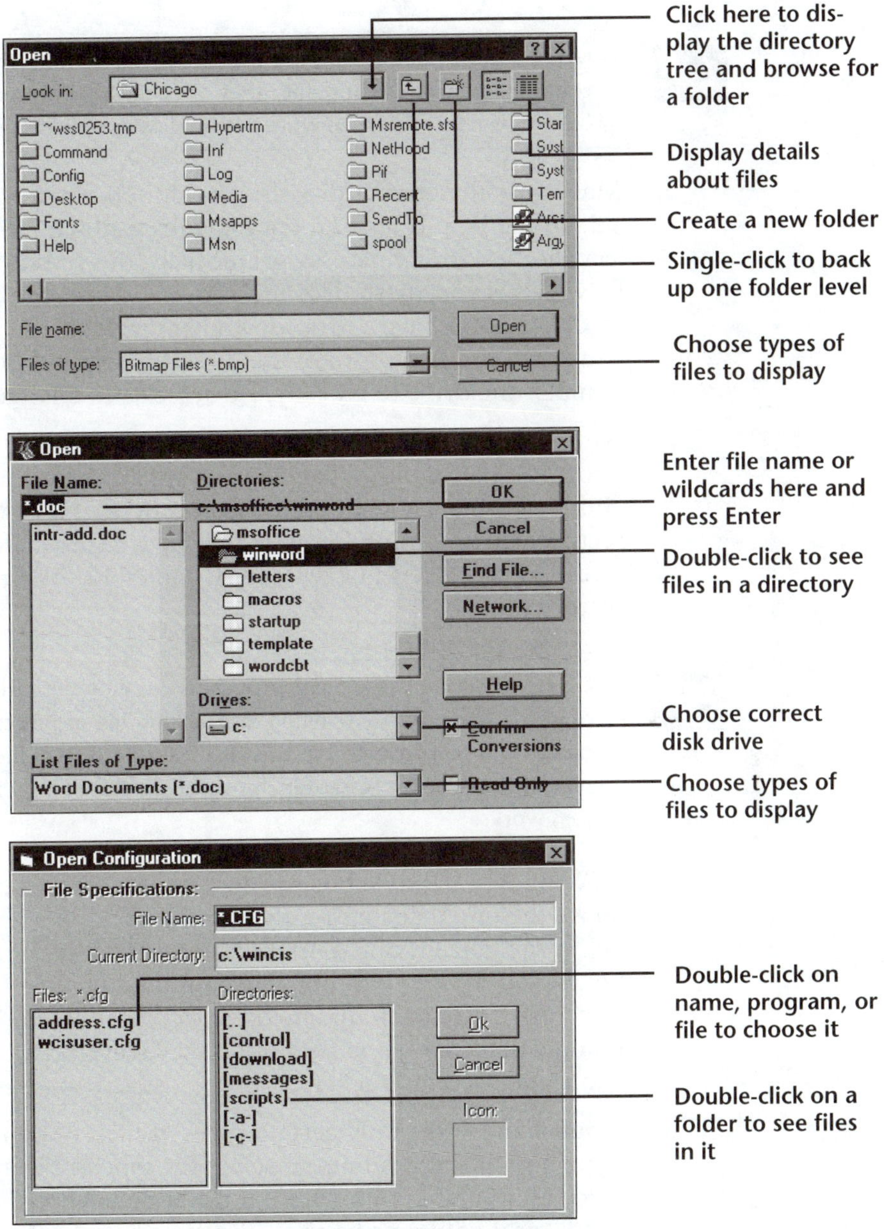
Click here to display the directory tree and browse for a folder
Display details about files
Create a new folder
Single-click to back up one folder level
Choose types of files to display
Open
Look in:
Chicago
File name:
Files of type:
Bitmap Files (*.bmp)
Open
Cancel
Enter file name or wildcards here and press Enter
Double-click to see files in a directory
Choose correct disk drive
Choose types of files to display
Open
File Name:
Directories:
*.doc
c:\msoffice\winword
intr-add.doc
msoffice
winword
letters
macros
startup
template
wordcbt
Drives:
c:
List Files of Type:
Word Documents (*.doc)
OK
Cancel
Find File...
Network...
Help
Confirm Conversions
Read Only
Double-click on name, program, or file to choose it
Double-click on a folder to see files in it
Open Configuration
File Specifications:
File Name:
*.CFG
Current Directory:
c:\wincis
Files: *.cfg
address.cfg
wcisuser.cfg
Directories:
[..]
[control]
[download]
[messages]
[scripts]
[-a-]
[-c-]
Ok
Cancel
Icon:

Figure 3.16 *A file dialog box lets you scan through directories to load or save a document. Here you see three typical file dialog box types. The upper one is the newer Windows 95 style. The middle one is the Windows 3.x style, and the lowest one is the moldy, oldy Windows 3.0 style.*

> **NOTE**   In this discussion, the words *directory* and *folder* are used inter-changeably because in reality they are the same thing. In the older dialog boxes, *directory* refers to what are now called *folders* under Windows 95.

1. Make sure the correct disk drive is chosen down in the lower-right side of the box. If it's not, open the drop-down *Drives* list box and se-lect another drive if necessary. Normally, this setting will be set to drive C, which is your hard disk and should be fine. On the oldest-style file box, you don't have a drop-down list for the drive. To change drives, you scroll to the bottom of the directory list and double-click on the name of the drive (e.g., [-a-], [-b-], [-c-]) to change drives.

2. Now select a directory on the right side by double-clicking on its little folder icon or name. Whatever files are stored in the directory you just chose will then show up in the list at the left. If you don't see the di-rectory you're aiming for, you may have to move down or back up the directory tree a level or two (see Chapter 12 for a review of DOS di-rectory theory).

> **NOTE**   Because these older programs were by definition written for Win-dows 3.x, their file boxes won't display long file or directory names. Long names will be converted to the "8.3" standard DOS file-name format for dis-play in these boxes. Chapter 1 covered details of how the conversion pro-cess works.

In Windows 3.1-style boxes, you'd double-click on the folder just above the one that's currently open to back up a level or on the folder below the current one to move down a level. In Windows 3.0-style boxes, you'd have to double-click on the two dots (..) at the top of the directory list to back up one directory level. Each double click backs up one directory level. To move down a level, click on any directory name enclosed in brackets.

3. If you want to see only certain types of files, open the List Files of Type box (if there is one) to select the type of files you want to see (such as programs, or all files). If the options offered don't suit your needs, or if you're using the older-style box, you can type in DOS-like wildcards in the File Name area, then press Enter to modify the file list accordingly. For example, to show only Lotus 1-2-3 worksheet files, you'd enter ***.WK?** in the File Name area and press Enter.

4. Once the file you want is visible in the file box at the left, double-click on it or highlight it, and click on OK.

When saving a file for the first time, the file won't exist on the drive yet, so it won't show up in the file list box; you'll be giving it a name. To do this, select the drive and directory as outlined above, then move the cursor to the File Name area and type in the file name and extension. Make sure to delete any existing letters in the text area first, using the Backspace and/or Delete keys. (For more information about selecting, editing, and replacing text, see Chapter 19.)

The Newer-Style File Box   The newer-style file box will show up in 32-bit programs written for Windows 95 and in portions of Windows 95 itself. Here's how to use this type of file box when you're opening or saving files.

> **NOTE** To see one of these new dialog boxes, you can run the Paint application found in the Accessories folder by clicking on the Start button, then choosing Start ➤ Programs ➤ Accessories ➤ Paint. Then choose File ➤ Open. (The ➤ symbol here indicates a chain of choices you make from the menus.)

1. First, notice the *Look in* section at the top of the box. This tells you what folder's contents is being displayed in the window below. You can click on this drop-down list to choose the drive or folder you want to look in. This will also list the folders you have on the Desktop so you can open or save files from/to the Desktop.

2. You can create a new folder using the Create New Folder button in the dialog box's toolbar if you want to save something in a folder that doesn't already exist. This can help you organize your files. The new folder will be created as a subfolder to the folder shown in the Look in area. (After creating the new folder, you'll have to name it by typing in a new name just to the right of the folder.)

3. The object is to display the target folder in the window and then double-click on it. So, if the folder you want is somewhere on your hard disk (typically drive C), one way to display it is to choose *C:* from the Look in area. All the folders on your C drive appear in the window.

4. In the large window, double-click on the folder you want to look in. If you don't see the folder you're aiming for, you may have to move down or back up the tree of folders a level or two (see Chapter 12 for a review of DOS directory theory). You back up a level by clicking on the Up One Level button. You move down a level by double-clicking on a folder and looking for its subfolders to then appear in the window. You can then double-click on a subfolder to open that, and so on.

5. Finally, click on the file you want to open. Or, if you're saving a file for the first time, you'll have to type in the name of the file. Of course, if you are saving a file for the first time, the file won't exist on the drive yet, so it won't show up in the list of files; you'll be giving it a name. To do this, select the drive and directory as outlined above, then click in the File Name area and type in the file name. Make sure to delete any existing letters in the text area first, using the Backspace

and/or Delete keys. (For more information about selecting, editing, and replacing text, see Chapter 19.)

6. If you want to see only certain types of files, open the Files of Type box to select the type of files you want to see (such as a certain kind of document or all files). If the options offered don't suit your needs, you can type in DOS-like wildcards in the File Name area, then press Enter to modify the file list accordingly. For example, to show only Lotus 1-2-3 worksheet files, you'd enter ***.WK?** in the File Name area and press Enter.

7. Once the file you want is visible in the file box at the left, double-click on it or highlight it, and click on OK.

Getting Help When You Need It

So far, you've gotten a fairly detailed overview of the Windows interface. Some of the things covered in this chapter will be helpful as reference once you are actually using Windows, though they might seem a little academic right now. Still, it's hard for the newcomer to Windows to begin using Windows without a little orientation to the basic elements of the Windows screen, and that's why I covered these topics right up front. Perhaps you've experimented on your own with dialog boxes and windows, or perhaps you have tried running some programs supplied with Windows 95 such as Notepad or Paint, which would provide additional opportunities for experimentation. (Running programs is covered in Chapter 4.)

Regardless of the extent of your computer know-how, there will be times when you don't remember or understand how to use an operation or command, or even what an element on the screen is for. Luckily, you don't always have to drag out a book or manual to get some quick help. The people at Microsoft have done a very good job of developing a built-in Help facility for this version of Windows. Once you learn how to use it, it'll answer many of your questions.

Many computer users still find books useful, which is lucky because it keeps us writers employed and our publishers, such as Sybex, in business. Books do provide an information source and style that can't be rivaled by computers. With a book, you intuitively know how many pages of material there are on a given topic, batteries are *not* required, and they don't break if you drop them. Using them doesn't really take much know-how (except the ability to read), and you can skim through a book very easily in hopes of searching for a given topic. In my opinion, books are bound (pun not intended) to be with us all for a long, long time.

Despite my probably biased stance on the superiority of books, let's face it: We don't always have a book with us or want to pore over an index to find the right reference (assuming the book even has a decent index!). So, online help (as it's called in the computer world)—especially *context-sensitive* help in which the computer guesses what you're trying to do— can be a great boon. Windows 95 has such a Help facility, as do virtually all Windows programs by this point. Some online help is useful, and some is downright lousy, telling you no more than the obvious. The good news is that because there is a standard for how programs are supposed to dish out help to you, once you learn how to get help with one program, you'll be equipped to take on others. So let's look at how Help works in Windows 95, and if you're an old-timer with Windows, you'll find the slightly modified Help system rather interesting.

To Start Help

There are several approaches to getting help, depending on what you want help *with*. There are two categories of help you can get: You can get help about using Windows itself and help about using one of your application programs. You can always get help about Windows to pop up on your screen whenever you're running Windows 95—which is to say whenever your computer is on. To get help with an application, though, the application has to be running. So, to get help with Word-Perfect for Windows, for example, you have to be running that program. Makes sense, right?

Let's first look at how Windows 95's own built-in Help facility works. Once you learn that, you'll be able to use any new programs that comply with this design. Then, we'll look at a typical Help screen or two from other programs.

The Windows 95 Help system uses a sensible layout that lets you look things up by topic (sort of like an index in a book) or by browsing a table of contents (also like a book). A third approach will scan through all the available Help text, searching for a specific word or phrase for you.

Here's how to get help with Windows topics—that is, help with how to use Windows itself, not specifically with Windows programs you might be running. If your computer is on, you might want to follow these steps to experiment a bit.

1. Click on the Start button at the bottom of your screen and then click on Help. A large window like the one you see in Figure 3.17 pops up.

2. Each of the little purple books on the left is like a chapter. You can "open" the chapter to see subtopics by clicking on it and then clicking

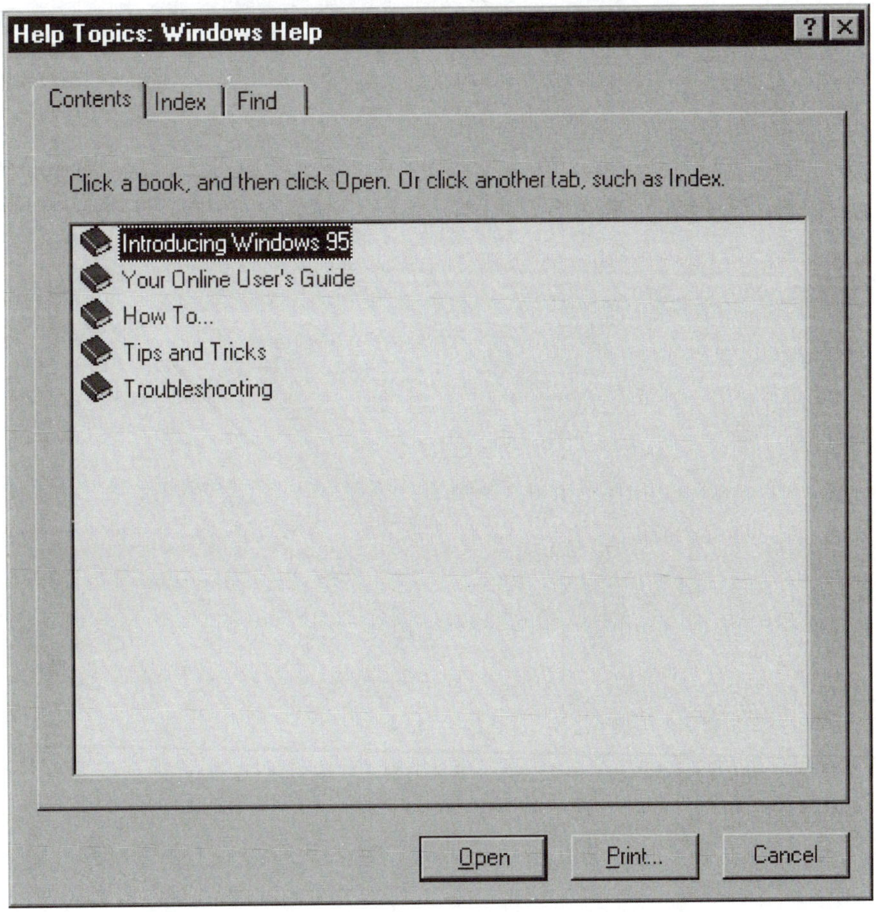

Figure 3.17   Your basic Windows Help screen. Notice the three tabs for doing three different types of topic searches.

on the Open button. (As a shortcut, you can simply double-click on the topic.) So, for example, click on Introducing Windows 95 and then click on Open. The topic opens up as you see in Figure 3.18. Some chapters will have subchapters beneath them that will open in the same way.

3. When you see a little icon that looks like a page of text, you can double-click on it (or click once and then click on Open) to read what it has to say. So, for example, try double-clicking on *Ten minutes to using*

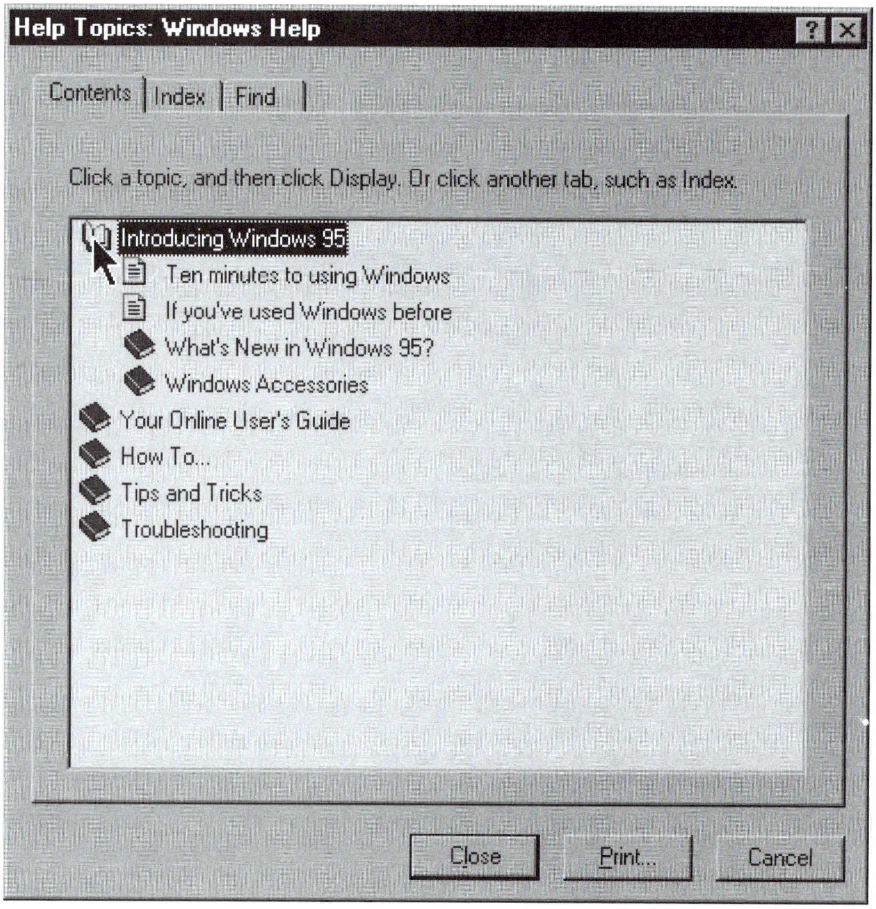

Figure 3.18   Double-clicking on a chapter opens it to display subtopics.

Windows. This brings up an illustrated Windows Tutorial that you might find educational (see Figure 3.19).

NOTE   This is the same tutorial that's an option on the Welcome to Windows 95 sign-on screen, which you will see when Windows 95 first boots up (unless you turned off the Welcome screen).

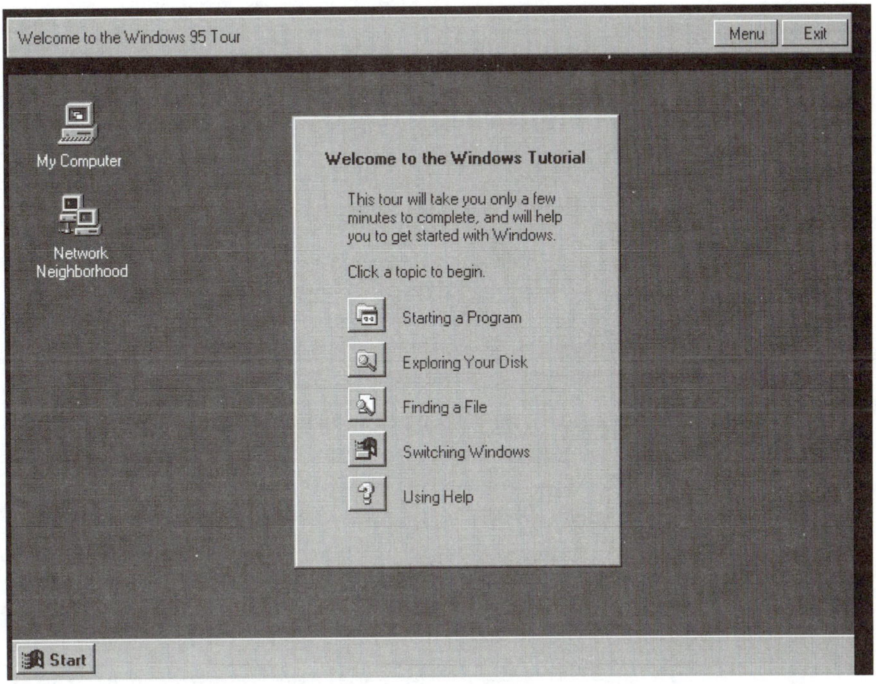

Welcome to the Windows 95 Tour   Menu   Exit

My Computer

Network Neighborhood

Welcome to the Windows Tutorial

This tour will take you only a few minutes to complete, and will help you to get started with Windows.

Click a topic to begin.

Starting a Program

Exploring Your Disk

Finding a File

Switching Windows

Using Help

Start

Figure 3.19   *The Windows Tutorial walks you through some of Windows 95's features. If you get confused, you can click on Exit.*

NOTE   In this book, I'll be covering all the skills that the tutorial addresses, but if you want to take a side trip right now, go ahead. If you want to quit the tutorial at any point, just click on Exit up at the top of the screen.

---

4.   Try double-clicking on one of the other Help topics, such as *If you've used Windows before* (or clicking once and then clicking on

Open). What you'll typically see is a little page of explanatory text, like this:

5. Notice that this little window contains buttons such as *How do I start programs?* To see how these work, you'll first have to maximize the window, otherwise you will miss the show (look back a bit in this chapter to the section on resizing a window if you have forgotten how to maximize).

6. After maximizing, click on the *How do I start programs?* button. You'll see the screen shown in Figure 3.20.

7. Try clicking on the other buttons to read related material and see additional illustrations.

8. When you're ready to return to the contents page, click on the Contents button at the top of the window:

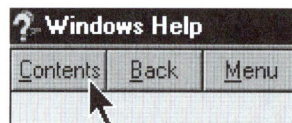

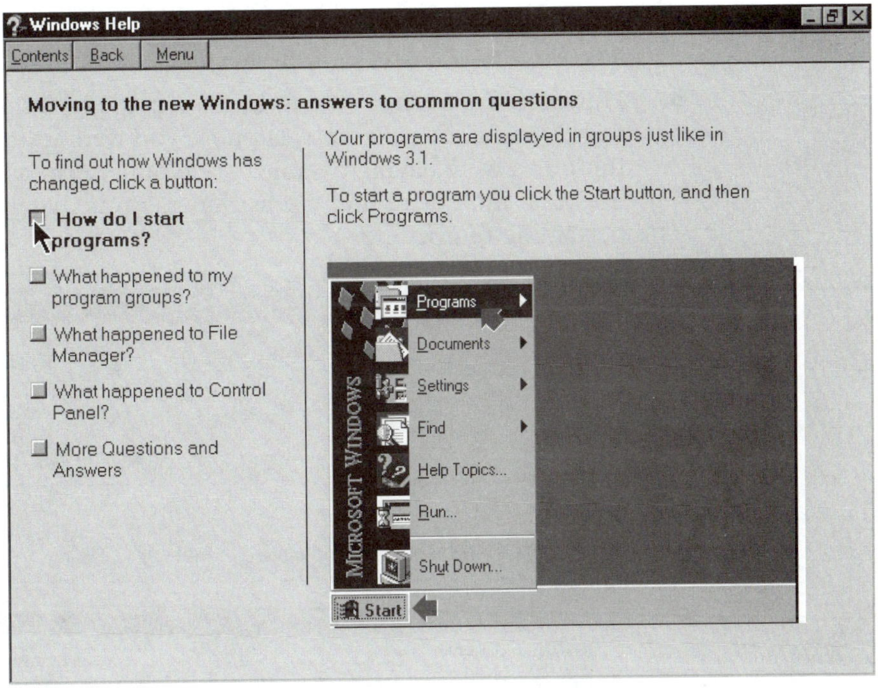

Figure 3.20   *Clicking on a topic button at the left displays an explanatory picture on the right.*

Using the Help Index

So much for the Table of Contents approach. Now check out the Index. Actually, when you're doing real work (rather than just passing the time reading about Windows and discovering new information about it), you'll use the Index. Just as in a book, the index can help you more quickly locate just the piece of trivia you need to get the job done. Of course, just as with a book index, the entry you need might not be there. It's sort of a potluck, but you're still likely to find something you need this way.

To use the index:

1. Run Help as you did in the above section.

2. Click on the Index tab this time. You'll see a new box listing a lot of topics. You can type in the topic you want information about or just click on a displayed topic and click on Display. Notice that there is a

scroll bar to the right of the list, so you can scroll the list to search for a topic.

3. However, the quicker way to find a topic is to simply start typing the topic's name. For example, suppose you were trying to print something and were having trouble. Try typing **print** as I did in Figure 3.21 and notice that the list jumps immediately to topics pertaining to printing.

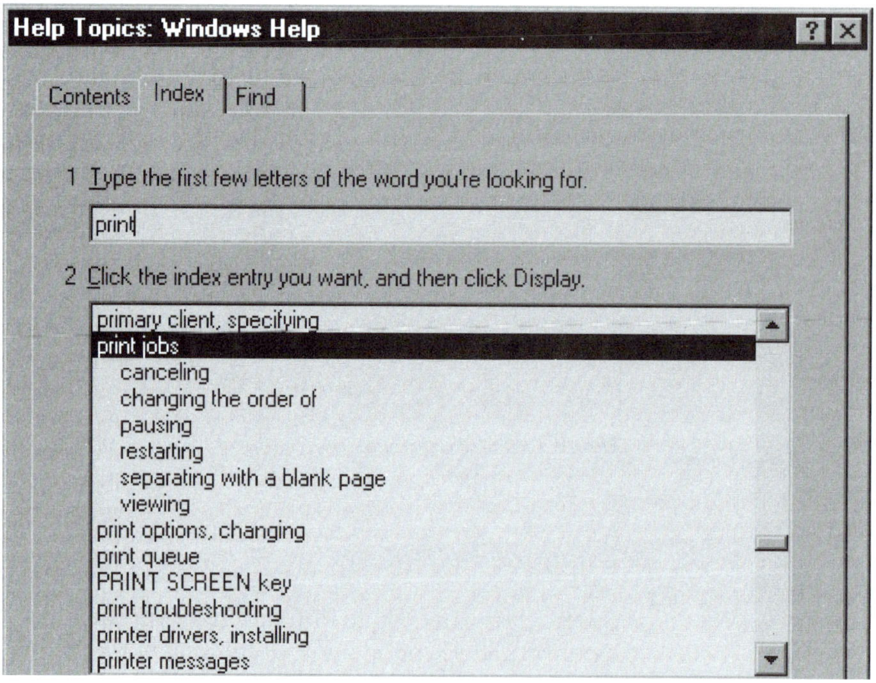

Figure 3.21   *The Index tab displays a long list of topics. Type in a topic and the list will jump to identically spelled topics as you type.*

4. Once the target is in sight, shoot! That is, double-click on it. A window will appear with helpful (you hope) information, possibly with other little buttons to click on for elaboration, and so forth. In some cases, before actually getting the help information, you'll be presented with a list of subreferences to choose from. You simply click on the one you want and click on Display.

TIP   Remember, when a Help topic is being displayed, you can always get back to the main Help screen by clicking on the Contents button, as explained above.

Searching for Help with Find

The third tab page on the basic Windows 95 Help screen is *Find.* This option is a last resort if you're really bummed trying to find some help on a topic and nothing is coming up. This command actually goes through all the Windows 95 Help files (there's one for each supplied application and for all major modules of Windows 95, such as Print Manager, Taskbar, system utilities, and so forth), looking for the word(s) you stipulate.

Here's how to do a Find:

1. Click on Start and then choose Help.

2. Click on the Find tab in the Help dialog box.

3. If this is the first time you have run a Find, a Wizard will run. That's right, a Wizard. If you've never met a Wizard, you're in luck. (Actually, you probably ran into one while setting up Windows 95.) Anyway, you'll see something such as that in Figure 3.22.

4. Follow the instructions on the screen. If you're short on disk space, use the Custom option. Otherwise click on Express and then on Next, followed by Finish. The computer now creates a database of words, and as this happens a cute little picture of a pen writing in a book appears:

5. After the database is created, the Find box appears, which is like the Index box on steroids. I mean, it's pretty powerful. Just as with the Index box, you simply type in the topic you're looking for, but in this

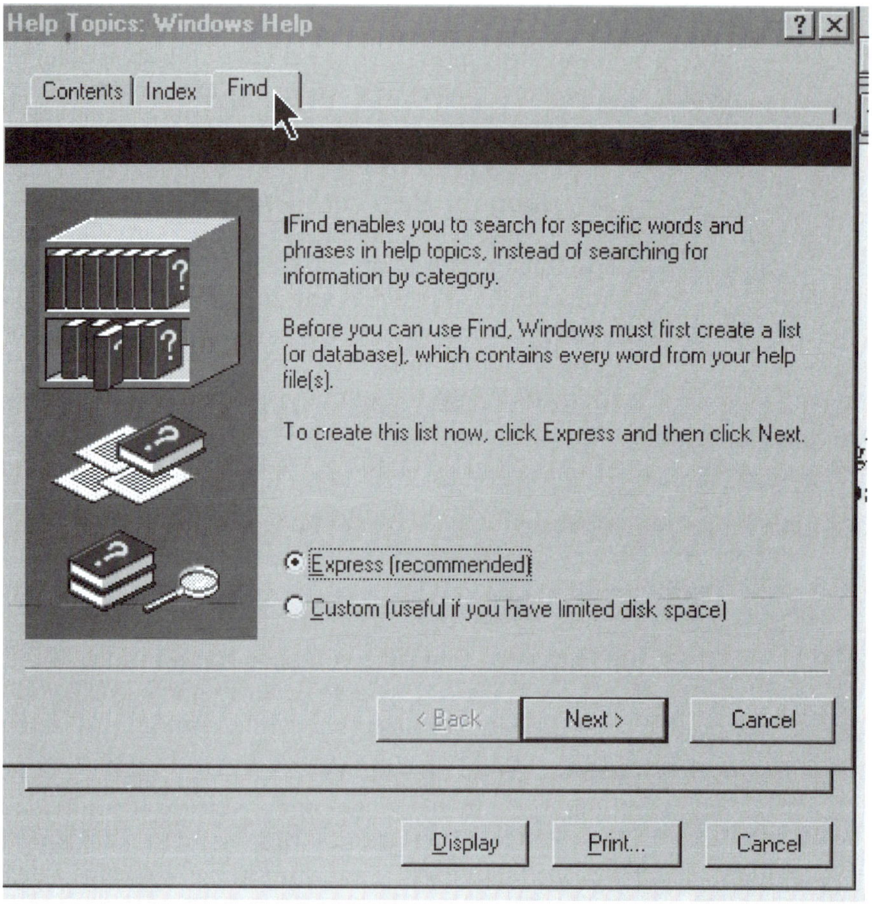

Figure 3.22   *The Wizard for setting up Find*

box you can type in multiple words and refine your search. For example, say you wanted to know how to change the speed at which the keys on your keyboard repeat. Just type in **keyboard repeat** and see what happens (see Figure 3.23).

TIP   If you type in a word followed by a space, a large list of optional words comes up that you can play with as options.

6. Now you can optionally select some additional modifiers that will narrow the search. Move to the second box (marked *2*) and click on any

Figure 3.23   *The Find box is like the Index box but with more options.*

words that have relevance to what you're looking for. By default, all the words in this list are selected, which is why they are all blackened. If you click on just one of these words, all others will become deselected.

7. The list of final contenders is shown in the bottom box. You can click on any items that appear there and then click on Display to read about the topic. You can also click in the little box to the left of a topic to select it for printing.

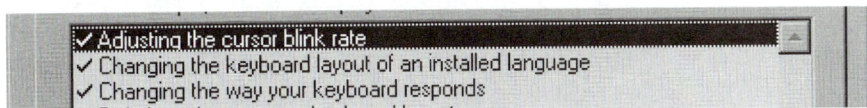

> **TIP** Remember when you're reading a topic to click on the Help Topics button in the topic's window to get back to the Find box so you can display any additional topics that you haven't yet viewed. Clicking on the Back button (when it appears) takes you back a step through the pages of information you have read.

8. Once some topics are check marked, you can print them by clicking on the Print button. You can also do one other strange thing. If you click on the Find Similar button, a list of sort-of-related topics (you'll find some of them a little far afield) pops up as shown in Figure 3.24.

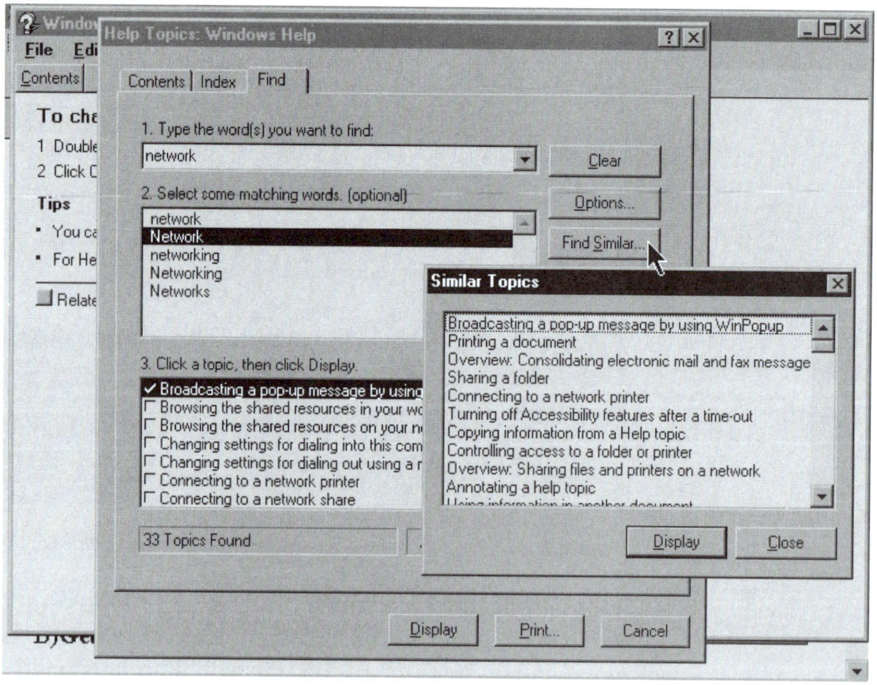

Figure 3.24 *Clicking on Find Similar will search for items that Help thinks are similar to the checkmarked topic(s).*

Two other options in the Find box are worth noting. The first is Rebuild. This simply rebuilds the database of words in case it got trashed or erased for some reason (like you accidentally erased the database file). Help database files have the extension .gid.

The second option is called Options. Clicking on this button lets you set some of the internal details controlling how the Find dialog box works. The settings in the box are self-explanatory should you decide to play with them. However, the default settings work fine in most instances.

Using Typical Help Screens

There are features common to many Help windows. You should be able to recognize them and know how they work. One thing to keep in mind is that Help screens come in many styles and formats. Help hasn't really been standardized to the point where all programs' Help facilities are going to behave in the same way. The best I can do here is to introduce you to the variety of elements you are likely to run into and let you take it from there. The good news is that there is virtually always the word "Help" at the far right side of any Windows program's menu bar. Clicking on this menu brings up some choices pertaining to online help. For example, Figure 3.25 shows a potpourri of such Help menus.

The majority of Help menus have a *Search for Help On* command or *Help Topics* command to help you narrow the topic search. Often, choosing one of these commands will present you with an Index box like the one described above. Other options (such as *Help with Procedures*) are pretty self-explanatory.

TIP If while looking at an application's Help screen you can't remember how to use Help, just press the F1 key. You'll then see a list of topics explaining how to use the Help system.

Because many of the programs you'll be running (at least for a couple of years after the release of Windows 95) will be Windows 3.x programs, you'll be seeing older Windows 3.x-style Help screens. Here's an example. Suppose you're using NetCruiser, a program for connecting to the Internet. Figure 3.26 shows NetCruiser's opening Help screen.

Notice the underlined words and the buttons just below the menu bar. These are just some of the elements to look for on Help screens. The following list describes these and other common Help-screen elements.

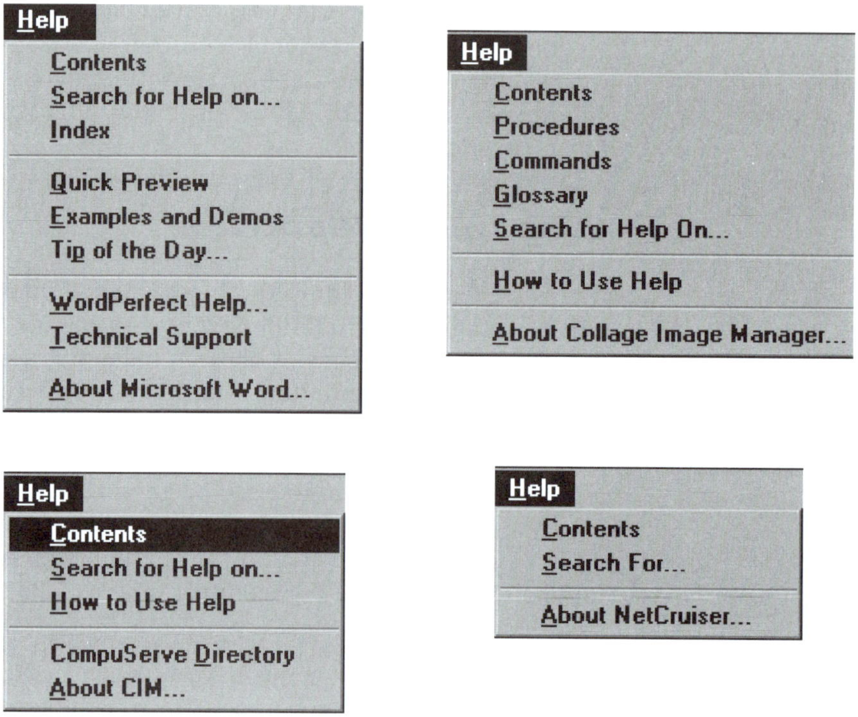

Help
Contents
Search for Help on...
Index

Quick Preview
Examples and Demos
Tip of the Day...

WordPerfect Help...
Technical Support

About Microsoft Word...

Help
Contents
Procedures
Commands
Glossary
Search for Help On...

How to Use Help

About Collage Image Manager...

Help
Contents
Search for Help on...
How to Use Help

CompuServe Directory
About CIM...

Help
Contents
Search For...

About NetCruiser...

Figure 3.25   *Most Windows programs have a Help menu, though each will have its own Help options. Here are a few typical Help menus.*

▶ Any word or phrase in a list that appears lighter (or green, if you have a color monitor) and is underlined with a solid line is a *topic*. Clicking on a topic jumps you to the section in the online help that is relevant to that word or procedure. You'll then see a new Help window with information about that topic.

▶ Occasionally you'll encounter hotspots (a hotspot is any item in the Help screen text that does something special if you click on it) that are graphics rather than words. They don't look any different from other graphics in the Help windows, but the pointer turns into the hand icon when it's positioned over them, meaning it's a hotspot. View information or activate this kind of hotspot the same way you do other hotspots—simply click. There are a few key combinations that highlight the hotspots in a Help window, making it easy to locate and select them. Pressing Tab advances to the next hotspot, Shift-Tab

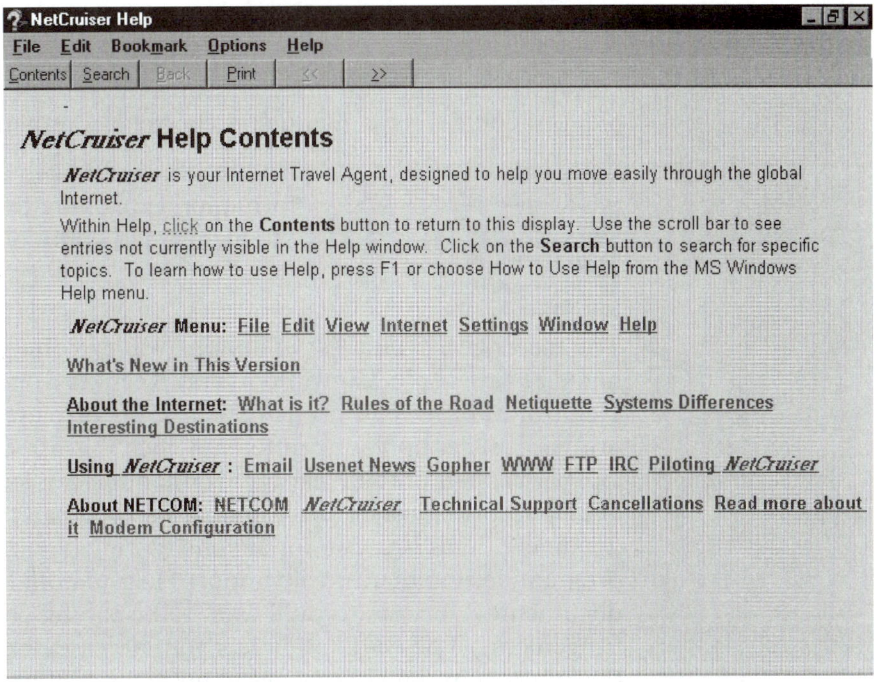

Figure 3.26   A typical Help screen. Read the topic by clicking on an underlined word or phrase. Click on a word underlined with a dotted line to see its definition.

moves to the previous hotspot, and Ctrl-Tab highlights all the hotspots for as long as you hold both keys down.

▶ Some words appear lighter (or green) and are underlined with a dotted line. Clicking on the word will typically bring up a box containing a definition of the word. To see the definition, position the pointer on the term (once again, the cursor changes to the hand icon) and click. The definition pops up in a window like that shown here. To close the box, just click again or press any key on the keyboard.

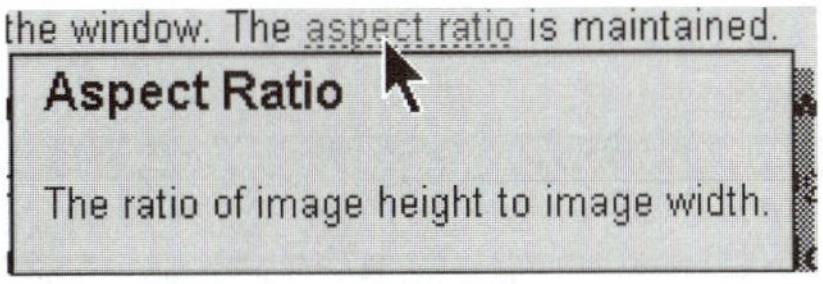

▶ The *What Is This?* button is the "?" button found on the toolbar or in the title bar of some programs. It looks like this:

or like this:

Clicking on this button turns the pointer into a question mark. Once that happens, you can click on an element on the screen that you're curious about, and you'll see an explanation of the element. For example, you could open a menu and choose a command, like this:

Spelling...	F7
Grammar...	
Thesaurus...	**Shift+F7**
Hyphenation...	
Language...	
Word Count	

The result would likely be a screenful of information explaining the ins and outs of the highlighted command.

▶ The menu gives you a list of options you can choose from such as Annotate, Print Topic, Copy, Font, and Keep on Top. Annotation is covered below. *Print Topic* prints the currently displayed topic on your printer. Just set up your printer and click this option. You'll then have a paper version of the Help topic at hand. *Copy* puts the current page of help information on the Clipboard so you can paste it into another document. This is useful for anyone writing documentation about a program, letting them easily import Help material into their own document. (Of course, you'll want to be careful about copyright infringement.) The *Font* option lets you increase or decrease the size of the lettering in the Help boxes to get more text in the window or to increase visibility. *Keep Help on Top* prevents the Help window from being obscured by other windows on the screen as they are selected or as you open new documents or applications (see below).

The Help Buttons

Many Help screens have a row of command buttons beneath the menu bar.

Some Help screens will have fewer buttons than this. It's also possible that you'll see more than this, but not likely. Here's what the command buttons do when you click on them:

Contents   This jumps you directly to the list of Help contents for the application you are using. The Contents list is a good starting point for getting help and a good place to return to after reading Help on one item if you want to see more on another, unrelated item. Incidentally, in some programs, pressing F1 takes you directly to this list.

Search   This button lets you look for a specific word or topic. There is a list of key words for each topic in the Help system. This command shows you those words in a list box. As explained above, you can select the subject you want to read about, or you can type in a word you want Help to look up. As you begin typing, the list will scroll to the word you've entered, assuming that there's a match. See the section above about using the Index and Find tab pages in this box. If you don't find the topic you want, click on the Cancel button (or press Esc).

Back   This lets you back up through the Help topics you have already viewed in the reverse order that you viewed them (meaning the most recent first). When you have backed up as far as you can go, the Back button is grayed.

History   This brings up a little box within the current Help screen that lists the Help screens you've consulted in the reverse order that you viewed them. The most recent is at the top of the list. By using the History box, instead of backing up to a previous topic by clicking on Back until the screen you want reappears, you can just double-click on the topic in the History box. If you click on Back while the History box is open, you'll see the topics you already looked at in the order that they appear in the list. Each topic is added to the top of the list as you view it again. If there isn't a History button, try opening the Options menu. There may be a choice there called Display History Window.

<<   This is the Browse Backward button. If the Browse buttons appear on a Help screen, it means that some topics related to the current one can be viewed one after another by pressing one of the Browse buttons. Each click on the button returns you to the previous topic in the series. When you reach the first topic, the button becomes grayed.

>>   This is the Browse Forward button. It advances you to the next screen in the series of related topics. When you reach the end of the series, the button is grayed.

Keeping a Specific Help Screen Handy

Help windows often "disappear" when you go back to the application that the Help screen is about. This is annoying because often you won't remember what you just read. It's not that the window really disappeared, it's simply that your application window has covered it up. With the new Help system, procedures appear in a little window that sits over to the right-hand side of your screen and doesn't go away (this is called *staying on top*) until you close it.

Sometimes the Help screen you're working with doesn't stay on top because this setting is turned off. Some older programs don't use the little Help window in the right-margin and aren't set to automatically stay on top. Even so, there are several ways to keep a windowful of specific help information in view or at least easily available.

▶ You can shrink the Help window down to a size where you can still read it but it doesn't take up the whole screen. Make it a small, wide band at the bottom or side of the screen, for example, and resize your other windows to accommodate it, as in Figure 3.27.

NOTE   Windows 95 allows Help for only one application to be open at a time. If you switch to another application and run Help from it, any Help that is already open will be closed and the new one opened. Implementing Help in this way was an economy decision on Microsoft's part. Limiting the number of simultaneously running Help files conserves memory and other resources, leaving more room for your applications and documents.

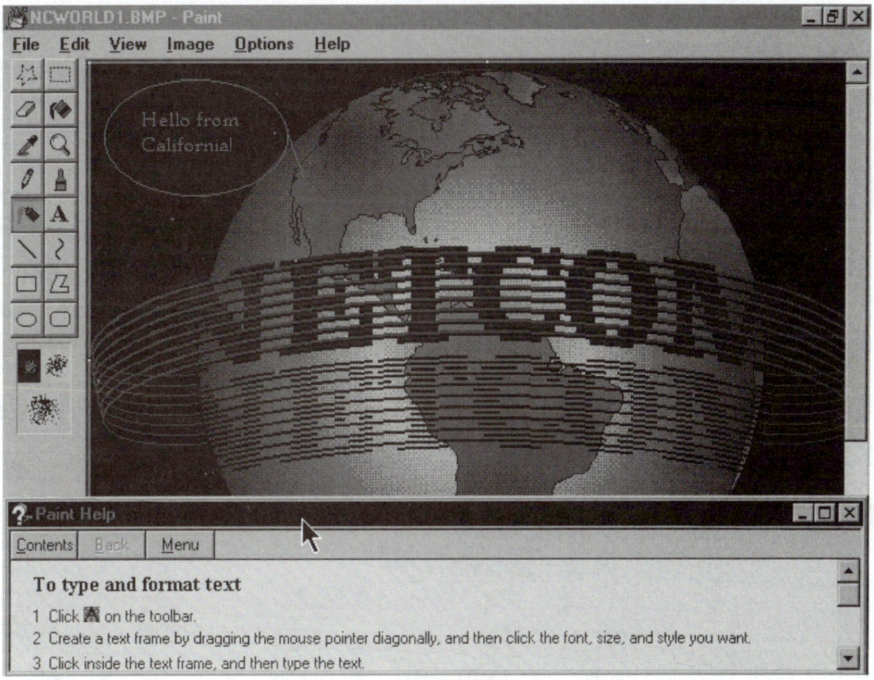

Figure 3.27   Keep Help windows handy while working in Windows.

▶ Another solution is to minimize it, which puts a button for it on the Taskbar. When you need to read the Help topic again, just click on the Help button's icon. This is particularly helpful for quickly recalling lists of key commands or other information that might be difficult to remember.

Using Bookmarks

Even within a given program's Help screen, you are limited to seeing one screen at a time. That is, you can't keep several of your favorite pages of Help information on screen at once. If you want to refer to a few topics' Help screens while you're working on a project, another feature, Bookmark, is a good tool for you to become familiar with. Bookmark allows you to create a list of the topics you most often refer to. Once you find a topic the first time and add it to the Bookmark list, you can jump to that Help screen quickly the next time simply by choosing the topic from your personal list.

To define your bookmarks:

1. Run the program you want to make up bookmarks for.

2. Open the Help menu and choose either Contents, Search for Help On, or Index, depending on how you want to locate your topics.

3. When the topic Help screen is open, open the Bookmark menu by clicking on it and choose Define.

4. In the Bookmark Define dialog box, shown below, you have the option of giving the bookmark a name or leaving it with the topic name. Type in a new name if you want to. Choose OK. The dialog box closes, and you return to the topic Help screen. If you open the Bookmark menu again, you will see your bookmark listed.

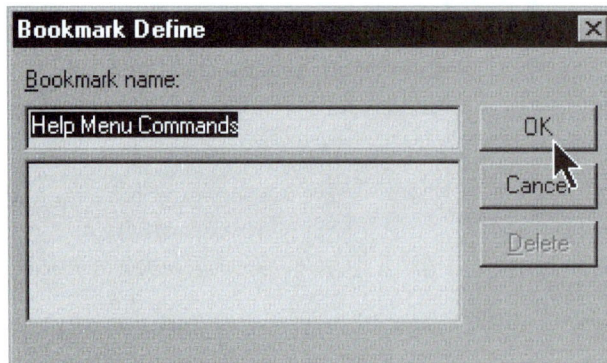

To quickly jump to one of your bookmarked topics later on:

1. Open Help for whatever program you have saved bookmarks in.

2. Up on the menu bar, click on Bookmark. The menu will list any bookmarks you have saved. Choose the desired topic by clicking on it. If more than nine topics are bookmarked, choose More from the Bookmark list, then click on the topic in the Go To dialog box.

To remove a bookmark from your list:

1. Run Help from the application in question. Then open the Bookmark menu and choose Define.

2. Click on the topic you want to delete.

3. Click on Delete. Repeat for each topic you want to delete from the list.

4. Click on OK when you're ready to close the box.

When Help Doesn't Help

In some cases, Help just won't tell you what you're interested in the first time around. In fact, probably 50 percent of the time Help doesn't help me. At least not the first time. Here's a general game plan to try when you can't seem to ferret anything useful out of Help.

First try spending some time wandering through the help screens. There is a lot of information in the Help files supplied with Windows and the Windows accessories. Sometimes the Search command won't find what you need to know, but the information is in the Help system in another context. Don't overlook playing with the Find tab page in the Contents dialog box as I described earlier.

> **TIP**   Though the Find tab page is a new feature for Windows 95, note that it works even with Help files from Windows 3.x applications. Any older Windows program with a standard Help file can be indexed using this command so you can search through it with a fine-tooth comb. If you're a veteran Windows user, you may want to revisit the Help files of your older applications now, searching through them in this new way. You just may discover tasty tidbits of information you didn't know existed.

Modifying the Help Screens

You can add your own notes to a Help topic. This is useful for reminding yourself of things you've figured out about an application program or of where to find information on some topic that eluded you last time you looked. Each topic can have only one annotation, but it can be quite long. An annotation is like a note that you "paper clip" to the topic. To make an annotation:

1. Get to the Help screen where you want to attach the note.

2. Open the Edit menu of the Help window and choose Annotate.

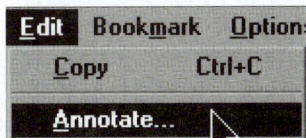

3. Type your notes into the dialog box that appears. You can edit the text using the Backspace key, the Delete key, and the arrow keys.

Annotate ? ✕

Current annotation:

> Jill:
>
> Also remember that you can select a word in the text by double-clicking on it. Then to copy it, just press Ctrl-C or click the Right mouse button and choose Copy.
>
> --Jack

Save

Cancel

Delete

Copy

Paste

4. When you are finished, click on Save. A paper clip now shows up before the topic title on the Help screen you're reading.

You can read the annotation on any help topic (if there is a paper clip there) by either clicking on the paper clip or choosing Edit ➤ Annotate. You can delete an annotation by opening the Annotation dialog box again and clicking on Delete.

When making an annotation, you can copy text from the Clipboard into the annotation window, or vice versa, using the Copy and Paste buttons in the box.

Copying the Help Screens

There may be occasions when you would find it useful to copy information from Help topics into a document or another application. For example, if you are preparing a training manual for employees in your company who are learning WordPerfect for Windows, you may find useful guidelines within WordPerfect's Help utility that you want to incorporate rather than retyping it all. This feature can also save you time using Help if you annotate one topic with related information from another topic.

Copying is done by way of Windows' Clipboard. The entire Help topic or only selected portions of it may be copied. (Graphics from a Help topic cannot be copied to the Clipboard, however.) For a complete discussion of Clipboard and text-selection techniques, see Chapter 6. I'll briefly outline the steps here for copying to the Clipboard from Help:

> **TIP**   Pressing Ctrl-Ins copies the entire contents of a Help topic to the Clipboard.

> **NOTE**   Text selection throughout Windows and in most Windows applications works the same way and is explained thoroughly in Chapter 19, which covers WordPad. The easiest way is to position the selection cursor—the blinking bar—at the beginning of the text. Then, keeping the mouse button depressed, move the mouse. Release the button when all the text you want to copy is highlighted.

1. Within the active Help topic window, use the mouse to select the text you want to copy.

2. Open the Edit menu and choose Copy (see Figure 3.28).

3. Switch to the document you want to paste the information into, open its Edit menu, and choose Paste.

> **TIP**   You can copy material from one Help screen onto the Clipboard, then paste it into an annotation box for another Help screen, as explained above. This way, you can, in essence, have the information from two Help screens in one place.

Exiting Windows

When you're finished with a Windows session, you should properly shut down Windows *before* turning off your computer. This ensures that Windows saves your work on disk correctly and that no data are lost. Even if you are running an application in Windows and you close that application, you'll have to exit Windows, too, *before* turning off your computer.

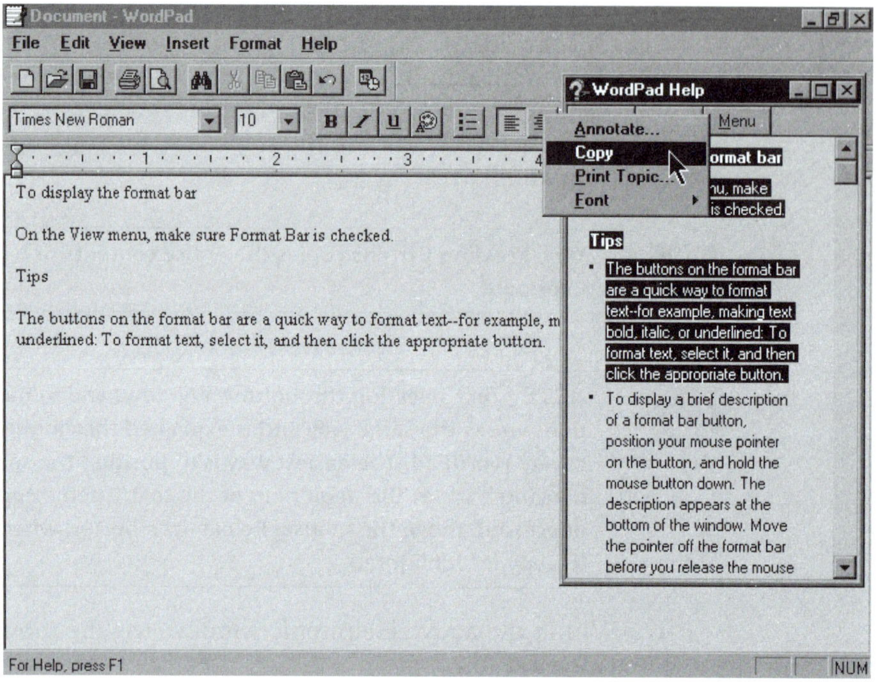

Figure 3.28   Copying text from a Help topic

CAUTION   Exiting Windows properly is very important. You can lose your work or otherwise foul up Windows settings if you don't shut down Windows before turning off your computer.

Here are the steps for correctly exiting Windows:

1. Close any program that you have running. (This can almost always be done from each program's File menu—choose Exit from the menu—or by clicking on the program's Close button.) If you forget to close programs before issuing the Shut Down command, Windows will attempt to close them for you. This is fine unless you were working on a document and didn't save your work. In that case you'll be prompted by a dialog box for each open document, asking you if you want to save your work. If you have DOS programs running, you'll have to close

them manually before Windows will let you exit. You'll also be reminded if this is the case by a dialog box telling you that Windows can't terminate the program and you'll have to do it from the DOS program. Quit the DOS program and type **exit** at the DOS prompt, if necessary.

2. Next, click on the Taskbar and choose Shut Down.

> 🗔 **Suspend**
> 🗔 **Shut Down...**
> 🗔 Start

THE SUSPEND OPTION FOR LAPTOPS

If your laptop computer has Advanced Power Manager (APM) built in, you may have a Suspend option in the Start button menu. This is like shutting down, only it lets you come right back to where you were working before you suspended. This means you don't have to exit all your applications before turning off your computer. You only have to choose Suspend. It also means you can get right back to work where you left off without rebooting your computer, finding the document(s) you were working on, and finding your place in those documents. I don't ever have to boot up Windows, run my favorite applications, and open my documents unless I want to. They are always up and running. I just pop open the lid to my laptop, enter my password, and I'm up and running right where I left off.

Though an increasing number of laptop computers now support a suspend function, they may not be APM-compatible. Also note that there is a limit to the amount of time a computer can stay in a suspended state. If the battery runs out, the computer will have to be rebooted when you turn it on, and your work may be lost.

Toshiba computers hold the record in terms of how long they will stay in Suspend mode. I have had five Toshibas thus far, precisely for their well-engineered *Auto Resume* feature. A typical Toshiba laptop will stay suspended on a full battery charge for several days to a week or more. Most other brands won't stay suspended for more than a couple hours. You'll want to check with the manufacturer of your computer about how long theirs will stay "alive" in a suspended state if you plan to use Windows 95's Suspend option.

Still, even if you have Suspend capability on your computer, you should save your work before suspending. You don't necessarily have to close the applications you're using, but you should at least save any documents you're working on.

3. You'll now see a dialog box like that in Figure 3.29. (If you are not on a network, you'll only see the first two options.)

4. Wait until Windows completely shuts down and tells you it's okay to turn off your computer. This may take about fifteen seconds.

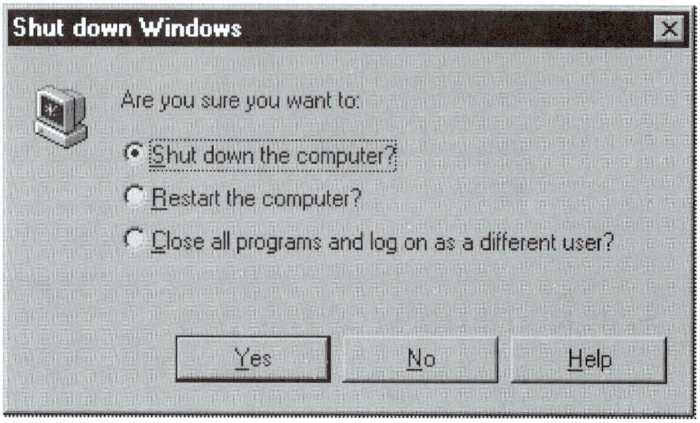

Figure 3.29   **Click on** *Shut down the computer?* **to end your Windows session.**

Chapter 4

Getting Down to Business: Running Your Applications

FEATURING

If you've just upgraded from Windows 3.1, you already know a lot about how to use Windows and Windows applications. A few things will be different with Windows 95, but you'll probably pick those up quickly. If you're new to Windows, then getting used to the turf might take a little longer, though you'll have an advantage—you won't have to unlearn any bad habits that Windows 3.x veterans have ground into their craniums.

What Can and Can't Be Run

As I discussed in the opening chapters, Windows 95 was designed to be *backward-compatible* with Windows 3.x and DOS programs and to be *forward-compatible* with most 32-bit programs designed for Windows NT. In a sense, Windows 95 is the best of all worlds when it comes to running your existing programs. You can pretty much bet that whatever is in your existing software arsenal won't be rendered obsolete by Windows 95.

Windows 95 will run your existing DOS programs quite nicely in scalable windows, offer them more conventional memory than previously possible, run many graphics programs in a window, and optionally give each DOS application its own custom DOS environment to run in. Likewise, most existing Windows programs will run just fine with smoother task switching and a more pleasant appearance, and (with a few workarounds I'll be telling you about) they can interact with the new Windows 95 Desktop. As new 32-bit programs for Windows 95 appear, you'll be able to run those, too, adding OLE 2.0 support and speedier performance. Any and all programs can be run from the DOS command line, not just DOS programs.

So, How Do I Run My Programs?

As with many of the procedures you'll want to do while in Windows, starting up your programs can be done in myriad ways. Here's the complete list of ways to run programs. You can:

▶ Choose the desired application from the Start button.

▶ Open My Computer, walk your way through the directories until you find the application's icon, and double-click on it.

▶ Run Explorer or File Manager, find the application's icon, and double-click on it.

▶ Run the old-style Windows 3.x Program Manager, open the group that contains the application's icon, and double-click on it.

▶ Find the application with the Find command and double-click on it.

▶ Locate a document that was created with the application in question and double-click on it. This will run the application and load the document into it.

▶ Right-click on the Desktop or in a folder and choose New. Then choose a document type from the resulting menu. This creates a new document of the type you desire, which, when double-clicked on, will run the application.

▶ Open the Documents list from the Start button and choose a recently edited document. This will open the document in the appropriate application.

▶ Enter command names from the MS-DOS prompt. In addition to the old-style DOS commands that run DOS programs and batch files, you can run Windows programs right from the DOS prompt.

For many users, the last three approaches will make the most sense because they deal with the document itself instead of the application that created it.

In deference to tradition, I'm going to cover the approaches to running applications in the order listed above. That is, application-centric first rather than document-centric. All the approaches are useful while using Windows, and you will probably want to become proficient in each of them.

Running a Program from the Start Button

Certainly the easiest way to run your applications is with the Start button. That's why it's called the Start button! Here's how it works.

When you install a new program, the program's name is added to the Start button's Program menu. Then you just find your way to the

RUNNING APPLICATIONS FROM THE COMMAND PROMPT

One of the nicest features of Windows 95 is that you can now run any application from the MS-DOS command prompt. If you're used to MS-DOS, you can open up a MS-DOS Prompt from the Start menu (Start ➤ Programs ➤ MS-DOS Prompt). If you use the command prompt frequently, you might want to create a shortcut on the Desktop to make access to the command prompt faster. To do this:

1.   Click on the Desktop with the right mouse button.

2.   Select New ➤ Shortcut.

3.   In the Create Shortcut dialog box's Command line edit box enter `command.com`.

4.   Click on Next.

5.   As a Program-Information File already exists for this program, the *Select Title for the Program* dialog box's *Select name for the shortcut* edit box should already have **MS-DOS Prompt** listed, but if it doesn't, go ahead and enter it now. If you want another title to be displayed, you can enter that instead.

6.   Click on Finish. A new shortcut should now be displayed on the Desktop.

7.   At this point you can change the default start-up directory (the MS-DOS Prompt's default directory) by right-clicking on the program icon and selecting Properties. Choose the Program tab, then change the entry in the Working edit box to your desired directory. I often change this to C:\ instead of the default C:\Windows so I can browse around from the root directory.

If you use a long–file-name directory, remember to enclose the entire text string in quotes. For instance, if you want to start your command prompt in the Program Files directory, it should look like **"C:\Program Files"** in the Working edit box.

Once you have a command prompt, you can use your familiar MS-DOS commands like **CD** to change directories or **MD** to make a new directory, or you can run your programs (any `.bat`, `.pif`, `.com`, or `.exe` file). And you can run either MS-DOS or Windows programs. Just type in the program name, and it will start up. For instance, if you want to run the Windows 3.x version of File Manager, type `winfile` and press the Enter key.

program's name, choose it, and the program runs. Suppose you want to run Notepad:

1.   Click on the Start button.

2.   Choose Programs because you want to start a program. Up comes a list of programs similar to what's shown in Figure 4.1. Your list will differ because this is the list of programs on *my* computer, not yours.

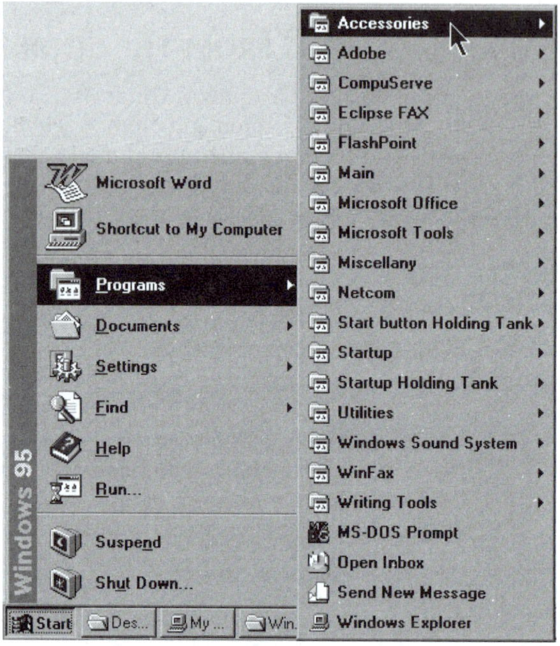

Figure 4.1 *The first step in running a program is to click on the Start button and choose Programs from the resulting list.*

Any selection that has an arrow pointer to the right of the name is not actually a program but a program *group*. If you've used Windows 3.x, you'll know that program groups are the collections of programs and related document files that were used to organize your programs in Windows 3.x's Program Manager. Choosing one of these opens another menu listing the items in the group.

3. I happen to know that the Notepad program lies amongst the accessory programs that come with Windows 95. Slide the pointer up or over to highlight Accessories. Now the rather long list of accessory programs appears. There are a lot of accessories, as you can see. Slide the pointer down to Notepad and click, as shown in Figure 4.2.

You've successfully run Notepad. It's now sitting there with a blank document open, waiting for you to start typing. Chapter 22 covers the

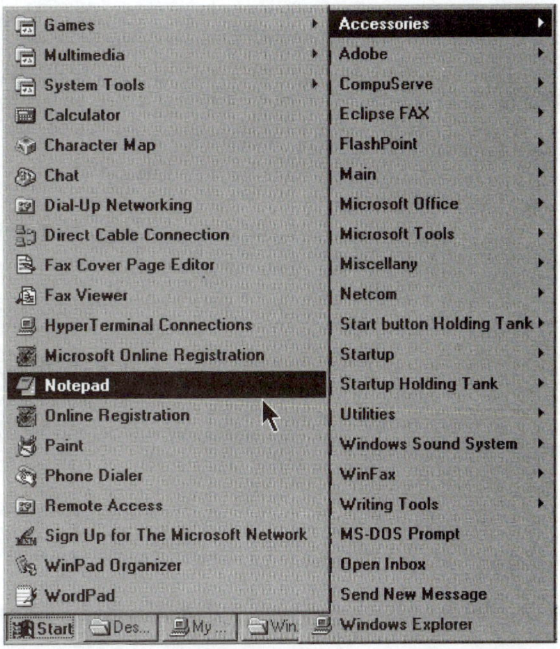

Games	▶	Accessories	▶
Multimedia	▶	Adobe	▶
System Tools	▶	CompuServe	▶
Calculator		Eclipse FAX	▶
Character Map		FlashPoint	▶
Chat		Main	▶
Dial-Up Networking		Microsoft Office	▶
Direct Cable Connection		Microsoft Tools	▶
Fax Cover Page Editor		Miscellany	▶
Fax Viewer		Netcom	▶
HyperTerminal Connections		Start button Holding Tank	▶
Microsoft Online Registration		Startup	▶
Notepad		Startup Holding Tank	▶
Online Registration		Utilities	▶
Paint		Windows Sound System	▶
Phone Dialer		WinFax	▶
Remote Access		Writing Tools	▶
Sign Up for The Microsoft Network		MS-DOS Prompt	
WinPad Organizer		Open Inbox	
WordPad		Send New Message	
		Windows Explorer	

Start | Des... | My ... | Win

Figure 4.2   *The second step in running a program from the Start button is to choose the program itself from the resulting Program list or to open a group such as Accessories and then choose the program.*

ins and outs of using Notepad, so I won't discuss that here. For now just click on the Close button.

Because Windows 95 lets you nest groups of applications and documents into multiple levels, you might occasionally run into multiple levels of cascading menus when you're trying to launch (that's computerese for *run*) an application. For example, in the instance above, I had to open the Accessories group to find Notepad. Open it again and notice that there are a couple of groups within Accessories up at the top—Games, Multimedia, and System Tools. Sometimes because of the length of a list, the list might wrap around the screen, open to the right or to the left, or otherwise scoot around your screen in some unexpected way. None of this matters. You simply look for the program or group name you want and click on it regardless of its orientation on the screen.

TIP   Sometimes spotting a program in a list is a visual hassle. Computers are smart about alphabetizing, so notice that the items in the lists are in order from A to Z. Folders appear first, in order, then programs after that. This ordering is something you'll see throughout Windows 95. To make things even simpler, you can press the first letter of the item you're looking for, and the highlight will jump to it. If there are multiple items starting with that letter, each key press will advance one in the list. This works fairly reliably unless the pointer is sitting on an item that has opened into a group.

Notice that if you open a Start button list that you don't want to look at—say, Documents—you can just move the pointer over to Programs, and that list will open. Pressing Esc also has the effect of closing open lists one at a time. Each press of Esc closes one level of open list. To close down all open lists, just click anywhere else on the screen, such as on the Desktop or another window.

Running a Program from My Computer

There are times when you might want to do a little sleuthing around using a more graphical approach as opposed to hunting for a name. The My Computer button lets you do this. My Computer is usually situated in the upper-left corner of your Desktop. Double-clicking on it reveals an interesting entry point to all the elements of your computer—hardware, software, printers, files, and folders.

The My Computer button is a little like a graphical version of File Manager, if you've used that. Getting to a program you want can be a little convoluted, but if you understand the DOS directory tree structure or you've used a Mac, you'll be able to grasp this fairly easily. Try it out.

1. Get to the Desktop by minimizing any windows that are on the screen. You can do this by clicking on each window's Minimize button (Chapter 3).

TIP   Another way to minimize all your windows and see the Desktop is to right-click on the clock in the Taskbar and choose Minimize All Windows.

2. Now double-click on My Computer. A window appears, looking something like this:

3. Typically, Drive C is where your programs will be located. Double-click on the drive icon, and your hard drive's contents will open up into another window as shown in Figure 4.3.

4. The object is to locate the folder containing the program you want and double-click on it. (Some programs are so ferreted away that it's difficult to find them. You may have to search around a bit.) The standard setting shows folders and files as *large icons*. If you want to see more folders on the screen at once to help in your search, you have several options. The large icon view can be annoying because it doesn't let you see very many objects at once. Check out the View menu.

5. Choose Small Icons, List, or Details. *Details* will show the sizes of files and other information about the files and folders, such as the date they were created. This is useful when looking for applications because the Type column will indicate whether the file is an application program.

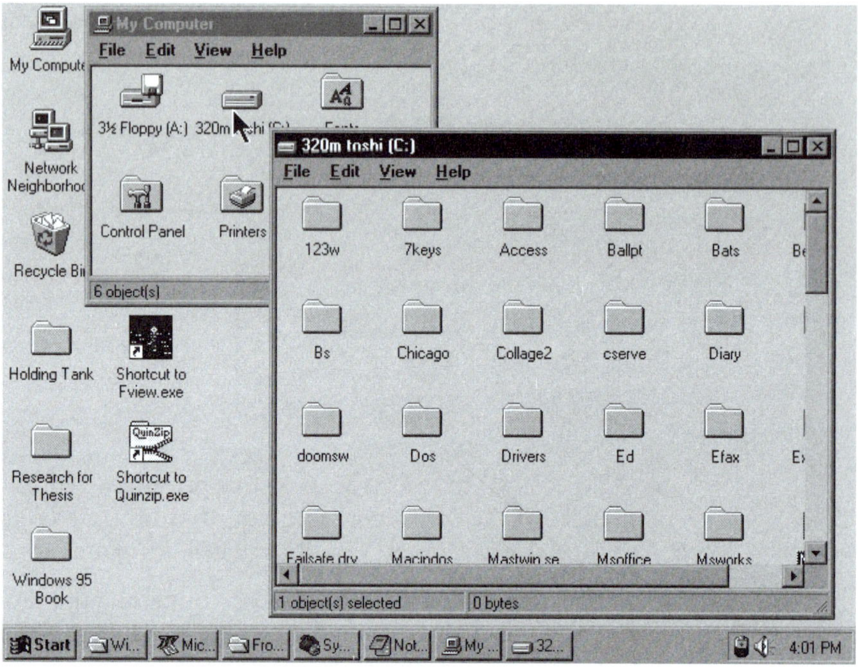

Figure 4.3   *Double-clicking on a drive icon displays its contents in a window. Here you see a portion of what I have on my C drive. Notice that folders (which used to be called directories) are listed first. Scrolling the listing would reveal any files in the folder. Here we are in essence looking at the root directory of the drive. Double-clicking on a folder will reveal its contents in another window.*

> **TIP**   Pressing Backspace while in any folder window will move you back one level. While in the C drive window, for example, pressing Backspace takes you back to the My Computer window. Or, if you're looking at a directory, Backspace will take you up to the root level.

6.   When you see the program you want to run, just double-click on it. For example, in Figure 4.4 I've found WinCIM.

Note that many of the files you'll find in your folders are *not* programs. They are documents or other kinds of files that are used by programs. Programs tend to have specialized icons such as the one for WinCIM in Figure 4.4. Documents, as you will learn later, look a bit different.

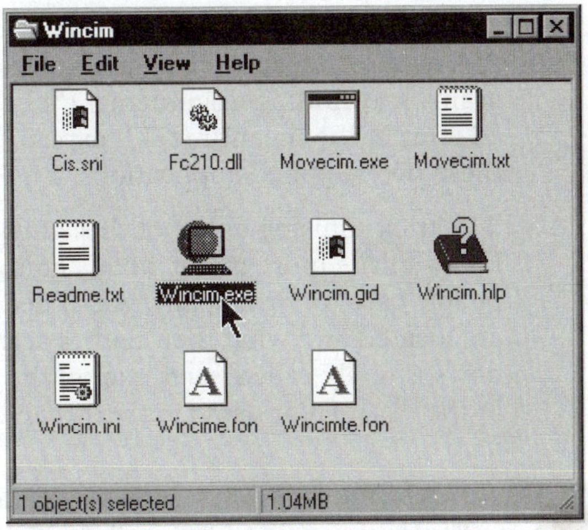

Figure 4.4 *Run a program by clicking on its icon. Regardless of whether the view is Large
Icons, Small Icons, List, or Detailed, double-clicking on a program will run it.*

TECH TIP Normally files with certain extensions (the last three letters of a
file's name) are hidden from display in your folder windows. Files with dll,
sys, vxd, 386, drv, and cpl extensions will not display. This choice was
made to prevent cluttering the display with files that perform duties for the
operating system but not directly for users. If you want to see all the files in
a folder, open the View menu on the folder's window, choose Options, and
select the File Types tab. Then turn on the appropriate check box. In Chapter 5 I'll explain all the options you can use when displaying folder windows.

Running a Program from
the Explorer or File Manager

On the Mac, all you get to work with to organize your documents and
programs is folders—essentially the same arrangement the last section
illustrated. This approach can be annoying when what you want is a grand
overview of your hard disk's contents. Working your way through a lot of
folder windows can get tedious and can clutter up the screen too much
to be efficient. There are ways to reduce the clutter when using this
approach, as I'll explain in Chapter 5. Even so, if you're the kind of person who prefers the *tree* approach (a hierarchical display of your disk's

contents) to your PC's hard disk, you might find the File Manager and its new replacement, the Explorer, a better means of running programs and finding documents. I'll be covering Explorer in Chapter 12. But in the meantime, I'll explain how to run your programs using these two supplied applications.

The trick to using either of these two programs is that you need to know a little more about what's going on in your computer than many people care to. Principally, you'll need to know where your programs are located and what their names are. For example, Word for Windows is really called word.exe on the hard disk and is typically stored in the Winword or Msoffice\Winword directory.

> **NOTE** Although not featured in Windows 95, the old-style Windows 3.x File Manager is actually supplied with Windows 95. It's not listed on the Start button menu, but it's most likely on your hard disk.

Here's how to use Explorer to run your programs (I'll explain File Manager next):

1. Because Explorer is a program itself, you have to run it before you can use it to run other programs. So click on the Start button, choose Programs, and point to Windows Explorer as shown in Figure 4.5.

> **TIP** Another way to run Explorer is to right-click on My Computer or a drive's icon in the My Computer window and choose Explore.

2. When the Explorer window comes up, adjust the window size for your viewing pleasure. It should look something like Figure 4.6.

3. The items on the left side are folders. Scroll down to the folder that contains the program you're looking for (folders are listed in alphabetical order). If a folder has a + sign next to it, it has subfolders. Clicking on the + sign displays the names of any subfolders.

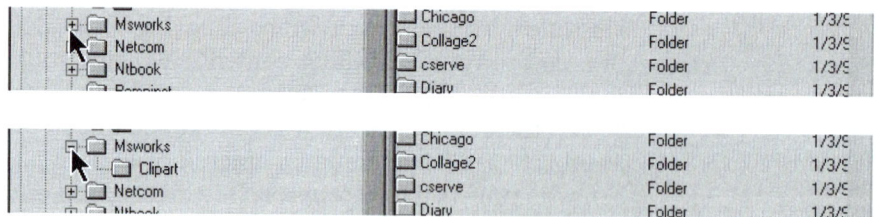

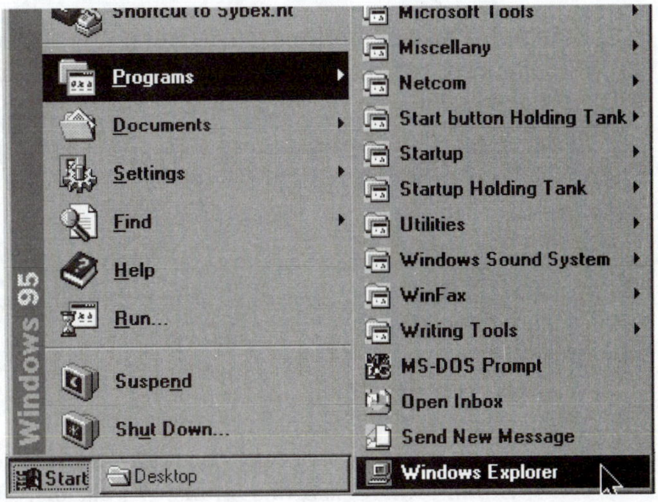

Figure 4.5   To run Explorer, click on Start, then Programs, then Windows Explorer.

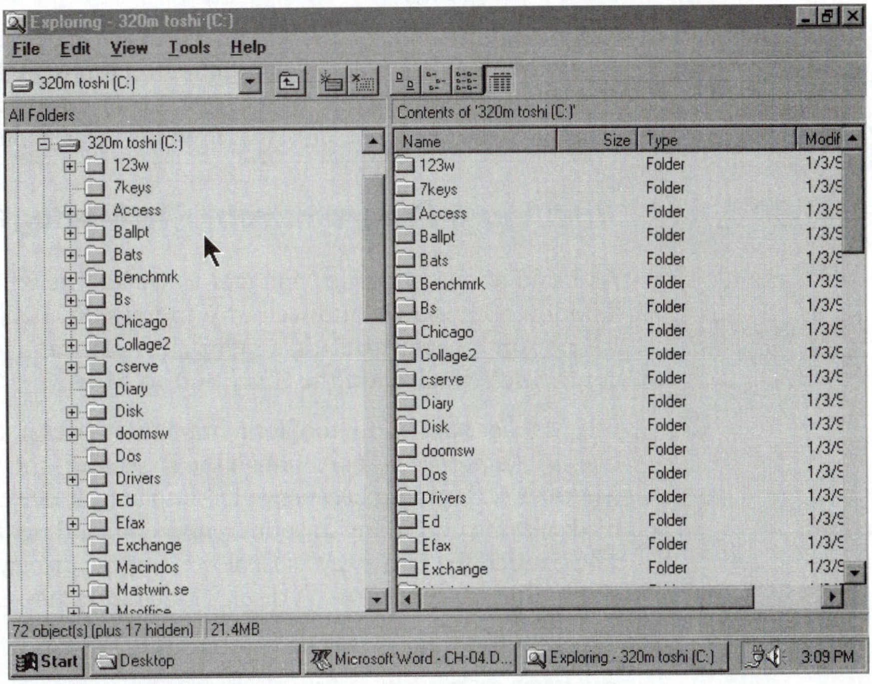

Figure 4.6   The Explorer window

4. Single-click on the folder containing the program you want to run. Its contents will appear in the right-hand side (called the right *pane*) of the window.

5. Then double-click on the program. Here I'm about to run Microsoft Works.

Notice that the items in the right-hand pane are displayed as large icons. Just as when using folders, you can change the appearance of listed items by opening the View menu and choosing Large Icons, Small Icons, List, or Details. It's easier to see which file is a program when the display is set to Large Icons (because you can see the icon clearly) or Details (because the third column will say *application* if the file is a program).

TIP   You can also use the four rightmost buttons on the toolbar to choose how items are displayed. They have the same effect as choosing Large Icons, Small Icons, List, or Details from the View menu.

Running a Program from File Manager

As I said above, the File Manager as we all knew it and love/hated it in Windows 3.x is alive and well in Windows 95. It's just sort of hidden. It's not on the Start button's menu, but you can run it with the Run command, which *is* on the Start button's menu.

File Manager is a useful tool for a number of tasks, including running programs (aka *applications*). Although the Explorer is more supercharged, File Manager is charming because of its simplicity. It doesn't confuse the issue by displaying everything in your computer including the kitchen sink. It works much the same way as Explorer, but the display is simpler. Unfortunately, File Manager doesn't display long file names.

To use File Manager to run a program:

1. Click on the Start button and choose Run.

2. In the resulting box, type **winfile** and click on OK.

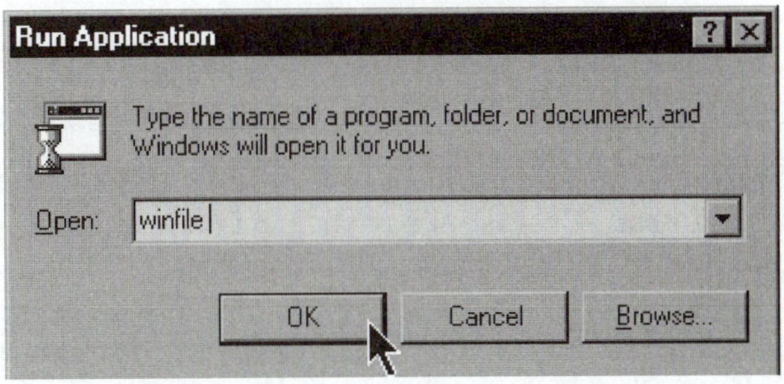

3. File Manager runs and appears in a window. Maximize the window, and File Manager will display as shown in Figure 4.7.

4. Select the folder you want by clicking on it. Normally, you won't see any indication of which folders have subfolders (subdirectories) under them. To see an indication of subfolders, you have to open the File Manager's Tree menu and choose Indicate Expandable Branches. After that, folders that have subfolders will be indicated by a + sign. Double-click on a + to display its subdirectories.

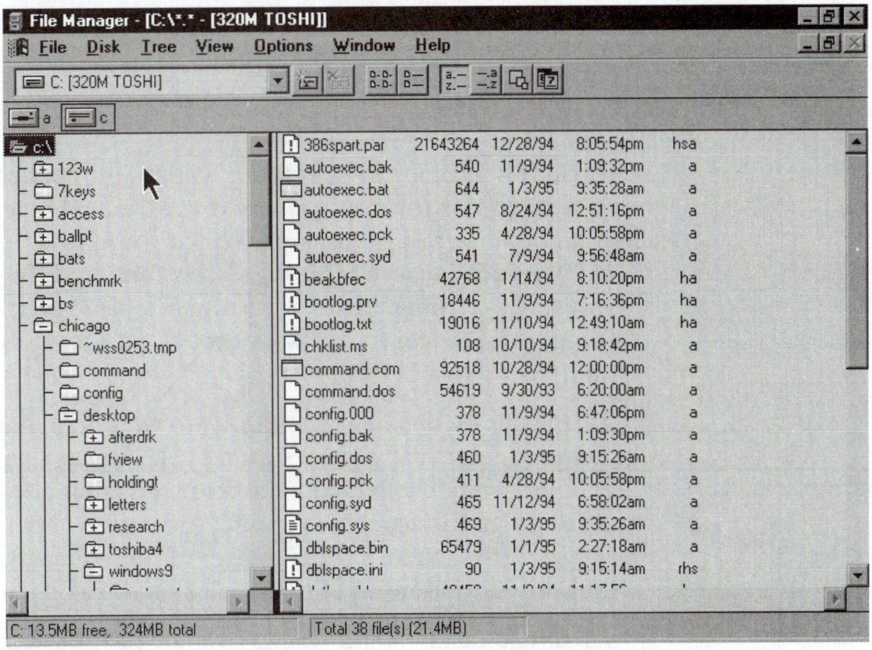

Figure 4.7   *To run a program from File Manager, double-click on it.*

NOTE   Even without the + sign showing, you can double-click on a folder to see any existing subfolders.

---

5. Scroll the display as necessary to show the name of the program you want to run. Programs have a special icon so you know which ones can be run. Here I'm about to run Works.

msoffice		maillabl.wps	673	10/14/93	11:30:30am	a
msworks		msworks.exe	1003456	3/20/92	12:00:20pm	a
netcom		msworks.hlp	1251061	3/20/92	12:00:00pm	a
ntbook		oldphone.wdb	3154	10/8/93	4:35:58pm	a

6. Double-click on the program file you want to run.

NOTE   As a general rule to remember, four kinds of files can be run using this method: Those with extensions of `exe`, `com`, `bat`, and `pif`. All other files will either not run when double-clicked on or will run their *associated* programs and load into them. For example, files with the extension `bmp` are graphics. Double-clicking on such a file (e.g., `arches.bmp`) will run the Paint program and load the graphic into the Paint window for editing.

Running a Program from Program Manager

If you're a Windows 3.x veteran, you might be most at home running your programs from the good old Program Manager. That's the program organizer that was supplied with Windows 3.x and is now essentially replaced by the Start button's submenus. To get new Windows 95 users over the hurdle of learning the new interface, they included Program Manager in the Windows 95 package. Like File Manager, though, it's sort of hidden away.

When you install a new program onto your computer (Chapter 5), the new program usually creates what's called a *program group*. A program group is a window that contains items pertaining to the program, such as the program's icon (for running it), various Readme files, a Help file, and so forth. To run a program from Program Manager, you just open the desired window and double-click on the icon you want.

When you install Windows 95 over an existing Windows 3.x setup, it does a little sleight of hand. All your preexisting Program Manager groups and icons end up on the Start button's Program lists. So clicking Start ➤ Programs will list your Program Manager groups.

Enough theory. Try this to run Program Manager:

1. Click on the Start button.

TIP You can press Ctrl-Esc to open the Start list from the keyboard at any time.

---

2. Choose Run. In the Run box enter **progman**.

3. Click on OK, and you'll see your old familiar Program Manager. Figure 4.8 illustrates.

4. The trick with Program Manager is that you have to find and display a group's window before you can run a program in it. If the screen is cluttered, sometimes the easiest way to do this is simply by opening the Window menu and choosing from there. Of course, you could just click on the window if it's in view, but the Window menu approach is a no-brainer.

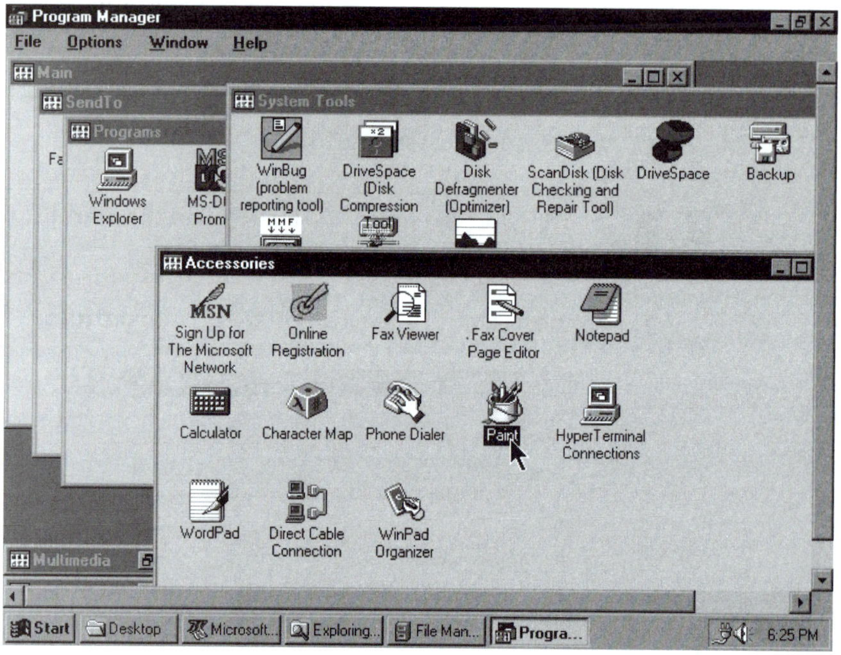

Figure 4.8   In Program Manager, double-clicking on a program's icon runs the program.

5. Once you've chosen the desired group, its window appears. Then double-click on the icon of the program you want to run. In Figure 4.8, for example, I'm about to run Paint from the Accessories group.

Running Applications from the Find Command

The Find command is covered in detail in Part V of this book, but I'll quickly mention how to use this indispensable little gadget. As with File Manager and Explorer, it helps if you know the file name of the program you're looking for, but at least Find cuts you some slack if you don't know the whole name. You can specify just part of it. Find will search a given disk or the whole computer (multiple disks) looking for something that looks like the program (or other file, such as a document) name you tell it. Once found, you can double-click on the program in the resulting list, and it will run. Pretty spiffy.

> **NOTE** The Run box technique (described above) is easier than Find if you know the exact name of the program. But the catch is that Run requires the program to be in the DOS *search path*. If it's not, the program won't run and you'll just get an error message saying the program can't be found. Of course, if you know the drive and directory the program is in, you *can* enter its entire path name, in which case it will probably run.

Here's an example. I have the program called Windsock somewhere on my computer. As it turns out, the Run command won't run this program because Windsock is stored in a folder that's not in my DOS search path. All I get when I try to find it is this message:

> **windsock** ⊠
>
> ⊖ Cannot find file 'windsock' (or one of its components).
> Check to ensure the path and filename are correct and
> that all required libraries are available.
>
> [OK]

So I cancel the Run dialog box and try the Find command. Here's how:

> **NOTE** From here on out, I'll use a shorthand notation to describe making multiple menu choices. Instead of: "Click on the Start button, choose Programs, then choose Accessories, and then choose Paint," I'll say: "Choose Start ➤ Programs ➤ Accessories ➤ Paint."

1. Choose Start ➤ Find ➤ Folders and Files.

2. The Find dialog box appears, and I fill in the top part with at least a portion of the name of the file I'm looking for. (See Figure 4.9—I've maximized the Find window to show you as much information as possible.) Note that I've set the *Look In* section to My Computer. As a default it will search your C drive, which is usually fine unless you have multiple hard disks on your computer and want Find to comb through them all.

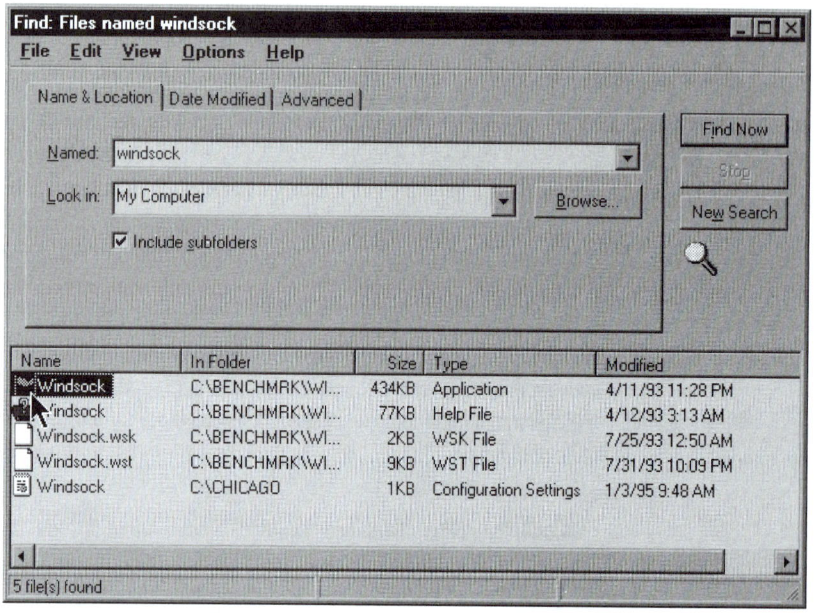

Figure 4.9   *Choosing Find from the Start menu lets you search the computer for a program. You don't have to enter the whole name as you do when using File Manager's Search command.*

3. I click on Find Now. In a few seconds any files or folders matching the search request show up in the bottom pane, as the figure illustrates. Note that several Windsock files were located, but that only one is an application (a program).

4. I double-click on the Windsock application, and it runs.

    When you want to run a program or open a document by clicking on it, don't double-click on its name slowly! If you do, this tells Windows that you want to change the object's name. You know this has happened when a little box appears around the name of the file like this:

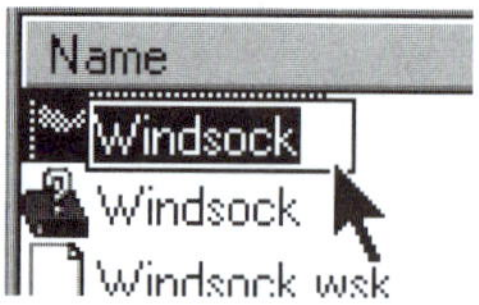

Just press Esc to get out of editing mode. To be safe, it's better to click on any item's icon (the picture portion) when you want to run it, open it, move it around, and so forth.

Running a Program
via One of Its Documents

As I mentioned above, some documents will open up when you click on their icons—if they are *registered*. Windows 95 has an internal registry (basically just a list) of file extensions that it knows about. Each registered file type is matched with a program that it works with. When you double-click on any document, Windows scans the list of registered file types to determine what it should do with the file. For example, double-clicking on a bmp file will run Paint and load the file.

The upshot of this is that you can run an application by double-clicking on a document of a known registered type. For example, suppose I want to run Word. All I have to do is spot a Word document somewhere. It's easy to spot one, especially in Large Icon view, because all Word documents have Word's telltale identifying icon. Unregistered documents have no discernible icon. Check out Figure 4.10. There I'm about to double-click on a Word document I came across in a folder. Notice that the icon just above it is what a nonregistered file icon looks like.

Once the program runs, you may decide you don't want to work with the actual document that you used as a trick to get the program going.

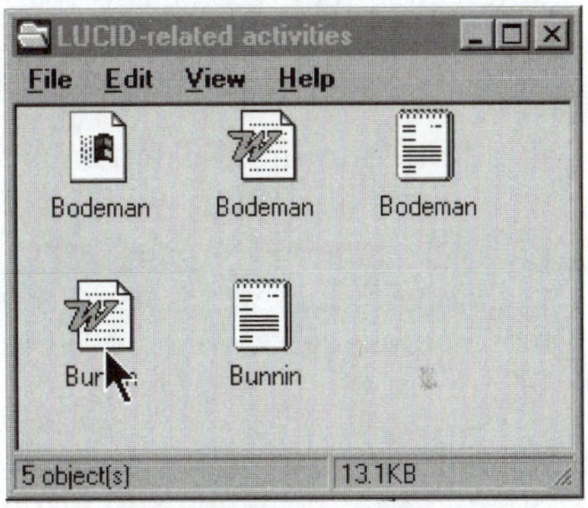

Figure 4.10 Double-clicking on a file of a registered type runs the program that created it.

That's OK because most programs will let you close the current document (try choosing File ➤ Close) and then let you open a new document (usually via File ➤ New) or an existing one with File ➤ Open.

TIP Try clicking on the Start button and choosing Documents to see a list of the files you've recently edited. Depending on what's on the list, you may be able to run the program you're looking for.

TECH TIP By default, file extensions of registered files are not displayed on screen. This cuts down on visual clutter, letting you see simple names that make sense, such as 1995 Report instead of 1995 Report.wk3. In later chapters I'll tell you how to turn off this option in case you always want to see and be able to change extensions at will.

How Do File Types Become Registered?

You may be wondering how documents with certain extensions become registered so they will run an application when double-clicked on. Some types are set up by Windows 95 when you install it. For example, hlp files (e.g., paint.hlp) are Help files and will open up in an appropriate window. Likewise, txt files will open in Notepad, pcx files in Paint, doc files in WordPad, ht files in HyperTerminal, and so on.

In addition to those extensions that are automatically established when installing Windows 95, some others might have been imported into your system from an earlier version of Windows. If you've upgraded to Windows 95 from Windows 3.x, then any previously registered types (called *associations* in Windows 3.x) are pulled into Windows 95.

Some programs register their file type when you install the program. So, for example, when you install Word, Windows 95 changes the registration list so that doc files will be opened by Word instead of by WordPad when double-clicked on.

And finally, you can register a file type yourself (Chapter 5) from any folder or Explorer window's View ➤ Options ➤ File Types command.

Running Applications
by Right-Clicking on the Desktop

When you don't want to bother finding some favorite program just to create a new document, there's an easier way. How often have you simply wanted to create a To Do list, a shopping list, a brief memo, little spreadsheet, or what have you? All the time, right? Microsoft figured out that people often work in just this way—they don't think: "Gee, I'll root around for Excel, then I'll run it, and then I'll create a new spreadsheet file and save it and name it." That's counterintuitive. On the contrary, it's more likely they think: "I need to create a 'Sales for Spring Quarter' Excel spreadsheet."

Just create a new *empty* document of the correct type on the Desktop and name it. Then double-clicking on it will run the correct program. Windows 95 takes care of assigning the file the correct extension so that internally the whole setup works. Try an experiment to see what I'm talking about.

1. Clear off enough windows so you can see your Desktop area.

> **TIP** Remember, you can right-click on the clock in the Taskbar and choose *Minimize all windows* to minimize all the open windows. You can reverse the effect by clicking again and choosing *Undo Minimize all*.

2. Right-click anywhere on the Desktop. From the resulting menu choose New. You'll see a list of possible document types. The types in my computer are shown in Figure 4.11 as an example.

3. Choose a document type by clicking on it. A new document icon appears on your Desktop such as this one that appeared when I chose *Sound*:

4. The file's name is highlighted and has a box around it. This means you can edit the name. As long as the whole name is highlighted, whatever you type will replace the entire name. When you create a new document this way, you don't have to worry about entering the extension. For example, a sound file normally has a wav extension, but you could just type in **Blam** for the name and press Enter (remember, you have to press Enter after typing in the name to finalize it). The actual file name will be Blam.wav because Windows 95 adds a hidden file extension for you.

5. Double-click on the icon and its associated program will run. In the case of the sound, Sound Recorder will run, waiting for me to record the sound.

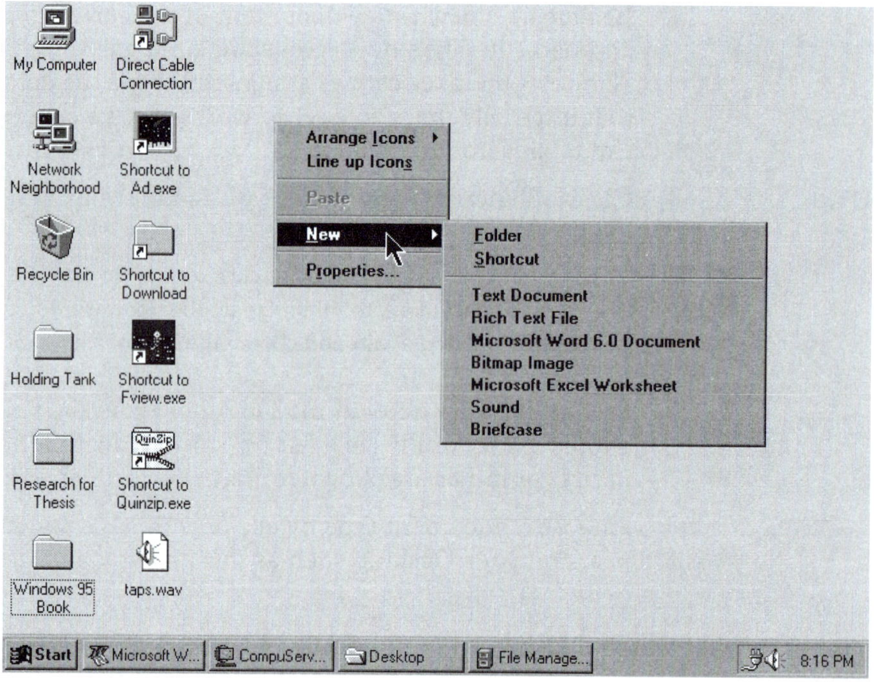

Figure 4.11 *You can create a variety of new document types by right-clicking on the Desktop. This creates a blank document that you then name and run.*

Using the Start ➤ Documents List

As I mentioned in a Tip above, choosing Start ➤ Documents lists the documents you've recently created or edited. It's an easy way to revisit projects you've been working on. This list is maintained by Windows 95 and is *persistent*, which means it'll be there in subsequent Windows sessions, even after you shut down and reboot. Only the last fifteen documents are remembered, though, and some of these won't be things you'd think of as documents. Some of them might actually be more like programs or folders. Check it out and see if it contains the right stuff for you. Figure 4.12 shows my list the day I wrote this section.

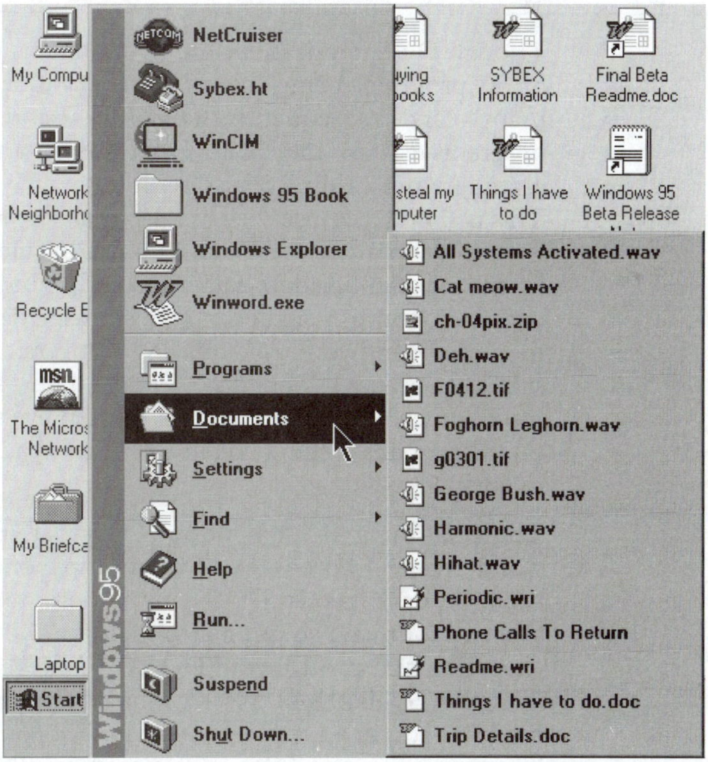

Figure 4.12 *The Document list from the Start button provides a no-brainer path to ongoing work projects.*

> **TIP**   Many Windows programs have a similar feature that lists your most recently edited documents at the bottom of their File menus. Because many of my favorite programs sport this feature, I tend to rely on that more than on the Document list.

> **TIP**   You can clear off the items in the Documents list and start fresh if you want to. Click on the Start button, choose Settings ➤ Taskbar ➤ Start Menu Programs, and click on the Clear button.

Running DOS Programs

Though DOS applications are by no means the preponderant genre of PC programs being sold in today's world, they certainly were for many years. Consequently, tens of thousands of useful and interesting programs exist for the IBM-PC DOS environment. Many of these programs are not easily replaced with popular Windows programs, either. This is simply because they were specialized programs custom designed for vertical market uses such as point of sale, transaction processing, inventory, scientific data gathering, and so on. It's safe to say that after a corporation invests significantly in software development, testing, implementation, and employee training, conversion to a Windows-based version just because it looks groovier isn't a very attractive proposition. As a result, much of the code that was written five to ten years ago and ran in DOS programs is still doing its job in companies and other institutions today.

The great thing about Windows 95 is that you can still run all those wonderful DOS programs, even multiple ones at the same time. And each can have its own DOS environment, tasking settings, window size and font, and so on, not to mention the ability to automate task execution and control with DOS *batch* files. Until Windows NT and Windows 95, batch files were not available for Windows users. They could be run in a DOS box but couldn't control Windows programs. Windows 95 can execute DOS programs, DOS batch files, and Windows programs from the command line. Therefore you can write batch files with Windows program command lines in them.

So How Do I Run My DOS Programs?

I'll explain briefly how you run DOS programs here.

You can run a DOS program by:

▶ clicking on the Start button, choosing Programs, and looking for the program on the resulting menus

▶ double-clicking on the program's name in a folder

▶ entering the program's name at the Run command

▶ double-clicking on the program in File Manager

▶ double-clicking on the program in Explorer

▶ running a "DOS session" and then typing in the program's name at the DOS prompt

▶ double-clicking on a document file with an extension that you've manually associated with the DOS program

I explained the first five of these techniques earlier when I told you how to run Windows programs. The only difference between running Windows programs and DOS programs using those techniques is that DOS programs don't normally have an identifying icon, such as a big "W" for Word. Instead, they tend to have a boring, generic icon that looks like:

Therefore, you have to rely on the icon's name alone. This one is for XTREE Gold, but because the actual program's name on disk is xtgold.exe, that's what you see. Well, actually, you don't see the exe part, because as I mentioned earlier, exe extensions are normally hidden from view.

Because the last two approaches in the above list differ from running Windows programs and haven't been covered, let's check those out. Then I'll tell you a bit about how DOS programs operate in Windows and what you can quickly do to modify their behavior.

First consider the option of running a DOS program from the good old DOS prompt.

NOTE   There isn't room in this book to discuss all the DOS commands and how DOS works. You should consult a book such as Sybex's *Mastering DOS 6.2* for more information about DOS commands. To get on-screen help with DOS, you can enter the command help at the DOS prompt and follow directions at that point.

To run a DOS session, do the following:

1. Click on the Start button.

2. Choose Programs, then MS-DOS Prompt, as shown in Figure 4.13.

3. The result will be what's sometimes called a *DOS box*—a window that operates just like you're using a computer running DOS. Try typing in **DIR** and pressing Enter. You'll see a listing of files on the current

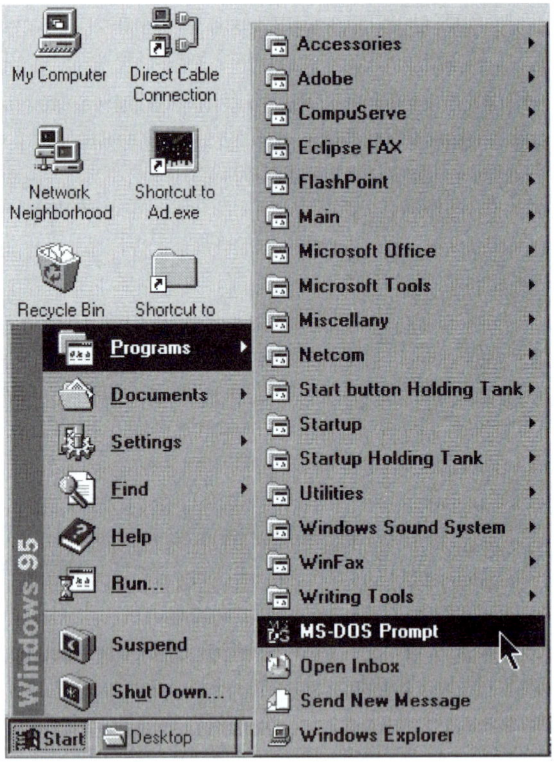

Figure 4.13   *You run a DOS session (get to a DOS prompt) by choosing MS-DOS from the Program list.*

drive, as shown in Figure 4.14. Note that short and long file names are both shown in this new version of DOS. Long file names are in the rightmost column, with corresponding short file names over on the left.

4. Enter the command **exit** when you are finished running DOS programs or executing DOS commands. This will close the DOS window and end the session.

> **TIP**   If no DOS program is actually running, clicking on the DOS window's Close button will also end the DOS session. If a DOS program is running, trying this results in a message prompting you to quit the DOS program first.

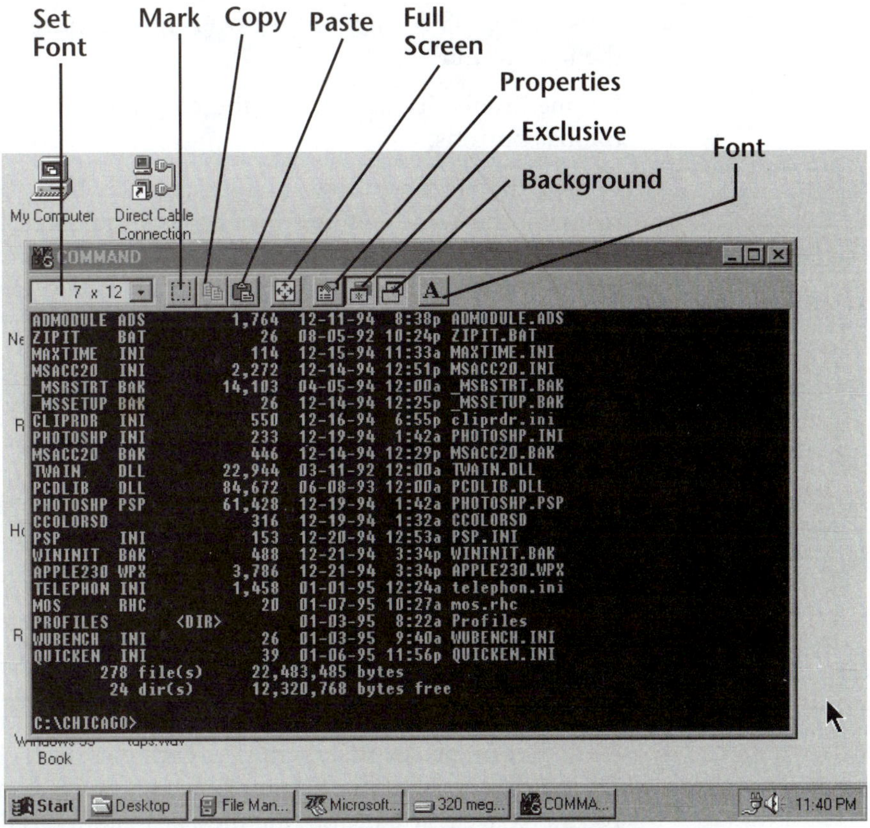

Figure 4.14 Enter any standard DOS commands at the prompt.

Options while Running a DOS Session

While running a DOS session, there are several easy adjustments you can make that are either cosmetic or actually affect the performance of the program. You can easily:

▶ toggle the DOS session between full screen and windowed

▶ turn the toolbar on or off

▶ adjust the font

▶ resize the DOS box

▶ allow the DOS session to work in the background

▶ cause the DOS session to take over the computer's resources when in the foreground

Let me briefly discuss each of these options. Refer to Figure 4.14 for toolbar buttons.

First, if the DOS window is taking up the whole screen (all other elements of the Windows interface have disappeared) and you'd like to have the DOS program running in a window so you can see other programs, press Alt-Enter to switch it to a window. Once windowed, you can return it to full-screen mode either by clicking on the Full Screen button or pressing Alt-Enter again.

Next, you can turn on the toolbar if you want easy access to most of the above features. Then you won't have to use the menus. If you don't see the toolbar (as in Figure 4.14), click in the upper-left corner of the DOS window and choose Toolbar. Choose the same command again, and the toolbar will turn off.

Once the toolbar is showing, you can set several useful options. A nice feature in Windows 95 is the adjustable font. Unlike in Windows 3.x, you can now use TrueType fonts in a DOS box. The easiest way to change the font is to open the Font drop-down list (rather than clicking on the "A" button). Fonts are listed there by the size of the character matrix (in pixels) that comprises each displayed character. The larger the matrix, the larger the resulting characters (and consequently the DOS box itself) will be. Setting the size to auto has the effect of scaling

Part
1

Up and Running
with Windows 95

the font automatically if you resize the DOS box from its lower-left corner. When resizing, don't be surprised if the mouse pointer jumps around a bit wildly. The box is not infinitely adjustable as Windows programs are, so as you're adjusting, the outline of the window jumps to predetermined sizes.

> **TIP** The *A* button on the toolbar lets you choose whether only bit-mapped fonts, TrueType fonts, or both will show in the Fonts listing on the left.

The Properties button we'll leave alone for the time being. Selections you make here are rather complicated and require some detailed discussion. So, moving right along, take note of the Exclusive button. This button determines whether your DOS program, when in the foreground, will receive all of your CPU's attention. That is, it will be run as though there are no other programs running in the computer that might need to be serviced. Some programs—such as data-acquisition programs that expect total control of the computer, the screen, keyboard, ports, and so forth—may require this. If you want to turn this option off, (which would allow other programs in the background to continue processing while this program runs), click on this button. It should pop out rather than look indented, meaning it's turned off.

The final button, Background, determines whether the DOS program will continue processing in the background when you switch to another program. As a default, this setting is on. You can tell it's on because the button looks indented. You can turn it off if you want your DOS program to temporarily suspend when it isn't the active window (the window in which you're currently working).

> **TIP** You can of, course, have multiple DOS sessions running at the same time in separate windows. This lets you easily switch between a number of DOS programs that can be running simultaneously.

> **NOTE** You can also Copy and Paste data from and to DOS applications. See Chapter 6 for details.

Additional Property Settings for DOS Programs

DOS programs were designed to run one at a time and are usually memory hogs. They often need at least 600K of free RAM, and some may require expanded or extended memory to perform well. Running a DOS program with several other programs (particularly other DOS programs) under Windows is conceptually like bringing a bunch of ill-mannered guests to a formal dinner.

The moral of this is simply that Windows has a lot of housekeeping to do to keep DOS programs happy. When running from Windows, DOS programs don't really "know" that other programs are running, and they expect to have direct access to all the computer's resources: RAM, printer, communications ports, screen, and so on.

In most cases, Windows 95 does pretty well at faking out DOS programs without your help, using various default settings and its own memory-management strategies. However, even Windows 95 isn't omniscient, and you may occasionally experience the ungracious locking up of a program or see messages about the "system integrity" having been corrupted.

TECH TIP   In reality, what Windows is doing when running DOS programs is giving each of them a simulated PC to work in, called a *VDM* (Virtual DOS Machine).

If a DOS program doesn't run properly under Windows 95 or you wish to optimize its performance, you must modify its PIF (Program Information File), declaring certain settings that affect the program within Windows. With Windows 3.x, making PIF settings for a program required using a program called the PIF Editor—a cumbersome program supplied with Windows. Things are simpler with Windows 95. The first time you run a DOS program, a PIF is automatically created in the same directory as the DOS program. It has the same name as the program but looks like a shortcut icon. Examining the properties of the icon will reveal it has a `.pif` extension.

To adjust a program's PIF settings, simply open the Properties box for the DOS program and make the relevant settings. This can be done by running the DOS program in a window and clicking on the

Properties button on the Toolbar or, without running the program, by right-clicking on its PIF icon and choosing Properties. When you close the Properties box, the new PIF settings are saved. From then on, those settings go into effect whenever you run the program from within Windows.

The PIF settings affect many aspects of the program's operation, such as, but not limited to:

▶ the file name and directory of the program

▶ font and window size

▶ the directory that becomes active once a program starts

▶ memory usage, including conventional, expanded, extended, and protected-mode memory usage

▶ multitasking priority levels

▶ video-adapter modes

▶ the use of keyboard shortcut keys

▶ foreground and background processing

▶ Toolbar display

▶ program-termination options

Some of these options were discussed above and are quickly adjustable from the DOS box Toolbar; others are not. To fine-tune the DOS environment for running a program:

▶ If the program will run without bombing:

1. Run it as explained above.
2. If it's not in a window, press Alt-Enter.
3. Click on the Properties button if the Toolbar is showing or, if it isn't showing, click on the Control Box in the upper-left corner of the window and choose Properties.

▶ If the program won't run without bombing:

1. Navigate with My Computer or Explorer to the folder containing the DOS program.
2. Find the program's icon and click on it.

3. Open the File menu and choose Create Shortcut. A new icon will appear in the folder, called "Shortcut to [*program*]."

4. With the new shortcut highlighted, open the File menu and choose Properties.

Now you'll see the DOS program's Properties sheet, from which you can alter quite a healthy collection of settings (Figure 4.15). Unfortunately, there isn't room in this book for an explanation of all the settings available from this box. Remember, you can get some basic information about each setting via the ? button.

NOTE In my upcoming book, *Windows 95 Secrets & Solutions* (Sybex, 1995), I'll discuss all of these settings in detail as well as the proper use of **DOS** device drivers and **DOS** TSR (terminate and stay resident) programs.

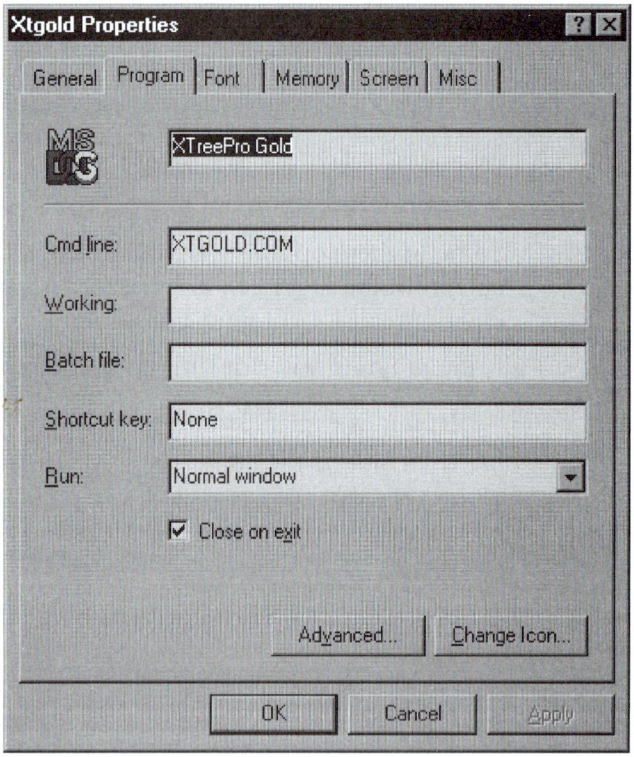

Figure 4.15 *The Properties box for the program XTreePro Gold*

Simply make your settings as necessary. When you're happy with them, click on OK in the Properties box to save the settings. The next time you run the program by double-clicking on the shortcut or the program's icon, the settings will go into effect.

TECH TIP When you run a DOS program by clicking on its icon or its PIF icon, the PIF settings go into effect and the program runs. However, if you run the program from the DOS command line (by typing in a command from a DOS box), the settings *don't* go into effect. *They simply aren't used.* Two other ways to ensure they are used are to use the Run command and enter the name of the PIF, such as `ed.pif`, and to use the Start command from the DOS prompt (e.g., start ed.exe). Also, aside from the active directory, only directories listed in the search path as set up by your `autoexec .bat` file are scanned for PIFs. If a PIF isn't found when a program is double-clicked on, it won't be loaded, and Window's default PIF settings will be used instead.

TIP If you are having trouble getting a DOS program to even check that the memory settings for the PIF match those required by the program (check the program's user manual) and if the program can't run in a window, set the screen usage to Full Screen.

TECH TIP PIFs are one of two types of shortcut files. Shortcuts for Windows applications and documents are given the LNK extension. Only shortcuts for DOS applications actually are given the PIF extension. Even if you elect to display the MS-DOS extensions of all files (from the View ➤ Options menu in Explorer or a folder), you won't see the PIF extension in listings. Use the Find utility to look for PIFs by extension, if you need to.

What I Didn't Tell You—
Shortcuts on the Desktop

A terrific feature of Windows 95 when it comes to running your pro-grams is called *shortcuts*. Shortcuts are alias icons (icons that represent other icons) that you can add almost anywhere, such as in folders or on the Desktop. Because a shortcut is really only a link or pointer to the real file or application it represents, you can have as many as you

AUTOMATING JOBS WITH BATCH FILES

Because I am not a 200-word-per-minute typist, I like to create batch files to automate repetitive jobs or to create jobs to run at Windows start-up. For instance, if you want to automate the process of checking your hard disk for errors with Scan-Disk every time you start Windows 95, try this:

1. Open up Notepad (Start ➤ Programs ➤ Notepad) or any other ASCII text editor.

2. To check just your C: drive, enter the following text:

    SCANDISK C: /n

To check all of your local disk drives, enter the following text:

    SCANDISK /a /n

3. Save the file with a `.bat` file extension. For instance, you might want to save it as `Check Disk Drives for Errors.bat`.

4. Then add this item to the Startup folder so that Windows 95 will run it every time you start it (see Chapter 5 for complete instructions on how to do this).

5. The check will now run automatically every time you start Windows 95. You can also run it anytime you desire by selecting it from the Start menu.

The really nice part about this process is that you can do this to automate any job. And you can make the process completely automatic by adding the batch file to the Startup group (as we did above), or you can choose to manually run it whenever you select it from the Start menu. For instance, I could have created a new folder under the Programs folder, called it `Batch Jobs`, and placed the Check Disk for Errors batch file there. Then anytime I wanted to run this process I would select Start ➤ Programs ➤ Batch Jobs ➤ Check Disk…. You can use this same process to automate any job or start up multiple applications to create your daily working set. For instance, I could have created a batch file to launch Microsoft Mail, Schedule Plus, Word for Windows, and Excel all at once. This would save several mouse or keystroke commands because I would not have to return to the Start menu to launch them individually.

want, putting them wherever your heart desires, without duplicating your files. So, for example, you can have shortcuts to all your favorite programs right on the Desktop. Then you can run them from there without having to click on the Start button, walk through the Program listings, and so forth.

In Chapter 5 I'll explain how you make, copy, and place shortcuts. I'll also cover how you can dump shortcuts of your favorite programs onto the Start button so they are right there on the first menu when you click on Start.

Switching between Applications

Remember, Windows lets you have more than one program open and running at a time. You can also have multiple folders open at any time, and you can leave them open to make getting to their contents easier. Any folders that are open when you shut down the computer will open again when you start up Windows again.

People often think they have to shut down one program before working on another one, but that's really not efficient nor true. When you run each new program or open a folder, the Taskbar gets another button on it. Simply clicking on a button switches you to that program or folder. For the first several programs, the buttons are long enough to read the names of the programs or folder. As you run more programs, the buttons automatically get shorter, so the names are truncated. For example:

You can resize the Taskbar to give it an extra line or two of buttons if you want to see the full names. On the upper edge of the Taskbar, position the cursor so that it turns into a double-headed arrow, then drag it upwards and release. Here I've added another line for my current set of buttons.

Note that as you increase the size of the Taskbar, you decrease the effective size of your work area. On a standard VGA screen, this means you'll be cutting onto your work area quite a bit if you go to two or three lines. Still, it's possible. Another nice feature is that you can set the Taskbar to disappear until you move the mouse pointer down to the bottom of the screen. This way, you sacrifice nothing in the way of screen real estate. You do this via the Settings menu from the Start button.

TIP If you prefer, you can also position the Taskbar on the right, left, or top of the screen. Just click on any part of the Taskbar other than a button and drag it to the edge of your choice.

Here's how to set the Taskbar options:

1. Click on Start and choose Settings.

2. Then choose Taskbar, as shown in Figure 4.16.

TIP A quick way to get to the Taskbar's Property settings is to right-click on an empty area of the Taskbar and choose Properties.

---

3. You'll now see the dialog box shown in Figure 4.15. Click on *Auto hide* to turn that option on—this is the one that makes the Taskbar disappear until you move the pointer to the edge of the screen where you've placed the Taskbar.

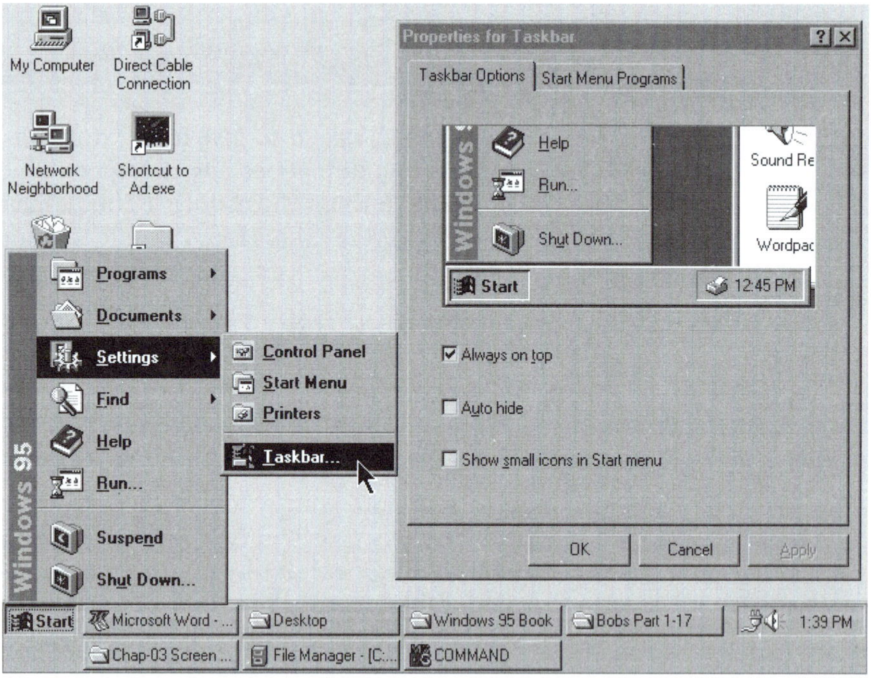

Figure 4.16 You set the Taskbar options from this box. The mostly likely choice you'll make will be Auto Hide.

4. If you'd like to see smaller icons in the first Start-up menu, set that option on, too.

5. OK the dialog box. Once you do so, the Taskbar will disappear. Try out the Auto Hide setting: Move the pointer down to the bottom and see how the Taskbar reappears.

TECH TIP Even when set to Auto Hide, the Taskbar still uses 1 or 2 pixels at the edge of the screen to indicate where it is and to act as a trigger zone to pop up the Taskbar when the pointer touches it.

Switching with Alt-Tab

Don't like the Taskbar? Are you a habituated Windows 3.x user? Okay. As you may know, there's another way to switch between programs and folders—the Alt-Tab trick. Press down the Alt key and hold it down. Now, press the Tab key (you know, that key just above the Caps Lock and to the left of the Q). You'll see a box in the center of your screen showing you an icon of each program or folder that's running, like this:

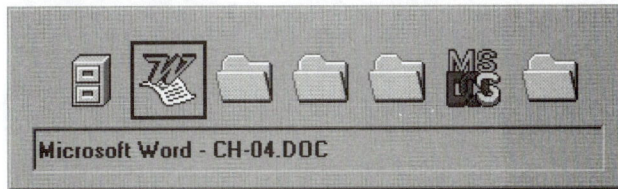

Microsoft Word - CH-04.DOC

Each press of the Tab key will advance the outline box one notch to the right. The outline box indicates which program you'll be switched to when you release the Alt key. If you want to back up one program (move the box to the left), you can press Alt-Shift-Tab. Note that the name of the program or folder is displayed at the bottom of the box, which is especially useful when choosing folders, as all folders look the same.

TECH TIP   In Windows 3.x, pressing Ctrl-Esc brought up the Task List. It no longer does: It opens the Start menu as though you clicked on the Start button. Likewise, double-clicking on the Desktop now fails to bring up the Task List. The only time you can get the Task List is when Explorer malfunctions and causes the Taskbar to cease functioning. At that point, double-clicking on the Desktop will bring up an updated version of the Task List. You can then use that to switch tasks or to shut down.

Chapter 5

Organizing Your Programs and Documents

FEATURING

n this chapter, we'll explore the best way to organize your own work within Windows 95 and just what steps to take to do so. I'll tell you how to use the Taskbar, the Windows 95 folder system, and the Explorer to arrange your programs and documents so you can get to them easily. With the techniques I'll show you in this chapter, you'll be ready to set up new folders and move your work files into them—just like setting up a new filing cabinet in your office. You'll also learn how to put your programs and projects on the Startup menus as well as on the Desktop so they are within easy reach.

Not obvious unless you opt to install Windows 95 with the Windows 3.x user interface (an option available when you do a custom install), the old-style Windows 3.x Program Manager and File Manager are both features of Windows 95. They are included with Windows for people who want to continue using a familiar interface to organize their files and programs while they're getting used to Windows 95.

Putting Your Favorite
Programs on the Start Button

One thing every Windows 95 user is bound to benefit from is knowing how to put their favorite programs and documents right on the Start button's menu. True, you can put your programs, folders, and documents right on the Desktop and just double-click on them to use them. But it's sometimes a hassle to get back to the Desktop because it can be obscured by whatever windows you might have open. Although there are ways around this (as in right-clicking on the Taskbar and choosing Minimize all Windows), dropping your favorite items on the Start button's first menu is easier. For example, Figure 5.1 shows you what my Start button's menu currently looks like.

With a single click of the mouse, no matter what I'm doing in Windows with my other programs, I can quickly see the programs, folders, and documents I use most and open them.

As with most things in Windows, there are several ways to add items to the Start menu. I'll show you the two that are the most straightforward—dragging onto the Start button, and using the Start ➤ Settings ➤ Taskbar ➤ Start Menu Programs command. The first technique is simply to drag the application, folder, or document's icon onto the

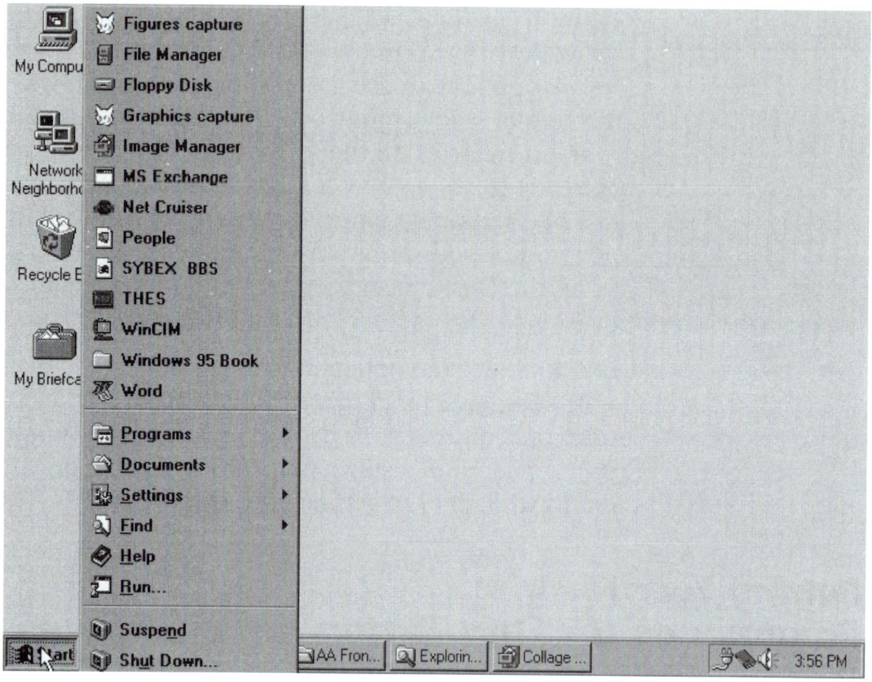

Figure 5.1   *You can add your favorite projects and programs to the top of the Start menu by dragging them onto the Start button.*

Start button. Windows 95 will then create a *shortcut* and place the shortcut on the Start button's opening menu.

> **NOTE**   A shortcut is not the application, folder, or document's *real* icon, it's a pointer to that icon. The result is the same either way. Double-clicking on a shortcut has the same effect as double-clicking on the object's original icon. In the case of the start button's menu, choosing the shortcut item from the menu will run the application, open the folder, or open the document.

1.   First, you'll need to find an icon that represents the object you want to put on the menu. The icon can be a shortcut icon or the original icon, either in a folder, on the Desktop, in the Find box, in Explorer, or displayed in any other window that supports drag-and-drop techniques.

The Find box is probably the easiest if you know the name of the file or document you're looking for.

2. Once you've located the object you want to add, drag it over the Start button and then release the mouse button. Figure 5.2 shows an example of adding a program to the Start button. I'm dragging a program called Wintach from the Wintac folder to the Start button.

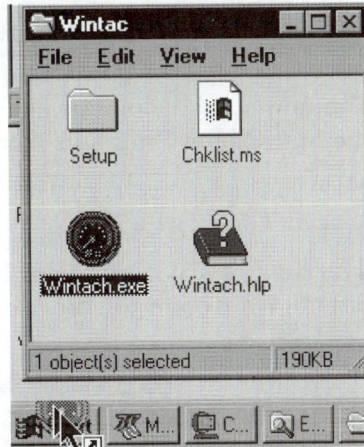

Figure 5.2   *Dragging from a folder to the Start button is simple. Just find the object you want to add, drag it over the Start button, and release.*

3. Now when you open the Start menu, you'll see the object has been added at the top of the list.

That's the easiest way to add new items to the Start button. When you want to remove items, you'll have to use another approach. You can't just select an item and press Del (see *Removing an Item from a Menu*, below).

Modifying the Start Button Menus

When you want a little more control over what you're adding to the Start menu, there's a command for it. This command also lets you add to and remove items from submenu folders. Here's how it works.

1. Click on Start and choose Settings ➤ Taskbar.

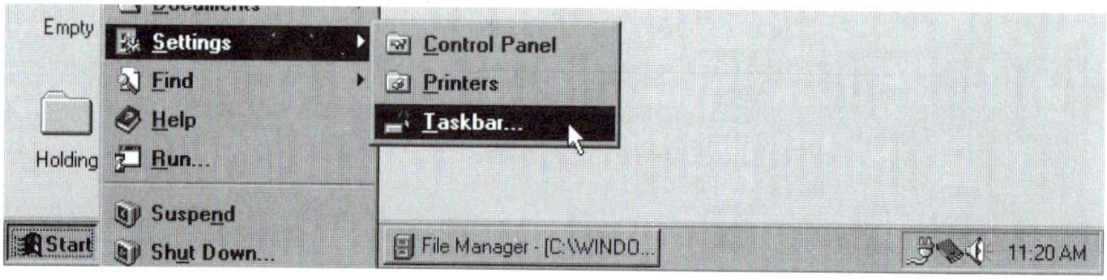

2. You now see a dialog box like the one shown in Figure 5.3. Click on the Start Menu Programs tab, then on OK.

3. Now you see a box from which you can choose Add, Delete, or Advanced. Click on Add.

4. The result is a Wizard dialog box that guides you though choosing the program you want to add (Figure 5.4).

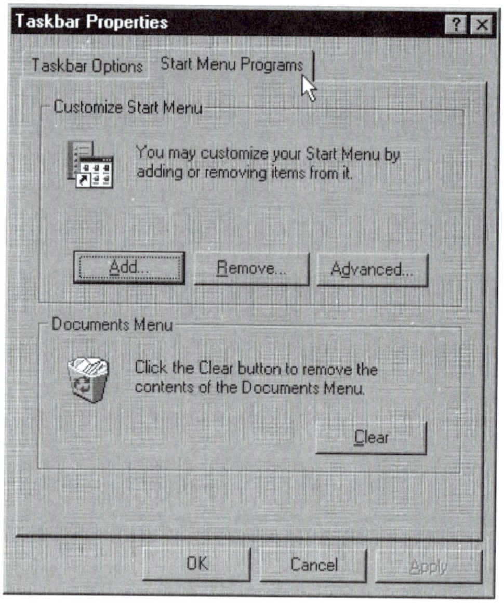

Figure 5.3   *Start menu setup is reached from this tab.*

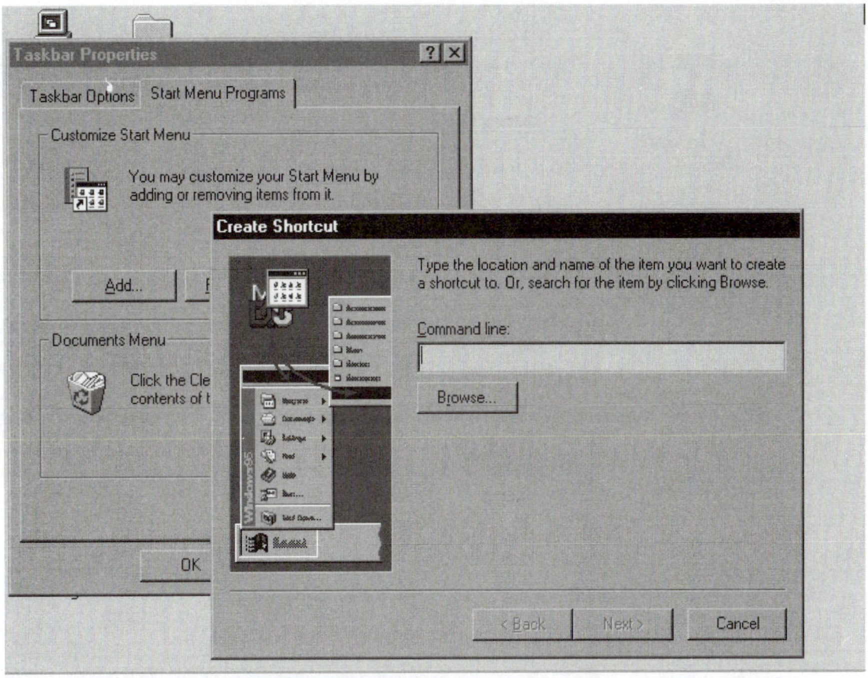

Up and Running
with Windows 95

Figure 5.4   *The Wizard walks you through adding an item to your Start button menu or sub-menus. Just fill in the name of the item or use the Browse button. Browse is probably easier.*

5.   If you know the name of the item, just enter it into the box. The problem is that you need to know the full path name of the item or it must be in your DOS search path. Otherwise, when you click on Next, you'll be told the file can't be found. Any program in the DOS root directory, your Windows directory, or DOS directory will work even without a full path name entered. For example, entering scandisk will work fine without specifying its full path name, which is \Windows\Command\scandisk.exe. To make life easier on yourself and cut down on possible typing or naming mistakes, click on the Browse button and browse for the item graphically. You'll see a typical File box. Normally, the box only displays *programs*. But if you're trying to add a *document* to your Start button menu, open the drop-down list and choose All Files. When you find the item you want, click on it, then click on Open.

TECH TIP   What if instead of adding a *program* or *document* to a Start menu you want to add a *folder?* Doing this can give you a shortcut to that folder as one of the options on your Start menu. The only catch is that you can't do it from the Browse box. You have to go back to Step 4. If the Browse box is open, close it by clicking on Cancel. Then enter the full path name of the folder.

6.   Now you're back to the Create Shortcut dialog box. Your item's name is now typed in. Click on Next.

7.   You'll see a large dialog box asking which folder you want the short-cut added to (Figure 5.5). Note that those listed in the box are the same folders and subfolders that are included on your Start ➤ Programs menu. As you can see, there's a lot of flexibility here. At this point you can choose to add the shortcut to any existing folder, to the Desktop, or to the Start menu. You can even create a new folder if you want to by clicking on New Folder. Just scroll the list and click on the folder you want to add the item to. If you're going to create a new folder, you have decide where you want it to be added. For example, if I wanted to add a subfolder under Berneze (see Figure 5.5), I'd first click on Berneze, then click on the New Folder button. A new folder is added there, waiting for me to edit its name.

8.   Click on Next.

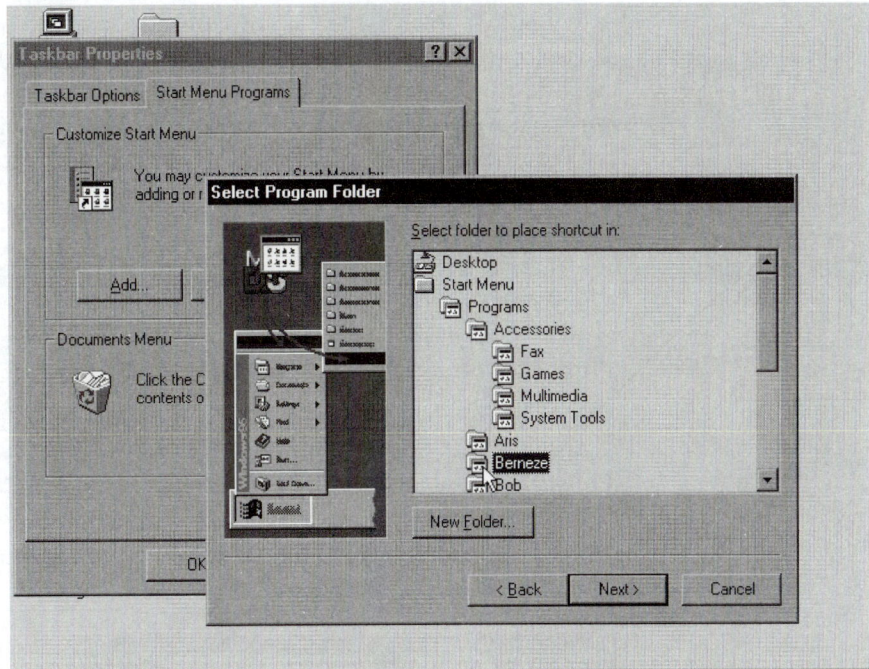

Figure 5.5   Choose which group or other location the new shortcut will be added to. If you want the item on the Start menu, choose Start Menu. To put the folder on the Desktop, scroll up to the top of the list.

9. Now you're asked to name your shortcut. This is thoughtful because it's more informative to have a menu item called Word Perfect 5.1 than WP51.EXE. (When you just drop an icon on the Start button, incidentally, you're stuck with whatever name the icon has.) Enter the name you want, but don't make it incredibly long because that will widen the menu appreciably, possibly making it difficult to fit on the screen.

10. Click on Finish.

11. Back at the Taskbar Properties dialog box, click on Close. The new items should now appear in the location(s) you chose.

A few points to consider: if you chose to add the item to the Desktop, it would appear there, not on one of the menus. Also, note that you can add more than one item to your lists at a time. Rather than closing the Taskbar Properties box in step 11, just click on Add and do the whole magilla over again for your next item, starting from step 2.

Removing an Item from a Menu

There will no doubt be times when you'll want to remove an item from one of your Start button menus, such as when you no longer use a program often enough to warrant its existence on the menu.

Note that moving an actual program or a document from one folder to another isn't reason enough to delete its choice on a Start menu. This is because shortcuts in Windows 95 are "self-healing." If an item that a menu item points to has been moved to another drive, directory, or computer, choosing the menu command results in a message similar to this:

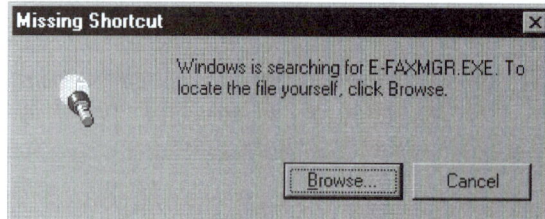

Windows 95 will automatically scan your hard disk(s) looking for the item. In most cases, if you've moved rather than deleted the displaced item, Windows 95 will find it, responding with a dialog box asking whether you want to repair the shortcut path.

Just click on Yes, and the shortcut on your Start menu will be repaired. Next time it will work flawlessly.

Here's how you remove an item:

1. Choose Start ➤ Settings ➤ Taskbar.

2. Click on the Start Menu Programs tab and click on Remove.

3. Wait a few seconds as Windows 95 updates your menus.

4. In the list that appears, scroll and otherwise maneuver the list until you get to the folder and item you want (see Figure 5.6). Note a

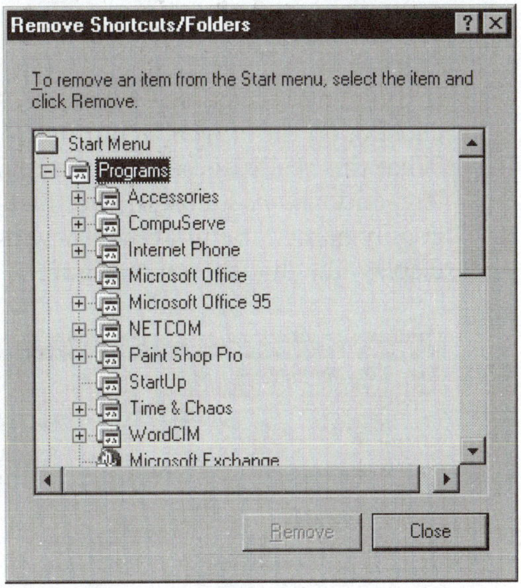

Figure 5.6 *Remove any folder or item from the Start menus using this box. Click on the item you want to remove, then click on Remove. Note that unless the folder is a short-cut removing a folder deletes everything in the folder, including any subfolders it might have.*

couple of things here. All items with plus signs are folders that have sub-items. For example, on your computer you'll certainly have an Accessories folder. Clicking on the + sign to the left of Accessories will display all the program items on the Accessories submenu. Clicking on the minus (−) sign closes up the folder. Items that normally list on the first Start button menu are at the *bottom* of the list. You may have to scroll down to see them.

5. Click on the item you want to remove. It can be a folder name or an individual item in the folder. Note that removing a folder removes all the sub-items in the folder.

> **NOTE** Just as with Program Manager icons in Windows 3.x, removing a shortcut from the Start button menus *never* removes the actual item from your hard disk. For example, if you remove a shortcut to Word for Windows, the program is still on your computer. It's just the shortcut to it that's been removed. You can always put the shortcut back on the menus again using the Add button.

Advanced Options

If you consider yourself a hotshot, you can wreak all kinds of havoc by clicking on the *Advanced* button from the Taskbar settings dialog box. What this really does is run the Explorer and let you copy, move, delete, and *rename* items on your menus. (This is *the* place to give any goofily named menu items a new name.) Clicking on it results in a display like that shown in Figure 5.7.

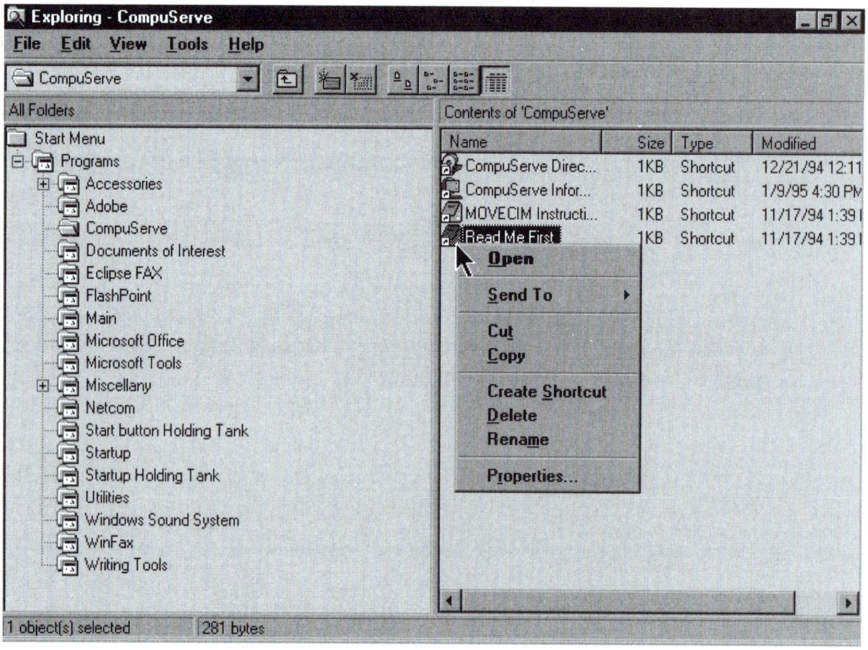

Figure 5.7   Exploring the Start button menus lets you easily modify them. You can use right-mouse clicks for a variety of purposes. Here you see the right-click menu as it appears for a shortcut in the CompuServe menu list. You can also drag and drop items if you want to move them between folders.

For details about using the Explorer, check out Part II of this book. For now, just note a few facts:

▶ Click on the topmost folder (Start Menu) to adjust the contents of the Start button's first-level menu.

▶ Change a name by clicking on the *name* once to highlight it, then once more. Alternatively, you can right-click on the name and choose Rename from the right-click menu.

▶ You can drag items in the right pane to destination menus in the left pane. Just drag and drop.

▶ You can create new submenus by clicking in the left pane on the menu you want to add to. Then right-click in the right pane and choose New ➤ Folder.

> **TECH TIP**   I know it doesn't make sense to choose New and then choose Folder, because you want to create a menu, not a folder. But actually everything in Windows 95 is *folders* or *files*, and in reality this whole menu thing is based on directories. Check out the directory structure under your \Windows\Start Menu directory, and you'll find directories that correspond to each menu, with .lnk (link) files for each shortcut.

> **TIP**   As a shortcut for modifying the contents of the Start button menus, right-click on the Start button. Then choose Open if you want to use the folder approach. Choose Explore if you like the Explorer approach.

Organizing Your Files and Folders

So much for adding items to the Start button menus. Now I'll show you a bit more about how you work with folders in Windows 95.

Making New Folders

As you may recall from the last chapter, you can create new documents simply by right-clicking on the Desktop, choosing New, then choosing the type of file you want and naming it. Then you double-click on it to start entering information into the document. Or, of course, you can create documents from within your programs and save them on disk using commands in the programs.

In either case you're likely to end up with a lot of documents scattered around your hard disk, or worse yet, a lot of documents lumped together in the same directory with no sense of organization. In interviewing users and teaching people about Windows over the years, I've found that most people haven't the foggiest idea where their work files are. They know they're on the hard disk, but that's about it.

TECH TIP   To some extent, Windows 95 will exacerbate this problem because every document or folder that's on the Desktop is actually stored in the `SystemRoot\Desktop` directory on the disk. Typically this will be the `C:\Windows\Desktop` directory. Even though each folder the user has on the Desktop will be a subfolder of the desktop directory, it still means that wiping out the `C:\Windows\Desktop` directory or doing a clean install of Windows by wiping out everything in the `\Windows` directory and below would wipe out anything on the Desktop. This normally won't be a problem for most people, as this kind of willy-nilly removal of whole directories or directory trees is something only power users are likely to do. If you are the kind of computer user who is going to be poking around on the hard disk, handle your `Windows\Desktop` directory with due respect.

Saving all your files in one directory without sorting them into folders makes creating backups and clearing off defunct projects that much more confusing. It's difficult enough to remember which files are involved in a given project without having to sort them out from all of Word's program and support files, not to mention all the other writing projects stored in that directory.

TECH TIP   Be cautious about storing a lot of files in the root directory of any disk. DOS and Windows 95 limits the number of file or directories in the root to 512. This limit doesn't apply to subdirectories. Also, because long file names take up additional space in the directory, economizing on name length in the root directory can be a good idea if you're pushing the 512-entry limit.

Admittedly, organizing files was a bit difficult in Windows 3.x, but with Windows 95, there's no excuse for bad organizing. And there's plenty of reasons to organize your files: You'll know where things are, you'll be more likely to make backups, and you'll be less likely to accidentally erase your doctoral dissertation because it was in the WordPerfect directory that you deleted so you could install a new word-processing program.

Probably the most intuitive way for most people to organize their work is to do it right on the Desktop. You can create as many folders as you like right there on the Desktop, name them what you like, and violà, you've done your homework.

If you want to get really tidy, you can pull all your subfolders into a single folder called something like My Work. To show you how to create folders and then move them around, I'm going to consolidate mine. First I'll create a new folder.

1. Right-click on the Desktop. Choose New from the resulting menu, then Folder.

2. A new folder appears, called New Folder. Its name is highlighted and ready for editing. Whatever you type will replace the current name. I'll enter the name *My Work*.

3. Now I'll open the folder by double-clicking on it.

So much for creating a new folder on the Desktop.

Incidentally, you're not limited to creating new folders only on the Desktop. You can create new folders within other folders using the same technique. That is, open the destination folder's window by double-clicking on it. Then right-click on an empty area inside the folder's window and choose New ➤ Folder.

Moving and Copying Items between Folders

Now that I've got a new folder on the Desktop, I can start putting stuff into it. Let's say I want to pull several of my existing Desktop folders into it to reduce clutter. It's as simple as dragging and dropping.

1. Open the destination folder. (Actually you don't even have to open the destination folder, but what you're about to do is more graphically understandable if you do.)

2. Size and position the destination folder's window so you will be able to see the folder(s) you put in it.

3. Repeatedly drag folders from the Desktop inside the perimeter of the destination folder's window. Be careful not to drop items on top of one another. Doing that will put the dropped item *inside* the item under it.

That's it. Figure 5.8 illustrates the process.

> **NOTE** You can drag and drop most objects in Windows 95 using this same scheme. Every effort has gone into designing a uniform approach for manipulating objects on screen. In general, if you want something placed somewhere else, you can drag it from the source to the destination.

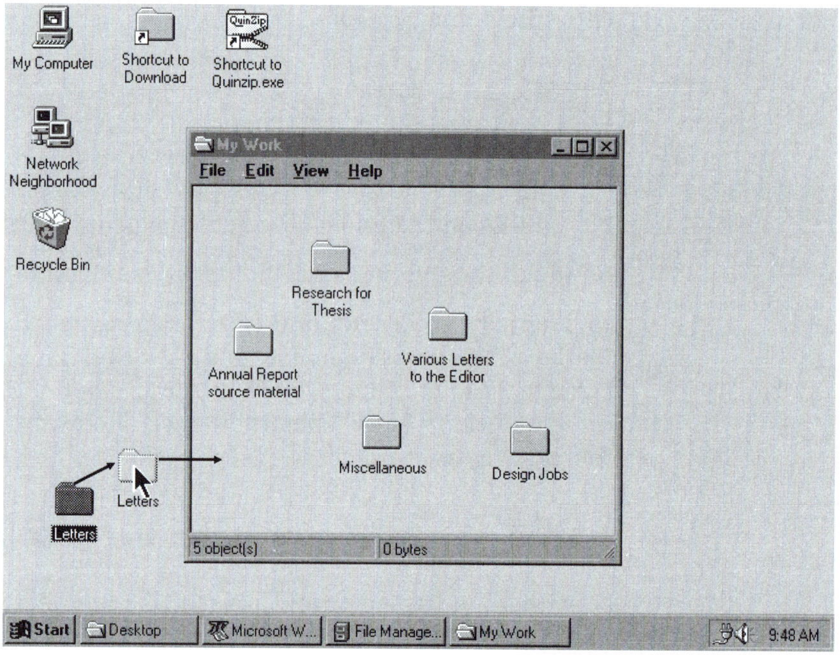

Figure 5.8　*Working with folder windows and objects is as simple as dragging and dropping. Rearranging your work is as simple as organizing your desk drawer.*

CAUTION   When dragging and dropping, aim carefully before you release the mouse button. If you drop an object too close to another object, it can be placed *inside* that object. For example, when moving folders around, or even re-positioning them on the Desktop, watch that a neighboring folder doesn't become highlighted. If something other than the object you're moving becomes highlighted, that means it has become the target for the object. If you release at that time, your object will go inside the target. If you accidentally do this, just open the target and drag the object out again, or, if the incorrect destination was a folder, open any folder and choose Edit ➤ Undo Move or right-click on the Desktop and choose Undo Move from the pop-up menu. Also, if you press Esc before you drop an object, the process of dragging is canceled.

Now all I have to do is close the My Work folder, and there's that much less clutter on my desktop.

Moving v. Copying

When you drag an item from one location to another, Windows 95 does its best to figure out if you intend to copy it or move it. As you might surmise, copying means making a replica of the object. Moving means relocating the original.

In the procedure above, Windows 95 assumed I wanted to move the folders from one location to another. This makes sense because it's not likely you'll want to make a copy of an entire folder. But you could.

The general rule about moving vs. copying is simple. When you *move* something by dragging, the mouse pointer keeps the shape of the moved object.

Design Jobs

But when you *copy*, the cursor takes on a + sign.

Design Jobs

To switch between copying and moving, press the Ctrl key as you drag. In general, holding down the Ctrl key causes a copy. The + sign will show up in the icon so you know you're making a copy. Pressing Shift as you drag ensures that the object is moved, not copied.

BUT ISN'T THERE AN EASIER WAY?

Here's a little technical tip you'll need to know regarding dragging. The easiest way to fully control what's going to happen when you drag an item around is to *right-click-drag*. Place the pointer on the object you want to move, copy, or make a shortcut for, then press the right mouse button (or left button if you're left-handed and have reversed the buttons) and drag the item to the destination. When you drop the object, you'll be asked what you want to do with it, like this:

Move Here
Copy Here
Create Shortcut(s) Here

Cancel

Being able to create a shortcut this way is pretty nifty. Often, rather than dragging a document file (and certainly a program) out of its home folder just to put it on the Desktop for convenience, you'll want to make a shortcut out of it. There are important considerations when using shortcuts, however, so make sure you understand what they do.

Organizing Document Files

Once you've thought out how to name and organize your folders, you'll naturally want to start stashing your documents in their rightful folders.

As you might expect, moving and copying documents works just like moving and copying folders—you just drag and drop. When you want to copy files, you press the Ctrl key while dragging. If you want to create a shortcut, you right-click drag and choose Shortcut from the resulting menu (see *But Isn't There an Easier Way?*). Here's an example you might want to try.

1. Clear off the Desktop by right-clicking on the clock in the Taskbar and choosing Minimize all Windows.

2. Create a new folder on the Desktop by right-clicking on the Desktop and choosing New ➤ Folder. Name it My Test Folder.

3. Now create a couple of new documents by right-clicking on the Desktop, choosing New, and then choosing a document type. Name the documents whatever you like.

Now let's say you want to put these three files into the new folder. You could just drag them in one by one. But here's a faster approach; you can select multiple objects at once. Selecting a number of objects can be useful when you want to move, copy, delete, or make shortcuts out of them in one fell swoop.

1. First, we're going to *snap a line* around the items we want to drag. Move the pointer to an empty area on the Desktop at the upper-left corner of the three documents and press the left mouse button. Now drag the mouse down and to the right. This draws a box on the screen, outlining the items you are selecting. You know which items you've selected because they become highlighted (see Figure 5.9).

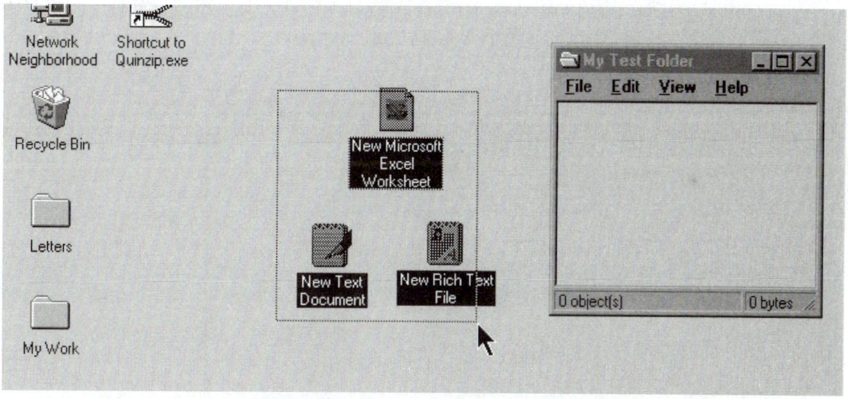

Figure 5.9 *You can select multiple objects by snapping a line around them.*

2. Once selected, you can perform a number of tasks on the group of items. For example, you could right-click on one and choose Open, which would open all three documents in their respective programs. In this case we want to move them. So while they are all selected, just drag one of them. The whole group will move (see Figure 5.10).

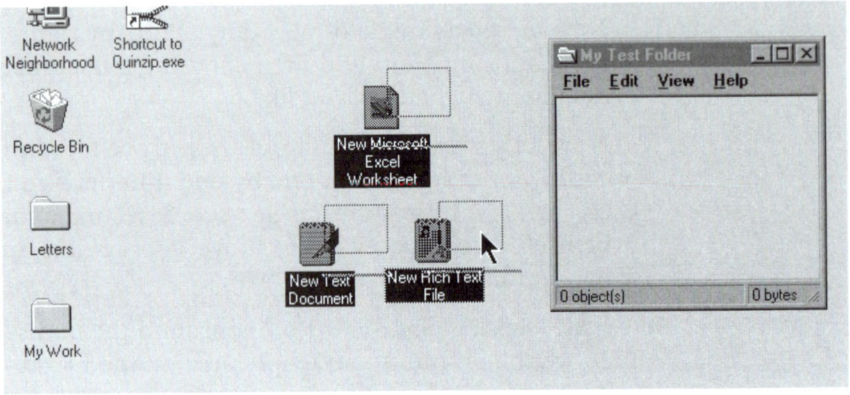

Figure 5.10   You can move or copy a group of selected items by dragging one of them. The others will come along. Notice the outlines of all three objects are moving.

3. Using this method, drag the items over the destination folder and release. They've all been moved into My Test Folder.

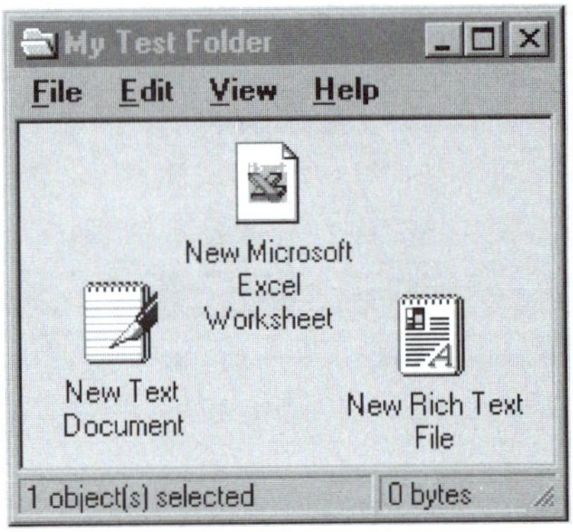

> **TIP**   Not all the outlines of the items you're moving need to fit into the destination folder before you release the mouse button. If just a single document's outline falls within the boundary of the target, all the selected items will move to the target folder.

Deleting Items

Of course there will be times when you'll want to delete items, like that old report from last year. Regular file deletion is very important if you don't want to become like everyone else—strapped for disk space. The same techniques will apply to deleting other objects as well, such as printers and fax machines you have installed, because all objects in Windows 95 are treated much the same way regardless of their type or utility.

To Delete a File

So how do you delete a file? Let me count the ways. Because Windows 95 has a Recycle Bin, that's one of the easiest ways, assuming you can arrange things on your screen to find the Recycle Bin. But there are other ways that are even easier though less graphically pleasing than dragging an item over the Recycle Bin and letting go.

To delete a file,

1. Just select the file in its folder, on the Desktop, in the Find box, or wherever.

2. Drag the item on top of the Recycle Bin, press the Del key on your keyboard, or right-click on the item and choose Delete from the resulting menu. Unless you drag to the Recycle Bin, you'll be asked to confirm the deletion.

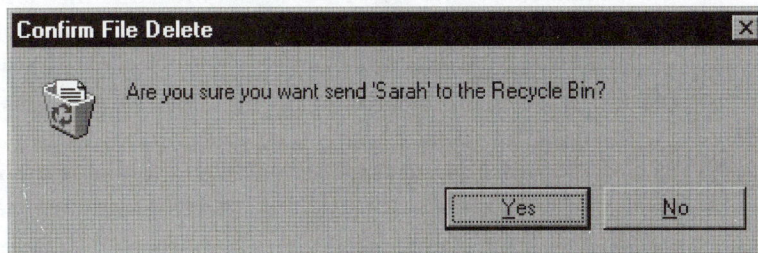

3. Choose appropriately. If you choose Yes, the item goes into the Recycle Bin.

> **TIP**   If you throw something away, you can get it back until you empty the trash, as explained in the section *Checking and Chucking the Trash* later in this chapter.

To Delete a Folder

Deleting a folder works much the same way as deleting a file. The only difference is that deleting a folder deletes all of its contents. When you drag a file over to the Recycle Bin, or delete it with one of the other techniques explained above, you'll see a confirmation message warning you that all the contents—any shortcuts, files, and folders (including files in those folders) will be deleted. Take care when deleting folders, as they may contain many objects.

> **CAUTION**   Before deleting a folder, you may want to look carefully at its contents. Open the folder and choose View ➤ Details or View ➤ List to examine what's in it, check on the dates the files were created, and so forth. Check the contents of any folders within the folder by double-clicking on them; you might be surprised by what you find.

Putting Items on the Desktop

The Desktop is a convenient place to store items you're working on regularly. Each time you boot up, the same files and folders you left there are waiting in easy reach. So how do you put things on the Desktop? You have probably figured out already that you simply drag them there from any convenient source such as a folder or the Find box.

> **TIP**   You can also drag files and folders to the Desktop from the Windows Explorer and File Manager. See Chapter 12 for more details.

However, there are a few details to consider when using the Desktop that aren't immediately obvious. First, some objects can't actually be *moved* to the Desktop—only their shortcuts can. For example, if you open the Control Panel (Start ➤ Settings ➤ Control Panel) and try pulling one of the icons (called Control Panel *applets*) onto the Desktop, you'll see this dialog box:

Shortcut   ☒

You cannot move or copy this item here.
Would you like to create a shortcut here instead?

     OK   Cancel

In the case of the Control Panel, setting up a shortcut is your only choice because Windows 95 won't let you move it. As you drag an icon from the Control Panel onto the Desktop or into a folder, the icon turns into a shortcut icon (it has a little arrow in it). But in some other cases, you'll have the choice of moving, copying, or creating a shortcut. How to choose? Here's a little primer about shortcuts.

Because a shortcut will work just as well as the real thing (the program or document file itself), in general shortcuts are a good idea. You can have as many shortcuts scattered about for a given item as you want. For example, suppose you like to use a particular set of programs. You can have shortcuts for them on the Start button menu, on the Desktop, and in a folder called My Favorite Programs. You still have only one copy of the program, so you haven't used up a lot of disk space.

TECH TIP   Shortcuts do consume *some* disk space. Each shortcut file has the .LNK (for Link) extension and contains information about where the program, folder, or document it represents is stored. LNK files will typically use up the smallest amount of space that the disk operating system (DOS) will allow. Most LNK files consume 1K, though some you'll find to be 2K.

The same holds true for other objects, such as folders or documents that you use a lot. You can have shortcuts to folders and shortcuts to documents. For example, try dragging a folder (the folder must be displayed as an icon) onto the Start button, and you'll see that a shortcut to the folder is created. A good way to create a shortcut to a document is, as I mentioned earlier, to right-click-drag it somewhere and choose Shortcut from the resulting menu.

I have to warn you of a few things when using shortcuts, however. Remember, shortcuts are *not* the real McCoy. They are *aliases* or pointers to an object only! Therefore, copying a document's shortcut to a floppy disk doesn't copy the document itself. A colleague will be disappointed if you copy only the shortcut of a document to a floppy and then give it to him or her, because there will be nothing in it. When you are in doubt about what is getting copied, look at the icon that results from the procedure. If it has a little arrow in it, it's a shortcut.

Shortcut to
Bart Simpson
portrait

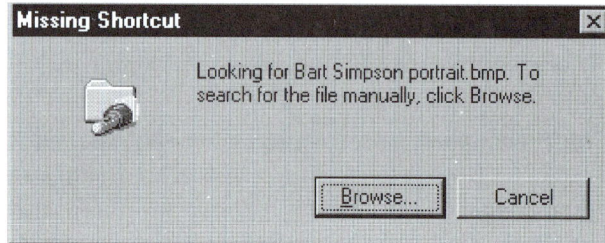

If no arrow, then it's the actual file.

And consider this: when you move the real McCoy around—whether a program, folder, or document—it may disable some shortcuts that point to it. For example, assume you've set up a bunch of shortcuts that expect your Annual Budget to be located in folder X. Then you move the budget document to folder Y. What happens? Nothing, until you try clicking on those shortcuts. Then you'll get an error message. Windows will try to find the missing object the shortcut is pointing to:

Bart Simpson
portrait

If the object is found, then the shortcut will be repaired and will work next time.

Another caution is that programs that are *installed* into Windows—these are typically big-time programs like those in Microsoft Office, Borland's or Lotus' office suites, database packages, communications packages, and so on—don't like to be moved around. Almost any program that you actually install with an install or setup program will register itself with Windows 95, informing Windows 95 of the folder it is located in. Moving the program around after that (i.e., actually moving it rather than moving the shortcuts that point to it) will bollix up something somewhere unless the program actually comes with a utility program for relocating it as, say, WinCIM (a program for working with CompuServe Information Service) does.

Saving Files to the Desktop from a Program

One of the features I like best about Windows 95 is the ability to use the Desktop as a sort of temporary holding tank. Here's one example. Suppose you want to copy some files from the floppy disk. It's as easy as opening the floppy disk window from My Computer, then dragging the desired file onto the Desktop. Violà, it's on the hard disk! (Actually, it's in a subdirectory of your Windows 95 directory, but for all intents and purposes it's simply on the Desktop.)

You can use the same kind of approach to move or copy items from one folder to another. Rather than having to open both folders and adjust your screen so you can see them both, you can just open the source folder and drag the items onto the Desktop temporarily. When you find or create the destination folder, you can later copy the items there.

But what about using the Desktop from your favorite programs? Although the Desktop is actually a subdirectory of your Windows directory, it's fairly easy to save a file to the Desktop. This is because the newer File dialog box lets you do so (Figure 5.11).

With programs written for Windows 3.x, there is no such option because the Desktop didn't exist in that version. Thus, saving a file to (or opening one from) the Desktop from a Windows 3.x program isn't so easy because the Save As dialog boxes don't have a Desktop option. Still, you can do it. Here's how:

> **NOTE** When your computer is set up for multiple users, there will be multiple Desktop directories, one for each user. They're located in subdirectories under `Windows\Profiles`. There will be one for each user who has an account. For example, for Joe, there will be a directory named `Windows\Profiles\Joe\Desktop`. These directories are *not* normally hidden and can be accessed from any program without modification.

1. Open the Save, or Save As, or Open dialog box from the File menu as usual.

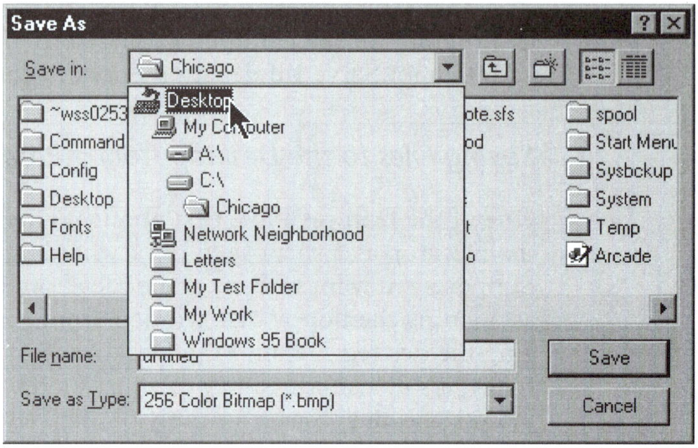

Figure 5.11   *Saving a file to the Desktop is easy with the newer File dialog box. Just scroll or click your way up to the Desktop in the Directory drop-down list box.*

2. In the dialog box, select the drive that contains Windows. This is probably your C drive.

3. Switch to the Windows directory. Then look for the Desktop subdirectory. Figure 5.12 shows an example.

4. Enter or choose the file's name or open one of the subfolders on the Desktop. Remember that subfolders that have long names will show up in the 16-bit File boxes with shortened names. For example, in Figure 5.14, notice the folder on the Desktop called holdingt. That's actually a folder called Holding Tank, something I like to use as a temporary storage area.

Copying Files and Folders to and from Floppy Disks

Whether you're sending a file to a colleague around the world, "sneaker-netting" some work down the hall, or simply making a backup of some important files, copying to and from floppy disks is one of those recurring computer housekeeping chores.

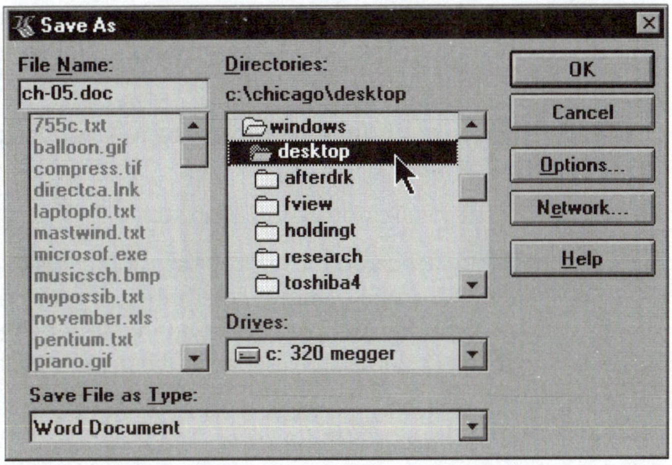

Figure 5.12   *Saving a file to the Desktop from Word for Windows (16-bit version)*

As you might expect, there are a number of ways to copy files to and from floppies. You can use:

▶ My Computer

▶ the Send-To option

▶ drag and drop on a floppy-drive's shortcut

▶ Explorer

▶ File Manager

▶ the Command prompt

Here I'll briefly cover the basics of the first three items. In Chapter 12 I'll cover use of the Explorer. Please refer to that chapter to learn more about copying files with that program. Refer to a book on DOS if you need help copying files by typing in copy commands at the DOS Command Prompt. Or open a MS-DOS window and type **copy /?** to read some help information about the Copy command.

Copying to and from a Floppy with My Computer

I've already explained in the sections above how to copy and move files between folders. Copying to or from a floppy disk works the same way. Your computer's floppy disk drives simply appear as icons in the My Computer window. Double-clicking on an icon brings up the contents of the floppy disk, displayed in the same format as a typical folder on your hard disk.

1. Clear off enough windows from your Desktop to see the My Computer icon.

2. Double-click on My Computer.

3. Double-click on the appropriate floppy disk icon. Typically you'll only have one, but some computers have two or more floppy disk drives. In Figure 5.13, I've double-clicked on the $3^1/_2$-inch floppy drive in my computer. (If you don't have a diskette in the drive, you'll see an error message.)

4. Once the floppy drive's window opens, you can easily work with it just as you do with other folders. Drag items from the window to other folders you might have opened on the Desktop, or vice versa.

TIP   When you replace one floppy diskette with another, the computer doesn't know about it automatically, as it does on the Mac. After you change the disk, the contents of an open floppy disk window will still be the same, even though the disk holds a completely different set of files. To update the contents of the floppy disk's window, press the F5 key. (This same technique is needed with File Manager and Explorer, incidentally, whenever you change a floppy.)

Remember, you're not limited to dragging between disk and folder windows. You can drop an item on a folder's *icon*, too. Here, I'm dragging Bart Simpson's portrait from the Desktop into My Test Folder.

Sometimes when using a floppy disk you'll see an error message alerting you that the disk has not yet been formatted, that the disk can't be read, or something else, such as the disk is *write protected*.

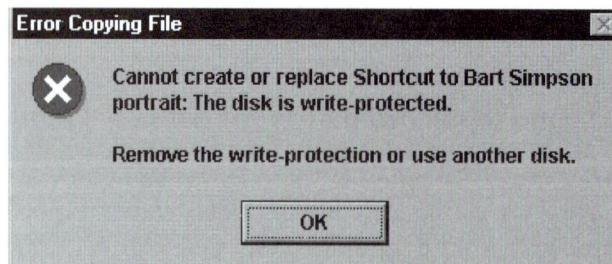

Error Copying File

Cannot create or replace Shortcut to Bart Simpson portrait: The disk is write-protected.

Remove the write-protection or use another disk.

OK

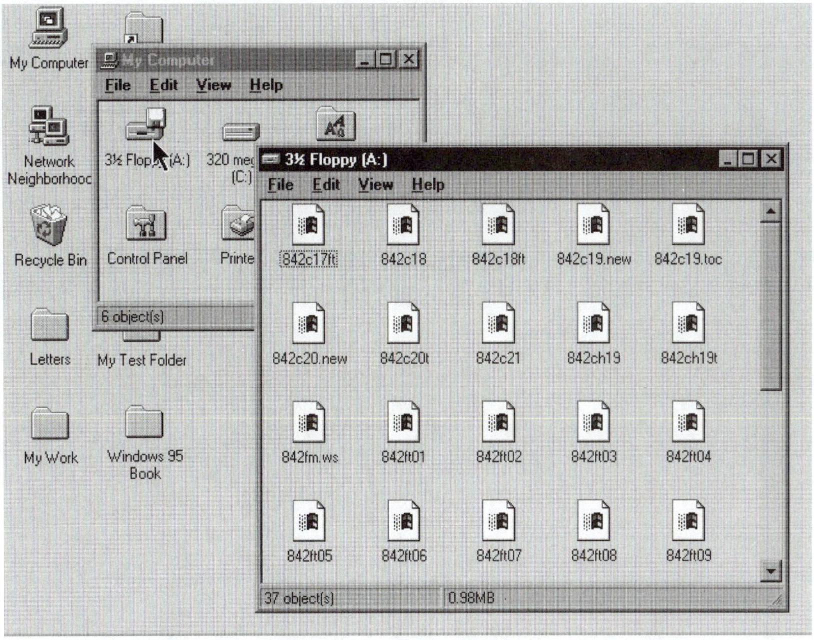

Figure 5.13   *You can examine the contents of the floppy drive by double-clicking on My Computer.*

On $3\frac{1}{2}$-inch diskettes, there's a little tab on the back of the disk that must be in the closed position for the disk to be written onto (new files put on it). On $5\frac{1}{4}$-inch diskettes, if a stick-on write-protect tab covers the write-protect notch, writing will not be allowed. You should know that a disk must be *write-enabled* (have no write protection) even to open or read files with certain programs such as Word or any program that creates temporary or backup files on disk while you are editing. See Figure 5.14.

If the disk isn't formatted—because you just bought it or it was used in another kind of computer or device, such as a Mac, and you want to use it on a PC—you simply can't write anything on it, regardless of the write-protect tab setting. You can format a floppy from:

► the DOS prompt's Format command

► the File Manager (using the Disk ► Format command)

► Explorer or My Computer by right-clicking on the floppy drive's icon and choosing Format

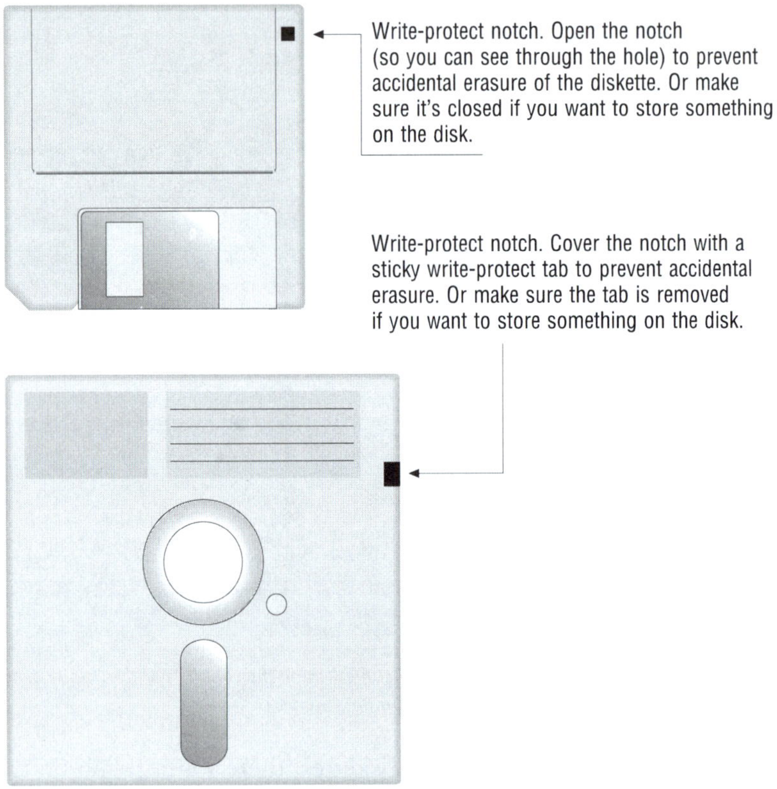

Write-protect notch. Open the notch (so you can see through the hole) to prevent accidental erasure of the diskette. Or make sure it's closed if you want to store something on the disk.

Write-protect notch. Cover the notch with a sticky write-protect tab to prevent accidental erasure. Or make sure the tab is removed if you want to store something on the disk.

Figure 5.14   Location of write-protect slider and notch on $3\frac{1}{2}$" and $5\frac{1}{4}$" floppies

▶ any floppy-disk shortcut icon by right-clicking on it and choosing Format

I'll cover formatting more in Chapter 12 when I talk about the file system.

TIP   To see how much room is left on any disk drive, including a floppy, right-click on the drive in My Computer and choose Properties. You'll see a display of the disk's free and used space. Disk properties are described more in Chapter 11, where I discuss right-clicking and property sheets.

Copying Files to a Floppy with Send To

Realizing that people wanted an easy way to copy a file or folder to a floppy disk, Microsoft has provided a cute little shortcut to the interface that copies to a floppy from almost anywhere.

1. Just right-click on any file or folder icon.

2. Then choose the Send To option.

Depending on your computer's setup, you'll have differing choices in the Send To list. You'll at least have one Floppy option.

3. Insert a floppy disk that has some free space on it and choose the desired drive. The file will be copied to the drive you specify.

The Send To option is very handy. Part III of this book, which covers Microsoft Fax, explains how you use this option to send a file to a fax recipient. You can also customize the Send To list for other purposes, such as sending a file to a viewer program, the Desktop, a file-compression program, a network destination, and so on.

Copying Files to a Floppy's Shortcut

Because a shortcut works just fine as a drag-and-drop destination, one convenient setup for copying items to a floppy is this:

1. Place a shortcut of the floppy drive on the Desktop. You can do this by opening My Computer and dragging the desired floppy drive to the Desktop.

2. Now, whenever you want to copy items to the floppy drive, insert a diskette in the drive, adjust your windows as necessary so you can see the drive's shortcut, and simply drag and drop objects on it. They'll be instantly copied to the diskette.

Of course, double-clicking on the shortcut will open a folder that displays the diskette's contents.

Setting Options
That Affect Viewing of Folders

In the interest of consistency, Microsoft has seen to it that all windows throughout the Windows 95 interface have the same menu options:

This menu provides a number of other useful features you might want to know about as you work with your files, folders, floppy disks, and so forth. I've already discussed the ways to create folders and files on the Desktop or within folders. The menu choices I want to discuss now are those found on the View menu. You can arrive at some of these commands by right-clicking and choosing View. Others are only reachable from the View menu. A couple of the settings I'll discuss here can be super useful, helping to keep your screen clear of clutter. From the View menu, you can control:

▶ The ordering of icons in the window

▶ Whether opening a new folder by clicking on it creates a new window or uses the existing one

▶ Whether file extensions (the last three letters after the period) will be displayed

▶ Which programs are associated with given file extensions

Sorting and Tidying Up the Listing

As you drag icons around, they have a way of obscuring one another, falling behind the edge of the window, or otherwise creating an unsightly mess. Once a bunch of icons become jumbled up, it's often difficult to see or find the one you want. A few commands let you quickly clean up, arrange, and sort the display of files and folders in a window.

1. If you want to tidy up the Desktop quickly, simply right-click on any free space on the Desktop and choose Arrange Icons.

```
Arrange Icons    ▶     by Name
Line up Icons          by Type
                       by Size
Paste                  by Date
Undo Rename
                    ✓  Auto Arrange
New              ▶

Properties...
```

2. Then choose the appropriate command.

By Name	Sorts the display of objects alphabetically based on the name. Folders always appear first in the listing.
By Type	Sorts the display of objects according to type. (The type is only visible when you list the objects' details.) Folders always appear first in the listing.
By Size	Sorts the display of objects in increasing order of size. Folders always appear first in the listing.
By Date	Sorts the display of objects chronologically, based on the date the object was last modified.
Auto Arrange	Keeps the objects lined up nicely at all times. It doesn't ensure that they'll be in any particular order, however. This is a toggle: choose it once to turn it on and again to turn it off.

If you have the display set to show Details, a convenient feature lets you sort all the objects without using any of these commands. Simply click on the *column heading control* over the desired column. For example, to sort by Name you'd click on the Name heading:

Clicking once on the heading sorts in ascending order (A to Z, 0 to 9). Clicking a second time sorts in descending order. This is particularly useful in the Size and Modified columns, letting you easily bring to the top of the list the files you've modified most recently *or* those you modified ages ago; or you can quickly find which files in a folder are very large and might be taking up significant space on your hard disk.

NOTE   Certain view settings you make in a folder pertain only to that folder. They don't affect other folders. The size, position, listing type and order, and auto-arrange setting are stored with the folder itself and will not affect other folders' settings. However, the single/multiple-window browsing option explained immediately below is global. Its setting will affect *all folder* windows.

Preventing Additional Windows from Appearing

When you're browsing around your hard disk and traversing folders, the Desktop can become cluttered with overlapping windows. If you like to nest your folders one inside another, the clutter will really become apparent as you walk your way though folders to get to a destination file or program. You can cut down on this annoyance by making a simple setting. Once set, the result will be a single window whose contents change as you browse from folder to folder.

1. Open any folder. It doesn't matter which one because this setting is *global*—that is, it affects all folders that you open in the future.

2. Choose View ➤ Options. You'll see the dialog box shown in Figure 5.15.

3. Choose the second option, as I'm about to do in the figure. Then OK the box.

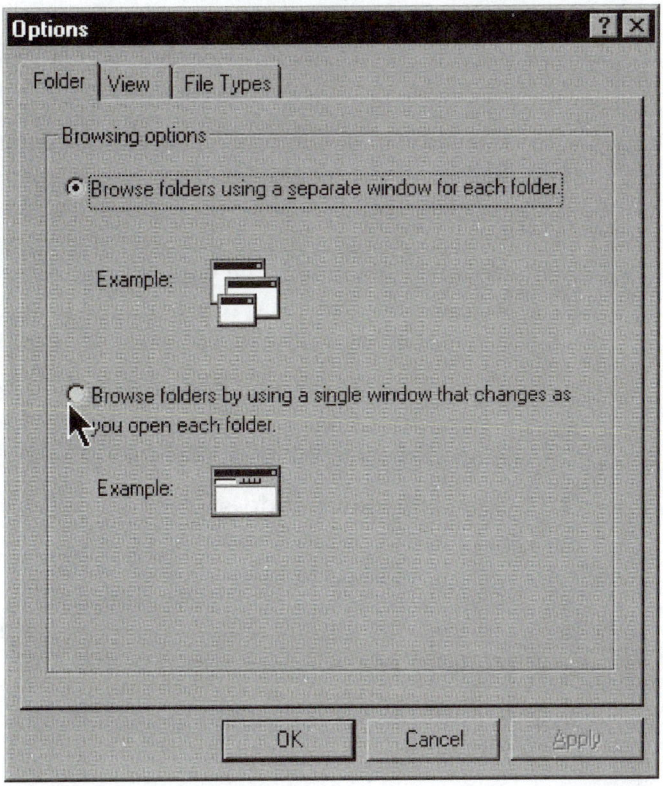

Figure 5.15   *Here you can set whether a new window will open for each folder as you browse.*

Until you change the setting again (remember you can do this from any folder window), the new scheme will stay in effect. Now when you double-click on a folder that's in a folder, a new window won't appear. Only the contents of the window will change.

File Extension Display and Other Options

If you're an old hand at Windows and DOS, you may have already been frustrated by the fact that file names don't always appear with the extension showing. So you might see a file displayed like the example on the left, rather than the one on the right.

Letter To Joe   Letter to Joe.txt

Extensions are normally not displayed for file types that are recognized by Windows 95. Recognized file types are referred to as being *registered.*

The reasoning behind hiding file extensions when possible is that it keeps extraneous information off the screen and makes life easier for normal mortals who don't want to be confused or hassled by file-name extensions. Once the extension is set and then hidden, you can rename a document file without fear of accidentally changing the extension and thus preventing the file from opening in the correct program when double-clicked on.

If you're a hard-core DOS type or want more control over when you see file extensions displayed in listings, folders, and whatnot, there are a few other options worth considering. Follow these steps to explore them:

1. Open any folder. It doesn't matter which one because this is a global setting.

2. Choose View ➤ Options.

3. Click on the View tab, and you'll see the dialog box shown in Figure 5.16.

4. Set the options as you see fit and OK the box. Options will stay in effect until you reset them. Here's what the settings mean:

Show all files	When set on, ensures that all files on your hard disks and floppy disks will be shown in folders, in the Explorer, in the Find box, and elsewhere.
Hide files of these types	When set on, the types of files shown in the list box won't be displayed in folders, in the Explorer, in the Find box, etc. You may want to scroll through the box to see the kinds of files that will be excluded.
Display the full MS-DOS path in the Title Bar	When set on, the entire *path name* of a document file that's open in a program will be displayed in the Title Bar at the top of the program's window. Normally, only the name of the file itself is shown. For example, a full path name might be C:\Windows\Desktop\budget.wks, whereas the file name alone would display as budget.wks.

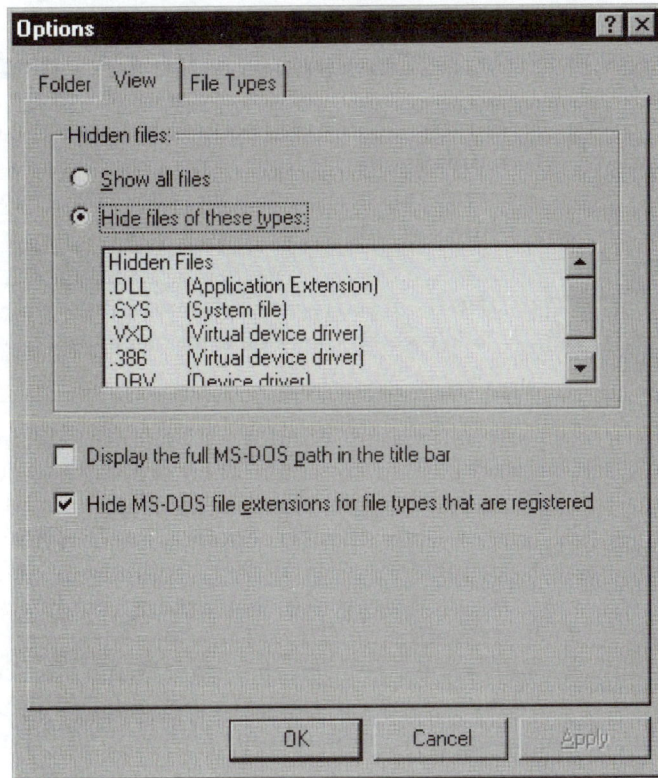

Figure 5.16 *This box, reachable from the View menu of any folder window, lets you set when file extensions will display. It also lets you hide altogether a preset list of file types.*

Hide MS-DOS file extensions for file types that are registered	When set on, files with recognized extensions won't have their last three letters (and the period) showing. Unrecognized (unregistered) file types will still show their extensions. Turn this off to see all extensions, even if they *are* recognized by Windows 95.

Of all these settings, the only ones I really concern myself with are the first two and the Hide MS-DOS extensions. The first two are worth playing with if you want to see all the files on your disk while browsing around.

Using the Cut, Copy, and Paste Commands with Files and Folders

You're probably well acquainted with the Cut, Copy, and Paste commands as they pertain to programs such as word processors. These commands let you remove, replicate, or move bits of data around while working on your documents.

> **NOTE** If you're *not* familiar with these concepts as applied to programs, don't worry. They'll be explained in Part IV, which covers the supplied accessory programs.

An interesting Windows 95 feature is its inclusion of the Cut, Copy, and Paste commands when browsing folders, files, and other objects (such as printers, fax machines, fonts, and so forth). To veteran Windows users, these commands might not make sense at first, because cutting and copying aren't commands that have been applied to files before. They're typically used within programs and apply to portions of documents. When I first saw this menu I wondered how *cutting* a file would differ from *deleting* it and why cutting it only made a file's icon grayed out rather than making it disappear. However, once you know how these commands work, you'll use them all the time.

As I mentioned earlier, the Desktop is a useful temporary storage medium when copying or moving objects between windows or folders. Having the Desktop available means you don't have to arrange *both* the source and destination windows on screen at once to make the transfer. Well, the Cut, Copy, and Paste commands do the same thing without the Desktop.

Here's how it works, using a real-life example. Today I downloaded a file from CompuServe called editschd.doc. My e-mail program dumped the file in my Download folder, but I want it in my Mastering Windows 95 folder instead. Well, I could open both folders, arrange them on screen, and drag the file from one to the other. Or I could drag the file first to the Desktop, then to the destination folder. But instead of either of these, I'll use the Cut and Paste commands to more easily accomplish the same task. Here are the steps I used:

1. First I opened the source folder—which in this case was the Download folder.

2. Next, I located the file in question, right-clicked on it, and chose Cut (not Delete, because that command actually trashes the file instead of preparing to put it somewhere else).

3. This turns the icon into a shadow of its former self, but it's still there in a ghostly form, which means it's waiting to be pasted into another location.

TIP At this point, failing to paste the file into a destination or pressing Esc will abort the cutting and copying process. Nothing will be lost. The file will remain in its original location.

4. Next, I can close the current folder, browse around to my heart's content until I find the proper destination for my file, whether it be a floppy disk, the Desktop, or another folder. In this case, I opened the Mastering Windows 95 folder.

5. I now position the pointer on an empty space within the folder, right-click, and choose Paste. The file's icon appears in its new home. That's it (see Figure 5.17).

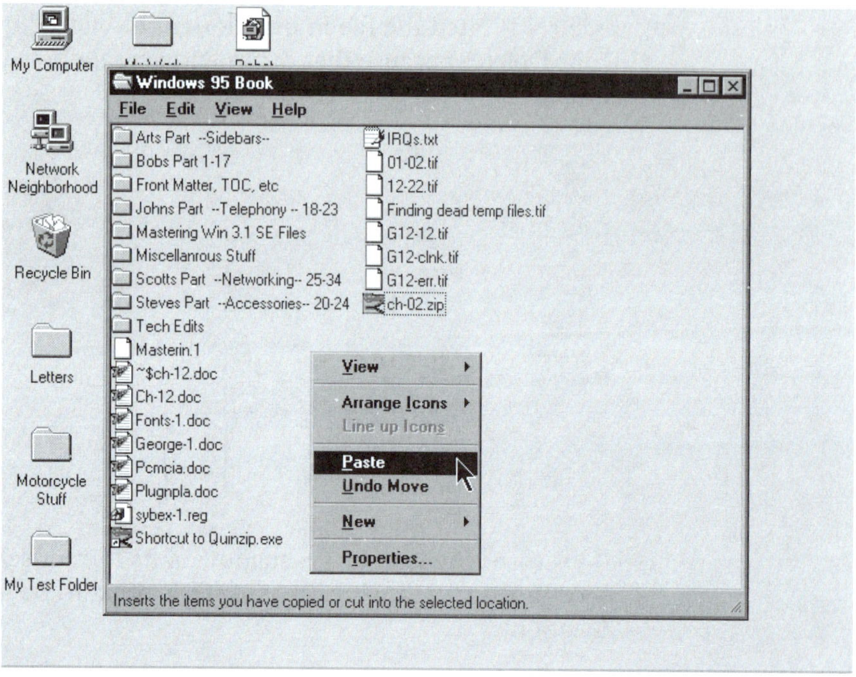

Figure 5.17   *Pasting the file into its new location*

NOTE   If, when you go to paste, the Paste command is grayed out, it means you didn't properly cut or copy the object. You must use the Cut or Copy commands on a file or other object *immediately* before using the Paste command, or it won't work. That is, if you go into a word processor and use the Cut or Copy commands in a *document*, then the Paste command for your *files* or other objects will be grayed out and won't work. (Chapter 6 discusses use of the Cut, Copy, and Paste commands within programs such as word processors.)

Now, a few points about cutting, copying, and pasting objects in this way. First, if you want to make a copy of the file rather than move the original, you'd choose Copy rather than Cut from the menu. Then, when you paste, a copy of the file appears in the destination location.

Second, you can cut or copy a bunch of items at once to save time. The normal rules of selection apply:

▶ Draw a box around them as I described in *Organizing Document Files*.

▶ Or press the Ctrl key and click on each object you want to select.

▶ Or click on the first of the items you want to select, hold down the Shift key, and click on the last of the items you want to select. This selects the *range* of objects between the two clicks.

Once a number of items is selected (they will be highlighted), right-clicking on any one of the objects will bring up the Cut, Copy, Paste menu. The option you choose will apply to *all* the selected items. Also, clicking anywhere outside of the selected items will deselect them all.

Take a look at the Edit menu in any folder window. There are two commands at the bottom of the menu—Select All and Invert Selection. These can also be useful when you want to select a group of files. Suppose you want to select all but two files; select the two you *don't* want, then choose Edit ➤ Invert Selection.

Finally, remember that you can cut, copy, and paste complete folders, too. When you paste a folder somewhere, you get all of its contents, including any other folders within it.

TIP What if you accidentally goof and realize that you didn't want to move an object or objects to the new location after all? After you perform the Paste, simply open the Edit menu in any folder and choose Undo Move.

Checking and Chucking the Trash

When right-clicking on an object, you may have noticed the Delete command in the menu.

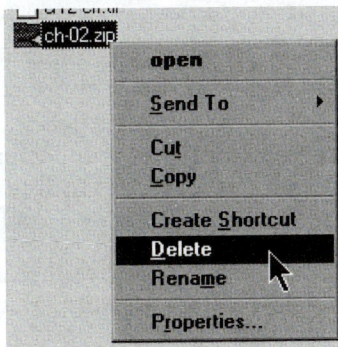

This command isn't the same as the Cut command. Delete sends the selected files, folders, or other objects to the Recycle Bin (essentially the trash can), while the Cut command puts the file on the Clipboard for pasting to another location.

When you delete a file, folder, or other item, it gets put into the Recycle Bin, which is actually a special folder on your hard disk. This folder or directory is called, as you might expect, `Recycled`, typically on your C drive.

TECH TIP   Each logical drive (drive with a letter name) has a `Recycled` directory on it. So, if you have a C and D drive, you'll have two Recycle Bins. `Recycled` directories are "hidden" system files, so they don't normally show up in Explorer or folders unless you set the View option as explained above in *File Extension Display and Other Options* You'll just have a Recycle Bin on the Desktop. If you have access to the root directory of a networked drive, whether mapped to a logical drive on your machine or not, it too will have a `Recycled` directory. CD-ROM drives, even though given a logical drive letter, do not have `Recycled` directories for the obvious reason that you can't delete their files or folders.

The Recycle Bin temporarily holds things that you delete. Because items are not actually *erased* from your computer when you delete them with the Delete command, you can get them back in case you made a mistake! This is a terrific feature. How many times have you accidentally erased a file or directory and realized you goofed? For most people even a single accidental erasure was enough. Now with the Recycle Bin, all you have to do is open its folder, find the item you accidentally deleted, and choose the File ➤ Restore command to undelete it.

Well, actually there's a caveat here. The Recycle Bin will hang onto your deleted items only until you empty the bin. Once you empty the bin, anything in it is *gone*. At that point your only hope is one of the undelete programs like those from PC Tools, Norton, or the one supplied with DOS 5 or 6. (From the Start button, check your Programs menu for a Microsoft Tools option. You may have an undelete program on it.) If that fails, look in your DOS folder (`C:\DOS`) for `undelete.exe` and run that. Or, for an easier approach, simply click on the Start button, choose Run, and enter **undelete**. If you have the program in the DOS directory, it should run. Refer to a book on DOS or the DOS help system (type **Help Undelete** at an MS-DOS prompt) for more information about how to use Undelete.

When you're doing your hard-disk housecleaning, merrily wiping out directories and files in hopes of regaining some needed disk space, you should be aware of one thing: Because files aren't actually erased until you empty the Recycle Bin, you won't increase your available disk space until you do just that.

Restoring Something You Accidentally Trashed

If there's one single thing you'll want to know about using the Recycle Bin, it's how to get back something you accidentally put there. (This page alone may make this book worth your investment!)

1. Get to the Desktop one way or another.

> **TIP** You can also reach items in the Recycle Bin via the Explorer. I'll discuss this approach in Chapter 12.

2. Double-click on the Recycle Bin icon. A folder will open, listing all the items you trashed since the last time the Recycle Bin was emptied. Figure 5.18 shows an example.

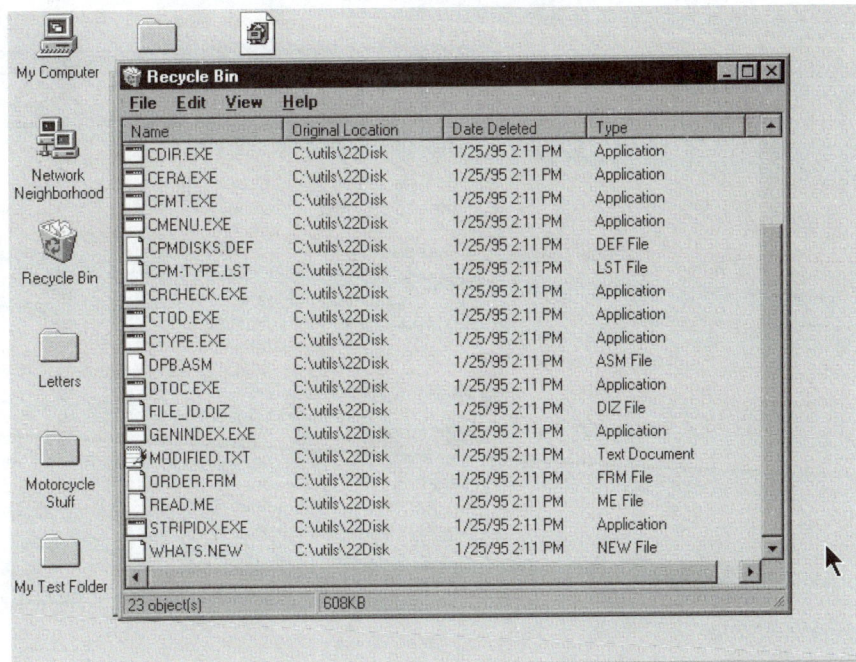

Figure 5.18   A typical Recycle Bin before emptying

3. Hunt around for the thing(s) you accidentally trashed. When you find it, highlight it by clicking on it. (You can select multiple items using the techniques I described earlier in this chapter.) If you want to know more about an item, click on it and choose File ➤ Properties. A dialog box displays when the item was created and when deleted.

> **TIP**   You can also restore an item in the Recycle Bin or Windows Explorer by right-clicking on the item and choosing Restore.

4. Choose File ➤ Restore. This will move all selected item(s) back to their original locations. Figure 5.19 shows an example.

Emptying the Recycle Bin

You've probably already noticed the command that empties the Recycle Bin. It's on the File menu. When you want to free up some disk space and are sure that all the contents of the Recycle Bin can be dispensed

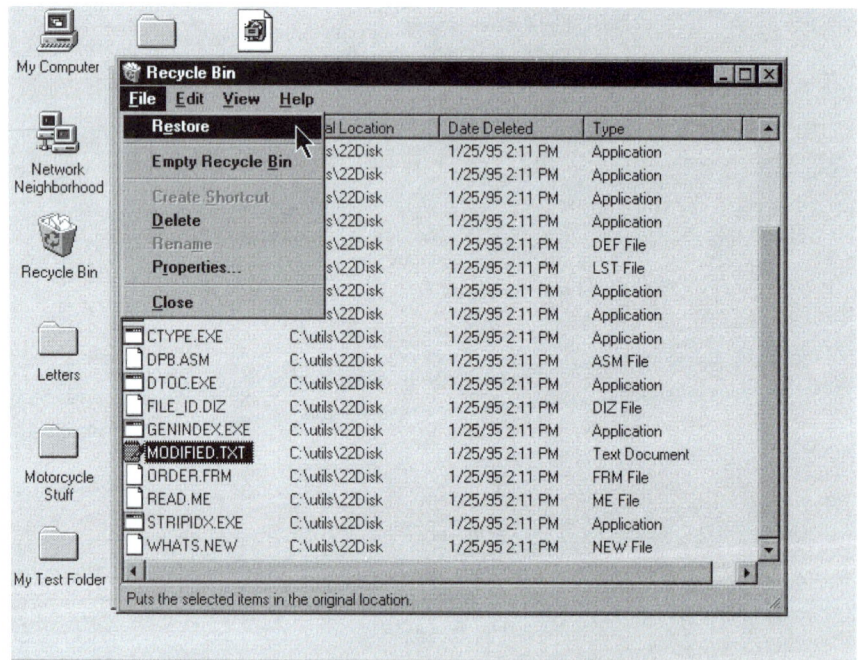

Figure 5.19   *Undeleting (restoring) a file that was accidentally erased*

Part
1

with, go ahead and empty it. It's always a good idea to have plenty of free disk space for Windows 95 and your programs to work with, so regularly emptying the trash, just like at home, is a good practice.

Here's the easiest way to empty the Recycle Bin:

1. Get to the Desktop.

2. Double-click on the Recycle Bin.

3. Examine its contents to make sure you really want to jettison everything.

4. Choose File ➤ Empty Recycle Bin.

5. You'll be asked to confirm the process (see Figure 5.20).

Up and Running
with Windows 95

TIP   You can quickly empty the Recycle Bin by right-clicking on it and choosing Empty Recycle Bin.

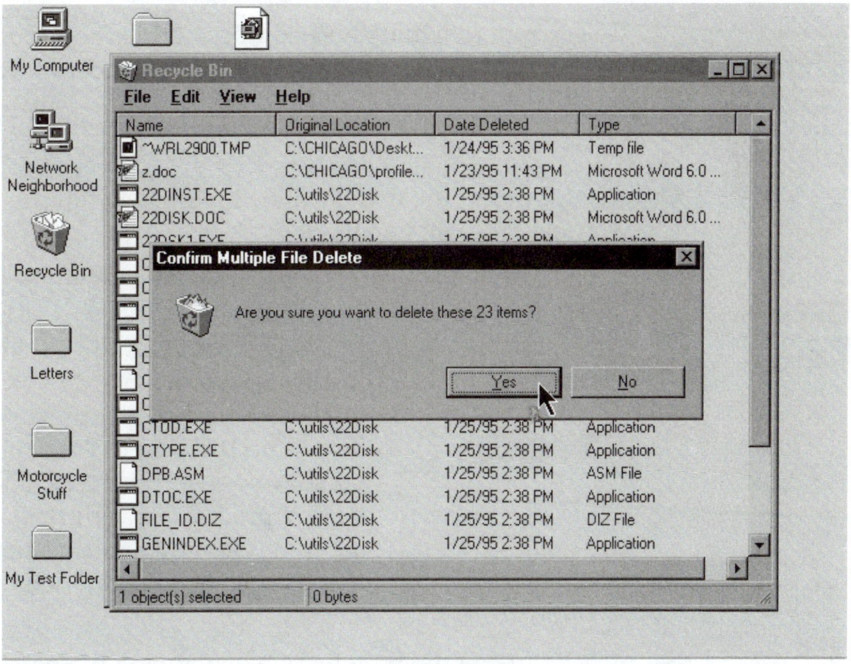

Figure 5.20   *Choosing File ➤ Empty Recycle Bin while viewing the Recycle Bin's contents results in a confirmation box. Once you confirm, the files are deleted from the disk.*

> **NOTE** We all love to accumulate junk on our hard disks. It doesn't matter whether the disk holds only 40 megabytes or a whopping gigabyte. It will fill up. When your hard disk can gets too crammed, Windows 95 starts to strangle. At that point, a dialog box reporting the sorry state of your disk housekeeping will pop up on your screen. If there is stuff in the Recycle Bin, the box will have a button you can click to empty the trash for you, reclaiming some precious space.

Renaming Documents and Folders

As you work with your files, folders, and other objects, you may occasionally need to rename them, either to more easily identify them later or because their purpose has changed and the current name is no longer valid. In any case, it's easy enough to change an object name. In fact, it's far easier than in Windows 3.x because you don't have to resort to the File Manager or DOS commands to do the renaming.

In general, renaming objects works similarly throughout Windows 95. The surest, though not necessarily the quickest, way is this:

1. Right-click on the object you want to rename and choose Rename from the resulting menu.

2. At this point, the name will be highlighted and the text cursor (small vertical bar) will be blinking.

3. Here's the tricky part. Because the whole name is highlighted, whatever you type now will replace the whole name. More often than not, this isn't what you want to do. Typically you'll just want to add a word or two, fix a misspelling, or something. So, just press ← (the left arrow key). This will deselect the name and move the cursor one space to the left. Now use the normal editing procedures with Backspace, Del, arrow keys, and regular typing to modify the name. (Chapter 19 details standard Windows editing procedures if you're in doubt about technique.)

4. Click outside the little text box encircling the name (or press ↵ once) when you're through; that will store the new name.

> **TIP**   A shortcut for editing a name is to do a *slow* double-click on the name. This puts the name into edit mode with the cursor blinking away and the name highlighted. Be careful not to double-click quickly or this will run the application or open the document.

If, when renaming a file, you see an error message about how changing the extension of the file may make it unworkable, you'll typically want to choose No. This message just means you forgot to give the file name an extension by typing in a period and the same three-letter extension it had before. So just rename it again, making sure to give it the same extension that it had before. So for example, let's say the file is named:

    Budget for Winter 1995.wks

and you change it to

    Budget for Spring 1995

You'll probably see an error message when you press the ⏎ key. Renaming the file to

    Budget for Spring 1995.wks

would prevent the error message.

As I discussed earlier in this chapter, extensions for registered file types are normally hidden. So a Word for Windows file named Letter to Joe, for example, will simply appear as:

    Letter to Joe

not

    Letter to Joe.doc

which is the name that's actually stored on the disk. When you change the name of a file that doesn't have an extension showing, you don't have to even think about what the extension is or about accidentally typing in the wrong one. So, when you change the name, it doesn't matter what you call the file or about typing in an extension. This is because the extension is hidden, and you can't accidentally change its name even if you tried.

Chapter 6

Sharing Data between Applications

FEATURING

As you know, you can run several programs at one time and switch between them with a click of the mouse or a press of Alt-Tab. You may also know that you can cut, copy, and paste information between programs and documents, embedding bits and pieces of information, graphics, sound, and video from multiple sources into a single destination source to create complex documents. Previously disparate types of information are beginning to merge into a new synthesis, evidenced by products such as CD-ROM–based interactive encyclopedias, in-car electronic guidance (map) systems, and voice-controlled telephone systems. All these capabilities are outgrowths of the desire to mix and match heretofore unrelated kinds of data.

In this chapter, we'll look at data sharing on the Windows 95 platform, paying particular attention to the techniques you can use to create complex documents, including the latest in Windows data sharing—OLE version 2.0.

OLE Overview

As a result of the standardization of the Windows interface and API, users have become accustomed to being able to cut, copy, and paste not only within a given program but between Windows programs. Nowadays, thousands of applications can easily share data with one another through these commands that use the Windows Clipboard.

We still have the problem of proprietary file and data formats—the kind of thing that makes a WordPerfect file different from a Word for Windows file, or an Excel file different from a 1-2-3 file. These proprietary formats often seem to be promoted by software developers as a means of pushing their own programs by locking users into a particular file format. Unfortunately, the proprietary-file-formats marketing strategy has backfired, leaving users grumbling and feeling held hostage by a particular brand of program.

For example, just try printing out, say, a JPEG graphics file from your favorite word-processing or desktop-publishing program. The situation becomes even thornier when multimedia files are thrown in. We are now seeing competing formats for live-motion video, audio recording, MIDI files, and the like.

Software developers have finally figured this out, though, and have made working with "foreign" file formats much easier. With each new month, more applications have built-in file-format converters to allow applications to share files. For example, Word for Windows 6.0 can read and write a whole gaggle of text and graphics file formats. Ditto for PageMaker, Ventura Publisher, Microsoft Access, and many others. Standards such as Rich Text Format (RTF), Windows Metafiles, and others are now emerging to facilitate data transfers between programs. Embedded TrueType fonts and utility programs such as Adobe's *Acrobat* even allow people to see and edit documents containing fonts not in their systems.

Windows 95 and Data Exchange

Actually, much more interesting than simply being able to use one program's document in another program is the ability to mix and match a great variety of document types, such as text, sound, graphics, spreadsheets, databases, and so forth. This lets you construct complex documents previously requiring physical cutting and pasting and possibly the aid of an art department.

Windows 95 offers three internal vehicles for exchanging data between programs: the Windows Clipboard (and Clipbook, which is an extension of Clipboard), Dynamic Data Exchange (DDE), and Object Linking and Embedding (OLE). In this chapter, I'll explain each of them, discuss how Windows 95's treatment of them differs from Windows 3.1, and then describe some special considerations for data sharing across the network.

TIP If you're new to Windows, you may only want to read the portion about the Clipboard. That's the part about the cut, copy, and paste commands. You'll use these commands much more often than the other stuff I talk about in this chapter. If you're using a network and want to share little bits of information with other people, then read about the Clipbook too. If you want to take full advantage of what Windows' OLE has to offer, read the entire chapter.

NOTE   Many of my examples in this chapter refer to Microsoft products. This isn't necessarily my endorsement of Microsoft products over other competing products! Competition in the software marketplace is a healthy force, ensuring the evolution of software technology, and I highly support it. But, because so many of you are bound to be familiar with the Microsoft product line, I use products such as Word, Excel, Graph, and Access in my examples in hopes of better illustrating the points I'm trying to make here.

The Clipboard

Though it's not capable of converting data files between various formats, such (such as `xls` to `wk3` or `rtf` to `doc`) the Windows Clipboard is great for many everyday data-exchange tasks. Just about all Windows programs support the use of the ubiquitous cut, copy, and paste commands, and it's the Clipboard that provides this functionality for you.

Clipboard makes it possible to move any kind of material, whether text, data cells, graphics, video or audio clips, and OLE objects between documents—and now, with Windows 95, between folders, the desktop, the Explorer, and other portions of the interface. The actual form of the source data doesn't matter that much, because the Clipboard utility and Windows together take care of figuring out what's being copied and where it's being pasted, making adjustments when necessary—or at least providing a few manual options for you to adjust. The Clipboard can also work with non-Windows (DOS) programs, albeit with certain limitations that I'll explain later.

How It Works

How does the Clipboard work? It's simple. The Clipboard is built into Windows 95 and uses a portion of the system's internal resources (RAM and virtual memory) as a temporary holding tank for material you're working with. For example, suppose you have cut some text from one part of a document in preparation for pasting it into another location. Windows stores the text on the Clipboard and waits for you to paste it into its new home.

The last item you copied or cut is stored in this no-man's-land somewhere in the computer until you cut or copy something else, exit

Windows, or intentionally clear the Clipboard. As a result, you can paste the Clipboard's contents any number of times.

You can examine the Clipboard's contents using the Clipbook utility supplied with Windows 95. If you've used Windows for Workgroups or Windows NT, you'll be familiar with this application. You can also use this application to save the Clipboard's contents to disk for later use or to share specific bits of data for use by others on your network.

Selecting, Copying, and Cutting in Windows Applications

In Windows 95, the Windows 3.1 standards and procedures for copying, cutting, and pasting apply because Windows 95 supports all the Windows 3.1 calls for these services. Even if you're mixing and matching 16- and 32-bit applications, the Clipboard will work just fine because in the internals of Windows 95, the 16-bit subsystem shares the same clipboard as the 32-bit section.

When running Windows 95, you simply use each application's Edit menu (or Edit menu's shortcut keys) for copying, cutting, and pasting (Figure 6.1). These tasks work just as they did in Windows 3.x.

Here are the steps for cutting, copying, or pasting within a Windows program:

1. First, arrange the windows on screen so you can see the window containing the source information.

2. Now *select* the information you want to copy or cut, such as text, a graphic, spreadsheet cells, or whatever. In many programs, simply clicking on an object, such as a graphic, will select it.

3. Once the desired area is selected, open the application's Edit menu and choose Copy or Cut depending on whether you want to copy the material or delete the original with the intention of pasting it into another location.

4. If you want to paste the selection somewhere, first position the cursor at the insertion point in the destination document (which may or may not be in the source document) you're working in. This might mean scrolling up or down the document, switching to another application using the Taskbar, or switching to another document within the *same* application via its Window menu.

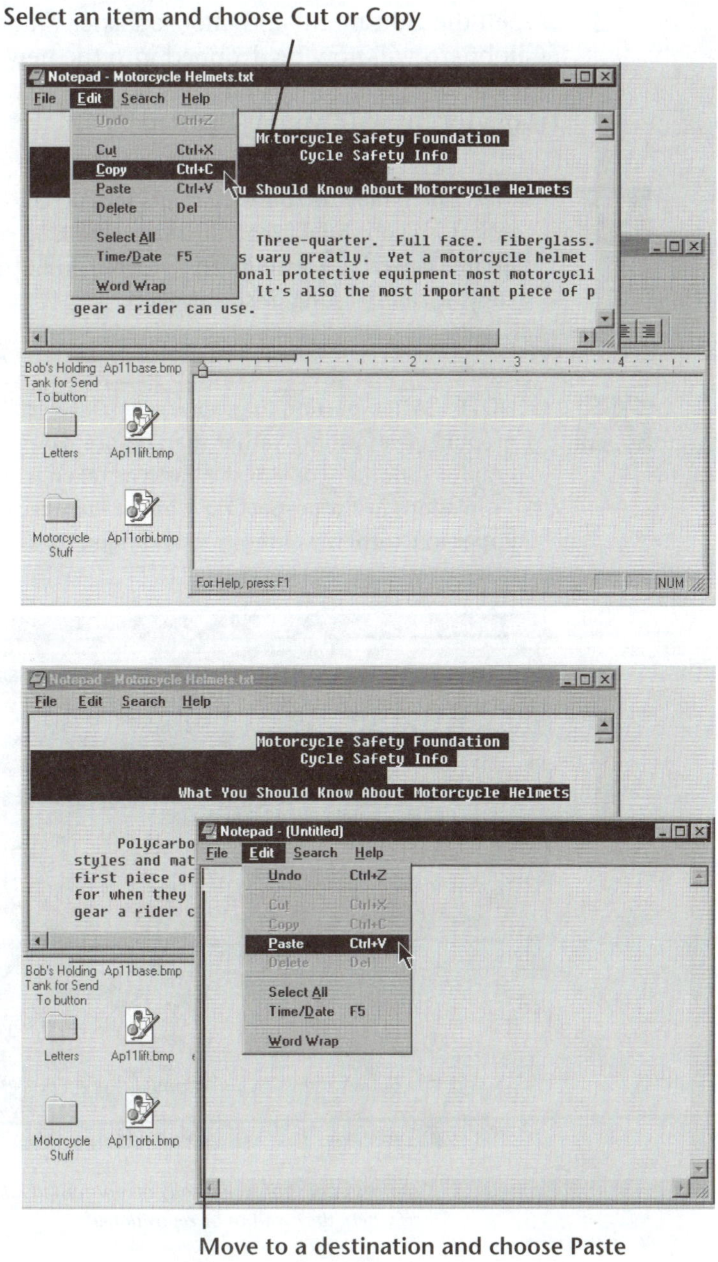

Select an item and choose Cut or Copy

Move to a destination and choose Paste

Figure 6.1   Copying and pasting in a Windows program

5. Open the Edit menu and choose Paste. Whatever material was on the Clipboard will now be dropped into the new location. Normally, this means any preexisting material, such as text, is moved down to make room for the stuff you just pasted.

TIP   There may be some shortcuts for cut, copy, and paste in specific programs, so you should read the manual or help screens supplied with the program. Generally, pressing Ctrl-X, Ctrl-C, and Ctrl-V are shortcuts for cutting, copying, and pasting, respectively.

NOTE   When pasting in graphics, you'll typically have to reposition the graphic *after* pasting, rather than before. For example, Figure 6.2 shows a graphic (another copy of the Earth as taken from the moon on the Apollo 11 mission) just after pasting it into a Paintbrush window. It appears in the upper-left corner, waiting to be dragged to its new home.

Figure 6.2   *Graphics applications typically accept pasted information into their upper-left corner, where they wait to be repositioned.*

Up and Running
with Windows 95

Copying Text and Graphics from a DOS Box

In Windows 95, as with Windows 3.x, copying selected graphics from DOS programs is also possible. This is a pretty nifty trick for lifting material out of your favorite DOS program and dropping it into a Windows document. There's only one caveat: the DOS program has to be running in a window, not full screen.

When you cut or copy selected material from the DOS box, it gets dumped into the Clipboard as text or graphics, depending on which mode Windows 95 determines the DOS box (*box* means window) was emulating. Windows 95 knows whether the application is running in character mode or graphics mode and processes the data on the Clipboard accordingly. If text mode is detected, the material is copied as characters that could be dropped into, say, a word-processing document. If the DOS application has set up a graphics mode in the DOS box (because of the application's video requests), you'll get a bit-mapped graphic in the destination document when you paste.

> **NOTE**   As you may know, some fancy DOS programs may look as though they are displaying text when they're really running in graphics mode. For example, WordPerfect for DOS and Microsoft Word for DOS can both run in a graphics mode that displays text attributes such as underline, italics, and bold, rather than as boring block letters displayed in colors that indicate these attributes. When you copy text from such a program and then paste it into another document, you'll be surprised to find you've pasted a graphic, not text. This means you can't edit it like text because it's being treated like a bit-mapped graphic. The solution is to switch the DOS application back to Text mode and try again. Refer to your DOS program manual for help.

Because of the Windows 95 DOS box's toolbar, the procedure for copying is simple to learn. You can use the menus or the toolbar almost as if you were using another Windows program. Figure 6.3 illustrates the simple technique. Here are the steps:

1. First, switch to the DOS application and display the material you want to work with.

2. Make sure the application is running in a window, rather than running full-screen. If it's not, press Alt-Enter. (Each press of Alt-Enter toggles any DOS window between full and windowed view.)

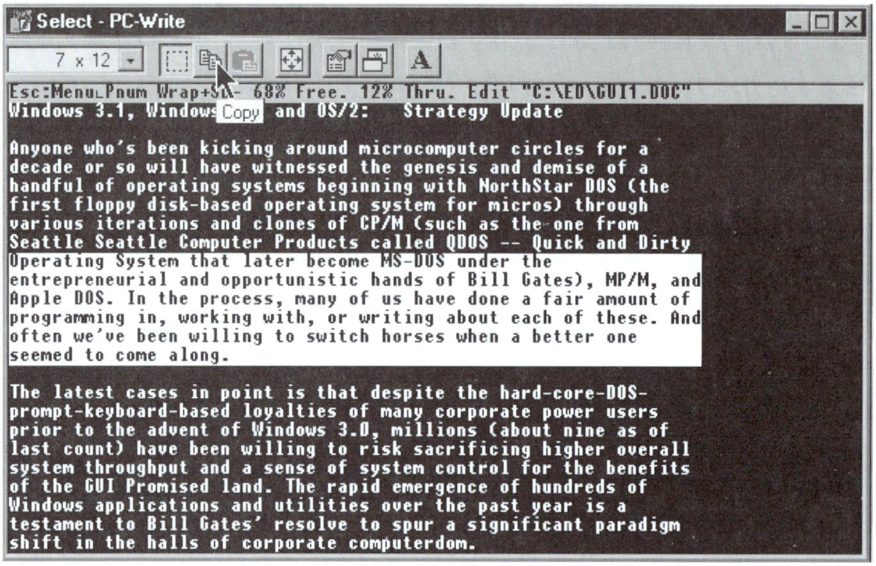

Figure 6.3   Copying text from a MS-DOS box is now a simple procedure. Click on the Mark button, click and drag across the desired text, and click on the Copy button.

3. If the DOS box's toolbar isn't showing, turn it on by clicking in the upper-left corner of its window (on the MS-DOS icon) and choosing Toolbar.

Part
1

Up and Running
with Windows 95

4. Click on the Mark button.

5. Holding the mouse button down, drag the pointer over the desired copy area, dragging from upper left to lower right. As you do so, the color of the selection will change to indicate what you're marking.

6. Release the mouse button. The selected area will stay highlighted.

7. Click on the Copy button. The information is now on the Clipboard.

> **NOTE** Notice that there isn't a Cut button because you can't cut from a DOS application in this way. Cutting has to be done using the DOS program's own editing keys, and it won't interact with the Windows Clipboard.

> **TIP** As soon as you click on the Mark button, the DOS box's title bar changes to read *Mark*. Once you start marking the selection, the word *Select* precedes the program's name in the title bar, indicating that you're in select mode. Typing any letter on the keyboard terminates the selection process.

That's all there is to copying information from an application that's running in the DOS box. Of course, the normal procedure will apply to pasting what was just copied. You just switch to the destination application (which, incidentally, can be a DOS *or* a Windows program), position the cursor, and choose Edit ➤ Paste to paste in the Clipboard's contents at the cursor position. (For a DOS application as the destination, you'd use the Paste button on the DOS box's toolbar. This is explained later in this chapter.)

Doing Screen Captures with Clipboard

As in Windows 3.x, you can capture all or part of the screen image while running an application. Screen captures are useful for creating program documentation, software education materials, or for putting out promotional material about software.

Clipboard is handy for capturing screen images in lieu of purchasing a special-purpose screen-capture program. The price is right, and it works, albeit with some limitations.

TECH TIP   Professional programs designed for screen capture help you organize, crop, and edit your screen captures, among other things. If you regularly do screen captures, you might want to check these programs out. I used Collage Complete for the screens in this book. Other programs you might want to explore are Tiffany, PixelPop, Hotshot, and Hijaak. These programs give you a lot of latitude with capture techniques, file formats, color settings, grayscaling, and so forth, none of which the old Clipboard workhorse affords you.

With Clipboard, you have just two options when capturing: you can capture the entire screen or just the active window. Whether you're capturing a DOS or Windows-based application, the capture is converted to bit-mapped format for pasting into graphics programs such as PageMaker, Paint, and so forth.

TIP   Though you can't edit your files or add borders and nice stuff like that using this economy approach to captures, you *can* save a file to disk for later use. The Clipboard and the Clipbook both let you save files on disk for later use. Please refer to *Saving the Clipboard's Contents in a File* and *Working with the Clipbook* later in this chapter.

To copy the active window's image onto the Clipboard, do the following (note that if a dialog box is open, this is usually considered the *active* window):

1. Get the desired application open and running in a window and adjust and size the window as needed.

2. Press Alt-PrintScreen. The image of the active window is copied to the Clipboard.

NOTE   All the computers I used this technique on responded as expected when these keys were pressed. However, some older PC keyboards use slightly different codes, requiring the user to press Shift-PrintScreen instead.

Instead of just copying the active window, you might want to capture a picture of the entire screen. There is a simple variation on the above theme for this purpose.

1. Set up the screen as described above.

2. Press PrintScreen (instead of Alt-PrintScreen). The image will be copied to the Clipboard. (See the discussion below about pasting the Clipboard contents.)

TECH TIP   Though object linking and embedding (OLE) is covered later in this chapter, I'll mention here briefly that you can use File Manager in conjunction with the Clipboard for embedding a file into a document. File Manager's Copy command results in a dialog box that lets you copy the file to the Clipboard instead of to another drive or directory. Then you'd use the destination application's Paste Special command to insert the object.

Using the Paste Command

Once you have some information on the Clipboard, Windows 95 offers you several options for working with it. In Windows 3.x only two of these were possible, but Windows 95 also incorporates the Clipbook facility previously part of Windows for Workgroups. Here are the three routes you'll be able to take:

▶ Paste the information into a document you're working with (or that you open subsequently).

▶ Save it to a Clipboard (.clp) file for using later.

▶ Save it on a Clipbook page for later use or for sharing over the network.

The last two choices are described later in this chapter. For standard pasting there are two options:

▶ You can paste information into Windows applications.

▶ You can paste into DOS applications (when they are in a window rather than running full-screen).

Let's look at these two individually because they require distinctly different techniques.

Pasting Information into Windows Applications   As you are probably aware, the great majority of Windows applications' Edit menus include a Paste command. As the name implies, this is the command you'll use to paste material from the Clipboard into your documents. Of course, this command won't be usable unless there is something already on the Clipboard that can be accepted by the document you're working with at the time.

TECH TIP   Some heavier-duty programs have their own internal Clipboard that's not connected at all to the system's Clipboard. This isn't usually the case, so you don't have to worry about it with most applications. However, to accommodate proprietary data types and large amounts of data, some programs do use their own. Word for Windows, for example, does have a so-called large clipboard that it uses when you cut or copy a sizable bulk of material. In such an application, data you thought you were making available to the entire Windows 95 system might not be. But this caveat will probably apply less to 32-bit applications than to 16-bit ones. We can expect the 32-bit internals of Windows 95—along with more intelligent memory management—to render its systemwide Clipboard both more intelligent and larger in capacity than its predecessor.

To successfully paste information from the Clipboard, here's what to do. Of course there may be some variation from application to application, but you'll figure that out as you use them. This basic approach works almost all the time.

1. First, you must set up the right conditions. That means cut or copy material onto the Clipboard.

2. Next, switch to the destination program or document—the one that will receive the information.

3. Now position the cursor or insertion point. In a text-based program this means position the I-beam cursor where you want it and click the primary mouse button.

4. Finally, choose Edit ➤ Paste or (in most programs) press Ctrl-V. The Clipboard's contents then appear in the destination window. Figure 6.4 shows an example.

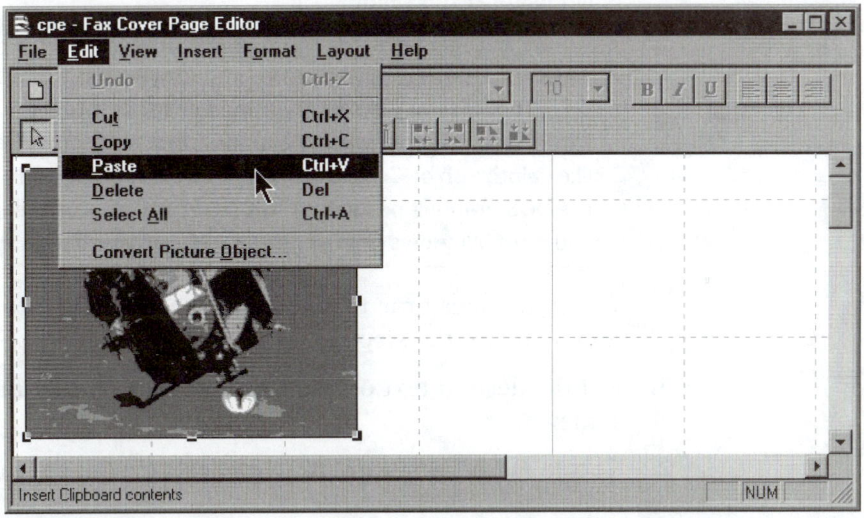

Figure 6.4   *Typical pasting operation, showing the Paste selection on the Edit menu*

NOTE   The Clipboard's contents remain static only until you copy or cut something new, so repeated pasting of the same material is possible. Just keep selecting insertion points and choosing Edit ➤ Paste.

Pasting into a DOS Box   As weird as this seems, you can also paste into DOS applications. I say weird because most DOS applications were invented way before the Windows Clipboard was even a twinkle in

Bill Gates' eye. There are certain limitations to this technique, such as only being allowed to paste text (no graphics). This is for obvious reasons—pasting graphics into a DOS application would be a nightmare. It simply wouldn't work because there is no standard agreement among DOS applications about treatment of on-screen graphics. Even with text, the results of pasting may be less than expected because DOS applications don't all accept data the same way.

> **NOTE**   You should be aware that all text formatting will be lost when you paste text into a DOS document. This is because formatting (bold, italics, fonts, bullets, and so forth) is application-specific information (specially coded for each program), and most applications just don't speak the same language at this point.

> **TIP**   Though you can't paste graphics directly into DOS applications, here's a workaround. Simply paste the graphic into a windows-based graphics program like Paintbrush or Corel Draw. Then save the graphic in a file that's readable by the DOS graphics program. Most DOS programs can read `.bmp` or `.pcx` files, and most Windows graphics programs can save files in these formats.

When it comes time to actually do the pasting into a DOS application, here are the steps:

1. Put the desired text on the Clipboard by cutting or copying it from somewhere.

2. Toggle the destination DOS application so it's a window (this can't be done full-screen).

3. Position the DOS application's cursor at the location where you want to insert the Clipboard's material. This *must* be the location where you would next type text into the DOS document.

4. Click on the DOS box's Paste button.

   Figure 6.5 shows an example in which I've inserted Clipboard text copied from a Help screen into a PC-Write file running in a window.

```
[■] WPOffice Editor                                    [_][□][✕]

  7 x 12  [▾]   [□][▣][▨]  [✥]   [▨][▨][🖨]   [A]

Esc:Menu Pnum Wrap+Sp-  88% Free.   9% Thru. Edit "C:\ED\GUI1.DOC"
various iterations and Paste s of CP/M (such as the one from
Seattle Seattle Computer products called QDOS -- Quick and Dirty
Operating System that later become MS-DOS under the
entrepreneurial and opportunistic hands of Bill Gates), MP/M, and
Apple DOS. In the process, many of us have done a fair amount of
programming in, working with, or writing about each of these. And
often we've been willing to switch horses when a better one
seemed to come along.

▮


The latest cases in point is that despite the hard-core-DOS-
prompt-keyboard-based loyalties of many corporate power users
prior to the advent of Windows 3.0, millions (about nine as of
last count) have been willing to risk sacrificing higher overall
system throughput and a sense of system control for the benefits
of the GUI Promised land. The rapid emergence of hundreds of
Windows applications and utilities over the past year is a
testament to Bill Gates' resolve to spur a significant paradigm
shift in the halls of corporate computerdom.
```

Figure 6.5   *To paste text into a DOS application running in a window, position the cursor and click on the Paste button.*

TECH TIP   The internals of the process of pasting into a DOS box are interesting. The text on the Clipboard is sent to the portion of the operating system that's responsible for buffering keyboard data entry. When you paste, the application thinks you have typed in the new text from the keyboard. For the procedure to work correctly, however, the recipient program has to be written in such a way that it doesn't balk at receiving information at the speed a supernormal typist could enter it.

Right-Click Shortcuts for Cut, Copy, and Paste

As mentioned earlier, the cut, copy, and paste scheme is implemented throughout Windows 95, even on the Desktop, in the Explorer, in folder windows, and so forth. This is done using right–mouse-button shortcuts. Some applications are starting to offer this feature too.

As explained in the last chapter, right-clicking on a file in a folder window and choosing Copy puts a pointer to the file on the Clipboard. Right-clicking on another location, such as the Desktop, and choosing

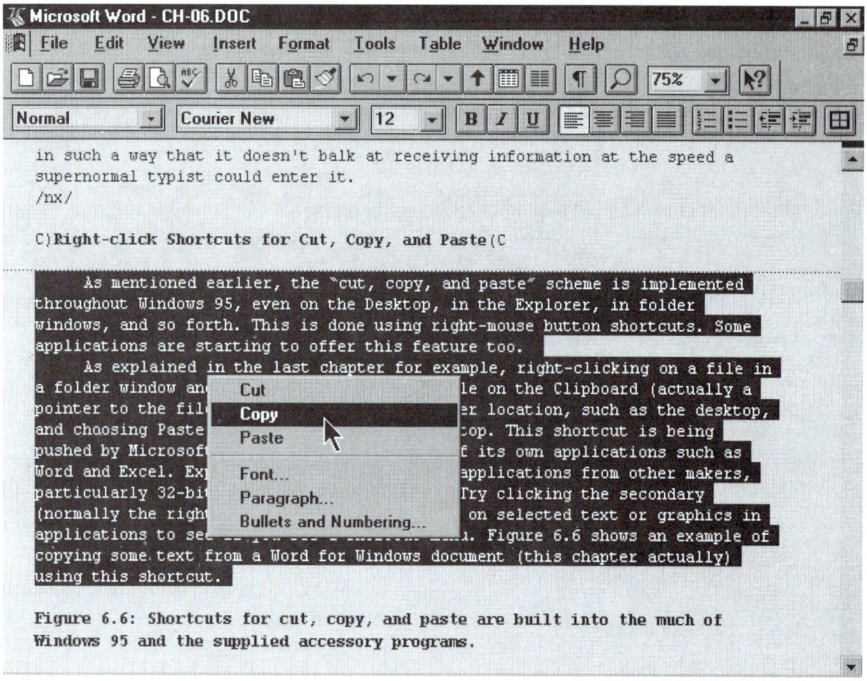

Figure 6.6: Shortcuts for cut, copy, and paste are built into the much of Windows 95 and the supplied accessory programs.

Figure 6.6   *Shortcuts for cut, copy, and paste are built into much of Windows 95 via the right-click menu. Windows applications are beginning to implement this feature, too, as you see here in Word for Windows.*

Paste drops the file there (e.g., on the Desktop). This shortcut is being pushed by Microsoft and is included in some of its applications such as Word and Excel. Expect to see it included in applications from other makers, particularly 32-bit Windows 95 applications. Try clicking the secondary (normally the right) mouse button on icons or on selected text or graphics in applications to see if there is a shortcut menu. Figure 6.6 shows an example of copying some text from a Word for Windows document using this shortcut.

Working with the Clipboard's Viewer

Once data is on the Clipboard, you may not want to paste it immediately, or you might want to see what's there. There are two programs supplied with Windows that make this really easy. One's called Clipboard Viewer, and the other is Clipbook Viewer. You can can find one or both of these in the Accessories folder (choose Start ➤ Programs ➤ Accessories ➤ Clipbook Viewer). These programs let you do some useful Clipboard-related things, such as:

▶ view the Clipboard's contents

▶ save and retrieve the Clipboard's contents to/from a file

▶ clear the Clipboard's contents

▶ set up pages of the Clipboard, each storing things you plan to use later or want to make available to networked colleagues

Let's look at each of these simple tasks in order.

Viewing the Clipboard's Contents

Sometimes you'll simply forget what information is on the Clipboard because you won't remember what you cut or copied last. And before you go ahead and paste it into an application (especially if that application doesn't have an Undo command), you might want to check out what's going to get pasted. Another time when viewing is useful is when you're trying to get a particular item into the Clipboard and don't know how successful you've been. Bringing up the Viewer and positioning it off in the corner of the screen can give you instant feedback as you cut and copy.

Here's how to view the Clipboard's contents.

> **NOTE**   Actually, there are two different utilities that let you examine the Clipboard's contents: Clipboard Viewer and Clipbook Viewer. Either one will work. You may have both of these programs in your Accessories folder, or only one, depending on whether you upgraded to Windows 95 over Windows for Workgroups or not. The procedure below explains the Clipbook approach. If you only have the Clipboard Viewer, the steps are actually quite similar. Simply run Clipboard Viewer instead of Clipbook Viewer and skip step 2, below.

1. Click on the Start button and choose Programs ➤ Accessories ➤ Clipbook Viewer.

2. The Clipbook Viewer window comes up. Double-click on the Clipboard icon in the bottom-left corner of the window or open the

Window menu and choose Clipboard. The iconized Clipbook icon turns into a window, displaying the Clipboard's current contents. Figure 6.7 shows typical Clipboard contents; in this case, a portion of an image I had just copied from the Paint program.

Changing the View Format

It's possible that the contents of the Clipboard will look different from how they look in the application you copied or cut from. For example, graphics may appear mottled or distorted, text may appear with incorrect line breaks, fonts, and so forth. You see, graphics and text can contain substantial amounts of formatting, such as font type and size, indents, colors, resolution settings, grayscaling, and so on. But there are some limitations to the amount of information that will actually be transferred through the Clipboard. It's the job of the source application to inform Windows 95, and thus the Clipboard, of the nature of the material. The Clipboard tries its best to keep all the relevant information, but it doesn't necessarily display it all in the Viewer window.

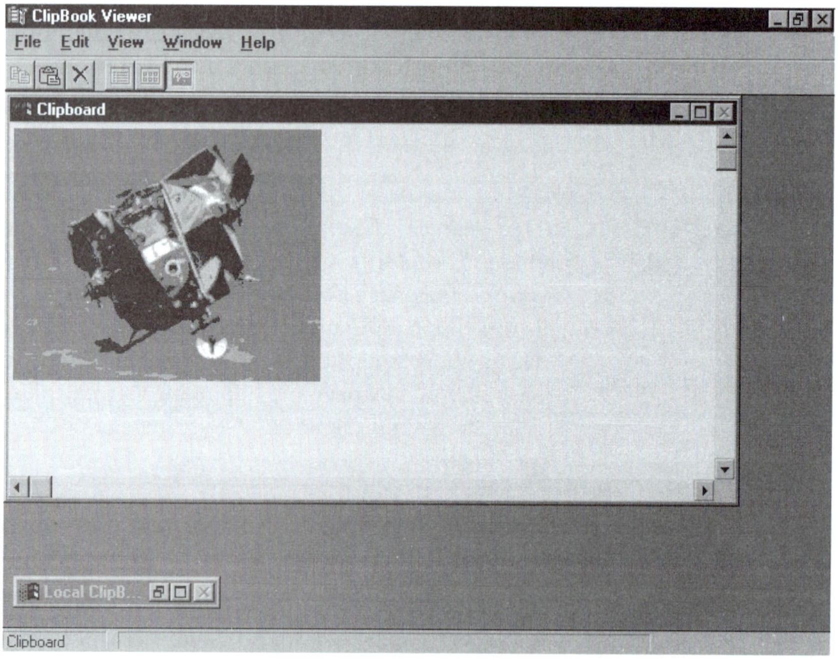

Figure 6.7   *The Clipboard's contents being displayed in a window within the Clipbook Viewer*

Let's take an example. A Paintbrush picture can be passed on to another application as what Windows 95 calls a bitmap, a picture, or a Windows Enhanced Metafile. (In addition to this, there can be information that pertains to Object Linking and Embedding, but these aspects don't appear in the Viewer window.)

When you first view the Clipboard's contents, the Viewer does its best to display the contents so they look as much as possible like the original. However, this isn't a fail-safe method, so there may be times when you'll want to try changing the view. To do this:

1. Open the View menu (or the Display menu in Clipboard Viewer).

2. Check out the available options. They'll vary depending on what you've got stored on the Clipboard. Choose one and see how it affects the display. The Default setting (called *default format*) returns the view to the original display format the material was first shown with. However, none of them will affect the Clipboard contents—only its display.

NOTE   When you actually go to paste into another Windows application, the destination program tries to determine the best format for accepting whatever is currently on the Clipboard. If the Edit menu on the destination application is grayed out, you can safely assume that the contents are not acceptable. (Changing the Clipboard's view format as described above won't rectify the situation, either. In fact, it doesn't have any effect on how things actually get pasted.)

Storing the Clipboard's Contents in a File

When you place new material onto the Clipboard, reboot, or shut down the computer, the Clipboard contents are lost. Also, because the Clipboard itself is not *network aware* (meaning it can't interact with other workstations on the network), you can't share the Clipboard's contents with other networked users. You'll want to take advantage of Clipbook pages for that (see below). However, there is one trick left. You *can* save the Clipboard's contents to a disk file. Clipboard files have the extension .clp. Once the Clipboard's contents are stored in a disk file, it's like any other disk file—you can later reload the file from disk. If you do a lot of work with clip art and bits and pieces of sound, video, text, and the like, this technique can come in handy. Also, if you give network users access to your .clp file directory, they can, in effect, use your Clipboard.

> **TIP**   The Clipboard CLP files use a proprietary file format that is readable by virtually no other popular programs. So, to use a CLP file, you have to open it in Clipboard and *then* paste it where you want it to appear. This might all seem like a hassle, and it is. Actually, the Clipbook Viewer, explained later in this section, offers a hassle-free way to archive little things you regularly want to paste.

In any case, here's how to save a Clipboard file:

1. First make sure you have run the Clipbook Viewer or Clipboard Viewer, as explained above.

2. Activate the Clipboard window within the Clipbook Viewer. The easiest way to do this is to choose Clipboard from the Window menu. You could also double-click on the Clipboard icon if you see it at the bottom of the Clipbook Viewer window.

3. Choose File ➤ Save As. A standard Save As dialog box will appear.

4. Enter a name. As usual, you can change the folder, name, and extension. Leave the extension as .clp because Clipboard uses this as a default when you later want to reload the file.

5. Click on OK, as you see in Figure 6.8. The file is saved and can be loaded again as described below.

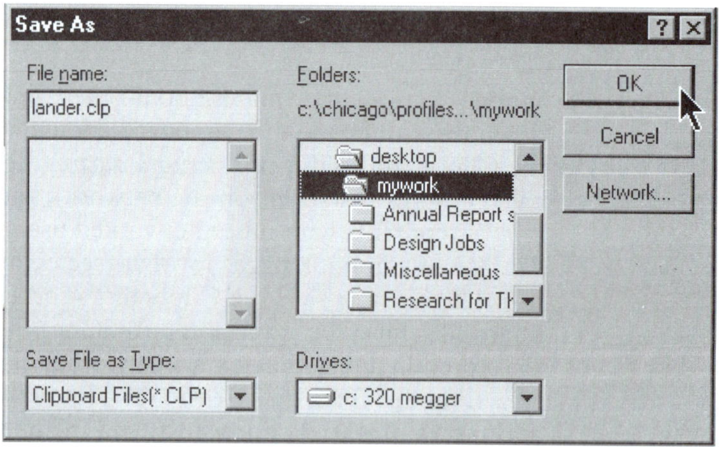

Figure 6.8   Saving a Clipboard file

Retrieving the Contents of a Stored Clipboard File

As I mentioned, once the CLP file is on disk, you can reload it. Use these steps.

CAUTION   When you reload a CLP file, anything currently on the Clipboard will be lost.

---

1. Run Clipbook Viewer.

2. Choose Clipboard from the Window menu.

3. Choose File ➤ Open. The Open dialog box will appear.

4. Select the file you want to pull onto the Clipboard. (Only legitimate CLP files can be opened.)

5. If there's something already on the Clipboard, you'll be asked if you want to erase it. Click on OK.

6. Change the display format via the View menu if you want to (assuming there are options available on the menu).

7. Paste the contents into the desired destination.

Clearing the Clipboard

You might want to keep in mind, while using the Clipboard, that the information you store there, even temporarily, can impact the amount of memory available for use by the system and other applications. If you're cutting and pasting small bits of text and graphics as most people do during the course of a workday, this shouldn't be a concern, especially because Windows 95's new memory management is more efficient than its predecessor's.

However, be aware that some items you might place on the Clipboard can be large. For example, graphics, video, sound samples, or large amounts of formatted text take up considerable space on the Clipboard. Some items are stored in a number of formats for pasting into different kinds of destinations and thus may hog more memory than you might expect.

The moral of the story is that if you're running into memory shortages, you may occasionally want to clear the contents of the Clipboard using the technique explained below.

NOTE   In Windows 3.1 you could get an idea of how much system memory an item on the Clipboard was occupying by switching to Program Manager or File Manager and choosing Help ➤ About. The resulting dialog box told you how much memory and User Resources were available. Windows 95 isn't as informative. Many *About* dialog boxes that under Windows 3.x reported free memory now simply report the total amount of RAM your system has. Windows 95 utility programs that monitor and report memory usage will probably begin to appear on the market. In the meantime, you can run the *System Monitor* program from the Accessories ➤ System Tools folder if you really need to keep track of memory (and many other system resource) usages.

To clear the Clipboard:

1. From Clipbook Viewer, select the Clipboard view by double-clicking on the Clipboard icon or clicking on its window.

2. Click on the X in the Toolbar or choose Edit ➤ Delete, as you see in Figure 6.9.

3. Click on OK in the resulting dialog box to actually clear the board. The Clipboard's contents will be deleted.

Using Clipbook

Though very handy, the Clipboard does have several drawbacks. The most obvious of these are:

▶ Information on the Clipboard can't be easily shared with network users.

▶ You're limited to one item being on the Clipboard at a time. Copying or cutting a new item erases the previous one.

▶ Saving and retrieving Clipboard files is a hassle. Accessing, say, a number of small sound clips or clip art pictures requires giving each one a CLP file name and later remembering their names so you can reload them.

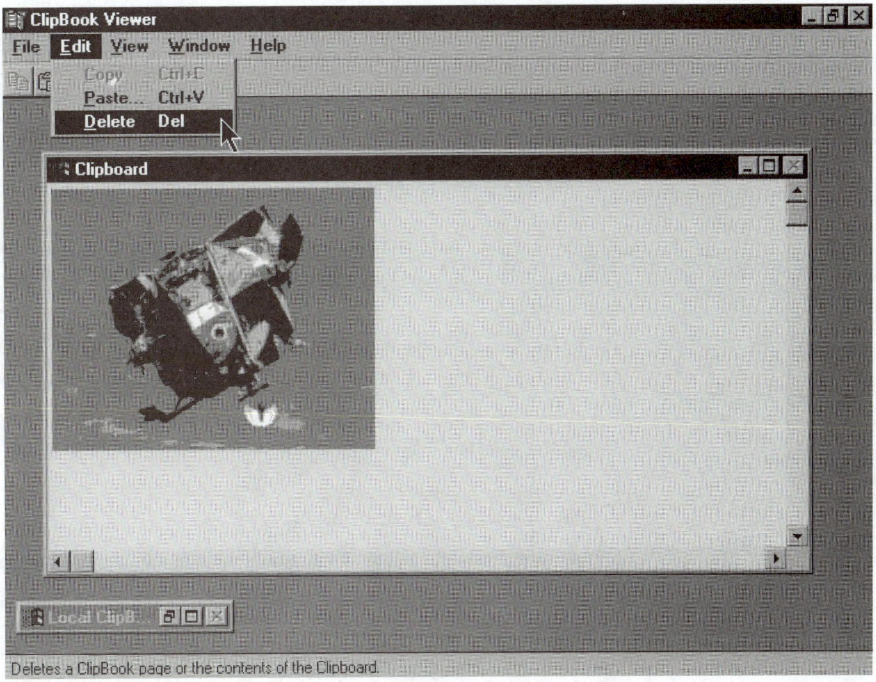

Figure 6.9   *Clearing the contents of the Clipboard*

So, what to do? Well, as I mentioned earlier, there's a thing called the Clipbook that works much like the Clipboard, but it's groovier. Clipbook first made an appearance in Windows for Workgroups. Then it came out in 32-bit form in NT, and now it's in Windows 95. Clipbook offers these advantages over Clipboard:

▶ You can store Clipboard memory on *pages* within the Clipbook. There can be as many as 127 of these pages, each one acting like a separate Clipboard.

▶ You can give each Clipbook page a description to help you remember what it is. The description can be up to 47 characters long. This is great for naming pages such things as *Joe's logo version 10*, and so forth.

▶ You can share all or selected pages of your Clipbook for use by colleagues at other network workstations.

▶ You can display thumbnail representations of each page so you can visually scan many pages of your Clipbook at once to find the one you want.

Running Clipbook

If you've been following the above section, you already know how to run Clipbook Viewer. This program is your connection to the Clipbook just as it is to the Clipboard. The only difference is that you select the Clipbook window rather than the Clipboard window. Do this from the Window menu by choosing Local Clipbook. Once you do, its window appears as you see in Figure 6.10. (It is probably empty unless you have saved some items to it in the past.)

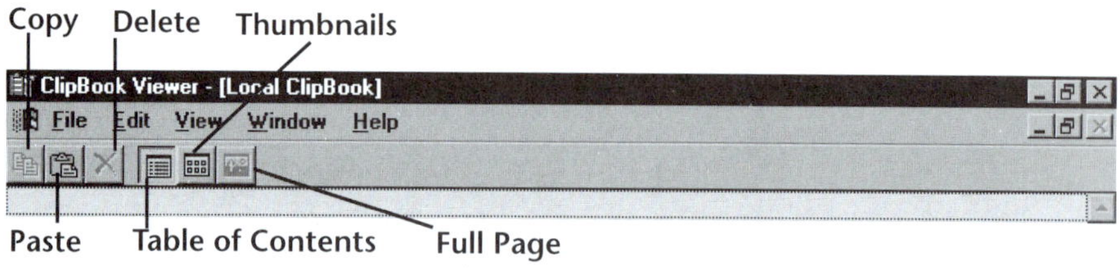

Figure 6.10 *Clipbook Viewer*

The following table explains the toolbar's buttons.

Button	Menu Command	Effect
	Copy	Paste selected Clipbook page to Clipboard
	Paste	Paste the contents of the Clipboard to Clipbook
	Delete	Delete contents of selected page (or of Clipboard if showing)
	Table of Contents	List the named pages in the Clipbook

| Button | Menu
Command | Effect |
| --- | --- | --- |
| ▦ | Thumbnails | Display thumbnails of
Clipbook's pages |
| ▦ | Full Page | Full display of selected
Clipbook page |

How It Works: Pasting into Clipbook

As you have probably suspected, the Clipbook doesn't actually re-place the Clipboard. It simply works in concert with it. In Windows 95, cutting, copying, and pasting within and between your various applications is still orchestrated by the Clipboard. What the Clipbook supplies is a convenient repository for Clipboard items—items that would normally be wiped out of the Clipboard when you shut down Windows or copy something new onto the Clipboard. Figure 6.11 illustrates the relationship of Clipboard to Clipbook.

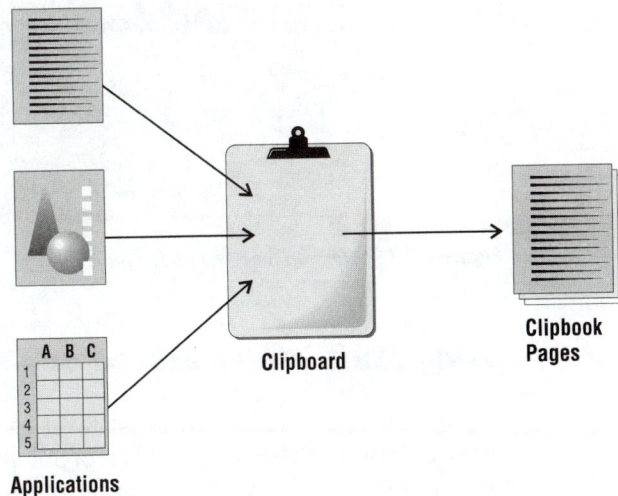

Figure 6.11 Items are added to the Clipbook by pasting them from Clipboard.

To use the Clipbook, you simply paste an item onto one of the 127 pages in your Clipbook. Then you give the page a name and description for later reference. Here are the steps:

1. First get the desired information onto the Clipboard.

2. Run or switch to the Clipbook Viewer.

3. At this point, it doesn't matter whether the Clipboard or Local Clipboard window is the active window. Just choose Edit ➤ Paste from within the Clipbook Viewer. A Paste dialog box now appears, asking for a name for the new page (Figure 6.12). Each time you paste into the Clipbook, you have to name the page. You can name the page anything you like, up to 47 characters in length. So you could name a page

   ```
   This is a silly picture of an elephant
   ```

4. Click on the Share Item Now box to turn it on, if you want to make the new Clipbook page immediately available to other users on the network (if you're on a network). (Sharing the item now will bring up another dialog box after you name the item, asking some things about how you want to share the item. This is explained below.)

Figure 6.12   *Naming a new Clipbook page*

Using Stuff You've Stored on Clipbook Pages

Once you've got your item(s) stowed away nicely on Clipbook pages, how do you use them again? No problem. You can easily paste them into documents on your computer or later share them for use by other computers on your network. Let's take these two situations separately.

First, here's how to paste something from a Clipbook into a document you're working on. Suppose you've saved a piece of clip art on a page and now you want to paste it:

1. Run Clipbook Viewer (or switch to it, if it's already running).

2. Display the Local Clipbook window by double-clicking on it, or easier, by opening the Window menu and choosing Local Clipbook. The display can be changed from Thumbnail view to List view from the View menu or from the Toolbar (see Figure 6.10 for the Toolbar button descriptions). Figure 6.13 shows a typical listing of pages.

3. Select the page containing the information you want by clicking on its thumbnail or name.

4. Within Clipbook Viewer, click on the Paste button, or choose Edit ➤ Copy. This copies the particular Clipbook page onto the Clipboard.

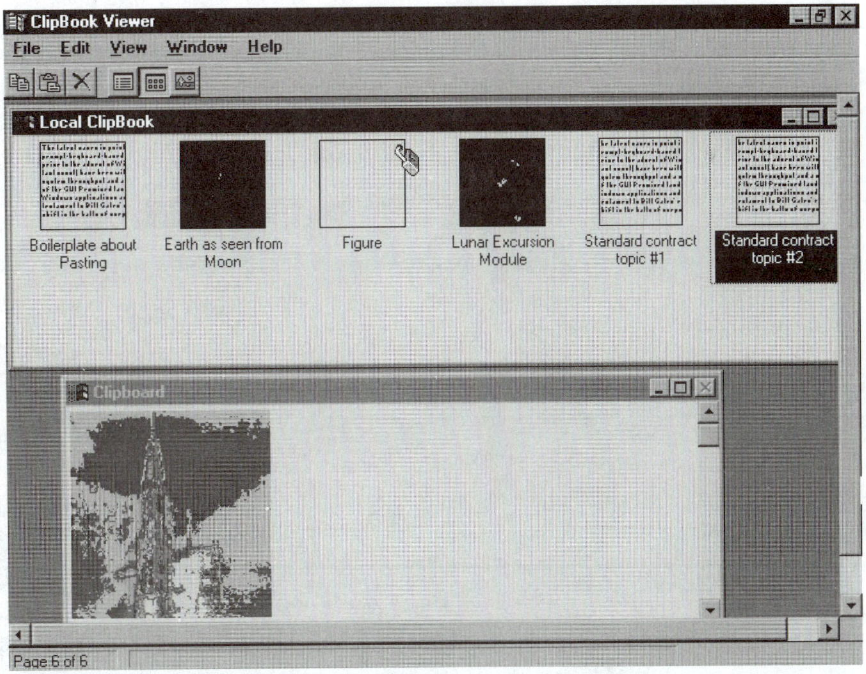

Figure 6.13 *Selecting a Clipbook page for reuse. You simply click on the page to use, copy, then paste it into the destination application. The Clipboard is used as an intermediary.*

5. Switch to the application you want to paste into. Position the cursor or do any setup in that application that might be necessary and then choose Edit ➤ Paste from that application. Windows should now paste in the item. Adjust as necessary.

Sharing Your Clipbook Pages with Network Users

When you want to share a Clipbook page so others on the network can link or copy it into their documents, do the following:

1. Run or switch to Clipbook Viewer.

2. View the Local Clipbook (via the Window menu).

3. Select the item you want to share. If you want to examine the item before sharing it, click on the Full Page button.

> **TIP**   You can quickly toggle between full-page and Thumbnail or Table of Contents view by double-clicking on an item.

4. Choose File ➤ Share. You'll see the following dialog box:

Note the *Start application on connect* check box. You have to set this check box *on* if the data on the Clipbook page is anything more complex than a bitmap or unformatted text. If you don't, network users won't be able to access the data. If you're in doubt about whether to turn this on, share the page with the setting turned *off* and let users try to use it. If this doesn't work, turn it *on*.

TIP   With the switch on, the source application will run when a remote user accesses the specific page. If you don't want the running of the application to interrupt your work by opening a window on the serving workstation, set the Run Minimized check box on.

5. Fill in the other options as you see fit. Unless you specify otherwise, pages are shared with a type of Full Access. This means other people can erase or edit the page as well as copy it. If you want to prevent others from editing or erasing the page, share it either as Read-only or require a password. If set to Read-only, remote users can only paste the information into documents. They can't edit what's on your Clipbook page. If you stipulate a password, then a remote user must enter the password before gaining access to the page or before altering the page's contents.

Connecting to a Shared Page

Connecting to another network station's Clipbook to use *its* pages is a relatively straightforward process. You simply use the File ➤ Connect command in the Clipbook Viewer to browse around the network and connect to the desired station and page. Then you use it as if it were your own. Here are the steps:

1. Run Clipbook Viewer.

2. Get to the Local Clipbook window.

3. Open the File menu and click on Connect.

4. Browse to, or type in, the name of the computer whose Clipbook has the information you want.

5. Click on OK. If a password is required for the remote Clipbook, you'll be prompted to enter it. The newly available page(s) will now

appear in a new window within your Clipbook Viewer. When you attempt to access one of its pages, you may be prompted for a password.

6. When you're through using another person's Clipbook, you may want to disconnect from it. Simply activate the particular remote Clipbook's icon or window within your Clipbook Viewer and choose File ➤ Disconnect.

Object Linking and Embedding under Windows 95

The ability to run numerous programs, simultaneously switching between them at will and copying data between documents, marked a major advance in desktop computing, especially on the PC. Merely for its task-switching capabilities, Windows has been embraced by thousands of DOS diehards who don't even like Windows per se. They use Windows just to switch between multiple DOS programs!

However, the Clipboard and Clipbook impose severe limitations on truly "transparent" data sharing between applications. If you've been following Windows developments over the past several years, you'll know that post-Windows 3.0 products (Windows 3.1, Windows for Workgroups, Windows NT, and now Windows 95) have taken data sharing several steps further with schemes called *Dynamic Data Exchange* (DDE), *Network DDE,* and *Object Linking and Embedding* (OLE).

If you've followed the computer magazines at all, you've likely been as inundated as I on the topic of OLE 2.0, the latest and greatest of data-sharing schemes, which is incorporated into Windows 95. In fact, you may already be quite familiar with its predecessor, OLE 1.0, using it to create fancy documents combining bits and pieces of data from a variety of programs scattered about on your hard disk or across your company's network.

By the same token, though, many veteran Windows users have only the barest awareness of OLE, considering it some kind of black art (along with, unfortunately, such simple tasks as using a modem or getting their printer to work). So why should they care about OLE? The vast majority of folks don't understand OLE or DDE's nuances and stick instead with the tried-and-true Clipboard when it comes to passing data between applications. (Want a chart in that report? Paste it in!)

And for good reason. *Live* data sharing such as that offered by Windows OLE and DDE is the stuff computer-science conventions are made of. There are some highly technical distinctions between DDE and OLE that are a bit difficult to grasp, not to mention that not all Windows applications are *OLE aware* or implement OLE in the same way when they are. Add to this some confusion concerning OLE's use over a PC network, and you've got a topic in need of clarification!

In hopes of dispelling some of the confusion, this section offers a brief OLE and DDE primer. I'll fill you in on why you won't be using DDE, why you'd want to use OLE, and actually how easy OLE 2.0 makes creating flashy documents that really take advantage of all that power your computer has under its hood.

Advantages of OLE

Just to give you an idea of what I'm even talking about here with all this technical talk, consider an example when the regular old Clipboard doesn't cut the mustard, and where you might want to use OLE instead.

Let's assume you're applying for a grant from an arts council and they want to see a professional-looking, attractive business plan as part of your application. You'll be using a Windows word processor such as WordPerfect, Word, or AmiPro to write the text, and you'll also need to incorporate financial projections for your project using data taken from a spreadsheet. Got the picture?

Okay. So you *could* just copy numbers from the spreadsheet into your text document. But there's a problem—your projections are changing daily as you update and refine your spreadsheet. What to do? Well you can just paste in the cells at the last minute before printing the grant application. But there's a more elegant solution. You can *link* the relevant cells from the live spreadsheet directly to the document. Then, whenever you alter any numbers in the spreadsheet, they'll be automatically updated in your grant application. Figure 6.14 shows an Excel spreadsheet linked to a Word for Windows document.

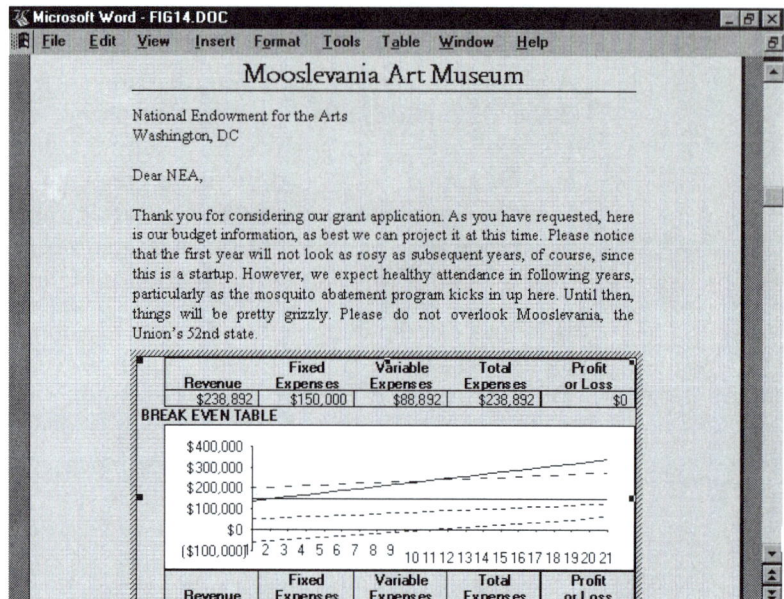

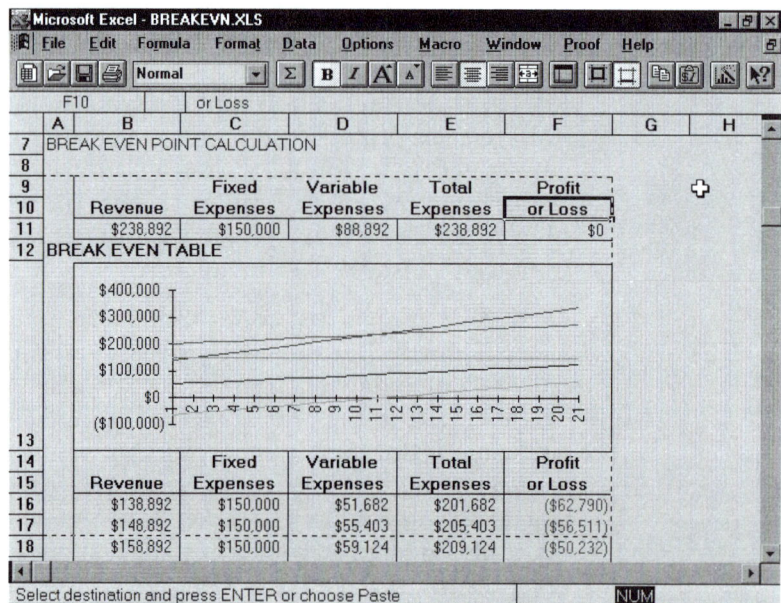

Figure 6.14   *Data linked between an Excel spreadsheet and a Word for Windows document*

This is basically what OLE is all about—splicing pieces of documents (called *objects*) from different applications into a single *compound* document. And this splicing (called *linking*) keeps the documents connected so editing one will affect any other documents that are linked to it.

There's one other major nicety of OLE: You can edit a linked addition to a document just by double-clicking on it. In the example above, this means if you wanted to enter new figures in the spreadsheet, there's no need to run Excel and open the source spreadsheet file. You just double-click on the portion of the spreadsheet that's in your word-processing document. Windows knows that Excel created this portion of the document and dishes up the correct tools for you to edit with. Once you've entered your changes, you save them, and you're dumped back into your word-processing document. Windows takes care of updating any related documents.

TECH TIP Technically, in the above example, Excel becomes the active application, not Word. Excel actually runs, takes over the active window, changes the menus, and accepts the edits. When you exit, the window returns to Word. To the user, it looks as though only the menus and toolbars have changed.

The catch is that programs must be intentionally designed with OLE. But more and more of them are these days, so you shouldn't have trouble finding chart, graphics, sound, and even video programs that'll all work together. For example, you might want to add a chart from that same spreadsheet program to your business plan to communicate the numeric information graphically or a sound clip that when clicked on explains a concept in the author's own voice. And because Windows 95 supports networks so well, linked documents can be spread out all over the network. The art department's latest version of the corporate logo could be loaded into the annual report you're about to print without your having to even make a phone call.

What Is DDE (Dynamic Data Exchange)?

Though OLE is getting all the attention these days, you might run into another term while reading about Windows' data-sharing methods. An older and less ambitious means for intercommunication between applications is called Dynamic Data Exchange (DDE), and it is also included in Windows 95. Some older applications used DDE to achieve some of the same results you get nowadays with OLE. Windows 95, Windows for Workgroups, and Windows NT have included an updated network version of DDE called NetDDE that allows applications to talk to one another over the network as well as on the same machine. And actually, OLE uses DDE as its communications link between programs.

The downside of DDE is that although it provides a way for applications to share information in a *live* way as OLE does (meaning that altering one document updates any linked documents too), how you, the user, set up the link varies too much from program to program. Another problem inherent in DDE is that the links it sets up between documents are too easy to sever. Simply moving a file to a new location or upgrading one of the source applications could result in a document losing one of its objects.

Since OLE's debut (with Windows 3.1), the bulk of serious Windows applications support OLE rather than DDE for user-created data sharing. Few programs actually used DDE internally to communicate between modules of a program or between multiple documents running under the same program. DDE has essentially been left to the domain of hackers working with such tools as Excel macros—one of the few DDE-enabled tools.

Basic OLE Concepts

It's important that you have a working understanding of OLE terms and concepts before you try creating documents with OLE. Also, it's important that you understand that there are differences between OLE 1.0 and OLE 2.0. As of this writing only a handful of applications are 2.0 enabled. Although OLE 2.0 is backward-compatible with 1.0, meaning you can mix and match the two, the techniques you'll use to create compound documents differ somewhat. In this section I'll explain all you need to know to use OLE 1.0 or OLE 2.0 to put together some fancy compound documents. I'll also explain what's so great about OLE 2.0.

So let's start with objects. What *is* an object, really? An *object* is any single block of information stored as a separate bundle but incorporated into a document. An object can consist of as little as a single spreadsheet cell, database field, or graphic element; or as much as an entire spreadsheet, database, or a complete picture or video clip.

Next, there's the issue of the differences between *linking* and *embedding*. With OLE, you have the option of using either one. You either link *or* embed an object—not both. Linking and embedding are different in functionality. Also you work with linked objects differently than you do with embedded ones. Study Figure 6.15 for a moment.

In the case of linking, two separate files exist—the spreadsheet and the word-processing files. The spreadsheet data can be edited either from within the word-processor document or separately from its source file in the spreadsheet application.

By contrast, the second figure displays an *embedded* object. The embedded graphic is more intimately connected to the word-processing document. In fact, it is contained *within* the word-processing file itself. Although the embedded picture can still be edited, it doesn't have a life outside of the word-processing document that contains it.

Regardless of whether the objects in the word-processing document are linked or embedded, the resulting larger document is called a *compound* document. A compound document is any document composed of two or more dissimilar document types joined via OLE.

Servers, Clients, Containers, and other Terms

Let's look a little more closely at how applications work together to create compound documents. First consider that there are two separate and distinct roles played by programs in the process of sharing information through OLE. One program originates the object that is to be embedded or linked. This is called the OLE *server*. The other program accepts the object. This is called the OLE *client*. For example, in Figure 6.14, Lotus 1-2-3 is the originating (server) program and the word processor is the accepting (client) program.

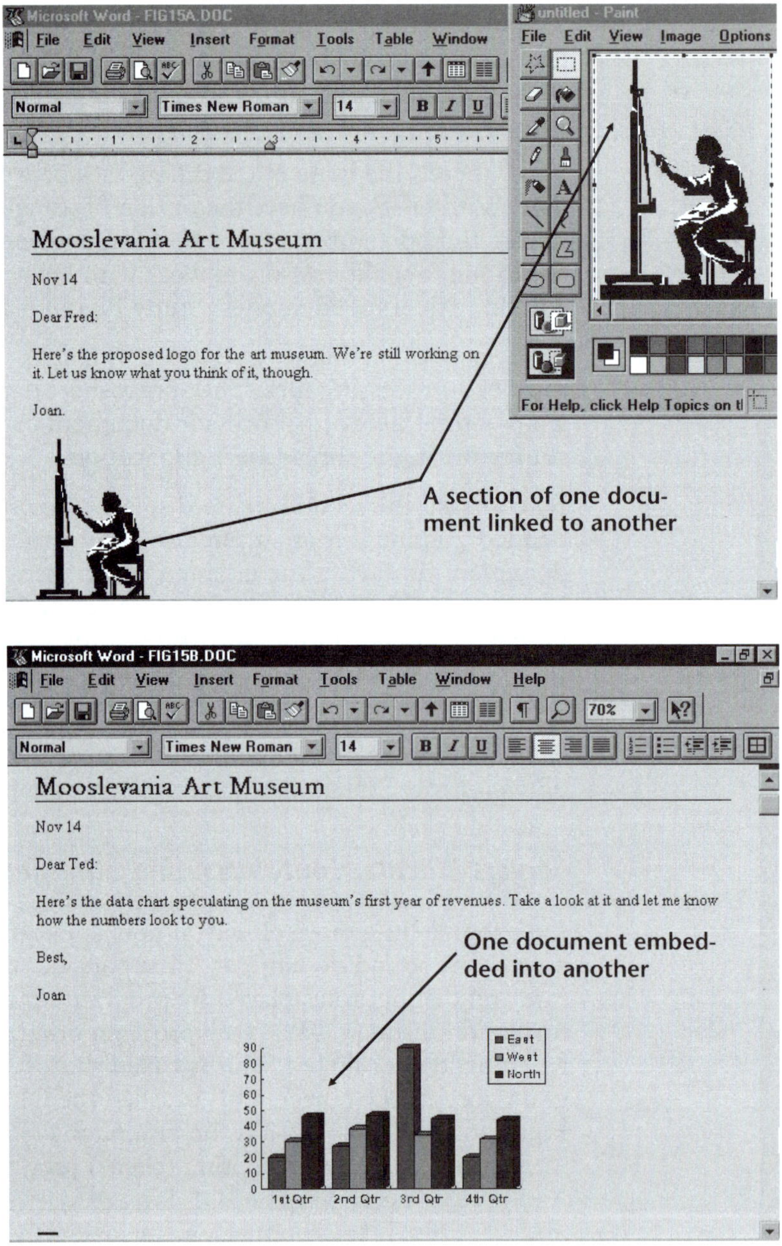

Figure 6.15   A linked and an embedded document

> **NOTE** To be absolutely precise, the terminology varies somewhat depending on whether you're speaking of OLE 1.0 or OLE 2.0. In OLE 2.0, the overall design model suggests the terms *container* and *component object* rather than *client* and *server*. The container is the receiver of any component object. For example, a word-processing document containing a graph would be the container, while the graph would be the component object. You'll probably be seeing these terms bandied about in the trade press, so the discussion here will incorporate these terms from time to time.

Sophisticated Windows applications usually will work both as OLE servers and as clients. As an example, consider a spreadsheet program such as Excel. This program can supply charts and worksheet objects to a word processor or desktop-publishing program—acting as an OLE server. Excel can also accept embedded database objects from, say, Access or Q+E.

This bidirectionality isn't always the case, however. For example, Windows Write, WordPad, and Cardfile can function only as clients while programs such as Paint, Media Player, and Sound Recorder can only behave as servers.

Two final terms you'll need to know are: the *source document* is the one in which an object is originally created, while a *destination document* is the one into which you place the object. I'll be using these terms in this chapter as we get into the procedures for creating compound documents.

Object Packages

In addition to the two basic OLE options I've described above—linking and embedding—there is a third variation of OLE called *packaging*. Packaging is a technique you can use to wrap up an object into a cute little bundle represented by an icon. Then you drop the icon into the destination document. For example, you might want to drop a sound clip or video clip into a document in this way. When the reader of the container document comes across the icon, he or she just double-clicks on it and it unwraps, so to speak. The video clip runs in a window, a sound clip plays, and so forth. Of course, this is only useful if the document is being viewed on a computer because nothing happens when you double-click on a piece of paper! It's particularly useful when sending e-mail messages because it keeps the messages smaller. Figure 6.16 shows an example of a WordPad document with a sound-file package embedded in it.

You add a package to a document using the Explorer, the File Manager, or the Object Packager program.

OLE 1.0 v. OLE 2.0

OLE 1.0 was a great stride forward in application integration when it was introduced with Windows 3.1. However, it still left much to be desired. For starters, creating and moving objects between applications was awkward, requiring use of the Clipboard. With OLE 2.0, you can use the ubiquitous drag-and-drop approach. By Ctrl-dragging, you can make a copy of the object.

Editing embedded objects is also much easier. In OLE 1.0, editing embedded objects confused users because double-clicking on an object brought up its source application in another window on the screen with the object loaded into that window. For example, clicking

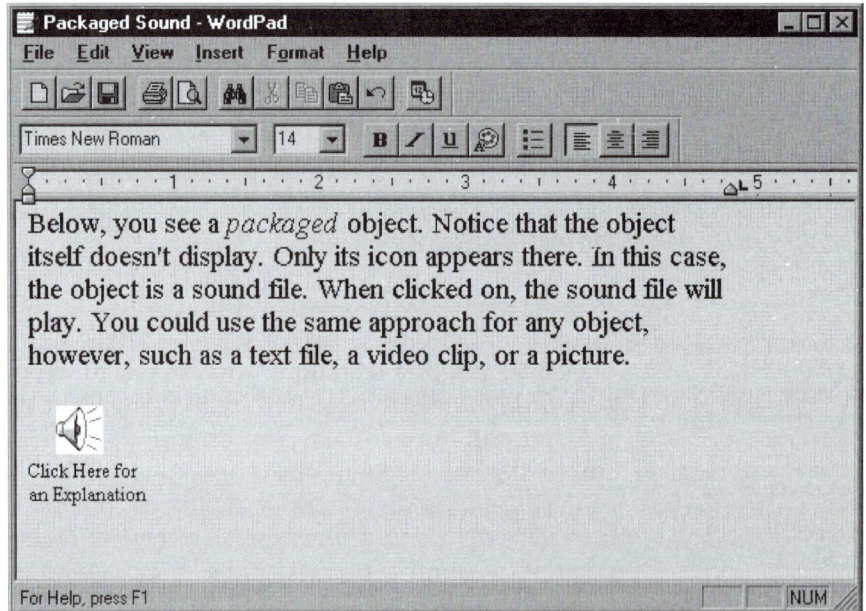

Figure 6.16   Packaging a document iconizes it for later replay when double-clicked on.

on spreadsheet cells embedded in a Word document brought up Lotus 1-2-3 in its own window, with the spreadsheet data loaded into it (see Figure 6.17). You'd use the 1-2-3 window to make changes to the data, then exit 1-2-3. This returned you to the original application with the data updated. This is not particularly intuitive because users feel as though they've left the report they were working on.

By contrast, with OLE 2.0 another window does *not* appear. You are still in the Word window. The two participating applications negotiate an arrangement whereby the menus, toolbars, menu commands, and palettes on the menus within the primary document's application window change. Figure 6.18 illustrates this.

This convenient arrangement has been dubbed *visual editing* and is much more intuitively obvious for users. Note however, that it only applies to editing embedded objects, not linked ones, and only works if both applications are OLE 2.0 enabled. Linked objects will be edited in separate windows, just as with OLE 1.0.

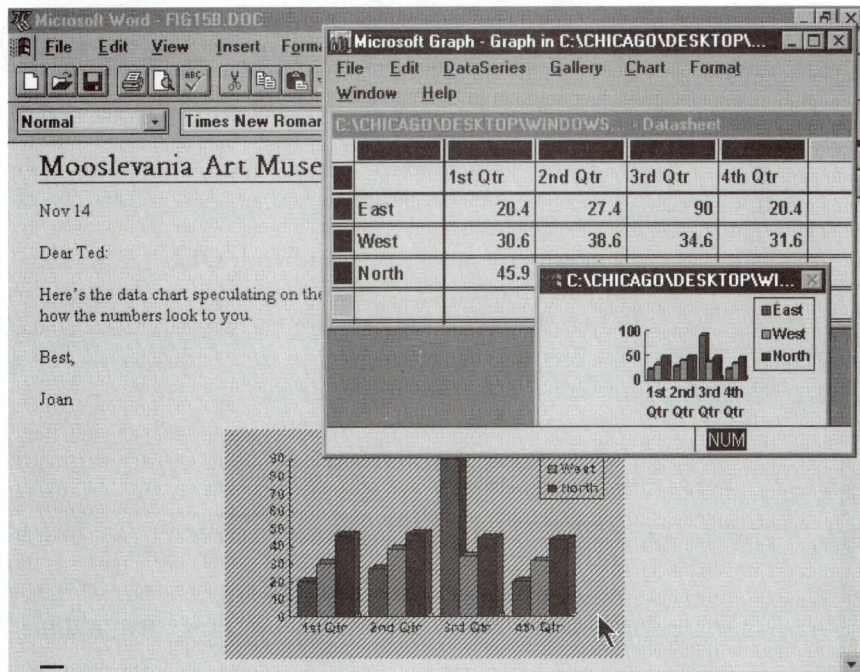

Figure 6.17 *In OLE 1.0, double-clicking on an embedded object brings up the source application in a window.*

Figure 6.18   *In OLE 2.0, double-clicking on an embedded object only changes the primary application's menus and commands to those of the object's source. In this case Word takes on certain characteristics of MSDRAW that allow editing of the embedded picture.*

The other primary problem with OLE 1.0 was that moving any of the linked object files would break the link, resulting in an error message when the compound document was opened. OLE 2.0 solves these problems by allowing you to move files to other drives or directories at will. As long as all the linked files are present in the directory, the compound document will still be intact. As another workaround to having to deal with multiple files in compound documents composed of many objects, OLE 2 allows you to easily convert all the links in a compound document to embedded objects. This in essence takes all the relevant data that was previously stored in separate files and squishes it into a single (albeit larger) one. With OLE 1.0, breaking the link meant losing the object altogether and having to reestablish it.

Another interesting feature of OLE 2.0 is that it conforms to a *transaction-based* I/O model. Thus, an OLE 2.0-enabled application can undo changes that were made to a compound document. For example, if you cut an embedded object, the application would be able to undo the cut, re-establishing the presence of the object in the file.

Next, OLE 2.0 specifies a new type of file format called the Compound File Format. This new format helps the operating system more efficiently store and edit complex documents that contain numerous objects. One advantage to this is that you can now edit a compound document object on an *incremental* basis rather than editing the entire object. For example, say you double-click on a series of spreadsheet cells embedded in your text-based report and start editing the cells. Only the cells you alter will be updated, rather than the whole series of cells. This makes for faster updating and overall performance.

Finally, the expanded OLE 2.0 specification not only allows document objects such as charts, pictures, video, and sound to communicate, but it also works with program modules. As you may know, many applications are composed of separate modules (each one usually stored in separate DLL files). A DLL typically will perform a specific function, such as spell checking, within a word-processing program. OLE 2.0 supplies a standard by which program modules can communicate with one another. As applications are written to comply with this standard, you'll have the option of mixing and matching your favorite program modules to create the "perfect" application. For example, you could buy a replacement spell checker for your favorite word processor, a favorite macro organizer for your spreadsheet, or add in some flashy graphics-manipulation tools to your favorite image-processing program.

OLE Inconsistencies

Developers, keen on building OLE compatibility into their products, are complying more and more with OLE conventions. There's been some leeway for interpretation of how an application will incorporate OLE, and so there are idiosyncrasies and slight variations in the way you work with OLE in different applications. Drag and drop isn't implemented everywhere, so it's not as simple as Microsoft might have you believe. You may have to do a little snooping in an application's manual, use online Help, or check out an application's menus to determine how to import or edit OLE items in your application.

For example, in the Windows 3.x Cardfile, you don't have to click on a linked picture before you edit it because Cardfile knows the picture is in the upper-left corner. Similarly, because you place a linked or embedded sound object in a destination document by double-clicking on the Sound Recorder icon, you can't use the double-click method to edit the object as you would in the case of, say, an embedded section of an Excel spreadsheet. Instead, you have to use the Edit menu's Sound Object command. As a general rule, one consistency you can usually count on is that an OLE-aware application has a Paste Special command on its Edit menu. If it's there, the application knows about OLE, and you'll almost certainly use this command to embed and link objects into your documents. Some applications (such as Word 6 and WordPad) also have an Insert menu that lets you embed all kinds of objects (Figure 6.19).

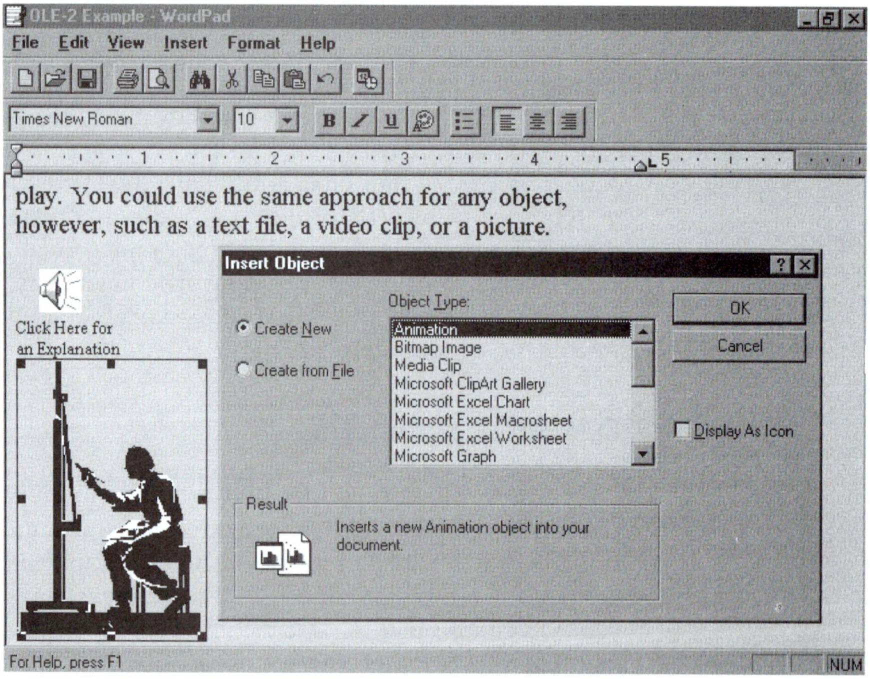

Figure 6.19 *WordPad has an Insert menu for embedding objects you create on the fly while still in WordPad. You can use the Edit ➤ Paste Special command or the Create from File option in this box for embedding and linking preexisting objects.*

You may have found the previous discussion a little daunting, what with all the hairy terms and such. Don't panic! OLE is a little confusing to everyone, especially because it's a scheme that's in flux. Once you experiment with embedding and linking a bit, you'll figure it out.

Now let's discuss the actual procedures for embedding, linking, and packaging objects in Windows 95. I'll also discuss some networking and security issues that pertain to linked objects.

Embedding Objects

The difference between linking and embedding throws people sometimes, so let's talk about that for a minute. It might help to think of embedding an object as almost identical to pasting a static copy of it from the Clipboard in a regular old non-OLE document. This is because neither embedding nor pasting involves a link to external files. Once a chart is embedded into your word-processing file, it becomes part of that file. The only difference between standard Clipboard cut and paste and OLE embedding is that once embedded, an object can easily be edited by double-clicking on it or via some other command. Even though the object (let's say a graph) isn't something the container application (let's say Word) knows how to edit, the object contains a pointer to a program that can edit it.

Here are the basic steps:

1. Open the source application and document. (The application must be able to perform as an OLE server.)

> **TIP** You might want to try this using some OLE applications, such as Word, Excel, AmiPro, 1-2-3, Wordpad, or Sound Recorder, just to name a few.

2. Select the portion of the document you want to embed in another.

3. Switch to the destination application and document. Position the insertion point and choose Paste Special. When you do so, you may see a dialog box giving you some choices about what you want to do. For example, here are two Paste Special boxes, one from Word and one from Excel.

As I said before, you might have to do a little head scratching to figure out which option to choose, but here are some tips. As a rule, if the option says just plain Paste, that won't get you anything more than a normal paste job—which isn't what you want. What you want is some choice that does *not* say Link, but *does* say something about an *object*. So, for example, in Word's dialog box you'd choose the first option and click on OK. In the Excel box you'd choose Object and click on Paste (not on Paste Link, because that will link the object rather than embedding it). Some dialog boxes will let you choose to display the pasted information as an icon rather than as the item itself. For example, normally an embedded video clip will appear in a box that displays the first video frame of the clip.

After doing the Paste operation, and assuming both applications are OLE aware, you might get what looks like a static copy of the material (such as a bitmap), but the destination application will know from whence it was received and thus it can be easily edited. Figure 6.20 shows an example of an MS-Graph file embedded in a Word document.

> **TIP** With some OLE applications you can embed an object using a command choice, such as Insert ➤ Object. This leads to a dialog box from where you choose the type of object (all the OLE-aware programs on your system are listed). When you choose, the source application runs and you can then create the object and exit. When you exit, the object is placed in the container document you were previously working in.

Editing an Embedded Object

Now assume you've got an object embedded in a document; anyone viewing the document can see it, or you can print it out, and so forth. If it's a video clip or sound clip, double-clicking on it brings up a suitable program—such as Sound Recorder or Media Player—running

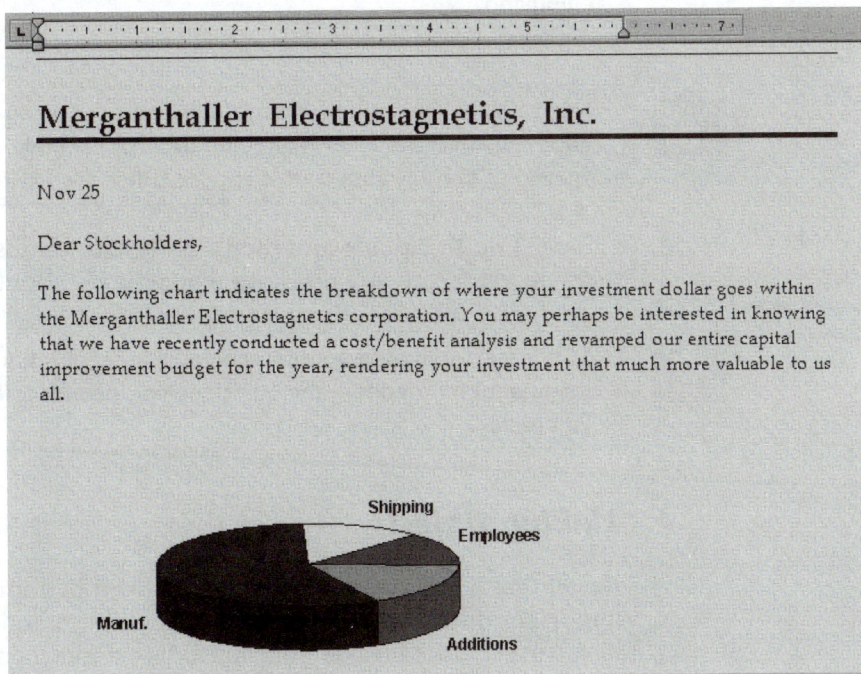

Merganthaller Electrostagnetics, Inc.

Nov 25

Dear Stockholders,

The following chart indicates the breakdown of where your investment dollar goes within the Merganthaller Electrostagnetics corporation. You may perhaps be interested in knowing that we have recently conducted a cost/benefit analysis and revamped our entire capital improvement budget for the year, rendering your investment that much more valuable to us all.

Figure 6.20   *After pasting an object into Word, the graph appears in the container document.*

the clip and allowing the reader of the document to pause, stop, rewind, and replay the clip as needed. For other types of objects, double-clicking makes the object really easy to edit. For example, say you have a graph in your Word document.

1. Double-click on the embedded item. Depending on whether the applications involved are OLE 1.0 or OLE 2.0, several different scenarios may occur. If both applications are 2.0 aware, what ideally happens is that the toolbar, menus, and commands in the application you're working with (the container application) change to those of the object. Use them just as if you were working in whatever program created the object. If one or both of the applications are only OLE 1.0 aware, the object's source application will run in its own window, and the object will be loaded into it. Edit as you normally would.

> **NOTE** Note that in some cases, such as a sound or video clip, double-clicking on an object will "play" the object rather than edit it. You'll have to edit it via another means, such as right-clicking on it and choosing Edit or selecting it, opening the File menu, and choosing Edit Object or some similar command.

> **NOTE** With some applications, double-clicking on an embedded file won't have any effect until you change modes. For example, with the Windows 3.x version of Cardfile you have to choose Edit ➤ Picture first.

2. Choose File ➤ Update and then File ➤ Exit, or just File ➤ Exit and then answer Yes to any resulting dialog boxes about updating.

> **TIP** As an alternative to this technique, an application may have an Edit menu option for editing the object. Select the object first, then check the Edit menu.

Linking Objects

Recall that linking an object is similar to embedding it, but there's one important difference! When linking, the object and the container both "live" in separate files on your hard disk somewhere. However, there is a connection between the linked document and the container it's linked to. This connection is called, not surprisingly, the *link*. So, instead of copying the object's data to the destination document, the link tells the destination application where to find the original source file.

As long as the link isn't broken, it is kept live by Windows, even between sessions. You can edit the linked object by double-clicking on it in the container document, just as you can an embedded object. However, the object will open in a separate window for editing—even if both the server and client applications are OLE 2.0 aware.

You can also edit the object separately using the program that created it, even if the container document isn't open. For example, if the linked item is a spreadsheet file, editing it at its source (say by running 1-2-3, opening the file, editing the spreadsheet, and saving it) will still work. What's more, any changes you make to the file independently will show up in any and all linked files. Because of this, linking is the technique to use when you want to use data that must always be identical in two or more documents.

To link two files:

1. Create or find the server document you want to link (the source document). For example, you could open Paintbrush and draw something.

> **NOTE** Before a file can be linked, it has to be given a name and saved on disk. Windows won't let you link a file that's still called Untitled (the default name of many documents before they are saved).

2. Select the portion of the document you want to pull into the container document.

3. Choose Edit ➤ Copy to put it onto the Clipboard.

4. Switch to the destination document.

5. Move the insertion point to the place where you want to insert the linked item.

6. Open the container's Edit menu and choose Edit ➤ Paste Link (not Paste). If there isn't a Paste Link command, look for Paste Special and the relevant linking option. You'll likely see a dialog box something like one of the two on the next page.

Choose options from the box as you see fit. Whatever the case, because you want to link rather than embed, choose a Paste Link option, as illustrated above.

NOTE   Some friendlier Paste Special dialog boxes explain what effect the various format options will have when you paste the link. The default choice (the one that comes up highlighted when the box first appears) is usually your best bet. However, you might prefer one of the other choices, particularly if you want the linked material to have the exact same look as the source. When linking to a spreadsheet, for example, if you want the headings, grid, and exact font in which the spreadsheet is displayed, you'd choose Bitmapped Picture. Note however, that linking data as a picture rather than text will take up much more room on the disk, making your file much larger. Importing data as formatted text is much more space efficient.

7. If you want to establish a second link, repeat steps 4 through 6, selecting a different destination document in step 4.

The linked item should now be added to the container document in the correct position. If everything went as planned, the object will appear in its original form. That is, a graphic looks like a graphic, cells look like cells, and so forth. In some cases, when OLE applications aren't communicating properly, you'll see the source application's icon instead. This can happen with older applications such as Windows 3.x's Write program and Word for Windows 2.0. If this happens, you're better off just pasting in the text as plain text. Otherwise what you get is essentially a packaged object (see the sections below on packaging).

Editing a Linked Object

Once you've successfully linked some object(s) into a container document, you can check out how well it works. Adjust both windows so you can see both sets of the same data (source and destination). Try altering the source and notice how, in a few seconds, the linked version of the data (stored in the container document) is updated as well.

But what about editing the linked stuff right from the container document? No problem. Just as with editing embedded objects, you simply double-click. The result, however, is different because changes you make to a linked object appear in all the documents you've linked it to.

Here's the basic game plan for editing a typical linked object.

1. In any of the documents the object has been linked to, simply double-click on the object. The source application will open in a window, with the object loaded. For example, Figure 6.21 shows some linked spreadsheet cells that opened in Excel when I double-clicked on them from a WordPad document.

> **TIP**   As an alternative, check the Edit menu. If you click on the object once and open the Edit menu, it may have an option such as Edit Object on it. Many Windows 95 applications are also supporting the right–mouse-click approach to editing. Click on the item, then click the right mouse button. You're likely to see an option such as Edit Lotus 1-2-3 Worksheet Link.

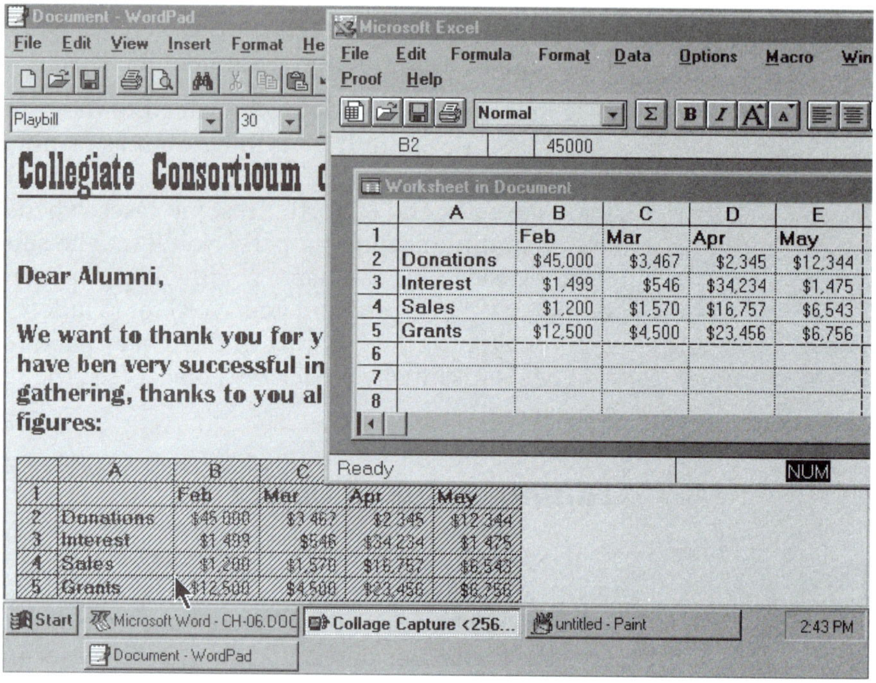

Figure 6.21   *Editing a linked object is usually as easy as double-clicking on it. You can also try right-clicking or check the Edit menu for a special editing command.*

2.   In the source application's window, make your edits.

3.   Choose File ➤ Save, then File ➤ Exit. Changes you made should appear in all destination documents containing links to this source material.

Maintaining Your OLE Links

As mentioned in Chapter 1, Windows 95 is better at maintaining the link between the server and client documents than was Windows 3.x. This is largely because of improvements in OLE 2.0. Still, nothing is perfect, and there are times when a link may be broken for some reason. A traditional example is when an application crashes before its links can be recorded properly. And although OLE 2.0 is intelligent about keeping your links in working order, it's not impossible to fake it out by copying source and destination files from folder to folder, erasing folders, and so forth. A broken link typically manifests itself as a hole where data was to appear in a document or as data that isn't up to date. In the next few sections I'll explain how to manually make changes to a link to modify its properties.

Manually Updating a Linked Object

Under normal circumstances, when you make changes to a server document (that is, a source document) your changes appear immediately in any other documents that contain copies of that object. (Actually, *immediate* updating requires that the other destination documents be open. If they aren't open, destination documents will be updated the next time you open them.)

In any case, there are times when you might want to delay the updating of objects linked to other documents. You can stipulate, if you want, that a given link will only update destination documents when you manually execute an update command. This might be useful when your source document is undergoing repeated revision that would cause the destination document to read inaccurately or appear unfinished or if the source document is linked to many destination documents and the automatic updating process slows down your computer too much, ties up the network (in the case of links to documents across the net), or is otherwise annoying.

To deal with this, just set up your link for manual updating. Here's how.

1. Open the destination document.

2. Click on the object to select it.

3. Choose Edit ➤ Links. You'll see a Links dialog box similar to Figure 6.22. (The box may vary somewhat depending on the application you're running.)

> **NOTE** If the Links dialog box lists two or more links, you can select multiple consecutive links by holding down the Shift key while you click with the mouse. You can also select multiple links that don't appear consecutively by pressing Ctrl while you click.

4. The Links dialog box lists all the links in your document, identifying each link by the source-document file name. Select the link whose automatic updating you want to turn off.

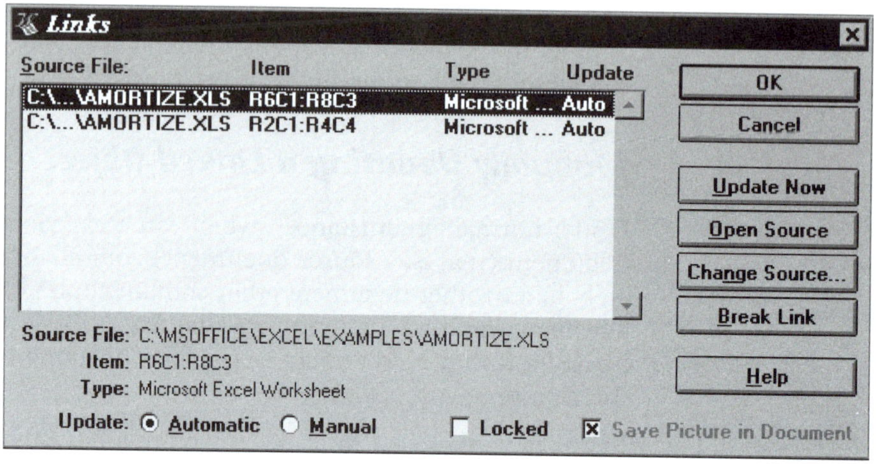

Figure 6.22   Changing details of a link

5. Click on the Manual button (down at the bottom of the box), then choose OK. The button should have an X or dot in it, indicating the setting is turned on.

If later you want to reset the updating to the automatic mode, open this box again and click on Automatic.

Note that once you've set a linked object to manual updating, no changes you make to the source document will be reflected in the destination until you manually update it. You'll have to open the Links dialog box, highlight the link in question, and choose Update Now.

Other Link-Management Tasks

You probably noticed that there are other buttons in the Link dialog box that suggest other possible link-related tasks. For example, you might want to break, delete, re-establish links, or alter existing links to refer to different source documents. Here's the rundown on each of these activities.

Canceling and Deleting Links

In certain circumstances you'll want to break a link between two documents. When you break a link, the data continues to appear in the destination document; it just can no longer be edited from within that document. If the destination application is capable of displaying the data, you will still see it. If it's not capable of displaying it, you will see an icon representing the material.

> **TIP** In most cases, double-clicking on an object whose link has been broken doesn't have any effect. That is, it doesn't bring up the source application or allow you to edit the object. But here's a workaround: Select the object, copy it to the Clipboard, and paste it back into the originating program. Then edit it as you need to, copy it onto the Clipboard again, and paste it back into the destination.

But now for the obvious question. Why would you want to break a link? You'd break a link if having the link is actually more of a hassle than it's worth, such as when you are going to separate the source and destination documents. For example, suppose you want to copy the destination document onto a floppy disk to send to someone. When the recipient opens the document, they'd come up with empty sections in the document and see a dialog box saying that parts of the document are missing. Breaking the link keeps the data in the document, with the only downside being that it's no longer editable.

Okay. What about *deleting* a link? Deleting a link actually wipes out the linked material in the destination document. The source document is left intact, of course, but the previously linked object is purged from the destination document.

How do you break a link or delete a link? Just use the Links dialog box.

1. Open the document containing the object with the link you want to break or delete.

2. Select the object and choose Edit ➤ Links to bring up the Links dialog box. (In some applications, such as Word, you don't have to select the object. All linked objects appear in the Edit ➤ Links dialog box.)

3. In the list of links, highlight the one whose connection you want to break or delete.

4. To cancel the link, click on the Cancel Link (or Break Link) button. To delete the link, press Delete.

5. OK the box.

Fixing Broken Links

As mentioned earlier, links can be broken inadvertently, especially on a network. Links made from within Windows 95 are robust and can survive even when you move source and destination documents around between directories or rename files. However, links will still sometimes be broken, especially in the case of documents composed of information on different workstations across the network. When a destination document can't find the file name and path name to locate a linked object, the application gets confused and breaks the link. The data may still appear in the destination document, but you won't be able to edit it, and the connection will no longer be live. Here's how to re-establish a link so the source and destination documents are once again connected:

1. Open the document containing the object whose link is broken.

2. Select the object and choose Edit ➤ Links. The Links dialog box appears with the object already highlighted in the list of links.

TIP You can also use Change Link to replace a link with a completely different one. Just select a different file name for the source document.

---

3. Click on the Change Link (possibly called Change Source) button. The Change Source dialog box appears.

4. Select the computer, drive, directory, and file as necessary to select the file name of the source document that contains the source material. Click on OK. The Links dialog box then reappears listing the updated location and name of the source document. If the source is on a workstation across the network, look for a Network button to click on.

5. Click on OK to finalize the new link information. When the box closes—and assuming the link is set for automatic updating—the current version of the linked object appears in the destination document.

Exploring Windows 95

2

Chapter 7

Basic Customizing with the Control Panel

FEATURING

Accessibility options

Adding new hardware

Adding and removing programs

Audio control

Setting the date and time

Customizing your screen display

Adjusting the mouse

There are numerous alterations you can make to customize Windows to your liking—adjustments to screen colors, modems, mouse speed, passwords, key repeat rate, fonts, and networking options, to name just a few. Most of these adjustments are not necessities as much as they are niceties that make using Windows just a little easier. Others are more imperative, such as setting up Windows to work with your brand and model of printer, setting up Microsoft Exchange preferences for your e-mail, or getting your mouse pointer to slow down a bit so you can reasonably control it.

Preferences of this sort are made through Windows 95's Control Panel. Once you change a setting with the Control Panel, alterations are stored in the Windows configuration Registry. The settings are reloaded each time you run Windows and stay in effect until you change them again with the Control Panel.

A few Control Panel settings can be altered from other locations throughout Windows. For example, you can set up printers from the Start ➤ Settings ➤ Printers command, you can make MS-Exchange settings from within Exchange, and you can change your screen's settings by right-clicking on the Desktop. However, such approaches essentially run the Control Panel option responsible for the relevant settings, so the Control Panel is still doing the work. Running the Control Panel to make system changes is often easier because it displays in one place all the options for controlling your system. This chapter discusses how you run and work with the Control Panel and delves into what the multifarious settings are good for.

Opening the Control Panel

You open the Control Panel by clicking on the Start button, choosing Settings, and choosing Control Panel. The Control Panel window then opens, as shown in Figure 7.1.

TECH TIP   The Control Panel can also be reached from My Computer or from the Explorer. From the Explorer, scroll the left pane to the top and click on the My Computer icon. Then double-click on the Control Panel in the right pane.

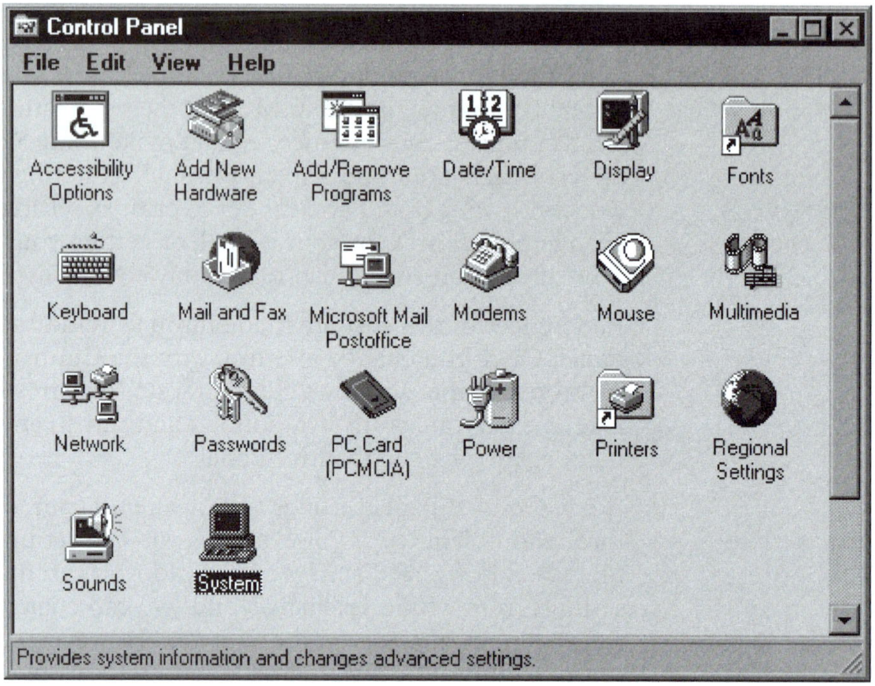

Figure 7.1 The Control Panel window. Each item opens a window from which you can make adjustments.

NOTE   Printers, Fonts, Multimedia, System, and Sound are not covered in this chapter. Refer to Chapter 8 for information about setting up printers, Chapter 9 for details about font management, Chapter 10 for help regarding installation and removal of video, audio, MIDI, and CD-ROM device drivers, and assigning system sounds, Chapters 15 and 16 for coverage of the Mail and Fax applet, Chapter 26 for information about the Network applet, and Chapter 31 for coverage of the System applet.

In your Control Panel there will be as many as twenty or so items to choose from, depending on the hardware in your computer and which items you opted for during installation of Windows 95. As you add new software or hardware to your system, you'll occasionally see new options in your Control Panel, too. Or your mouse icon might look different from the one you see in the figure. My computer has a

Microsoft Ballpoint mouse, so the icon looks like a trackball rather than a tabletop mouse.

Each icon in the Control Panel represents a little program (called an *applet*) that will run when you double-click on it, typically bringing up one or more dialog boxes for you to make settings in. Below is a list of all the standard Control Panel applets and what they do.

Accessibility Options   Lets you set keyboard, mouse, sound, display, and other options that make a Windows 95 computer easier to use by those who are visually, aurally, or motor impaired.

Add New Hardware   Installs or removes sound, CD-ROM, video, MIDI, hard- and floppy-disk controllers, PCMCIA sockets, display adaptors, SCSI controllers, keyboard, mouse, printers, ports, and other device drivers.

Add/Remove Programs   You can add or remove modules of Windows 95 itself and sometimes add or remove other kinds of programs. Also lets you create a start-up disk to start your computer with in case the operating system on the hard disk gets trashed accidentally.

Date/Time   Sets the current date and time and which time zone you're in.

Display   Sets the colors (or gray levels) and fonts of various parts of Windows' screens, title bars, scroll bars, and so forth. Sets the background pattern or picture for the Desktop. Also allows you to choose the screen saver, display driver, screen resolution, and energy-saving mode (if your display supports it).

Fonts   adds and deletes typefaces for your screen display and printer output. Allows you to look at samples of each of your fonts. Fonts are discussed at length in Chapter 9.

Keyboard   sets the rate at which keys repeat when you hold them down, sets the cursor blink rate, determines the language your keyboard will be able to enter into documents, and lets you declare the type of keyboard you have. Covered in Chapter 31.

Mail and Fax   As explained in Chapters 15 and 16, profiles are groups of settings that control how your faxing and e-mail are handled. This applet lets you manage these profiles.

Microsoft Mail Postoffice   If you are connected to a network that has a Microsoft Mail Postoffice, this applet lets you administer the postoffice or create a new postoffice. Postoffices are used as a central repository for mail on a network. This is covered in Chapter 17.

Modems   Lets you add, remove, and set the properties of the modem(s) connected to your system. Covered in Chapter 15.

Mouse   Sets the speed of the mouse pointer's motion relative to your hand motion and how fast a double-click has to be to have an effect. You can also reverse the functions of the right and left buttons, set the shape of the various Windows 95 pointers, and tell Windows 95 that you've changed the type of mouse you have.

Multimedia   Changes the Audio, MIDI, CD music, and other multimedia device drivers, properties, and settings. See Chapter 10 for details.

Network   Function varies with the network type. Typically allows you to set the network configuration (network card/connector, protocols, and services), add and configure optional support for Novell, Banyan, Sun network support, and network backup hardware, change your identification (workgroup name, computer name), and determine the manner in which you control who gains access to resources you share over the network, such as printers, fax modems, and folders. This applet is covered in Chapter 26.

Passwords   Sets up or changes log-on passwords, allows remote administration of the computer, and sets up individual profiles that go into effect when each new user logs onto the local computer. Passwords and security are covered in Chapter 31.

PCMCIA   Lets you stop PCMCIA cards before removing them, set the memory area for the card service shared memory (very unlikely to be needed), and disable/enable the beeps that indicate PCMCIA cards are activated when the computer boots up. This applet is discussed in Chapter 31.

Power   If you have a battery-powered portable computer, provides options for setting the Advanced Power Management and viewing a scale indicating the current condition of the battery charge. This is covered in Chapter 30.

Printers   Displays the printers you have installed on your system, lets you modify the property settings for those printers, and lets you display and manage the print *queue* for each of those printers. Use this applet to install *printer drivers*. (Installing new printer drivers and managing the print queue are covered in Chapter 8.)

Regional Settings   Sets how Windows displays times, dates, numbers, and currency (covered in Chapter 31).

Sounds   Turns off and on the computer's beep or adds sounds to various system events if your computer has built-in sound capability. Lets you set up sound *schemes*—preset collections of sounds that your system uses to alert you to specific events.

System   Displays information about your system's internals—devices, amount of RAM, type of processor, and so forth. Also lets you add to, disable, and remove specific devices from your system, set up hardware profiles (for instance, to allow automatic optimization when using a docking station with a laptop), and optimize some parameters of system performance such as CD cache size and type. This applet also provides a number of system-troubleshooting tools. The use of the System applet is rather complex and thus is covered in Chapter 31.

I'll now discuss the Control Panel applets in detail. Aside from the Accessibility settings, the applets here are the ones you're most likely to want to adjust.

Part 2

Exploring Windows 95

NOTE   All the Control Panel setting dialog boxes have a ? button in their upper-right corner. Remember from Chapter 3 that you can click on this button, then on an item in the dialog box that you have a question about. You'll be shown some relevant explanation about the item.

Accessibility Options

Accessibility means increasing the ease of use or access to a computer for people who are physically challenged in one way or another. Many people have difficulty seeing characters on the screen when they are too small, for example. Others have a disability that prevents them from easily typing on the keyboard. Even those of us who hunt and peck at the keyboard have it easy compared to those who can barely move their hands, are limited to the use of a single hand, or who may be paralyzed from the neck down. These people have gotten the short end of the stick for some time when it came to using computers unless they had special data-entry and retrieval devices (such as speech boards) installed in their computers.

Microsoft has taken a big step in increasing computer accessibility to disabled people by including in Windows 95 proper, features that allow many challenged people to use Windows 95 and Windows programs without major modification to their machines or software. (Accessibility add-ons for Windows 3.x and NT have been available for some time, but as add-ons.)

The Accessibility applet lets you make special use of the keyboard, display, mouse, sound board, and a few other aspects of your computer. To run the Accessibility option, double-click on its icon in the Control Panel. The resulting dialog box looks like Figure 7.2.

Keyboard Accessibility Settings

Probably all of us have some difficulty keeping multiple keys depressed at once. Settings here help with this problem and others.

1. Click on the Keyboard tab (if it's not already selected). There are three basic setting areas:

StickyKeys	Keys that in effect stay pressed down when you press them once. Good for controlling the Alt, Ctrl, and Shift keys.
FilterKeys	Lets you filter out quickly repeated keystrokes in case you have trouble pressing a key cleanly once and letting it up. This prevents multiple keystrokes from being typed.

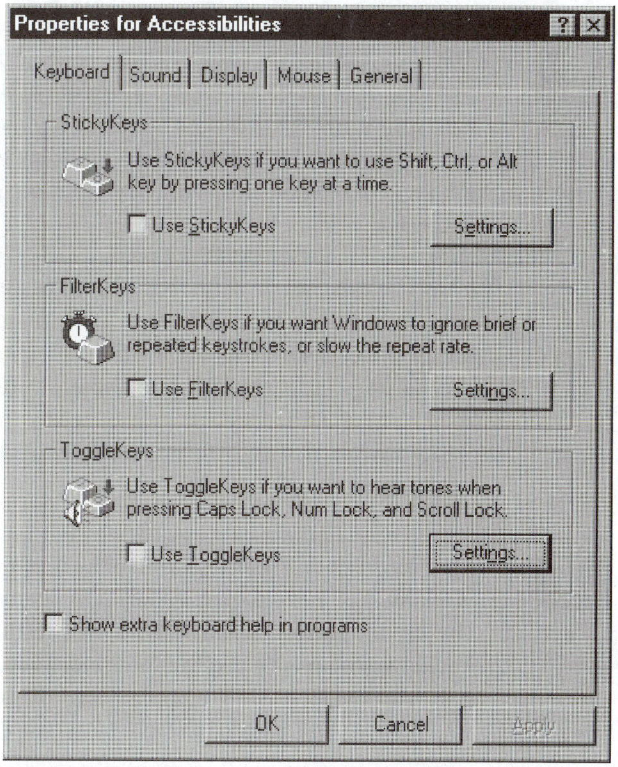

Figure 7.2 *Accessibility dialog box*

ToggleKeys	Gives you the option of hearing tones that alert you to the Caps Lock, Scroll Lock, and Num Lock keys being activated.

2. Click on the box of the feature you want your Windows 95 machine to use.

3. Note that each feature has a Settings button from which you can make additional adjustments. To see the additional settings, click on the Settings button next to the feature, fine-tune the settings, and then click on OK. The most likely setting changes you'll make from these boxes are to turn on or off the shortcut keys.

4. After you have made all the keyboard changes you want, either move on to another tab in the Accessibility box or click on OK and return to the Control Panel.

> **TIP**   You can turn on any of these keyboard features—StickyKeys, FilterKeys, or ToggleKeys—with shortcuts at any time while in Windows 95. To turn on StickyKeys, press either Shift key five times in a row. To turn on FilterKeys, press and hold the right Shift key for eight seconds (it might take longer). To turn on the ToggleKeys option, press the Num Lock key for five seconds.

When StickyKeys or FilterKeys are turned on, a symbol will appear on the right side of the Taskbar indicating what's currently activated. For example, here I have the StickyKeys and FilterKeys both set on. StickyKeys is indicated by the three small boxes, representative of the Ctrl, Alt, and Shift keys. FilterKeys is represented by the stopwatch representative of the different key timing that goes into effect when the option is working.

> **TIP**   Turning on FilterKeys will make it seem that your keyboard has ceased working. You have to press a key and keep it down for several seconds for the key to register. If you activate this setting and want to turn it off, the easiest solution is to use the mouse or switch to Control Panel (via the Taskbar), run the Accessibility applet, turn off FilterKeys, and click on OK.

Unless you disable this feature from the Settings dialog box, you can turn off StickyKeys by pressing two of the three keys that are affected by this setting. For example, pressing Ctrl and Alt at the same time will turn StickyKeys off.

Sound Accessibility Settings

There are two Sound Accessibility settings—Sound Sentry and Show Sounds (see Figure 7.3). These two features are for the hearing impaired. What they do is simply cause some type of visual display to occur in lieu of the normal beep, ding, or other auditory alert that the program would typically produce. The visual display might be something such as a blinking window (in the case of Sound Sentry) or it might be some kind of text caption (in the case of ShowSounds).

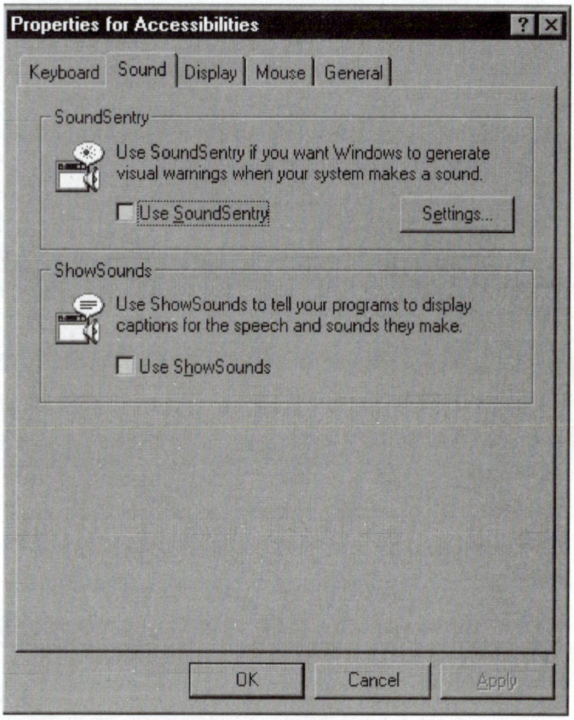

Figure 7.3   *The two Sound Accessibility settings*

The Settings button for Sound Sentry lets you decide what will graphically happen on screen when a program is trying to warn you of something. For example, should it flash the window, flash the border of the program, or flash the whole screen? If you really don't want to miss a beep-type warning, you might want to have it flash the window. (Flashing the whole screen doesn't indicate which program is producing the warning.)

NOTE   Not all programs will work cooperatively with these sound options. As more programs are written to take advantage of these settings, you'll see more *closed captioning*, for example, wherein sound messages are translated into useful captions on the screen.

Part 2

Exploring Windows 95

Display Accessibility Settings

The Display Accessibility settings pertain to contrast. These settings let you set the display color scheme and font selection for easier reading. This can also be done from the normal Display setting, described below, but the advantage to setting it here is that you can preset your favorite high-contrast color scheme, then invoke it with the shortcut key combination when you most need it. Just press Left-Alt, Left-Shift, Prnt-Scrn. This might be when your eyes are tired, when someone who is sight impaired is using the computer, or when you're sitting in an adverse lighting situation. Figure 7.4 displays the dialog box:

1. Turn on the High Contrast option box if you want to improve the contrast between the background and the characters on your screen. When you click on Apply or OK, this will kick in a high-contrast color scheme (typically the Blue and Black) scheme, which will put black

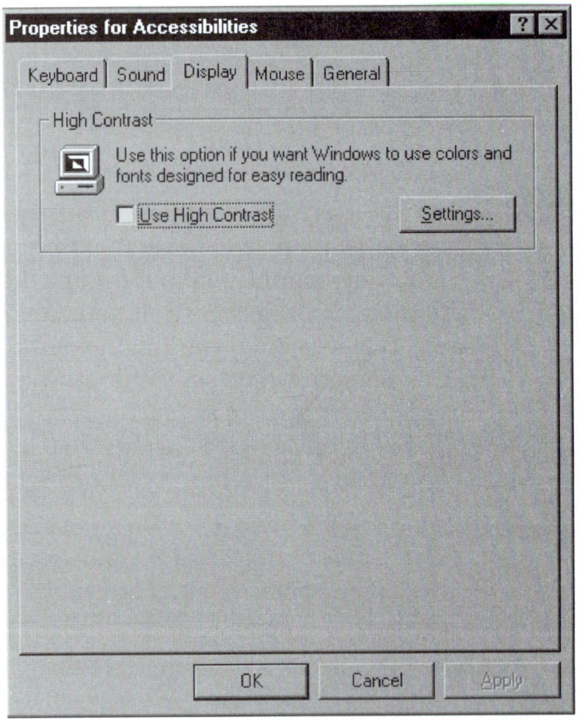

Figure 7.4   The dialog box for setting Display Accessibility features

letters on a white work area. (You can't get much more contrast than that!)

2. Click on the Settings button if you want to change the color scheme that'll be used for high contrast or if you want to enable or disable shortcut-key activation of this feature. This option may come in handy because some of the schemes have larger fonts than others and some might show up better on your screen than will others.

> **TIP** You can experiment more easily with the schemes in the Display applet than here. You can even create your own custom color scheme with large menus, title bar lettering, and dialog box lettering if you want. I explain how to do all this in the Display section.

3. Click on Apply if you want to keep making more settings from the other tab pages or on OK to return to the Control Panel.

Mouse Accessibility Settings

If you can't easily control mouse or trackball motion, or simply don't like using a mouse, this dialog box is for you. Of course, you can invoke most commands that apply to dialog boxes and menus throughout Windows and Windows programs using the Alt key in conjunction with the command's underlined letter. Still, some programs, such as those that work with graphics, require you to use a mouse. This Accessibility option turns your arrow keys into mouse-pointer control keys. You still have to use the mouse's clicker buttons to left- or right-click on things, though. Here's what to do:

> **TIP** This is a great feature for laptop users who are on the road and forgot the mouse. If you have to use a graphics program or other program requiring more than simple command choices and text entry, use the Mouse Accessibility tab to turn your arrow keys into mouse-pointer keys.

1. Click on the Mouse tab in the Accessibility dialog box. You'll see the box displayed in Figure 7.5.

2. Turn on the option if you want to use the arrow keys in place of the mouse. You'll probably want to adjust the speed settings for the arrow

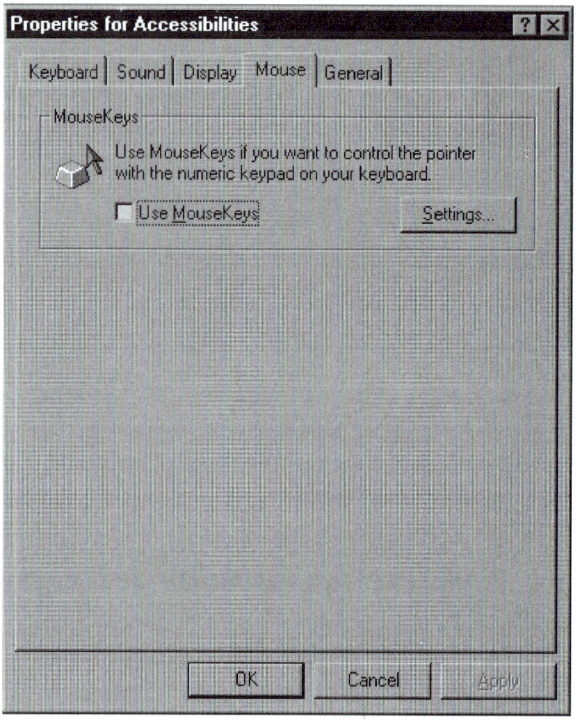

Figure 7.5   *The Mouse Accessibility dialog box*

keys, though, so the pointer moves at a rate that works for you. The
Settings button brings up the box you see in Figure 7.6. Note that
you can also set a shortcut key sequence to activate MouseKeys.

3. Play with the settings until you like them. The Top Speed and Acceleration settings are going to be the most important. And note that you
have to set them, click on OK, then click on Apply in the Mouse dialog box before you can experience the effect of your changes. Then go
back and adjust your settings if necessary. Notice that one setting lets
you change the tracking speed on the fly while using a program, by
holding down the Shift key to slow down the pointer's motion or the
Ctrl key to speed it up.

4. Click on Apply if you want to keep making more settings from the
other tab pages or on OK to return to the Control Panel.

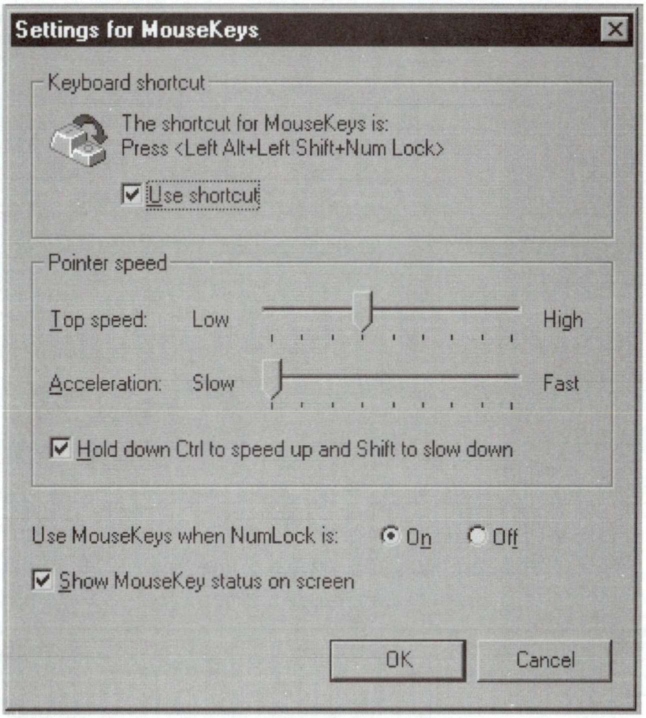

Figure 7.6 *Additional Mouse Accessibility settings*

TIP　The pointer keys that are used for mouse control are the ones on a standard desktop computer keyboard's number pad. These are the keys that have two modes—Num Lock on and Num Lock off. These keys usually have both an arrow and a number on them; for example, the 4 key also has a ← symbol on it. Most laptops don't have such keys because of size constraints. However, many laptops have a special arrangement that emulates these keys, providing a ten-key numeric keypad (and arrows when NumLock is off).

Other Accessibility Settings

The last tab in the Accessibility box is called General (Figure 7.7).

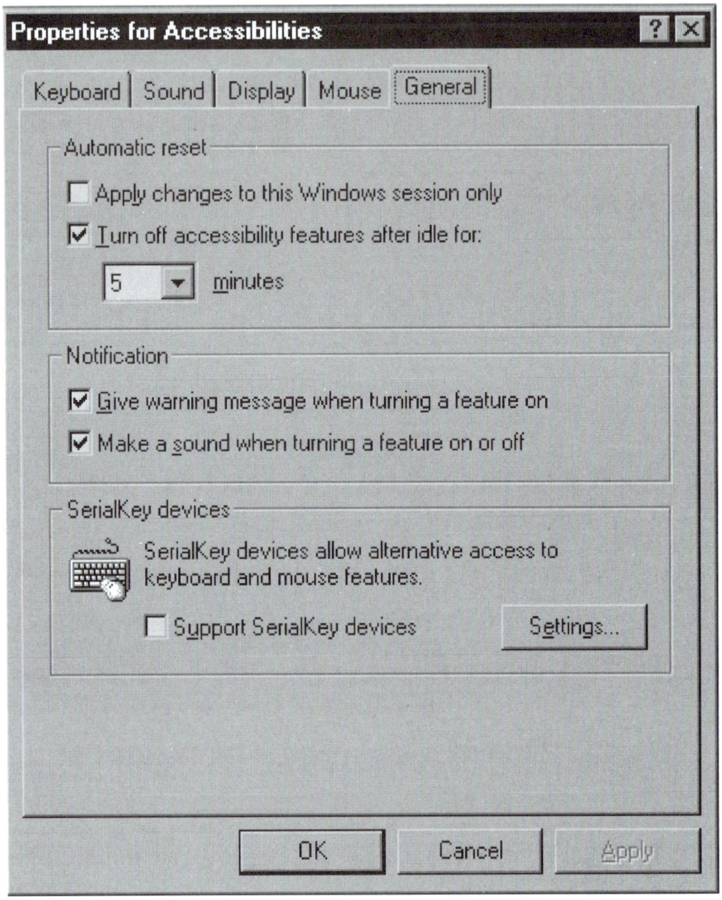

Figure 7.7 *The last of the Accessibility settings boxes*

The box is divided into three sections pertaining to:

▶ When Accessibility functions are turned on and off. Notice that you can choose to have all the settings you've made during this Windows session apply only to this session (that means until you restart Windows 95).

▶ How you are alerted to a feature being turned on or off. You have the choice of a visual cue (a little dialog box will appear) and/or a sound.

StickyKeys

By pressing the SHIFT key five times you have turned on the StickyKeys feature. With this feature, you can lock down the CTRL, ALT, or SHIFT keys. This is useful if you are unable to hold down more than one key at a time.

Do you want to continue?

[OK]   [Cancel]   [Settings...]

▶ Acceptance of alternative input devices through the serial (COM1 through COM4) ports on your computer.

Adding New Hardware

If you have a computer that is Plug-and-Play compatible, this section won't be of a lot of use to you, and you should celebrate. That's because, as I discussed in Chapter 1, Plug and Play ensures that by simply plugging a new card or other device into your computer, it will work. The Plug-and-Play software in Windows 95—in concert with software coding in the computer and add-on cards and devices—takes care of installing the appropriate hardware device driver file and making the appropriate settings so your new device doesn't conflict with some other device in the system. That's the good news.

TECH TIP Of course, there are a limited number of IRQs, ports, and DMAs. Plug in enough Plug-and-Play cards, and one or more is guaranteed not to be installed by the system because Plug and Play will not enable a device unless resources are available for it.

The bad news is that there are a zillion non–Plug-and-Play PC cards and devices floating around in the world and just as many pre–Plug-and-Play PCs. This older hardware isn't designed to take advantage of Windows 95's Plug-and-Play capabilities. The upshot of this is that when you install such hardware into your system, most computers won't detect the change. This will result in disappointment when you've carefully installed some piece of new and exciting gear (such as a sound card) and it just doesn't work—or worse, it disables things that used to function just fine.

Microsoft has added a nifty feature that tries its best to install a new piece of hardware for you. All you have to do is declare your new addition and let Windows 95 run around and try to detect what you've done. Luckily, the Add Hardware applet is pretty savvy about interrogating the hardware you've installed—via its Install Hardware Wizard—and making things work right. You can also tell it exactly what you have to save a little time and ensure Windows 95 gets it right.

> **NOTE**   Notice the applet is only for adding new hardware, not for removing hardware and associated driver files. Removing drivers is done through the System applet, covered in Chapter 32. Note that there are other locations throughout Windows for installing some devices, such as printers, which can be installed from the Printers folder via My Computer. However, the effect is the same as installing these devices from this applet.

> **TIP**   Microsoft maintains a Windows 95 Driver Library that contains new, tested drivers as they are developed for printers, networks, screens, audio cards, and so forth. You can access these drivers through CompuServe, GEnie, or the Microsoft Download Service (MSDL). You can reach MSDL at (206) 936-6735 between 6:00 AM and 6:00 PM Pacific Standard Time, Monday through Friday. As an alternative, you can order the library on disk from Microsoft at (800) 227-4679.

Running the Install Hardware Wizard

If you've purchased a board or other hardware add-in, first read the supplied manual for details about installation procedures. There may be installation tips and an install program supplied with the hardware. If there are no instructions, then install the hardware and follow the steps below.

NOTE I suggest you install the hardware before you run the Wizard, or Windows 95 won't be able to validate that the hardware is present. Also, simply putting new hardware into your computer will rarely result in anything unless you follow these procedures. This is because Windows has to update the Registry containing the list of hardware in your system, it has to install the appropriate device-driver software for the added hardware, and it often has to reboot before the new hardware will work.

1. Close any programs you have running. You're probably going to be rebooting the machine, and it's possible that the detection process will hang up the computer, possibly trashing work files that are open.

2. Look up or otherwise discover the precise brand name and model number/name of the item you're installing. You'll need to know it somewhere during this process.

3. Run the Control Panel and double-click on the Add New Hardware applet. You'll see its dialog box, looking like the one in Figure 7.8.

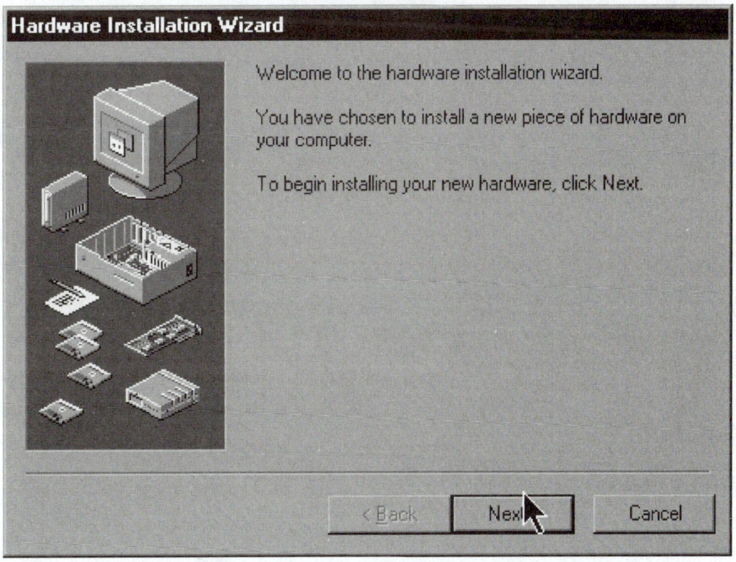

Figure 7.8 *The Add Hardware Wizard makes installing new hardware pretty easy, usually.*

4. There's nothing to do but click on Next. The next box, as shown in Figure 7.9, requires some action on your part, though.

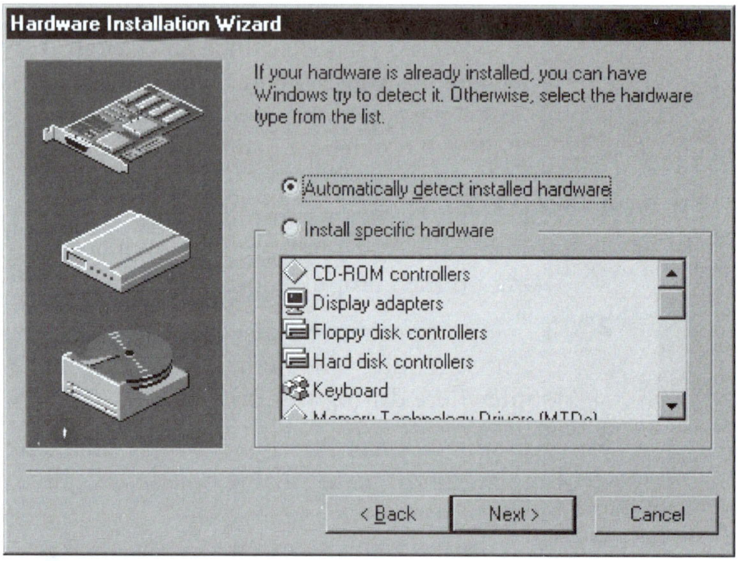

Figure 7.9 *Choose the type of hardware you want to install.*

5. Now, if you want the Wizard to run around, look at what you have, and notice the new item you installed, just leave the top option button selected and click on Next. You'll be warned that this could take several minutes and be advised to close any open programs and documents. Keep in mind that the Wizard is doing quite a bit of sleuthing as it looks over your computer. Many add-in cards and devices don't have standardized ID markings, so identifying some hardware items isn't so easy. The Microsoft programmers had to devise some clever interrogation techniques to identify myriad hardware items. In fact, the results may even be erroneous in some cases. Regardless, while the hardware survey is underway, you'll see a gauge apprising you of the progress, and you'll hear a lot of hard-disk activity. In rare cases, the computer will hang during this process, and you'll have to reboot. If this happens repeatedly, you'll have to tell the Wizard what hardware you've added, as explained in the next section.

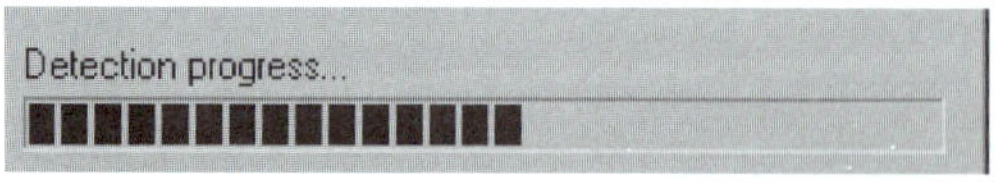

6. When completed, you'll either be told that nothing new was found or you'll see a box listing the discovered items, asking for confirmation and/or some details. Respond as necessary. You may be prompted to insert one of your Windows 95 diskettes or the master CD-ROM so the appropriate driver file(s) can be loaded. If nothing new was found, click on Next, and the Wizard sends you on to step 2 in the section below.

Telling the Wizard What You've Got

If you're the more confident type (in your own abilities rather than the computer's), you might want to take the surer path to installing new hardware. Option two in the second Wizard box lets *you* declare what the new hardware is. This option not only saves you time, but even lets you install the hardware later, should you want to. This is because the Wizard doesn't bother to authenticate the existence of the hardware: It simply installs the new driver.

1. Follow steps 1 through 4 above.

2. Now choose the second option button, *Install specific hardware*.

3. Scroll through the list to get an idea of all the classes of hardware you can install via this applet. Then click on the category you want to install. For this example, I'm going to install Creative Lab's Sound Blaster sound card because that's a popular add-in item.

> **TIP**   If you don't know the class of the item you're installing, you're not sunk. Just choose the last item in the list—Unknown Hardware. Find and click on the manufacturer's brand name in the left-hand list; most popular items made by that manufacturer will be displayed in the right-hand list. Then choose your new hardware from this list.

4. Click on Next. This brings up a list of all the relevant drivers in the class you've chosen. For example, Figure 7.10 lists the sound cards from Creative Labs, the people who make the Sound Blaster cards.

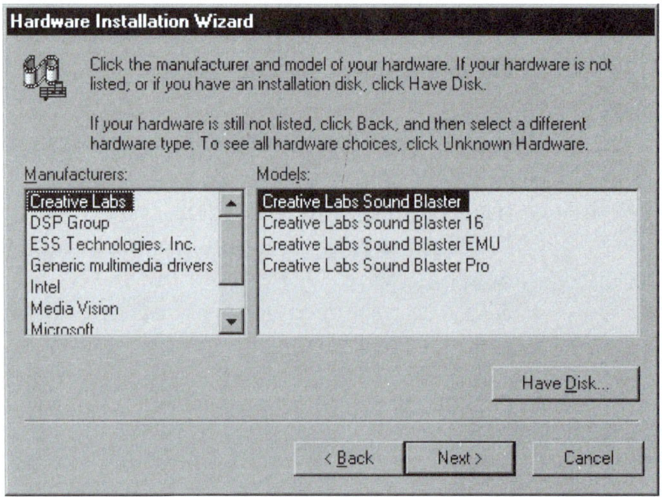

Figure 7.10   After choosing a class of hardware, you'll see a list of manufacturers and models.

5. First scroll the left list and click on the manufacturer. Then find the correct item in the Model list and click on that.

6. Click on Next. What happens at this point depends on the type of hardware you're installing:

▶ If the hardware is Plug-and-Play compatible, you'll be informed of it, and the Wizard will take care of the details.

▶ For some non–Plug-and-Play hardware, you'll be told to simply click on Finish, and the Wizard will take care of installing the necessary driver.

▶ In some cases, you'll be shown the settings that you should adjust your hardware to match. (Add-in cards often have switches or software adjustments that control the I/O port, DMA address, and other such geeky stuff.) For example, Figure 7.11 shows the message I got about the Sound Blaster card. Your job is to read the manual that came with the hardware and figure out how to adjust

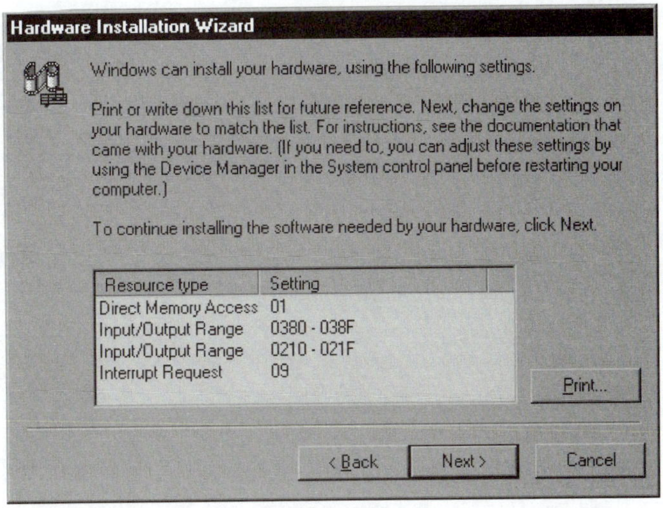

Figure 7.11 *For hardware that has address or other adjustments on it, you may be told which settings to use to avoid conflicts with other hardware in the system.*

the switches, jumpers, or other doodads to match the settings the Wizard gives you.

> **TIP** If for some reason you don't want to use the settings suggested by the Wizard, you can set the board or device otherwise. Then you'll have to use the System applet's Device Manager to change the settings in the Windows Registry to match those on the card. See Chapter 31 for coverage of the Device Manager.

▶ In some cases, you'll be told there's a conflict between your new hardware and what's already in your computer (Figure 7.12). Despite the dialog box's message, you have *three* choices, not two. In addition to proceeding or canceling, you could also back up and choose a different piece of hardware, such as a different model number or a compatible make or model that might support a different port, DMA address, or whatnot. If you decide to continue, you'll have to resolve the conflict somehow, such as by removing or readdressing the conflicting board or device. In that case you'll be shown a dialog box that lets you run the *conflict troubleshooter.*

Part 2

Exploring Windows 95

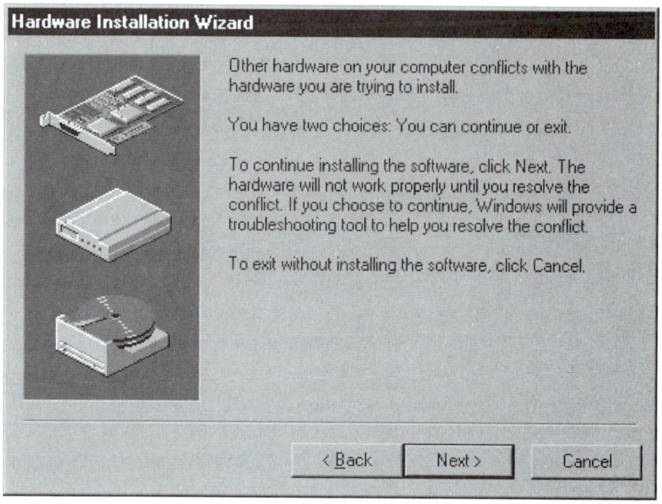

Figure 7.12   If you try to install a piece of hardware that conflicts with preexisting hardware, you'll see this message.

This is a combination of a Help file and the System applet's Device Manager. The Help file walks you through a series of questions and answers.

7. Next, you may be prompted to insert a disk containing the appropriate software driver. Windows remembers the disk drive and directory you installed Windows 95 from, so it assumes the driver is in that location. This might be a network directory, your CD-ROM drive, or a floppy drive. In any case, just supply the requested disk. If the driver is already in your system, you will be asked if you want to use the existing driver. This is okay assuming the driver is up to date and you aren't trying to install a new one.

8. Finally, a box will announce that the necessary changes have been made and you can click on Finish. If you haven't physically installed the hardware already, you'll see this message:

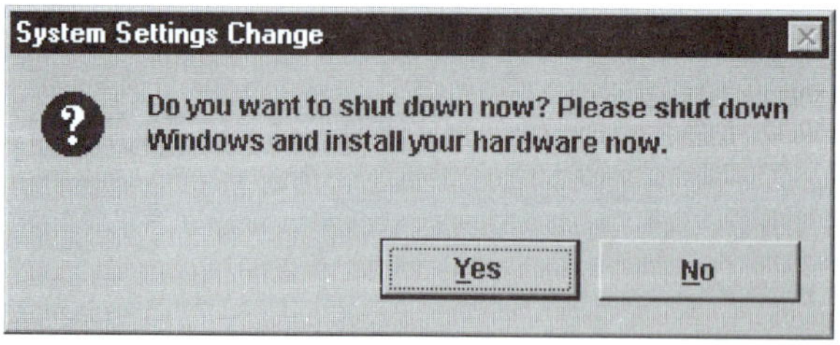

If the hardware is already installed, you'll probably see a message asking you to shut down and restart.

When Your Hardware Isn't on the List

Sometimes your new hardware won't be included in the list of items the Wizard displays. This means that Microsoft hasn't included a driver for that device on the disks that Windows 95 came on. This is probably because your hardware is newer than Windows 95, so it wasn't around when Windows 95 went out the door from Microsoft. Or it could be that the manufacturer didn't bother to get its product certified by Microsoft and earn the Windows "seal of approval." It's worth the few extra bucks to buy a product with the Windows 95 logo on the box rather than the cheapie clone product. As mentioned above, Microsoft makes new drivers available to users through several channels. However, manufacturers often supply drivers with their hardware, or you can get hold of a driver from a BBS, an information service such as CompuServe, or Microsoft Network.

If you're in this boat, you can just tell the Add New Hardware Wizard to use the driver on your disk. Here's how:

1. Run the Add New Hardware applet.

2. Click on Next, then choose the correct class of hardware.

3. Click on the Have Disk button.

4. Enter the location of the driver (you can enter any path, such as a directory on the hard disk or network path) in this box.

Part 2

Exploring Windows 95

Install From Disk

OK

Cancel

Browse...

Insert the manufacturer's installation disk into the drive selected, and then click OK.

Manufacturer's information located in:

A:\

Typically, you'll be putting a disk in drive A, in which case you'd use the setting shown here. However, don't type the file name for the driver, just its path. Usually this will be just A:\ or B:\. If the driver is on a hard disk or CD-ROM and you don't know which letter drive or which directory it is, use the Browse button and subsequent dialog box to select the source drive and directory. When the path is correct, click on OK.

5. Assuming the Wizard finds a suitable driver file (it must find a file called OEMSETUP.INF), choose the correct hardware item from the resulting dialog box and follow on-screen directions (they'll be the same as those I described above, beginning with step 6).

TECH TIP If you're not sure which ports and interrupts your other boards are using, rather than use the old trial-and-error method, Windows 95 comes with a great tool for sleuthing this out—see Chapter 31 for a discussion of the Control Panel's System applet. Double-clicking on the Computer icon at the top of the Device Manager page in that applet will reveal a list of IRQs and ports that are currently in use.

Adding and Removing Programs

The topic of adding and removing programs is discussed in Chapter 5, in the context of the Program Manager and ways to organize your programs and documents. The applet has three functions:

▶ Installing and uninstalling programs that comply with Windows 95's API for these tasks. The API ensures that a program's file names and locations are recorded in a database, allowing them to be reliably erased without adversely impacting the operation of Windows 95.

▶ Installing and removing specific portions of Windows 95 itself, such as Microsoft Exchange.

▶ Creating a start-up disk that will start your computer in case the operating system gets trashed beyond functionality for some reason. With a start-up disk, you should still be able to gain access to your files and stand a chance of repairing the problem that prevents the machine from starting up.

Installing New Programs

The applet's first tab page is for installing new programs:

1. Run Control Panel, then the Add/Remove Software applet. You'll see the box shown in Figure 7.13.

2. Click on Install. Now a new box appears, telling you to insert a floppy disk or CD-ROM in the appropriate drive and click on Next. Assuming an appropriate program is found (it must be called *install* or *setup* and have a `.bat`, `.pif`, `.com`, or `.exe` extension), it'll be displayed as you see in Figure 7.14.

3. Click on Finish to complete the task. The new software's installation or setup procedure will now run. Instructions will vary depending on the program. If your program's setup routine isn't compatible with the applet, you'll be advised of this. After installation, the new program will appear in the list of removable programs only if it's compatible with Windows 95's install/remove scheme.

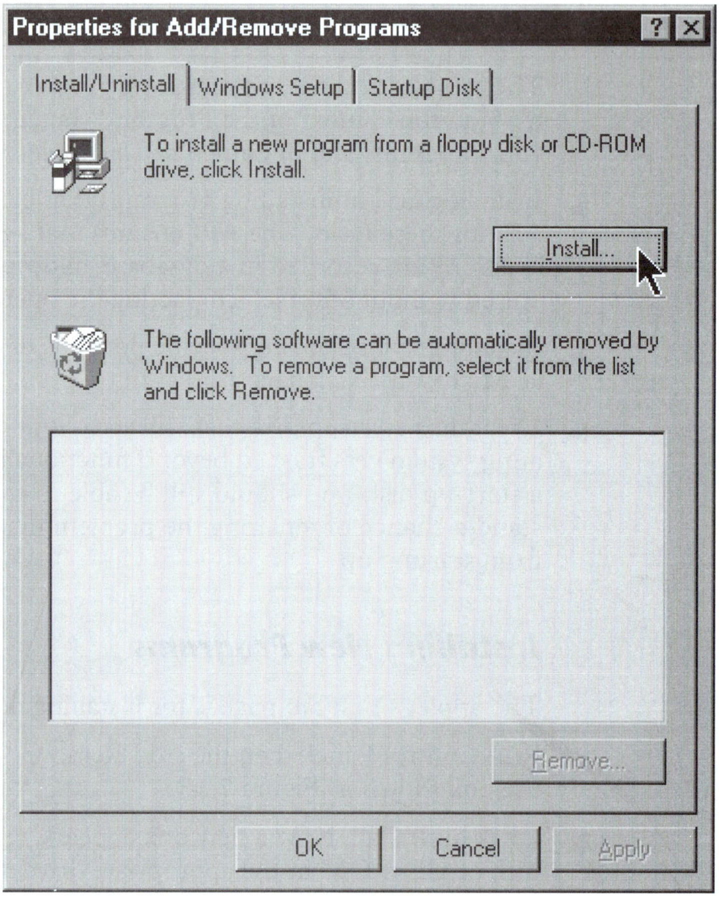

Figure 7.13   *The Wizard for adding and removing software can be reached from the Add/Re-move Programs applet. Only programs that were installed using the applet will be listed in the box. Programs installed using other means (such as before you upgraded to Windows 95) will not appear here.*

Removing Existing Programs

With time, more programs will be removable via the Control Panel. This is because the PC software industry at large has heard much kvetching from users and critics about tenacious programs that once installed are hard to remove. Some ambitious programs spread them-selves out all over your hard disk like olive oil in a hoagie, and there's

Install Program From Floppy or CD-ROM

Windows found a setup program on 3½ Floppy (A:). If this is the correct program, click Finish. Otherwise, click Back.

Setup.exe

< Back   Finish   Cancel

Figure 7.14 *The Wizard looks for a likely installation program on your CD-ROM or floppy and displays the first one it finds.*

no easy way of reversing the process to return your system to a pristine state. The result is often overall system slowdown, unexplained crashes, or other untoward effects.

To this end, aftermarket utilities such as Uninstaller have become quite popular. Uninstall utility programs monitor and record just exactly what files a new software package adds to your hard disk and which internal Windows settings it modifies. It can then undo the damage later, freeing up disk space and tidying your Windows system.

In typical fashion, Microsoft has incorporated such a scheme into Windows 95 itself. Time will tell if its mousetrap is as good as the competition's. Probably not, but it will be "close enough for jazz," as the saying goes. If programmers write installation routines that work with Windows 95's Add/Remove Software applet, we'll all be in luck.

Use of the uninstall feature of the applet is simple:

1. In the bottom pane, select the program(s) you want to uninstall.

2. Click on Remove.

3. Answer any warnings about removing an application as appropriate.

Part 2

Exploring Windows 95

> **NOTE** Once removed, you'll have to reinstall a program from its source disks to make it work again. You can't just copy things out of the Recycle Bin to their old directories because settings from the Start button—and possibly the Registry—will have been deleted.

Setting the Date and Time

> **NOTE** You can also adjust the time and date using the TIME and DATE commands from the DOS prompt.

The Date/Time icon lets you adjust the system's date and time. The system date and time are used for a number of purposes, including date- and time-stamping the files you create and modify, scheduling fax transmissions, and so on. All programs use these settings, regardless of whether they are Windows or non-Windows programs. (This applet doesn't change the format of the date and time—just the actual date and time. To change the *format*, you use the Regional applet as discussed in Chapter 31.)

1. Double-click on the Date/Time applet. The dialog box in Figure 7.15 appears.

2. Adjust the time and date by typing in the corrections or clicking on the arrows. Note that you have to click directly on the hours, minutes, seconds, or am/pm area before the little arrows to the right of them will modify the correct value.

3. Next, you can change the time zone you are in. Who cares about the time zone, you ask? Good question. For many users it doesn't matter. But because people fax to other time zones, and some programs help you manage your transcontinental and transoceanic phone calling, it's built into Windows 95. These programs need to know where in the world you and Carmen Sandiego are. So, click on the Time Zone tab and you'll see a world map (Figure 7.16).

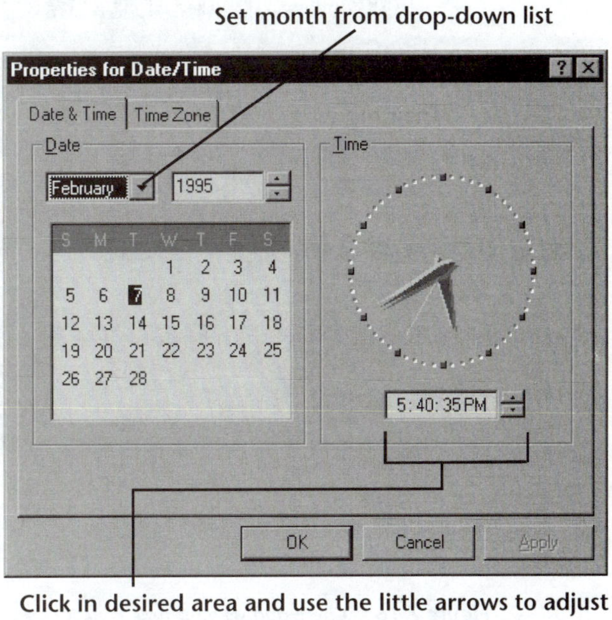

Set month from drop-down list

Click in desired area and use the little arrows to adjust

Figure 7.15   *Adjust the date, time, and local time zone from this dialog box. A shortcut to this box is to double-click on the time in the Taskbar.*

Customizing Your Screen Display

> **TIP**   The Display icon is accessible either from the Control Panel *or* from the Desktop. Right-click on an empty area of the Desktop and choose Properties.

The Display applet packs a wallop under its hood. For starters, it incorporates what in Windows 3.x were the separate Color and Desktop Control Panel applets for prettying up the general look of the Windows screen. Then, in addition, it includes the means for changing your screen driver and resolution—functions heretofore (in Windows 3.x) available only from the Setup program. If you were annoyed by getting at all these areas of display tweaking from disjunct venues, suffer no more. Microsoft has incorporated all display-related adjustments into the unified Display applet. If you

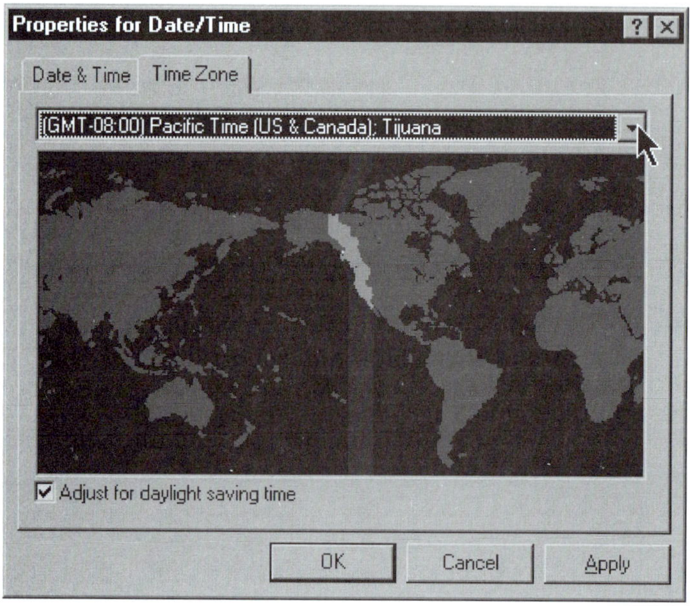

Figure 7.16   *Check and set your time zone if necessary. Some programs will use this information to help you schedule mail or fax transmissions to other time zones. For laptop users who travel, this can be a great boon. Just point to your new location and click: The computer's time is automatically adjusted.*

are among the blessed, you will even have the option of changing screen resolution on the fly.

Here are the functional and cosmetic adjustments you can make to your Windows 95 display from this applet:

▶ set the background and wallpaper for the Desktop

▶ set the screen saver and energy conservation

▶ set the color scheme and fonts for Windows elements

▶ set the display device driver and adjust resolution, color depth, and font size

Let's take a look at this dialog box page by page. This is a fun one to experiment with and will come in handy if you know how to use it.

First run the applet by double-clicking on it.

Setting the Background and Wallpaper

The *pattern* and *wallpaper* settings simply let you decorate the Desktop with something a little more festive than the default screen. Patterns are repetitious designs, such as the woven look of fabric. Wallpaper uses larger pictures that were created by artists with a drawing program. You can create your own patterns and wallpaper or use the ones supplied. Wallpapering can be done with a single copy of the picture placed in the center of the screen or by *tiling*, which gives you multiple identical pictures covering the whole screen. Some of the supplied wallpaper images cannot be used if you are low on memory. This is because the larger bit-mapped images take up too much RAM.

Loading a Pattern

To load a new pattern,

1. Click on the first tab page of the applet's dialog box.

2. Scroll the Pattern list to a pattern you're interested in and highlight it. A minuscule version of the pattern will show up in the little screen in the dialog box (Figure 7.17).

> **NOTE**   For a pattern to show up, wallpaper has to be set to None. This is because wallpaper always sits on top of the Desktop's pattern.

3. To see the effect on the whole screen, click on the Apply button. This keeps the applet open and lets you easily try other patterns and settings. (If you want to leave it at that, click on OK. Then the applet will close, and you'll be returned to the Control Panel.)

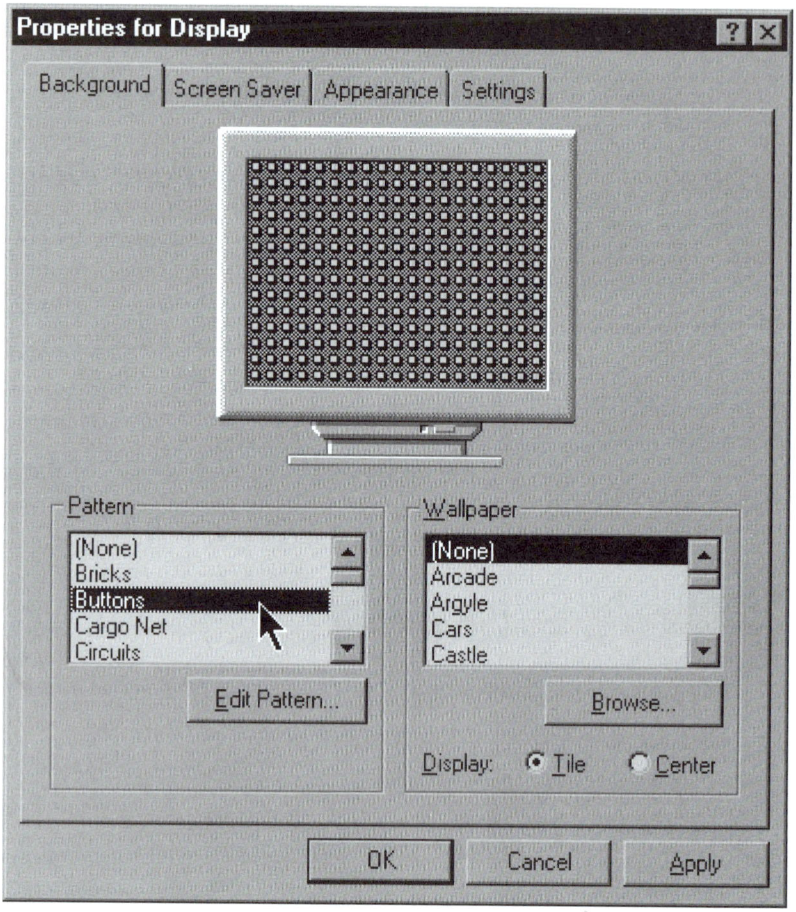

Figure 7.17 *Simply highlighting a pattern will display a facsimile of it in the dialog box's tiny monitor screen.*

Editing a Pattern

If the supplied patterns don't thrill you, make up your own with the built-in bitmap editor. You can either change an existing one or design your own. If you want to design your own, choose None from the Name drop-down list before you begin. Otherwise, choose a pattern you want to play with:

1. Click on the Edit Pattern button. A new dialog box appears.

2. In the Name text box, type in a name for the new pattern.

3. Create the pattern by clicking in the box on the left. What you are doing is defining the smallest element of the repeated pattern (a cell). It is blown up in scale to make editing easier. Each click reverses the color of one pixel. The effect when the pattern is applied across a larger area and in normal size is shown in the Sample section to the right.

4. When you like the pattern, click on Add and the pattern will be added to your list of patterns.

5. Click on Done when you're through creating new patterns.

If you later want to remove a pattern, select the pattern while in the editor and click on Remove. If you want to edit an existing pattern, get into the editor, select an existing pattern, make changes to it, and click on Change.

TIP If you want to abandon changes you've made to a pattern, click on the Close button (X) and answer No to the question about saving the changes.

Loading a New Slice of Wallpaper

The images used in wallpaper are .bmp files. These are bit-mapped files created by programs such as Paintbrush. Other programs create

.bmp files too, so the sky's the limit as far as what you can use as wallpaper. For example, you could use a scanned color photograph of your favorite movie star, a pastoral setting, some computer art, a scanned Matisse painting, or a photo of your pet lemur. Figure 7.18 shows an example of a custom piece of wallpaper.

You can also edit the supplied .bmp files with Microsoft Paint if you want. Just load one into Paint by selecting File ➤ Open. In the Open dialog box, open the List Files of Type drop-down list box and choose BMP file (*.**bmp**) to display available .bmp files. Then choose the desired file and click on OK. Also note that in Microsoft Paint's File menu there's a choice for setting the currently open bit-mapped file to Wallpaper.

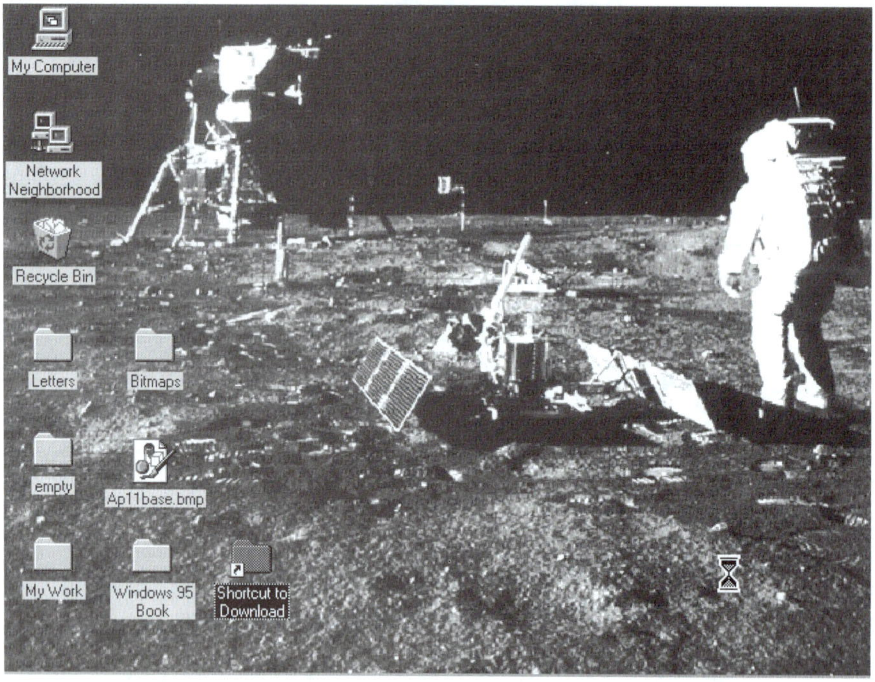

Figure 7.18   *A custom piece of wallpaper Arthur Knowles, the technical editor of this book, sent to me over the Microsoft Network. This is a* .bmp *file of the Apollo 11 base camp on the Earth's moon.*

> **TIP** If you have some other form of picture file, such as a `.gif` or `.pcx` file that you want to use, you can, but you'll have to convert the file to `.bmp` format first using another graphics program such as Collage Image Manager, Publisher's Paintbrush, Paintshop Pro, or other.

Here's how to load a new `.bmp` file and display it as wallpaper:

1. Create or otherwise obtain the image with whatever program you want, as long as it saves the image as a `.bmp` file.

2. Run the Display applet and click on the Browse button in the Wallpaper section of the dialog box.

3. Switch to the directory containing your `.bmp` file. Select it and click on OK.

4. Click on Apply to see the effect and keep the dialog box open, or on OK to apply the new wallpaper and close the dialog box.

Setting the Screen Saver

A Screen Saver will blank your screen or display a moving image or pattern if you don't use the mouse or keyboard for a predetermined amount of time. Screen savers can prevent a static image from burning the delicate phosphors on the inside surface of the monitor, which can leave a ghost of the image on the screen for all time no matter what is being displayed.

Many modern computer monitors have an EPA Energy Star, VESA, or other kind of energy-saving strategy built into them. Because far too many people leave their computers on all the time (although it's not really true that they will last longer that way), efforts have been made by power regulators and electronics manufacturers to devise computer–energy-conservation schemes. If your monitor has an Energy Star rating and your video board supports this feature, the screen saver in Windows 95 can power the monitor down after it senses you went out to lunch or got caught up at the water cooler for a longer-than-expected break.

TECH TIP   For an energy-saving screen saver to work properly, you'll have to turn on the Energy Star option from the Control Panel ➤ Display ➤ Settings ➤ Change Display Type dialog box. Also, the monitor must adhere to the VESA Display Power Management Signaling (DPMS) specification or to another method of lowering power consumption. Some LCD screens on portable computers can do this. You can assume that if your monitor has an Energy Star emblem, it probably supports DPMS. Energy Star is a program administered by the U.S. Environmental Protection Agency (EPA) to reduce the amount of power used by personal computers and peripherals. The Energy Star emblem does not represent EPA endorsement of any product or service. If you notice that your screen freaks out or the display is garbled after your power-management screen saver turns on, you should turn off this check box.

The screen-saver options allow you to choose or create an entertaining video ditty that will greet you when you return to work. You also set how much time you have after your last keystroke or mouse skitter before the show begins.

Loading a Screen Saver

Here's how it's done:

1. Click on the Screen Saver tab. The page appears as you see in Figure 7.19.

2. Choose a name from the drop-down list. The saver will be shown in the little screen in the dialog box.

3. Want to see how it will look on your whole screen? Click on Preview. Your screen will go black and then begin its antics. The show continues until you hit any key or move your mouse.

4. If you want to change anything about the selected screen saver, click on Settings. You'll see a box of settings that apply to that particular screen saver. For example, for the Mystify Your Mind saver, this is the Settings box:

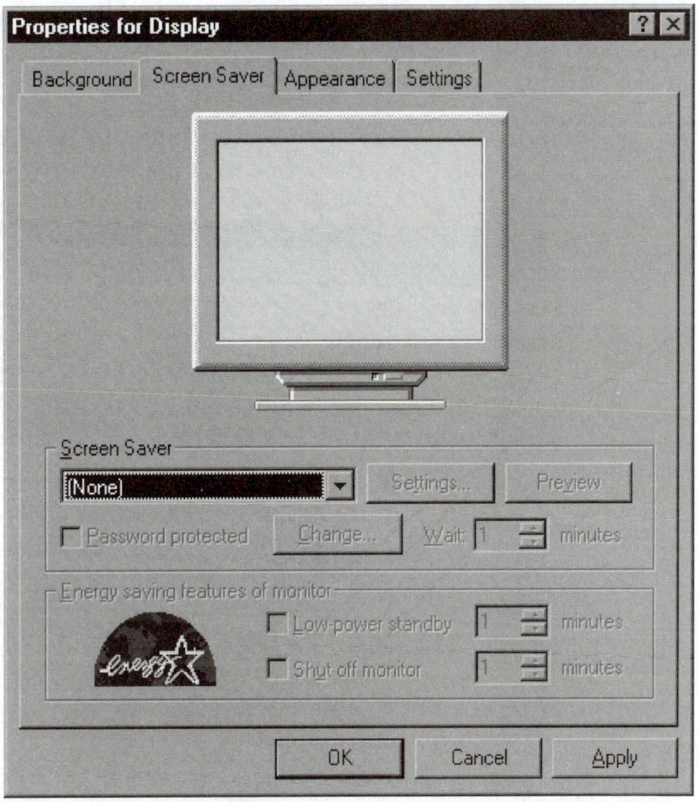

Figure 7.19   *Setting up a screen saver*

Most of the option boxes have fun sliders and stuff you can play with to get an effect you like. Depending on which screen saver you chose, you'll have a few possible adjustments, such as speed, placement, and details pertinent to the graphic. Play with the settings until you're happy with the results and OK the Setting box.

5. Back at the Screen Saver page, the next choice you might want to consider is Password Options. If you set password protection on, every time your screen saver is activated you will have to type your password into a box to return to work. This is good if you don't want anyone else tampering with your files or seeing what you're doing. It can be a pain, though, if there's no particular need for privacy at your computer. Don't forget your password, either, or you'll have to reboot to get back to work. Of course, anyone could reboot your computer

and get back into it anyway, so this means of establishing security is somewhat limited. Click on the Password Protected check box if you want protection and go on to the next two steps. Otherwise skip them.

6. Click on the Change button to define or change your password. In the dialog box that appears, type in your new password.

You won't see the letters, just an asterisk for each letter (to preserve confidentiality). For confirmation that you typed it correctly, *type it again* (don't copy the first one and paste it; a mistake in the first one can result in your being locked out of your computer) in the Confirm New Password text box. If there is a discrepancy between the two, you'll get an error message. Reenter the password. (If you're changing a password, the steps will be approximately the same. Enter your old password first, then the new one and its confirmation.) When it is correct, click on OK.

7. Back at the Desktop dialog box, set the number of minutes you want your computer to be idle before the screen saver springs into action. Next to Wait, either type in a number or use the up and down arrows to change the time incrementally.

8. Next you have the Energy Star options. Energy Star monitors need an Energy Star-compatible video card in the computer. If your screen setup supports this, the options will not be grayed out. Otherwise they will be. Assuming you can gain access to the settings, you have two choices: when the low-power mode kicks in and when total power off kicks in. You don't want total power down to happen too quickly because the screen will take a few seconds (like about ten) to come back on when you move the mouse or press a key, which can be annoying. So make the two settings something reasonable, such as 15 minutes and 30 minutes.

9. When all the settings are correct, click on Apply or OK.

Adjusting the Appearance

The Appearance page lets you change the way Windows assigns colors and fonts to various parts of the screen. If you're using a monochrome monitor (no color), altering the colors may still have some effect (the amount will depend on how you installed Windows).

Windows sets itself up using a default color scheme that's fine for most screens—and if you're happy with your colors as they are, you might not even want to futz around with them.

However, the color settings for Windows are very flexible and easy to modify. You can modify the color setting of just about any part of a Windows screen. For those of you who are very particular about color choices, this can be done manually, choosing colors from a palette or even mixing your own with the Custom Colors feature. Once created, custom colors and color setups can be saved on disk for later use or automatically loaded with each Windows session. For more expedient color reassignments, there's a number of supplied color schemes to choose from.

On clicking on the Appearance tab, your dialog box will look like that shown in Figure 7.20. The various parts of the Windows graphical environment that you can alter are shown in the top portion and named in the lower portion. As you select color schemes, these samples change so you can see what the effect will be without having to go back into Windows proper.

Loading an Existing Color Scheme

Before playing with the custom color palette, first try loading the supplied ones; you may find one you like:

1. Click open the drop-down Color Schemes list box.

> **TIP**   You can always toggle a drop-down list box open and closed from the keyboard by pressing Alt-↓ or Alt-↑.

2. Choose a selection whose name suits your fancy. The colors in the dialog box will change, showing the scheme. Try them out. Some are garish, others more subtle. Adjusting your monitor may make a

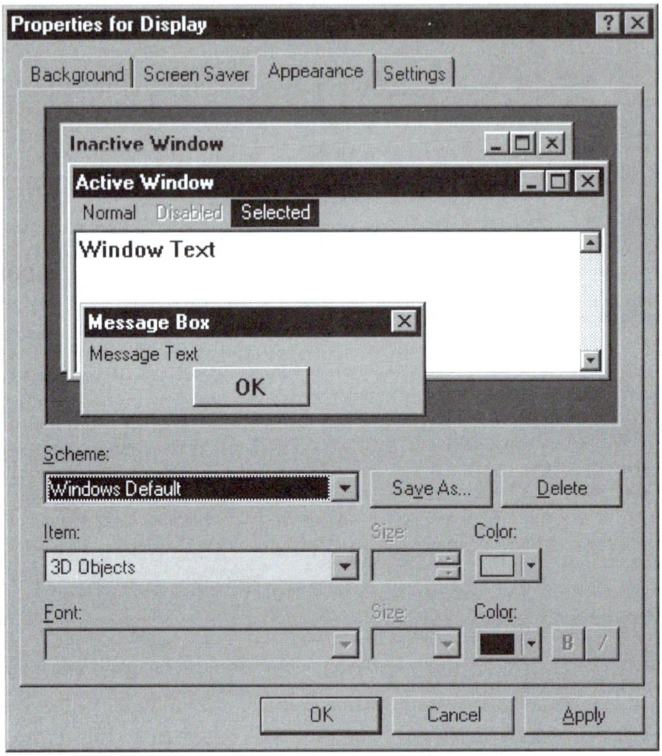

Figure 7.20 *The dialog box for setting the colors, fonts, and metrics of the Windows environment*

difference, too. (You can cycle through the different supplied color schemes without selecting them from the drop-down list: with the Color Schemes space highlighted, just press the ↑ and ↓ keys. The sample screen elements will change to reflect each color scheme as its name appears in the Color Schemes box.)

3. Click on Apply or OK to apply the settings to all Windows activities.

Microsoft has incorporated a few color schemes that may enhance the operation of your computer:

▶ On LCD screens that you'll be using in bright light, you might try the setting called High-Contrast White.

▶ If your eyes are weary, you may want to try one of the settings with the words Large or Extra Large in the name. These cause menus, dialog boxes, and title bars to appear in large letters.

Choosing Your Own Colors and Other Stuff

If you don't like the color schemes supplied, you can make up your own. It's most efficient to start with a scheme that's close to what you want and then modify it. Once you like the scheme, you may save it under a new name for later use. Here are the steps:

1. Select the color scheme you want to modify.

2. Click on the Windows element whose color you want to change. Its name should appear in the Item area. You can click on menu name, title bars, scroll bars, buttons—anything you see. You can also select a screen element from the Item drop-down list box rather than by clicking directly on the item.

3. Now click on the Color button to open up a series of colors you can choose from.

4. Click on the color you want. This assigns it to the item. Repeat the process for each color you want to change.

5. Want more colors? Click on the Other button. This pops up another 48 colors to choose from. Click on one of the 48 colors (or patterns and intensity levels, if you have a monochrome monitor) to assign it to the chosen element.

6. Once the color scheme suits your fancy, you can save it. (It will stay in force for future Windows sessions even if you don't save it, but you'll lose the settings next time you change colors or select another scheme.) Click on Save Scheme.

7. Type in a name for the color scheme and click on OK.

TIP If you want to remove a scheme (such as one you never use), select it from the drop-down list and click on the Delete button.

Before I get into explaining custom colors, there are two other major adjustments you can make to your display—the fonts used for various screen elements, and Windows *metrics,* which affect how big or small some screen elements are.

In Windows 3.x this wasn't possible, but now you can choose the font for elements such as title bars, menus, and dialog boxes. You can get pretty wacky with this and make your Windows 95 setup look very strange if you want. Or, on the more practical side, you can compensate for high-resolution monitors by making your menus more easily readable by using large point sizes in screen elements. In any case, you're no longer stuck with boring sans serif fonts such as Arial or MS Sans Serif. For an example, see Figure 7.21.

1. On the Appearance page, simply click on the element whose font you want to change.

2. In the lowest line of the dialog box, the current font for that element appears. Just open the drop-down list box and choose another font if you want. You may also change the size, the color, and the style (bold or italic) of the font for that element.

3. Be sure to save the scheme if you want to keep it.

Finally, consider that many screen elements—such as the borders of windows—have a constant predetermined size. However, you might want to change these settings. If you have trouble grabbing the borders of windows, for example, you might want to make them larger. If you want icons on your desktop and in folders to line up closer or farther apart, you can do that, too.

Figure 7.21   You can use any installed fonts when defining your screen elements.

Part
2

Exploring Windows 95

1.   Simply open the list and choose the item whose size you want to adjust. Some of the items are not represented in the upper section of the dialog box. They're things that appear in other parts of Windows 95, such as *vertical icon spacing* or *selected items*. You'll have to experiment a bit to see the effects of these items.

2.   Click on the up or down size buttons to adjust.

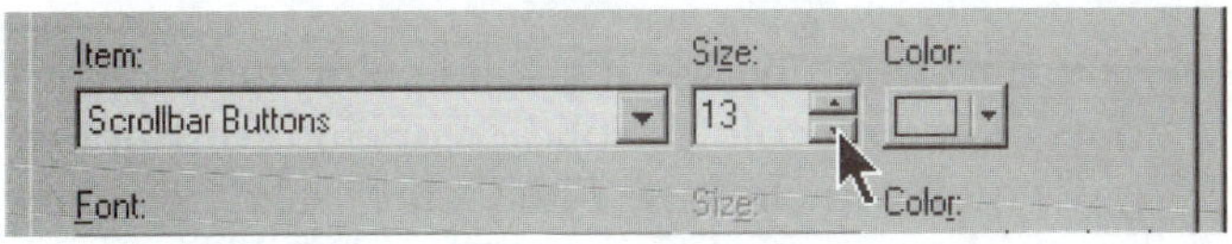

3. Click on Apply to check out the effects of the changes. You might want to switch to another application via the Taskbar to see how things look.

4. If you don't like the effects of the changes you've made, just return to the Control Panel and click on Cancel. Or you can just select another color scheme, because the screen metrics are recorded on each color scheme.

Making Up Your Own Colors

If you don't like the colors that are available, you can create your own. There are 16 slots at the bottom of the larger color palette for storing colors you set using another fancy dialog box called the color refiner. Here's how:

1. Click on the Color button and then choose Other. This opens the enlarged color-selection box.

2. In that box, click on Define Custom Colors. Now the Color Refiner dialog box appears (see Figure 7.22).

   There are two cursors that you work with here. One is the *luminosity bar* and the other is the *color refiner cursor*. To make a long story short, you simply drag these around one at a time until the color in the box at the lower left is the shade you want. As you do, the numbers in the boxes below the color refiner will change. *Luminosity* is the amount of brightness in the color. *Hue* is the actual shade or color. All colors are composed of red, green, and blue. *Saturation* is the degree of purity of the color; it is decreased by adding gray to the color and increased by subtracting it. You can also type in the numbers or click on the arrows next to the numbers if you want, but it's easier to use the cursors. When you like the color, click on Add Color to add the new color to the palette.

   You can switch between a solid color and a color made up of various dots of several colors. Solid colors look less grainy on your screen but give you fewer choices. The Color|Solid box shows the difference between the two. If you click on this box before adding the color to the palette, the solid color closest to the actual color you chose will be added instead of the grainier composite color.

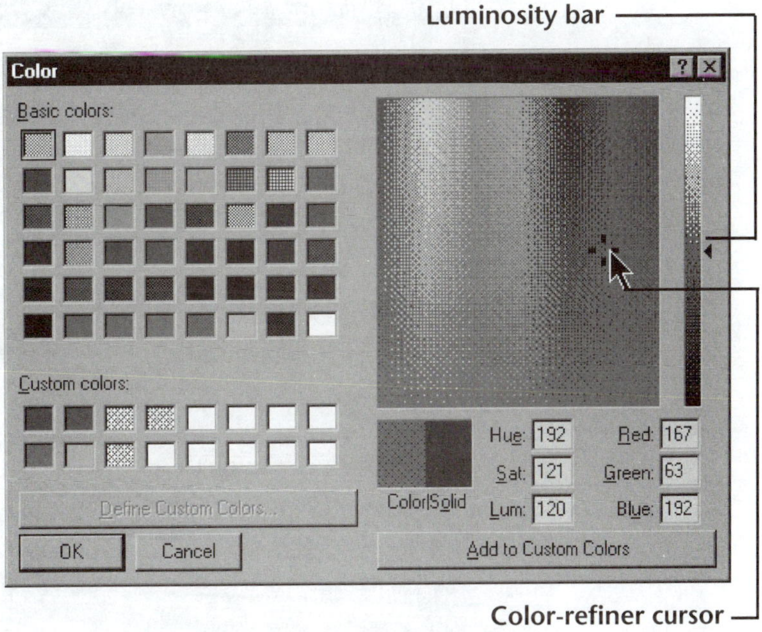

Luminosity bar ——

Color-refiner cursor ——

Figure 7.22   *The custom color selector lets you create new colors.*

Once a color is added to the palette, you can modify it. Just click on it, move the cursors around, and then click on Add Color again. Click on Close to close the dialog box. Then continue to assign colors with the palette. When you are content with the color assignments, click on OK. If you decide after toying around that you don't want to implement the color changes, just click on Cancel.

Driver Settings

The last tab page of the Display applet tweaks the video driver responsible for your video card's ability to display Windows. These settings are a little more substantial than those that adjust whether dialog boxes are mauve or chartreuse because they load a different driver or bump your video card up or down into a completely different resolution and color depth, changing the amount of information you can see on the screen at once (see Figure 7.23). This option is also the

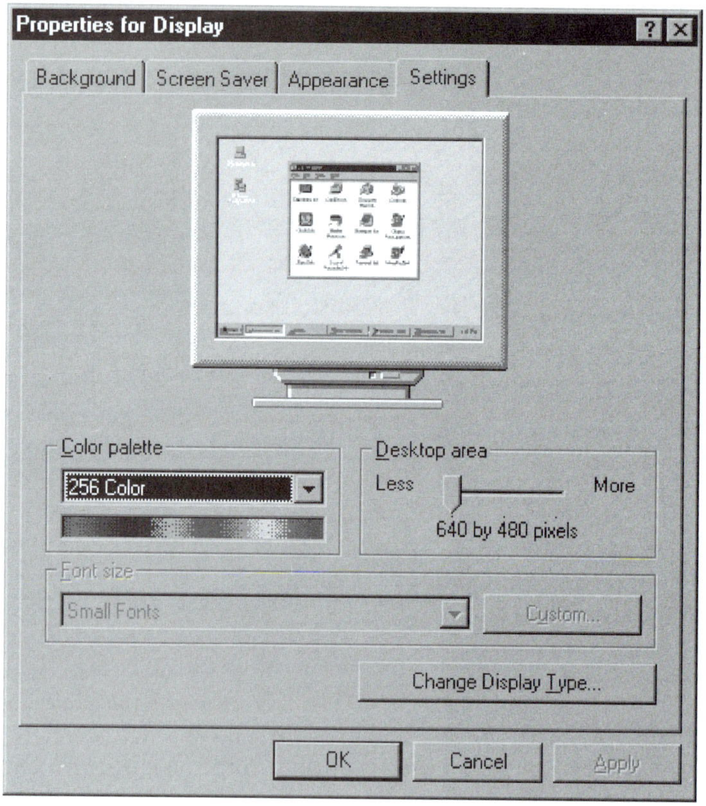

Figure 7.23   *The Settings page of the Display applet controls the video card's device driver. With most video systems, the slider lets you adjust the screen resolution on the fly. Changing color depth requires a restart, however.*

one to use for installing a Windows 3.x video driver for your video card just in case there isn't a Windows 95 driver for it.

Color Palette

Let's start with the color palette. Assuming your video card was properly identified when you installed Windows 95, this drop-down list box will include all the legitimate options your card is capable of. As you may know, different video cards are capable of displaying differing numbers of colors simultaneously. Your monitor is not the limiting factor here (with the exception of color LCD screens like those on laptops, which do have limitations); the limitations have to do with how much RAM is on your video card. All modern analog color monitors for PCs are capable of displaying 16 million colors, which is dubbed True Color.

It's possible that the drop-down list box will include color amounts (called *depths*) that exceed your video card's capabilities, in which case such a choice just won't have any effect. On the other hand, if your setting is currently 16 colors and your screen can support 256 or higher, Windows will look a lot prettier if you choose 256 and then choose one of the 256-color schemes from the Appearance tab page.

TECH TIP When you change the setting in the color palette and OK the box or click on Apply, you'll be prompted to reboot. This is because Windows 95 has to load in a different video driver altogether, not simply adjust the one currently running.

Desktop Area

The Desktop Area setting is something avid Windows users have been wanting for years. With Windows 3.x, changing this parameter (essentially the screen resolution) meant running Windows Setup, choosing a different video driver, and rebooting the machine and Windows. Now, with the right video card, you can change the resolution as you work. Some jobs—such as working with large spreadsheets, databases, CAD, or typesetting—are much more efficient with more data displayed on the screen. Because higher resolutions require a tradeoff in clarity and make on-screen objects smaller, eyestrain can be minimized by going to a lower resolution, such as 640-by-480 pixels (a pixel equals one dot on the screen). Note that there is a relationship between the color depth and the resolution that's available. This is because your video card can only have so much RAM on it. That RAM can be used to display extra colors *or* extra resolution, but not both. So, if you bump up the colors, you won't have as many resolution options. If you find the dialog box won't let you choose the resolution you want, try dropping the color palette setting to 16 colors.

To change the Desktop area:

1. Run Control Panel and run the Display applet.

2. Choose the Settings tab page.

3. Grab the slider and move it right or left. Notice how the little screen in the box indicates the additional room you're going to have on your real screen to do your work (and also how everything will get relatively smaller to make this happen, because your monitor doesn't get any larger!). Figure 7.24 illustrates.

NOTE   As of this writing, virtually all laptop computers have screens that can only display one resolution—640-by-480 pixels. (There are a few exceptions that run at 800 by 600.) Unless the computer is hooked up to an external monitor, this will be the only workable choice. If you try a higher resolution, the choice won't work, and the applet will revert to the previous setting. Check the computer's manual if in doubt about which external monitor resolutions are supported by your laptop.

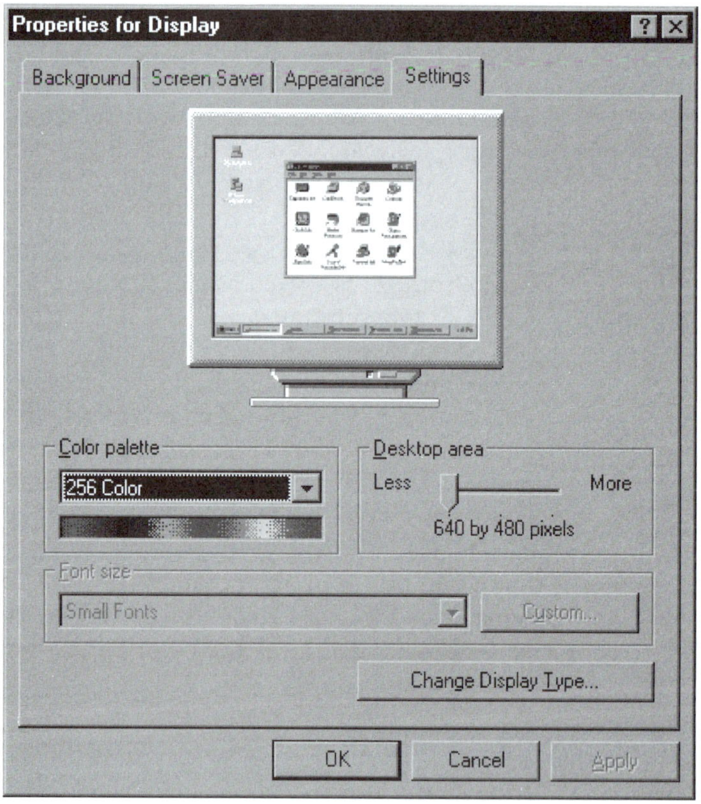

Figure 7.24   *Change your screen resolution by dragging the slider. Here I've chosen 800 by 600.*

4.   Click on Apply. You'll now see this message:

> **Settings**   ☒
>
> ⓘ   Windows will now resize your desktop. This could take a
>   few seconds, during which your screen might flicker. If
>   Windows does not reappear correctly, wait 15 seconds,
>   and your original settings will be restored.
>
>   [OK   ]   [Cancel]

Go ahead and click on OK to try the setting. If your screen looks
screwy and you can't read anything, don't worry. It will return to normal in about 15 seconds. If, on the other hand, you like what you see,
there will be another dialog box asking you to confirm that you want
to keep the current setting. Confirming that box makes the new setting permanent until you change it again.

TIP   If you don't change the Palette setting, you should be able to change
the Desktop area without restarting Windows.

Font Size

As you may know, some screen drivers use different size fonts for
screen elements such as dialog boxes and menus. When you switch to
a high Desktop-area resolution, such as 1,280 by 1,024, these screen
elements can get quite small, blurry, and difficult to read. For this reason, you can adjust the font size. Of course, you can do this via the
Fonts settings on the Appearance page as discussed earlier. But doing
it here is a little simpler. If you select a Desktop area above 640 by
480, you'll have the choice of Small Fonts or Large Fonts. Especially
for resolutions of 1,024 by 768 or above, you might want to check out
the Large Fonts selection from this drop-down list box. If you want,
you can also choose a custom-size font by clicking on the Custom button, which lets you declare the amount that you want the fonts scaled
up. The range is from 100 to 200 percent.

**Part
2**

Exploring Windows 95

Display Type

Finally, the Settings box allows you to actually change the type of video card and monitor that Windows 95 thinks you have. If you install a new video card or monitor, you should update this information.

> **NOTE**   As discussed earlier in this chapter, you can also do this from the Add New Hardware and System applets.

1. Click on the Change Adaptor button. The box shown in Figure 7.25 appears.

2. Check the settings to see that they correspond to what you have. The adaptor type may not make sense to you because it often lists the type of video chip rather than the brand of video board you have.

3. If you want to change either of the settings, just click on the Change button. In the resulting box, the Show Compatible Devices option is normally selected and will result in a list of video adaptors or monitors that are compatible with what you have. Because the computer doesn't actually know what type of monitor you have (unless it's a fancy Plug-and-Play monitor), you'll have to take its assumption with a grain of salt. You can tell it otherwise. Click on Show all Devices and choose from the resulting list. In case you don't know what kind of

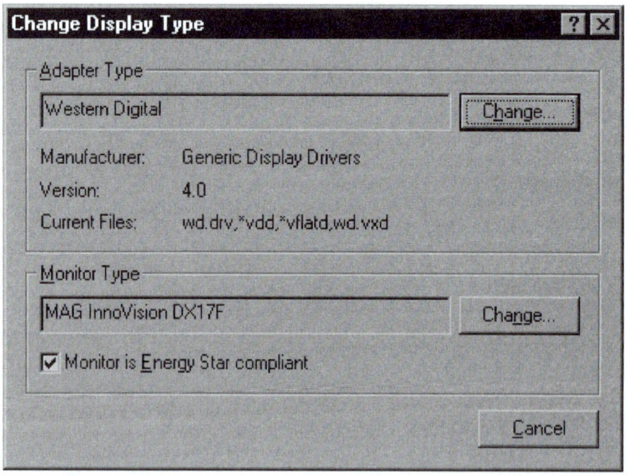

Figure 7.25   *Changing the video adaptor and display type is necessary when you install new video hardware.*

monitor you have because it doesn't have a name or the name isn't in the list of monitors (there are many no-name monitors around), choose Generic Monitor. Then narrow down the description by choosing one from the right-hand list that matches yours. You'll have to look in your monitor's manual to figure this out. Choose the highest resolution the monitor can support at the refresh rate listed. For example, if your monitor can do 1,280 by 1,024 at a refresh rate of 70 Hz, choose that.

CAUTION If you specify a refresh rating that is too high for your monitor, trying to expand the Desktop area to a larger size may not work. You'll just get a mess on the screen. If this happens, try using a setting with a lower refresh rate, such as 60 Hz or *interlaced*. The image may flicker a bit more, but at least it will be clearly visible.

4. If you have just received a new driver for your video adaptor card and want to use that instead of the one supplied with Windows 95 (or Windows 95 doesn't include a driver), click on the Have Disk button and follow the directions.

Adjusting the Mouse

You can adjust six aspects of your mouse's operation:

▶ left-right button reversal

▶ double-click speed

▶ look of the pointers

▶ tracking speed

▶ mouse trails

▶ mouse type and driver

Switching the Buttons and Setting Double-Click Speed

If you're left-handed, you may want to switch the mouse around to use it on the left side of the computer and reverse the buttons. The main button then becomes the right button instead of the left one. If

you use other programs outside of Windows that don't allow this, however, it might just add to the confusion. If you only use the mouse in
Windows programs and you're left-handed, then it's worth a try.

1. Run the Control Panel and double-click on Mouse. Then click on the
   first tab page of the dialog box (Figure 7.26).

2. Click on the Left-handed button as shown in the figure. Then click on
   Apply to check it out. Don't like it? Revert to the original setting and
   click on Apply again.

On the same page, you have the double-click speed setting. Double-
click speed determines how fast you have to double-click to make a
double-click operation work (that is, to run a program from its icon, to
open a document from its icon, or to select a word. If the double-click
speed is too fast, it's difficult for your fingers to click fast enough. If it's
too slow, you end up running programs or opening and closing

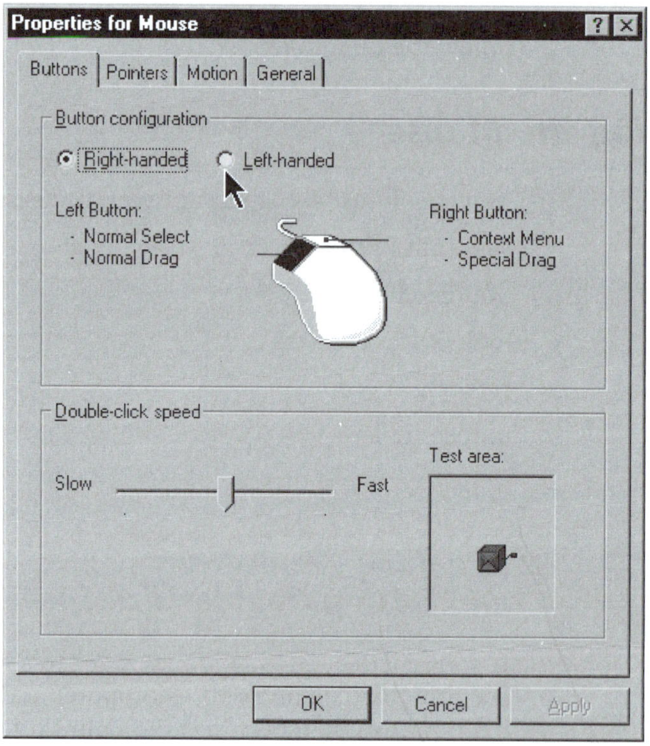

Figure 7.26   *First page of the Mouse settings. Here you can reverse the buttons for use by
left-handed people. You can also adjust the double-click speed.*

windows unexpectedly. Double-click on the Jack-in-the-box to try out the new double-click speed. Jack will jump out or back into the box if the double-click registered. If you're not faring well, adjust the slider and try again.

> **NOTE**   You don't have to click on Apply to test the slider settings. Just moving the slider instantly affects the mouse's double-click speed.

Setting Your Pointers

Your mouse pointer's shape changes depending on what you are pointing at and what Windows 95 is doing. If you are pointing to a window border, the pointer becomes a two-headed arrow. If Windows 95 is busy, it becomes a sandglass. When you are editing text, it becomes an I-beam, and so on.

You can customize your cursors for the fun of it or to increase visibility. You can even install animated cursors that look really cute and keep you amused while you wait for some process to complete.

> **TIP**   Animated cursors don't come with Windows 95. But you can get some from anyone with Windows NT. Just copy the ANI files from the NT machine into your Windows 95 directory. You'll probably be able to find ANI files on BBSs and information services such as Microsoft Network and CompuServe. See Chapter 32 for information about the animated cursors included in Microsoft Plus.

To change the cursor settings:

1. Click on the Pointers tab page of the Mouse dialog box (see Figure 7.27).

2. The list shows which pointers are currently assigned to which activities. To change an assignment, click on an item in the list.

3. Next, if you've changed the shape and want to revert, click on Use Default to go back to the normal pointer shape that Windows 95 came shipped with. Otherwise, choose Browse and use the Browse box to load the cursor you want. When you click on a cursor in the Browse box, it will be displayed at the bottom of the box for you to examine in advance—a thoughtful feature. Even animated cursors will do their thing right in the Browse box.

Part
2

Exploring Windows 95

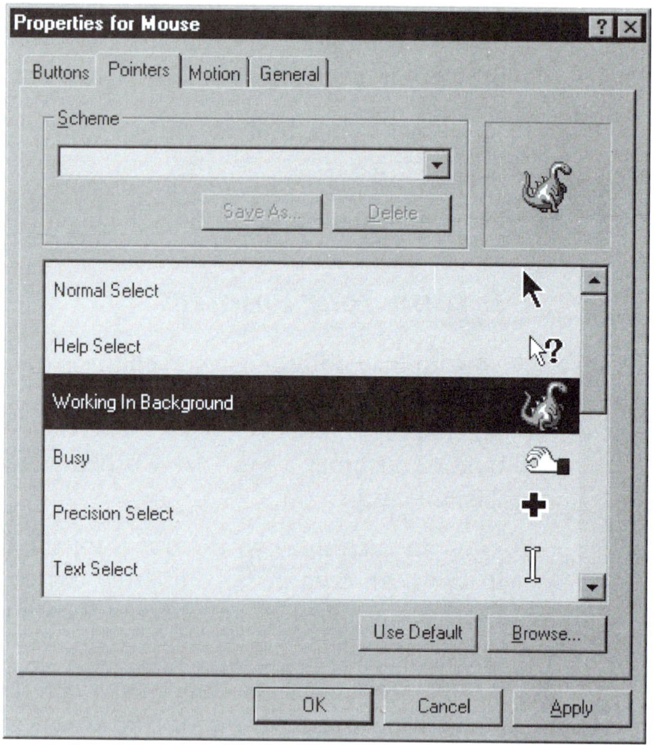

Figure 7.27   Choose pointer shapes for various activities here. As you can see, I have a couple of weird ones installed, such as the walking dinosaur instead of the sandglass.

4. Click on Open. The cursor will now be applied to the activity in question.

You can save pointer schemes just as you can colors. If you want to set up a number of different schemes (one for each person in the house, for example), just get the settings assigned the way you like, enter a name in the scheme area, and click on Save As. To later select a scheme, open the drop-down list box, select the scheme's name, and click on Apply or OK.

Setting the Pointer Motion

Two very useful adjustments can be made to the way to the mouse responds to the motion of your hand—speed and trails (Figure 7.28).

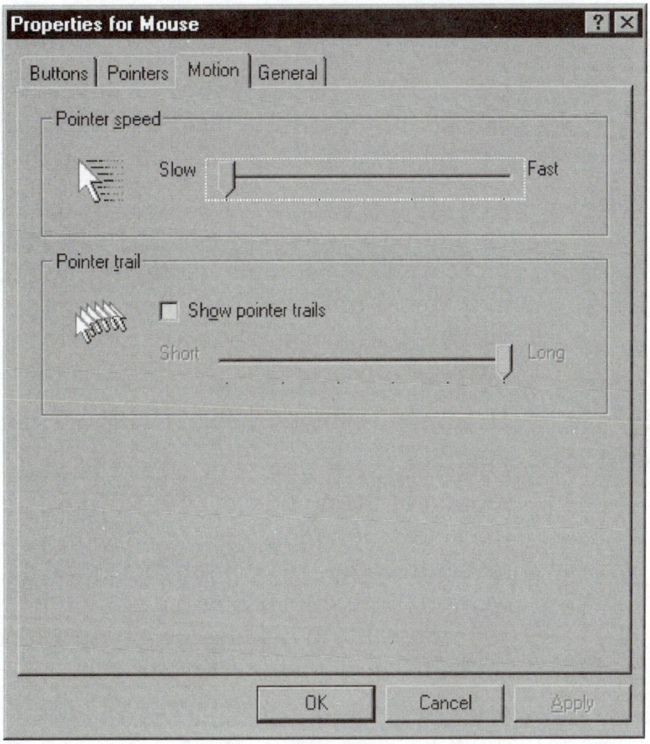

Figure 7.28   *You can adjust the speed at which the mouse pointer moves and whether you'll see trails.*

Pointer speed is the speed at which the mouse pointer moves relative to the movement of the mouse. Believe it or not, mouse motion is actually measured in *Mickeys*! (Somebody out there has a sense of humor.) A Mickey equals $\frac{1}{100}$ of an inch of mouse movement. The tracking-speed setting lets you adjust the relationship of Mickeys to pixels. If you want to be very exact in your cursor movement, you'll want to slow the tracking speed, requiring more Mickeys per pixel. However, this requires more hand motion for the same corresponding cursor motion. If your desk is crammed and your coordination is very good, then you can increase the speed (fewer Mickeys per pixel). If you use the mouse with MS-DOS programs that use their own mouse driver, you might want to adjust the Windows mouse speed to match that of your other programs so you won't need to mentally adjust when you use such non-Windows programs.

Incidentally, if you think the mouse runs too slowly in your non-Windows applications, there may be a fix. Contact your mouse's maker. For example, if you're using a Logitech mouse, a program called Click that is supplied with the Logitech mouse lets you easily control its tracking. See the Logitech manual for details.

The other setting—Mouse trails—creates a shadow of the mouse's path whenever you move it. Some people find it annoying, but for those who have trouble finding the pointer on the screen, it's a blessing. Mouse trails are particularly helpful when using Windows on passive-matrix or dual-scan laptop computers, where the pointer often disappears when you move it.

Here are the steps for changing these items:

1. Drag the speed slider one way or another to increase or decrease the motion of the pointer relative to your hand (or thumb in the case of a trackball) motion. Nothing may happen until you click on Apply. Adjust as necessary. Try aiming for some item on the screen and see how well you succeed. Having the motion too fast can result in straining your muscles and holding the mouse too tight. It's ergonomically more sound to use a little slower setting that requires more hand motion.

2. If you want trails, click the option box on and adjust the slider. You don't have to click on Apply to see the effects.

3. Click on OK or Apply to make it all official.

General Mouse Settings

The last tab page lets you change the mouse's software driver and possibly make changes that the driver has built in. The type of mouse is listed in the box. If this looks wrong or you're changing the mouse to another type, click on Change and choose the desired mouse type from the resulting Select Device box. See the discussion about changing the Display Adaptor, above, if in doubt about how to use the Select Device dialog box.

In some cases, you'll have an Options button on this tab page. The options will vary from mouse to mouse. They may include such things as choosing to have the mouse pointers be black rather than white or be transparent rather than opaque. For example, the Options for my Ballpoint mouse are shown in Figure 7.29.

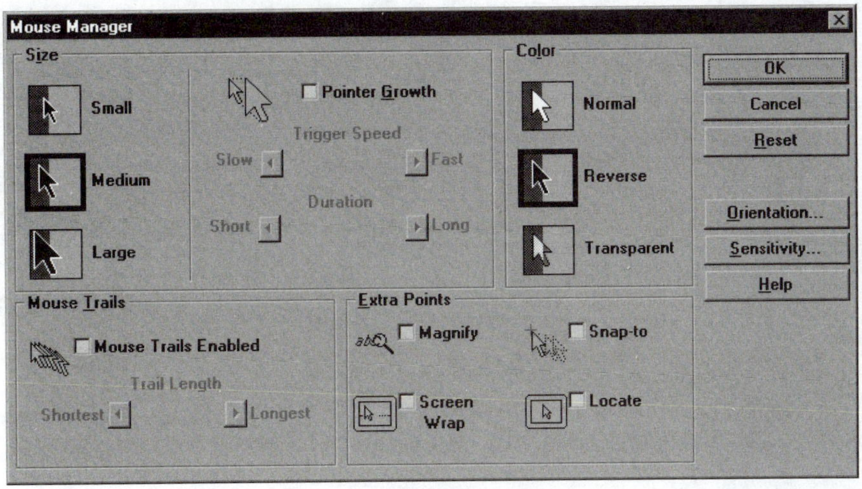

Figure 7.29   *Some mouse drivers have additional options built in. The last tab page of the Mouse applet gives you access to them.*

Chapter 8

Printers
and Printing
with Windows 95

FEATURING

If your printer is of the Plug-and-Play variety, your Windows 95 system will have a so-called default printer driver already installed. This means you'll be able to print from any Windows program without worrying about anything more than turning on the printer, checking that it has paper, and choosing the File ➤ Print command from whatever programs you use. If your printer isn't Plug-and-Play compatible, wasn't plugged in at the time of installation, or you weren't upgrading over a previous version of Windows for which you had printers set up already, you'll have to manually set up your printer before you can print. This chapter tells you how to do that and how to manage the use of your printer to get your work done.

As with Windows 3.1, unless you specify otherwise, Windows programs hand off data to Windows 95, which in turn *spools* the data to a specified printer. Spooling means temporarily putting on the hard disk the information that's really headed for the printer. Your document then gets sent out to the printer at the slow speed that the printer can receive it. This lets you get back to work with your program sooner. You can even print additional documents, stacking up a load of jobs for the printer to print. This stack is called a *queue*.

In Windows 3.x and Windows NT, a program called Print Manager is responsible for doing the spooling and managing the print jobs. Windows 95 nomenclature dispenses with the term "Print Manager," even though the same functionality is provided. Now you simply look at what's "inside" a printer by clicking on the printer's icon. This opens a window and displays the print queue for that printer. In reality, however, there *is* a spooler program and Print Manager-like thing in Windows 95, and that is how I'll refer to the window that displays and works with the print queue.

TECH TIP Unlike Windows NT, Windows 95 doesn't always prevent a program from writing directly to the printer port. (In Windows NT, any such attempt by programs to directly write to hardware, such as an LPT port, is trapped by the security manager.) Windows 95 offers less security in this regard. Unless a port has a printer associated with it, an application can directly access that port. Also, if you shell out of Windows 95 and run MS-DOS mode, direct port access is allowed.

> **NOTE**   MS-DOS programs can also be spooled so you can get back to work with your DOS or Windows programs while printing happens in the background.

When you print from a Windows program, Print Manager receives the data, queues up the jobs, routes them to the correct printer, and, when necessary, issues error or other appropriate messages to print-job originators. As in Windows 3.11 and NT, you can use the Print Manager user interface to manage your print jobs. Print Manager makes it easy to check out what's printing and see where your job(s) are in the print queue relative to other people's print jobs. You may also be permitted to rearrange the print queue, delete print jobs, or pause and resume a print job so you can reload or otherwise service the printer.

In Windows 3.11, printer-driver installation and configuration (making connections) are done through the Printers applet in Control Panel, while print-job management is done through the Print Manager program. Windows 95 combines both functions in the Printers folder. (The Control Panel still has a Printers icon, but it simply calls up the Printers folder.) Each printer you've installed appears in the Printers folder, along with an additional icon called Add Printer that lets you set up new printers. Printer icons in the folder appear and behave like any other object: You can delete them at will, create new ones, and set their properties. Double-clicking on a printer in the folder displays its print queue and lets you manipulate the queue. Commands on the menus let you to install, configure, connect, disconnect, and remove printers and drivers.

This chapter explains these features, as well as procedures for local and network print-queue management. Some basics of print management also are discussed, providing a primer for the uninitiated or for those whose skills are a little rusty.

A Print-Manager Primer

Windows 95's Print Manager feature mix is quite rich. Here are the highlights:

▶ You can add, modify, and remove printers right from the Printers folder (available from My Computer, Explorer, the Start button, or Control Panel).

▶ An object-oriented interface using printer icons eliminates the abstraction of thinking about the relationship of printer drivers, connections, and physical printers. You simply add a printer and set its properties. Once added, it appears as a named printer in the Printers folder.

▶ Once set up, you can easily choose to share a printer on the network so others can print to it. You can give it a useful name such as *LaserJet in Fred's Office* so people on the network know what it is.

▶ If you're on a network, you can manage network-printer connections by displaying available printers, sharing your local printer, and connecting to and disconnecting from network printers.

▶ Because of Windows 95's multithreading and preemptive multitasking, 32-bit Windows 95 programs will print more smoothly than under Windows 3.x. You can start printing and immediately go back to work; you don't have to wait until spooling for Print Manager to finish. (This won't be true for 16-bit programs.)

▶ While one document is printing out, other programs can start print jobs. Additional documents are simply added to the queue and will print in turn.

▶ Default settings for such options as number of copies, paper tray, page orientation, and so forth are automatically used during print jobs so you don't have to manually set them each time.

▶ For the curious, a window can be opened displaying jobs currently being printed or in the queue waiting to be printed, along with an indication of the current print job's progress.

▶ You can easily rearrange the order of the print queue and delete print jobs.

▶ You can choose whether printing begins as soon as the first page is spooled to the hard disk or after the last page of a document is spooled.

▶ You can temporarily pause or resume printing without causing printer time-out problems.

Adding a New Printer

As I mentioned, the Setup program prompts you to install a printer. If you elected to do so, or if you've installed printers in Windows 3.1, you'll be somewhat familiar with the procedure. If your printer is already installed and seems to be working fine, you probably can skip this section. In fact, if you're interested in nothing more than printing from one of your programs without viewing the queue, printing to a network printer, or making adjustments to your current printer's settings, just skip down to *Printing from a Program*, below. However, if you need to install a new printer, modify or customize your current installation, or add additional printers to your setup, read on to learn about how to:

▶ add a new printer

▶ select the printer port and make other connection settings

▶ set preferences for a printer

▶ install a printer driver that's not listed

▶ set the default printer

▶ select a printer when more than one is installed

▶ delete a printer from your system

About Printer Installation

As I mention in the Appendix, before installing hardware, including printers, you should read any last-minute printed or on-screen material that comes with Window 95. Often such material is full of useful information about specific types of hardware, including printers. Because these are last-minute details, I can't include them in this book. Look for a Readme file or something else similar on your Desktop that you can open by double-clicking on it. Then look through the file for information about your printer.

With that said, here is the overall game plan for adding a new printer. It's actually a really easy process thanks to the Add a Printer Wizard that walks you through it.

▶ Run Add a Printer from the Printers folder.

▶ Declare whether the printer is local (directly connected to your computer) or on the network.

▶ Declare what kind of printer it is.

▶ Select the printer's port and relevant port settings.

▶ Give the printer a name.

▶ Print a test page.

▶ Check and possibly alter the default printer settings, such as the DPI (dots per inch) setting and memory settings.

After these steps are complete, your printer should work as expected. Once installed, you can customize each printer's setup by modifying its properties, such as:

▶ specifying the amount of time you want Windows to keep trying to print a document before alerting you to a printer problem

▶ specifying the share name for the printer so other network users can find it when they search the network for printers

▶ setting job defaults pertaining to paper tray, two-sided printing, and paper orientation

▶ stipulating a *separator file* (a file, usually one page long, that prints between each print job)

▶ selecting the default printer if you have more than one printer installed

▶ choosing whether your printer should substitute its own fonts for certain Windows TrueType fonts

▶ selecting printer settings relevant to page orientation, color matching, greyscaling, size scaling, type of paper feed, halftone imaging, and when file-header information (such as a PostScript "preamble") is sent to the printer

Part 2

Exploring Windows 95

▶ set whether you want to share the printer for use by others on the network

▶ set whether documents will go directly to the printer or will go through the spooler

The good news is that normally you won't have to futz with any such settings. The other good news is, unlike in Windows 3.x and NT, getting to any one of these settings is now a piece of cake. You don't have to wind your way through a bevy of dialog boxes to target a given setting. The Properties dialog box has tab pages, so it's a cinch to find the one you want.

TIP   The Properties box has context-sensitive Help built in. Click on an element in a dialog box and press F1, or click on the ? button, then on the item. A relevant Help topic will appear.

NOTE   Advanced printer-security issues—such as conducting printer-access auditing and setting ownership—are not features of Windows 95. Windows 95 *does* support use of a password when sharing a printer, however, which is explained later in this chapter.

About Adding Printers

Before running the Wizard, let's consider when you'd need to add a new printer to your Windows 95 configuration:

▶ You didn't tell Windows 95 what kind of printer you have when you first set up Windows.

▶ You're connecting a new printer directly to your computer.

▶ Someone has connected a new printer to the network and wants to use it from your computer.

▶ You want to print to disk files that can later be sent to a particular type of printer.

▶ You want to set up multiple printer configurations (preferences) for a single physical printer so you can switch between them without having to change your printer setup before each print job.

Notice that a great deal of flexibility exists here, especially in the case of the last item. Because of the modularity of Windows 95's internal design, even though you might have only one physical printer, you can create any number of printer definitions for it, each with different characteristics.

> **TECH TIP**   These definitions are actually called printers, but you can think of them as printer names, aliases, or named virtual devices.

For example, you might want one definition set up to print on legal-sized paper in landscape orientation while another prints with normal paper in portrait orientation. Each of these two "printers" would actually use the same physical printer to print out on. While you're working with Windows 95's manual, online help, and this book, keep this terminology in mind. The word "printer" often doesn't really mean a physical printer. It usually means a printer setup that you've created with the Wizard. It's a collection of settings that typically points to a physical printer, but it could just as well create a print file instead.

About Printer Drivers

And finally, consider that a printer can't just connect to your computer and mysteriously print a fancy page of graphics or even a boring old page of text. You need a printer *driver*. The printer driver (actually a file on your hard disk) translates your text file to commands that tell your printer how to print your file. Because different brands and models of printer use different commands for such things as *move up a line*, *print a circle in the middle of the page*, *print the letter A*, and so on, a specialized printer driver is needed for each type of printer.

> **NOTE**   Because some printers are actually functionally equivalent, a driver for a popular brand and model of printer (for example, an Epson or a Hewlett-Packard) often masquerades under different names for other printers.

> **TECH TIP**   DOS programs require a print driver for the application, too. For instance, WordPerfect 5.1 running in a DOS session under Windows 95 will use a DOS printer driver *and* a Windows 95 printer driver to work under Windows 95.

When you add a printer, unless you're installing a Plug-and-Play–compatible printer, you're asked to choose the brand and model of printer. With Plug-and-Play printers, if the printer is attached and turned on, Windows 95 queries the printer and the printer responds with its make and model number. This is because Windows 95 can't usually detect this information on its own. Eventually all printers will be Plug-and-Play compatible, but until then, you'll typically have to tell Windows what printer you have so it knows which printer driver to install.

A good printer driver takes advantage of all your printer's capabilities, such as its built-in fonts and graphics features. A poor printer driver might succeed in printing only draft-quality text, even from a sophisticated printer.

If you're the proud owner of some offbeat brand of printer, you may be alarmed when you can't find your printer listed in the box when you run the Wizard. But don't worry, the printer manufacturer might be able to supply one. The procedure for installing manufacturer-supplied drivers is covered later in this chapter.

> **NOTE**   If your printer isn't included in the list, consult *When You Don't Find Your Printer in the List,* later in this chapter.

Running the Wizard to Add a New Printer

Microsoft has made the previously arduous chore of adding a printer something that's much more easily mastered by a majority of computer users. Here's what you have to do:

1. Open the Printers folder by clicking on the Start button and choosing Settings ➤ Printers. Two other paths are from My Computer and from Control Panel.

TECH TIP   Depending on the type of access control you stipulate from the Access Control tab of the Network applet in the Control Panel, you may want to password-protect your printer when you share it on the network. This helps guard against a printer being continually tied up with print jobs from an unauthorized user somewhere on the network. Just share your printer with password protection as discussed later in this chapter, or if part of an NT domain, restrict access to your resources via the Control Panel applet mentioned above (see Part V of this book).

2. Double-click on Add Printer, as shown in Figure 8.1.

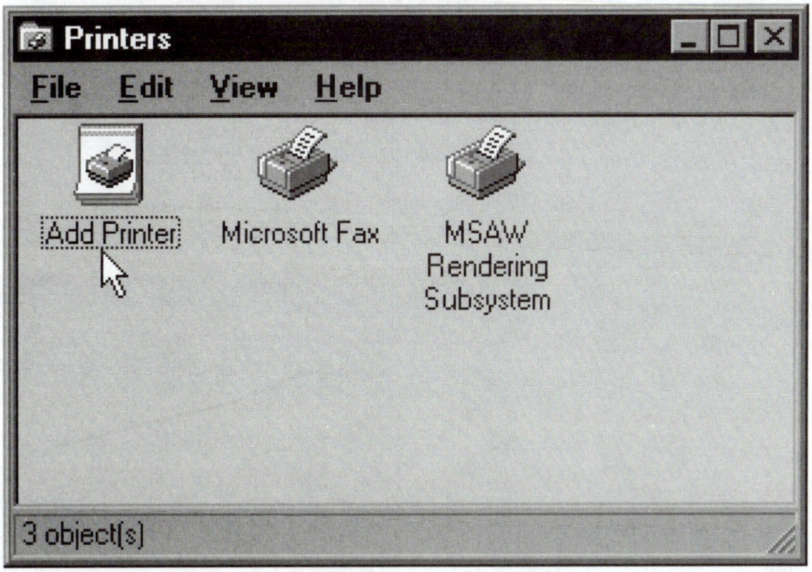

Figure 8.1 **Run the Wizard to add a printer.**

3. A dialog box like that in Figure 8.2 appears. Click on Next.

4. You're asked whether the printer is *local* or *network*. Because here I'm describing how to install a network printer, choose Network, then click on Next. (If you are setting up a local printer that is connected directly to your computer, at this point you should skip down to the next section, *Adding a Local Printer.*)

5. You'll now be asked two questions, as shown in Figure 8.3.

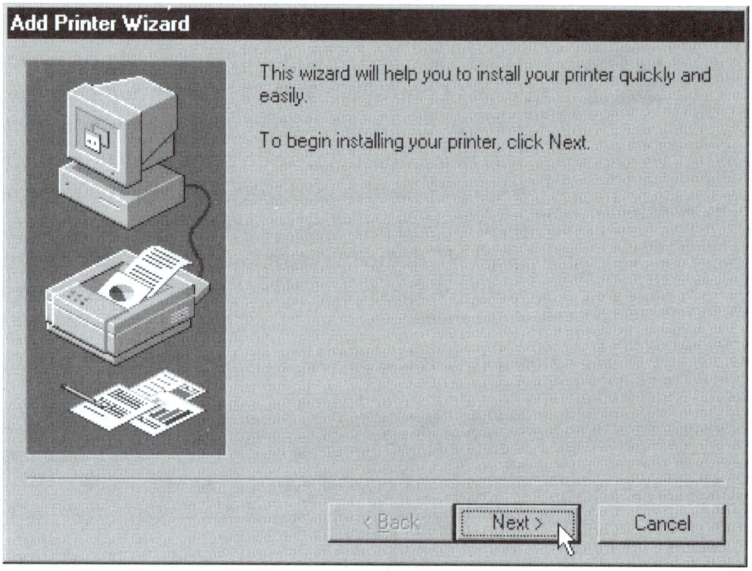

Figure 8.2   *Beginning the process of adding the printer*

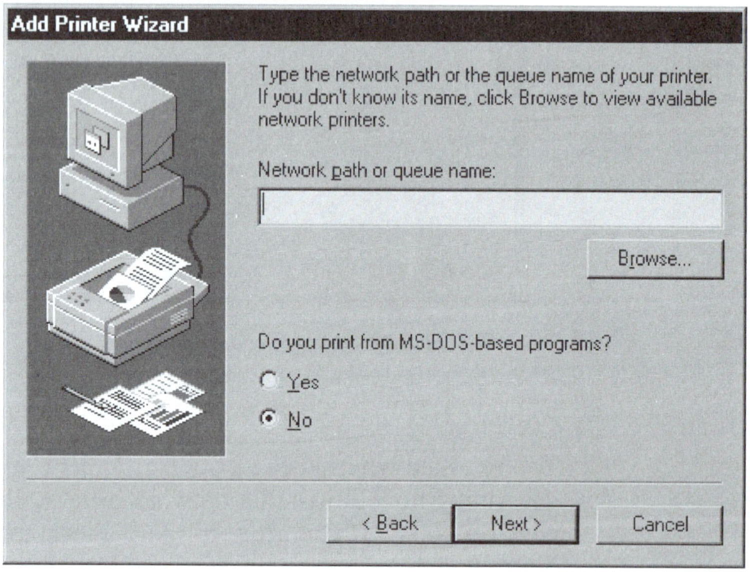

Figure 8.3   *When choosing a network printer, you have to specify the printer's path and declare whether you want to print from DOS programs.*

> **NOTE**   For a printer to appear in the network listing, it has to have been added to the host computer's setup (the computer the printer is directly attached to) using the steps in *Adding a Local Printer*, below. It must also be shared for use on the network.

6. You don't have to type in the complicated path name for the location of the printer on the network. Just click on Browse, and up comes a list of the printers on the network. For example, in Figure 8.4 you see the network printer *Apple*. You may have to double-click on Entire Network or click on the + sign next to a computer to display the printer(s) attached to it. Either way, just highlight the printer you want to connect to and click on OK.

If the network printer is currently *offline*, you'll be told that you have to wait until it comes back online before you can use it but that you can go ahead and install it if you want. However, as long as it's offline, you'll be asked to specify the brand and model of the printer because

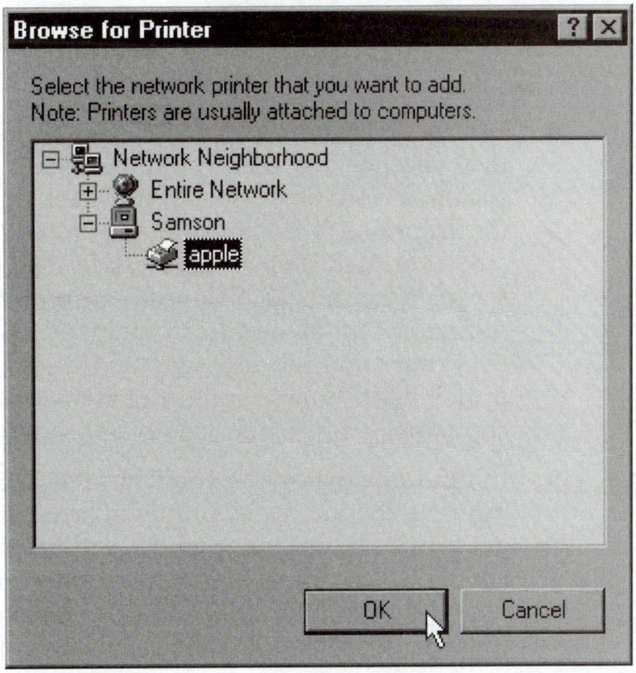

Part
2

Exploring Windows 95

Figure 8.4   *The Browse box graphically displays computers that have shared networked printers available for others to use. Click on the printer you want, then click on OK.*

the Wizard can't figure out what kind of printer it is when it is unavailable for your computer to question. If you can alert the owner of the printer to put it online (they have to right-click on the printer's icon at their computer and turn off the Work Offline setting), then you won't have to specify these settings. If this isn't possible, just select the brand name and model from the resulting list.

7. Back at the Wizard dialog box, decide whether you want to print from DOS applications or not.

   ▶ If you choose Yes, click on Next, and you'll be asked to choose a printer port to associate the output with (such as LPT1, LPT2, and so on). Usually this will be LPT1. However, if you have a local printer attached to your computer using LPT1, you should choose a different port, such as LPT2. This doesn't mean the printer has to be connected to your LPT (parallel) port, it only tells Windows 95 how to fake the DOS program into thinking that it's printing to a normal parallel port. Click on Capture Printer Port, choose accordingly, and click on OK. Then click on Next.

   ▶ If you won't be printing from DOS applications to this new printer, choose No, and you won't be asked about the port. Just click on Next.

8. Now you're asked to name the printer (Figure 8.5). This is the name that will show up when you're setting up to print from a program such as a word processor, spreadsheet, or whatever. Type in a name for the printer; the maximum length is 32 characters. Typically, the type of printer, such as HP Desk Jet 320, goes here. There's also a description line in which you can be even more descriptive about the printer, accepting up to 255 characters. Specifying the location of the printer in this box is a good idea so network users can find a printer when browsing and will know where to pick up their hard copy when a print job is completed.

9. In this same dialog box you'll have to decide whether you want the printer to be the *default* printer. The default printer is the one that programs will assume you want to print to. Some programs don't let you choose which printer a document will print out on, so setting the default printer can be important. If you want this network printer to be the default printer, remember that the computer the printer is directly

connected to (in the example here, that would be the computer called Samson) has to be up and running for the printer to work. So, if you have a local printer on your machine as well, it's better to make that the default printer.

10. Finally, you're asked if you want to print a test page. It's a good idea to do this. Turn on the printer, make sure it has paper in it, and click on Finish. You may be prompted to supply a printer driver for the printer, depending on the type of network you're connecting to and whether a driver is already on your machine. If you're told that a driver file for the printer is already on your machine, you'll be asked if you want to use it or load a new one from the Windows 95 CD-ROM or floppy disks. It's usually easier to use the existing driver. If the driver isn't on your hard disk, you'll be instructed to insert the disk containing the driver.

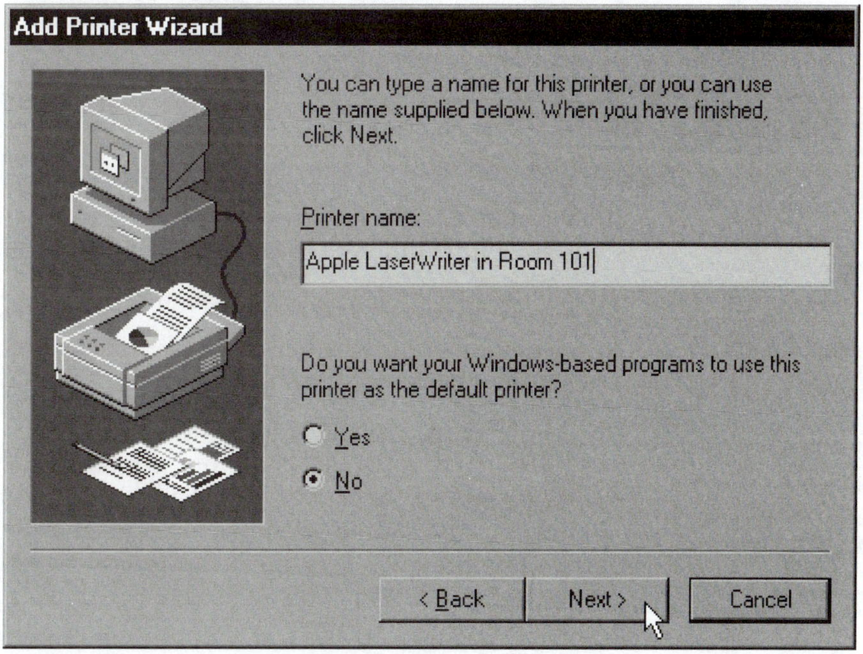

Figure 8.5 *Name the printer and choose whether it's going to be your default printer.*

11. The test page will be sent to the printer; it should print out in a few minutes. Then you'll be asked if it printed OK. If it didn't print correctly, click on No, and you'll be shown some troubleshooting information containing some questions and answers. The most likely fixes for the malady will be described. If the page printed OK, click on Yes, and you're done.

If all went well, you now have a network printer set up and ready to go. The new printer appears in your Printers folder.

Adding a Local Printer

If you want to add a local printer rather than a networked printer, the steps are a little different from what I explained above.

1. Follow the first three steps in the section above.

2. In the box that asks whether the printer is local or networked, click on Local. Then click on Next.

3. You're presented with a list of brands and models. In the left column scroll the list, find the maker of your printer, and click on it. Then in the right column choose the model number or name that matches your printer. Be sure to select the exact printer model, not just the correct brand name. Consult your printer's manual if you're in doubt about the model. What you enter here determines which printer driver file is used for this printer's definition. Figure 8.6 shows an example for an HP LaserJet IV.

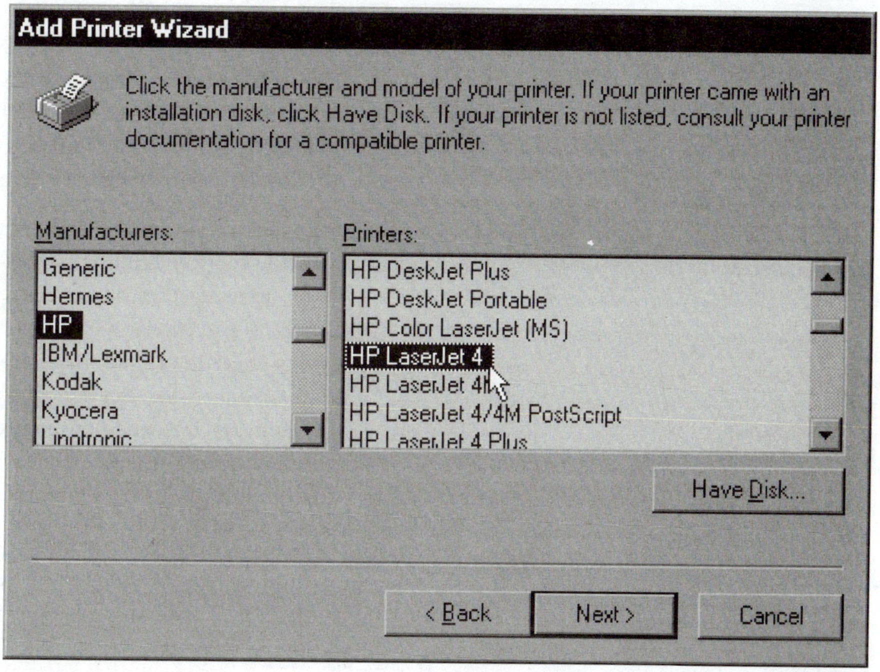

Figure 8.6   *Choosing the printer make and model; here I'm choosing a Hewlett-Packard Laser-Jet IV.*

4. Click on Next: Now you'll see a list of ports. You have to tell Windows which port the printer is connected to. (A port usually refers to the connector on the computer.)

Most often the port will be the parallel printer port called LPT1 (Line Printer #1). Unless you know your printer is connected to another port, such as LPT2 or a serial port (such as COM1 or COM2), select LPT1 as in Figure 8.7.

5. Click on Next. Now you can give the printer a name (see Figure 8.8).

> **NOTE**   If the printer will be shared with DOS and 16-bit Windows users (such as people running Windows for Workgroups 3.11), you might want to limit this name to twelve characters because that's the maximum length those users will see when they are browsing for printers.

Port	Notes
LPT1, LPT2, LPT3	The most common setting is LPT1 because most PC-type printers hook up to the LPT1 parallel port. Click on Configure Port if you want to turn off the ability to print to this printer from DOS programs.
COM1, COM2, COM3, COM4	If you know your printer is of the serial variety, it's probably connected to the COM1 port. If COM1 is tied up for use with some other device, such as a modem, use COM2. If you choose a COM port, click on Configure Port to check the communications settings in the resulting dialog box. Set the baud rate, data bits, parity, start and stop bits, and flow control to match those of the printer being attached. Refer to the printer's manual to determine what the settings should be.
File	This is for printing to a disk file instead of to the printer. Later, the file can be sent directly to the printer or sent to someone on floppy disk or over a modem. When you print to this printer name, you are prompted to enter a file name. (See the section in this chapter titled *Printing to a Disk File Instead of a Printer.*)

Table 8.1   **Printer Ports**

6. Also set whether the printer will be the default printer for Windows programs.

7. Finally, you're asked if you want to print a test page. It's a good idea to do this. Turn on the printer, make sure it has paper in it, and click on Finish. If the driver file for your printer is in the computer, you'll be asked if you want to use it or load a new one from the Windows 95 CD-ROM or floppy disks. It's usually easier to use the existing driver. If the driver isn't on your hard disk, you'll be instructed to insert the disk containing the driver.

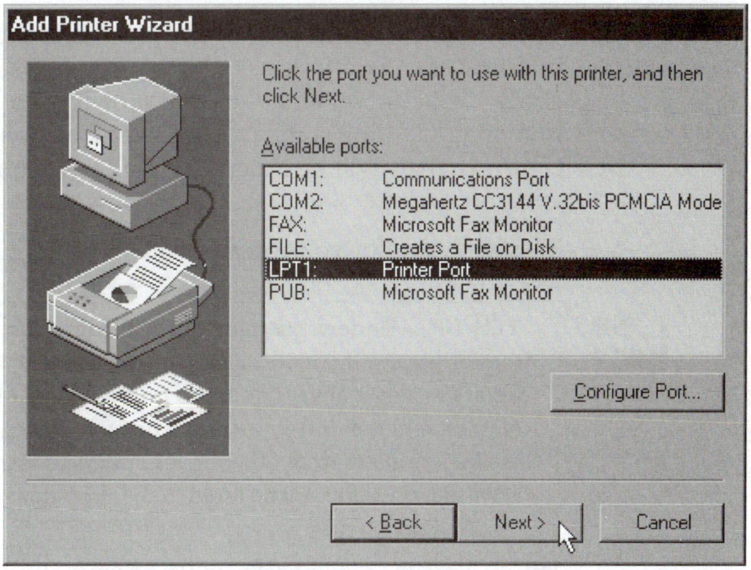

Figure 8.7 Choosing the port the printer's connected to is the second step in setting up a local printer.

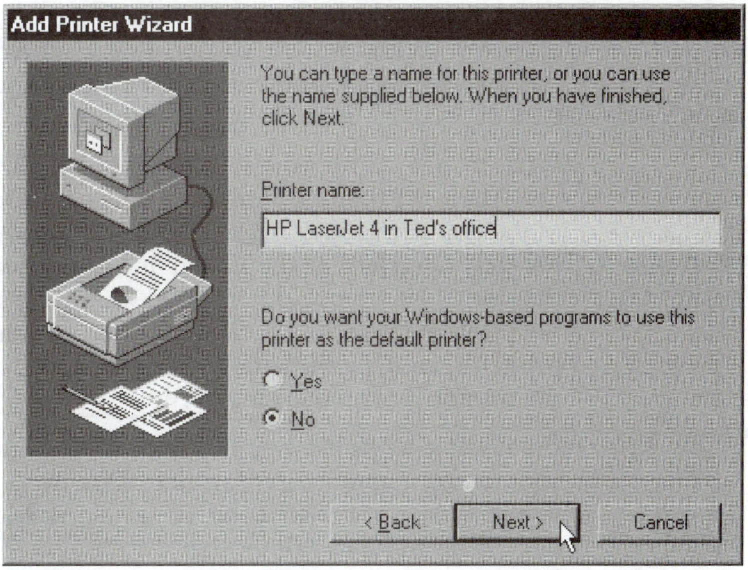

Figure 8.8 Give your new printer a name that tells you and other people something about it.

8. The test page will be sent to the printer. It should print out in a few minutes, then you'll be asked if it printed OK. If it didn't print correctly, click on No, and you'll be shown some troubleshooting information containing some questions and answers. The most likely fixes for the malady will be described. If the page printed OK, click on Yes, and you're done.

The new icon for your printer will show up in the Printers folder now.

TECH TIP Windows 95 remembers the location you installed Windows 95 from originally. If you installed from a CD-ROM, it's likely that the default location for files is always going to be the CD-ROM drive's logical name (typically some higher letter, such as E or F). If you have done some subsequent installs or updates from other drives or directories, those are also remembered by Windows 95 and will be listed in the drop-down list box.

When You Don't Find Your Printer in the List

When you're adding a local printer, you have to supply the brand name and model of the printer because Windows 95 needs to know which driver to load into your Windows 95 setup to use the printer correctly. (When you are adding a network printer, you aren't asked this question because the printer's host computer already knows what type of printer it is, and the driver is on that computer.)

What if your printer isn't on the list of Windows 95-recognized printers? Many off-brand printers are designed to be compatible with one of the popular printer types, such as the Apple LaserWriters, Hewlett-Packard LaserJets, or the Epson line of printers. Refer to the manual that came with your printer to see whether it's compatible with one of the printers that *is* listed. Some printers require that you set the printer in compatibility mode using switches or software. Again, check the printer's manual for instructions.

Finally, if it looks like there's no mention of compatibility anywhere, contact the manufacturer for their Windows 95-compatible driver. If you're lucky, they'll have one. It's also possible that Microsoft has a new driver for your printer that wasn't available when your copy of Windows 95 was shipped. Contact Microsoft at (206) 882-8080 and ask for the Windows 95 Driver Library Disk, which contains all the latest drivers.

Also remember that Windows 95 can use the 16-bit drivers that worked with Windows 3.x. So, if you had a fully functioning driver for your printer in Windows 3.x (that is, your printer worked fine before you upgraded from Windows 3.x to Windows 95), you should be able to use that driver in Windows 95.

> **NOTE**   All existing printer setups should actually have been migrated from Windows 3.x to Windows 95 when you upgraded, so if it was working under Windows 3.x, it will probably work fine under Windows 95. This is true for other types of drivers, too, such as video display cards, sound boards, and so on. However, whenever possible, you should bag any 16-bit drivers you have from Windows 3.x and use the drivers supplied with Windows 95.

Locate the Windows 3.x driver disk supplied with your printer or locate the driver file. (Sometimes font or other support files are also needed, incidentally, so it's not always as simple as finding a single file.) One source might be CompuServe, which has a listing of Microsoft's latest driver library online. Try **GO**ing WIN95, WINADV, or WDL (Windows Driver Library) for more info.

Assuming you do obtain a printer driver, do the following to install it:

1. Follow the instructions above for running the Add a Printer Wizard.

2. Instead of selecting one of the printers in the Driver list (it isn't in the list, of course), click on the Have Disk button. You'll see this box:

3. The Wizard is asking you to enter the path where the driver is located (typically a floppy disk). Insert the disk (or make sure the files are available somewhere), enter the path, and click on OK. Enter the correct source of the driver. Typically, it'll be in the A or B disk drive.

> **TECH TIP**   The Wizard is looking for an file with an `.inf` extension, incidentally. This is the standard file extension for manufacturer-supplied driver-information files.

4. Click on OK.

5. You might have to choose a driver from a list if multiple options exist.

6. Continue with the Wizard dialog boxes as explained above.

> **TECH TIP**   If none of the drivers you can lay your hands on will work with your printer, try choosing the Generic *text-only* driver. This driver prints only text—no fancy formatting and no graphics. But it will work in a pinch with many printers. Make sure the printer is capable of or is set to an ASCII or ANSI text-only mode, otherwise your printout may be a mess. PostScript printers don't have such a text-only mode.

Altering the Details of a Printer's Setup—The Properties Box

Each printer driver can be fine-tuned by changing settings in its Properties dialog box. This area is difficult to document because so many variations exist due to the number of printers supported. The following sections describe the gist of these options without going into too much detail about each printer type.

The settings pertaining to a printer are called *properties*. As I discussed earlier, properties abound in Windows 95. Almost every object in Windows 95 has properties that you can examine and change at will. When you add a printer, the Wizard makes life easy for you by giving it some default properties that usually work fine and needn't be tampered with. You can change them later, but only if you need to. It may be worth looking at the properties for your printer, especially if the printer's acting up in some way when you try to print from Windows 95.

1. Open the Printers folder.

2. Right-click on the printer's icon and choose Properties. A box such as the one in Figure 8.9 appears.

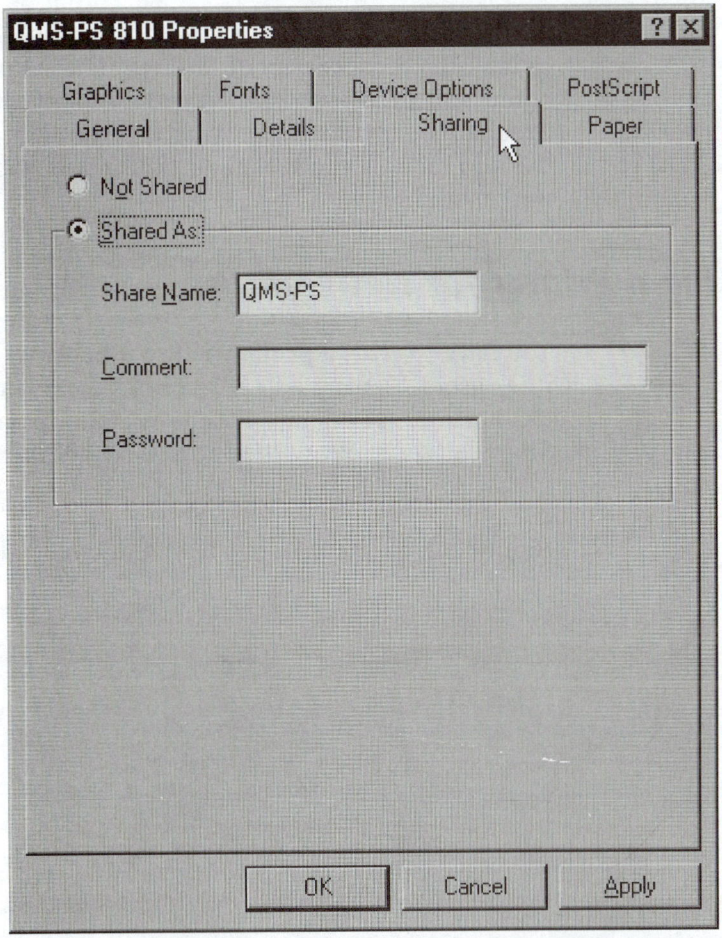

Figure 8.9   *Each printer has a Properties box such as this, with several tab pages. Options differ from printer to printer.*

> **TIP**   You can also type Alt-Enter to open the Properties box. This is true with many Windows 95 objects.

3. Notice that there is a place for a comment. This is normally blank after you add a printer. If you share the printer on the network, any text that you add to this box will be seen by other users who are browsing the network for a printer.

Part
2

Exploring Windows 95

4. Click on the various tab pages of your printer's Properties box to view or alter the great variety of settings. These buttons are confusing in name, and there's no easy way to remember what's what. But remember that you can get help by clicking on the ? in the upper-right corner and then on the setting or button whose function you don't understand.

Sharing a Printer for Network Use

You have to *share* a printer before it becomes available to other network users. Sharing is pretty simple: First you add the printer as a local printer. Then you share it by right-clicking on it and choosing Share, or via its Properties box. Here are the details:

1. Add the printer as described earlier in this chapter.

2. Right-click on the printer's icon and choose Properties or Sharing.

3. Now you'll see the box in Figure 8.9. Click on the Sharing tab if it's not selected.

4. On the Sharing page, click on Shared As.

5. A *share name* based on the Printer Name is automatically generated. You can leave the share name as is or give it another name. DOS-based network users see this name, which must conform to DOS file-naming rules. Other users will see this name, too, though some may see the other comments about the printer. This name can't be more than twelve characters long and mustn't contain spaces or characters not acceptable in DOS file names, such as ?, *, #, +, |, \, /, =, > , < , or %.

6. Fill in a comment about the printer, such as the location of the printer so users know where to pick up their printouts.

7. Fill in a password only if you want to restrict the use of the printer. If a password is entered here, other network users will be prompted to enter it at their machine before they can print to your printer. Make a list of people whom you want to give printer access to and tell them what the password is. This is one way to prevent overuse of a given printer. If you don't enter a password, protection is not in effect.

TIP Another approach to preventing overuse of a given printer (at least temporarily) is to right-click on its icon and choose Pause Printing. Not a very elegant way to deter people from printing to your printer, but it *will* stop print jobs.

---

8. Click on OK. If you entered a password, you'll be prompted to verify it by reentering. Then click on OK, and your printer is shared! Its icon now has a hand under it. Pretty soon you'll QMS-PS 810 start to see unexpected print jobs rolling out of your printer.

To unshare your printer, open the Properties box again, choose the Sharing page, and click on Not Shared.

TIP If you forget the password, don't worry. You can change it by simply entering a new password from the Share tab page.

Connecting to a Network Printer

Assuming your Windows 95 network system is successfully cabled and running, network printing should be possible. Before a network user can access a network printer, the following must be true:

▶ The printer must be cabled to the sharing computer.

▶ The printer must be created and working properly for local use.

▶ The printer must be shared.

▶ The printer's security settings and network users wishing access must match.

Part 2

Exploring Windows 95

> **TIP** By default, new printer shares are given a security setting that gives all users access for printing. Only the creator and administrators can *manage* the printer, however. Managing the printer means rearranging the print-job queue: starting, stopping, and deleting print jobs.

How to Delete a Printer from Your Printers Folder

You might want to decommission a printer after you've added it, for several reasons:

▶ You've connected a new type of printer to your computer and you want to delete the old setup and create a new one with the correct driver for the new printer.

▶ You want to disconnect from a network printer you're through using.

▶ You've created several slightly different setups for the same physical printer and you want to delete the ones you don't use.

In any of these cases, the trick is the same:

1. Open the Printers folder (the easiest way is using Start ➤ Settings ➤ Printers).

2. Right-click on the icon for the printer setup you want to delete and choose Delete (or just press Del).

You will see at least one confirmation box before the printer is deleted. You may see another warning if there are print jobs in the queue for the printer.

> **NOTE** If you have stipulated that the computer can keep separate settings for each user (via Control Panel ➤ Passwords ➤ User Profiles), the removal process removes only the printer setup from Windows 95's Registry for the currently logged-in user. Also note that the related driver file and font files are not deleted from the disk. Therefore, if you want to re-create the printer, you don't have to insert disks, and you won't be prompted for the location of driver files. This is convenient, but if you're tight on disk space, you might want to remove the printer fonts and drivers. To remove fonts, use the Fonts applet in the Control Panel, as described in Chapter 9.

How to Print Out Documents from Your Programs

By now your printer(s) are added and ready to go. The procedure in Windows 95 is really no different from Windows 3.x, Windows NT, or even Mac programs. Just open the document, choose File ➤ Print, and make a few settings, such as which pages to print. (You might have to set the print area first or make some other settings, depending on the program.) If you're already happy with the ways in which you print, you might want to skim over this section. However, there *are* a couple of conveniences you might not know about, such using drag and drop to print or right-clicking on a document to print it without opening the program that created it.

About the Default Printer

Unless you choose otherwise, the output from both Windows and DOS programs are shunted to the Print Manager for printing. If no particular printer has been chosen (perhaps because the program—for example, a DOS app or Notepad—doesn't give you a choice), the default printer is used.

> **NOTE** The default printer can be set by right-clicking on a printer icon and choosing Set as Default.

Exactly how your printed documents look varies somewhat from program to program because not all programs can take full advantage of the capabilities of your printer and the printer driver. For example, simple word-processing programs like Notepad don't let you change the font, while a full-blown word-processing program such as Ami Pro can print out all kinds of fancy graphics, fonts, columns of text, and so forth.

> **TIP**   Here's something to consider. If you choose as a default a printer that your DOS programs can't work with, your print jobs could bomb. Suppose you're running WordPerfect 5.1 for DOS and have it installed to print to an HP LaserJet, but the default printer is a Postscript laser printer. This would cause your printouts to be nothing but a listing of PostScript commands, such as `ERROR: undefined`, `OFFENDING COMMAND: |ume STACK {–pop–`, and so on. On another type of printer, you might see garbage printouts such as `@#$@$%G$V%B^YB&M(OM` instead of readable text. Just make sure your DOS 95 programs can work with your default printer (or change the default printer).

When you print from any program, the file is actually printed to a disk file instead of directly to the printer. Print Manager then spools the file to the assigned printer(s), coordinating the flow of data and keeping you informed of the progress. Jobs are queued up and listed in the Print Manager window, from which their status can be observed; they can be rearranged, deleted, and so forth.

Printing from a Program

To print from any program, including Windows and Windows 95 programs, follow these steps (which are exact for Windows programs but only approximate for other environments):

1. Check to see that the printer and page settings are correct. Some program's File menus provide a Printer Setup, Page Setup, or other option for this. Note that settings you make from such a box temporarily (sometimes permanently, depending on the program) override settings made from the Printer's Properties dialog box.

2. Select the Print command on the program's File menu and fill in whatever information is asked of you. For example, in WordPad, the Print dialog box looks like that in Figure 8.10.

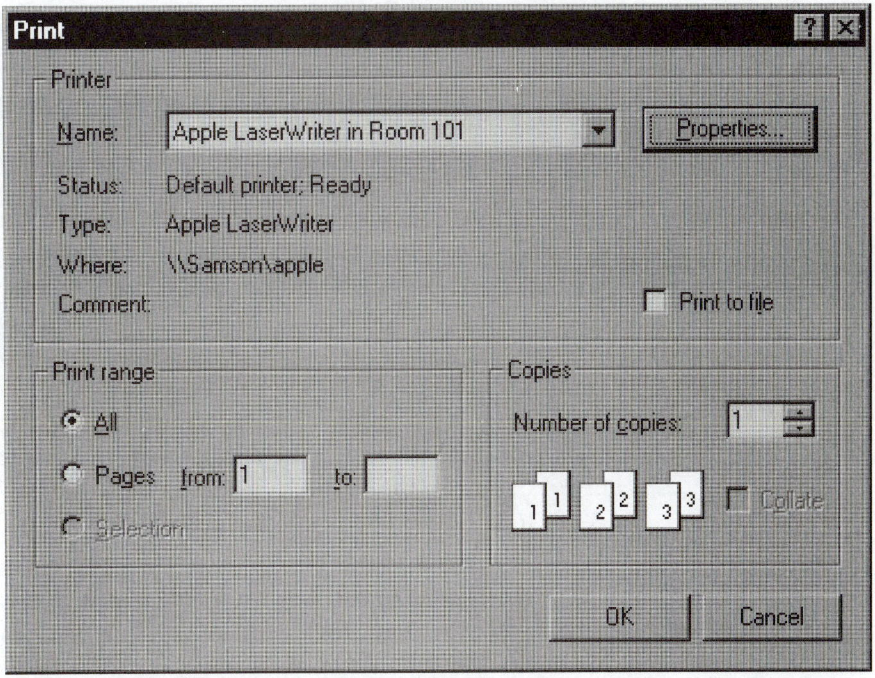

Figure 8.10   *When you choose Print from a Windows program, you often see a dialog box such as this that allows you to choose some options before printing. This one is from WordPad, a program supplied with Windows 95.*

Some programs have rather elaborate dialog boxes for choosing which printer you want to print to, scaling or graphically altering the printout, and even adjusting the properties of the printer. Still, you can normally just make the most obvious settings and get away with it:

▶ correct printer

▶ correct number of copies

▶ correct print range (pages, spreadsheet cells, portion of graphic, etc.)

▶ for color printers, which ink cartridge you have in (black & white or color)

3. Click on OK (or otherwise confirm printing). Windows 95 intercepts the print data and writes it in a file, then begins printing it. If an error

occurs—a port conflict, the printer is out of paper, or what have you—
you'll see a message such as this:

```
┌─────────────────────────────────────────────────────────────┐
│ Print Manager                                            [X] │
├─────────────────────────────────────────────────────────────┤
│                                                             │
│   ⬤?   Error writing to LPT1: for printer (QMS-PS 810):    │
│         Printer is not ready. Make sure it is on and online.│
│         Click Retry to continue printing.                   │
│         Print Manager will automatically retry after 5 seconds.│
│                                                             │
│                   ┌──────────┐   ┌──────────┐               │
│                   │  Retry   │   │  Cancel  │               │
│                   └──────────┘   └──────────┘               │
└─────────────────────────────────────────────────────────────┘
```

Check the paper supply, check to see that the printer is turned on,
that it's online (there may be a switch on the printer for this). If it's a
network printer, make sure it's shared and that the computer it's connected to is booted up and has shared the printer for use.

> **TIP**   When printing commences, a little printer icon will appear in the Task-
> bar next to the clock. You can double-click on this icon to see details of your
> pending print jobs.

Printing by Dragging Files onto a Printer Icon or into Its Window

You can quickly print Windows program document files by dragging
them onto a printer's icon or window. You can drag from the Desktop,
a folder, the Find box, the Explorer, or the File Manager window into
the running Print Manager. This will only work with documents that
have an association with a particular program. (See Chapter 3 for a
discussion of associations.) To check if a document has an association,
right-click on it. If the resulting menu has an Open command on it
(not Open With), it has an association.

1. Arrange things on your screen so you can see the file(s) you want to
    print as well as either the printer's icon or its window (you open a
    printer's window by double-clicking on its icon).

> **TIP** You can drag a file into a shortcut of the Printer's icon. If you like this way of printing, keep a shortcut of your printer on the Desktop so you can drag documents to it without having to open up the Printers folder. Double-clicking on a shortcut provides an easy means of checking its print queue, too.

2. Drag the document file(s) into the Print Manager icon or window (Figure 8.11 illustrates). The file is loaded into the source program, the Print command is automatically executed, and the file is spooled to Print Manager. The document isn't actually moved out of its home folder, it just gets printed.

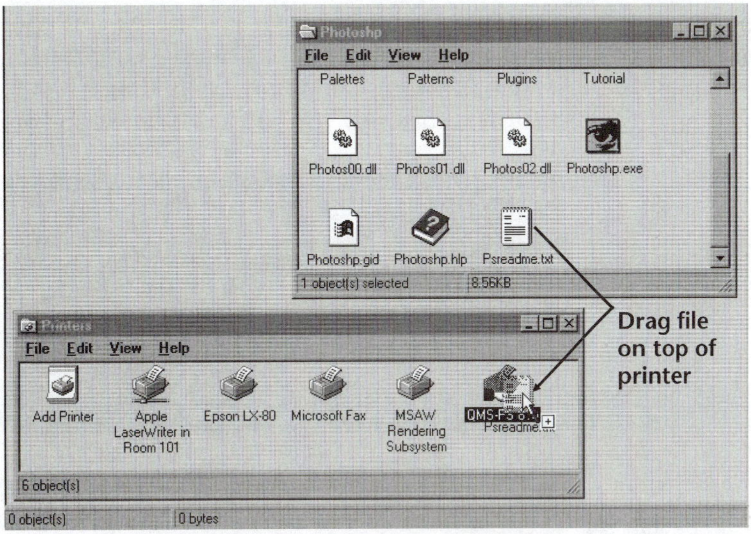

Figure 8.11   *You can print a document by dragging it to the destination printer's icon or window.*

If the document doesn't have an association, you'll see an error message:

Also, a nice feature of this approach is that you can drag multiple files onto a printer's icon or open window at once. They will all be queued up for printing, one after another, via their source programs. You'll see this message asking for confirmation before printing commences:

Printers

ⓘ You are trying to print multiple files at once. Are you sure you want to do this?

| Yes | No |

One caveat about this technique: as you know, some programs don't have a built-in facility for printing to a printer other than the default one. Notepad is a case in point: Try to drag a Notepad document to a printer that isn't currently your default printer, and you'll see this message:

Printing Error

ⓘ This program requires you to print documents with the default printer. Do you want this printer to become your default printer? If you click No, this document will not be printed.

| Yes | No |

TIP The drag-and-drop method can be used with shortcuts, too. You can drag shortcuts of documents to a printer or even to a shortcut of a printer, and the document will print.

Printing by Right-Clicking on a Document

Finally, you can print some documents using another shortcut that doesn't even require you to have a printer icon in view; instead, you use the right-click menu. Here's how:

1. Right-click on the icon of any document you want to print and notice whether the right-click menu has a Print command on it.

2. If there's no Print command, press Esc to cancel the menu. You can't print the document using this technique. If there is a Print command, choose it. The file will open in its source program and start printing right away. Once spooled to the Print Manager, the document will close automatically.

Working with the Print Queue

If you print more than a few files at a time, or if you have your printer shared for network use, you'll sometimes want to check on the status of a printer's print jobs. You also might want to see how many jobs need to print before you turn off your local computer and printer if others are using it. Or you might want to know how many other jobs are ahead of yours.

You can check on these items by opening a printer's window. You'll then see:

Document Name: Name of the file being printed and possibly the source program

Status: Whether the job is printing, being deleted, or paused

Owner: Who sent each print job to the printer

Progress: How large each job is and how much of the current job has been printed

Start at: When each print job was sent to the print queue

Figure 8.12 shows a sample printer with a print queue and related information.

To see the queue on a printer:

1. Open the Printers folder.

2. Double-click on the printer in question.

Part 2

Exploring Windows 95

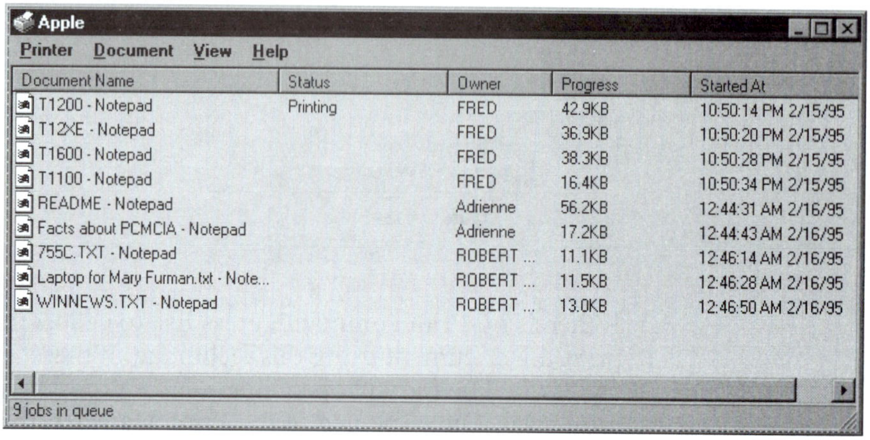

Figure 8.12   *A printer's window with several print jobs pending*

3. Adjust the window size if necessary so you can see all the columns.

NOTE   If the print job originated from a DOS program, the Document Name will not be known. It's listed as Remote Downlevel Document, meaning that it came from a workstation that doesn't support Microsoft's RPC (Remote Procedure Call) print support. Additional cases in point are Windows for Workgroups, LAN Manager, Unix, and Netware.

TIP   You can resize the columns in the display to see more data in a small window. Move the pointer to the dividing line in the header display and drag the line left or right.

TIP   If the printer in question is a network printer, and the printer is offline for some reason, such as its computer isn't turned on, you'll be forced to work *offline*. An error message will alert you to this, and the top line of the printer's window will say *User intervention required—Work Offline*. Until the issue is resolved, you won't be able to view the queue for that printer. You can still print to it, however.

Refreshing the Network Queue Information

The network cabling connecting workstations and servers often is quite busy, so Windows 95 usually doesn't bother to add even more traffic to the net by polling each workstation for printer-queue information. This is done when necessary, such as when a document is deleted from a queue. So, if you want to refresh the window for a printer to get the absolute latest information, just press F5. This immediately updates the queue information.

Deleting a File from the Queue

After sending a file to the queue, you might reconsider printing it, or you might want to re-edit the file and print it later. If so, you can simply remove the file from the queue.

1. Open the printer's window.

2. Select the file by clicking on it in the queue.

> **NOTE** I have found, especially with PostScript laser-type printers, that after deleting a file while printing, I'll have to reset the printer to clear its buffer or at least eject the current page (if you have a page-eject button). To reset, you'll typically have to push a button on the printer's front panel or turn the printer off for a few seconds, then on again.

3. Choose Document ➤ Cancel Printing, press Delete, or right-click and choose Cancel Printing. The document item is removed from the printer's window. If you're trying to delete the job that's printing, you might have some trouble. At the very least, the system might take some time to respond.

> **NOTE** Of course, normally you can't delete someone else's print jobs on a remote printer. If you try to, you'll be told that this is beyond your privilege and that you should contact your system administrator. You *can* kill other people's print jobs if the printer in question is connected to *your* computer. But if you want to be able to delete jobs on a remote computer, someone has to alter the password settings in the remote computer's Control Panel to allow remote administration of the printer. Remote administration is covered in Part V.

Part 2

Exploring Windows 95

> **NOTE** Pending print jobs will not be lost when computers are powered down. Any documents in the queue when the system goes down will reappear in the queue when you power up. When you turn on a computer that is the host for a shared printer that has an unfinished print queue, you will be alerted to the number of jobs in the queue and asked whether to delete or print them.

> **TIP** When an error occurs during a print job, Windows 95 tries to determine the cause. For example, the printer might be out of paper, or the printer might be offline or unplugged from the AC outlet. You may be forced to work offline until the problem is resolved. Opening the printers queue should display an error message approximating the nature of the problem to the best of Print Manager's capabilities. Check the printer's File menu to see if the Work Offline setting has been activated. When you think the problem has been solved, turn this setting off to begin printing again.

Canceling All Pending Print Jobs on a Given Printer

Sometimes, because of a megalithic meltdown or some other catastrophe, you'll decide to bail out of all the print jobs that are stacked up for a printer. Normally you don't need to do this, even if the printer has gone wacky. You can just pause the queue and continue printing after the problem is solved. But sometimes you'll want to resend everything to another printer and kill the queue on the current one. It's easy:

1. Select the printer's icon or window.

2. Right-click and choose Purge Print Jobs, or from the printer's window choose Printer ▶ Purge Print Jobs. All queued jobs for the printer are canceled.

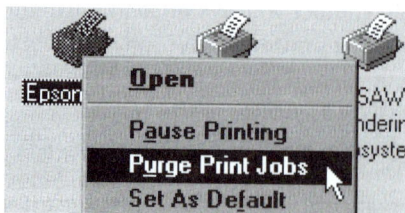

CAUTION   Make sure you really want to cancel the jobs before you do this. This is a good way to make enemies if people on the network were counting on their print jobs being finished anytime soon.

Pausing (and Resuming) the Printing Process

If you're the administrator of a printer with a stack of jobs in the print queue, you can temporarily pause a single job or all jobs on a particular printer at any time. This can be useful for taking a minute to add paper, take a phone call, or have a conversation in your office without the noise of the printer in the background. The next several sections explain the techniques for pausing and resuming.

Pausing or Resuming a Specific Print Job

You can pause documents anywhere in the queue. Paused documents are skipped and subsequent documents in the list print ahead of them. You can achieve the same effect by rearranging the queue, as explained in the section titled *Rearranging the Queue Order*. When you feel the need to pause or resume a specific print job:

1. Click on the document's information line.

2. Choose Document ➤ Pause Printing (or right-click on the document and choose Pause Printing as you see in Figure 8.13). The current print job is temporarily suspended, and the word "Paused" appears in the status area. (The printing might not stop immediately because your printer might have a buffer that holds data in preparation for printing. The printing stops when the buffer is empty.)

3. To resume printing the document, repeat steps 1 and 2 to turn off the check mark next to Pause Printing.

Pausing or Resuming All Jobs on a Printer

In similar fashion, you can temporarily pause all jobs on a given printer. You might want to do this for a number of reasons including:

▶ to load paper or otherwise adjust the physical printer

▶ to alter printer settings from the printer's Properties dialog box

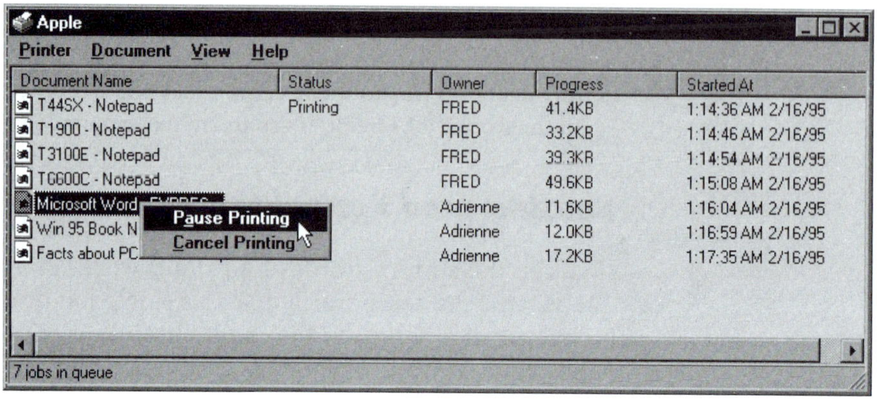

Figure 8.13 *Pause the printing of a single document with the right-click menu. Other documents will continue to print.*

Follow these steps to pause or resume all jobs for a printer:

1. Deselect any documents in the printer's window; press the Spacebar if a document is selected.

2. Choose Printer ➤ Pause Printing. The printer window's title bar changes to say "Paused."

3. To resume all jobs on the printer, choose Printer ➤ Pause Printing again to turn off the check mark next to the command. The *Paused* indicator in the title bar disappears, and printing should resume where the queue left off.

Rearranging the Queue Order

When you have several items on the queue, you might want to rearrange the order in which they're slated for printing.

1. Click on the file you want to move and keep the mouse button depressed.

2. Drag the file to its new location. The name of the document moves to indicate where the document will be inserted when you release the mouse button.

3. When you release the mouse button, your file is inserted in the queue, pushing the other files down a notch (see Figure 8.14).

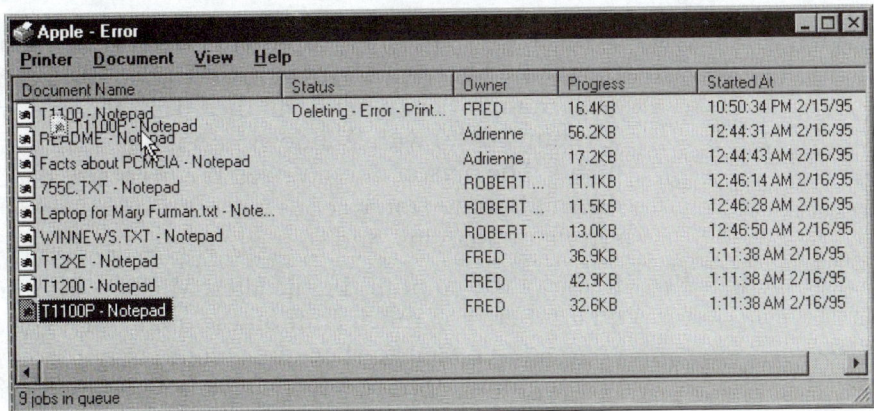

Figure 8.14 *You can shift the order of a document in the queue by dragging it to the desired position and dropping it.*

Printing to a Disk File instead of a Printer

There are times when you may want to print to a disk file rather than to the printer. What does this mean? When you print to a disk file, the codes and data that would normally be sent to the printer are shunted off to a disk file—either locally or on the network. The resulting file typically isn't just a copy of the file you were printing; it contains all the special formatting codes that control your printer. Codes that change fonts, print graphics, set margins, break pages, and add attributes such as underline, bold, and so on are all included in this type of file. Print files destined for PostScript printers typically include their PostScript preamble, too—a special file that prepares the printer to receive the instructions that are about to come and the fonts that are included in the document.

Why would you want to create a disk file instead of printing directly to the printer? Printing to a file gives you several options not available when you print directly to the printer:

▶ Print files are sometimes used by programs for specific purposes. For example, printing a database to a disk file might allow you to more easily work with it in another application. Or you might want to print an encapsulated PostScript graphics file to be imported into a desktop-publishing document.

▶ You can send the file to another person, either on floppy disk or over the phone lines, with a modem and a communications program such as Terminal. That person can then print the file directly to a printer (if it's compatible) with Windows or a utility such as the DOS **copy** command. The person doesn't need the program that created the file and doesn't have to worry about any of the printing details—formatting, setting up margins, and so forth. All that's in the file.

▶ It allows you to print the file later. Maybe your printer isn't hooked up, or there's so much stuff on the queue that you don't want to wait, or you don't want to slow down your computer or the network by printing now. Print to a file, which is significantly faster than printing on paper. Later, you can use the DOS **copy** command or a batch file with a command such as **copy *.prn lpt1 /b** to copy all files to the desired port. This way you can queue up as many files as you want, prepare the printer, and then print them without having to be around. Be sure to use the **/b** switch. If you don't, the first Ctrl-Z code the computer encounters will terminate the print job because the print files are binary files.

In some programs, printing to a disk file is a choice in the Print dialog box. If it isn't, you should modify the printer's configuration to print to a file rather than to a port. Then, whenever you use that printer, it uses all the usual settings for the driver but sends the data to a file of your choice instead of to the printer port.

1. In the Printers folder, right-click on the printer's icon and choose Properties.

2. Select the Details tab page.

3. Under *Print to the following port,* choose FILE:

Print to the following port:

```
LPT1: (Printer Port)          ▼

\\Samson\apple
COM1: (Communications Port)
COM2: (Megahertz CC3144 V.32bis PCMCIA
FAX: (Unknown Local Port)
FILE: (Creates a File on Disk)
LPT1: (Printer Port)
PUB: (Unknown Local Port)
```

4. OK the box. The printer's icon in the Printers folder will change to in-
    dicate that printing is routed to a disk file.

Now when you print a file from any program and choose
this printer as the destination for the printout, you'll be
prompted for a file name.

Epson LX-80

TIP If you want to print the file as ASCII text only, with no special control
codes, you should install the Generic/Text Only printer driver. Then select
that as the destination printer.

TIP If you want to print to an encapsulated PostScript file (`.eps`), print to
a printer that uses a PostScript driver (the Apple LaserWriter or the QMS
PS-810, for instance) or set up a phony printer that uses such a driver. (No
physical printer is needed.) When prompted for a file name, specify an EPS
extension.

Chapter 9

Using Fonts Effectively

FEATURING

One of the most compelling characteristics of Windows—possibly even the single ability that most ensured the acceptance of Windows as *the* PC standard GUI—is the convenience of having a single system for displaying and printing text that works with all Windows programs. Though at the time Windows 3.0 appeared some ordinary MS-DOS programs could display and print high-quality fonts, they have had to rely on a bewildering hodgepodge of different printer drivers and font formats to achieve any success in this arena. Worse yet, each program solved font dilemmas in its own way, not sharing their wealth of fonts or font-management utilities with other MS-DOS programs.

By contrast, Windows programs (especially as of Windows 3.1, when True Type fonts were introduced) need only a single printer driver and one pool of fonts. Thus, Lotus 1-2-3 for Windows, Ami Pro, Paradox, Microsoft Access, Power Point, and Ventura Publisher programs on a Windows system can all share the same fonts and print with them to a number of printers without difficulty. Because fonts are so readily available at this point—in shareware packages, on BBSs, or on those economy CD-ROM packages down at the local computer discount store—getting your paws on some interesting fonts is a cinch.

Like other Windows versions, Windows 95 comes with a set of stock fonts such as Courier New, Times New Roman, and Arial. You may be happy with these relatively banal, though useful, choices and possibly never feel the need to add to them. More likely, though, you'll want to augment these rudimentary fonts with a collection of your favorites to spruce up your documents. In this chapter I'll explain how to add and remove fonts from your system, how to choose and use fonts wisely, ways to procure new fonts, and even how to create fonts of your own.

Font Management in Windows 95

Fonts are highly desirable to most users. Suddenly having the Gutenbergian power to lay out and print aesthetically sophisticated correspondence, books, brochures, newsletters, and the like is one of the great joys of computerdom. But installing, removing, and managing fonts threw a kink in the works for many Windows 3.x users, especially once they installed a zillion fonts and realized how much that slowed down their system. Windows 3.x initially loads much more slowly once you've hyped up your system with a lot of fonts because all the fonts, font names, and font directories have to be checked out and loaded.

Once font-related boondoggles became common knowledge, font-management programs started popping up in the marketplace. These programs improved on the rudimentary Font utility supplied in the Windows 3.x Control Panel. For example, they'd display all your fonts, let you print sample pages of your fonts, manage fonts in groups that could be easily installed and removed from the system, and so on. Some of these packages also had built-in font-conversion capabilities, producing TrueType fonts from other types such as Adobe Type 1 or bit-mapped fonts, and could create novel display type by applying special effects to fonts you already had installed.

Microsoft has included much-improved font management in Windows 95. It's not perfect, but it's better. Choosing Fonts from the Setting menu or My Computer, or selecting the Fonts directory in Explorer will present options such as:

- installing and removing fonts
- viewing on screen or printing an example of each font in various point sizes
- listing only font families rather than each variation of a font, eliminating redundant listings (for instance, Times New Roman, Times New Roman Bold, and Times New Roman Italic)
- listing all fonts similar in appearance to a given font, such as all fonts similar to Arial
- toggling between a listing of actual font file names and the font's common name

What Are Fonts and What Is TrueType?

Fonts are the various type styles that you can use when composing a document, viewing it on the screen, or printing it on paper. Fonts add visual impact to your documents to help you express your words or numbers in a style that suits your audience. They can also increase readability.

As an example of some fonts, Figure 9.1 shows several popular type styles. Fonts are specified by size as well as by name. The size of a font is measured in *points*. A point is $\frac{1}{72}$ of an inch. In addition, fonts styles include **bold,** *italic*, and underlining.

Times New Roman
12 point

Brush Script
33 point

Times New Roman Italic
12 point

Gill Sans
28 point

Shelley Allegro
30 point

Casper Open Face
20 point

Figure 9.1   *Various fonts and point sizes*

Windows comes supplied with a reasonable stock of fonts, some of which are installed on your hard disk and integrated into Windows during the setup procedure. The number and types of fonts installed depend on the type of screen and printer you have. When you install a printer into your Windows setup (see Chapter 8), a printer driver is installed. The printer driver includes a set of basic fonts for your printer.

Some programs, such as word processors, may have additional fonts supplied with them—fonts not included with Windows—that you may want to use. Fonts can also be purchased separately from companies that specialize in typeface design, such as Bitstream, Inc., Adobe Systems, Inc., and Microsoft.

Font packages usually come with their own setup programs, which will automatically install the fonts into your Windows system for you. When installing fonts with these programs, just follow the instruction manual supplied with the font package. If there is no such installation program, use the Control Panel's Fonts applet as explained later in this chapter.

General Classes of Fonts

There are several basic classes of fonts that are used in Windows, and an understanding of them will help you manage your font collection. Windows fonts break down into the following groups:

Screen fonts control how text looks on your screen. They come in predefined sizes, such as 10 points, 12 points, and so forth.

Printer fonts are fonts stored in your printer (in its ROM), stored on plug-in cartridges, or downloaded to your printer by Windows when you print. Downloaded fonts are called *soft fonts*.

Vector fonts use straight line segments and formulas to draw letters. They can be easily scaled to different sizes. These are primarily used on printing devices that only draw lines, such as plotters.

TrueType fonts are generated either as *bitmaps* or as soft fonts, depending on your printer. The advantage of TrueType fonts is that they will print exactly as seen on the screen. (TrueType fonts were first introduced with Windows 3.1 to solve problems associated with differences between how fonts appear on screen and how they print.)

Before Windows 3.1, both printer and screen fonts often had to be added for each type style you wanted to add to your setup. TrueType fonts simplify matters because adding a TrueType font installs both printer and screen fonts simultaneously. In addition, TrueType fonts will look identical (though perhaps with differences in smoothness or resolution) regardless of the printer with which you print them.

When you print a document, Windows checks your printer driver file to see if it includes the fonts you put in the document. If the printer or printer driver does not supply the font, Windows attempts to find a happy solution. In most cases, Windows will handle day-to-day printing jobs just fine. If your printer has a soft font already in it (from plug-in font cartridges or in its ROM) and Windows doesn't have a screen font of that type, Windows will usually substitute another, similar screen font with the correct size for displaying your work on screen. Even though it might not look exactly like the final printout, the line length and page breaks on your screen should be accurate.

About TrueType Fonts

With the addition of TrueType fonts in Windows several years ago, typefaces could be scaled to any size and displayed or printed accurately on virtually all displays and printers—without the addition of any third-party software. And because of the careful design of the screen and printer display of each font, TrueType provides much better WYSIWYG (What You See Is What You Get) capabilities than previous fonts. Furthermore, you no longer have to ensure that you have fonts in your printer that match the fonts on screen.

In the past, if you used a printer like the LaserJet II, you might have been limited to the two fonts that come standard with that printer (Courier and Line Printer). If you wanted to print any other fonts, you had to buy a cartridge containing a few additional fonts, or you had to buy soft fonts. These fonts had to be individually rendered by the vendor in each size that might be required. This was often costly and required a tremendous amount of hard-disk space. If you wanted to display the fonts on screen, you had to create yet another set of screen fonts that matched the printer fonts.

With TrueType, any printer that can print graphics can print the full range of TrueType fonts—all orchestrated by Windows 3.1. And the results will look more or less the same, even on different printers. Although different printers provide different resolutions, the essential characteristics of a TrueType font will remain consistent whether it is printed on a 9-pin dot-matrix printer or a high-resolution image setter.

TrueType also allows users of different computer systems to maintain compatability across platforms. For example, because TrueType is also integrated into System 7, the Macintosh operating system, a document formatted on a Macintosh using TrueType fonts will look exactly the same on a Windows 3.1-equipped PC.

Finally, because TrueType is an integrated component of Windows, any Windows program can make use of TrueType fonts. These fonts can be easily scaled (increased or decreased in size), rotated, or otherwise altered.

TECH TIP   You can only use TrueType fonts if you have a Windows 3.1 or later printer driver.

Comparing TrueType Fonts to Bit-Mapped and Vector Fonts

So much for TrueType fonts. Now let's consider other types of fonts, namely bit-mapped and vector fonts. First let's see how these two kinds of fonts work as screen fonts. Then I'll discuss printer fonts.

NOTE   Recall from the list above that printer fonts are those built into the printer or those sent to the printer by the computer to print a document. Screen fonts are the fonts Windows uses to display text on the screen.

There are two types of screen fonts: bit-mapped and vector. Each is quite different from the other and serves a distinct purpose.

Bit-Mapped Fonts

Bit-mapped fonts are essentially a collection of bitmaps (pictures), one for each character you might want to type. These bitmaps cover the entire character set and range of styles for a particular typeface in a limited number of sizes. Examples of bit-mapped fonts in Windows 3.1 are Courier, MS Serif, MS Sans Serif, and MS Symbol. When you install Windows, these fonts are automatically copied to the appropriate Windows FOLDER by Setup. Windows comes with a number of versions of these fonts. Based on the resolution of your video adapter, Windows chooses the font files that take best advantage of your particular display. Figure 9.2 shows a character map of a bit-mapped font (MS Serif).

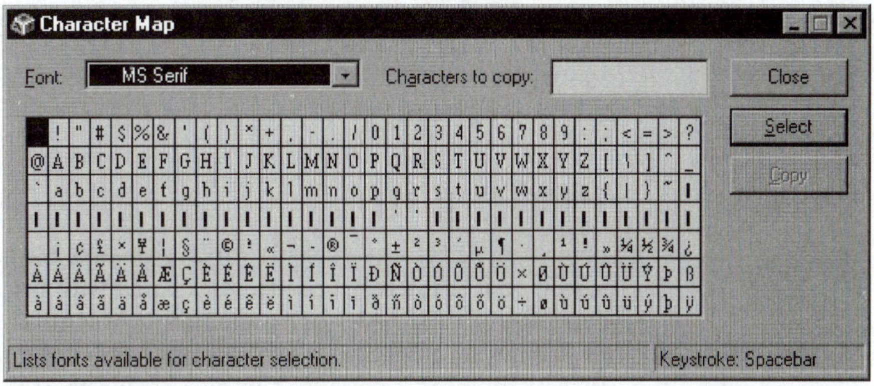

Figure 9.2 *A bit-mapped font*

NOTE   Some of your programs may not display the list of bit-mapped fonts in their Font boxes. They may only show a list of TrueType fonts. This doesn't mean they aren't there, only that your program isn't displaying them. If you try other programs, such as MS Paint (when using the Text tool), you'll see a larger list, including such bit-mapped fonts as MS Serif.

Because bit-mapped fonts are dependent on the bitmaps included in their font files, you are limited to displaying these fonts in the sizes provided or in exact multiples of their original sizes if you want the font to look good. For example, MS Serif for VGA resolution includes bitmaps for display at 8, 10, 12, 14, 18, and 24 points. Opening the Size box for a bit-mapped font will display a limited list of sizes such as this list for Courier:

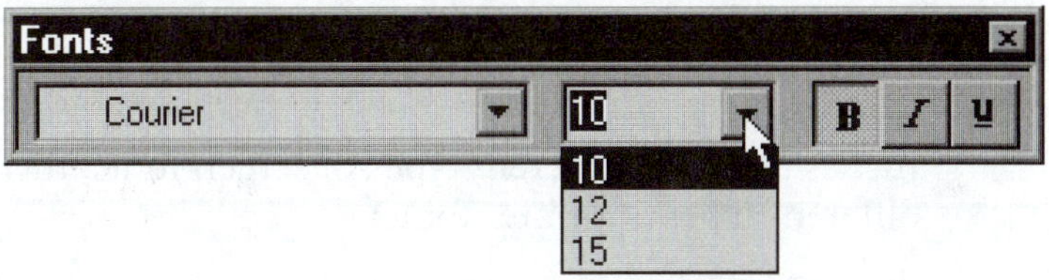

Even though the list of sizes for a bit-mapped font is usually limited, you can type in any number you want. Windows will do its best to scale the font to the approximate size you ask for, but it will likely look pretty icky. There's one exception to this: bit-mapped fonts can scale acceptably to exact multiples. So if 10 is on the list (as in the example above), you could get decent-looking 20-, 30-, or 40-point renditions, although the results will not look as good as a TrueType font at the same size.

Vector Fonts

Vector fonts are more suitable for devices like plotters that can't use bit-mapped characters because they draw with lines rather than dots. Vector fonts are a series of mathematical formulas that describe a series of lines and curves (arcs). They can be scaled to any size, but because of the process involved in computing the shape and direction of the curves, these fonts can be quite time consuming to generate. PostScript fonts are actually vector fonts, but because the PostScript printer itself is optimized to do the computing of the font sizes and shapes, performance is fairly good. Examples of vector fonts are Modern, Roman, and Script.

Variations of Printer Fonts

Just as there are different types of screen fonts, there are also several different types of printer fonts:

▶ device fonts

▶ printable screen fonts

▶ downloadable soft fonts

Device fonts are those fonts installed in your printer, either factory defaults or members of a font-cartridge collection. Printable screen fonts are bit-mapped and vector fonts that can be used not only on screen but also sent to the printer. Downloadable soft fonts are fonts that, like TrueType, are stored on your PC's hard disk and can be sent to the printer as needed. Unlike TrueType fonts, though, they are specific to your printer and are generally provided in limited styles and sizes.

How Does TrueType Work?

TrueType fonts are similar to both bit-mapped and vector fonts. They contain a description of the series of lines and curves for the typeface—like a vector font. When you press a key in a Windows word processor, for example, that application asks Windows to generate the bitmap of the appropriate character in the right font and size at a particular spot on screen. Windows' Graphical Device Interface (GDI) creates a bitmap in memory that best represents that character. But the job of creating the character is only half done.

Like bit-mapped fonts, TrueType fonts include a number of bit-mapped "hints" that help Windows when rendering the font in smaller point sizes. Hints are an extremely important element of TrueType. Because the resolution of a VGA monitor is considerably less than that of a 300-dpi laser printer, many fonts simply don't look right on screen. There just aren't enough pixels to accurately reproduce the font at smaller point sizes.

When Windows displays a character at a small point size, it uses the hinting instructions located in a TrueType font to cheat a bit by reshaping the character so lines or curves aren't missing or misshapen. But hints are not just important for screen display. Look closely at a page of small text generated by your printer. If it prints 300 dots per inch, chances are you'll notice slight imperfections in characters. An *O* may not be perfectly round; the slant of a *W* may not be truly straight. Hinting ensures the highest possible quality of fonts despite the resolution limits of most common output devices.

You may notice that when you select a different font or a new point size that Windows pauses for a moment. During this delay, it creates bitmaps for the entire character set in the new size or style. This happens only once during a Windows session. After first generating the bitmaps, Windows places them into a memory cache where they can be quickly accessed the next time they are required.

> **TIP** If you have a number of documents you created using fonts that you no longer have, you don't need to go through the documents and change your formatting. You can force Windows to substitute appropriate replacements. Load `win.ini` into an editor like Notepad. If you look at the [FontSubstitutes] section of the file, you'll notice lines like `TmsRmn=MS Serif`. Add any associations you like, keeping the old name on the left of the equation and the new name on the right. Windows will automatically fill requests for the old font with the new font.

Elements of TrueType Typography

As discussed earlier, *font* is now used freely to describe a number of different typographical elements. Font is often used to mean the same thing as *typeface*, a group of fonts that are closely related in design. Technically, a font is a specific set of characters, each of which shares the same basic characteristics. For example, Arial is a typeface. In turn, Arial comprises the fonts Arial, Arial Bold, Arial Bold Italic, and Arial Italic. When you pick Arial from your word processor's font dialog box and then choose to italicize text, you are selecting the font Arial Italic.

Basic TrueType Font Families

As with other types of fonts, all TrueType fonts can be generalized into font families. These are a group of typefaces with similar characteristics but that are much more loosely related than the members of a typeface. Windows recognizes five font families: Decorative, Modern, Roman, Script, and Swiss.

The most common of these families are Roman and Swiss. The Roman font family contains the majority of serif fonts. Sans-serif fonts like Arial are generally members of the Swiss family. Figure 9.3 shows fonts from the Roman and Swiss families. (Serifs are discussed below, in *Classes of Font Styles*.)

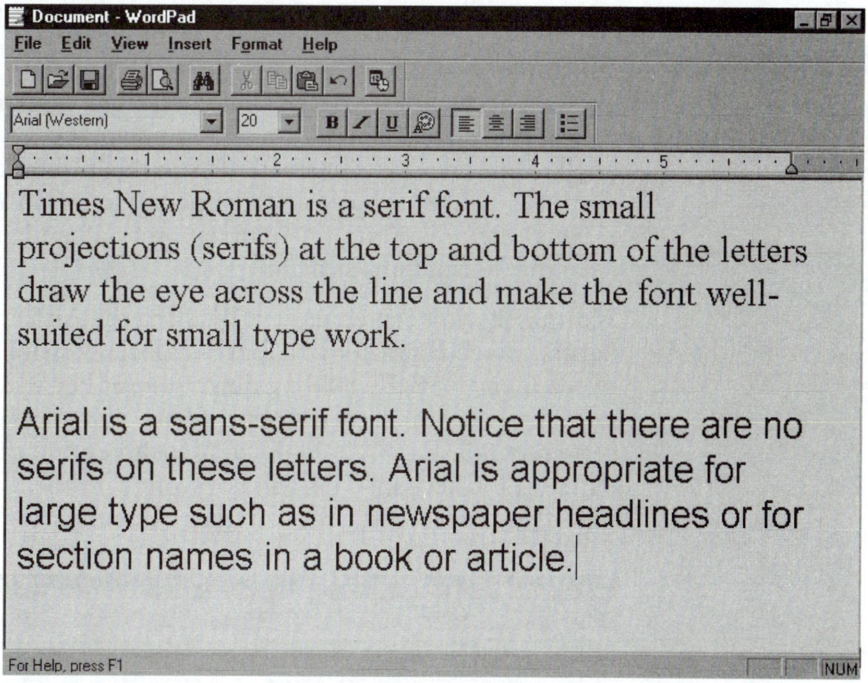

Figure 9.3   *A Roman font (Times New Roman) and a Swiss font (Arial)*

Special Characters

Each TrueType font contains a number of special characters like trademark (™) and yen (¥), punctuation such as the em dash (—) and curly quotes (""), and foreign (æ) and accented (ñ) characters. But Windows 95 also includes two special fonts you should become familiar with: Symbol and WingDings.

Symbol contains a number of mathematical symbols such as not-equal-to (≠) and plus or minus (±). It also contains a complete Greek alphabet for scientific notation.

WingDings is quite a bit more versatile. It contains a wide range of symbols and characters that can be used to add special impact to documents. Instead of printing *Tel.* next to your phone number, why not place a telephone symbol? WingDings includes several religious symbols: a cross, a Star of David, and a crescent and star, as well as several zodiac signs. Figure 9.4 displays all of the characters of these two fonts.

You can access these special characters in several different ways. The easiest is to select WingDings or Symbol in any TrueType-compatible application, then type characters from the keyboard. For example, the universal symbol for *airport* corresponds to a *Q* in WingDings. This method requires a bit of memorization or a handy reference chart to keep the associations straight.

Alternately, you can enter keys by using the Alt key with your numeric keypad. Each character in a font is associated with a numeric value between 0 and 255. By holding down the Alt key while entering that number, you can insert the appropriate character. For example, to insert an em dash (—), hold down the Alt key and press the numbers 0151 on the keypad. This will not work with the number keys at the top of your keyboard, and you must remember to preface the number

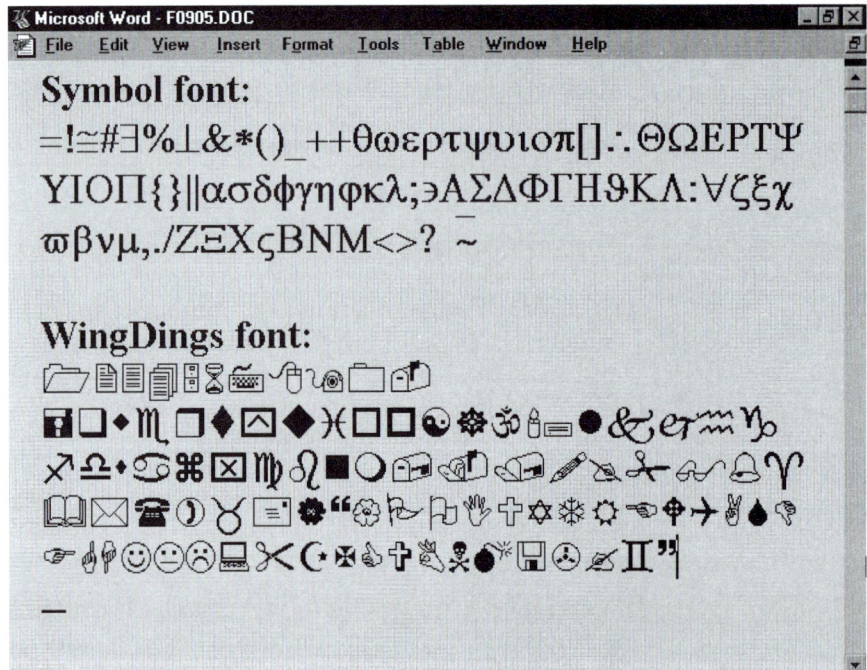

Figure 9.4   *Symbol and WingDings are two TrueType fonts worth checking out. They contain characters you might find useful in your documents. You may even want to use one of these for your personal or corporate logo.*

with a 0. Again, you will need a reference chart for the particular font you're using to take advantage of this method.

> **TIP**   The Fonts option from the Control Panel lets you examine all the characters in a font, too. You can read about that later in this chapter, under *Adding and Removing Fonts Using Control Panel* .

Many word processors include a function called Insert Symbol. This feature allows you to choose a character from a table of all the characters in a particular font. You just highlight the character you want and click on OK (or double-click on the character), and it appears instantly in your document. This is not the quickest way to enter a symbol, but it is the easiest if your word processor offers it. Figure 9.5 shows the Insert Symbol table in Word for Windows 6.0.

If your application lacks an Insert Symbol feature, you can open the Character Map accessory discussed in Chapter 22 and copy the symbols you want to the Clipboard. Then switch back to your application and paste the symbols where you want them. While not the easiest way to insert symbols, this method is adequate for most uses. However, sometimes the font "loses" its font family name when it's copied in this way; once pasted, you may have to select the character and reset its font.

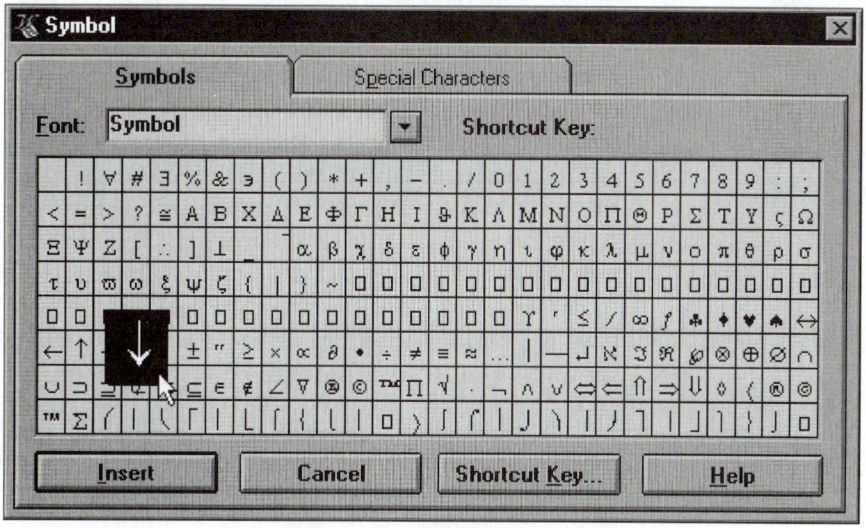

**Part
2**

Exploring Windows 95

Figure 9.5   *A typical Insert Symbol table in a word-processing application*

TrueType Font Embedding

What if you get a document from a friend or a business associate that was formatted with TrueType fonts you don't have on your system? One of the most important features of TrueType is the ability to *embed* fonts in documents. So when you send a document to someone else, the fonts you use go with it.

> **NOTE**   Beware: although Windows itself supports embedded TrueType fonts, not all Windows applications do. Most programs will be able to display embedded TrueType fonts, though an occasional program won't be able to embed them.

When you load a document that contains embedded TrueType fonts, Windows copies those fonts into memory temporarily. They can then be used in conjunction with that document specifically. Depending on the attributes set by the font vendor, a font can have one of three embedding options—read-only embedding, read-write embedding, or no embedding at all.

The most common type of font will most likely be read-only. If you load a document containing read-only fonts—and you don't have those fonts yourself—you will only be able to print or view the document. You won't be able to alter it. This prevents nonowners of a font from using it without paying for it.

However, the fonts supplied by Microsoft in Windows 95 as well as those in Windows 3.x and Microsoft's TrueType Font Pack are read-write fonts. Documents containing these fonts can be printed, viewed, and edited regardless of whether the fonts themselves are installed on the system. Also, Windows provides the ability to save the fonts themselves for use with future documents. Obviously, this approach is not popular with commercial developers who make their livings selling their fonts, but a quick scan of public-domain TrueType fonts that have popped up on online services like CompuServe and GEnie shows that most free fonts are read-write enabled.

On the other end of the spectrum, vendors may choose to disallow embedding of their fonts. If you try to save a document that contains one of these typefaces, your word processor will simply not include the fonts.

Essentially, this would create documents similar to those containing no font information other than the name of the original font.

TrueType's greatest advantage is that it ensures that the fonts you see on screen are the fonts you get on paper. Embedded TrueType takes this one step further by ensuring that the fonts used to create a document are the ones used to view, edit, and print it.

TECH TIP   If when you send another person a document, you want to ensure that he or she will be able to actually edit the document using the fonts you have used to create it, either use popular fonts that all Windows users have on their systems, such as Times New Roman, Arial, or Courier New; or check that your application is set to embed fonts. For example, in Microsoft Word this is done with the Tools ➤ Options menu.

Which Fonts Should I Use?

You can install bit-mapped, vector, and scalable fonts into Windows. But as long as your printer can print graphics and is not a plotter, you should stick to scalable fonts like TrueType and ignore bit-mapped and vector fonts entirely—in fact, you can remove them from your system, as discussed later.

Bit-mapped fonts look good on your screen, but only at the particular size they're designed for; when you display them at another size, they appear distorted and jagged. In addition, because you need one file for every size of a given typeface you want to display, one set of bit-mapped fonts can consume a great deal of valuable territory on your hard disk. It's also inconvenient to keep track of all the files involved.

Vector fonts are worth using only if your output device is a plotter. While the files aren't overly large, and while you can print vector fonts at any size, they have an unattractive, noticeably angular appearance. One plus: vector font files are quite small.

TrueType and other scalable fonts, by contrast, look great when displayed or printed at any size. If you decide that a particular document requires, say, a 13.5-point rendition of Times, all you have to do is request it, and Windows will generate it automatically. Although True-Type font files are fairly large, typically around 60K, you only need one file for each typeface. Font files of other scalable font formats such as Type 1 PostScript and FaceLift tend to be somewhat smaller.

How Your Fonts Get Used by Windows

Most Windows programs that print text let you specify the font you want.

In some cases, as in most word-processing programs, you can change fonts with every text character, while other programs restrict you to one font for each block of text or field or impose some other limitation. For example, in the accessory program Paint, once text is laid into a picture, its font can't be altered.

Ideally, Windows should let you select only from the fonts your printer can actually print. Unfortunately, this isn't always the case if you install more than one printer driver. In this situation, many Windows programs offer you all the fonts available with every installed printer driver, leaving it to you to figure out which ones are appropriate for your printer. Or they might switch the list of fonts available when you change the default printer to a new printer, but a list of MRU (most recently used) fonts may still display fonts from the previous default printer. Word 6 has such a list at the top of its font list.

All the fonts above the double line are recently used fonts.

In any case, once you've chosen a font, what you see on the screen depends on the class in which the font falls. If you've selected a True-Type or other scalable font, Windows will generate the appropriate screen font for you so you'll always get a close match between the screen and the final printout. On the other hand, if you're using a nonscalable font, Windows must look for a screen font that corresponds to the one you'll be printing with. If it can't find a match, Windows will substitute the most similar screen font it can find. Depending on the font you've chosen and your screen font collection, this substitute screen font may not look anything like the printed version. Nevertheless, at least the line lengths and page breaks you see on your screen will be accurate.

When you print the document, Windows checks your printer driver file and the win.ini file, looking for the fonts you specified. If the fonts exist, Windows will know whether they're already resident in the printer or must be scaled or downloaded from the hard disk. If a font is missing, Windows will again make an effort to substitute a similar one.

Building a Font Collection

Windows comes with a set of very attractive TrueType fonts that will serve you well in most situations, whether you're writing letters, preparing reports or grant proposals, or adding text to charts or graphics. So why buy more fonts?

Broadly stated, the reason to enlarge your font collection is simple: to improve your ability to communicate. Typographers claim the fonts you use can influence the impact of your message on your readers, even if they're not consciously aware of their reactions. With more fonts to work with, you'll be better able to select ones that suit the mood of whatever document you're preparing. Some fonts, such as Bodoni or Times New Roman, have a decidedly formal appearance, ideal for serious business correspondence. But these same fonts are just too stuffy for a letter to a friend; for this you'd be better off using a font with a casual look, such as Dom Casual or Tekton.

In addition, looking beyond the stock Windows fonts helps you create an identifiable style for your printed documents. Like a logo, the typefaces you choose become associated with you or your business in the minds of those who read your documents regularly. Using the same typeface that everyone else does will make it harder to establish your own typographic identity.

What About Other Scalable Type Alternatives?

TrueType fonts are the most convenient kind of scalable fonts for anyone who uses Windows because TrueType technology is built right into the Windows environment. However, you have several other choices in scalable-font formats.

TrueType's biggest competitor is the Type 1 or PostScript format. Type 1 fonts produce very high quality screen fonts and printed output. Vast numbers of fonts are available in the Type 1 format from many different manufacturers, including some of the most respected typographic houses, and they cover an extremely wide range of beautiful designs.

NOTE PostScript fonts used with Adobe Type Manager are referred to as Type 1 fonts to distinguish them from another PostScript font format, Type 3. Don't get Type 3 fonts unless you have a PostScript printer or a way to convert them to Type 1.

Since the release of Windows 3.1, TrueType has become very popular, even to the point of being implemented widely on the Macintosh. Although the selection of TrueType fonts was limited only a few years ago, this is no longer the case. Still, there is at least one other reason to consider using Type 1 fonts instead of TrueType fonts: PostScript is still the established standard for very high resolution typesetting devices used in professional publishing. If you stick with Type 1 fonts, you can use the exact same fonts for printing drafts on a desktop laser printer and outputting final typeset copy on a Linotronic or other digital typesetter. This means you can be confident that, aside from lower resolution, your draft will look exactly like your final document.

To use Type 1 fonts to your best advantage, you need a utility program called Adobe Type Manager (ATM). ATM scales Type 1 fonts to the requested size faster than Windows does. It also provides a number of useful options for handling the fonts that you don't get with Windows' built-in font manager.

Other scalable font choices for Windows are less attractive, though you might want to consider them in special circumstances. If you have access to a library of fonts in another scalable font format, it may make sense to purchase a font-scaling utility that allows you to use your font collection with Windows. Like ATM, other font-scaling utilities take over from Windows the job of creating the correctly sized final fonts for the screen and printer.

The runner-up font-scaling utility with the broadest appeal for Windows users is probably Intellifont-for-Windows (by Hewlett-Packard). It works with the Intellifont scalable-font format designed for the LaserJet III family of printers. If you have a LaserJet III, IIID, or IIISi and use Intellifont fonts with your non-Windows programs, it may make sense to use Intellifont-for-Windows and stick with a single set of fonts.

Another choice is Bitstream's FaceLift. Although FaceLift produces high-quality output, the only reason to prefer it to TrueType is if you have already purchased a large FaceLift font library for use with the non-Windows programs that require this format.

SuperPrint (by Zenographics) is the Rosetta stone of font-scaling utilities. It works interchangeably with most of the major font formats—including Type 1, FaceLift, Intellifont, Fontware, and Nimbus Q—although reviews have judged output quality to be lower than that from ATM or FaceLift. As a bonus, SuperPrint speeds up Windows graphics printing significantly and allows you to print sophisticated graphics on non-PostScript printers.

Finally, if you have a limited font budget, consider Publisher's Power-pak for Windows (by Atech Software) and MoreFonts (by Micro-Logic Software, Inc.). The fonts that work with them are much, much less expensive than most TrueType, Type 1, and FaceLift fonts.

NOTE   As of this writing, all of these products were available in versions for Windows 3.11 but had not yet been rewritten for Windows 95. Though Windows 3.11 versions may work correctly under Windows 95, you should acquire up-to-date versions.

Choosing Specific Fonts

Once you've settled on the font format you're going to use, your next task is to decide which specific fonts to buy. The number of typeface designs available for Windows totals in the thousands and is still growing. With that much variety, selecting a set of fonts that's right for you can be a daunting proposition.

For this reason, it makes sense to stick to the tried-and-true favorites of typographic professionals when you're starting to build a font library. Figure 9.6 offers a few suggestions; you can't go wrong with any of the fonts shown here. Another simple solution is to buy one of the font sets available from vendors such as Adobe Systems and Monotype. Each of these packages comes with several fonts chosen for a specific type of document, along with design tips for using the fonts appropriately.

Classes of Font Styles

As Figure 9.6 suggests, fonts can be classified into various styles, or looks, too. Even if you choose your fonts from a style chart, such as Figure 9.6, a basic understanding of the classifications is a good idea before you start buying fonts and designing your own documents.

The simplest division in the font kingdom is between serif and sans-serif designs. As a look at the table will show you, serifs are the little bars or lines that extend out from the main parts of the characters. A

Serif typefaces for body text

Baskerville   Caslon
Garamond   Palatino

Sans-serif faces for general use

Futura   Gill Sans
Optima   Univers

Display and decorative faces

Benguiat   Bernhard Modern
LITHOS   Peignot

Figure 9.6   *The typefaces in the top two groups are proven designs that work well in many types of documents. To be safe, start with these faces. It's more difficult to recommend display faces because you must choose them carefully for the particular mood you want to convey. Still, they are high-quality designs, popular among professional designers, and they cover a considerable range of moods.*

sans-serif font lacks these lines. It's important to choose a few fonts from each category because almost any combination of a serif and a sans-serif font will look good together, but two sans-serif or two serif fonts will clash.

Another simple classification for fonts depends on the space allotted to each character. In a *monospaced* font, every character occupies the same amount of space in the horizontal dimension. That is, an *i* takes up just as much room on a line of text as a *w*. In a *proportionally spaced* font, characters occupy differing amounts of space. Proportional fonts are easier to read and allow you to fit more text in a given space. (The typefaces in this book are proportional.) The only reason to use monospaced fonts is when you're printing reports or tables in which the alignment of columns is determined by spaces (by pressing the space-bar on the keyboard).

NOTE The numerals in most proportionally spaced fonts are monospaced, allowing you to line up columns of numbers easily.

Still another way to classify fonts has to do with their intended purpose, such as for:

▶ body text

▶ headlines

▶ ornamental special effects

▶ nonalphabetic symbols

Body fonts have highly legible characters and work well for long blocks of text. Although any body-text font can be used for titles and headlines, display or headline fonts are specifically meant for that purpose (such as those used in this book). They boast stronger, more attention-getting designs, but for that reason don't work well for body text.

Two remaining font types—*ornamental* and *display* fonts—aren't shown in Figure 9.6 because they don't have universal application. The distinction between ornamental (or novelty) fonts and display fonts is arbitrary. Still, the idea is that an ornamental font is so highly stylized that it might distract the reader's attention from your message. Use ornamental fonts with care when you want to set a special mood. Symbol or pi fonts contain special symbols such as musical notes, map symbols, or decorations instead of letters, numbers, and punctuation marks, as explained earlier.

Procuring Fonts

The explosion of interest in typography generated by desktop-publishing technology has, in turn, resulted in a proliferation of font vendors. Even Microsoft is offering its TrueType Font Pack, a $99 collection of 44 fonts designed by the same group that produced Arial, Courier New, and Times New Roman—the TrueType fonts included with Windows 95.

Many other leading font vendors, including Bitstream and SWFTE, have brought out TrueType versions of their font collections. You can find these in most software stores. Shareware sources of TrueType fonts abound. Be aware though, that not all TrueType fonts have sophisticated hinting built in and may not look as good as fonts from the more respectable font foundries. Also, some users report that badly formed TrueType fonts can sometimes wreak havoc on your system.

If you're looking for fonts on the cheap side, check out one of your local BBSs or an online service like CompuServe or GEnie. The Windows sections of these networks hold a number of free fonts that are yours for the taking. Many of the fonts are PostScript Type 1 fonts that have been converted to TrueType. The quality of these fonts is generally not as good as the commercial fonts, but in most cases, you'll be hard-pressed to notice the difference. I've seen numerous cheapie CD-ROMs that pack hundreds of TrueType fonts on them in several computer stores.

Adding and Removing Fonts Using Control Panel

Now that you have the basics of fonts under your belt, let's get down to the business of managing and maintaining your font collection. As mentioned earlier, the Control Panel's Fonts applet (also available from Explorer if you display the \Windows\Fonts directory) is the tool for the job. The Fonts applet lets you:

▶ add fonts to your system so your programs can use them

▶ remove any fonts you don't use, freeing disk space

▶ view fonts on screen or print out samples of each font you have

▶ display groups of fonts that are similar in style

Adding Fonts

If no installation program came with your fonts or if you want to add some TrueType fonts to your system that you downloaded from some BBS or otherwise acquired, here's how to do it.

1. Run Control Panel by clicking on Start ➤ Settings ➤ Control Panel.

2. Double-click on the Fonts icon. A window now appears as shown in Figure 9.7. All your installed fonts appear in a folder window that

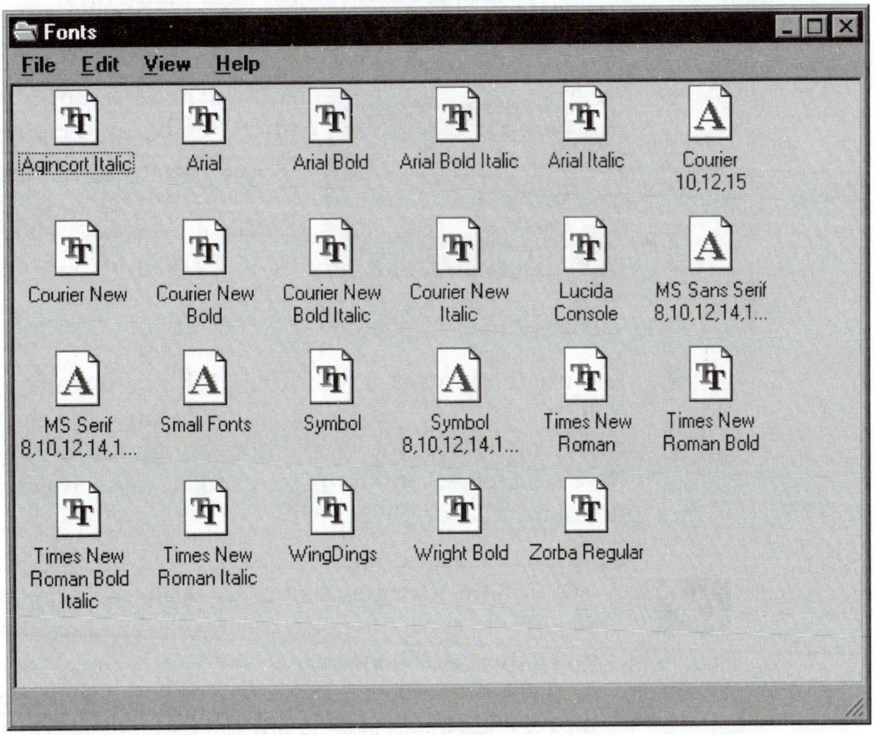

Figure 9.7 *All of your installed fonts are displayed when you choose Fonts from the Control Panel. Because fonts are actually files, they appear the same way other files on your disks do. The TrueType fonts have the TT icon. The fonts with the A icon are bit-mapped or vector fonts.*

looks like any other folder. (This is a departure from Windows 3.x, which had a nonstandard Font dialog box.) You can choose the form of the display from the View menu as with any other folder, too. There are a couple of extra menu options, though, as you'll see.

> **NOTE**   If you have installed special printer fonts for your particular printer, these fonts may not appear in the Fonts folder. They will still appear on font menus in your programs. They just won't show up in the Fonts folder because they probably aren't stored in that folder.

> **NOTE**   Bit-mapped and vector fonts are stored on disk in files with the extension .fon; TrueType font files have the extension .ttf.

3. Open the File menu and choose the Install New Font option.

A file dialog box appears, as shown in Figure 9.8. Choose the correct drive and directory where the fonts are stored. Typically the fonts you'll be installing are on a CD-ROM or on a floppy disk drive, so you'll have to select the correct drive by clicking on the drive selector.

4. Choose the fonts you want to add. If you want to select more than one, extend the selection by Shift-clicking (to select a range) or Ctrl-clicking (to select individual noncontiguous fonts). Noticed that I have selected several fonts to install at once. If you want to select them all, click on Select All.

> **NOTE**   If the fonts you want to install are on a network drive somewhere, you have to choose the correct network drive from the Drive list. If the drive isn't in the list, this means you have to *map* the network drive to a local hard-disk name (D, E, F, and so forth) by clicking on Network and filling in the resulting box (mapping drives is covered in Part V).

5. When fonts are installed, they're normally copied to the \Windows \Fonts directory. However, font files are pretty large. If the fonts you're installing are already on your hard disk in another folder, you

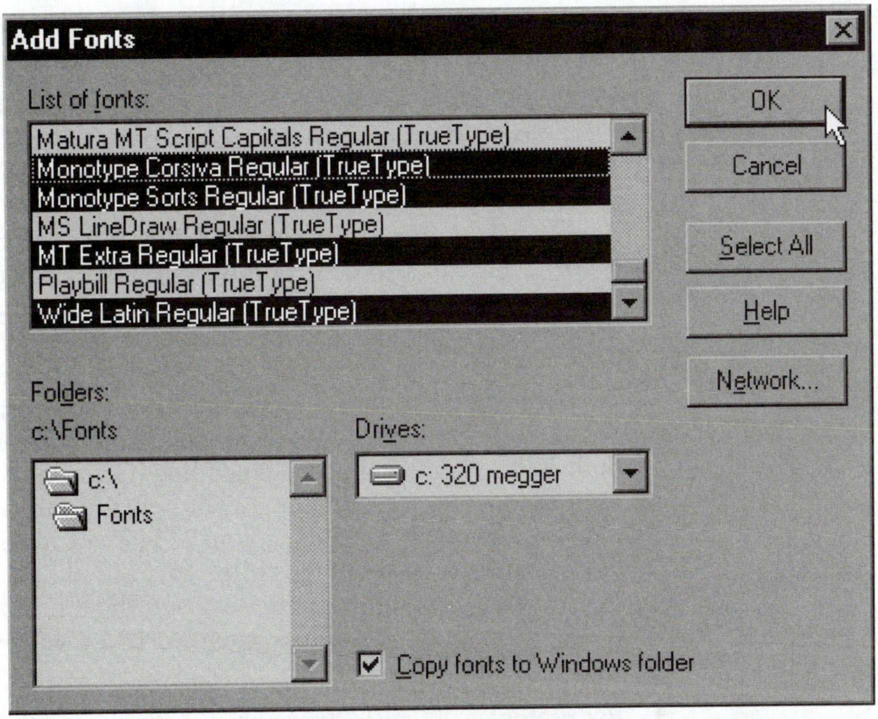

Figure 9.8 *Choose the drive, directory, and fonts you want to install. Consider whether you want the fonts copied into the Windows font directory, typically* \Win- dows\Fonts. *You can select multiple fonts to install at once, using the Shift and Ctrl keys.*

might want to leave them in their current home, especially if your hard disk is low on space. If this is the case, turn off the Copy Fonts to Windows Folder check box. The fonts will still be installed, but they'll be listed in the Fonts folder with shortcut icons rather than normal font file icons.

> **TIP** You should *not* turn off this box if the files are being installed from a CD-ROM, a floppy, or from another computer on the network (unless the network drive is always going to be available). You'll want the fonts on your own hard disk so they'll always be available.

6. Click on OK. The font(s) will be added to your font list, available for your Windows applications.

If you try to install a font that's already in your system, the installer won't let you, so don't worry about accidentally loading one you already have.

TrueType Options

As mentioned above, TrueType fonts take up a fair amount of disk space. They can also be slower to print than fonts that are built into your printer. For example, PostScript printers often have 35 or so built-in fonts that are very similar to popular TrueType fonts like Courier, Times New Roman, and Arial. If you use the basic cast of TrueType fonts a lot, you may be able to speed your print jobs by telling Windows 95 to use a font-substitution table that uses the printer's built-in fonts rather than downloading TrueType fonts to the printer each time you print something. The substitution table will, for example, use the internal Helvetica font in place of the TrueType font Arial. Line breaks and page appearance should print as you see them on the screen, though minute details of the font may differ a bit. Some other kinds of printers, such as HP LaserJet's for example, have TrueType options too.

For examples of typical dialog boxes with options that affect TrueType printing, study Figure 9.9. It shows the TrueType options for a PostScript printer (such as an Apple Laserwriter) and for an HP LaserJet IV.

These dialog boxes are reached via the Printers folder. Open the folder, right-click on a printer, choose Properties, and then choose the Fonts tab.

NOTE Font options will vary from printer to printer, depending on the printer driver. Some printers won't even have a font tab page.

TIP Normally you will do just fine by not even adjusting the settings in these boxes. If you are curious, you can click on the buttons such as the Edit Substitution Table button or Send Fonts As button. You'll see a lot of options, many of which may be confusing at first. You can always click on the ? button on the title bar of the dialog box, then on the item in question to learn about the options. Some interesting bits of information about the options will pop up, including advice about how best to set them.

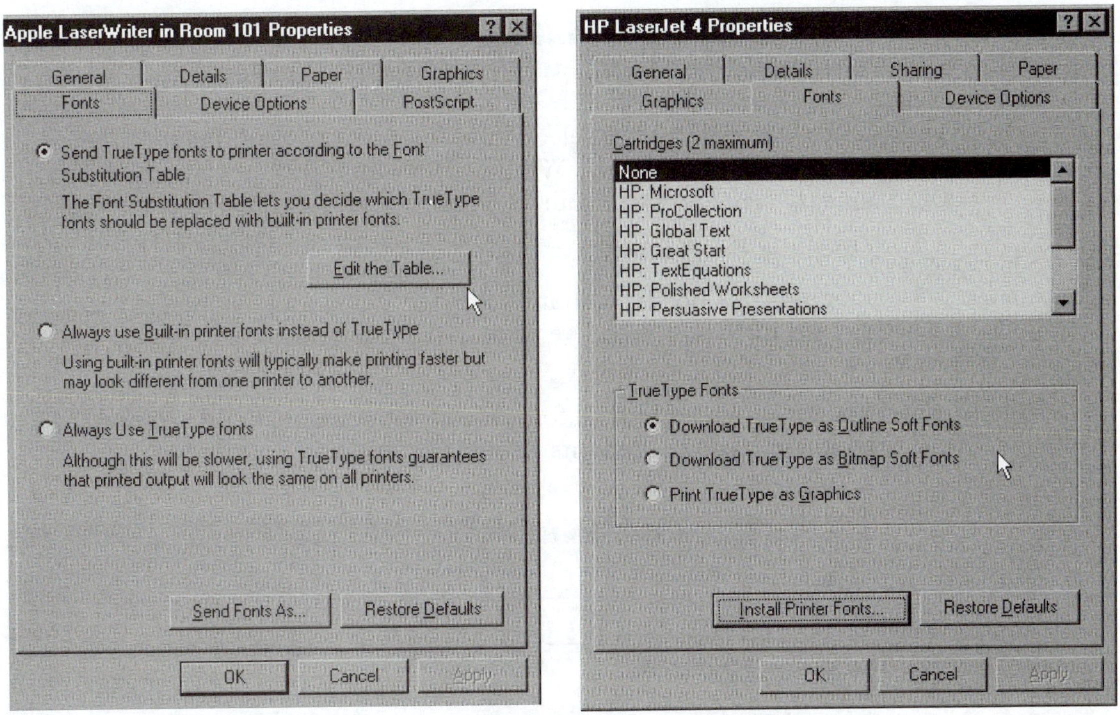

Figure 9.9   *Options for TrueType printing are available for some printers. Setting these correctly can speed up printing. As a rule, these settings have already been optimized when you install Windows 95.*

One last point about TrueType font options: in Windows 3.x, the Fonts applet in the Control Panel gave you two systemwide options controlling TrueType fonts. You could disable TrueType fonts to economize on RAM usage, and you could elect to show only True-Type fonts in your applications, eliminating confusion on the font menus by hiding vector and bit-mapped fonts. Both of these options have been dropped in Windows 95, mostly because of improvements in Windows 95's memory management and the standardization of TrueType fonts industrywide. Windows 95 just doesn't bog down as much when TrueType fonts are enabled, and because the majority of Windows machines these days are using TrueType fonts, disabling other fonts isn't as advantageous as it once was.

Displaying and Printing Examples of Fonts with the Font Viewer

Once you have a large selection of fonts, it can be difficult to remember what each looks like. Windows 95's built-in font viewer provides an easy way to refresh your memory.

1. Open the Fonts folder.

2. Double-click on any icon in the folder. The font will open in the font viewer. In Figure 9.10 I've displayed a font called Desdemona and maximized the window.

3. You can open additional fonts in the same manner and arrange the windows to compare fonts to one another.

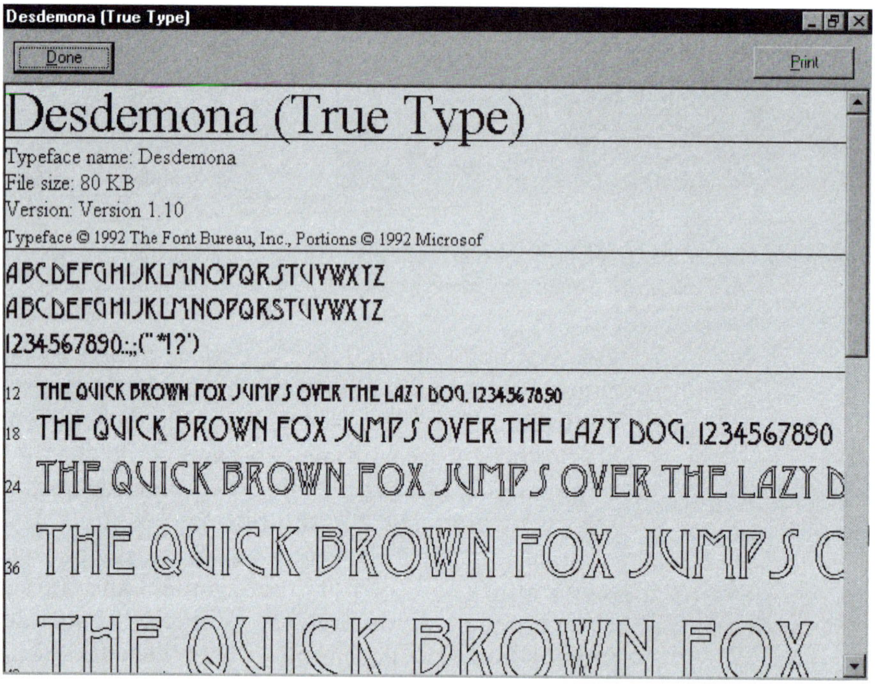

Figure 9.10   *The font viewer kicks in when you double-click on any font in the Fonts folder. The small numbers in the left margin indicate what point size is displayed to the right. Information about the font's maker appears in the upper portion of the window.*

4. Sometimes it's useful to have a printout of a font. You can compile a hard-copy catalog of all your fonts for easy reference if you work with a healthy stable of fonts regularly. To print a single font, double-click on it and click on Print (or right-click on it and choose Print).

> **TIP** To print all your fonts (or multiple fonts) in one fell swoop, select them in the Fonts window with Edit ➤ Select All. Then choose File ➤ Print (or right-click on one of the selected icons and choose Print). You'll get a one-page printout for each font.

> **TIP** Actually, the font viewer will work from any directory. So, if you have a floppy with some fonts you're thinking of installing but you want to see each font first, just open the floppy disk folder and double-click on the fonts one at a time.

> **TIP** Like other objects in Windows 95, fonts have properties. Right-click on a font's icon and choose Properties to view details about the font's size, creation date, location, type, DOS attribute settings, and so forth. Chapter 11 discusses object properties in detail.

Viewing Font Families

Each variation on a typeface is stored in a separate file. That means a separate font file is required for normal, bold, italic, and bold italic versions of each font.

When you're viewing the contents of the Fonts folder, it can be helpful to see only one icon per font family instead of four. This way, you can see more clearly and quickly just which fonts you have. To do this, open the View menu and choose Hide Variations:

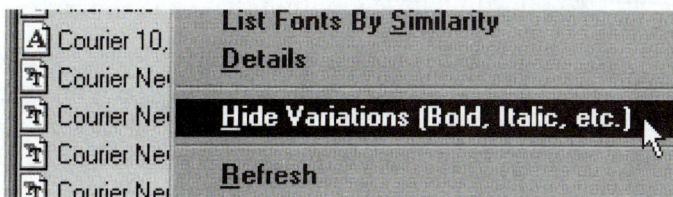

Try it with your fonts and notice how it clears up the display. Unless all four files required for a complete font family are installed, a name won't appear in the listing now. So, if you've installed only Garamond Bold but not Garamond, Garamond Italic, and Garamond Bold Italic, you won't see Garamond listed at all. You will still see an icon for the one type you installed, but such icons won't be named. Double-clicking on an unnamed icon will still display the font in the font viewer so you can identify it.

To return the view to showing all font files listed separately, choose the command again to toggle the check mark off in the menu.

Viewing Fonts by Similarities

Many TrueType fonts contain within them something called *Panose* information. Panose information helps Windows 95 classify a font by indicating a font's general characteristics, such as whether it is a serif or sans-serif font. Based on this information, Windows 95 can group together fonts that will appear somewhat similar on screen and when printed. It can be a boon to have Windows 95 list the fonts that are similar in look to, say, Arial, in case you're looking for an interesting sans-serif font that everyone hasn't seen already.

> **NOTE**   Some older TrueType fonts, as well as all bit-mapped and vector fonts, won't have Panose information stored in them. This is also true of symbol fonts, such as WingDings and Symbol. The font folder will simply display *No Panose information available* next to the font in this case.

To list fonts according to similarity:

1. Open the Fonts folder, one way or another. You can do this most easily from the Control Panel, as described earlier, or from Explorer.

2. Choose View ➤ List Fonts by Similarity. If the folder's toolbar is turned on, you'll have a button that will render the same effect.

3. The folder window will change to include column headings and a drop-down list. The list box is for choosing which font will be the model to which you want all the others compared. Open this list box and choose the desired font. The font must be one endowed with Panose information, otherwise Windows 95 will have nothing with which to compare other fonts. The results will look like Figure 9.11.

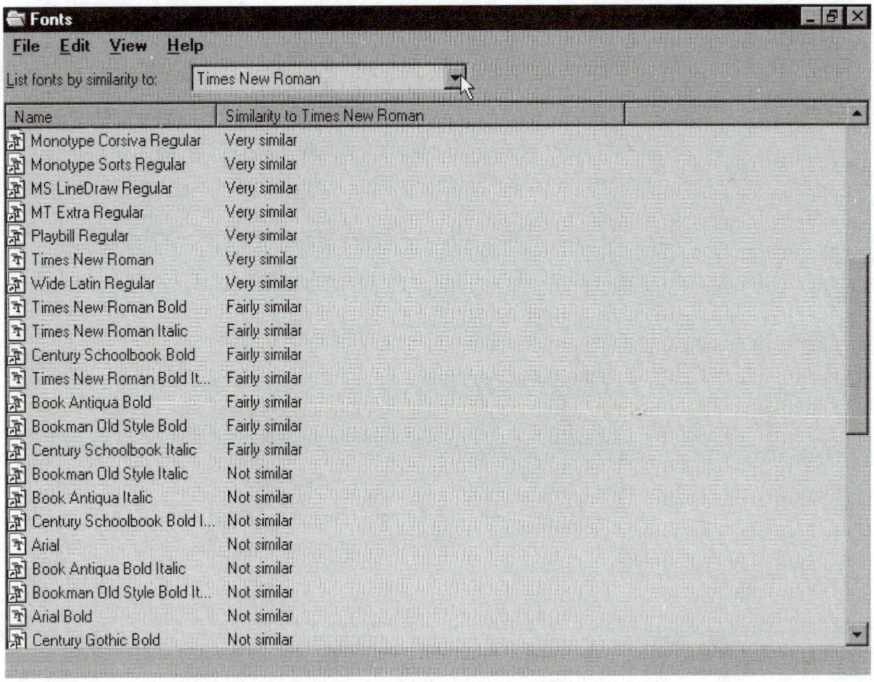

Figure 9.11   Font listing by similarity. Notice three categories of similarity: Very similar, Fairly
similar, and Not similar.

4.   You may want to turn off the Hide Variations setting on the View
     menu to eliminate unnamed icons in the window.

Removing Fonts

Fonts consume space on your hard disk. A typical TrueType font consumes between 50 and 100K (one thousand bytes) of disk space. Deleting individual fonts or font sets increases the available memory in
your computer, letting you run more programs and open more documents simultaneously. If you are having memory-limitation problems,
you could gain some room by eliminating fonts you never use. If you
never use the Italics versions of some fonts, for example, you might
want to remove the Italic and Bold Italic versions specifically, leaving
the normal version installed. A little-known fact is that even if an italic
or bold font has been removed, Windows 95 can still emulate it on the
fly. It won't look as good as the real thing, but it will work.

To remove a font, follow these steps:

1. Open the Fonts folder. All the installed fonts are displayed.

2. To remove an entire font family (normal, Bold, Italic, and Bold Italic), turn on the View ➤ Hide Variations setting. If you want to remove individual styles, turn this setting off so you can see them.

3. Select the font or fonts you want to remove.

4. Choose File ➤ Delete or right-click on one of the selected fonts and choose Delete.

> **CAUTION**   Don't remove the MS Sans Serif font set; it's used in all the Windows dialog boxes.

5. A dialog box asks you to confirm the removal. Choose the Yes button. The font is moved to the Recycle Bin.

> **CAUTION**   You shouldn't remove or install fonts just by dragging them from and to the Fonts folder. Using the Install command from the File menu ensures that the fonts will be registered properly in the Windows 95 Registry and the internal list of fonts that applications draw on for displays in their menus and dialog boxes. Always use the Install New Font command to add fonts and the Delete command to remove them.

Some Basic Guidelines for Using Fonts

Whether you rely on the fonts supplied with Windows or put together a sizable font collection, you should follow a few simple guidelines when formatting your documents. Attractive fonts by themselves aren't enough—the chief goal is readability:

▶ Allow plenty of space between lines. The space between two lines of text should be about 20 percent greater than the size of the font. Thus, if you're using a 12-point font, you should set the line spacing or *leading* to 14 points. This guideline doesn't hold true for headlines, in which the line spacing should usually be about the same as the font size.

▶ Don't mix too many fonts in one document. It's often best to stick with one font for the main body of your text and a larger, bold version of the same font for headlines. If you want to mix fonts, use a serif font for the body of your text and a sans serif for the headlines, or vice versa. You can get away with using a third font for sidebar text, but you'll run the risk of clashing font designs.

▶ If you use two or more font sizes, be sure they contrast adequately. If your main text is in 12-point Times New Roman, use at least 14-point type for the subheadings.

▶ Use italics or boldface type to indicate emphasis. Avoid underlining and capitalizing letters, both of which make it harder to read your text.

▶ Make your margins generous. One of the most common mistakes that causes an amateurish-looking document is text that crowds too closely to the edge of the paper. Allow plenty of space between columns as well.

Following these few guidelines will help you avoid the most glaring errors of document layout. For more detailed advice, consult your bookstore or library for treatises on the topic of desktop publishing or graphic and printing design.

Deleting Font Files from Your Hard Disk

While a variety of high-quality fonts can definitely lend a professionally typeset look to your printed documents and make it easier to understand the information on your screen, a big font collection isn't necessary to run Windows. In fact, you don't even need all the fonts that come with Windows.

In Windows 3.x there were three critical system fonts you had to have on your hard disk; Windows simply wouldn't work if you deleted certain important fonts used in dialog boxes, menus, and DOS boxes. In Windows 95, because you can use TrueType fonts for just about every aspect of a window, including DOS boxes, you can bag any fonts you're not using. Remember, however, that I don't just mean fonts you're not using in your documents; your Windows 95 screen display (set or checked via the Control Panel's Display applet) uses fonts as well. But if disk space is at a premium and the appearance of your text isn't critical for the work you do with Windows, you can remove unused fonts from your Windows setup, saving valuable disk space in the process.

Using Control Panel's Fonts applet, you can remove all the fonts you find unnecessary from your Windows installation and delete their files on disk at the same time. The procedure is detailed in *Removing Fonts* in Chapter 5. However, I recommend you keep at least the fonts that have the *A* icon (bit-mapped fonts)—such as all the ones that start with *MS*, as in MS-Sans Serif—in the dialog box because various error dialog boxes and some programs will use these from time to time. If they are missing, Windows 95 will substitute a system font that you may find harder to read.

After removing all the fonts from the Control Panel list, you can then check your disk for any remaining `.fon` or `.ttf` files. They may be scattered around in different directories. You can use Start ➤ Find to assist you in the search.

Font Utility Programs

If you are a font nut, you might like to know about a few classes of font programs that can assist you in managing and expanding your type library. This section describes some of them.

Managing Large Numbers of Fonts

Font aficionados and typography professionals typically have no trouble acquiring a bevy of typestyles that range from the sublime to the absurd. The upside of this method is that you'll always have just the right typestyle available when you need it. But managing hundreds of fonts can be tedious, and Windows' performance can be negatively impacted if you have a large number of fonts installed in the system and active at one time. Windows start-up time can become sluggish, and some applications may also be bogged down by too many installed fonts. Aside from performance issues, scrolling through a gargantuan font list in your word-processing program just to find a common font such as Times New Roman is a nuisance. If you have a healthy font collection (more than 50 fonts), you'll want to lay your hands on a good font-organizer program. There are a number of programs on the market for Windows 3.x as of the time of this writing, and those for Windows 95 are appearing.

TECH TIP   Some Windows 3.x font-utility programs expect to find fonts in the `\Windows\System` directory. Windows 95 now places fonts in the `\Windows\Fonts` directory, which could throw a wrench into some font-manager programs. You should contact the manufacturer of a font-utility program about its compatibility with Windows 95 before purchasing or using it.

Although there are shareware font managers available that you might hunt around for if you're on a budget, Ares Software's FontMinder at $79 probably offers the most attractive commercial font-management product. In fact, Ares provides just about anything you could want in the way of font utilities. But I'll get to that later.

Ares FontMinder gives you several advantages over manually managing font installation and removal. First, it lets you preview fonts and print type samples before loading them onto your hard disk. Second, you can create font *packs*—predefined groups of fonts that can contain any number of fonts in the TrueType or PostScript Type 1 format. A single font can be included in any number of font packs without duplicating the font file itself. Typically, a professional would have font packs associated with a given design job or area of work, such as word processing, database, spreadsheet, CAD, and so forth. Once packs are set up, FontMinder lets you install or uninstall them on the fly (without having to reboot Windows). Most applications will recognize the changes to the system font arsenal as they occur. You can even associate a font pack with a given document so installing the pack automatically launches the application and document (such as a design job), ready to go to work. A font pack can be moved to a floppy disk, too, so you can take it to a service bureau in preparation for typesetting.

As discussed above, Windows 95's Font Viewer lets you print out samples. But the printout is rather pedestrian. FontMinder prints six different styles of font summary pages, including complete characters sets, font capabilities, sample text in a variety of user-definable sizes, and a "family" page showing columns of each font in the family (bold, italic, and so on). You can easily print batches of font samples (something I've had trouble getting Windows 95 to do).

As another benefit, you can sort all your fonts, arranged by six preset categories: serif, sans serif, script, monospaced, symbol, and decorative. If a font isn't already assigned to a category, you can add it using the included properties editor. You can create additional custom categories should you need to.

Finally, because so many people in the document-design field work on a LAN, a Network Administrator option for FontMinder is designed to help control and manage burgeoning font libraries on client/server networks. TrueType, PostScript Type 1, and PostScript multiple master fonts can be controlled on three different levels of network support, depending on your needs. The upshot is that management of shared fonts over the network is possible, eliminating unnecessary duplication of fonts and the resulting loss of disk space.

NOTE   Some fonts are copyrighted and not in the public domain. It is illegal to copy and use these fonts without buying them or buying site licenses for them.

The other primary font-management program of note is called FontHandler, from Qualitype. This program also lets you set up packs (groups) of predefined fonts and subgroups of fonts, much like the Explorer has folders and subfolders. It provides an elegant means for viewing, printing, searching for, installing and uninstalling, and viewing details about each of your fonts. Four different sample page styles can be printed. Figure 9.12 shows one of the installed fonts being displayed.

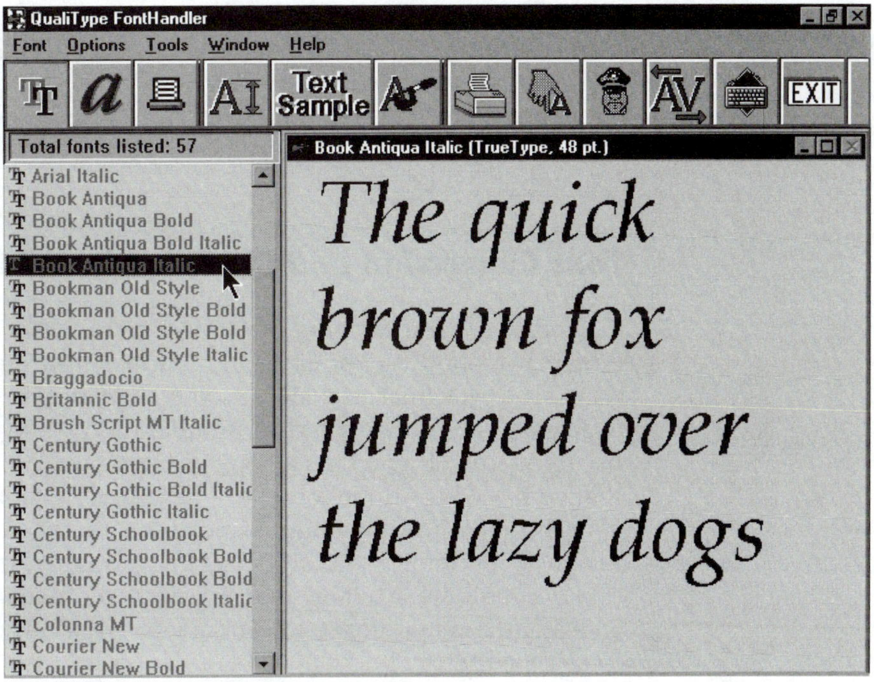

Figure 9.12   *FontHandler lets you quickly scroll through and display fonts.*

Up to nine fonts can be displayed at once, which is a nice feature, allowing quick comparison. ATM, Printer, and TrueType fonts are supported.

Beyond this, FontHandler offers something not found elsewhere. Unless a document has embedded TrueType fonts, a problem arises when you try to open a document that includes a font not currently installed in your system. Windows will do its best to locate a font that will suffice as a replacement, but it rarely looks very good. If the font called for in the document is actually on your computer, but not installed, a utility in FontHandler called *Font Sentry* can save the day. It sits in the background, quietly watching and waiting for any program or document to request a font that is not currently available. When a request for a missing font is detected, Font Sentry goes out and *AutoInstalls* the needed font on the fly, with the application or document never missing a beat or being aware of anything having been wrong.

Once a font is installed in this way, it will appear as available in all Windows programs. Such AutoInstalled fonts can be declared *temporary* or *permanent*, defined by the user, so that AutoInstalled fonts are either automatically forgotten when Windows is restarted or fully installed as if you'd done it from the Control Panel's Fonts applet or Explorer.

Font Conversion and Modification Utilities

The other general category of font programs deals with conversions of one sort or another. For example, you may have aquired fonts other than TrueType ones. If you've used type managers like Adobe Type Manager, you probably have a number of PostScript fonts that you use frequently. If you own a copy of CorelDRAW or another program that comes with Adobe fonts, you have more than a hundred fonts at your disposal. You can convert such fonts to TrueType format using various conversion tools, salvaging your font investment. Some other popular tools are available that will help you manage your fonts by organizing them into collections or create variations of your existing TrueType fonts. The sections below describe a few of the available programs.

Ares FontMonger can convert fonts—and it does a great job at it. It also provides support for TrueType, PostScript Type 1 and Type 3, Nimbus Q, and Intellifont; as well as CorelDraw WFN and Laser-Master formats.

But FontMonger goes far beyond simple format conversion. Font-Monger is a full-featured type-manipulation and editing tool. It becomes clear after just a few minutes with the product that format conversion is just a side benefit of FontMonger.

Fonts can be converted by FontMonger as a batch or individually. When you select File ➤ Convert Batch, you are presented with a batch list containing the names of the fonts in your last conversion batch (see Figure 9.13).

When you press the Find button, FontMonger will scan the directories you specify for all the font types it knows. You just select the files you want to convert, tell FontMonger what format to convert them into, and off it goes.

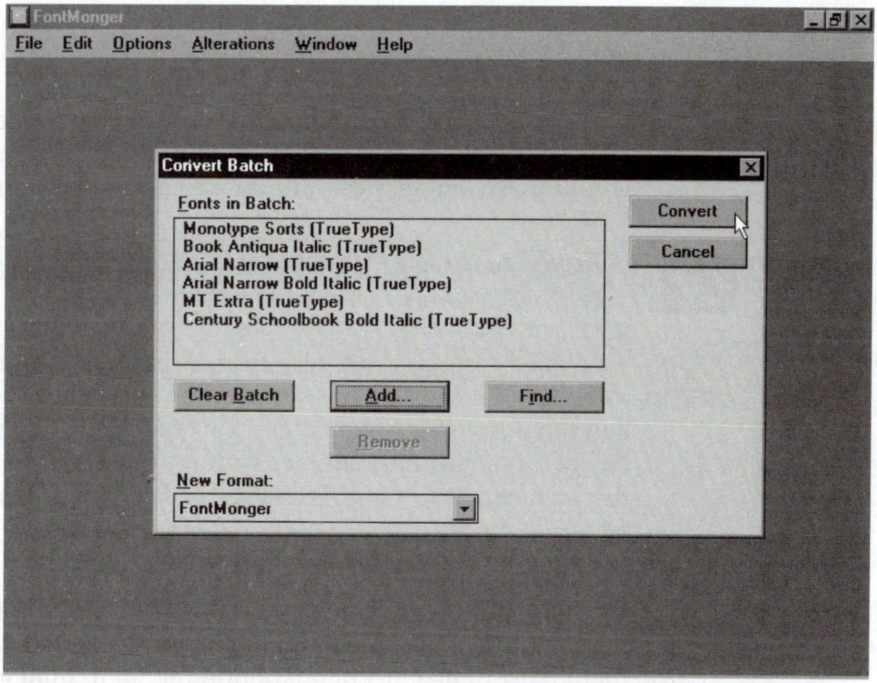

Figure 9.13 shows the FontMonger "Convert Batch" dialog box, containing a list titled "Fonts in Batch:" with the following entries:

- Monotype Sorts (TrueType)
- Book Antiqua Italic (TrueType)
- Arial Narrow (TrueType)
- Arial Narrow Bold Italic (TrueType)
- MT Extra (TrueType)
- Century Schoolbook Bold Italic (TrueType)

Buttons: Convert, Cancel, Clear Batch, Add..., Find..., Remove. New Format: FontMonger.

Figure 9.13   *FontMonger eases font conversion by allowing you to convert a batch of fonts in one fell swoop. Here's a list of fonts about to be converted.*

FontMonger provides facilities to set font information such as font name and family relationship (normal, bold, italic, bold italic, or other). Once you've set the selections appropriately, you can set the font-protection level (meaning whether your font should have read-only or read-write embedding). Unless you want to customize further, you can then choose File ➤ Build Font to create a new font. Select the new format for the font, and you're done.

FontMonger looks at the font itself and generates new hinting rules based on the characteristics of the font. The result is clean, crisp-looking screen fonts that can be recognized as distinct designs even at small point sizes.

But the real strength of FontMonger is its full complement of font-editing tools. FontMonger will easily perform a number of alterations to a font, including Small Caps, Slant (italicize), Superior (superscript),

and Inferior (subscript). You can even create your own custom alterations by simply dragging the font's outline in an editing box. Font-
Monger also lets you import characters designed in Adobe Illustrator
or saved in Encapsulated PostScript. You can develop a logo or symbol in a drawing package such as Illustrator, Micrografx Designer, or
CorelDRAW and assign your logo to a key in a standard font.

NOTE   FontMonger is available for about $149 from Ares Software in Fos-
ter City, California. Call 415-578-9090.

Two other font products also from Ares are worth noting. The first,
dubbed Font Fiddler, has some of the capabilities of FontMinder,
handling three font-related chores: renaming and changing the properties of fonts, printing samples without installing the font, and setting
the kerning pairs of any TrueType or Postscript Type 1 fonts.

The second, Font Chameleon, is a positively reviewed program that
lets you easily create custom fonts. And you don't have to do this me-
ticulously, character by character. Instead, Chameleon comes with a
number of flexible highest-quality, hinted fonts and lets you combine
them (sort of like morphing photographs) in millions of different com-
bintations, tweaking weight, width, x-height, and ascender and de-
scender sizes as you go. The upshot is that you can have an incredibly
small type library (each flexible font takes up only 4K of disk space)
rather than tie up tons of disk space with hundreds of fonts. When
you need a new font, just create it on the fly with Font Chameleon.
Then save it as a Type 1 or TrueType font and install it. The fonts you
design can also be used under OS2/Warp or on a Mac. As of this writing, Font Chameleon was priced at $55 with 45 flexible fonts, or
$295 with 200 fonts.

Finally, here's an interesting category of font manipulation: what the
marketing people call *special effects*. If you have Microsoft Office or
Word, you'll have a font special-effects program called WordArt that
lets you create fun and interesting shadow effects, rotated text, 3-D
looks, and such. An example of some WordArt is shown in Figure 9.14.

Another font-effects product is TrueEffects from MicroLogic. This
program works differently than WordArt. Like Chameleon, it generates whole new TrueType fonts based on existing TrueType fonts in
your system. WordArt just lets you insert a small snippet of text into

Figure 9.14 Microsoft's WordArt add-on to Microsoft Office lets you insert fancy text into any OLE-aware document. In Word, for example, choose Insert ➤ Object and click on WordArt.

an otherwise normal document. With TrueEffects, you choose which of a zillion effects you want to apply to an existing TrueType font. For example, effects such as 3-D shading, patterned fills, and various thicknesses of outline can be applied. You then give the new font a name, save it on disk, and install it into your system. This is a convenient way to generate novel display fonts for posters, flyers, banners, or newsletters. For information, call MicroLogic at (800) 888-9078 or (510) 652-5464.

Part
2

Exploring Windows 95

Chapter 10

Windows Multimedia

FEATURING

As of version 3.1, Windows has been *multimedia-ready*. Though it could be argued that Windows' multimedia capabilities are still a bit sketchy, PC-based multimedia has nevertheless grown dramatically in the last several years and affords users impressive benefits by this point. Even mainstream products such as Lotus 1-2-3 and Paradox for Windows, when purchased in their CD-ROM format, provide online multimedia help. Multimedia PCs, which are very affordable and highly compatible, are capable of:

▶ displaying television-quality video

▶ recording, editing, and playing stereo CD-quality sound

▶ responding to voice commands; playing MIDI sequences on your synthesizer or other MIDI device

▶ playing fancy CD-ROM titles such as interactive encyclopedias that talk, play music for you, and have moving pictures

All such considerations and the hardware and software that make them work fall into the category of *Windows multimedia*. This chapter will answer your questions about Windows 95's multimedia abilities and how you can best take advantage of them. Please keep in mind while reading that talking about Windows multimedia is like shooting at a moving target. Changes are taking place so rapidly in the field that book publishers would need unrealistically brisk turnaround times (akin to that of magazines) to accurately reflect the state of the industry. Therefore, in the interest of sparing you the annoyance of reading out-of-date material, I'll focus this chapter on the multimedia features of Windows 95 itself and deal only fleetingly with issues of secondary, aftermarket products.

What Is Multimedia?

Multimedia—alias *interactive media* or *hypermedia*—is difficult to define, which accounts for much general confusion on the topic. At the simplest level, in today's use of the term, it simply means adding sound to your programs. At the most advanced level, it is the amalgamation of animation, graphics, video, MIDI, digitally recorded sounds, and text— with all of these presentation media controlled by a single PC.

Some multimedia applications are *interactive* and some are not. Interactivity means that through some input device such as keyboard, mouse, voice, or external controller—for example a Musical Instrument Digital Interface (MIDI) keyboard—you interact with the system to control aspects of the presentation. Most of today's software is still primarily based on text display, perhaps supplemented by simple graphics such as a chart or piece of clip art. With the added capabilities of stereo sound, animation, and video, multimedia computing offers a much richer and more efficient means for conveying information.

As an example of a simple interactive program, consider the Windows tour, which demonstrates Windows fundamentals for the newcomer, reachable from the Start ➤ Help button. The tutorial demonstrates rudimentary multimedia, integrating small moving graphics and text. It does not incorporate speech or live-action video clips. Now imagine expanding such a tutorial to include spoken instructions, music, realistic animation, and moving video images just as if you were watching TV. As you probably know by now, animators, musicians, designers, writers, programmers, audio engineers, industry experts, and video producers are beginning to join forces to create multimedia applications such as:

▶ A WordPerfect document that lets you paste in video clips (with audio) from a VCR tape; instead of displaying just a still graphic, the document will be "alive" with sight and sound.

▶ A music-education program on a CD-ROM from Microsoft that plays Beethoven's Ninth Symphony while displaying informative and educational text about each passage and about the composer.

▶ A dictionary, thesaurus, book of quotations, and encyclopedia on a CD-ROM from Microsoft that not only contains a huge amount of textual information but actually pronounces the dictionary entries; reads quotations aloud in the voices of Robert Frost, Carl Sandburg, T.S. Eliot, e.e. cummings, Dylan Thomas, and JFK; and illustrates scientific phenomena with animation.

▶ Programs that teach you how to play the piano using a MIDI keyboard connected to your PC. The computer senses whether you play the lesson correctly and responds accordingly with a recorded high-quality voice. Similar programs teach music theory.

▶ Multimedia magazines on CD-ROM that let you choose what news topics you want to read. News is displayed like television, with high-fidelity sound and video.

▶ Interactive company annual reports, product demonstrations, presentations, or corporate training manuals for new employees.

▶ Interactive real-time video conferencing (*videotel conferencing*) on your desktop computer, where you can see your colleagues at several remote office locations while working interactively on your company's newsletter, also displayed on the screen.

▶ *Moving catalogs* from mail-order houses, displaying everything from cars to coats via high-quality video and audio.

▶ An interactive geography test used at the National Geographic Society Explorer's Hall in Washington, D.C.

▶ Interactive high-speed, random-access books, newspapers, or catalogs for the blind, using high-quality voice synthesis or recorded voices.

▶ Interactive training for hard-to-teach professions such as medical diagnosis, surgery, auto mechanics, and machine operation of various types.

▶ Complex interactive games that incorporate stereo sound effects, flashy visuals, speech synthesis, and speech recognition, where you interact with the game by speaking.

▶ A program that uses popular sound cards to record your voice, then compresses it on the fly and pumps it across the Internet, allowing two-way conversations with users around the globe without the phone charges.

Most of these applications (often called *multimedia titles*, *information titles*, or simply *titles*) already exist. Others are still in the making. The explosion of multimedia CD titles has been enormous in the last two years, and mail-order CD-ROM catalogs are becoming ubiquitous. One PC Magazine disk includes an entire year's articles, easily searchable.

Upgrading to Multimedia

With Windows 3.0, working with multimedia required purchasing Microsoft's Multimedia upgrade kit or buying an expensive and hard-to-find MPC (multimedia PC). MPCs were manufactured by several

Part 2

Exploring Windows 95

vendors and were not generally available on the clone market. Whether upgrading an existing computer or buying an MPC, the results were about the same: you got the Microsoft multimedia extensions (drivers), a CD-ROM drive, audio card, and a good VGA video card.

Either solution was pricey, often amounting to thousands of dollars. Some people didn't want to shell out for the hardware because they only needed a specific hardware addition, such as a sound card. More often than not, people just wanted the software drivers so they could use the hardware they already owned. In response to this interest, Microsoft decided to bundle some popular drivers and a couple of utility programs with the Windows 3.1 package in the hopes that this would accelerate the development of multimedia Windows applications. Microsoft also included the programming *hooks* (called APIs—Application Programming Interfaces) in Windows 3.1 that allow multimedia applications to run on it.

The MPC specification helped set some standards for what a multimedia PC should look and act like, and the PC add-on market did the rest. A vast profusion of multimedia hardware, applications, and utilities have subsequently become prevalent. The magazines now inundate us with ads for newer and faster CD-ROM drives, 64-bit coprocessed video cards, high-resolution energy-efficient monitors, and fancy sound cards—even ones with samples of real orchestral instruments built in. The MPC moniker has sort of fallen by the wayside, and now what's really more important is whether a system is Windows 95-compatible or not. After that, the rest is icing on the cake: How big is the screen, how good do the speakers sound, how clear is the image, and overall, how fast does the *whole system* (not just the CPU chip) perform. You'll have to rely on the magazines for these kinds of test comparisons. Don't rely on the guys in the store. One brand of 50-MHz 486 machine might actually be faster than another one that's got a 75-MHz 486 under the hood, due to the vagaries of hard-disk controllers, type of internal bus, memory caching, or speed of the video card.

If you're already in possession of a multimedia-ready machine with a couple of speakers and a CD-ROM drive, you might as well skip this section and move down to the next major section in this chapter, *Supplied Multimedia Applications and Utilities*. But if you're thinking about endowing your machine with the gift of gab, some fancy video graphics capabilities, and the ability to run all those groovy-looking CD-ROM-based games or educational packages your kids are bugging you about, read on.

There are three basic ways to upgrade your computer: buy a whole new computer, buy an "upgrade-in-a-box," or mix and match new components that exactly fit your needs. As of this writing, there were about twenty upgrade-in-a-box products to choose from. You'll typically get a CD-ROM drive, speakers, a sound card, and maybe some CDs in the package. The sound card has the SCSI connector that hooks the CD-ROM drive to the computer. Mixing and matching is for us total control-freak geeks who must have the best or who don't like the idea of other people controlling our purchase decisions. The obvious downside is that sorting through the sea of components in the marketplace is a big waste of time. I've spent too many hours testing video boards, trying to get a SCSI upgrade to my sound card to work with my CD-ROM drive, or running around listening to speakers. In any case, here are a few points about the pros and cons of the three upgrade routes:

NOTE   You might want to check out Chapters 2 and 31 for more about choosing and adding hardware to your system because some of those topics apply to multimedia.

In your shopping, you may wonder what the minimal requirements of a multimedia system should be. With the technology changing so quickly, it's hard to predict what the pickings will look like a year from now and what the latest and greatest version of Star Trek (the interactive CD-ROM game) or Myst will want your system to have. As a rule, though, the best balance between price and performance lies just in the wake of the technology wave. Don't bother being on the cutting edge. Brand new cutting-edge gear is too expensive and usually still has some bugs to be worked out or ends up being dropped by the industry at large. When a product hits the mainstream, that's the time to buy; prices usually take a nosedive at that point, often about 50 percent.

Question	New Computer	Kit in a Box	Mix and Match Components
What is it?	A whole computer that is designed for multimedia Windows 95 from the ground up and includes a fairly zippy computer, color screen, speakers, sound card, and CD-ROM drive.	A box of stuff you get at a computer store or by mail order. Everything works together and costs less than $500. Includes a sound card, CD-ROM drive, and speakers.	CD-ROM drive, sound board, speakers, cabling, and any necessary software drivers that you research and purchase separately.
Who should buy?	Owner of a mid-level computer who has already decided to purchase a new computer either because existing computer isn't worth upgrading to a faster CPU and larger hard disk or because an additional computer is needed.	Average owner of nonmultimedia computer that's well endowed in the CPU and hard-disk area (e.g., a 486 and 250-MB hard disk or larger) but needs multimedia capability to run multimedia games and standard productivity applications.	Power user who wants the best selection of components—or who already has one or two essential components, such as a CD-ROM drive, and now wants the rest. May be a professional such as a musician, application developer, or graphic artist who needs one element of the multimedia upgrade to be very high quality.
How much hassle?	No hassle. Everything is installed and working. Get the system with Windows 95 installed and working if you can, and you're really set.	You'll have to remove the cover to the computer, remove some screws, insert a couple of cards, hook up some cables and the CD-ROM drive if the drive is the internal type then hook up the speakers. If the cards and computer are not Plug-and-Play compatible, you'll have to make IRQ and DMA settings.	About the same amount of hassle as a box upgrade, but you'll have to deal with separate documentation for each component and figure out how to get everything working together, unless they are Plug-and-Play components.

Table 10.1   Approaches to Multimedia Upgrading

Question	New Computer	Kit in a Box	Mix and Match Components
		This may take some homework. You might have conflicts with existing hardware; then you have Windows 95 detect and install drivers for the new hardware, or you use supplied drivers.	IRQ and DMA conflicts are likely otherwise.
Advantages?	Low hassle factor. You can start getting work done instead of poring over magazines and manuals. Your church (or kid) gets your old computer, you get a tax write-off, and you get more sleep.	You don't have to sell your existing computer. You might even get some free CD-ROM software in the box.	You can have exactly what you want. 24-bit TrueColor graphics, direct video capturing, video conferencing, great sound, superfast display at 1,600 by 1,280—you name it.
Disadvantages?	You have to buy a whole new system. You'll probably be compromising somewhat on the components for the low hassle factor.	It will take some work to install it, unless it comes from the same people who made your computer (e.g., a Dell upgrade to a Dell computer). Again, some compromise on the components is likely. You may not have the best-sounding speakers, fastest video, greatest color depth, or CD-ROM drive.	Price and installation hassle is high.
Price?	Not much more for a multimedia system than for those without multimedia. A few hundred additional dollars is typical.	Typically between $200 and $500, though some high-class upgrades are closer to a thousand.	Difficult to predict. Bottom-of-the-line but functional clone parts could run you as little as a few hundred dollars. Or you could pay well into the thousands for the best brands.

Table 10.1 **Approaches to Multimedia Upgrading** (continued)

What does that mean in the current market? Well the MPC specification requires at least a machine with 4 MB of RAM, a 130-MB hard disk, and a fast processor such as a 486 or Pentium. Here are my thoughts when you're shopping for multimedia components and systems:

Computer   I'd suggest at least a 486DX2/50 CPU, a local bus video card, and a 500-MB hard disk (E-IDE or SCSI), with 8 MB (preferably 16 MB) of RAM. SCSI is the better bet because you can also hook up as many as seven devices to a SCSI controller, not just hard disks.

CD-ROM Drive   Get at least a double-speed drive. Double-speed drives will do most anything you need, albeit slower than triple- or quad-speed drives. Windows 95 caches your CD-ROM drive, so that will help with slower drives. Quad-speed drives are getting cheap and you will notice the difference, so get one if you can afford it. If you want to be able to connect to a laptop or move the drive between computers, get a lightweight portable external job. You'll pay more for it, but prices are plummeting anyway, so the difference won't be that much. If you change disks a lot, get the *caddyless* type. Make sure the drive supports *multisession* Kodak photo format. This lets you not only view photographs in CD-ROM format on your computer but also take an existing photo CD-ROM to your photo developer down at the pharmacy and have them add new pictures to it. You might want up-front manual controls on the player so you can listen to audio CDs without running the CD Player program.

Speakers   The larger the better, usually. Little speakers will sound tinny by definition. Listen before you buy if possible. Listen to a normal, speaking human voice—the most difficult instrument to reproduce. Does it sound natural? Then hear something with some bass. If you're going to listen to audio CDs, bring one with you to the store and play it. Speakers that are separate (not built into the monitor) will allow a nicer stereo effect. Separate tweeter and woofer will probably sound better, but not always. It depends on the electronics in the speaker. Magnetic shielding is important if the speakers are going to be within a foot or so of your screen; otherwise, the colors and alignment of the image on the screen will be adversely affected. (Not permanently damaged, though. The effect stops when you move the speakers away.) Of course, instead of buying speakers you can use your stereo or even a boom box if it has high-level (sometimes called *auxiliary*) input. Some boom boxes and virtually all stereos do have such an input. Then it's just a matter of using the correct wire to attach your sound card's *line* output to the stereo's or boom box's Aux input and setting the volume appropriately. The easiest solution is to purchase a pair of amplified speakers designed for small recording studios, apartments, or computers. For about $150 you can find a good pair of smaller-sized shielded speakers (4- or 5-inch woofer, separate tweeter) with volume, bass, and treble controls. For $300 you can get some that sound very good. If you like real bass, shell out a little more for a set that comes with a separate larger sub-woofer you put under your desk.

Sound Board   This should have 16-bit 44.1-KHz sound capability for CD-quality sound. You'll want line-in, line-out, and microphone in jacks at least. Typical cards also have a joystick port for your game controller. The card should be compatible with Windows 95, with the General MIDI specification, and with Sound Blaster so it will work with popular games. This means it should have protected-mode 32-bit drivers for Windows 95 either supplied with Windows 95 or with the card. If it doesn't, you'll be stuck using 16-bit drivers that take up too much conventional memory space, preventing many DOS-based games and educational programs from running. I've seen this problem with cards, such as the Sound Blaster Pro, prevent a number of games such as the Eagle-Eye Mystery series from running. Fancy cards such as those from Turtle Beach don't sound like cheesy synthesizers when they play MIDI music because they use samples of real instruments stored in *wave tables* instead of using synthesizer chips, but you'll pay more for them.

Video Card and Monitor   (The video card goes inside the computer and produces the signals needed to create a display on the monitor. A cable runs between the video card and the monitor.) For high-performance multimedia, you'll want a *local bus* video card (typically VLB or PCI) capable of at least 256 colors at the resolution you desire. Local bus cards only work in computers that have a local bus connector slot, so check out which kind of slots your computer has. Standard resolution (number of dots on the screen at one time, comprising the picture) for a PC is 640 (horizontal) by 480 (vertical). Most new video cards these days will support that resolution at 256 colors. If you have a very sharp 15-inch screen or a 17-inch screen, you may opt for a higher resolution, such as 800 by 600 or 1,024 by 768. When shopping for a video card, make sure they display at least 256 colors (and preferably in the thousands of colors) at the resolution you want *and have at least 70-Hz noninterlaced refresh rate at that resolution and color depth.* The correct refresh rate ensures the screen doesn't flicker and give you a headache. Video cards with graphics co-processor chips on them will run faster than those that don't. Fast speed is necessary when you move objects around on the screen or display video clips. Make sure the board will work well with Windows 95, preferably with the 32-bit video driver that comes with Windows 95, not an old driver designed for Windows 3.x. You don't have to worry about any monitor's ability to display colors because any color monitor will display all the colors your card can produce. What you have to check out are the monitor's dot pitch, controls, and refresh rate. The monitor should ideally have a dot pitch of .25 or .26, be at least 17 inches (though 15 inches will do), and run all your desired resolutions at 70-Hz refresh or higher to avoid flicker. Beware of the refresh-rate issue: False or misleading advertising is rampant. Many monitors and video cards advertise 72-Hz or higher refresh rates, but the fine print reveals that this is only at 640 by 480. Bump up the resolution, and the refresh on cheaper cards or monitors drops to a noticeable 60 Hz. Get a monitor that has low radiation emissions, powers down automatically when isn't being used (a so-called green monitor), and has a wide variety of controls for size, picture position, pincushion, and barrel, brightness, contrast, color, and so forth.

That's the basic rundown on multimedia upgrading. Now let's look at what's supplied with Windows 95 in the way of multimedia programs and utilities.

The Supplied Multimedia Applications and Utilities

Here's what you get in the way of multimedia programs and utilities with Windows 95:

Sound Settings   This Control Panel applet lets you assign specific sound files (stored in the .wav format) to Windows system events such as error messages, information dialog boxes, and when starting and exiting Windows.

Media Player   This application, which you'll find in the Accessories ➤ Multimedia folder from the Start button, lets you play a variety of multimedia files on the files' target hardware. In the case of a device that contains data, such as a CD-ROM or video disk, Media Player sends commands to the hardware, playing back the sound or video therein. If the data are stored on your hard disk (as are MIDI sequences, animation, and sound files), Media Player will send them to the appropriate piece of hardware, such as a sound board, MIDI keyboard, or other device.

> **TECH TIP**   The Media Player only works with MCI devices (Media Control Interface) and thus requires MCI device drivers.

Sound Recorder   This is a little program for simple recording of sounds from a microphone or auxiliary input and then editing them. Once recorded, sound files can be used with other programs through OLE or used to replace or augment the generic beeps your computer makes to alert you to dialog boxes, errors, and so forth. It is also the default program used to play back WAV files.

CD Player   Assuming your computer's CD-ROM drive and controller card supports it (most do), this accessory program lets you play back standard audio CDs. This can be great boon on long winter nights when you're chained to your PC doing your taxes or writing that boring report. You'll find coverage of this program in Chapter 22 along with the other Accessory odds and ends.

Adding Drivers   The System and Add New hardware applets in the Control Panel let you install drivers for many add-in cards and devices such as CD-ROMs, MIDI interface cards, and video-disk controllers. Drivers for most popular sound boards such as the Sound Blaster (from Creative Labs, Inc.) and Ad Lib (Ad Lib, Inc.) and popular MIDI boards such as the Roland MPU-401 (Roland Digital Group) are supplied. Other drivers can be installed from manufacturer-supplied disks using this option. Even if your hardware is physically installed, it won't work unless the proper driver is loaded.

A few programs have either been covered elsewhere in this book or were seen in Windows 3.x but have been dropped from Windows 95. They are:

Volume Control   The volume control accessory, available from the Taskbar, simply lets you control the balance and volume levels of the various sound sources that end up playing through your computer's speakers. This is covered in Chapter 22.

MIDI Mapper   This was included as a separate Control Panel applet in Windows 3.1 and NT but has been hidden in Windows 95 because it is rarely used. Its purpose was to declare settings for your MIDI device, such as channel assignment, key remapping, and patch-number reassignment for nonstandard MIDI instruments. The assumption now is that most MIDI instruments comply with the General MIDI standard for these parameters and thus the Mapper is rarely needed. If you have a nonstandard MIDI instrument that you're running from Windows programs (this won't affect DOS programs), check out the Control Panel's Multimedia ➤ MIDI ➤ Add New Instrument button. It will lead you to the rather complex remapping facilities.

Assigning Sounds with the Control Panel's Sound Utility

The Control Panel's Sound utility is for designating sounds to system events, such as warning dialog boxes, error messages when you click in the wrong place, and so on. Once you've installed a sound board, you can personalize your computer's beep to something more exciting. If your computer had a sound card when you installed Windows 95, it's likely Windows 95 established a default set of rather boring sounds for your system, most of which you're probably tired of already. Aside from making life more interesting, having different sounds for different types of events is also more informative. You know when you've made an error as opposed to when an application is acknowledging your actions, for example.

Of course, to add basic sounds to your Windows setup, you need a Windows 95-compatible sound card. The sounds you can use must be stored on disk in the .wav format. Most sounds you can download from BBSs or get on disk at the computer store are in this format. Also, the Sound

Recorder program explained later in the chapter records sounds in WAV format. Windows 95 comes with more than a few sound files now, a big improvement over the measly assemblage of WAV files supplied with Windows 3.x. In fact, just as with the color schemes you can create and save with the Control Panel's Display applet (covered in Chapter 7), you can set up and save personalized sound schemes to suit your mood. Microsoft has supplied us with several such schemes, running the gamut from happy nature sounds to futuristic, mechanistic robot utterances to the sonorities of classical musical instruments.

> **NOTE**   You have to do a Custom installation to get all the sound schemes loaded into your computer. You can do this after the fact by running Control Panel ➤ Add/Remove Programs ➤ Windows Setup. Then click on Multimedia to select it and click on the Details button. The sound schemes are located near the bottom of the list.

Part
2

Exploring Windows 95

Despite this diverse selection, you may still want to make or acquire more interesting sounds yourself or collect them from other sources. To record your own, you'll need a sound board such as Sound Blaster or another digital sampler board. I have messages in my own voice, such as, "You made a stupid mistake, you fool," which—for a short time—seemed preferable to the mindless chime. If your system lets you play audio CDs, you should be able to directly sample bits and pieces from your favorite artists by popping the audio CD into the computer and tapping directly into it rather than by sticking a microphone up to your boom box and accidentally recording the telephone when it rings. Check out the Volume Control applet and adjust the slider on the mixer panel that controls the input volume of the CD. Then use the Sound Recorder applet to make the recording.

Like any good sound-o-phile, I'm always on the lookout for good WAV files. You'll find them everywhere if you just keep your eyes open: cheap CDs at the local Compu-Geek store, on the Internet, on CompuServe, even on other people's computers. Usually these sound files aren't copyrighted, so copying them isn't likely to be a legal issue. Most WAV files intended for system sounds aren't that big, either. But do check out the size, using the Explorer or by showing the Details view in a folder, before copying them. Sound files *can* be super large, especially if they are recorded in 16-bit stereo. As a rule you'll want to keep the size to a minimum for system sounds because it can take more than a few seconds for a larger sound file to load and begin to play.

Once you're set up for sound and have some WAV files, you assign them to specific Windows events. Here's how:

1. Open the Control Panel and run the Sounds applet. The dialog box shown in Figure 10.1 appears:

2. The top box lists the events that can have sounds associated with them. There will be at least two classes of events—one for Windows

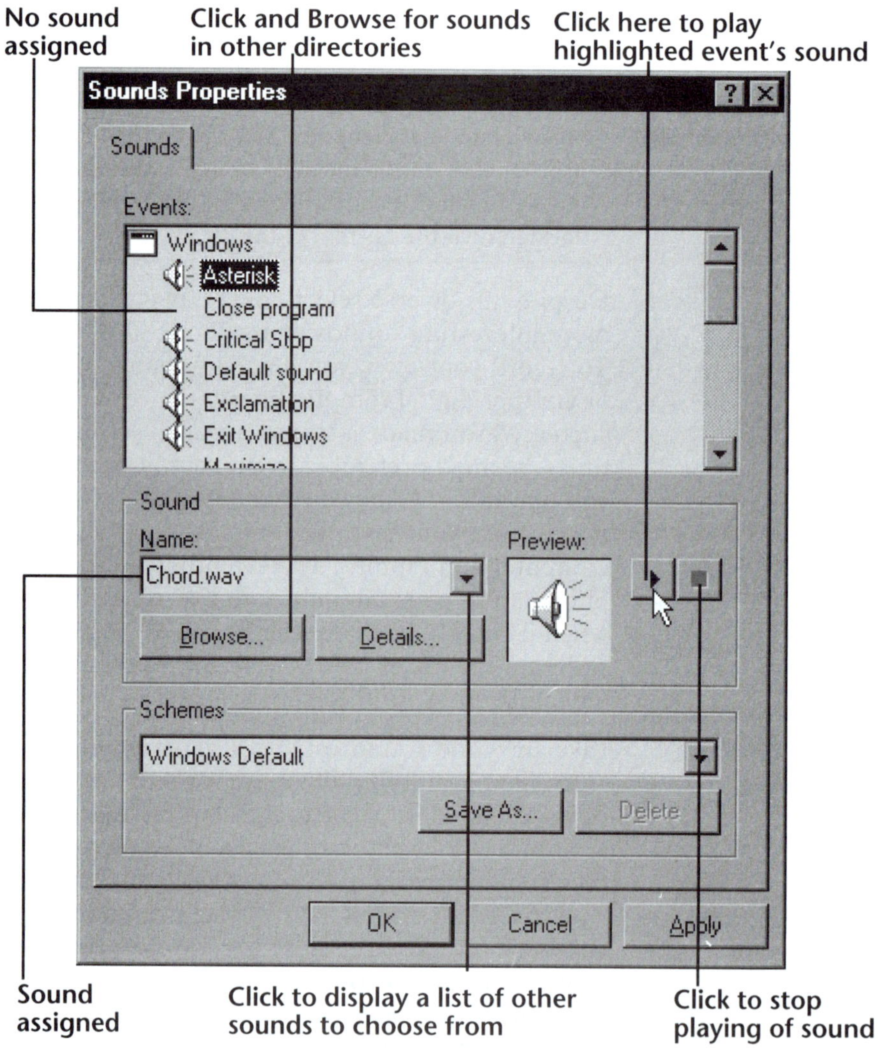

No sound assigned   **Click and Browse for sounds in other directories**   **Click here to play highlighted event's sound**

Sound assigned   **Click to display a list of other sounds to choose from**   **Click to stop playing of sound**

Figure 10.1   Use this dialog box to choose which sounds your computer makes when Windows events occur.

events and one for Explorer events. (Scroll the list to the bottom to see the Explorer events.) As you purchase and install new programs in the future, those programs may add their own events to your list. An event with a speaker icon next to it already has a sound associated with it. You can click on it and then click on the Preview button to hear the sound. The sound file that's associated with the event is listed in the Name box.

3. Click on any event for which you want to assign a sound or change the assigned sound.

4. Open the drop-down Name list and choose the WAV file you want to use for that event. Some of the event names may not make sense to you, such as Asterisk, Critical Stop, or Exclamation. These are names for the various classes of dialog boxes that Windows 95 displays from time to time. The sounds you're most likely to hear often will be Default beep, Menu Command, Menu Popup, Question, Open Program, Close Program, Minimize, Maximize, Start Windows, and Exit Windows.

> **TIP** The default directory for sounds is the \Windows\Media directory. That's where the WAV files that come with Windows 95 are stored. If you have WAV files stored somewhere else, you'll have to use the Browse button to find and assign them to an event. I find it's easier to copy all my WAV files into the \Windows\Media directory than to go browsing for them when I want to do a lot of reassigning of sounds.

5. At the top of the list of available sounds there is an option called <none> that has the obvious effect—no sound will occur for that event. Assigning all events to <none> will effectively silence your computer for use in a library, church, and so forth. You can also quickly do this for all sounds by choosing the No Sounds scheme as explained below.

6. Repeat the process for other events to which you want to assign or reassign sounds.

7. Click on OK.

Keep in mind that different applications will use event sounds differently. You'll have to do some experimenting to see when your applications use the default beep, as opposed to the Asterisk, Question, or the Exclamation.

Clicking on the Details button displays information about the WAV file, such as its time length, data format, and copyright information (if it's copyrighted).

Loading and Saving Sound Schemes

Just as the Control Panel's Display applet lets you save color schemes, the Sounds applet lets you save sound schemes so you can set up goofy sounds for your humorous moods and somber ones for those gloomy days—or vice versa. The schemes supplied with Windows 95 are pretty nice even without modification.

To choose an existing sound scheme:

1. Click on the drop-down list button for schemes, down at the bottom of the box:

2. A list of existing schemes will appear. Choose a sound scheme. Now all the events in the upper part of the box will have the new sound scheme's sounds. Check out the sounds to see if you like them.

3. If you like them, click on OK.

    You can set up your own sound schemes by assigning or reassigning individual sounds, as I've already explained. But unless you *save* the scheme, it will be lost the next time you change to a new one. So, the moral is: once you get your favorite sounds assigned to system events, save the scheme. Then you can call it up any time you like. Here's how:

1. Set up the sounds the way you want. You can start with an existing scheme and modify it or start from scratch by choosing the No Sounds scheme and assigning sounds one by one.

2. Click on the Save As button.

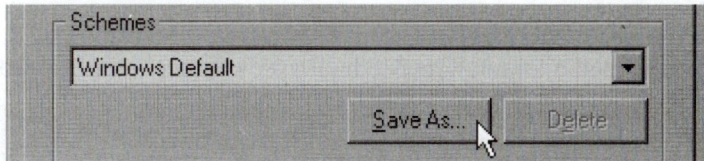

Schemes

Windows Default

Save As...   Delete

3. In the resulting dialog box, enter a name for the scheme. For example, here's one I made up and saved:

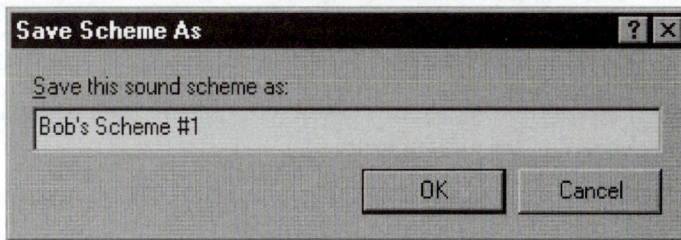

Save Scheme As   ? X

Save this sound scheme as:

Bob's Scheme #1

OK   Cancel

4. OK the little dialog box, and your scheme is saved. Now you can create additional schemes and save them or just OK the large dialog box to activate the new scheme.

You can delete any existing sound schemes by choosing the doomed scheme from the list and then clicking on the delete button. You'll be asked to confirm the deletion.

Playing Multimedia Files with Media Player

Media Player is a little application that plays multimedia files, such as digitized sounds, MIDI music files, and animated graphics. It can also send control information to multimedia devices such as audio CD players or video disk players, determining which tracks to play, when to pause, when to activate slow motion, and so on.

Obviously, you can only use Media Player on devices installed in your system and for which you've installed the correct device drivers (see *Installing New Drivers*, below), so first see to that task. Then follow these instructions for playing a multimedia file:

1. Run Media Player from the Start ➤ Programs ➤ Accessories ➤ Multimedia folder. The Media Player's control panel appears, as shown here:

2. Open the Device menu and choose the type of device that's going to receive the information.

3. If the type of device you've chosen has an ellipsis (…) after it, a File Open dialog box will appear, asking for the name of the file you want played and displaying the files with the correct extension for the selected device. This only happens with devices that play a file stored in a disk file (this type of device is called a *compound* device). Choose the file you want played. If the device you selected has no ellipsis after it, it's a *simple* device. This means the data to be played are already in the drive—as in the case of a CD-ROM or video disk—and don't have to be chosen (no File Open box will appear). When you load a file for a compound device, the Media Player's appearance will change slightly to display a scale and tick marks indicating the length of the item:

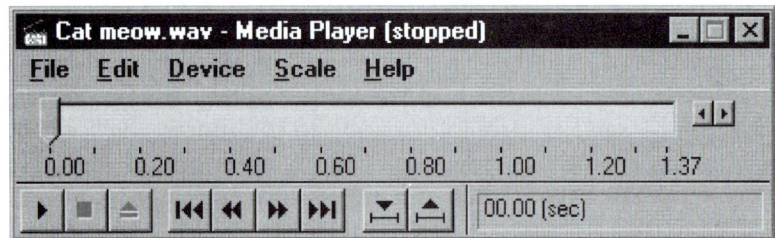

> **TIP**   You can jump to a particular location in the piece by dragging the scroll bar, clicking at the desired point in the scroll bar, or using ↑, ↓, ←, →, PgUp, and PgDn. Also, check the Device menu for options pertaining to the device you are using.

4. Now you can use the buttons in the dialog box to begin playing the piece. The buttons work just as on a VCR or cassette deck; if in doubt, the buttons have pop-up descriptions. The Eject button only works for most devices with an Eject feature, like an audio CD player. However, not all devices will respond to the eject button. It depends on the device and the driver.

5. If you want to open another file for the same device (in the case of compound devices), use the File ➤ Open command to do so. If you want to play a file intended for another device, you'll have to change the device type first from the Device menu, which will then bring up the File ➤ Open command for you to open a new file.

6. You can change the scale (tick marks) above the scroll bar to show *tracks* instead of time. Track display may be useful when you're playing audio CDs or video disks arranged by track. Do this from the Scale menu. Track tick marks will then replace the time tick marks. To change tracks, drag the scroll bar, click on the scroll buttons, or use →, ←, PgUp, and PgDn.

7. When you're done playing, close the application from the Exit menu.

NOTE Compound devices will stop as soon as you quit Media Player; simple devices will continue to play.

Media Player has a few options worth noting. Check out the Edit ➤ Options and Device ➤ Configure options. Choose Device ➤ Volume control to bring up the volume control and mixer for your particular sound board.

NOTE Use of the Volume Control is covered in Chapter 7 of this book.

Recording and Editing Sounds with Sound Recorder

Sound Recorder is a nifty little program that lets you record your own sounds and create WAV files. To make it work, you need a digital sampling card such as the Sound Blaster with a microphone. The program also lets you do some editing and manipulation of any WAV files you might have on disk. You can do this even if you don't have a microphone.

The resulting WAV files can be put to a variety of uses, including assigning them to system events or using them with other multimedia applications, such as Media Player. Once a file is recorded, you can edit it by removing portions of it. Unfortunately, you cannot edit from one arbitrary spot to another, only from one spot to either the beginning or the end of the file. You can also add an echo effect to a sample, play it backwards, change the playback speed (and resulting pitch), and alter the playback volume.

Playing a Sound File

Follow the steps below to play a sound file:

1. Make sure you've installed the correct driver and that your sound board works (Chapter 7 discusses how to add new hardware and drivers).

2. Run Sound Recorder by choosing Start ➤ Programs ➤ Accessories ➤ Multimedia ➤ Sound Recorder. The Sound Recorder window will appear, as shown here.

3. Choose File ➤ Open and choose the file you want to play. Notice that the length of the sound appears at the right of the window and the current position of the play head appears on the left.

4. Click on the Play button or press Enter to play the sound. As it plays, the wave box displays the sound, oscilloscope style. The Status Bar also says *Playing*. When the sound is over, Sound Recorder stops and the Status Bar says *Stopped*. Press Enter again to replay the sound.

You can click on Stop during a playback to pause the sound, then click on Play to continue.

5. Drag the scroll button around (see below) and notice how the wave box displays a facsimile of the frequency and amplitude of the sample over time.

You can also click on the rewind and fast-forward buttons to move to the start and end of the sample or press the PgUp and PgDn keys to jump the play head forward or backward in longer increments.

Recording a New Sound

This is the fun part, so get your microphone ready. Suppose you want to make up your own sounds, perhaps to put into an OLE-capable application document such as Write or Cardfile so that it talks when clicked on. Here's how:

1. Choose File ➤ New.

2. You may want to check the recording format before you begin. Choose File ➤ Properties. Select Recording Formats, then click on Convert Now. A dialog box appears, asking some details about the recording format as shown in Figure 10.2. A combination of data-recording format (e.g., PCM, Microsoft's ADPCM, and so forth) and sampling rate (e.g., 8-KHz 4-bit mono) are shown. Together these comprise a *format scheme*.

Part 2

Exploring Windows 95

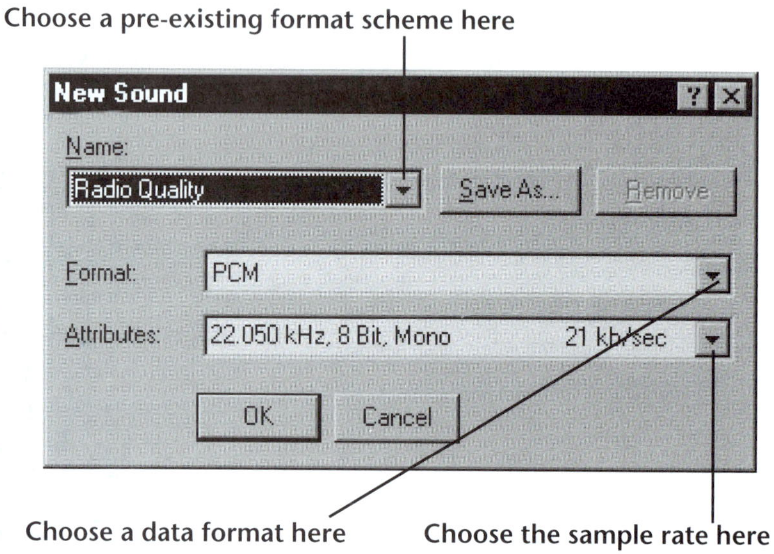

Choose a pre-existing format scheme here

Choose a data format here   Choose the sample rate here

Figure 10.2   Choosing a data scheme for a new sound recording

NOTE   The Attributes list shows the amount of disk space consumed per second of recording. You'll want to consider this when making new files, as recording in high-fidelity stereo can suck up precious disk room, rendering sound files quite unwieldy. Also, for most purposes, you are best served by choosing one of the preexisting sound schemes—CD-Quality, Radio Quality, or Telephone Quality—for your recordings. All three use the PCM recording technique but employ different sample rates. If you are recording only voice, use either the Radio or Telephone setting. The CD-quality setting will only use up more disk space than you need to. If you are planning to record from an audio CD player, you'll probably want to choose the CD-quality setting unless you want to conserve disk space. If you accidentally record at a higher quality level than you wanted to, don't worry. You can convert to a lower quality and regain some hard disk space via the File ➤ Properties ➤ Convert Now button. You can save recording and playback settings with the Save As button in the dialog box if you want or not save it if you don't mind choosing a setup each time you want to change from the default settings.

3. Click on the Record button. The clock starts ticking, counting the passing time. Begin talking into the microphone that's plugged into your sound card, playing whatever is connected to your AUX input (aka *line in*) on the sound card, or playing the audio CD that's in the CD-ROM drive. You'll have to use the volume control applet to set the relative balance of the various devices. Typically you'll be able to mix these disparate audio sources into a single recording if you use the mixer deftly. The maximum recording time will vary, depending on your recording format. In the default setting (PCM, 22.050-KHz 8-bit mono) you can record for up to one minute. Be cautious about the length of your sounds, as they tend to take up a large amount of disk space. For example, a one-second sample at CD Quality in stereo consumes about 172K.

4. Click on Stop when you are finished recording.

5. Play back the file to see if you like it.

6. Save the file with File ➤ Save As. You'll see the familiar File dialog box. Enter a name (you don't have to enter the WAV extension; the program does that for you).

When recording a voice narration, make sure to speak loudly and clearly, particularly if you notice that playback is muffled or buried in noise.

> **TIP** A simple way to create a new sound file is to right-click on the Desktop and choose New ➤ Sound File. Name the file, then double-click on it. Then click on the Record button.

Editing Sounds

You can edit sound files in several ways. For instance, you can:

▶ add echo to a sample

▶ reverse a sample

▶ mix two samples together

▶ remove unwanted parts of a sample

▶ increase or decrease the volume

▶ increase or decrease the speed and pitch

Part 2

Exploring Windows 95

NOTE You may run out of memory if your file becomes very long because of inserting files into one another. The amount of free physical memory (not virtual memory) determines the maximum size of any sound file.

To edit a sound file:

1. Open the sound file from the File menu.

2. Open the Effects menu to add echo, reverse the sound, increase or decrease volume, or increase or decrease speed. All the settings except echo are undoable, so you can experiment without worry. You undo a setting by choosing its complementary setting from the menu (e.g., Increase Volume v. Decrease Volume) or by choosing Reverse. Some sound quality can be lost by doing this repeatedly, however.

3. To cut out the beginning or ending of a sound—i.e., to eliminate the lag time it took you to get to the microphone or hit the Stop button—determine the beginning and ending points of the sound, get to the actual starting position of the sound, and choose Edit ➤ Delete Before Current Position. Then move the scroll button to the end of the desired portion of the sample and choose Edit ➤ Delete After Current Position.

4. To mix two existing sounds, position the cursor where you'd like to begin the mix, choose Edit ➤ Mix with File, and choose the file name. This can create some very interesting effects that are much richer than single sounds.

5. To insert a file into a predetermined spot, move to the spot with the scroll bar, choose Edit ➤ Insert File, and choose the file name.

6. To put a sound on the Clipboard for pasting elsewhere, use Edit ➤ Copy.

7. To return your sound to its original, last-saved state, choose File ➤ Revert.

Note that not all sound boards have the same features. Some won't let you save a recording into certain types of sound files. Also the quality of the sound differs from board to board. Some boards sound "grainy," others less so. This is determined by the sampling rate you've chosen, the quality of the digital-to-analog converters (DAC), and the analog amplifiers on the board.

Playing Tunes with CD Player

The CD Player accessory turns your computer's CD-ROM drive into a music machine: With it, you can play standard audio CDs with all the controls you'd expect on a "real" CD player, and then some. Of course, you'll need speakers (or at least a pair of headphones) to hear the music. Here's what CD Player looks like:

Part
2

Exploring Windows 95

With CD Player, you can:

▶ play any CD once through or continuously while you work with other programs

▶ play the tracks in sequential or random order, or play only the tracks you like

▶ move forward or in reverse to any desired track

▶ fast forward or rewind while a track is playing

▶ stop, pause, and resume playback, and (if your CD-ROM drive has the capability) eject the current CD

▶ control play volume if you're playing the CD through a sound card (this only works with some CD-ROM drives)

▶ control the contents of the time display (you can display elapsed time, time remaining for the current track, or time remaining for the entire CD)

▶ catalog your CDs (after you've typed in the title and track list for a CD, CD Player will recognize it when you load it again, displaying the titles of the disk and the current track)

Getting Started with CD Player

To run CD Player, begin from the Start menu and choose Programs ► Accessories ► CD Player. Load your CD-ROM drive with an audio CD, turn on your sound system or plug in the headphones, and you're ready to go.

CD Player can tell when your CD-ROM drive is empty or doesn't contain a playable audio CD. In this case, it will display the message:

```
Data or no disc loaded
Please insert an audio disc
```

in the Artist and Title areas in the middle of the window.

Basic Playing Controls

The CD Player window looks much like the front panel of a typical CD player in a sound system. The large black area at the top left displays track and time information. On the left, the faux LED readout tells you which track is currently playing, while on the right it keeps a running tally of how many minutes and seconds have played in the track (you can change the contents of the time display as detailed below).

If you've ever worked a standard CD player, the control buttons (to the right of the track and time display) should be immediately familiar.

On the top row are the essential stop/start controls:

Play: The largest button with the big arrow starts or resumes play.

Pause: The button with the two vertical bars pauses play at the current point in the track.

Stop: The button with the square stops play and returns you to the beginning of the current track.

On the second row, the first four buttons have double arrows pointing to the left or right. These let you move to other parts of the disk.

TIP   You can move directly to a specific track by choosing it from the list in the Track area near the bottom of the CD Player window. See *Playing Discs with the Play List* later in the chapter.

Previous and *Next Track:* At either end of this set of four buttons, the buttons with the vertical bars move to the beginning of the previous or next track. The one at the left end—with the left-pointing arrows—moves to the beginning of the previous track (or if a track is playing, to the beginning of the current track). The one at the right—with the right-pointing arrows—moves to the beginning of the next track.

Skip Backwards and *Skip Forwards:* The two center buttons in the set of four have double arrows only; these are for moving quickly through the music while the disc plays in the reverse or forward direction.

The *Eject* button is the last button at the far right of the second row, with the upward-pointing arrow on top of a thin rectangle. Click here to pop the current disk out of your CD-ROM drive. Of course, this will only work if your drive is capable of ejecting automatically.

Display Options

Modern Windows program that it is, CD Player has a *Toolbar* with buttons for other common commands (we'll cover these in a moment). The Toolbar may not be visible when you first run the program. Choose View ➤ Toolbar to turn it on and off. Here's how the CD Player window looks with the Toolbar visible:

Part 2

Exploring Windows 95

When the Toolbar is on, you can get a brief description of each button's function by placing the mouse pointer over the button.

Two other elements of the CD Player window can also be turned off and on via the View menu. These are the Status Bar and the area displaying the artist and disc and track titles.

When visible, the Status Bar runs along the bottom of the window. It offers Help messages when the mouse pointer passes over a menu choice or rests over a button on the Toolbar for a few moments. Otherwise, it displays the total play time for the disc and current track. To turn the Status Bar off or on, choose View ➤ Status Bar.

Once you've cataloged a disc, CD Player displays the artist, disc title, and title of the current track in the middle of its window. If you want to hide this information, perhaps to make the window small enough to stay on your screen while you work with another program, choose View ➤ Disc/Track Info.

TIP   You can choose between two font sizes for the numerals in the track and time readout. See *Setting CD Player Preferences* below.

You can also control what time information appears in the main readout of the CD Player window. The standard display setting shows elapsed time for the track currently playing. If you prefer, you can instead see the time remaining for the current track or for the entire disk. To select among these options, open the View menu and choose one of the three relevant options: Track Time Elapsed, Track Time Remaining, or Disk Time Remaining. The currently active choice is checked on the View menu. Or, if the Toolbar is visible, you can click on the button corresponding to your time-display choice.

Other Play Options

You have several commands for determining the play order for a disc's tracks. Three of these are available as items on the Options menu or as buttons on the Toolbar:

Random order: Plays the tracks randomly. This is often called *shuffle* mode on audio-only CD players.

Continuous play: Plays the disc continuously rather than stopping after the last track.

Intro play: Plays only the first section of each track. You can set the length of this intro with the Preferences command, covered below.

> **NOTE** If you have a multiple-disc CD-ROM drive, you'll find an additional **Multidisc Play choice on the Options menu. Select this if you want to hear all the discs loaded in the drive rather than just the currently active disc.**

You can select these playback options in any combination. To turn them on or off, open the Options menu and choose the desired item; they are active when checked. Alternatively, click on the button for that command (the button appears pressed when the command is active). Here are the buttons you use:

If none of these commands are active, CD Player plays the tracks in full and in sequence, stopping after the last track.

Other play options include whether or not the current disc keeps playing when you close CD Player (covered in *Setting CD Player Preferences,* below) and playing a custom list of tracks, covered in the next section.

Cataloging Your CDs and Creating Play Lists

If you're willing to do a little typing, CD Player will keep a "smart" catalog of your disc collection. Once you've entered the catalog information, such as the disc title, the artist, and the track titles, CD Player automatically displays these details whenever you reload the disc:

Artist:	George Jones	<K:>
Title:	Super Hits	
Track:	Why Baby Why	<02>

Note that if you have a multidisc CD-ROM drive (or more than one unit), you can choose from the available drives by letter using the list in the Artist area.

Cataloging a Disc   When you load a disc that hasn't been cataloged, CD Player displays generic disc information. The Artist area reads *New Artist*, and the Title area says *New Title*. Tracks are titled by number (*Track 1*, *Track 2*, and so on).

To enter the actual information for the current disc, choose Disc ➤ Edit Play List, or, if the Toolbar is visible, click on the corresponding button (the one at the far left, shown here on the left). The dialog box shown in Figure 10.3 will appear.

The top area in this dialog box, labeled Drive, identifies the location of the disc being cataloged. If you have a multidisc player, you can double-check whether you're working with the correct disc here.

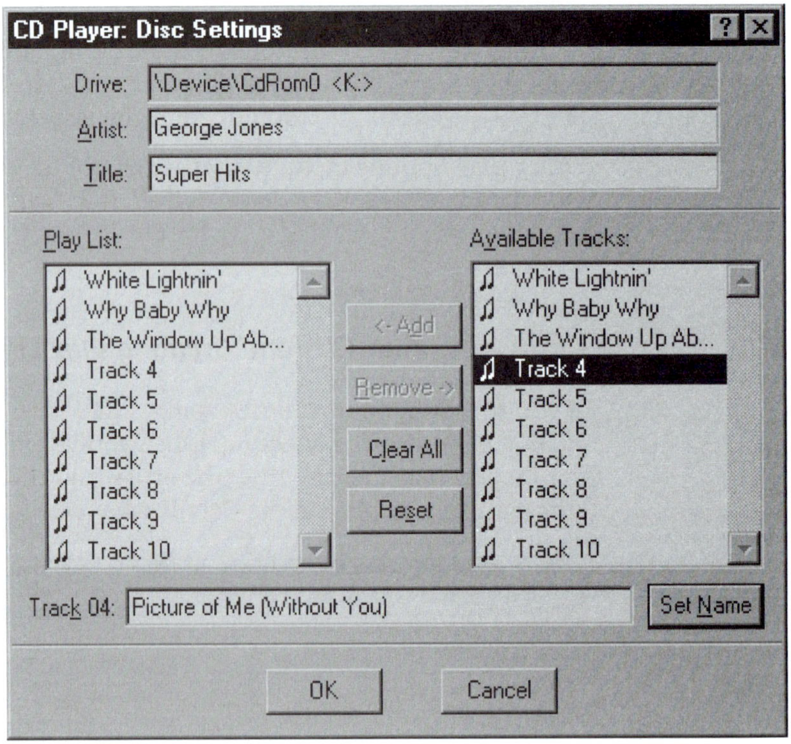

Figure 10.3   *The Disc Settings dialog box*

Type in the artist and title of the CD in the appropriate areas at the top of the dialog box. To type in track titles:

1. Select a track in the Available Tracks box (the one at the *right* of the dialog box).

2. Type in the track title in the Track area at the bottom of the dialog box.

3. Click on the Set Name button to change the current name.

You can change any of this information at any time. When you're satisfied with your entries, go on to create a play list as described below or click on OK to return to CD Player. The disc information will appear in the appropriate areas of the window.

Creating a Play List   The typical CD has some great songs, a few that are good to listen to but aren't favorites, and one or two that are just terrible. CD Player lets you set up a custom play list for each disc so you never have to hear those dog songs again. If you like, you can even play your favorites more often than the others (be careful, you might get sick of them).

Here's how to create a play list:

1. In the Disc Settings dialog box (Figure 10.3), the Play List box on the left side of the window displays the tracks in the play list. Initially, the box displays all the tracks on the disc in order.

2. If you just want to remove one or two tracks, drag each track off the list as follows: Point to the track's icon (the musical notes) in the Play List box, hold down the mouse button, and drag to the Available Tracks box. Alternatively, you can highlight each track in the Play List box and click on the Remove button. To remove all the tracks and start with an empty list, click on Clear All.

3. You can add tracks to the play list in two ways:

   ▶ Drag the track (or tracks) to the Play List box using the same technique for deleting tracks but in the reverse direction: Starting from the Available Tracks box, drag the track to the desired position in the play list. You can add a group of tracks by dragging across them to highlight them, releasing the mouse button, then dragging from the icon area to the play list.

▶ Use the Add button: Highlight one or more tracks in the Available Tracks box and click on Add. In this case, the added track always appears at the end of the list.

4. If you want to start again, click on Reset. The Play List box will again show all the tracks in order.

5. Click on OK when you've finished your play list to return to the main CD Player window.

Playing Discs with the Play List CD Player always selects the tracks it plays from the play list. Before you make any modifications, the play list contains all the tracks on the disc, and you'll hear every track when you play the disc. Once you've created your own play list, though, CD Player plays only the tracks on the list. If you select Random Order play, the program randomly selects tracks from the play list, not from all the tracks on the disc.

The play list tracks are accessible individually in the Track area near the bottom of the CD Player window. To move to a particular track, just select it in the list. If the disc is already playing, the selected track will start. Otherwise, click on the Play button to start it.

Setting CD Player Preferences

Use the Preferences dialog box to change miscellaneous CD Player settings. To display it, choose Options ➤ Preferences. Here's what the Preferences dialog box looks like:

Here are the available preferences settings and their effects:

Stop CD playing on exit: When this box is checked, CD Player stops the CD-ROM drive, halting audio playback. If you clear this box, the current disc plays through to the end.

Save settings on exit: When this box is checked, the settings you make on the View and Options menu and in the Preferences dialog box are saved when you close the program. If you clear this box, changes in settings affect only the current session—the previous settings are restored the next time you start CD Player.

Show tool tips: Check this box if you want pop-up descriptions and Help messages in the Status Bar when the mouse pointer rests on a button for a few moments. Clear it if you find these messages annoying.

Intro play length: Use the arrow controls to set the number of seconds at the beginning of each track that CD Player will play when you activate the Intro Play command.

Display font: Choose a large or small font for the LED-like track and time readout by choosing the appropriate radio button.

Managing Multimedia Drivers

When you add a new piece of hardware to your system, such as a sound board, CD-ROM controller, MIDI board, or other piece of paraphernalia, you'll have to alert Windows to this fact by installing the correct software device driver for the job. Some drivers simply control an external player as though you were pushing the buttons on the device's control panel by hand. These types of devices are called Media Control Interface (MCI) devices and include audio CD players, video disc players, and MIDI instruments. Other drivers actually send the sound or video data to the playback card or hardware, as well as control the playback speed and other parameters.

You use the Add New Hardware option in the Control Panel to install the device driver. Drivers for popular multimedia items are included with Windows and will often be detected when you've added the hardware, especially if the hardware is Plug-and-Play compatible.

Chapter 7 covers the use of the Add New Hardware applet; refer to that chapter if you have added new multimedia hardware to your system and it isn't being recognized.

If you are having trouble running your multimedia hardware or need to make adjustments to it, you'll have to examine the Properties of the item and its driver. Device property dialog boxes can be reached from several locations. For example, the Edit menu in the Sound Recorder applet will take you to your sound card's Properties settings, though you could also use the System applet in the Control Panel to get there. Properties are discussed in Chapter 11.

Information Sources

Magazines are great sources of quickly changing computer-product information. Visit your local smoke shop or magazine rack to look for multimedia intelligence. One magazine speaks directly to the issues herein—*MPC World*, available nationwide.

For online assistance, files, and general chitchat on multimedia, try CompuServe's Multimedia Forum (**GO MULTIMEDIA**) and Multimedia Vendor Forum (**GO MULTIVEN**); they contain the latest gossip, hints, trivia, and tips on the subject. Also try the Windows Advanced Forum (**GO WINADV**) and The Microsoft Network.

Windows Information Manager (*WIM*) is a periodical that's offered in a hypertext multimedia format, incorporating sound and animation.

Finally, there is at least one book that looks at Microsoft's multimedia development tools and discusses the processes involved in integrating image, sound, and text within a multimedia title. *Microsoft Windows Multimedia Authoring and Tools Guide* (Microsoft Press) is intended for publishers, managers, and developers who are considering writing their own multimedia titles. It doesn't touch on other vendors' authoring languages (of course). Still, it should be required reading when planning and preparing your sound, MIDI, graphics, animation, text, and CD-ROM data for use with any authoring language front end. Logistics of project planning and coordination are also covered.

Multimedia PC Marketing Council

These are the companies involved in establishing multimedia standards for PCs. They also market multimedia products and are good sources of information on MPC systems and software:

AT&T Computer Systems
1 Speedwell Ave.
Morristown, NJ 07960

CompuAdd Corp.
12303 Technology Blvd.
Austin, TX 78727

Creative Labs, Inc.
2050 Duane Ave.
Santa Clara, CA 95054

Media Vision, Inc.
47221 Fremont Blvd.
Fremont, CA 94538

Microsoft Corp.
One Microsoft Way
Redmond, WA 98052-6399

NEW Technologies, Inc.
1255 Michael Drive
Wood Dale, IL 60191

Olivetti
Via Jervis 77
10015 Ivrea
ITALY

Phillips Consumer Electronics Co.
1 Phillips Drive, P.O. Box 14810
Knoxville, TN 37914

Software Publishers Association
1730 M St. N.W., Suite 700
Washington, DC 20036

Tandy Corp.
700 One Tandy Center
Fort Worth, TX 76102

Video Seven
46221 Landing Parkway
Fremont, CA 94538

Zenith Data Systems
2150 East Lake Cook Road
Buffalo Grove, IL 60089

Chapter 11

Object Properties and the Right-Click

FEATURING

Right-clicking to reveal quick menu choices

Object Properties boxes

In this chapter, I'll discuss Properties boxes and the use of the right-click as a means for getting your work done faster and for adjusting object properties. Let's start with a brief recap of right-clicking.

Right-Clicking around Windows

As you are well aware by now, right-clicking on objects throughout the Windows 95 interface brings up a shortcut menu with options pertaining to the objects at hand. The same options are typically available from the normal menus but are more conveniently reached with the right-click.

> **NOTE** These button names will, of course, be reversed if you are left-handed or have reversed the mouse buttons for some other reason. If you have a trackball, a GlidePoint, or other nonstandard pointing device, your right-click button may be somewhere unexpected. You may have to experiment a little to find which one activates the right-click menus.

Right-clicking isn't only part of the Windows 95 interface; it's being incorporated into recently written Windows programs, too. For example, Microsoft Office programs such as Word 6 and Excel have had right-click menus for some time. Some of the accessory programs supplied with Windows 95 have context-sensitive right-click menus, too. In general, the contents of the right-click menus change depending on the type of object. Options for a table will differ from those for a spreadsheet cell, frames, text, graphics, and so on.

As a rule, I suggest you start using the right-click button whenever you can. You'll learn through experimentation which of your programs do something with the right-click and which don't. Many 16-bit Windows programs won't even respond to the click; others may do the unexpected. But in almost every case, right-clicking results in a pop-up menu that you can close by clicking elsewhere or by pressing Esc, so don't worry about doing anything dangerous or irreversible.

A good example of a right-clickable item is the Taskbar. Right-click on an empty place on the Taskbar, and you'll see this menu:

Now right-click on the Start button, and you'll see this menu:

Here are a few other right-clicking experiments to try:

▶ Right-click on My Computer and notice the menu options.

▶ Right-click on a document icon. If you right-click on a DOS batch file (any file with a BAT extension), you'll have an edit option on the menu. What an easy way to edit a batch file!

▶ Right-click on a program file, such as Pbrush.exe in the Windows directory or on a DLL (Dynamic Link Library) file. The Quick View option lets you read information about the program, such as how much memory it requires to run and when it was created. A Properties option may tell you even more.

▶ When you right-click on a printer in the Printer's folder, you can quickly declare the printer to be the default printer or to work offline (not actually print yet even though you print to it from your applications) or go online with accumulated print jobs. Right-click on the Desktop to set the screen colors, screen saver, and so forth.

▶ Right-click on any program's title bar and notice the menu for resizing the window or closing the application.

▶ Right-click on a minimized program's button down in the Taskbar. You can close the program quickly by choosing Close.

▶ Right-click on the time in the Taskbar and choose Adjust Date/Time to alter the date and time settings for your computer.

Right-click menus will often have Cut, Copy, Paste, Open, Print, and Rename choices on them. These are discussed in Chapters 4, 5, and 6.

Many objects such as folders, printers, Network Neighborhood, and Inbox have a right-click menu called Explore that brings up the item in the Explorer's format (two vertical panes). This is a super-handy way to check out the object in a display similar to the Windows 3.x File Manager. You'll have the object in the left pane and its contents listed in the right pane. In some cases the contents are print jobs; in other cases they are fonts, files, folders, disk drives, or computers on the network. The Explorer is covered in Chapter 12.

Sharable items, such as printers, hard disks, and fax modems will have a Sharing option on their right-click menus. The resulting box lets you declare how an object is shared for use by other users on the network. Sharing a printer is covered in Chapter 8, and those general rules apply here. Additional discussion of sharing can be found in Part 5.

Property Sheets

Just as most objects have right-click menus, many also have property sheets. Properties pervade all aspects of the Windows 95 user interface, providing you with a simple and direct means for making settings to everything from how the screen looks to whether a file is hidden or what a shared printer is named.

Virtually every object in Windows 95—whether a printer, modem, shortcut, hard disk, folder, networked computer, or hardware driver—has a *property sheet* containing such settings. These settings affect how the object works and, sometimes, how it looks. And property sheets not only *display* the settings for the object, but usually allow you to easily *alter* the settings.

You've probably noticed that many right-click menus have a Properties choice down at the bottom. This choice is often the quickest path to an object's property sheet—not that there aren't other ways. Many dialog boxes, for example, have a Properties button that will bring up the object's settings when clicked on. And the Control Panel is used for setting numerous properties throughout Windows 95. Still, as you become more and more comfortable with Windows 95, you'll find the right-click approach most expedient.

Who Will Use Property Sheets?

The majority of Windows 95 users will rarely bother viewing or making changes to property-sheet settings because Windows 95 is well-enough behaved to govern itself (for example, repairing shortcuts when the target file or folder has been moved) and to prompt you when necessary for details about objects. As a case in point, when you install Windows 95 for the first time, or when you add new hardware or create a new printer, Wizards conscientiously assume the responsibility of setting up properties appropriately. The upshot is that tweaking Windows 95's internals and objects isn't nearly as necessary as it was in Windows 3.x. And in those rare instances when it is, unearthing the required dialog box for the job isn't an exercise reminiscent of dismantling a Chinese box puzzle.

Certainly any self-respecting power user will want to know all about properties for easily performing tasks such as sharing a folder on the network, changing the name of a hard-disk volume, checking the status of the computer's ports, displaying a font or other file's technical details, or checking the amount of free disk space on a hard disk.

> **TIP**   To even more quickly see an object's properties, highlight the object and press Alt-Enter.

Trying Out a Few Properties Boxes

The Properties option is always the last command on a right-click menu. For example, if you right-click on My Computer, you'll see this menu:

Or right-click on the clock in the Taskbar, and you'll see this:

```
Adjust Date/Time
Cascade
Tile Horizontally
Tile Vertically

Minimize All Windows
Undo Cascade

Properties...                    PM
```

Just choose the Adjust Date/Time command to easily set the time, date, and time zone for your computer, ensuring that all your files are properly date and time stamped and your Taskbar displays the time correctly.

Here's another everyday example. Suppose you're browsing through some folders (or the Explorer) and come across a Word document. Wondering what it is, when it was created, and who created it, you just right-click and choose Properties. The file's property sheet pops up, as shown in Figure 11.1. Notice that there are several tab pages on the sheet. That's because this is a Word file, and Word stores information in such files.

Property sheets for other kinds of files may only have a single tab page with less than a copious amount of information. In fact, most document property sheets are truly useful only if you want to examine the history of the file, determine its shorter MS-DOS file name, or set its DOS attributes such as whether it should be read-only (to prevent others from using it), hidden from view in folders, or if its *archive bit* should be set. (A check mark in the Archive box means the file hasn't been backed up since it was last altered or since it was created.) My point is that you can usually only *view* the status of the document, not *alter* it.

Property sheets for objects other than documents often let you make more substantive changes to them. A shortcut's property sheet, for example, lets you adjust some goodies about how the shortcut works, the file it points to, and so on, as shown in Figure 11.2.

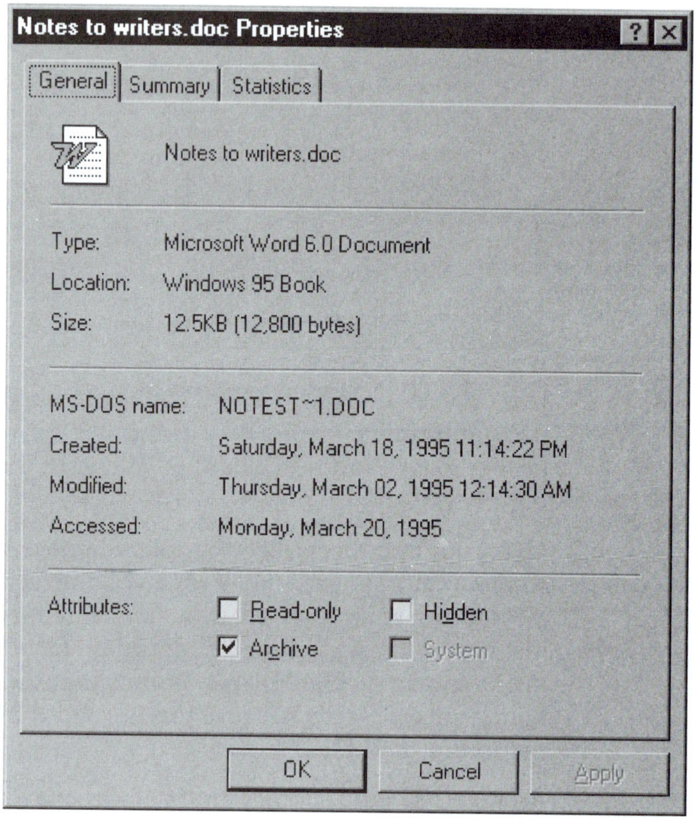

Figure 11.1   *A typical property sheet for a document file. This one is for a Word 6 file, so it has several pages listing its editing history, who created it, keywords, title, and so forth.*

TIP   There is now a way to ensure that a program (whether DOS *or* Windows) defaults to a certain directory. In the dialog box shown in Figure 11.2, you can use the Start In field to set the default directory for a program. When you start the application from the shortcut, the File ➤ Open and File ➤ Save As commands will then default to this directory. In Windows 3.x, setting this variable was only possible for DOS programs. Now it's possible for Windows programs too.

This property sheet is somewhat similar to the old PIF files in Windows 3.x, though those only affected the running of DOS programs.

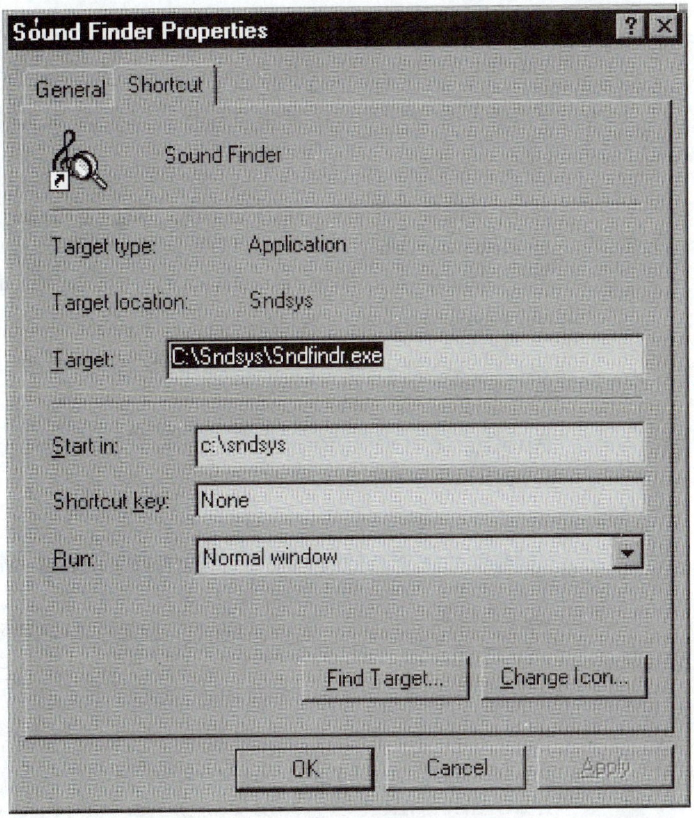

Figure 11.2 *Shortcuts have property sheets with a second tab page listing the particulars of the shortcut and allowing modification. Here you can change settings that control how the document or program will run when the shortcut is double-clicked on.*

Shortcut property sheets can affect any program or document. You can use the ? button for help on any of the options, but I'll just say that the two handiest items here are Shortcut Key and Run. Shortcut Key lets you assign a key combination that will run the shortcut from anywhere. For example, to jump to My Computer without having to minimize all your other windows first:

1. Get to the Desktop. Then right-click on My Computer and choose Create Shortcut. This creates a new shortcut on the Desktop called Shortcut to My Computer.

2. Right-click on the new shortcut and choose Properties.

3. In the Properties dialog box, click on the Shortcut tab, then click in the Shortcut Key field.

4. Press Ctrl-Alt-C to assign the shortcut key to Ctrl-Alt-C.

5. OK the box.

Now whenever you want to open My Computer, just press Ctrl-Alt-C. It takes a little manual dexterity, but it's quick. Use the same trick for any object you use regularly and find you're fishing around to open.

The Run field in a Shortcut's property box just determines whether the object will open in a maximized, minimized, or normal (floating) window.

Another interesting property sheet belongs to the Recycle Bin. See Chapter 31 for details.

Making Property Settings from My Computer

Probably the most powerful property sheet is reachable directly from My Computer. Clicking on My Computer and choosing Properties brings up the box shown in Figure 11.3.

Examine the four tab pages here. The first page tells you some useful information about the version of Windows 95 you are running, how much memory your computer has, and what type of CPU chip is in your machine. This will come in handy the next time someone asks you what's in the computer you're running: Instead of drumming your fingers on the desk, feeling like a dufus, you can open this box and read what it says.

The second tab page lists all the devices in the whole computer, many of which you probably didn't even know you had. Clicking on a + sign opens up a device to display more attributes about it. Clicking on a device and then on the Properties button tells you more about the highlighted device.

The third and fourth tab pages are about setting up specialized system profiles (collections of settings to match different hardware arrangements, such as when a laptop is docked into a base unit or running around in the field) and for fine-tuning your system's virtual memory management, file system, and video graphics display speed. These are covered in Chapter 31.

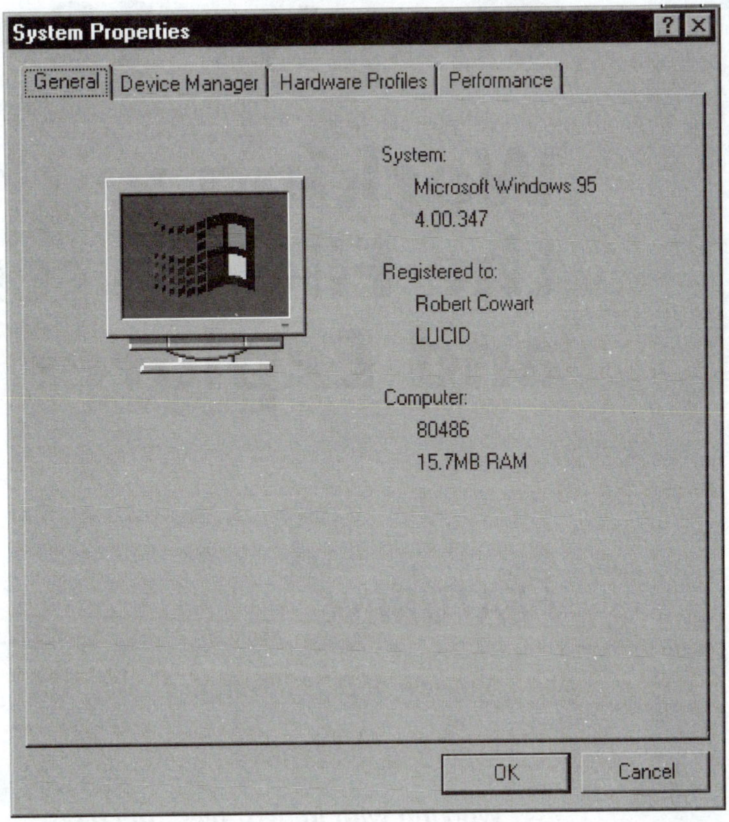

Figure 11.3 *A grand overview of your computer's attributes is available by right-clicking on My Computer and choosing Properties. Use some caution with these settings. This box is also available from the System applet in the Control Panel.*

CAUTION As a rule, don't toy with the System Properties settings unless you know what you're doing. Examining all the dialog boxes is fine if you just cancel them. But adjusting the file system and virtual memory settings will more likely negatively impact your system's performance than accelerate it.

Chapter 12

Working with the File System and Explorer

FEATURING

Most application programs nowadays consist of numerous files. Add to this the plethora of documents and programs you're likely to collect, and suddenly your hard-disk directory looks like that ugly snake-filled chamber in *Raiders of the Lost Ark*. With the advent of affordable high-capacity hard disks (300 MB, 500 MB, even 1 or 2 gigabytes), one of the more challenging maintenance issues with any computer operating system is the job of managing your files.

If you find that the folder system is a nuisance because of the circuitous routes it takes you through at times, read on, because in the following pages, I'm going to reveal the pleasures of the Windows Explorer—a sort of supercharged Windows 3.x File Manager. It's a very powerful tool that does almost any Windows 95 system task, from making Control Panel settings to adding printers, viewing and mapping network drives, creating and managing folders and documents, and running programs. If you want to truly master Windows 95, the Explorer is *the* vantage point from which to do it. You'll benefit greatly in your day-to-day tasks by understanding how to use it.

A Review of DOS Directories

But first a little review. For the most part this chapter assumes you understand the basics of the DOS directory structure. However, if you're a little rusty on the topic, here's a thumbnail primer of directory (folder) workings.

> **NOTE**   Keep in mind that although Microsoft would like us all to forget we ever heard the terms "directory" and "subdirectory," any discussion of the Explorer has to at least acknowledge that most of what the program does is display and manipulate your DOS directories. In Windows 95 lingo we're now to think of these as *folders* and *subfolders*, as those terms conform more with the new paradigm of the file/folder approach to organizing your work. If it serves you to think in the new terms, have at it. As a compromise, I'll use the terms "folders" and "directories" interchangeably, though I'll favor the new terms.

DOS stores all files in folders on your disk. As you know, a folder is simply a collection of files, whether they are programs, documents, fonts, or what have you. Even Windows with all its bells and whistles is nothing but a bunch of files spread out across many folders. As you also know, folders let you keep related files nested together. With occasional limitations imposed by specific programs, you can organize your files however the spirit strikes you.

Folders are organized in a system analogous to a tree, as illustrated in Figure 12.1. In fact, the organization of folders is called the *directory tree*. The folders are organized in a hierarchical manner, from the *root* (the most basic level) to various branches off the root (folders) and branches off those branches (subfolders).

It is possible that you've never used folders before, because, theoretically, you can put all your files in the default folder (aka the *root directory*), though there is a limit to the number of files you can store in

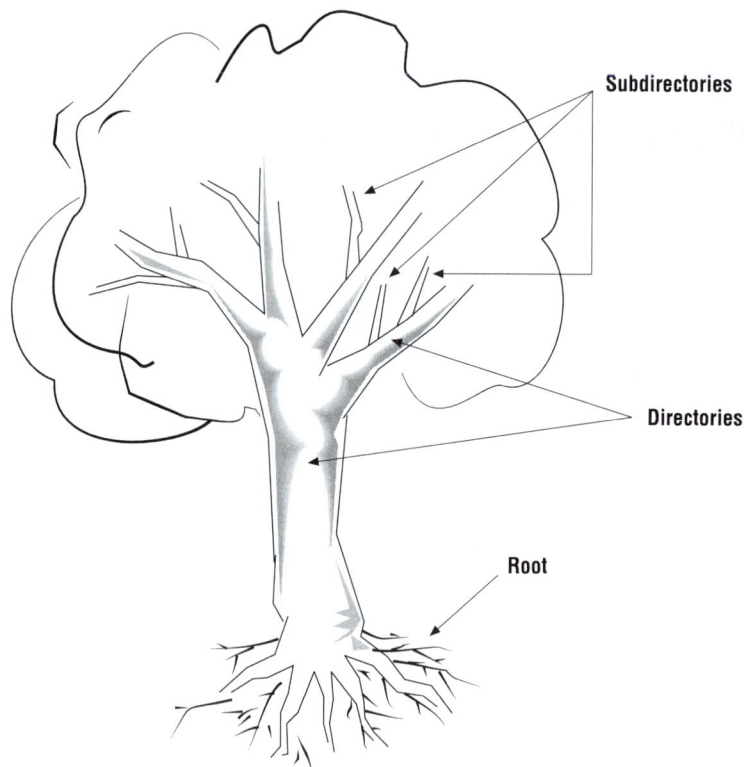

Figure 12.1   *The DOS directory-tree structure. Folders are organized from the root outward.*

the root folder (512 using short files names, fewer with long names). If you've never created a new folder, it's possible (though not likely) that all your files are stored in the root folder. However, as discussed in Chapter 5, it's much wiser to divide things up according to projects.

The root folder in DOS and File Manager was indicated by a single backslash (\). In Explorer it's indicated by the drive's icon:

All other folders have names that you or some program (such as a program's installation program) create. For example, the Windows Setup program created a folder branch called Windows. Subordinate to Windows, it created another branch called System. The official name of the system folder is C:\Windows\System. This is called the folder's path name. The name describes the path you'd take to get to the folder, just as if you were climbing the tree—from the root up to the particular branch. Notice that the \ (indicating the root) precedes the folder name and that branches in the path name are also separated by a backslash.

In working with folders, the main thing to keep in mind is the *you can't get there from here* rule. To switch between distant branches, there are times when you have to remember their relationship to the root; I explain this in Chapter 3 in *File Dialog Boxes*. For example, if you were working in the \Windows\System folder and wanted to save a file in the \Letters\Personal folder, you'd typically have to back up to the root level first, select the Letters folder, and finally select the Personal folder. Just like when climbing a tree, if you want to get from one branch to the next, you have to go back to the trunk, *then* out the other branch.

Exploring the Explorer

To run the Explorer, click on the Start button and choose Programs ➤ Windows Explorer. The Explorer will load. Maximize the window and it will look something like Figure 12.2. Of course, the folders in your window will be different from those shown here.

Unlike the File Manager, Explorer doesn't let you open multiple windows. On the other hand, it's not necessary because Explorer is more flexible in design. You can actually copy files, folders, or other objects from anywhere to anywhere without needing multiple windows.

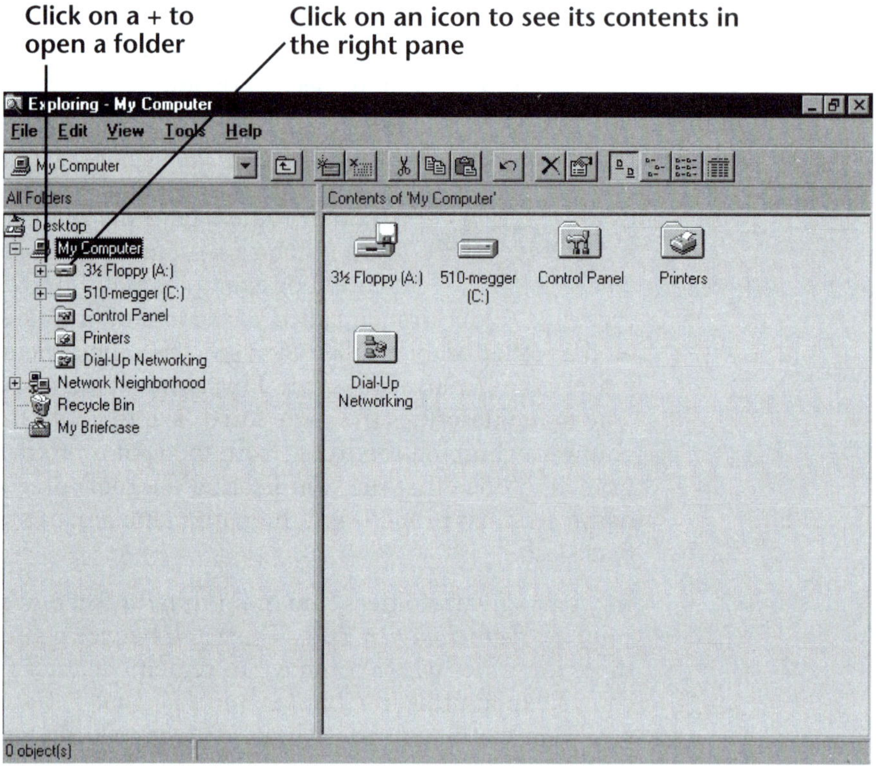

Click on a + to
open a folder

Click on an icon to see its contents in
the right pane

Figure 12.2 *The basic Explorer screen, showing the major items on the left and the contents on the right*

TIP Actually, there are two workarounds that will give you multiple windows for a drive or folder. The first is to put multiple shortcuts for a drive on your Desktop. Then you can double-click on them all and adjust the size and placement of the windows as necessary. This uses the folder system, not Windows Explorer, though. If you prefer to use Explorer, you can run it more than once and adjust the windows as necessary to see the multiple instances of it.

Displaying the Contents of Your Computer

When you run the Explorer, all the objects constituting your computer appear in the list on the left. Some of those objects may have a plus sign (+) next to them, which means the object is *collapsed*; it contains sub-items that aren't currently showing. For example, my hard disk drive in Figure 12.2 is collapsed. So is Network Neighborhood (which you won't see unless you're on a network) and the floppy drive (drive A). Here's how to check out the contents of such an item:

1. Click on the item itself, not on the + sign. For example, click on your C drive's icon. Now its contents appear in the right pane as a bunch of folders.

2. Another approach is to click directly on the + sign. This opens up the sublevels in the left pane, showing you the relationship of the folders in a tree arrangement as in Figure 12.3.

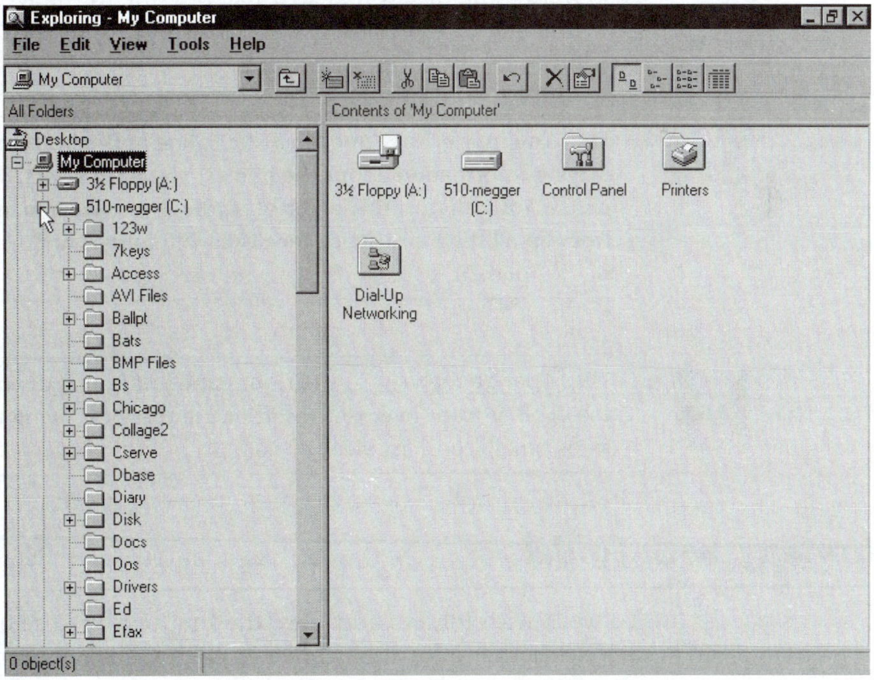

Part 2

Exploring Windows 95

Figure 12.3   Click on a + sign to display folders and other sub-objects.

3. Notice that the + is replaced with a − sign, indicating that the object's display has been *expanded*. Click on it again, and it collapses.

4. To collapse everything, click on the − sign next to My Computer.

5. Click on the Desktop icon up at the top of the tree. Notice that all the objects on your Desktop appear in the right pane.

The tree is a graphical representation of your disk layout. Each file folder icon symbolizes one folder, and the straight lines connecting them indicate how they're related. The name of each folder appears after the icon. If you have more folders than can be seen at one time, the window will have a scroll bar that you can use to scroll the tree up and down. Notice that there are two scroll bars—one for the left pane and one for the right. These scroll independently of one another, a feature that can be very useful when you are copying items from one folder or drive to another.

Also notice that a Toolbar just like the one in the My Computer window is at the top of the Explorer window. Refer to Chapter 4 for a discussion of the buttons' functions.

> **TIP**   You may or may not see a status line at the bottom of the window displaying information about the item(s) you have selected in the right or left panes. You can turn this on or off through the View menu. Turning it off frees up a little more space for displaying folders and files. The same is true of the Toolbar.

> **TIP**   Change the view in the right pane just as you do in any folder. Click on the Toolbar icons over to the left or use the View menu to display large icons, small icons, list view, or details.

Working with Folders

To work with folders and files, the first task is to select the correct drive, whether a local hard disk, a floppy drive, or a networked drive. Once you have the correct drive selected, you can drag and drop files, run programs, open documents that have an association, and use right-click menu options for various objects. For example, you can right-click on files or folders and choose Send To ➤ 3^{1}/$_{2}$ Floppy to copy items to a floppy disk.

Selecting the Correct Drive and Choosing a Folder

To select the drive whose contents you want to work with:

1. Scroll the left pane up or down until you see the drive you want. Use the scroll bar in the middle of the window to do this. If the drive you want isn't showing, you may have to expand the My Computer icon by clicking on its + sign. At least one hard drive (and probably a floppy) should be visible.

> Desktop
> My Computer
>   3½ Floppy (A:)
>   510-megger (C:)

2. Click on the name or icon of the drive whose contents you want to work with. The right pane then displays its contents. On a hard disk, you'll typically see a bunch of folders there, not files. (Floppies often don't have folders on them.) Folders are always listed first, followed by files. If you scroll the list a bit, you'll reach the files. Remember, at this point you are in the root directory of the selected drive. You have to find a specific folder before you get to see what's in it.

3. If the drive has folders on it, you now have a choice. You can double-click on one of the folders in the right pane, or you can expand the drive's listing in the left pane by clicking on its + sign. Which option you choose doesn't really matter. You can get to the same place either way. The advantage of expanding the drive in the left pane is simply that it gives you more of a graphical view of how your disk is organized and also lets you drag items from the right pane into destination folders. Go ahead and click on the drive's + sign if it's showing (Figure 12.4). Note that I've changed the right pane's view to show small icons so I can see more items at once.

> Desktop
> My Computer
>   3½ Floppy (A:)
>   510-megger (C:)
>   Control Panel

4. Now suppose you want to see which fonts you have in your Fonts folder. This folder is a subfolder of the Windows folder. Finding it from My Computer would take a little hunting around, but with Explorer it's easy. If necessary, scroll the left list down, using the scroll box in the left pane's scroll bar, until you see the Windows folder.

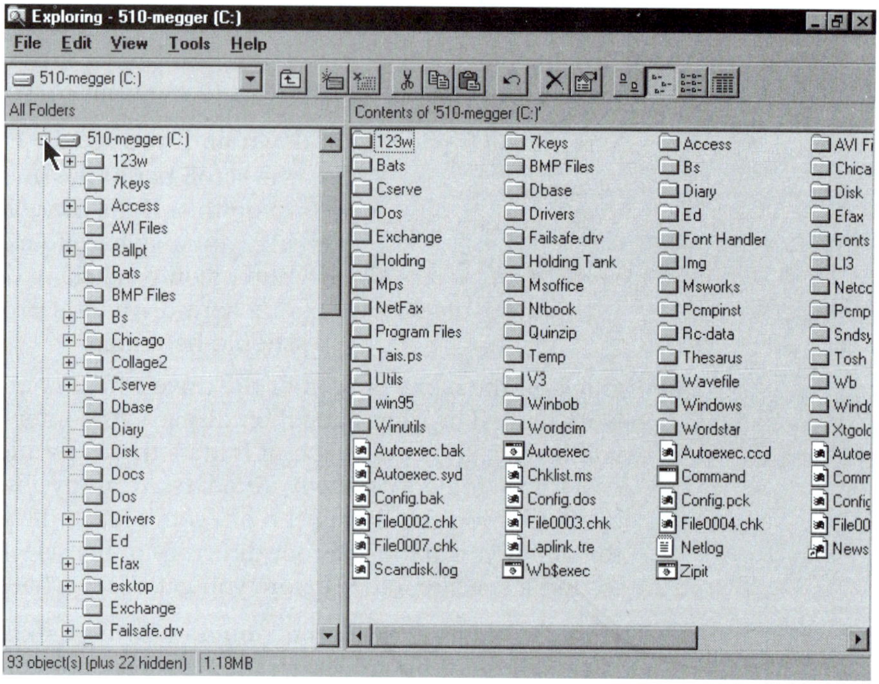

Figure 12.4   Clicking on a drive's + sign opens it. Here you see my C drive.

5. Because the Windows directory has subfolders, click on the + sign. Its subfolders now show.

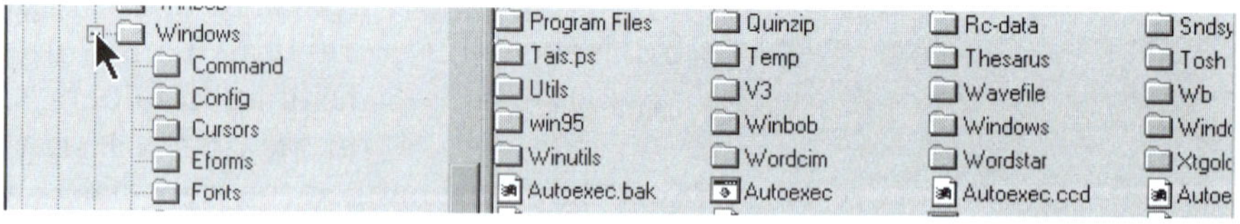

6. Fonts is one of the subfolders under Windows. Click on it to see which font files are in the directory and consequently which fonts are installed on your system. The Fonts directory works a little differently than other directories, letting you install and display fonts by similarity. You'll notice some menu commands that are different from other directories.

7. Click on the Cursors folder to see which cursors are in your system. These are the shapes Windows has available for your mouse pointer.

Here are a few tips when selecting folders:

▶ Only one folder can be selected at a time.

▶ When a folder is selected, its icon changes from a closed folder to an open one.

▶ You can select a folder by clicking on it, typing its first letter, or moving the highlight to it with the arrow keys. When selected, the folder icon and name become highlighted.

▶ You can jump quickly to a folder name by typing its first letter on the keyboard. If there is more than one folder with the same first letter, each press of the key will advance to the next choice.

▶ Click on the + sign to expand a folder tree one level down. Click on the - sign to collapse a folder's tree up a level.

▶ The fastest way to collapse all the branches of a given drive is to click on the drive's – sign.

Notice that every time you select a folder, its contents are displayed in the folder-contents side of the window. The contents will include subordinate folders (listed first and looking like little folders just as they do in the left window), followed by the list of files.

If you want to change the order in which files are sorted (by name, extension, etc.), you can only do it in Details view. Change to Details view via the View menu, the right-click menu, or the Toolbar, then click on the appropriate column heading. For example, to sort files by size, click here:

All Folders		Contents of 'Windows'			
		Name	Size	Type	Modified
⊞ 📁 Tosh Utils		🗿 Win386.swp	20,992KB	SWP File	3/22/95 1:1
📁 Toshiba		🗿 Msn.pst	801KB	PST File	3/20/95 5:3
⊞ 📁 Utils					

The first time you click, the files list in ascending size. A second click reverses the order. And just as with most column headings of this style, you can resize any column by dragging the dividing line between two column headings.

Name	Size	Type	Modified
Arrow_1.cur	1KB	Cursor	3/2/95 12:0
Arrow_l.cur	1KB	Cursor	3/2/95 12:0

Creating a New Folder

As explained in Chapter 5, organizing often involves making up new folders. You already know how to do this using My Computer. In keeping with Windows 95's consistency, Explorer uses the same techniques.

TECH TIP   Technically, the folder system is also the Explorer. They both are part of the same program.

Creating a folder is easy, and because of the graphical nature of the folder tree, for many people it's easier to visualize what you're doing in Explorer than when creating folders from My Computer when you have windows scattered all over the screen.

1. From the left (tree) pane, select the folder in which you want to create a subfolder. If you select the A drive icon at the top of a tree (the root), the folder will be created directly off of it. Make sure you click on the folder, not just on its + or – sign. The folder icon has to open up, and the name must be highlighted.

2. Now here's the trick. Click in any empty space in the *right* pane, then create a new folder just as you do from My Computer. That is, choose File ➤ New or right-click and choose New ➤ Folder.

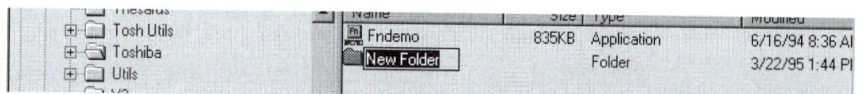

	Name	Size	Type	Modified
Thesaurus				
Tosh Utils	Fndemo	835KB	Application	6/16/94 8:36 A
Toshiba	New Folder		Folder	3/22/95 1:44 P
Utils				

3. Type in the name for your folder, replacing the default name *New Folder*, which is really only a placeholder. When you finalize the name by pressing Enter, it will show up in the left pane when you expand its parent folder branch.

Deleting a Folder

As you may know, deleting a folder in DOS can be a pain. You have to remove all the files first, then delete the folder. After DOS 6, the **deltree** command made this much simpler. And in Explorer, just as from My Computer, it's even more simple; you can do it in one step. But because it's so easy, you should be careful—you can easily trash an entire directory. The good news when using Explorer or My Computer rather than DOS is that you can reverse the action with the File ➤ Undo command—at least until you delete something else. And of course, you can examine the Recycle Bin and return individual items to their former locations until you empty the trash.

> **CAUTION**   You should know that only programs designed to take advantage of the Recycle Bin will safely move files there rather than irrevocably deleting them. Deleting a file in the old File Manager or from the MS-DOS prompt, for example, will definitely erase the file.

You'll be asked if you want to delete an item or group of items before it gets trashed; you have the option of turning the confirmation request off, but it's a reasonable safeguard. Techies who don't want to be bothered with the Recycle Bin or confirmation messages may turn off from the Recycle Bin's property sheet (Global Settings tab page).

> **TIP**   To quickly erase an entire floppy, right-click on the drive's icon and choose Format ➤ Quick erase ➤ Start.

1. In the left pane *or* the right pane, right-click on the folder you want to delete and choose Delete. As an alternative, left-click on it, then

Part
2

Exploring Windows 95

choose File ➤ Delete or press Del. A confirmation box such as this
will appear, asking for your permission:

> **Confirm Folder Delete**   ☒
>
> Are you sure you want to remove the folder 'DBASE' and move all its
> contents to the Recycle Bin?
>
> [Yes]   [No]

2.   If you really want to delete the folder and all its files, click on Yes. The
contents of the folder (*including* any and all subfolders!) will be moved
to the Recycle Bin.

If you click on Yes in the above dialog box with the confirmation messages set on, you will need to keep clicking on Yes for each file before
it is deleted. If you click on *Yes to All*, all files will be deleted with no
further ado, with one exception. When Windows 95 detects that you
are trying to erase an application program (any file with an EXE,
COM, or BAT extension), it will ask for additional confirmation:

> **Confirm File Delete**   ☒
>
> The file 'wp5.exe' is a program.
>
> If you remove it, you will no longer be able to run this program or edit
> some documents. Are you sure you want to move it to the Recycle
> Bin?
>
> [Yes]   [Yes to All]   [No]   [Cancel]

Click on Yes to delete the named program. Click on Yes to All to not
be hassled by such messages for the duration of the folder's deletion.

Moving Folders

In addition to enabling you to move files easily, the Explorer lets you move complete folders or folder branches. When you move a folder, all the files in the folder are moved automatically.

You can select the folder to be moved either from the tree pane or from the folder (file) pane. Just drag the folder from either pane to the new destination:

▶ When you move a folder to another folder, Windows adds it below the destination folder.

▶ When you move a folder from one drive into another drive's icon, it gets added below the current folder in the destination drive.

More often than not, people want to move folders around on the same drive, a bit like rearranging their living-room furniture. This is extremely easy with the Explorer. After using this feature, you'll wonder how you ever did without it:

1. Select the folder you want to move (in either pane) and drag it to its new location. As you slide the mouse over possible targets, the target becomes highlighted, indicating where the folder will land if you release the mouse button.

2. When you release the mouse button, the folder will be added as a subfolder one level below the destination folder (and any subfolders will be arrayed below it as before).

Moving Multiple Folders Simultaneously

You can move the contents of more than one folder at a time, but unless they are connected by a descending branch, you have to do this from a folder (file) pane, not from the tree pane. For example, suppose you wanted folders named 1994 Reports, 1995 Reports, and 1996 Reports to be subfolders under a folder called All Reports. You could do this by dragging one folder at a time as explained above. But it's faster to do it in one fell swoop. Select the three folders in the folder pane. Drag them as a group to All Reports in the tree pane. Figure 12.5 shows one way of doing this and the resulting dialog box.

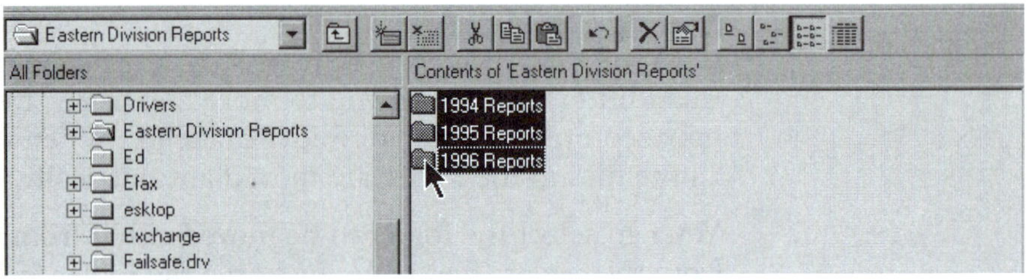

Figure 12.5   *Dragging multiple folders into a destination folder. The source folders will become subfolders of the destination folder.*

Figure 12.6 shows the change to the folder tree. Notice that 1994 Reports, 1995 Reports, and 1996 Reports were added under All Reports as subfolders.

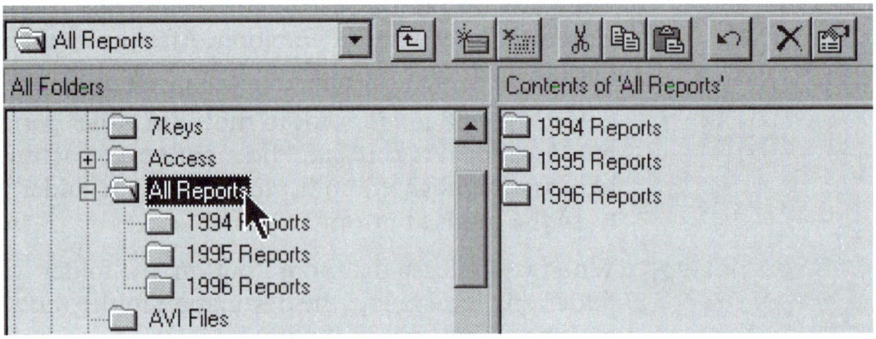

Figure 12.6   *The result of moving* 1994 Reports, 1995 Reports, *and* 1996 Reports *into* All Reports. *Notice the altered folder tree.*

TIP   Though not a skill often needed, you *can* copy a complete directory. Simply click on a folder (either in the left or right pane) and choose Edit ➤ Copy. Then click on the destination drive or folder icon and choose Edit ➤ Paste.

Working with Files

So what about working with files? It's simple. All the rules of working with files in standard folders (as discussed in Chapter 5) apply to Explorer. Once you've selected the correct drive and folder, you do all your work with files by selecting them in the right pane. Just select the file(s) and then cut, copy, paste, run, open, print, quick view, or change properties of the files using the right-click menu or commands from the File and Edit menus. You can also drag files around to relocate them or right-click-drag them to move, create shortcuts, or copy them.

All these techniques were covered in Chapter 5. But to give you a feel for dragging a file from one folder to another, here's a little exercise. Try moving a file, using the drag-and-drop approach.

1. In the left pane, click on the Windows folder. Then make sure it's expanded to show its subfolders.

2. Then click on the Media folder, which is a subfolder of Windows. In the right pane, you should see a lot of sound (WAV) files.

3. Now scroll the right pane until you see the file Canyon.mid. We can experiment with this file because it's not terribly important. It's a MIDI sound file.

4. Now let's say you wanted to move this file to the Cursors folder. Scroll the left pane up or down until you see Cursors (another subfolder of Windows).

5. Now drag Canyon.mid *on top* of the Cursors folder. The Cursors folder is the *target* folder and must be highlighted before you release the mouse button, so keep the mouse button depressed until the word *Cursor* is highlighted, then release.

Name	Size	Type	Modified
Canyon.mid	20KB	MIDI Sequence	3/2/95 12:0
Chimes.wav	16KB	Wave Sound	3/2/95 12:0
Chord.wav	25KB	Wave Sound	3/2/95 12:0

6. Just to check that it worked, now view the contents of the Cursors folder by clicking on it. In amongst all your icon files you'll now have the Canyon file.

7. Now, for purposes of good housekeeping, you should return the file to its origin. Choose Edit ➤ Undo Move (or drag the file from the right pane onto the Media folder in the left pane).

Refreshing the Directory

Sometimes other programs will affect the contents of an open drive window. For example, you might switch away from Explorer into an application window such as Word, Paradox, or whatever, and create a new document in a folder that's displaying back in the Explorer. Or you might edit a file that's also displayed in the folder's window, changing its size (in bytes). Normally Windows takes care of updating the information in the display; however, there are times when this doesn't happen reliably. Particularly when you are connected to a network, Windows may have trouble detecting that a folder's contents have changed. This will also be an issue if you change floppy disks and want to see the folder on the new disk. If you suspect that a folder may have been changed in some way that isn't reflected in the folder pane, just choose Window ➤ Refresh or press F5.

Selecting Files

Before you can work with the files in a folder, you have to select one or more of them. As with other objects in Windows, you select files by highlighting them. Here are various methods of selecting (and deselecting) files:

To select one file: Click once on the file. Notice that the status line (the last line in the File Manager window) indicates that one file is selected.

To select multiple nonconsecutive files: Click on the first file to select it and Ctrl-click on additional files.

To select a group of consecutive files: (This is easiest in the List or Details view because objects are in a list.) Click on the first file in the series, then Shift-click on the last item you want to select. As an alternative, you can draw a box around the files you want to select.

To select several groups of consecutive files: Select the first group as described above. To select the second group, hold down the Ctrl key and click on the first file in the second group. Press the Shift and Ctrl keys simultaneously and click on the last file in the second group. Repeat for each additional group.

To select all the files in a folder: Choose File ➤ Select All. You can then deselect specific files by Ctrl-clicking.

To invert the selection of files: Select the files you want to omit from the selection. Then choose Edit ➤ Invert Selection.

Once highlighted, a file or group of files can be operated on via the mouse or by using the commands on the File and Edit menus. For example, you can drag a group of files into another folder, delete them, copy and paste them somewhere else, or print them (assuming they are documents). All these commands are covered in Chapter 4, but here's a quick recap of the commands and clicks:

▶ *Run* a program or *open* a document by double-clicking on it. Alternatively, highlight a file and press Enter.

▶ *Print* a document by choosing File ➤ Print. Alternatively, right-click and choose Print.

▶ *View* a file (document, program, font, etc.) with File ➤ Quick View or by right-clicking and choosing Quick View.

▶ *Edit* a BAT file with File ➤ Edit or by right-clicking and choosing Edit.

▶ *Send* selected file(s) to a floppy drive, fax recipient, or your Briefcase with File ➤ Send To or by right-clicking and choosing Send To. (Briefcase is covered in Chapter 30.)

▶ Create a *new* document or shortcut or certain types of registered documents with File ➤ New or by right-clicking and choosing New. You can also create a new shortcut for the selected item(s) with File ➤ Create Shortcut.

▶ *Paste a shortcut* for the selected item(s) by first copying, then choosing Edit ➤ Paste Shortcut. Alternatively, right-click-drag and choose Shortcut from the pop-up menu when you release the mouse button.

▶ *Delete* the selected item(s) with File ➤ Delete, the Del key, or by right-clicking and choosing Delete. This sends items to the Recycle Bin. Clicking on the X button in the Toolbar has the same effect.

▶ *Rename* items with File ➤ Rename, by right-clicking and choosing Rename, or by a slow double-click on their name. Edit the name with the edit keys, then press Enter to finalize the new name.

▶ Check a file's *Properties* with File ➤ Properties or highlight it and press Alt-Enter. (Properties are covered in Chapter 11.)

▶ *Copy* a file by choosing Edit ➤ Copy, selecting the destination (folder or drive), and choosing Edit ➤ Paste. You can right-click and choose Copy followed by right-clicking and choosing Paste as a shortcut or use the Copy and Paste buttons in the Toolbar.

▶ *Move* selected item(s) from one location to another by dragging and dropping or with Edit ➤ Cut followed by Edit ➤ Paste. (Again, the Cut and Paste buttons on the Toolbar will work.)

▶ *Undo* your last action with the Edit ➤ Undo command or the Undo button on the Toolbar.

For viewing options, setting up associations, or refreshing the directory listing, please refer to Chapter 5.

TIP   In Explorer and in My Computer folders, pressing Backspace always moves you up a level in the folder hierarchy. This is an easy way to move back to the parent directory of the current folder. After several presses, you'll eventually end up at the My Computer level, the top level on any computer. At that point, Backspace won't have any effect.

When moving files around, keep these points in mind: The new destination can be a folder window that you opened from My Computer, a folder in the left pane of Explorer, or a folder in the right pane. Many programs that support drag and drop will let you drag from Explorer into them, too. To open a Word file in an existing Word window, for example, drag the file onto the Title Bar of the Word window. You can even drag a document onto a printer's window, icon, or shortcut. The general rule is this: If you want to move it, try selecting it and dragging it to the new location. If the action isn't allowed, Windows will inform you and no damage will have been done. If you're trying to move the item and get a shortcut instead, right-click-drag the item and choose Move from the resulting menu.

Moving Files to Another Disk Drive

Moving or copying files to another disk drive uses much the same technique as when moving or copying to another folder on the same drive. The basic game plan is that you select the source files and drag them into the destination drive icon as described below.

1. Open the source drive and folder and select the files in the right pane.

2. If it's not showing, scroll the tree pane so you can see the destination drive's icon.

3. Click open the drive if you need to target a particular folder on it.

4. Drop the files on the target. If you're moving the folders or files to a floppy drive, make sure you have a formatted disk in the drive, or you will get an error message.

> **NOTE**   When you drag files (or folders) between *different* drives, Windows 95 assumes you want to copy them, not move them. That is, the originals are left intact. When you drag files between folders on the *same* drive, Windows 95 assumes you want to move them, not copy them.

Working with Disks

Explorer has a few features that apply specifically to managing your disks, particularly floppy disks. These commands make the process of formatting disks and copying disks a bit simpler. There's also a way to easily change the volume label of a disk, the optional name that each floppy or hard disk can be assigned (typically for archival purposes).

Formatting Disks and Making System Disks

> **CAUTION**   Formatting erases all data from the disk! Reversing the process is difficult if not impossible.

As I mentioned in Chapter 5, floppy disks must be formatted before they can be used in your computer. Many disks you buy in the store are preformatted, so this isn't an issue. Some are not, however. Also, you more than likely have many disks with old defunct programs and files on them that you'd like to re-use. To gain maximum room on such a disk, you'll want to erase all the old files, something you can most efficiently achieve with a *quick format*. Finally, you may want to create a disk that is capable of booting the computer. In this section I explain how to do all these things.

> **NOTE** What with the myriad disk capacities and sizes around these days, formatting a floppy disk from DOS can turn out to be quite an exercise. The DOS manual is usually not much help either. There are enough options to the format command to choke a rhino. You might become a real fan of Windows just for its formatting command.

Here's how to format a disk:

1. Put the disk to be formatted in the floppy drive.

2. Right-click on the floppy disk in the My Computer window or in Explorer and choose Format.

3. The dialog box shown in Figure 12.7 appears. Use the drop-down lists to set the drive and disk capacity of the floppy.

4. In the *Format type* and *Other options* section of the box, choose the appropriate options.

   ▶ *Quick:* simply deletes the file-allocation table and root folder of the disk, but the disk is not scanned for bad sectors. It doesn't actually erase the whole disk and reinitialize it or check for errors in the disk medium itself. Quick formatting can only be done on a disk that has been formatted in the past.

   ▶ *Full:* checks the entire disk's surface to make sure it's reliable. Any bad spots are omitted from the directory table and won't be used to store your data. This kind of format isn't fast, but it better ensures that valuable data is stored properly on the disk.

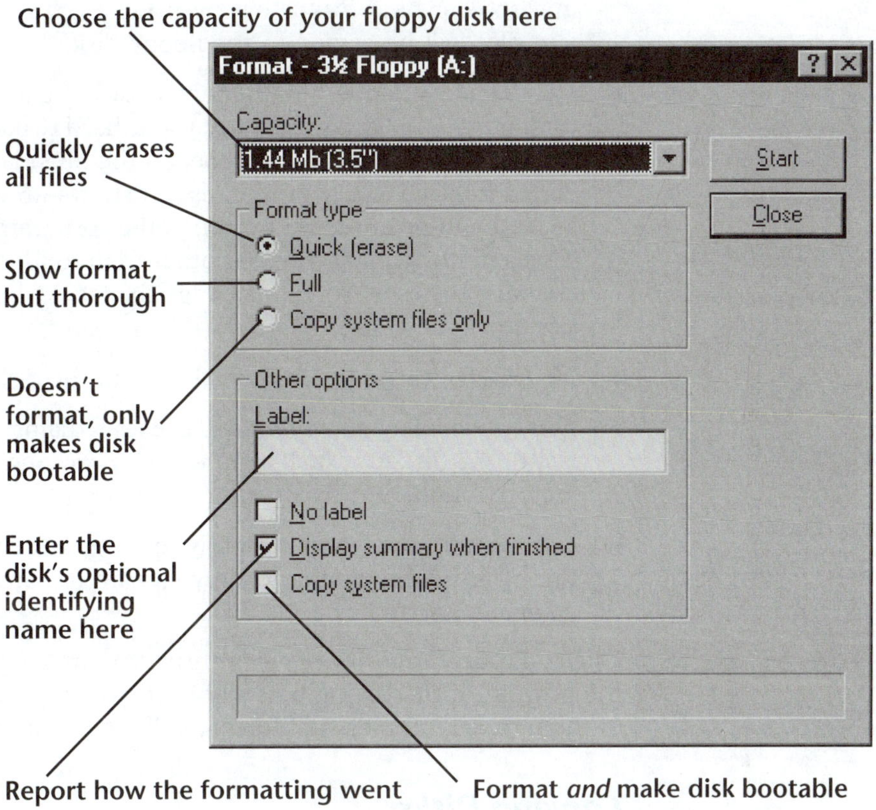

Choose the capacity of your floppy disk here

Quickly erases
all files

Slow format,
but thorough

Doesn't
format, only
makes disk
bootable

Enter the
disk's optional
identifying
name here

Report how the formatting went   Format *and* make disk bootable

Format - 3½ Floppy (A:)   ? X

Ca_pacity:
1.44 Mb (3.5")   ▼   _S_tart

Format type   _C_lose
  ⦿ _Q_uick (erase)
  ○ _F_ull
  ○ Copy system files _o_nly

Other options
Label:

  ☐ _N_o label
  ☑ _D_isplay summary when finished
  ☐ Copy _s_ystem files

Figure 12.7   *Right-click on a floppy drive and choose Format to reach this dialog box. A disk
must be formatted before you can store files on it.*

NOTE   Disks can actually lose some of their formatting information with
time. If you are going to use an old disk, it's better to full format it rather
than quick format it to prevent data loss down the road. And if you do not
know where it has been, it's a good idea to full format it to prevent any possible viruses from spreading.

▶ *Copy system files only:* doesn't format the disk. It just makes the disk
   bootable. That means it can start up your computer from the A drive

in case your hard disk is having trouble. The necessary hidden system files will be copied to the floppy disk.

▶ *Label:* lets you enter a name for the diskette if you're really into cataloging your disks. All floppy and hard disks can have a volume label. This is not the paper label on the outside, but a name encoded into the folder on the disk. It shows up when you type **DIR** at the DOS prompt and in some other programs. The label really serves no functional purpose other than to identify the disk for archiving purposes. You can change the label from the disk's Properties box at any time.

▶ *No Label:* clears any existing label from the disk.

▶ *Display summary when finished:* causes a dialog box listing particulars of the diskette, such as how much room is available on it, bad sectors found, and so on, after formatting.

▶ *Copy system files*: works similarly to Copy system files only, except that you use this option when you want to copy the system files in *addition* to formatting the disk.

5. Click on Start. You may see a confirmation message. A gas gauge at the bottom of the dialog box will keep you apprised of the progress of the format. A typical full format will take a minute or so.

Copying Disks

You can make copies of disks four basic ways—from My Computer, Explorer, the DOS prompt, and the old Windows 3.x-style File Manager.

For many, the DOS-prompt approach is probably the easiest way.

1. Choose Start ➤ Programs ➤ MS-DOS prompt.

2. Type the following command:

```
diskcopy x: y:
```

where *x* is the drive that contains the disk you want to copy and *y* is the drive that contains the disk you want to copy to. For example:

```
diskcopy a: b:
```

TIP   You can use the same drive letter for both drives if you have only one floppy drive. For more information, type diskcopy /? at the command prompt.

Using Explorer or My Computer will work fine as well. Just right-click on a floppy drive's icon, and you'll see a Copy Disk command. Choose it, and a little dialog box pops up asking for the destination drive. If you only have one drive, that's okay. You may have to swap the source and destination disks, but you'll be prompted if this is necessary.

Finally, you can also use the Windows 3.x File Manager to copy disks if the disk formats and sizes are the same. Run File Manager by choosing Start ➤ Run and entering **winfile** in the Run box. Click on the floppy drive up in the menu bar and choose Disk ➤ Copy Disk. If you have two drives, you'll have to choose the destination drive from the dialog box. If you only have one drive, you'll have to swap the disks a few times.

Part
2

Exploring Windows 95

CAUTION   Be aware that all of these methods erase everything on the destination disk before creating an exact copy of the source disk.

The Explorer has no built-in command for copying a disk. However, you could do it by creating a directory on your hard disk, copying the files from the floppy there, switching floppies, then copying from the hard-disk directory to the floppy.

Making Sure There's Enough Room on a Floppy Disk

When you are moving files about, particularly to a floppy disk, there may not be enough room on the floppy for all the source files. Explorer shows you how many bytes you've got selected in the Status Bar of its window. So, select the files you're going to copy, then look at the Status Bar.

`8 object(s) selected        619KB`

Remember this number for a moment. Then in the left pane, click on the destination drive and check its properties before doing the copy.

Using Network Drives, Files, and Disks

Assuming you are on a network, the Explorer lets you browse around and explore it, too. This is a brilliant feature of Explorer. Networks are covered in great detail in Part 5, but here I'll just introduce you to simple use of Explorer for examining and working with networked objects.

Here's the general game plan. You can *share* your drives and folders (printers and fax machines, too, as discussed in Parts 3 and 5) for use by coworkers on the net. Likewise, you can hook up to the resources other people have shared. With Explorer, scanning the network to see what's available is straightforward. It's just like looking at your own hard disk or computer's contents.

Many everyday tasks such as using a document or program on another workstation's hard disk can be done right from the folder system or the Explorer without any fancy footwork. You just open Network Neighborhood from the Desktop or from the Explorer (open the drop-down list in Explorer or any folder and choose Network Neighborhood) and see who's on the net:

Then double-click on a computer and start browsing. Examining someone else's drives and folders is *exactly* like looking at your own. For example, I double-clicked on Samson and saw the contents of Figure 12.8.

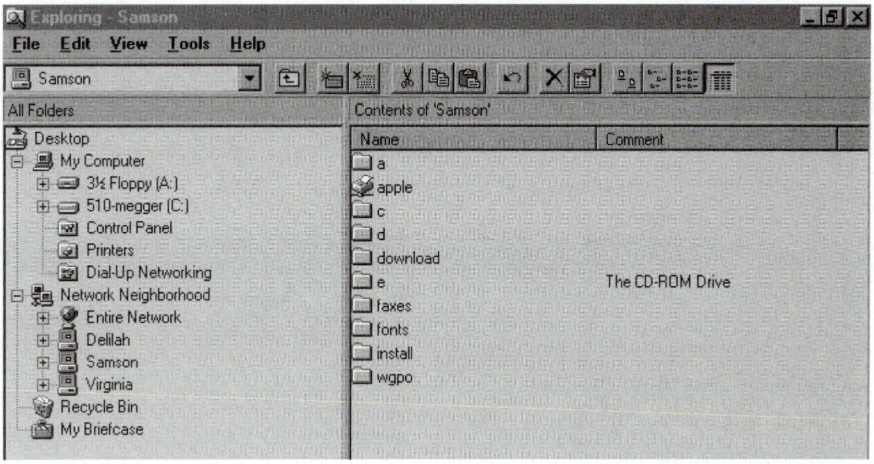

Figure 12.8   *Here you see the shared folders and drives on the networked computer named Samson.*

Note that you'll only see *shared* items on any networked computer, not *everything* in or on that computer. This scheme allows users to protect confidential items. Password protection is another option, limiting access of shared objects to specific users. Each of the folders in Figure 12.8 (as well as the printer) were intentionally shared by the person who maintains Samson.

Another point about using Explorer on the network concerns *connecting* to networked drives. If you are familiar with Windows for Workgroups 3.11, you'll note that with Explorer you don't have to connect to a networked drive before you can examine it. You simply browse any networked computer to see what's been shared on it. Some programs may need you to *map* a shared folder to a drive letter so you can open a document or perform some other action, but there's an easy way to do this from Explorer, from folders, and from some older-style Windows 3.x File dialog boxes that have a Network button on them.

Virtually all Windows 95 programs will let you use networked drives and folders with no hassle. For example, say I wanted to open a Notepad file that's stored on someone else's computer. I simply find the file and double-click, just as if it were on my computer. If I'm already in, say, WordPad and I want to use its File ➤ Open command to open a file, no problem. Consider this dialog box:

Notice that I've selected Network Neighborhood in the drop-down list, and the stations on the net show up. Just double-click on a workstation and look for the document you want. Of course, the same approach applies to saving a document with File ➤ Save.

Mapping a Drive from a Windows 3.x File Dialog Box

With Windows 3.x-style applications, you won't have the same luxuries because the File dialog boxes aren't as savvy about networking. You'll more often see something like the dialog box on the following page.

To gain access to a workstation's shared folder, you first have to map the network folder to a drive letter (such as D, E, F). Basically, mapping is just a way to fake your computer and your applications into thinking it has another hard disk on it so you can use older File dialog boxes with networked folders. Mapping is also necessary for some other procedures such as when an application expects to find support files on a logically lettered drive. In any case, the necessity is a throwback to DOS days.

Click on Network, then fill in the dialog box below. In the lower text area, type in the network path name of the shared directories. You can also use the drop-down list of previous mappings, assuming you've made this connection before. Then select or choose the disk letter you want to assign this folder to.

When you OK this box, you'll have a new disk-drive letter to choose from when you open or save a document from any application. Here's what happened when I mapped Delilah's drive C to my local drive D:

```
┌─────────────────────────────────────────────────────────────────┐
│ File Open                                               [?] [X]   │
├─────────────────────────────────────────────────────────────────┤
│ File name:                  Folders:                             │
│ [*.bmp              ]       d:\                    ┌─────────┐    │
│                                                    │   OK    │    │
│ ┌──────────────────┐ ▲     ┌──────────────┐ ▲     └─────────┘    │
│ │                  │       │ 📂 d:\        │                     │
│ │                  │       │ 📁 accbook2   │      ┌─────────┐    │
│ │                  │       │ 📁 afterdrk   │      │ Cancel  │    │
│ │                  │       │ 📁 chicago    │      └─────────┘    │
│ │                  │       │ 📁 cserve     │                     │
│ │                  │ ▼     │ 📁 disk      ▼│      ┌─────────┐    │
│ └──────────────────┘       └──────────────┘      │ Network │    │
│                                                   └─────────┘    │
│ List files of type:         Drives:                             │
│ [Bitmaps (*.BMP)     ▼]     [💻 d: \\delilah\drive c  ▼]        │
└─────────────────────────────────────────────────────────────────┘
```

> **NOTE**   Now even Explorer and My Computer will show the newly mapped drive as a "network" drive D until you disconnect it as explained below.

Mapping a Drive from Explorer—The Easy Way

The approach explained above is necessary at times, and it's handy because many dialog boxes have a Network button right there. But it's sometimes a hassle to remember the network path name of a particular folder and to enter it. Notice above that the path name syntax is `\\computer name\path`. In a complex path name there are a lot of slashes to enter and potential for typos. Also, there's no Browse button to let you cruise the network and find a folder to map.

Opening Network Neighborhood from the Desktop or Explorer makes mapping a network drive way simpler.

1. Open Network Neighborhood.

2. Browse to the folder you want to map.

3. Right-click on it and choose Map Network Drive (or click on the Map Network Drive icon in the Toolbar).

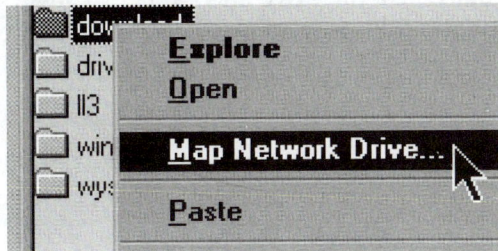

4. Choose the drive letter.

5. Click on Reconnect at Logon if you want to always have this mapping made when you boot up your computer. Of course, the remote work-station will have to be running when you boot up for this to work properly, but it won't harm anything if it isn't. You just won't have ac-cess to the drive.

NOTE   If the folder you're trying to connect to is password protected, you'll be prompted to enter a password.

Now you'll have an additional icon in Explorer and in your My Com-puter folder, representing the new drive letter. For example:

Network drives have their own style of icon, similar to the hard-disk icon but with a network cable attached. Not that it will behave as a lo-cal drive would. For example, open its Properties box to see how much free space is left on it.

Disconnecting from a Network Drive or Folder

When you're through with a mapped network drive, you'll probably want to disconnect from it. There's no sense in staying connected unless you regularly use the drive and expect to always have the setup available. Use the following steps to disconnect a network drive:

1. Click on the mapped networked drive either from My Computer or Explorer.

2. Choose Tools ➤ Disconnect Network Drive, right-click and choose the same, or click on the Disconnect Network Drive icon in the Toolbar.

If you currently have any files open on the mapped drive, attempting to disconnect will result in a warning. Make sure you're not running a program, editing a file, or otherwise accessing the logical drive that you're about to disconnect. If you get such a warning, cancel the box, close any suspicious programs or documents, and try again. In my experience, this warning can actually be erroneously triggered (i.e., when no files are open). As long as you know you're not going to lose data, go ahead and disconnect.

Sharing Folders and Drives

As implied above, you and others can share folders on the network for others to use. Before other workgroup members can use your files, though, you have to share the directory containing them. Shared directories can have passwords, and they also can have specific privileges (read-only or read-write). If you have a bunch of files that you want people to be able to see but not alter, just put them into a new folder and share it as read-only. If you want only specific people to be able to alter the files, share them protected by a password. The following section discusses how to share your folders.

1. In My Computer or Explorer, right-click on the folder or drive you want to share.

> **CAUTION** Because sharing a hard disk itself allows network users into all directories on the disk, doing so can be dangerous. Clicking on a disk icon in the Explorer or My Computer and sharing it is certainly the easiest way to share all files and folders on your computer. However, it allows any connected user to alter or erase everything you have on your hard disk.

2. Choose Sharing. A dialog box appears, as shown in Figure 12.9. Click on Shared As.

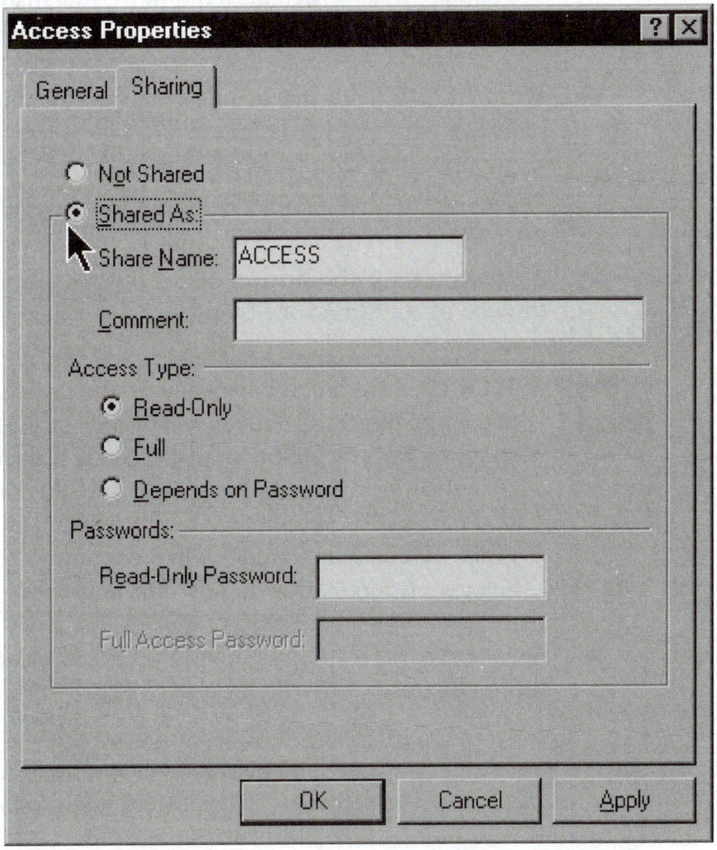

Part
2

Exploring Windows 95

Figure 12.9 *To share a folder or drive, just click on Shared As and OK the box.*

3. You don't have to do anything other than click on OK. The icon of the folder or drive will change to include a little hand under it, a suggestion of sharing.

The other options in the dialog box are useful to better control details of how the object is shared. Here's some discussion on each of those settings:

▶ The Share Name is, by default, the same name as the directory itself. This should be limited to a DOS 8.3-character name if others on the network will be using an operating system that doesn't display long file names, such as Windows 3.11 or DOS.

TIP   Even if you choose to limit the Share Name to the DOS 8.3 file-naming convention, you might want to elaborate on the directory name a bit. For example, while still conforming to DOS file-naming conventions (spaces and some characters are illegal), you could lengthen `Reports` to `Reports.96`.

▶ You can add a comment line that network users will see, perhaps explaining who the file is for or what is in the shared folder. This will show up when someone checks out your computer in Network Neighborhood or Explorer in the Details view. This line can be approximately 50 characters long and include spaces and punctuation.

▶ Next, you have the option of setting specific permissions to restrict the use of the directory by others.

TECH TIP   If you don't manually set the permissions, although anyone can access the directory, nobody will be able to edit the files in it or make other changes that an application might require, such as recording changes to a style sheet or creating a temp file in the directory. If you are sharing a folder that has applications in it for use by workers on the net, this could cause a problem. Consider carefully whether you should share the directory with Full permission to prevent potential application or document problems.

▶ Set the Access Type by clicking on the appropriate button. You have three choices:

Read   Enables viewing file names, copying information, running applications in the directory, and opening document files.

Full	All permissions listed above, plus the ability to delete files, move files, edit files, and create new subdirectories.
Depends on Password	The type of access will be determined by which password option is chosen and which password is entered by the person attempting to use the disk or folder.

> **CAUTION** Note that a user has the same rights to all the subdirectories of a shared parent directory. Be careful not to share directories that have subdirectories unless you want those to become accessible with the same level of restriction.

▶ Finally, there are the password settings.

With Read-Only or Full selected, you can enter a password in the appropriate spot. Anyone trying to use the folder will be prompted to enter a password. If you choose the Depends on Password option, the level of access the remote user is granted (Read-only or Full) is determined by the password he or she enters.

> **NOTE** Access to shared objects can be further controlled from the Network applet in the Control Panel. Using this applet, you can control whether access is granted on a user-by-user basis or on a group basis. Group access control is discussed in Part 5 of this book.

Changing a Share's Properties

You can change permissions or other settings pertaining to the share after the fact, if necessary. For example, you might decide to limit the number of people who use the shared folder by requiring passwords to be entered. You might want to change the passwords on a regular basis to ensure security. Or you might decide to stop sharing a folder altogether.

1. Right-click on the directory or disk in Explorer or My Computer's File Manager and choose Sharing.

2. The Share dialog box that appears, letting you make changes, is the same one that appeared when you originally shared the directory.

3. Click on Not Shared to stop sharing the object. If workgroup users are currently connected to the directory, you see a message indicating this and warning you against terminating the share. If you really want to terminate, click on Yes, but be aware that other users might lose their data—particularly if the dialog box indicates that files are open. Closing a shared directory like this is a great way to lose friends, so normally you would click on No, get the other user to sign off from your directory, then try again later.

> **TIP**   You might want to contact users of the directory to alert them of your intention to remove the drive from the network.

If you want to know what's really going on with a directory (that is, who's using it and whether files are open), run the NetWatcher program found in the Programs ➤ Accessories ➤ System Tools folder. This program isn't installed by default, so you might have to load it from your master Windows 95 disk(s).

Working with Other Objects in Explorer

As I mentioned at the top of this chapter, Explorer has many talents. You can explore and set properties for not only files, folders, and disks, but also Printers, Control Panel, the Recycle Bin, Dial-Up Networking (an option with Microsoft Plus; see Chapter 32), and Briefcase. Try experimenting with each of these objects by clicking on them. You'll find most of them at the bottom of the Explorer's tree in the left pane. As you'd expect, the Explorer simply provides another view of these items, even though functionally the effect is no different from working with them in ways discussed elsewhere in this book. For example, look at Figure 12.10, which shows the result of clicking on

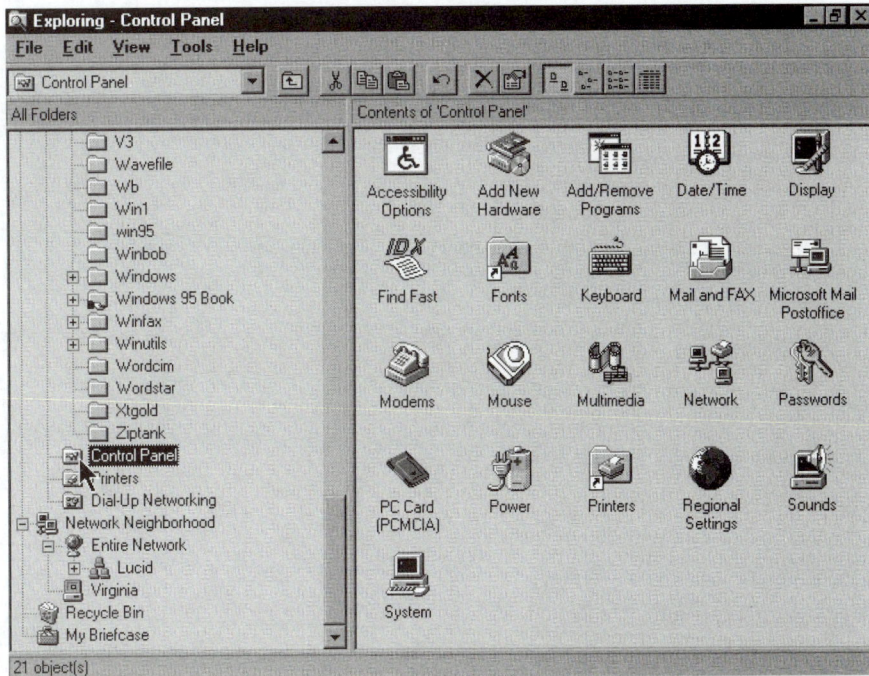

Figure 12.10   _Other computer-related objects such as the Control Panel can be accessed via Explorer, too._

the Control Panel. You can run the Control Panel applets from the right pane by double-clicking as usual.

Part
2

Exploring Windows 95

Managing Communications with Windows 95

3

Chapter 13

Introduction to Windows Communications

FEATURING

What's new in Windows 95 communications

The Windows Telephony Interface

Installing a modem

When you first got your computer, you probably planned to do things like word processing, financial record keeping and analysis, and maybe play some games. You would tap information into the keyboard, the computer would do its thing, and after a while, it would print the result on a piece of paper or display it on your screen. At that point, your computer was probably a standalone device, not connected to any other computers. If you needed to exchange data with somebody else, you could use a floppy disk to move files from one machine to the other (this technique is sometimes called "sneakernet").

But when you start connecting them together, standalone computers become extremely flexible communications tools. Relatively early in the development of computer technology, people figured out that it wasn't particularly difficult to transfer information through a wire from one computer to another. As long as the computers on both ends use the same technical standards, you can move messages, programs, text, and data files back and forth. And when you connect a *lot* of computers together through a network, you can communicate with any other computer on the same network, just as you can reach any other telephone connected to the global telecommunications system from the one on your desk.

Under the broad category of "communications," your PC can send and receive text, program files, sounds, and images. It can also exchange images of fax pages with a distant fax machine. This data can enter and leave your PC through a modem, a network interface card, or a direct cable connection to another computer.

Communications capability has been part of DOS and Windows since the earliest IBM PCs. Windows 95 includes an extensive set of communications tools that can allow you to exchange electronic mail with other computers, to send and receive faxes, and to use your computer to control telephone calls. This chapter contains information about the communications features of Windows 95 and tells you how to configure Windows to work with your modem. You can find more specific information about communications applications, Microsoft Exchange, and Microsoft Network in the remaining chapters of this section. HyperTerminal, the new communications program, is discussed in Chapter 20. Finally, Chapter 17 describes how to use Windows 95 to connect your computer to the Internet.

What's New in Windows 95 Communications?

Windows 95 includes some major improvements over the way Windows 3.x handled communications—it's a lot happier about sending and receiving data at high speeds, transferring data in the background doesn't interfere with other applications, and you don't have to shut down a program that waits for incoming messages or faxes before you try to use the same modem to place an outgoing call. In addition, Microsoft has replaced the old Terminal program in Windows 3.x with a completely new set of applications for connecting to distant computers through a modem; for sending, receiving, and managing messages, data files, and faxes; as well as a "Telephony Applications Program Interface" (TAPI) that integrates your PC with a telephone system. Microsoft has also included access to its own online information service, called the Microsoft Network. Overall, Windows 95 goes a long way toward turning your standalone computer into a tool that can be linked to other computers, fax machines, and other communications devices anywhere in the world.

The Windows Telephony Interface

Windows 95 includes a new set of software "hooks" to applications that control the way your computer interacts with the telephone network. TAPI is an internal part of the Windows 95 operating system rather than a specific application program—it provides a standard way for software developers to access communications ports and devices such as modems and telephone sets to control data, fax, and voice calls. Using TAPI, an application can place a call, answer an incoming call, and hang up when the call is complete. It also supports things like hold, call transfer, voice mail, and conference calls. TAPI-compliant applications will work with conventional telephone lines, PBX and Centrex systems, and with specialized services like cellular and ISDN.

By moving these functions to a common program interface, Windows prevents conflicting demands for access to your modem and telephone line from multiple application programs. Therefore, you no longer need to shut down a program that's waiting for incoming calls before you use a different program to send a fax.

Windows Telephony is part of the base Windows 95 operating system; it's not a separate program. Unless you're planning to write your own communications applications, you won't ever have to deal directly with TAPI, but you will see its benefits when you use the communications programs included in the Windows 95 package—such as HyperTerminal, Microsoft Exchange, Phone Dialer, and Remote Access—and when you use new, Window 95-compatible versions of third-party communications programs such as ProComm and WinFax. In addition, Microsoft is planning a separate Windows Telephony application product (code name Tazz—short for Tasmanian Devil) that will use TAPI to integrate your PC with the telephone network.

Windows 95 includes a relatively simple telephony application called Phone Dialer, but that just scratches the surface of what TAPI will support. In the same way that Windows 95's faxing capabilities are not as extensive as those of a program like WinFax or that WordPad has fewer bells and whistles than Word for Windows, Phone Dialer is much simpler than some of the other programs that will appear in the near future.

Eventually you can expect to see a lot of new Windows Telephony products that will move control of your telephone to the Windows Desktop; for example, you might be able to use the telephone company's caller ID service to match incoming calls to a database that displays detailed information about the caller before you answer, or use an on-screen menu to set up advanced call features like conference calling and forwarding that now require obscure strings of digits from the telephone keypad.

Installing a Modem

Every time you installed a new communications application in Windows 3.x, you had to go through another configuration routine—you had to specify the port connected to your modem, the highest speed the modem could handle, and so forth. Because there was no central modem control, each program required its own setup.

This has changed in Windows 95, which uses a *universal modem* driver called *Unimodem*. Unimodem is the software interface between all of your computer's 32-bit Windows 95-compatible communications applications (including the ones that use TAPI) and your modem or other communications hardware. It includes integrated control for port selection, modem initialization, speed, file-transfer protocols, and terminal emulation. The modem configuration is handled by Unimodem, so you only have to specify setup parameters once.

If you're using third-party communications applications left over from earlier versions of Windows, they'll work with Windows 95, but you'll still have to configure them separately. When you replace them with newer, Windows 95-compatible updates, they'll use the settings already defined in Windows.

In most cases, you will need a modem to use Windows 95's communications features. Your modem might be an internal expansion board, an external modem plugged into a serial port, or a credit-card-n-sized PCMCIA modem. If the modem is already in place when you install Windows, the Windows Setup routine will automatically try to detect your modem for you. To install your modem later, you can use the Windows Control Panel, or you can configure it from a communications application such as Phone Dialer or HyperTerminal.

Follow these steps to install a modem from the Control Panel:

1. Click on the Start button and open the Control Panel from the Settings menu.

2. If you're using an external modem, turn it on and make sure it's connected to both the telephone line and a serial port on your computer.

3. Double-click on the Modems icon. The Modems Properties dialog box in Figure 13.1 will appear.

4. Click on the Add button to open the Install New Modem wizard.

5. Because you turned on the modem in step 2, you can let the Modem Wizard try to identify your modem type. Click on the Next> button.

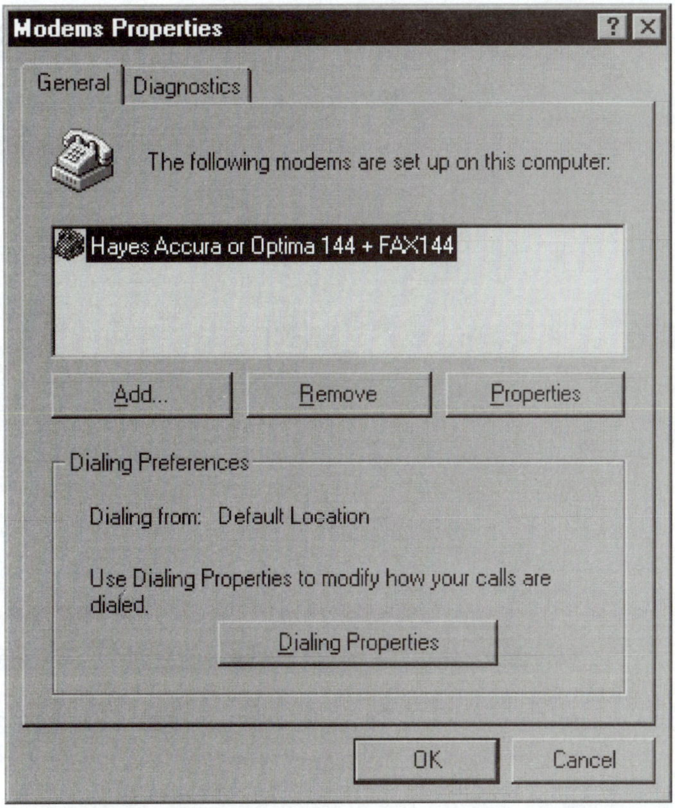

Figure 13.1   *This is the Modems Properties dialog box: click on the Add button to install a new modem.*

6.   If you have an external modem, you will see the lights flash on the front panel while the Wizard tests it. When the tests are complete, the Wizard in Figure 13.2 displays the Verify dialog box.

7.   If the Wizard is not able to identify your modem, click on the Change button and choose its make and model from the list. If your modem is not listed, look in the modem manual for an equivalent type or select the Generic Modem Drivers item in the Manufacturers list. When Windows 95 is in wide use, modem manufacturers will probably supply drivers on diskette with their modems. In that case, use the Have Disk button to install the driver.

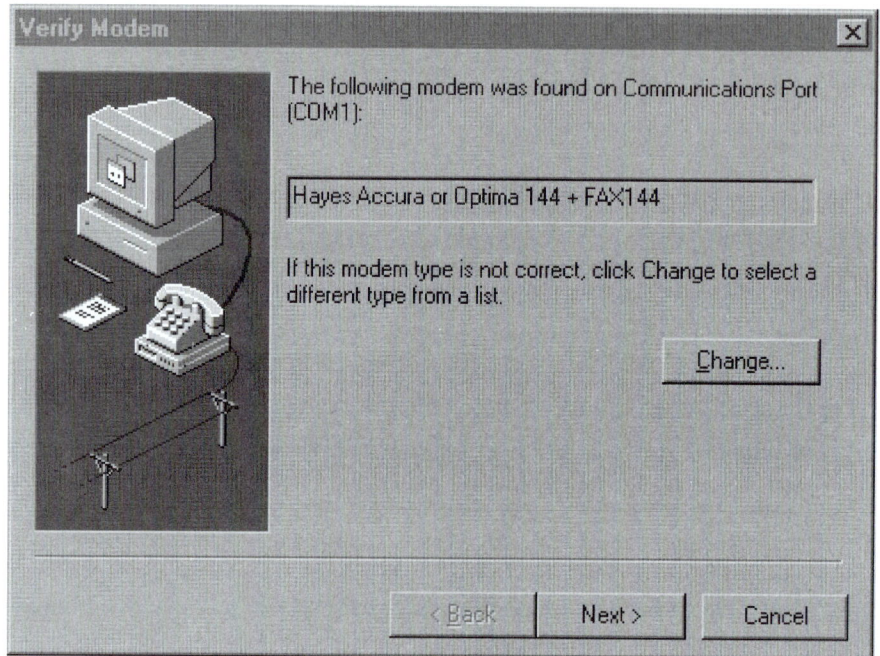

Figure 13.2   The Verify Modem dialog box: if the modem type is correct, click on the Next> button.

8. Click on the Next> and Finish buttons to complete the modem instal-
    lation. If you haven't already entered your location and area code, the
    Location Information dialog box in Figure 13.3 will ask for this
    information.

    If your modem is connected to a line that uses Touch-Tone™ dialing,
    choose *Tone*. If not, choose *Pulse*.

Changing Modem Properties

Once you've installed your modem, all of your Windows 95 communications programs will use the same configuration settings. When you
change them in one application, those changes will carry across to all
the others. In general, you won't want to change the default modem
properties, which specify things like the loudness of the modem's

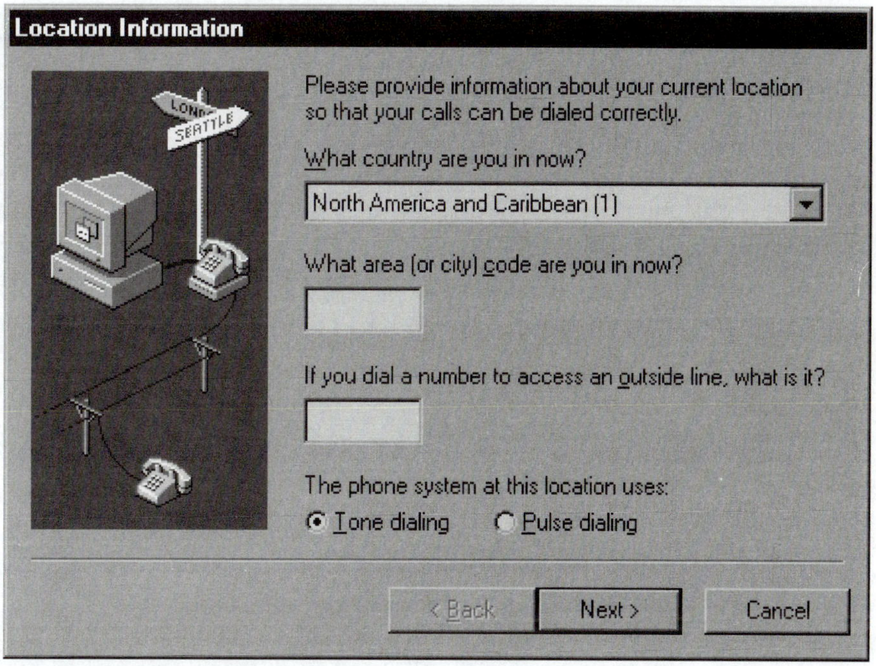

Figure 13.3 *The Location Information dialog box: choose your location from the drop-down menu and type in your area code.*

speaker and the maximum data-transfer speed. If you replace your modem, or if you use different modem types in different locations, you can install an additional modem from the Control Panel.

To change the modem properties after installation is complete, open the Control Panel and double-click on the Modems icon. When the Modems Properties dialog box appears, click on the Properties button to display the dialog box in Figure 13.4.

General Properties

The General tab has three settings:

Port Use the drop-down Port menu to specify the COM port to which your modem is connected.

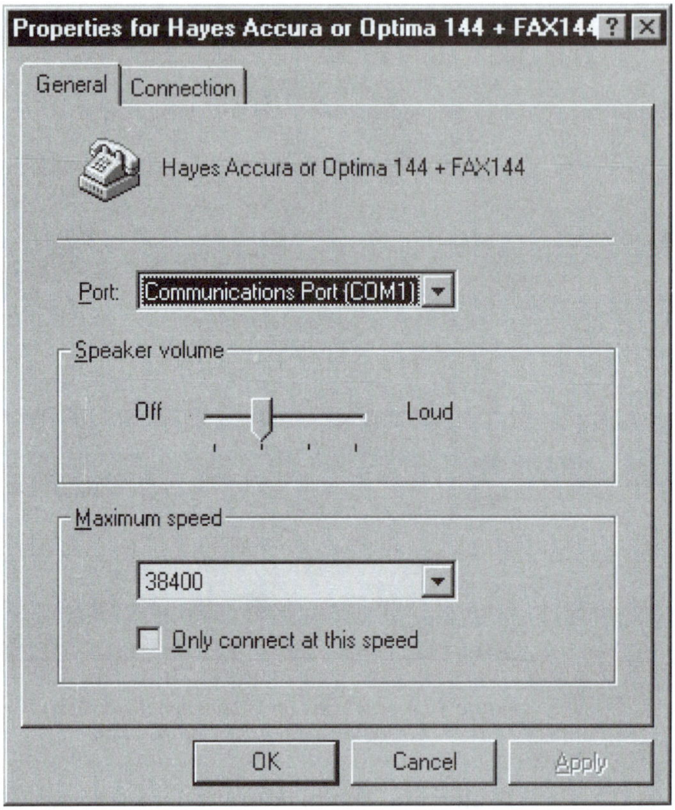

Figure 13.4   *Use this Properties dialog box to change your modem configuration.*

Speaker Volume   The Speaker Volume control is a slide setting that sets the loudness of the speaker inside your modem.

Maximum Speed   When your modem makes a connection, it will try to use the maximum speed to exchange data with the modem at the other end of the link. As a rule, if you have a 9,600 bits-per-second (bps) or faster modem, the maximum speed should be three or four times the rated modem speed (e.g., set your modem speed to 38400) to take advantage of the modem's built-in data compression.

If you don't want to accept a slower connection, check *Only connect at this speed*.

Choose the Connection tab to display the dialog box in Figure 13.5.

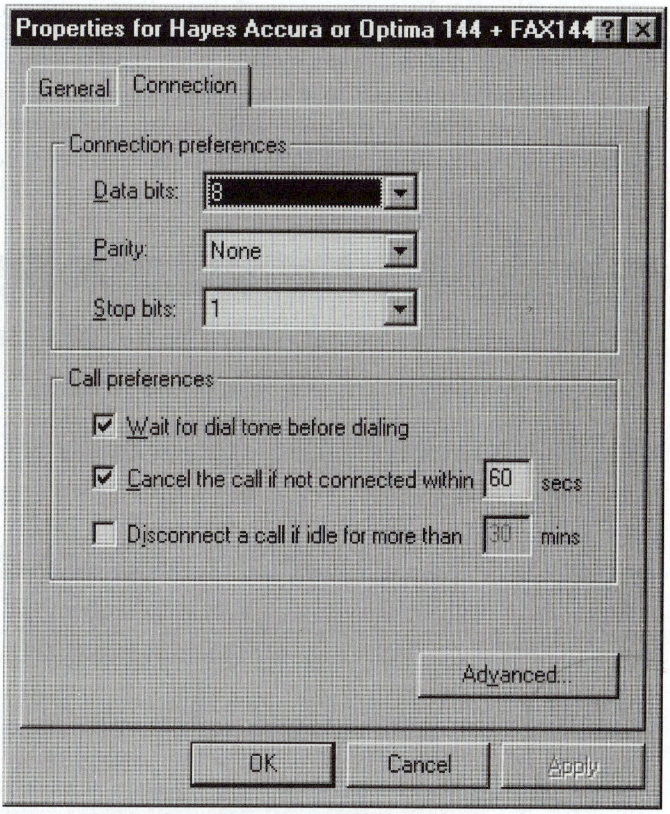

Figure 13.5 *Use the Connection dialog box to change communication parameters.*

The Connection dialog box has several options:

Connection Preferences   The Data bits, Parity, and Stop bits settings must be the same at both ends of a data link. The most common settings are 8 data bits, no parity, and one stop bit.

Call Preferences   The three *Call preferences* options control the way your modem handles individual calls. Place a check mark in each box if you want to use that option.

Advanced Options   The Advanced Connection Settings are options that you will probably set once and then leave alone. They manage error control, flow control, and additional special settings.

Figure 13.6 shows the Advanced Connection Settings dialog box.

The *Extra settings* section is a place to send additional AT commands to your modem. In most cases, you won't need to add any special commands. Because different modem manufacturers use slightly different command sets, you'll have to consult your modem manual for specific commands.

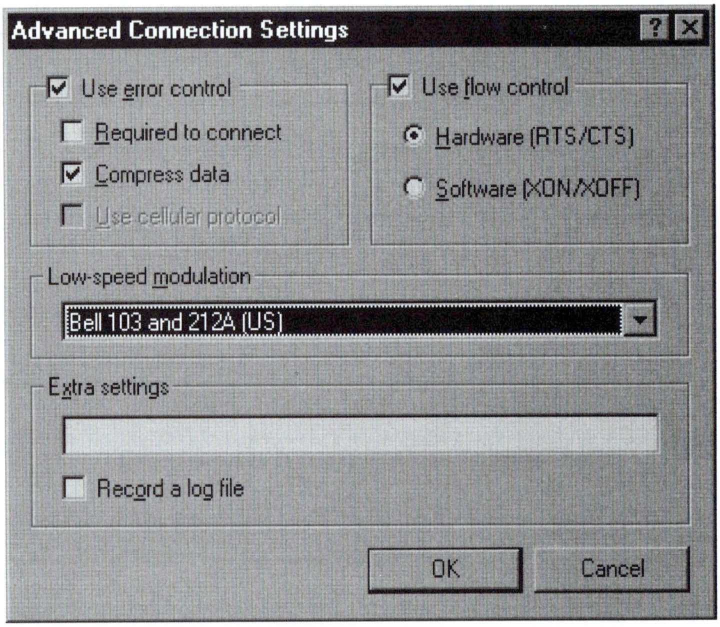

Figure 13.6   Use the Advanced Connection Settings dialog box to specify error control and flow control.

Diagnostic Properties

Click on the Diagnostics tab back in the original Properties for Modems dialog box to display the dialog box in Figure 13.7. The Diagnostics dialog box identifies the devices connected to each of your COM ports.

Click on the Driver button to see information about the Windows communications driver program. Highlight a COM port and click on

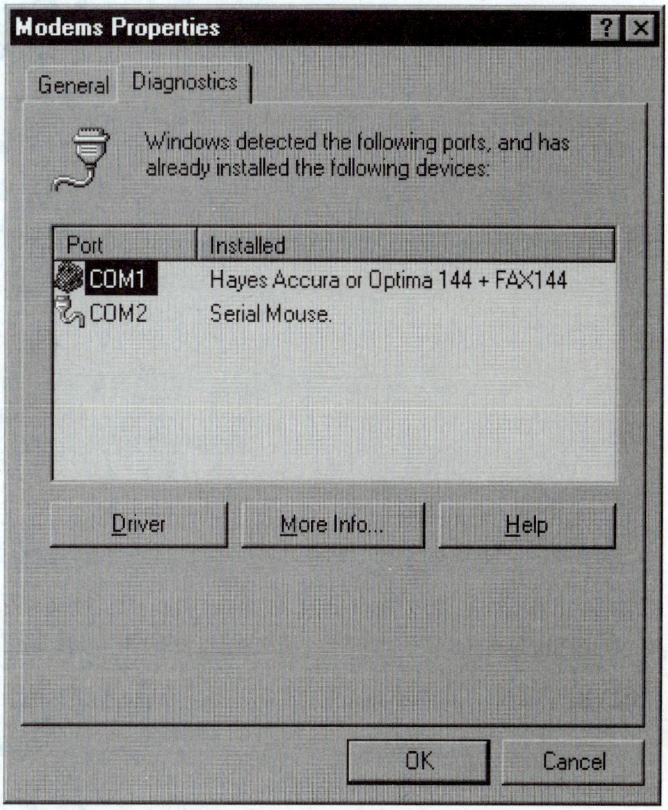

Figure 13.7 *Click on the Diagnostics tab to see the devices connected to your COM ports.*

the More Info button to display the information in Figure 13.8. This information can be extremely useful when you are trying to configure additional communications devices.

Dialing Properties

If you're using a portable computer, you may need to change the information about your location. You can open the Dialing Properties dialog box in Figure 13.9 from any Windows 95 communications application.

Part
3

Managing
Communications

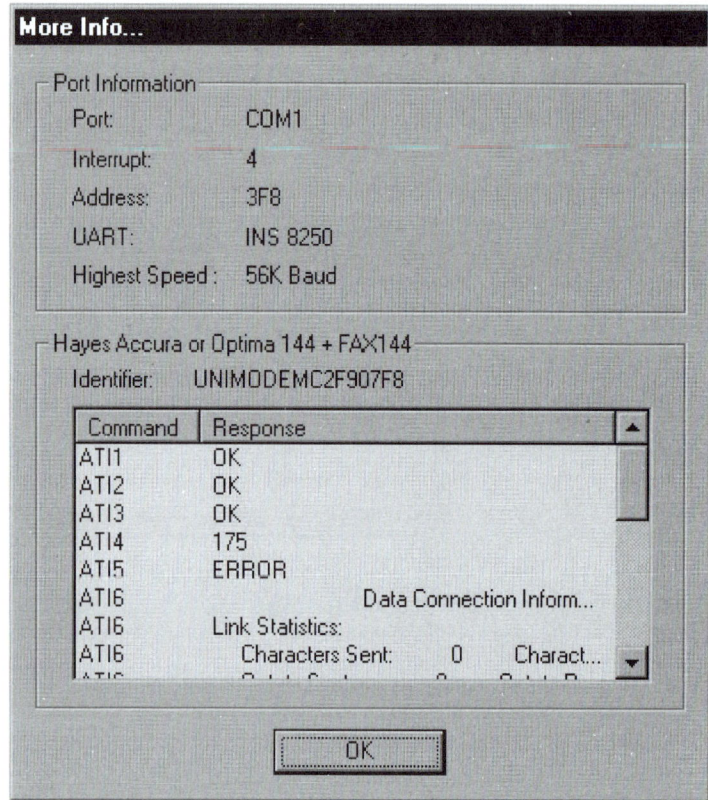

Figure 13.8   *The More Info window shows detailed information about a COM port configuration.*

The Dialing Properties dialog box includes these fields:

I Am Dialing From   This field specifies the name of each configuration set. To create a new configuration, use the New button and type a name in the Create New Location dialog box.

The Area Code Is   Type your own area code in this field.

I Am In (Country Code)   This field contains a drop-down menu that lists the international dialing codes for most countries of the world. Choose the name of the country from which you will be originating

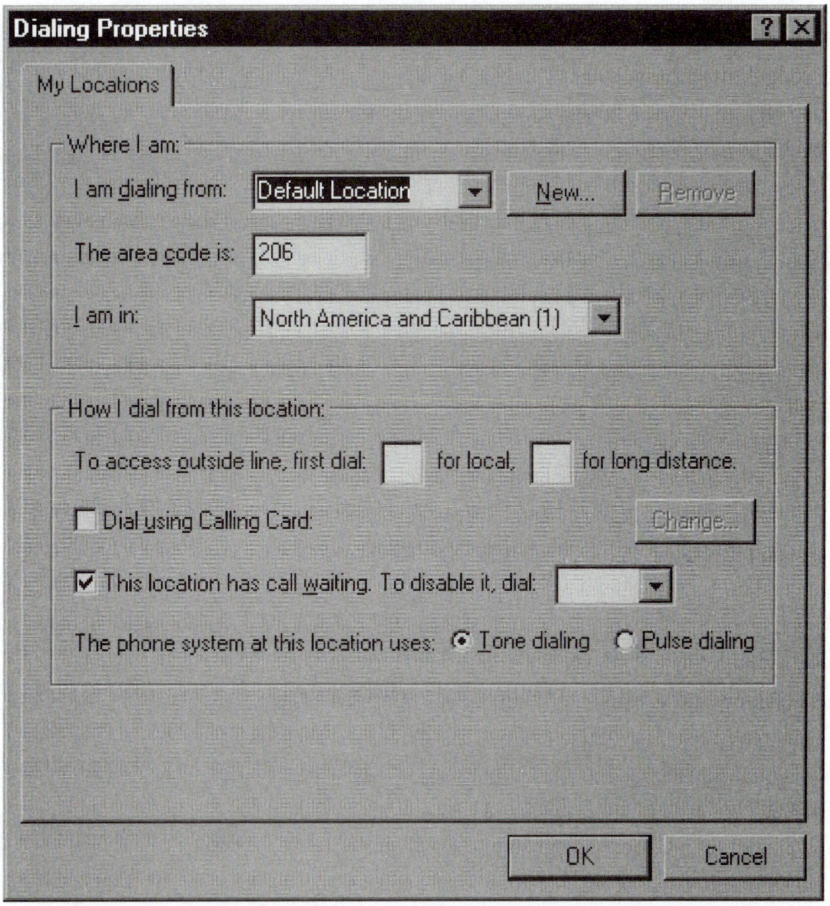

Figure 13.9 *The Dialing Properties dialog box controls the way communications programs place telephone calls.*

calls. The United States, Canada, and many Caribbean countries all use the same Country Code.

How I Dial From This Location If your modem line is in an office where you must dial **9** for an outside line or some other code for long distance, type those number in these fields. If you have a direct outside line, leave these fields blank.

> **NOTE**   The only time you will need to use the *long distance* field is when your modem is connected to a PBX or other telephone system that uses a special code for toll calls. Do not use this field for the "1" prefix that you dial before long-distance calls. The dialer will add that code automatically.

Dial Using Calling Card   To pay for a call with a calling card (a telephone company credit card), you must dial a special string of numbers that includes a carrier access code, your account number, and the number you're calling. In some cases, you have to call a service provider, enter your account number, and wait for a second dial tone before you can actually enter the number you want to call.

To use your calling card, select the Calling Card option to display the Change Calling Card dialog box in Figure 13.10. Either select your calling-card type from the drop-down menu or type the name of the card in the *Calling Card to use* field. Enter your complete calling-card number or account number in the *Calling Card number* field.

The drop-down Calling Card to use menu includes the most commonly used telephone credit cards in the United States—those issued by AT&T, MCI, and Sprint. If you choose a calling card from the menu, the program automatically uses the correct calling sequence for that long-distance carrier. But if you need a special calling sequence,

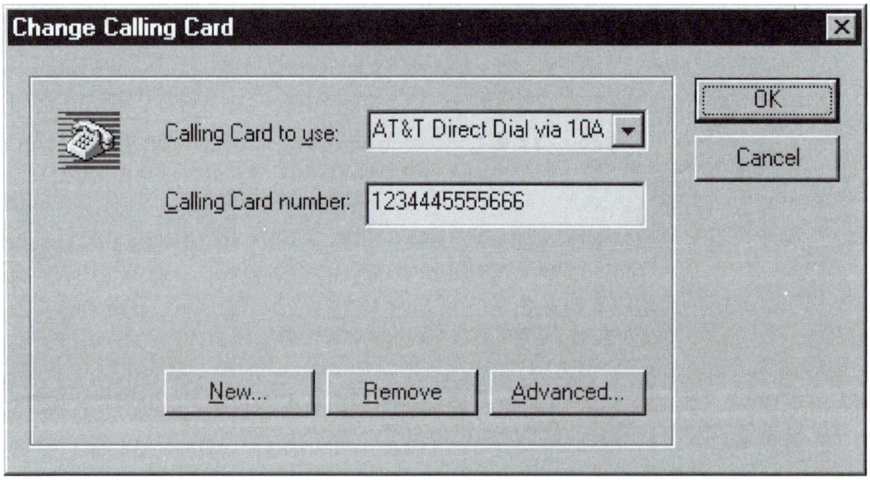

Figure 13.10 Use the Change Calling Card dialog box to specify your telephone credit-card type and number.

choose the Advanced button and type the sequences for local, long distance, and international calls in the Dialing Rules dialog box.

Use these codes for variables within a calling sequence:

E	Country Code
F	Area Code
G	Destination Local Number
H	Calling-card number
W	Wait for second dial tone
@	Wait for a ringing tone followed by five seconds of silence
$	Wait for a calling-card prompt tone (the "bong" tone)
?	Display an on-screen prompt

For example, the default calling sequence for long-distance calls using an AT&T calling card is 102880FG$H:

10288	specifies AT&T as long distance carrier
0	specifies a credit-card call
F	specifies the area code
G	specifies the local telephone number
$	specifies a wait for the calling-card prompt
H	specifies the calling-card number

This Location Has Call Waiting   Call waiting is an optional service offered by many local telephone companies to let you know that a second call has arrived while you are on the telephone. Unfortunately, the call-waiting signal can break a modem connection, so you must disable call waiting before placing a call through your computer.

If your telephone line uses call waiting, click on the call-waiting option to disable it. Look in the front of your local telephone directory or call your telephone business office to find out which code you need to use and select that code from the drop-down menu.

Tone v. Pulse Dialing

Most push-button telephones use tone dialing (known in the United States as Touch-Tone™ dialing). However, older dial telephones and some cheap push-button phones use pulse signaling instead. Tone dialing is a lot more efficient because it takes a lot less time. Chances are, your telephone line will accept tone dialing even if there's a dial telephone connected to it. Therefore, you should go ahead and select Tone dialing and place a test call to see it if works. If it doesn't, choose Pulse dialing instead.

Because all Windows 95 application programs use the same modem-configuration information, you'll probably have to worry about the stuff in this section only once, when you install your modem for the first time. After that, TAPI uses the existing information when you load a new program.

In the next couple of chapters, you can find more specific information about using the communications applications that are included in the Windows 95 package, including the Phone Dialer, Microsoft Exchange, and The Microsoft Network online service.

Chapter 14

Using
Phone Dialer

FEATURING

Phone Dialer is a simple application that places outgoing voice telephone calls through your modem. You can tell Phone Dialer what number you want to dial by typing the number, choosing it from a Speed Dial list, or clicking numbers on an on-screen keypad. After you've called a number, you can select it from a list of recent calls. After it dials the call, Phone Dialer connects the line through to the telephone set plugged into the phone jack on your modem so you can pick up the handset and start talking.

You'll have to decide for yourself whether pressing keys on your computer keyboard is any improvement over pressing buttons on a telephone, but the speed-dial feature can be quite convenient for frequently called numbers. Of course, you're out of luck if you normally use separate telephone lines for voice and data.

Starting Phone Dialer

Phone Dialer is in the Windows Accessories menu, so you can start it by clicking on the Start button and then choosing Programs ➤ Accessories ➤ Phone Dialer. If you use Phone Dialer frequently, you can create a shortcut for this application.

When you start the program, the main Phone Dialer screen in Figure 14.1 appears. To make a call, either type the number or click on the numbers on the on-screen keypad. If you want to call a number you've called before, you can display recently dialed numbers in a drop-down menu by clicking on the arrow at the right side of the *Number to dial* field. When the complete number you want to dial is in this field, click on the Dial button.

Dialing a number with Phone Dialer is exactly like dialing the same number from your telephone. Therefore, you must include all the prefixes required by the phone company for this kind of call, such as a **1** for prepaid long-distance calls or a 0 for operator-assisted calls. On the other hand, if you're using an office telephone that requires **9** or some other access code for an outside line, you can use the Dialing Properties dialog box to add the code for all calls. You can open the Dialing Properties dialog box from Phone Dialer's Tools menu (Chapter 13).

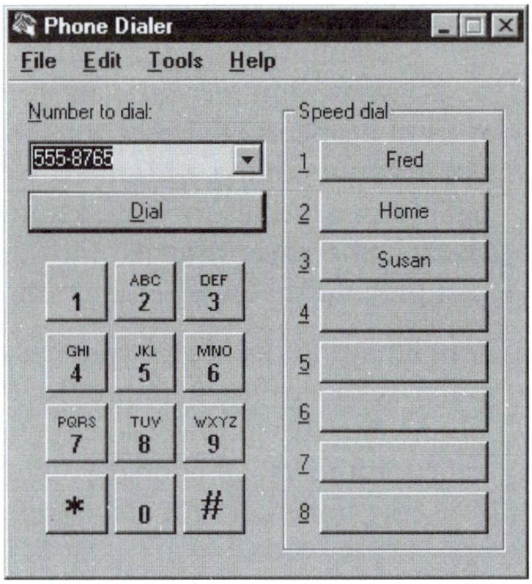

Figure 14.1   *The Phone Dialer screen offers several ways to enter a telephone number.*

Programming the Speed Dial List

The eight entries in the Speed Dial list are push buttons. Click on one of the names in the list to dial that person's number. When you click on an unassigned button, the Program Speed Dial dialog box in Figure 14.2 appears. Type the name you want on the button in the *Name* field and the complete telephone number in the *Number to dial* field. Click on the Save button to save the new number and return to the main Phone Dialer screen or the Save and Dial button to call the number from this dialog box.

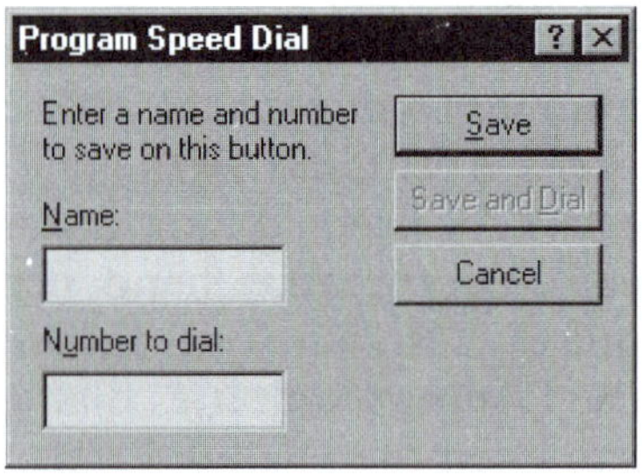

Figure 14.2   *Use the Program Speed Dial dialog box to assign names and numbers to the Speed Dial list.*

You can program several Speed Dial buttons at one time or change the name or number of a previously assigned button by choosing Speed Dial from the Edit menu. When the Edit Speed Dial dialog box in Figure 14.3 appears, click on the button you want to change and then type the name and number you want to assign to that button. After you have configured as many of the eight buttons as you want to use, click on the Save button.

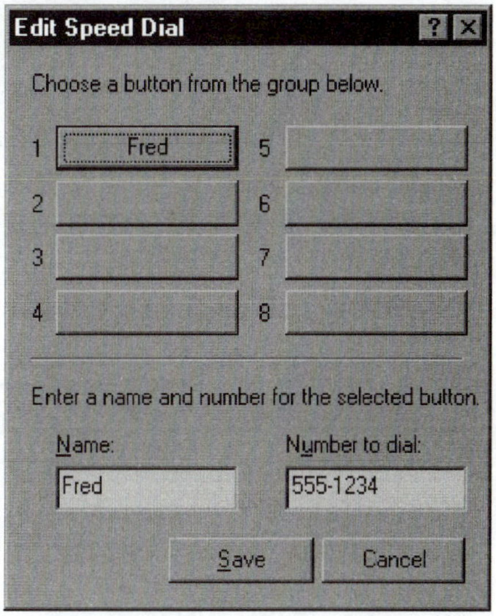

Figure 14.3   *Use the Edit Speed Dial dialog box to add or change Speed Dial items.*

Placing a Call

When you place a call through Phone Dialer, the Dialing dialog box in Figure 14.4 appears. If you entered the number from the Speed Dial list, the dialog box will display the name of the person you're calling. Otherwise, it will report the call destination as *unknown*. If you wish, you can type the recipient's name and a few words about the call to keep a record of this call in the Phone Dialer log.

As Phone Dialer places the call, you will hear the dialing tones (or pulses) and the ringing signal or busy signal through the modem's speaker. A *Call Status* window will let you know when the call has gone through. To transfer the call to your telephone set, click on the Talk button and pick up the handset or click on Hang Up to break

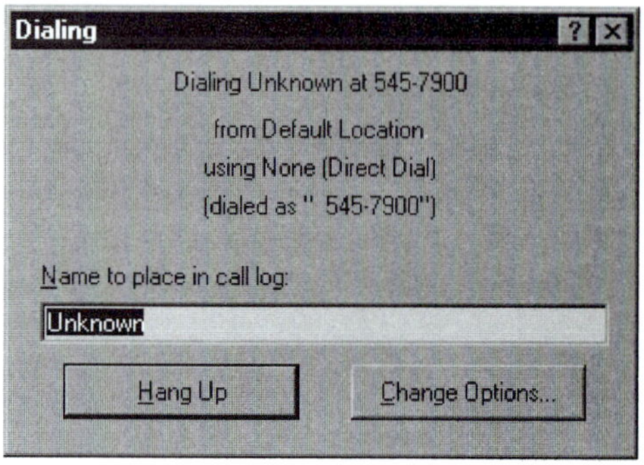

Figure 14.4 This dialog box appears when you place a call with Phone Dialer.

the connection. If the modem detects a busy signal, you will see a *Call Failed* window instead.

After you pick up the receiver and click on the Talk button, your call passes through the modem to your telephone set. At this point, there's no real difference between a Phone Dialer call and one placed directly from the telephone itself. To end the call, hang up the telephone.

Chapter 15

E-Mail and Microsoft Exchange

FEATURING

The Microsoft Exchange client is the central control point for Windows 95's messaging components, including electronic mail and fax. When you use Microsoft Exchange instead of separate application programs, a list of all of your messages and faxes appears in one window, regardless of the way your computer received them. You can send and receive messages, files, and faxes through several different services while using just one common on-screen client window.

Initially, the Exchange client supports three messaging services: Microsoft Mail, the Microsoft Network online service, and direct fax transmission through a fax modem. Microsoft will offer Exchange support for additional messaging services, including CompuServe and the Internet, in the Microsoft Plus accessory (see Chapter 32) and in their planned quarterly upgrades to Windows 95.

It's likely that other messaging services such as America Online and MCI Mail will offer add-on integration with Microsoft Exchange. And as new technologies such as voice mail become available, Microsoft Exchange will support them as well. The ultimate goal is to handle all kinds of messages through a single front end.

The Exchange client is a trade-off between the convenience of a single control center for many kinds of messages and the flexibility and features offered by single-purpose programs like WinFax and Lotus Notes. If you're committed to using the built-in Windows 95 messaging services, you may think of Exchange as the heart of Windows messaging. On the other hand, if you prefer using third-party messaging applications and services, you don't need to use Exchange at all.

In addition to the message-handling front end in Windows 95, Microsoft also uses the name *Exchange* for the separate network-messaging product that will probably be released some time in 1996 as Microsoft's answer to Lotus Notes. The Exchange client in Windows 95 will work seamlessly with the Exchange server product.

The Microsoft Exchange client is the most visible part of Windows 95's Messaging Subsystem, but it's just one piece of the puzzle. The Messaging Subsystem in Windows 95 also includes these elements:

The Messaging Applications Program Interface (MAPI) MAPI is the interface between Microsoft Exchange or other compatible applications and the drivers that communicate with many information services.

Personal Address Book   Your Personal Address Book contains names, e-mail addresses, telephone and fax numbers, and other information about potential recipients of messages, even if you reach them through different services. E-mail and fax applications consult the Personal Address Book through MAPI, so you can keep a single address book for all the people to whom you send messages.

Personal Folders   Personal Folders is a database that contains messages, forms, and documents. Microsoft Exchange uses Personal Folders to store incoming and outgoing messages. If more than one user shares the same PC, each can use a separate Personal Folder.

Microsoft Mail Postoffice and Drivers   The Microsoft Mail Postoffice server is similar to the one in the separate Microsoft Mail product except that it does not provide access to Microsoft Mail gateways, it only supports a single post office, and it has fewer, less-extensive administration tools. The Microsoft Mail drivers are the interface between Microsoft Mail and MAPI.

Fax Drivers   In addition to conventional e-mail messages and files, Exchange can also handle fax pages to and from standalone fax machines or fax modems. Chapter 16 describes Windows 95's fax functions in detail.

Drivers for the Microsoft Network   The Microsoft Network is the new online information service that Microsoft is introducing along with Windows 95; Exchange can automatically connect to the Microsoft Network (MSN) to send and receive e-mail messages. And because MSN has gateways through the Internet to most other electronic mail services, you can use Exchange and MSN to process e-mail to many other destinations.

Windows 95's messaging architecture is similar to the telephony architecture described in Chapter 13: It uses an application programming interface (API) between the front-end programs the user sees and the individual drivers for various messaging services. The software flow looks like this:

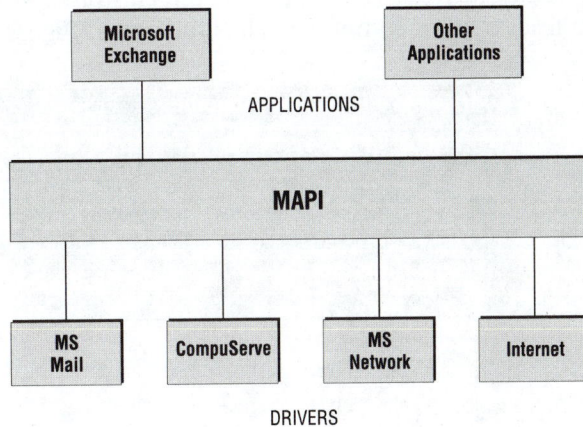

This modular structure allows outside software developers to create new drivers to work with existing applications or new front-end applications that will work with existing drivers. As a user, you can install new features and services without the need to completely relearn the messaging system.

Microsoft Exchange

All the messaging applications in Windows 95 use Microsoft Exchange to process inbound and outbound messages. The advantage of this approach is that it provides a single point of access.

Installing Microsoft Exchange

There are two ways to install Microsoft Exchange: during Windows 95 Setup or separately. If you want to load the Messaging System (including Microsoft Exchange) when you load the rest of Windows 95, you must select Custom rather than Typical setup. If you took the program's on-screen advice and used Typical Setup, you'll have to figure out where you've put the Windows 95 software disks before you can load Microsoft Exchange and the other communications programs.

To perform a separate installation, click on the Control Panel's Add/Remove Programs icon and choose the Windows Setup tab. If you're installing Windows from scratch, choose the Custom Setup option. Either way, you'll see a list of components like the one in Figure 15.1.

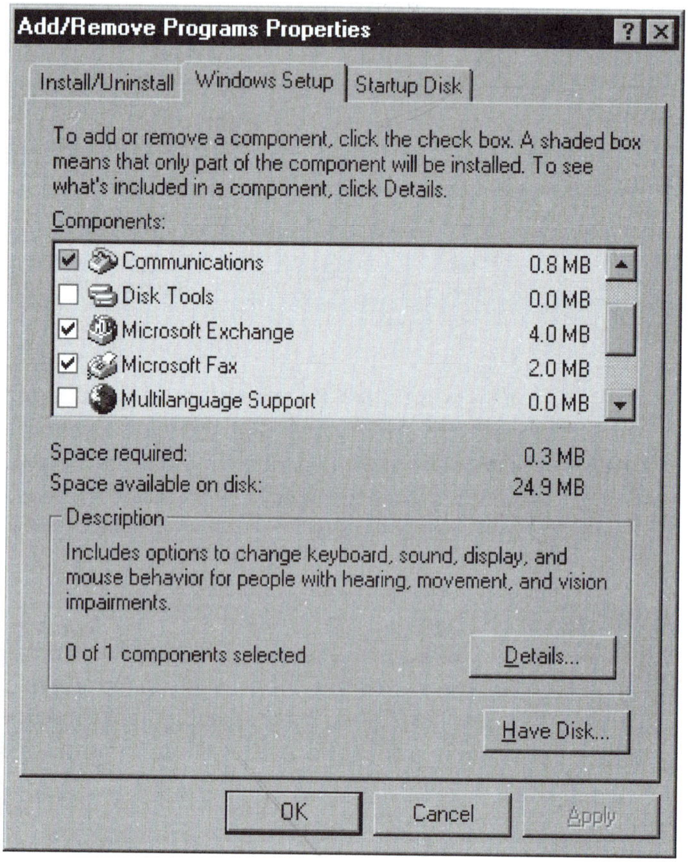

Figure 15.1   *Choose applications from the Windows Setup tab of the Add/Remove Programs Properties dialog box.*

Check the services you want to install. If you choose one or more of the messaging applications, such as either Microsoft Fax, Microsoft Network, or both, the Wizard will also force you to install Microsoft Exchange.

After you specify the services you want Microsoft Exchange to manage, the Wizard completes the installation for you.

Working with User Profiles

Microsoft Exchange uses configuration profiles to specify each user's messaging services and other options. If more than one person shares a single computer, or if you use the same computer in more than one location, it's a simple matter to create multiple profiles.

A single profile may include one or more messaging services, and each profile manages the features of all of the services in that profile. Depending on the way you want to manage your mail, you can either create one central profile that handles all your mail, or you can create separate profiles for different services.

The first time you run Exchange, a Configuration Wizard creates a profile for you. When you install the Microsoft Network software, Windows automatically creates a new profile.

To modify an existing profile or create a new one, follow these steps:

1. Open the Control Panel and double-click on the Mail and Fax icon.

2. When the Properties dialog box appears, click on the Show Profiles button. The Exchange Setting Properties dialog box in Figure 15.2 will appear. It will display a list of all the profiles that have previously been created on your system.

3. Highlight the name of a profile and choose one of these options:

   Add: creates a new profile.

   Remove: deletes the profile whose name is highlighted.

   Properties: defines the way Exchange will handle messages in the currently highlighted profile.

   Copy: creates a new profile with the same properties as the currently highlighted profile. After you copy a profile, you can use the Properties option to personalize the new profile.

NOTE   If you create more than one profile, you should assign a name to each profile that describes the way you plan to use it, such as the name of the person using it or the name of the service that the profile controls.

4. When you open Microsoft Exchange, it will start with the default profile active. To change the default profile, drop down the menu in the *When starting, use this profile* field and highlight a profile name.

Part
3

Managing
Communications

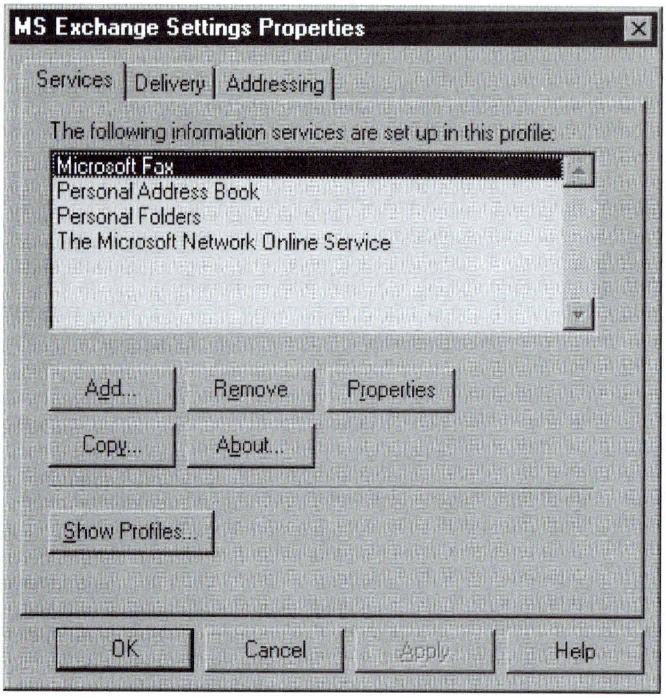

Figure 15.2   *The Exchange Setting Properties dialog box shows all current profiles.*

Defining Properties in an Exchange Profile

Each of the services in a profile has a specific set of properties that defines the way Exchange uses that service. To view or change the default settings, double-click on the Mail and Fax icon in the Control Panel to open the Properties dialog box. Highlight the name of the service whose properties you want to view or change and click on the Properties button.

Fax Properties

The Microsoft Fax Properties dialog box in Figure 15.3 controls the way Exchange handles fax messages. Chapter 16 contains detailed information about configuring Fax Properties.

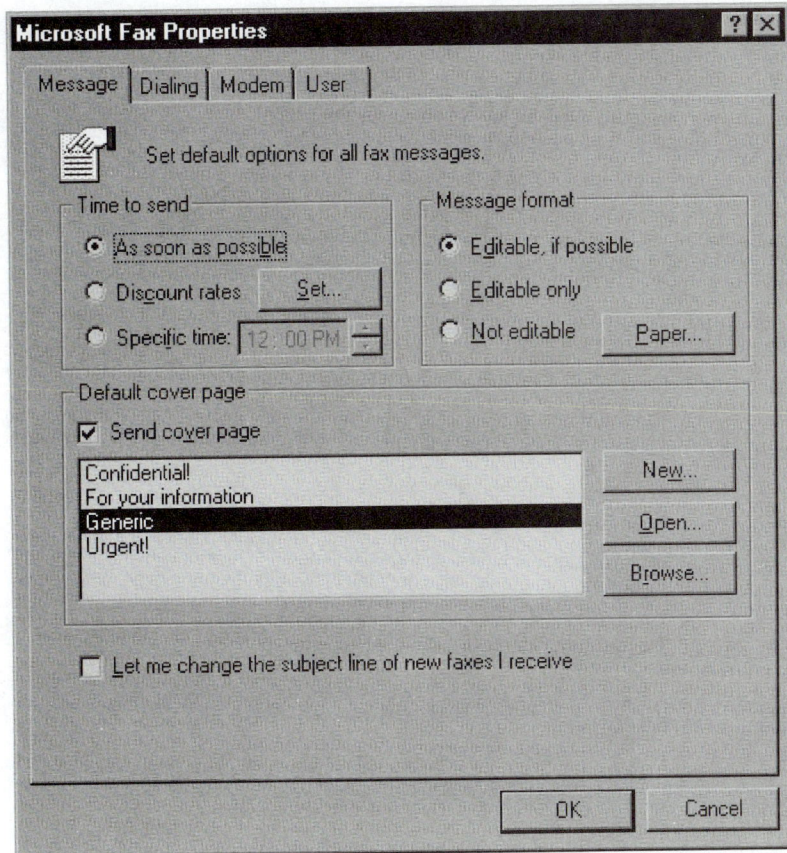

Figure 15.3   *Use the Fax Properties dialog box to select features of outbound faxes.*

Microsoft Mail Properties

To send and receive messages through a Microsoft Mail post office, you must add Mail to your Microsoft Exchange profile. The Microsoft Mail dialog box has eight tabs:

Connection   To use Microsoft Mail, you must specify the full path for the post office that handles your messages on the Connection tab page shown in Figure 15.4. The post office may be located on your computer or on another computer connected to yours through a network.

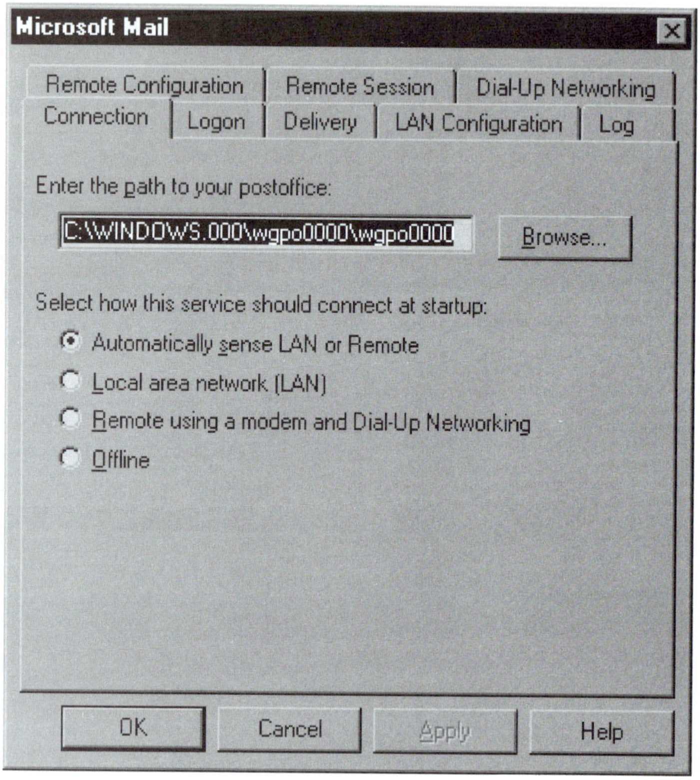

Figure 15.4 *The Connection tab defines the connection to your post office.*

You can connect to your post office through a LAN or a modem and telephone line. Select the radio button that describes the type of connection you're using.

Logon   Use the Logon tab to specify the name and password that your post office uses for your account.

Delivery   The Delivery tab in Figure 15.5 controls the way messages move between your post office and the Exchange client.

The *Enable incoming* option must be active to receive mail. The *Enable outgoing* option must be active to send mail.

Many Microsoft Mail installations have gateways to other messaging services, including fax and MCI Mail, among many others. If you don't want to use Mail to send messages to one or more of these

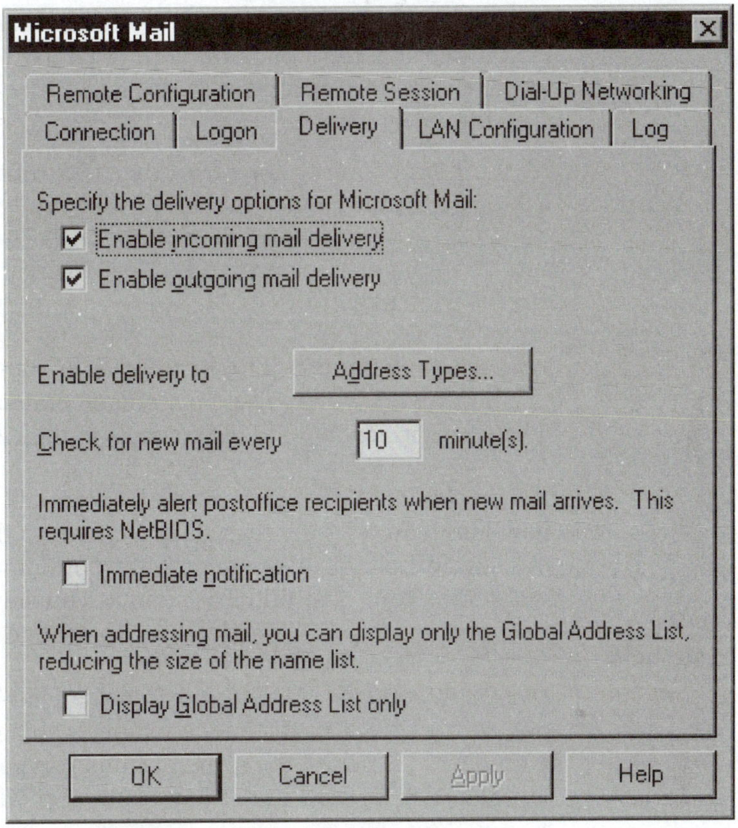

Figure 15.5 *Use the Delivery tab to specify delivery options.*

services, click on the Address Types button and remove the check mark from the name of the service. For example, if you want to send faxes through your fax modem rather than through your LAN, remove the check mark next to Fax.

LAN Configuration The LAN Configuration options all require a connection to a LAN. If you connect to your post office through a modem, you can ignore these options.

When *Use remote mail* is active, Exchange automatically transfers the headers of new incoming messages rather than the full text of the messages. When you want to read a message, use the Remote Mail command in Exchange's Tools menu.

Part
3

Managing
Communications

When the *Use local copy* option is active, Exchange stores a copy of the post office's address book on your local hard drive and uses that list rather than connecting you to the post office every time you request an address.

If your connection to the post office is extremely slow, the external delivery agent may reduce the amount of time needed for mail delivery.

Log   Use the options on the Log tab to create a history file for Microsoft Mail activity.

Remote Configuration   The Remote Configuration tab controls options that apply when you're using a modem connection to your post office. These options are similar to the ones on the LAN Configuration tab.

Remote Session   Use the Remote Session tab to specify when and for how long you want Exchange to connect to the post office through a modem. When the *Automatically start* option is active, Exchange will dial out to your post office as soon as you start Exchange. The *Automatically end* options specify when Exchange breaks the connection.

Dial-Up Networking   The options in the Dial-Up Networking dialog box control the way Exchange connects to a remote network through a modem. These are the same options you can reach through the Dial-Up Networking icon in the My Computer window.

Personal Address Book Properties

Your Personal Address Book is a combined listing of people to whom you send messages, regardless of the service that you use to reach that person. When you choose a name from your Personal Address Book, Exchange automatically routes the message through the service specified for that name. For example, your address book might include some people with Microsoft Network addresses, others with fax numbers, and still others who are on your Microsoft Mail system. By using the address book, you won't have to specify which service to use every time you send a message.

You can use as many separate Personal Address Books as you want. For example, if you share the computer with somebody else, each of you might want your own address book. Or you might want to use separate address books for personal and business purposes.

The Personal Address Book dialog box in Figure 15.6 specifies the file that contains your Personal Address Book and the order in which Exchange displays the contents of the address book (first name first or last name first).

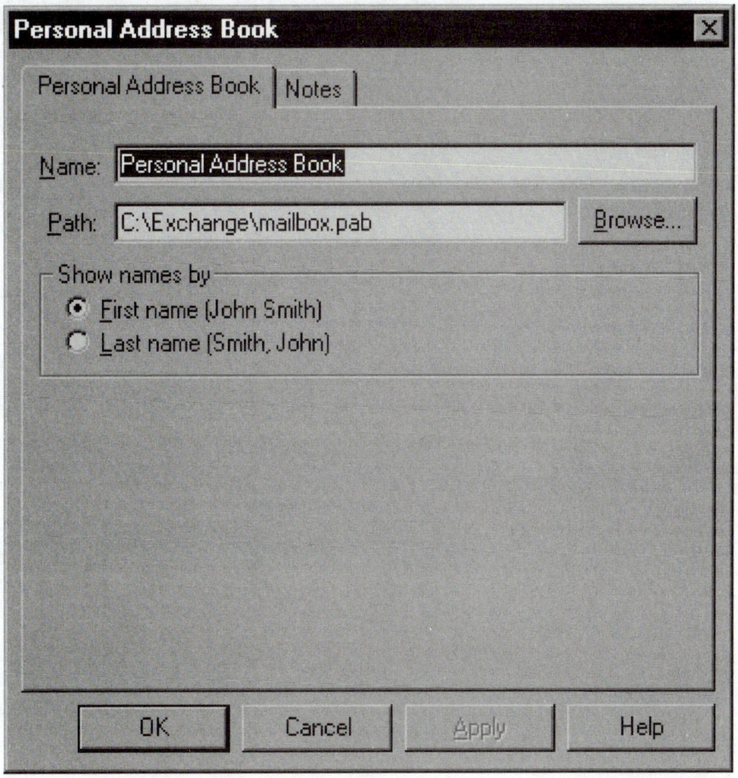

Figure 15.6 *The Personal Address Book dialog box controls the location and format of address books.*

The Notes tab displays any comments you might want to save about each Personal Address Book on your computer. If you have more than one address book, you can use these comments to remind yourself what each one contains. If you have only one address book, you can leave the Notes field blank.

Part 3

Managing Communications

Personal Folders Properties

Personal Folders are folders on your hard drive where you store messages. The Personal Folders dialog box shown in Figure 15.7 controls the way Exchange manages these folders. Most of the fields in the Personal Folders dialog box are fixed.

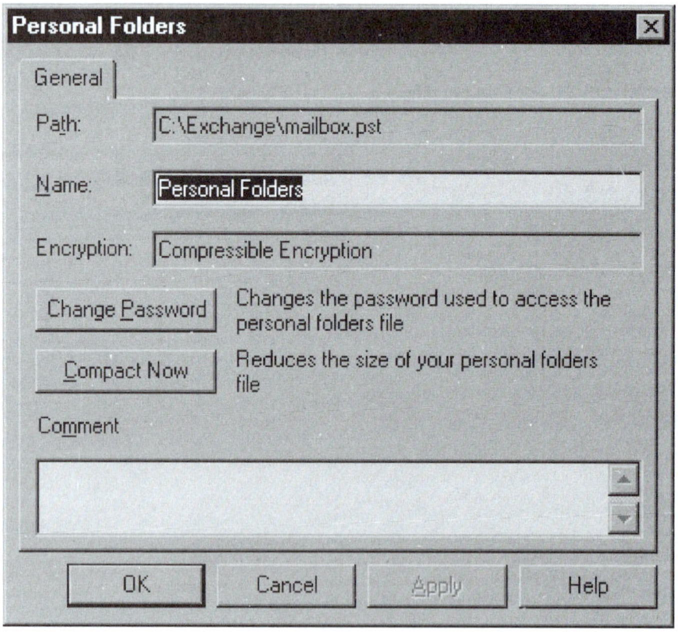

Figure 15.7   *The Personal Folders dialog box specifies the way Exchange stores messages.*

Microsoft Network Properties

The Microsoft Network Properties dialog box controls the way Exchange sends and receives messages from MSN. Use the Transport tab shown in Figure 15.8 to specify when you want Exchange to retrieve your MSN mail.

The Address Book tab turns address verification on and off. If *Connect to MSN to check names* is active, Exchange will automatically call MSN to confirm that names in your Personal Address Book with MSN addresses are current MSN subscribers.

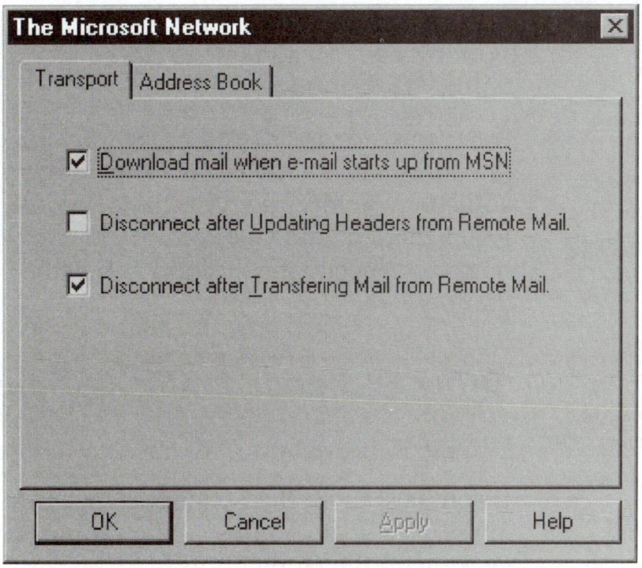

Figure 15.8 *The MSN dialog box lets you choose when Microsoft Network downloads your messages.*

Adding New Services to an Exchange Profile

To add a new service to an existing profile, click on the Add button to open the Add Service dialog box in Figure 15.9.

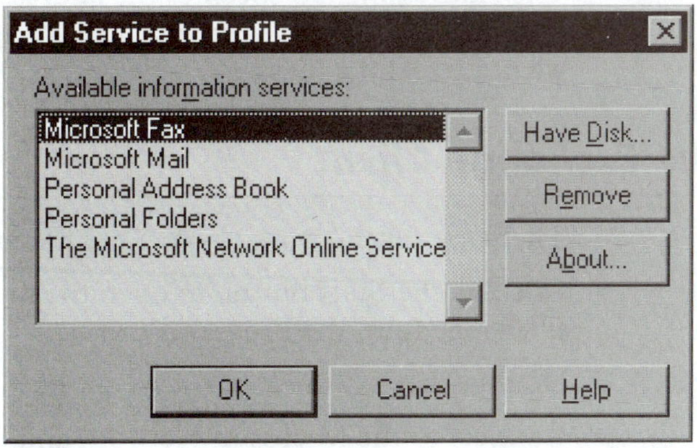

Figure 15.9 *Use the Add Service dialog box to add a messaging service to an Exchange Profile.*

The services in the *Available services* field are the ones included with Windows 95. To add one to the current profile, highlight it and click on the OK button.

Over time, Microsoft and other software developers and service providers will integrate other messaging services into Exchange. To add a new service to an Exchange profile, place the diskette or CD-ROM that contains the software in a drive and click on the Have Disk button to specify the location and name of the directory that contains the software.

Other Exchange Profile Options

Use the Remove button to delete a service from a profile.

If you have more than one Exchange profile, you can copy a messaging service, including its configuration, from one profile to another by clicking on the Copy button.

The About button opens an information window that shows details about all of the DLL files that control the currently highlighted messaging service.

The Delivery tab controls the location where Exchange will deliver new messages and the order in which Exchange polls messaging services.

The Addressing tab specifies the address book that Exchange uses as a default and the order in which Exchange consults address books when you send a message.

Using the Exchange Client

There are several ways to open the Exchange client:

▶ Click on the Start button to open the menu bar and choose Microsoft Exchange from the Programs menu.

▶ Double-click on the Inbox icon on the Windows Desktop.

▶ Connect to the Microsoft Network and click on E-Mail in the MSN Central screen.

The default Exchange screen in Figure 15.10 shows a list of messages in the current folder. You can customize the way Exchange organizes information in folders and the specific information that appears on your screen. I'll talk about other screen layouts later in this section.

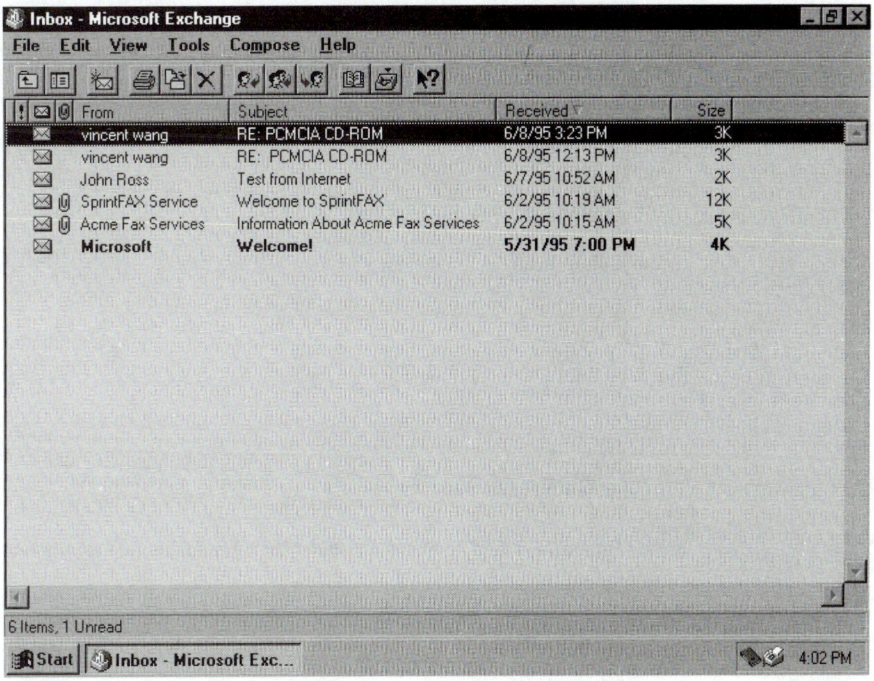

Figure 15.10 *Microsoft Exchange uses an Explorer-like screen layout.*

When you click on the Show/Hide Folder List button in the Toolbar or select the Folders command in the View menu, a graphic display of Exchange folders appears to the left of the list of messages. This layout is very similar to the Windows Explorer. Figure 15.11 shows a folder list.

Exchange calls each user's mailbox a *Personal Folder*. Each Personal Folder may contain an unlimited number of subfolders, but at a minimum they all must include an Inbox, an Outbox, and folders for deleted items and sent items. You can use the subfolders in a Personal Folder to hold the items that you send and receive through Exchange,

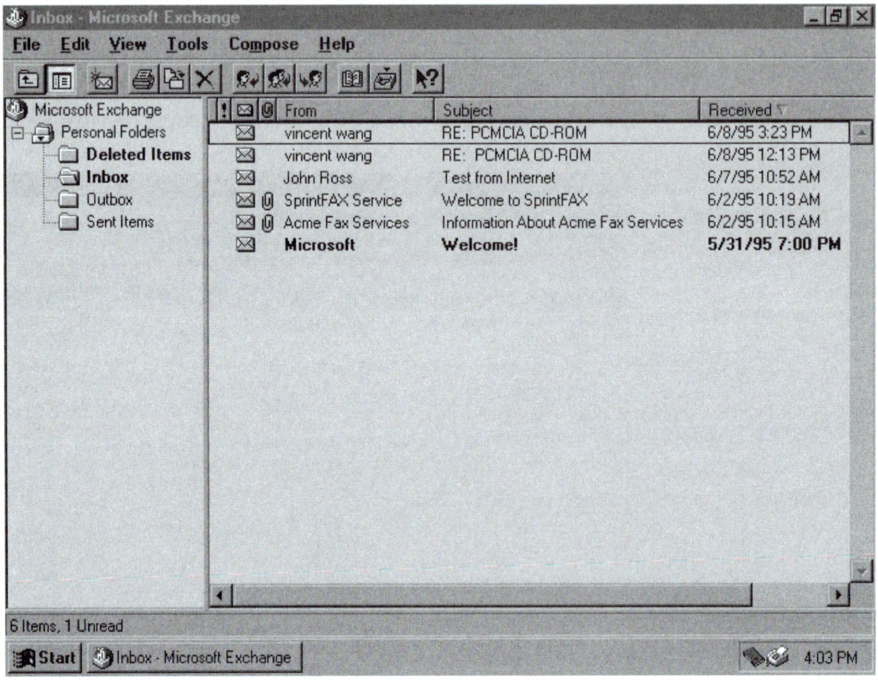

Figure 15.11   The Exchange folder list is similar to the list in Windows Explorer.

including e-mail messages, files, and faxes. As a general rule, you should have one Personal Folder in each user profile.

Like Explorer screens, the Exchange Viewer shows folders on the left and the contents of the currently highlighted folder on the right. You can move a message or other item to a new folder by dragging it to the destination folder or by highlighting it and using the Move or Copy command in the File menu or the menu that appears when you click the right mouse button. If you have more than one Personal Folder, it's also possible to move or copy an entire subfolder from one Personal Folder to another; however, you can't move or copy one sub-folder to another subfolder within the same Personal Folder.

There are several possible ways to arrange the display of files and mes-sages in the right pane of the Exchange Viewer: You can define the spe-cific information that will appear in each column, the order in which the columns appear, and the way the Viewer sorts messages and other items.

The headings across the top of the pane identify the information in each column. Click on a heading button to sort the messages according to that heading; for example, click on the From heading to arrange the messages and other items by source. To change the order from ascending (earliest or smallest first) to descending (latest or largest first), use the Sort command in the View menu or right-click on the column heading.

To change the set of headings in the Viewer or the order in which the headings appear, use the Columns command in the View menu to open the dialog box shown below. To add a heading, choose it from the *Available columns* list and click on the Add button; to remove a heading, highlight it in the *Show the following columns* list and click on the Remove button. The columns appear in the Viewer in the same order they appear in the list; to change the order, highlight an item and use the Move Up or Move Down button.

Searching for a Message

If you send and receive a lot of messages, you will eventually have either a bunch of folders with many messages in each one or one folder with a huge amount of stuff in it. Finding a month-old memo by looking through subject lines could take hours; fortunately, there's an easier method. Exchange has a message finder that can search through all the messages in a folder or in an entire Personal Folder to find messages that match one or more search criteria.

Part 3

Managing Communications

Follow these steps to search for messages:

1. Choose the Find command in the Tools menu.

2. When the Find window in Figure 15.12 appears, fill in the fields you want to use to search for messages:

> **Look in:** This field specifies the folder whose contents you want to search. Use the Folder button to choose a different folder.

> **Find items containing:** Use one or more of these fields to specify the contents or other characteristics of the message you want to find.

> **Advanced:** Click on the Advanced button to display the dialog box shown on the next page. You can use this dialog box to specify the size, date, and other characteristics of the messages.

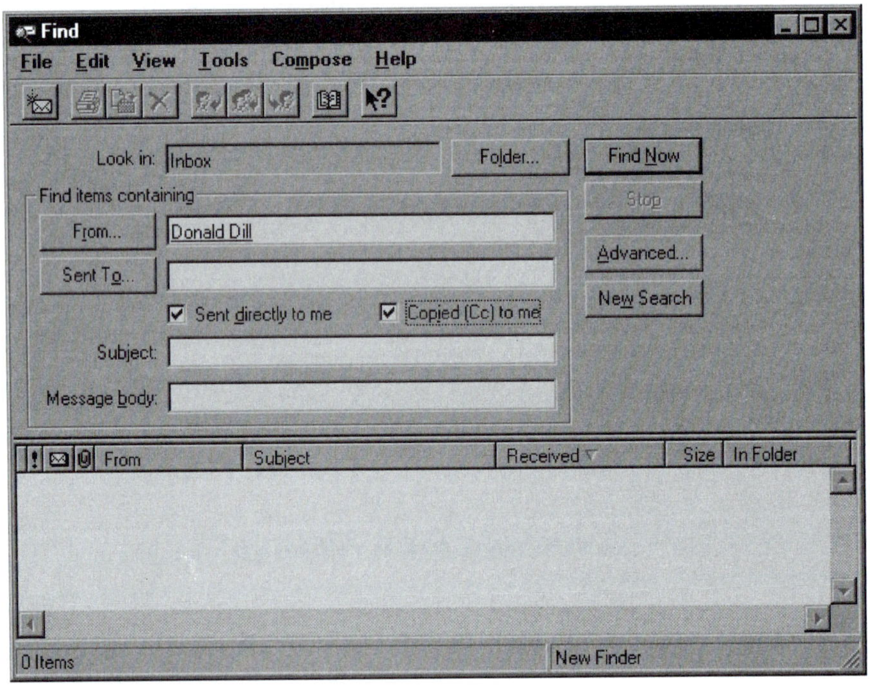

Figure 15.12   *Use Find to search for messages.*

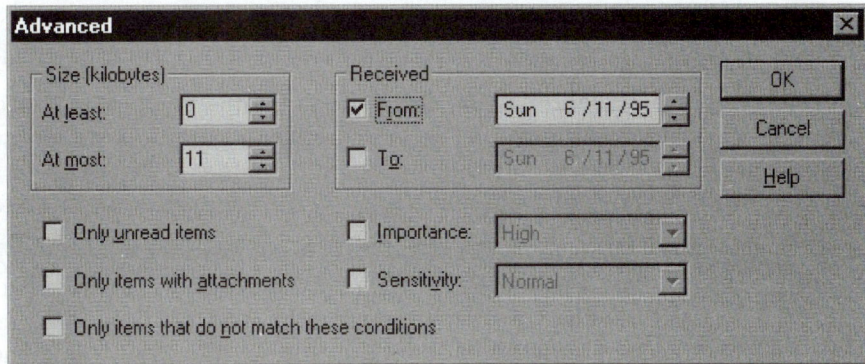

3. Click on the Start button to begin the search.

4. If the Finder locates any messages that match your search criteria, it will list them in the bottom half of the Finder window.

5. To cut off a search before it is complete, use the Stop button.

You can work with messages in the Finder the same way you work with them in the Exchange Viewer window. Double-click on a listing to display the contents of the message. Use the commands in the menu and the Toolbar to arrange columns; sort messages; use groups, filters, and views; and compose new messages.

Changing the Exchange Window

Most of the elements of the Exchange screen can be adjusted to meet your own needs and preferences. The Customize Toolbar command in the Tools menu opens a dialog box that controls the set of buttons in the Exchange Toolbar. The Services and Options commands in the Tools menu open the same dialog boxes that you used to configure Exchange from the Control Panel. And the commands in the View menu display, hide, or rearrange many specific screen elements.

Address Books

An address book is a list of names of potential recipients of Microsoft Exchange messages. Because each address-book entry specifies the messaging service you use to reach that person, you can create a single list that includes people with whom you communicate through several services.

When you want to send a message, you can choose the recipient by name and let Exchange worry about the transmission details.

If several users share the same machine, each user can have one or more personal address books. In addition, many messaging servers—such as Microsoft Mail and Microsoft Network—also provide directories of their subscribers in the same address-book format.

You can open an address book from the Compose Message window by clicking on the To or Cc buttons, or directly from the Microsoft Exchange screen by using the Address Book command in the Tools menu or clicking on the Address Book button in the Toolbar.

Figure 15.13 shows the Address Book window. The Type Name field is a smart search tool that will home in on the name you want as you type it. In most cases, it will find the name you want by the time you

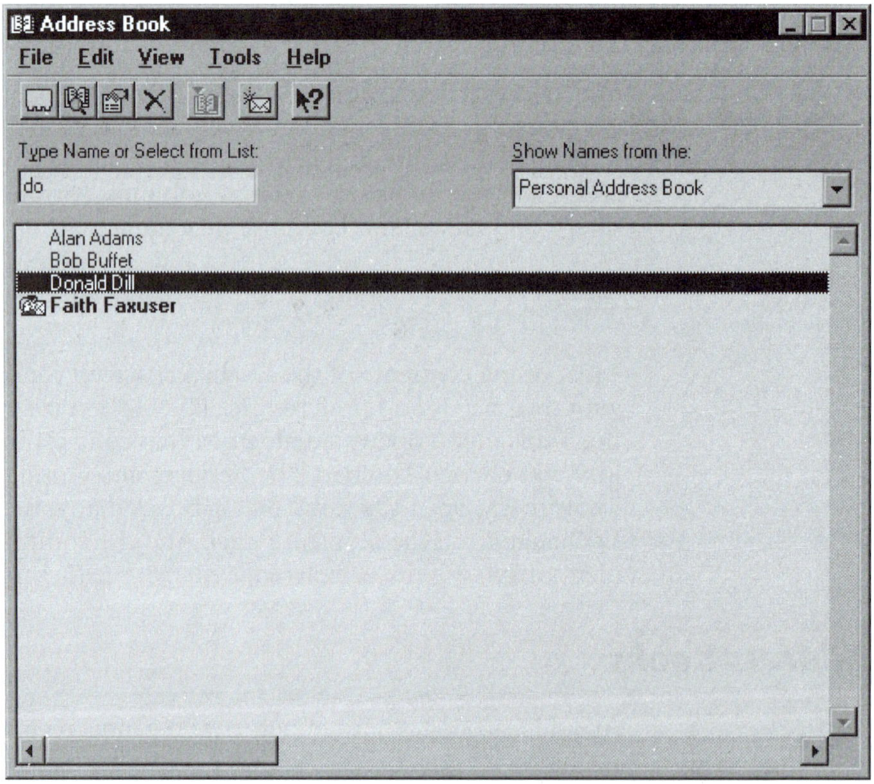

Figure 15.13   *A single Exchange address book can list subscribers to several messaging services.*

type three or four letters. If you prefer, you can point directly to a name in the list and click to highlight it. Double-click on an address-book listing to change the properties assigned to that name. To select a different address book, drop down the menu in the Show Names field.

To add a name to your address book, use the New Entry command in the File menu or on the Toolbar. Choose the service you want to use to communicate with this person and click on OK to open a Properties dialog box. The Exchange client in Windows 95 does not support direct connection to the Internet, but you can send e-mail to Internet addresses through the Microsoft Network.

The Properties dialog box asks different questions for each type of messaging service. For example, if you specify an MSN e-mail address, the dialog box in Figure 15.14 will appear.

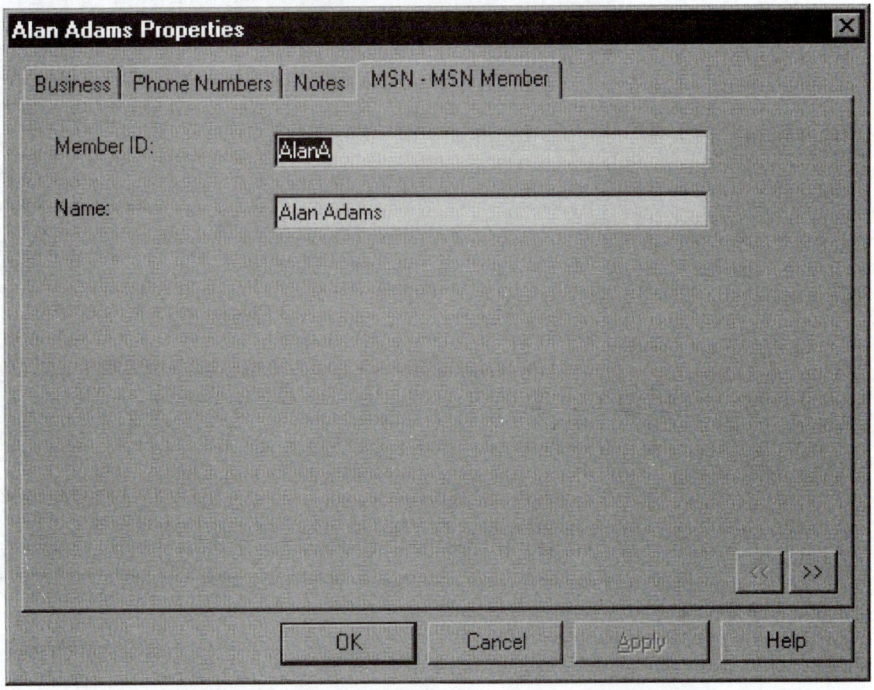

Alan Adams Properties ☒

| Business | Phone Numbers | Notes | MSN - MSN Member |

Member ID: AlanA

Name: Alan Adams

≪ ≫

OK   Cancel   Apply   Help

Figure 15.14   *The Properties dialog box for a Microsoft Network address includes space for the recipient's name and MSN Member ID.*

Part
3

Managing
Communications

The other tabs provide space for you to add additional information about this party, including full name and address, up to eight different telephone numbers, and other notes.

Besides using Address Book listings to send messages through Microsoft Exchange, you can also use the Address Book to set up voice telephone calls through Phone Dialer. To place a call, double-click on the name of the person you want to call and click on the Phone Numbers tab to display the dialog box in Figure 15.15. Choose the location you want to call and click on the Dial button next to that telephone number. When the call goes through, Phone Dialer will tell you to lift the handset and start talking.

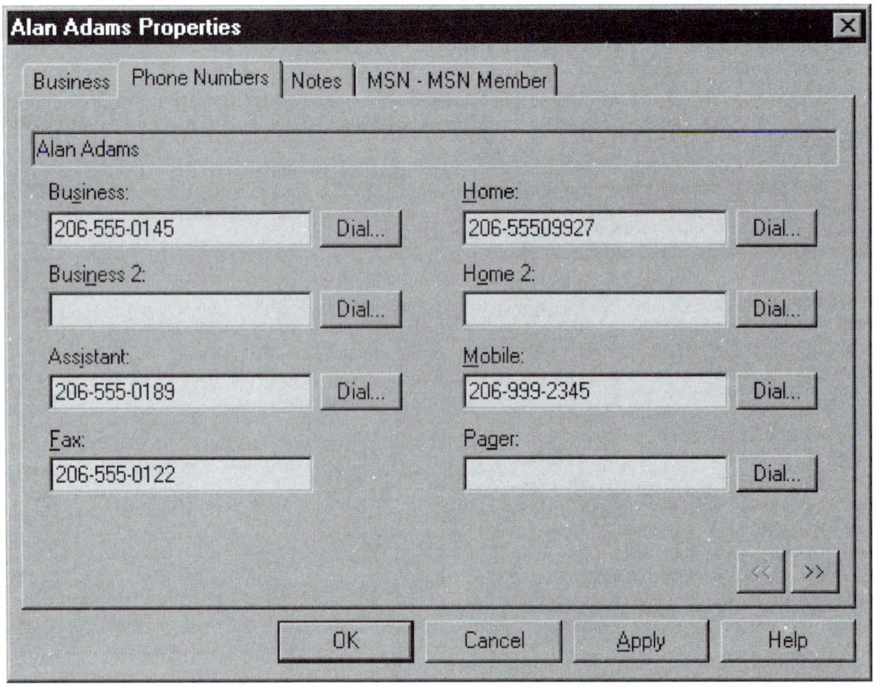

Figure 15.15   *The Exchange Address Book may contain multiple telephone numbers for the same person.*

Creating and Sending Messages

Everything I've talked about so far in this chapter is about getting Microsoft Exchange organized. In this section, I'll explain how to use it to do something actually useful. It's easy to forget that Microsoft Exchange isn't really about profiles or address books—it's a tool for sending and receiving messages. All of its other features and functions support those activities.

Here's the procedure for sending a message through Microsoft Exchange:

1. Start Microsoft Exchange from the menu bar or the Desktop Inbox icon.

2. When the Inbox - Microsoft Exchange screen appears, choose the New Message command from either the Compose menu or the Toolbar.

3. When the New Message screen in Figure 15.16 appears, either type the names of the recipients in the To field or click on the To button to select names from an address book. If you want to send this message to more than one person, use semicolons to separate the names.

   ▶ If you want to send duplicate copies of this message, tab or mouse to the Cc field in the New Message box and type the names. Alternatively, in the Address Book dialog box click on the Cc-> button to select from the list.

   ▶ If you want to send a blind copy of this message, use the Bcc Box command in the View menu.

4. Point and click on the Subject field and type a subject line for this message.

5. Move your cursor to the large box at the bottom of the screen and type the text of your message. You can find more detailed information about formatting messages, adding inserts, and attaching files in the next part of this chapter.

6. When the text and format of your message are complete and ready to go, use the Send command in the File menu or the Send button in the Toolbar to place the message in the Exchange Outbox.

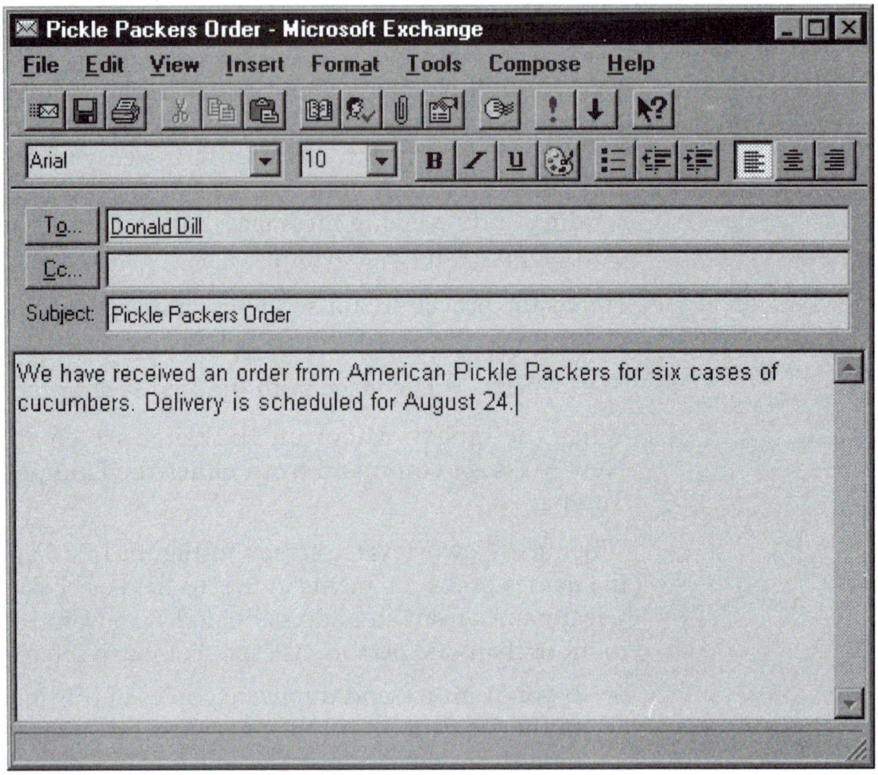

Figure 15.16   *Use this screen to compose e-mail messages for many services.*

7. After you have finished composing messages, open the Outbox folder and choose the Deliver Now command in the Tools menu. If all the messages in your out box are for the same message service, you can choose that service from the Deliver Now submenu, but it's generally easier to use the All Services command.

8. After Exchange has uploaded your message, it automatically transfers the message from the Outbox folder to the Sent Items folder. You can move the message to a different folder by dragging and dropping it in the Exchange window.

Formatting Messages

The message editor in Microsoft Exchange uses the same formatting tools as WordPad, including a Toolbar with buttons to control font, character size, style, color, indentation, and justification. To change the format of all or part of a message, highlight the text you want to format and click on the appropriate button in the Toolbar.

Just because it's possible to do all kinds of fancy formatting tricks with your messages, it doesn't mean you have to use them in every message. In most cases, you send a message to communicate information, and a screen with three different colors and four different typestyles doesn't contribute anything to the reader's understanding of your message—it's just hard to read. Sending an e-mail message that looks like a ransom note does not convey a businesslike image, but it might be exactly what you want when you send a birthday greeting to a ten-year-old.

It's also a good idea to think about the type of hardware and software the person receiving your messages will use. Unless the recipient is also using Microsoft Exchange, all your special effects will be lost if the other mail reader does not recognize formatting information.

Attaching a File to a Message

In addition to new text, you can also include existing text files in the body of your message and accompany your message with one or more binary files. An attached file can appear in the body of your message as an icon with a name. As in the Explorer and the Windows Desktop, clicking on an icon in a message opens the attached file.

It's also possible to create a link to a file that already exists on the recipient's computer or network. For example, you might have a program on your computer that reports your company's daily sales volume. If other people on the same LAN have access to your computer through the network, you could send them a message like the one in Figure 15.17.

Part
3

Managing
Communications

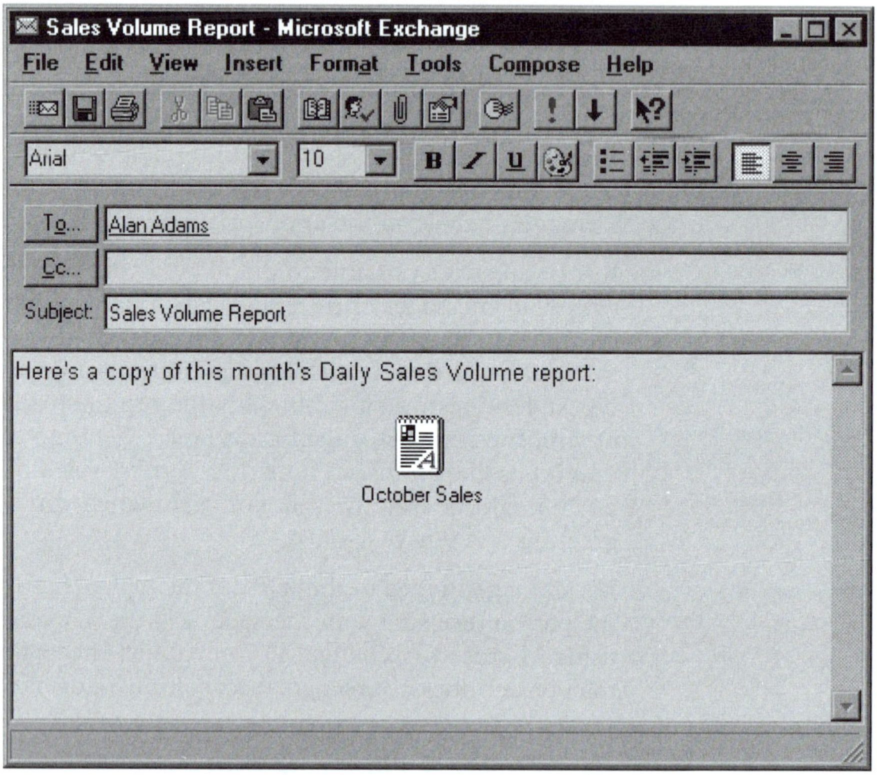

Figure 15.17   Microsoft Exchange messages may include embedded files.

Follow these steps to include a file with a message:

1. Move your cursor to the place in the message where you want the file.

2. Select the File command in the Insert menu. The Insert File window in Figure 15.18 will appear.

3. Locate the file you want to attach and highlight it.

4. Choose a method from the Insert As box:

> **Text only:** inserts the text contained in the file into your message as text.
>
> **An attachment:** attaches a copy of the file to your message and places an icon in your message at the current cursor location.

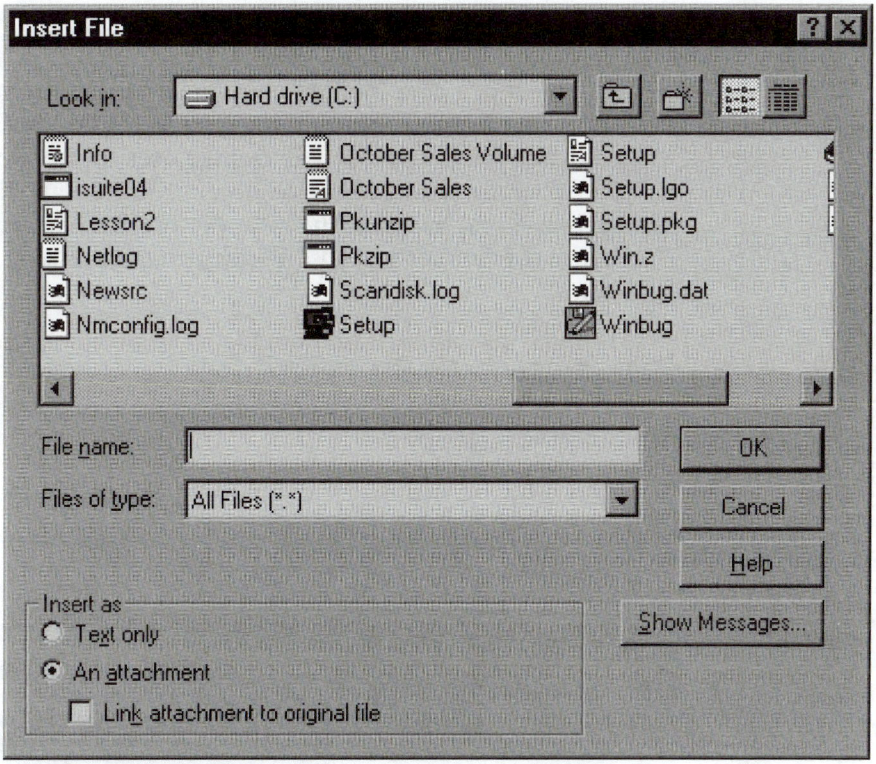

Figure 15.18   Use the Insert File dialog box to attach a file to a message.

Link attachment to original file: inserts an icon that points to the file's location rather than making a copy of it. A linked file must be located in a place where the recipient can get to it. Therefore, you should generally limit linked files to recipients who are on the same computer or network.

5. Click on the OK button or double-click on the icon for the file you want to insert.

6. If you want to insert or attach another file, repeat steps 3, 4, and 5.

7. To close the Insert File dialog box, click on OK.

Part
3

Managing
Communications

Embedding an Object in a Message

An object is a data file that contains information formatted for a particular application. When the recipient reads a message with an embedded object, Microsoft Exchange uses the application to open the file. Therefore, an embedded object could be any kind of data file, such as a graph, spreadsheet, or picture. Like an attached file, an object may be either pasted directly into the message or displayed as an icon.

You may use an existing data file as an object or create a new one especially for your message. If you choose to create a new object, Exchange will open the application program associated with the type of object you specify.

Here's the procedure for embedding an object in a message:

1. Move your cursor to the place in the message where you want the embedded object or icon to appear.

2. Select the Object command from the Insert menu.

3. The Insert Object dialog box shown below has two options:

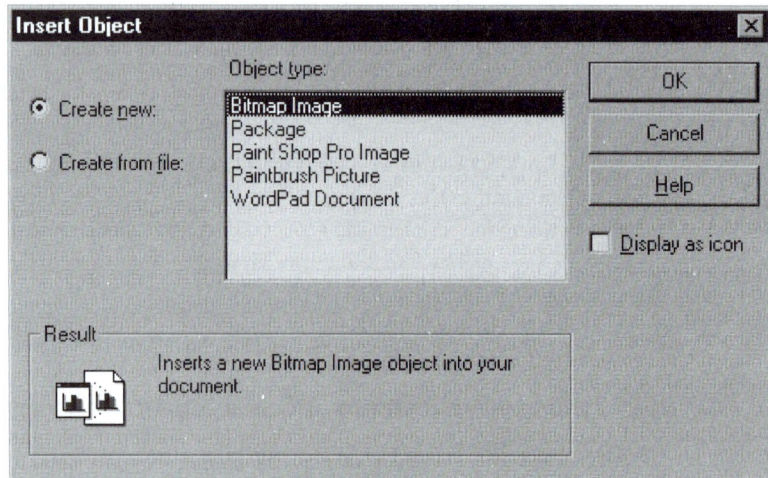

Create New: Use this option if the object does not already exist.
Create from File: Use this option to select an existing object.

4. If you want the object to appear in the body of your message as an icon, check Display As Icon.

5. If you're creating a new object, select the object type from the list. The application associated with that object type will open.

6. If you're embedding an existing file, choose Create from File to display the dialog box shown below. Either type its full path and name in the File field or use the browser to find the file you want.

7. When the Link option is not active, the embedded object is part of the message you actually send. When Link is active, Exchange displays the latest version of the file, even if the file changes after you send your message.

> **NOTE** A linked object file must be located in a place where the recipient can get to it. Therefore, you should generally limit linked objects to recipients who are on the same computer or network that you use.

8. Click on the OK button to embed the specified object file.

Part
3

Managing
Communications

Receiving Messages

Exchange checks for new mail at the same time it delivers outgoing messages to the messaging services that relay them to their ultimate destinations. To connect to your messaging services, use one of the Deliver Now commands in the Tools menu.

When Exchange receives new messages, it stores them in the Inbox folder. It displays descriptions of unread messages in boldface type. After you read a message, the description changes to normal type. To read a newly received message, open the Inbox folder and double-click on the description.

Fax messages are a special case. Unlike most e-mail services, which are store-and-forward systems that hold your messages until you go looking for them, fax messages might arrive at any time. Chapter 16 contains detailed information about using Exchange to send and receive faxes.

Moving Messages and Files to Other Applications

Microsoft Exchange is an OLE-compatible application. Therefore, you can drag messages and other items in the Exchange Viewer to and from other applications, including the Windows Desktop. When you drag a message from an Exchange folder to a drive or directory on the Desktop, Windows will save the message as a file with an .msg file extension.

It's also possible to drag files from other applications into Microsoft Exchange. If the file was created with an application that uses Summary Info dialog boxes, you can use the Summary fields as column headings for sorting, searching, or filtering in Microsoft Exchange.

Microsoft Mail

Microsoft Mail is one of the information services that can use MAPI and Microsoft Exchange to move messages to and from your PC. Microsoft Mail uses a post office located on one of the computers in a workgroup to hold messages until the Mail client on the recipient's own machine retrieves it. You may know Microsoft Mail as a separate product or as an element of Windows for Workgroups. Windows 95 includes both a Microsoft Mail client and a Mail post office that are completely compatible with other products that support Mail. Therefore, you can operate a mixed workgroup that includes both Windows 95 and Windows 3.x systems along with Microsoft Mail clients for other platforms.

It's important to remember that a workgroup may have only one post office, so you should not create a new post office if you're adding a new Windows 95 machine to an existing workgroup. The post office in Windows 95 is limited, which means that it can't communicate with other post offices. If you're planning to move mail through more than one post office to other workgroups, you'll have to use the complete version of Microsoft Mail. This version comes as a separate product, and it will be included with the standalone Microsoft Exchange product.

Earlier in this chapter, I explained that Microsoft Exchange uses a Personal Folder to hold messages from many different information services. A Microsoft Mail post office is a similar information store that holds messages for all the members of a workgroup. When the recipient receives a message, the post office removes its copy of the same message. If a message is addressed to more than one recipient, the post office deletes it after the last recipient retrieves it.

Microsoft Mail can deliver mail to three kinds of Windows 95 clients:

▶ a Personal Folder located on the same computer that holds the post office

▶ a Personal Folder located on a computer connected through a network to the computer that holds the post office

▶ a Personal Folder located on a mobile or remote computer that makes a temporary connection to the computer that holds the post office

Installing a Microsoft Mail Post Office

The first time Exchange runs, it will ask for the location of your post office. If your workgroup already has a post office, you should not install another one from Windows 95. If you don't have access to an existing post office, you should create one on your PC. All Microsoft Mail users must use a post office, even if they are not connected to a LAN.

Follow these steps to create a new post office:

1. From the Control Panel, click on the Microsoft Mail Postoffice icon to start the Postoffice Admin Wizard.

2. Choose the Create a New Postoffice option and click on the Next button.

3. Type a path for the post office folder.

4. When the dialog box shown below appears, fill in the details for your Administrator account. You will need this name and password to add or remove additional accounts in this post office.

5. When the Administrator account is set up, go back to the Control Panel and click on the Microsoft Mail Postoffice icon again. This time, choose the Administer radio button and click on Next. The Wizard will display the location of your post office. Click on Next.

6. Type your Administrator password in the Password field and click on Next.

7. When the Postoffice Manager window in Figure 15.19 appears, click on the Add User button to create new accounts for the other people in your workgroup. Use the Details button to see information about existing users.

8. After you have created an account for every user in your workgroup, click on the Close button.

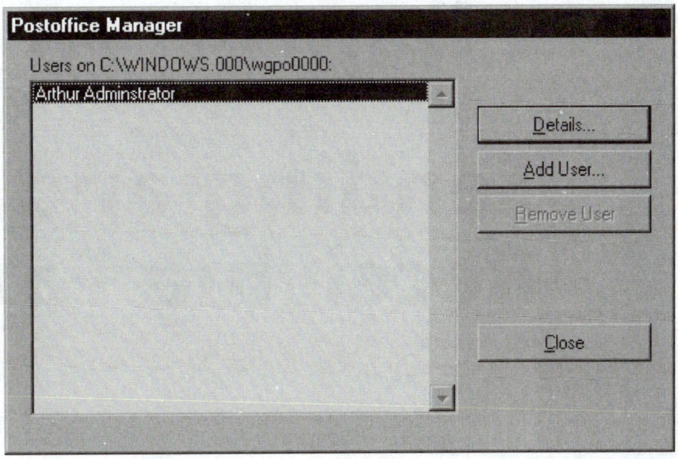

Figure 15.19   Use the Postoffice Manager dialog box to add, remove, or modify user accounts.

Shutting Down Microsoft Exchange

Once you start Microsoft Exchange, it will run in the background, waiting for incoming messages, until you use the Exit or the Exit and Log Off command in the File menu.

By this time, you're thinking that Microsoft Exchange seems incredibly complicated. You're right. Because Exchange and MAPI can control so many different message services, it has a very large set of configuration options. But in practice, you will probably use no more than a few services at the same time—maybe just fax and Microsoft Network or Microsoft Mail. It's really not as complex as it looks.

The great advantage of Microsoft Exchange over a separate application for each service is that you can store and manage all your messages in one place and use the same set of commands to send and receive messages through many services. Once you've got Exchange configured the way you want it, you can spend your time thinking about the content of your messages.

In the next two chapters, I'll explain how to use two specialized communication services: fax and the Internet. Both of these services can use Microsoft Exchange as a front end, but that's just one of several options—there's a lot more to sending and receiving faxes and to connecting your PC to the worldwide Internet.

Chapter 16

Sending and Receiving Faxes

FEATURING

If you're in business today, a fax machine is as essential as an office copier or a coffeepot. The most common tool for facsimile communication is still the standalone fax machine, but there are some real advantages to using your PC as a personal fax machine instead.

Here's what you need to do to send a fax through a fax machine: create the document; print a copy on paper; write up a cover sheet; carry the document and cover sheet to the fax machine; wait for your turn to use the machine; dial the recipient's fax number; feed the document and cover sheet through the fax machine; and finally, walk back to your office. When somebody sends you a fax, it spills out of the machine and waits for you to come get it—meanwhile, everybody who walks past the fax machine has a chance to read your messages before you do.

On the other hand, you can send and receive faxes through your PC and a fax modem without leaving your chair. If you have a home office or a *really* small business with a tight budget, you can do PC-based faxing without spending two-hundred dollars or more for a separate machine. And when you're traveling with a portable computer, you can use it to exchange faxes with your office and your customers.

In this chapter, you can find out how to use Microsoft Fax to send faxes from Microsoft Exchange, from the Windows 95 desktop, and directly from application programs. You'll also learn how to create cover pages for your outgoing faxes, how to receive faxes through your modem, and how to use the Fax Viewer program.

Installing Microsoft Fax

Before you can send or receive faxes, you must configure Windows 95 to recognize Microsoft Fax as a virtual printer. You can load the fax software when you install Windows 95 by choosing Custom Setup and checking Microsoft Fax from the list of components. Since the fax program uses the Microsoft Exchange client, you'll also have to load Exchange if it's not already present on your computer. If you've already installed Windows 95 without the Microsoft Fax component, you can add it by using this procedure:

1. From the Control Panel, double-click on the Add/Remove Programs icon.

2. Choose the Windows Setup tab.

3. Scroll down the list of components until you see the listing for Microsoft Fax in Figure 16.1.

4. Check the box for Microsoft Fax and click on the OK button.

5. Insert and remove the Windows 95 software disks as the on-screen Wizard instructs you to do so.

6. Open the Control Panel again and double-click on the Mail and Fax icon. The dialog box in Figure 16.2 will appear.

7. Either click on the Add button to create a new Exchange profile for fax messages or highlight the name of an existing profile and click on Properties to add Fax to an existing profile.

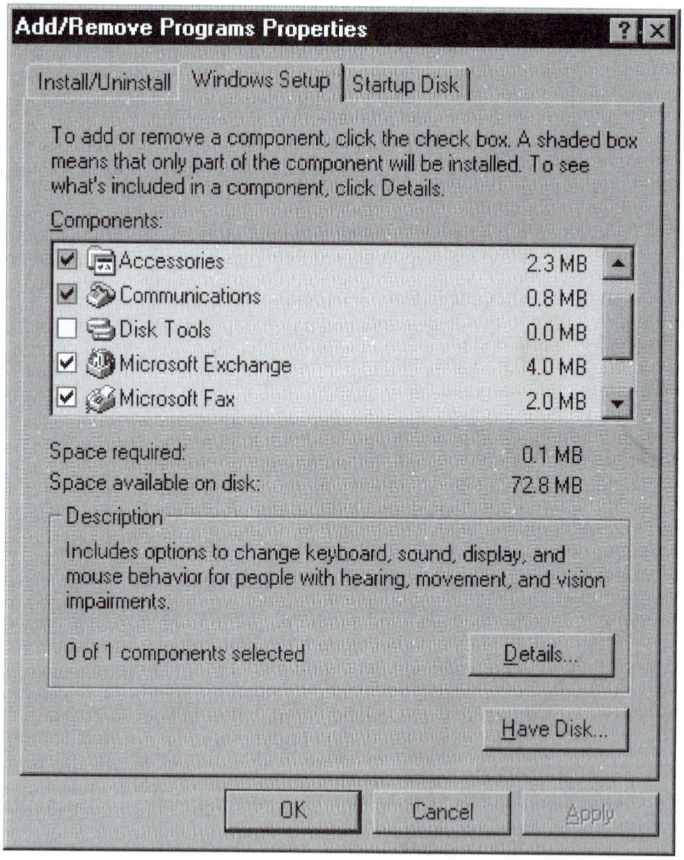

Figure 16.1 *Check Microsoft Fax to send and receive faxes.*

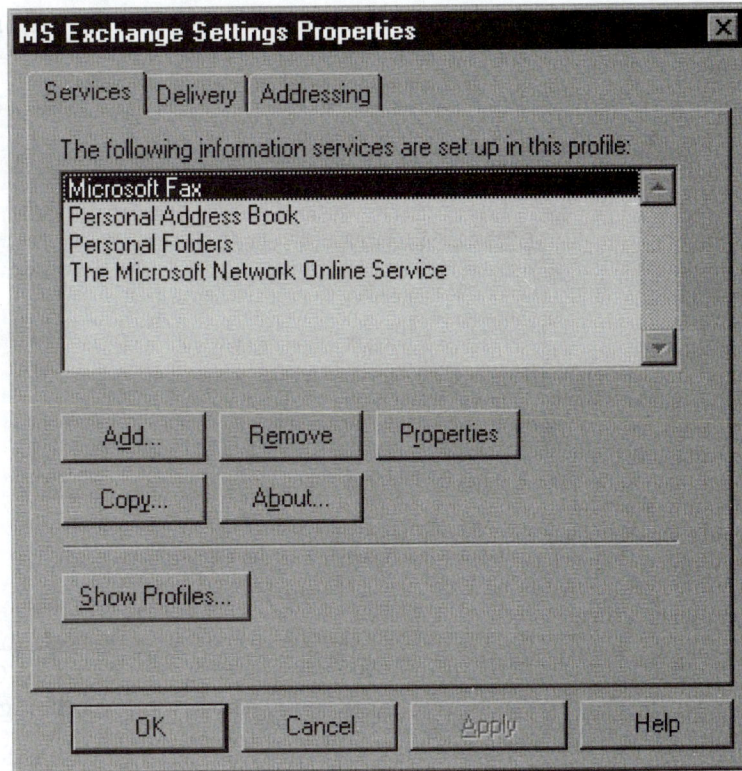

Figure 16.2 *You may add Microsoft Fax to an existing profile or create a new one.*

8. If you're creating a new profile, the Exchange Setup Wizard will ask you to identify the services you want in this profile. Check the box next to Microsoft Fax.

9. Click on the Next button and fill in each field as the Wizard asks for information about this new profile.

To add Microsoft Fax to an existing profile, follow these steps:

1. Open the Control Panel and double-click on the Mail and Fax icon or use the Shortcut to Mail and Fax icon on your Desktop. The Properties dialog box in Figure 16.2 will appear.

2. Click on the Show Profiles button to display a list of profiles.

3. Highlight the name of the profile to which you want to add Fax and click on the Properties button. The dialog box in Figure 16.2 will

Part
3

Managing
Communications

appear again, this time with the name of the profile you just selected in the title bar.

4. Click on the Add button to display the dialog box below.

Add Service to Profile

Available information services:

Microsoft Fax
Microsoft Mail
Personal Address Book
Personal Folders
The Microsoft Network Online Service

Have Disk...
Remove
About...

OK   Cancel   Help

5. Highlight Microsoft Fax in the list of available Information Services and click on the OK button.

6. A warning message will appear advising you that Microsoft Fax needs information about your fax number. Click on OK in the warning message window to open the Fax Properties dialog box.

7. The Microsoft Fax Properties dialog box has four tabs: Message, Dialing, Modem, and User. You can accept the default settings under the Message, Dialing, and Modem settings, but you'll have to type the name and fax number that you want on your fax cover sheet in the User dialog box.

8. The Message tab opens the dialog box in Figure 16.3. It includes these fields:

Time to send: These radio buttons control the time of day when Microsoft Fax will send your faxes. The three options are:

As soon as possible: Microsoft Fax tries to send your fax immediately.

Discount rates: Microsoft Fax holds your faxes until the long-distance rates are lower, usually in the evening. Use the Set button to specify the times of day when discount rates begin and end.

Specific time: Microsoft Fax waits for the specified time before sending your faxes. To change the time, highlight the hour or minute and use the up and down arrows.

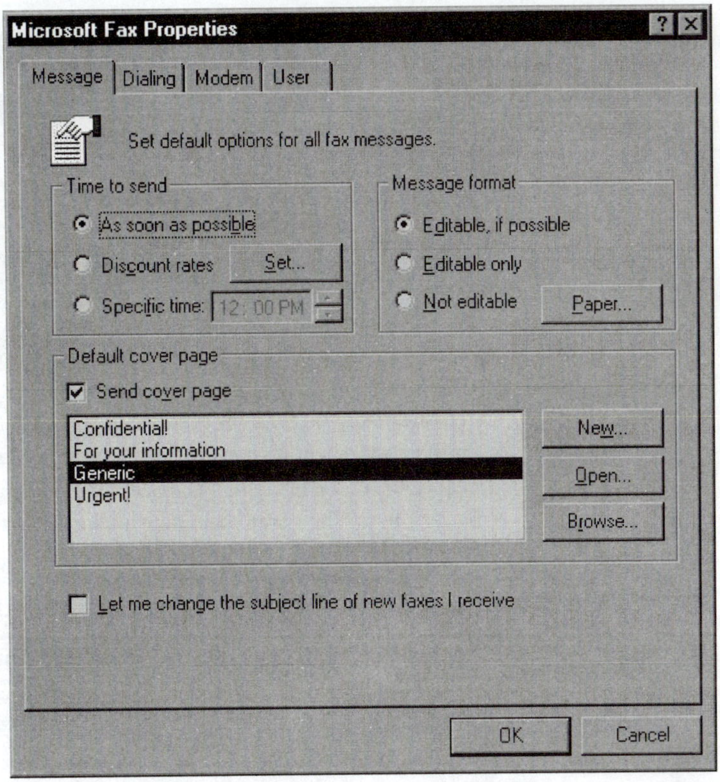

Figure 16.3 *Use the Message tab to change the default format, time, and cover page of your faxes.*

Message format: The message format is not only the layout of the page, as you might expect, but it's also the way Microsoft Fax sends the message: as either a binary file that the recipient can edit with a word processor or text editor, or as a bit-mapped image.

Editable, if possible: Microsoft Fax will automatically use the binary editable format when the receiving system can recognize it.

Editable only: Microsoft Fax will try to send all faxes as binary files and refuse to send the message if the receiving system can't accept that format.

Not editable: Microsoft Fax will send faxes as bit-mapped images.

Paper: This button opens the dialog box on the next page, which controls the layout of the fax page.

Part 3

Managing Communications

Default cover page: This section controls whether Microsoft Fax normally sends a cover sheet with every fax message, and if so, which one. Each time you prepare to send a fax, you will specify the name and fax telephone number of the recipient. The cover sheet may include information about both the sender and the recipient of each fax message.

9. The Dialing tab opens the dialog box in Figure 16.4.

   Dialing Properties: This button opens the same Dialing Properties dialog box as most other communications applications. Chapter 13 explains this dialog box.

   Toll Prefixes: This button opens the dialog box in Figure 16.5. If you must dial your own area code when you dial an in-state long-distance call, you can use this dialog box to specify the telephone numbers that require an area code.

   If Microsoft Fax does not successfully connect and send your fax on its first attempt, it will use the Retries information to make additional attempts.

10. The Modem tab opens the dialog box in Figure 16.6. The top half of the dialog box contains the same information that you saw when you ran the modem-setup routine. The other options are:

   Set as Active Fax Modem: If you have more than one modem attached to your computer, highlight the one that you want to use to send and receive faxes, and click on the Set as Active button.

   Let other people on the network use my modem to send faxes: If your PC is connected to a LAN, you can allow other people to send faxes through your fax modem by making this option active.

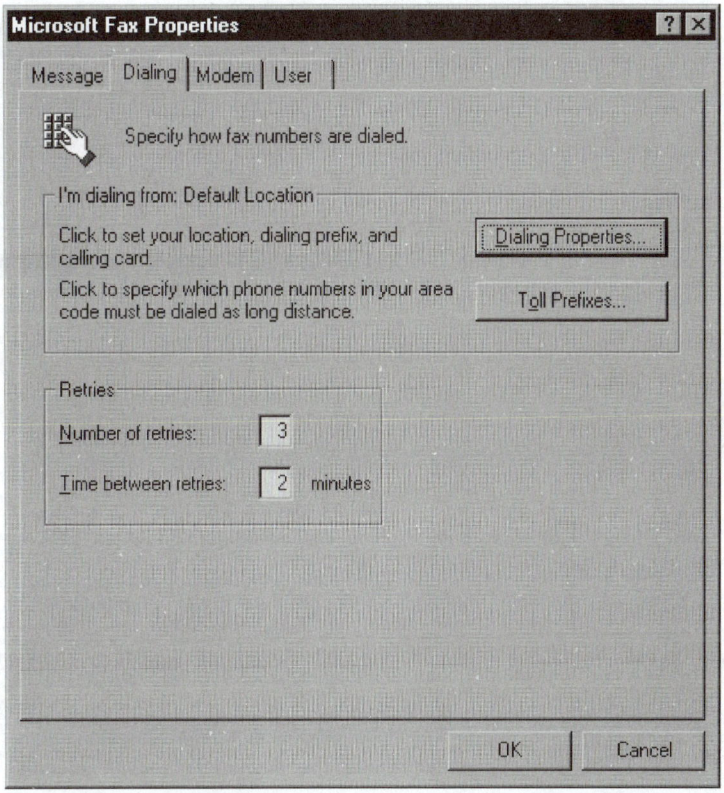

Figure 16.4   *Dialing properties control the way Microsoft Fax places fax calls.*

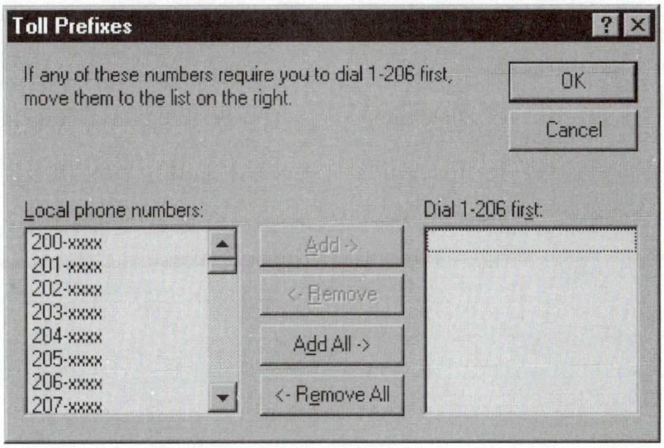

Figure 16.5   *Use the Toll Prefixes dialog box to identify nearby telephone numbers that require an area code.*

Part
3

Managing
Communications

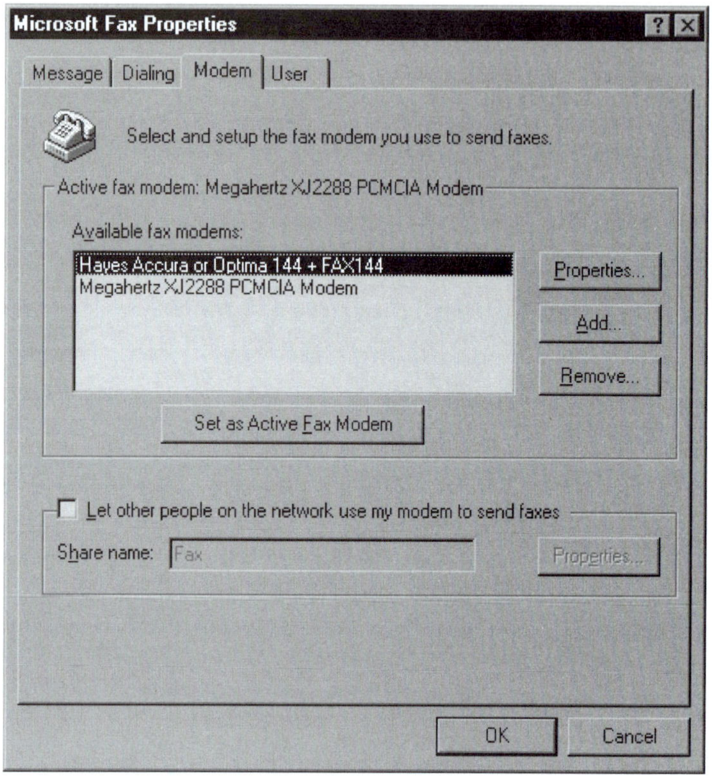

Figure 16.6 *Use the Modem tab to choose a fax modem.*

Work offline: When this option is active, Microsoft Fax will not send or receive fax messages, but you can still create new faxes and store them in Exchange. This option could be useful to portable computer users for creating faxes when no telephone line is available.

11. The User tab opens the dialog box in Figure 16.7.

12. Click on the OK buttons in the Fax Properties dialog box and the Settings Properties dialog boxes and the Close button in the Exchange Profiles dialog box to save the changes to this profile and return to the Control Panel.

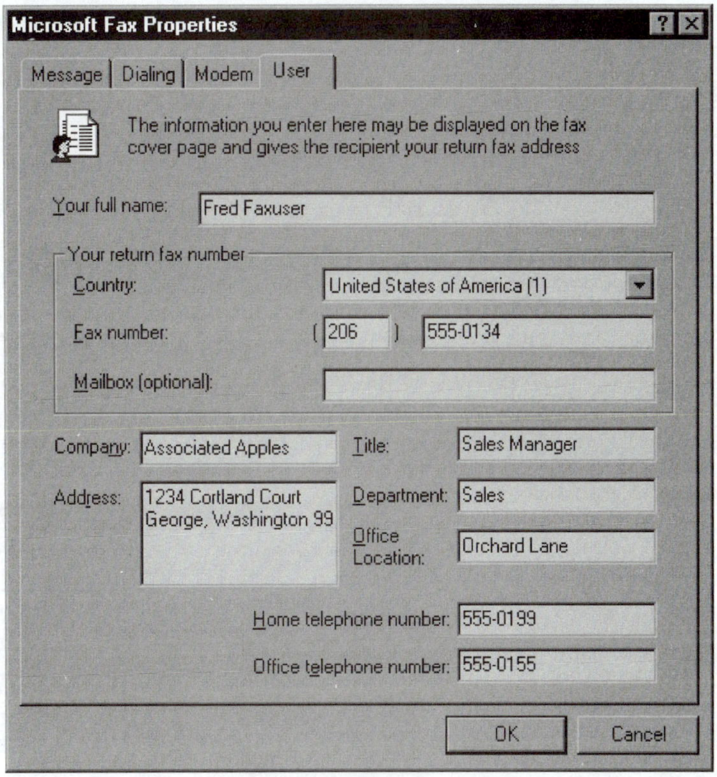

Figure 16.7   *Microsoft Fax uses information from this dialog box in your fax cover sheet.*

Sending Faxes

There are four ways to send faxes from Windows 95:

▶ Drag a text or graphics file to the Microsoft Fax icon in the Printers folder.

▶ Right-click on an icon and choose the Send to Fax Recipient command.

▶ Select Microsoft Fax as the printer in any application program.

▶ Fax from Microsoft Exchange.

All of these methods lead you to the Compose New Fax Wizard. However, if you use the Message Editor in Exchange, you won't see the Wizard if you choose a fax recipient from your address book.

Part
3

Managing
Communications

The Print to Fax Wizard

When you "print" a document to the fax driver, Windows 95 uses the Compose New Fax Wizard to take you through the steps needed to specify the recipient's fax telephone number and add a cover sheet to the document.

When the Compose New Fax Wizard opens the dialog box in Figure 16.8, either type the recipient's name in the To field and the fax number in the Fax # field or click on the Address Book button to choose a recipient from your address book. Click on the Add button to place this name in the list of recipients. You can send the same fax message to more than one recipient by adding more names to the list. Click on the Next button to move to the next dialog box.

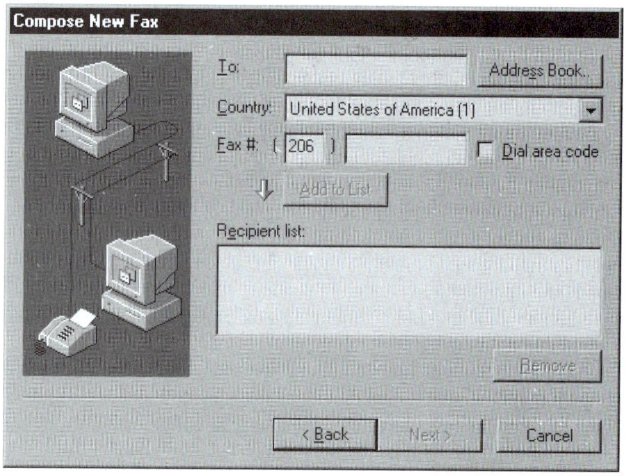

Figure 16.8   Use the Compose New Fax Wizard to choose a fax recipient.

The dialog box in Figure 16.9 specifies the cover sheet that will accompany this fax, if any. To add a cover page, click on the *Yes, Send this one* radio button and highlight the description of the cover page you want to use. To schedule delayed transmission or change any of the other default options, click on the Options button.

If you chose to include a cover page, the next dialog box in the Compose New Fax Wizard (Figure 16.10) includes space to type a subject header and message.

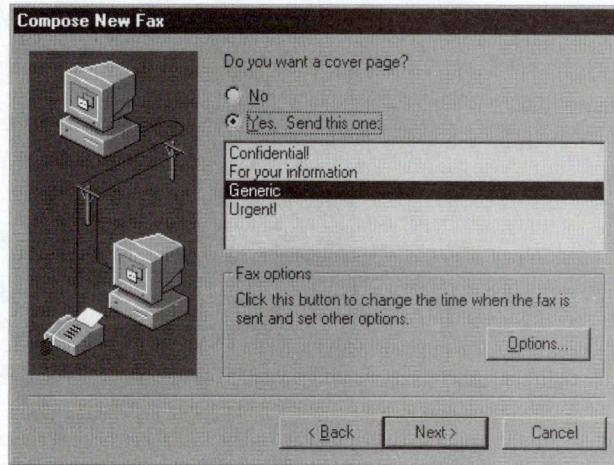

Figure 16.9   *Use the Compose New Fax Wizard to add a cover sheet to your fax message.*

Figure 16.10   *Type your subject line and cover-page message in this dialog box.*

It's possible to attach a file to a fax message, but people who use standalone fax machines won't be able to receive them. If you know that the recipient of your fax is using a PC with a fax modem and software that can handle attached files, use the Compose New Fax function in Exchange. The New Fax Wizard dialog box in Figure 16.11 specifies the file you want to send with your fax message. Click on the Add File button to open a File Selector window.

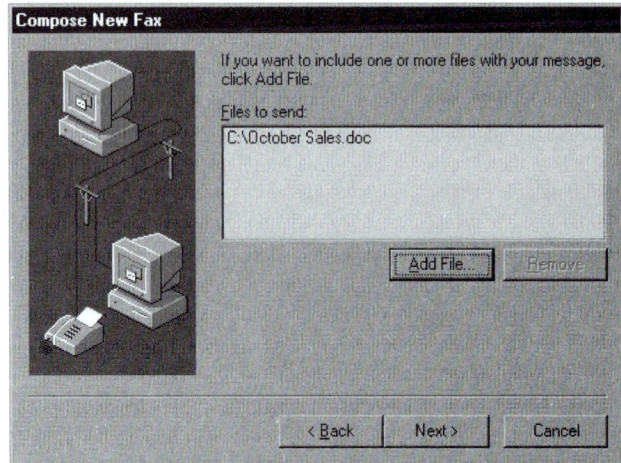

Figure 16.11 *Use this dialog box to attach one or more files to your fax message.*

Some users may find that attaching files to fax messages is easier than using a data communications program such as HyperTerminal, especially if the recipient is not familiar with file-transfer protocols.

Dragging an Icon

Because Windows treats the fax driver like a printer, you can drag and drop a file to the *fax printer* in the Printers window to send that file as a fax. When you drop a text file or image file on the fax printer, Windows automatically starts a Fax Wizard where you can specify the recipient and create a cover page.

If you plan to use this technique frequently, you might want to create a Microsoft Fax shortcut icon on the Windows 95 Desktop rather than opening the Printers window every time you want to send a fax. To create a shortcut, right-click on the Microsoft Fax icon in the Printers folder and select the Create Shortcut command.

Follow these steps to send a fax by dragging an icon:

1. Open the folder that contains the file you want to send as a fax.

2. Move your mouse to the icon for the file you want to send and hold down the left mouse button while you drag the icon to the Microsoft Fax icon in the Printers window or on the Desktop.

3. Windows will open the application associated with the file type you want to send, format the file, and print it to Microsoft Fax. The Print to Fax Wizard will start.

Right-Clicking on an Icon

As you know, clicking the right mouse button opens a menu that contains a set of commands appropriate to the current location of the cursor. If the file is an object that can be printed (such as a document or a bit-mapped image), the right-click menu includes the Send To command shown below, which opens a submenu with a list of destinations.

```
Open
Print
---------------------
Send To         ▶    ⊟ 3½ Floppy (A)
---------------------
Cut                   Fax Recipient
Copy                  Mail Recipient
---------------------
Create Shortcut
Delete
Rename
---------------------
Properties
```

When you click on Fax Recipient, Windows starts the Compose New Fax Wizard. If you have more than one profile, or if you have defined a profile as your default, Windows asks you which Messaging Profile you want to open.

Sending a Fax from Within an Application

Because Windows treats Microsoft Fax as a printer, it's a simple matter to send a fax by designating Microsoft Fax as your printer in an application. For example, when you enter the Page Setup command in WordPad and then click on the Printer button, it displays the dialog box in Figure 16.12. To send a fax, drop down the Printer Name menu to select Microsoft Fax. In other applications, such as Notepad, you must use the Print Setup command to specify the Fax printer driver before you enter the Print command.

The Properties button opens a set of dialog boxes that control details about printing. Most of the tabs are common to many printers, as

Part 3

Managing
Communications

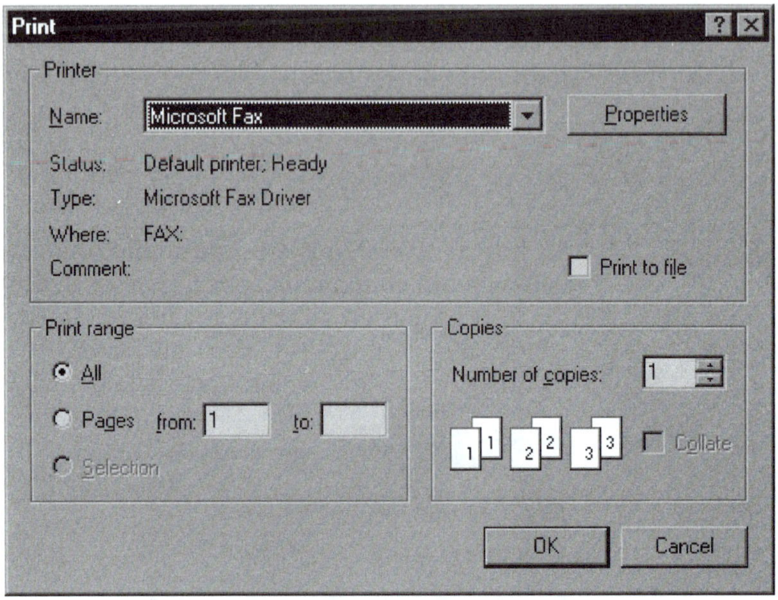

Figure 16.12 Use the WordPad Print dialog box to choose Microsoft Fax as a printer.

detailed in Chapter 8, but the Graphics tab in Figure 16.13 is specific to the fax driver.

The Graphics Properties dialog box includes these options:

Dots Per Inch: The number of dots per inch determines the resolution of the transmitted document. If you use a higher resolution, the fax will look better, but it will take longer to transmit. If the fax machine at the receiving end can't handle 300 dpi, Microsoft Fax will step down to 200 dpi.

Grayscale - Halftoning: Choose one of the radio buttons in this option to define the way Microsoft Fax will handle colors other than either solid black or solid white. As a general rule, Patterned Grays is a good choice, because an image with big solid black areas will be very hard to read.

Darkness: If you want the fax to appear darker or lighter at the receiving end, use the slide control to increase or decrease darkness. For most faxes that you send from a PC, you should leave the slider in the middle, which is the default setting, but if you have a particularly muddy bit-mapped image, or if the recipient asks you to re-send the page, you might want to experiment with other settings.

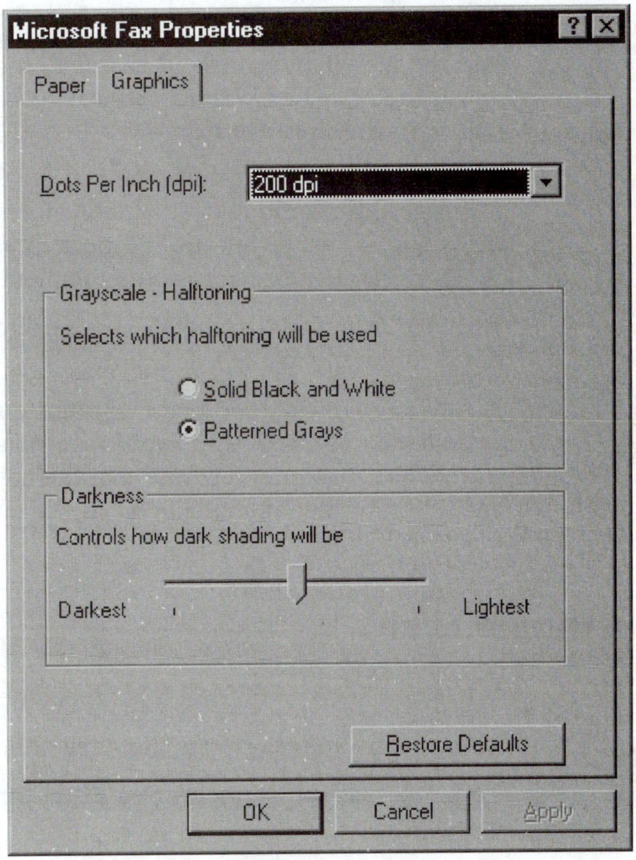

Figure 16.13   *Graphics Properties dialog box*

The exact command may be different from one program to another, but every Windows application that can print to paper can also print by sending a fax. When you specify Microsoft Fax as your printer, the application's Print command will start the Compose New Fax Wizard.

Sending a Fax from Microsoft Exchange

In most cases, you'll want to send faxes from your word processor or other application, but you can also originate faxes from Microsoft.

There are two ways to send a fax from Exchange:

▶ Use the New Fax command in the Compose menu to open our old friend the New Fax Wizard. After you complete the Wizard, Exchange will open the Message Editor.

▶ Use the New Message command in the Compose menu to open the Message Editor and choose one or more fax recipients from your address book. This technique is especially convenient when you want to send the same message to some recipients via e-mail and others by fax.

Write your message in the Message Editor, format it, and use the Send command in the File menu.

This is probably a good place to point out that it will do absolutely no good to send somebody a multicolor message by fax if the recipient is using a fax machine; regardless of the colors going in, the image that spews out of the fax machine at the receiving end will be in boring black and white.

Sending Binary Files

When you send a fax from a fax machine, three things happen:

1. Your fax machine converts the image on the paper to digital form.

2. Your fax machine connects to a distant machine and transmits the digital data.

3. The distant fax machine converts the digital data back to an image, which it prints onto paper.

A fax modem connected to a PC is really only concerned with step 2 of this process—it receives digital data from the PC and transmits it to a distant fax machine (which may be a standalone machine or another modem). Your PC converts the image to digital form before it gets to the fax modem.

The fax modem doesn't care where that digital data came from—it could just as easily have been from a data file or a program file instead of a fax image. As long as there's similar software at the receiving end to convert it back to its original form, you can send any kind of binary data file by fax. Some fax software, including Delrina's WinFax Pro, calls this method *binary file transfer*.

Binary file transfer via fax is a technology whose time has not yet come; no standalone fax machines and few fax programs will accept binary files. Unless you know that the recipient has a fax modem and software that knows how to deal with binary files, your transmission will fail.

Exchange treats fax transmission as just one more type of e-mail, but fax protocols are completely different from the protocols used for other kinds of data transfer, even if they use the same modem. You can't use a terminal program (such as HyperTerminal) to receive a binary fax message. Therefore, you will probably find it easier and more consistently reliable to use HyperTerminal or some other data communications program to move programs or data files over a telephone line.

That said, if you know that the recipient can receive and process binary files, you can attach any file to a fax message just as you would attach it to an e-mail message. There are three ways to do it:

▶ Right-click on the icon and choose the Send to Fax Recipient command.

▶ Drag the file icon to the Fax icon in the Printers folder.

▶ Open Microsoft Exchange and use the Compose New Fax command in the Fax menu. When the message-editor window appears, select the File command in the Insert menu.

Cover Sheets

A cover sheet serves several purposes: in an office where several people receive faxes through the same machine, it identifies the intended recipient; it tells recipients how many pages to expect; and it lets them know who to call if there's a transmission problem. A cover sheet can also contain a comment about the document that it accompanies.

Unless it's absolutely obvious who is supposed to receive your fax and who sent it, you should include a cover sheet as the first page of every fax you send. Your cover sheet should include this information:

▶ the name, fax number, and voice telephone number (or extension) of the recipient

▶ the name, fax number, and voice telephone number of the sender

▶ the number of pages in the fax message

▶ the date and time of transmission

Part 3

Managing Communications

Windows 95 includes a handful of standard cover pages and a Cover Page Editor program that produces *templates* that automatically insert information about the sender, the recipient, and the message into information fields. You can choose the cover page you want to add to each fax in the Compose New Fax Wizard. After Windows 95 is released, there will probably be an assortment of additional fax cover-sheet templates available for downloading from Microsoft Network, CompuServe, and other online information services.

To create a new cover-sheet template, follow these steps:

1. Start the Cover Page Editor program from the Programs ➤ Accessories ➤ Fax menu.

2. Use the Insert commands to add the information fields you want to include in your cover sheet. Figure 16.14 shows the Cover Page Editor screen.

   Click on a menu item to add it to your cover-sheet template. Don't worry about the position right now; you can move items around the page after you have chosen them.

   When you send a fax, Windows will use information from your Fax Setup dialog box and address book to fill in the information fields.

   The Insert menu includes these fields:

Recipient:	Name	Zip Code	Home Telephone
	Fax Number	Country	Number
	Company	Title	Office Telephone
	Street Address	Department	Number
	City	Office Location	To: List
	State		CC: List
Sender:	Name	Title	Home Telephone
	Fax Number	Department	Number
	Company	Office Location	Office Telephone
	Address		Number
Message:	Note	Time Sent	Number of
	Subject	Number of Pages	Attachments

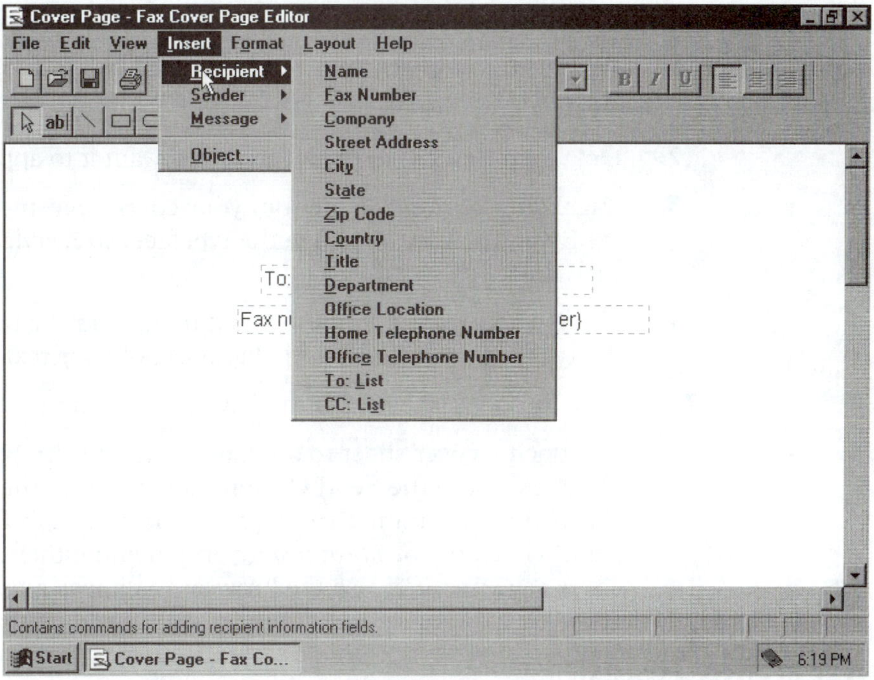

Figure 16.14 *Use the Insert commands to place information fields in your fax cover sheet.*

3. Drag each information field to the position you want it to appear in on the page.

4. To add text to your cover-sheet template, click on the arrow key in the Drawing Toolbar and drag your mouse to create a box, click on the text button, and then click inside the new box to create a cursor. Type the text at the cursor. If you need more space, move your mouse to the edge of the box and expand the box by dragging one or more edges. Don't worry about the exact position of your text; you can fix it later.

5. To add new graphics to your cover page, click on the arrow key in the Drawing Toolbar and drag your mouse to create another box. Use the line, rectangle, polygon, and ellipse buttons in the Toolbar to choose a shape and place the figure in the new box. You can change the characteristics of a figure with the Line, Fill, and Color command in the Format menu.

6.   To import an existing text file or graphics object into your cover sheet, use the Insert ➤ Object command. You can also use this command to create a graphics object with another application.

7.   Drag each element to the location you want it to appear in on the page.

8.   Highlight each text element of your cover page and use the buttons in the Style Toolbar to change the typeface, size, style, and alignment of each item.

9.   Use the commands in the Format menu and the toolbars to change the typeface, type style, and alignment of your text.

10.   Save the cover sheet with the Save command in the File menu.

To attach a cover sheet to a fax message, answer *Yes* when the Fax Wizard asks, or use the Send Options command in the Message Editor's File menu. When the Send Options dialog box in Figure 16.15 appears, check the *Send cover page* option and either drop down the cover page menu or use the browser to choose a template.

Receiving Faxes

If you plan to use your PC to receive faxes as well as send them, you will probably want to leave your computer and modem on all the time, with Microsoft Fax running in the background, because it's not always possible to predict when somebody will try to send you a fax. If you share the same telephone line for voice, data, and fax calls, you must either use a line-sharing device to direct voice calls to your telephone set and fax/data calls to the modem, or you will have to accept calls manually when you hear a fax calling tone through the handset.

To set up Microsoft Exchange to automatically receive fax calls, follow these steps:

1.   If it is not already set up, add Microsoft Fax to the active Exchange Profile. See Chapter 15 for information about configuring your Exchange Profile.

2.   Start Microsoft Exchange. Within a minute or two, the minimized Fax Modem Status button will appear in the Taskbar. When the Fax Modem Status is Idle, Microsoft Fax is ready to accept incoming calls.

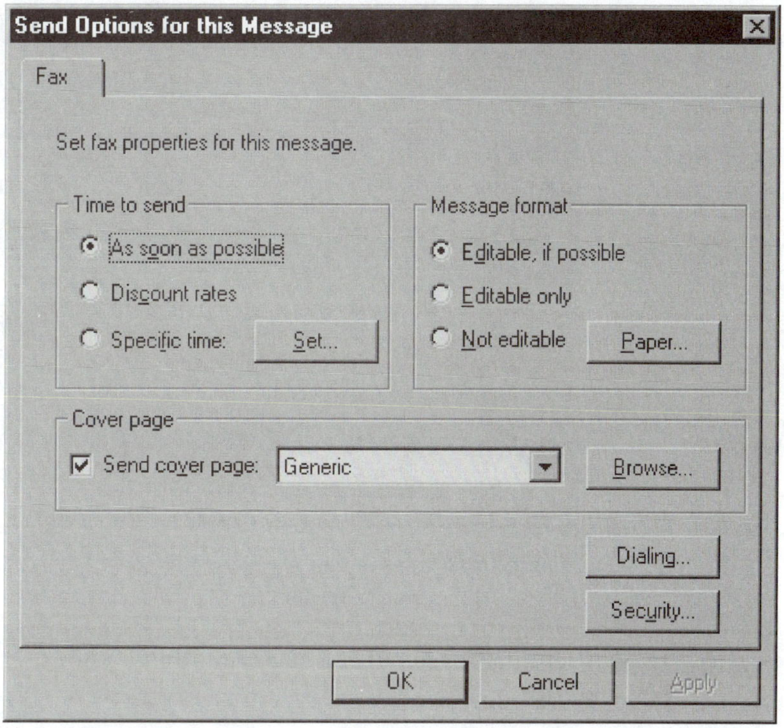

Figure 16.15   *Use the Send Options dialog box to choose a cover page.*

3. Click on the Fax machine icon in the Taskbar to open the Status window shown below.

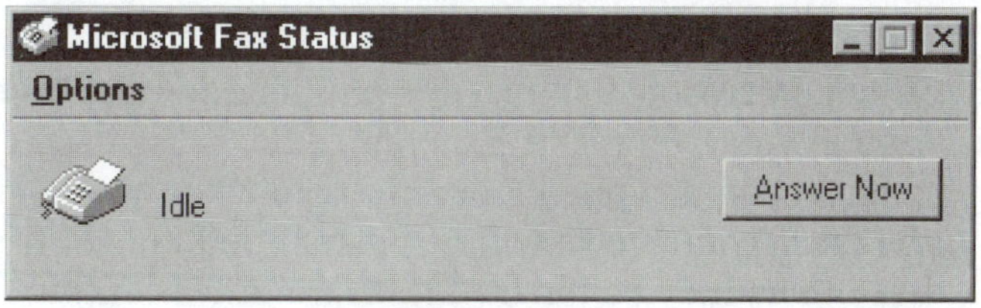

4. Select the Modem Properties command in the Options menu to open the Fax Modem Properties dialog box in Figure 16.16.

5. If you have a dedicated fax/data telephone line, click on the *Answer after* radio button. If you use the same telephone line for incoming voice calls, click on the Manual radio button. If you use this computer for

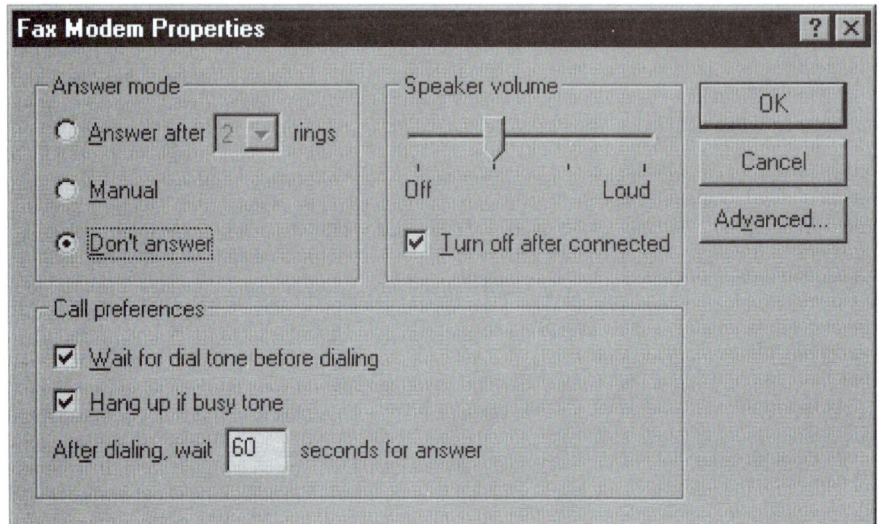

Figure 16.16 The Fax Modem Properties dialog box controls inbound and outbound Microsoft Fax calls.

sending faxes but not receiving them, choose the *Don't answer* radio button.

6. Click on OK to close the Fax Modem Settings dialog box and then minimize the Fax Modem Status window.

If Microsoft Fax is set to automatically answer, it will show the progress of incoming and outgoing calls in the Status window or button. If Manual Answer mode is active, Microsoft Fax will display a message when it receives a call.

When Microsoft Fax receives an incoming message, it places the message in your Microsoft Exchange inbox. Like any other message in Exchange, you can open a fax message by double-clicking on it. Most of the faxes you receive will be bit-mapped images from fax machines, but others may be binary files from other computers with fax modems. When you double-click on a bit-mapped image, Exchange opens the Fax Viewer; when you double-click on a binary file for which an association exists, Exchange opens a program that can read and edit the file. Because Exchange automatically recognizes both types of fax messages, you can open all fax messages the same way.

Using Fax Viewer

Fax Viewer is a tool for viewing and printing bit-mapped fax pages. Fax Viewer opens automatically when you double-click on a bit-mapped image entry in Microsoft Exchange. Figure 16.17 shows the Fax Viewer window.

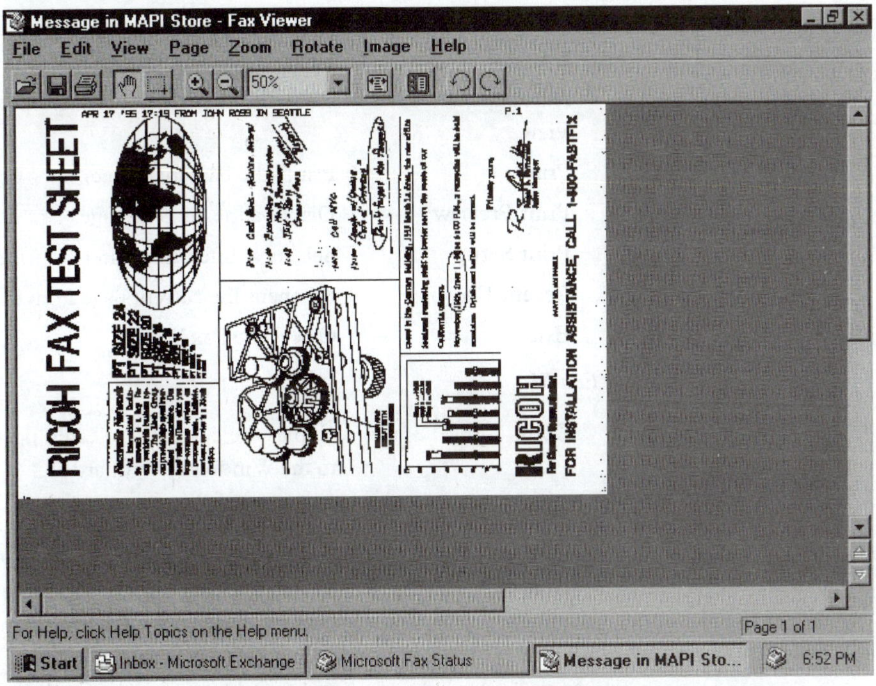

Figure 16.17   *Use the Fax Viewer to read and print bit-mapped fax pages.*

When you open Fax Viewer from Exchange by double-clicking on the name of a fax, Fax Viewer automatically loads the first page of the fax message. To load a different message, use the Open command in the File menu. Almost all of the commands in the Fax Viewer menus and Toolbar control the way the Viewer displays fax images.

Fax Viewer Command Summary

File Menu

Open	Loads a new fax message. Choose the fax file (with a `.awd` or `.dcx` file extension) from the browser.
Save	Stores the current fax message with the original name.
Save As	Saves the current image with a new file name.
Automatically Save View	Saves the zoom, rotation, and image settings.
Print	Prints the current image.
Print Preview	Displays the current page.
Print Setup	Selects a different printer or print option.
Recent File	Re-opens the current page from the version on disk.
Exit	Closes the Fax Viewer.

Edit Menu

Copy	Copies the currently selected portion of the image to the Windows Clipboard.
Copy Page	Selects the entire current page.
Select	Highlights an image.
Drag	Moves the image in the Viewer to a new position. Because the Viewer window is smaller than the fax page within the window, you will need the Drag command to read an entire page.

View Menu

Toolbar	Displays or hide the Fax Viewer Toolbar.
Status Bar	Displays or hide the Status Bar at the bottom of the Fax Viewer window.
Thumbnails	Displays small "thumbnail" views of several pages of a fax message, rather than a larger view of a single page.

Page Menu: Use the commands in the Page menu to move between pages in a multiple-page fax message.

Zoom Menu

Fit Width	Expands the image horizontally to the full current width of the Viewer window.
Fit Height	Expands the image vertically to the full current height of the Viewer window.
Fit Both	Distorts the shape of the image to fit the current dimensions of the Viewer Window.
25% 50% 100%	Expands or contracts the size of the image in the Viewer window. The percentage numbers are the relative sizes of the image that will appear when you choose one of these commands.
Zoom In	Changes the view to the next larger size.
Zoom Out	Changes the view to the next smaller size.

Rotate Menu

Right	Rotate the current image 90 degrees to the right.
Left	Rotates the current image 90 degrees to the left.
Flip Over	Turns the current image upside down.

Image Menu

Invert	Replaces the current image in the Viewer with a mirror image of the same page.

Most of the faxes you will receive will be images of pages, which Windows stores as bit-mapped files. Even though a page may contain text and graphics, it is really a picture of the page that the sender placed in his fax machine or printed to her fax modem. Sometimes it would be nice to be able to export text from a fax to an editor or word processor, either to make changes to the text or to incorporate it into another document. Likewise, you might want to use a picture or diagram from a fax in another document.

Unfortunately, the Windows 95 fax utility does not include any tools for exporting or modifying received faxes. However, there are many separate fax programs that provide these services. Among others, Delrina's WinFax Pro has an extensive set of fax-management features, including converting images to Paintbrush, TIFF, and Windows Bitmap formats and converting words to ASCII text.

Chapter 17

The Microsoft Network

FEATURING

The Microsoft Network (MSN) is the software giant's new entry in the online information-service wars currently dominated by CompuServe, America Online, and Prodigy. Like its competitors, MSN offers electronic mail, conferences about a wide variety of subjects, technical support from Microsoft and other hardware and software vendors, data files and programs available for downloading, general and specialized news services, and live *chat* channels where you can exchange messages with other users and with experts and celebrity guests. In addition, MSN offers a gateway to the Internet, including access to Usenet news groups and e-mail. MSN is closely integrated with the Windows 95 user interface, so you can use online resources as if they were located on your own PC.

Even more than the rest of Windows 95, the Microsoft Network is still a work in progress. At this stage in its development, MSN does not include many of the features and services that will (Microsoft hopes) make it attractive to millions of users. By the time Windows 95 is actually released, MSN will probably have signed up a long list of additional information providers. This chapter explains how to connect your PC to MSN and how to use its features and services. It is not a definitive guide to content areas, because most of them are not yet in place at the time of this writing. But by using the tools and procedures you find here, you will be able to explore MSN and take advantage of everything it has to offer.

The only way to connect to MSN now is through a modem and telephone line, but eventually you can expect it to be accessible through the same cable TV service that brings you all those wrestlers and music videos today. TCI, the largest American cable company, owns 20 percent of the Microsoft Network.

Installing and Signing Up for the Microsoft Network

To join MSN, you must have a modem connected to your PC. Chapter 13 describes the procedure for installing Windows 95 modem support.

You can install the Microsoft Network support when you install Windows 95 by choosing Custom Setup; you can also install it after Windows 95 is running. To add the Microsoft Network to an already installed system, double-click on the Add/Remove Programs icon in the Control Panel and choose the Windows Setup tab. Either way, when the dialog box in Figure 17.1 appears, scroll down the Components list until you see the listing for the Microsoft Network.

Check the box next to the Microsoft Network listing. If you haven't previously installed Microsoft Exchange, Setup may force you to install it at the same time. When you click the OK button, Setup will ask you to load the disks that contain the MSN software.

After the software is loaded, follow these steps to set up your account with the Microsoft Network:

1. Click on the Microsoft Network icon on your desktop. An MSN start-up screen will appear.

2. Click on the OK button to move to the screen in Figure 17.2.

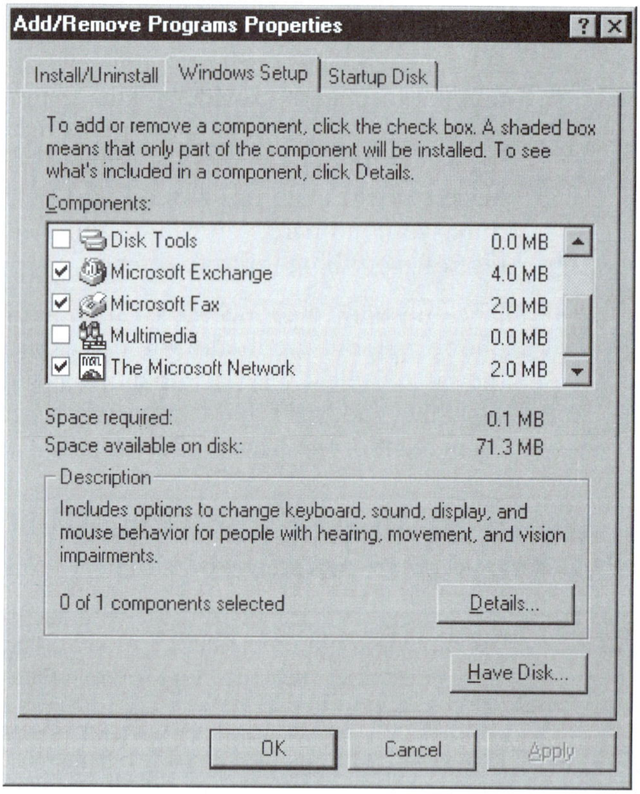

Figure 17.1 Use the Windows Setup dialog box to install the Microsoft Network.

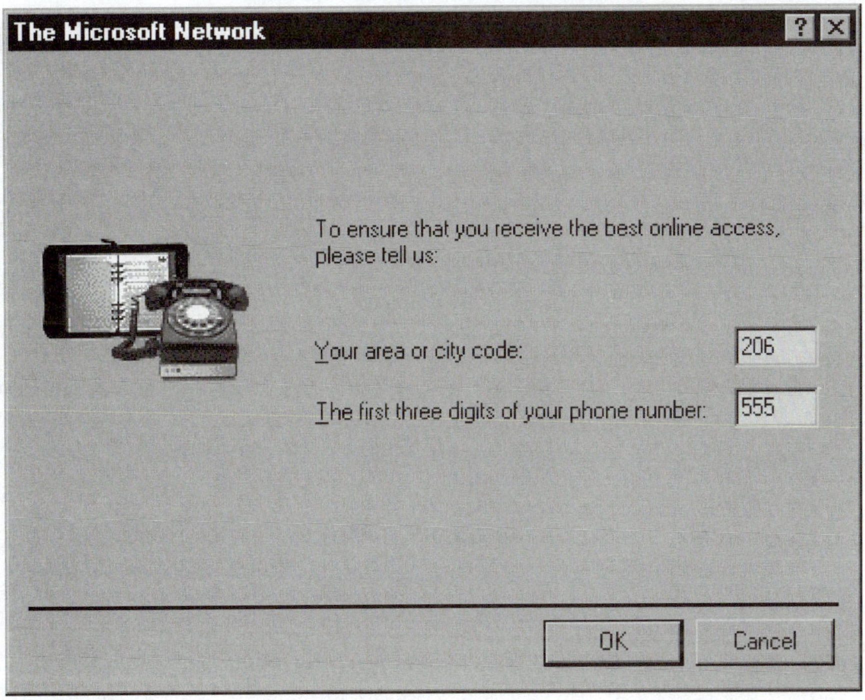

Figure 17.2 *Use this screen to find the nearest local telephone number for the Microsoft Network.*

3. Fill in the area-code portion of your own telephone number (or if you're outside North America, your city code) and the first three digits of your telephone number. This information will guide the program to find the nearest access telephone number for MSN. Click on the OK button.

4. If you have an external modem, make sure it is turned on and connected to your PC. If you have an internal modem, it's always on. Make sure the modem is connected to your telephone line.

5. Click on the Connect button in the Calling screen. The program will call Microsoft and download the current list of access numbers for your area and the current subscription rates.

6. Your computer will display the window in Figure 17.3 with the three steps needed to join MSN. Click on the *Tell us your name and address* button.

Part 3

Managing Communications

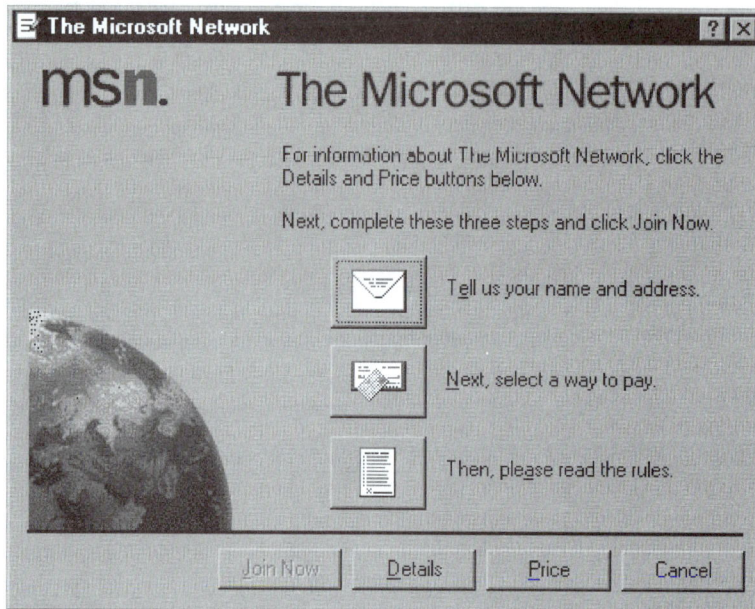

Figure 17.3   *Complete these three steps to join the Microsoft Network.*

7.   Complete all of the fields in the next dialog box, shown in Figure 17.4, and click on OK.

8.   Click on the *Next, select a way to pay* button and fill in your credit card number or other billing information in the dialog box shown in Figure 17.5. Click on OK to return to the previous screen.

9.   Click on the *Then, please read the rules* button. After you have read the fine print, click on the I Agree button.

10.   When you have big check marks next to all three steps, click on the Join Now button. Based on the telephone number you specified in Step 3, two nearby access numbers will appear in the dialog box in Figure 17.6. If the number is a local call, the software will ignore the area code even though it appears in this dialog box.

If there's no local number for your area, it might be less expensive to use a number different from the one the program automatically assigns you. For example, the rates for calling across a state line might be cheaper than an in-state call. To choose different access numbers,

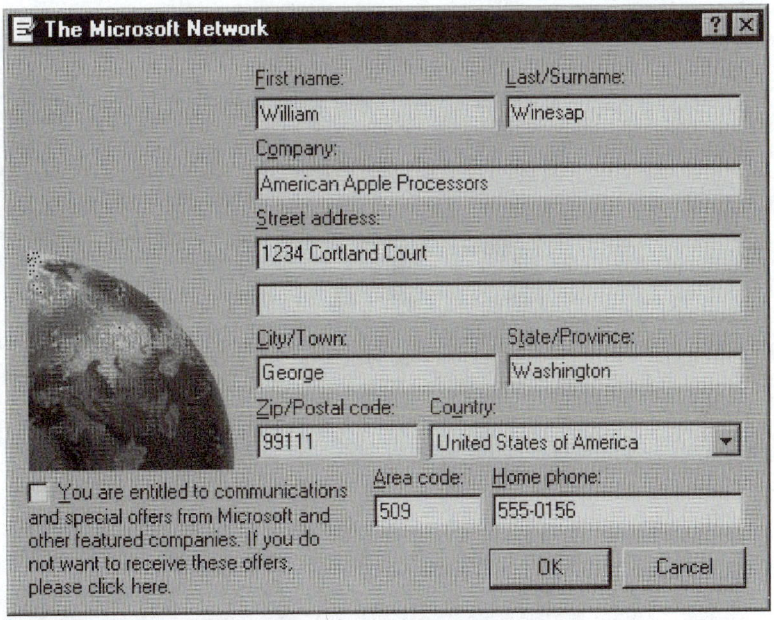

Figure 17.4   *Fill in your name and address in this dialog box.*

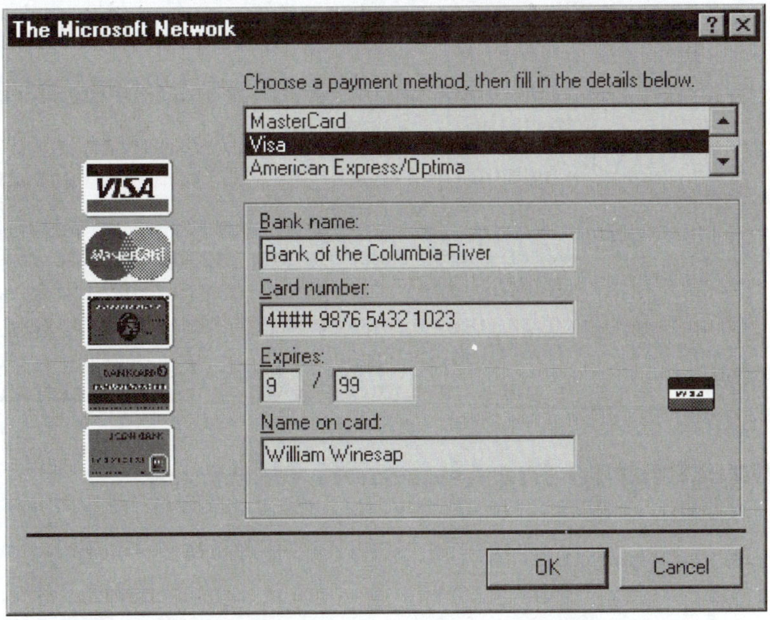

Figure 17.5   *Use this dialog box to send MSN your credit card number.*

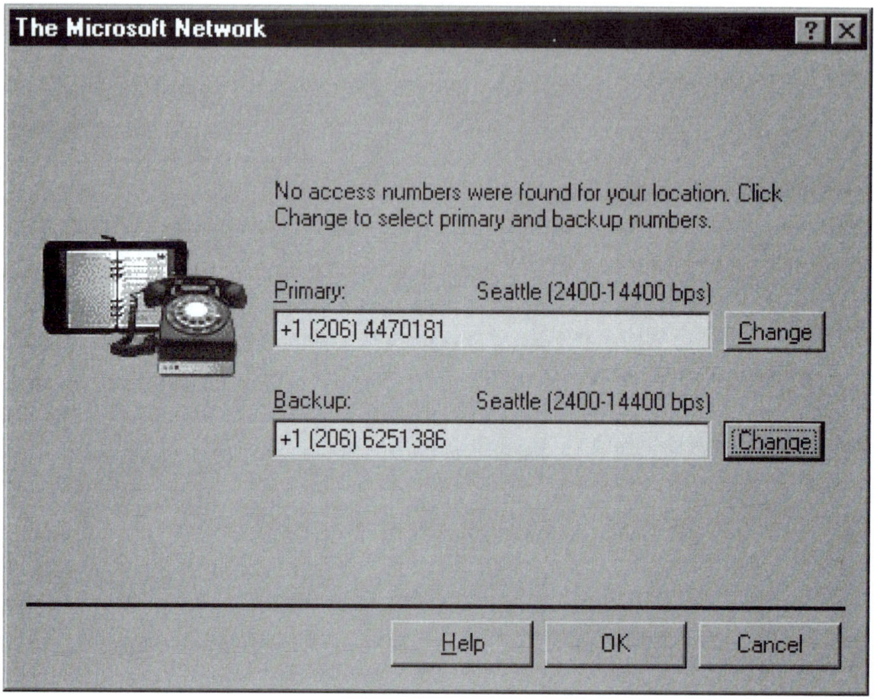

Figure 17.6 *The telephone numbers for access to MSN*

click on the Change buttons and find the location you want to call from the drop-down menus.

11. Click on the OK button and then the Dial button to call MSN and set up your account.

12. When the connection goes through, MSN will ask for a member ID (log-in name) and password using the dialog box in Figure 17.7. Because you will need both of these items to sign in later, you should write them down somewhere. But don't paste them on your computer or put them someplace where other people can see them.

Connecting to the Microsoft Network

Follow these steps to connect your PC to the Microsoft Network:

1. Make sure your modem is turned on and connected to a telephone line.

2. Double-click on the Microsoft Network Icon on your Desktop.

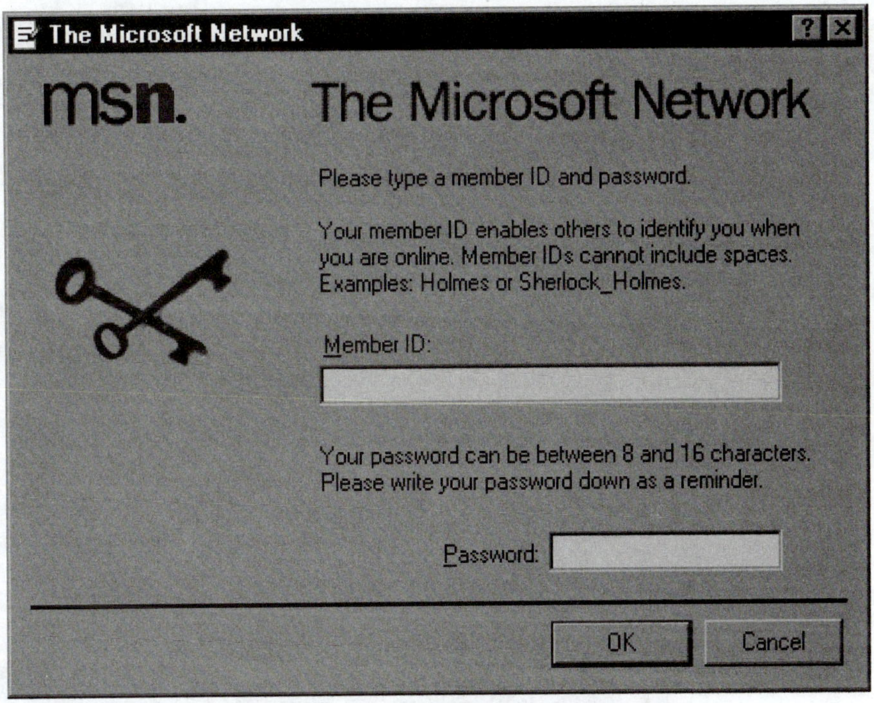

Figure 17.7 *Type your log-in name and password in this dialog box.*

3. When the Sign In screen in Figure 17.8 appears, type in your member ID and your password. If you are the only person using your PC, you can check the *Remember my password* box so you won't have to type it again the next time you log in.

4. Click on Connect to start dialing. The Sign In window will show the progress of your call as it dials and verifies your account. When it completes the log-in, it will display the MSN Central screen in Figure 17.9.

    While you're connected to MSN, a little modem icon with two red dots is visible on the lower right side of the Taskbar. The left dot duplicates the RD (Receive Data) light on an external modem. It turns green when your PC is receiving data from MSN. The right dot corresponds to the SD (Send Data) light on your modem. It turns green when your PC is sending data to MSN. If you move your cursor to

Figure 17.8 Type your ID and password to log into MSN.

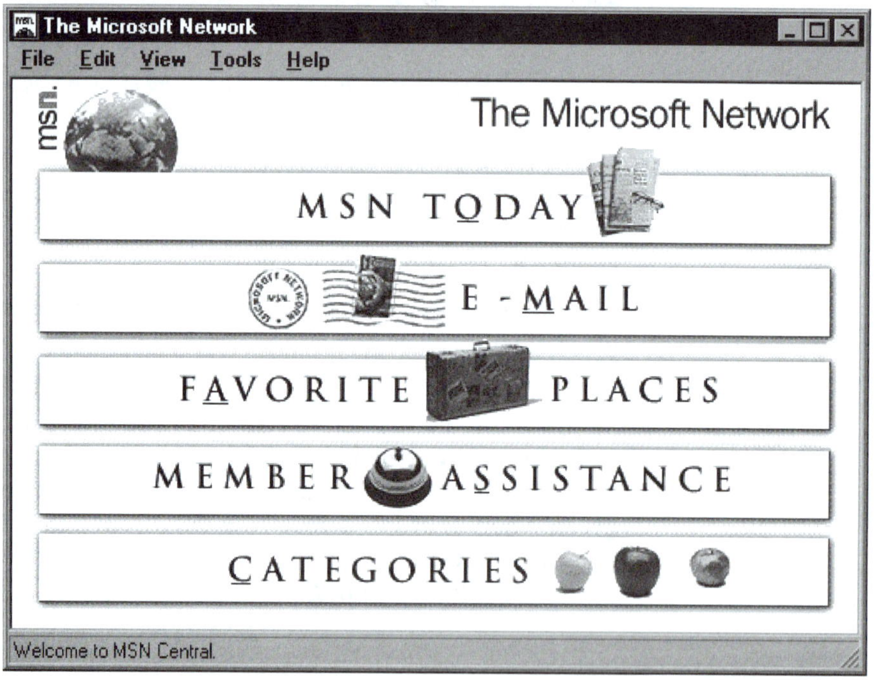

Figure 17.9 The MSN Central screen

the modem icon, MSN will display the number of bytes received and sent during the current online session as shown below.

41058 bytes received 4767 bytes sent
12:24 PM

For more details about your connection to MSN, double-click on the modem icon to display the window shown below.

Megahertz XJ2288 PCMCIA Modem

4780 bytes sent
41065 bytes received

Connected at 14400 bps for 15 minutes.

OK

When Microsoft Exchange transfers a message to or from MSN, a tiny envelope with an arrow pointing in the direction the message is traveling appears between the MSN icon and the modem icon. When Exchange has received one or more messages, it shows envelope icons without any arrow.

When you're connected to MSN, you can right-click on the MSN icon in the Toolbar (next to the time of day) to open the menu of shortcuts shown below.

Send Mail...
Find ...

Go to MSN Central
Go to Favorite Places
Go to...

Sign Out

12:30 PM

Navigating the Microsoft Network

The first window you see when you connect to Microsoft Network is called *MSN Central* and contains links to various online areas. When your cursor is on a link, it changes from the usual arrow to a pointing finger. To link to one of the areas listed in the MSN Central window, click on the area's name.

The Options command in the View menu is the same as the Options command in other windows used for browsing folders on your computer. The Folder tab offers a choice of either using a separate window for each new folder you open or using a single folder that changes when you move from one folder to another.

There are five areas you can reach from MSN Central:

MSN Today

MSN Today is a daily list of special events and services that MSN wants to promote, such as scheduled live appearances and new resources. Figure 17.10 shows a typical MSN Today window. To jump to one of the items promoted in MSN Today, move your cursor to the icon and single-click your mouse. To return to MSN Central, close the MSN Today window.

E-Mail

The E-Mail button in MSN starts Microsoft Exchange and downloads any messages that might be waiting for you at MSN. The E-Mail command starts the default Exchange profile, including any other message services that might be in that profile. Therefore, you might want to make sure that MSN is the first item in the profile so Exchange doesn't waste your time trying to set up fax or other online services while you're connected to MSN.

MSN E-Mail is closely integrated with Exchange. The Options for Microsoft Network command in Exchange's Tools menu opens the dialog box in Figure 17.11.

Figure 17.10 *MSN Today offers jumps to other MSN resources.*

The Transport dialog box includes these options:

Download mail when e-mail starts up from MSN	When this option is active, MSN automatically opens Exchange and downloads your messages when you start the MSN E-Mail program.
Disconnect after updating headers	When this option is active, Exchange copies the headers of any waiting messages and then disconnects from MSN. When you select a message header, Exchange will reconnect to MSN and download the whole message. This allows you to reduce your connect-time charges because you can preview messages offline before deciding to transfer them to your PC.

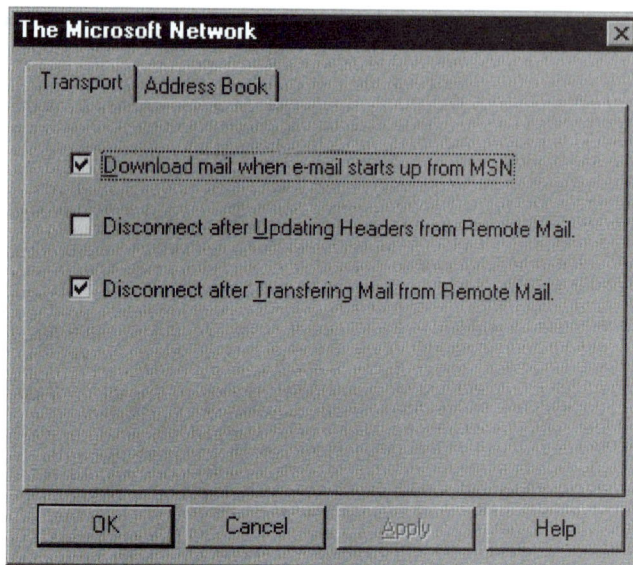

Figure 17.11   *Open the Transport tab of the Microsoft Network dialog box from Exchange's Tools menu.*

Disconnect after Transferring Mail	Make this option active to break your connection to MSN after Exchange has downloaded your mail.

Favorite Places

Favorite Places is an area you can use to place shortcuts to the MSN services you regularly use in a single convenient window. When you join MSN, your Favorite Places area will be empty. To include an area in your list of Favorite Places, use the Add to Favorite Places command in the File menu, the right mouse button menu, or the MSN toolbar.

To add a forum, BBS, or other MSN area to your Favorite Places list, use the Add to Favorite Places command in the File menu or toolbar, or right-click on an icon and select the Add to Favorite Places command.

If you have multiple MSN windows open, you can also drag and drop icons from other parts of MSN to your Favorite Places window or to the Windows Desktop.

Member Assistance

Member Assistance is a specialized set of conferences and documents directly related to MSN itself. If you're looking for online help in using MSN, Member Assistance is a good place to start looking for help.

Categories

The Categories window in Figure 17.12 is the subject guide to MSN services. Each category icon opens a set of conferences, kiosks, chat areas, file archives, additional subcategories, and other resources related to that category. Double-click on an icon to open a category.

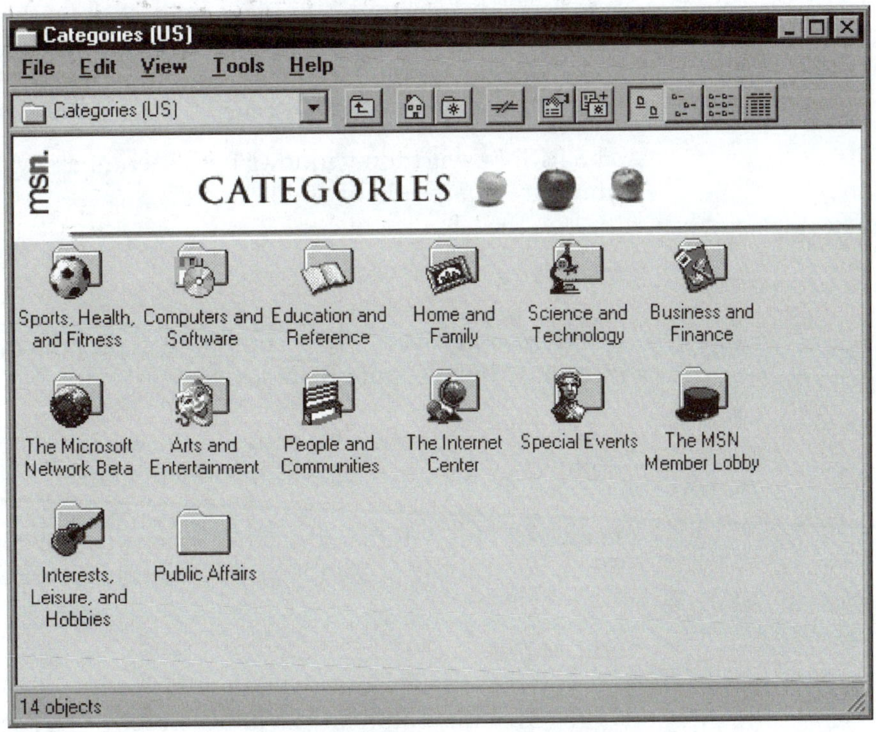

Figure 17.12   *The Categories window is a starting point for finding new MSN services.*

Moving Around MSN

Microsoft Network has a hierarchical file structure that will be familiar to anybody who has used DOS and Windows. MSN Central takes the place of the root directory, and each subdirectory may contain many different kinds of files and services, including additional subsubdirectories. To move to a subdirectory or open a file or service, double-click on the icon. The icons in MSN work exactly the same way as those in Windows 95; you can create shortcuts and place MSN icons on your Desktop or in folders.

MSN navigation commands are like the ones in other Windows toolbars. The two unfamiliar buttons are: one that moves you back to MSN Central and one that adds an item to Favorite Places.

If you find yourself hopelessly lost, you can always return to MSN Central by clicking on the toolbar button with the house on it. You can also open a new MSN Central window by clicking on the MSN icon on your Desktop. When you right-click on the MSN icon in the Taskbar at the bottom of your screen, you will open a menu with several common commands, including jumps to MSN Central and Favorite Places, as well as sign-out.

The MSN navigation windows have menu bars with these commands which are not in other windows:

File Menu

Add to Favorite Places   This command copies the currently highlighted icon into your Favorite Places window.

Sign In   This command is active if you are not currently connected to MSN. Click on it to dial MSN and log yourself in.

Sign Out   This command is active when you are connected to MSN. When you choose it, Windows disconnects your PC from MSN.

Edit Menu

Go To   Use this command to jump directly to a specific MSN service. Go Words in MSN are like GO commands in CompuServe or keywords in America Online. To find the Go Word for any MSN service, highlight the icon for that service and use the Properties command in the File menu or the right-mouse-button menu. For example, Figure 17.13 shows the Properties for the Windows 95 forum. In this example, the Go word for this forum is "Windows."

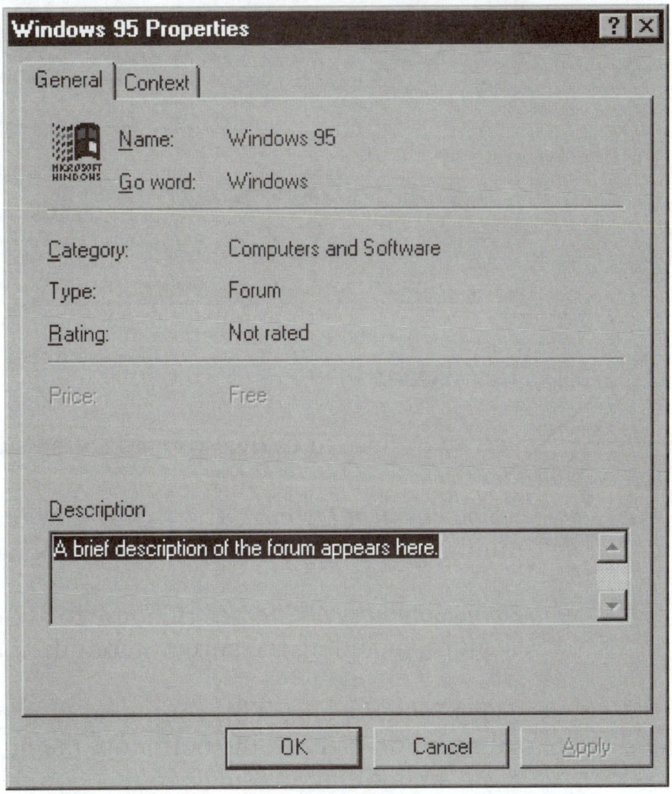

Figure 17.13   *The Go Word for the Windows 95 Forum is "Windows."*

View Menu

Options   The General tab within the Options dialog box opens the dialog box below. You can use this command to set the number of minutes MSN waits before shutting down automatically and specify whether you want to see the MSN Today message every time you connect to the Microsoft Network. The Content view menu lists groups of bulletin boards, chat rooms, files, and other services organized by language or geographical region. If you want to see content groups for a region other than your own, click on that content view item. The next time you connect to MSN, it will display the new content view.

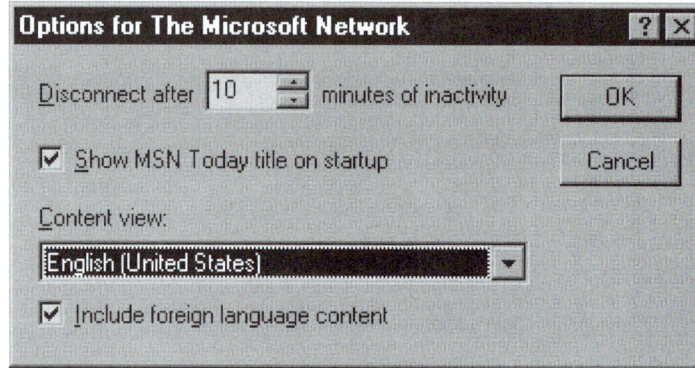

Options for The Microsoft Network

Disconnect after `10` minutes of inactivity

☑ Show MSN Today title on startup

Content view:

`English (United States)`

☑ Include foreign language content

OK

Cancel

Tools Menu

Password   Use to change your MSN password.

Billing Payment Method   Choose to view or change the credit card number or other information that MSN uses to bill you for service.

Billing Summary of Charges   Choose to see the current status of your account, including the current monthly charge.

Billing Subscriptions   This command displays information about your subscription plan. At the bottom of the dialog box, you can set a maximum amount for any single transaction. If you try to download something that costs more than this amount, MSN will ask for confirmation.

At the time this was written, Microsoft had not yet announced how it plans to charge for MSN, so this dialog box may change by the time Windows 95 is released.

Connection Settings   Use to choose a different access telephone number or modem configuration. You can also get to the Connection Settings dialog box before you log into MSN by clicking on the Settings button in the Sign In window. If you are running MSN on a portable computer, this is the place to set up access after you arrive at a different location. Figure 17.14 shows the Connection Settings dialog box.

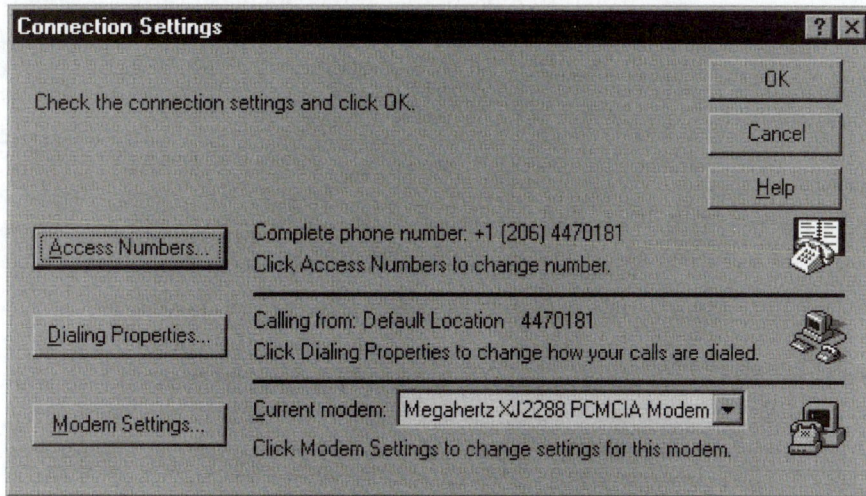

Figure 17.14 *Use the Connection Settings dialog box to change details about your MSN connection.*

Help Menu

Member Support Numbers If you need assistance, choose this command to display a list of telephone numbers for Customer Service and Technical Support. Of course, if you can't log into MSN, you won't be able to reach MSN Central, so it won't be possible to use this command when you need help making the connection. However, you can also display the same list of telephone numbers by clicking on the Settings button in the MSN Sign In window, clicking on the Help button, and choosing the Customer Service Phone Numbers item at the bottom of the MSN Member Support Help window.

Right-Click Menus Like those in other windows, the icons in MSN windows all display context-sensitive menus when you move the cursor to an icon and click the right mouse button.

Conferences and File Libraries

Many of the items you will see in MSN windows are conferences (which MSN calls Bulletin Boards or BBSes) and file libraries devoted to a particular topic, such as household improvements or Windows communication. When you double-click on one of these icons, you will see a message folder window like the one in Figure 17.15. The commands and toolbar buttons that control the appearance of the screen have special functions in a message folder window—the three options are Conversation view, List view, and Attached Files view. In all three views, listings change from boldface type to normal type after you view them, but you can display a listing again by clicking on the message description.

When you visit a BBS, MSN will display a list of all messages and downloadable files that have been added since the last time you looked at that BBS. It will also show you older items for which there are new replies. To display message listings you've seen before, use the Show All Messages command in the Tools menu.

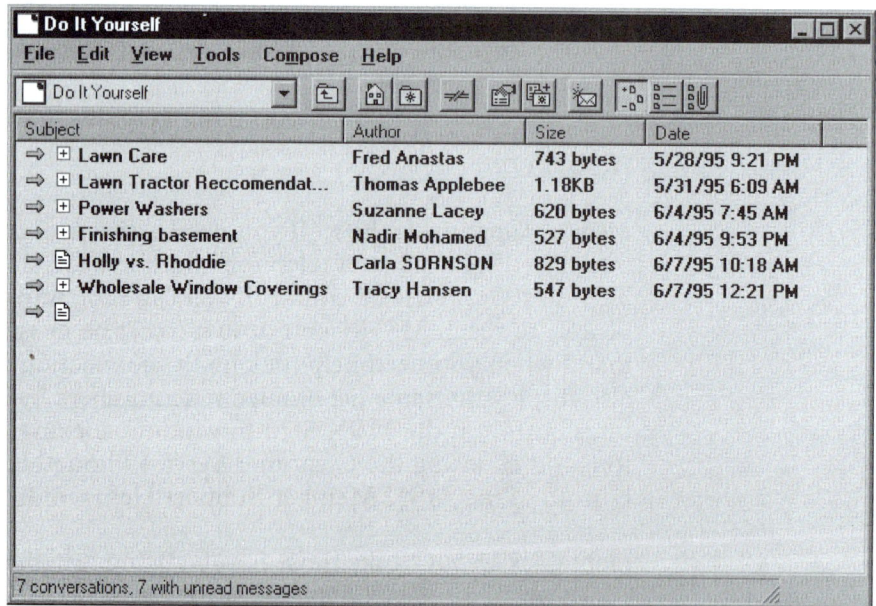

Subject	Author	Size	Date
Lawn Care	Fred Anastas	743 bytes	5/28/95 9:21 PM
Lawn Tractor Reccomendat...	Thomas Applebee	1.18KB	5/31/95 6:09 AM
Power Washers	Suzanne Lacey	620 bytes	6/4/95 7:45 AM
Finishing basement	Nadir Mohamed	527 bytes	6/4/95 9:53 PM
Holly vs. Rhoddie	Carla SORNSON	829 bytes	6/7/95 10:18 AM
Wholesale Window Coverings	Tracy Hansen	547 bytes	6/7/95 12:21 PM

7 conversations, 7 with unread messages

Figure 17.15   The Conversation view is the default layout for message folder windows.

In Conversation view, you only see the top item in each thread until you click on an icon, which displays all the items that are replies to the original item. If there are replies to replies, you will see another plus sign inside the icon, which you can click to expand the list. You can expand all the lists at one time with the Expand All Conversations command in the View menu. An arrow at the left side of a listing indicates that there are unread messages in this thread. Figure 17.16 shows the same BBS with all replies visible.

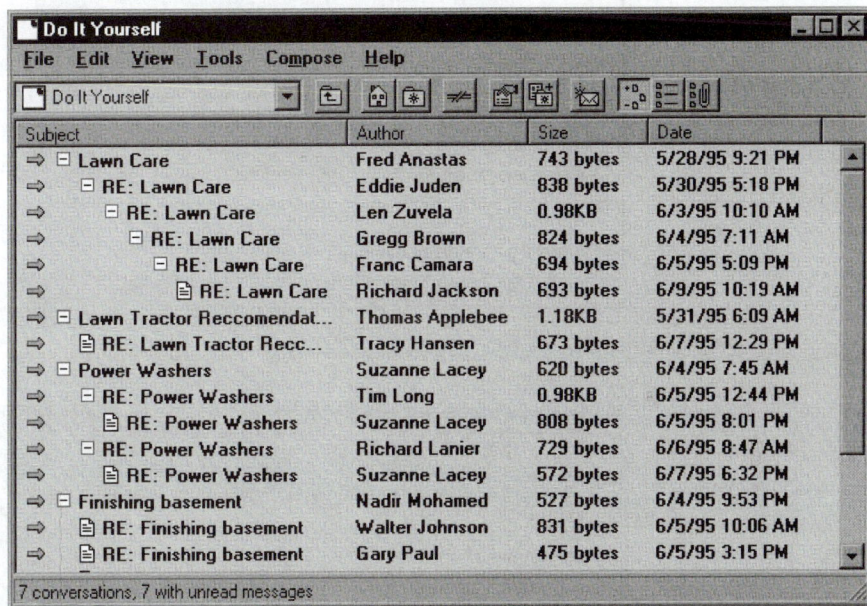

Subject	Author	Size	Date
Lawn Care	Fred Anastas	743 bytes	5/28/95 9:21 PM
RE: Lawn Care	Eddie Juden	838 bytes	5/30/95 5:18 PM
RE: Lawn Care	Len Zuvela	0.98KB	6/3/95 10:10 AM
RE: Lawn Care	Gregg Brown	824 bytes	6/4/95 7:11 AM
RE: Lawn Care	Franc Camara	694 bytes	6/5/95 5:09 PM
RE: Lawn Care	Richard Jackson	693 bytes	6/9/95 10:19 AM
Lawn Tractor Reccomendat...	Thomas Applebee	1.18KB	5/31/95 6:09 AM
RE: Lawn Tractor Recc...	Tracy Hansen	673 bytes	6/7/95 12:29 PM
Power Washers	Suzanne Lacey	620 bytes	6/4/95 7:45 AM
RE: Power Washers	Tim Long	0.98KB	6/5/95 12:44 PM
RE: Power Washers	Suzanne Lacey	808 bytes	6/5/95 8:01 PM
RE: Power Washers	Richard Lanier	729 bytes	6/6/95 8:47 AM
RE: Power Washers	Suzanne Lacey	572 bytes	6/7/95 6:32 PM
Finishing basement	Nadir Mohamed	527 bytes	6/4/95 9:53 PM
RE: Finishing basement	Walter Johnson	831 bytes	6/5/95 10:06 AM
RE: Finishing basement	Gary Paul	475 bytes	6/5/95 3:15 PM

7 conversations, 7 with unread messages

Figure 17.16   *Expand the conversations in a BBS to see all replies.*

In the List view shown in Figure 17.17, all messages and files appear in a single column. To rearrange the order in which entries appear, click the heading you want to use to sort the listings—subject, author, or date. Items with attached files appear in the list with a paper-clip icon at the left side of the description instead of a piece of paper.

Attachment view, shown in Figure 17.18, limits the display to items that have embedded files. If you're looking for a file to download, Attachment view is probably the easiest way to find it.

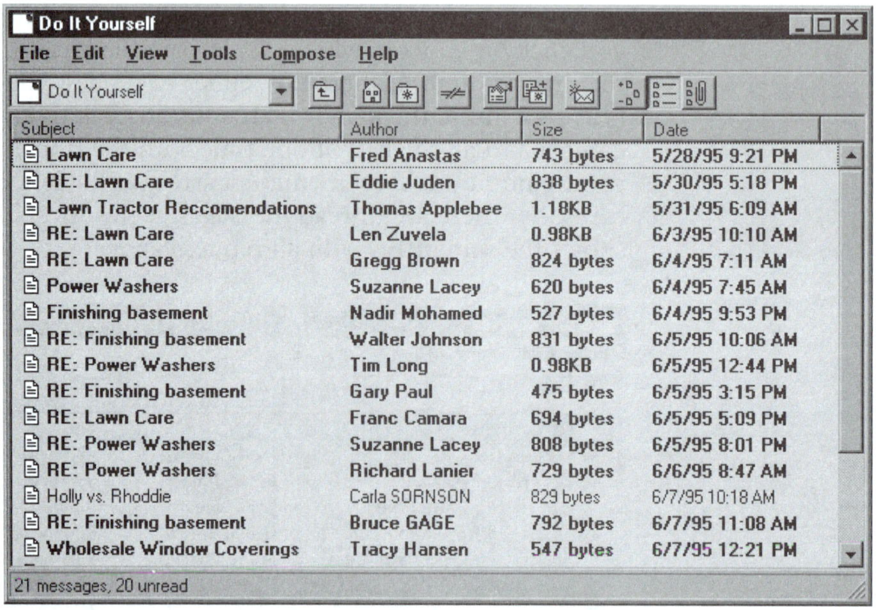

Figure 17.17 List view displays all messages in a flat list.

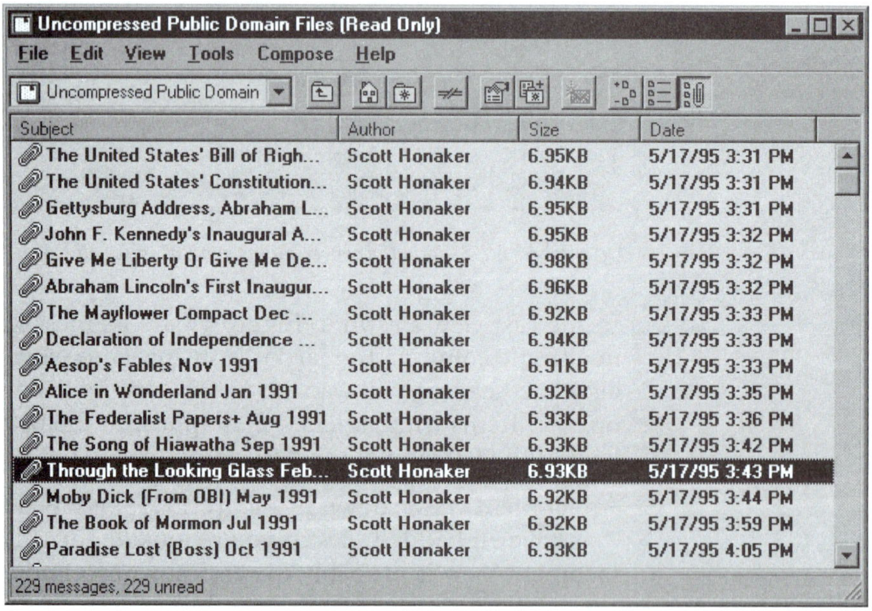

Figure 17.18 Attachment view shows only those messages with attached files.

Adding a new message to a thread or creating a new message is very much like creating a message in Microsoft Exchange: Use the Compose ➤ New menu command to open a message editor. Chapter 15 contains detailed information about the Message Editor.

Message Folder Commands

The menu bar in a message folder window includes these special commands:

File Menu

Open This command opens the currently highlighted message.

Save As Use to save a message as a file.

Properties This command opens a panel with more detailed information about the currently highlighted item, including the additional cost, if any.

Up One Level This command moves you to the parent window for the current window.

Edit Menu

Go to These commands move you directly to MSN Central, Favorite Places, or to any other location in MSN using a Go Word.

View Menu

Conversation This command displays messages in a threaded list, with replies indented under the original message.

List This command displays all messages in a flat list, arranged alphabetically by subject or author, or chronologically by date.

Attached Files This command displays a flat list of only those messages with attached files.

Arrange Messages   These commands specify the order in which MSN displays the messages in a BBS—by subject, author, size, or date.

Expand All Conversations   This command displays all the threads of all conversations in nested form, with replies indented under original messages. This command only works in Conversation view.

Collapse All Conversations   This command is the opposite of Expand All Conversations. It hides listings of message replies and shows only the top-level message in each conversation.

Refresh   Use to obtain a new copy of the current message list.

Tools Menu

Use one of these commands to change the status of one or more messages.

Mark Message as Read

Mark Message as Unread

Mark Conversation as Read

Mark Conversation as Unread

Mark All Messages as Read

Show All Messages   Use to include messages that you've seen before in MSN's display of a BBS, even if there are no new replies to those messages.

Compose Menu

New Message   Use to open the Message Editor. To send a reply to an existing message, open the message and use the Reply command in the Compose menu.

Reading Messages

To read a message, double-click on the listing. The Message Viewer window in Figure 17.19 will appear. The Message Viewer looks and works very much like the Message Editor; you can change the

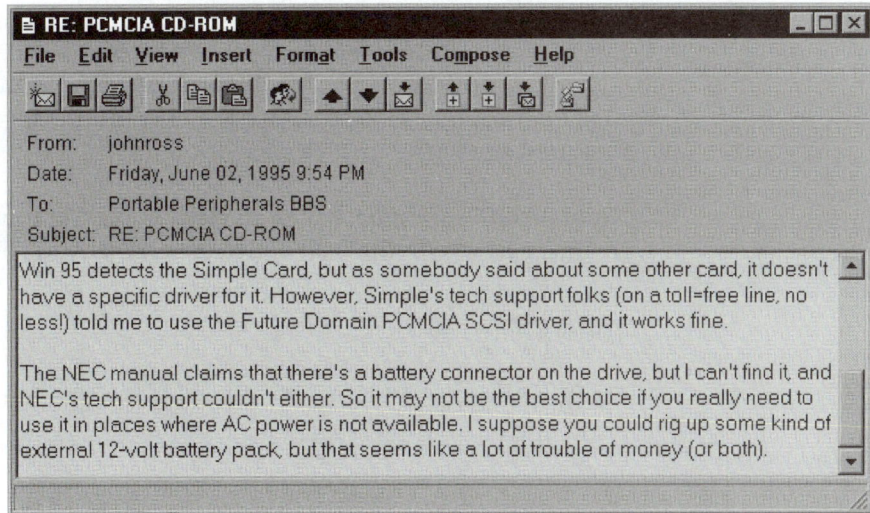

Figure 17.19   *The Message Viewer displays messages from MSN conferences.*

typestyle, size, color, or alignment of the text as it appears on your screen.

To reply to a message, use the Compose ➤ Reply to BBS command. If you prefer to send a private reply, use the Reply by E-mail command. A Message Editor will appear, and you can type your text, attach a file, or copy text from another message or other document.

The Message Viewer includes these commands that don't appear in other Windows menus:

View Menu

Previous Message   Use to close the current message and open the preceding message immediately before it in the message folder.

Next Message   Use to close the current message and open the next message.

Next Unread Message   Use to close the current message and open the next message that you haven't read yet.

Previous Conversation   Use to close the current message and open the first message in the previous conversation.

Next Conversation   Use to close the current message and open the first message in the next conversation.

Next Unread Conversation   Use to close the current message and open the first message in the next conversation that you haven't already seen.

Tools Menu

Member Properties   Use to display information about the person who wrote the current message.

Compose Menu

New Message   Use to create and post a message that is not related to the current message.

Reply to BBS   Use to create a new message and send it as a public reply to the current message.

Reply by E-Mail   Use to send an e-mail message to the person who posted the original message.

Forward by E-Mail   Use to send a copy of the current message to another user as an e-mail message.

The Message Viewer also has two optional toolbars. The first contains commands related to sending and receiving messages. The message toolbar is shown in Figure 17.20.

Downloading Files from MSN

Figure 17.21 shows a message with an embedded file icon. You can obtain more information about a file by double-clicking on its icon to open the Properties window for that file. Figure 17.22 shows a typical Properties window. Notice the information in the Price field; some files cost additional money to download.

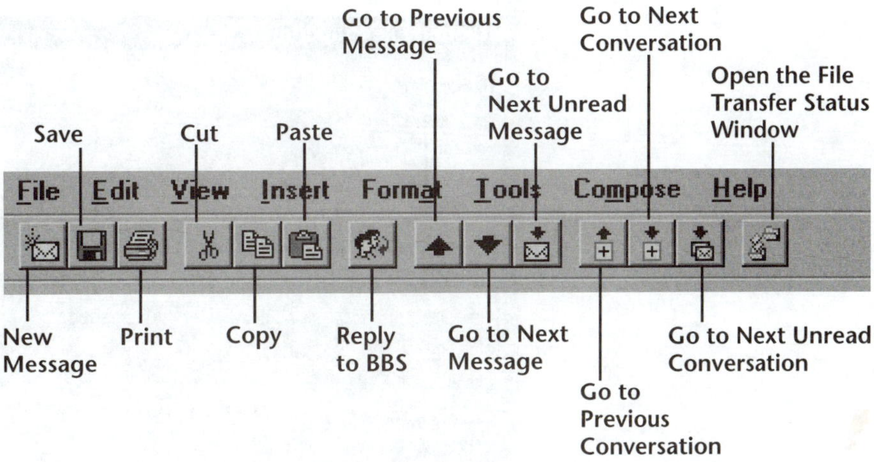

Go to Previous
Message

Go to Next
Conversation

Go to
Next Unread
Message

Open the File
Transfer Status
Window

Save   Cut   Paste

File   Edit   View   Insert   Format   Tools   Compose   Help

New   Print   Copy   Reply   Go to Next   Go to Next Unread
Message   to BBS   Message   Conversation

Go to
Previous
Conversation

Figure 17.20   *The message toolbar*

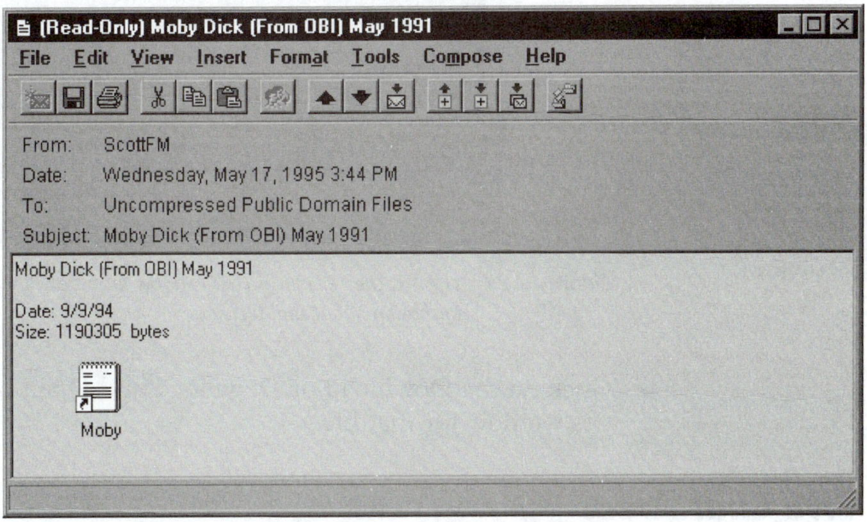

(Read-Only) Moby Dick (From OBI) May 1991

File   Edit   View   Insert   Format   Tools   Compose   Help

From: ScottFM
Date: Wednesday, May 17, 1995 3:44 PM
To: Uncompressed Public Domain Files
Subject: Moby Dick (From OBI) May 1991

Moby Dick (From OBI) May 1991

Date: 9/9/94
Size: 1190305 bytes

Moby

Figure 17.21   *Downloadable files may be embedded in MSN messages.*

There are several ways to download a file:

▶ Use the Save As command in the File menu or the toolbar.

▶ Right-click on the icon and select Download from the File Object
submenu.

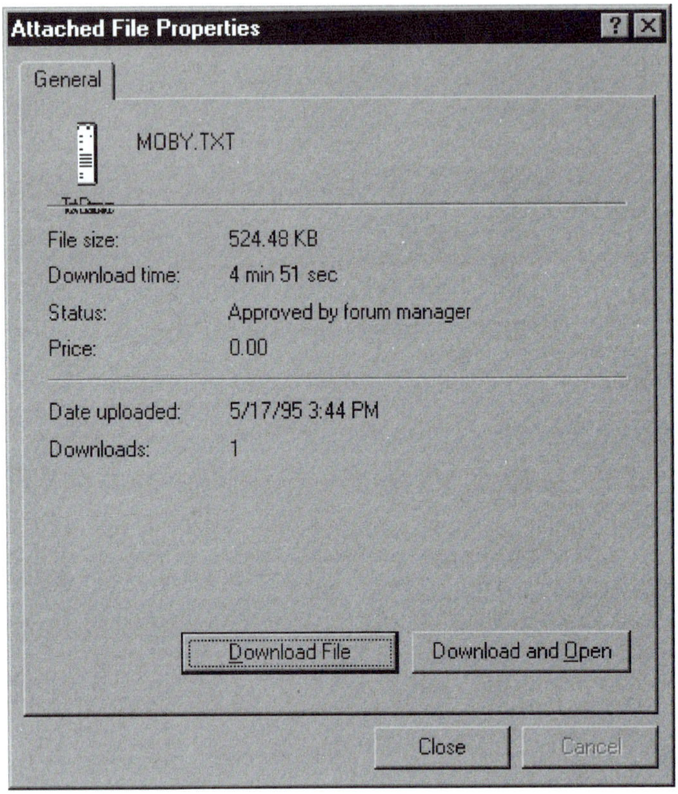

Figure 17.22   *The Attached File Properties window for a downloadable file shows detailed information about that file.*

▶   Click on the Download or Download and Open button in the Properties window for that file.

Live Chat Areas

The Message Folders described in the previous section are a store-and-forward method for sending and receiving messages and files. The Microsoft Network also supports real-time conversations in which other people see your messages as soon as you type them.

MSN calls these conversations *chats*. Some chats are dedicated to informal conversation around a specific topic, while others provide an opportunity to ask questions of experts who presumably know what they're talking about. Chat rooms are identified in MSN subject windows by icons with speech balloons.

Figure 17.23 shows a chat window. The text of the ongoing conversation appears in the Chat History pane in the upper-left part of the window. The Member List on the right side of the window shows the names of the current participants in this chat room. At the bottom of the screen there's a Compose Pane where you can type your own comments or questions. When you click on the Send button, you transmit the text in the Compose Pane to the chat room, and you should see it in the Chat History pane within a few seconds.

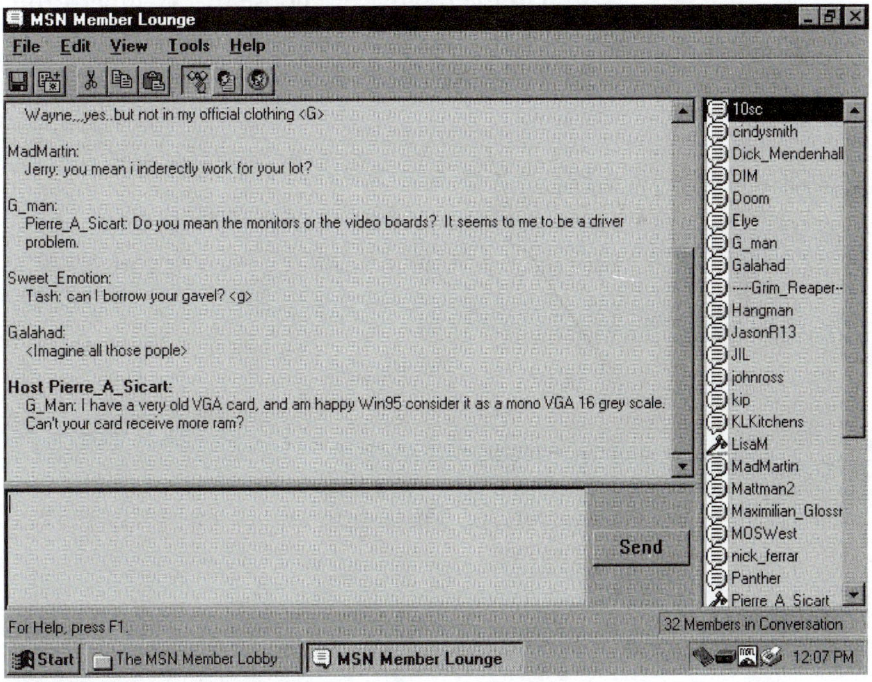

Figure 17.23   *Chat rooms contain live online conversations.*

Part 3

Managing Communications

You can change the relative sizes of panes by moving the cursor to the space between the panes and dragging the border. If you like, you can even make one or more of the panes disappear from the window completely.

The Member List displays an icon next to each name. This icon identifies the person as a host, a participant, or a spectator. The Host is generally the first person to enter a chat room. Participants can send and receive comments, but spectators may only read comments from other people. The Host can change a user's status from Participant to Spectator and back again.

Sometimes it's useful to learn more about the other people participating in a chat with you. To see information about a person listed in the Member List, highlight the name and either click the Member Profile button in the toolbar or choose the Member Profile command in the Tools menu.

Chat rooms have these commands in their menus that aren't in other windows:

File Menu

Save History   Use to store the current conversation in a text file.

Save History As   Use to assign a new name to the text file that contains the current conversation.

Edit Menu

Clear History   This command deletes all of the text in the Chat History Pane.

View Menu

Move Split Bar   Use to change the relative sizes of the panes within the chat window. You can do the same thing by moving your cursor to the boundary between panes and dragging the edge to a new position.

Show Spectators When active, the member list shows both participants and spectators. When it is not active, it lists participants only.

Ignore Members   Highlight one or more names and use this command
if you don't want to see postings from certain people who are participating in a chat.

Member Properties   Use to open the dialog box below for the currently
highlighted name. If you check the Ignore Messages box, you will not
see messages from this person.

Member Options

Selected members:

johnross

☐ Ignore messages from selected members

OK

Cancel

Tools Menu

Select Members   This command opens a submenu with options for selecting all names in the Member List and for inverting the current selection. When you invert a selection, all of the currently unselected
names will be selected, and the selected names will be unselected.

Host Controls   You can't use this command unless you're host of the
current conference. If you are a host, you can use the command to
change the status of other members from Participant to Spectator
or Spectator to Participant.

Options   This command opens the Options dialog box on the next
page. Use this dialog box to change message spacing, automatically

save a conversation when you leave a chat room, and see notices when a member joins or leaves the chat room.

Options

Notify me when members

☐ Join the chat

☐ Leave the chat

☐ Save chat history before clearing or exiting

☐ Insert blank line between messages

OK   Cancel

The chat room toolbar has three icon buttons that are not in other windows:

Show Spectators   Use this button to display the names of spectators as well as participants in the Member List.

Member Properties   Use this button to display information about the currently highlighted name in the Member List.

Ignore   Use the Ignore button to omit messages from the currently highlighted name in the member list. When you Ignore a name, that name appears in the Member List with a line through it.

Internet Access through the Microsoft Network

In addition to its own services, Microsoft Network will also incorporates a variety of Internet functions. MSN's Internet services are now limited to e-mail and newsgroups. By early 1996, Microsoft has promised to incorporate a World-Wide Web browser into MSN. (See Chapter 32 for a discussion of the Web browser available with Miscrosoft Plus.)

Internet Newsgroups

MSN treats Internet newsgroups as one more source for bulletin-board conferences. In the main Categories window, there's a folder called *The Internet Center*. You may also see an icon in many folders, labeled *Related Internet Newsgroups*. When you click on one of these icons, you open sub-folders that eventually lead you to individual newsgroups.

MSN displays the contents of Internet newsgroups exactly the same way as it shows the bulletin boards and conferences that originate within the Microsoft Network. The important difference is that messages posted to an Internet group will be distributed to readers on many other networks around the world.

Sending and Receiving Internet E-Mail

The only difference between e-mail to another MSN user and messages to foreign addresses is the address format. Follow these steps to send a message through the Internet from MSN:

1. Starting at MSN Central, click on the E-Mail button.

2. Click on the compose button and choose the New Message option.

3. Type the Internet e-mail address of your intended recipient in the To field.

4. Compose and send the message just as you would for any other service.

Disconnecting from the Microsoft Network

To disconnect your PC from the Microsoft Network, use the Sign Out command in either the File menu, the toolbar, or the menu that appears when you left-click on the MSN icon on the Taskbar.

Because Microsoft wants you to spend as much time as possible on MSN with the meter running, the final version will have all kinds of interesting areas to occupy your attention and tempt you to download files and use special services for a "slight additional cost." Unless you have an unlimited budget, you will want to keep a close eye on the amount you spend online each month, or you'll have a *really* unpleasant surprise when you receive your credit card bill.

Part
3

Managing
Communications

Chapter 18
Internet Access Tools

FEATURING

Connecting to the Internet

Internet utilities

Other Internet applications

As you probably know by now, the Internet is the worldwide interconnection of computers and computer networks that permits exchange of messages and files among millions of users around the world. Windows 95 includes the networking utilities necessary to connect your PC to the Internet, along with a couple of very basic Internet application programs.

This chapter will tell you how to connect to the Internet, how to use the built-in applications, and how to use those applications to obtain some free or almost-free applications that will make your life online a great deal more pleasant.

Connecting Your PC to the Internet

There are at least four common methods for connecting a PC to the Internet: as a remote terminal on a host computer already connected to the Internet, through a Network Interface Card (NIC) to a local-area network, through a dial-in TCP/IP connection to an Internet access provider, and through an online information service such as America Online or Microsoft Network.

> **NOTE** An Internet access provider is a business or nonprofit organization that supplies dial-in or private line connections to the Internet.

To understand the differences among these connection methods, it's helpful to know that the Internet uses a common set of rules, commands, and procedures called TCP/IP (transmission-control protocol/Internet protocol), which allows many different kinds of computers to communicate with one another. To send and receive data through the Internet, you must either use TCP/IP software on your own computer or move the data through another computer that converts it to and from TCP/IP.

Figure 18.1 shows a remote-terminal connection. Your PC uses a conventional communications program such as HyperTerminal or Pro-Comm to exchange data with a second computer, called a *host*, that is connected to the Internet. As far as the host is concerned, your PC is just like a terminal that does not have its own computer processor. For this reason, communications programs like HyperTerminal are also called *terminal-emulation* programs. Unless the host is located in the same building, you probably use a modem to connect to the host through a telephone line. You may also see this kind of Internet access called a *shell account* because many host computers use a user interface called a *shell*.

Remote-terminal access to the Internet has both advantages and disadvantages. It's frequently less expensive than other types of Internet connection because a single host can support many remote terminals at the same time. And because the TCP/IP programs are located on the host, not on your PC, you can use a slower modem and less powerful computer (but if your computer has enough power to run Windows 95, it should have no trouble with TCP/IP software). However, remote access generally uses a command line (like the DOS prompt) rather than a graphic interface, it limits you to the Internet tools loaded on the host, and it takes a lot longer to transfer files from a distant computer because you have to relay it through a host.

Figure 18.2 shows a connection through a local-area network (LAN), and Figure 18.3 shows a direct TCP/IP link through a SLIP (serial-line Internet protocol) or PPP (point-to-point protocol) connection. The Internet tools that control such functions as mail, news, and file transfer all run on your own PC. If you're already connected to a LAN, it's generally more efficient to connect the whole network to the Internet because a network connection is faster than a modem link.

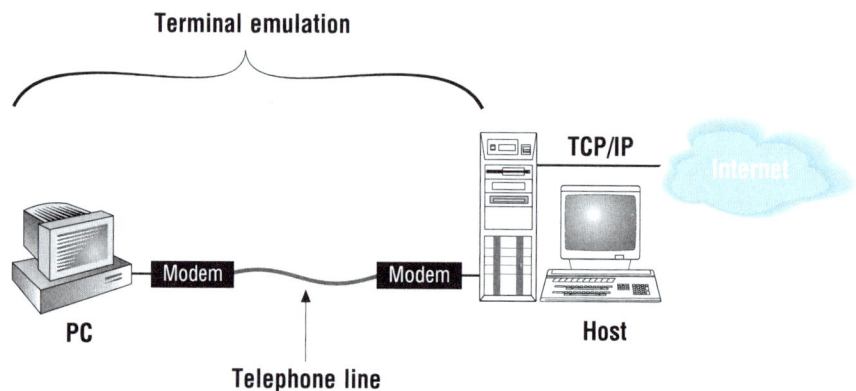

Figure 18.1   *A remote-terminal connection to the Internet uses TCP/IP programs on a host computer.*

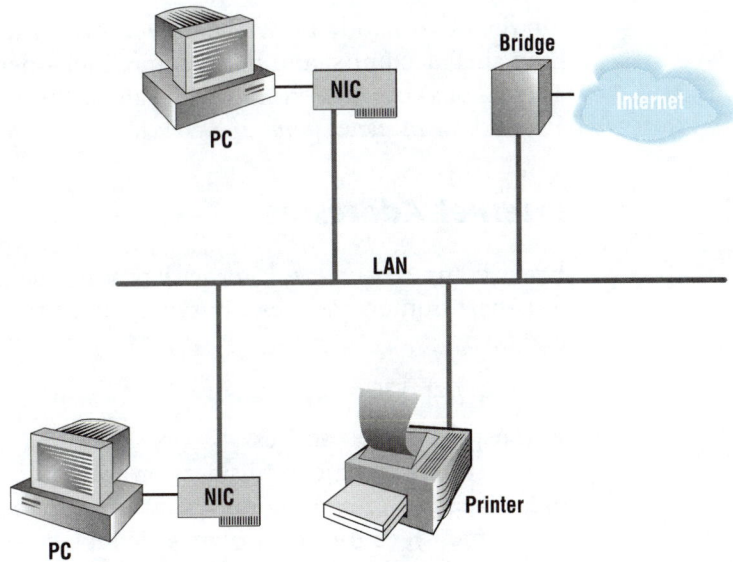

Figure 18.2   *A LAN connection to the Internet provides access to all of the computers on a local-area network through NIC (the Network Interface Card).*

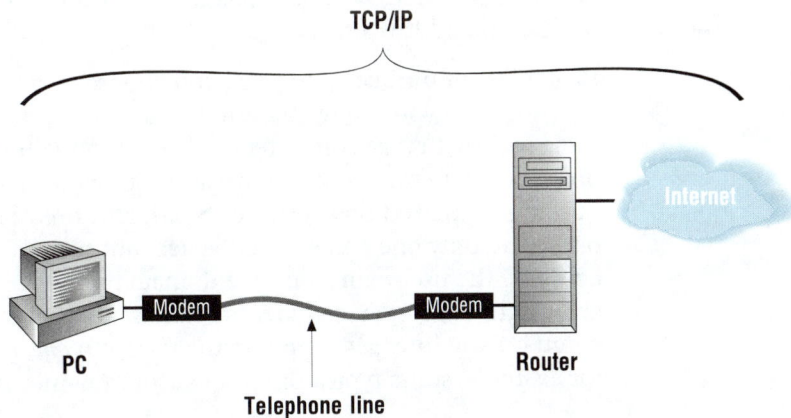

Figure 18.3   *SLIP and PPP connections to the Internet communicate directly to the Internet using TCP/IP protocols.*

The advantages of a direct TCP/IP connection to the Internet are speed and flexibility. There are many Windows application programs that provide graphical displays, drag-and-drop file transfer, and other features that are not available through a remote-terminal connection.

On the other hand, TCP/IP connections are usually more expensive than shell accounts, and they require high-speed modems (at least 14,400 bps) or other kinds of (usually costly) data links between your PC and an Internet *point of presence.*

Internet Addresses

Every computer on the Internet has a unique identity in the form of a four-part numeric address. For example, a typical address would look like this:

```
132.163.135.130
```

In most cases, that address also exists as a name, with a *domain* that shows either the type of business or other institution that uses this address (such as .com for commercial, .edu for educational, or .gov for government), or the country in which it's located. For example, Microsoft's domain address is microsoft.com, while Mindlink, an Internet service provider in Vancouver, British Columbia, Canada, uses mindlink.bc.ca as its address. Your Internet access provider uses a database called a *Domain Name Server* to convert from domain names to numeric addresses.

Regardless of the access method you choose, you will need to obtain an account from your network administrator or service provider. In the same way that every computer connected to the Internet has its own address, every user has a distinctive account name. Therefore, if the same business employed both Frances Smith and Fred Smith in the same department, only one could have the account name fsmith. When you combine the user name with the domain name, the two are separated by an *at* sign (@) so you can identify (and send mail to) anybody with an account on any Internet system in the format *name@address.domain.* So, for example, some typical Internet account names would be

```
bluebottle@finchley.uk
yokum@dogpatch.com
snorkel@swampy.mil
```

In addition to your own account name, address, and password, your service provider or network administrator may also give you several other pieces of information that you will need to set up your Internet account. These may include the dial-in Internet host's telephone number and the numeric addresses of the servers for name conversion, mail, and network news.

Connecting as a Remote Terminal

When you use a communications program such as HyperTerminal to dial into a host computer, your PC becomes a terminal on that host. If the host is connected to the Internet, you must use Internet programs resident on the host.

The most common remote-terminal access to the Internet is through a Unix host, or a host that recognizes Unix-like Internet commands such as telnet, ftp, and so forth.

> **NOTE**   Unix is a widely used computer operating system that is available for many different kinds of computers, including desktop systems, mainframes, and everything in between. Unix allows more than one program to run at the same time and multiple users to share a single computer.

As far as Windows is concerned, when you use a shell account, your PC is running a modem communications program to move ASCII characters or binary files through a modem. All the TCP/IP activity is happening at the host. In other words, when you type commands on your PC's keyboard, those commands pass through your computer to the host, which runs the programs that communicate with the Internet.

If you have a remote-terminal connection to the Internet, you don't need to worry about network configuration, because the administrator of the host has taken care of all those things for you. Once you know your own account name and password and the host's Internet address, you're ready to go.

Configuring Windows for TCP/IP Internet Connection

Windows 95 includes support for dial-in TCP/IP access to the Internet through a PPP account. To use this function, you must have a PPP account with an Internet service provider. If you have a SLIP account, you will have to install SLIP support separately. I'll explain how to do that later in this chapter.

This kind of connection is not your only option for connecting to the Internet. There are many add-on Internet access products, including Microsoft Plus (Chapter 32), that offer easier ways to set up a TCP/IP connection.

When you set up your Internet access account, you will need to obtain the following information from your service provider:

▶ your log-in name and password

▶ the service provider's access telephone number

▶ the service provider's host name and domain

▶ the numeric IP address of your service provider's name server

If your service provider does not use dynamic address assignment (most do), you will also need to obtain your IP address, subnet mask address, and gateway address from the service provider.

With this information in hand, follow these steps to load and configure dial-in Internet access:

1. If you haven't yet installed Windows 95, run Setup and choose Custom Setup. If Windows has already been installed, open Add/Remove Programs from the Control Panel and click on the Windows Setup tab.

2. Click on Communications to put a check mark in the box and then click on the Details button.

3. Check the Dial-Up Networking option in the component list shown in Figure 18.4 and click on the OK button. Insert the disks as Windows asks for them.

4. After loading the software, double-click on the Network icon in the Control Panel.

5. When the Network dialog box in Figure 18.5 appears, click on the Add button.

6. Click on the Protocol option and the Add button.

7. When the Select Network Protocol menu in Figure 18.6 appears, choose Microsoft from the Manufacturers menu and TCP/IP from the Network Protocols menu. Click on OK.

8. When the Configuration dialog box appears again, highlight the Dial-Up Adapter and click on the Properties button.

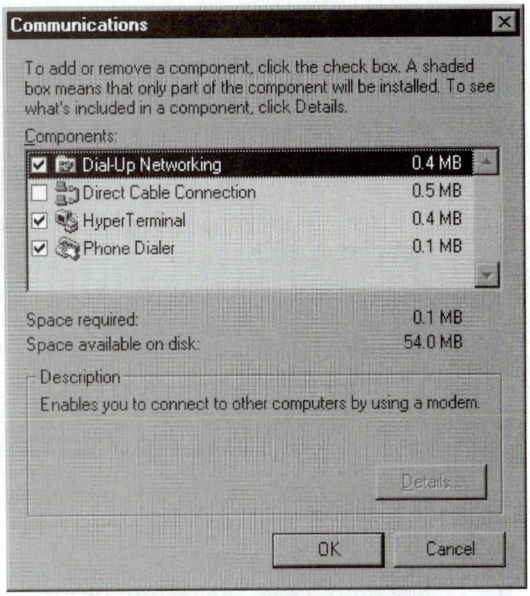

Figure 18.4 Check Dial-Up Networking to install the Internet access software.

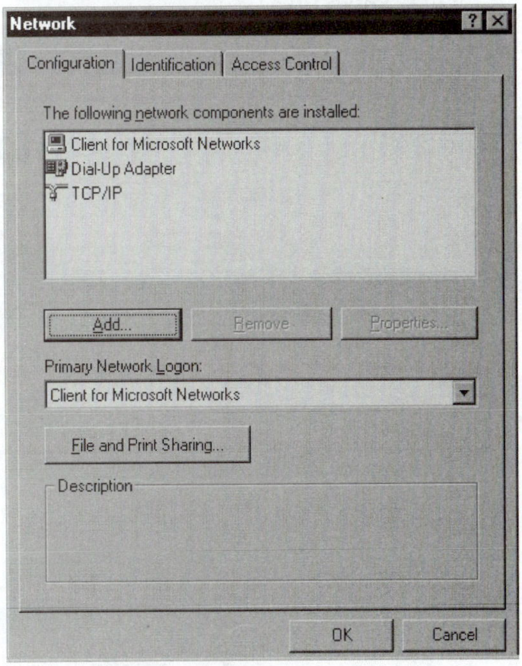

Figure 18.5 Click on the Add button to install TCP/IP support.

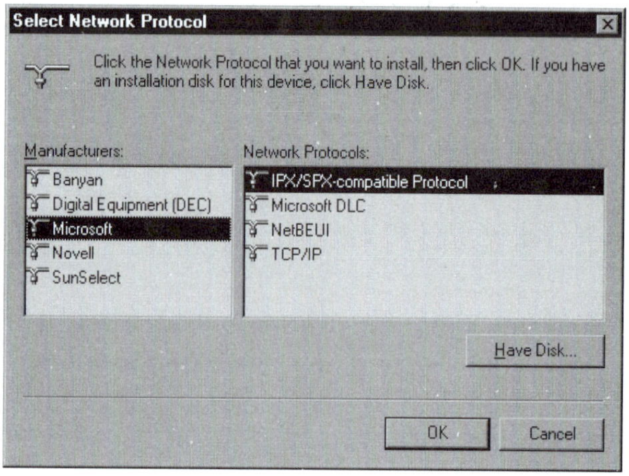

Figure 18.6 Choose the TCP/IP network protocol to set up a PPP connection to the Internet.

9. Click on the Bindings tab to display the list of protocols in Figure 18.7. Confirm that there's a check mark next to the TCP/IP protocol listing. Click on OK.

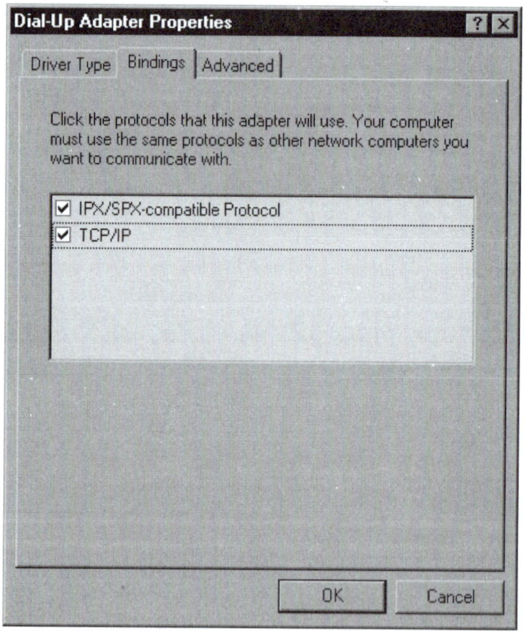

Figure 18.7 Confirm that TCP/IP is active.

10. Once again, the Configuration dialog box appears. Highlight TCP/IP in the Network Components menu and click on the Properties button.

11. Choose the IP Address tab to display the dialog box in Figure 18.8. If your Internet access provider supplies a different IP address each time you log in, choose the *Obtain an IP address automatically* radio button. If your service provider has given you a permanent IP address, choose the *Specify an IP address* radio button and type your address and subnet mask (if any) in their respective fields.

12. If your service provider gave you a gateway address, click on the Gateway tab and type the gateway address in the New Gateway field.

13. Click on the DNS Configuration tab to display the dialog box in Figure 18.9. Click on the Enable DNS radio button and type your service provider's host name and domain. Type the Domain Name Server's IP address in the *DNS server search order* field and click on the Add button.

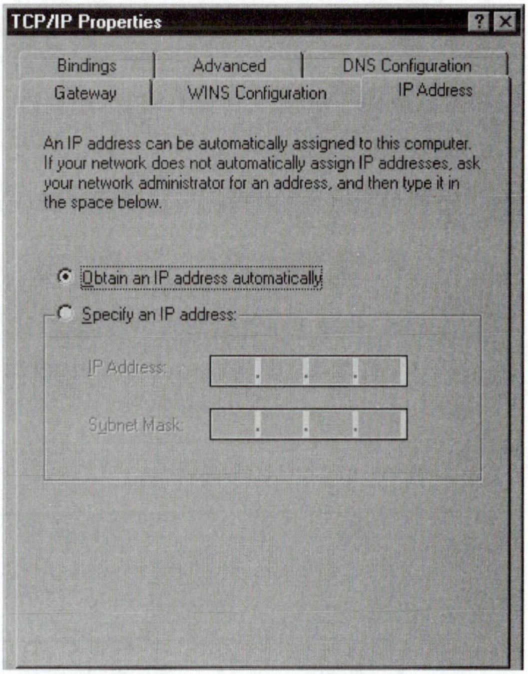

Figure 18.8   *Use this dialog box to specify your IP address.*

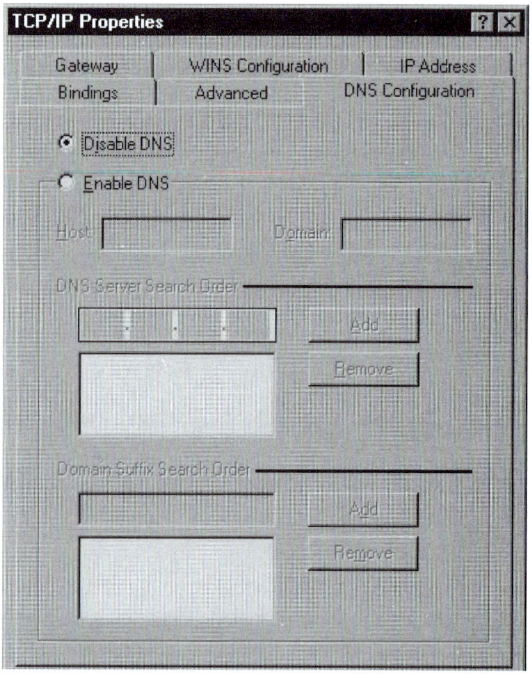

Figure 18.9   Use this dialog box to identify your service provider's Domain Name Server.

14. Click on OK to return to the Network dialog box and OK again to return to the Control Panel. Windows may ask you to load one or more disks at this point.

15. Close the Control Panel and restart Windows 95.

16. After Windows has restarted, double-click on the My Computer icon and choose the Dial-Up Networking icon, or click on the Start menu, open the Programs menu, and choose Dial-up Networking from the Accessories menu.

17. If you haven't already installed a modem, the program will give you a chance to install it now.

18. Double-click on the Make New Connection icon to start the New Connection Wizard. In the first screen of the Wizard, shown in Figure 18.10, replace "My Connection" in the *Type a name for the computer you are dialing* field with the name of your service provider or with something like *Internet Access*. Click on the Next> button.

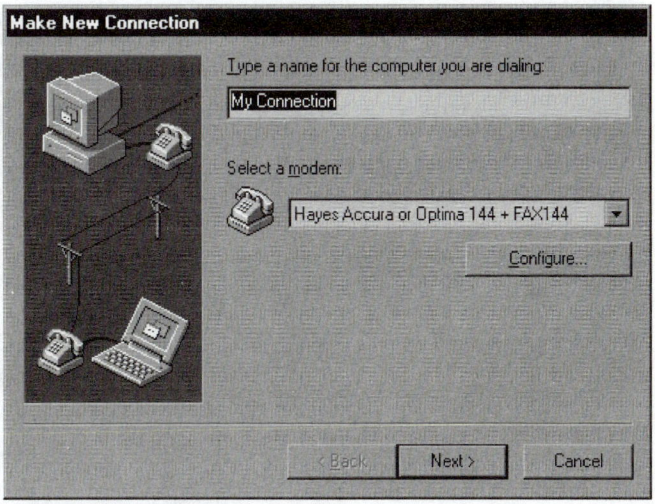

Figure 18.10   Type a name for the command that connects you to the Internet.

19. In the next screen of the New Connection wizard, type your service provider's telephone number for dial-in access.

20. The Dial-Up Networking window will now have a second icon with the name you specified, as shown below. Right-click on the new icon and select the Properties command.

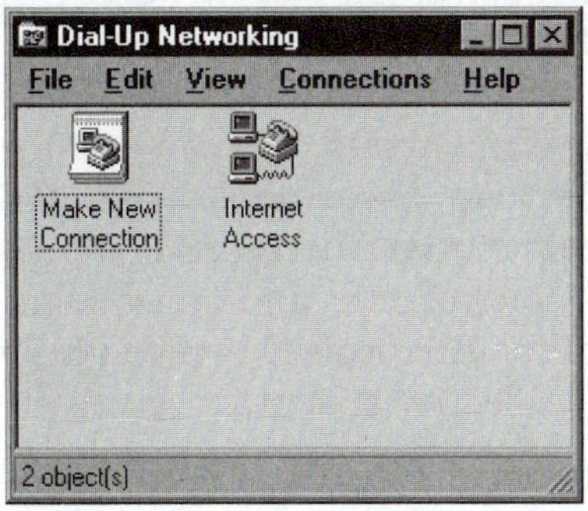

21. Click on the Configure button and select the Options tab to display the dialog box in Figure 18.11. Under *Connection control*, make the *Bring up terminal window after dialing* option active.

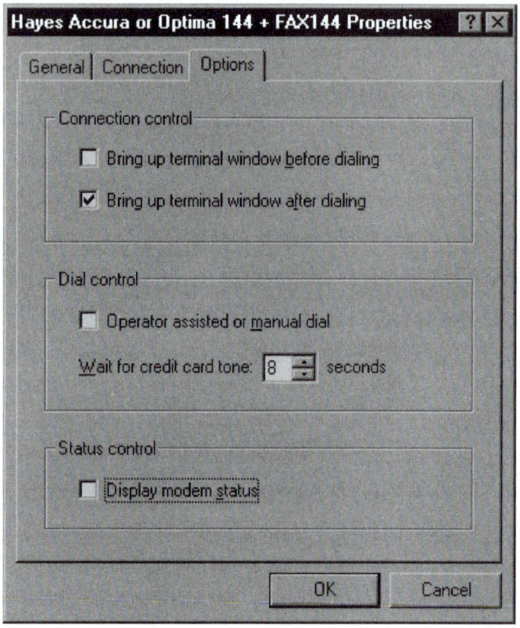

Figure 18.11 **Be sure to choose the After Dialing option and not Before Dialing.**

Configuring a SLIP Connection

If your TCP/IP connection to the Internet uses SLIP rather than PPP, you'll need a separate setup information file called `rnaplus.inf` that is not automatically installed during Windows setup. If you have the CD-ROM version of Windows 95, you can find the file in the directory `\admin\apptools\slip`. If you don't have a CD-ROM, you'll have to download the file from Microsoft. It should be available on Microsoft Network, CompuServe, and other online information services, as well as from the Microsoft Download Service at 206-936-6735. Look for a file called `rnaplu.zip`.

Follow these steps to install a SLIP connection:

1. Copy the `rnaplus.inf` file to a floppy disk. Leave the diskette in the drive.

2. Open the Windows 95 Control Panel and select Add/Remove Programs.

3. When the Add/Remove Programs Properties dialog box appears, choose the Windows Setup tab and click on the Have Disk button.

4. When the Install from Disk dialog box shown below appears, make sure the path of the drive that contains the `rnaplus.inf` file is in the Copy From field and click on OK.

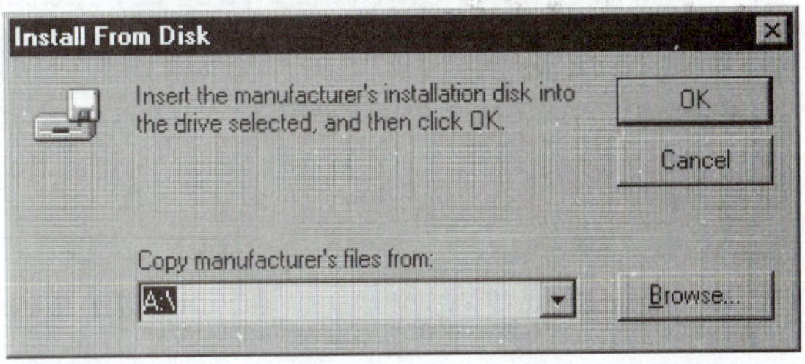

Install From Disk

> Insert the manufacturer's installation disk into the drive selected, and then click OK.
>
> OK
>
> Cancel
>
> Copy manufacturer's files from:
>
> A:\   Browse...

5. The Have Disk dialog box in Figure 18.12 lists setup information files in the path you specified in step 4. Click on the box next to Unix Connection for Dial-Up Networking to put a check mark in the box and click on Install.

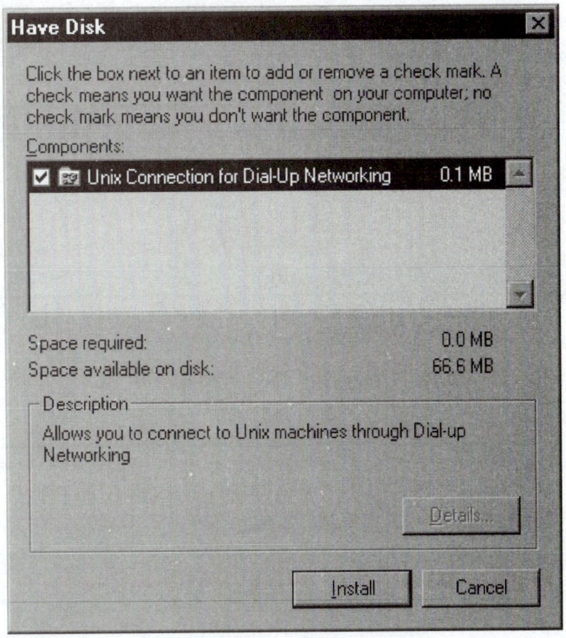

Have Disk

> Click the box next to an item to add or remove a check mark. A check means you want the component on your computer; no check mark means you don't want the component.
>
> Components:
>
> ☑ Unix Connection for Dial-Up Networking   0.1 MB
>
> Space required: 0.0 MB
> Space available on disk: 66.6 MB
>
> Description
> Allows you to connect to Unix machines through Dial-up Networking
>
> Details...
>
> Install   Cancel

Figure 18.12   *The Unix Connection item adds SLIP access to Dial-Up Networking.*

Part 3

Managing Communications

6. Windows will copy the Unix Connection component from the diskette. When the Add/Remove Programs Properties dialog box appears again, scroll to the bottom of the Components list and make sure there's a check mark next to Unix Connection for Dial-Up Networking.

7. Close the Control Panel and restart your computer.

8. When the Windows Desktop re-appears, click on the Start button, open the Programs menu, and choose Dial-Up Networking from the Accessories submenu.

9. Double-click on Make New Connection.

10. Step through the New Connection Wizard until you see the screen in Figure 18.13.

11. Click on Next and then Finish to complete the New Connection Wizard.

12. Click on My Computer in your Desktop and open the Dial-Up Networking Window.

13. Right-click on the new icon for Internet Access (or whatever you chose to name it) and select the Properties command.

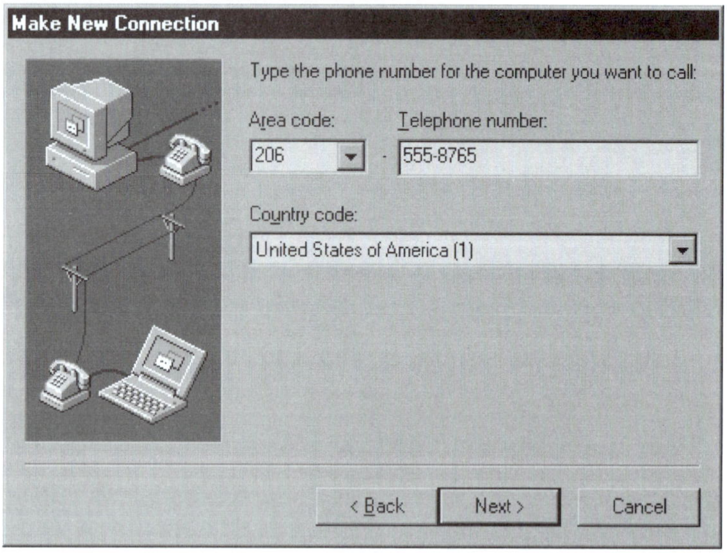

Figure 18.13   *Type your Internet service provider's access number in this screen.*

14. Click on the Server Type button to open the dialog box in Figure 18.14.

15. Drop down the Type of Dial-Up Server menu and choose either the CSLIP or SLIP option, depending on the kind of connection your service provider supplies. If you're not sure which option to choose, ask your service provider.

16. Click on OK to save your configuration and again to close the Properties dialog box.

Making the Connection

The good news about network configuration is that you only have to do it once. After that, you can make your Internet connection by simply making a network connection.

Follow these steps to connect your computer to the Internet through a PPP or SLIP account:

1. Make sure your modem is turned on.

2. Open the Dial-Up Networking window from either My Computer or the Programs Accessories menu.

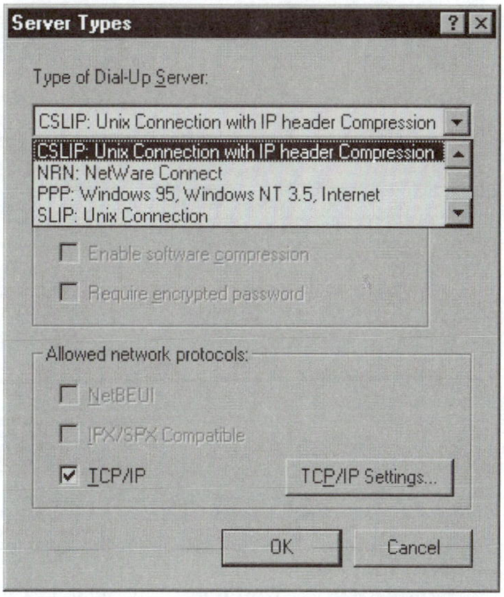

Part

3

Managing
Communications

Figure 18.14   *Specify either CSLIP or SLIP as your server type.*

3. Double-click on Internet Access (or whatever you named your Internet-access command).

4. When the Connect To dialog box in Figure 18.15 appears, fill in any blank fields and click on Connect. Windows will start dialing.

5. When your modem connects to the network host, Windows will open a Terminal window like the one in Figure 18.16. If the host asks for your log-in and password, type the information requested and press the Enter key.

6. If you're using a SLIP account, the host may tell you your IP address for this session. Make a note of the address; you'll need it in a minute.

7. Click on the Continue button or press the F7 key.

8. If a dialog box asking you to confirm your IP address appears, type the number you copied from the host and click on the OK button.

9. Your computer now has an active connection to the Internet. When you start an Internet application, such as ftp, Mosaic, or telnet, the application will automatically send and receive data through this connection.

When you have finished your interaction with the Internet, click on the Disconnect button to take your computer offline.

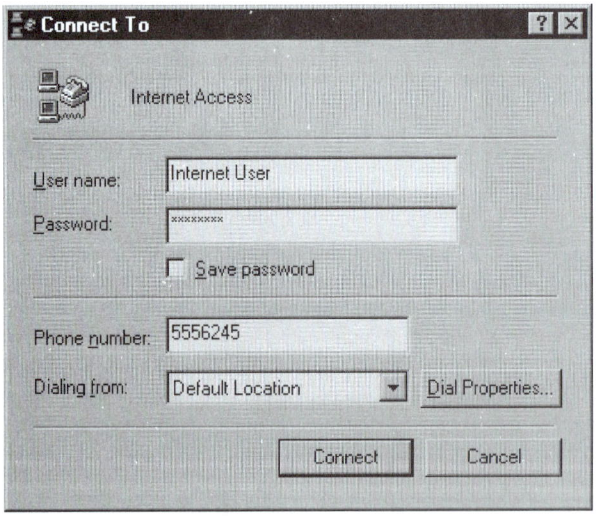

Figure 18.15   The Connect To dialog box

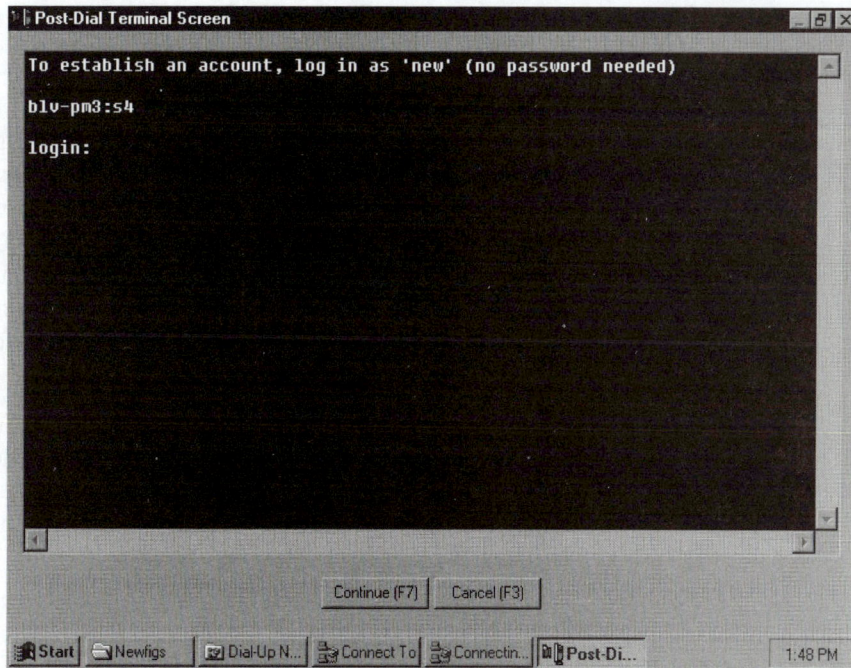

Figure 18.16 Type your name and password in the Terminal window.

If you have access to the Internet through a LAN, follow these steps to make your connection:

1. Click on the Network Neighborhood icon in the Windows Desktop.

2. Select the icon for your Internet connection.

3. Start the Winsock-compatible application you want to run. The application will communicate to the Internet through `winsock.dll` and your network connection.

Regardless of the type of connection you're using, your Winsock applications will automatically find your connection to the Internet. If you close one application and start another or run more than one application at the same time, the second (and subsequent) application will use the same Winsock connection to the Internet.

If you're using a dial-in connection, remember to break the connection when you're finished doing whatever you're doing online.

Internet Utilities

Window 95 includes several Internet utilities—an FTP (file-transfer protocol) program, a telnet program for remote log-in to distant computers, and a handful of programs for testing Internet connections. Both the FTP and the telnet programs are *clients*, which means they can communicate with computers configured as FTP and telnet servers. Most of these applications are character-based programs that operate from within a DOS window. Therefore, you need to use the DOS Prompt command in the Program menu before you can use them.

Some of these utilities may not work with other Winsock stacks, such as the ones in Internet Chameleon, Internet in a Box, or Trumpet Winsock. This really isn't a problem because most Internet packages include other utilities that do the same job as the ones in the Windows 95 package, only better.

File-Transfer Protocol

FTP is the standard TCP/IP file-transfer protocol used for moving text and binary files between computers on the Internet. If you have an account on a distant computer on the Internet, you can use FTP to download files from the other computer to your PC and to upload files from your PC to the host. In addition, there are hundreds of *anonymous* FTP archives all over the Internet that accept log-ins from anybody who wants copies of their files.

The Windows 95 FTP program is located in the \Windows directory, which is in your Path statement. Therefore, you don't have to specify the path when you enter an ftp command. To connect to an FTP server, follow these steps:

1. Use the Run command in the Start menu to enter this command: **ftp \<host name>**.

2. A terminal window will open with an ftp> prompt.

3. When FTP connects to the server, the server will ask for your user name and password. If you're connecting to an anonymous FTP server, type **anonymous** as your user name and your Internet address as your password. Use the standard *name@address.domain* format.

Most FTP servers use the same system of directories and subdirectories that you know from DOS and Windows. To see the contents of the current directory, type **dir** at the ftp> prompt. Figure 18.17 shows an FTP directory.

A "d" as the first letter in a listing indicates that the item in that line is a directory. If there's a dash as the first character, the item is a file. The name of the file or directory is at the extreme right.

To move to a subdirectory, use the command **cd *name***.

To move up to the next higher level, use the command **cd ..**

When you download a file from an FTP server, you must specify that it is either an ASCII text file or a binary file. As a general rule, binary files that you can read on a PC will generally have a DOS file extension (other than .txt for a text file or .ps for a Postscript print file), but you really can't be certain. ASCII text files may or may not have a file extension.

When you make your initial connection to an FTP server, you're in ASCII mode. Before you try to transfer a binary file, you'll have to change modes. To switch to binary mode, use the command **binary**.

```
FTP                                                                _ | 8 | X
 Auto        ▼   [ ]  🗎 🗎  🔲  🗎 🗎  A
ftp> dir
200 PORT command successful.
150 Opening ASCII mode data connection for /bin/ls.
dr-xr-xr-x   1 owner    group            0 Mar 30 18:03 bussys
dr-xr-xr-x   1 owner    group            0 Oct  7  1994 deskapps
dr-xr-xr-x   1 owner    group            0 Dec 21  1994 developr
-r-xr-xr-x   1 owner    group         7656 Mar 31 15:29 dirmap.htm
-r-xr-xr-x   1 owner    group         4375 Mar 31  9:32 dirmap.txt
-r-xr-xr-x   1 owner    group          712 Aug 25  1994 disclaimer.txt
-r-xr-xr-x   1 owner    group          860 Oct  5  1994 index.txt
dr-xr-xr-x   1 owner    group            0 Apr 18 14:10 KBHelp
-r-xr-xr-x   1 owner    group      5827261 Apr 19  3:51 ls-lR.txt
-r-xr-xr-x   1 owner    group       711577 Apr 19  3:52 ls-lR.Z
-r-xr-xr-x   1 owner    group       554310 Apr 19  3:52 LS-LR.ZIP
-r-xr-xr-x   1 owner    group        28160 Nov 28  1994 MSNBRO.DOC
-r-xr-xr-x   1 owner    group        22641 Feb  8  1994 MSNBRO.TXT
dr-xr-xr-x   1 owner    group            0 Oct  7  1994 peropsys
dr-xr-xr-x   1 owner    group            0 Nov  2  1994 Services
dr-xr-xr-x   1 owner    group            0 Apr 21 10:48 Softlib
-r-xr-xr-x   1 owner    group         5095 Oct 20  1993 support-phones.txt
-r-xr-xr-x   1 owner    group          802 Aug 25  1994 WhatHappened.txt
226 Transfer complete.
1271 bytes received in 3.68 seconds (0.35 Kbytes/sec)
ftp>
```

Figure 18.17   *The FTP directory shows files and subdirectories.*

To switch back to ASCII mode, use the command **ASCII**. The host will acknowledge your mode-change command.

To download a file from the server, use the command **get** *filename*. If you want to store the file on your PC with a different name, use the command **get** *filename newname*. When the file transfer is complete, the host will send you another message, shown below.

```
ftp> get index.txt
200 PORT command successful.
150 Opening ASCII mode data connection for index.txt.
226 Transfer complete.
860 bytes received in 0.88 seconds (0.98 Kbytes/sec)
ftp>
```

When you are finished with your FTP session, use the command **disconnect** to break the connection to the server. You can connect to another host by typing the new server's address.

To close the FTP utility, type the command **quit**.

Telnet Remote Log-In

When you connect through a telnet connection, your PC becomes a terminal on the distant system. In most cases, a telnet log-in requires an account on the host (remote) machine, but there are also many systems that accept log-ins from anybody who wants to connect. Among the most common public telnet sites are online library catalogs. Other public telnet sites let you use character-based Internet services that may not be available on your own computer, such as *Gopher* or *Finger*.

To set up a telnet connection, follow these steps:

1. Click on the Telnet icon in the Windows directory. The Telnet window in Figure 18.18 will open.

2. Open the Connect menu and select the Remote System command to display the Connect dialog box shown below.

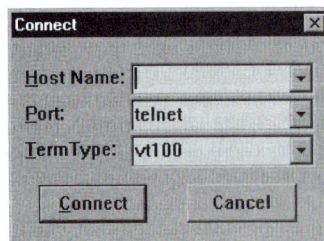

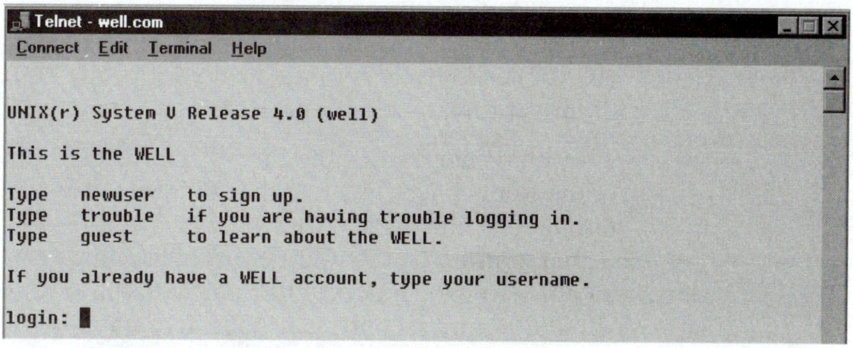

Figure 18.18 Use the Telnet window to connect to remote computers across the Internet.

3. Type the name of the host to which you want to connect in the Host Name field. Click on the Connect button.

    If you prefer, you can use the Run command in the Start menu and type **telnet** *hostname*, using the domain name or IP address of the computer to which you want to connect in place of *hostname*.

    Telnet will connect your computer to the host whose name you supplied and display messages from that host in the Telnet window.

    Most telnet hosts display a series of log-in prompts as soon as you make the connection. If you're connecting to a public telnet host, it will probably tell you how to log in.

Ping

Ping is a diagnostic utility that tests your ability to connect your computer to another device through the Internet by sending an echo request and displaying the number of milliseconds required to receive a reply.

To set up a Ping test, follow these steps:

1. Use the MS-DOS Prompt command in the Start ➤ Programs menu to open a DOS window.

2. At the C:\Windows> prompt, type **ping** *destination*. Use the domain name or the IP address of the host you want to test in place of *destination*.

Part
3

Managing
Communications

3. Ping will send four sets of Internet Control Message Protocol (ICMP) echo packets to the host you specify and display the amount of time it took to receive each reply, as shown in Figure 18.19.

The important part of the Ping display is the "time=*nnn*ms" section of the Reply lines. The fact that Ping was able to connect to the distant host at all tells you that your own connection to the Internet is working properly; the number of milliseconds can tell you if you have an efficient connection to this particular host (anything less than about 800 milliseconds is usually acceptable).

Network Configuration

The Network Display diagnostic command opens an information window that shows your current TCP/IP configuration values. To open the information window in Figure 18.20, type **winipcfg** at the DOS prompt or the Run window. For additional details, click on the More Info>> button.

Protocol Statistics

Use the **netstat** command to display a list of currently active connections to other computers across the Internet.

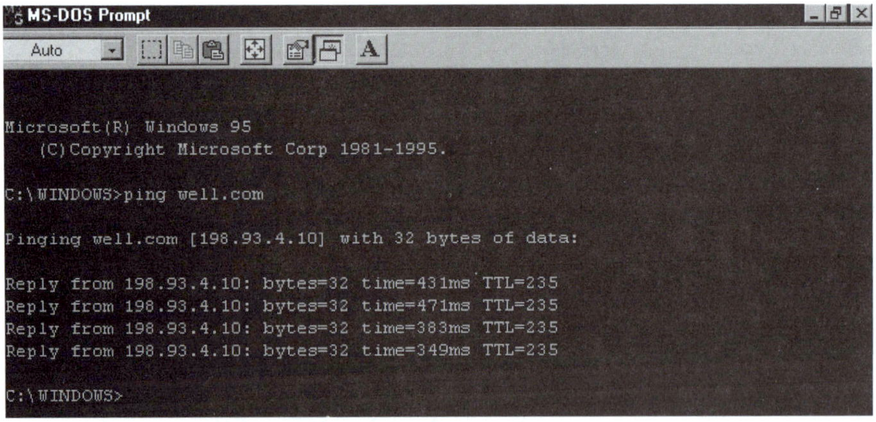

Figure 18.19   *A successful Ping test shows the amount of time needed to send and receive several echo packets.*

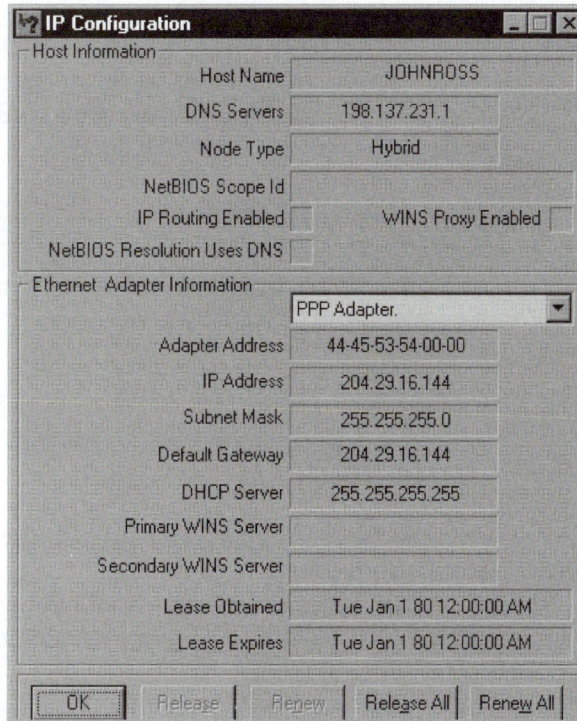

Figure 18.20   The IP Configuration window shows the current TCP/IP configuration values.

1. Use the MS-DOS Prompt command in the Start ➤ Programs menu to open a DOS window.

2. At the C:\Windows> prompt, type **netstat**. A list of connections similar to the ones shown below will appear.

A Netstat report includes the following information:

Proto   Shows the networking protocol in use for each active connection. For PPP or SLIP connections to the Internet, the Proto column will always be "TCP," which specifies a TCP/IP connection.

Local Address   The identity of your PC on the network.

Foreign Address   Shows the address of each distant computer to which a connection is currently active.

State   Shows the condition of each connection.

Trace Route

In most cases, when you set up a connection to a distant computer through the Internet, your signal path passes through several routers along the way. Because this is all happening in a fraction of a second, these intermediate routers are usually invisible. But when you're having trouble making a connection, the trace route command can help isolate the source of the problem.

To run a trace route test, complete these steps:

1. Use the MS-DOS Prompt command in the Start ➤ Programs menu to open a DOS window.

2. At the C:\Windows> prompt, type **tracert <*target*>**. In place of *target*, type the address of the distant system. A trace route report will appear in the DOS window.

In many cases, your connection will pass through one or more backbone networks between your own connection to the Internet and your ultimate destination. For example, the tracert report in Figure 18.21 shows a route from a PC in Seattle to The WELL, near San Francisco. In this case, the connection passes through backbone networks operated by Sprintlink and AlterNet.

Tracert steps through the connection route, one step at a time. For each step, it shows the amount of time needed to reach that router, in milliseconds. If an intermediate router, or a connection between two intermediate routers fails, tracert will not display any steps beyond that point in the route. If that happens, you can assume that the failed site is the reason that you are unable to connect to your intended destination.

Obtaining Other Internet Applications

With the exception of telnet and e-mail through Microsoft Network, the Internet tools included with Windows 95 are pretty primitive. They're all character-based programs that use the klunky old DOS command line. If you plan to use the Internet more than once every three or four months, you really ought to replace them with some of the Windows-based graphic applications that are available from several software archives on the Internet. You can use the Windows FTP program to obtain another, easier-to-use FTP program, and then use that program to download other Winsock-compatible Internet application programs. If you prefer, you can use the Internet Tools in Microsoft Plus (see Chapter 32) or one of the commercial all-in-one

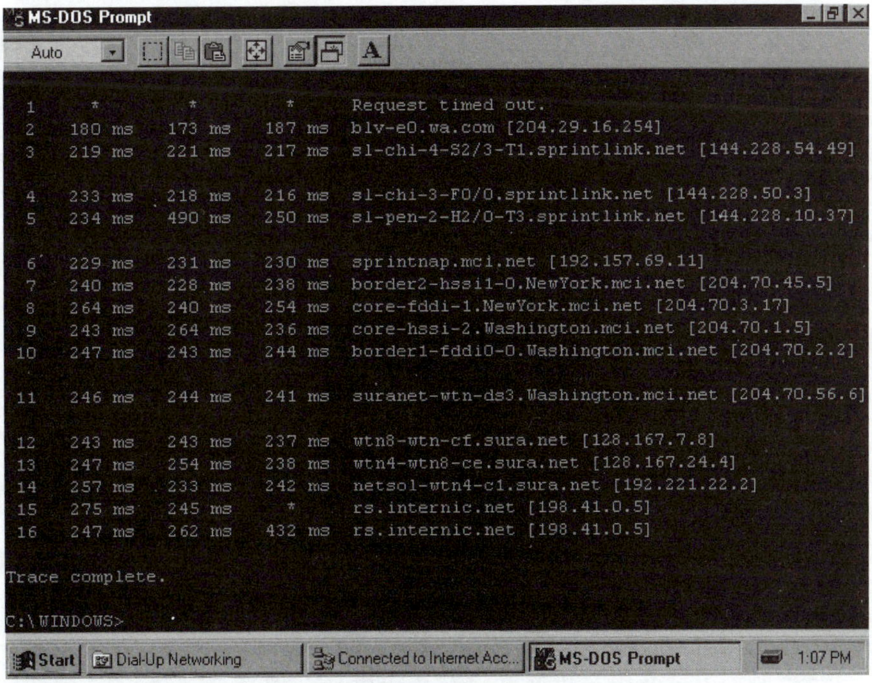

Figure 18.21   *The* tracert *command produces a list of intermediate routers between your PC and an Internet host.*

Part
3

Managing
Communications

Internet-access products, such as Internet in a Box or SuperHighway Access.

Winsock FTP is a free FTP application that is a lot easier to use than the one included with Windows 95. Figure 18.22 shows the main Winsock FTP window. You can obtain it via anonymous FTP from `ftp.usma.edu`, in the directory `/Pub/Msdos/Winsock.files`. The file is called `ws_ftp.zip`. You'll need an unzip program such as PK-Zip to uncompress the file after you download it. Winsock FTP includes a list of other FTP archives that contain additional Winsock applications.

A few *whiteboarding* programs are available, which let you and other users exchange drawn or hand-printed ideas in real time in a manner similar to using the whiteboard at your company's conference center. When a user draws on his or her screen, the other's screens are all updated to show the new addition. Typically, each connected user can have a different color "marker," and pictures or documents can be loaded into the whiteboard when needed.

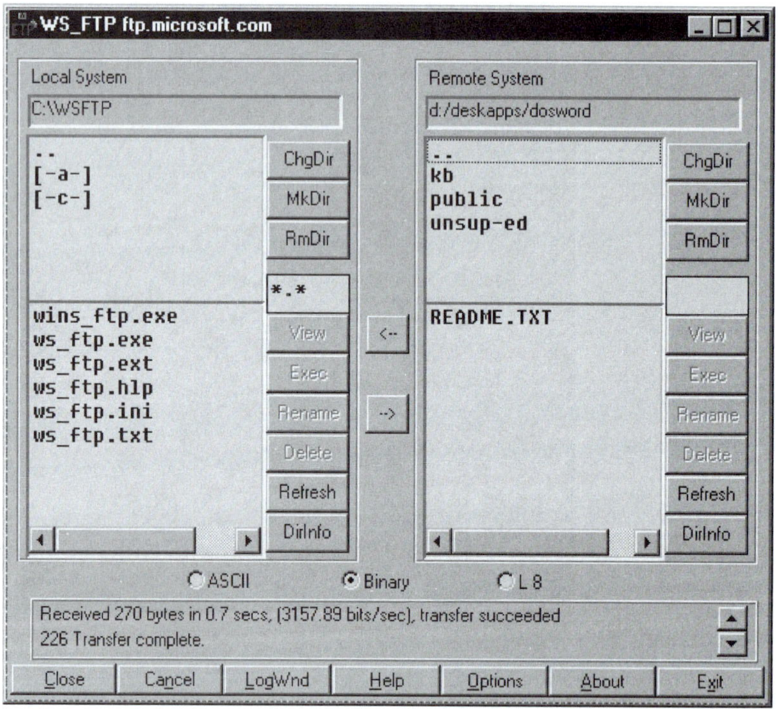

Figure 18.22 *Winsock FTP is a great improvement over the FTP utility supplied with Windows 95.*

If you literally want to chat across the network, try VocalTec's IPhone (see Figure 18.23) or Camelot's Digiphone. These products let you talk with anyone else over a TCP/IP connection and require only the software, almost any sound card, and an inexpensive microphone. The amazing thing about these products (aside from the fact that they actually work) is their relatively low bandwidth; for example, you can be chatting with someone while simultaneously viewing Web pages with Mosaic or Netscape over even a 14.4K Internet connection.

Taking the above ideas a step further, video-conferencing applications—such as CU-SeeMe and VidPhone—let you send still or motion video to other users. Besides the software, you will need either a camcorder (usually on a tripod) or a small designed-for-videoconferencing camera that perches on your monitor. In addition, you will need a video capture card, typically used to convert video from a VCR or camcorder into a signal you can display on your computer monitor, which can also be used to create movie or graphics files. For less-than-full-motion video, even a 14.4K modem connection can be used to send a few frames a second; on a faster network connection, these video-conferencing applications can meet or exceed movie-quality video.

Another relatively new arrival in the multimedia-over-TCP/IP category is RealAudio. This product gives you the equivalent of AM-radio–quality continuous (but one-way) sound across a TCP/IP connection. Currently the Deutsche Welle (national radio of Germany), Radio Canada, a few U.S. radio stations, and other individuals are experimenting with simulcasting parts of their normal radio broadcasts over

Figure 18.23 *Internet Phone (IPhone) from VocalTec lets you communicate with voice over any TCP/IP connection.*

the Internet. Again, the bandwidth is low enough that you can receive their broadcasts even over a 14.4K audio connection.

As you can see, the Internet is a virtual hotbed of new multimedia and client-server technology, and by adopting TCP/IP as your network protocol, you can ensure easy expansion into a wide-area network, plus have the freedom to assimilate Internet media technologies to your own network, even if you decide not to connect your company's network to the Internet.

Coming Attractions: Accessing the Internet through Microsoft Network

It won't be available until the end of 1995 (or later), but Microsoft has announced that it plans to offer full Internet access through the Microsoft Network, including a licensed version of NCSA Mosaic. This version of Mosaic won't look exactly like the screen in Figure 18.24, but it will provide a similar set of graphical Internet navigation tools, including browsers for FTP, Gopher, and the World Wide Web.

The advance publicity for the MSN Internet service describes it as "seamless access," which suggests that the user interface will be an extension of the Microsoft Network architecture. You can expect to see Internet tools in Home Base and Internet resources in other MSN screens and menus. It won't be necessary to find a separate Internet service provider because an Internet connection will be closely integrated with MSN.

Obviously, this kind of Internet access will be a great deal easier to use than the primitive TCP/IP tools bundled with the earliest release of Windows 95, but because Microsoft hasn't revealed how much going to charge for Internet access, it's too soon to know if MSN will be a better deal than any of the other ways to connect to the Internet. In the meantime, there are about half a dozen shrink-wrapped products and several shareware programs available today that provide easier Internet access than the tools in Windows 95.

Microsoft also includes a World Wide Web browser and a mail reader that uses Exchange in the add-on Microsoft Plus package (see Chapter 32).

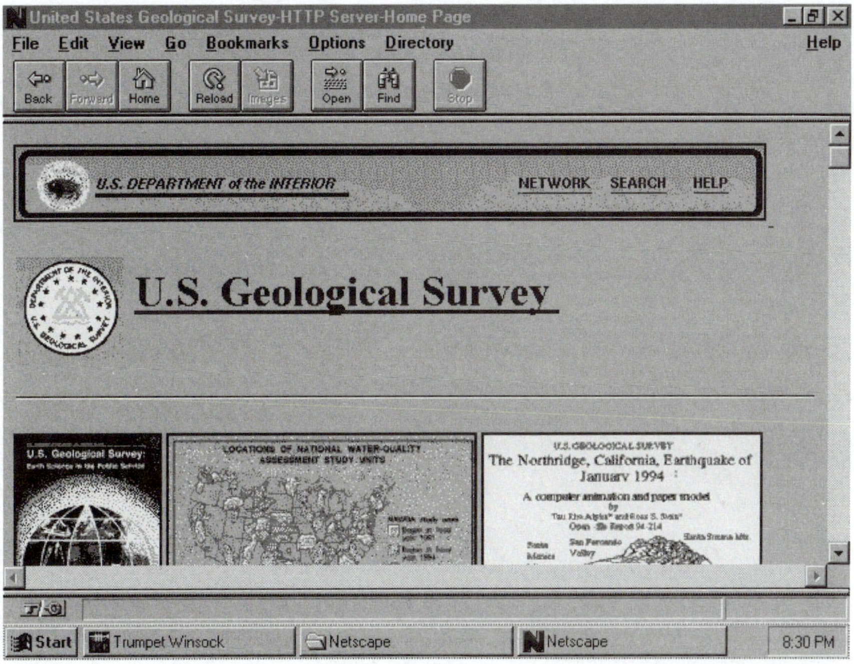

Figure 18.24   Microsoft Network will eventually include an Internet browser similar to this one.

The Internet can connect you to a huge and growing number of resources, including thousands of programs and data files, newsgroup discussions on almost every imaginable subject, and much more. For a more detailed guide to exploring the Internet, check out *Access the Internet!* (Sybex, 1995) or *The Internet Roadmap* (Sybex, 1994).

The Supplied Applications

4

Chapter 19

Using WordPad for Simple Word Processing

FEATURING

Creating a document

Entering and editing your text

Inserting the date or time in a document

Formatting paragraphs and characters

Adding graphics to your WordPad document

Saving your work

Printing your document

f you're like most people, you'll end up using Windows for writing more than for any other task. Writing letters, memos, and reports with your computer is much more efficient—and much more fun—than banging them out on a typewriter. To get you started, Windows 95 comes with a simple yet capable *word processor*, called WordPad, for editing and printing text documents.

WordPad lacks the frills of the hefty word-processing programs like Microsoft Word for Windows, WordPerfect, or Ami Pro, but it works fine for most everyday writing chores. WordPad gives you all the essential tools you'll need for editing word-processing documents of virtually any length; it is limited only by the capacity of your disk drive. Like the high-end programs, it even lets you move text around with the mouse, a feature called drag-and-drop editing. WordPad accepts, displays, and prints graphics pasted to it from the Clipboard; it also lets you edit those graphics right in your document using OLE (see Chapter 6 for more about OLE). WordPad may not offer all the bells and whistles of the market leaders, but it's no toy—and besides, the price is right.

This chapter begins with a tutorial that gives you the opportunity to learn how to create and edit a word-processing document. Along the way, you can experiment with the major procedures involved in a simple Windows-based word processor. Many of the techniques discussed in this chapter are applicable to other Windows programs as well.

After entering and editing your document, I'll discuss the various formatting features you can easily apply to your documents. Included in the discussion is information on how to

▶ format individual characters with font, style, and size alterations

▶ format paragraphs by changing line spacing, indents, and margins

▶ set the tab stops to aid you in making tables

▶ quickly search for and replace specific text

▶ include headers and footers

▶ paginate your document correctly

▶ incorporate and edit graphics

▶ copy text between two WordPad documents

▶ save and print files

TIPS FOR WINDOWS 3.1 USERS

If you have ever used Windows Write, the word processor included with earlier versions of Windows, you know how crude it seems compared to WordPad. But while WordPad would clobber Write in a beauty contest and WordPad's fancier button bars make it easier to use, Write actually has several important features that WordPad lacks. If your word-processing needs don't justify buying a high-end program such as WordPerfect or Microsoft Word, you should consider keeping Write handy in case you need these capabilities.

Present in Write but missing from WordPad are:

▶ Repeating headers and footers for information you want to display on every page. Write lets you insert a page-number marker that automatically numbers each page for you.

▶ Full paragraph justification (so that text is flush on both the left and right sides of a paragraph).

▶ Double-spacing and $1^1/_2$-spacing for paragraphs (WordPad permits only single-spaced paragraphs).

▶ Decimal tabs, allowing you to line up columns of decimal numbers.

▶ Superscript and subscript character formats.

▶ A *Regular* character format command, allowing you to remove all styles (bold, italic, underlining, super- and subscripts) from selected text with a single command.

▶ A *page break* command, allowing you to force text that follows to the top of a new page, regardless of how you edit previous text (useful for creating documents with sections).

▶ The ability to find text that matches the capitalization (case) of your entry in the Find dialog box and the ability to find text that is found only if it occurs as a separate word (not as part of a longer word).

▶ The ability to search for paragraph markers, page breaks, and tabs with the Find command. Among other uses, this lets you reformat DOS-style plain text documents much more easily.

By the way, you should know that although WordPad can open Write documents, items that WordPad doesn't recognize are converted or discarded. For example, WordPad converts decimal tabs to ordinary tabs, and it simply discards headers or footers.

Creating a Document

To start a new WordPad document, begin from the Taskbar. Choose Programs ➤ Accessories ➤ WordPad. Within a few moments, the WordPad window will appear with a new, empty document window open for you. If the WordPad window isn't already maximized, maximize it so it fills the whole screen. Your screen should now look like that shown in Figure 19.1.

Getting Help in WordPad

Before going any further, it bears repeating that on-screen help is always a mouse-click or key press away while you're working in WordPad. To activate WordPad Help, press F1 or choose Help ➤ Help Topics. When the standard Windows Help application appears, choose the Contents, Index, or Find tabs, then locate the topic you need help with and double-click on it.

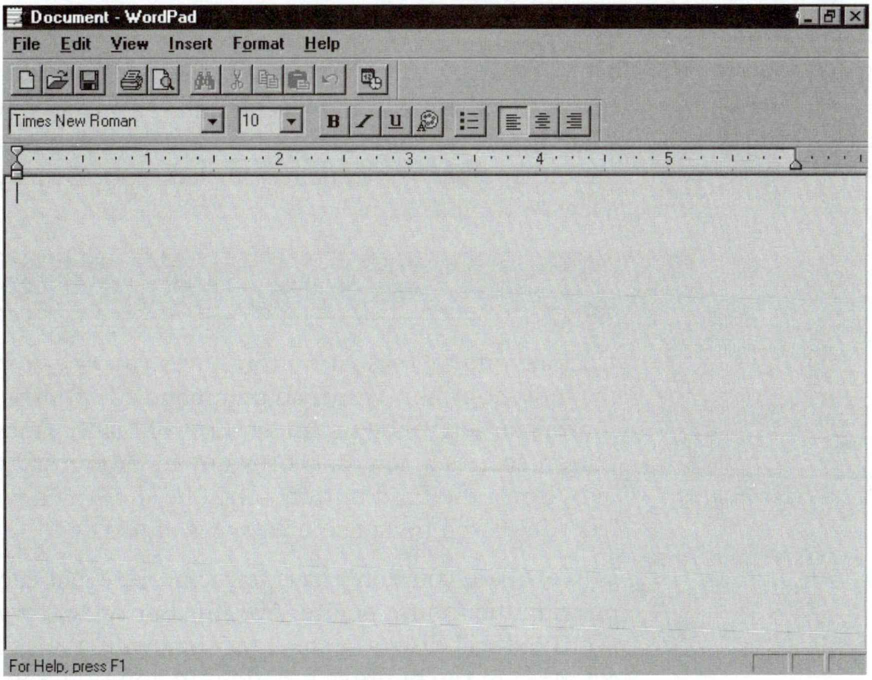

Figure 19.1   The initial WordPad screen with no text in the document

You can also get help for any item in a dialog box by using the right mouse button. Click over the item with the right button to pop up the *What's this?* button. Click on the button to display a short help message.

Finally, WordPad displays brief help messages when you pass the mouse pointer over certain items on the screen. These include menu choices and the buttons on the Toolbar and Status Bar (those rows of buttons at the top of the screen).

Working with the WordPad Window

There are several things to notice on your screen. As usual, up at the top of the WordPad window you see the menu and Title bars. The menu bar offers options for writing, editing, and formatting text.

Referring to your screen or to Figure 19.1, notice that the Title Bar shows *Document* as the file name because you haven't named the document yet.

The Toolbar

Just below the menu bar you should see a row of buttons, each with a small graphical icon. This is the *Toolbar,* shown below. (If you don't see the Toolbar, someone has turned it off. Display it by choosing View ➤ Toolbar.)

Clicking on the Toolbar buttons gives you one-step access to some of the most common WordPad commands. For instance, the first button (on the far left) shows a single sheet of blank paper. Clicking on this button creates a new, blank document. About halfway across the row of buttons, the Find button—the one showing a pair of binoculars—lets you search for specific passages of text.

In WordPad, you don't have to memorize what each button does. Just position the mouse pointer over the button and wait a few seconds. WordPad will display a small text box with a one- or two-word description of the button's function. In addition, the Status Bar at the bottom of the screen displays a longer help message.

Displaying and Hiding Control Bars with the View Menu

WordPad offers several other bar-like sets of controls and readouts to speed your work and give you quick information on your document. The View menu lets you display or remove each of these control bars individually. If the item isn't currently visible, choose its name from the View menu to display it. Do exactly the same to remove the item if it's already displayed (if, for example, you want more space for editing text).

Notice that when you display the View menu, you'll see a check mark to the left of each control bar that is currently visible. If there's no check mark, the corresponding bar is currently hidden.

The Format Bar

Like the Toolbar, the *Format Bar* offers a set of graphical buttons, but it also contains (at the far left) two drop-down list boxes for selecting font and type size:

| Courier New ▼ | 10 ▼ | **B** | *I* | U | 🎨 | ☰ | | ☰ ☰ ☰ |

All of the Format Bar's controls affect aspects of your document's appearance. Besides the font and type-size controls, various buttons let you set such characteristics as type style (such as boldface and italics) and paragraph alignment (such as left aligned or centered).

The Ruler and the Status Bar

The *ruler*, another control bar available from the View menu, lets you see and modify paragraph indents and tab stops. See *Formatting Paragraphs* below for instructions on working with the ruler. The *Status Bar* is a thin strip at the very bottom of the WordPad window. It displays messages from WordPad on the left. On the right are indicators showing when the Caps Lock and Num Lock keys are depressed.

Repositioning the Toolbar and Format Bar

You can reposition the Toolbar and Format Bar if you like. Just position the mouse pointer over any part of the bar that's not a button and drag the bar where you want it. If you drag the bar to the bottom of the WordPad window, the bar will merge with the lower portion of the window. You can also drag the Toolbar to the right side of the window so it becomes a vertical strip fused with the right window edge (this won't work with the Format Bar because the list boxes for typeface and size are too wide to fit in the narrow strip). If you drag either bar into the document area or outside the WordPad window altogether, it becomes a separate moveable window with its own title bar (as shown in Figure 19.2).

Entering Text

Notice the main document area of the WordPad window. Because you haven't typed in anything yet, the only item to look at here is the blinking cursor in the upper-left corner. This *insertion point* indicates the place where new text will appear when you type.

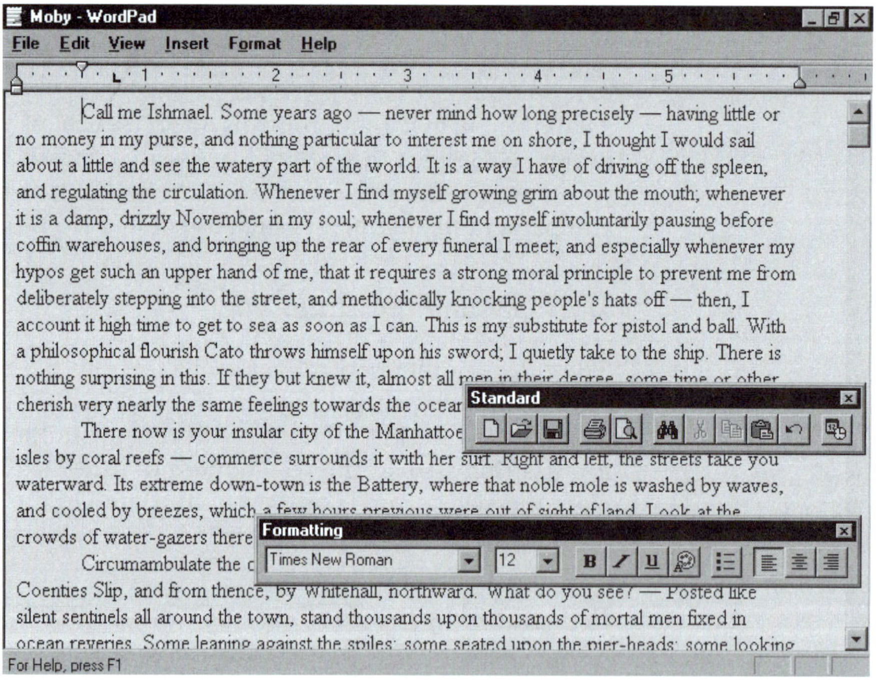

Figure 19.2   *Here's how the Toolbar and Format Bar look when you "tear" them from their standard locations, thereby turning them into separate, moveable windows.*

Now begin creating a document. Of course, you're free to type in anything you want. However, to establish a consistent text to refer to later on in this chapter, try entering the following text, a hypothetical news story. (For later steps in the tutorial, keep the two misspelled words, *Pizza* and *sight*, as they are.) If you are at all unfamiliar with word processors, first read the steps that follow this text:

NEWS FLASH

Society for Anachronistic Sciences
1000 Edsel Lane
Piltdown, PA 19042

The Society for Anachronistic Sciences announced its controversial findings today at a press conference held in the city of Pisa, Italy. Pizza was not chosen as the sight for the conference because of its celebrated position in the annals of Western scientific history. The Society has made public its annual press conferences for well over 300 years and, as usual, nothing new was revealed. According to its members, this is a comforting fact and a social service in an age when everything else seems to change.

Begin entering the text into your new file, following the steps outlined here. If you make mistakes while you are typing, use the Backspace key to back up and fix them. If you don't see an error until you have typed past it, leave it for now—you'll learn how to fix any mistakes later:

1. Type **NEWS FLASH** on the first line.

2. Next, press Enter twice to move down a couple of lines to prepare for typing the address. Notice that pressing Enter is necessary to add new blank lines in a word-processing document. Pressing the ↓ key will not move the cursor down a line at this point or create new lines; you will only hear an error beep from your computer if you try this.

> **TIP** Don't double-space between sentences as you would with a typewriter. WordPad will automatically add enough space to clearly separate each sentence. If you double-space, your text will print with unsightly gaps between sentences.

3. Enter the first line of the address, then press Enter to move down to the next line. Repeat this process for the last two lines of the address.

4. Press Enter twice to put in another blank line.

5. Begin entering the body of the story. Don't forget to leave in the spelling mistakes so we can fix them later on. When you get to the end of a line, just keep typing. You shouldn't press Enter because WordPad will automatically move text that overflows to the next line for you. This is called *word wrapping*. All you have to do is keep typing—and leave only one space between sentences, not two.

When you've finished entering the sample text, the WordPad window should look something like Figure 19.3.

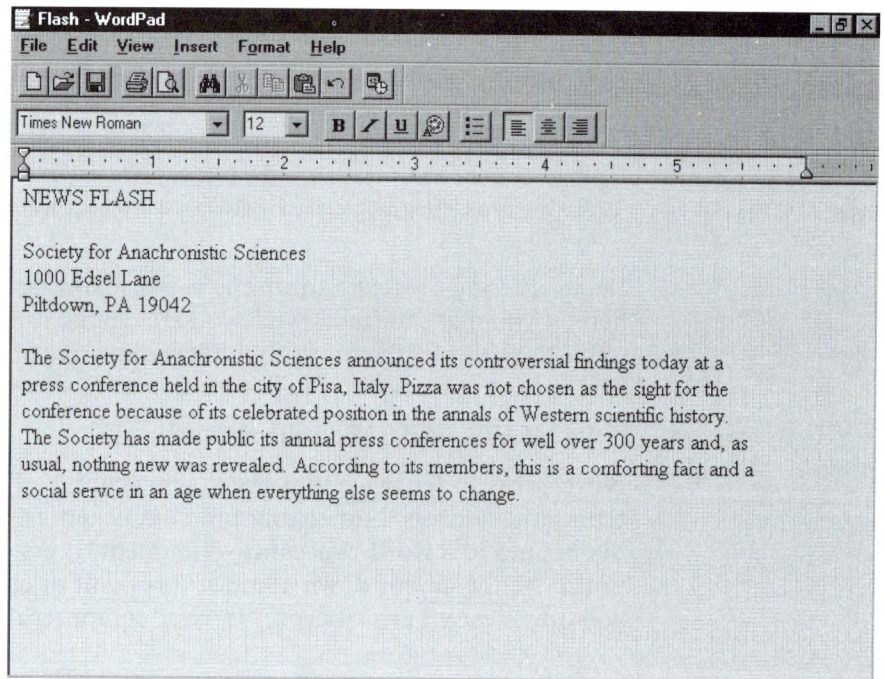

Figure 19.3   The WordPad window after you've entered the sample text

Editing Your Text

The first step in editing is learning how to move around in the text. If you followed the instructions above, you moved the cursor only by pressing Enter and, perhaps, by pressing Backspace to delete a character or two after you had mistyped. For the most part, you left the cursor alone and it moved along by itself as you typed. But now you'll want to move up and down to fix misspelled words and make other changes. After all, it's the ability to move around freely in your document and make changes at will that makes a word processor so much more capable than a typewriter.

Moving the Cursor

The *cursor* marks the position where letters appear when you type—the *insertion point*. Editing your text involves moving the insertion point to the correct location and then inserting text, removing words, fixing misspellings, or marking blocks of text for moving, copying, or deletion.

The easiest way to move the cursor is just to point and click. When the mouse pointer is over the document window, it looks like a large letter *I* or a steel beam (this shape is often called the *I-beam pointer*). Move the I-beam pointer so that the vertical line is over the place in the text where you want to begin editing or typing. When you click, the blinking insertion point will jump from wherever it was to this new position.

NOTE   After positioning the cursor with the mouse, don't forget to click; otherwise, you'll end up making changes in the wrong place.

You can also use the arrow keys to move the cursor. This is often quicker than using the mouse when you only need to move the cursor by a few characters or lines.

Here are some exercises in cursor movement using both the mouse and the keyboard:

1. Move the mouse pointer to the second line of the story and click immediately to the left of the *t* in the word *sight*.

2. Press → and hold it down for a few seconds. Notice that the cursor moves one character to the right, pauses briefly, and then moves rapidly to the right. When it gets to the end of the first line, it wraps around to the start of the second line, continuing to the right from that point. Now press ← and hold it down. The cursor moves steadily to the left until it reaches the beginning of the line, then jumps to the end of the previous line. When the cursor gets to the beginning of the document, your computer starts to beep because the cursor can't go any farther.

3. Press ↓ to move the cursor down a line. If you hold down the key, the cursor will keep moving down until it reaches the last line in the text. (If a document has more text than will fit in the window, the text will scroll up a line at a time until the document end is reached.) To move up one line at a time, press ↑. Again, the text will scroll when you get to the top of the window until the cursor reaches the very first line.

4. Press Ctrl-→. Each press of the arrow key moves the cursor ahead one word. Ctrl-← moves it a word at a time in the other direction.

5. Press Ctrl-Home. The cursor jumps to the very beginning of the document. To jump to the end of the text, press Ctrl-End.

Because writing relies heavily on the keyboard, WordPad provides several keyboard combinations that can be used to move the insertion point. These are listed in Table 19.1.

Key combination	Moves the insertion point...
↑	Up one line
↓	Down one line
←	Left one character
→	Right one character
Ctrl-←	Left one word
Ctrl-→	Right one word
Ctrl-Home	Beginning of document
Ctrl-End	End of document
Ctrl-PgUp	Top left of current window
Ctrl-PgDn	Bottom right of current window

Table 19.1   Keyboard Combinations for Moving the Insertion Point

Scrolling in the Document

Like other Windows programs, WordPad gives you a variety of ways to scroll through your document when the entire text doesn't fit in the window. Depending on the size of your WordPad window, the sample press release you've typed in probably does fit.

With the mouse, you scroll using the scroll bars. You can also use the arrow (cursor) keys to move right and left a character at a time or up and down a line at a time. Use the PgUp and PgDn keys to scroll your text a screen at a time.

Scrolling with the Mouse

When your entire document won't fit in the WordPad window, scroll bars appear in the work area along the right edge or at the bottom. A vertical scroll bar indicates the text is *longer* than the window, a horizontal bar means the text is *wider*. Because the sample document you've entered in this chapter fits in the maximized WordPad window, scroll bars will only be visible if you make the window smaller, as shown in Figure 19.4.

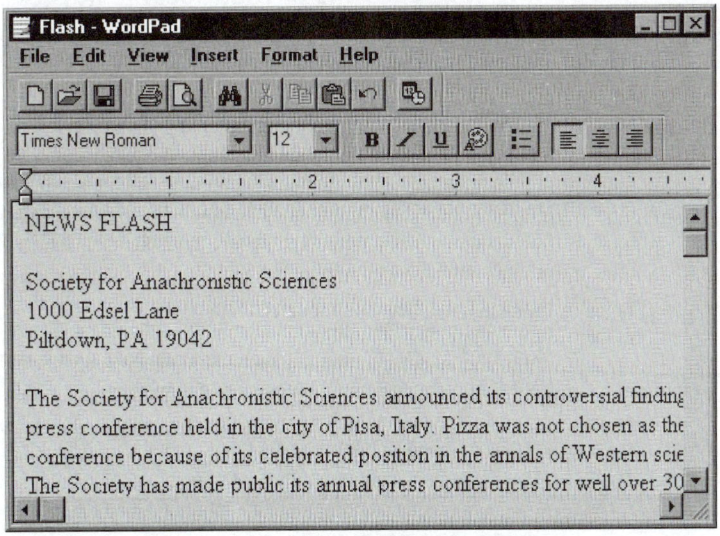

Figure 19.4   *This resized window has both horizontal and vertical scroll bars.*

Consider the vertical scroll bar to be a sort of measuring stick for your document, with the top of the bar representing the beginning of your document and the bottom of the bar the end. The elevator, that rectangular object that you slide along the scroll bar, shows you the relative position of the current window's text within the document.

By dragging the elevator to the approximate relative position you want to scroll to, you can get close to your desired spot quickly. You can also scroll by clicking in the scroll bar above or below the elevator.

The horizontal scroll bar works the same way as the vertical bar but is only useful if your document is more than a page wide.

Scrolling with the Keyboard

Scrolling with the keyboard can be more efficient than using the mouse because you don't have to take your hands off the keyboard.

1. Hold down the ↑ or ↓ key to move one line at a time. When you reach the top or bottom of the window, the text scrolls a line at a time as long as you hold down the key.

2. Press the PgUp key. Pressing PgUp moves you up one window toward the beginning of your document. Pressing PgDn has the opposite effect.

Making Selections in WordPad

Much of editing with a word processor centers around manipulating blocks of text. A *block* is a section of consecutive text characters (letters, numbers, punctuation, and so on). Blocks can be of any length. Many of the commands in Windows programs use this idea of manipulating blocks of information.

You must *select* a block before you can work with it. When you select a block, it becomes the center of attention to WordPad. As shown in Figure 19.5, WordPad highlights the block. Until you deselect it, WordPad treats the block differently than the rest of the document. For example, some menu commands will affect the selection and nothing else.

There are two main ways to select a text block: with the mouse, by dragging over the area you want to select, and with the keyboard, by holding down the Shift key while you move the cursor. We'll cover

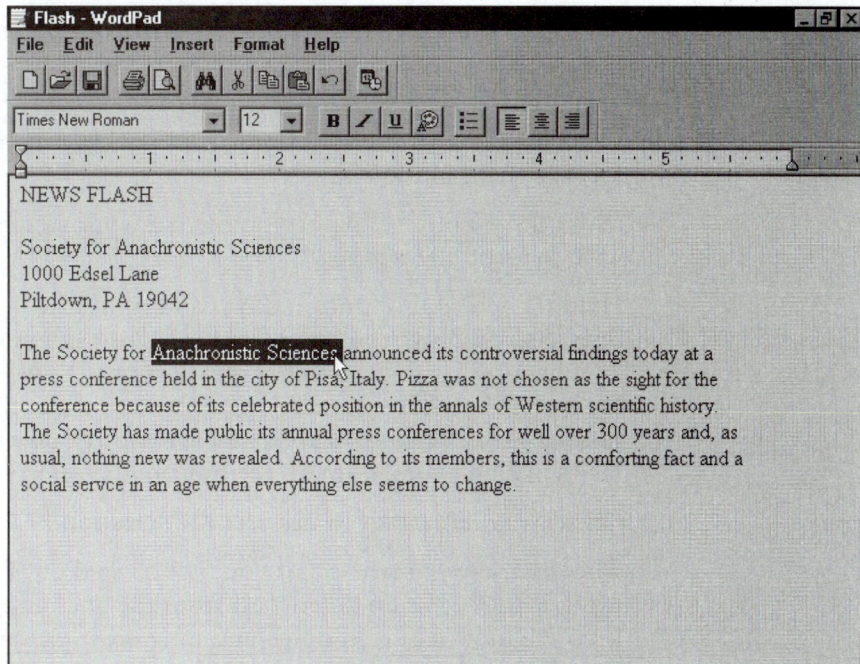

Figure 19.5   *The highlighted passage is a selected block of text.*

both methods in detail in a moment. You *deselect* when you click elsewhere, select elsewhere with the mouse, or move the cursor after letting up on the Shift key.

Once you've selected a block, be careful about the keys you press. If you type **A**, for example, the text of the whole block (the *selection*) will be replaced by the letter *A*. If this happens accidentally, choose Edit ➤ Undo or click on the Undo button on the Toolbar *before doing anything else*, and your text will be returned to its previous state.

After selecting a block of text, you can manipulate it in any number of ways: you can cut or copy it, change its font size, alter the paragraph formatting, and so forth. Try the following exercises to get the hang of selecting blocks.

Selecting an Arbitrary Text Area with the Mouse

Selection is particularly intuitive and simple with the mouse. Try this:

1. Deselect any possible selections you may have made already by clicking anywhere in the text.

2. Move the pointer to the beginning of a word somewhere (you may have to scroll the window).

3. Hold the left mouse button down and move the pointer down several lines. As you move the mouse, the selection extends. You'll notice that as soon as the pointer touches any part of each word in turn, the entire word becomes selected (unless someone has changed the relevant setting—see *Selecting Measurement Units and Controlling Word Selection* below). When you let up on the button, the selection is completed.

4. Click anywhere again to deselect the selection.

   The *anchor point* is the point you first clicked on. Dragging downward extends the selection downward from the anchor point. If you were to keep the mouse button down and drag *above* the anchor point, the selection would extend from the anchor point upward.

Selecting an Arbitrary Text Area with the Shift Key

You can also use the Shift key in combination with the arrow keys or the mouse to select an arbitrary amount of text:

1. Deselect anything you have already selected.

2. Move the cursor to the beginning of any word in the first paragraph. Now press Shift-→. The selection advances one letter with each press (unless you hold the key down too long, in which case it moves by itself and selects several letters).

3. Press Shift-↑ five times. Notice that as you move up past the anchor point, the selection reverses, moving upward in the text.

4. Press Shift-Ctrl-→. As the cursor jumps a word to the right, WordPad removes the selection highlighting from the characters it passes over.

5. Release the keys and click somewhere to deselect.

6. Click on the first word in the second paragraph (with the method you're testing now, this sets a new anchor point there).

7. Hold down the Shift key.

8. Click on a word in the middle of the paragraph. This changes the selection: It now extends from the new anchor point to the point where you clicked.

Selecting a Word or a Paragraph at a Time

Often you'll want to select a word or paragraph quickly, either to delete it or to change some aspect of it, such as its font size. You can do this easily by double-clicking (to select a word) or triple-clicking (for a paragraph). If you keep clicking rapidly, the selection alternates between the whole paragraph and the word under the pointer.

Selecting a Line or Series of Lines

There's a shortcut for selecting an entire line or quickly selecting a series of entire lines:

1. Move the mouse pointer into the left margin. It changes into an arrow pointing to the top right. This margin is called the *selection area*.

2. Position the pointer to the left of the first line of the first paragraph and click the mouse to select the entire line.

3. Starting from the same place, hold down the mouse button and drag the pointer down along the left margin. This selects each line the pointer passes.

Selecting an Entire Paragraph: An Alternative Method

Here's another shortcut for selecting an entire paragraph:

1. Move the cursor into the selection area (left margin) next to the first paragraph.

2. Double-click. The entire paragraph will be highlighted.

Holding down the Shift key while you drag the pointer in the margin selects additional paragraphs.

Selecting an Entire Sentence

If you need to change a particular sentence in its entirety, you can do so easily:

1. Hold down the Ctrl key.

2. Click anywhere in the document. The whole sentence containing the location you clicked on will be selected.

Selecting an Entire Document

Sometimes you'll want to select the whole document. This can be useful for changing the font size or type of all the text or changing other attributes, as discussed below. You have several choices for selecting an entire document. From the menu, you can choose Edit ➤ Select All. But try these simpler methods as well:

▶ Move the pointer into the selection area (the left margin of the document window). Hold down Ctrl and click the mouse. The entire document will be selected. Click anywhere in the text to deselect it.

▶ Move the pointer back to the selection area. This time, triple-click to select the whole document. Again, deselect it by clicking elsewhere.

▶ The keyboard shortcut for selecting the whole document is Ctrl-A.

Making Some Changes to the Text

Now that you know how to get around and select portions of text, you can begin to correct some of the typos in your letter.

Deleting Letters

Let's start with the second sentence of the first paragraph, where the word *site* is misspelled as *sight*:

1. Position the cursor between the *i* and *g* in *sight*.

2. Press Del. This removes the misplaced *g*. Notice also that the space closed up where the *g* was when you deleted the letter, pulling the letters to the left to close the gap.

3. Press Del again to remove the *h*.

4. Move the cursor one character to the right and add the *e*.

Notice that the line opened up to let the *e* in. Unlike on a typewritten page, lines on a computer screen are flexible, letting you insert the letter—in fact, so flexible that you may have noticed that WordPad re-wraps all the lines of the paragraph almost instantly as you insert text.

Many simple errors can be fixed using the Del or Backspace key. But suppose you wanted to delete an entire word, sentence, or paragraph. You could do this by moving to the beginning or end of the section you wanted to erase and then holding down Del or Backspace, respectively, until the key repeated and erased all the words, letter by letter. But this is a slow and potentially risky method. If you're not careful, you may well erase more than you intended to. This where selecting a text block comes in.

Deleting Words

For our second change, find the word *not* in the second sentence, the one that now begins "Pizza was not chosen..." So the paragraph makes more sense, delete the *not* as follows:

1. Select the word *not* with one of the techniques you learned earlier.

2. You have several choices for removing the word. You can press Del or Backspace to remove the offending word permanently. Choosing Edit ➤ Clear has the same effect, it just takes a little longer.

TIP   If you delete a word accidentally with any of these techniques, you can retrieve it by choosing Edit ➤ Undo or clicking on the Undo button before you make any other changes. And if you want to remove a word but save it on the Clipboard for later use, you would cut it—you'll learn how to cut se-lected blocks a bit later.

But what if you want to *replace* a word, not just delete it? WordPad gives you a shortcut method for doing just that.

1. Select the misspelled *Pizza* in the first sentence.

2. With *Pizza* highlighted, type in **Pisa**. Notice that as soon as you type the first letter, *P*, it replaces the entire selection. This saves the extra

step of pressing Del or choosing Clear from the Edit menu. (You may have to add a space after the word, depending on how you selected *Pizza*.)

All of this may seem like a lot of work just to change a few letters, but for larger selections you will find it's worth the effort.

Inserting Letters

You can insert any number of letters, words, or paragraphs wherever you want within a document. This is called *inserting* because as you type new characters, they appear within the existing text, which is pushed to the right as you type.

Some word processors allow you to deactivate insertion in favor of *overwriting*, where newly typed letters replace the old ones instead of pushing them to the right. WordPad does not let you do this. The advantage is that you will never accidentally type over some text you want to keep. The disadvantage is that you will have to take action to delete unwanted text.

TIP If you need to insert characters that aren't available on your keyboard—such as ™, ©, or ¥—use the Character Map accessory, covered in Chapter 22.

Moving Selected Blocks

The editing process often involves moving large portions of text, such as sentences and paragraphs, within a document. Rather than inserting a block of text by retyping it, you can pick it up and move it from one place to another with the Cut, Copy, and Paste commands covered here. And WordPad also gives you a snazzy drag-and-drop method for moving text around with the mouse.

Moving Blocks with Cut and Paste Commands

Here's an example of the Paste command that will reverse the order of the first two paragraphs in our letter:

1. Move to the top of the document.

2. Select the "News Flash" line (this is a one-line paragraph) with what-
    ever technique you prefer—and carefully select the blank line immedi-
    ately below the paragraph, too, because you want a blank line between
    the paragraphs after the move. This second line is also a *paragraph* as
    far as WordPad is concerned. If you're selecting by dragging, just drag
    the mouse a little further down. If you double-clicked in the margin
    to select the first paragraph, press Shift to retain the paragraph selec-
    tion and then double-click to the left of the blank line. You'll know the
    blank line is selected when a thin strip at the left margin becomes
    highlighted (this is the normally invisible *paragraph mark* associated
    with the blank line):

NEWS FLASH

Society for Anachronistic Sciences
1000 Edsel Lane
Piltdown, PA 19042

TIP   Every paragraph has a paragraph mark. Paragraph attributes such as
alignment, tab settings, and margins are contained in it. Copying this mark
is an easy way of copying attributes from one place to another.

---

3. Now it's time to cut the block. You have three choices: You can choose
    Cut from the Edit menu, click on the Cut button on the Tool-
    bar, or press Ctrl-X on the keyboard.

4. Move the insertion point to the place where you want to insert the
    paragraph, which happens to be just before the *T* of the word *The* in
    the first main paragraph.

5. Paste the paragraph back into your document. You can click on the
    Paste button on the Toolbar (the one that shows a small piece
    of paper and a clipboard), choose Edit ➤ Paste, or press Ctrl-V.

Sometimes after moving paragraphs around, you may have to do a little adjusting, such as inserting or deleting a line or some spaces. You
can always insert a line with Enter. If you have extra blank lines after
a move, you can delete them by putting the insertion point on the

first space of a blank line (the far-left margin) and pressing the Backspace key.

Just a reminder: once you've placed text (or any other information) on the Clipboard, you can reuse it as many times as you like because it stays on the Clipboard until you replace it with new information by using the Cut or Copy commands.

Moving Blocks Using the Right Mouse Button

In WordPad, clicking the right mouse button over the document pops up a small menu offering immediate access to the most common editing commands, as shown in Figure 19.6.

Here's how to move the paragraph back with this method:

1. Select the paragraph again.

2. Click the right mouse button anywhere over the selected block. The pop-up menu shown in Figure 19.6 appears.

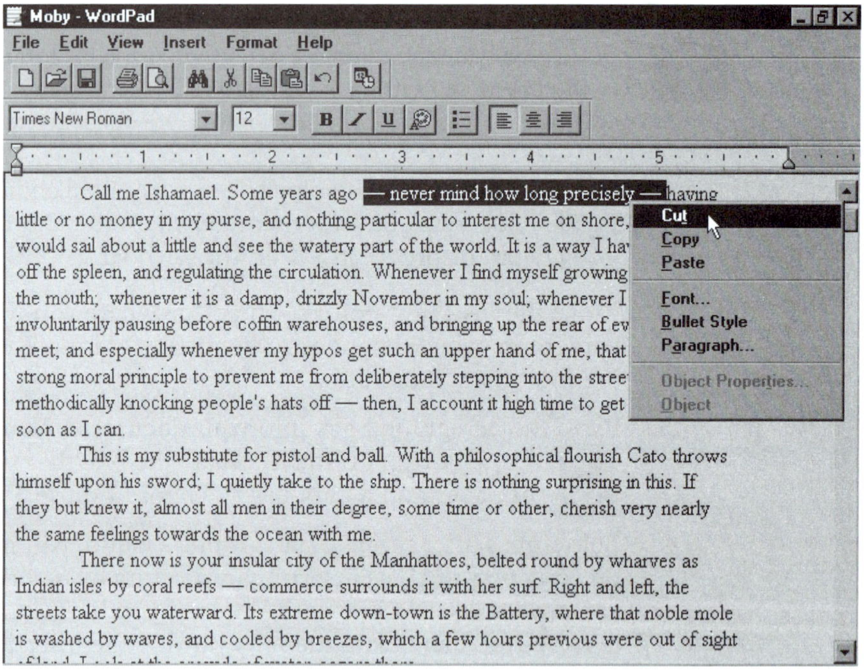

Figure 19.6 *WordPad's pop-up menu, displayed when you click the right mouse button*

3. Choose Cut from the pop-up menu.

4. Position the pointer where you want the text to go and click, again with the right button. From the pop-up menu, choose Paste.

Copying Blocks of Text

There are times when you want to move existing text to a new location without deleting the original. That's when you need the Copy command. After selecting a block of text, use Copy instead of Cut to place a copy of the passage on the Clipboard. Then move the cursor to the spot where you want the copy and Paste it in. As usual, you have several alternatives for copying a selected block to the clipboard. You can

▶ click on the Copy button, the one that shows two overlapping pieces of paper

▶ click the right mouse button, then choose Copy from the pop-up menu

▶ choose Edit ➤ Copy

▶ press Ctrl-C

After you've copied the text to the Clipboard, you paste it in just as you would when moving a text block.

Moving Blocks with Drag and Drop

WordPad gives you yet another method for moving a block of text within a document. With drag-and-drop editing, you *pick up* the block with the mouse and *drop* it into place without ever having to fuss with menus, buttons, or keyboard commands.

This time, move the third full paragraph in the story to the very end of the document. Here's how:

1. Select the paragraph.

2. Click anywhere within the selection and hold the button down.

3. Very slowly (just for this exercise), begin to move the pointer while holding the button down. Notice that the pointer becomes a white arrow with a dotted line at its tip and a small dotted rectangle at its base as soon as you begin to move it.

4. Move the pointer so that the dotted line is over the very end of the document (when you get to the bottom of the window, the text will scroll automatically if the end isn't visible) and release the button. The paragraph reappears at its new location.

A couple of points about drag-and-drop editing bear mentioning. First, no matter where you click on a selected block as you start to drag it, the entire block will appear—beginning at the pointer location—when you let go of the mouse button.

Second, don't panic if you realize you've made a mistake after you've started dragging a block. One way out is to press the Esc key before releasing the mouse button. You can also move the pointer back to the original block, releasing it anywhere in the block. The insertion point moves to the spot where the pointer is, but the block itself remains in place. Finally, you can let up on the mouse button wherever you happen to be when you discover your mistake and immediately use Undo to restore the block to its original location.

Inserting the Date or Time in a Document

One of WordPad's few frills is a special command that automatically inserts today's date or the current time into your document. For dates, you have many choices for the style WordPad uses. Depending on the document's intended audience, you can pick an abbreviated format such as 12/12/95 or let WordPad write out the full date, as in December 12, 1995. For the time, you can choose between two versions of the 12-hour AM/PM format that most people use and the 24-hour military format.

> **NOTE** WordPad always records the complete current time—down to the second—in your text. You probably won't want the seconds to appear in most documents, so you'll need to delete them after the Insert Date and Time dialog box has closed.

To insert the date or time:

1. Choose Insert ➤ Date and Time; or, if the Toolbar is visible, click on the Date and Time button shown below. The Insert Date and Time dialog box appears.

2. In the dialog box, choose your preferred style for the date or time from the list. The list offers more choices than will fit in the box, so you should scroll through if you don't see the style you want.

3. Click on OK to insert the chosen information in your document.

Formatting Paragraphs

Paragraphs are the most essential division of your text when it comes to *formatting*, which simply means controlling the looks of your document. A paragraph is defined by WordPad as any text terminated by pressing the Enter key. So even a single letter, line, or word will be treated as a paragraph if you press Enter after typing it. For that matter, pressing Enter on a completely blank line creates a paragraph, albeit an empty one.

WordPad handles each paragraph as a separate entity, each with its own formatting information. The press release you created early in the chapter uses a standard block-paragraph format typical of many business letters. In that format, a paragraph's first line is not indented, so you separate paragraphs with an empty paragraph. Also notice that the right margin is *ragged*, rather than aligned evenly—or *justified*—as it is on the left.

These and other qualities affecting the looks of your paragraphs can be altered while you are entering text or at any time thereafter. As you change the format settings, you immediately see the effects. Bold letters will look bold, centered lines centered, italic letters look slanted, and so forth.

For most documents, you may find that you are happy with Word-Pad's default format. WordPad applies the standard default format for you, carrying it from one paragraph to the next as you type. If you decide you'd rather use a different format for a new document, just alter some settings before typing anything. Then everything you type into the new document will be formatted accordingly until you change the settings again.

The *ruler* helps you keep track of where you are typing on the page, much like the guide on a typewriter. It also lets you alter the format of paragraphs by clicking on various symbols displayed within its boundaries. These alterations can also be made from the Paragraph menu and from the pop-up menu displayed when you click the right mouse button, but making changes on the ruler is probably easiest. The ruler and its sections are shown below.

The ruler may be off (*hidden*), but you can turn it on or off at will: Choose View ➤ Ruler. This command is a *toggle*: if the ruler is off, choosing the command displays it; if it is already on, choosing this command hides it.

Hiding the ruler lets you see extra lines of your text in the document window, but the ruler is useful to have around. The ruler has markings on it to help you gauge where your text will fall across the printed page and to help you set up tab stops. Each inch is marked with a number, and each tenth of an inch is marked by a small line. (You can change the ruler to show centimeters or other units via the Options dialog box.)

Notice the small markers at either end of the ruler. On the left are two triangular shapes: one along the top of the ruler, the other along the bottom; the lower one rests atop a small block. At the right side of the ruler, there's a single upward-pointing marker.

The lower markers at either end indicate the current paragraph's left and right indents (these are sometimes called *margin settings*, but remember that they affect the current paragraph, not the whole page). The upper marker on the left indicates the setting of the first-line indent for each paragraph. Actually, these markers do more than mark the current settings—you can use them to change the settings as well.

The ruler also shows tab settings. WordPad's built-in tab stops are marked by tiny gray dots along the lower border of the ruler. When you set your own tab, it appears on the ruler as a heavy black L-shaped mark in the ruler proper.

Viewing and Altering Paragraph Settings

Paragraph formatting falls into three categories with WordPad: *alignment*, *spacing*, and *indents*. The following sections explain and illustrate these categories. Unless otherwise noted, the examples here use inches as the basic unit of measure. If you wish to indicate another unit, such as centimeters, you can use the View ➤ Options command to do so.

Alignment

Alignment refers to where the text in a paragraph sits within the margins. *Left* is the default, causing text to be flush with the left margin (and ragged right). *Center* centers every line of the paragraph. *Right* causes text to be flush with the right margin (and ragged left).

Figure 19.7 shows three paragraphs, each one with a different type of alignment. To display or modify the settings for a given paragraph, click anywhere on it and then view or change the setting either from the Format Bar or from the Format Paragraph dialog box. Anytime you position the insertion point in a paragraph, the rulers and menu will reflect that paragraph's current settings.

CAUTION   WordPad does not permit you to create fully justified paragraphs, that is, paragraphs whose text is flush on both the right and left. If you need justified paragraphs, you'll have to use another word processor.

Viewing Paragraph Alignment

1. Move the insertion point to the paragraph in question and click.

2. If the Format Bar is visible, look at it. The alignment buttons will indicate the current setting—the button for that setting looks like it has been pressed, as shown below.

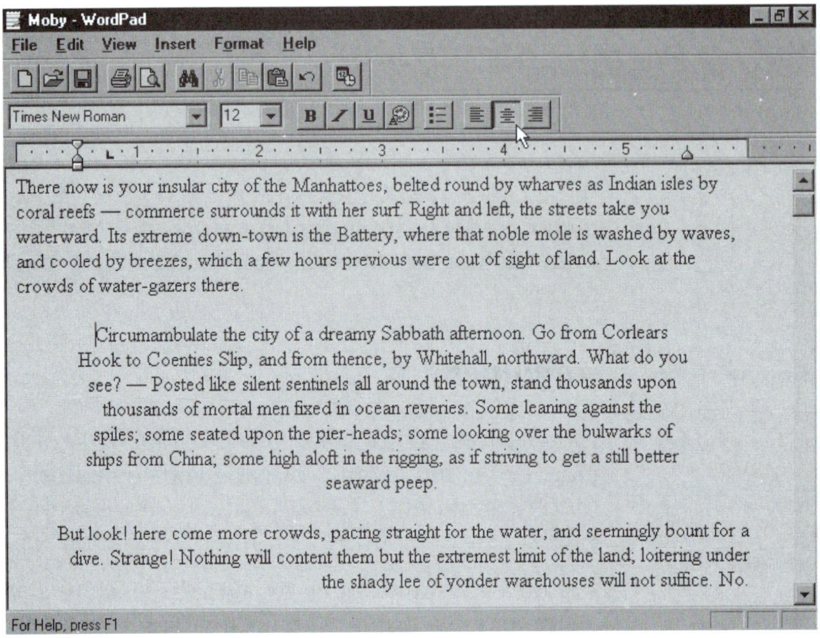

Figure 19.7 *Three types of alignment (from top to bottom): left, centered, and right*

3. To open the Format Paragraph dialog box (Figure 19.9) you can choose Format ➤ Paragraph or click the right mouse button with the pointer over the paragraph and then pick Paragraph from the pop-up menu. At the bottom of the Format Paragraph dialog box you'll see the current paragraph's alignment setting. On the next page you can see how the dialog box looks for a centered paragraph with a first-line *outdent* (true, that's an unlikely combination, but notice that outdents are specified by typing negative numbers).

Changing Paragraph Alignment

You can change the settings for a paragraph almost as easily as you can display them:

1. Move the insertion point to the paragraph or select several paragraphs (even a portion of each paragraph will suffice).

Paragraph ? ✕

Indentation

Left: 0.5"

Right: 0.25"

First line: -0.25"

OK

Cancel

Alignment: Left ▾

2. Open the Format Paragraph dialog box (choose Format ➤ Paragraph or right-click and choose Paragraph). In the Alignment drop-down list box, choose the alignment setting you want.

3. As an alternative, if the Format Bar is showing, click on one of its three alignment buttons (this is faster).

Indents

Indents fall into three categories: *right*, *left*, and *first-line indent.* Every paragraph has settings for each, and each paragraph's settings can be different. As with the other paragraph settings, these are carried from one paragraph to the next as you type, or you can change them after the fact. You set indents via the Paragraph menu's Indents command or by dragging the indent symbols on the ruler shown below to change the left, first line, and right indents.

The settings determine how far in from the left and right margins your text will appear. (They do not determine how far from the edge of the page the text will appear, however. That's established by the *margins*, discussed later in this chapter.) The first-line indent determines the starting position of the first line of each paragraph.

Setting the Left or Right Indent

You can change the left or right indent by either typing new settings into the Format Paragraph dialog box or using the ruler. Here's the first method:

1. Place the insertion point in a paragraph or select several paragraphs whose settings you want to change.

2. Choose Format ➤ Paragraph or right-click and choose Paragraph from the pop-up menu. The Format Paragraph dialog box (shown in Figure 19.9) will appear. Type in the desired indent and click on OK. If you just type in a number, it's assumed to be in inches. You can type **cm** after the number to indicate centimeters, **pt** to indicate typesetter's points, or **pi** for typesetter's picas.

    If the number you enter isn't acceptable, WordPad will tell you. This usually happens when you accidentally enter a value that is too large for the paper your printer driver is set up for.

    You can also use the ruler to change the left or right indent:

1. Place the insertion point in the paragraph or select several paragraphs whose settings you want to change.

2. Turn on the ruler, if it's off, by choosing View ➤ Ruler.

3. Drag the left-indent marker in the ruler—the lower triangular symbol—to its new position. First, try grabbing the block *underneath* the triangular portion of the marker. This moves the block, the triangle that rests on it, *and* the other triangular marker, the one at the top of the ruler. When you let go of the mouse button, the paragraph's left indent moves to the new location. Notice that the first line has moved too, even if it had been indented or outdented. It retains its indent relative to the left indent of the other lines.

4. Now try dragging the left-indent marker by grabbing the lower triangle. This time, the top triangle remains where it is; when you release the button, all the other lines move to align with the new left indent.

Setting the First-Line Indent

On a typewriter, you have to hit the Tab key if you want to indent the first line of each paragraph. It's easier to let WordPad do it for you with its first-line indent setting. This also lets you modify the look of a letter after you've written it because you can adjust the first-line indents.

The first-line indent setting establishes the relative indent for the first line of each new paragraph. Note that the setting is *in addition to* the left indent. So if the left indent is 1 inch and the first-line indent is 0.5 inch, the first line will start 1.5 inches from the left margin. Incidentally, setting the first-line indent to a negative number, such as -0.5, will cause it to hang out that amount from the left indent. This is sometimes called a *hanging indent* or an *outdent*. To change the first-line indent:

1. Place the insertion point in the paragraph—or select several paragraphs—whose settings you want to change.

2. Choose Format ➤ Paragraph or right-click and choose Paragraph. The Format Paragraph dialog box will appear. Type in the first-line indent amount and click on OK.

As an alternative, drag the first-line indent marker (the upper triangle on the left side of the ruler) to the new indent position.

In either case, WordPad will immediately reformat the paragraph in accordance with the new settings. Figure 19.8 shows examples of three different indent setups.

Creating Bulleted Paragraphs

One of the most common conventions in business and technical writing is the use of *bullets* to set off the items in a list. The standard bullet—and the one WordPad uses—is a heavy circular spot, though a bullet can be any symbol offset to the left of a paragraph. Bulleted text is useful for, and illustrated by, the following items:

▶ calling attention to the individual benefits or features of a product or service

▶ listing a set of options

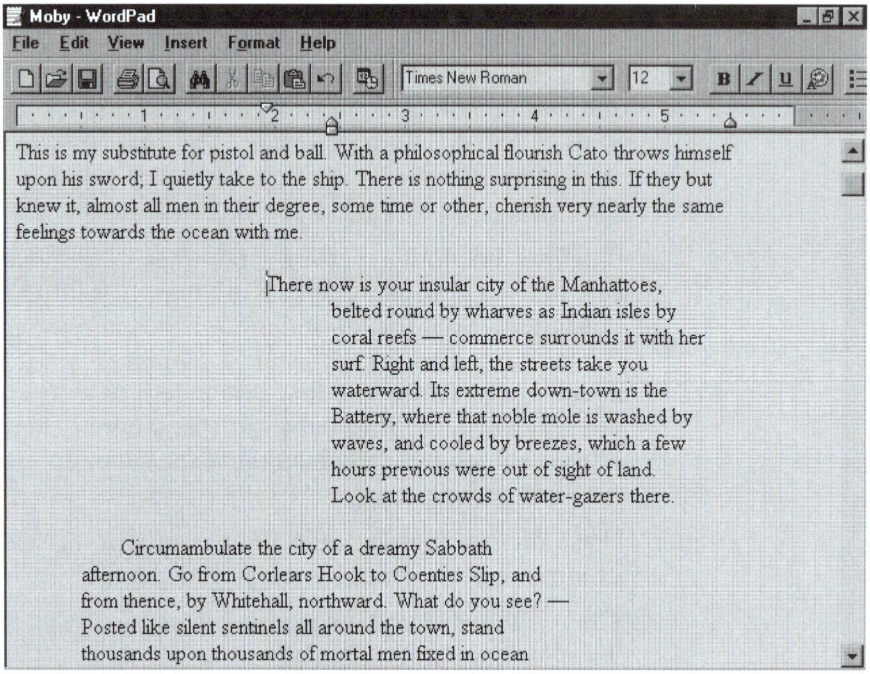

Figure 19.8   **Paragraphs with three different indent setups**

▶ itemizing the parts or supplies needed for a given job

WordPad can automatically add a bullet to any paragraph or to each paragraph in a selected block of text. WordPad places the bullet at the original left indent of the paragraph, shifting the rest of the paragraph to the right (the position changes are accomplished by adjusting the left indent and first-line indent settings, as you can see on the ruler).

The Bullet Style command works as a toggle: If the paragraph already has a bullet, the Bullet command removes the bullet.

To apply bullets to an unbulleted paragraph or group of paragraphs:

1. Place the cursor in the paragraph to be bulleted or select a group of paragraphs.

2. Choose Format ➤ Bullet Style or, if the Format Bar is visible, click on the Bullet button shown below.

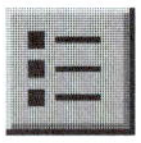

Reformatting the Whole Document

You'll often want to reformat an entire document. That is, you'll print out the document, look at it, and realize you should have used larger (or smaller) type or perhaps that it should have smaller (or larger) first-line indents.

Select the whole document first, then change the settings.

Formatting Characters

WordPad includes commands for altering the look of the individual letters on the printed page. This is called *character formatting*. You can use character formatting to emphasize a section of text by making it bold, underlined, or italicized, or you may want to change the size or the font.

> **NOTE** As with all Windows programs, WordPad measures character sizes in *points*. Typical point sizes are 9 to 14 for ordinary text. (This book is printed in 11 point Plantin.) Newspaper headlines may appear in anything up to 60 points or so.

Just as with paragraph formatting, WordPad starts you off with a standard character format: a conventional, unobtrusive font (Times New Roman) at a standard size (10 points). But you can change character formatting to your heart's content. WordPad gives you three ways to modify character formatting:

▶ from the Format bar

▶ from the Fonts dialog box

▶ with shortcut Ctrl-key combinations to change type styles

You can change the formatting of individual characters, selected blocks of text, or the whole document. Character formatting applies to paragraphs as a whole only if they're actually selected.

Formatting Existing Characters

To change the formatting of characters you've already typed, begin by selecting the text character(s) to be altered. You can select a single letter, a sentence, a paragraph, the whole document, or any arbitrary sequence of characters. Now you have three choices:

▶ Use the controls on the Format Bar to alter individual format characteristics (font, size, and so forth). This is a quick way to control any aspect of character format.

▶ Use keyboard shortcuts to modify the text style (boldface, italics, or underlining). This is the quickest way to change these styles, but you have to memorize the shortcuts and you can't control other aspects of character format.

▶ Use the Fonts dialog box to set all the format characteristics from a single window. This lets you see a sample of how your text will look as you experiment with different formatting choices.

> **CAUTION**   Expect lower print quality if you add boldface or italics when you don't have separate fonts installed for those styles. Windows lets you add boldface or italics to any installed font, even if you haven't installed the bold or italics versions of the font. When the actual bold font is missing, Windows just makes the characters thicker. When the italics font is missing, it simply slants the regular font. See Chapter 9 for details on how fonts work in Windows 95.

Changing Character Format with the Format Bar

Here's how to use the Format Bar to change character formatting:

1. If the Format Bar isn't already visible, choose View ➤ Format Bar to activate it.

> **NOTE**   The icon next to the font name tells you whether it is a TrueType or Printer font. Note that the type of font you choose affects the range of available sizes. Scalable fonts such as TrueType and PostScript (Type 1) fonts can be used in virtually any size, while other fonts have a set number of specific font sizes available.

2. To change the font of the selected text, choose the new font name from the drop-down list box at the left side of the Format Bar.

3. To change the text size, you can pick a new size from the next list box or type in the size you want (WordPad only allows integer font sizes—fractional values won't work).

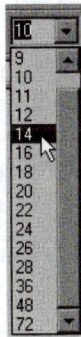

4. To turn styles (boldface, italics, or underlining) on or off, click on the appropriate button. When the style is active, the appropriate button looks like it has been pressed.

Finally, to change the color of the selected text, click on the button that displays an artist's palette and pick your color from the list that appears.

Note that you can change these settings in any combination. For example, a single selection can be italicized, underlined, and displayed in fuschia—if you're willing to take some serious liberties with typesetting etiquette.

After you've returned to your document and deselected the block, the Format Bar shows you the current formatting of the character or selection. If the character or selection has been italicized, for example, the button for italics appears pushed.

You can see at a glance if a selected block contains more than one style, font, or font size. For example, if only part of the block is set to bold, the Format Bar button for bold appears translucent. If the block contains two or more different fonts, the entry in the box for fonts will be blank.

Changing Character Format with the Fonts Dialog Box

If you're willing to give up the space on your screen to display the Format Bar, you might want to use the Fonts dialog box to see a sample of your character-formatting choices before you apply them. Otherwise, if your formatting experiments prove unsuccessful, you'll have to reset all the settings for the selected block individually.

To modify character formatting with the Fonts dialog box:

1. With the text selected, choose Format ➤ Fonts or right-click and choose Fonts. You'll see the Fonts dialog box.

2. In the dialog box, you can make changes to any of the character-formatting settings you wish. When you're through, click on OK.

Changing Character Formats with Keyboard Shortcuts

You can also use keyboard shortcuts (these also are toggles) to modify the character styles (bold, italics, and underlining) of a selected block. Use Ctrl-B for bold, Ctrl-I for italics, and Ctrl-U for underlining.

Formatting Characters as You Type

You can also change the appearance of text as you type. Subsequent characters will be entered with the new settings—and the settings will remain in force until changed. For instance, you would press Ctrl-B once to start typing bold characters and then press it again when you're ready to type more unbolded text.

Working with Tabs

As with a typewriter, you can vary WordPad's tab settings to suit your needs. For complex multicolumn tables, you'll probably want to set up your own custom tab stops. Default tabs are already set up across the page in half-inch increments. If you haven't set tabs yourself, the half-inch markers—small gray dots on the ruler's lower border—indicate the locations of the default tabs.

For each paragraph—or any selected group of paragraphs—you can also place as many as 32 of your own tabs. These show up as heavy L-shaped markers in the ruler, as you can see in this detailed view:

> **NOTE** When you set a tab manually, WordPad automatically eliminates all default tab stops to its left.

You can set and alter tabs from the Tabs dialog box or from the ruler.

Setting Tab Stops from the Ruler

If you're good with the mouse, setting tabs is much easier and faster with the ruler. Here's how to do it:

1. Get the ruler on screen (choose View ➤ Ruler if it's not already visible).

2. To position a tab, click inside the ruler at the place where you want the tab. You can drag the tab marker left and right to adjust its placement any time. The text affected will be adjusted immediately.

Setting Tab Stops from a Dialog Box

To set tabs from a dialog box, choose Format ➤ Tabs or right-click over the paragraph or selection and choose Tabs from the pop-up menu. A dialog box appears, as shown below.

All you need to do is type in the exact location for each new tab stop and choose Set. You can set tabs in any order (for example, you could set a tab at 4.5 inches, then set a second at 2.5 inches). When you choose Set, WordPad inserts the tabs in order.

Type the position in inches (or whatever measurement unit you're using in the Options dialog box). Three custom tabs are shown above: .75 inches, 1.2 inches, and 2.69 inches.

After you click on OK, the tabs will be set. The ruler will have new tab markers in it to indicate the new tab positions, and the text will be adjusted immediately.

Repositioning Existing Tab Stops

It's easy to adjust existing tabs to improve the layout of a table or list without ever having to retype columns or add or delete spaces between them. The quickest way to change a tab's location is with the ruler. Just drag the tab to its new location. If you want more precision, you can use the Tabs dialog box—but you have to first clear the existing tab stop, then set a new one at the desired location.

Clearing Custom Tab Stops

You can clear any of your custom tab stops at any time, either from the ruler or from the dialog box. To clear a tab from the ruler, simply drag the tab marker from the ruler down into the document as though you were pulling it off the ruler. It will disappear.

Any text formerly aligned at that tab will move right to the next custom tab stop. If there are no remaining custom tab stops, the text moves to the appropriate default tab.

To clear tabs from the dialog box:

1. Choose Format ➤ Tabs. The Tabs dialog box appears.

2. Find the tab stop you want to clear in the list box and click on it. It will appear in the entry box above the list.

3. Choose Clear to zap the tab stop, removing it from the screen.

4. Click on OK. Any text aligned at deleted tabs will move right to the next one.

To remove all your custom tab stops in one step, choose the Clear All button in the Tabs dialog box.

Using Undo to Reverse Mistakes

WordPad makes allowances for our imperfections via the Undo command. In a split second, a slip of the mouse—choosing Clear instead of Cut—can send a large block of text to oblivion instead of to the Clipboard.

Undo is, quite understandably, the first selection on the Edit menu. But you can access Undo even faster if the Toolbar is visible: Just click on the button showing an arrow with a curved stem.

Undo can reverse the following:

▶ block deletions made with the Delete command from the Edit menu or the Del key on the keyboard

▶ individual or multiple letters that you erased using the Del or Backspace keys. Unfortunately, it will return only the last letter or series of letters erased. Once you move the cursor to another location using any of the cursor-movement keys and delete again, the text in the previous deletion is lost.

▶ selected blocks directly deleted and replaced by typing new text on the keyboard

▶ new text you typed in. This can be undone back to the last time you issued a command.

▶ character- and paragraph-formatting changes (if you select the Undo command immediately after making the change)

When you realize you've done something that you regret, select Edit ➤ Undo or click on the Undo button on the Toolbar. Remember, though, that the Undo command can only recall the last action. If you decide you have made a mistake, either while entering or deleting, you must undo the damage before using any other editing or formatting commands.

Searching for and Replacing Text

WordPad offers Find and Replace commands to look for specific letters, words, or series of words in your text. Once the word processor finds the text, you can have it automatically replace that text with other text if you wish. Though WordPad calls these searching commands Find and Replace, this type of operation is also referred to as *search and replace*.

You can also use searching to get to a particular place in your document quickly. If you put unique markers (for example, *##1* or *aaa*) in your text, you can search for them to move from one part of a document to another specific point.

Using Find and Replace together, you can replace abbreviations with words. For example, in preparing the manuscript for this book, I replaced *W* with *Windows* and *wp* with *word processor*. This eliminated a lot of repetitive typing.

Finding a Specific Word or Text String

Here's how to use Find to locate a specific word or group of words:

1. Choose Edit ➤ Find, press Ctrl-F, or, if the Toolbar is visible, click on the Find button (the one showing binoculars). The dialog box you see in Figure 19.9 will appear.

2. Type the text you're searching for and press Enter or click on Find Next. The cursor moves to the next instance of that text.

3. To find out if there are any other occurrences of the text, click on Find Next again or just press Enter. WordPad will try to find the text again. WordPad always remembers the last word you searched for so you can repeat the action more easily. It also scrolls the document for you so you can see the text if and when it's found.

> **TIP** Here's a shortcut for finding other occurrences of text in your document: Select the text, then bring up the Find dialog box. WordPad will have entered the text for you in the *Find what:* area, so you can immediately click on Find Next.

When there are no further occurrences of the text you're searching for and the entire document has been searched, a dialog box will appear saying:

```
WordPad has finished searching the document.
```

Just press Enter or click on OK.

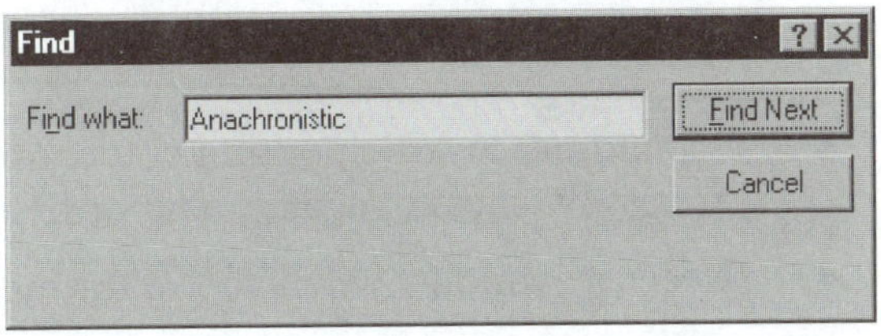

Figure 19.9 *The Find dialog box. Type the word you want to find—here, it is* Anachronistic.

The Find command always starts at the current cursor location and searches to the end of the document. Then it wraps around to the beginning and continues until it reaches the cursor again.

Keep in mind that you can move the Find dialog box around the screen. Although WordPad automatically moves the Find window so you can see text that has been found, you may want to move the Find window so you can see other parts of the document. The Find window stays on the screen, ready for searching, until you close it.

Another handy command lets you repeat the previous search without the Find dialog box. After using Find to search for your text the first time, close the box. Now whenever you want to repeat the search, either choose Edit ➤ Repeat Last Find or simply press F3.

Replacing Specific Words

To replace a text string with another text string, you use the Replace dialog box:

1. Choose Edit ➤ Replace or press Ctrl-H. A Replace dialog box appears, slightly larger than the one for Find. There is an additional text area in the dialog box called Replace With. This is where you type in the text that you want the found text to be changed to.

2. Now click on Find Next, Replace, or Replace All. Here's what each does:

Find Next	Finds the next occurrence of the word, but doesn't change anything.
Replace	Changes the next or currently highlighted occurrence of the word and then moves on to find and highlight the next occurrence.
Replace All	Automatically finds and changes all occurrences of the word. You don't get to see what's happening.

3. Depending on which option you chose, you may want to continue the process by clicking again on a button.

4. Close the window when you're through by clicking on Close.

Copying between Two Documents

You may often need to copy portions of text between two documents. Many professionals use word processors because they can use *boiler-plate text* to piece together new documents from existing ones. This is particularly useful for constructing legal documents or contracts that regularly include standard clauses or paragraphs. A more domestic example is creating a series of somewhat similar letters to a number of friends.

Because Windows lets you have multiple programs running at once, you have a fair amount of flexibility here. Though WordPad doesn't let you open more than one *document* at a time, Windows *will* let you run more than one *session* of WordPad. So you can run WordPad for each document you want to open.

Once your documents are open, you can select text from one, copy or cut it, and then open another window, position the cursor, and paste it in. Adjust the windows so you can see enough of each document to easily select and insert text. Figure 19.10 shows an example of two WordPad documents open simultaneously.

Of course you can use the multiple WordPad windows for simply writing or viewing more than one document at a time, too. For example, you may be working on several news stories, several letters, or several chapters of a book. Just minimize the documents you're not actively working on but want to have close at hand.

Here are the general steps for opening two WordPad documents and transferring material between them:

1. Minimize any other running applications. The quick way to do this is to click with the right button over any empty part of the Windows Taskbar and choose Minimize All Windows from the pop-up menu that appears.

2. Run WordPad and open the first document (or just leave the window as is if you're creating a new document).

3. Run another copy of WordPad from the Start menu and open the file from which you're going to be cutting or copying.

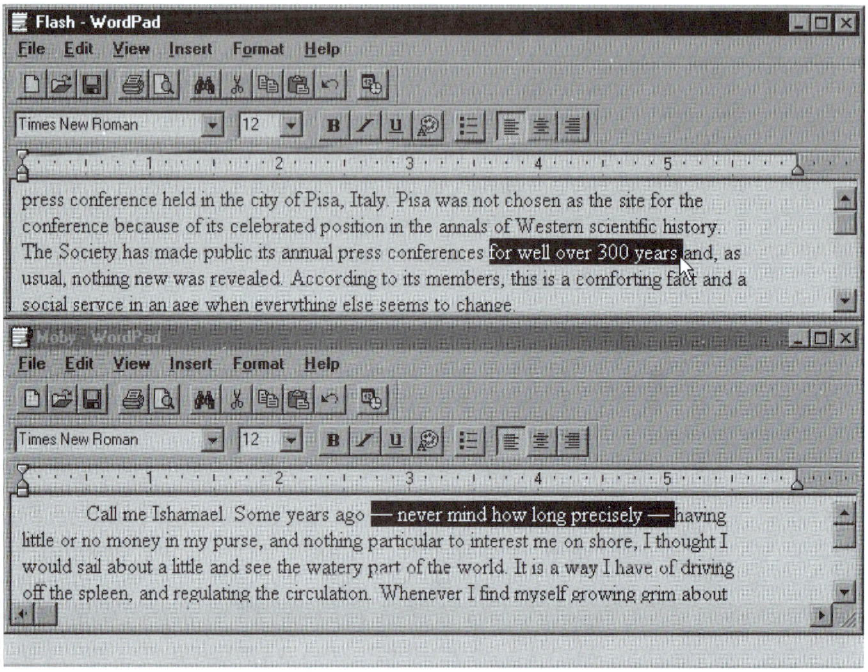

Figure 19.10   *You can run multiple copies of WordPad and load a different document into each window. This lets you transfer material easily between them or switch between writing tasks.*

4. Adjust the windows so you can see both. Again, the quick way is to right-click on the Taskbar, then choose Tile Horizontally from the pop-up menu.

5. You can now move information between the windows to your heart's content.

Hyphenating

WordPad does not hyphenate your text automatically. As a result, some lines will be too short because WordPad has to push an entire large word to the next line. In WordPad, the only cure for such layout problems is to insert the missing hyphens manually. You should do this as the very last step you take before printing a document. Otherwise, if you make any further changes in your text—whether it's adding or deleting text or changing paragraph or character formatting—the line layout will likely change, and the entire word you hyphenated will now appear on a single line with the hyphen still visible (if this happens, just delete the hyphen).

Here's what you should do:

1. Find the optimal hyphenation point in the long word at the beginning of the next line, move the cursor to that point, and type a hyphen.

2. Then move the cursor to the beginning of the line and press Backspace. The newly hyphenated word will split, with the first section being pulled up to join the last word on the previous line. Press the Spacebar to separate the two words again.

You may find that when you press Backspace, the last word from the previous line jumps down to join the hyphenated word. If this happens, it means that even the first part of the hyphenated word will not fit on the previous line. Go back to the word and remove the optional hyphen.

> **TIP** If you edit your text or change the formatting after hyphenating it, be sure the changes don't cause hyphenated words to move to locations where the hyphens are inappropriate. The easiest way to check for this is to use the Find command to search your document for all occurrences of a hyphen.

Adding Graphics to Your WordPad Document

Although it's sort of a bare-bones word processor, WordPad *does* allow you to insert pictures or graphics—and all kinds of other *objects* such as charts, video sequences, and sounds—into your documents. We'll focus on graphics for the moment, but the steps you'll learn here apply to other types of objects as well.

With this insertion feature you can add your company logo to every letter you print, put your picture on your letterhead, or put a map on a party announcement. Figure 19.11 shows examples of graphics inserted into WordPad documents.

You can't *create* graphics with WordPad itself—you have to get them from other Windows applications such as Paint. But you can use just

Figure 19.11   Examples of graphics in WordPad documents. Graphics are imported from the Clipboard and then can be moved and sized.

about any kind of image in your WordPad documents. To add a photo, for example, you would have the photograph digitized with a scanner, then copy the picture onto the Clipboard and paste it into WordPad.

Once you've inserted graphics in the document, you can then cut, copy, or paste them. You can also change a graphic's size or move it around.

The simplest way to handle graphics in WordPad is to treat them as isolated items copied as independent chunks directly into the document via the Clipboard. But with a little more effort, you can maintain a connection between the graphic and the other application that created it. That way, you can edit the graphic from within WordPad—you don't have to return to the application that created the picture to make changes and then recopy the graphic to WordPad. Windows calls this feature *object linking* and *embedding*, or OLE. Chapter 6 covers object linking and embedding in detail.

Importing a Graphic from the Clipboard

To import a graphic into your document, follow these steps:

1. Place the picture on the Clipboard by switching to the source application, such as Paint, and choosing the Copy or Cut commands (in Paint and many other applications, you'll have to select the portion of the image you want before you copy or cut). You can then paste almost any image that can be cut or copied into WordPad.

2. Open the WordPad document or activate its window.

3. Position the insertion point on the line where you want the picture to start and select Edit ➤ Paste.

The graphic will be dropped into the document at the insertion point. Figure 19.12 shows an example. Now you can move it or resize it with the methods explained next.

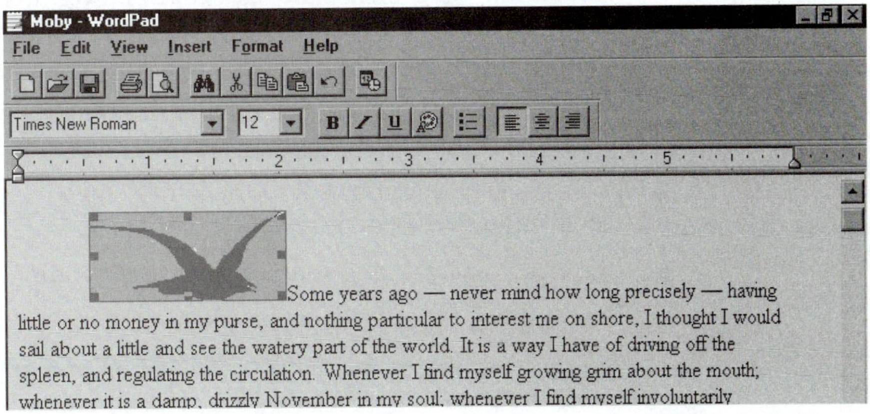

Figure 19.12   A graphic copied from Paint into a WordPad document. The small squares at the corners and along the edges are the handles.

Positioning the Graphic

Once you've pasted a graphic into WordPad, you have only crude control over positioning it where you want it in the document. You can't move a graphic around with the mouse, and there's no menu command for this purpose. Instead, you must "push" the picture around in your document with ordinary typing.

NOTE WordPad automatically adjusts the spacing between lines so that the graphic fits without overlapping the line above it—just as it does if you change the text size.

It helps to know that WordPad treats an inserted graphic or other object as if it were a single text character. The bottom edge of the graphic sits on the line of text marked by the insertion point.

If you insert a graphic into a separate paragraph—so that it's the only "character" in the paragraph—you can use WordPad's paragraph alignment commands to position the image. With the insertion point on the same line as the graphic, click on any of the alignment buttons on the Format bar or use the Format ➤ Paragraph command to choose the correct alignment.

Otherwise, you can move the graphic by typing characters to the left or right on that same line. If the right edge of the graphic passes the right-indent setting for the current paragraph, WordPad wraps the graphic down a line, repositioning it on the left side just as when wrapping text.

To move a graphic, then, begin by positioning the insertion point to its left. Now:

▶ Press Backspace to move it to the left (or up a line, if it's already at the left side of the paragraph).

▶ Press the Spacebar or Tab to move it to the right.

▶ Press Enter to move it down in the file.

Another way to change the *vertical* location of a graphic is to select it (by clicking on it), cut it to the Clipboard, click where you want to move the graphic, and paste it into place.

Sizing the Graphic

You can resize a graphic, too. Here's how:

1. Select the graphic by clicking on it. The rectangular frame indicating the boundaries of the graphic appears, with small black squares called *handles* at the corners and at the center of each side.

2. Drag the handles to resize the graphic. You can resize in both the horizontal and vertical dimensions by dragging a corner handle. Drag a side handle if you want to resize in one dimension only.

3. When you're finished stretching or shrinking the image, release the mouse button. If you don't like the results, Undo will return the graphic to its previous size.

Notice that you can distort the picture if you want to by making it long and skinny or short and fat. In general, you'll get best results by trying to maintain its original proportions, or *aspect ratio*, by changing both width and height by the same percentage.

> **TIP**   To avoid distortion when the picture is printed, keep the x and y values (in the status line) the same and keep them in whole numbers rather than fractions.

Also, be aware that bit-mapped images, such as Paint pictures and scanned photos, never look as good when resized. If you shrink them, you lose detail; if you stretch them, curved edges look blocky.

Inserting Graphics as Objects

When you place a graphic into a WordPad document using the Clipboard, the connection between the image and Paint (or whatever application created it) is broken. If you need to edit the graphic, you'll have to delete it from WordPad, then start all over in Paint.

Unless you're sure the graphic is final, it makes more sense to insert it using Windows' OLE (object linking and embedding) capability. That way, the graphic remains *live* in your document—you can edit it in place without having to leave WordPad at all. See Chapter 6 for step-by-step instructions on how to link and embed objects into your documents.

Saving Your Work

WordPad stores your document in memory while you work on it. However, memory is not a permanent storage area; you will lose your work when you turn off your computer unless you first save it.

You save your documents with two commands: File ➤ Save and File ➤ Save As (there are two shortcuts for the Save command: the Save button on the Toolbar and the Ctrl-S keyboard shortcut). The first time you save a document, WordPad will ask you for a name to give your document—in this situation, the Save and Save As commands work the same. After the initial save, WordPad assumes you want to use the current name unless you indicate otherwise by using the Save As command.

Remember to save your work frequently. Nothing hurts like losing forever an afternoon's inspired writing. Taking a few moments to save your document every five or ten minutes is much easier on the psyche.

Again, there are three ways to save a file: File ➤ Save, the Save button—the one with the picture of a floppy disk—and Ctrl-S.

No matter which of these methods you use to start the process, the Save As dialog box (Figure 19.13) appears because this is the first time you've saved this file. WordPad has assigned a generic name, Document, but you can change it. Finish saving your file as follows:

1. Type in a more descriptive name in the File name box.

2. Ensure that the correct drive and directory are selected.

3. If you wish to change the type of file you'll be saving, do so by picking a new choice from the *Save as Type* drop-down list box.

4. Click on OK.

The Save as Type drop-down list box is normally set to store your document in the Word for Windows 6 format. Different programs use different coding systems, or *formats,* to store the document's text, its character and paragraph formatting, any graphics or other objects, and other miscellaneous information.

NOTE   There are two distinct uses for the term "format": It can refer to the way a document is stored in a disk file or to the appearance of text in a document.

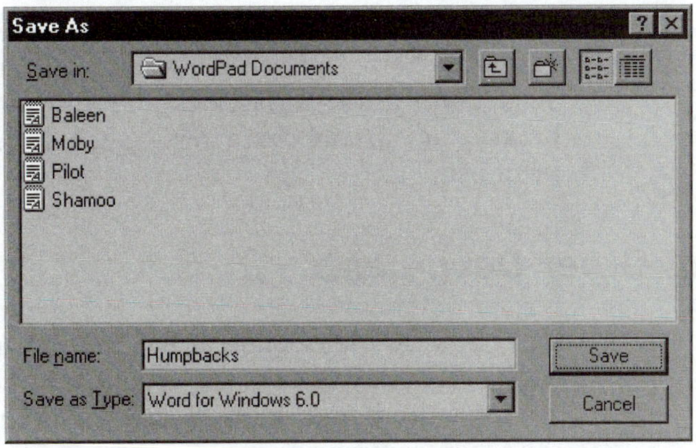

Figure 19.13   *The Save As dialog box. After making sure the drive and directory are right, type in the file name.*

The various formats in which you can save a document are discussed below. You shouldn't alter this setting unless you want to create a document that other word processors or other types of programs can read:

Word for Windows 6.0

This choice stores the document in the same format used by Microsoft Word for Windows, version 6.0. This full-featured word processor is the most popular Windows application. If you open the document with Word, all the text, character and paragraph formatting, graphics, and other objects will be preserved.

Rich Text Format

The Rich Text Format is used as a common format for exchanging documents between word processors, but none of them use it as their primary format (it's sort of like Esperanto for word processors). The Rich Text Format preserves the appearance as well as the content of your document. Graphics and other objects are saved in the file along with the text but may be lost when you open the file with another application.

Text Files

Files saved with this option contain only text without any of the character and paragraph formatting you've added. Such files are also known as *plain* text files. They can be opened by a text editor such as Notepad. You can also open them with DOS text editors such as PC-Write, WordStar, or Sidekick, though you may have to add line breaks, and special characters—such as bullets—will not display or print properly.

Opening Other Documents

Once a WordPad document has been saved on disk, you can come back to it at any future time. To *open* a document—moving the information stored on disk into RAM so you can work with it again—use the Open command.

Keep in mind that in WordPad, unlike fancier word processors, you can only work with one document at a time. When you open a document, it replaces the one you were working with, if any. If you want to keep the changes you made in a document, you must save that document before opening a new one. But don't worry—WordPad will remind you to save before it lets you open another document.

As usual, you have several options for opening existing documents: choose File ➤ Open, press Ctrl-O, or on the Toolbar click on the Open button, which shows a picture of a file folder opening.

Regardless of which technique you use, you'll see the Open dialog box. After listing any subdirectories, this dialog box shows you all the files in the current directory matching the setting in the *Files of type* drop-down list box. Unless someone has changed the entry, you'll see a list of all files stored in the Word for Windows format, WordPad's preferred format.

To open a document, double-click on it in the list or click once on the document and then click Open. At this point, if you haven't already saved the previous document, WordPad asks if you want to do so. Choose Yes or No, as you prefer.

A Shortcut for Opening Recent Documents

WordPad lists the last four documents you've opened on the File menu. If you want to reopen any of these documents, do it the quick way: Open the File menu, then choose the document by name from the menu. WordPad will open the document immediately without displaying the Open dialog box (you'll still receive a message asking if you want to save the current document if you haven't done so yet).

Opening Documents Stored in Other Formats

Although WordPad's standard format for storing documents on disk is the Word for Windows 6.0 format, WordPad can also open documents stored in several other formats. Formats WordPad can open include:

▶ the Windows Write format (Write was a simple word processor included with earlier versions of Windows)

▶ the Rich Text Format

▶ *text only* files

If you know the format of the document you want to open, select that format in the Files of Type drop-down list box. If you're unsure of the format, choose All Files instead—Windows will now display all the files in the current directory. Once you locate the correct document in the list, double-click on it to open it.

WordPad automatically opens Word for Windows, Windows Write, and Rich Text Format files, even those incorrectly named. If someone has improperly renamed say, a Word for Windows-format document, the Open dialog box may not show it even when the Files of Type setting is correct. However, WordPad can still open the document if you locate it with All Files selected in the Files of Type box (or if you type in the document's name at *File name*).

All other documents are opened as text-only files. If the document contains formatting information from some other application, WordPad will display the entire document, including the formatting information, as ordinary text. You'll likely see gibberish mixed in with intelligible text.

Converting ASCII Files

When opening most text-only files created by DOS programs, WordPad interprets each line of text as a separate paragraph (in these *ASCII* files, paragraphs are typically set apart by a blank lines).

The only way to fix the problem is to delete the unwanted paragraph dividers once you open the document into WordPad. It's best to do this systematically immediately after opening the document.

Follow these steps to fix each paragraph. Skip paragraphs that are only one line long:

1. Move the cursor to the end of the first line of the paragraph. Press Del to remove the paragraph division. This will pull up the previous line to the cursor.

2. Press the Spacebar to add a space between the two words on either side of the cursor, if necessary.

3. Repeat the above steps on all lines of the paragraph *except* the last one.

Opening a New Document

Whenever you start WordPad, the program opens a new, empty document for you. To create a new document after working with an existing one, however, you need the New command. Here's how to do it:

1. Choose Edit ➤ New, press Ctrl-N, or click on the New button on the Toolbar—it's the one that looks like a blank sheet of paper.

2. If you haven't already saved the current document, WordPad gives you a chance to do so.

3. WordPad now asks you what format you want to use for the new document: Word for Windows, Rich Text, or Text Only. Select the desired format in the list and choose OK. The new document will appear in the window.

Display Options

You have some choices about the way the WordPad window looks and works. As you learned earlier, the View menu lets you turn on or off any of the individual control bars (the Toolbar, the Format Bar, the ruler, and the Status Bar). Other display options are available via the Options dialog box.

To open the Options dialog box, choose View ➤ Options. You'll see the window shown in Figure 19.14.

The Options dialog box is tabbed. One tab covers general options, while the remaining tabs apply to the various document types (file formats) that WordPad can handle.

Selecting Measurement Units and Controlling Word Selection

Click on the tab labeled Options in the Options dialog box to set measurement units for your document. You can choose from inches, centimeters, points, and picas (the last two units are used by typesetters). If the ruler is visible, it will be displayed with the selected measurement units. In addition, spacing settings in the Paragraph Spacing and Page Setup dialog boxes will be listed in the chosen unit.

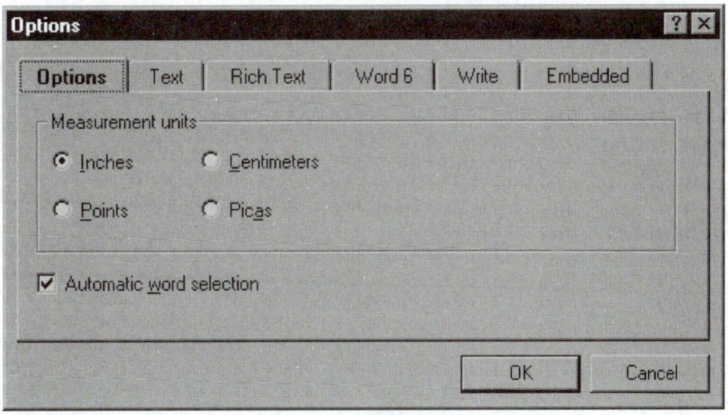

Figure 19.14   *The Options dialog box. It lets you set measurement units for the ruler and for spacing settings, among other choices.*

> **TIP** Regardless of the *Measurement units* setting in the Options tab, you can enter new settings in the Paragraph Spacing and Page Setup dialog boxes in any unit by typing the unit abbreviation after the value. For example, type 1.5 in to enter a left margin of 1.5 inches, 2.3 cm to enter a right margin of 2.3 centimeters.

The only other choice on the Options tab is a check box labeled Automatic Word Selection. With this setting checked, the mouse selects entire words when you drag the pointer across two or more words. You can still select a group of characters within a single word by holding down Shift while pressing the arrow keys.

Uncheck the Automatic Word Selection box if you want the selection to cover only the characters you actually drag the pointer across.

Choosing Display Options for Each Type of Document

Aside from the page labeled Options, the other pages in the Options dialog box pertain to the various types of documents that WordPad can open—Word for Windows 6.0, Windows Write, Rich Text Format, and Text-only files, as well as WordPad documents embedded via OLE in other documents. Each of these pages offers identical choices, shown in Figure 19.15.

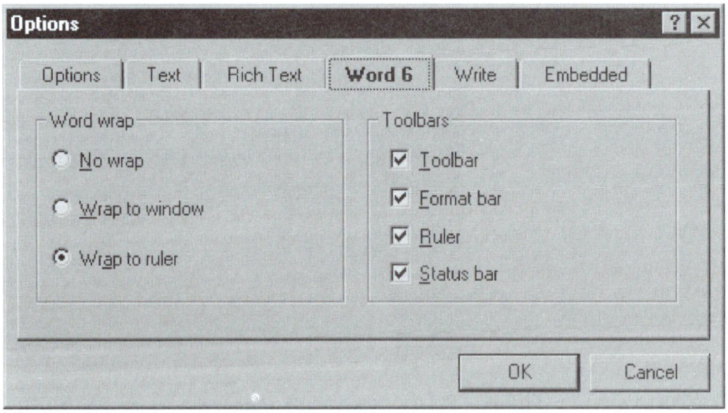

Figure 19.15   *The Options dialog box offers these choices for each type of file WordPad can handle.*

Check boxes on the right of each tab let you select which of the control bars (the Toolbar, Format Bar, ruler, and Status Bar) WordPad will display automatically when you open a document of the type indicated by the tab.

On the left side of each tabbed panel are radio buttons for selecting the way WordPad wraps your text from line to line on the screen. Note that none of these choices affects the way your document prints:

No Wrap   If this button is selected, WordPad doesn't wrap your text at all. As you add text anywhere within a line, the line keeps expanding toward the right regardless of the right indent and right margin settings. On printed copies, though, the text still wraps according to the indent and margin settings.

Wrap to Window   With this button selected, WordPad wraps the text to fit within the document window, ignoring the right indent and margin settings. Choose this setting to see all your text even when the WordPad window is narrower than the paragraph width set by the ruler. Again, this doesn't affect printed documents.

Wrap to Ruler   When this button is selected, the displayed text wraps according to the right indent and right margin settings as shown on the ruler (whether or not the ruler is visible).

Printing Your Document

Generally speaking, the ultimate goal of all your typing and formatting is a printed copy of your document. Printing a WordPad document is a straightforward process. Like the major-league word processors, WordPad lets you see a preview of your document as it will appear in print, and you can fix your mistakes before they appear on paper.

Seeing a Preview of Your Printed Document

Instead of wasting paper on a document with an obvious layout mistake, use WordPad's *print preview* command to inspect your work before you print. The print preview command displays your document on screen just as it will look when printed. You can look at entire pages to check the overall layout or zoom in on a particular portion to check details.

To use print preview, choose File ➤ Print Preview. (Alternatively, you can click on the Print Preview button if the Toolbar is visible—it's the button with the picture of a magnifying glass over a sheet of paper.)

The WordPad window fills with a mock-up of your document, fitting two full pages into the available space, as shown in Figure 19.16. A special Toolbar offers quick access to a number of special commands, and the mouse pointer becomes a magnifying glass.

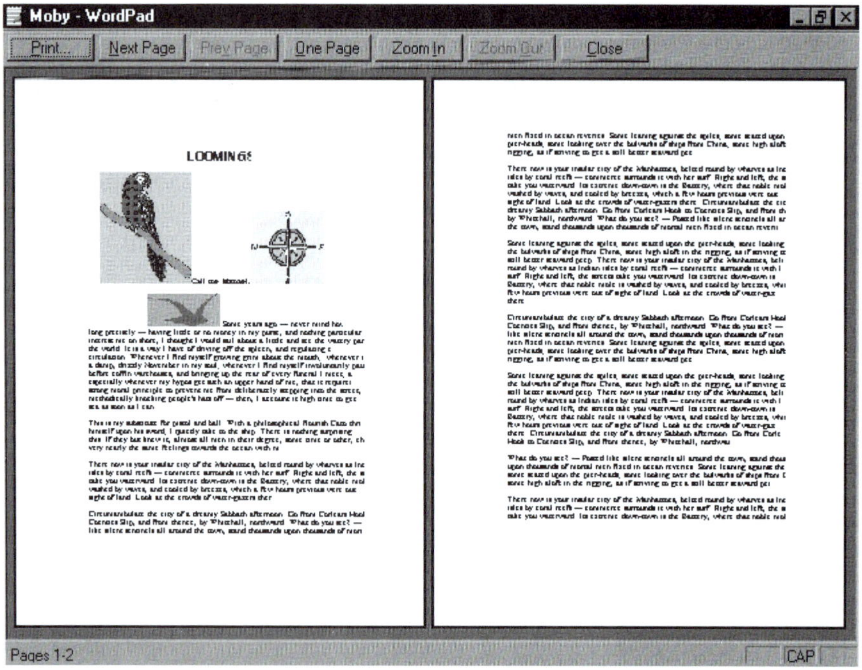

Figure 19.16 *WordPad's Print Preview window*

At this level of magnification, you can't read ordinary-size text, but you can check for problems with page margins, paragraph alignment, and spacing. Clicking anywhere on the document window changes the magnification, cycling through the three available levels. Starting from the full-page view, the first click zooms you in on the portion of the page you clicked on, the second gives you a life-size close-up of a still smaller area, and the third click returns you to the full-page view. You can also change the magnification by clicking on the Zoom In or Zoom Out buttons in the Toolbar.

To page through the mock-up of your document, click on the Next Page button. You can move back toward the beginning with the Prev Page button. To display only a single page of the document instead of two, click on the One Page button; you can switch back to the two-page view by clicking on the same button, which will now read Two Page. You can also page through the mock-up with the PgUp and PgDn keys.

When you're satisfied that the document looks as you expected, click on the Print button to begin the actual printing process, covered in the next section. On the other hand, if you find mistakes, click on the Close button to return to editing the document.

Printing

When you are about ready to print, don't forget to save your file first just in case the computer or the printer goes berserk in the process and you lose your file. If you want to print only a portion of your document, select that portion. And don't forget to turn on the printer and make sure it has paper and is ready to print (in other words, that it is *online*).

Then, to print just choose File ➤ Print (or you can press Ctrl-P or click on the Print button from Print Preview). You'll be presented with a dialog box asking you about the following options:

Name (of Printer)   If the printer you plan to use isn't already chosen in this box, choose it from the drop-down list of your installed printers.

Properties   This button takes you to the Printer Properties dialog box for the selected printer. From this dialog box, you can choose the paper orientation (portrait or landscape), paper size and feed, print quality (for text) and resolution (for graphics), and other options available for your printer. See the discussion of printer properties in Chapter 8 for full details.

Print Range   If you want to print all the pages, click on All. If you want to print specific pages only, click on Pages and type in the range of page numbers you want to print in the *From* and *to* boxes. If you want to print only text that you selected, click on Selection.

Copies   The number of copies of each page to be printed.

Collate   Whether each complete copy should be printed one at a time, in page order (more convenient but slower), or all copies of each page should be printed before moving on to the next page (quicker but requires you to hand collate). Applies only if you're printing more than one copy of the document.

When you've made your choices, press Enter or click on OK. If the printer is connected and working properly, you should have a paper copy of your document in a few moments.

The Print Button

If you're sure the settings in the Print dialog box are already correct and you want a copy of the entire document, you can streamline the printing process via the Toolbar's Print button. It's the one showing the picture of a printer ejecting a page.

When you click on the Print button, WordPad immediately begins sending your document to the printer via Windows' Print Manager—you won't have to deal with the Print dialog box.

Chapter 20

Communicating Using HyperTerminal

FEATURING

The HyperTerminal program supplied with Windows lets you and your PC make contact with other computers to exchange or retrieve information. With HyperTerminal and the right hookups, you can communicate with other computers whether they are in your own house, around the block, or on the other side of the world. The kinds of information you might share in this way run the gamut from electronic mail through instant stock quotes to complete document files (such as word-processing or spreadsheet documents). More and more people use communications programs to connect to their company's computer so they can work from home—a style of work called *telecommuting*.

There are countless types of information you can access with your PC and a communications program such as HyperTerminal. You've probably heard of the Internet, a web-like international network of computers that has become the most talked-about telecommunications phenomenon of the '90s. If you subscribe to an Internet access service, you can tap news, scientific data, and commentary and discussions on almost any topic imaginable via HyperTerminal. Commercial information (online) services such as CompuServe, Prodigy, and Genie offer a lot of information, too, but they also provide shopping, investing, and even dating services. Nowadays, many clubs and organizations have their own dial-up Bulletin Board Systems (BBSs) where members can leave messages and read notices of interest. Numerous BBSs also provide a wide variety of public-domain software and shareware that anyone with a computer, a modem, and a communications program can have just for the taking.

Working with HyperTerminal

We'll get into the details of how to operate HyperTerminal in a moment, after a summary of the steps required to set up your system for telecommunications. For now, I owe you a quick answer to a question you may have: Why is the choice on the Start menu called HyperTerminal *Connections*, instead of plain HyperTerminal? The reason is that HyperTerminal needs a different setup to communicate with each different connection (information service, BBS, computer, or what have you). But after you've set up for a given connection, connecting again is as simple as double-clicking on its icon in the HyperTerminal Connections folder. In the example on the next page, I'm just a double-click away from the Internet, CompuServe, MCI Mail, and the chemistry lab at the university.

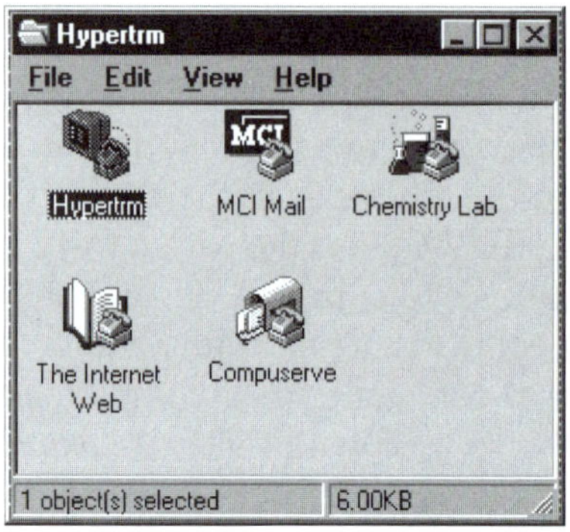

HyperTerminal is usually set up to display its Dial dialog box (or the prerequisite setup dialog boxes) when the program starts. For this reason, you may not see HyperTerminal's *main window* for a while. Just so you'll know, Figure 20.1 shows how the main window looks. Like many other Windows programs, it has a Toolbar at the top full of buttons for one-click access to common commands. At the bottom is the Status Bar, which keeps you informed of the progress of your

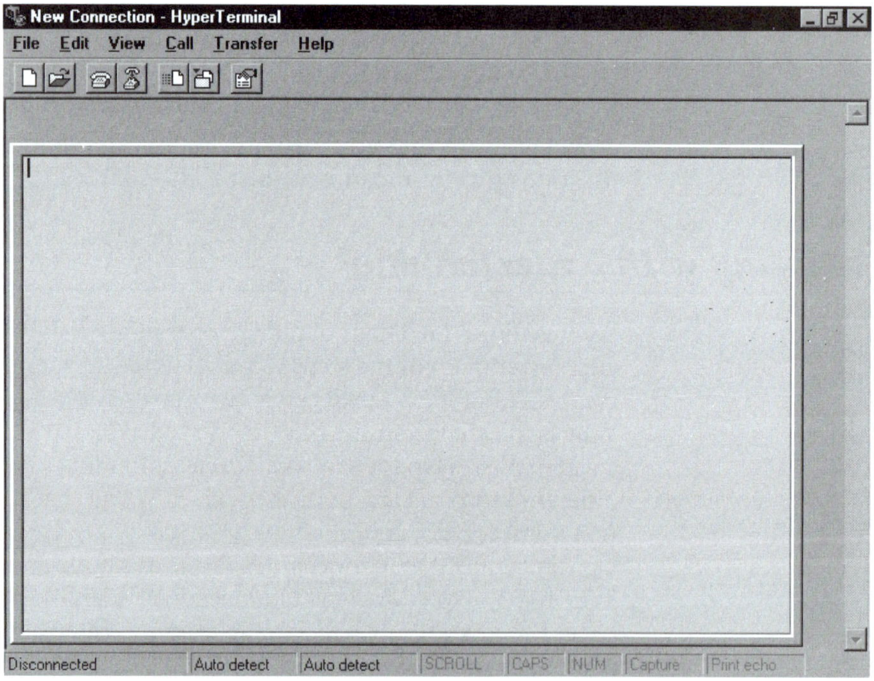

Figure 20.1   *The main HyperTerminal window*

communications session. (You can shut the Toolbar and Status Bar off if you prefer—we'll talk about that below.)

Within dialog boxes, you can click on the Help button at the upper right and then on a button or setting of interest to get a quick help message.

Finally, an apologetic explanation is in order here: The information in this chapter is necessarily somewhat general. Because a communications program such as HyperTerminal can be used to connect to an almost endless variety of information services and computers, it's impossible to cover all the specific situations. What's more, each service typically has its own way of logging on, transmitting and receiving files, and so on. So, instead of demonstrating exact procedures, I'll discuss all the aspects of the HyperTerminal program and explain the general steps you'll have to understand to use it effectively.

FOR WINDOWS 3 USERS

If you've been relying on the Terminal program supplied with previous versions of Windows, making the transition to HyperTerminal will be easy. But before you decide to switch to HyperTerminal, you should compare the two programs to see which really fits your needs best. You may find that sticking with Terminal makes more sense, especially if you're already very familiar with how it works.

While HyperTerminal offers a few meaty improvements over Terminal, most of the changes have to do with making your communications sessions easier and better looking. On the other hand, some of Terminal's most useful features aren't available in HyperTerminal.

One thing you won't sacrifice if you stick with Terminal is speed: When it comes to telecommunications, the limiting factor is modem speed, always far less than the speed of your software.

For my money, the most important additions to HyperTerminal are the new file-transfer protocols, especially Zmodem. Zmodem's speed, its ability to communicate the name and size of a file, and its talent for recovering gracefully from interruptions make it the best of the widely used protocols. Zmodem's absence from Terminal is that program's Achilles heel.

Another substantive improvement is in the area of complicated dialing sequences. While Terminal can remember a phone number in each setup file, there is no way to configure it to automatically access outside lines, dial credit-card numbers, or shut off call waiting. HyperTerminal does all this with aplomb.

(continued on next page)

Other new features address convenience and cosmetics. For example, the Toolbar buttons are a nice addition for one-click access to commands, and the reorganization of the various settings into a set of concise tabbed dialog boxes is much less confusing for the newcomer.

Now comes the bad news. If you're used to Terminal, here's what you'll miss in HyperTerminal:

▶ Function key commands. In Terminal, you can assign sequences of commands and typed characters to the function keys on your keyboard and then play back the command sequences by pressing the keys. For example, you can assign to a function key the sequence of characters you have to type each time you log on to an online service or BBS (usually your name or ID number and a password). This can be a big time-saver if you telecommunicate frequently. HyperTerminal has no comparable feature.

▶ The ability to view text files from within the program. HyperTerminal lacks Terminal's View Text File command, meaning you have to switch to another application such as Notepad or WordPad to examine disk files (so you can figure out which one to send, for example).

▶ The ability to send selected text without copying it to the Clipboard first. Terminal's Edit menu has a Send command for selected text, but HyperTerminal lacks a counterpart.

▶ Tabular text format for received text. Terminal can be set up to recognize incoming text as a table and format it accordingly; HyperTerminal can't.

▶ Some advanced communications settings. A number of the settings available in Terminal have been dropped in HyperTerminal. These include Carrier Detect, Flow Control for text files, word wrap for outgoing text files, and the ability to set the number of columns in the window. While these aren't necessary very often, they do come in handy from time to time.

If you do plan to switch to HyperTerminal, you can make the transition as efficient as possible by importing the settings from your Terminal setup (.TRM) files. To open a Terminal setup file:

1. Choose File ➤ Open.

2. At the bottom of the Select Session File dialog box, choose Terminal files from the list in the *Files of type* box.

3. Locate the Terminal file you want, select it, and click on Open. HyperTerminal reads its settings.

4. Make any necessary adjustments to the settings via the Properties dialog boxes.

5. Choose File ➤ Save As to save the settings as a HyperTerminal connection (session file).

Once you've completed these steps, you can use the new settings just as you would any other HyperTerminal connection.

Setting Up Your Communications System

In most cases, you'll be using HyperTerminal to communicate across a telephone line. You might connect to the Internet, to a commercial dial-up service such as CompuServe, Dow Jones News/Retrieval, the Source, or MCI Mail, or you might call up a friend's or colleague's computer to exchange files. The other computer can even be of a different type, such as a Macintosh.

> **NOTE** *Telecommunications* is the term used for communication over telephone lines or via cellular phone systems.

To communicate in this way from a distance via the telephone line (as opposed to communications between computers connected directly together with a cable), you'll need a modem. A *modem* is a device that provides the electronic connection between a computer and the phone line. The modem attached to your computer converts digital information from the computer into an *analog* signal that travels over the phone line. On the other end of the line, the receiving modem does just the reverse (see Figure 20.2). The word *modem* stands for *modulator/demodulator*, as the process of converting digital information to an analog signal is called modulation.

Though you can always run the HyperTerminal program to experiment with it, you can't use it over the phone line without a modem.

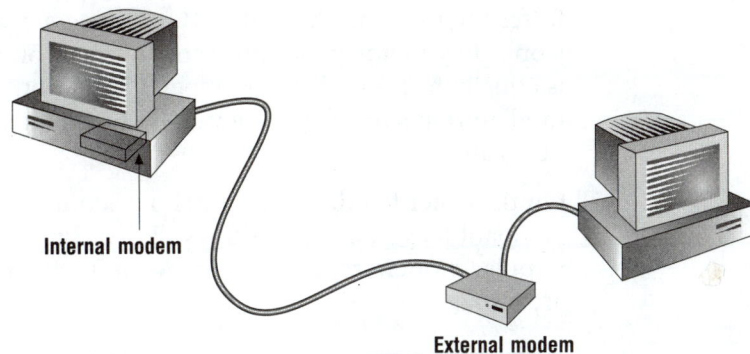

Internal modem

External modem

Figure 20.2 *A telecommunications setup, which consists of two computers, two modems, and interconnecting wires*

To connect a modem, you'll need either:

▶ an external modem, a cable, an unused serial port (where you plug in the cable), and an unused COM port (the electronics that permit communications at a specific computer *address*)

▶ an internal modem installed inside your computer plus an unused COM port

In either case, the general installation procedures are similar. You install the modem, plug your telephone line into it, and run a communications program (in this case, HyperTerminal).

The main distinguishing factor among modems is the speed at which they can transfer data over the phone lines. As of this writing, modems that transmit data at 14,400 bits per second are the most popular, though many slower modems are still in use and faster ones are available. (When it comes to bits-per-second ratings, the larger the number, the faster the transmission.)

NOTE   You're likely to see the word *baud* used as a synonym for bits per second as a rating of modem speed. Technically, the two terms aren't strictly synonymous, and you can avoid confusion by sticking with *bits per second*.

Because I can't cover all the ins and outs of modem purchasing here, I'll leave the purchase and installation details to you. Comparative reviews in computer magazines are a great source of up-to-date consumer information. A few quick pointers: in theory, of course, the faster the modem, the better. But buying a brand-new superfast unit won't do you any good unless the modem on the *other* end of the line is equally fast—so don't overspend. And don't let anyone sell you a modem that's not *Hayes compatible*. Fortunately, though, most modems are.

On the other hand, if you somehow acquire a modem that isn't Hayes compatible, you can probably still use HyperTerminal because other popular modem types—such as MultiTech and TrailBlazer models—are also supported.

NOTE   *Hayes compatibility* lets you take advantage of some useful features of HyperTerminal (and most other communications programs) such as the ability to dial the phone for you automatically, redial busy numbers, and so on.

Make sure you have your modem connected to, or installed in, your computer properly, following instructions in the modem's manual, before continuing. Incorrect modem installation (most often caused by improper switch settings) is a frequent cause of communications problems.

Once the modem is installed, Windows should be able to set it up properly for you. If there's a glitch in the setup process, the most likely solution will be to manually change the settings for the COM port to which you've connected the modem. Of course, you'll need to know which COM port that is. Beyond that, Chapter 26 will point you in the right direction when it comes to manually configuring the ports.

Setting Up a HyperTerminal Connection

Your most basic rule in communicating holds true in HyperTerminal: You have to know how to reach the other party. Before doing anything else, find the telephone number your modem must dial to connect to the information service, BBS, or computer you're trying to reach. Be sure you have the number for modem communications—in printed material it may be labeled the *modem* or *data* number. *Voice* or *fax* numbers won't work.

While you're looking for the number, see if you can locate any details on the communications setting in force at the computer you want to connect to. Your system must be set up to match, as detailed later in this chapter.

Starting HyperTerminal

To access HyperTerminal, begin from the Start menu and choose Programs ➤ Accessories ➤ HyperTerminal Connections. This will display the contents of the HyperTerminal folder. This window will look like the one shown earlier in this chapter except that the first time you use it, the HyperTerminal icon is the only icon you'll see.

Double-click on the HyperTerminal icon to run the program and prepare to set up a new connection. Once a specific connection has been set up, you'll be able to double-click on its icon to start a communications session with that connection.

Defining a New Connection

When you start from the program icon (rather than from an existing connection icon), HyperTerminal asks you to define a new connection in the dialog box shown here:

Connection Description

New Connection

Enter a name and choose an icon for the connection:

Name:

Icon:

OK   Cancel

You can also set up a new connection once you're working with the main HyperTerminal window by choosing File ➤ New Connection or clicking on the New button on the Toolbar to display the above dialog box.

Your first step is to give the new connection a name. Keep it simple—something like *MCI* or *Bill's office PC* will do. Then pick out an appropriate icon for the connection from the scrolling list and click on OK to go on.

Entering a Phone Number

Next you must supply the phone number your modem should dial to make the connection. HyperTerminal displays the Phone Number dialog box, shown on the next page.

Type in the phone number for the new connection. You have your choice of styles:

1-(510)-555-1111

1-510-555-1111

15105551111

555-1111 (if you are calling a local number)

In case you're wondering, HyperTerminal ignores dashes and parentheses in the main phone number.

If the phone number for the new connection is local, that's all you have to do—Windows has already entered your settings for the country code and area code. If you're dialing out of the area or out of country, use the first two boxes to set the correct country and area code. And if you have more than one modem connected to your computer, choose the one you want to use for this connection from the list at the bottom of the dialog box.

OK the Phone Number box when all the settings are correct.

Setting Dialing Properties

Once you've set the phone number, HyperTerminal assumes you want to dial it and presents you with the following dialog box:

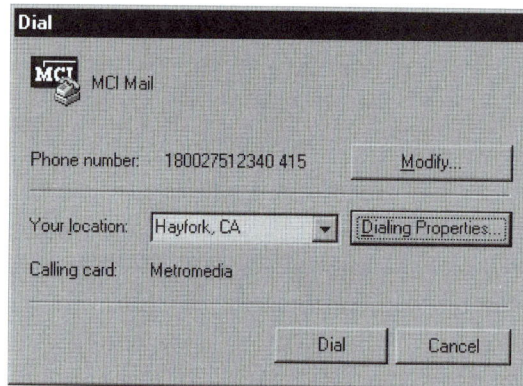

At this point, it's safe to go ahead and click on OK to see if the setup works. But don't be too surprised if nothing happens. In many cases, you'll need to change other settings before you can connect successfully.

Take a look at the area labeled *Your location*. Here, you should select the choice that describes where you are at this moment. The first time you use HyperTerminal, the only choice available is the nondescript selection *Default location*. This corresponds to the area code and country you entered when you set up Windows itself, so if you haven't moved, it may well be correct for those items.

If you use a portable computer, however, you may be thousands of miles from your default location. And besides, there are other considerations: Do you have to dial 9 to get an outside line? Are you dialing from a customer's office, so it will be necessary to use your telephone credit card? Or are you at a friend's place who doesn't believe in high technology and never installed a push-button phone? If so, tone dialing won't work.

To change any of these properties for the default location or to set up new locations from scratch, click on Dialing Properties. You'll see the dialog box shown in Figure 20.3.

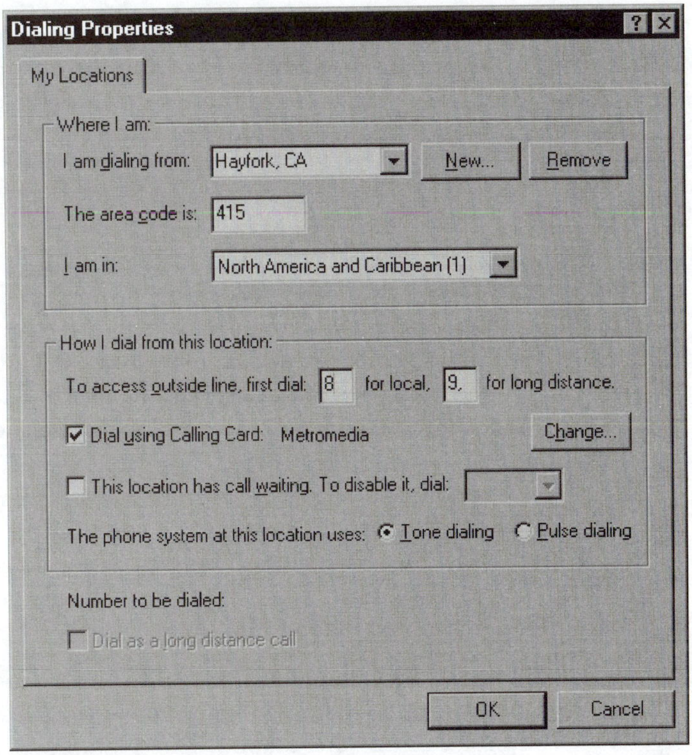

Figure 20.3   *The Dialing Properties dialog box*

NOTE   The Dialing Properties dialog box controls dialing settings for the Phone Dialer accessory, too. Phone Dialer is covered in Chapter 14.

Follow these instructions to set up or change a location and its dialing properties:

1.   First comes a group of settings collectively titled *Where I am*. In the area labeled *I am dialing from*, choose the name for the location settings you want to work with. To create a new location, click on New and type in the name. For example, if you move around from place to place with your computer, you'll want to create locations, say, for your home, for your office, and for each customer site. After you create a new location, it will automatically appear in the *I am dialing from* area.

2. In the next area, type in the area code for the location you're setting up. Remember, you're identifying *your* location—the location where you'll be when you use these settings. (Don't type in the area code of the number you're dialing.)

3. Likewise, choose the location's country code from the list in the *I am in* area.

TIP   Insert commas into the phone number to tell your modem to pause before moving ahead to the next digit. On Hayes-compatible modems, each comma results in a two-second pause. At least one comma is necessary when you have to dial a special number to reach an outside line. So a typical entry in the boxes for accessing an outline line would be **9 , .**

---

4. Next comes a group of settings titled *How I dial from this location*. On the first line in this group, type the numbers you must dial to reach an outside line for local and long-distance calls. By the way, the dialer knows enough to add a 1 before long-distance numbers—you don't need to enter it here.

5. If you use a calling card to dial from this location, check the box on the next line. When you do—and if the location wasn't previously set up for calling-card dialing—the Change Calling Card dialog box appears:

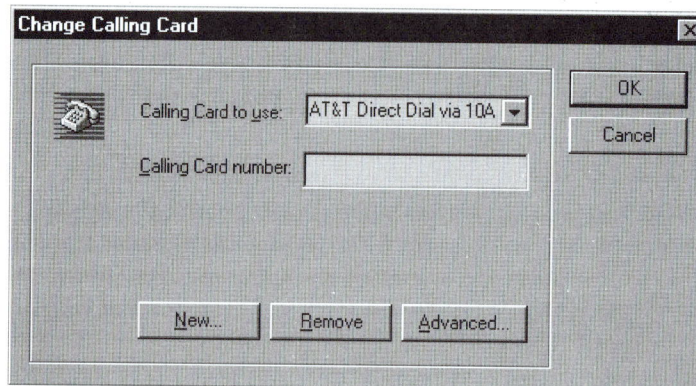

Here, choose the type of calling card you have from the list. Then type in your card number (your *PIN*), the number you must dial so the phone company can bill you. If your card isn't listed, use the instructions in *Customizing Calling Card Settings* below.

TIP Again, you may need to add one or more commas in a calling-card dialing sequence to create pauses. Often it takes several seconds for the second dial tone to come on after the connection to the service is made.

---

6. If the phone line at this location has the call waiting "service" (I regard call waiting as a punishment), be sure to check the box labeled *This location has call waiting*. Then choose the sequence of characters that must be dialed to disable call waiting at this location (if the correct sequence isn't available in the drop-down list, just type in the characters yourself). If you don't disable call waiting, calls that come in during a communications session will likely interrupt the connection, forcing you to start the session all over again.

7. Click on the radio button for the type of phone line at the location, tone or pulse (pulse is the type of dialing used by rotary-dial phones). If you're dialing from a location with a rotary phone, you will still be able to use tone dialing—which is faster—if the line is set up properly. If you don't know, you can always try tone dialing first and switch to pulse if tone doesn't work.

8. Check the display at *Number to be dialed*, which shows the actual digits that will be dialed. If you find an error, go back to the appropriate section and re-enter the correct codes.

9. The last option in the Dialing Properties dialog box is the check box labeled *Dial as a long distance call*. This choice is available only if the number you're dialing has the same area code as your current location. If you check this box, the dialer adds a 1 before the number and any other special access numbers you've specified for long-distance calls. When the box is unchecked, the number is dialed as a local call.

10. Click on OK to close the Dialing Properties dialog box and return to the Dial dialog box.

At this point, you may be ready to proceed with making the connection to another computer. On the other hand, there is a reasonable chance that you will need to modify one or more of the rather technical settings that pertain to communicating via a modem. See the next major section, *Choosing Communications Settings*, if you want to check your settings now or if your attempt to connect fails.

Customizing Calling-Card Settings

The dialer comes set up for several popular telephone calling (credit) cards, but with so many different carriers, yours may not be on the list. Here's how to set up your own calling card or modify the settings for an existing card:

1. Display the Dialing Properties dialog box (Figure 20.3) by clicking on the Dialing Properties button on the Dial dialog box in HyperTerminal (or by choosing Tools ➤ Dialing Properties in Phone Dialer).

2. Check the *Dial using Calling Card* box if it's not already checked. If the Change Calling Card dialog box appears automatically, go on to step 3; otherwise, click on the Change button to display the new dialog box.

3. If you're adding a new calling card—one that's not on the list at *Calling card to use*—click on the New button. In the little dialog box that appears, type in the name of your card and click on OK. The new name appears as the selected card in the Create Calling Card dialog box.

4. To customize the dialing sequence for the currently selected card, click on Advanced in the Change Calling Card dialog box. Another small dialog box appears:

You use the Dialing Rules dialog box to enter the sequence of numbers that you must dial to place a call using your calling card. There are three entry areas allowing you to enter different dialing sequences (*rules*) for local, long-distance, and international calls. You can enter the actual digits that must be dialed, plus codes for various sequences such as the calling-card number (the PIN) and the phone number itself. Table 20.1 summarizes the entries you can make in a dialing rule. An example of a typical rule is shown below.

5. Click on OK to return to the Dialing Properties dialog box. If you're working in HyperTerminal, the calling-card sequence is added to the actual digits to be dialed displayed at *Number to be dialed*. For a bit of security, however, your private calling-card number is indicated by the name of the card in brackets. Check to ensure that the sequence shown is correct; if not, click on the Change button again to edit the calling-card settings. When the sequence is right, click on OK to close the Dialing Properties dialog box.

Here's an example showing how to build up a custom dialing rule using the characters in Table 20.1. Let's say your card requires the following dialing sequence: You begin by accessing your long-distance carrier by dialing 1-800-555-2000. After you hear the bong tone, you dial the phone number, beginning with the area code. You then wait for a second bong tone and finally dial your calling-card number.

Your entry in the Dialing Rules dialog box would look like this:

```
18005552000$TFG$H
```

Here's a breakdown of the entry's parts, in order:

▶ First comes the access number.

▶ After the access number, the first *$* tells the dialer to wait for the bong tone.

▶ The *T* tells the dialer to switch to tone dialing at this point in the dialing sequence. That way, you can when necessary set the dialer to initiate calls with pulse dialing on the main Dialing Properties dialog box. With the T command, your calling card—which depends on tone dialing—will still work.

▶ The *F* tells the dialer to dial the area code of the phone number you're calling.

Character(s)	Results
0-9	Dialed as typed
*	Dialed as typed (works only on tone dialing lines)
#	Dialed as typed (works only on tone dialing lines)
A–D	Dialed as typed (the letters A-D are used to control some phone systems; they work only on tone dialing lines)
E	Dials the country code for the phone number you're calling
F	Dials the area code for the phone number you're calling
G	Dials the phone number (without the area code or country code)
H	Dials the calling card number (PIN)
T	Dials digits that follow via tone dialing
P	Dials digits that follow via pulse dialing
,	Pauses for a fixed time (2 seconds on most modems)
!	*Flashes* the connection (same as hanging up for half a second or pressing the Flash button on your phone)
W	Waits for a second dial tone
$	Waits for the bong tone that indicates the system is waiting for a calling-card number or other entry
@	Waits for an answer followed by 5 seconds of silence as required by some systems

Table 20.2 *Valid Entries for Calling-Card Dialing Rules and Their Effects*

▶ The *G* tells the dialer to dial the phone number itself.

▶ The second *$* tells the dialer to wait again for another dial tone.

▶ The *H* at the end tells the dialer to dial your card number.

Choosing Communications Settings

Unfortunately, there are no set standards covering all aspects of the technology required for modem communications. But look on the bright side: Once you've figured out the correct settings for a given connection, HyperTerminal will remember them. From then on, all you have to do is start up the connection, and you're guaranteed success.

If you are in doubt about how to set these options, there's a simple solution. Just find out what the settings are on the computer at the other end of the line and set yours accordingly. If you can't find out what those settings are, go ahead and try the standard settings by dialing the connection and seeing if you can communicate. If that doesn't work, then start systematically altering the settings one at a time, testing for a good connection each time.

To change the communications settings, choose File ➤ Properties or click on the Properties button on the Toolbar.

This works even if the Dial or Dialing Properties dialog box is active. You can also click on Modify in the Dial dialog box. After any of these steps, you'll see the Properties dialog box showing settings for the current connection, as shown in Figure 20.4.

NOTE To alter settings for another connection, you must open the Properties dialog box for that connection first. You can set the Properties for any connection from the HyperTerminal folder (the fast way: right-click on the connection's icon and choose Properties from the pop-up menu). Alternatively, when HyperTerminal is already running, switch to another connection by choosing File ➤ Open, then choose File ➤ Properties or click on the Properties button on the Toolbar.

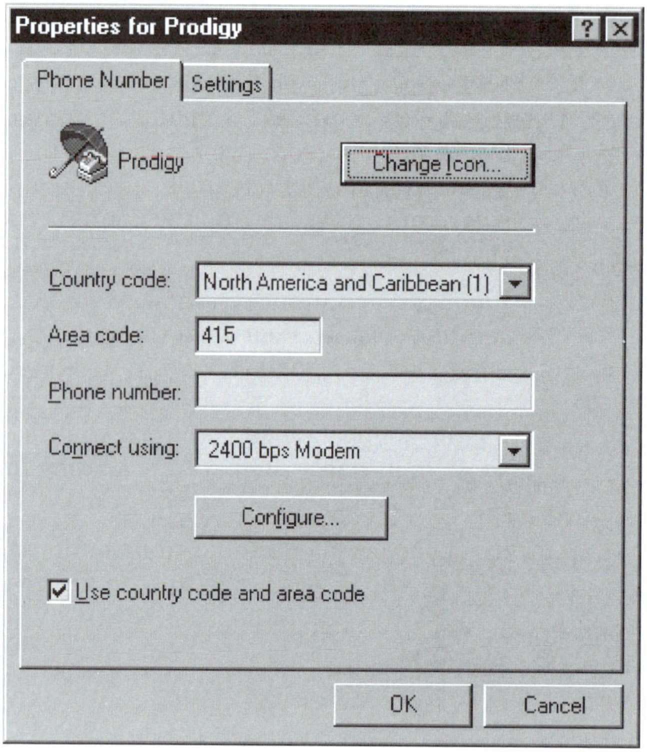

Figure 20.4   *Use the Properties dialog box to change communications settings*

Changes you make here apply only to the specific connection you're working with at the time. As you can see, the Properties dialog box has two tabs, one called Phone Number, the other called Settings.

The settings you may need to change to connect successfully fall into the following categories:

Basic Communications	For setting the speed and format for commands and data sent between the two connected computers.
Terminal Emulation	For choosing between the types of terminals that HyperTerminal can simulate (terminals are defined below). Both the remote computer and your software must be set to the same terminal type to communicate correctly.

In addition, you can control a variety of settings that are a matter of preference, detailed at the end of this section.

Choosing Basic Communications Settings

What I'm calling basic communications settings control the fundamental "language" of modem-to-modem communications. They determine such critical characteristics as how fast information flows between the modems, how they signal each other, and how each modem can tell one nugget of information from another.

One fundamental principle bears repeating: Most of these settings must be identical on both ends of the communications link (I'll note the exceptions as they come along). Because you probably have no control over the settings at the other end of the line, you're stuck with making sure your settings match. Actually, most connections will work without any changes—HyperTerminal's standard settings are the most popular ones, in use by most of the major commercial information services. But if you experience problems or if you know the other computer's settings are different, you'll need to alter the standard settings.

All the basic communications settings are controlled via the modem Properties dialog box. Access it as follows:

1. Display the Properties dialog box for the connection you're working with (Figure 20.4).

2. In the list labeled *Connect using*, choose the modem you want to use for the connection.

3. Click on the Configure button. You'll see the Properties dialog box for this particular modem, as shown in Figure 20.5.

   The modem Properties dialog box has three tabbed pages: General, Connection, and Options.

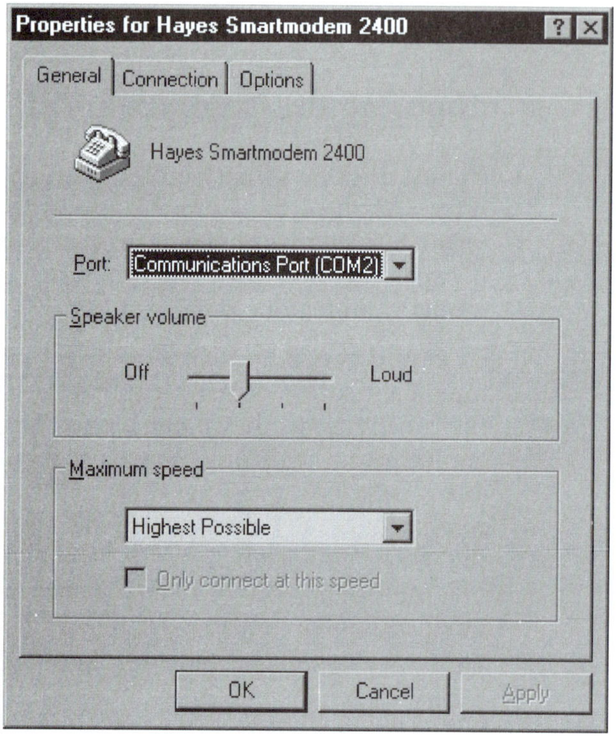

Figure 20.5　The Properties dialog box for modem settings

The Port Setting

> **NOTE**　There's a subtle but important distinction between the communications or COM ports, which are circuits that permit communications at a particular computer address, and the *serial* ports on the back of your computer, which are the physical receptacles into which you plug devices like external modems. Each serial port is assigned to a specific COM port. On the other hand, you may not have a serial port for every COM port—devices such as internal modems can access a COM port directly.

The first setting on the General page of the modem Properties dialog box is Port. Here, you tell HyperTerminal which *port* your modem is connected to. Most PCs have at least two communications ports, called COM1 and COM2. Many systems have COM3 and COM4 ports as well. Each modem is assigned to one of these ports when you first install the modem. If the port has changed, you can change the setting to match by choosing from the list here.

CAUTION Don't change this setting unless you know what you're doing. It's uncommon for the port to which your modem is connected to change—often, you would have had to plug the modem into a different place on the back of your computer or change little switches on the modem. If you change the port setting incorrectly, HyperTerminal won't be able to access your modem at all.

This is an exception to the rule about your settings needing to match those of the other computer. The port setting pertains exclusively to communications between *your* computer and *your* modem, and doesn't affect interactions between your system and another modem.

Setting Modem Speed

The speed at which your modem transfers information makes a big difference in how much work you can get done during a communications session. Just how fast information can travel between two modems depends on two things: the top speed of the *slower* modem and the quality of the telephone line.

NOTE As discussed before, modem speed is measured in bits per second, or *bps*. Typical modem speeds at this writing range from 1,200 and 2,400 bps at the low end through 9,600 and 14,400 bps, available with most modems now being sold, to 28,800 bps for the latest reasonably priced models. At any given speed, some modems achieve even faster transmission rates by *compressing* the data. When you set the modem speed in Windows, use the value for the actual speed (with compression turned off).

In any connection, the theoretical speed limit is set by the slower modem—obviously, it won't do you any good to have a super-fast modem when you're communicating with an old, slow unit. Usually, though, you don't need to worry about the speed of the other modem. Because most modems can sense the speed of the other modem, automatically adjusting themselves to match, you may be able to leave yours set to its maximum speed. If your modem cannot auto-adjust, though, you'll have to set its speed to match the other unit (consult your modem's instruction manual to see if it can auto-adjust). If the two modems are mismatched for speed, you will fail to get a connection, or you may see weird characters or punctuation marks on your screen instead of normal text.

In practice, the top speed you actually achieve may be less than the theoretical limit, depending on the quality of the phone line. If there's much static or distortion on the line—still a problem on some long-distance calls—you may need to drop your speed setting down a notch (from, say, 14,400 bps to 9,600 bps or from 2,400 to 1,200) to avoid data loss.

Also, many information services, such as CompuServe, charge more for your connection time when you use a fast modem. You'll save money if you take advantage of the faster communications speed to get your work done quicker. On the other hand, if you just like to dial up and browse through the available options, you may save money at a slower speed.

To change the speed setting, display the modem Properties dialog box (Figure 20.5). Then:

1. In the Maximum speed area, choose the speed you want. The setting is labeled *Maximum speed* on the assumption your modem can auto-adjust to lower speeds to match its counterpart on the other end of the line. If your modem lacks that feature—this is unlikely—the speed you choose here will be used exclusively. If you choose the Highest Possible option, Windows will try to connect at the fastest speed your modem and computer can handle.

2. If you're sure you don't want to connect at a slower speed than the one you've set, check the box labeled *Only connect at this speed*. This can be useful if you'd rather call back later to take advantage of a higher speed if the receiving modem is too slow at the moment. This choice is available only if your modem's auto-adjust feature can be turned off.

Specifying the Data Format Settings

Three key settings pertain to the way the two modems in a connection define and detect individual chunks of data. The two modems must agree on the same format for data, or they will speak completely different languages.

The individual data-format settings—data bits, parity, and stop bits—are described in separate paragraphs below. To change any of these settings:

1. Display the Properties dialog box for the connection you're working with (Figure 20.4).

2. In the list labeled *Connect using*, choose the modem you want to use for the connection, then click on the Configure button. In the Properties dialog box for this modem (Figure 20.5) click on the Connection tab. The dialog box should now display the page shown in Figure 20.6.

3. For each of the three settings in the *Connection preferences* area, select the choice you want from the list.

Setting Data Bits   The *Data bits* setting refers to the number of *bits* (the smallest division of computer information) you want to send out in each separate chunk of data. For example, each letter is typically

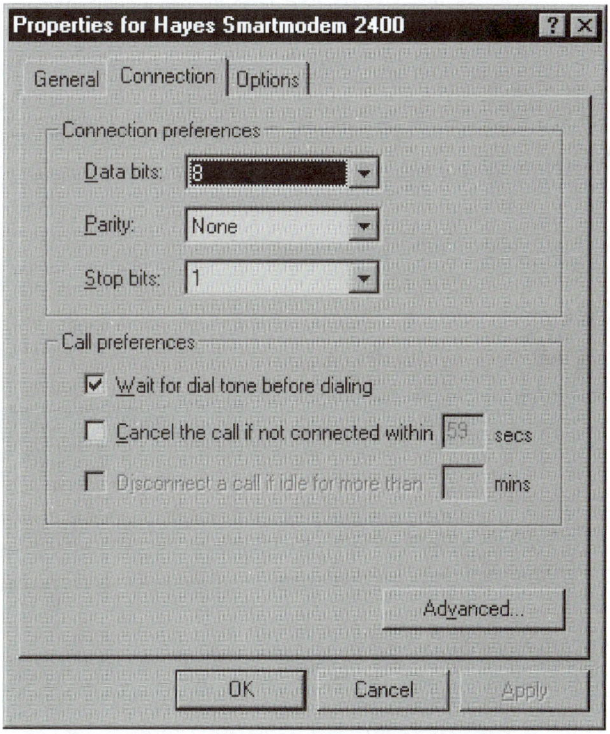

Figure 20.6 *The Connections page of the modem Properties dialog box*

stored in your computer as eight bits. (Eight bits is called a *byte*.) Suffice it to say that this setting is almost always going to be 8 and must be 8 if you are intending to transfer binary files between computers. Binary files include all programs and any documents that consist of more than plain ASCII characters. Thus, formatted word-processing documents, spreadsheets, and graphics documents are binary files. The other popular standard is 7 bits, which allows you to send plain text files slightly faster. The 4-, 5-, and 6-bit options are rarely used. Change this setting only if you are specifically told that the other system uses a setting other than 8 bits.

Setting Parity   *Parity* is a means by which the communications software can perform a rudimentary check to see if an error has occurred in the transmission of each byte of data. Parity checking isn't commonly used, and the standard setting is None. If you are specifically told that the system with which you're communicating uses parity checking, change this setting to match.

Setting Stop Bits   *Stop bits* are used by the computers on both ends to indicate the end of one character and the beginning of the next. You can probably leave this set to 1. Change this setting if you are specifically told that the other system uses 2 or 1.5 stop bits.

Special Dialing Settings

> **NOTE**   Because they only affect your own modem, these dialing settings are an exception to the rule about matching your settings to those at the other end of the line.

Two settings control the way your modem interacts with the telephone line. You'll need to change these settings if your modem is unable to dial for you even when other settings are correct. This can happen with certain types of phone systems that have nonstandard dial tones—or no dial tone at all—or that require you to dial outside calls via the operator.

The two settings are:

Wait for dial tone before dialing: This check box is located on the Connection page of the modem Properties dialog box. It's available only if Windows knows how to control your modem's ability to recognize the dial tone. The box should be checked if there's a delay before the dial tone comes on—otherwise HyperTerminal will start dialing too soon. Clear the box if the system uses a nonstandard dial tone, if there is no dial tone at all, or if you will be dialing yourself or with the operator's help.

Operator assisted or manual dial: This check box is located on the Options page of the modem Properties dialog box. Check it only if you need to dial the phone yourself or via the operator. When this box is checked, HyperTerminal displays a message telling you to dial the number after you click on Dial on the Dial dialog box:

As the message indicates, you should then dial the number (directly, or with the operator's help). When you hear the modem at the other end of the line answer, click on the Connect button and hang up the receiver.

Specifying Advanced Settings

A number of the basic communications settings are accessible in a separate window for advanced settings. These settings are perhaps more technically complex than the ones described above, but they can be just as critical to successful communications. They include:

▶ error-control settings

▶ flow-control settings

▶ low-speed settings

▶ custom-initialization commands

To access these settings, begin from the Connection page on the modem Properties dialog box (see Figure 20.6). Click on the Advanced button to display the Advanced Connection Settings dialog box, shown here.

When you're through making changes to the advanced settings, click on OK to return to the modem Properties dialog box. From there, you can change other settings or click on OK again to return to HyperTerminal.

Selecting Error-Control Settings   Some modems come with built-in circuits that detect and correct errors in transmission and that *compress* data, reducing the amount of information that must be sent and, in turn, speeding up the transfer process. If your modem has these features, you can turn them on or off in the Advanced Connection Settings dialog box. Use the four check boxes in the area labeled *Use error control*.

To access any of these error-control features, you must first check the *Use error control* box. The remaining choices are:

> *Required to connect:* Even if your modem has error-control features, you may not be able to use them for a given connection—the modem at the other end of the line may not have them or some other problem may interfere. Check this box if you don't want to proceed with a connection unless the error-control features are working. If the box is clear, HyperTerminal will go ahead and connect even if error control isn't available.

Compress data: Check this box if you want to use the data-compression feature if it's available. At each end of the connection, information is compressed by the sending modem and then *decompressed* by the receiving modem. Data compression speeds up transmission significantly and appears to work reliably, so this box should be checked unless you have some specific reason to do otherwise.

Use cellular protocol: Some modems include a special error-control method for cellular communications, which are prone to more glitches than communications over standard phone lines. If you're communicating "cellularly," checking this box may be necessary for a successful connection. On the other hand, the extra error-control procedures will slow you down, so clear the box when you return to a regular phone line.

Setting the Flow-Control Method

> **NOTE** This setting has no effect on the interaction between your modem and the remote computer, so you don't need to match the other computer's setting.

In the process of receiving and sending data, your computer often has to attend to other tasks as well, such as storing information on disk. Sometimes these tasks can distract the computer from handling incoming data. The *Use flow control* setting in the Advanced Connection Settings dialog box determines how *your* computer interacts with *your* modem to manage such situations. It provides a way for the computer and the modem to agree when to stop and start the sending process so other contingencies can be dealt with.

Unless you know the system will work otherwise, leave the *Use flow control* box checked. Beneath the check box, choose one of the available flow-control protocols. The hardware method is more reliable, so choose its radio button unless your modem isn't able to respond via hardware.

Setting the Low-Speed Modulation Protocol   At speeds above 2,400 bps, modems use a standard international signaling (modulation) protocol. At 1,200 bps and 2,400 bps, however, there are two sets of signaling protocols in wide use: Bell and CCITT. The Bell protocols are the ones to use in the United States, while the CCITT are for Europe and many other parts of the world (outside the United States and

Europe, you'll need to check locally). Choose the appropriate radio button in the Advanced Settings dialog box.

Specifying Initialization Settings

NOTE   The initialization command may or may not pertain to settings in effect at the other end of the line.

If you need to send special commands to your modem before you begin a communications session—*initialization* commands—type them into the area labeled *Extra settings* in the Advanced Connection Settings dialog box. For example, you may want to tell your modem how many rings to try before giving up trying to connect with the remote computer. Or, if you don't have Touch Tone™ service, you can tell the modem to use pulse dialing instead. Check your modem's manual for the commands it uses.

By the way, you can send commands to your modem at any time from the main HyperTerminal window. Just type the command and press Enter. As an example, you can set up the modem to answer an incoming call after four rings with the command ATS0=4.

Choosing Terminal Settings

Before PCs were invented, people used *terminals* to communicate with large mainframe computers. Terminals are essentially nothing but a screen and keyboard with which data can be entered and displayed. They have no internal computing power or disk storage as does your PC. Because more than one manufacturer made terminals, conflicting standards developed regarding how data were displayed on the terminal screens and how keyboards worked.

These standards remain valid today. They apply to communications setups using PCs as well as to terminals. As its name implies, HyperTerminal can make your PC act like an old-style terminal. But because your computer has more brains and storage capabilities than a terminal, your PC is something of a chameleon—it can *emulate* more than one type of terminal with a change of options in a dialog box.

> **NOTE** Some of the settings on the Settings page have more to do with personal taste than ensuring successful communications. Still, because HyperTerminal lumps them together, I'll cover them in this section.

For successful telecommunications, two computer systems must use the same terminal standard. This almost always means that you'll be setting up your connection to match the terminal standard used by the remote system.

To set or check the settings pertaining to *terminal emulation* and related attributes in HyperTerminal, begin by choosing File ➤ Properties or clicking on the Properties button on the Toolbar. In the Properties dialog box for this connection, click on the Settings tab to display the page shown in Figure 20.7.

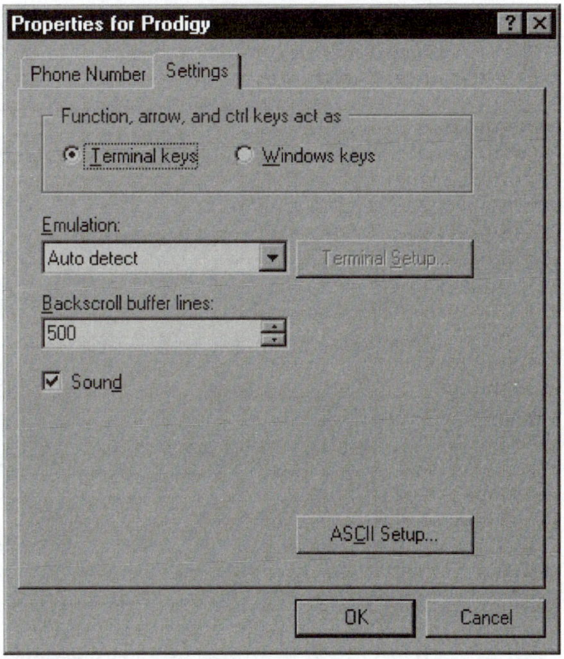

Figure 20.7 *The Settings page for a HyperTerminal connection in the Properties dialog box*

Controlling the Function, Arrow, and Ctrl Keys

HyperTerminal gives you a choice around how some of the keys work when you're communicating with another computer. In the area labeled *Function, arrow, and ctrl keys act as*, choose the Terminal keys radio button if you want HyperTerminal to send the codes for these keys to the other modem. Choose the Windows keys radio button to have HyperTerminal *trap* these keys so they're still available to control Windows. For example, pressing Ctrl-Esc would still work to open the Start menu.

Selecting a Terminal-Emulation Setting

The Emulation setting lets you choose which type of terminal Hyper-Terminal should emulate (work like) for this connection. The standard setting, Auto detect, usually works—HyperTerminal can tell what type of terminal the remote computer expects and sets everything up for you automatically. If the Auto detect setting doesn't work or if you simply want manual control over your system, choose the correct terminal type from the drop-down list.

Here are descriptions of some of the more popular terminal standards:

TTY (for teletype): is the least sophisticated choice and therefore has the highest level of compatibility. It makes your PC emulate what's known as a *dumb* terminal, meaning that the only formatting codes it uses in communicating to the remote computer are carriage return, Backspace, and Tab characters. If you do not know which terminal emulation to use or if you see strange characters on your screen during a session, try this.

VT52: emulates the DEC VT-52 terminal. Use this for information services such as CompuServe, BBSs, electronic mail services, and so on.

VT100: emulates the DEC VT-100 terminal. Select this for communicating with mainframes as though you were using a DEC VT-100, VT-220, or VT-240 terminal or compatible.

ANSI: recognizes a set of standard commands, or *escape sequences*, governing screen displays. Most BBSs optionally allow you to use these ANSI escape sequences to display their menus and other screen elements in color. ANSI stands for American National Standards Institute, an industry body that establishes voluntary standards for many products.

Choosing Options for a Specific Terminal Emulation If you choose a specific type of terminal in the Emulation area, you can then set various
options concerning its operation. To do this, click on the Terminal
Setup button. The available options are different for each terminal-
emulation setting. Here's an example:

```
VT52 Terminal Settings                    ? X
 ┌─Cursor──────────────────────────────────┐
 │                                          │
 │  ⦿ Block    ○ Underline    □ Blink       │
 │                                          │
 │  □ Alternate keypad mode                 │
 │                                          │
 │            ┌─────────┐  ┌─────────┐      │
 │            │   OK    │  │ Cancel  │      │
 │            └─────────┘  └─────────┘      │
 └──────────────────────────────────────────┘
```

Often, as in the above example, you can choose whether the Hyper-
Terminal cursor appears as a block or underline and whether or not it
blinks. When you change the cursor setting, it changes for all the
other terminal emulations. Settings unique to a given terminal emulation remain even after you select a different emulation; when you
change back to the first emulation, the previous settings are restored.

Setting the Backscroll Buffer Size

HyperTerminal records all the text that it displays in its main window,
storing it so you can scroll back to see earlier material at any time.
The recorded text is preserved in a backscroll buffer even when you exit
HyperTerminal so you can see text from a previous day's communication
sessions.

You can control how many lines of text the program records on the
Settings page of the Properties dialog box for the current connection.
The standard setting is the maximum, 500 lines. To change it, type in
a new number or click on the small arrow controls to increase or decrease the value.

Turning Sound On or Off

The Sound check box at the bottom of the Settings page toggles Hyper-
Terminal's beep off and on. Sometimes the remote computer will send

your computer the code that causes a beep sound. You may want to disable this if you find it annoying. To do so, clear the Sound check box.

Controlling How Text Is Sent and Received

Five settings control the way HyperTerminal handles text transferred between your modem and its counterpart at the other end of the line. To access these settings, click on the ASCII Setup button, found on the Settings page of the Properties dialog box. The ASCII Setup dialog box appears, as shown here:

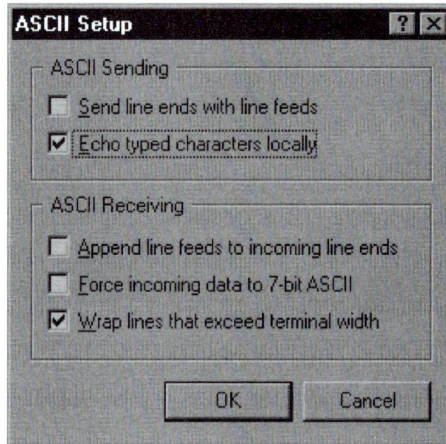

All five choices are check boxes, meaning you can turn them on or off individually by checking or clearing the box. Here's how they work:

Send line ends with line feeds: Computer systems differ in how they register the end of a line of text. Sometimes the system you're sending text to won't be able to detect the end of a line unless HyperTerminal sends a special character called a *line feed* after each line. If that turns out to be the case, check this box.

Echo typed characters locally: When this box is checked, the characters you type on your keyboard appear on your screen so you can see what you're typing. It may sound strange, but in some communications sessions you may find you can't see what you're typing unless this setting is turned on. That's because the remote computer isn't sending the characters it receives from you back to your screen. On the other hand, if you see double characters on the screen (such as *HHEELLLLOO!!*), clear this box.

Append line feeds to incoming line ends: If all the incoming text appears on a single line that gets continually rewritten, or if the cursor moves to the right margin and seems to get stuck, try checking this box. What's happening is that the other computer isn't sending the special line-feed character to move the cursor down after each line is complete. When you turn this setting on, HyperTerminal moves the cursor down every time it receives a finished line. If this box is checked and the text you receive is double-spaced, clear the box.

Force incoming data to 7-bit ASCII: On a PC, each character is represented by 8 bits of data, providing a total of 256 different characters. Although the first 128 characters have been standardized internationally, characters numbered 128 and above (*high-ASCII characters*) vary from country to country and from computer system to computer system (in fact, they are different in DOS and Windows). So if you see strange characters on your screen, it may help to check this box. HyperTerminal will then translate high-ASCII characters according to the International Standards Organization (ISO) 7-bit codes. Normal letters, numbers, and punctuation marks are left as is.

Wrap lines that exceed terminal width: Checking this box causes incoming text that is longer than the width of your screen to wrap to the next line.

Setting Other HyperTerminal Preferences

A smattering of other settings control various aspects of HyperTerminal's operation according to your preferences—these settings don't affect your ability to transfer information successfully. You can:

▶ control your modem's speaker volume

▶ control how long HyperTerminal waits to make a connection

▶ have HyperTerminal hang up automatically if no information is being transferred

▶ control the display

▶ change the font for the main window

Setting Speaker Volume

Many modems are equipped with speakers, allowing you to monitor the progress of a call audibly. If your modem has a speaker and Windows knows how to control the speaker (this varies by type of modem), you can change the volume as follows:

1. Choose File ➤ Properties or click on the Properties button to display the Properties dialog box for this connection (Figure 20.4).

2. Click on Configure to display the Properties dialog box for the selected modem (Figure 20.5).

3. Change the volume with the sliding *Speaker volume* control.

Setting Call Preferences

Two settings let you set waiting periods governing HyperTerminal's behavior in certain calling and communications situations. When dialing, you can specify the number of seconds HyperTerminal waits for a connection before giving up. After a connection is made, you can tell HyperTerminal to disconnect if no information has been transferred after a specified number of minutes.

Change these settings as follows:

1. Choose File ➤ Properties or click on the Properties button to display the Properties dialog box for this connection (Figure 20.4).

2. Click on Configure to display the Properties dialog box for the selected modem (Figure 20.5).

3. Click on the Connection tab.

4. To have HyperTerminal stop trying to connect after a given waiting period, check the box labeled *Cancel the call if not connected within* and type in the number of seconds. To have HyperTerminal disconnect after a period of inactivity, check the box labeled *Disconnect a call if idle for more than* and type in the number of minutes. (If Windows can't control the settings in question, they will be unavailable.)

Controlling the HyperTerminal Display

Several settings are available for controlling what you see in HyperTerminal and when.

For one thing, you can choose whether or not to display the Toolbar or the Status Bar. Just choose the appropriate item on the View menu to turn either bar on or off.

You can also decide whether the Dial dialog box appears when you first start HyperTerminal and whether to view a window showing modem status when HyperTerminal dials a number. To access these settings:

1. Choose File ➤ Properties or click on the Properties button to display the Properties dialog box for this connection (Figure 20.4).

2. Click on Configure to display the Properties dialog box for the selected modem (Figure 20.5).

3. Click on the Options tab. You'll see the settings shown in Figure 20.8.

4. The check boxes in the area labeled *Connection Control* determine whether or not HyperTerminal displays the terminal window (the main portion of the HyperTerminal display) before dialing the connection or after the call is concluded. In the *Status control* section, the check box labeled *Display modem status* turns on and off the message

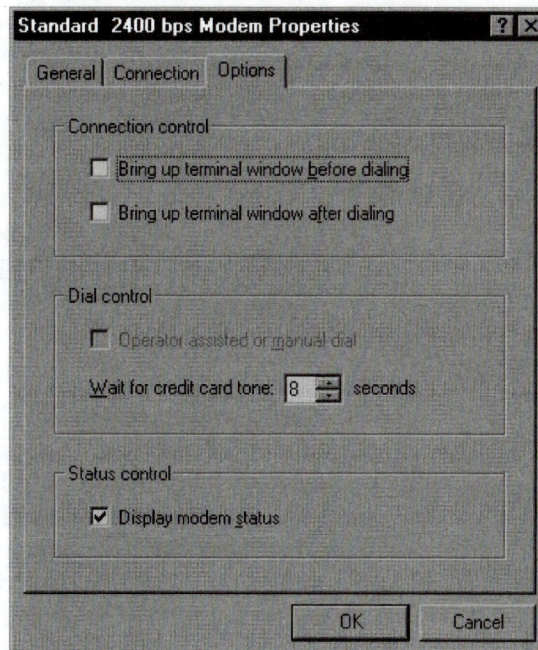

Figure 20.8   *The Options page of the Properties dialog box*

window (shown below) that tells you how a connection is progressing when HyperTerminal dials. (The *Dial control* settings on the Options page are covered earlier in this chapter.)

Choosing a Font

Another cosmetic option, this one determines which font and type size HyperTerminal will use to display both incoming and outgoing characters. This is actually a thoughtful feature, giving tired eyes a break when you're doing a lot of telecommunications. If you increase the font size beyond a size that will allow a complete line of text to fit in the window, scroll bars will allow you to scroll horizontally to see it. However, it's rather a nuisance to do this, and it's better to stick with a smaller size, such as 12 or 14 points.

To make a font change, choose View ➤ Fonts. Select the font, style, and size in the standard Fonts dialog box that appears, then click on OK.

Saving Your Settings

HyperTerminal automatically saves the changes in settings you make as soon as you click on OK in the Properties dialog box for the current connection as well as in the modem Properties dialog box. However, you can save the settings yourself just to be sure they're recorded. More practically, you can save the current settings as a new connection. That makes it easy to use existing settings to connect with a different service or computer—all you have to do is change the phone number and then use the Save As command.

To save the current settings for the connection that's already active, just choose File ➤ Save. To save them as a new connection, choose File ➤ Save As. The familiar Save As dialog box will appear. Give your connection a name, preferably one that will help you remember which information service or computer the settings are for, and click on OK.

Making Connections

NOTE By the way, if HyperTerminal has displayed the Dial dialog box but you don't want to make the connection at this time, just click on Cancel to go to the main HyperTerminal window.

Assuming you've completed all the setup steps properly, the process of actually making a connection couldn't be simpler. All you do is click on the Dial button on the Dial dialog box:

HyperTerminal displays the Dial dialog box first each time you start the program from an existing connection. There are other ways to bring up the Dial dialog box to start a new communications session:

▶ When you're creating a new connection, the Dial dialog box will appear after you've named the connection, chosen its icon, and typed in a phone number.

▶ Once you're working with the main HyperTerminal window—perhaps after completing a previous communications session—you can display the Dial dialog box again by choosing Call ➤ Connect or clicking on the Dial (Connect) button.

TIP   If you want to stop the dialing process, click on Cancel in the Connect window.

When you click on the Dial button, HyperTerminal immediately starts the dialing process. You'll see the Connect message window, informing you of the progress of the call:

Behind the scenes, HyperTerminal begins by sending a series of commands to the modem to prepare it for dialing. These are determined by the settings you've chosen, as detailed in the previous section.

Then HyperTerminal sends the command to dial the number. At this point, if your modem's speaker is on, you'll hear the telephone being dialed. When the phone on the other end is answered, you may hear some high-pitched tones indicating that the modems are "talking" to each other.

If the connection is successful, the message *Connected* will appear briefly in the Connect window and you'll hear three quick beeps. The Connect window will then disappear. If you have the Status Bar visible, you'll see the message *Connected* at its far left followed by a time indicator showing how long your computer has been connected to the remote machine in hours, minutes, and seconds.

At this point, if both modems are set up properly, and depending on how the other computer is programmed, you're likely to see messages from the connection on your screen. From now on, everything you type on the keyboard will be sent to the other computer. You can respond to these messages—or initiate messages of your own—by simply typing whatever you like. And you're now ready to transfer files from disk in either direction, as discussed later in the chapter.

What Might Go Wrong

A variety of problems can prevent you from successfully communicating. Here are the broad categories and some brief tips on how you can track down the specific problem:

▶ If you receive a message that no lines are available, or if the Connect window never displays the *Dialing* message, something is wrong with your modem or its connection to your computer. The modem may not be connected properly, it may not be turned on, or the COM port settings may be incorrect. Your modem could even be broken, though this is by far the least likely problem.

▶ If HyperTerminal is able to dial your modem, but can't establish a connection, it will eventually give up. You'll see the message *Busy* in the Connect window. Typical reasons for failure at this point are the following:

   ▶ There was a busy signal.

   ▶ The call didn't go through. Check to be sure the phone number is correct and that you've set up the Dialing Properties dialog box to dial the proper numbers to connect you to an outside line and to dial using your calling card, if you're using one.

   ▶ The other phone never answered.

   ▶ The other phone was answered, but not by a modem (you dialed a voice line or a standard fax machine, or the other modem was turned off). You may have entered the wrong number or area code.

   ▶ The modems are set at different speeds so they didn't recognize each other.

When any of these problems occur, the Connect window remains on your screen. The Dial Now button becomes active, so if you want to try again, just click on it.

▶ If a connection is made but you see gibberish on your screen, your modem settings don't match those of the other party. See *Choosing Communications Settings* above for details on changing modem settings.

Disconnecting

After you've completed a communications session, it's time to break the connection between your system and the other modem. When possible, the graceful way to do this is by telling the other computer you want to end the session. Most information services and BBSs let you type a command such as **EXIT** or **BYE** for this purpose. When you do, the other computer sends the *disconnect* command to your modem, and you are disconnected automatically.

Sometimes, though, it's necessary to break off a connection manually. All you have to do is click on the Disconnect button on the Toolbar or choose Call ➤ Disconnect.

When HyperTerminal disconnects, you'll hear three quick beeps. The message *Disconnected* appears at the far left of the Status Bar.

Making a Different Connection

Of course, after opening HyperTerminal from one connection icon and completing your communications session with that computer, you don't have to shut down the program to call a different destination. All you need do is choose File ➤ Open or click on the Open button on the Toolbar. Pick the connection (session) file you want to open, click on Open, and click on the Dial button to place the call.

Connecting via Cable

> **TIP** If you are connecting two computers directly to each other (without using modems), you might want to refer to *The RS-232 Solution (Second Edition)* (Sybex, 1994).

While you'll usually use HyperTerminal to communicate over the telephone lines, the program will also work to transfer information when you connect your computer to another computer directly, via a *serial cable*. All you need is the right type of cable: a *null-modem* cable, with jacks that fit the serial ports on the backs of the two computers (a modem is not required and shouldn't be used).

When you plug in the cable to your computer, be sure you know which COM port you've connected it to. Then, in HyperTerminal, proceed as follows:

1. Open the Properties dialog box for this connection to set up the program for that port. On the Phone Number page, select the correct COM port from the list at *Connect using*.

2. Click on the Configure button. You'll see the dialog box full of settings for this COM port shown in Figure 20.9. Select the maximum speed the two computers can reliably handle—direct connections are usually much faster than modem-based connections. The other settings work the same as they do for modems and are described earlier in the chapter. All of them should be set the same on both computers.

3. Click on OK twice to return to the main HyperTerminal window.

4. Click on the Connect button or choose Call ➤ Connect to establish the connection. HyperTerminal immediately proceeds with the connection—you won't see a Dial dialog box or anything similar. If all the settings are correct, you should be able to send messages back and forth between the two computers by typing on their keyboards. You can now send and receive text and files just as in a modem-based connection.

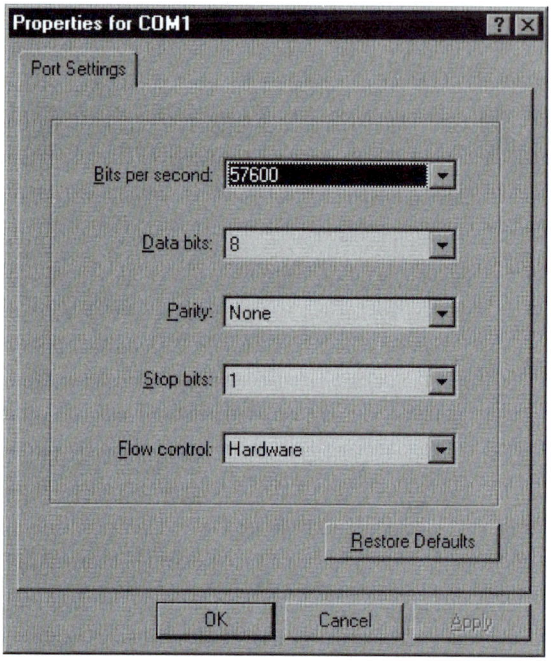

Figure 20.9   *Configure the COM port with the settings in this dialog box.*

Sending and Receiving Data

Once you've made a successful connection, you can begin to transfer data between the two computers. What you do now depends entirely on what the other computer expects from you. If you are calling an information service, BBS, or a mainframe computer, you will typically have to sign on to the remote system by typing your name and possibly a password. If you are calling a friend's or associate's computer, you can just begin typing whatever you want to say. In any case, once the initial connection is made, there are several ways that you can begin to transfer data between the two computers. The next several sections describe these techniques and how to use them.

Communicating in Interactive Mode

The simplest way to communicate information is directly from your keyboard. As mentioned earlier, once you're connected to the other computer, everything you type is automatically sent to the other end of the connection. Conversely, characters typed at the other computer will be sent to your computer, showing up on your screen. Sending and receiving data this way is called working in *interactive* or *terminal* mode. Communication sessions often begin in terminal mode, with each person typing to the other's screen.

Terminal mode is often used, too, when connecting to many of the information services and electronic-mail services that are interactive in nature. With these, you type certain commands to the host computer, and it responds by sending you some data. As information comes over the line to your computer, it will appear on the screen, as shown in Figure 20.10. As you type, your text will appear on the screen as well.

How HyperTerminal Displays and Stores Text

As each new line of text is received or typed in by you, the cursor moves down a line in the HyperTerminal window. Once it reaches the

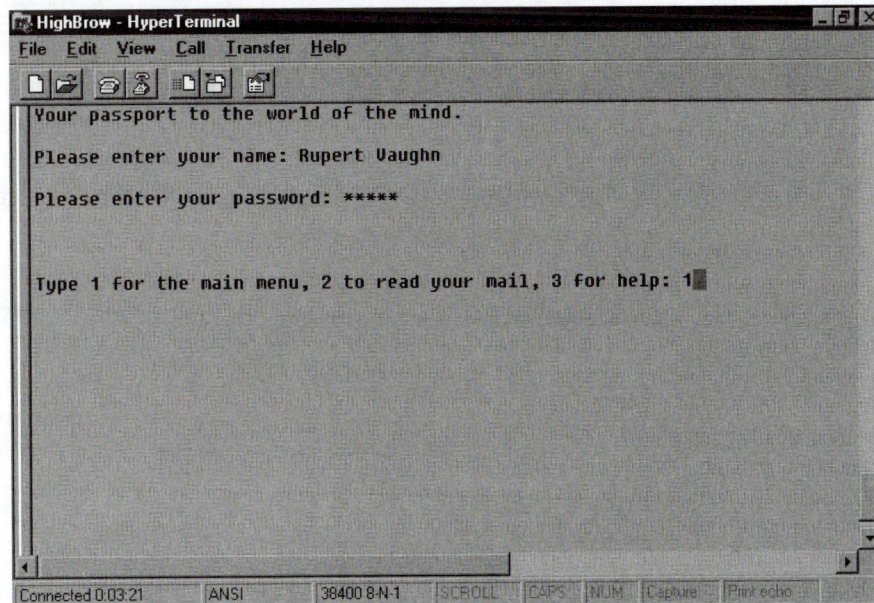

Figure 20.10 *A typical interactive session. Notice that the user entered the number 1 at the bottom of the screen in response to the prompt from the sender.*

bottom of the window, each new line shifts the previous text up so the oldest line disappears from view. This is just as text behaves in a word-processing program such as WordPad (Chapter 19).

But the older text isn't gone forever. HyperTerminal remembers the last 500 lines in its *backscroll buffer*. To see text that has scrolled off the screen, use the vertical scroll bar or the standard cursor-movement keys. Then scroll back down to continue interacting with the other computer. (You can scroll through previous text when you're not connected, too.)

Capturing Text

There will be times when you'll want a way to save data you see on your screen while you're working in terminal mode so you can work with it later. You can *capture* incoming text at any time during a communications session with the Receive Text File command on the Transfer menu and save it in a disk file for later reading, printing, or editing. Here is the basic procedure for capturing text:

1. Choose Transfer ➤ Capture Text.

2. A small dialog box appears, asking you to name the file in which you want the captured text stored. Type in the name (you can use the Browse button to select a new directory) but don't press Enter yet.

3. Click on OK. The file will be opened. If the Status Bar is visible, the Capture message becomes highlighted, indicating the capture is in progress.

4. Continue with your session. All incoming text, along with whatever you type as well, will be captured in the file you chose. When you want to stop capturing text, choose Transfer ➤ Capture Text again to display a new submenu (only available when a capture is currently in progress). Here, choose either:

   ▶ *Stop* to close the file or

   ▶ *Pause* to temporarily discontinue capturing text while leaving the file open for more. To resume the capture, choose Transfer ➤ Capture Text ➤ Resume.

By the way, after you stop a capture, you can add or append more text to the same file by simply restarting the capture process and specifying the file again. If you don't want the new text to go into the previous capture file, you must enter a different file name when you restart the capture process.

Capturing Selected Portions of Text

During text capturing there may be sections of text you don't want to save interspersed with portions you do. There are two ways to selectively capture portions of the text that appears in the HyperTerminal window:

▶ You can use the Pause feature of the Capture command to stop the capture process whenever you're receiving information you don't want to keep. When you expect more "good" information, use Resume.

▶ Alternatively, you can dispense with the Capture command and just allow HyperTerminal to store the text in its backscroll buffer. You can then scroll through the buffer to copy the information you want to keep to a document in a text-editing program such as Windows Notepad. See *Manipulating Text in the HyperTerminal Window* below for details.

Sending and Receiving Text Files

Receiving text files sent from the other computer is easy: You just use the Capture command described in the previous section. When you're connected to a BBS or information service, you'll first have to type whatever commands are needed to get the other computer to send you the file you want.

It's convenient to *send* short messages by typing them on your keyboard, but obviously, this would be an inefficient way to send larger quantities of text. HyperTerminal gives you an alternative: You can send documents already prepared by a word processor or other program and stored on disk. By composing your messages first with a word processor or text editor, you can drastically reduce the connection time (and resultant cost). And it's much easier than typing them using the primitive editing features of HyperTerminal.

There are two ways to do it. One method uses error correction to ensure that the other computer receives your file without any loss of data, and it also allows you to transfer complete documents. This is discussed in the next section. The other technique does not use error correction and can send *only* text, but it is compatible with a wider variety of computers.

> **CAUTION**   You cannot use the Send Text File command to send formatted documents or to send programs. Send such files as binary files as described in the next section.

The Send Text File command on the Transfer menu is the method for sending text only, *without* error correction. Use this command to send memos, letters, and so forth when the content alone of your text, without any fonts or formatting, will suffice.

Files you can send with this command are called, of all things, *text-only* files, also known as ASCII files. (Sometimes they're just called *text files*, but this can be a little confusing because a word-processing document might also be considered a text file.) Text-only files are standard means of communicating on most electronic-mail services such as MCI Mail. There are several ways to create text-only files:

▶ You can use a text editor such as Windows Notepad (see Chapter 22).

▶ Most word-processing programs, including WordPad, let you save a document as a text-only file. Remember that when you save a word-processing document as a text-only file, all formatting—including fonts, type styles, and spacing settings such as margins and indents—are lost.

▶ Files stored with HyperTerminal's Capture Text File command (described in the previous section) are also text-only files, and they'll work too.

Checking Settings for Text-File Transfers

Before sending or receiving a text file, you might want to check the pertinent settings for this connection. To do so:

1. Choose File ➤ Properties or click on the Properties button on the Toolbar. When the Properties dialog box for this connection appears, switch to the Settings page.

2. Click on the ASCII Setup button. A small dialog box appears.

ASCII Setup   ? ✕

ASCII Sending
- ☐ Send line ends with line feeds
- ☑ Echo typed characters locally

ASCII Receiving
- ☐ Append line feeds to incoming line ends
- ☐ Force incoming data to 7-bit ASCII
- ☑ Wrap lines that exceed terminal width

[OK]   [Cancel]

Only the first choice, *Send line feeds with line ends*, pertains to sending text-only (ASCII) files. If you need to add a line feed to the end of each line of text you send, check this box. You might have to talk with the person running the other computer to determine whether line feeds should be added or not. The three choices in the section labeled *ASCII Receiving* pertain to receiving text-only files. You can figure out which settings are correct based on the appearance of the text you receive.

3. Click on OK twice to close the dialog boxes.

Sending a Text File

Once you've selected the correct settings, you're ready to actually send the text file. Connect to the other computer if you haven't already done so. Then follow these steps:

1. Prepare the other computer to receive the text. If you're sending an e-mail letter via a BBS or commercial service, for example, type whatever command the service requires to prepare itself for the message. You might need to enter a command such as *Create* or *Send mail*, and then enter the name and electronic address of your recipient. Consult the service for details.

2. When the other computer is ready to receive your text, choose Transfer ➤ Send Text File.

3. A standard Windows file dialog box will appear. Select the file you want to transfer, then click on OK. The text from the file will appear on your screen as it is sent to the other computer.

4. When the entire file has been sent, type whatever command the other computer requires to indicate the end of the message or go on to send another file.

Sending and Receiving Documents and Other Files

Most of the files stored on your computer's disks do *not* consist of only text. Instead of simple sequences of characters arranged in lines, the typical file—whether it's a document created by your word-processing or spreadsheet program or the program itself—contains all sorts of information in encoded form. This information is perfectly understandable by your computer (with the right software), but it usually looks like complete gibberish to you and me.

> **TIP** There is a way, with a little legwork to send non-text files to another person through an electronic-mail service that only accepts text-only files. You have to use a utility program that converts binary files into a special type of encoded 7-bit "text" file before sending it. The receiving party will then have to reconvert the file on their end with the same utility program. Such utilities are available as shareware on many BBSs.

That's why you can't transfer most files with HyperTerminal's Capture Text and Send Text File commands. You need the Send File and Receive File commands instead. These commands transfer the entire document just as it is, without trying to interpret it as text. In the bargain, they detect and correct errors that have crept in during the transfer.

> **TIP** By the way, it's perfectly okay to send and receive text-only files via the Send File and Receive File commands to get the benefits of error correction. The only drawbacks: you won't see the text on your screen, and the process takes a tad longer.

It's not uncommon for data to be lost or corrupted during the transmission process over telephone lines, particularly when long distances are involved. As we all know, long-distance lines often suffer from noise, static, or even other people's conversations accidentally being crossed with ours. Usually we just put up with the noise, asking the other party to repeat their last sentence, or we redial the call.

Computers are less tolerant of such maladies. Noise on the line between two computers can cause a plethora of erratic data alterations during a file transfer. In response to this, computer scientists have devised numerous error-detection and error-correction schemes to determine whether errors have occurred in transmission and to correct them if possible. These schemes are referred to as *file-transfer protocols* because they also manage other aspects of the file-transfer process. HyperTerminal lets you choose from several of the most popular of these file-transfer protocols with its Receive File and Send File commands.

Understanding File-Transfer Protocols

To detect and correct errors, file-transfer protocols divide a file into a series of small sections, called *blocks*. The blocks are then sent sequentially, and each one is accompanied by a mathematically calculated code based on the contents of the block. After getting the block, the receiving computer sees whether its contents match this calculated code. If they do, the sending computer is advised to send the next block. If there is a discrepancy, the receiving computer asks the sending computer to retransmit the block until it's received properly. This process continues until the entire file is transmitted error free.

Some file-transfer protocols, such as Zmodem, keep track of how far along the file transfer is from moment to moment. If the connection is broken, they can pick up the file transfer where it left off so that you don't have to start all over again from scratch.

Choosing a File-Transfer Protocol

When you transfer a file with the Send File or Receive File commands, HyperTerminal lets you choose which of several file-transfer protocols to use for the transfer. Although each of the file-transfer protocols has its own characteristics, the critical point should sound familiar by now: To send or receive a file successfully, you need to use the same protocol as the other computer.

Often, when you're transferring files to or from a commercial service or BBS, you'll be able to tell the other computer which protocol to use. Whether or not you select the other computer's protocol, just be sure to set HyperTerminal to match.

Here's a list of the file-transfer protocols available in HyperTerminal:

Xmodem was the first widely used error-detection and correction scheme. It was devised by Ward Christensen, who placed it in the public domain in 1977 for use on microcomputers, which were just then becoming available. Xmodem is available on most information services, such as CompuServe. The 1K version is a bit faster than the standard version.

Ymodem is similar to Xmodem but a little faster and more reliable.

Kermit may be the only protocol available when you communicate with some larger computers such as the minicomputers at a university. It's usually slower than the others, so this protocol would be a second or third choice.

Zmodem is the fastest and most capable of HyperTerminal's protocols. Use this choice if the other computer permits it.

Sending Files

> **NOTE**   You can't pause a binary transfer, but you can stop it in midstream by clicking on Stop or choosing Stop from the Transfers menu.

To send a file, follow these steps:

1. Make sure you're online (connected).

2. Make sure the receiving computer is ready to receive the file. How you do this depends on the computer system, BBS, or information service to which you are connected. If you are sending a file to another PC, you may want to type a message in HyperTerminal mode telling the operator of the other computer to do what is necessary to prepare for receiving the file.

3. Choose Transfer ➤ Send File or click on the Send button on the Toolbar.

A small dialog box appears:

```
Send                                    ? X
 ┌─────────────────────────────────────────┐
  Filename:
  C:\WIN95\HYPERTRM\Hypertrm.exe    Browse...

  Protocol:
  Zmodem                              ▼

                        Send      Cancel
 └─────────────────────────────────────────┘
```

4. Enter the name of the file you want to send (or click on Browse, locate and select the file, and click on OK to go back to the Send dialog
   box). Then choose the error-detection protocol you want (the one in
   use by the receiving system).

5. Click on OK to begin the file transfer.

NOTE By the way, you won't see the contents of the file on the screen (if
it's not all text, it would look like garbage anyway).

You'll now see a large window reporting the progress of the transfer as
shown in Figure 20.11. At the top, the name of the file being sent is
displayed. Next come several readouts on the error-checking process—
these are pretty technical, and you can usually ignore them. If something goes seriously wrong, HyperTerminal will halt the transfer. At
that point, you may be able to diagnose the problem by reading the
message displayed at *Last error*.

The (slightly) more interesting part of the display is the lower half.
Here, HyperTerminal shows you graphically and in numbers how
quickly the transfer is going. The bar graph at File expands to the
right giving you a quick sense of how much of the file has been sent
so far, relative to its total size. Next to the graph, you're shown how
much of the file has been sent in numbers. Below are counters showing how much time has elapsed since the transfer began, how much
time is remaining (assuming all goes well, and if HyperTerminal is
able to calculate this), and, in the Throughput area, your current
"speed." By clicking on the cps/bps button, you can set the display

units for throughput speed: characters per second (cps) or bits per second (bps). Characters per second is actually a measure of the number of bytes (8-bit information units) being transferred each second.

To cancel a file transfer before it has finished, click on the Cancel button at the bottom of the window. If the transfer completes normally, you'll hear a single beep as the window disappears.

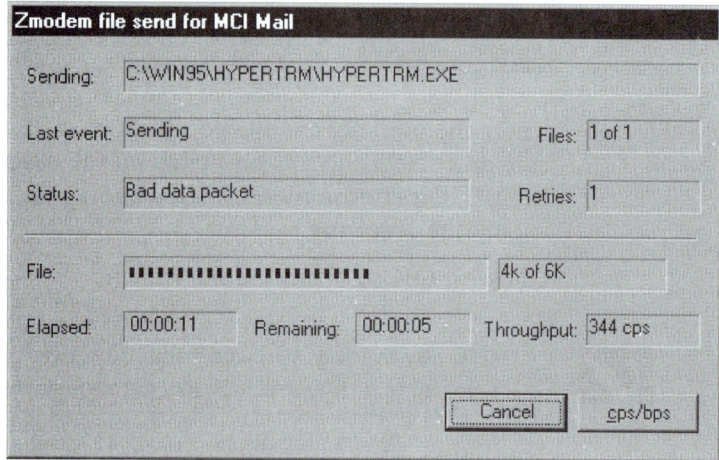

Figure 20.11   *You'll see a window like this during file transfers.*

As a recap of sending binary files, consider the following: a binary file will arrive just as you sent it, with no modifications (for example, no adding or stripping of line feeds). All types of files, including program files, can be sent and received as binary files. Formatted text as well as program files must be transmitted as binary files, or information will be lost.

Receiving Files

You'll want to use the Receive File command to transfer document and program (non-text) files to your computer from the computer at the other end of the line. The process of receiving such a file is very similar to sending one:

1. After connecting to the other computer, tell the sending computer to send the file and which file-transfer protocol to use in the process. How you do this depends on the computer and program(s) involved. If you're connected to a BBS or information service, you can usually

control the process from your computer. If you're connected to another individual's computer, you ask the person at the other end of the line to type in the command to send you the file.

2. Choose Transfer ➤ Receive File or click on the Receive button on the Toolbar.

The Receive File dialog box appears. Choose the *directory* where you want HyperTerminal to store the received file (not the actual file name, which will be set by the other computer). Type in the directory name or use the Browse button to find it. Then select the file-transfer protocol that matches the one used by the other computer. And do all this quickly because the other computer is already trying to send the file. It will wait, but usually not too long.

3. Click on OK or press Enter, and the transmission should begin.

Once the transfer is underway, a window that looks and works very similar to the one you see when sending files (Figure 20.11) will appear. See the previous section for details on its use.

> **CAUTION**   Depending on the file-transfer protocol you're using, HyperTerminal may not know the size of the file being sent to it. In this case, you won't be able to check to see whether you have enough disk space for the file, and you may run out of disk space while receiving it. This is a real hassle, particularly if you've spent half an hour receiving most of a large file only to get an error message saying there isn't enough room on your disk for the rest of it. When this happens, HyperTerminal will abort the receiving process. So make sure the disk you choose to store the file on has enough free space on it before you begin the transfer.

Manipulating Text in the HyperTerminal Window

You can manipulate the text in the document window in various ways while in a HyperTerminal session. You can:

▶ copy it to the Clipboard

▶ transmit selected text or the Clipboard's contents to the other computer as though you were typing it

▶ print incoming or selected text

▶ clear all the text in the window

Copying Text to the Clipboard

Any text you can see on screen or that is still in the backscroll buffer can be copied to the Clipboard. Once there, it can be pasted into other applications or sent to the other system:

1. Select text with the mouse, just as in any other program, such as WordPad or Notepad. (Refer to Chapter 19 for instructions on selecting text in WordPad.) To select all the text in the buffer, choose Edit ➤ Select All.

2. Choose Edit ➤ Copy.

   The text is now on the Clipboard, and you can place it in any open document in another application with the Paste command.

Transmitting Text from the Clipboard

Sometimes you'll want to send text from a different application to the other computer you're currently connected to. If the document containing the text is open in a window, this is very easy. You don't have to create and send a new file. Just follow these steps:

1. In the other application, copy the text to the Clipboard. It can be text in any other application window, such as Microsoft Word, Excel, Write, Ami Pro, PageMaker, and so forth. You can also copy text from the HyperTerminal window.

2. Switch back to the HyperTerminal window (if you're not already there) and choose Edit ➤ Paste to Host. The contents of the Clipboard will be sent, unchanged, to the other computer. If the other computer is using Windows, the user could then select the information, copy it to the Clipboard, and paste it into another document.

CAUTION   Only text can be transferred in this way. If a graphic is on the Clipboard, you cannot paste it.

Printing Incoming Text

If you want to print text as it comes onto your screen from the remote computer, follow these steps:

1. Set up your printer and put it online. If necessary, select the correct printer by choosing File ➤ Print and then choosing the printer by name.

2. Choose Transfer ➤ Capture to Printer. A check mark will appear next to the menu selection. All received text will be printed. (If you've set up the connection to echo characters you type to the screen, everything you type will be printed, too.)

3. Choose Transfer ➤ Capture to Printer again to turn off this function.

Printing Selected Text

You can't print selected text directly from HyperTerminal. However, here are two ways you can print what's come over the line:

▶ Select the text you want to print and copy it onto the Clipboard. Then open WordPad, Notepad, or another word processor and paste the text into the document, edit it, and print it as usual.

▶ Save the incoming text as a file, as explained earlier. Exit HyperTerminal and then open the text file in a word processor and print it.

Background Communications with HyperTerminal

Like other Windows programs, HyperTerminal remains active even when you switch to another application. Not only does the HyperTerminal program itself continue running, but any communications connection you've made remains *live*. In other words, information can continue to flow between the two computers in the background while you're working with other programs.

This is a great feature because it allows you to do constructive work with your computer while HyperTerminal transfers files, conducts on-line searches, or carries out other time-consuming communications chores. Otherwise you'd just have to twiddle your thumbs during such activities.

To take advantage of background communications, just start your file transfer or other procedure as you normally would and switch out to whatever other application you want to use. HyperTerminal notifies you when a file transfer is complete by sounding a quick beep. If the connection is broken while you're working with another program, you'll hear the three-beep disconnect signal.

> **NOTE** Of course, you can hear these audible messages from HyperTerminal only if the Sound setting is turned on. You'll find this check box on the Settings page of the Properties dialog box for this connection.

Running Multiple Communications Sessions

There probably aren't too many times that you'd want to run multiple communications sessions, but it is possible to have two sessions connected at the same time. To do this, run HyperTerminal a second time by double-clicking on a different connection icon while you still have the first session open. Change any settings as necessary and dial. You must *not* use the same communications port as you're using for the first session. From the Communications dialog box you'll have to select the unused COM channel (1 or 2) as the port for the second session. Of course, you'll need another modem (or cable in the case of direct connection) connected to the second port, as well. By using the Pause command wisely and jumping between windows, you could juggle the two communications sessions.

Ending a Communications Session

Once you've finished your work (or play) during a session, you should end it by following some simple rules:

1. If you want to save the settings you've made, choose File ➤ Save and name the file.

2. If you are logged on to an information service, electronic mail provider, or BBS, follow the system's instructions for signing off. This may be important to free up a connection for other users or to ensure that the service will cease billing you for connect time.

3. Choose Call ➤ Disconnect.

4. Close HyperTerminal by double-clicking on its Control box.

Troubleshooting

Despite great strides in the field of communications, mostly due to conveniences spurred by the personal computer market, communications is still a bit of a black art. Chances are good that you'll run into some problem or other while transferring files, sending mail, or whatever it is you end up doing with HyperTerminal. The fault will not necessarily lie with HyperTerminal (or yourself), but much more likely will be the result of improper wiring, faulty modems, noisy telephone lines, incorrect log-on procedures, or incompatible software on the other end of the line. If you're trying to connect to a BBS or information service, don't hesitate to call them (the old-fashioned way) for help with making things work right. You can also get help from your company's computer expert, your computer store, or an experienced friend.

Chapter 21

Painting Pictures with Windows Paint

FEATURING

Basic painting techniques

Manipulating areas of a picture

Zooming in for detail work

Editing the color scheme

Printing

Paint is a program for the artist in you. It's a simple but quite capable program for painting and drawing images on your computer screen. You can brush on colors free-form, draw lines and geometric shapes, and even add text to your pictures. A variety of nifty special effects are at your command, too.

Here are some ideas for things you can do with Paint:

► create printed signs

► create illustrations for printed matter

► create images for use in other Windows programs

► design invitations

► enhance digitized images or photographs

► draw maps

► make wallpaper images for your Windows Desktop

► edit clip art (pre-drawn images you can buy in collections)

► clean up "digital dust" from scanned images

► edit graphics embedded or linked into documents created by other programs (see Chapter 6)

Starting a New Document

To bring up Paint:

1. Beginning from the Taskbar, choose Start ➤ Programs ➤ Accessories ➤ Paint.

2. The Paint window appears. Maximize the window. Figure 21.1 shows the Paint window and its component parts.

The *work area* is the main part of the window where you do your painting. Along the left side, the *Tool Box* provides a set of buttons for activating the tools you use to paint. You choose colors from the *Color Box* at the bottom of the window. The Status Bar offers help messages on menu choices and displays the coordinates of the mouse pointer.

FOR WINDOWS 3.X USERS

Compared to its Windows 3.x predecessor, Paintbrush, Paint has more features, it looks a little snazzier, and some of the commands and buttons have changed. Still, Paint will seem very familiar if you've worked with Paintbrush. The one big difference that you might not notice is this: You can paint with the *right* mouse button, not just the left (using the right button paints with the background color). Aside from that, most of the tools work about the same as they did in Paintbrush.

Though they aren't earth shattering, new features are plentiful in Paint. You get two new tools: the eyedropper and the pencil. Manipulating selections is much easier now that they have resize handles, and you can rotate them or even use them as a brush shape. Print Preview lets you check your work before you print, saving paper and time. It's easier to work with text by virtue of the Text Toolbar (for setting font, size, and style). And you can Undo three previous commands, not just one.

You give up some features, too. The color eraser tool is gone. You can't save files in the PCX (PC Paintbrush) format, and you can't use shadow or outline styles with text. Paintbrush let you print headers and footers, Paint does not. But if you are enamored of any of these features, you don't have to give them up. Because both programs can open the same files, you can keep Paintbrush on your hard disk and use it when the need arises.

Here's a list of some of the tools and menu commands that have changed:

In Paintbrush	In Paint
Paint roller	Paint Can
Shrink and Grow	Stretch
Tilt	Skew
Inverse	Invert Colors

Understanding Computer Art

Before going any further, let's pause a minute for a little background on how Paint works—it will help you to get the results you want from your artistic creations. In the personal-computer world there are two basic classes of pictures, or *graphics*: *bit-mapped* and *object-oriented*.

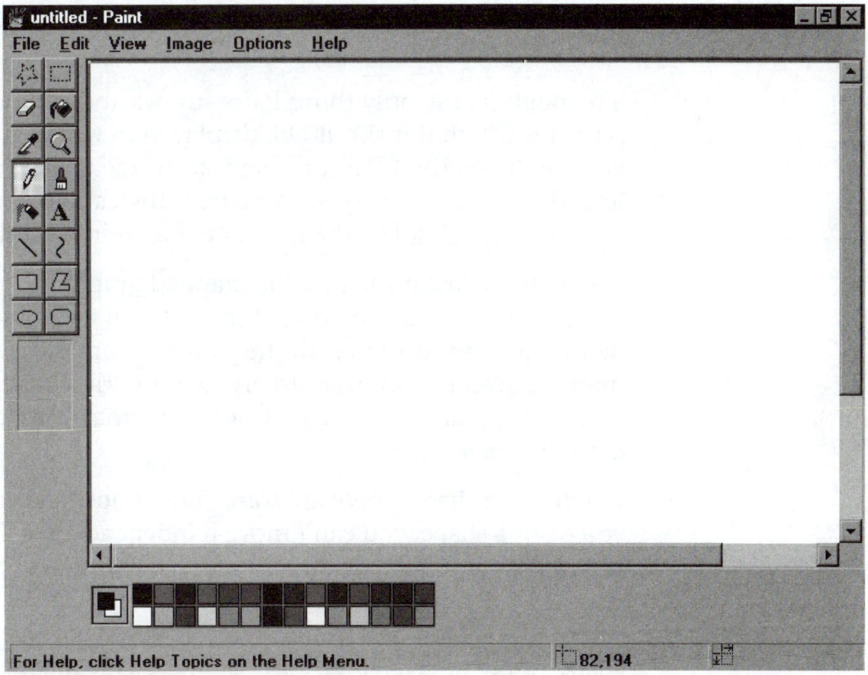

Figure 21.1   *The Paint window*

Paint can create and edit only bit-mapped graphics, so let's focus there (more on object-oriented graphics in a moment).

In programs like Paint, you create a picture on the computer screen as if you were painting on a canvas with paint. Imagine yourself painting the Mona Lisa. With each stroke of the brush, the paint you apply to the canvas sticks irreversibly, covering up whatever was there before.

In Paint, you use colored dots on the screen as your paint, but the process is otherwise quite similar. Once you've placed anything on the screen (and unless you use Undo immediately), it becomes an integral part of the image. It remains there until you cover it up with something else.

Here's why Paint works this way. Your computer's screen is divided into very small dots (*pixels* or *pels*) that are controlled by the smallest division of computer information—bits. A bit map is a collection of bits of information that creates an image when assigned (*mapped*) to dots on the screen. This is similar to a sports scoreboard that can display the score, a message, or even a picture by turning on and off specific lightbulbs in a grid.

The point is, the only thing Paint knows about the image on your screen is which dot should be displayed in which color. When you change the picture, Paint doesn't keep track of whether you paint a line, draw a circle, or type some text. Instead, it simply changes its map of colored dots—the new dots blend into all the other ones.

What all this means is that bit-mapped graphics can be incredibly detailed because you can control the color of each and every dot in your picture if you want to (with the Zoom command). That's why bit-mapped graphics are used to create artwork with the rich detail of a real painting and to store photographic images that have been recorded by a scanner.

On the other hand, there are some limitations to keep in mind. Once you paint a shape, you can't move it independently. True, you can use the computer to remove an area of the painting and place it somewhere else—as if you were cutting out a piece of the canvas and pasting it elsewhere. But *all* the dots in the area get moved, not just the ones in the shape you're interested in. Also, because a bit-mapped graphic has a fixed number of dots, its resolution is fixed—you can't make it look sharper by printing it on a higher-resolution printer, for example.

By contrast, in object-oriented graphics, the computer stores each shape as a separate entity—it's something like those felt boards you used in grade school. Each line, circle, and text character retains its identity as a separate object. These objects can later be moved, sized, cut, copied, and otherwise altered without affecting anything else in the picture. In addition, object-oriented graphics always display and print at the maximum possible resolution of the device you're using.

With object-oriented graphics it's harder to do detailed work, especially involving random shapes and color blends, than with bit-mapped graphics. On the other hand, this type of computer art is great for line drawings, logos, and poster-like illustrations.

Windows 95 doesn't come with an object-oriented graphics program. Popular programs of this type include Corel Draw, Adobe Illustrator, and Micrografx Designer. Also, simple object-oriented graphics modules are included in many word processors and spreadsheets.

Enough theory.

Opening an Existing Picture

To open, or *load*, an existing picture, do the following:

1. Choose File ➤ Open.

2. Select the picture by name in the Open dialog box. Windows 95 comes with many Paint-style pictures in the main Windows directory. Figure 21.2 shows a picture of weightless chess pieces open in Paint.

Now you can edit the picture and save it again or copy any part of it to the Clipboard for use with other programs.

> **TECH TIP**   Paint remembers the last four pictures you've opened or saved, listing them by name at the bottom of the File menu. To open one of these pictures without slowing down for the Open dialog box, just choose the picture from the File menu.

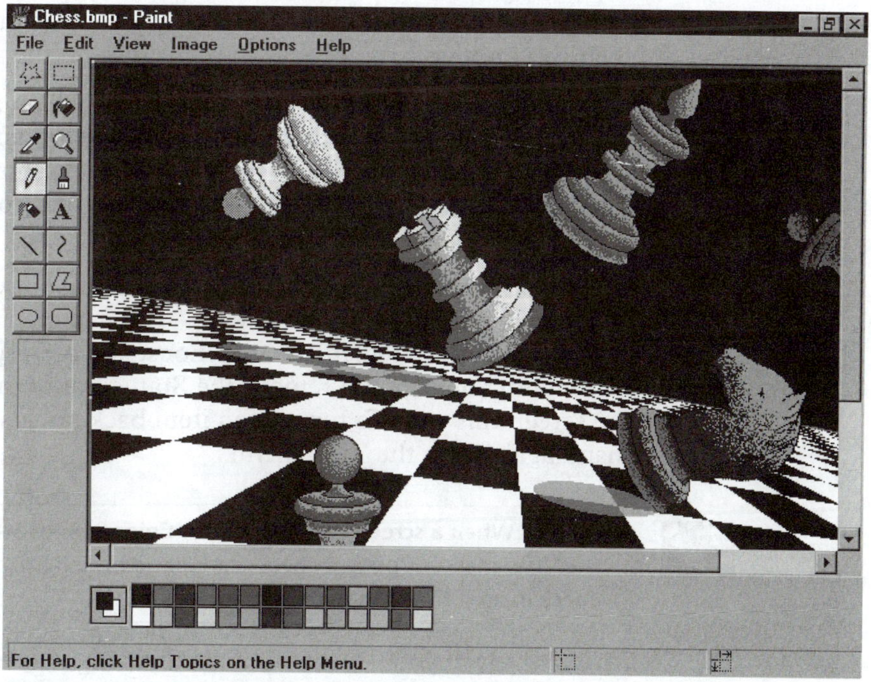

Figure 21.2   *A picture file opened and displayed in the work area*

Paint can only open pictures stored in its own format (also known as the BMP format). If you want to open pictures stored in other formats, such as PCX or TIF, you'll have to translate them to the BMP format with conversion software first.

Seeing More of the Picture

If the picture is too big to fit in the work area, you can, of course, scroll to see any part of the image. But scrolling is a nuisance. You can also take steps to see more of the picture all at once, as detailed in the following sections.

Removing and Tearing Off the Tool and Color Boxes

The simplest method to increase your viewing area is to remove the tools along the left side and bottom of the Paint window. Actually, you don't have to give them up entirely—you can "tear them off" as floating windows that are easy to reposition on the screen.

To tear off the Tool Box or the Color Box, click on any part of the box's background. Hold down the mouse button and drag the window outline that appears into the work area. As shown in Figure 21.3, the box becomes a separate floating window that you can move around as needed to work with your picture.

If you don't need the Tool Box or Color Box—not very likely, but once in a while this may be the case—you can turn them off altogether. Open the View menu and choose the corresponding menu command. You can also remove the Status Bar at the very bottom of the screen this way. To turn on an item back on, just choose its command again from the View menu.

NOTE   When a screen item (Tool Box, Color Box, or Status Bar) is visible, the View menu displays a check mark beside the item's command; there's no check mark if the item has been turned off.

Alternatively, if you've torn off a box, making it a separate window, you can remove it from the screen by clicking on its close box. To turn

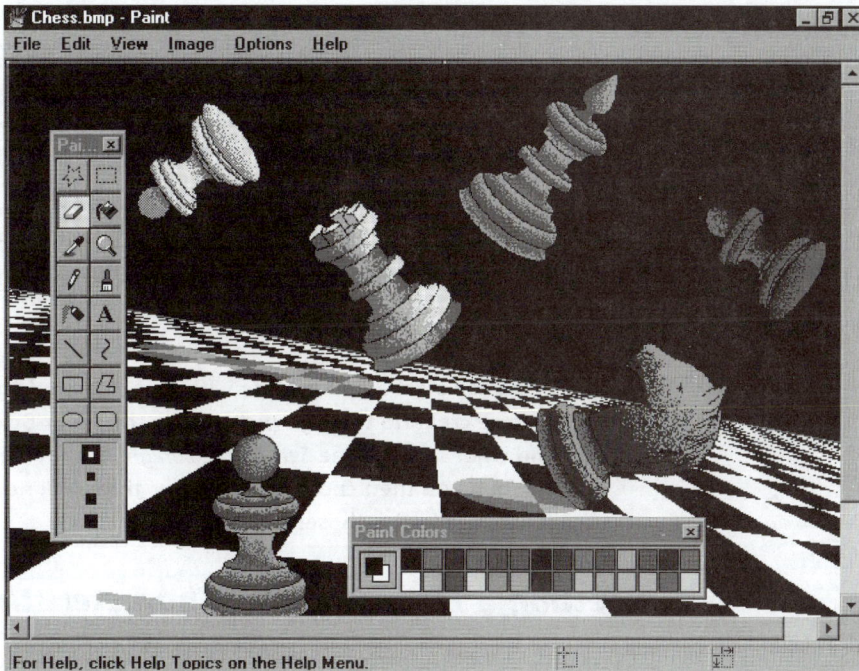

Figure 21.3 *The Paint window after you've "torn off" the Tool Box and Color Box*

it on again, choose the corresponding item on the View menu. It will appear on the screen in its last location.

Displaying Only the Picture

If you just want to look at as much of your picture as possible, choose View ➤ View Bitmap. The picture fills the entire Paint window—all the other screen elements, including the title bar, menu bar, and scroll bars disappear. You still may not be able to see the whole picture, of course, but this is as good as it gets. And all you can do is look at the picture—you can't make any changes. Clicking anywhere on the screen or pressing any key returns you to the working screen.

Creating a New Picture

To start a new picture, choose File ➤ New to erase the previous image, then choose Image ➤ Attributes to set the picture size and select *color* or *black and white*.

If another picture is open, choose File ➤ New to begin work on a new, blank "canvas." If you haven't already saved the previous picture, Paint will ask if you want to do so. The existing image will then disappear, leaving the work area empty.

> **TIP**   You can start a new picture with a background color other than white. Just before creating the new picture, use the Color Box to change the background color setting (see *Setting the Foreground and Background Colors* below). When you then choose File ➤ New, the blank new picture comes up in the work area in the chosen color.

Setting a Picture's Baslc Characteristics

Before you actually start painting, decide whether you want to change any of Paint's standard settings governing the picture's basic characteristics: its size and whether it's a color or black-and-white image. When you use Paint for the first time, it sets up each new picture as a color image with a size equal to that of your screen (not the Paint work area, but the entire screen).

To change the settings for either of these characteristics, choose Image ➤ Attributes to display the Attributes dialog box shown below. You can also change a picture's size with the mouse.

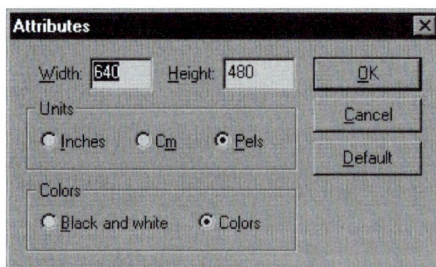

Setting Picture Size

The first thing you should decide when starting a new picture is how big it should be. If you're creating a picture to fit snugly into another document, or if you have an idea of how much room you'll need to express your ideas, defining the picture's size now may save you some work down the road. It's easy to change the size of a picture, so don't spend much time on this decision.

Keep in mind that the size of the image you see is tied to the resolution of your screen. Actually, the size settings control only the number of dots in the picture (even though you can set the size in inches or centimeters in the Attributes dialog box). If you increase the resolution of your screen (see Chapter 7), the picture will look smaller because each component dot is smaller.

Likewise, the image will almost certainly print smaller than it appears on your screen because most printers have much higher resolution than even a Super VGA monitor.

TIP If you're planning to print the image, choose size settings according to the printed size you plan, not the screen size. For example, if you want the image to be 3×5 inches on the printed page and your printer's resolution is 300 dots per inch, you would enter a width of 900 pixels and a height of 1,500 pixels. Remember too that if your picture is wider than it is tall, and if its printed width is more than about 8 inches, you'll need to change the page orientation for printing from Portrait to Landscape. Choose File ➤ Page Setup and select the appropriate button.

NOTE The maximum size of a picture is limited by the amount of memory available in your computer. Maximum size also depends on the color scheme: black-and-white pictures use far less memory than color pictures do, so they can be much larger. Paint will let you know if you set a picture size that's too large to fit in memory.

NOTE   When you change the size of a picture, Paint remembers the new dimensions. From then on—until you make further size changes—Paint uses these dimensions whenever you choose File ➤ New to create a new picture. This is so even if you open other larger or smaller pictures in the meantime.

You can resize a picture with the mouse or by typing entries in the Attributes dialog box. Using the mouse is easier if the entire picture fits in the work area, but many pictures are bigger than that. Besides, the mouse isn't very accurate, whereas you can type exact dimensions. At any rate, you use the same resizing techniques whether you're working with a brand new picture or an existing one.

To set the size of your picture with the Attributes dialog box:

1.   Choose Image ➤ Attributes. The Attributes dialog box appears.

2.   Decide on the measurement units you want to use and click on the corresponding radio button. Pixels (screen dots) is the standard unit, but you can choose inches or centimeters instead.

3.   Type in new width and height values. At any time, you can return to the standard size values—equal to the size of your screen—by clicking on Default.

4.   Click on OK to return to Paint. The size of your canvas will change according to your entries, though you can only see this if the entire canvas fits within the work area.

To resize a picture with the mouse:

1.   Find the picture's sizing handles, the small squares at the bottom-right corner of the picture and along the bottom and right edges. If the picture is larger than the work area, you'll have to scroll down or to the right to see the sizing handles. (The handles at the other three corners and along the other edges do nothing.)

2.   To change the picture's width, drag the handle on the right edge to the left (to make the picture narrower) or to the right (to make the picture wider). To change the height, drag the bottom-edge handle up or down. To change both dimensions simultaneously, drag the handle at the bottom-right corner.

Setting the Image to Color or Black and White

> **NOTE** Paint's black-and-white setting restricts you to two "colors" only, black and white (the speckled-looking choices on the color palette are patterns of black and white dots). A black and white image is *not* the same thing as a gray-scale image, in which you can paint with 16 or more separate shades of gray. To create a grayscale image, you must place the desired shades of gray on the palette—see *Editing the Color Scheme* later in this chapter.

Paint can handle both color and black-and-white images. Of course, if you want to create a cartoon or line drawing, you can do it with a color picture by painting with a black brush only. The only real reason to set the picture itself to a black-and-white "color" scheme is to save memory or disk space. Black and white pictures consume one-fourth as much memory and disk space as the simplest color pictures. If you need a very large image, and memory or disk space is limited, black and white may be your only choice.

You're not likely to get great results when converting an existing color image to black and white. Paint converts light colors to white and darker colors to black, and you have no control over the process. In most cases, you'll lose much of the image detail.

> **CAUTION** You can't undo a change from color to black and white. Be sure you want to make the change. If you're working with an existing color picture, make a backup copy before you convert it to black and white.

To set up a new black-and-white picture, or to convert an existing color picture to black and white:

1. Choose Image ➤ Attributes to open the Attributes dialog box.

2. Choose the *Black and white* radio button and click on OK. Any existing colors in the picture will be converted to either black or white.

Remember, this change is permanent.

> **NOTE** New pictures always open in color, even if you changed a previous picture to black and white.

Basic Painting Techniques

Once you've created a new, empty painting, you're ready to try your hand at computer art. Feel free to play with the tools as much as you want—you can't hurt anything, and the learn-by-doodling approach is fun.

In this section I'll explain each of the on-screen controls in the Color Box and Tool Box and suggest some tips and tricks to make your work easier. You might want to sit at your computer and work with each of the tools as you read, changing colors to suit your fancy along the way. Pretty soon you'll have a good high-tech mess on your screen, at which point you can just choose File ➤ New again to clear it and be ready for more experimentation. (When asked about saving your work, click on No unless you really like it.)

Setting the Foreground and Background Colors

> **NOTE** The term *color* describes either a color or a colored pattern selected from the Color Box. If you are using a black-and-white screen, colors in the Color Box may appear as shades of gray or varying densities of dot patterns.

One of the most fundamental techniques to learn is selecting a color to paint with. In Paint, you control both foreground and background colors independently.

Understanding Foreground and Background Colors

The foreground or drawing color is the main color you paint with. For example, when you add strokes with Paint's paintbrush, draw lines or shapes, or even when you type text, these items appear in the currently selected foreground color.

The term *background color* is somewhat misleading. True, if you select a background color just before you start a new painting, this will be the color of the canvas or backdrop for the entire picture.

NOTE   It may help to understand that creating a new picture with a specific background color is exactly equivalent to painting the entire picture with that color. There's nothing special about the background color as far as Paint is concerned—a picture is just a set of dots that happen to be all one color when you first create it.

On the other hand, once you have a picture on your screen, many of the tools (such as the Brush, Pencil, and the shape tools) let you paint with the so-called background color just as you would with the foreground color. All you have to do is hold down the right mouse button instead of the left one as you paint. The background color also determines the fill color for circles, squares, and other enclosed shapes, the fill color inside text frames, and the color with which you erase existing parts of the picture.

The key thing to remember: after you've started work on a picture, changing the background color doesn't affect the picture directly in any way. If any of the original background color is still visible, it remains the same.

Choosing a Color Scheme: Basic Tips

You'll get the best results if you stick with solid colors. Here's the scoop: the number of separate solid colors you can use depends on the capabilities of your display hardware and the specific software driver setting you've chosen. A standard VGA screen can display only 16 discrete colors, while more sophisticated displays can handle 256 on up to 16.7 million colors.

Paint uses patterns made up of dots of different colors to represent hues that it can't display as solid colors. These patterns tend to look murky or fuzzy in your pictures. Avoid them when possible.

Also, keep in mind the color capabilities of your printer when you choose colors for your picture. An image that looks great on your screen can become a blurry gray soup when you print it out on a black-and-white printer. When Windows prints to a black-and-white printer, it attempts to translate colors into contrasting shades of gray (actually, gray shades are simulated with different densities of black dots). Sometimes the translation gives you good results, but if not, experiment with the color scheme until you find one that produces a clear image in print—even if the colors clash horribly on the screen. If that doesn't work, just stick with painting in black on a white background.

Viewing and Changing Color Settings

The current settings of the foreground and background colors are shown in the area at the left side of the Color Box. In this area, the box on top toward the upper left shows the foreground color. The box in back, toward the lower right, shows the background color. The default colors are a black foreground on a white background, and they always come up that way when you open a new or existing picture.

You choose new foreground and background colors by selecting them in the Color Box, as described below. Alternatively, you can use the Eyedropper tool, described later, to use a color from the picture as the new foreground or background color.

Setting the Foreground Color

Set the foreground color as follows:

1. Point to the color or pattern you want.

2. Click the *left* mouse button. Now whatever you paint with the tools using the left mouse button will appear in this color. Notice that the foreground color box at the left side of the Color Box reflects your color choice.

Setting the Background Color

To set the background color:

1. Point to the color or pattern in the Color Box.

2. Click the *right* mouse button. The background color box at the left side of the Color Box changes accordingly.

If you want to apply a background color to an entire picture, you must choose the desired background color, then immediately choose File ➤ New to create the new picture. Note, though, that the background color becomes white again as soon as Paint creates the new picture.

> **CAUTION**   You can't change the color of an existing picture's actual background by changing the background color with the Color Box.

> **TIP**   If you start a new picture with the wrong background color, there's an alternative to starting all over again. Before painting anything on the picture, choose the correct background color and click anywhere over the work area with the Paint Can tool, described below. The entire picture area will change to the background color. Alternatively, after choosing the desired background color, choose Image ➤ Clear Image.

Selecting Colors with the Eyedropper Tool

We haven't yet covered the use of the Tool Box—that's the subject of the very next section. Still, this is the appropriate place to mention an alternative technique for selecting colors: the Eyedropper tool.

The Eyedropper lets you "suck up" a color that already appears in the picture. That color becomes the new foreground or background color for use with any of the painting tools.

Be aware, though, that the Eyedropper can only detect solid colors. If the shade you're interested in is a composite of two or more solid colors, the Eyedropper will select only one of those colors, not the shade.

Here's how to use the Eyedropper:

1. Click on the Eyedropper tool in the Tool Box. When you move the mouse pointer into the work area, the pointer becomes an eyedropper.

2. In the picture, locate the color you want to use. Click over that color with the left button to select it as the foreground color, with the right button to make it the background color. The Color Box display changes accordingly.

You can now paint with the chosen color using any of the painting tools as detailed in the next section.

Using the Painting Tools

To use any of the tools in the Tool Box:

1. Click on the tool you want to use. This selects the tool.

2. Position the pointer in the work area where you want to start painting, selecting, or erasing and then click and hold the mouse button.

3. Drag to paint, select, or erase. Release the mouse button when you are through.

Paint's Tool Box offers a slew of useful controls to help you realize your artistic vision. Here's the Tool Box:

To choose a tool, you simply click on its button in the Tool Box. The tool is then activated (and highlighted), and the pointer changes shape when you move back into the work area. In most cases, the tool stays selected until you choose another one.

Most of the tools are for making modifications to your picture, but one lets you select colors (the Eyedropper), and one is for zooming, or magnifying, the screen image of the picture (the Magnifier tool). Two other tools let you select areas that you can then move around in the picture or modify with other commands. These selection tools and the commands you can use with them are covered in *Manipulating Areas of a Picture*.

When some of the tools are selected, the area below the grid of buttons provides options for the selected tool. The options are different for each tool. For example, if you're drawing with the line tool, you can choose how thick the line should be by clicking on an icon in this area. If there are no options associated with a tool, this area is empty.

The following sections will describe each of the painting tools, referring to the names in Figure 21.4.

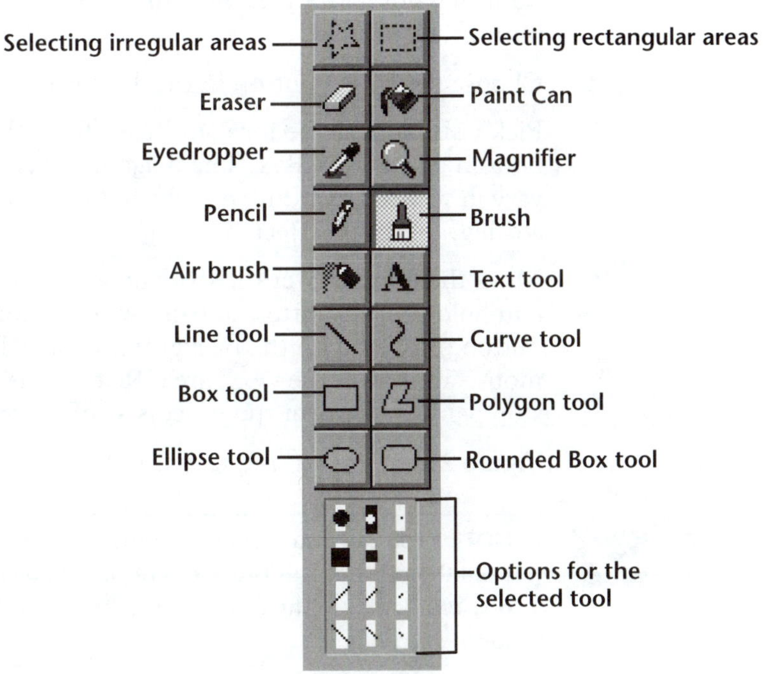

Selecting irregular areas — Selecting rectangular areas
Eraser — Paint Can
Eyedropper — Magnifier
Pencil — Brush
Air brush — Text tool
Line tool — Curve tool
Box tool — Polygon tool
Ellipse tool — Rounded Box tool
Options for the selected tool

Figure 21.4   *The Paint Tool Box with its many tool buttons*

The Brush

The Brush is the basic painting tool.

It works like a paint brush, pen, or marker. Use this tool to create freehand art.

With the Brush, you can paint in either the foreground or the background color, switching between the two by simply changing which mouse button you press. All of the painting tools that add lines, strokes, or enclosed shapes work this way.

Here's how to use the Brush:

1. In the Color Box, select the foreground and background colors you want to paint with by clicking on them with the left button and right buttons, respectively.

2. Choose the Brush button in the Tool Box.

3. Pick a size and shape for your brush from the tool options area in the bottom of the Tool Box. The diagonal brush shapes produce lines that vary in width depending on which direction you move the brush—it's a calligraphic pen effect.

4. Move the pointer over the work area so it becomes a crosshair. Press and hold the left button to paint with the foreground color, the right button to paint with the background color. Paint by dragging the mouse around in the work area. Release the button when you want to stop painting. Repeat the process as often as you like.

Figure 21.5 shows a simple brush design.

> **NOTE**   You can also paint with a custom brush that you create by copying it from the picture. This brush can be any shape and can contain multiple colors. You don't use the Brush tool for this—see *Sweeping* later in this chapter for the technique.

Doing Precision Work   Although painting is usually a free-form act of creativity, there may be times you want to position your work with precision, perhaps to align a series of shapes along an imaginary horizontal

Figure 21.5   *A freehand design made with the brush*

line. You can use the Status Bar for this purpose. To the right of center, the Status Bar always displays a readout of the mouse pointer's location in pixel coordinates. The first value represents the horizontal location, in pixels, from the left edge of the picture. The second number is the vertical location from the top.

A second readout farther to the left is only active when you're drawing shapes such as boxes, ellipses, and polygons or when you're selecting an area of the picture. This set of coordinates tells you where the mouse pointer is relative to the location where you started drawing the shape or where you began selecting.

Undoing Mistakes   Each addition you make to a picture ultimately loses its identity, blending seamlessly into the rest of the image. However, Paint does keep track of the most recent additions as separate items, giving you a chance to undo your mistakes. Otherwise, if you accidentally covered up part of the picture you wanted to keep, you'd be stuck having to recreate it—if you could.

You can use the Undo command to eliminate the last *three* additions to the picture. Each time you make a new change, Paint "forgets" the fourth most recent change, and it becomes permanent.

To activate Undo, choose Edit ➤ Undo or press the keyboard shortcut, Ctrl-Z.

Paint will even let you redo changes you've removed with Undo. To restore what you previously undid, choose Edit ➤ Repeat or press F4. Again, you can restore as many as three changes.

Here's another way to undo your mistakes: If you realize something is wrong in the middle of any painting operation, such as using the Brush, drawing a line, or even using the Eraser, click the *right* mouse button *before* you release the left button. Whatever changes you were in the process of making disappear—it's as if you never started.

> **TIP**   This little trick gives you a fourth level of Undo: You can erase whatever you're currently drawing by clicking the right mouse button—and still undo three previous changes.

The Eraser

The Eraser works like the eraser on a pencil—only you don't have to rub.

Just pass it across an area, and it erases whatever it touches, leaving nothing but the background color behind. Use the Eraser whether you want to obliterate a major section of your picture or just touch up some stray dots or lines.

Actually, of course, the Eraser doesn't remove anything from your picture—it just replaces the existing dots with dots of another color. In fact, you can think of the eraser as just another brush tool, but one that paints with the background color (that is, the background color that's currently selected—the Eraser doesn't know what background color you started the picture with).

Of course, there's nothing that special about the Eraser—after all, the other tools apply the background color if you paint with the right mouse button instead of the left. It's just that with the Eraser, you access the background color with the left button, which you're probably more used to (the right button has no effect with the Eraser). The Eraser can paint wider lines than the brush, too.

Here's how to use the Eraser:

1. Set the background color (in the Color Box) to the color you've chosen for the background (of your picture) or to the color you want to paint wide strokes with.

2. Select the Eraser.

3. In the tool options area at the bottom of the Tool Box, set the eraser size. For fine work, use the smallest setting.

TIP Even the smallest Eraser size covers more than a single dot in your picture. To erase (change) individual dots, use the Pencil tool (see the next section), setting the *foreground* color to the desired erasure color.

---

4. The mouse pointer will change to a hollow box when moved into the work area. Drag it over the material you want to erase. Hold the Shift key down while moving the mouse if you want to limit your movement to just the vertical or horizontal direction.

Below you can see the effect of dragging the Eraser over a solid colored area.

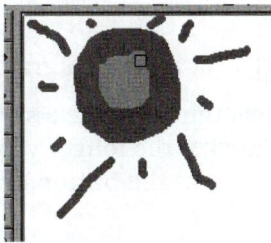

The Pencil

The Pencil works much like the Brush for freehand art, except that it only paints lines that are one dot (pixel) wide.

You can produce essentially the same effect with the Brush by choosing the smallest circular shape for the Brush (at the top right of the Brush-shape display), but the Pencil is often a convenient way to draw fine lines freehand while leaving the brush for wider swaths.

In addition, you can force the Pencil to draw straight vertical, horizontal, or diagonal lines, something you can't do with the Brush. After selecting the Pencil tool, hold down the Shift key while you drag the mouse. The direction you initially move establishes the line's direction—as long as you hold down Shift, you can only lengthen the line, not change directions (this is different from the way the Line tool works, as described below).

The Pencil is your best bet for doing fine touch-up work, including erasures. To erase individual dots with the pencil, set either the foreground or background color in the Color Box to the background color of your picture. Then click with the corresponding mouse button on stray dots one at a time to erase them. (Like the Brush, the Pencil applies the foreground color when you paint with the left button, the background color when you paint with the right.)

> **TIP**   For precise, dot-by-individual-dot editing, make it easy on yourself—zoom in on your picture to see the detail. See *Zooming In for Detail Work* below.

The Airbrush

Here's a tool that's a legal outlet for repressed graffiti artists.

The Airbrush works like the real thing, or like a spray can, spraying a mist of paint that gets thicker the longer you hold it one place. Think of the mouse button as the button on the top of the spray can:

1. Set the foreground and background colors to taste.

2. Click on the Airbrush tool (the button with the spray-can icon).

3. Select the spray size in the tool options area at the bottom of the Tool Box.

4. Position the cursor in the work area—it now looks like an airbrush—and press the mouse button for the desired color (left for foreground color, right for background color). Hold it down.

5. Move the mouse around and spray the color onto the work area. Note that the speed of movement affects the density of the spray, just as it does with a real spray can: moving the mouse quickly results in a finer mist, while letting it sit still or moving very slowly plasters the paint on.

Figure 21.6 shows an example of some airbrushed painting.

Figure 21.6 *The Airbrush works like a spray can. Just point and spray.*

The Line Tool

Use the Line tool to draw straight lines (and only straight lines):

> **TIP** Hold the Shift key down to force the line to be vertical, horizontal, or at a 45-degree angle.

1. Select the foreground and background colors you want to draw with.

2. Select the Line tool.

3. Choose from one of the five line widths offered in the tool options area at the bottom of the Tool Box.

4. Move into the work area. The cursor becomes a crosshair.

5. Press and hold one of the buttons and move the mouse. Use the left button to draw with the foreground color, the right button for the background color. A straight line will appear between the point you started drawing (the anchor point) and the current location of the mouse pointer. (Actually, the line won't look perfectly straight because computers can't draw straight diagonal lines.)

6. Move the endpoint around until you are satisfied with its location (you can make a full circle around the anchor point if you like). Release the button.

Below is an example of a drawing made up only of lines.

The Curve Tool

Use the Curve tool for drawing curves, of course.

But don't expect to master this tool quickly—it will seem downright strange at first.

You start by laying down a straight line, just like you would with the Line tool. Then you get two chances to "stretch" that line into a curve—once from one location and once from another. The result might be an arc, an *S* curve, or even a pretzel-y shape:

1. Select the foreground and background colors you want to draw with.

2. Choose the Curve tool.

3. Select the line size from the tool options area at the bottom of the Tool Box.

4. Begin the curve with a straight line, using the same techniques as you would with the Line tool covered earlier. When the line is finished, release the mouse button.

5. Move the cursor to one side of the line, hold down the mouse button, and drag the cursor away from or towards the line. As you do so, the line will stretch like a rubber band. Release the button when the bend is correct. (How will you know when it's correct? That's another book...)

6. If the curve already looks right, finish it by clicking on the endpoint (the end opposite where you started the line). If you do want to stretch it some more, move to another position in the work area, perhaps on the other side of the line, and drag the mouse again. The line will stretch further. When you are satisfied with the final shape—or give up—release the mouse button.

Figure 21.7 shows the process of drawing a curve.

The Box Tool

The Box tool draws, well, boxes—or rectangles, if you prefer.

You can draw three types of boxes:

Hollow boxes with borders only: In this type of box, the border is the only addition to the picture, enclosing whatever was already there in the picture. The border appears in the currently selected foreground color.

Filled, bordered boxes: This type of box has a solid-color interior that covers up whatever had been there plus a surrounding border. The solid interior appears in the currently selected background color, while the border appears in the foreground color.

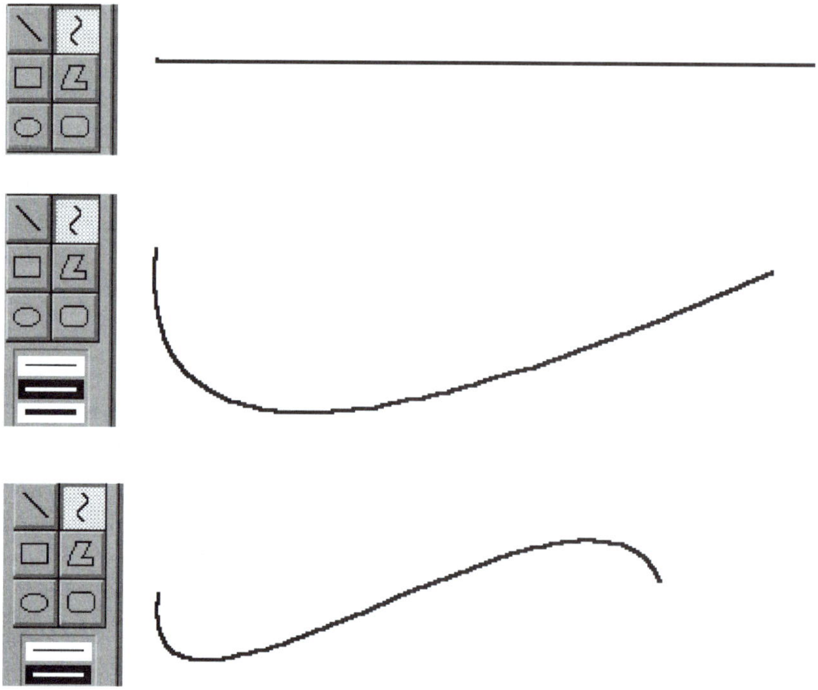

Figure 21.7   *The three steps in creating a curved line: draw a straight line, bend it one way, then bend it another.*

Solid boxes without borders: This type of box appears as a solid rectangle drawn in the currently selected background color.

The above descriptions apply if you use the left mouse button to draw the box. If you use the right button instead, the border and interior colors are reversed. This applies to the other tools for drawing enclosed shapes as well.

Here's how to create boxes of any type:

TIP   To constrain boxes to be perfect squares, hold down the Shift key as you draw. This applies to filled boxes as well as to hollow ones.

1. Set the background and foreground colors to taste, as necessary (see the discussion above).

2. If you're drawing a bordered box, select the Line tool and then set the line width from the choices in the tool options area at the bottom of the Tool Box.

3. Select the Box tool.

4. Click where you want one corner of the box to start. This sets the anchor.

5. Drag the crosshair down and to one side. As you do, a rectangular outline will appear.

6. Release the mouse button when the size is correct.

The Rounded Box Tool

The rounded Box tool works exactly like the regular Box tool described in the previous section, but it creates boxes with rounded corners, rather than crisp right angles.

The Ellipse Tool

This tool also works just like the Box tool, except that it creates ellipses (ovals).

Use the same basic drawing technique. The rules regarding the fill and border colors of boxes apply to ellipses, too. Below you'll see a gaggle of bubble-like objects created with the Ellipse tool. As you might guess, the perfect circles were created by holding down the Shift key while drawing with the Ellipse tool.

The Polygon Tool

With the Polygon tool you can create an endless variety of polygonal shapes.

It works something like the Line tool and something like the Box tool.

As with the Line tool, you manually draw straight lines—the difference being that you keep adding endpoints until you complete the polygon's edges. Paint then connects all the endpoints into a single shape with an unbroken boundary.

As with the Box tool, you can choose from three types of polygons: hollow ones (with borders but no solid filling); filled, bordered polygons; and solid polygons with no border.

> **TIP**   To constrain any line of the polygon to be vertical, at 45 degrees, or horizontal only, hold down the Shift key as you draw.

1. Select the colors you want for the polygon's border (the foreground color) and filling (the background color) as appropriate.

2. If you're drawing a bordered polygon, select the Line tool and choose a line width for the border.

3. Select the polygon tool and choose the type of polygon you want to draw (border only, filled and bordered, or solid with no border).

4. Click where you want the anchor point of the first side and hold the button down.

5. Drag the mouse pointer to the endpoint for the side and release the button. The line you've drawn defines the first side of the polygon.

6. Press and hold the mouse button again as you drag to the endpoint of the next side (or just click over this next endpoint). Paint draws the second side. Continue adding sides in this way, but *double-click* to mark the endpoint of the next-to-the-last side (for example, the fourth side of a pentangle). Paint connects this endpoint with the original anchor point, filling in the polygon if appropriate.

Note that a polygon's sides can cross. The polygons don't have to be symmetrically shaped the way hexagons or octagons are. You can haphazardly click all over the screen, and, until you double-click, Paint will keep connecting the dots regardless.

You can create a cubist artistic effect with this tool because of the way Paint calculates an enclosed area. It starts at the top of the screen and begins filling areas. If your polygon has a lot of enclosed areas from multiple lines overlapping, Paint alternates the fills. Thus adjacent enclosed areas will not all be filled. Using the tool with the cutout tools and the Invert command can lead to some rather interesting geometrical designs (inverting is covered later in the chapter). Figure 21.8 shows an example of the possibilities.

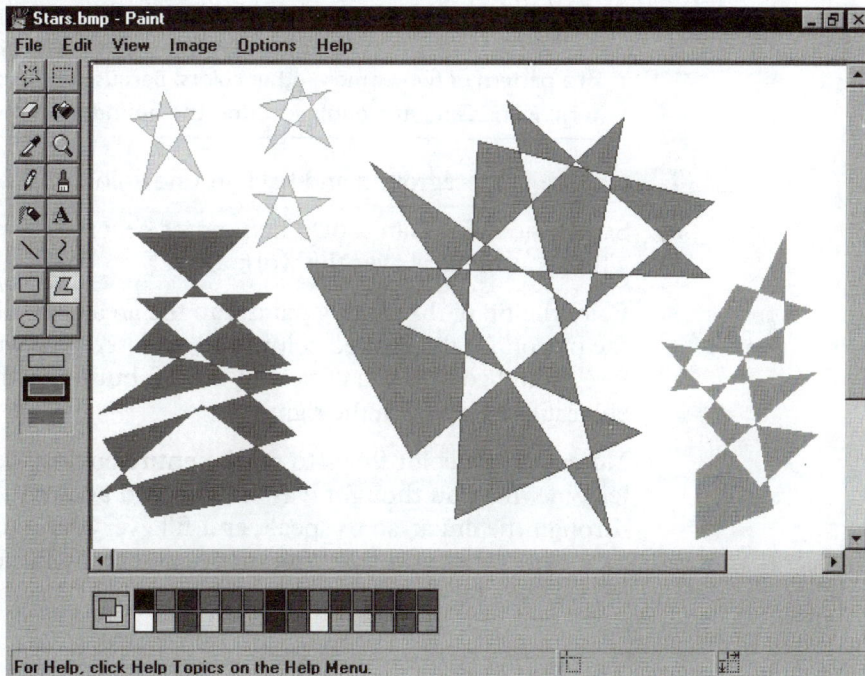

Figure 21.8 *A geometric design created with the Polygon tool using filled polygons*

Filling Areas with the Paint Can

The Paint Can will fill in any enclosed area with the foreground color. An *enclosed area* can be defined by any lines or curves in the work area. So three separate lines set up to form a triangle constitute an enclosed space just as much as a box's border does. Because the entire work area is also considered an enclosed space, you can use the Paint Can to change the background of the picture. Letters you create with the Text tool (discussed next) can be filled, too:

CAUTION   There's one situation where the Paint Can doesn't work as expected. If you've previously filled an enclosed area with one of the "grainy" shades, Paint Can may not be able to replace the current filling or may do so inaccurately. The problem is that these grainy colors are actually made up of a pattern of two or more other colors. Because of the complexity of the pattern, Paint Can has trouble locating the boundaries of the area.

1. Choose the foreground and background colors you want to use for fills.

2. Select the Paint Can tool. The pointer becomes a spilling paint can when you move it over the work area.

3. Point the tip of the spilling paint into the area to be filled and click with the button for the desired color. The enclosed area will be filled with the foreground color if you click with the left button, with the background color if you click with the right.

Note that the color flows to fill the entire enclosed area. If there is a leak in what you thought was an enclosed area, the paint will seep through the crack, so to speak, and fill everything until it is stopped by a complete boundary. You may accidentally fill the entire work area. If this happens, just choose Undo.

The Text Tool

The Text tool lets you add words to your pictures, which is great when you're designing flyers, invitations, maps, instructions, and the like.

Before you actually start typing, you define a rectangular *frame* for the text. You can resize or reposition this frame or change its color at any time until you finalize your text entry by clicking elsewhere in the picture.

Oh yes, about the color of the text frame. You can add text in two ways: as text only, so that only the characters you type are added to your picture; and as text on a solid rectangular background that covers up whatever was there in the picture. These two styles are also called *transparent* and *opaque*.

1. Choose the color for the text by clicking in the Color Box with the left button (text always appears in the selected foreground color). If you plan to add opaque text (on a solid-color background), choose the color for the background by clicking on it with the right button.

2. Choose the Text tool in the Tool Box.

3. In the tool-options area at the bottom of the Tool Box, choose the icon for opaque or transparent text. The top one turns on the opaque style. Alternatively, you can switch between opaque and transparent styles by choosing Options ➤ Draw Opaque. When the Draw Opaque menu choice is checked, the opaque style is active.

4. Draw your text frame using either mouse button. When you let go, *handles* appear on the dashed rectangular frame at the corners and along the edges, and, if you chose the opaque text style, the frame fills with the background color. In addition, a large flashing vertical bar (cursor) marks the text-insertion point. And a small window titled Paint Font Tool (also known as the Text Toolbar) appears. Figure 21.9 shows a text frame and the Text Toolbar.

5. Choose the font, size, and styles for your text from the Text Toolbar. You can use bold, italic, and underline in any combination.

> **TIP**   If the Text Toolbar isn't visible, choose View ➤ Text Toolbar to restore it to the screen.

6. Click again over the new text frame to make the insertion-point cursor reappear. Now type whatever you like. When your text reaches the right edge of the text frame, Paint wraps down to the next line. You can use standard Windows text-editing techniques to move the insertion point, select characters or words, and cut, copy, and paste (see the section on Notepad in Chapter 22 for a summary).

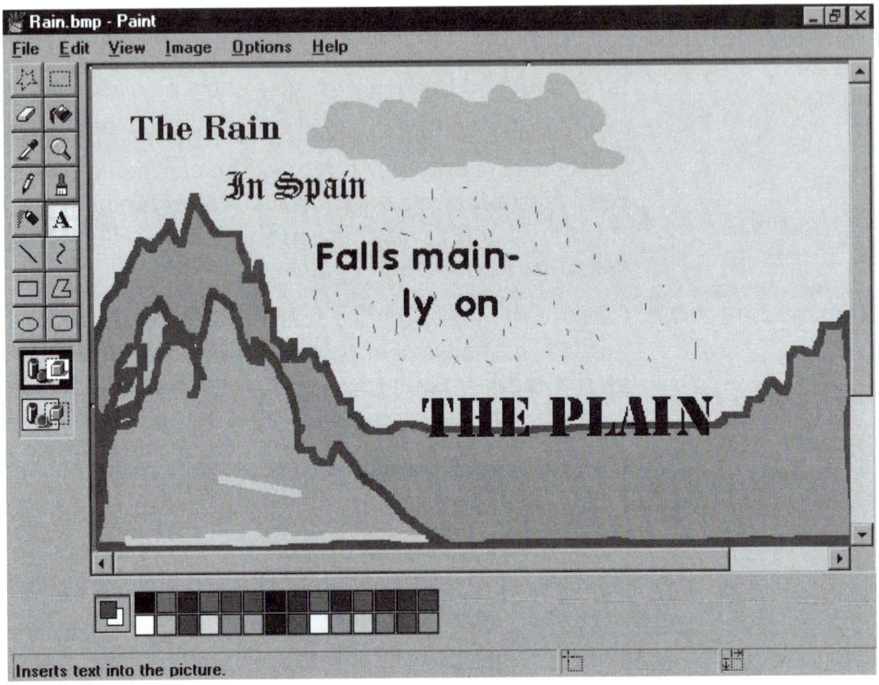

Figure 21.9 *Some type styles produced with the Text tool on my system. They may differ from yours.*

NOTE Even though you can select individual words in a text frame, Paint permits only one font, size, and style combination for *all* the text within the frame.

---

7. As long as the rectangular outline of the text frame remains on the screen, you can change its size and location and the colors of the text and the frame background:

To resize the frame: Drag any of the handles, the little squares at the corners and along the sides of the frame. The mouse pointer becomes a double-headed arrow when it's directly over a handle, indicating that you can move the handle.

To move the frame: Drag any part of the frame outline that isn't a handle. The mouse pointer becomes an arrow when it's over the outline. As you drag, a solid gray rectangle represents the moving frame, which appears at the new location when you release the button.

To change colors: On the Color Box, click the left button to change the color of the text, the right button to change the frame background's color. You can also switch between a transparent and opaque text frame by clicking on the appropriate icon in the tool-options area or by choosing Options ➤ Draw Opaque.

8. Click outside the text frame to finalize your text entry.

Once you've completed a text entry, it loses its separate identity, becoming just another set of dots in the picture. While you can select the text area for other operations (as described in the next section), you can't select, cut, copy, or otherwise manipulate the individual characters as such.

Manipulating Areas of a Picture

So far, you've learned how to add and change colors and shapes with the various painting tools. But your creative options don't stop there. Paint gives you a variety of tools and commands for working with a specific portion of the picture as a unit. Of course, you must first define, or *select*, the area you want to work, as detailed in the next section. If you don't select an area (see Figure 21.10), many of the commands covered in this section will affect the entire picture.

Selecting an Area

The Tool Box offers two tools for selecting specific portions of a picture for further manipulation. Appropriately enough, they're collectively called the *selection tools*. They are the top two buttons on the Tool Box. The one on the left with the star-shaped outline is for selecting irregular shapes; it's called the Free-Form Selection tool. The one on the right with the rectangular outline, the Select tool, is for selecting rectangular areas.

Once you've selected an area with either tool, you can "cut out" the area, either by cutting it to the Clipboard or simply by moving it around in the picture. For this reason, selections are also called *cutouts*. You can also perform many other manipulations on a selection, such as inverting its colors or rotating it.

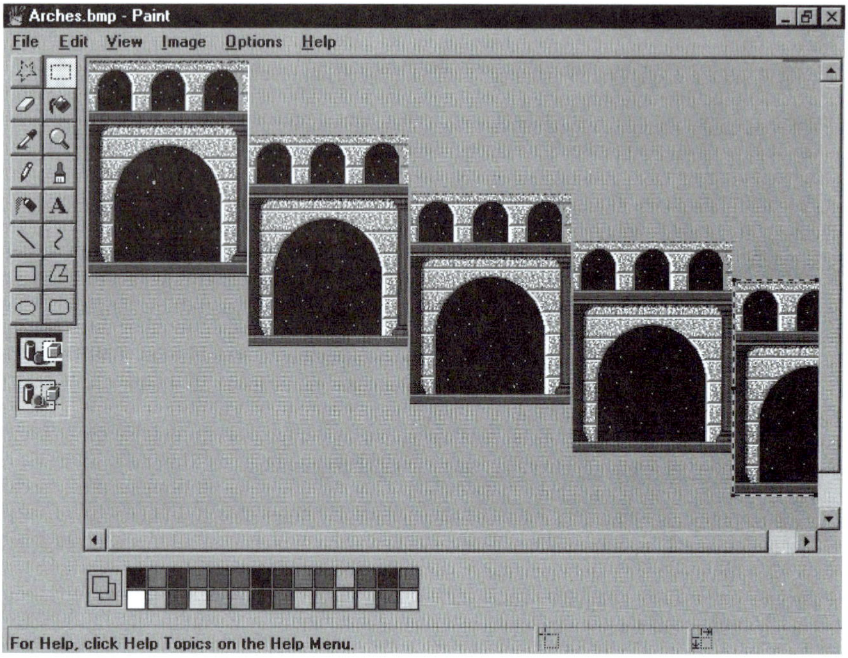

Figure 21.10   *Once you select an area, you can manipulate it in a variety of ways. Here you see brick archways copied and placed across the picture.*

Selecting Rectangular Areas

The easiest way to select an area—or define a cutout, if you prefer—is with the Select tool, the one with the dotted rectangular outline at the top right of the Tool Box.

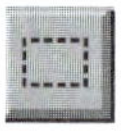

All you have to do is drag the mouse to define a boxed area. You can easily select the entire picture if you need to:

1. Select the Select tool (how's that for computerized English?).

2. Move to the upper-left corner of the boxed area you want to select. Click and hold down the left mouse button.

3. Drag the mouse down and to the right. As you draw, a dotted rectangular outline indicates the selection area.

4. Release the button. After a moment, the dotted outline reappears, but it now has handles on all four corners and along each edge (see Figure 21.11). Don't use the handles to redefine the selection area—they're for resizing the image within the area.

Once you've selected an area, it remains selected until you click outside the dotted outline around it (the *selection rectangle*) or until you choose another tool.

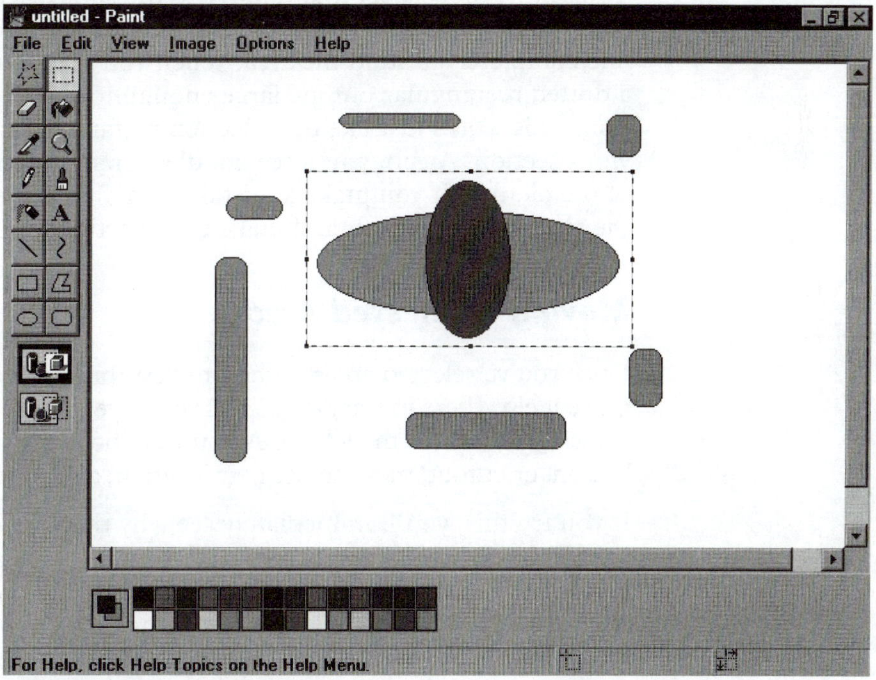

Figure 21.11 *A selection is marked by this dotted outline, the selection rectangle.*

Selecting Irregular Areas

The Free-Form Select tool lets you select any area of the picture by drawing a line freehand around the area.

It allows you to select exactly the part of the picture you're after, hugging the edges of the element that interests you.

That way, the commands you use on the selection affect only that element, not the nearby dots. And if you plan to cut or copy an area and then paste it elsewhere, using this tool to select the area ensures that you won't paste an unwanted border that might overlap other items. The only drawback: it's hard to draw the selection outline accurately.

To use this tool, select it and move to the spot where you want to start defining the area. As you hold the mouse button down, draw a line completely around the area. When you're through, Paint displays a dotted rectangular outline large enough to contain the entire selection. This works just like the selection rectangle described in the previous section. Again, you'll see handles for stretching the selected part of the picture. If you make a mistake in defining the selection, press the right mouse button and make the selection again.

Moving a Selected Area

Once you've selected an area, the simplest thing you can do with it is to move it elsewhere in the picture. All you have to do is drag it where you want it to go: Press the left mouse button down anywhere within the selection, or cutout, move to the new location, and release the button.

If you try this, you'll immediately see why they call a selection a cutout: The selection is neatly removed from its original location, just as if you'd cut it out with a straightedge and tacked it down in the new spot. Again, it remains selected until you click outside the selection rectangle, so you can move it again or perform other manipulations.

TIP   Actually, this is both a tip and a caution, depending on the results you're after. When you move a cutout by dragging it, without leaving a copy behind, Paint colors the area you cut it out from. The area is covered with the currently selected background color. So if you want to move a cutout and leave behind a colored "shadow" at the same time, change the background color first (*before* you select the area). On the other hand, if you previously changed the background color for an interim operation, be sure to change it back to the "real" background color, or you'll get shape of an unwanted color in your picture.

To move a *copy* of the selection, leaving the original in place, just hold down the Ctrl key while you drag the cutout to its new home. Figure 21.12 shows the results of moving a copy of the selection by dragging it.

> **TIP** There's even a way to create special effects by dropping multiple copies of the cutout along the path you move the mouse on as you drag. See the *Sweeping* section below.

Opaque v. Transparent Placement

When you move a selection by dragging it, you can choose between *opaque* and *transparent* placement at the new location. In opaque placement, the selection will completely replace whatever you place it on top of in the picture—nothing of what was previously there will show through.

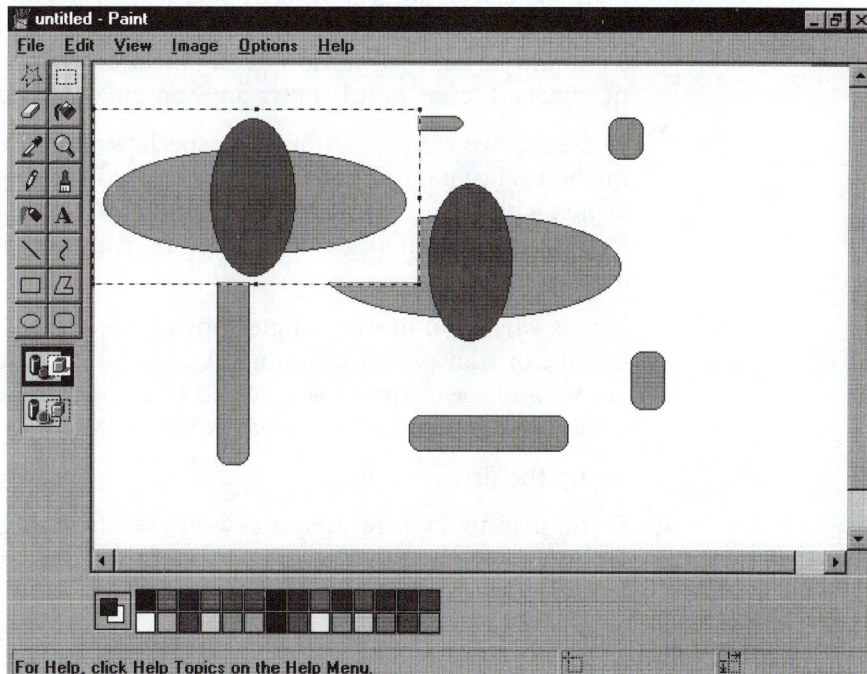

Figure 21.12　*In this picture, a selection has been copied to another location, leaving the original intact, by dragging it with the Ctrl key held down.*

In transparent placement, the selection's background disappears, so only the foreground elements in the selection appear at the new location. But this only works if you select the background color of the cutout as the background color in the Color Box (by clicking in the Color Box with the right button). Select the correct background color before you move the selection.

NOTE   In transparent placement, what actually happens is this: Paint ignores all parts of the selection having the background color currently active in the Color Box. Of course, you're free to set the Color Box background color to match part of the selection's *foreground.* In that case, these elements, not the selection's background, would drop out when you place the selection.

Sweeping

Sweeping a selection is a neat trick that deposits multiple copies of the cutout across the picture as you move the mouse. You can use this technique to suggest motion of an object or to create interesting artistic effects. Figure 21.13 shows an example of sweeping.

There are two ways to perform this special sweeping effect. The first method is just a modification of the standard technique for moving a selection with the mouse. With the second technique, you convert the selection into a brush, more or less, that remains active until you choose another tool.

Just as when you move a single copy of a selection, you can do opaque or transparent sweeping. Again, the background color of the cutout and the current background color have to be the same for transparent sweeping to work as you'd expect.

To try the first technique:

1. If you plan to do a transparent sweep, set the background color in the Color Box to match what you consider to be the background color in the selection.

2. Choose either of the selection tools and set it to opaque or transparent operation.

3. Select the area.

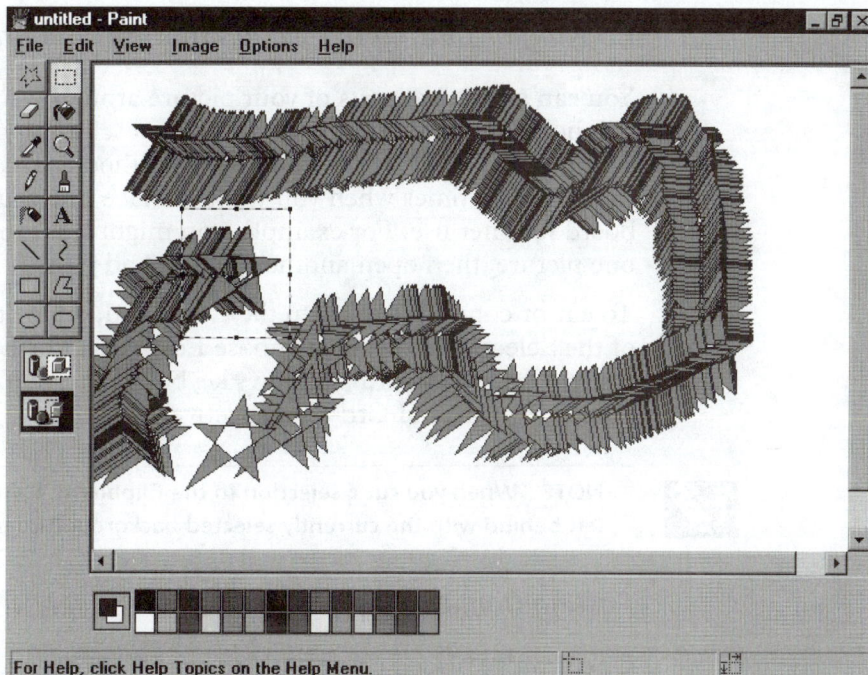

Figure 21.13   *Sweeping a cutout makes numerous copies on a single sweep of the mouse.*

4. Drag the selection while holding the Shift key down. Copies of the cutout are made as you drag the cursor around.

In the second sweeping technique, you use the selection as if it were a brush tool:

1. Choose the background color in the Color Box, choose a selection tool, and choose a setting: opaque or transparent.

2. Select the area.

3. Press Ctrl-B. A copy of the selection appears on the screen, slightly offset from the original selection.

4. Paint with the left mouse button to sweep with the actual colors you see in the selection. If you paint with the right mouse button, the Brush paints with the background color selected in the Color Box. Details of how this works are complicated to explain, so if you're interested, just try it.

Copying or Cutting a Selection to the Clipboard

You can also move parts of your picture around using the Windows Clipboard as an alternative to dragging a selection directly to a new location as described above. The latter method is usually easier, but there may be times when you want to place a selection on the Clipboard for later use. For example, you might want to cut a design from one picture, then open another picture and paste it in.

To cut or copy a selection to the Clipboard, define the area with one of the Selection tools, then choose Edit ➤ Cut or Edit ➤ Copy, or just press the standard Windows keyboard shortcuts for these commands (Ctrl-X and Ctrl-C, respectively).

> **NOTE** When you cut a selection to the Clipboard, Paint fills in the space left behind with the currently selected background color.

Pasting from the Clipboard

Once you've placed a selection on the Clipboard, you can paste it back into any picture at any time. To paste the Clipboard contents, choose Edit ➤ Paste or press Ctrl-V. The selection appears in a selection rectangle at the top left of the work area, and you can drag it into place wherever you want it. Just as with new selections, pressing Ctrl while you drag leaves a copy of the original selection behind.

Saving and Retrieving a Cutout

You can save a selection as a disk file for later use. Using this technique, you can create a stockpile of little graphics (like clip art) that you can call up from disk to drop into new pictures. Here are the steps to save and retrieve a selection:

1. Define the selection with either of the selection tools.

2. Choose Edit ➤ Copy To. A file box pops up. Name the file as you wish.

3. When you want to reload the cutout, choose Edit ➤ Load From and click on the picture file containing the selection from the file box. It will appear in the upper-left corner of the current picture on screen.

4. Reposition the selection by dragging it.

Flipping and Rotating Selections

Paint lets you rotate any selected area within the plane of the picture or *flip* the selection on its vertical or horizontal axis. Flipping reverses the pattern within the selection, producing a mirror image. If you flip horizontally, the pattern is still right-side up, while if you flip vertically, it's upside down. Rotating simply turns the pattern on its side or turns it upside down, but it doesn't create a mirror image.

You'll understand better how these commands work if you just play with them:

1. Select an area with one of the selection tools.

2. Choose Image ➤ Flip and Rotate. The Image Flip and Rotate dialog box appears.

3. Choose the appropriate radio button: Flip horizontal, Flip vertical, or Rotate. If you choose Rotate, an additional set of three radio buttons becomes available. Choose 90° to lay the area on its side, rotating to the right; 180° to stand the selection on its head, so to speak; or 270° to lay the image on its left side.

4. Click on OK to close the box. Paint transforms the selection according to your choices.

You can use these commands to create symmetrical patterns by defining a selection, copying it to the Clipboard, and then pasting it repeatedly into the same picture. Each time you paste, position the new copy where you want it, then flip or rotate it. Figure 21.14 shows an example.

Inverting Colors

The Invert Colors command *reverses* the colors in the selected area (or, if nothing is selected, in the entire picture). Black turns to white and white will turn to black. If you're working in color, the colors will turn to their complements. *Complementary colors* are defined here as being the color on the opposite side of the RGB (Red, Green, Blue) color wheel. This is a really fun tool. Try selecting several slightly overlapping squares of a picture and inverting them in sequence. An example is shown in Figure 21.15.

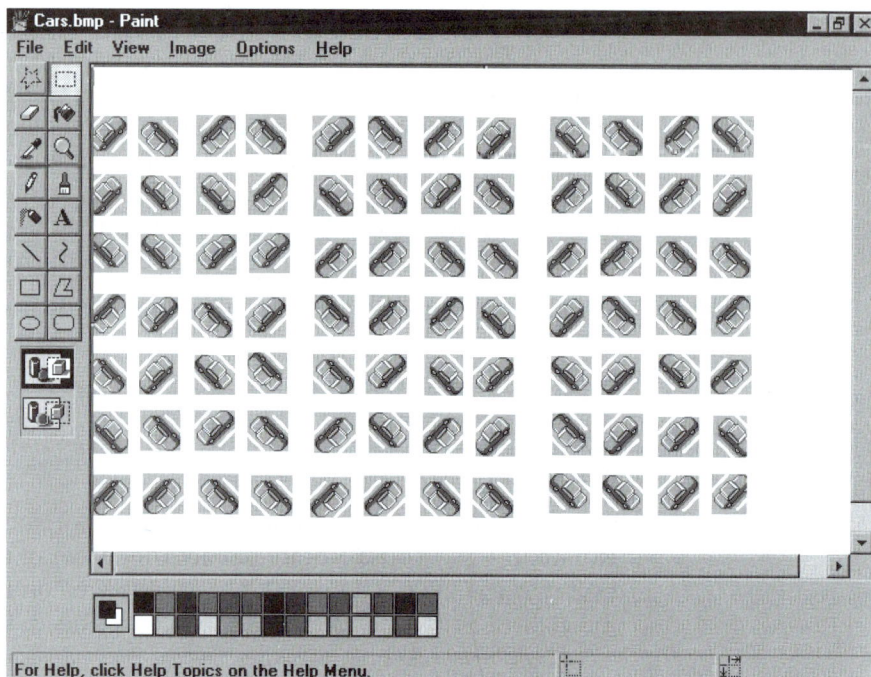

Figure 21.14   Cutouts flipped horizontally and vertically

To try this:

1. Select the area to have its colors inverted.

2. Choose Image ➤ Invert Colors.

Stretching and Shrinking a Selected Area

Paint lets you change the size of a selection with the mouse, for convenience, or by typing values into a dialog box, for accuracy. Figure 21.16 shows a selection that has been stretched and shrunken to several different sizes. (Using the dialog box, you can slant the selection at the same time you resize it, as described in the next section.)

You can repeatedly resize a selection as many times as you like until you click elsewhere to deselect the area. Just remember that the more you stretch or shrink the area, the more distorted it will look.

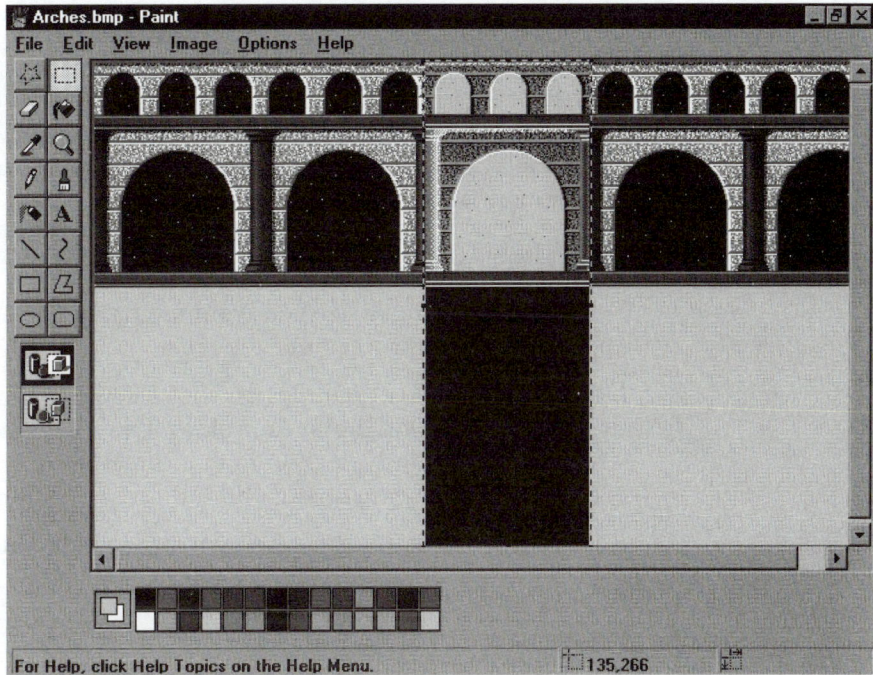

Figure 21.15   *Invert a section of a picture by selecting the cutout area and then choosing Image Invert ➤ Colors.*

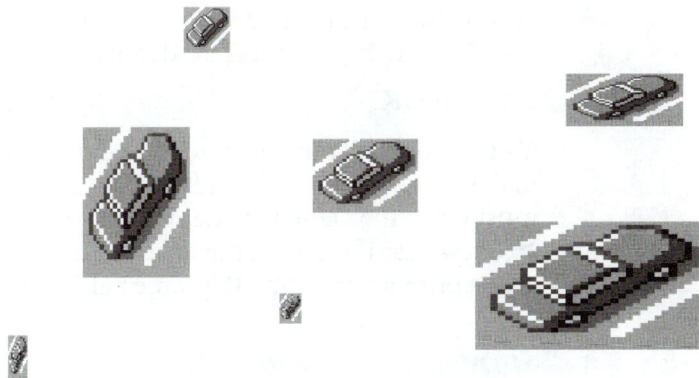

Figure 21.16   *In this picture, a selection has been pasted in several times, with each copy stretched or shrunken to a different size.*

CAUTION   When you change the size of a bit-mapped image (or any part of it), you create unavoidable distortions in the image look. Even if you maintain the area's proportions perfectly, shrinking it will result in loss of detail and a coarse appearance, while enlarging it will make curved lines appear more jagged.

To change a selection's size with the mouse:

1. Select the area whose size you want to change. The selection rectangle appears as an outline around the area.

2. Drag any of the eight handles on the selection rectangle (located at the four corners and along each side). Dragging a side handle lets you stretch or shrink the selection in one direction only, while dragging a corner handle lets you change both dimensions at once.

3. Release the mouse button when you're satisfied with the size change.

To resize a selection with the dialog box:

1. Select the area you want to resize.

2. Choose Image ➤ Stretch ➤ Skew. Select one of the top two radio buttons, Horizontal or Vertical, then type in the percentage by which you want to resize the selection in that dimension. Negative numbers make the area smaller.

3. If you also want to slant the selection, enter values in the Skew area now (see the next section for details).

4. Click on OK.

You can only change the size in one dimension each time you use the dialog box. If you want to resize the area in both dimensions, you must enter the value for one dimension, then choose Image ➤ Stretch ➤ Skew again to repeat the process for the other. To maintain the area's proportions, type the same value for both dimensions.

Slanting a Selected Area

You can slant, or *skew*, a selection horizontally or vertically, as shown in Figure 21.17. Here's how:

1. Select an area.

2. Choose Image ➤ Stretch ➤ Skew. The Image Stretch and Skew dialog box appears.

3. Choose the radio button for Horizontal or Vertical skewing. Horizontal skewing slants the selection to the right; vertical skewing slants it upward.

4. Type in the skew angle in degrees. You can type any integer between 1 and 89 (negative numbers aren't allowed).

Zooming In for Detail Work

Sometimes you need a magnified view of your picture, either to see fine detail or to make precise changes more easily. In Paint, you can choose from five magnification levels: normal, 2×, 4×, 6×, and 8×. Figure 21.18 shows a picture at highest magnification, 8× (800%).

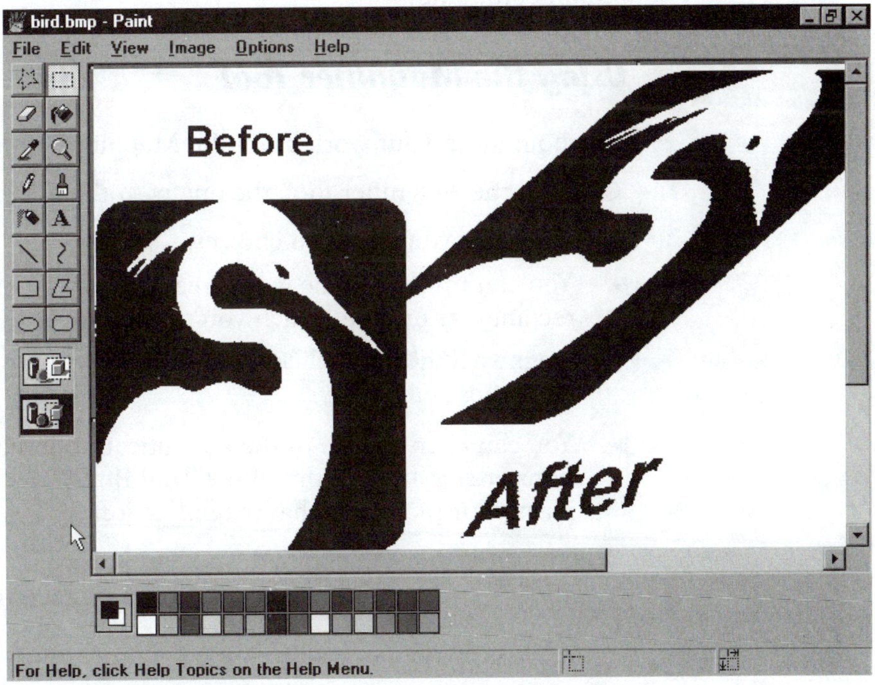

Figure 21.17   *Examples of skewing. Notice that skewing can distort the appearance of text as well as graphics.*

At the normal level, a dot on the screen corresponds to a dot on your picture. At the magnified levels, a dot in the picture is represented by a group of four or more dots on your screen that act as a unit. At any zoom level, the tradeoff is between how much you can see of the whole picture versus how detailed a view you have.

You can use any of the standard painting tools at any magnification level. By viewing things close up, you'll be able to do more precise work. But for the ultimate in precision, you can edit individual dots with the Pencil tool, covered earlier, which lets you change the color of one dot at a time.

The highest magnification is best for editing individual dots. This kind of microsurgery is useful for smoothing out lines, creating minute patterns, and eliminating single stray dots that often appear in scanned images.

You can change the magnification level with the Magnifier tool or the Zoom command.

Using the Magnifier Tool

To zoom in on your work using the Magnifier tool:

1. Click on the Magnifier tool, the one with the magnifying glass.

2. At this point, you have two choices:

   ▶ You can move into the work area. The mouse pointer displays a rectangular outline, which you position over the area you want to magnify. When you click, Paint displays this area at 4× (400%) magnification.

   ▶ You can click on one of the magnification levels in the tool-options area at the bottom of the Tool Box. Paint immediately displays your picture at that magnification.

When the picture is magnified, you can restore it to the normal, unmagnified size by selecting the Magnifier tool and clicking anywhere in the work area.

Magnifying with the Zoom command

To change the magnification level with the Zoom command:

1. Choose View ➤ Zoom to open a submenu of Zoom commands.

2. To display the picture at 4× (400%) magnification, choose Large Size. To display it at any other level, choose Custom to display the View Zoom dialog box. Click on the radio button for the desired magnification, then click on OK.

When you're zoomed in, you can go directly back to the normal, unmagnified view by choosing View ➤ Zoom ➤ Normal.

Seeing the Big Picture When You're Zoomed In

Although magnifying your picture lets you see and work with the fine details, you can lose your sense of how the picture will look at normal size. That's why Paint provides a little window that displays a normal-size view of the magnified area. This Paint View window is visible in Figure 21.18.

You can move the Paint View window around as necessary, and you can turn it off or on at will. To close the window, just click on its close box. To turn it on again, choose View ➤ Zoom ➤ Show Thumbnail.

Displaying a Grid for Precision Editing

At higher magnification levels (4× and above), Paint lets you display a grid of lines that indicates the location of each individual dot in your picture. With the grid visible, you'll find it easier to do very detailed, accurate work with your painting tools.

To turn the grid on, choose View ➤ Zoom ➤ Show Grid. The grid is shown in Figure 21.18.

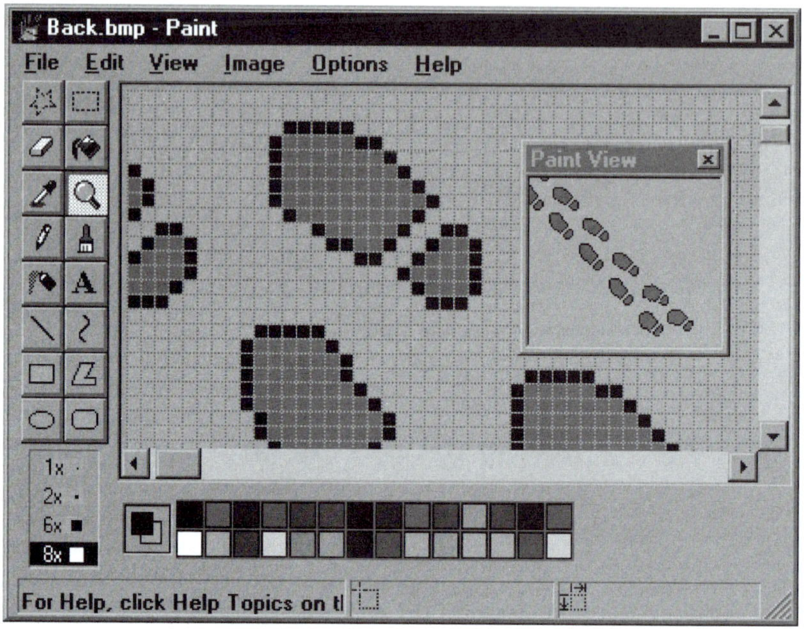

Figure 21.18   *Here's a screen image showing what a magnified picture looks like. The network of horizontal and vertical lines is Paint's grid, designed to make precision editing easier. The little Paint View window shows some of the magnified area at its normal, unmagnified size.*

Editing the Color Scheme

If you are working in color, you may want to create custom colors. If you are working in black and white, you may want to create a new pattern. To do either:

1. Start by selecting the color you want to change in the Color Box. Click on the chosen color to make it the foreground color.

> **TECH TIP**   Double-click on a color in the Color Box to open the Color dialog box.

2. Choose Options ➤ Edit Colors (or you can just double-click on the chosen color in the Color Box). The Color dialog box, shown in Figure 21.19, appears.

3. The Basic Colors area shows more colors than are available in the Color Box. If you find a suitable color in the grid, click on it to select it and then click on OK to close the dialog box. The chosen color replaces the previously selected color in the Color Box.

4. If none of the basic colors will do, click on the Define Custom Colors button. The dialog box expands to show a color-editing area.

5. In the large color-editing area, drag the crosshair cursor to choose the desired color (it appears in the smaller area below). Once you have the basic hue, you may find it easier to select the exact shade you want with the slider at the far right.

6. When you're satisfied, click on the Add to Custom Colors button. The new color appears in the area for custom colors. When you click on OK, it also appears as a choice in the Color Box.

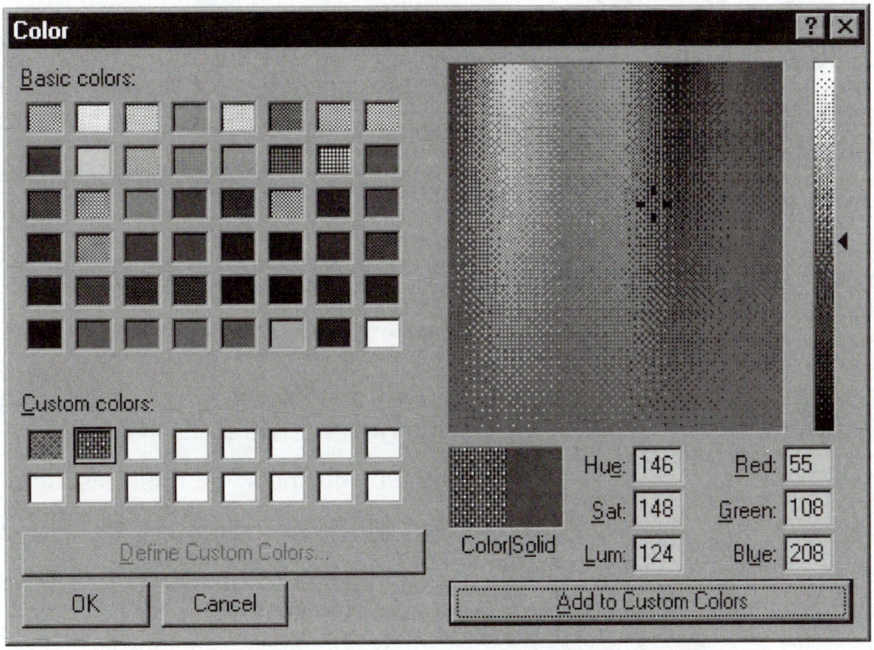

Figure 21.19   *Here's where you edit the colors that appear in the Color Box. In this illustration, the Define Custom Colors button has already been clicked on; when the Color dialog box first appears, you'll see only the left half.*

Note that the changes you make do not affect the picture's existing colors.

A custom color set remains active only with the current picture. When you open a different picture, Paint uses the color set that was active when the picture was last saved. If you start a new picture, Paint restores the standard, or default, color set.

Saving and Loading Your Own Color Schemes

Once you've created a custom color set, you can save it for use with other pictures using the Options ➤ Save Colors command. And once you've saved a custom color set, you can use it again in other pictures with the Options ➤ Get Colors command.

Saving Your Work

If you're painting for posterity—or at least have some use in mind for your work other than doodling—remember to save your work to disk regularly. Of course, you can open pictures you've worked on before for further editing—or just to admire them.

Saving Files

You can save pictures as disk files in several formats, all of them variations of the basic Paint (BMP) format. Normally, you can just let Paint choose the correct format for you. But there may be times when knowing which format to use comes in handy.

Here are the available formats and their descriptions:

Monochrome Bitmap: Use when you have only two colors (black and white) in your picture.

16-Color Bitmap: Use when you have 16 colors or fewer in your picture.

256-Color Bitmap: Use when you have more than 16 and fewer than 257 colors in your picture.

24-Bit Bitmap: Use when you have more than 256 colors in the picture.

Why change a picture's format? The most common reason: you have a picture and you like its design, but it looks cartoon-ish because it has too few colors. By saving it in a format with more colors, you'll be able to modify it with a much richer, more realistic color palette. But this only works if your screen can display the additional colors and is set up in Control Panel to do so (see Chapter 7 for instructions). Note that the more colors you save, the larger the files become and the more disk and RAM space they'll need.

CAUTION   Saving a picture with a format that has fewer colors may ruin it. When you save (for example, if you save a picture with 16 colors as a monochrome bit-mapped file), Paint translates each color in the original picture into the closest match in the new format. Clearly, you're likely to lose a significant amount of detail, especially when going to the monochrome format—the picture may well come out looking like a sea of black with a few white dots, or vice versa.

Using Your Picture as Windows Wallpaper

After you've saved a new picture, or if you're working with a picture you opened from disk, Paint can tell Windows to use the picture as wallpaper. From then on, the picture will appear as the backdrop for your Windows Desktop. Paint handles the details for you—you don't need to use the Control Panel at all. (See Chapter 7 for more on wallpaper.)

To set the current picture as wallpaper:

1. Save the picture to disk if you haven't already done so.

2. Choose File ➤ Set as Wallpaper (Tiled) if you want multiple side-by-side copies of the image on your Windows Desktop. Choose File ➤ Set as Wallpaper (Centered) if you want a single copy of the image centered on the Desktop.

Printing

Finally, you might want to print out your artwork! Here's how you do it:

1. Open the picture document, if it's not already open.

2. Turn on the printer and get it ready to print.

3. If you want to change the page margins or paper orientation, choose File ➤ Page Setup and make the necessary entries in the dialog box.

4. To see how the picture will look on the printed page, choose File ➤ Print Preview. You'll see a mock-up of the printed page on your screen. This works exactly like the Print Preview function in WordPad (see Chapter 19).

5. When you're ready to print, choose File ➤ Print, or, from Print Preview, click on the Print button. The standard Windows Print dialog box will appear, allowing you to choose the correct printer, specify which pages should print and how many copies, and change the printer's settings (by clicking on the Properties button).

Chapter 22

The Other Windows Accessories

FEATURING

In this chapter, you'll learn about the miscellaneous accessories included with Windows 95. These accessories are fairly modest programs, but each is genuinely useful in its special niche. If you take the time to acquaint yourself with their basic functions, you'll know where to turn when you need help with a problem they can solve.

Jotting Down Notes with Notepad

Like WordPad, Notepad lets you type and edit text. But the two programs have different missions. Notepad is a tool for text editing *only*, while you use WordPad to make the text you type look good (that is, to *format* your text). To use the appropriate jargon, Notepad is a *text editor,* while WordPad is a *word processor.* (WordPad is covered in Chapter 19.)

In Notepad, you can type text, but you can't change the fonts, add bold, italics, or color, modify the tab settings, center a paragraph—well, you get the point. So why bother with Notepad? After all, you could type your text in WordPad and simply not use that program's formatting features.

Notepad's main advantage over WordPad is that it's *lean*—it takes up much less memory than WordPad, and it starts up faster, too. It's small enough to keep open all the time so you can jot down quick notes whenever you need to. And it's a perfect tool to call up whenever you need to view a text file. So what's a text file?

Understanding Text Files

Notepad can only open and save *text-only* files—files that contain only text characters. That is, text-only files *don't* contain any of the formatting codes used by word processors to store information about the looks and layout of a document. Text-only files are also known as plain text files, ASCII or plain ASCII files, or simply as *text files,* which is what Windows calls them.

Before I explain more about text files, here is some practical information: Windows recognizes a text file as such only if it is stored on disk with the file-name extension .txt. Files having the .txt extension appear in your folders with the text-file icon, shown to the left. Text files often have other extensions, however. Note that Windows will recognize files having the .doc extension as WinPad documents even if they actually contain plain text only. You may wish to rename such files to avoid this conflict.

Though text files look fairly boring, they do have some important advantages over fancier, formatted text documents. The most important one is their universality: Text files provide the lowest common denominator for exchanging text between different programs and even between different types of computers. Every system has a way to create and display text files. That's why they remain the medium for most of the electronic-mail messages passed back and forth on the Internet and other information services, as well as those posted to electronic bulletin boards.

In addition, most programs have text files on the installation disk named something like READ.ME, README.TXT, or README.DOC. Such files usually contain important information about the software that was added after the manual was printed, including tips on installation, details on new features or bugs in the software, and corrections of errors in the manual. Again, these messages are stored as text-only files because that way, everyone can read them.

Text files are also good for storing the "source code" used to generate computer programs. When a programmer writes the source code, he or she types it in using a text editor such as Notepad, saving the work in a text file. That way, the instructions needed to create the final program aren't mixed up with extraneous formatting information that would confuse the *compiler* (software that converts the source code into a working program).

You may not be a programmer, but you do sometimes deal with program files of a sort—your system-configuration files, including win.ini, sys.ini, protocol.ini, config.sys, and autoexec.bat. These text files qualify as programs because they tell your system how to operate. You can edit them with Notepad.

Notepad's Limitations

Just so you won't use it for the wrong tasks, here's a summary of Notepad's limitations:

▶ It has no paragraph- or character-formatting capability. It can wrap lines of text to fit the size of the window, however, which is a nice feature.

▶ Files are limited to text only. Notepad can't open formatted documents created with WordPad, Microsoft Word for Windows, WordPerfect, or any other word processor (actually, it can open the files, but they won't look right).

▶ Files are limited in size to about 50K. This is fairly large, accommodating approximately 15 pages of solid single-spaced text—20 or so pages of regularly spaced material.

▶ It doesn't have any fancy pagination options, though it will print with headers and footers via the Page Setup dialog box.

Running Notepad

> **TIP**   If you have Notepad files that you use regularly—for example, a file for your random notes—you might want to put them into a folder for easy access. If you use them very regularly, put them into the start-up folder so they are loaded when you start up Windows. You can assign each one a shortcut key for rapid access.

To run Notepad, double-click on the Notepad icon; it's in the Accessories group. Notepad will appear on your screen, and you can immediately begin typing in the empty work area (Figure 22.1).

Alternatively, you can double-click on any document that Windows recognizes as a text file. As it starts up, Notepad will open that file automatically, and you'll see the text in the work area.

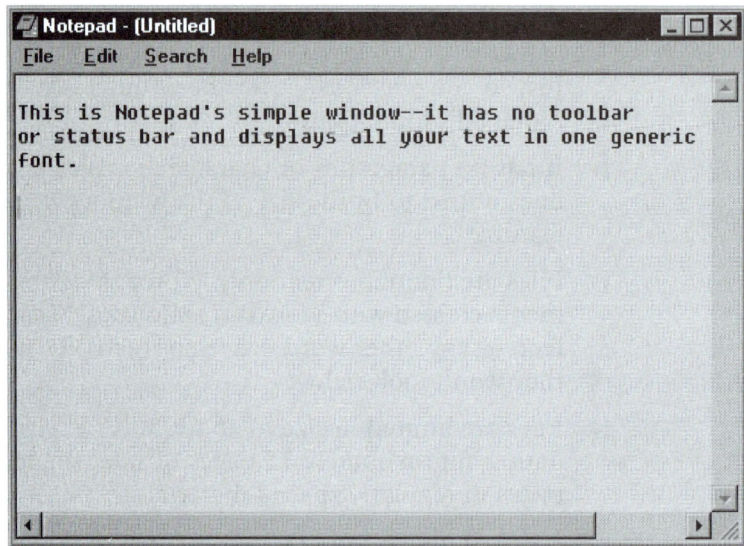

Figure 22.1   The Notepad window

Opening Files

NOTE Of course, you can choose File ➤ New to start a new file at any time. If you've made changes in the previous file, Notepad gives you the expected opportunity to save it before creating the new file.

Once Notepad is up and running, opening another text file is as simple as choosing File ➤ Open and selecting the file you want from the Open dialog box.

Keep in mind, though, that Windows may not recognize the file you want to open as a text file. When you initially bring up the Open dialog box, it's set to display only files stored with the .txt extension (note the setting in the *Files of type* area). To locate a text file with another extension, choose All files in the Files of type area.

If you try to open a file that is too large, Notepad will warn you with the message:

```
This file is too large for Notepad.
Would you like to use WordPad to read this file?
```

Clicking on Yes will automatically run WordPad, which will open the chosen file.

> **CAUTION**   Be careful about opening non-text files with Notepad. While it's fine to browse through a non-text file to see if you can make sense of it, don't make any changes and, above all, *don't save the file*. If you do, the file may be unusable even by the program that originally created it.

Notepad will go ahead and open any file you specify, even if it doesn't contain only text. If you open a non-text file, it will probably look like unintelligible garbage.

Entering and Editing Text

You can enter and edit text in Notepad as you would expect, with a few exceptions. To enter text, just start typing. The insertion point will move, just as it does in WordPad. However, as you reach the end of the window, the text will not wrap. Instead, Notepad just keeps adding new text to the same line, scrolling the window to the right so that the insertion point is always visible. When you press Enter, the window will pan back to the far left again, ready for the next line of text. Figure 22.2 shows an example of text in this state.

This is a rather inconvenient way to enter your text because you can't see much of what you just typed. To fix the problem, choose Edit ➤ Word Wrap. When you do, the text will wrap within the constraints of the window. If you resize the window, the text will rewrap to fit the available space. Figure 22.3 shows the same long line of text reformatted with Word Wrap turned on.

> **NOTE**   Certain types of program files, such as .bat, .ini, and config.sys files, are line-oriented and are better edited with Word Wrap off. This allows you to distinguish more clearly one line from the next in the case of long lines.

Note that the word-wrap setting doesn't affect the text file itself. That is, Notepad does not insert line feeds or carriage returns at the points where the lines wrap.

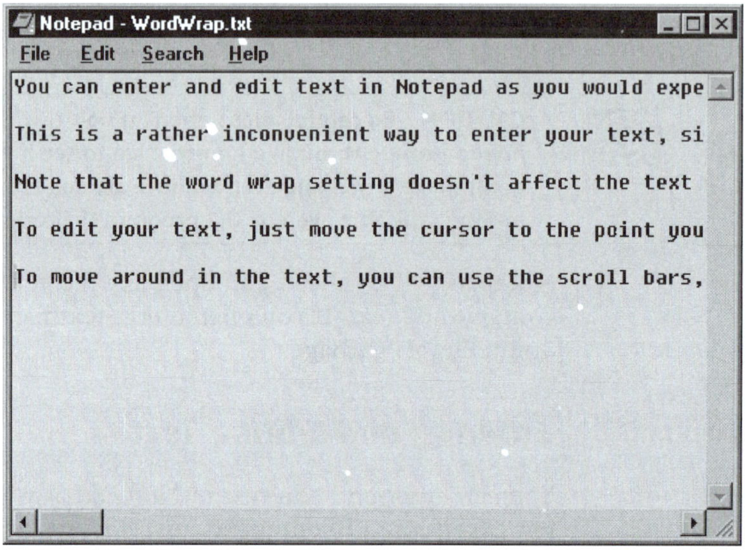

Figure 22.2   *Each paragraph of text will normally stay on one long line unless Word Wrap is turned on.*

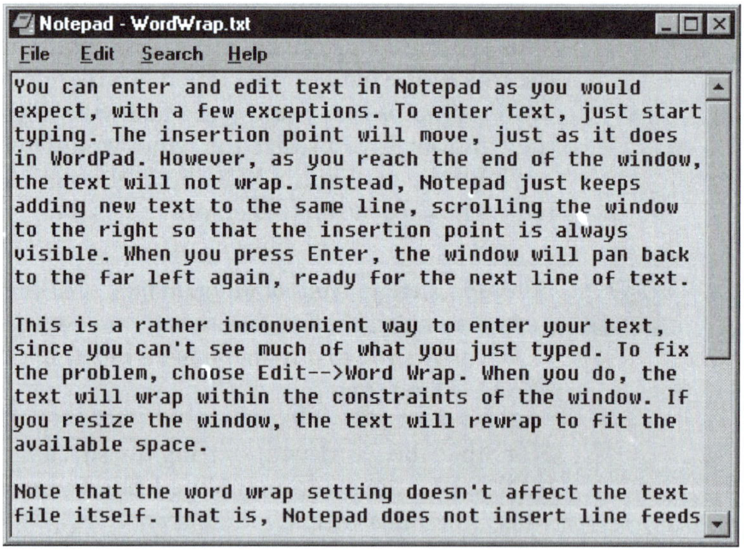

Figure 22.3   *Text will wrap within a window if Word Wrap is turned on.*

To edit your text, just move the cursor to the point you want to change. You can select, cut, copy, and paste text with the mouse, using the same techniques described in Chapter 19. To select all of the text in the file, choose Edit ➤ Select All.

To move around in the text, you can use the scroll bars, of course. You can also use the following keys:

Key	Moves Insertion Point to
Home	Start of the line
End	End of the line
PgUp	Up one window
PgDn	Down one window
Ctrl-Left Arrow	Start of previous word
Ctrl-Right Arrow	Start of next word
Ctrl-Home	Start of the file
Ctrl-End	End of the file

Entering the Time and Date in Your Text

A common use of a Notepad-type program is to take notes pertaining to important phone conversations or meetings with clients or colleagues, or to type up memos. Typically, you'll want to incorporate the current time and date into your notes to document developments as they happen. The Time/Date command on the Edit menu does this quickly.

To enter the time and date at the cursor:

1. Position the insertion point where you want the time and date inserted.

2. Choose Edit ➤ Time/Date or press F5.

Searching for Text

You can search for specific text in a Notepad file, but you can't replace it automatically. Follow these steps to search:

1. Choose Search ➤ Find. The dialog box shown on the next page will appear.

Find

Find what: | jelly beans

Direction: ○ Up   ● Down

☐ Match case

Find Next   Cancel

2. Type in the text you want to search for.

3. Check the Match Case box if you want to find text only having the same capitalization as your text. If you want the search to ignore capitalization, leave the box clear.

4. Click on Up if you want to search the portion of text above the current insertion point. Down is the default setting—Notepad searches from the insertion point to the end of the file and stops. Unlike Word-Pad, Notepad does not wrap around to the top of the file and continue the search down to the insertion point.

5. If you want to search again for the same word, choose Search ➤ Find Next or, better yet, press F3.

Setting Margins and Adding Headers and Footers

While its formatting capabilities are crude, Notepad does let you change the page margins and set up headers and footers. Here's how:

1. Choose File ➤ Page Setup command. You'll see the small dialog box shown here:

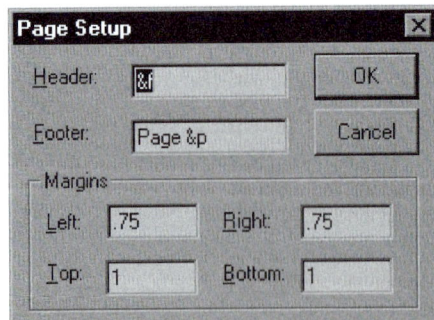

Page Setup

Header: &f

Footer: Page &p

Margins
Left: .75   Right: .75
Top: 1   Bottom: 1

OK   Cancel

2. To change the margins, type in the new settings in inches.

> **NOTE**   Margin changes and header and footer settings aren't visible on the screen but will show up in your printed document.

3. To add a header or footer, type in any text you want to appear on every page. You can also use special codes to have Notepad place various information in the header or footer for you. Note the standard header and footer settings in the Page Setup dialog box shown above. These standard settings print the file name at the top of the page and the page number at the bottom. Here's a list of the codes you can enter:

Code	Effect
&d	Includes the current date
&p	Includes the page number
&f	Includes the file name
&l	Makes the subsequent text left align at the margin
&r	Makes the subsequent text right align at the margin
&c	Centers the subsequent text
&t	Includes the time of the printing

You can enter as many of these codes as you like.

Printing a Notepad File

To print a Notepad file, do the following:

1. Make sure the printer is ready.

2. If you're not sure that the correct printer is selected or if you want to make changes to its settings, choose File ➤ Page Setup, then click on the Printer button. You can now choose a different printer (if more than one is installed) or change settings by clicking on the Properties button.

3. Choose File ➤ Print to print the file. Notepad immediately starts the printing process and always prints the entire document—you don't have an opportunity to select which pages will print or how many copies.

Performing Calculations with the Calculator

The Calculator is a pop-up tool that you can use to perform simple or complex calculations. There are really two calculators in one—a Standard Calculator and a more complex Scientific Calculator for use by statisticians, engineers, computer programmers, and business professionals.

To run the Calculator, find it in the Accessories group on the Start menu and select it from the menu. A reasonable facsimile of a hand-held calculator will appear on your screen, as shown in Figure 22.4. If your Calculator looks larger, it's the Scientific one. Choose View ➤ Standard to switch back to the basic calculator. The program always remembers which type was used last and comes up in that mode.

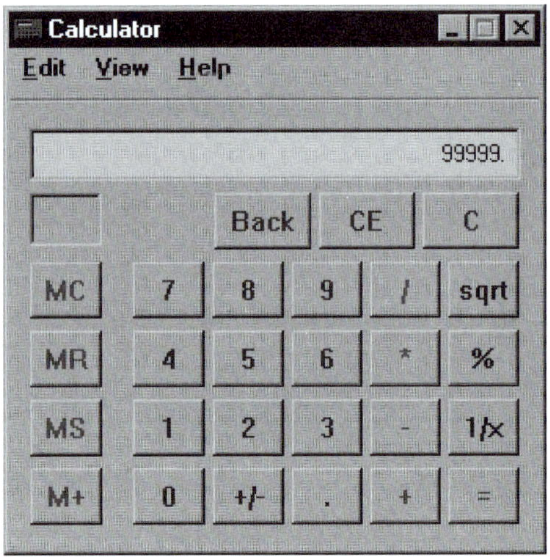

Figure 22.4   The Standard Calculator

Getting Help with the Calculator

For quick tips on how to use any calculator button, just click the right mouse button over the calculator button of interest. A little *What's this* button appears. Click on this, and you'll see a pop-up Help window. Of course, you can also choose Help ➤ Help Topics to display the main Help text.

Calculating a Result

TIP To add up a series of numbers or to find their mean, you may prefer to use the statistical functions on the Scientific Calculator. This way, you can see all the numbers in a list before you perform the calculation instead of having to enter them one at a time. And don't let the idea of statistics make you nervous—the technique is very simple.

To perform a typical calculation, follow these steps:

1. Clear the calculator's display by pressing Esc or clicking on the C button.

2. Enter the first value in the calculation by clicking on the numbers or using the keyboard. (If you set the keypad's Num Lock setting on, you can use it to enter the numbers and the four mathematical operators. This is easier than using the number keys across the top of the keyboard.) You can use the Backspace key to fix mistakes, click on C to clear the calculator and start again, or click on CE to clear only the current entry but preserve the previous result.

3. After entering the first number, click on the mathematical operator you want to use. (The asterisk represents multiplication, SQRT calculates the square root, and 1/x calculates the reciprocal. The others are self-evident.)

4. Enter any additional numbers followed by the desired operators. In this way, you can perform a sequence of operations using the result of each computation as the beginning of the next.

5. Press Enter or click on the calculator's equals (=) button. The answer appears in the display.

Most of the operations on the standard calculator are self-explanatory, but a couple of them—square roots and percentages—are just a bit tricky. They are explained below, as are the functions of the scientific calculator.

Using the Memory Keys

The memory keys work just like those on a standard calculator. MS stores the displayed number in memory, MR recalls the memory value to the display for use in calculations, M+ adds the current display value to the existing memory value, and MC clears out the memory, resetting it to zero.

When the Calculators' memory contains a value, an *M* appears in the small area just above the MC button. If no value is in memory, this area is empty.

Copying Your Results to Other Documents

To enter the number displayed in the Calculator readout into another document, just use the standard Windows copy and paste commands. Use the Calculator for your computations, and then, when the result you want is in the display, choose Edit ➤ Copy (or press Ctrl-C). The value will be copied to the Clipboard. Then switch back to your document, position the cursor where you want the result, and paste it in.

Copying Calculations from Other Documents to the Calculator

Although the Calculator doesn't keep records of your computations for reference or reuse, you can get around that limitation via the Clipboard and a text editor such as Notepad or your word processor. Here's what to do:

1. In the text editor, type in the entire equation using the special symbols listed in Table 22.1.

2. Copy the equation to the Clipboard.

3. Switch to Calculator.

4. Click on the C button to clear the Calculator, then press Ctrl+V or choose Edit ➤ Paste.

   If you've written out the equation correctly, the Calculator will compute the answer for you.

Calculator button	Equivalent keyboard key
%	%
(	(
)	)
★	★
+	+
+/−	F9
−	−
.	. or ,
/	/
0–9	0–9
1/x	r
=	= or Enter
A–F	A–F
And	&
Ave	Ctrl-A
Bin	F8
Byte	F4
Back	Backspace
C	Esc
CE	Del
cos	o
Dat	Ins
Dec	F6

Table 22.1   *Keyboard Shortcuts for the Calculator*

Calculator button	Equivalent keyboard key
Deg	F2
dms	m
Dword	F2
Exp	x
F–E	v
Grad	F4
Hex	F5
Hyp	h
Int	;
Inv	i
ln	n
log	l
Lsh	<
M+	Ctrl-P
MC	Ctrl-L
Mod	%
MR	Ctrl-R
MS	Ctrl-M
n!	!
Not	~
Oct	F7
Or		
PI	p

Table 22.1 Keyboard Shortcuts for the Calculator (continued)

Calculator button	Equivalent keyboard key
Rad	F3
s	Ctrl-D
sin	s
SQRT	@
Sta	Ctrl-S
Sum	Ctrl-T
tan	t
Word	F3
Xor	^
x^2	@
x^3	#
x^y	y

Table 22.1   *Keyboard Shortcuts for the Calculator (continued)*

Here's how a simple calculation might look, ready for copying from the text editor to Calculator:

    ((2+4)+16)/11=

or

    (2+(4+16))/11=

Note that you must surround each pair of terms in parentheses to in-dicate the calculation sequence. This is true even if you would have gotten the right answer had you typed in the numbers into the Calcu-lator without the parentheses.

If you don't like the parentheses, you can try this format instead:

    2+4=+16=/11=

Note that this time you have to insert a = after each arithmetic opera-tion; the Calculator gets confused if you don't.

You can use the following special characters in an equation to activate various Calculator functions:

:c	Clears the Calculator's memory
:e	If the Calculator is set to the decimal system, this sequence indicates that the following digits are the exponent of a number expressed in scientific notation; for example, 1.01:e100 appears in the Calculator as 1.01e+100
:m	Stores the number currently displayed in the Calculator's memory
:p	Adds the number currently displayed to the number in memory
:q	Clears the calculator
:r	Displays the number stored in the Calculator's memory
\	Places the number currently displayed into the Statistics box, which must already be open

Computing Square Roots and Percentages

To find a *square root*, just enter the number whose square root you want and click on the SQRT button. That's all there is to it—the only thing to remember is that this is a one-step calculation. You don't need to click on the = button or do anything else.

Percentages are a little trickier. Let's say you want to know what 14 percent of 2,875 is. Here's how to find out:

1. Clear the Calculator of previous results. This is a key step—you won't get the right answer if you leave a previous result in memory when you start.

2. Enter the number you're starting with, 2875 in this case.

3. Click on or type * (for multiplication) or *any* of the arithmetic operators. It actually doesn't matter which one you use—this step simply separates the two values you're entering.

4. Enter the percentage; in this case, 14. Don't enter a decimal point unless you're calculating a fractional percentage, such as 0.2 percent.

5. Now click on or type %. The Calculator reports the result.

Using the Scientific Calculator

In the Standard view, the Calculator may seem a fairly simple affair, but wait 'til you see the Scientific view—this is an industrial-strength calculating tool that can handle truly sophisticated computations. Figure 22.5 shows how the Scientific calculator appears on your screen. To display it, choose View ➤ Scientific.

The term "scientific" is somewhat misleading because the functions available here cover programming and statistics as well as the operations traditionally used by scientists. With the Scientific Calculator, you can:

▶ perform complex computations, grouping terms in up to 25 levels of parentheses

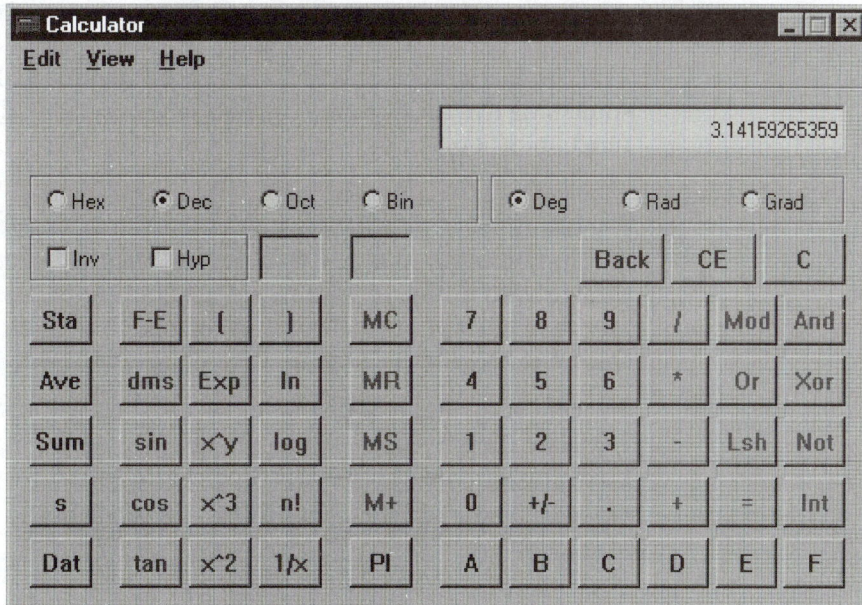

Figure 22.5   *The Scientific Calculator*

▶ display and perform calculations on values expressed in scientific (exponential) notation

▶ raise numbers to any power and find any (nth) root

▶ calculate logarithms and factorials

▶ perform trigonometric functions such as sine and cosine, displaying values as degrees, radians, or gradients

▶ insert the value of pi into your calculations

▶ perform calculations in four bases (hexadecimal, octal, and binary, in addition to decimal) and translate values between the bases

▶ perform bitwise operations (logical and shift operations on individual bits in a value) such as And, Or, Not, and Shift

▶ calculating standard deviations and other statistical computations

Details on the individual functions of the Scientific Calculator are beyond the scope of this book—if you're rocket scientist enough to use them, you probably don't need me to explain them to you. An introduction to operating the program is in order, however.

Accessing Additional Functions with the Inv and Hyp Check Boxes

The Inv check box at the left side of the Scientific Calculator functions something like the Shift key on your keyboard: checking it alters the function of some of the Calculator's buttons. This means you have access to additional functions that aren't obvious from the button labels.

For example, to find the arcsine of the value currently displayed in the readout, you would check the Inv box, then click on the sin button. Similarly, to find a cube root, enter the number, check the Inv box, and then click on the x^3 button. Instead of raising the value to the third power, you've calculated the cube root.

As you can guess, Inv stands for *inverse*, and it causes most buttons to calculate their inverses. With some buttons, though, checking the Inv box simply accesses a related function.

The Inv box is automatically cleared for you after each use.

Immediately to the right of the Inv box is the Hyp (for hyperbolic) check box, which works similarly. Its function is to access the corresponding hyperbolic trigonometric function when used with the sin, cos, and tan buttons.

Working with Scientific Notation

To enter a number using scientific (exponential) notation:

1. Begin by entering the significant digits (the base number).

2. When you're ready to enter the exponent, click on the Exp button. The display changes to show the value in exponential notation with an exponent of 0.

3. If you want to enter a negative exponent, click on the +/– button.

4. You can now enter the exponent. The Calculator accepts exponents up to +/– 307. If you enter a larger number, you'll get an error message in the display and you'll have to start over.

You can switch back and forth between exponential and standard decimal notations for numbers with absolute values less than 10^{15}. To do so, just click on the F–E button.

Working with Different Number Bases

The Scientific Calculator lets you enter and perform calculations with numbers in any of four commonly used number base systems: decimal (base 10), hexadecimal (base 16), octal (base 8), and binary (base 2). To switch to a different base, click on the appropriate radio button from the group at the upper left. The value currently in the display will be translated to the new base.

Many of the Scientific Calculator's operators and buttons work only while the decimal numbering system is active. For example, you can only use scientific notation with decimal numbers. The letter keys (A–F) at the bottom of the Scientific Calculator's numeric button pad are for entering the hexadecimal digits above 9 and only work in hexadecimal mode.

You have three display options when each number base system is active. The choices appear as radio buttons at the right side of the Calculator.

When the decimal system is active, you can display values as degrees, radians, or gradients. These are units used in trigonometric computations, and for other work you can ignore the setting.

> **NOTE**   If the display is set for Degrees, you can use the dms button to display the current value in the degree-minute-second format. Once you've switched to degrees-minutes-seconds, you can translate back to degrees by checking the Inv box, then clicking on the dms button.

The choices for the other three bases are:

Dword, which displays the number as a 32-bit value (up to 8 hexadecimal places)

Word, which displays the number as a 16-bit value (up to 4 hex places)

Byte, which displays the number as an 8-bit value (up to 2 hex places)

When you switch to an option that displays fewer places, the Scientific Calculator hides the upper (more significant) places but retains them in memory and during calculations. When you switch back, the readout reflects the entire original number, as modified by any calculations.

Grouping Terms with Parentheses

You can use parentheses to group terms in a complex calculation, thereby establishing the order in which the various operations are performed. You can *nest* parentheses inside other parentheses to a maximum of 25 levels.

Aside from the math involved, there's nothing tricky about using parentheses—except keeping track of them as your work scrolls out of the display area. In this regard, the Scientific Calculator does provide one bit of help: It displays how many levels "deep" you are at the moment in the small area just above the right parenthesis button.

Performing Statistical Calculations

The Scientific Calculator can also perform several simple statistical calculations, including standard deviations, means, and sums. Even if you're not savvy with statistics, the statistical functions provide a good way to add or average a series of values. You get to enter the numbers in a list, where you can see them all, and then click on a button to get the result.

You access the statistical functions via three buttons at the left of the Scientific Calculator: Ave, Sum, and s. These buttons only work when you display the Statistics box, as detailed in the general instructions below. The functions of each button are listed after the instructions.

Now you're ready for the general method for performing any statistical calculation:

1. Click on the Sta button to display the Statistics box, shown here:

```
┌─────────────────────────────────────┐
│ Statistics Box                   [X] │
│ ┌─────────────────────────────────┐  │
│ │ 85.                             │  │
│ │ 651.                            │  │
│ │ 102.36                          │  │
│ │                                 │  │
│ └─────────────────────────────────┘  │
│                                      │
│  [RET]   [LOAD]   [CD]    [CAD]      │
│                n=3                   │
└─────────────────────────────────────┘
```

2. Position the Statistics box and the Calculator on your screen so you can see the box and have access to the Calculator buttons and readout.

3. Place each value in the Statistics box by entering the value and clicking on Dat. Repeat this for all the values you want to perform the calculation on.

4. To delete an entry in the Statistics box, highlight it, then click on CD (clear datum). You can delete all the entries by clicking on CAD (clear all data).

5. When you've entered all the correct values, click any of the three statistics buttons to perform the selected calculation. The answer appears in the Calculator's main readout.

Each of the statistical function buttons performs two functions: one "regular" function and a second function if you check the Inv box above before clicking on the button. Here are the buttons' functions:

Button	Normal function	Function with Inv
Ave	Calculates the mean	Calculates the mean of the squares
Sum	Calculates the sum	Calculates the sum of the squares
s	Calculates the standard deviation using $n-1$ as the population parameter	Calculates the standard deviation using n as the population parameter

Never heard of the population parameter? You're not alone....

Entering Special Symbols with Character Map

The Character Map program lets you choose and insert into your documents those oddball characters such as foreign alphabetic and currency symbols and characters from specialized fonts such as Symbol and Wingdings. With Character Map, you can easily view and insert these symbols even though there aren't keys for them on your keyboard.

Here are some everyday examples. Suppose that instead of the standard straight quotes (like "this") you'd prefer to use real open and close quotes (like "this") for a more professional-looking document. Or perhaps you regularly use the symbols for Trademark (™), Registered Trademark (®), Copyright (©); Greek letters such as α, β, δ; or the arrow symbols ↑, ↓, ←, and → that we use in this book. These, as well as fractions and foreign-language accents and the like, are included in your Windows fonts and can most likely be printed on your printer.

Character Map is a small dialog box that displays all the symbols available for each font. You select the symbol(s) you want, and Character Map puts them on the Clipboard for pasting into your document. Figure 22.6 displays some examples of special characters.

Figure 22.6   Sample characters inserted into a WordPad document using Character Map

Using Character Map

Here's how to use Character Map:

1. Run Character Map (it's in the Accessories group). The Character Map table comes up, showing all the characters included in the font currently selected in the Font list (a font can contain up to 224 characters).

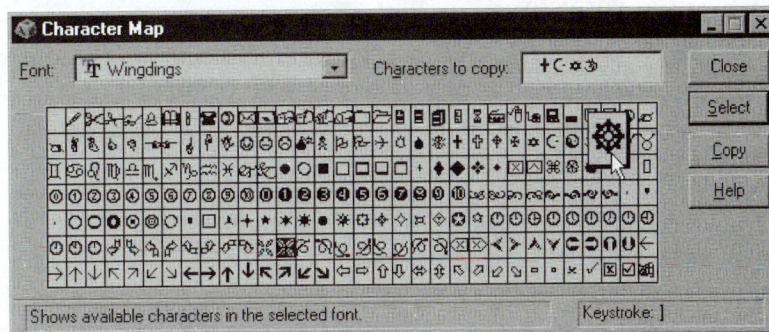

2. In the Font list, choose the font you want to work with. Most of the fonts have the same characters, but some special fonts have completely different *character sets*. For example, the Symbol font includes all sorts of special math and Greek symbols, while the Wingdings font consists of a wacky set of little pictures.

3. To make it easier to see the individual characters, you can click on a character box and hold the mouse button down to magnify the symbol. You can accomplish the same thing with the keyboard by moving to the character using the arrow keys. With this technique, each character is magnified as you select it.

4. Double-click on a character to select it, transferring it to the *Characters to copy* box. Alternatively, once you've highlighted a character, you can click on the Select button or press Alt-S to place it in the Characters to copy box.

NOTE You can change fonts at any time. Just be aware that this will affect the characters you previously placed in the Characters to copy box, not just new characters.

---

5. If you want to grab more than one character, keep adding them in the same way. Each new character is added to the end of the string in the Characters to copy box.

6. Click on the Copy button. This places everything in the Characters to copy box onto the Clipboard.

7. Switch back to your destination application and use the Paste command (typically on the application's Edit menu) to insert the characters into your document. You may then have to select the inserted characters and choose the correct font to format the characters correctly.

Of course, once you've entered a character in this way, you're free to change its font and size as you would any character you typed in.

Entering Alternate
Characters from the Keyboard

Notice that the bottom of the Character Map dialog box includes a
line that reads

Keystroke:

When you click on a character in Character Map, this line displays
the keys you would have to press to enter the character directly from the
keyboard rather than from Character Map. For the characters in the first
three lines—except the very last character on the third line—the keystroke shown will be a key on your keyboard. If you're working with a
nonstandard font such as Symbol, pressing the key shown will enter the
selected symbol into your document. With Symbol, for example,
pressing the *a* key enters α. With Wingdings, pressing *J* enters
the cheery symbol shown at left.

For all the other characters, Character Map instructs you to enter a sequence of keys in combination with the Alt key. For example, say you
wanted to enter the copyright symbol (©) into a Windows application
document. Note that with a standard text font like Arial or Times
New Roman selected in Character Map, the program lists the keystrokes for the copyright symbol as Alt-0169. Here's how to enter the
character from the keyboard:

1. Press Num Lock to activate the numeric keypad on your keyboard if
   the keypad is not already active.

2. Press Alt and as you hold it down type 0 1 6 9 (that is, type the 0, 1,
   6, and 9 keys individually, in succession). When you release the Alt
   key, the copyright symbol should appear in the document.

Not all Windows application programs accept characters in this way,
but it's worth a try as a shortcut to using the Character Map.

Character Sets: ANSI v. IBM

Normally you'll be using Character Map with Windows applications.
However, you may have some success dropping special characters into
non-Windows applications. The basic technique is simple:

1. Copy the desired characters to the Clipboard.

2. Display the non-Windows application in a window if it isn't windowed already.

3. Paste the Clipboard contents into your application using the application window's Control menu (choose Edit ➤ Paste or click on the Paste button).

That's easy enough, but whether or not you see the desired characters depends on several factors. Here's the situation: Windows uses the American National Standards Institute (ANSI) character set to display characters on the screen and assign them to the keyboard. This includes 256 characters, numbered 0 to 255. By contrast, when your PC runs DOS *text mode* or *character-based* programs, the computer uses a different character set called the IBM extended character set.

In the United States, at least, the ANSI and IBM sets are identical for the characters numbered between 32 and 127, which correspond to the letters, numbers, and symbols on a standard U.S. keyboard. However, the two sets differ dramatically when it comes to the other characters. For example, in the ANSI set the British pound symbol (£) is character 163, whereas in the IBM extended character set it is 156.

With me so far? Okay, here's how Character Map and your non-Windows programs interact. When you copy a character from a standard Windows text font to a non-Windows application, Windows tries to translate the character into one that the non-Windows program can display. Sometimes this works, sometimes it doesn't. Here are the possible scenarios:

▶ If the symbol is present in the IBM character set, you may be in luck—it should appear in the non-Windows document as is. For example, if you select and copy the British pound symbol, Windows translates it to the correct code for that same symbol in the IBM character set. So far so good. But what happens when that code gets pasted into your non-Windows program is up to the program. Some programs can accept any character code you throw at them. Others display some codes as expected but react strangely to others, perhaps by executing some menu command. Still others ignore all characters except the standard ones.

▶ If Windows has no exact equivalent in the IBM character set, Windows converts it to the character it thinks is the closest. Thus, a copyright symbol becomes *c*, the registered trademark becomes *r*, and so on. Again, depending on the character code after the conversion, your non-Windows application may or may not accept it when you paste it in.

By the way, Windows performs these translations on all Clipboard text you paste to a non-Windows program, not just characters copied from Character Map.

It's usually easier to enter the non-keyboard characters into a non-Windows application directly, rather than copying them from Windows—that way, you'll avoid all the pitfalls I've just described. Check your non-Windows application's manual to see whether it includes information about entering non-keyboard characters from the keyboard. If you don't find any specific advice, you can try entering them as follows:

1. Look up the code for the character you want to insert. There are several places to look:

   ▶ In Character Map's Font box, select the font called Terminal, which is used to display text in your windowed non-Windows programs. This font includes all the characters of the IBM set, although Character Map doesn't display the first 31 of them. Again, the necessary code appears at the bottom of the Character Map window.

   ▶ Character codes are usually listed in your computer's manual or your DOS manual.

   ▶ You can get pop-up utilities (I'm talking non-Windows utilities) that display the characters and their codes on the screen. Usually referred to as *ASCII tables*, these utilities are available as shareware or freeware from many bulletin boards and shareware distributors.

2. Once you've found the code, press Num Lock to activate the numeric keypad on your keyboard if the keypad is not already active.

3. To enter the character, press the Alt key, hold it down, and type the three-digit code on the numeric keypad. Note that these are *three*-digit codes, not four-digit codes as in Windows. All Windows keycodes require entry of an initial 0, the fourth digit. For example, to enter the British pound symbol in a non-Windows program, you would enter Alt-156, *not* Alt-0156. If the three-digit code does start with a 0, go ahead and enter that.

Note that you can use a Windows program such as WordPad or Notepad to open text files saved by a non-Windows application, even if they contain extended characters. In general, however, the extended characters will be represented by small solid or hollow boxes—in other words, you'll lose them. The rest of your text should remain intact, however.

Audio Control

This accessory is a pretty simple one. When you run it, it pops up volume controls, balance controls, and the like for controlling your sound card, if you have one. If you don't have a sound card, this accessory won't be available, or won't do anything. There are two sets of controls—one for recording and one for playback.

1. Run the accessory from Start ➤ Programs ➤ Accessories ➤ Multimedia ➤ Volume Control. You can more easily run it by double-clicking on the little speaker icon in the Taskbar. Your sound system's capabilities will determine the format of the volume control(s) you'll see. On first running the accessory on my machine, I see:

2. Change any volume control's setting by dragging the volume up or down. Change the balance between right and left channels by dragging the Balance sliders left or right.

3. Check out the Properties menu. It may have options that will provide an expanded view of the volume controls. The graphic below shows a typical Properties box allowing alteration of which volume controls display.

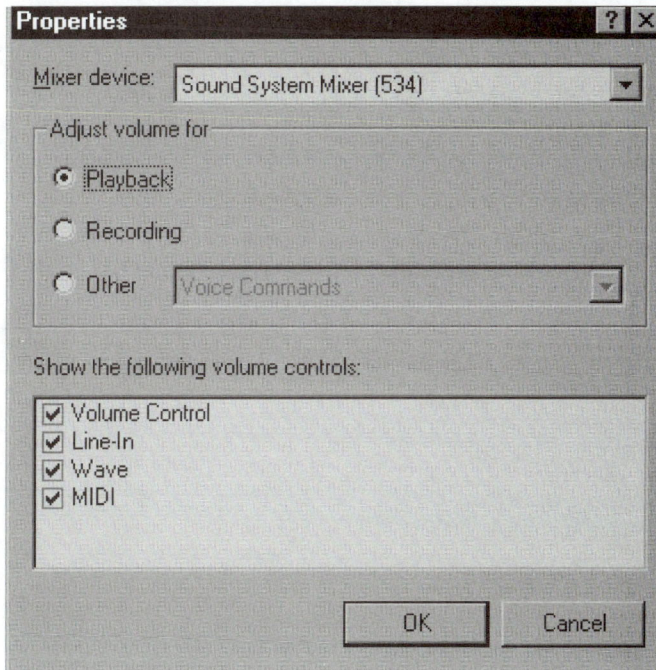

NOTE Some of the sliders in one module are linked to sliders in other modules. Adjusting the Volume setting on one will affect Volume settings on the other mixers, for example.

Because audio controls operate differently for different sound cards, check out any Help files that might be available from your audio controls. Typically there will be a Help button to press.

Two little tips here: if you're using the Microsoft sound system, you can adjust the recording volume by clicking on the microphone or line slider and speaking into the microphone. As long as you keep the mouse button depressed, the input signal will be displayed in the VU meter bar.

Second, to quickly kill the sound output from your system (useful when the phone rings), click on the little speaker icon in the Taskbar:

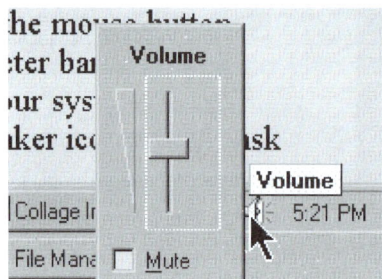

You'll be able to adjust the master volume from here and even mute the sound by clicking on the Mute box.

Chapter 23

Using the System Tools

FEATURING

Correcting disk errors with ScanDisk

Backing up files with Backup

Increasing disk capacity with DriveSpace

Disk Defragmenter

Tracking system resources with System Monitor

Windows 95 comes with a full set of software tools designed to improve the performance of your system and protect your vital information against breakdowns, damage, theft, or loss. The tools include:

ScanDisk: for detecting and correcting errors on your disks that might otherwise cause you to lose information or waste disk space.

Backup: for making backup copies of the files on your hard disks onto floppy disks or tape. If your computer or hard disks ever break down or get stolen, you'll be able to retrieve the files using Backup and the backup copies.

DriveSpace: for increasing the amount of storage space available on your disks by compressing the information in your files.

Disk Defragmenter: for speeding access to the files on your hard disks. It works by reorganizing the disks so each file is stored as a single block on one area of the disk instead of in sections scattered over different parts of the disk.

System Monitor: for displaying technical information about the activity of your system, showing you how your system resources are being used on a moment-to-moment basis (this is only available if you install Network Administrator Tools).

Correcting Disk Errors with ScanDisk

While your PC's disks give you a reliable place to store vast amounts of information, they are vulnerable to glitches of various types that can make the information unusable or reduce the space available for storing new data. The ScanDisk accessory can find these problems and take remedial action either by correcting the problem directly or locking out problem areas on the disk. It can't fix all possible errors, but it will notify you of every problem it discovers.

NOTE This version of ScanDisk performs functions similar to those of the non-Windows programs SCANDISK and CHKDSK (SCANDISK was included with MS-DOS 6, and CHKDSK is available in every version of DOS and comes with Windows 95 as well). The big difference is, you can use the new version of ScanDisk while you're working with Windows.

To run ScanDisk, begin from the Start menu and choose Programs ➤ Accessories ➤ System Tools ➤ ScanDisk. You'll see the main Scan-Disk window, shown in Figure 23.1.

> **TIP** If something has gone seriously wrong with your hard disk, it may help to run ScanDisk more than once. In some cases, the program is able to find and repair additional errors on each of several passes.

You have only a few choices to make in this window. Choose the disk you want to analyze from the list at the top of the window. Check the Automatically Fix Errors box if you want ScanDisk to correct the errors it finds for you without any further input from you. Clear this box if you want a chance to determine how ScanDisk handles each error.

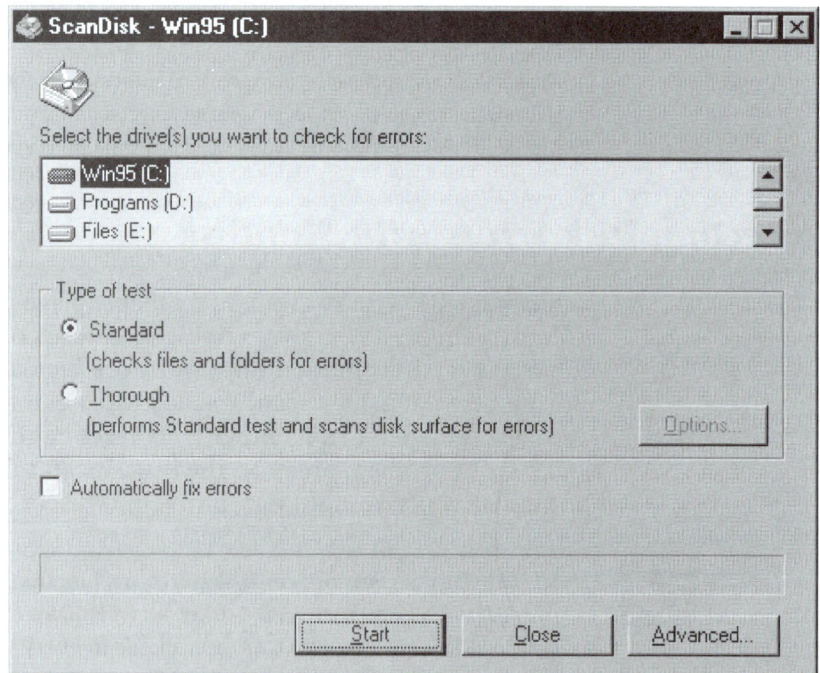

Figure 23.1   *The main ScanDisk window*

The two radio buttons in the center let you select either a standard test, which simply checks for errors and inconsistencies in the records Windows keeps on folders (directories) and the files they contain; or a "thorough" test which in addition checks the actual disk surface itself for problems with the magnetic media on which information is stored.

I'll explain more about the various types of checks that ScanDisk performs and why they're necessary in a bit. For now, a quick word of advice on how to choose between these two options is in order. The standard test is *much* faster than the thorough test, and the problems it detects occur far more frequently than flaws in the disk surface. You should run the standard test regularly—every day when you start your PC, if you're a heavy user, or once a week if you only use your computer occasionally. Running the thorough test once a week (for heavy users) to once a month (for occasional users) should be enough to catch most disk-surface errors before you lose data.

Testing a Disk

To begin a disk test, click on the Start button at the bottom of the ScanDisk window. As the program analyzes your disk, it reports its progress in the area above the buttons near the bottom of the window. You'll see messages explaining what ScanDisk is doing at the moment plus a graphical meter of how much of the analysis is complete.

You can stop a test at any time by clicking on the Cancel button. Otherwise, ScanDisk displays the message "Complete" when it finishes the analysis. Depending on how you've set the display options, you may see a summary of its findings.

Setting ScanDisk Options

ScanDisk's standard settings are best for most users, and you probably won't need to change them. But choice is the name of the game. ScanDisk lets you select settings for a variety of options pertaining to both standard and thorough tests.

To review and change the settings for standard disk tests, click on the Advanced button in the ScanDisk window. You'll see the ScanDisk Advanced Options dialog box, shown here:

The dialog box is divided into four main areas: one for specifying display options, one for controlling how files are analyzed, and two for specifying how ScanDisk handles specific types of errors. In addition, there's a check box near the bottom of the dialog box that pertains only to compressed drives.

Setting Display Options

The Display Summary area offers radio buttons for three settings that determine when you will see a summary of ScanDisk's findings. Choose:

Always: if you want to see the summary when ScanDisk finishes testing a disk, whether or not it finds any errors.

Never: if you never want to see the summary.

Only if errors found: if you want to see the summary only if ScanDisk found any errors.

Handling Cross-Linked Files

One long-familiar PC problem that can still bedevil your Windows disks is *cross-linked files*. Because of quirks in the way DOS and Windows store information about files, errors can creep into the master record that shows where each file is located on the disk. When files are cross-linked, the record shows that two or more files share a common part (cluster) of the disk. Files are always supposed to be independent entities, so this is clearly a mistake. When the system tries to access a cross-linked file, it will likely read the wrong information. Your documents may open looking like garbage, or your whole system may come to a halt.

ScanDisk lets you decide how to handle the cross-linked files it discovers as it combs through the disk's master record. However, these settings only apply if you have checked Automatically Fix Errors in the main ScanDisk window (if not, ScanDisk will let you decide how to handle each cross-linking problem on a case-by-case basis as described just below).

Choose one of the radio buttons in the Cross Linked Files area as follows:

Delete: if you want ScanDisk to erase the cross-linked files. You won't have to worry about them again, although you'll lose the data they contain.

Make copies: if you want ScanDisk to copy each cross-linked file to a new location on the disk in hopes of preserving the original information. When two or more files are cross-linked, the disk cluster they have in common contains valid information from only one of the files, at most. (In some cases, all of the information in the shared cluster is garbage.) If you're lucky, copying the files will restore one of them to its original condition. In any case, you may be able to retrieve some of the contents if they are copied word-processor or database files. To try this, open them in a text editor or word processor and copy any valid information you find to a new file.

Ignore: if you want ScanDisk to leave the cross-linked files as is. This is a choice for advanced users who may wish to use other disk tools to examine the contents of the problem files in hopes of retrieving more of their data. Normally, you shouldn't select this option—if you leave the cross-linked files in place, you're very likely to lose even more of the information they contain, and the problem may spread to other files.

If Automatically Fix Errors is not checked, ScanDisk displays a dialog box similar to this one when it detects cross-linked files:

```
ScanDisk Found an Error on 3½ Floppy (A:)          ?  X

The following files or folders are cross-linked:

 ┌─────────────────────────────────────────────┐
 │ A:\1WINPAD.DOC                               │
 │ A:\sybex-1.reg                               │
 │                                              │
 │                                              │
 └─────────────────────────────────────────────┘

A crosslink occurs when two or more files use the same
cluster (area of a disk) at the same time. Except in unusual
circumstances, the data in the crosslinked cluster(s) is correct
for only one of the files.


 ⊙ Give each file a separate copy of the shared cluster(s).
 ○ Delete all affected files.
 ○ Truncate all files at the point of the crosslink.
 ○ Keep selected file and delete others
 ○ Keep selected file and truncate others
 ○ Ignore this error and continue

      ┌──────────┐       ┌──────────┐
      │    OK    │       │  Cancel  │
      └──────────┘       └──────────┘
```

Handling Lost File Fragments

Lost file fragments are portions of the disk containing information that doesn't belong to any specific file. Somehow, the master record for the disk has gotten muddled. While the record indicates that these areas hold data, it doesn't show which files they belong to. As Scan-Disk checks the master record, it finds these free-floating chunks of information by checking the entry for each cluster against the list of files and their locations.

If you have checked the Automatically Fix Errors box in the main ScanDisk window, ScanDisk will deal with the lost file fragments it finds according to the setting in the Lost File Fragments area. Choose:

Free: if you want ScanDisk to delete the lost file fragments, freeing up the space on disk for other files.

Convert to files: if you want ScanDisk to convert the fragments to valid files. Scan-Disk names the files according to the pattern `file0000.chk`, `file0001.chk`, and so on, placing them in the top-level folder (the root directory) of the current disk drive. After you finish with ScanDisk, you can use a file-viewing program to examine their contents.

If the Automatically Fix Errors box isn't checked, you'll receive a message when ScanDisk encounters lost file fragments, allowing you to decide then how to deal with the situation.

File-Checking Options

The Check Files For area has two check boxes having to do with the types of errors ScanDisk checks for when analyzing individual files. You can check them in any combination. Choose:

Invalid filenames: if you want ScanDisk to find files with invalid characters in their names.

Invalid dates and times: if you want ScanDisk to find files whose date and time information is invalid.

If you have checked the Automatically fix errors box on the main ScanDisk window, ScanDisk will fix the types of errors you've chosen automatically. If not, you'll be shown a message describing the problem and giving you options for dealing with it, as in this example:

ScanDisk Found an Error on 3½ Floppy (A:)　　　? ✕

The A:\ folder contains incorrect information about the Ö?Ç?????.??? file.

The file's MS-DOS name (I?I?????.???) contains invalid characters, as represented by question mark(s). This may prevent you from using the file. ScanDisk repairs the error by changing lowercase letters to uppercase letters and by replacing invalid characters with hyphens.

　◉ Repair the error.
　◯ Delete the affected file.
　◯ Ignore this error and continue.

　　[OK]　　[Cancel]

Options for Compressed Drives

The check box labeled *Check host drive first* in the ScanDisk Advanced Options dialog box applies only to compressed drives. If you're testing a drive that has been compressed for more storage space by DriveSpace (included with Windows 95) or DoubleSpace (included with DOS 6), you might want to change this setting.

When the box is checked, ScanDisk tests the actual disk—the *host* drive—where the compressed drive is located before checking the files and folders of the compressed drive. You should leave this box checked for most work because the host drive may be hidden and because errors on a compressed drive are commonly caused by problems with the host drive. Clearing the box will make the test run faster.

Options for Thorough Disk Tests

If you select a thorough test on the main ScanDisk window, the Options button becomes available. Click on it to display the Surface Scan Options dialog box, shown here:

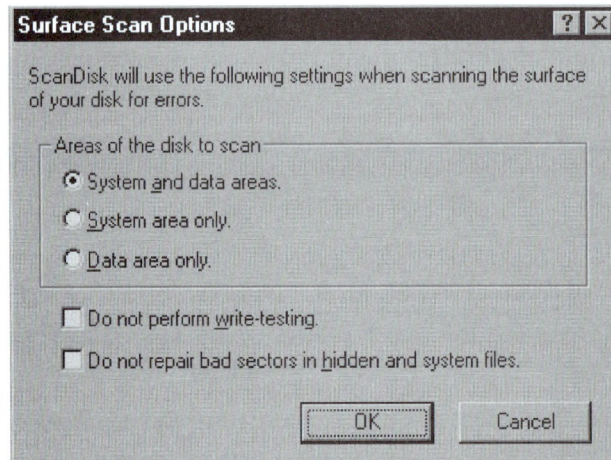

Surface Scan Options   ? X

ScanDisk will use the following settings when scanning the surface of your disk for errors.

Areas of the disk to scan

- System and data areas.
- System area only.
- Data area only.

☐ Do not perform write-testing.

☐ Do not repair bad sectors in hidden and system files.

OK   Cancel

In the bordered area labeled *Areas of the disk to scan*, choose the radio button for the type of test you want to perform:

System and data areas: if you want to scan the entire disk.

System area only: if you want to scan only the sections of the disk that store system information, such as the boot (start-up) programs and the master records of the file and folders. Much of the information stored here cannot be moved, so Scan-Disk will be unable to fix problems here. If errors in the system area are found, the disk probably should be junked.

Data area only: if you want to check the bulk of the disk area, where your files can be stored, but not the system area. This choice scans the entire data area, including areas not currently storing files. When it finds a faulty location, ScanDisk can often preserve the information stored there by moving the data elsewhere. The faulty location is then marked as "bad" so it won't be used in the future. If the problem isn't caught early enough, however, data at the faulty location may be unreadable, in which case it's gone for good (ScanDisk will still mark the bad spot).

Because the system area occupies only a small part of the entire disk, testing the system area only takes much less time than testing the data area or the full disk.

The Surface Scan Options dialog box also has two check boxes:

Do not perform write-testing: when this box is cleared, ScanDisk tests each location on the disk exhaustively. It reads the data stored at that location, writes the data back to the same spot, then rereads the information to check it against the original copy. If you check the box, ScanDisk simply checks to be sure it can read the data. This may not be enough to catch and correct some errors before the information becomes unusable.

Do not repair bad sectors in hidden and system files: when this box is cleared, Scan-Disk attempts to relocate the data stored in all damaged locations on the disk, even if the information belongs to a hidden or system file. The problem is, some programs expect to find certain hidden system files in a specific disk location. If these files (or any part of them) are moved, the program stops working. In the early days of the PC, this was a fairly common *copy-protection scheme,* a technique to keep people from making unauthorized copies of software. If you have such programs, you may wish to check this box. ScanDisk will then leave hidden and system files where they are even when they are found on damaged areas of the disk. The programs will find their special files in their expected locations—but because of the disk problems, they may not work anyway.

Backing Up Your Files with Backup

You're probably sick of people telling you how important it is to back up the work you do with your computer. Well, as far as I'm concerned, whether or not you back up is your business. My job is to tell you how to do it with the Backup program included with Windows 95.

NOTE In case you're new to computers, you should know that backing up is a critical everyday task. Any information you store on a disk is vulnerable to damage or loss from a host of dangers, ranging from theft, fire, and water to magnetic or mechanical failure of the disk itself. The greatest threat to your data is you—choosing the wrong command can wipe out hours of work in an instant. Your most effective weapon in the battle to protect your data is to make backup copies of everything you keep on your disks, especially the documents and other files you create yourself. Should disaster strike and wipe out your frontline data, you can fall back on the backups—but only if you've made them.

Backup simplifies the process of backing up your disks and of *restoring* the backed-up files should the originals ever be lost. With Backup you can:

▶ back up to floppy disk or on tape

▶ specify which files are backed up

▶ create sets of files for repeated backup as groups

▶ compress the backed-up files so fewer floppy disks or tapes are required

▶ restore the backed-up files to their original folders or to new locations

▶ compare the backed-up files with the current versions on disk

One caveat is important to mention here: don't rely on your backups until you've tested the entire process of backing up and restoring data. Back up a set of files including programs and some data. After restoring them, check that the programs still run properly and that the other files will still open and still contain valid information. This is the only way you can be sure that Backup and your backup hardware are working properly.

Also, be aware that backup tapes and floppies can go bad as they age. Although it should be fine if your daily backup sessions only back up files that are new or have changed, I urge you to back up *all* your files at regular intervals.

Running Backup

To run Backup, begin from the Start menu and choose Programs ➤ Accessories ➤ System Tools ➤ Backup. Backup's window appears on your screen as shown in Figure 23.2.

> **TIP** If you install a new tape drive after running Backup for the first time, you must choose Tools ➤ Redetect Tape. Backup will re-initialize itself, repeating the search for a working tape drive.

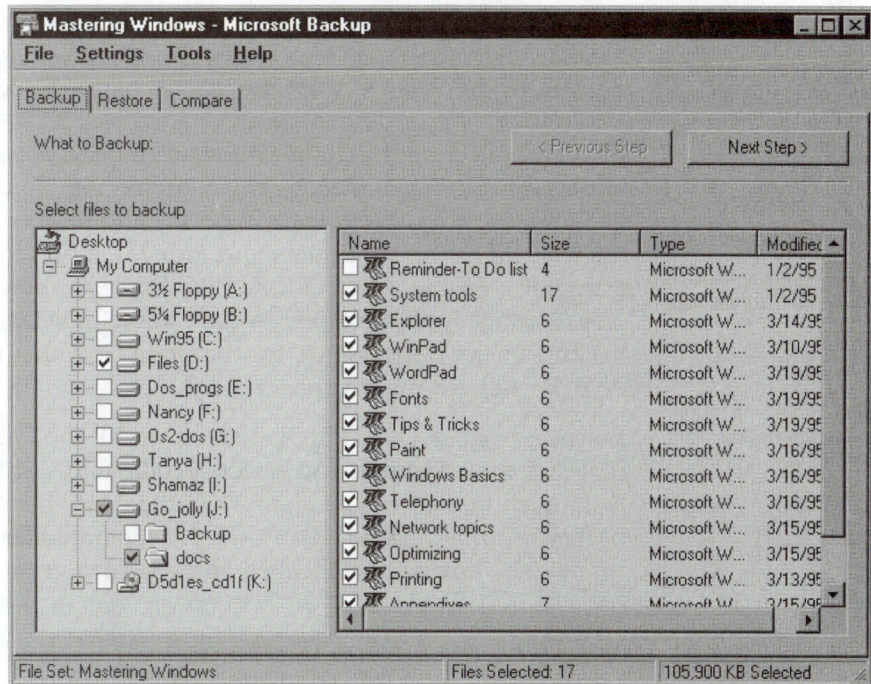

Figure 23.2 *The main Backup window, displaying the first step on the Backup page*

The first time you run Backup it examines your system, looking for a working tape drive. You may hear some gruesome noises from your floppy drives as Backup probes to see just what kind of devices they really are. If Backup can't find a working tape drive, you won't be able to access the tape-related commands.

The main window is tabbed and has three pages: one for backing up files, one for restoring them, and one for comparing the versions on disk with their backed-up counterparts.

Backing Up Your Files

The first page of the Backup window is the Backup page, appropriately enough. You use this page to choose the information you want to back up and where you want to store it as well as to initiate the actual backup process.

> **NOTE**   Backup lets you set a variety of optional settings controlling details of the backup process. See *Setting Backup Options* below.

Begin by selecting the items you want to back up: entire disks, their folders, or individual files, in any combination. The display works just like the one in Explorer, showing disks and folders in a tree view on the left and listing subfolders and individual files in the currently selected disk or folder on right. Unlike Explorer, however, Backup displays a small check box next to each item. To select an item for backup, click on the square for that item (in either side of the window) so a check mark appears there.

As you can guess, checking a disk selects all the folders and files on that disk for backup. If you select specific folders rather than an entire disk, Backup places a check mark in the disk's box, too, but on a gray background. Similarly, if you pick out separate files within a folder, the folder's box will be checked and will turn gray.

Specifying the Backup Destination

When you've chosen all the information you want to back up, click on Next Step to select the destination for the backups. The Backup window changes, as shown in Figure 23.3.

Here, use the tree on the left to locate the disk and directory in which you want to store your backups. When you click on your choice, it will show up in the Selected Device or Location area at the right.

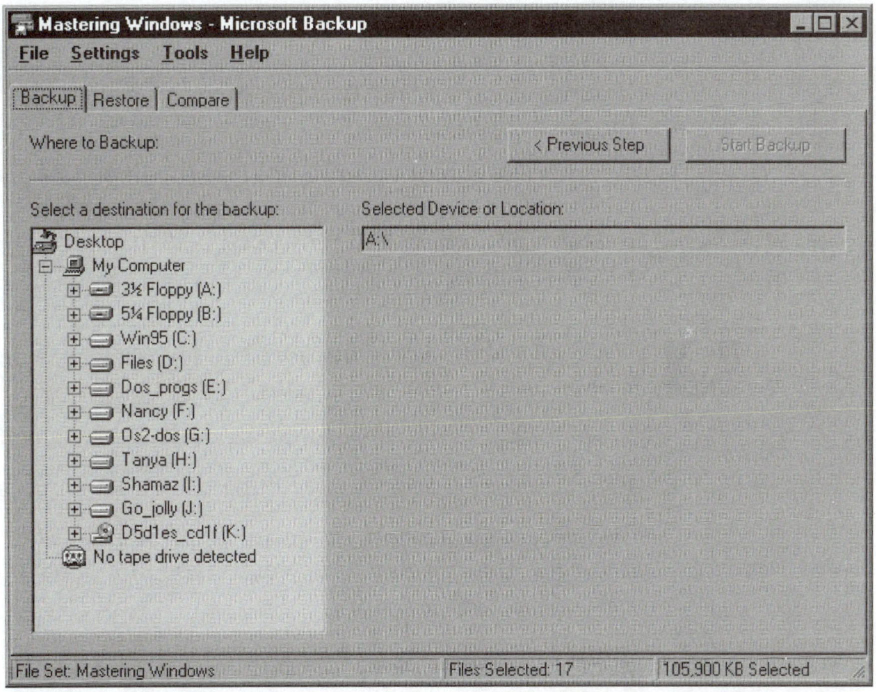

Part
4

Supplied Applications

Figure 23.3   *The Backup page lets you choose a destination for your backups after you click on Next Step.*

> **NOTE**   Although the File menu offers a Save As choice when you're selecting the files to back up, you can't save a file set until you specify a backup destination.

Saving and Using Backup File Sets

Once you've selected the information you want to back up and the backup destination, you have the option of saving these choices in a reusable *file set*. When you want to back up the same files again—a common necessity—just open the file set and proceed with the backup.

To save a file set, choose File ➤ Save As, type in a name, and click on OK. To open a file set you previously saved, choose File ➤ Open File Set.

Finishing the Backup

Before you go any further, prepare the disks or tapes you'll be using for the backup:

1. Get out enough of them to hold all the data. (Backup displays the total size of all the selected files at the bottom right. If you turn the compression option on, you may need half this much capacity or less on your backup tapes and disks.)

TIP If you need to format your tapes or erase existing data from tapes or disks, use the commands on the Tools menu described in *Formatting and Erasing the Backup Media* below.

---

2. Label the first tape or disk with the date, a set name, and the number 1.

To proceed to the actual backup step, click on Start Backup at the upper right. Backup first asks you to type in a descriptive name for the backed-up files as a unit:

Before you go on, you have the option of protecting the whole set of files with a password. If you assign a password, Backup will ask you to enter it again before you can restore files in the set to replace a damaged or missing original.

To set a password, click on Password Protect in the Backup Set Label dialog box. You are required to type in the password twice to ensure that you've entered it correctly.

Back at the Backup Set Label dialog box, click on OK to proceed. Backup creates a new file on the destination device and begins copying the information from your files there. You'll see a series of message windows that keep you posted on how far along the backup has gone from moment to moment.

NOTE If Backup encounters any problems during the backup process, you'll see error messages describing the glitch.

If all the files won't fit on the first floppy disk or tape, Backup notifies you and asks you to insert another disk or tape (before you do, label it with the date and set name and number it in proper sequence). The process continues in this way until all the files in your file set have been backed up.

Formatting and Erasing the Backup Media

Backup can format blank tapes for you. To format a tape, insert it in the drive and choose Tools ➤ Format Tape, following the instructions provided. If you always back up to new, blank tapes, you can set up Backup to format all the tapes automatically. See *Changing Backup Settings* below.

You can also use Backup to erase existing data from the tape currently in the tape drive by choosing Tools ➤ Erase Tape. By the way, you can set up Backup so that it *always* automatically erases existing data from tapes and/or from floppy disks before each new backup operation. See *Changing Backup Settings* below.

Quick Backups from the Desktop

Once you've created a backup file set, you can back up the files in the set directly from the Desktop without starting the Backup application first. You can set up and perform these quick backups in two ways:

▶ You can place a shortcut for the Backup application on the Desktop. Then, whenever you want to back up a given file set, just locate the set in any file display, drag it to the Desktop, and drop it onto the Backup shortcut.

▶ Alternatively, you can place a shortcut for one or more particular file sets on the Desktop. To start the backup, you just double-click on the shortcut.

Use the first approach if you've created a number of Backup file sets and want to keep the Desktop from becoming too crowded. If you use only one or two sets, the second approach is faster. Of course, you can combine the two methods, placing a shortcut for your most commonly used file set on the Desktop and using the drag-and-drop technique for the sets you back up only occasionally.

With default settings, you never see the main Backup window when you start a backup using either quick method. Instead, you're simply informed that the procedure is starting and asked whether you want to continue. As the backup proceeds, other messages let you monitor Backup's progress as it finds and selects the files in the set and then backs them up. Error messages appear if anything goes wrong.

Setting Drag-and-Drop Options

You have three simple choices for controlling the way Backup operates during quick backups from the Desktop. You can:

▶ decide whether or not Backup runs minimized so you never see the main Backup window on your screen during a quick backup

▶ choose whether or not you'll be asked to OK the backup before it begins

▶ decide whether or not Backup closes after carrying out the backup

To change any of these settings, choose Settings ➤ Drag and Drop and, in the resulting dialog box shown below, clear or check the relevant box.

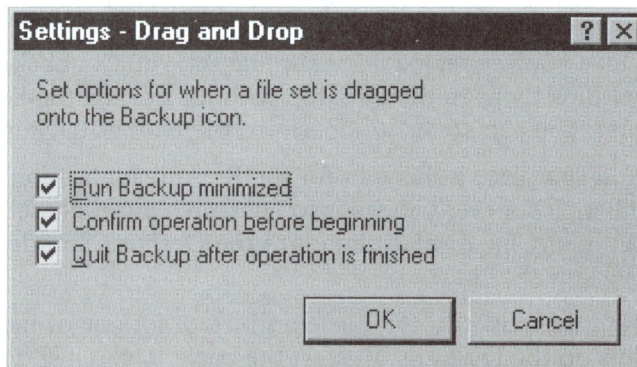

```
┌─────────────────────────────────────────────────┐
│ Settings - Drag and Drop              [?] [X]    │
├─────────────────────────────────────────────────┤
│                                                  │
│   Set options for when a file set is dragged     │
│   onto the Backup icon.                          │
│                                                  │
│   ☑ Run Backup minimized                         │
│   ☑ Confirm operation before beginning           │
│   ☑ Quit Backup after operation is finished      │
│                                                  │
│                    ┌────────┐   ┌────────┐       │
│                    │   OK   │   │ Cancel │       │
│                    └────────┘   └────────┘       │
└─────────────────────────────────────────────────┘
```

Restoring Files from Your Backups

You may never need the backups you've so diligently made, day after day, week after week. If your hard disk never breaks down, if you never delete a file by mistake, if your computer never gets stolen, consider yourself lucky and the time you spent backing up as inexpensive insurance.

But if you ever do lose data, your backups suddenly will seem to you precious jewels of infinite value. After your computer is running again—or you've gone out and bought another—slip the backup disk or tape into the machine, and a few minutes later your vanished files will be miraculously restored.

With Backup, restoring files is a piece of cake. Find the set of tapes or disks containing the lost files and insert disk or tape #1. Then, in Backup:

1. Switch to the Restore page, shown in Figure 23.4.

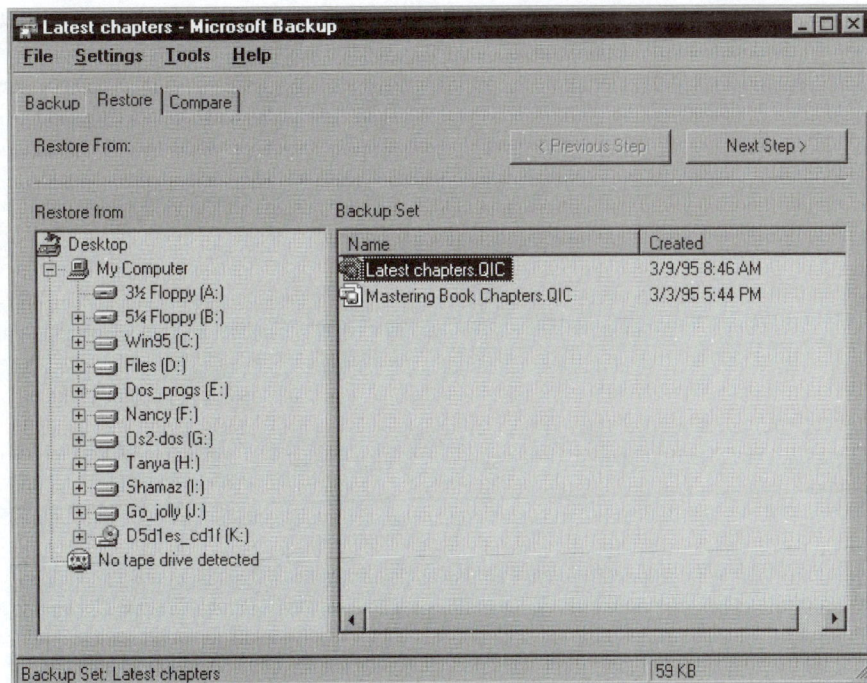

Figure 23.4 *Use this page to restore damaged or lost files.*

2. Navigate in the disk-and-directory tree on the left to the disk or tape drive containing the backups. When you're there, Backup finds and displays on the right the backup file set or sets (there may be more than one if you back up fairly small files in separate sets).

3. Double-click on the set you want to restore from. After Backup checks the set, the window changes to show the set's disks and folders (Figure 23.5). To select the information you want to restore, click in the little boxes next to each displayed item just as you did to select files for backup. If you check the box of the top item in the left-hand list, all the disks, folders, and files contained in the set will be restored. Otherwise, you can check individual disks, folders, and files in any combination. To display an item's contents in the right side of the window, click on the item (not its check box).

4. When you've selected the correct files, click on Start Restore to proceed. If you assigned a password when you created the backup, you'll be asked to type it in now. Depending on the option settings, you may

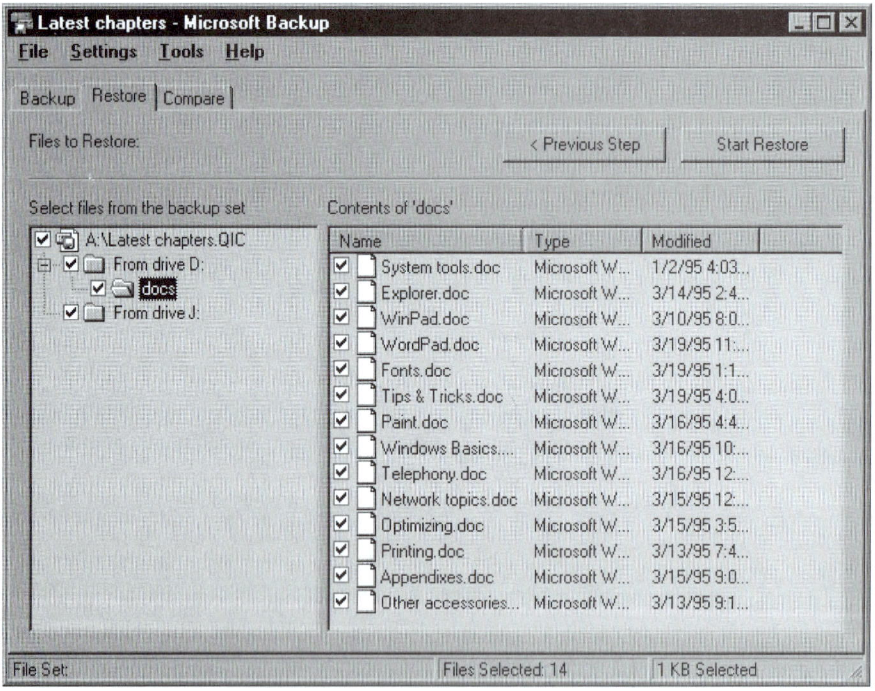

Figure 23.5   *Backup shows you the contents of the selected set in this view.*

also need to specify a destination for the restored files (if the standard settings are active, Backup restores the files to their original disks and directories, if possible).

5. The restoration begins. You'll be informed of its progress and notified when it completes. Depending on how you've set the options, you may be asked for permission to overwrite existing files with the same names as the ones you're restoring.

Comparing Backups against the Originals

Once you've backed up a set of files, use the Compare function to ensure that the backup copies contain exactly the same information as the originals. This step takes a significant amount of time, but without it you can't be sure the backup copies are actually protecting you against data loss.

Here's how to compare backups and their originals:

1. Insert the tape or floppy disk containing the backed-up files you want to compare into the proper drive.

2. On the main Backup window, switch to the Compare page (see Figure 23.6).

3. Use the disk-and-directory tree on the left to locate the backup set containing the files you want to compare and click on it so it is listed on the right.

4. Click on the desired backup set, then click on Next Step at the top right. The Backup window changes to display the set you've chosen on the left.

5. Now select the specific folders or files in the backup set you want to compare:

   ▶ If you want to compare the entire contents of the set, just click in the box to its left.

   ▶ To select individual folders, click on the icon for the set so folder icons appear, then click on the boxes for each folder you want.

   ▶ To pick out individual files, open the folders one at a time to display their contents on the right side of the window, then click on the box for each file.

Figure 23.6 Backup's Compare page

6. Click on Start Compare at the top right. Backup displays its progress in the Compare window, shown below.

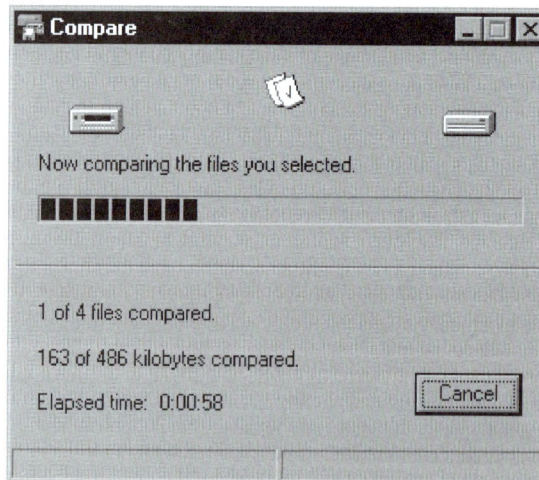

7. When the comparison is complete, you'll see a little message box to that effect. Click on OK to return to the Compare window, where you'll see a summary of the operation.

Using Filters to Select Files and Folders

To speed file selection for a Backup, Restore, or Compare operation, you can use a *filter* to automatically select or reject files that match criteria you specify. You can exclude particular types of files, even if they're in a selected folder, or specify a range of dates for the files to be selected. Choose Settings ➤ File Filtering to display the dialog box shown in Figure 23.7.

The top portion of the dialog box lists many common types of files. To exclude a particular type, select it in the list and click on Exclude.

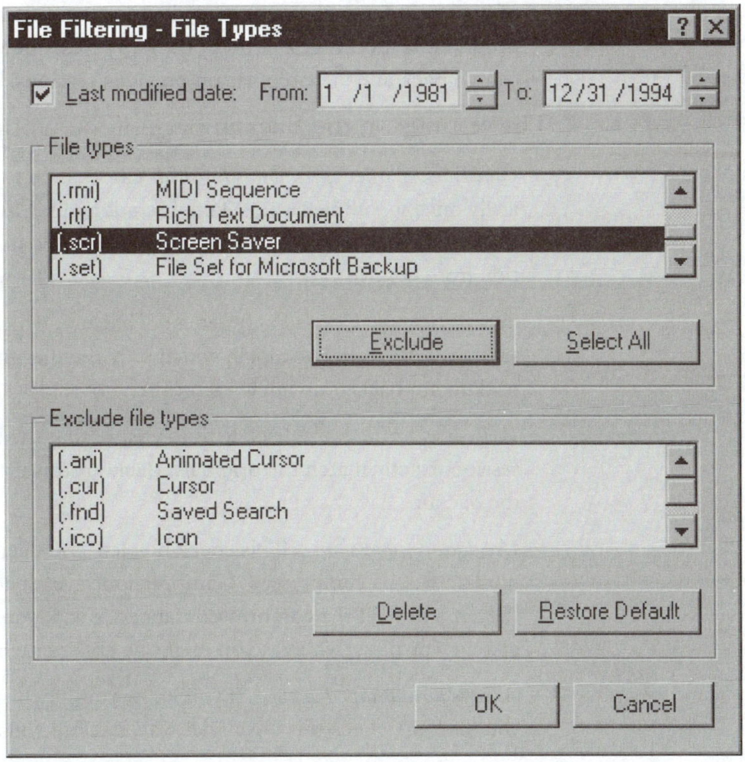

Figure 23.7   *Set filters for various file types and dates here.*

It will appear in the exclude list in the lower part of the dialog box. To specify a date range for selected files, check the Last Modified Date box and then set the From and To dates as desired.

Changing Backup Settings

You can control Backup's operating characteristics by choosing Settings ➤ Options to display the Options dialog box.

The Options dialog box is tabbed and has four pages, one each for General settings and for options pertaining to the Backup, Restore, and Compare functions. Here are the settings on the General page:

Turn on audible prompts: Check this box if you want Backup to sound a tone when your input is required.

Overwrite old status log files: Check here if you want Backup to replace the contents of the status log with a report on the most current session each time you use the program. With this box cleared, Backup saves a new status log each time so you can go back and view reports on previous sessions.

The settings on the Backup page of the Options dialog box include:

Quit Backup after operation is finished: Check here to have Backup close automatically once it completes a backup operation. This frees the memory and resources Backup uses as soon as the program has finished its work without further intervention from you.

Type of Backup: Choose between a *full* backup, which backs up all files in the file set, or a *differential* backup, in which only the files that have changed since the last backup are backed up anew each time.

Verify backup data…: Check here to ensure that the backup copies created during a session exactly match the originals. Backup runs its Compare function as soon as the backups have been made.

Use data compression…: This check box lets you decide whether or not the backed-up data will be compressed. Compression saves space, but it can have drawbacks: If even a little of the compressed data goes bad, your backups may become completely worthless, whereas you might be able to salvage uncompressed files.

Always format tape backups: If you know you'll be using fresh, blank tape every time you back up, check this box. That way, Backup will automatically format the new tape before it starts copying information to it. If you clear this box, you'll need to format new tapes with the Format Tape command on the Tools menu.

Always erase on…: The last two check boxes let you specify whether Backup erases all existing data on your backup tape or floppy disk before proceeding with a new backup.

Options on the Restore page include:

Quit Backup after operation is finished: Check this box to have Backup close automatically after any restore procedure finishes.

Restore backed up files to: The three radio buttons here tell Backup where to put the restored files: in their original disks and folders (directories); in an alternate location (disk and folder) of your choice, preserving the original hierarchy of subdirectories; or in an alternate location, with all the restored files placed in a single directory.

Verify restored data…: Check this box if you want Backup to perform a Compare operation after it completes the restore to ensure that the restored files match the data stored on the backup tapes or disks.

<Overwrite options>: The last three radio buttons on this page let you tell Backup what to do when a file it is restoring is already present on the destination disk. Choose *Never overwrite* to preserve the disk file no matter what; *Overwrite older files only* to replace only those disk files that are older than the ones being restored; or *Overwrite files* if you want Backup to replace the disk files with those from the backup set. If you pick the last choice, you can then check the box beneath it, *Prompt before overwriting files*. When this box is checked, Backup will ask you for permission before replacing an existing disk file.

Here are the options on the Compare page:

Quit Backup after operation is finished: Check this box if you want Backup to close automatically after completing any compare operation.

Location of Compare: These three radio buttons tell Backup where to find the disk files it compares to the files in the backup set. Select the radio button for the desired choice: in the same disks and folders that were used to create the backup set; in another location (disk and folder) that otherwise has the same subfolder hierarchy as the original; or in another location with all the files in a single folder. The two latter options are especially useful for comparing a backup set against copies of the files you've already restored from backup disks.

Increasing Disk Capacity with DriveSpace

The DriveSpace system tool helps you stay ahead of the ever-increasing demand for information storage capacity. DriveSpace *compresses* the files on your disk, storing them in an encoded form so they take only about half as much space as they normally would.

No matter how big a hard disk you buy, it always fills up faster than you expected. It's easy to see why. Windows 95 itself takes up 50 MB of hard disk space or more, depending on which components you install—that's roughly five times as much as Windows 3.1. Programs are constantly growing larger, too. And if your system software and programs haven't eaten up all the available room, wait 'til you save a few of those multimedia files everybody talks about. A high-resolution still image with a color palette of 16-million-plus colors can easily consume many megabytes of disk space. And when you're talking about full-motion video sequences or CD-quality digital sound files, look out (remember, an audio CD that plays only an hour of music holds about 600 megabytes).

With DriveSpace, there *is* a free lunch: It roughly doubles the available space on any disk, leaving you with a compressed disk that operates exactly as normal and *maybe even faster*. Of course, you'll still run out of disk space faster than you planned.

FOR WINDOWS 3.X USERS

Windows 95's version of DriveSpace recognizes and works fine with existing compressed disks created by the non-Windows version of DiskSpace that came with MS-DOS 6.22 or the DoubleSpace utility included with MS-DOS 6.0 or 6.2. You'll no longer need your DOS-based tools to manage these disks because DriveSpace can handle compression-related chores, while ScanDisk (covered earlier in this chapter) can check for and repair errors on the compressed disks.

Windows 95 will recognize disks compressed with other compression software such as Stacker. However, keep two limitations in mind: ScanDisk can't check these "foreign" compressed disks for compression errors, and you can't use DriveSpace and another compression utility at the same time.

> **NOTE** See Chapter 32 for a discussion of DriveSpace 3, the enhanced version of DriveSpace in Microsoft Plus.

Using DriveSpace

To run DriveSpace, begin from the Start menu and choose Programs ➤ Accessories ➤ System Tools ➤ DriveSpace. You'll see the main Drive-Space window, consisting simply of a menu bar and a list of the disk drives on your system:

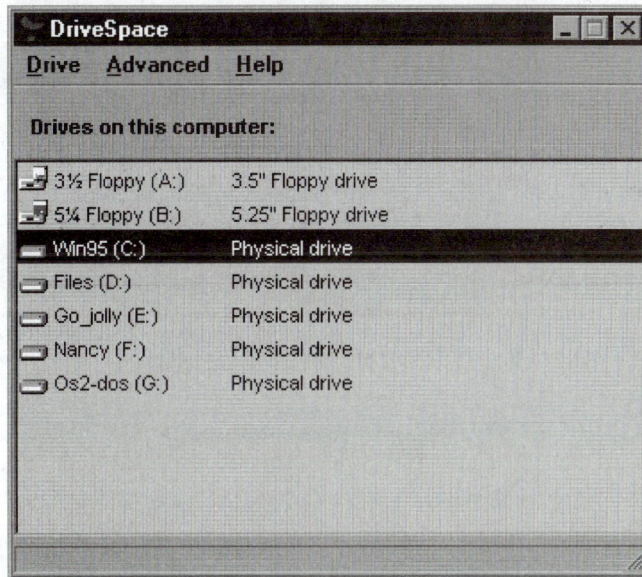

The DriveSpace menu choices let you compress new disks, activate and deactivate them, remove existing compressed disks, and adjust various settings. These options are covered in detail below.

To see information about any disk in the list, double-click on the entry for the disk or choose Drive ➤ Properties. You'll see the window shown in Figure 23.8.

The window tells you whether or not the disk is compressed and displays a pie graph showing how much space is in use and how much is

Compression Information -- Drive I

Compressed drive I is stored on uncompressed drive E in the file E:\DBLSPACE.001.

| | Label: | COMPRESSED |
| | Type: | Compressed drive |

| ■ Free Space: | 31.15 MB | Est. Compression Ratio: 2.0 to 1 |
| ■ Used Space: | 3.87 MB | Compression Ratio: 2.9 to 1 |

Capacity: 35.03 MB

Drive I

OK

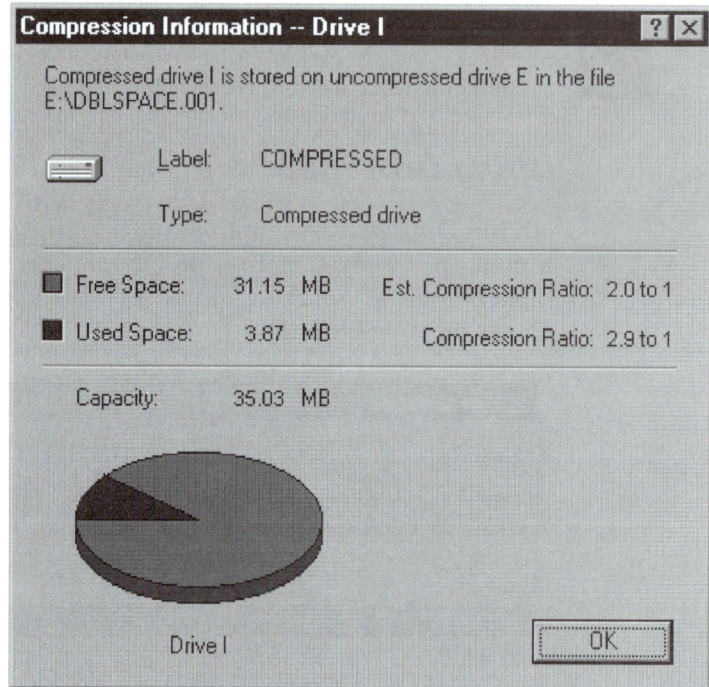

Figure 23.8 *The Compression Information window*

free for new programs and documents. You also get a numeric readout of the used and free space and of the total disk capacity. OK the window to close it.

How DriveSpace Works

Disk compression is essentially a coding system for the information in your files. As it stores a file on disk, DriveSpace examines the data for repeated sequences that it can represent with shorter codes. Files containing long repeating sequences wind up more compressed than files in which the information has no consistent pattern. When it reads a compressed file, DriveSpace translates the codes back into the original sequences. DriveSpace works with all your files, programs and documents alike.

NOTE Compression utilities such as PKZIP and LHA work by encoding and decoding files the way DriveSpace does, but only when you specifically tell them to. Such utilities can create significantly smaller compressed files than DriveSpace does, which is great for storing large files you rarely use. Because you have to operate them manually, though, these utilities are far too time consuming and inconvenient for ordinary use.

DriveSpace works behind the scenes without any intervention on your part. When you run a program, copy a file, or save or open a document, Drive-Space steps in automatically to handle the compression or decompression. In the jargon of the day, DriveSpace provides *on-the-fly* compression.

As the discussion implies, DriveSpace actually compresses files, not disks. When it "compresses" a disk, it creates one large special file on the disk to hold the compressed files it then stores there. This special file is set up to act just like a real disk in Windows. It is assigned a letter, just like any other disk drive. The original disk that contains the special file is called the *host* drive.

The file containing the compressed disk must exist on a single unbroken area of the hard disk (that is, it must not be *fragmented*—see *Disk Defragmenter* later in this chapter for more on fragmentation). For this reason, DriveSpace must defragment the hard disk to consolidate its free space before the actual compression process. It also checks the disk for errors before proceeding.

When to Use DriveSpace

My advice is to go ahead and use DriveSpace on all your hard disks, but to preserve some uncompressed space—say about 10 to 20 megabytes—on the C drive that's used to boot your computer. Disk compression really does work, it's very reliable, it doesn't slow your system down, and it's free—so why not take full advantage of it?

Although DriveSpace can compress floppy disks, keep in mind that you can only use these floppies on computers that also have DriveSpace.

Compressing a Drive

Before you compress a disk for the first time, it makes a lot of sense to back up the entire disk just in case something goes wrong during the compression process. After all, you should be backing up regularly anyway, so just think of this as a good time to do your regular backup. You can use the Backup utility, covered earlier, to do the job.

CAUTION Be prepared to wait a long time—possibly many hours—if you compress a disk that already contains a lot of files. And don't think you can walk away from your computer while it works because you may need to respond to messages from the program many times during the process. Why does it take so long? DriveSpace starts by creating a small, uncompressed disk from the available free space. It then goes through a cycle of copying some uncompressed files to the compressed disk, erasing them from the uncompressed disk, and enlarging the compressed disk, repeating this sequence over and over. The best time to compress a disk drive is *before* you install programs other than Windows.

When you use the standard method for compressing a drive, DriveSpace converts nearly all of the original (host) drive to the new compressed drive. All existing files are copied to the compressed drive, leaving only about 2 megabytes of free space uncompressed on the host. If you like, however, you can control how much free space is left uncompressed. You can also use an alternative method, covered later, to create a compressed drive using only the remaining free space on the host.

To compress a drive using the standard method, select the drive from the list in the DriveSpace window, then choose Drive ➤ Compress. You'll see the window shown in Figure 23.9.

This before-and-after window shows you graphically and in numbers how much more room you'll have on the disk after you compress it.

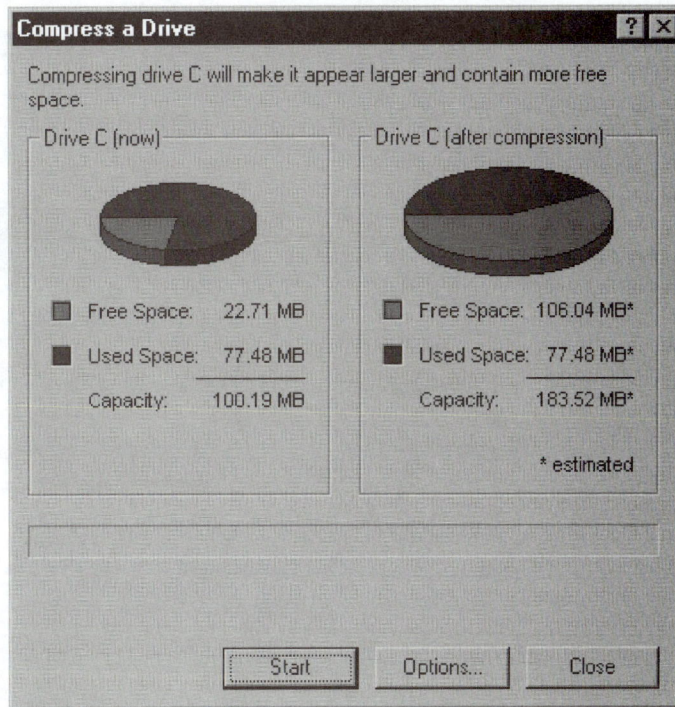

Figure 23.9   *The Compress a Drive window*

To go ahead and compress the drive using the standard settings, click on Start.

When DriveSpace compresses a drive with this standard method, the new compressed drive is assigned the drive letter that had been used by the original uncompressed drive, the host. The host receives a new letter but is then *hidden* so it won't appear in Windows Explorer, My Computer, and File dialog boxes such as Open and Save As (after all, the host hardly has any usable space).

Setting Compression Options

To review the compression settings and change them if you like, click on Options in the Compress a Drive window. You'll see the small dialog box shown here:

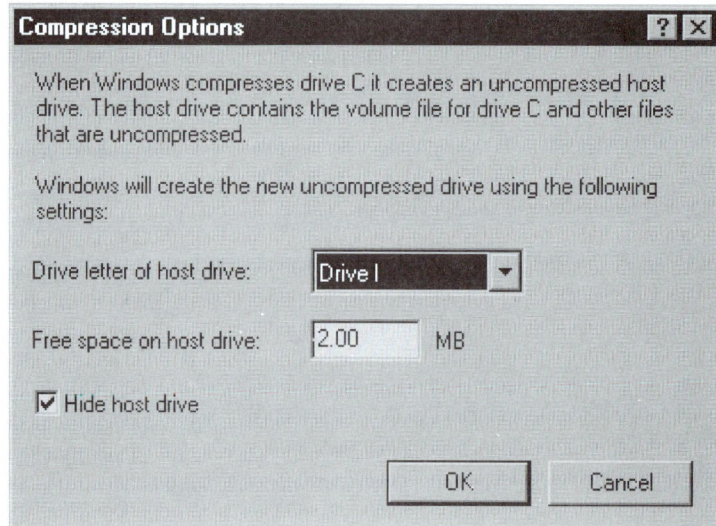

```
┌─────────────────────────────────────────────────────┐
│ Compression Options                          [?][X]  │
├─────────────────────────────────────────────────────┤
│                                                       │
│  When Windows compresses drive C it creates an        │
│  uncompressed host drive. The host drive contains     │
│  the volume file for drive C and other files that     │
│  are uncompressed.                                    │
│                                                       │
│  Windows will create the new uncompressed drive       │
│  using the following settings:                        │
│                                                       │
│  Drive letter of host drive:    [Drive I      ▼]      │
│                                                       │
│  Free space on host drive:      [2.00    ]  MB        │
│                                                       │
│  ☑ Hide host drive                                    │
│                                                       │
│                              [   OK   ] [ Cancel ]    │
└─────────────────────────────────────────────────────┘
```

Your choices include:

Drive letter of host drive: DriveSpace will automatically assign the next available drive letter to the host drive. If you want to assign a different drive letter, select it from this list. For example, if you know the letter DriveSpace has chosen will be used by a network drive or a new, real hard disk you plan to install, you would select another letter.

Free space on host drive: If you want to change the amount of uncompressed free space DriveSpace automatically preserves on the host drive, type in the new amount here.

TIP   I recommend that you keep at least 5 MB uncompressed on the drive used to start your system (originally drive C). After the compression process is complete, you should copy some essential utility programs such as a non-Windows text editor and a disk manager such as Xtree to the noncompressed drive, just in case something ever goes wrong with DriveSpace and you need a way to get at your machine without Windows. (As a safeguard against even more serious problems, make sure you have made two or more start-up diskettes). If you're using a program that requires uncompressed disk space for its work files, as some do, you'll need to increase this amount. The other host drives require little or no free space.

Hide host drive: Check this box to have DriveSpace hide the host (the uncompressed original drive) in Windows. The host won't appear in Explorer, dialog boxes, and other lists of available disk drives. Clear the box if you don't want the host drive hidden.

TIP   To "unhide" all hidden drives, choose Advanced ➤ Options and click on Show all hidden drives.

Click on OK to confirm any new settings you've made and return to the Compress a Drive dialog box, then click on Start to compress the drive.

Adjusting the Amount of Free Space

After you've compressed a drive, it may turn out that you need more uncompressed free space on the host. Or perhaps you realize that you don't need as much uncompressed space as you thought you would and you really should compress the surplus to get more capacity. Fortunately, DriveSpace lets you shift unused capacity back and forth between a compressed drive and its uncompressed host.

To change the distribution of free space, highlight either the compressed drive or its host in the main DriveSpace window. Then choose

Drive ➤ Adjust Free Space. You'll see a window like the one shown in Figure 23.10.

The window shows you graphically and in numbers how much free space is currently available on the two drives. Use the slider control at the bottom of the window to shift free space between them. You can set the slider with the mouse or by pressing the → and ← keys. As you do, the graph changes to show you how free space would be distributed with the new settings.

When you're satisfied, change the setting in the *Hide this host drive* box if you like and then click on OK. DriveSpace makes the necessary adjustments and returns you to its main window.

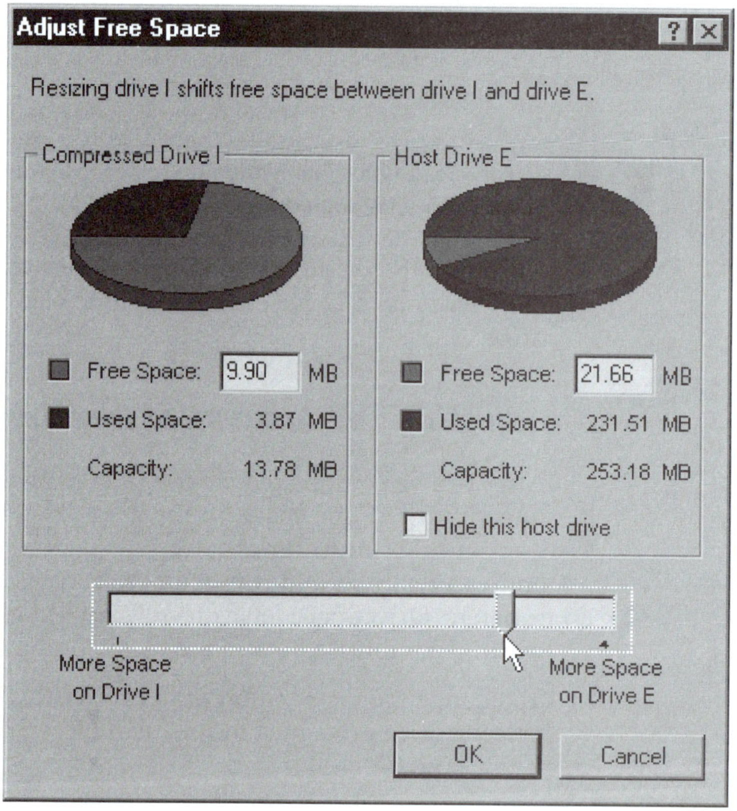

Figure 23.10   The Adjust Free Space window

Uncompressing a Compressed Drive

Just in case you ever need to, you can restore a compressed drive to its original, uncompressed state. (Actually, what you would be doing is removing the compressed drive from its host, but let's not get bogged down in technicalities.) DriveSpace will transfer the files contained on the compressed drive to the host, reset the host to its original drive letter, and show the host if it was hidden.

There's only one potential fly in the ointment, but unfortunately it's rather large: If you've been using the compressed drive for its intended function—storing files—there's a good chance those files won't fit on the uncompressed drive. In this case, if you want to go through with uncompressing the drive, you'll need to move the excess files to another disk somewhere before uncompression can proceed. If your computer is connected to a network, a drive somewhere else on the network may be a good place to try.

To uncompress a compressed drive, highlight it in the main DriveSpace window, then choose Drive ➤ Uncompress. DriveSpace displays a window showing a before-and-after graph of the used and free space on the compressed drive and the host. If the projected results meet your expectations, click on Start to proceed.

Creating an Empty Compressed Drive from Free Space

If you prefer, you can have DriveSpace compress only the free space on an existing drive rather than compressing the entire drive. This is often a *much* quicker way to get more space because DriveSpace doesn't have to copy all the existing files to the new compressed drive. On the other hand, if the existing disk contains a lot of files, you won't have much free space to work with and the compressed drive will be relatively small.

Because it is created from free space, the new compressed drive is empty. The host drive retains its original letter while the compressed drive is assigned a new letter. This is the opposite of the way things work when you compress a drive with the standard method as described above.

To create an empty compressed drive from free space, select the uncompressed drive where the free space is located in the main DriveSpace window. Choose Advanced ➤ Create Empty. You'll see the dialog box shown in Figure 23.11.

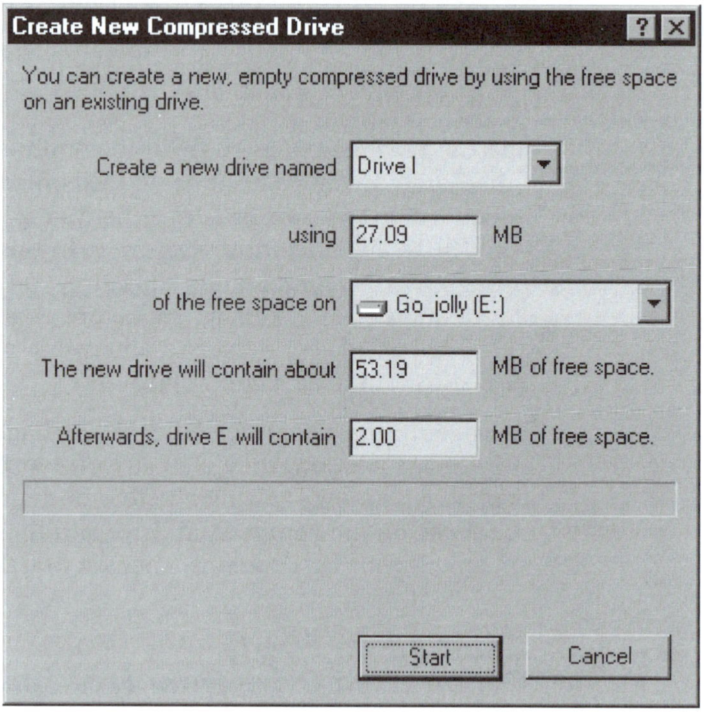

Create New Compressed Drive   ? ✕

You can create a new, empty compressed drive by using the free space on an existing drive.

Create a new drive named   Drive I   ▼

using   27.09   MB

of the free space on   Go_jolly (E:)   ▼

The new drive will contain about   53.19   MB of free space.

Afterwards, drive E will contain   2.00   MB of free space.

Start   Cancel

Figure 23.11   The Create New Compressed Drive dialog box

DriveSpace assumes you want the new drive to occupy all but 2 MB of the free space now available on the uncompressed drive. You can change the new drive's size in any of the three areas listing megabyte amounts. The first of these three areas, labeled *using*, indicates the amount of uncompressed free space to be compressed; the second area, *The new drive will contain about*, gives an estimate of how much space will be available on the compressed drive; while the third area, *Afterwards, drive "X" will contain*, shows you how much free space will be left on the host. Typing a new number into any of these areas changes all three areas. If you enter a value that's too large, DriveSpace adjusts it to the maximum valid value.

You can choose a different drive letter for the new drive if you need to in the first area. When you're through making changes, click on Start to create the new compressed drive.

Deleting a Compressed Drive

If you know you won't ever need the information on a compressed drive, or if you've backed up all the files you want to preserve, you can summarily delete the drive. This is a quicker way of restoring the host drive to its original state than using the Uncompress command because DriveSpace doesn't have to copy all the compressed files back to the host.

To delete a compressed drive, select it in the main DriveSpace window, then choose Advanced ➤ Delete. DriveSpace will warn you that this command will delete all the information on the drive. To proceed, click on Yes.

Mounting and Unmounting Compressed Drives

Mounting a compressed drive means to activate it so that the drive and the files it contains are accessible. Normally, DriveSpace automatically mounts all compressed drives, including those on floppy disks and removable hard-disk cartridges. If you turn off this automatic mounting feature, however, you'll have to mount the drives yourself. This doesn't make much sense for most people.

To mount a compressed drive, select its uncompressed host drive in the list in the main DriveSpace window. Then choose Advanced ➤ Mount. DriveSpace will search the disk for the special files that contain compressed disks. If it finds any unmounted compressed drives, it displays them in a list box (if there are two or more of these files, you can pick the one you want to mount from the list). DriveSpace shows you which drive letter it plans to assign to the selected disk. You can select a different letter by clicking on Options and choosing the desired letter from the list box that appears at the bottom of the same window.

Of course, you can *unmount* any compressed drive any time you like. Each mounted compressed drive uses a small amount of system memory, so if you're not using the drive, you may want to unmount it. You might also unmount a drive to keep other people who use the computer from accessing it, though anyone familiar with DriveSpace could find and mount the drive. The best reason to unmount a drive is when you need to change its letter designation, because you can't select a new letter for a drive that is currently mounted.

Changing the Estimated Compression Ratio

Because the amount of compression varies from file to file, Drive-Space can only estimate how much free space is available on a compressed drive. When you store an average mix of files, DriveSpace's standard estimate is about as good as you can expect. If you store many files of a particular type, however, you can improve on the estimate's accuracy. This will help you figure out how much more information the compressed drive will hold.

Select the compressed drive and choose Advanced ➤ Change Ratio. DriveSpace displays this window:

Here you can see the actual compression ratio for the files currently stored on the drive, along with DriveSpace's current setting for the estimated ratio it uses to calculate the remaining free space. If the actual ratio varies from the estimate and you're pretty sure you'll be using the disk in about the same way, you should change the estimated ratio. Use the slider control, dragging it to the new value with the mouse or pressing the ← and → keys.

Automatic v. Manual Activation

Choose the Advanced ➤ Options command to display the following dialog box:

Normally, DriveSpace automatically activates, or mounts, new compressed drives immediately after you create them. If you want to mount new compressed drives manually, clear the *Automatically mount new compressed drives* box.

The *Driver currently in use* box simply lists the version number of the DriveSpace software installed on your system. Before installing a new version, check to make sure it has a later version number—if not, leave the existing driver in place.

Disk Defragmenter

Disk Defragmenter keeps your system performing at its best by detecting and correcting *fragmentation* on the hard disks. The term "fragmentation" sounds a little scary—after all, who wants their hard disk to break into little pieces? Actually, though, it refers to the files stored on the disk, not the disk itself.

When Windows stores information on your disk in a file, it begins *writing* the information onto the first place it can find that isn't already occupied by another file. If the disk already contains a lot of other files, however, that location may not be large enough for the whole file Windows now wants to store. If this is the case, Windows must search for another open spot on the disk for the next section of the file. The process goes on in this way until the entire file has been written to the disk into as many pieces, or fragments, as necessary. Of course, Windows keeps track of the location of all the fragments, and when you need the file again, it can find all the pieces for you without your ever knowing where they are stored.

Actually, this system for breaking files up into fragments when necessary has important performance benefits. If Windows had to stop and find a single section of the disk big enough for each entire file, your system would steadily slow down as the hard disk filled up. Also, you would wind up with less usable disk space. Eventually there would come a time when the disk still had many free areas, but none of them big enough to fit a reasonably sized file.

So what's the problem? Well, fragmentation also slows your hard disk down. To access information stored on a disk, the disk drive must move mechanical parts over the location where the information is stored. It takes only a fraction of second to move these parts, but those fractions add up when a file is broken into many fragments. As more and more files become fragmented, you may begin to notice the slowdown, especially when Windows opens and saves files.

Disk Defragmenter remedies the problem by reorganizing the disk so that each and every file is stored as a complete unit on a single area of the disk. To do this, it identifies any remaining free areas, moves small files there to open up more space, and uses this newly opened space to consolidate larger files. It continues to shuffle files around in this manner until the entire disk is defragmented. All of this takes place behind the scenes. Though the files have been moved physically on the disk, they remain in exactly the same place "logically"—you'll find all your files in the same folders they were in before running Defragmenter.

When Should You Use Disk Defragmenter?

After wading through this long technical explanation, you may feel let down when I tell you that you may not ever really need to defragment your hard disk. Yes, it's true that fragmentation puts a measurable drag on file access if you time the system electronically. But in real life, you'll probably detect a slowdown only if you have very large, very fragmented data files. The reason is simply that today's hard disks are so fast.

Keep in mind also that the defragmenting process itself can take quite a bit of time (on the other hand, you can run Disk Defragmenter overnight or while you're out to lunch). Anyway, the point is simply that you shouldn't worry about a drastic performance loss if you don't defragment your disk regularly.

All that said, here are some tips for deciding when to use Disk Defragmenter:

▶ Disk Defragmenter itself can help you decide when to defragment. When you run the program, it analyzes the disk to detect fragmentation and offers a recommendation about whether or not to proceed (more on that in a moment).

▶ The slower your hard disk, the more you'll notice the performance hit caused by fragmentation and the more often you should defragment it. If you're still using a disk with an access time of 25 milliseconds or greater, you'll probably detect an improvement after defragmenting a heavily fragmented disk.

▶ The greater the percentage of data files (documents, pictures, database files, and so on) on your hard disk—as compared to program files—the more likely you'll need to defragment. After you install them, your program files stay put. Data files, on the other hand, are constantly being revised and saved anew, and are much more vulnerable to increasing fragmentation. (If you frequently install and then remove programs, the risk for significant fragmentation also rises.)

Running Disk Defragmenter

To run Disk Defragmenter, begin from the Start menu and choose Programs ➤ Accessories ➤ System Tools ➤ Disk Defragmenter. A small Window appears:

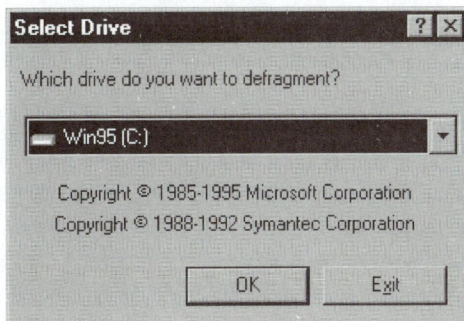

Choose the hard disk you want to defragment from the drop-down list and click on OK. You can switch to another disk later as necessary.

Disk Defragmenter analyzes the chosen disk for fragmentation, then displays another small window informing you of its findings:

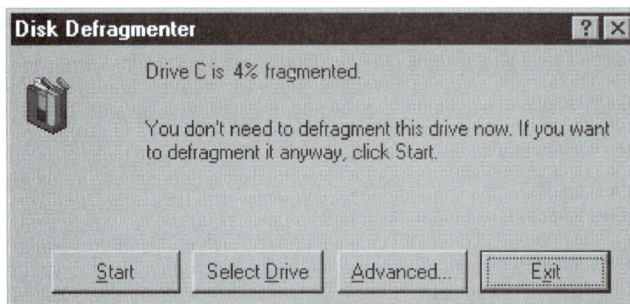

This dialog box has four buttons:

Start: begins the defragmentation process. If Disk Defragmenter recommends against defragmenting the disk at this time, the button will be labeled *Defragment Anyway,* but it does the same thing.

Select Drive: returns you to the Select Drive dialog box shown above so you can choose another drive to defragment.

Advanced: lets you set defragmentation options.

Exit: closes Disk Defragmenter.

The Defragmentation Process

Click on Defragment (or Defragment Anyway) in the Defragmentation dialog box to begin the process. You'll see yet another little dialog box informing you of the program's progress:

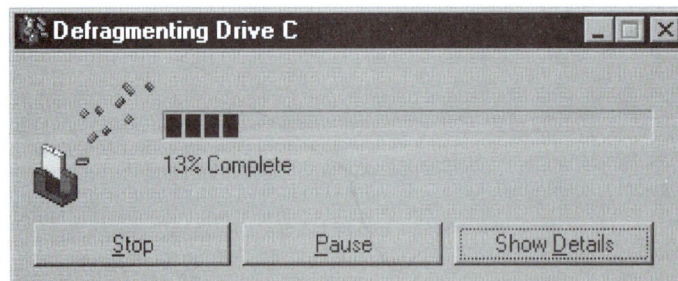

As Disk Defragmenter does its work, the indicator at the right shows you graphically how far along you are in the process, and the percentage complete is displayed as well. Three buttons are available:

Stop: stops the defragmenting process and returns you to a dialog box titled Are You Sure. The choices are similar to those of the Defragmentation dialog box: You can click on Resume to return to defragmenting, Select Drive to pick another drive to defragment, Advanced to set defragmentation options, or Exit to close Disk Defragmenter.

Pause: temporarily stops the defragmenting process. The Pause button appears pushed in while Disk Defragmenter remains paused. To continue where you left off, click on it again.

Show Details: displays a large window showing you exactly what's going on during the defragmentation process (Figure 23.12). This window represents the disk contents as a grid of little colored boxes, each of which stands for a single *cluster* (usually 2,048 bytes). The various colors signify the status of each cluster: those containing information that needs to be moved, those that are already defragmented, those that are free (containing no file information), and so on. To see a legend showing the meanings of the block colors, click on the Legend button:

Defrag Legend

▦ Optimized (defragmented) data
Unoptimized data that:
  ☐ Belongs at beginning of drive
  ▦ Belongs in middle of drive
  ▦ Belongs at end of drive

☐ Free space
◰ Data that will not be moved
◩ Bad (damaged) area of the disk
☐ Data that's currently being read
■ Data that's currently being written

Each box represents one disk cluster.

[Close]

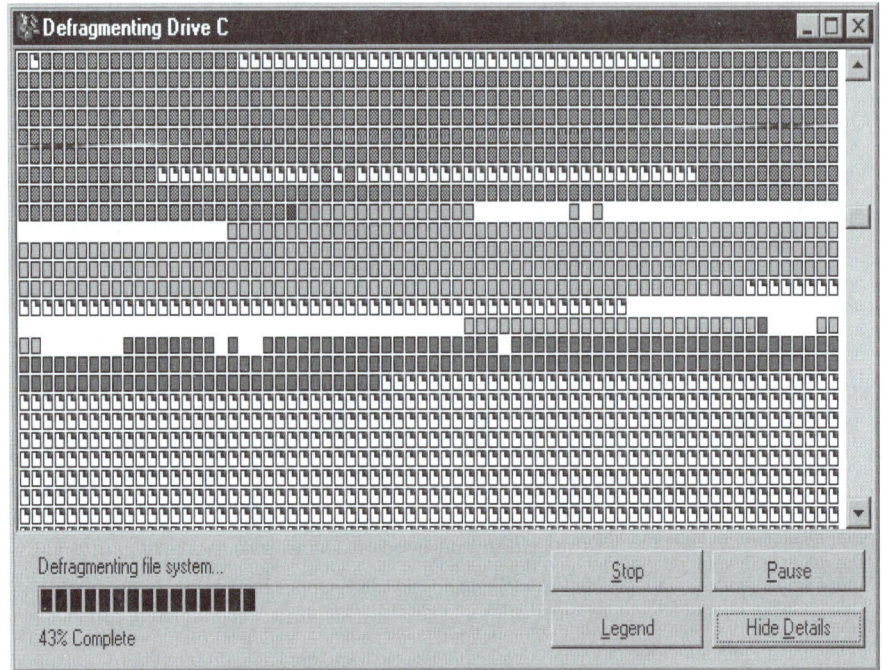

Figure 23.12   This is the window you'll see if you choose Display Details during defragmentation.

As Disk Defragmenter moves information around, the map gives you a moment-by-moment readout of which clusters are being read and written to, and the resulting disk organization. The bottom of the window displays a progress indicator and readout and includes Stop and Pause buttons. You can close the large map window at any time by clicking on Hide Details.

Because Disk Defragmenter continues its work whether or not the program window is visible, you can switch to another program to continue your work. You'll hear the hard disk chattering more or less continuously during the defragmentation process, and your system will probably seem a little sluggish at times when it waits for Disk Defragmenter to give it access to the disk. Otherwise, however, you can use Windows just as you normally would.

Setting Disk Defragmenter Options

Disk Defragmenter's standard settings ensure that your disk is fully defragmented, which can take quite a while. You can often speed things up considerably with a partial defragmentation targeted for the characteristics of your disk. You should get most of the performance benefits of a full defragmentation.

To change the defragmentation settings, click on the Advanced button in the Defragmentation dialog box (or in the dialog box you see when you stop an earlier defragmentation). You'll see the Advanced Options dialog box, shown in Figure 23.13.

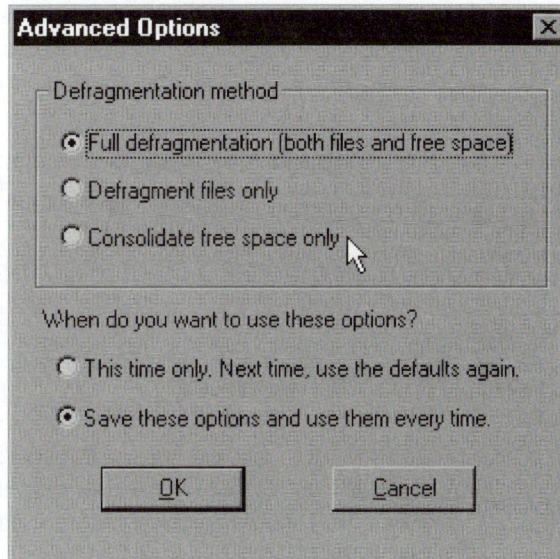

Figure 23.13   *Use this dialog box to set Disk Defragmenter options.*

In the top part of the dialog box, choose the radio button for the type of defragmentation you want:

Full defragmentation (both files and free space): This is the standard setting. All the files are defragmented, and, in addition, they are placed one after another on the disk so all the remaining free space is available on a continuous section of the disk.

Defragment files only: When this choice is selected, Disk Defragmenter moves information on the disk only enough so every file is stored in its entirety on a continuous area of the disk. Free space between these continuos files is left where it is. This setting is faster than a full defragmentation because the files don't have to be rearranged as much. But depending on how much free space there is between the files, files you save in the future will be vulnerable to fragmentation.

Consolidate free space only: Use this option to move existing files around just enough so all the available free space on the disk is placed in one continuous area. Files you save from now on will be less likely to become fragmented. Again, this is quicker than a full defragmentation. The downside is that fragmented files remain fragmented and the existing files may be more vulnerable to fragmentation when they are changed and saved again. This can be a good choice if you know you're about to save some large files that would otherwise be broken up into fragments. It can also be useful if you have just copied many files to a new disk (or installed a number of programs); the files are unlikely to be fragmented, but there may be gaps of free space between them.

The two radio buttons in the lower portion of the Advanced Options dialog box let you specify whether the defragmentation method you select is stored for future use or is used only for the current session. Choose the appropriate button before you OK the dialog box.

Tracking Your System Resources with System Monitor

System Monitor is a *real-time* analysis tool that lets you monitor Windows' activities from one moment to the next. If you are trying to track down a performance problem, say with unexpected memory shortages, or if you just want to keep tabs on what Windows is up to, try System Monitor. You can use it on your own system or across a network to monitor other computers.

There's a good chance System Monitor is not yet installed on your hard disk. If you need to install it, begin by placing the install disk in your floppy or CD-ROM drive, choosing Add/Remove Programs in the Control Panel, and switching to the Windows Setup page. Highlight Accessories, then click on Details. In the list that appears, check the box for System Monitor. When you click on OK, the program will be installed.

Once System Monitor has been installed, run it by choosing Programs ➤
Accessories ➤ System Tools ➤ System Monitor from the Start menu.
You'll see the System Monitor window, as shown in Figure 23.14.

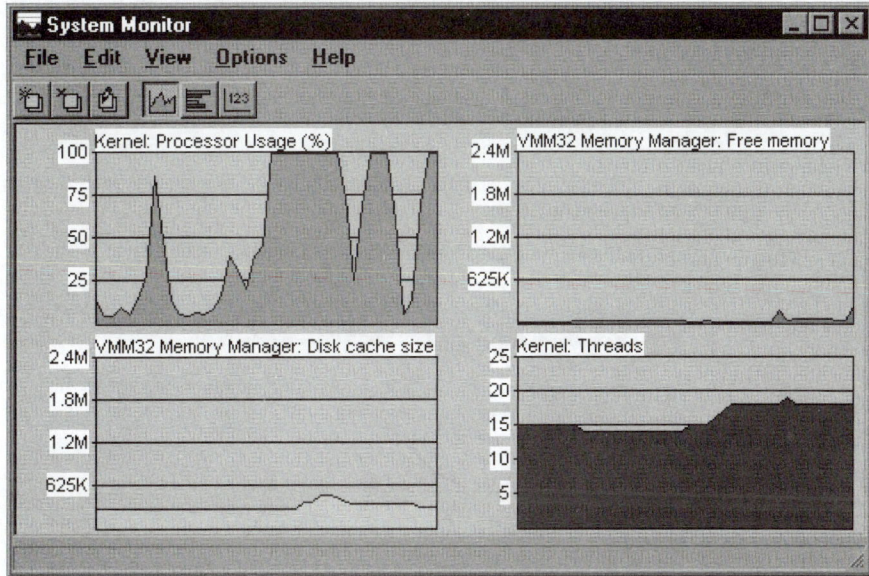

Figure 23.14   *The System Monitor window. The specific items displayed when you first start*
the program will be different from those shown here.

The main part of the window is divided into areas for each type of information you choose to monitor. When you first run the program, it
displays its reports as shaded line graphs, but you can select bar
graphs or numeric displays instead. You can click on any displayed
item to get a report of its last and peak values in the Status Bar at the
bottom of the window.

Note that System Monitor has its own little button bar for quick access to commonly used commands. The buttons are displayed in two
groups of three buttons each. The first group (on the left) includes
buttons for adding, removing, and editing individual items on the

display; the second group lets you pick between the two graph types and a numeric readout.

System Monitor continuously updates the information it displays at a rate you can control. To change the frequency of updates, choose Options ➤ Chart and use the slider to set the Update Interval.

Choosing Items to Display

You have your choice of twenty-odd types of system information you can track with System Monitor. To add a new item, click on the Add button or choose Edit ➤ Add Item. You'll see the dialog box shown here:

Select a category of system information from the list on the left. When you do, a list of the individual items available for display appear on the right. Be forewarned: Unless you're technically oriented, the terms you see here may look completely foreign to you. You can learn something about what an item means by selecting the item and clicking on Explain. System Monitor will then display a slightly longer—but also highly technical—description of the term.

When you're ready to choose one or more items, select them in the list. You can select more than one item at a time by dragging across consecutive items with the mouse or by holding down the Ctrl key while you click on individual items anywhere on the list. However, you can only select items from one category at a time.

Click on OK to return to System Monitor. The items you chose will now appear, each in its own area on the screen. As you add more items, System Monitor reduces the size of each item's graph.

Editing an Item's Display Properties

System Monitor lets you control some aspects of the graphical display of each item. To see or change the current settings:

1. Click on the Edit button or choose Edit ➤ Edit Item. You'll see a list of all the items currently displayed.

> **TIP** You can double-click on the item you want to edit to move directly to the Chart Options dialog box for that item.

2. Select the item you want to work with and click on OK. A Chart Options dialog box appears:

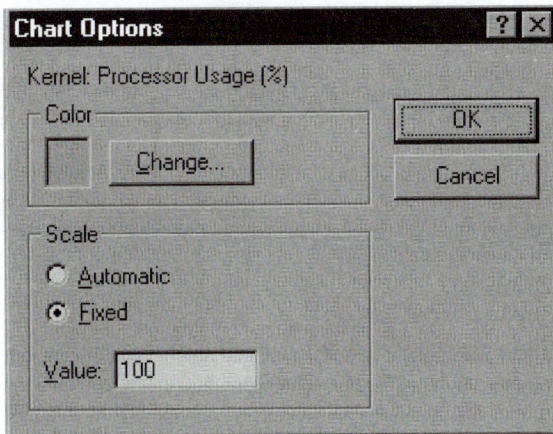

```
┌─ Chart Options ──────────────────── ? ✕ ─┐
│  Kernel: Processor Usage [%]              │
│  ┌─ Color ──────────────┐  ┌──────────┐   │
│  │                      │  │    OK    │   │
│  │  ┌──┐  ┌─────────┐   │  └──────────┘   │
│  │  │  │  │ Change… │   │  ┌──────────┐   │
│  │  └──┘  └─────────┘   │  │  Cancel  │   │
│  └──────────────────────┘  └──────────┘   │
│  ┌─ Scale ──────────────┐                 │
│  │  ○ Automatic         │                 │
│  │  ◉ Fixed             │                 │
│  │                      │                 │
│  │  Value: ┌────────┐   │                 │
│  │         │ 100    │   │                 │
│  │         └────────┘   │                 │
│  └──────────────────────┘                 │
└───────────────────────────────────────────┘
```

3. Here you can choose the graph color and control its scale. The pair of radio buttons on the left let you switch between letting System Monitor adjust the scale automatically based on the current values for the item and fixing the scale to cover a range you specify by typing in the

scale maximum at Value. The right pair of radio buttons switches between linear and logarithmic display.

4. Click on OK to confirm your choices. System Monitor adjusts the item's graph to match.

Choosing the Display Type

To select a different type of display for all the items in the window, click on the button for the type of display you want (line graph, bar graph, or numeric). Alternatively, you can choose the desired type from the View menu.

Removing Items from the Window

To remove an item from the System Monitor display, click on the Remove button or choose Edit ➤ Remove Item. You'll be presented with a list of all the items currently displayed. Choose the item or items you want to remove and click on OK.

Other Display Options

To reset all items to zero, removing all the current graphs and starting the analysis again from scratch, choose Edit ➤ Clear.

You can control whether the Toolbar and Status Bar are visible. Choose the corresponding command on the View menu to turn either item off or on.

To remove System Monitor's title bar, menu bar, Toolbar, and Status Bar so only the graphs remain visible, press Esc or choose View ➤ Hide Title Bar. To restore the window to its normal state, double-click anywhere in the window or press Esc again.

To keep the System Monitor visible no matter what other programs you use, choose View ➤ Always on Top. If you choose this option, you may wish to resize the window so it won't block your view of your other programs.

Networking
with Windows 95

5

Server Administrator

Chapter 24

An Overview of Windows 95 Networking

FEATURING

The OSI reference model

The Windows 95 networking model

Windows 95 has been endowed with all the features necessary to make it the perfect network citizen. Right out of the box—with no additional software required—your PC with Windows 95 installed is capable of connecting to and interoperating with all major network operating systems (NOSs) and can function either as a client, a server, or as both simultaneously. Because of its modular approach to networking software and its true multitasking ability, it is capable of simultaneously speaking multiple network languages (called *protocols*) and even using multiple network interface cards. You could, for example, simultaneously access a database on your company's mainframe, print a report on your office's Novell print server, and cruise the Web on the Internet, all while one or more other users are accessing files located on your PC's hard drive. Moreover, these various network connections can be made via any combination of the following: standard network adapters and cable, high-speed digital phone lines, "normal" phone lines and modem, or even directly attached to your PC via either a serial or a parallel port. And because the networking features are truly integrated parts of Windows 95, you can access drives and printers located on a variety of different networks from any Windows application—always in the same way, regardless of the type of computer or network you are connected to. Being able to network—or rather, *internetwork*—with other computer systems in exactly the same manner, whether you're at the office, at home, or even on the road using your laptop, opens almost endless possibilities for extending the usefulness of your computers.

These networking possibilities supplied by Windows 95 truly are exciting—never before have so many ways to so easily network with other computers been brought together like this in one product—let alone within a popular, graphical, operating system. In this and following chapters, we will look closely at the networking capabilities of Windows 95 and discuss step by step how to install, configure, and use them. If you are interested less in the details and more in how to quickly set up your networking components, just skip ahead to the "how-to" sections in the following chapters.

Windows 95, as I have said, can share your local hard drive(s) and printer with other users, acting as a server on a peer-to-peer network. In this role, a Windows 95 workstation allows other computers to use its resources such as files, printers, and (in certain respects) modems. Additionally, Windows 95 can act as either a Dial-Up Networking client or as a host so you can use regular phone lines to extend the reach of your network. This allows you to be on the road (or at home—or anywhere) and dial into your office network and have the same resources available as if you were sitting right at your desk.

If your computer supports Plug and Play, when you install a Plug-and-Play–compatible network adapter card, Windows 95 will automatically load and configure all the necessary software to place your computer on a network—all with no user intervention apart from selecting the desired protocols.

Roughly, protocols can be thought of as the various languages that different networks use to communicate. The protocol implementation manages such tasks as requesting data from file and application servers, providing resources to other workstations, and placing data onto the network. Each of these tasks uses a specific protocol or layer of a protocol, and Windows 95's networking software ensures that it uses the correct protocol at the correct time. While this may sound complex (and behind the scenes, it is), Windows 95 makes it very easy to choose, install, and make use of the protocol(s) you will need. In the next section, we will discuss protocols in more detail. You *can* configure and use Windows 95 without a thorough knowledge of networking protocols, but having at least a passing familiarity with networking protocols and related concepts will be helpful in getting the best performance out of your network.

A protocol, in general, is really nothing more than a set of rules and conventions for accomplishing a specific task. In the case of computer networking, a protocol defines the manner in which two computers will communicate with each other. As an analogy, consider the protocol you use to place a phone call. Before you dial, you first make sure no one else is using the phone line. Next you pick up the phone and listen for a dial tone. If you are at your office, you might have to dial 9 and again wait for a dial tone. Then you can dial either a 7-digit number for a local call or a 1 followed by a 10-digit number for a long-distance call. You then wait for the other person to answer. But if you do not follow this protocol correctly—for example, you do not dial a 9 for an outside line when at the office—you will be unable to place your phone call.

In the world of computers, a protocol works exactly the same way. If a client does not structure and send a request in the exact manner in which the server expects it—and we all know how particular computers can be—it will never establish the connection.

When you first activate the networking component on your computer, Windows 95 installs the NetBEUI and IPX/SPX protocols by default. Besides these two, Windows 95 allows you to install several other protocols that—depending on the design of your network and type of applications you run—might provide better performance or have other advantages. To help you make the best choices possible for your Windows 95 network, I will next present an overview of how LANs work—both in theoretical and practical terms. I will do this by first talking about networking models and then looking at how Windows 95 implements these concepts. Finally, I will delve into the most common protocols themselves and help you choose which is or are the best for your particular environment.

The OSI Reference Model

In the early years of networking, each vendor defined its own standard for communication between its computers. The primary goal was to maximize the performance on a particular vendor's hardware (and lock you into their products) rather than to provide compatibility with other vendors' products. This caused problems as these systems did not share a common protocol and so could not interact with each other. In the late 1970s, the networking community came together in an effort to replace these closed systems with open systems. This would allow IS (Information Systems) shops to mix and match their hardware so end users could access the desired resources on other vendors' products. The end result was the Open System Interconnect (OSI) model developed by the International Standards Organization (ISO). While no network fully implements this model in the exact manner described by the ISO committee, it is a very common framework for discussing networking in theoretical terms. Its strongest asset is that it provides an excellent way of comparing two different networking technologies because it provides a common measuring stick.

The OSI reference model (often referred to simply as the OSI model) takes a modular approach to networking by identifying and defining seven separate processes that any network—whether local- or wide-area—must accomplish. In OSI lingo, each process is a layer. Figure 24.1 shows the seven layers of the OSI model.

Each of these seven layers is responsible for a specific and discrete aspect of networking. The OSI model describes the flow of network data from the top layer—the user's application—to the bottom layer—physical connections of the network. Because no network follows the OSI model exactly, some networks may use only four separate pieces to cover the same functionality as the seven layers of the OSI model. Others may segment it into nine parts.

As data flow across a network, the OSI model stipulates that each layer only communicate with the layers immediately above and below it. This serves two purposes. First and foremost, it creates modularized layers. Each layer needs to know none of the details of how the other layers work; it only needs to know what its input will look like and how it must format its output so the next layer can understand it. Second, modularizing prevents *feature creep*—layers growing excessively complex and taking on the functions that other layers should accomplish.

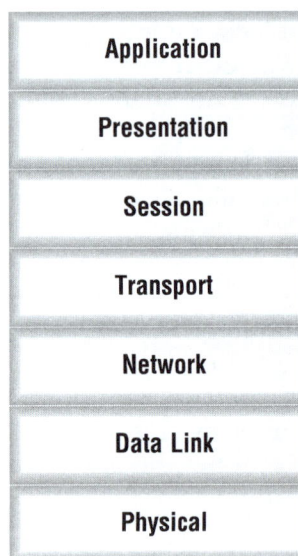

Figure 24.1   *The seven layers of the OSI reference model*

When creating a message, each layer assumes that it is in direct communication with its peer layer on the other side. For example, when the transport layer needs to send an error across the network, it sends the message directly to the transport layer on the other side. This virtual communication further streamlines the process.

Before we delve into the individual layers of the OSI model, let's look at the process of network communication in everyday terms. A good way to look at network communication is simply as a message: requesting a database row, opening a file for access, or sending someone an e-mail note. Now imagine that this message is nothing more than a letter to Gramma Gertrude that needs to pass through several layers to get from you to her.

After deciding to write the letter, you need to get out some paper and a pen and write the message: "Thanks for the lovely dress, I wear it to church every Sunday." Now you must place it in a container—an envelope. Next you place a stamp on the envelope. After that, you address it so it can get to the correct place. Finally you drop it into the mailbox and from there the post office bundles it with all the other messages and delivers it. If you want to ensure that the letter was delivered, you might send it via certified or registered mail with a return receipt; otherwise, you have no guarantee that the letter will be delivered.

The Application Layer

The application layer is at the top—closest to the end user—of the OSI model. This layer directly supports any application that wants to access a network resource for any reason—be it a file, a printer, or another application. In other words, anytime any user's application—regardless of type—needs to communicate with any resource across the network, it must begin here.

In the example of the letter to Gramma Gertrude, this layer systematically encompasses your decision to write the letter thanking her for the dress. Explorer, Exchange, and Dial-up Networking provide application-layer services in Windows 95.

The Presentation Layer

The presentation layer acts primarily as a translation agent. In doing so, it determines the best way for two computers to communicate with one another. When data are going down to the physical layer, the application layer relies on the presentation layer to translate the data sent from the application layer into an intermediary format. Here the presentation layer resolves character set (ASCII, EBCDIC, Unicode) differences, adds any security, and compresses the data. Conversely, when data come up from the physical layer, the presentation layer reverses the process and removes the encryption, re-expands the data, and gives it to the application layer using a data set that the application layer can directly use.

Back in the Gramma Gertrude example, translating the message content from your mind to written words represents the activities of the presentation layer. When you first start up your computer and log into an NT network, Windows 95 encrypts your password so no one can steal it as it goes across the network wire—this is the presentation layer at work.

The Session Layer

The session layer manages the dialogue between two logical addresses. It allows applications on a network to initiate, use, and terminate a connection—called a session—with another computer or another process. The layer also is responsible for name recognition between computers.

Once two computers have established a session, the session layer synchronizes the communication between them. Essentially, it sets the ground rules defining whose turn it is to send data and sets a limit on how long one side may monopolize the communication before it must yield to the other computer.

When you place the letter to Gramma Gertrude in the envelope, you are, in OSI terminology, *initiating a session*—passing control over to the session layer.

The Transport Layer

The transport layer ensures end point–to–end point data integrity by managing error recognition and, if necessary, correction and recovery throughout the data transfer. This layer ensures accuracy by adding Error Correcting Code (ECC), typically a Cyclic Redundancy Checksum (CRC). This CRC is a calculated value based on an accumulation on a byte-per-byte basis of the data being sent.

Once the transport layer receives a packet, it first calculates the Cyclic Redundancy Checksum (CRC). If the CRC calculated in real time does not match the CRC the other side originally placed in the data packet, it knows there has been an error in the transmission. If an error occurred, the data will be sent again until an acknowledgment is received. If several attempts to transmit the data fail, an error message will be displayed.

In our letter example, placing a stamp on the envelope and requesting the return receipt is the proxy for the transport layer. Here you are providing a means of ensuring the message gets through snow, sleet, and rain. If it encounters an error along the way, you will get the message back; otherwise, you will get a signed receipt indicating that your grandmother received (and hopefully read) your letter.

The Network Layer

The network layer manages addressing the message. Once it has resolved the address, it routes the message using a cost-based algorithm. On the addressing side, the network layer translates the logical address it originally received from the session layer into a physical address the data layer can understand. When data come back up the chain, the network layer reverses the process, replacing the physical address with a logical one. By doing so, it provides connections between two open systems regardless of the type of physical link between the two. Packages coming from the upper layers need only contain the logical address, thus freeing these layers from concerning themselves with the peculiar addressing schema of various network technologies.

In your letter to Gramma, you performed the task of the network layer when you put the address on the letter. If you wanted to send it via the U.S. Postal Service, you would include a zip code and possibly the carrier route.

The Data Link Layer

The data link layer is responsible for providing error-free transmission of this frame between any two destinations over the physical layer. (This differs from the data integrity provided by transport layer. The transport layer, remember, is concerned with the data throughout the transmission.) As a data frame flows down to the physical layer, the data link layer takes the frames sent to it from the network layer and places them bit by bit onto the physical layer.

The address in the data link layer differs from that in the network layer in that it is a simpler address, one that the data link layer on the other side will recognize. To understand the difference between the addresses, you can think of the network layer address as the street name and the data layer address as the street number.

The Physical Layer

The physical layer's job is to send individual bits—usually impulses of light or electricity—from one end of the physical medium (the wire) to the other. The physical layer defines the data-flow rate, the type of cable over which the data flow, the topology, the number of pins, and the voltage flowing through those pins. Common specifications for the physical layer include 10Base-T Ethernet, Token Ring, and FDDI (optical fiber). In the letter example, the mail carrier would be considered our network physical layer as he or she drives down to your grandmother's house to deliver your letter.

The Windows 95 Networking Model

Now that I have covered networking on the theoretical level, I can discuss the networking architecture built into Windows 95 and the protocols it supports. Just like the OSI model, Windows 95 takes a layered approach to networking as shown in Figure 24.2.

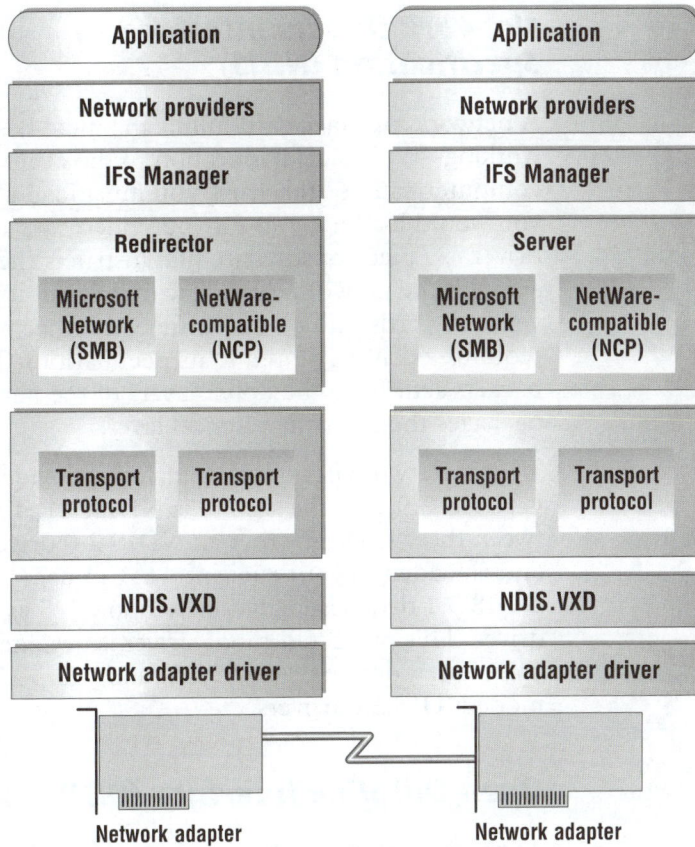

Figure 24.2   *Layers of the Windows 95 Networking model*

The Network Drivers Interface Specification (NDIS) is key to Microsoft's layered network. It provides the vital link between the protocol and the network interface card driver. While the protocol and the network interface card drivers provide separate functions, they remain fundamentally linked. The protocol (discussed in more detail in a later section) determines how your computer structures data sent across the network. The network adapter card drivers define how your computer interacts with the card, which, in turn, actually places the data on the network.

Network Drivers Interface Specification (NDIS)

A network interface card fulfills the most basic requirement of networking—a physical connection to the other computers. Before your computer can use this card, you must load a device driver for it just as you would load a driver for your video card or CD-ROM drive. The driver is a piece of software that instructs the computer how to interact with the network card; how to drive it, if you will. Because each vendor's cards differ from those of another vendor, each type of card requires a driver tailored to its peculiarities. This driver takes the data packets sent from the upper layers of the network architecture and packages them for the physical layer.

There are two types of NDIS drivers provided by Microsoft. The first is NDIS 2.0, and the second is NDIS 3.1. The primary difference between these drivers is that an NDIS 2.0 driver is a real-mode driver and is loaded in your `autoexec.bat` or `config.sys` files, while an NDIS 3.1 driver is loaded in Windows 95 as a 32-bit protected-mode driver. This protected-mode driver is designed as a dynamically loadable virtual device driver (VxD) and will perform better than the real-mode NDIS 2.0 drivers.

Open Datalink Interface (ODI)

As a universal client, Windows 95 also supports the Open Datalink Interface (ODI) standard put forth by Novell and Apple in addition to NDIS. Essentially, ODI and NDIS provide the same functionality in different ways. The only practical difference from an end-user perspective is that Windows 95 implements ODI as a real-mode device driver where NDIS is a 32-bit protected-mode driver. If you plan to connect to a NetWare server, you might need to stick with the ODI drivers for compatibility reasons as some network applications are very particular about the network drivers. I would recommend trying NDIS drivers first, though, keeping in mind you may need to change to ODI if any of your networking applications begin misbehaving. The performance gain of using the 32-bit protected-mode NDIS drivers makes having to use ODI (which executes in real-mode) rather undesirable, but if you absolutely need the most compatibility, the ODI drivers are there and can be installed just as easily as the NDIS drivers can.

With an understanding of Windows 95's networking model, we can now go on to look at the various transport protocols available to you as you set up your Windows 95 network.

Which Protocol to Use?

Right out of the box, Windows 95 gives you a choice of twelve transport protocols. These protocols fall into two broad groups. First, there are the open-systems protocols such as NetBEUI and IPX/SPX that you can use to connect to several vendors' networks. With them you can communicate over a Windows 95 peer-to-peer network or over another vendor's network. The second type are the proprietary protocols used to support specific vendors' networks such as Banyan Vines and DEC Pathworks. Because the choice of protocols only becomes important in open systems (if you have DEC Pathworks for example, you already know what protocol you are going to use), I will discuss the open protocols in this chapter. In Chapter 28 I will cover these other (proprietary) protocols.

> **NOTE**   Although it is somewhat confusing, when a network manager refers to a *transport protocol,* he or she usually means the functions provided by both the transport and network layers. The reason these two layers are combined into one term (besides sloppiness) is that they are interrelated; between the two of them they are responsible for transporting your data through the network. The upper layers are more closely tied to the application requesting the network services. The lower physical layer, because it is the only layer with a tangible presence (unless you are using a wireless net where there is no tangible presence except for the network interface card), is not lumped into *transport protocol.*

Whenever you are installing Windows 95 Networking support (either initially or at any later point), Windows 95 allows you to select protocols as shown in Figure 24.3. Here Windows 95 gives you the choice of five built-in, open protocols: IPX/SPX, DLC, NetBEUI, TCP/IP, and IPX/SPX with NetBIOS.

Before I go into more detail on the particulars of each protocol, I'll quickly look at the typical uses of each protocol.

▶ IPX/SPX is the protocol used by Novell to connect to their NetWare file servers.

Part 5

Networking with Windows 95

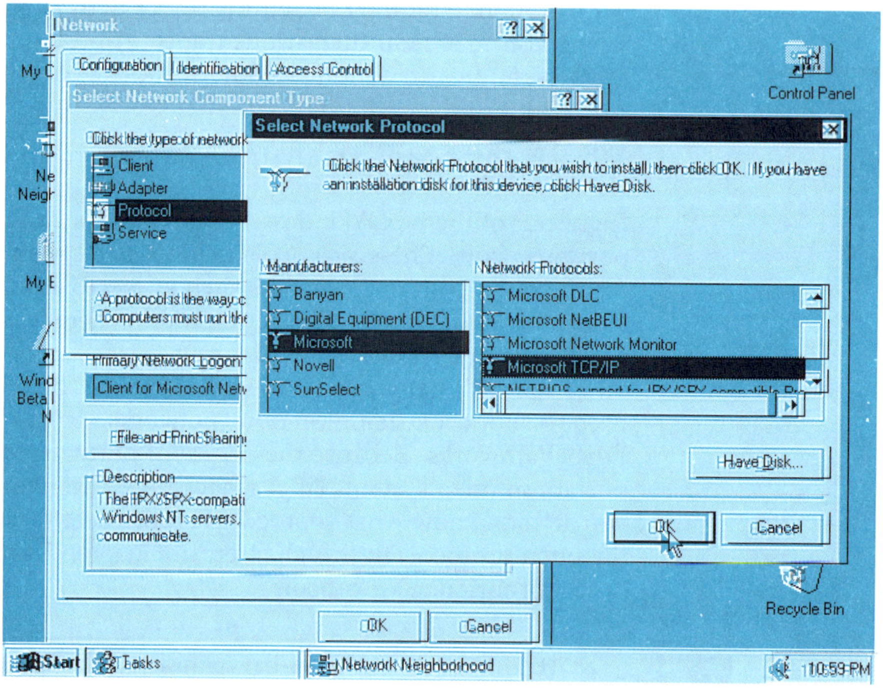

Figure 24.3   *List of Microsoft-supplied protocols when installing a network*

▶ IPX/SPX with NetBIOS adds support for the NetBIOS application programming interface (API) to the standard IPX/SPX protocol stack.

▶ DLC (data link control) provides an interface between Windows 95 machines and mainframes as well as network printers.

▶ NetBEUI is a protocol originally developed by IBM and used by Windows for Workgroups and LAN Manager.

▶ TCP/IP is a protocol often used over wide-area networks and for communicating with computers running some flavor of the Unix operating system.

IPX/SPX and IPX/SPX with NetBIOS Protocols

Xerox originally developed the Internetwork Packet Exchange/Sequenced Packet Exchange (IPX/SPX or just IPX) protocol as part of its XNS protocol suite. Novell decided to use it as the base protocol for connecting to its NetWare file servers and currently maintains the specifications and ongoing enhancements to the protocol. In Windows 95 you can use the IPX protocol to connect to NetWare 2.x, 3.x, and 4.x (with bindery emulation) servers. You can also use it to connect to Windows for Workgroups 3.x, Windows NT 3.x, and of course Windows 95 computers running the IPX protocol.

> **NOTE**   Windows 95 allows you to install either Microsoft's own version of IPX/SPX or one supplied by Novell. I will discuss the ins and outs of these two flavors in Chapter 28; for the time being, however, we will treat them both as simply IPX/SPX.

Where NetBEUI used to be the default protocol in Windows 3.x, Windows 95 now uses IPX as the default. IPX works for small to medium-size networks because it is small and fast, besides being *routable*. A routable protocol is one that you can use to send data to computers on different LAN segments. (I will discuss what constitutes a LAN segment in the following chapter.)

The IPX protocol can support larger networks than can other non-routable protocols because it allows network managers to break down larger networks into smaller segments to achieve significant performance gain, with packets being automatically forwarded (routed) to the correct segment. However, IPX is not suitable for networks consisting of more than 500 workstations or networks connected over a WAN, because IPX workstations regularly send out "hey, I'm still here" messages, called broadcasts, which tell other servers and stations on the network that their connection is still active. On large networks, these broadcasts alone generate quite a bit of network traffic and thus reduce the performance of the network as a whole.

Network Basic Input/Output System (NetBIOS) is a programming interface that implements many of the functions provided by the session layer. Sytek originally developed it for IBM's broadband computer networks and included it in the ROM of its network adapter cards. Since then, many other companies have developed their own version of NetBIOS, making it a de facto standard.

NetBIOS allows applications to communicate over any protocol that is compliant with NetBIOS. Many server-based applications, such as Lotus Notes, use NetBIOS to communicate with clients over a network. Because IPX does not directly support NetBIOS, you must load it separately. Previously, to use NetBIOS over the IPX protocol, you had to use a Novell-provided terminate-and-stay-resident (TSR) driver called netbios.exe. Like all other TSRs, you had to load it before starting Windows if you wanted any of your Windows applications to take advantage of it. As such, it not only took up valuable conventional memory (below the 640K limit), but it also forced Windows to switch into real mode to communicate with NetBIOS applications.

Fortunately, Windows 95 provides a full 32-bit protected-mode implementation of NetBIOS for use with the IPX protocol called NWNBLink (NetWare NetBIOS Link). It is fully compatible with the Novell version and provides significantly improved performance simply because it is 32-bit and executes in protected mode. In addition, Windows 95 can support Windows *Sockets* over IPX. (Like NetBIOS, Windows Sockets is another network programming interface—in this case, based on the sockets standard used on several other operating systems, Unix in particular.) When communicating with other computers using NWNBLink, Windows 95 can support sliding windows and PiggyBackAck (acknowledging previous frames in later response frames).

In Windows NT 3.5 (both flavors), the service that allows it to act as a peer-to-peer server (not to be confused with the product NT Server) supports IPX without NetBIOS. The service that provides peer-to-peer *workstation* support (not to be confused with the product NT Workstation), however, does *not* support IPX without NetBIOS. Therefore, a Windows 95 client running IPX without NetBIOS can connect to a Windows NT *server*; however, a Windows NT *workstation* will not be able to connect to a Windows 95 machine running IPX without NetBIOS. If you install IPX with NetBIOS support on both sides, you will always be able to communicate over the IPX/SPX protocol.

Advantages of IPX/SPX	Disadvantages of IPX/SPX
Compatible with Novell products	Not as fast as NetBEUI
Routable	Not as routable as TCP/IP
Single protocol support for mixed NetWare and Microsoft networks	More overhead than NetBEUI
	Regular broadcasts take up limited bandwidth

DLC (Data Link Control)

Networks based on IBM Token Ring claim most of the users of the Data Link Control protocol. Actually, DLC really is not properly a transport protocol; rather it is a data link layer protocol that behaves much like a transport protocol. You cannot, for example, use DLC to share files and printers on Windows 95 networks; however, Windows 95 machines can use DLC to send print jobs to printers located directly on the network (rather than attached to a printer server), such as HP LaserJet IVs with a JetDirect card installed. And Microsoft has also included DLC to enable your Windows 95 machines to connect directly to IBM mainframe computers.

Advantages of DLC	**Disadvantages of DLC**
Compatible with IBM mainframes	Not compatible with standard Microsoft file and print services

NetBEUI

The NetBIOS *Extended User Interface* (or NetBEUI), first introduced by IBM in 1985, is a protocol written to the NetBIOS interface. Microsoft first supported NetBEUI in MS-Net, its first networking product, when it introduced the product in the mid-1980s. It used to be the default protocol for all Microsoft networks from Windows for Workgroups to LAN Manager up through Windows NT 3.1. NetBEUI is a small and very fast protocol—in fact, the fastest protocol shipped with Windows 95—because it requires very little overhead. Overhead in this context refers to the additional network-control information such as routing and error checking that the protocol adds to the data that the application layer wishes to send across the network.

NOTE   NetBEUI is not NetBIOS. It is easy to confuse NetBIOS and NetBEUI (NetBIOS Extended User Interface). The confusion stems not only from the similar naming but from the fact that earlier implementations of NetBEUI provided NetBIOS as an integral part of the protocol driver. When I refer to NetBEUI here, I am referring to the transport-layer protocol, not the NetBIOS programming interface. NetBEUI is a sufficient but not a necessary requirement for using NetBIOS because other protocols also support NetBIOS. In other words, if you use NetBEUI, you can run NetBIOS applications. On the other hand if you have another protocol such as IPX *with* NetBIOS (which obviously includes support for NetBIOS), you can completely remove the NetBEUI protocol and still run your NetBIOS applications.

One reason for NetBEUI's lower overhead is that NetBEUI only provides what is called *unreliable communication*. Don't worry, unreliable is something of a misnomer; the connection is still reliable. Unreliable communication means that the protocol does not require an explicit acknowledgment (ACK) of each frame before it sends the next. Rather, the receiving computer bundles up several acknowledgments and sends them all at once. In our example of the letter to Gramma Gertrude, you would have had unreliable communication had you decided not to send the letter registered but waited to hear that she had received your card as part of some future message like a holiday card.

Were a protocol to require an ACK for each packet, it would waste the majority of the networks' resources because an ACK is so small it would use very little of the network's bandwidth. Rather than require an acknowledgment for each frame, NetBEUI dynamically determines (through a process called Sliding Windows) the number of frames the sender can transmit before receiving an ACK, based on the current network conditions.

> **NOTE**   Actually, the NetBEUI shipped with Windows 95 and Windows NT is not really NetBEUI. Rather, it is a NetBIOS Frame protocol (NBF), sometimes referred to as NetBEUI 3.0. NBF is completely compatible with the "real" NetBEUI used in Windows for Workgroups and LAN Manager. In addition to supporting the NetBEUI specification, NBF is completely self-tuning, provides better performance across slow links such as telephone lines, and eliminates the 254-session limit of the original NetBEUI. Because the Windows 95 documentation refers to NBF as NetBEUI, we will too; for all practical purposes, they are identical.

Because of its speed and ability to self-tune through Sliding Windows, NetBEUI provides an excellent protocol for small networks such as regional sales offices. While NetBEUI is fast on small networks, you cannot use it effectively on large networks. The main reason for the poor performance over large networks is its addressing scheme. For NetBEUI, your computer's address is the very name you entered as your computer's name in the Network Identification dialog. Obviously, this prevents a network from having two computers with the same name—something quite difficult to achieve on a large network while still giving computers meaningful names. Another, not quite as obvious, implication is that you cannot route it although you can bridge it. A bridge provides the same basic functionality as a router by providing the ability to combine multiple network segments into one logical segment.

Advantages of NetBEUI	Disadvantages of NetBEUI
Compatible with Windows for Workgroups and LAN Manager	Not routable
Small memory footprint	Poor performance on large networks
Good error checking	Difficult to give meaningful names to computers on large networks
Fastest protocol in Windows 95	Tuned for small networks

TCP/IP

Quite simply, Transmission Control Protocol/Internet Protocol (TCP/IP) is the most complete, most widely accepted protocol in the world. And strictly speaking, TCP/IP is not a single protocol but a suite of protocols, usually referred to singularly as TCP/IP, that defines various interactions between computers sharing the protocol. TCP/IP originated as the protocol the U.S. Department of Defense developed in the late 1970s to connect computers to the Advanced Research Projects Agency Network (ARPANet), the precursor to the Internet. In 1983, in an effort to ensure that all its computers could talk to one another, the Department of Defense mandated that all its new networking products support TCP/IP. Overnight, it created an instant market for TCP/IP. Soon after, one of the three major Unix vendors, Berkeley Software Distribution (BSD), released Unix version 4.2BSD, which incorporated TCP/IP into its core operating system, thus making it the lingua franca of midrange computers.

Until recently, that's where TCP/IP stayed—on midrange computers. In the last few years, however, the PC began to replace the dumb terminal as the standard in desktop computing. This forced network managers to find ways of integrating PCs into the rest of their corporate network, which included TCP/IP-based midrange computers.

Because PCs use an open architecture rather than the proprietary ones in legacy systems, the obvious choice was to bring the PCs to the legacy systems via TCP/IP. Thus, just like the Department of Defense, many network administrators began demanding TCP/IP support for all their new PCs.

Windows 95 includes an easy-to-configure version of all the standard TCP/IP connectivity applications (FTP, telnet, etc.) as well as the diagnostic tools (arp, ipconfig, ping, route, etc.).

> **NOTE**   For an in-depth discussion of TCP/IP, see Chapter 18.

While TCP/IP has a reputation as a difficult protocol to configure and manage, new implementations are making it easier. In the TCP/IP arena, support for servers running Dynamic Host Configuration Protocol (DHCP) represents probably the most important advance in Windows 95 over Windows 3.x. Without DHCP, network managers have to manually assign the four-byte IP addresses to each machine. With DHCP enabled, a DHCP server manages a range of IP addresses and assigns one to each workstation as it logs onto the network.

> **NOTE**   Currently only Windows NT Server 3.5 provides the Dynamic Host Configuration Protocol server required by the DHCP client in Windows 95. Windows NT Server 3.5 also provides the Windows Internet Name Service (WINS) server to resolve NetBIOS computer names to IP addresses. WINS provides the same functionality as the Unix Domain Name System (DNS) service.

The TCP/IP protocol included with Windows 95 supports Windows Sockets 1.1. Windows Sockets is a programming interface similar to NetBIOS but specifically designed for client/server applications because of its scalability. Microsoft TCP/IP supports NetBIOS by encapsulating—providing a wrapper—around the NetBIOS request within the TCP/IP protocol.

Advantages to TCP/IP	Disadvantages to TCP/IP
Most widely used	More overhead than NetBEUI
Routable	Can be difficult to administer
Interoperates across hardware and software platforms	Not as fast as NetBEUI on small networks
Provides Internet connectivity	
Supports Windows Sockets 1.1	

Subsequent chapters examine many of the networking features in much more detail to help you either to design a new network around Windows 95 workstations or to integrate Windows 95 clients into your existing network.

Chapter 25

Planning Your Windows 95 Network

FEATURING

Ethernet networks and cabling technologies

Which LAN topology to implement

Choosing your cards

This chapter is a fast track to designing your Windows 95 network. While there are several network-technology choices you can make, I am only going to look at Ethernet networks. This is because Ethernet networks are less expensive to implement than token ring and easier to manage. Token-ring networks require more hardware than Ethernet, are more expensive to implement, and are only advantageous if you have to interface your network clients with IBM mainframes.

I will first take a look at the two most likely network-cable topologies that will be used by home consumers and small-business owners, and then I will help you pick the best network interface card (NIC) for your computer.

If you are setting up a brand new Windows 95-based network, one of the first things you will have to decide on is the technology you will use to physically connect your computers. If you are integrating Windows 95 computers into an existing network (or if someone else has specified the network technology), you can skip ahead to the section on selecting your network adapter card.

If your network will have more than 30 or 40 workstations, you will probably need to split it into multiple sections, called *segments*. You then connect each segment to the other segments of the network through a series of routers or bridges. While I will mention the implications your decisions will have on both segmented and nonsegmented networks, segmented networks are outside the scope of this book. While there are indeed several excellent books on the subject, I have found that enterprise-wide network specialists design more successful networks than network managers who try to do everything themselves. Because these sorts of networks are exceedingly complex and there are no clear guidelines, many consultants resort to trial and error as a design methodology. When looking for a network consultant, try to find one who has done a trial-and-error period with a previous client.

Ethernet Networks and Cabling Technologies

Ethernet is what network professionals call a Carrier-Sense Multiple Access with Collision Detection (CSMA/CD) network. The University of

Hawaii developed this model in the late 1960s when it was trying to place multiple computers on a campus-wide wide-area network (hence *Multiple Access*). Their network controlled access by requiring each computer to listen to the wire and wait until no one else was transmitting (the *Carrier Sensing* part). Once the network was free, a station could go ahead and send its data. If another station tried to send at the same time and the transmissions collided, the computers realized this (*Collision Detection*), and each waited a random period of milliseconds before trying to resend. Whichever computer had the shorter random period of time got to transmit first.

When designing the physical side of your local-area network (LAN), you have two main decisions to make. You need to select which type of cable you will use to connect your computers together, and you need to choose which LAN technology you will employ to send data over this cable. In the next section I will deal with the first question— the wiring. After that I will discuss in more detail each of the technologies I highlighted above.

Which Type of Cable to Use?

In the past decade or so, network managers have installed LANs that run on every type of wiring imaginable. We will limit our discussion to looking at coaxial cable, often referred to as Thin Ethernet, and unshielded twisted-pair cable. These two cabling mediums are most widely used today and each offers unique strengths and weaknesses.

Coaxial Cable

Up through the late 1980s, almost every LAN (at least every one that I saw) used coaxial cable, usually referred to as coax. Coax has only a single center conductor—usually solid copper wire—with a thick insulation surrounding the center and a layer of wire-mesh braid over this insulation. A final, outer layer of plastic insulation covers the wire braid and is what you normally see when you look at a piece of coax. The purpose of the wire-braid layer is to further insulate the inner conductor from possible interference. As you can see on the next page, this coax looks very much like the round cable that connects your TV set to your antenna. In fact, network coax (especially thin coax) is quite similar to the coax used by ham and CB radio and TV antennas.

solid conductor
dialectric (plastic insulator)
foil shielding
wire-braid shielding
insulation

Coax is fairly inexpensive and very easy to install. One complicating factor, however, is that each LAN technology uses a slightly different specification (called an RG number—such as RG-58). As a result, your existing cabling may or may not work with a new technology. However, for a home consumer or small-business owner this technology will provide usable network services for many years to come.

Part
5

Advantages of Coax	Disadvantages of Coax
Simple to install	Low security, easy to tap
Good signal-to-noise ratio, particularly over medium distances	Difficult to change topologies
Low maintenance costs	Limited distance and topology
	Easily damaged

Unshielded Twisted Pair

Unshielded twisted pair (UTP) is similar to the cable that connects your phone to the wall jack. Each pair of wires is twisted around each other, as shown below, to create a magnetic field that provides better transmission capabilities. Because the wire is unshielded, it is open to

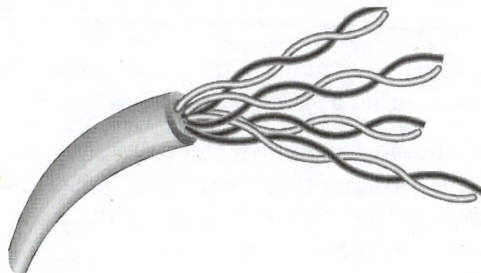

Networking
with Windows 95

electrical interference, so you should be careful about how you route the cable. For instance, never run your cables next to a power transformer or an overhead lighting system.

You should never use a low-quality cable type for your network. For instance, never use a telephone patch cord in your network segment. While a telephone cable looks just like a network cable (RJ-45), they have different properties. Telephones will run on almost anything that carries a current; high-speed data networks, however, are very finicky. If the cable is not perfect, the data will garble up and bring your network to its knees. A single six-foot patch cable constructed from the standard untwisted telephone cabling that runs between your wall jack and phone (called *silver satin*) will usually prevent the entire LAN from sending any data across the entire segment.

To clean up the confusion over what constitutes acceptable network cable and to prevent installation mistakes, the Electronics Industries Association/Telecommunications Industry Association (EIA/TIA) released a system differentiating the varieties of unshielded twisted pair. The EIA/TIA system ranks cable from Grade 1 at the low end to Grade 5 at the high end.

▶ Levels 1 and 2: These grades are not appropriate for high-speed digital transmissions and should only be used for voice.

▶ Level 3: You can safely use Level 3 for low- to moderate-speed data such as 4-Mbps token ring and 10-Mbps 10Base-T. If your network is in a location where it will be subjected to a great deal of electrical interference, you probably will want to use at least Level 4 even for speeds of 10 Mbps.

▶ Level 4: When you start getting up above 10-Mbps speeds such as 16-Mbps token ring, you must use at least Level 4.

▶ Level 5: This top-of-the-line cable can be used for all transmission speeds, even up to the 100-Mbps rate of Fast Ethernet. One word of caution: when you start using the new, high-speed technologies, be sure to use a top-rated cable-installation firm; a high-quality installation becomes essential at these speeds.

So what level should you choose? For the past year or so, I have been recommending nothing other than Level 5. Because installing cable is labor-intensive (at least three-quarters of the total installation cost is directly related to labor; even more in complex, multifloor jobs), it only makes sense to make sure that whatever you use will last as long as possible. By saving a few hundred dollars in cable costs, you run the risk of having to rip it all out and pull all new cable if your cable is not up to supporting the newest LAN technologies. Remember, like any physical plant, you would like your cable to last at least ten years, so it behooves you to plan for your network's future traffic.

> **NOTE** Every now and then one of my clients tells me that one of their (usually previous) vendors told them they could not use Level 5 for token ring and 10Base-T because the specification called for Level 3. This misunderstanding is due to a misreading of the spec that sets the minimum acceptable EIA/TIA grade rather than the required grade. You can—and usually should—use a higher grade anytime a lower grade is specified.

The following table lists the maximum data-transfer rates for each of the EIA/TIA grades for unshielded twisted pair.

EIA/TIA Level	Maximum Data-Transfer Rate
1	0 Mbps
2	1 Mbps
3	10 Mbps
4	10 Mbps
5	100 Mbps

Advantages of Unshielded Twisted Pair	Disadvantages of Unshielded Twisted Pair
Easy to add additional nodes to the network	Limited bandwidth
Well-understood technology	Limited distance
Inexpensive	Low security, easy to tap
Can be used to support phones	Requires hubs
Supports many topologies	

All told, unshielded twisted pair is probably your best choice if you are using a cabling contractor to install your network cable in a business office or if you are building a new home and can have the cable installed before you put the wallboard up. If you are just trying to connect several computers in the same room or have short cable runs between rooms, coax cable is the better choice.

Which LAN Topology to Implement

Now that you understand the physical media, you need to decide which LAN topology you will use to create your network. There are basically two types to be considered in our discussion: either a bus topology for thin Ethernet or coax cabling, or a star topology for unshielded twisted pair.

Thin Ethernet (10Base-2)

Thin Ethernet uses the main network cable, or bus, to connect each person's PC to the network. Each PC connects to this main cable by splicing the cable and terminating it with a bayonet nut connector (BNC), which is then connected to a T connector on the back of the network card. This essentially creates a single network cable that runs from the first PC to the last PC on the network.

You can create a Thin Ethernet segment for up to 185 meters (about 600 feet) and connect up to 30 stations to it. The cable itself must have an impedance of 50 ohms and be terminated with a $\frac{1}{2}$-watt 50-ohm (±1 ohm) resistor at each end. To prevent ground loops, you should also ground one (and only one) end of the cable as shown in Figure 25.1.

Thin Ethernet quickly became one of the most popular LAN technologies primarily because of its high performance-to-cost ratio and also because of its relative ease of installation. In the early 1990s it began to lose favor to a newer variant of Ethernet, which runs on twisted pair rather than coax.

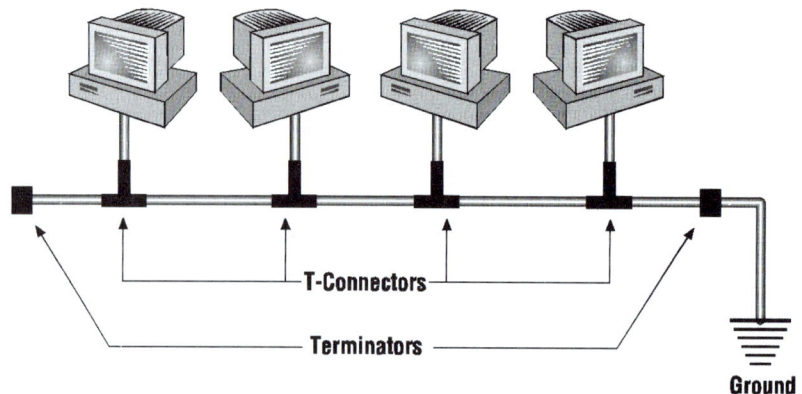

Figure 25.1   *A typical Thin Ethernet segment*

The real problem with 10Base-2 comes not from the coax cable but from the bus topology, where every computer is connected to a single cable. Whenever a computer wants to send data, it places a signal on the wire. This signal or *bus* then travels the length of the cable. As the bus passes each computer, the computer checks the destination address to see if it matches its own. If it matches, it reads the message; otherwise, it ignores it. If the cable breaks or otherwise becomes inoperable, suddenly every computer between the break and the terminator can no longer communicate with any of the stations on the other side of the break.

This is the primary reason I no longer recommend Thin Ethernet for business use outside of training rooms. If you only have three or four computers to connect or the network cable can be easily routed from computer to computer and is very accessible, thin Ethernet is a good choice. Otherwise, by all means go with 10Base-T.

Twisted-Pair Ethernet (10Base-T)

In the late 1980s, LANs moved out of the domain of the tightly controlled corporate MIS departments and into the departmental workgroup where everyone was connected to the network. Not only did the likelihood of the cable breaking increase as more computers were put on the network but so did the costs of downtime as more and more users began to depend on consistent network access.

In an effort to address these problems, vendors began offering Ethernet running on twisted pair using a star bus topology. In a star bus network, each workstation is connected directly to a multiport repeater, sometimes called a *hub* or a *concentrator*. The concentrator basically acts as a traffic cop, directing incoming messages out to the correct computer. Each hub usually supports either eight or sixteen computers, but some hubs can handle up to 128. If you need to add more computers than your concentrator can handle, or if you want to segment network traffic, you can connect several concentrators together.

The benefit of a star topology (see Figure 25.2) is that if the cable fails at any point, only the computer directly served by that cable loses its connection. The downside, however, is that if the multiport repeater (*hub*) fails, then all the workstations attached to it lose their

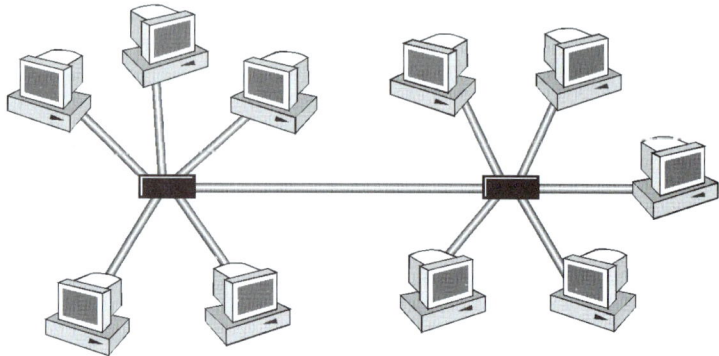

Figure 25.2   *A network based on the star bus topology*

connection to the network also. In my opinion, you should not view this as a deterrent to installing a star bus rather than a bus network.

A failed hub in a star bus topology has the same effect as a cable break in a regular bus-style network: a lot of people lose their connection to the network. However, a failed hub is almost always easier to troubleshoot than a broken cable. With bus-style networks, you have no idea where your cable might have broken; it may be right at someone's computer or it may be up in the ceiling between the third and fourth floors. Once you have located the point of failure, hub problems are easy to fix—just swap in a new one. It is not that easy with cable because you cannot replace it; you need to fix it by splicing in a good piece of cable.

While twisted-pair Ethernet only requires two pairs, typical networks use 8-pin (four pairs) cable with an RJ-45 connector. Some networking professionals suggest using the extra wires for voice so you do not have to pull separate cables for your phones. While this is technically possible, I don't think it's a good idea. Rather than use the extra wires for voice, use them for future expansion or as a backup in case a wire breaks. Better yet, you may be able to use them as part of your new 100-Mb Ethernet cabling.

With twisted-pair starting to catch on, computer managers quickly jumped at the opportunity to upgrade their cables to twisted-pair Ethernet, and the IEEE 802.3 committee created a new specification for Ethernet called 10Base-T. Among other things, this specification stipulates that a workstation running 10Base-T must be within 100 meters (330 feet) of a concentrator and connected to it by cable meeting or exceeding the EIA/TIA UTP Level 3 grade.

As for the hubs themselves, you are better off sticking with the eight- or sixteen-port variety rather than going with the larger ones. By using more hubs, you can reduce the workload on each one. As of this writing, you can get these hubs for around $20 per port. In addition to the RJ-45 jacks for the twisted pair, each will usually have a BNC or AUI (attachment unit interface) connector on the back so you can attach it to ThickNet or fiber backbones.

As your network grows, you will want to look at hubs with built-in management features. While costing more, they are a great benefit to the harried network manager because they allow him or her to remotely check the status of and administer each port on the hub.

I would recommend 10Base-T for your Ethernet network; unless you have a huge investment in thin Ethernet, or you have a small network with an even smaller budget, the other options just are not worth it.

The following table summarizes the specifications of each of the LAN technologies discussed.

	ThinNet (10Base-2)	Twisted Pair (10Base-T)
Topology	Bus	Star Bus
Cable	RG-58	UTP
Impedance	50 ohm	N/A
Termination	50 ohm ± 2 ohm	UTP 85–115 ohm
Maximum length per segment	185 m	100 m
Maximum segments	5	N/A
Maximum stations per segment	30	N/A
Minimum distance between stations	.5 m	2.5 m (between hub and station)

Choosing Your Cards

Now, with the LAN, protocol, technology, and topology decisions behind you, you only have one more decision to make before you can start installing your network: How will you connect your PCs to this physical network you have just designed?

Four years ago network designers agonized over this decision. They would pore over manufacturers' spec sheets, then dutifully design a whole set of tests so they could compare the performance of various cards from various manufacturers. Finally, they would spend days laboriously putting the cards into each model computer on site and running the tests.

Why put forth such an effort for a $300 (that's what they cost then) piece of silicon? Well, while the costs of cards only varied by about 25 percent, the performance difference between a good card and a bad card could vary as much as 300 percent. Nowadays, most manufacturers use standard chip sets so the performance difference is quite small.

When choosing a card, by far the most important factor should be whether there is an NDIS 3.1 driver available for the card. If not, you will either not be able to use the card with Windows 95, or you will have to use 16-bit real-mode drivers rather than the faster 32-bit protected-mode drivers.

Really, if the card does not have a NDIS 3.1 driver available, don't even consider buying the card. Using 16-bit real-mode drivers will deprive you of one of Windows 95's major benefits—the speed of 32-bit protected-mode drivers—every time you need to access the network.

Microsoft ships Windows 95 with drivers for many of the most popular token ring and Ethernet cards on the market. But if you find that Windows 95 does not have a driver for an existing card, you do have a few options. First, check to see if Microsoft has recently released a driver. You can get all the latest Microsoft drivers from the following sources:

▶ CompuServe: Windows 95 Driver Library

▶ CD-ROM: \Drivers subdirectory (some but not all drivers)

▶ Internet: FTP to ftp.microsoft.com (131.107.1.11)

▶ Microsoft Download Servers: Data (206) 936-6735 (N81)

▶ Microsoft Product Support Services: Voice (206) 637-7098 if you do not have a modem

In addition, you will probably be able to download the drivers from the Microsoft Network.

If Microsoft does not have a driver available, you can contact your card's manufacturer directly. Be warned, however, this is a real hit-or-miss prospect. In some cases, the hardware manufacturers produce excellent drivers for their hardware—they, after all, know its ins and outs better than anyone else. In other cases, the manufacturer will have put very little effort into producing a quality driver. Rather, it simply wants to say Windows 95 supports its hardware with little regard for how buggy the hardware is and how often it crashes your system.

You will also want to consider the flexibility of your cards. You want a card that supports multiple network media and one you can configure with software. Until recently, manufacturers made separate cards for Thin coax and twisted pair. Now many manufacturers offer cards that support both of the popular media. If your network runs on multiple technologies, you definitely want cards that will support all of them.

I refuse to purchase a manufacturer's cards if I cannot configure them on the fly with software. As recently as two years ago, you could only change a card's configuration—interrupt, I/O address, DMA channel—by getting the forceps out and changing the jumpers. Most leading manufacturers now allow you to either hard configure your NIC with jumpers or soft configure with software. Until all your cards are Plug-and-Play compliant, soft configuration is the best available option.

You also need to match your network adapter card to your computer's system bus. Bus types are fairly easy to identify as there are only five from which to choose:

► 16-bit Industry Standard Architecture (ISA)

► 32-bit Extended Industry Standard Architecture (EISA)

► 16- and 32-bit Micro Channel Architecture (MCA)

► VESA (VL-Bus) Local Bus

► Intel Peripheral Component Interconnect (PCI) Local Bus

If you are not sure what type of bus you have, chances are it is an Industry Standard Architecture (ISA) machine. Currently ISA (sometimes called AT-bus or AT-compatible because it originated when IBM first released the IBM Personal Computer AT) is by far the mostly widely used architecture. ISA machines have both 8- and 16-bit slots. If you have any 16-bit slots still available, get a 16-bit network adapter card. While it will not double your throughput, switching from an 8- to a 16-bit card will produce a noticeable improvement.

The Extended Industry Standard Architecture (EISA) standard was *supposed* to be the successor to the ISA standard. In addition to the standard 8- and 16-bits slots used in ISA machines, EISA adds support for 32-bit cards. Unfortunately, it never gained market acceptance because the additional performance failed to justify the (substantial) extra cost. These days you only see EISA machines in file and database servers. While you can use both 8- and 16-bit ISA cards in an EISA machine, you should take advantage of the EISA bus and use 32-bit EISA cards. (But see the comments below about EISA network cards.)

IBM also tried to create the successor to ISA with MCA. Like EISA, the costs outweighed the benefits. To make matters worse, if you have an MCA machine, you *must* use MCA cards (unlike EISA, which supports ISA cards). If you have an IBM P/S or any other computer that requires a reference disk, you probably have an MCA bus and therefore must use MCA cards.

If you purchased your computer in the last year or two, you might have local bus slots in addition to ISA or EISA slots. A local bus interface card can send and receive data at the full speed of your system bus (usually 25 or 33 MHz); it doesn't have the 8-MHz limit of standard ISA and EISA slots. Because of their faster throughput, local bus slots are a perfect candidate for I/O-intensive interface cards such as video and disk controllers.

There are two types of local bus machines on the market; those adhering to the VESA local bus standard (VL-Bus) and the PCI bus produced by Intel for its Pentium machines. If you have a VL-Bus machine, the benefits of a local bus network card are unclear. For reasons outside the scope of this discussion, the VL bus requires a great deal of your CPU's resources. In some cases you may even get slightly better performance from a standard EISA or even an ISA network card. Besides the possible performance hit, a computer can only have a maximum of three VL bus cards. Because of this limit and the ambiguities surrounding VESA performance, I recommend you save your local bus slots for other cards such as video accelerators, where you know you will get improved performance.

Pentium machines built around the PCI local bus show much more promise when it comes to increasing network performance. First off, they support a full 64-bit data path, as opposed to the VL Bus' 32-bit path. Second, you can have any number of PCI local bus cards in your computer. Lastly, there is no uncertainly about the performance of PCI: it is definitely faster. If you have a PCI machine and find network cards that Windows 95 supports, buy them.

When choosing a manufacturer, I recommend that all my clients purchase a card from a leading vendor. For Ethernet you cannot go wrong with 3Com, Eagle, Intel, National Semiconductor, or SMC. These are the market leaders: almost all software supports them, and they have the widest variety of drivers available. While you might save a bit purchasing the GarageTech clone, it is not worth the possible incompatibilities to save 20 percent on a $100 card.

Now that you have your physical network planned, in the following chapter we will take a look at setting up a simple-yet-complete Windows 95 peer-to-peer network.

Part 5

Networking
with Windows 95

Chapter 26

Setting Up a Simple-Yet-Complete Peer-to-Peer Windows 95 Network

FEATURING

In this chapter I will walk through setting up a simple peer-to-peer network of Windows 95 workstations. I will start with obtaining, configuring, and installing a network adapter card, then installing and configuring the correct network drivers, go on to discuss pros and cons of installing Windows 95 before or after installing your network card, and finally set up a small workgroup of at least two Windows 95 stations, which will be able to easily access each other's disk drives, printers, and modems.

Getting Acquainted with Peer-to-Peer Networking

Peer-to-peer refers to the fact that each station on the network treats each other station as an equal or a peer. There is no special station set aside to only provide file and print services to all the other stations. Instead, any printer, CD-ROM drive, hard drive, or even a floppy drive located on any one station can (if you wish) share access with all the other stations on the network. When you share a resource, such as a disk drive or printer, the computer that shares the resource becomes the server, and the computer that accesses the shared resource becomes the client. In a peer-to-peer network you can both share resources and access shared resources equally. In effect, your computer can be both a server and a client at the same time. Figure 26.1 illustrates a peer-to-peer network arrangement.

> **NOTE** A modem, too, can be shared with other stations on the network— but only when configured as a dedicated fax server. In this way, stations without a fax modem can both send and receive faxes. For detailed instructions on configuring and sharing a fax server, see Chapter 16.

Of course, there are security features as well, which will allow you to grant or remove access to shared resources on your computer. But first let's get the network up and running.

> **NOTE** For step-by-step instructions on setting up a direct-cable network connection, see Chapter 28.

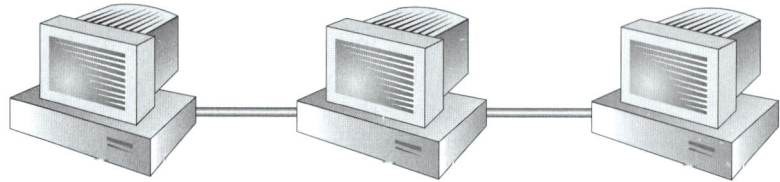

Figure 26.1   *A typical peer-to-peer network topology: notice that no particular station is designated as a standalone server.*

NETWORKING WITHOUT A NETWORK CARD

Amazingly, with Windows 95, it is *possible* to set up a peer-to-peer network of two computers with no additional hardware except a $5 cable! By installing the Direct Cable Connection (DCC) network driver supplied in Windows 95 and connecting a cable between available printer or serial ports on two PCs, you can quickly set up a simple yet full-featured, two-station network, actually sharing drives and printers just like the bigger networks.

The main drawback to this approach is that it is slow—copying a 1-MB file, for example, takes about one minute via a null-modem serial cable or about 25 seconds via a parallel cable. While this is much faster than networking via modem (an option that is also supported), it is significantly slower than most network interface cards (NICs). Generally, if you want to network two or more PCs on a regular basis, it will be worth the money to just buy network cards and cable and network the normal way. But whenever you need a convenient but temporary network connection, DCC provides you with a slick and easy built-in solution.

I was *amazed* the first time I connected my laptop to desktop via parallel port and discovered I suddenly had several "neighbors" in my Network Neighborhood. Not only could I access resources such as my Desktop's CD-ROM drive and 5$\frac{1}{4}$-inch floppy drive, I also could print from my laptop directly to any network printer at the office, send faxes using another station's fax modem, and send and receive e-mail from the network mail server—all of this just using the parallel (printer) port. (The serial port could be used just as easily but is somewhat slower than using the parallel port, and it's usually easier to find an available printer port as serial ports tend to be already occupied by mice and/or modems.) In Chapter 28 I discuss DCC and its cousin—Remote Access Service (RAS)—in greater detail.

Setting Up the Network

By way of example, let's assume in this chapter that we are setting up a new Windows 95 peer-to-peer network from scratch. For now, our goal will be to connect two or three stations together so we can share various drives and printers from each station to its peers. Based on our reading of the previous chapter, we have decided to go with a 10Base-2 (coax) configuration. Accordingly, here is our shopping list of equipment and hardware we will need—other than Windows 95 and our soon-to-be-networked computers:

▶ one network interface card (NIC) for each station we want on the network

▶ one premade coax (RG-58) cable with BNC connectors on each end for each workstation to be connected. Cable-length requirements will be based on the distance between workstations, between 6 and 50 feet.

▶ one T-connector per network card

> **TIP** Look in your local computer store for a Microsoft Windows 95 starter kit. Currently Microsoft sells just such a kit for Windows for Workgroups 3.11, and I expect that when Windows 95 is made available to the public, Microsoft will continue these starter kits. The kit includes everything you need, aside from the computer, to get your network up and running: two software-configurable network cards, two T-connectors, a 25-foot roll of coax cable, two licenses for your operating system, and complete instructions. You can purchase additional add-on kits that include another network card, T-connector, coax cable, and software license to add additional single workstations as well.

Let's take a closer look at each of these items.

Buying Your Network Cards

First you'll need a network card for each station. If you're buying network cards for the first time, please note that these are also frequently referred to as network adapters or network interface cards (NICs). Your network cards will have a thin Ethernet connector (also called a BNC connector) on them, and you might want the flexibility of also having RJ-45 connectors and/or thick Ethernet connectors, if you foresee ever having to use these types of cable. You may find that the two- or three-connector cards cost almost as much individually as buying two separate single-connector network cards. But again, if you think you need the flexibility, nothing beats the convenience of being able to change cable type without (in many cases) even having to change software or card settings. Figure 26.2 shows what a typical NIC (network interface card) looks like.

At the time of this writing, typical 16-bit single-connector network cards range from $45 to $60 or more, with dual-connector (and triple-connector) cards ranging from $120 to $140, and high-speed PCI, VESA, and other 32-bit cards selling for around $130 or more. Be sure your cards either come with NDIS 3.1 drivers on diskette or (ideally) are supported with a Windows 95 built-in driver. Last, remember you want Plug-and-Play adapter cards (if available) or at least software-configurable cards, as these can save a lot of grief and aggravation when you start installing and configuring driver software.

Installing the Network Hardware

In this section I'll describe how to install and connect the basic hardware elements of your peer-to-peer network—the NIC and the cables.

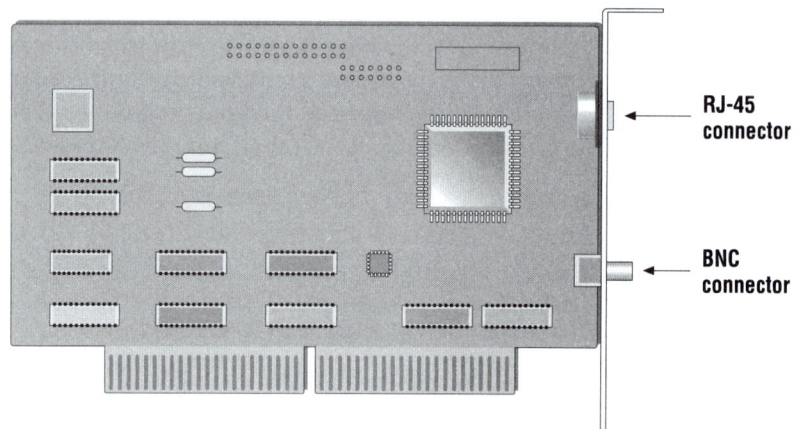

RJ-45 connector

BNC connector

Figure 26.2   This is a typical Network combo-card, sporting both RJ-45 and BNC thin coax connectors.

TIP   If you happen to be adding a non–Plug-and-Play network card (or any other hardware, for that matter) *after* Windows 95 is already running on your system, first use Windows 95 to print out a current System Summary Report, then shut down your system. This report can be printed by going into My Computer ➤ Control Panel ➤ System applet and clicking on the Device Manager tab. Click on the Print button, choose System Summary for report type, and click on OK. This will give you a handy listing of all current IRQs, DMA channels, port I/O addresses, and upper memory the memory between 640K and 1024K) currently being used in your system.

Installing the Network Interface Card (NIC)

In the unlucky event you are working with a network card that still uses jumpers to configure it, we have a little work to do. First, open the card's manual to where it shows how to set the jumpers or switches to configure the card's settings. For now, don't make any changes, but do write down the current IRQ (interrupt) number, DMA channel, and memory address, as you will need these to configure the driver. Even if you have a card that doesn't have switches but lets you make changes to settings via software, you'll have to install the card. Follow these steps to do so:

1. Select your first PC "victim," make sure the power is turned off, unplug it to be really safe, and remove the PC's case. If you have questions about how to remove your computer case, refer to your owner's manual for a complete description.

CAUTION   Don't forget to unplug your PC from the AC outlet before opening up the cover. This ensures you have the PC's power turned off, plus reduces to zero any chance of electric shock. Having come this far, I don't want to lose you. Also, before you install the network card, be sure to ground yourself by touching the metal case of the computer to eliminate the possibility of static electricity zapping your network card.

2. You likely have all too much experience inserting and removing cards, but in any case, you'll have to remove the screw that holds the thin metal slot cover behind the connector you intend to use for your card. Don't drop the screw into the machine! If you do, you must get it out one way or another, such as by turning the machine over.

3. Insert the card gently but firmly until it is completely seated in the slot. You may have to wiggle the card a bit from front to back to ensure it seats firmly into the connector.

4. Next, store the metal slot cover somewhere for future use and screw the card in securely (this can be a hassle sometimes as the screw may not line up with the hole too easily).

> **CAUTION**   After installing your network card, it is imperative that you take the time to put the screw back in the bracket and tighten the card down securely. Otherwise, once you have the network cable attached to the card, a little tug on the cable could easily uproot the NIC, damaging it and your computer's motherboard (if the power is on). This is not fun. So take the extra time to put the screw back in.

5. If the PC in question is a laptop computer or a desktop that accepts PCMCIA cards, your chores are much easier. Simply plug the card into an available PCMCIA slot. Your computer (and Windows 95) can even be running while you do this. (You might want to verify this first, however, by reading the manual or asking the salesperson, as there are a few early PCMCIA cards that should only be inserted when the unit is off.) And, of course, it won't hurt to insert the card before turning on the laptop. If the card is in next time Windows 95 starts up, the appropriate driver will be loaded immediately. But the ability to insert the card *while* Windows 95 is running is Plug and Play at its finest. If all goes well, network drivers appropriate to your card will get automatically loaded when you insert the card and unloaded when you remove it. The first time you plug the card in, however, you may be prompted to insert one of the master Windows 95 diskettes (or the CD-ROM) to load the correct network card driver.

> **NOTE**   Some network cards may come with updated Windows 95 drivers included on a diskette. Read the documentation that came with your card (or call the manufacturer) to determine whether this is the case, and if so, insert this driver diskette into your drive when you are prompted to do so.

6. Repeat the above process with each PC you intend to network. When finished, place each PC's cover back on but do not put all the screws back into the case yet—anyone who's done this before will tell you that screwing the case back on before making sure everything works is

the best way to ensure that things will *not* work. Unfortunately, even with Plug-and-Play network cards, you may still end up having to get back inside your PC to reconfigure that Sound Blaster or some other card that happens to be using a needed IRQ or DMA channel and is not itself Plug-and-Play compatible. (In my experience, sound cards are the most frequent problem.)

Installing the Cables

Connect the T-connectors to the back of each network card, then connect each workstation to the next with lengths of coax cable. The first and last stations must have a terminator attached to the free end of their T-connector. Be sure to ground one, and only one, terminator to prevent ground loops.

With a network card installed in each of your stations and each card connected via cable to the next, you are now ready to install and configure your Windows 95 software for networking. If all goes well, the hard part of your job is already complete.

Installing and/or Configuring Windows 95 for Networking

If you have not yet installed Windows 95 on your stations, you'll need to do so before continuing (see the Appendix for installation instructions). If all goes well, Setup will automatically detect your newly installed network card and, if you're lucky, will even determine the type of card and configure it for you. If it does neither, you have two choices—either manually tell it during setup which network card you have or wait until Windows 95 is finished installing and then add the network drivers. If you take the opportunity during setup to configure your network drivers, use the following procedure. Otherwise, skip down to *Installing Network Drivers After You've Installed Windows 95*.

Installing Network Drivers During Windows 95 Install   If you want to declare the settings for your network while you are installing Windows 95, start the normal Windows 95 Setup program and follow these steps as Windows 95 is installing:

1. When you get to the Select Components screen, make sure the *accessories* option is checked. If you are certain you do not want the accessories, you may still at least want the Communications features, which include

Microsoft Fax, Dial-Up Networking, and Direct Cable Connect. If you think you will need these, either include the accessories or double-click on accessories and enable the Communications check box.

NOTE   If you leave out an option during installation, don't worry—it can be added quite easily after Windows 95 is installed and running.

---

2. When you get to the Network Configuration part of the setup (see Figure 26.3), you will want to verify that the following network components get installed:

   ▶ Client for Microsoft Networks

   ▶ a driver specific to your network card (if not listed, just let Setup finish for now)

   ▶ NetBEUI

   ▶ File and Printer Sharing for Microsoft Networks

   If you need to add anything to this list, just click on the Add button, select Client, Adapter, Protocol, or Service, then select the manufacturer and type. Don't worry about IPX/SPX and other protocols now, these can easily be added later. And unless you want them immediately, the Dial-Up and Direct-Cable connection can probably wait

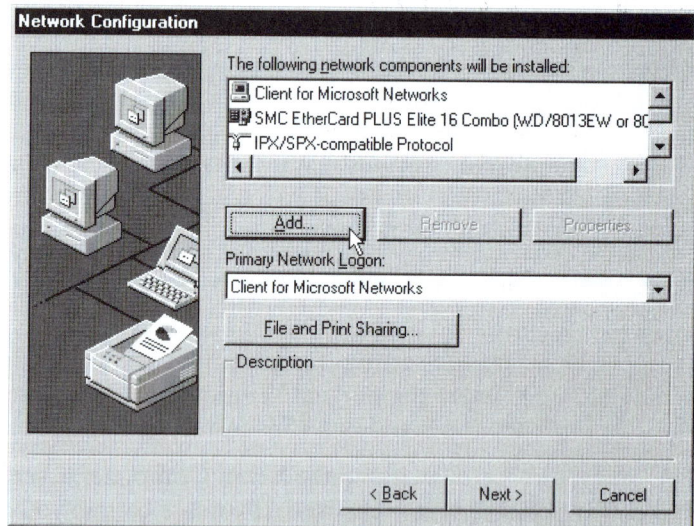

Figure 26.3   *The Network Configuration dialog box*

and be added later as well. Keeping your network components to a minimum right now may make it easier to get your initial network connections operating.

3. Click on the File and Print Sharing button and make sure both options are checked: *I want to be able to give others access to my files* and *I want to be able to give others access to my printer(s)*. These will probably be on by default, but check to make sure. Again, if you accidentally skip this step, you can do it later. Just remember that file and printer sharing will not even appear on menus if these options are not enabled.

> **NOTE** Because Windows 95 (unlike Windows for Workgroups) includes support for Novell networks right out of the box, the Client for Novell Networks as well as IPX/SPX (its default protocol) will probably show up in your *network components to be installed* list. To keep things simple, remove the Client for Novell Networks and the IPX/SPX for now—unless you plan to connect to a Novell Network—and make sure NetBEUI is selected as the only protocol to be installed. Installing additional clients and protocols can only complicate matters right now, and can also slow down your network to a small degree.

4. When asked for your machine name, choose a name descriptive of the computer—the important thing is to make this name different for each station. Fortunately, the machine name can be very easily changed later, so don't worry too much about being creative at this point. Select a descriptive name for your workgroup: this *does* need to be the same for each station—in Chapter 8 I discussed making multiple workgroups.

5. Continue through the rest of the install process, and if you've configured the networking components appropriately, you can skip ahead to *Network Neighborhood*.

Network operability should be complete now. However, if you already have Windows 95 running but have not installed your network card yet, shut down Windows (perhaps print out a system-configuration report first), then turn off the computer and install the network card. (See *Installing the Network Interface Card*, above, for details on installing your card.) You'll want to note the IRQ, I/O, and memory address of your card in case you need to manually enter these settings later. Most likely, however (especially if your card is new), after turning your computer back on, Windows 95 will come up and detect that you've added a network card, detect what kind it is, and configure it for you. If this is the case, you can skip down to *Network Neighborhood* now.

Installing or changing Network components after Windows 95 is up and running is also quite easy. You can access the network-configuration options in Windows 95 via the Control Panel by choosing My Computer ➤ Control Panel ➤ Network, as shown in Figure 26.4.

Installing Network Drivers After You've Installed Windows 95

Assuming you have opened the Network applet under the Control Panel, you should see the Network Properties dialog box (see Figure 26.5).

1. Under *The following network components are installed* on the Configuration tab, make sure you have the following:

▶ Client for Microsoft Networks

▶ a driver specific to your network card

▶ NetBEUI

▶ File and Printer Sharing for Microsoft Networks

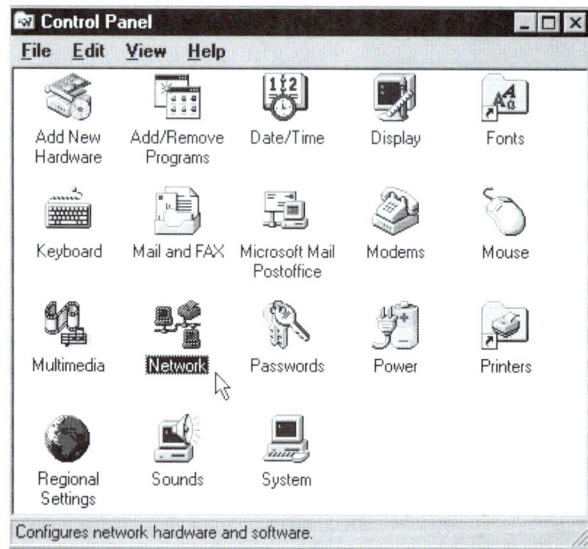

Figure 26.4   *Accessing network options once Windows 95 is installed*

Because Windows 95 includes support for Novell networks right out of the box, the Client for Novell Networks and IPX/SPX (its default protocol) will show up in your *network components to be installed* list if you didn't uncheck them earlier. Remove the Client for Novell Networks and the IPX/SPX for now—unless you plan to connect to a Novell Network—and make sure NetBEUI is selected as the only protocol to be installed.

If you need to add anything to this list, just click on the Add button, select Client, Adapter, Protocol, or Service, then select the manufacturer and type.

> **NOTE** Sometimes the diskette that shipped with your network card will contain drivers for a variety of different operating systems, each in a different subdirectory. If Windows 95 cannot find the correct drivers in the root directory of the diskette, you may have to help it along a little. Click on the Browse button and double-click on the correct subdirectory before letting Windows 95 continue.

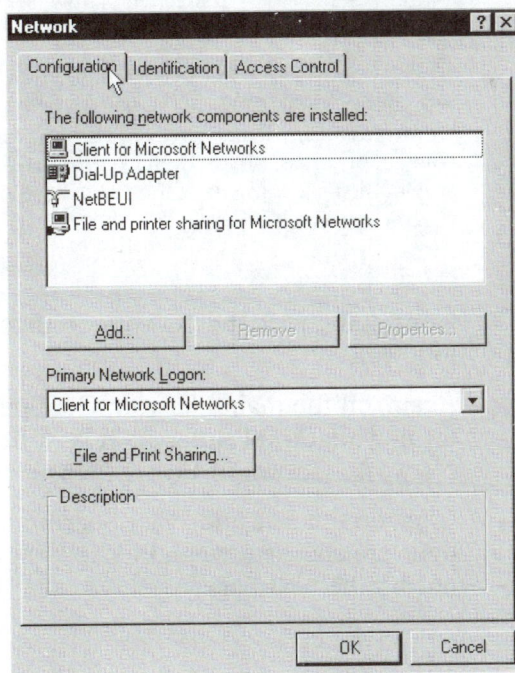

Figure 26.5   *The Network Properties dialog box*

IF WINDOWS 95 DOESN'T DETECT YOUR NETWORK ADAPTER TYPE

If Windows 95 did not detect your adapter correctly (or at all), do the following, making sure you have the diskette containing your network card's drivers:

1. Choose Control Panel ➤ Network and click on the Configuration tab.

2. Click on Adapter. If you see an incorrect network card driver installed, remove it by selecting it and then clicking on the Remove button.

3. Press the Add button to add your new driver.

4. Now click on Have Disk in the Select Network Adapters dialog box.

5. When prompted, insert the driver disk and press Enter.

6. For some cards, you will next be shown the desired settings for your network card. Make sure you write these down, because as soon as the drivers are installed, you will need to shut down Windows 95, remove your card, and make sure all the jumpers are set to configure the card for the required settings. If your card is software configurable, just run the card's configuration program and verify that the settings are what Windows 95 wants them to be.

7. Windows 95 will probably let you know it needs to restart (reboot) to load your network drivers. Choose Yes to restart.

When Windows 95 comes back up, the newly installed drivers will hopefully detect your network card and be able to communicate with it. If you do not see any error messages, you can proceed with the Network configuration procedure already in progress. (If you do have problems—an error message comes up, for example—first see if the message points to anything obvious you can fix; otherwise, flip to Chapter 29.)

Continuing with the network-configuration procedure, next do the following:

2. Again, on the main Network Configuration property sheet, make sure for now that the Primary Network Logon says Client for Microsoft Networks (shown in Figure 26.5).

3. Click on the File and Print Sharing button and make sure both options are checked; when finished, the dialog box should look like the one on the next page.

File and Print Sharing

☑ I want to be able to give others access to my files.

☑ I want to be able to allow others to print to my printer(s).

OK   Cancel

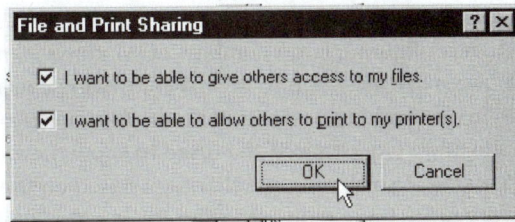

4. Now click on the Network Identification tab (see Figure 26.6). For the computer name, enter something descriptive of the computer—the important thing is that this name be different from others on the network. Select a descriptive name for your workgroup: This name needs to be the same for each station. Finally, add a computer description, if you like.

Part 5

Networking with Windows 95

Network

Configuration | Identification | Access Control

Windows uses the following information to identify your computer on the network. Please type a name for this computer, the workgroup it will appear in, and a short description of the computer.

Computer name: MARYSDESK

Workgroup: WORKGROUP

Computer Description: Mary C.'s Desktop

OK   Cancel

Figure 26.6   *The Network Identification Properties sheet lets you specify how your computer will be known to other users and which workgroup you are a member of.*

> **TIP** When configuring large numbers of Windows 95 machines, you may want to give more attention to the machine name you assign to each workstation. While the machine name itself is easy to change later, doing so can confuse all the other workstations that used to know the workstation under a different name. Also all resource sharing is based on the computer name. Therefore, if your office has a high turnover rate, you do not want to be naming machine names after employees using each machine; rather, give each machine a name descriptive of its function within the workgroup it belongs to.

5. Now click on the Access Control tab. Again, at least for now, select the share-level access control. We'll look at user-level access control at the end of this chapter, under *Security Features*.

When finished setting these options, be sure to click on the OK button at the bottom of the Network Property dialog box. After the dialog box closes, you may be prompted to shut down and restart Windows 95. If so, go ahead and do this.

Repeat this network-configuration procedure on any other stations that need it.

If all goes well, either you or Windows 95 has successfully installed the appropriate network drivers on each of your peer-to-peer stations, and you are now ready to begin testing and configuring your network. (If all has *not* gone well, the most likely problem will be incorrect network-card settings. Check Chapter 29.)

Network Neighborhood (aka The Hood)

Start up Windows 95 on each of your stations, and you should now see the Network Neighborhood icon on each station's Desktop. Double-click on the icon, and you should see a number of computer-shaped icons with names matching those unique machine names you assigned to each station.

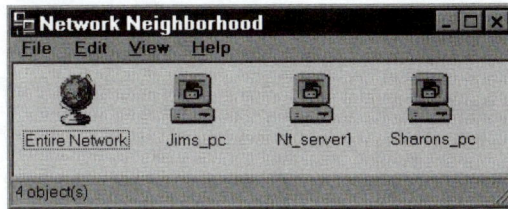

Each station on your network should appear in this Neighborhood folder. If any are missing, or worse, if you do not *have* a Network Neighborhood on your Desktop, you'll have to do some troubleshooting. The most common problem, aside from missing protocol(s) and incorrectly configured network cards, will be that one or more of your stations are not set to the same workgroup as all the others.

Sharing Resources on the Network

To make the resources from one station accessible to other stations on the network, you need to *share* the drive or printer. First we will look at sharing drives, then sharing printers, and, finally, we will look at how to use security features to restrict access to your shared resources.

> **NOTE** File and Print Sharing must be enabled before you can share files or printers to your network.

Sharing Drives and Subdirectories

Using the Explorer and manipulating folders both provide an easy way to share information with other people on your network. In the following example, I'll share a station's hard drive. (If you are not currently on a station that has a hard drive, you may wish to switch to one on your network that does so you can try the example.)

Sharing from a Folder   The easiest way to share a folder object is to point to an object in the folder you wish to share and right-click on it. As shown on the next page, this will bring up the right-click menu for that object, and you will see a menu option labeled Sharing. Select this, and you will go to the Properties dialog box (see Figure 26.7). Then just follow these steps.

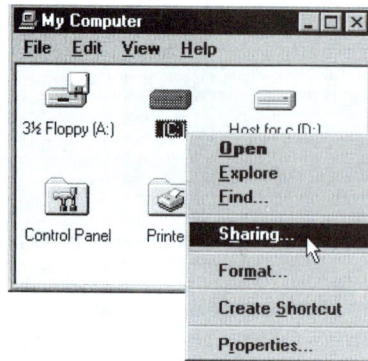

1. Click on the Sharing tab.

2. Type in a share name or just keep the default share name. If you like, you may add a comment describing the contents of this share.

3. Next you need to set the access type. Note the default is read-only, which only allows other users to open and view the contents but not to change them. The Full option lets anyone on the network both read and make changes to this folder. Keep in mind, by the way, that sharing a drive or folder shares all the subfolders below it as well.

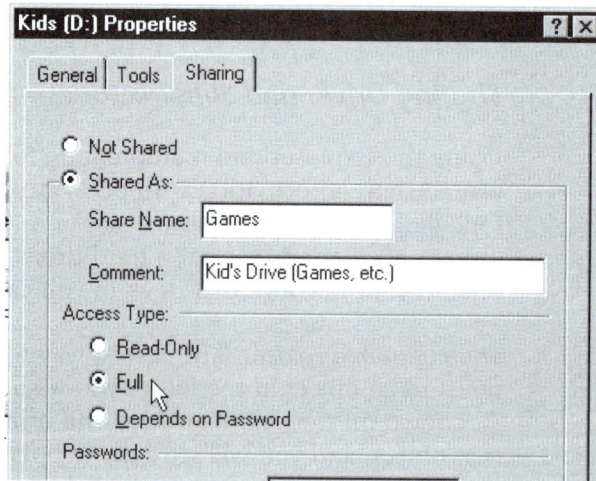

Figure 26.7 *The Sharing dialog box lets you specify how a shared drive (or folder) will be known to others on the network. It also allows you to specify a password and even which users and groups of users will be allowed to access the shared resource.*

4. If you want to restrict access to the share, assign a password. For now, let's leave access set to Full. We'll cover security shortly.

Another way you can bring up the share options is via the File menu. If you click on the drive or folder to be shared, then select the File menu option, you will see Sharing on this menu as well. Selecting this sharing option produces the same results as right-clicking and selecting Sharing.

Note the change in appearance of your drive or folder. When it is shared, the same icon appears, but as if held out in someone's hand.

Sharing from Explorer   If you understand the above-mentioned ways to share from a folder, then you also know how to share using Explorer. Both sides of the Explorer window support right-clicking to bring up property sheets (and from there you can select Sharing), and the File menu will also have the Sharing option, provided you've selected an object on the right side of the Explorer window (see Figure 26.8).

Before you go to another station to see if you can access the shared drive, bring up an MS-DOS prompt and type **NET VIEW \\Com-puterName** where *ComputerName* is the name of your computer. This will display a list of all the resources you have shared on your computer. If you can see the new shared resources, then go to another workstation and open Network Neighborhood, then open the computer that has the shared drive. If you now see the shared resource,

Part 5

Networking with Windows 95

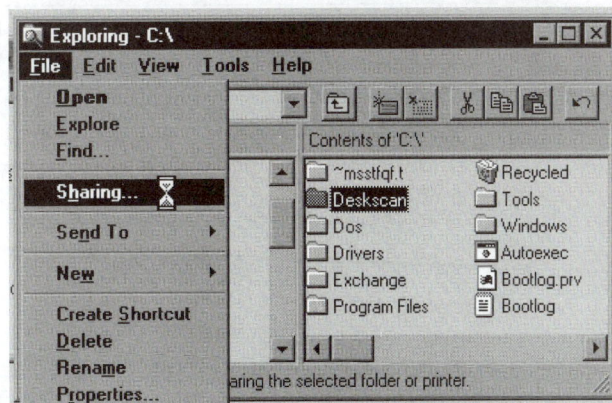

Figure 26.8   *Resources can also be shared via the Explorer applet—either using the menu or via the right-click method just mentioned.*

congratulations. You can now go to each station and add shares to any local drive you want accessible from the network.

Don't forget you can also share floppy drives and CD-ROM drives in exactly the same way. Perhaps only one station has a $5\frac{1}{4}$-inch floppy or a CD-ROM drive. Share it via the network, and anyone now has access to both sizes of floppy drive and the CD-ROM drive. Of course, network etiquette will likely preclude frequent use of someone else's floppy or CD-ROM drive, but for occasional use—installing software, for example—having the ability to share even removable media drives can be wonderfully helpful. Here, I am about to share a CD-ROM drive:

NOTE   If you are going to share a read-only resource such as a CD-ROM drive, be sure to set the network access to read-only (the default). This will prevent a remote user from attempting to write to the CD-ROM drive. If you do not do this, your remote software may hang while attempting to write to read-only media, so it's best to make sure that read-only access is enabled.

Sharing Printers

Sharing printers is just about as easy—and is certainly as much fun— as sharing drives and subdirectories. Before a printer can be shared, of course, its driver must be installed on the station to which the printer is physically attached. Additionally, other stations needing to use this printer across the network must have the same printer driver installed on their stations. Therefore, let's next look at how to install the printer driver.

Installing the Printer Driver for a Shared Printer   Go to a station that has a local printer attached. If you haven't yet installed the driver for this printer, you will need to do this first. To install it, just open My Computer ➤ Printers ➤ Add printer, and select the appropriate printer brand and model. If you are asked whether this is a network or local printer, select local. Depending on which printer you have, you might be asked for a Windows 95 driver diskette.

Once the printer driver is installed, the printer should show up in the Printers folder (located in My Computer). Using the right-click method, share the printer. Note that printers can also be shared from Explorer, just as drives and folders can.

Now, to share the printer, do exactly what you did to share a drive—namely, after right-clicking on the printer's icon, select the Sharing menu option. You have a set of sharing options quite similar to those for drive sharing. Type the name you want your printer known as on the network, provide a descriptive comment, if you like, and note the option to provide a password. If you do enter a password, your printer will only be available to users on the network who know the password. For now let's leave the password off, as this will make testing easier.

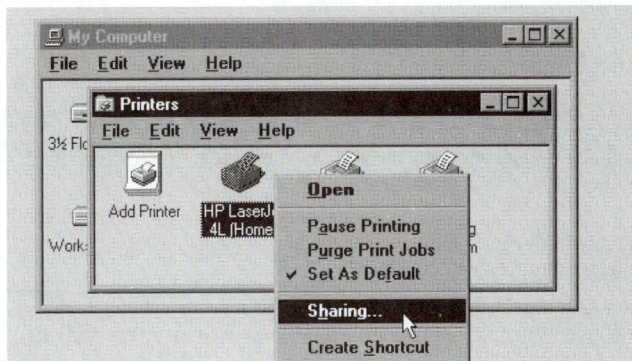

After you've shared the printer, go to another station—preferably one that has no local printer attached—and open Network Neighborhood. Double-click on the computer icon that has the shared printer, and you should now see the printer, plus any shared drive(s) for that station. If so, congratulations are once more in order. You can now go to any other stations that have a local printer and share those as well. Here's an example of what a shared printer will look like:

Having shared those printers you want accessible on the network, your users will now be able to print to any of them simply by choosing the Print option from any Windows application that supports printing. Of course, with more than one printer on the network, the desired printer can also be selected from any Windows application, usually by selecting File ➤ Print Setup from the application's menu. Additionally, note that any printer (local or network) can be set on each station as that station's default printer.

Now that your network printers are printing correctly (at least I hope they are!), I'll discuss using security features to control access to your shared drives and printers. For more about printers and printing with Windows 95, refer to Chapter 8.

Security Features

Although we've disabled all of them for clarity's sake, Windows 95 does have several means of restricting access to a station's shared resources.

Hiding Share Names

Let's start with the easiest (but not a very well known) technique. In any Share As name, if you add a dollar sign ($) to the end of the share name, that resource becomes invisible but still accessible to those who know both its existence and name. For example, if you want to make your CD-ROM drive accessible anywhere on the network but not have everyone using it, you might type CDROM$ as the drive's share name. Then, whenever you need to access this drive from another station, you would need to specify the share name and the machine name to map to the drive or otherwise access it. The access path would look similar to this: `\\CD_STATION\CDROM$`.

Obviously this technique is only as secure as the knowledge of the resource's share name (and location).

Share-Level and User-Level Access Control

A second means of restricting access is to use passwords with share-level control. This means you supply one password for each shared resource, and that password remains the same for all users who access the resource. Again, there are limitations to this.

Although the simple effectiveness of the above two methods might be all that is needed on smaller networks, eventually you will need to consider using user-level access control. This more-sophisticated security relies on Windows 95 verification of users by their log-on password. In other words, you specify exactly which users and groups of users are to have access to a given network resource, and then those users, once they have logged in, automatically gain access to that network resource. For Windows 95 to make use of user-level access, it must use a Windows NT Server user database.

Read-Level and Read-Write-Level Access Control

Both the user- and share-level control methods also allow read-only access as distinct from read-write access. Read-only access makes perfect sense for memoranda, static databases (perhaps a zip code database?), and backups.

Obviously, any such security is only as good as the confidentiality of the passwords. If security is of more than passing interest to you, you should encourage proper choice of user passwords. There are several good computer security books that discuss guidelines for selecting difficult-to-guess passwords. Additionally, keep in mind that you may want to combine share-name hiding with share-level or user-level passwords. In this way, even if someone logs on with a stolen ID and password, he or she may not know a particular resource exists. I wouldn't count on this, but on the other hand, I wouldn't discredit or overlook even small additional layers of security where they are called for.

Please bear in mind that Windows 95 was not designed to be a really secure operating system. If you do need something more secure, strongly consider using Windows NT—it is one of only a few operating systems that has security incorporated in it at every level, earning it a C2-level security rating. We will look at these and other features of Windows NT in the next chapter.

Chapter 27

Internetworking Windows 95 Workstations with NT

FEATURING

Domains

Adding Windows 95 workstations to the network

As you connect more stations to your Windows 95 peer network, you will sooner or later want to interconnect with one or more Windows NT Workstations or Servers. My goal in this chapter is to learn how to network Windows 95 stations with one or more Windows NT stations functioning as a server for files, printers, and applications. Adding one or more Windows NT servers to your network provides you with an array of powerful options and tools that can help maximize the usefulness and productivity of your Windows 95 workstations—especially in the areas of security, performance, and network administration.

Some Networking Philosophy

In the preceding chapter you saw how each networked peer showed up in the Network Neighborhood as a computer icon. Each station's shared printers and folders were available to anyone who double-clicked on a particular computer or created a map to one of the shared drives or printers. This is great as far as it goes, but consider how it would be if you had two hundred, a thousand, even several thousand stations on the network all appearing in Network Neighborhood. Clearly, the neighborhood concept would become very confusing to use and a *nightmare* for the network administrator. What is needed then is a way to organize these stations into groups, and perhaps groups of groups, so visualizing and working with the stations becomes both more manageable and efficient: thus the concept of *workgroups.* First introduced in the Windows for Workgroups product, the subdividing of Windows workstations into workgroups helps free the members of each workgroup to maintain, support, and use only those resources needed by their workgroup. All other network resources may still be *physically* connected, but the workgroup sees and makes use of only those resources directly relevant to their area. From the user's vantage point, 95 percent of the clutter is removed from Network Neighborhood, and the neighborhood becomes a familiar metaphor once more. And where security is needed, passwords can be assigned within the workgroup on either a per-resource or a per-user and groups-of-users basis.

Smaller networks—say fifty or fewer workstations total—might find that this workgroup approach is a sufficient and easy enough means of organizing the network resources and users, assuming subdivision into multiple workgroups. But with very large networks, workgroups are not adequate either because there's no way to oversee all the different workgroups. Management of at least the centralized networking resources on larger networks requires being able to access and configure user accounts and network resources in a way that transcends the boundaries of individual workgroups.

Domains

For ease of organizing and managing larger networks, Microsoft came up with the idea of *domains*. Domains are similar to workgroups but provide the ability to group all users in a single user database. This database resides on the Windows NT Server domain controller. For more specific information on NT Server, take a look at *Mastering Windows NT Server 3.5* (Sybex, 1995). When you log onto a domain from the Windows 95 log-on dialog box, you are authenticated as a specific user with specific access rights. These access rights are the basis for your ability to access shared resources on the network such as a directory or printer.

NOTE   Throughout this chapter, I am speaking of NT version 3.5 or later. If you are still running NT or NT Advanced Server version 3.1, you will notice a marked performance increase by upgrading to version 3.5 or later.

NT Workstation v. NT Server

Although in this chapter I will be primarily concentrating on Windows NT in its capacity as a server, NT can also be used as a workstation and as a peer of Windows 95 stations. In fact, Microsoft emphasizes these dual uses by currently selling two different "flavors" of NT, appropriately labeled NT Workstation and NT Server. While both can be used as servers and both can be used as workstations, each has certain optimizations that better suit it to one of the two uses. Why, you may wonder, would you want to use NT on a workstation? If you plan to run NT services software or certain high-end graphics software, need beefed-up security or support for non-FAT file systems, or have a non-Intel-compatible workstation, you will need Windows NT rather than Windows 95. Software developers, CAD users, and scientists doing math-intensive work might need or prefer Windows NT over Windows 95 for a combination of these features. Some programmers, for example, will have both Windows 95 and Windows NT installed on their stations and can boot to either operating system to develop and test their software. So without further ado, let's look at the differences between NT Workstation and NT Server.

While NT Workstation can certainly function as a server, it (unlike NT Server) has the following limitations:

▶ It cannot function as a domain controller.

▶ It has a maximum of ten simultaneous client connections.

▶ It does not provide gateway services to Novell Netware.

▶ It does not provide network services for Apple workstations.

▶ It has a limit of two CPUs (for Symmetric Multiprocessing).

Let me clarify these briefly. First, and perhaps most notably, NT Workstation cannot be used as a domain controller. As mentioned above, a domain controller is where the user database resides. NT Workstation can, however, log onto a domain and can function as an additional server within an existing domain. Despite this limitation, I do want to emphasize that NT Workstation can perform very ably as a server for a workgroup of Windows 95 stations. Where cost is an issue and the ten-client limit is not a problem, NT workstation might well be the best choice. The ten-connection limit, by the way, does not prevent NT Workstation from having more than ten user accounts or from recognizing more than ten other stations on a network. It simply means that no more than ten other workstations or servers can be *simultaneously* connected to its disk and printer resources. If you do have one or more Novell Netware servers, consider installing NT Server.

NT Workstation (and of course Windows 95 stations themselves) can easily connect to and use Novell resources—and Windows 95 can even share files and printers back to Novell stations. But for the ultimate in all sorts of connectivity options between Windows and Novell network resources, you definitely want NT Server. And if you have Apple workstations connecting to your network or have a server computer with more than two CPUs, you will need NT Server. NT Server also provides for centralized administration because all the user accounts and groups reside on the domain controller rather than on each individual NT workstation. The above differences between NT Server and Workstation are by no means the only differences, but they are the main points to keep in mind if you're considering buying NT. For the rest of this chapter, I'll be discussing NT Server unless otherwise mentioned.

> **NOTE**   One other interesting point about Windows NT Server is that it can operate as a super workgroup server. When NT Server is configured to run in server mode, instead of as a domain or backup controller, it does not perform any user authentication. In this mode it essentially works just like NT Workstation but with unlimited user connections, and it still includes the rest of the NT Server functionality, like the Novell Gateway Service and Macintosh Services.

Adding Windows 95 Workstations to the Network

To allow your Windows 95 stations to communicate with an NT server, you must make sure they are using one of the protocols used by the NT server. In most cases, this will probably be either NetBEUI or IPX/SPX—or if you have a really big network, you may be using TCP/IP. Remember, on a small Windows-only network (where no connections to Novell or other systems are needed) NetBEUI will be your fastest protocol. Again, you just need to make sure the Windows 95 stations are talking the same language as your server.

Adding Windows 95 Workstations to an NT Server

Once the protocols have been configured, you need to take the following steps so your Windows 95 stations can share network resources with an NT server.

1. Use the right-click ➤ Share Properties dialog box on your Windows 95 stations to share any printers, drives, and/or folders that you want the NT station (and the other Windows 95 stations) to be able to access. Add any security restrictions (either share level or user level) desired.

> **NOTE** To use user- or group-level access rights, you must be part of a Windows NT domain.

2. Use NT's File Manager applet to share any drives or folders you want your Windows 95 stations to access.

3. Use NT's Print Manager applet to share any printer(s) you want your Windows 95 stations to access. Note that NT can share not only any locally attached printers, but also any printers it has access to if they are located on another NT station (either Workstation or Server).

4. If the NT server is a domain server, you will also need to create a user account on the NT server for each Windows 95 user needing access to resources on the NT server. Use NT's User Manager for Domains to create these accounts and then set any desired file restrictions using NT's File Manager and any desired printer or printing restrictions using NT's Print Manager.

5. Choose as appropriate:

   ▶ If you are using NT Server, set each Windows 95 station to log onto the NT domain and enter the correct domain in the domain field at each station. To do this, open Control Panel ➤ Networks and double-click on Microsoft Client for Windows Networks. Click on the Domain check box and type in the name of your NT domain (see Figure 27.1).

   ▶ If you are using NT Workstation, simply make sure you have the same workgroup name specified on the NT workstation as you do for each Windows 95 station that will be part of this workgroup.

After performing these steps, you should be able to open Network Neighborhood on any Windows 95 stations in the workgroup (or domain) and see an icon for the NT server. Using the server browsers in either NT's Print Manager or File Manager, you should now also see your Windows 95 stations appear as additional servers in the workgroup (or domain).

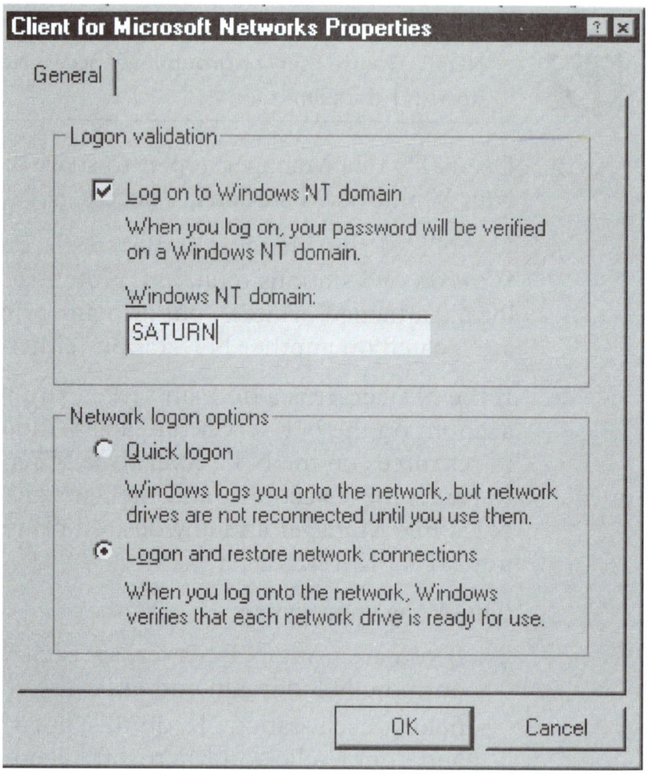

Figure 27.1 *Configuring a Windows 95 station to log onto an NT Server domain*

> **NOTE** If your office has one or more Novell Netware print servers and you are running NT Server, you can use Print Manager to share Netware print servers as well. You must first install and configure the Netware Gateway Services software (supplied with NT Server) and then connect to the Netware print queue before trying to share it. In this way, Windows 95 stations (and even DOS, Windows 3.1, and Windows for Workgroups stations) will not need Novell-specific network drivers loaded to print on the Novell print queue, although you will need to use a printer driver for each printer you use.

Using Shared Printers

One of the major benefits of using Windows NT or Windows 95 is that they both provide the ability to connect to a network printer without installing a printer driver. You will of course need to install a printer driver on the computer that has the local printer attached to it, but your NT and Windows 95 clients do not need to have a printer driver installed. Instead, they will access the remote printer and use the printer driver installed on the remote computer. The only time you will need to install a printer driver is when you connect to a different type of print server, such as a Windows for Workgroups, Novell Netware Server, or Unix server. If you are unfamiliar with how to install a printer or connect to a networked printer, take a look at Chapter 8.

Mapping Windows 95 and Windows NT Shared Drives

You might also at this point wish to establish *persistent* drive mappings on either the NT server or your Windows 95 stations, or both. This will allow you to always have the same drive letters assigned to shared drives (or folders).

For Windows 95 stations, the fastest and easiest way (in my opinion) to map to any drive is simply to right-click on Network Neighborhood's icon, then select the Map Network Drive option. Just select the drive letter you want to refer to the drive as, type in the correct *machine name\drive name*, and press the OK button. Note that the Reconnect on Login option is enabled by default; this is probably what you want. If not, you can also disconnect from a shared drive quite easily. Right-clicking on Network Neighborhood is again one way to do this, but for disconnecting mapped drives, I find the most straightforward way is to open Network Neighborhood and right-click on the shared drive's icon. Choose the Disconnect option, and you're done.

For NT stations, mapping drive letters to network (shared) drives is accomplished using (again) NT's File Manager. The disk-connecting and mapping procedure for NT is as follows:

1. Open File Manager.

2. Click on the Drives menu option.

3. Select the Connect option.

4. Select the drive letter you want to map to, then use the server browser (the list box in the lower half of the dialog box) to select which server and which shared drive to connect to. Or just type in the *machine name\drive name*.

5. Press the OK button.

6. At this point you may also need to enter a password if the directory share includes share-level password protection.

Assuming your NT station is going to function primarily as a server, you will probably place some or all of your workgroup's most frequently accessed data on the NT server, both to free up your workstations' loads somewhat and also to get the best performance because you now have a dedicated server. Just keep in mind that NT Workstation can only provide ten simultaneous connections, so its use as a dedicated server will only work well for very small networks.

Chapter 28

Extending Your Networking with Dial-Up Networking

FEATURING

Remote access

Windows 95 and Dial-Up Networking

DCC using a serial or parallel port

In the past few years, the number of mobile computer users has increased dramatically. Both advances in computer technology—in both the hardware and software arenas—and changes in the business climate have driven this sea change. Improved manufacturing techniques have allowed miniaturization only dreamed of ten years ago—clearly, there would be far fewer mobile users if everyone still had to carry around a seventeen-pound Compaq luggable. And improved communication interfaces have allowed users to access other computers without having to memorize obscure Unix or AT modem commands.

On the business side, the near-universal reliance on computers has driven the cost of being disconnected from the network so high that technology managers have had to provide remote access to their off-site users. That, coupled with the downsizing and reengineering trends that forced users out of the office and off to client sites, created the demand for remote access at about the same time advances in computer technology provided the means.

Mobile users are everywhere. Because computer-toting travelers are so ubiquitous these days, few self-respecting motels and hotels fail to provide RJ-11 data jacks on their phones. I no longer ask if a hotel is modem-friendly; I simply assume that because they are still in business they provide data jacks. While I still carry a telephone patch cable with alligator clips on one end, it has been more than a year since I stayed in a hotel so far in the Dark Ages that I actually had to splice their phone cord and use it.

In this chapter, I will first cover the options Windows 95 provides for remote connections and help you choose the best one for your particular circumstance. Next, I'll examine the hardware requirements for effective remote commuting over phone lines and take an in-depth look at *Dial-Up Networking*, as Microsoft Plus' remote-node client is called. Finally, I will cover specific issues you need to address when using remote access, such as security.

NOTE Dial-Up Networking is an option available in Microsoft Plus, an add-on product for Windows 95. Please see Chapter 32 about procuring and installing this product.

Remote Access, Your Computer, and You

If you need to allow off-site users to connect to your network, you essentially have two choices: remote control or remote node.

Remote-control programs use standard telephone lines and provide on-demand connections. Remote control works just as you would expect from the name. You sit down at the remote computer, it dials into a host computer, and then you can actually control the computer you dial into from the computer you have dialed in from. The leading remote-control products include Norton PCAnywhere, Carbon Copy, and Co-Session. When you type or move the mouse on the remote computer, the software sends the keystrokes and mouse movements to the host computer for processing. In turn, the software transmits any screen updates such as dialog boxes or drop-down menus from the host back to the remote computer for display. If the user wants to run an application, he or she launches the application on the host computer.

Remote node works on an on-demand basis just like remote control, but rather than taking over the host computer, the remote computer uses the host computer as a server. This places the remote node directly on the network. In other words, the phone line becomes an extension of the network cable. This allows the user to request file and print services just as if he or she sat right next to the file server. When a user starts an application, it runs on his or her local computer, not on the host computer as in remote-control systems.

Remote node and remote control both provide network connectivity, but they use two entirely different approaches to providing remote access. The primary difference between these two types of remote-access software is that remote-control software actually takes over complete control of the host system, while remote-node software just uses the modem to provide a network interface to the host system.

Windows 95 and Dial-Up Networking

A mobile user can use Dial-Up Networking, Microsoft Plus' remote-node software, to seamlessly connect remote resources. While early versions of Windows included a version of Dial-Up Networking, called Remote Access Services (RAS), it was clearly an add-on feature. To use it, you had to start it separately before accessing shared resources on a remote computer. Installing Dial-Up Networking from Microsoft Plus (see Chapter 32) places the remote-node software directly into the core operating system so you can access remote resources just as you can local ones. Whenever you try to open a remote file (whether through the File ➤ Open dialog box or by double-clicking on the file), Windows 95 automatically starts Dial-Up Networking and establishes the remote connection with the host computer.

Dial-Up Networking uses the Telephone Application Programming Interface (TAPI), Microsoft's proposed standard for integrating telephones and computers. Because TAPI allows multiple applications to share a single line, one application can wait for a call while another dials out.

What is the point, you may ask; when one application dials out the line is busy, so waiting applications can't receive a call anyway. Suppose, for example, you have Microsoft Fax waiting to receive incoming faxes and you want to use Dial-Up Networking to download a file from a computer in a satellite office. In earlier versions of Windows, you would have had to shut down the fax software before you could use the modem for any other purpose. Because Dial-Up Networking uses TAPI, you can leave Fax running in the background as you connect to a remote computer. As soon as you finish with Dial-Up Networking, Fax will pick up any incoming faxes.

Another benefit of TAPI is its support of Dial Helper, shown below, which allows you to define phone numbers in location-independent fashion.

This way, you can associate a single number with any resource. If you change locations, you simply change the Dial Helper location rather than having to reenter the number. When you want to call that number from the office, Windows 95 will prefix it with a 9 so your PBX can distinguish it from an internal call and thus give it an external line. When at home, Windows 95 will prepend a *70 to turn off call waiting. Finally, when on the road, it will enter your calling-card information for you.

Along with its support of TAPI, Windows 95 further simplifies Dial-Up Networking by supporting the unimodem infrastructure. You can think of unimodem as the modem equivalent of the Windows printer subsystem. Rather than require each application to manage its own printing, Windows 95 allows the application to send a print job to the printer subsystem, which then passes the job to a printer driver specifically designed for the printer in use. Unimodem does the same thing; it provides a single interface for any application requiring communication services. When an application wants to access a modem, it sends a packet or *communication job* to Unimodem. Unimodem then passes the packet off to the modem-specific driver.

Anytime you want to connect to a remote computer, you must keep three questions in mind. What type of server or host do you want to connect to, how will you connect with it, and what communication protocol will you use? Luckily, Windows 95 supports the majority of the options available. Better yet, Dial-Up Networking will negotiate with the host and automatically configure itself using the best set of options that both it and the host support.

Windows 95 supports the following remote-node servers:

▶ Windows 95 Dial-Up Server

▶ Windows NT 3.x RAS

▶ Novell NetWare Connect

▶ Microsoft LAN Manager Remote Access Servers

▶ Windows for Workgroups 3.x RAS (if you have the separate WFW RAS server installed)

▶ Shiva LanRover (and compatibles) dial-up router

▶ Third-party PPP and SLIP servers, including Internet access providers

NOTE   At the time this was written, Dial-Up Server support was removed from Windows 95. It will be provided as an add-on package in Microsoft Plus (see Chapter 32).

If you are like the vast majority of Windows 95 users, you will use standard modems to establish asynchronous connections over Plain Old Telephone Service (POTS)—residential and business phone lines. To accommodate users with additional requirements, Dial-Up Networking also supports:

▶ PBX modems

▶ Integrated Systems Digital Network (ISDN)

▶ Parallel port or null modem over a serial connection

Just as you have a choice of protocols when plugging directly into your local-area network, Dial-Up Networking can communicate with any of the following protocols:

▶ NetBEUI

▶ TCP/IP

▶ IPX/SPX

If your network has either an NT Server or NetWare server, Windows 95 will fully support user-based security, allowing you to grant different users varying levels of access to your computer and the rest of the network. If your server is running NT, Windows 95 additionally supports domain-trust relationships and centralized network security administration.

TIP   If you plan to dial into a computer running either Windows NT 3.x (Advanced) Server or Workstation, make sure the computer's owner or the network administrator has granted you dial-in access. When you first install Remote Access Services (RAS) it does not give dial-in privileges to anyone, not even the administrator. You can start up the RAS server and, unless you have explicitly granted someone dial-in rights, it will be useless.

Once you have connected to a remote computer, you can use any of its shared resources, be they files, printers, or other modems (for faxing), just as if you were in the same office building connected with Ethernet or Token Ring.

Besides the resources on the single computer you're dialed into, you may also use the services of any other computer in the workgroup (or the NT domain)—assuming you've been given access. In other words, if you dialed into your office computer from home, you could copy the files from any computer that your office computer can see or print a report on any printer your office desktop can access. You can, of course, restrict access to the rest of the network if you choose.

Setting Up Your Modem for Dial-Up Networking

As with all other hardware, Windows 95 provides a Wizard for installing your modem(s). You can activate it either through the Hardware Installation Wizard or by double-clicking on the Modems icon in the Control Panel. The following steps use the Hardware Installation Wizard:

1. If you have an external modem, make sure it is properly connected to your computer and turned on.

2. Open up the Control Panel by selecting it from the Start ➤ Settings menu.

3. Double-click on Add New Hardware.

4. This will bring up the Hardware Installation Wizard welcome screen. Select Next.

5. From the next screen, select Modem from the list of specific hardware, then press Next.

6. The next window asks you whether you want Windows 95 to automatically detect the modem type or select from a list of modems. I usually let Windows 95 try to detect the new modem, so go ahead and press Next. (This is the first screen you would have seen had you double-clicked on the Modems icon in the Control Panel.)

7. Once the Hardware Installation Wizard has finished, it will ask you to verify the modem type. If Windows 95 failed to detect your modem correctly, press the Change button and the Hardware Installation Wizard will take you to the window shown in Figure 28.1. If Windows 95 correctly identified your modem, which is usually the case, skip to step 11.

8. First, select the manufacturer of your modem. If it is not listed and you have an installation disk from the manufacturer, press the Have Disk button. If you do not have a disk, try using the Generic Modem driver appropriate for your modem speed. These drivers will work for most Hayes-compatible modems.

9. Next choose the specific model or modem speed.

10. Press OK.

11. Press Finish, and you are done.

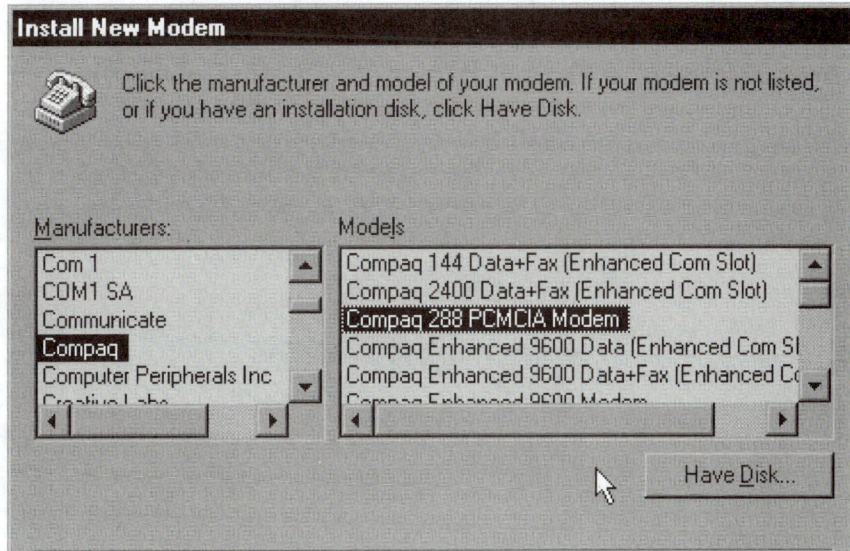

Install New Modem

Click the manufacturer and model of your modem. If your modem is not listed, or if you have an installation disk, click Have Disk.

Manufacturers:

- Com 1
- COM1 SA
- Communicate
- **Compaq**
- Computer Peripherals Inc
- Creative Labs

Models:

- Compaq 144 Data+Fax (Enhanced Com Slot)
- Compaq 2400 Data+Fax (Enhanced Com Slot)
- **Compaq 288 PCMCIA Modem**
- Compaq Enhanced 9600 Data (Enhanced Com Sl
- Compaq Enhanced 9600 Data+Fax (Enhanced Co
- Compaq Enhanced 9600 Modem

Have Disk...

Figure 28.1   Selecting a specific modem

> **NOTE** If you have a PCMCIA modem, you may find that Windows 95 installs a generic modem driver for it. This is because many modem manufacturers use modems designed by someone else.

Now that you have installed your modem, you can install and set up both a Dial-Up Networking client and server. The client allows you to dial into other computers. The server portion allows other computers to dial into yours.

Setting Up Dial-Up Networking on Your Computer

To install Dial-Up Networking, choose it when you install Microsoft Plus (see Chapter 32). Once you have the Dial-Up Networking component installed, you need to set it up.

1. Select Dial-Up Networking from the Start ➤ Programs ➤ Accessories menu. Alternatively, you can double-click on the Dial-Up Networking folder in My Computer. Either way, you get to the screen below.

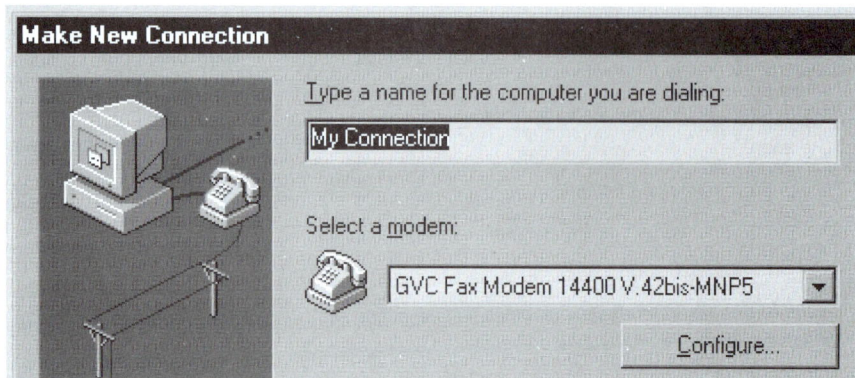

2. Give your connection a name, such as *Al's Desk in the East Wing*.

3. If you have more than one modem, select the modem you want to use.

4. Press Next. This leads you to the screen shown on the next page where you enter the particulars for this connection.

5. Enter the area code and phone number.

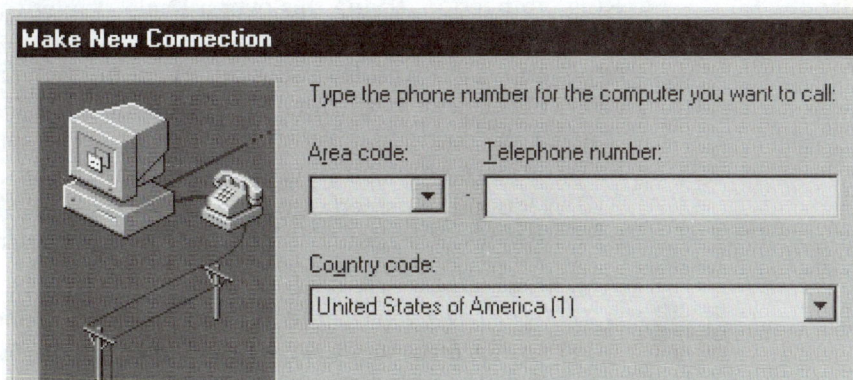

6. If necessary, change the country code.

7. Press Next.

8. You are now done. Verify the name and press Finish to save the connection.

Now that you have set up Dial-Up Networking, whenever you open up the Dial-Up Networking folder there will be two icons: the connection you just created—Al's Desk in the East Wing in my example—and Make New Connection. If you select this second icon, Windows 95 will use the same Wizard to lead you through setting up a connection to another remote-node server.

Now that you have Dial-Up Networking installed and configured, you can use the Dial-Up Networking client to dial into other computers. You are now ready for the next section where you will learn how to take full advantage of Dial-Up Networking.

Using Dial-Up Networking

As noted earlier, Dial-Up Networking allows you to leverage the near-universal reach of the phone system to extend your network to any location with a phone line. But just because you can, it does not mean you should. You will need to exercise some caution when using remote resources over a dial-up connection because your connection is much slower than a normal network connection. While you might not think twice about SUMing an XBase table (DBF) across a Token

Ring connection, trying this over a Dial-Up Networking link will produce a very disappointing performance. The same goes for starting up applications that reside on the remote computer. In both cases, the cause of the poor performance is the same: Dial-Up Networking must transfer the entire file over the phone link. For example, starting Fox-Pro from a remote computer requires the transfer of the entire 2.5-MB executable. Instead of taking a few seconds to load from a local hard disk, it takes about 20 minutes over a 14.4K modem connection.

> **TIP**   Whenever you want to run any application during a Dial-Up Networking session, make sure you have the application on your local hard drive *and* in your path. This will ensure that you run the local version and avoid passing the entire executable across the wire.

With Windows 95 you have three ways to establish a remote connection:

- explicit
- application initiated
- implicit

With an explicit connection, you must manually initiate the connection. As you might expect, an application-initiated connection is started by an application calling the remote-node software. As for implicit connections, Windows 95 starts these when it can find a resource neither locally nor on the physical network (i.e., via your network adapter card).

Explicit Connections

Connecting to a remote computer with an explicit connection is very similar to creating a RAS connection with Windows for Workgroups 3.11 or Windows NT.

When you create an explicit connection, you manually dial up the remote computer and log on. Once you have done this, the remote computer and all its share points show up in your Network Neighborhood.

You can manipulate these resources just as you would any other computer's resources—except that it's much slower.

To use Windows 95 Dial-Up Networking to explicitly connect to a remote computer:

1. Open up the Dial-Up Networking folder by selecting Dial-Up Networking from the Start ➤ Programs ➤ Accessories menu. Alternatively, find the Dial-Up Networking folder in My Computer and double-click on it.

2. Double-click on the icon you created in the previous section. This will bring up a dialog box like the one shown in Figure 28.2.

3. Enter the password, if any, for this resource. If you are connecting to a computer with user-based security, enter your log-in name and password.

4. Click on the Connect button.

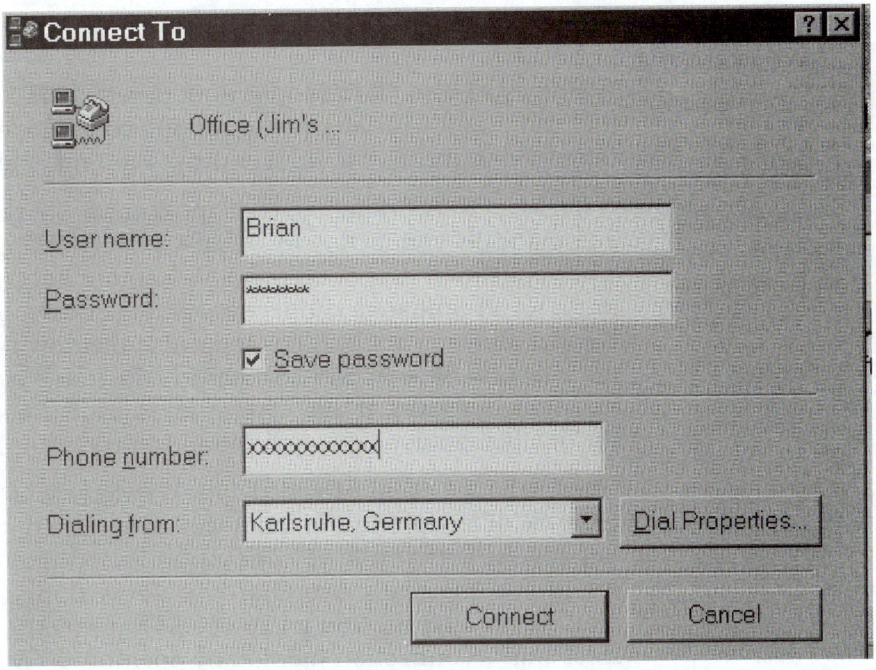

Figure 28.2 *Connecting to a remote network*

Windows 95 will now initiate a process that will result—if all goes well—in a connection to the remote computer. As the negotiation between the two computers progresses, Windows 95 gives you periodic updates to reassure you the process has not gone awry.

Now that you have manually initiated the connection, you will remain connected until you click on the Disconnect button or time out your session connection.

Application-Initiated Connections

Windows 95 also allows application developers to create programs that will establish Dial-Up Networking connections themselves rather than forcing the user to initiate the session manually.

A Dial-Up Networking-enabled application will take responsibility for automatically connecting to a Dial-Up Networking server as needed. The application uses Windows 95's Remote Access Session API to select a server, initiate a connection, and later disconnect the session. Besides allowing applications to initiate their own connections, the Remote Access Session API also reports the status back to the calling application. This way, if the server is unavailable for some reason (like the line being busy), the application can try again later.

The Exchange client provided with Windows 95 serves as an excellent example of an application that takes advantage of the Remote Access Session API. If you have configured Exchange for remote access, it will automatically use Dial-Up Networking to connect to your mail server anytime you try to access your mailbox. You can change Exchange's connection method by opening up Microsoft Exchange Profiles in the Control Panel and then selecting Properties ➤ Microsoft

Mail ➤ Properties ➤ Connection (for more information on Exchange, see Chapter 15). As soon as it is connected to the mail server, Exchange will send all your outgoing mail, retrieve any new messages, and then disconnect.

Implicit Connections

Establishing a Dial-Up Networking implicit connection to a remote computer is just like connecting to that same computer in the office—simply double-click on the network object. Depending on the type of object you clicked on, Windows 95 may try to automatically create an implicit Dial-Up Networking connection. Whenever you have Dial-Up Networking installed, the following circumstances will cause Windows 95 to establish an implicit connection:

▶ You double-click on a link pointing to a remote resource.

▶ You try to use a network resource while disconnected from a network.

▶ Either you or an application you are using specifies a resource using a Universal Naming Convention (UNC) name (i.e., *serve name\share point*), and Windows 95 cannot find it on the local-area network. Remember that Windows 95 references printers via their UNC names (*server name\printer name*), so printing to a remote printer will also trigger an implicit connection.

▶ You try reconnecting to a remote OLE object not located on the local network.

▶ An application tries to connect to a named pipe.

Whenever you try to access a resource either by directly double-clicking or through an application request, Windows 95 first tries to find it locally on your computer or out on your LAN. If it fails to locate the resource, Windows 95 gives you the dial-in dialog box shown in Figure 28.3, asking if you want to connect to the resource through Dial-Up Networking.

It then checks the Registry for the Dial-Up Networking entry for the server associated with the object. If it finds a server, it establishes the connection automatically. If it cannot find a server associated with the object, it prompts the user to either select the proper Dial-Up Networking connection for the object or to enter a new one, as shown

Part
5

Networking
with Windows 95

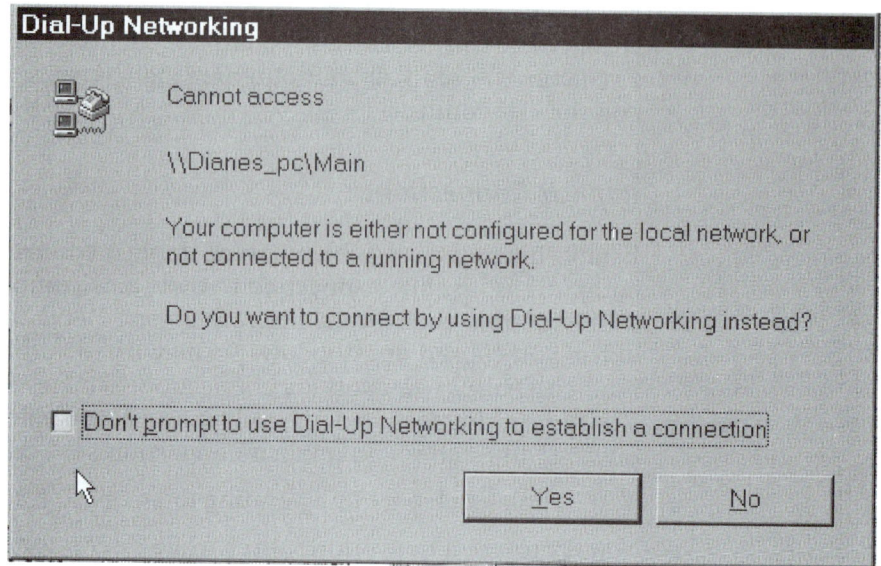

Figure 28.3 *Windows 95 asks the user if it should connect to a remote resource via Dial-Up Networking.*

below. With this information, Dial-Up Networking tries to establish a connection to the server.

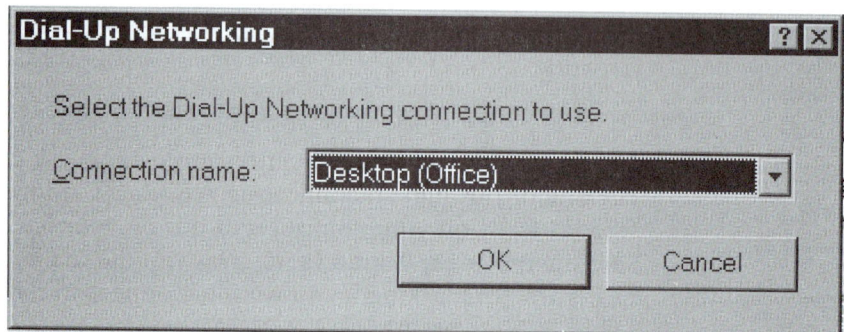

If it succeeds and successfully establishes a Dial-Up Networking connection, Windows 95 stores the name of the connector in the Registry so the next time you click on the object or enter its name in a File ➤ Open dialog box, it does not have to prompt you to select the server.

NOTE According to the documentation, when prompted for the name of a remote server, you can either select an existing server or enter a new one. (In the beta used to write this book, however, there is no means to enter a new server save for going back to the Dial-Up Networking folder and double-clicking on New Connection.)

Which of the three connection modes you use most often depends on the type of work you do. If you are a network manager and your job requires you to manage several remote networks, you will probably find yourself using explicit connections most often, as they give you the greatest amount of control over your remote session. Less technical users will probably rely on implicit connections because they are less hassle. Whether you use application-initiated connections depends on whether you purchase any remote-access–enabled applications. Even so, you might end up establishing the connections yourself rather than relying on the application to do it for you; this way, once you have a connection to a remote server, you can do several tasks online rather than having the enabled application simply hang up when it is done with the first task.

Advanced Configurations for Dial-Up Networking

In this section I will cover the advanced settings you will find most useful. When configuring Dial-Up Networking, there are three sets of parameters you can edit:

▶ dialing locations

▶ server type

▶ modem configurations

You can select a dialing location each time you establish a connection. Whenever you change locations, your location selection only remains in effect for that one connection. You set the other two parameters— server type and modem configuration—in the Connection property sheet. Any change you make there affects all subsequent connections to that server. Modem configuration is covered in Chapter 13.

Server Type

Changing the server type is the last of the Dial-Up Networking settings we will discuss. With the exception of ensuring you have the line speed set to the modem's maximum data rate, the Server Type options will have the greatest impact on the performance of Dial-Up Networking.

To bring up the Server Type Properties:

1. Open the Dial-Up Networking folder from My Computer.

2. Right-click on the connection you want and select Properties from the drop-down menu. This brings up the Dial-Up Networking Connection Properties box.

3. Select the modem whose Properties you wish to edit. Remember, Dial-Up Networking will use whichever modem you select to establish your connection. As with the Modem Configuration Properties, you can set the Server Type options on a per connection, per modem basis.

4. Click on the Server Type button to open up the dialog box shown in Figure 28.4.

As you can see, Windows 95 allows you to configure three properties:

Server Type: Windows 95 will connect to four types of Dial-Up Networking servers: NetWare Connect; Point-to-Point Protocol (PPP) servers such as Windows 95, Windows NT 3.5, and Internet access providers; Serial-Line Internet Protocol (SLIP) hosts; and Windows for Workgroups 3.x and Windows NT 3.1. By default, whenever Windows 95 establishes a Dial-Up Networking connection, it assumes the computer on the other end is a PPP server. If it isn't, Windows 95 cycles through the other three possibilities until it succeeds in making a connection or fails on all four. If you know the type of server to which you will connect (and you probably do), you will reduce connection time by selecting the proper type in this field. A warning, however: if you select the incorrect type of server, Windows 95 will not cycle through the other options. Rather, it will give up after trying your selection.

Enable software compression: As a rule, data compression will increase the effective data-transfer rate. These days, most modems support compression themselves, so you can have either the software (your computer) or the hardware (the modem) compress the data for you. For almost all types of data, software compression will

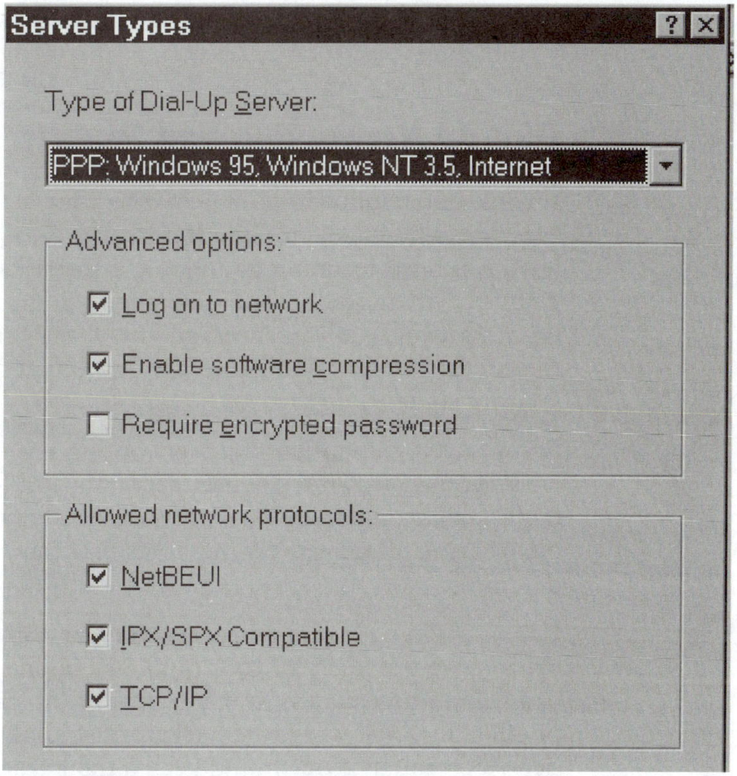

Figure 28.4   Editing the Server Type Properties

provide superior performance to hardware compression. As you probably know, data compression works through a pattern-recognition algorithm that reduces redundancies in the data. Because Windows 95 provides more memory for storing patterns than your modem, software compression has a better chance of recognizing complex patterns and thus of compressing the data as much as possible. The only time data compression does not increase performance—and in fact may reduce it—is when you transfer already highly compressed data such as ZIP files. If you plan to transfer ZIP files in a given Dial-Up Networking session, turn off software compression. Along the same lines, if you choose to use software compression, be sure to turn hardware compression off.

Require encrypted passwords: This is a security feature. By checking this box, Windows 95 will scramble your password as it transmits it across the phone lines so no one tapping your line can steal your password. (For additional information about

Dial-Up Networking and security, see the following section.) If you check this box, make sure the server can understand and decrypt the password.

Dial-Up Networking and Security

Whenever you allow dial-in access to your network, you open it up to everyone who has a modem. Before you set up a Dial-Up Networking host, you need to take a good look at the risks involved and design your security model to minimize them. Some network managers go so far as to forbid dial-up access to any of their machines, regardless of the circumstances. While this is a Draconian step, you do need to give security some thought.

Before setting up a Dial-Up Networking server, your first level of network security was not the user accounts and log-ins, but the more difficult hurdle of gaining physical access to your network. Dial-Up Networking effectively removes this first (and probably most effective) deterrent.

For a system with remote access, your first line of defense becomes the relative obscurity of your modem's phone number. Before anyone can gain remote access to your network (at least through the telephone lines), the would-be hacker must know your data phone number. Accordingly, you should keep a tight grasp on who knows this number. You cannot, however, keep your modem number a secret. Hackers can (and will) set their modems to dial every number in a given prefix just looking for modems.

The next level in your security model is supplied by the user accounts and passwords. Regardless of how open your company is with its data, instituting a policy of secure log-ins and passwords on any network is a good precaution. This becomes essential when physical access is no longer a requirement for logging onto your network.

You can add security to your network by using Dial-Up Networking's callback feature. When using a Windows 95 Dial-Up Networking server with the callback facility turned on, as soon as the server authenticates a user, Windows 95 drops the line. It then calls the user back at a prearranged phone number. The obvious advantage being that simply figuring out the modem number and guessing the log-in and password combination is not enough to gain access to your network. An unauthorized user must also be at the prearranged phone number.

This scenario also has an obvious drawback: It will not work for users, such as members of your sales force, who move around and thus do not have a consistent phone number. There is also a less obvious security hole: The phone system is not all that secure, and talented phone hackers (phreakers) can reroute a phone call to any location.

> **NOTE**   Many companies implement RAS callback features primarily as a means of controlling phone costs. Callback enables you to control who pays for the call and therefore provides a means of tracking costs. With callback, companies are able to centralize their telecommunications costs to one line (or a group of lines) so they can easily tell how much money they are spending to provide their free-spirited users with ready access to corporate resources. Additionally, callback allows them to route calls through the least-expensive channels available, whether it be WATS lines or lines purchased though a reseller.

On top of these security measures, you can use several third-party security devices such as random-number generators and encrypted-access modems with Dial-Up Networking to further bolster your security.

The best method for maintaining a secure environment is to regularly monitor your network's activity; not only the dial-in portion, but *all* activity. When you notice something unusual, such as repeated (yet unsuccessful) log-in attempts or abnormally high traffic at strange times, investigate it at once to find out the cause. While the answer may be simply an employee working late or someone who forgot their password, it may also be someone trying to break into your system.

Direct Cable Connect (DCC) Using a Serial or Parallel Port

When you installed the Dial-Up Adapter in your Control Panel ➤ Networks dialog box, you may not have realized that this same driver is used for both RAS and for Direct Cable Connect (DCC) support. Windows 95's DCC is a wonderful little feature that lets you have a fully operational network connection between any two PCs connected only by their serial (modem/mouse) ports or parallel (printer) ports.

If you find working over a RAS connection at 14.4K usable but still really slow, you may be pleasantly surprised at the networking performance DCC provides—considering you are not actually using a networking card. To be sure, RAS and DCC were designed for different uses, and each can be an ideal tool for the job, depending on the circumstances. RAS is great when you need to connect to a computer (or network) that is some distance away and your only connection can be via phone line or digital or leased line. DCC, on the other hand, is most helpful when you need a temporary network connection between two PCs where one or both of them do not have network interface cards installed.

If you're one of the growing numbers of laptop users, you probably appreciate having the mobility of the laptop but still find times when you could really use a $5\frac{1}{4}$-inch floppy drive, or a CD-ROM drive, or just wish you could copy files up to the network or down to your laptop faster than with floppies. Using DCC, you can very easily and quickly connect that laptop to any other computer running Windows 95 as long as you have either a serial-to-serial or a parallel-to-parallel cable designed for data transfer between two computers (LapLink-style cables). There's a place near where I live that sells nice, long parallel cables for only $5, and if you find a similar deal, I'd recommend buying at least a few. Leave one cable connected to a parallel port on your desktop PC at home and another at the office, and when you go on trips with your laptop, pack a cable along with it. It is really a joy to simply connect the cable to the printer port on your laptop, start DCC on both PCs, and within seconds actually have a network connection, allowing you to access any shared resources on whichever PC is configured as the host.

The first thing you will need to do to set DCC up on your system, if you haven't done so already, is add the Dial-Up Adapter driver to your list of network components. Just open My Computer ➤ Control Panel ➤ Networks, click on Add, click on Adapter, select Microsoft, and select Dial-Up Adapter. Click on OK, and you're all set. To start up the DCC applet, look in your Accessories folder or click on Start ➤ Programs ➤ Accessories, then choose Direct Cable Connect.

When you start up DCC for the first time, it will ask you to select whether this PC will be configured as a Guest or Host PC, as shown in Figure 28.5. Usually it makes sense to make your desktop PC the host and the laptop the guest, but remember that the guest PC is the

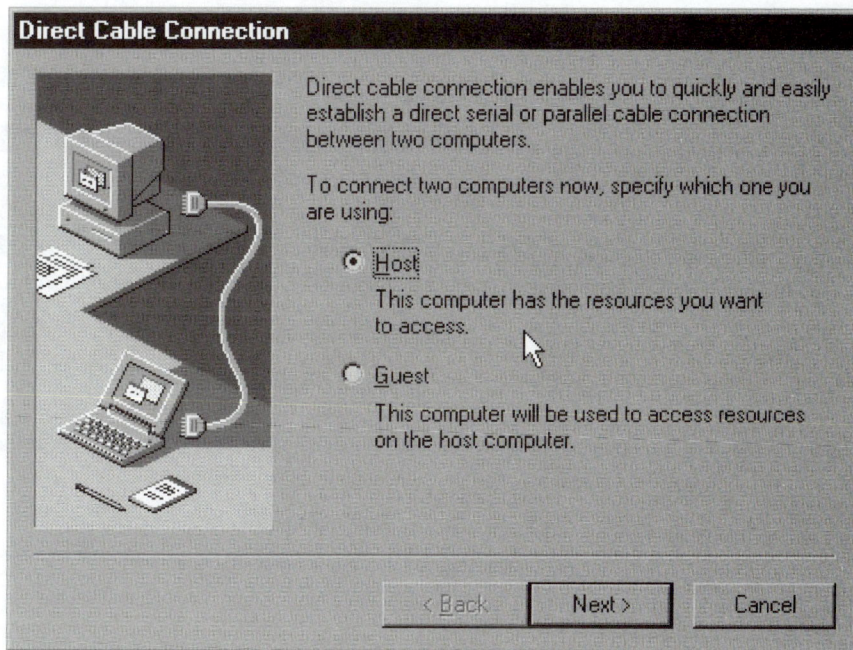

Figure 28.5   *Configure one PC as Host, the other as Guest. The guest PC is the one that will access the host PC's shared resources.*

one that will need to use the folders, drives, and/or printers located (and shared) on the host PC. Also, if one PC happens to be on a network, you might want that one to be the host because it will allow the guest to access any resources the host normally can.

Finally, you have to select which port you want to use with DCC (see Figure 28.6). If at all possible, you want to use a parallel port. Not only is it quite a bit faster, it will also usually be easier to find an available parallel port on the computers you'll be connecting to.

> **TECH TIP**   One time I was installing DCC, no parallel ports showed up in the ports list. After checking out my Device Manager list in Control Panel ➤ Devices, I discovered that the parallel port was disabled because it conflicted with a sound card. After reconfiguring the sound card to a different IRQ, the printer port showed up in DCC's list of available ports.

Part 5

Networking with Windows 95

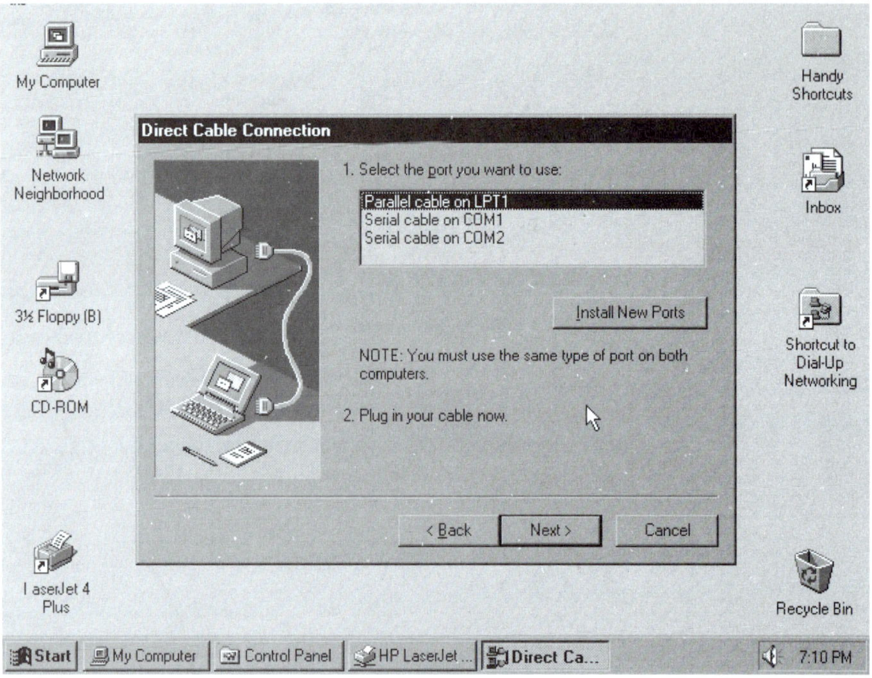

Figure 28.6 *Configuring DCC to use a parallel port. Note that both PCs will need to be using the same type of port (either serial or parallel).*

Now that you've configured one PC, you need to do the same on the other one, of course making sure you choose the same port type (either serial or parallel), and set one PC to Host and the other to Guest. Then, connect your cable between the two ports, click on Listen on the host PC, and click on Connect on the guest PC. After a few seconds, you should see a message similar to this:

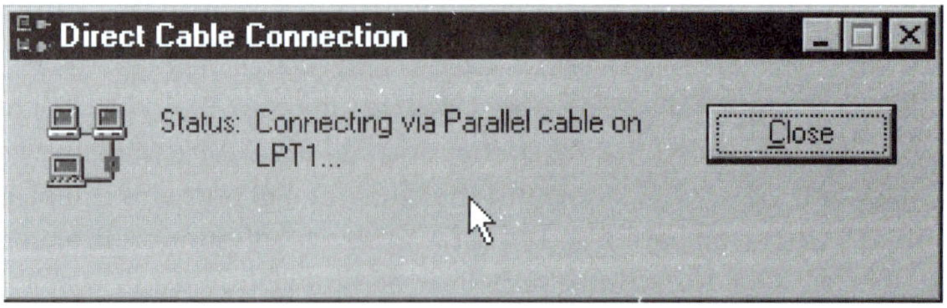

If you've entered a password (on both sides), you will next see *Verifying user id and password*, and then the connection will be established. Once the connection has been established, you can minimize the DCC status dialog box on both PCs to get them out of the way.

At this point, you will be able to access the host PC from Network Neighborhood and thus can map drives, install a printer driver corresponding to any printers on the host side, and so on—just like we did back in Chapter 26 while setting up the peer network.

TIP   If you will be using DCC frequently on a particular PC, you may want to drag the DCC icon onto your Desktop for easy access. Or, if you prefer, drag and drop the DCC icon onto your Start button; the next time you click on Start, you will have DCC as one of the Start menu options.

By now you should have a good understanding of the many options Windows 95 gives you for interconnecting (networking) your computers. In the next chapter I'll discuss troubleshooting.

Chapter 29

Troubleshooting Your Windows 95 Network

Featuring

Diagnosing cable problems

Diagnosing NIC and driver problems

Restoring from a downed hard drive

What to do if your system can't boot

Aside from reducing your system bottlenecks, running backups, and dealing with daily user issues—such as creating new accounts, setting up new stations, adding servers, and so on—much of a network administrator's time is typically spent fixing various network problems. In this chapter, I will look first at the process of troubleshooting network problems, then step through several of the most frequent types of problems and show how to resolve them. At the end of this chapter, I'll discuss some procedures for getting a Windows 95 station back into operation after a hard-drive failure.

Not only are networking problems sometimes difficult to track down, they also typically require a quick resolution because frequently a network problem means downtime for one or more network users. When you first learn of a problem, it helps to assign it a priority by taking into account criteria such as the following:

▶ How many users are (or will be) affected?

▶ What type of work (emergency, critical, or lower priority) is affected?

▶ How difficult does the problem appear to be?

▶ Does the problem have a known solution (at your organization) or are you dealing with something new?

Part 5

> **TIP** It is a very good policy to always log problems as they occur. Include the time and date, who reported the problem, initial prognosis, and estimated time to resolution. And, most importantly, be sure to add a detailed description both of the problem and the steps taken to fix the problem. While such a log requires a certain time (and discipline) investment, it can pay off significantly the next time a problem occurs. Be sure to make frequent backups of your log—including regular printed copies. (Keeping it on the computer gives you the ability to do quick searches.)

Dealing with networking problems—and with computer problems in general—is largely a matter of deduction, eliminating possibilities through questioning, trial and error, and adverting to past experience. This is why keeping a problem-and-resolution log can be so effective. If someone else is reporting the problem to you, write down what they say and ask questions while the situation is still fresh in their memory. Almost always, the first thing you should ask is, "When was the last time this equipment, software, or whatever, worked correctly?"

The second most helpful question to ask—assuming someone else is explaining the problem to you—is, "What were you doing when you noticed the problem?" (Avoid giving this question an accusatorial tone—you just want to know what led to the problem.) Besides helping to narrow your focus, these questions sometimes point you directly to the root cause of the problem. Sometimes, for example, users will try tightening the keyboard or mouse cables and end up loosening the network cable. Perhaps they turned off the computer without first shutting down. About half the time, the problem was caused by operator error, but if so, rather than chastising the user, show them how to avoid this problem in the future. As much as you may enjoy using computers, don't forget that to some users, they are probably a mystery and even an object of fear. Try to pass on your appreciation of computers whenever possible. A thorough and positive introduction to the computer and occasional user training can go a long way toward eliminating accidental damage to cables, keyboards, and other hardware and software.

Troubleshooting is also helped by having a good memory (or a good set of notes). When was the software on this station upgraded? Which network adapter (and drivers) is it using? When was this cable run? Again, knowing what to look for greatly reduces the number of possibilities you need to look at.

Certain applications may indirectly cause extra troubles for your organization. Maybe an older communications program insists on using an earlier version of Winsock, thus conflicting with Windows 95's built-in version of Winsock. Perhaps some application is opening files in exclusive mode, preventing other users from opening the same file.

Has a new piece of hardware or software recently been added to the station? If so, this is a good place to start looking. Until every system is fully Plug-and-Play aware and has only Plug-and-Play components installed, interrupt and I/O address conflicts will be an ongoing source of problems. The best weapons against such conflicts are these: using identical hardware for all workstations, using the same interrupts and I/O addresses for the same devices in each workstation as much as possible, documenting the card settings on a sheet of paper taped inside each computer, and lastly, making use of a POST (power-on self test) diagnostics card. Such a card fits into the bus of a problem PC and can perform a large array of tests on the computer, reporting the results via LEDs on the card. The Discovery Card from

JDR Microdevices costs about $99 and can find IRQ- and DMA-related conflicts, while a more complex card may cost $1,200 to $1,500 and can identify all devices set to the same IRQ, bad SIMMs, errors on the motherboard, as well as problems with the power supply, serial and parallel ports, and so on. Such errors might otherwise take half a day or longer to diagnose, besides the productivity time wasted while the system is down. I have seen completely configured systems delivered with two serial ports configured to the same address, a network card conflicting with video memory, and even two parallel port adapters, both configured to LPT1, in the same PC. Obviously whoever configured these systems was not using a POST diagnostics card.

For the rest of this chapter, I'll look at some of the most common problems that can plague your Windows 95 network and how you can resolve them most efficiently.

Diagnosing Cable Problems

One of the nicest things about star-topology networks (such as 10BaseT) is the relative ease of diagnosing and fixing cable problems. If all stations on a particular hub suddenly lose their network connection, you should check out your hub. Check the connection from the hub to the server, in particular—assuming you have a dedicated server. If none of the cable connections have pulled loose, try swapping in a different hub. If the stations now connect to the network again, you've found the problem. You can see the practicality of keeping a spare hub around—ideally one identical to what's in use so you can immediately replace the hub if it ever becomes necessary. For diagnostic purposes though, even a hub with a small number of ports lets you try connecting a few stations. If it works, you know there's a problem with the other hub.

On a network using thin coax, however, things are a bit more hairy. First of all, it's much more likely for the whole segment to go down, because of the nature of the connection. Typically what you'll have to do then is perform *binary searching* for the location of the cable break by splitting the network segment in half, seeing which half still works when you connect it to the server, then splitting the bad subsegment in half and repeating this process until you locate the offending cable portion.

On a thin-net coax network, some additional things you'll want to check include making sure the terminators are still connected to each end and that one end is properly grounded, and verifying that the complete length of cable has the same RG number. I have seen strange connection problems surface only months later, and then only intermittently, when someone used a length of cable somewhere in the network that had slightly different impedance than the rest of the network cable.

When single stations lose their connection on a star-type configuration, again the problem-solving process is much easier. The first thing to do (obvious, but frequently effective) is to check that both ends of the cable are connected tightly. If this doesn't take care of the problem, try connecting the hub end of the cable to a different jack on the hub.

NOTE   One thing I really appreciate about Windows 95 and NT is their ability to auto-reconnect when a connection is temporarily broken. This may seem like a small thing, but it's nice not to have to reboot the station each time; I can just double-click on Network Neighborhood or reopen a folder on a network drive.

If you still aren't able to establish a connection, try whichever of these is less trouble: either swap in a different cable or connect a different PC to the end of the existing cable (use a PC known to have no trouble getting on the network). Using these two tests, you can determine either that the cable is bad (if the new cable worked or the new PC did not) or that the original PC has a network-card problem (if the new PC worked, but the new cable did not work with the original PC). If you determine that the cable is the problem, you might try replacing the cable connector if you are adept at this and think it's a quicker solution than running a new length of cable.

Finally, if you are able to connect to the network, but transferring data across the network seems slow as molasses, you are likely dealing with an inferior quality (or damaged) network cable. Remember, nowadays you want level 5 cable, if possible (and at least level 3); otherwise, you can expect all sorts of problems with throughput on your network.

Diagnosing Network Interface Card (NIC) and Driver Problems

If you have reason to believe a network card may not be functioning properly, here are several things you can try in the order in which you'll most likely want to try them. First, if Windows 95 is already running, go into Control Panel ➤ Networks and check that all network components that should be installed actually are. If not, add them, shut down and restart Windows 95, and again try to get on the network. If this doesn't work, then just to get everything working, you could remove any network (software) components other than these three:

▶ the driver for the installed network card

▶ the protocol(s) you need to get on the network

▶ the appropriate client service (for example, Client for NetWare Networks or Client for Microsoft Networks)

The most important thing is to verify that the card settings match those configured on the driver. To do this, double-click on the card driver (while looking at the installed–network-components list). This should bring up the network card's Properties dialog box (see Figure 29.1). Click on the Resources tab and verify that the settings are correct. Also write down these settings in case you need to pull your network card later to verify that its settings correspond to these.

Another common problem is that the memory-address settings required by the adapter card are not excluded from use by the expanded memory manager. In our example above we would also want to make sure that the `DEVICE=EMM386.EXE` line in `config.sys` also included an `X=E000-E3FF` entry. Otherwise the expanded memory manager would map the NIC memory address to be used as upper memory and could cause connectivity problems. As a quick and easy test to determine an upper memory block (UMB) problem, comment out the expanded memory manager in `config.sys`. This can be accomplished by placing a REM statement in front of the `DEVICE=EMM386.EXE` if using Microsoft's expanded memory manager or `DEVICE=QEMM386.SYS` if using Quarterdeck's QEMM.

**Part
5**

Networking
with Windows 95

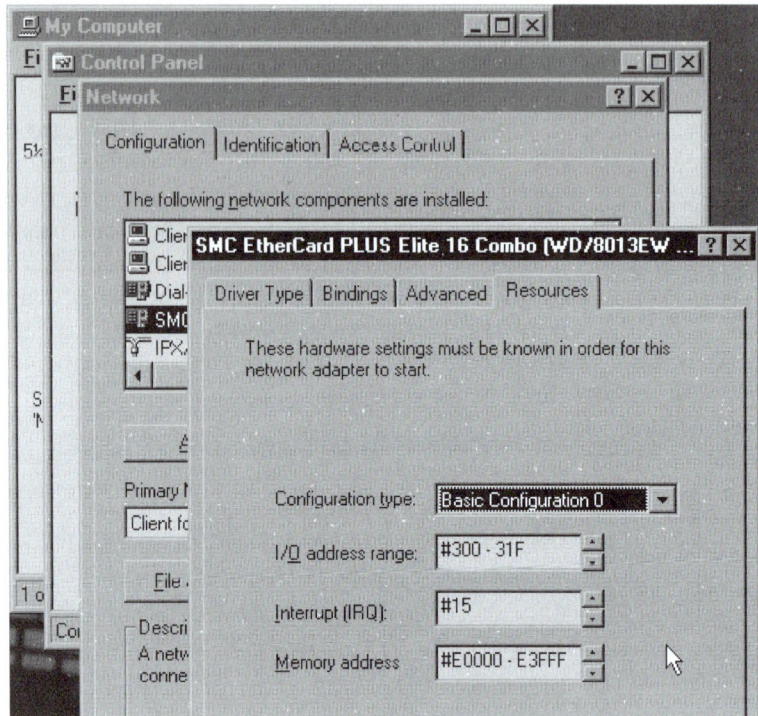

Figure 29.1 *Verifying and configuring network-card settings*

Next, click on the Driver Type tab. In almost all cases, you'll want the first radio button, *Enhanced mode (32 bit and 16 bit) NDIS driver*, selected—the only reason you ever need real-mode drivers is if you happen to be using a network card for which you cannot find Windows 95 protected-mode drivers or if you want to test network-connectivity problems. For instance, when attempting to solve a connectivity problem, you can install an NDIS 2.0 (real-mode) driver, boot Windows 95 to a command prompt, then try and log onto the network with a **NET LOGON** command. If that works, but the NDIS 3.1 (protected-mode) driver failed, you have at least identified the problem and can begin troubleshooting the protected-mode driver installation. In any case, make sure the setting matches what you need. Also, click on the Bindings tab and verify that a check mark is placed next to the protocol(s) you will need to get on your network.

If you notice any incorrect settings, after changing these you will next want to restart Windows 95 and see if you are now able to connect to the network. Otherwise, the next thing I'd recommend doing is printing out a handy list of equipment and resource settings, which can be done by going to Control Panel ➤ System ➤ Devices and clicking on Print.

If your network card is one that lets you software-configure the IRQ and I/O address, open a DOS window and run this software now. If the settings match what they should be, good. Otherwise, adjust them accordingly.

> **NOTE** Some cards that let you run a software-configuration utility also have one or more jumper settings that need to be set to enable this feature. If your card is like this, you may find your configuration software will not work: either it won't run at all, or when you try to make changes, they won't stick. In this case, refer to your card's documentation for information on enabling the software-configuration option.

Part 5

If your network card is not software configurable, you'll need to remove the network card to visually inspect it and possibly make changes to it. Again, first print out the system summary report, as it will definitely be helpful in setting your card. Next, shut down Windows 95, turn off the PC and unplug it, remove the PC's cover, and take out the network card. If you're lucky, the network card will have the jumper settings silk-screened near the jumper pads. Otherwise, dredge up your card's documentation and flip to the jumper-settings diagram. Verify that the settings match what your driver is configured to. If not, make changes to the jumpers.

Networking with Windows 95

> **NOTE** If your network-card settings match your network-driver settings and you are *still* not able to connect to the network, it's likely either the IRQ or I/O address conflicts with another card. In this case, refer to your system-configuration report and select a different (unused) IRQ and I/O address for your network card.

When you've got your network card configured, gently reinstall it and tighten down the edge bracket with a screw. Replace the PC's cover (you don't want to replace all the screws holding the cover just yet—wait until your network card is verified operational). Then turn the computer back on and make any changes to the network-card driver to synch it with the changes you've made to the card. If you're prompted to shut down and restart Windows 95, do so.

NOTE When attempting to get network support operational, you may want to start Windows 95 in *safe mode with networking support*. This disables other drivers that may conflict with your network card, reducing the number of factors that can interfere with initially connecting with the network. To boot Windows 95 in this mode, press the F6 key when the computer is first starting (when you see the Starting Windows 95 prompt), before you see the logo screen. (Alternatively, you can press F8, then select Safe Mode with Network Support.)

If you've got any patience left, and you're *still* not able to talk to the network at this point (you're probably a saint!), you might try swapping this network card into a PC that is talking to the network—and perhaps swap that PC's card into the problem PC. This, finally, will tell you one way or another what you need to know. Either the NIC from the bad PC will now work in the good PC, meaning there's still a conflict with another card in the bad PC, or the bad card will also refuse to work in the good PC. If it's a conflict, start removing other cards from the bad PC one by one, bringing up Windows 95 after each time, until you're able to get back on the network. If you're with a large-enough organization to have a POST diagnostic card, you will have put it to use before now, I am sure. Otherwise, you'll be wishing you had one at this point.

If you continue to have no success after futzing with IRQs and I/O addresses some more, try installing a different network card, preferably from a different vendor. If the first card was a jumpered card, do yourself a favor and try a newer card. By the time you're reading this, just about any new network card should at least be software configurable, if not fully Plug-and-Play. Just choose one of the top five or six brands, and you should be up and running again in no time. If not, your problems are way outside the scope of this book and you certainly deserve a prize of some sort for having come this far.

Restoring from a Downed Hard Drive

When you have a station that has undergone a disk crash or for other reasons has damaged system files, you will likely find the system refuses to get further than the initial logo screen before issuing an error message and then hanging at the system prompt. Of course the ideal thing at this point is to simply restore the system files from those back-ups you make every night. Here are the files you will need most if you need to restore from a damaged drive:

From the root directory of the boot drive:

▶ config.sys (if used)

▶ autoexec.bat (if used)

▶ io.sys (hidden, read only, system)

▶ msdos.sys (hidden, read only, system)

▶ command.com

From the \Windows directory (the directory where Windows 95 is installed):

▶ win.ini

▶ system.ini

▶ protocol.ini

NOTE   These next two are the most important (or the most likely to be damaged).

▶ user.dat (hidden, system)

▶ system.dat (hidden, system)

Try booting Windows 95 using the boot menu and selecting Safe Mode. To bring up the boot menu, press the F8 key while the system is first booting. The first thing I usually try running is the *logged to file* option, which tries starting Windows 95 again normally and also creates a file in the Windows 95 directory called BOOTLOG.TXT, which shows each step as it's trying to boot.

NOTE   If BOOTLOG.TXT isn't in your Windows 95 directory, look in the root directory of the boot drive. If you find it here, it will be marked as a hidden file.

If your system fails again while starting Windows 95, reboot, select *System Prompt only*, go into the Windows 95 directory, and check BOOTLOG.TXT for clues to why Windows wouldn't start. If this doesn't help, try booting using Safe Mode. As a last resort, try booting using *safe mode with command prompt only*. This will at least let you try the following technique.

TECH TIP   When a Windows 95 station will not start Windows 95, the single most likely way to get the station up again fast is to go to the directory Windows 95 is installed in (usually \Windows or \Win95), run attrib -s -h on SYSTEM.* and USER.*, and then make a backup of SYSTEM.DAT and USER.DAT. Finally, copy SYSTEM.DA0 to SYSTEM.DAT, and USER.DA0 to USER.DAT. What this does is restore the backup copies of the system Registry files. If you're lucky, rebooting after doing this will allow you to get back into Windows 95.

If you still cannot get Windows 95 to start, and you've tried replacing the Registry files SYSTEM.DAT and USER.DAT from the backups automatically made by Windows 95, it's looking rather grim. You need to start thinking about reinstalling Windows 95. If you do have a recent full-system backup, try restoring all the files from the Windows 95 directory and all directories under it. If restoring from a backup won't work, your best bet is to dust off your Windows 95 CD-ROM or disks and run the install again.

TIP   If you are only able to boot to a system prompt, do not have a CD-ROM drive locally attached, but have been (up 'til now) part of a network and using an NDIS 2.0 (real-mode) network driver, try going into the Windows 95 directory and typing NET START WORKSTATION. With luck, this will get you on the network and allow you to copy the Windows 95 install files from some other station on the network that *does* have a CD-ROM drive. Of course, you will need to have sufficient disk space (around 35 MB) available, plus space for installing Windows again.

> **TIP**   For those systems on your network that can afford 30-some MB of disk space better than they can afford to be down for some time, copy the contents of the **\Win95** install directory from your CD-ROM or diskettes into a unique directory on the hard drive and then reinstall from this directory if you ever need to reinstall Windows 95. You will find this to be noticeably faster than even the fastest CD-ROM drives. And if you want to save even more time, look at creating a setup script file so you can run the reinstall without any prompting for options. (This is an advanced option; you will need to run the NetSetup program, click on Make Script, and then set all the options as you would normally set them interactively.)

When reinstalling Windows 95, first try installing to the same directory you originally installed to. This usually works fine and will let you keep most of your system settings (assuming they haven't been damaged).

What to Do If You Cannot Even Boot to a System Prompt

While rather rare, it is possible to have your system in such a state that it won't even boot but says *invalid system* or some such message. Before taking the extreme measure of reformatting your drive, try booting with the Windows 95 start-up disk you made during setup. If you don't have one of these, go to another station on the network and make one. In case you're not familiar with the process, open Control Panel ➤ Add/Remove Programs, click on the Startup Disk tab, and click on the Create Disk button (after inserting a blank diskette).

Once you've booted with the Windows 95 start-up diskette and are at the command prompt, do the following:

1. Change to the System directory, which is under the Windows 95 directory.

2. Copy the file sys.com to your Windows 95 start-up diskette.

3. Switch to drive A (or B if appropriate) and type **SYS C:**—this should allow your hard drive to at least boot to a Windows 95 command prompt.

4. Remove the diskette and attempt to reboot system.

5. If Windows 95 doesn't start normally, reboot and use the Safe Mode with command prompt only.

At this point, follow the above instructions for restoring the SYS-TEM.DAT and USER.DAT Registry files. If this doesn't work, read the above section about reinstalling Windows 95.

Ideally, you are reading this before any troubles arise and can see some ways to practice preventive medicine, such as keeping an extra hub, cables, and network cards handy for quick replacements in time of failure. You may realize that it makes more sense to use several smaller hubs rather than one or two large ones. And I'm sure you can now better see the utility of making Windows 95 start-up diskettes and regular backups of the system Registry files.

Customizing and Traveling with Windows 95

6

Chapter 30

Using Your Laptop with Windows 95

FEATURING

An increasing premium is being placed on portability in the computing arena. Whether you are a traveling salesperson, writer, programmer, teacher, student field scientist, or corporate manager, the freedom that portable computing affords in achieving your goals is hard to rival. As a freelance writer, I've been an advocate of portable computing since its inception. The idea of being chained to a desk is tantamount to incarceration—merely an extension of the oppressive office cubicle that I quit my nine-to-five job years ago to escape.

I went portable as soon as the first viable mobile computer hit the streets sometime about ten years ago. It was the Radio Shack Model-100. With its puny 8-line display (and only 40 characters wide at that) and performance-challenged programs, it wasn't much to write home about. On the other hand, at least you *could* write home *with* it. You could even write home via *e-mail*, using the built-in 300-bps modem and the free CompuServe starter account that came with the machine.

Portable-computing technology has come a long way since then; experts estimate that at the end of 1995, 33 percent of PC computing will be performed on mobile machines. Nowadays a clear majority of PC sales are of the mobile variety. The competition is fierce, the technical developments rapid. Thanks to the feeding frenzy, the last year has brought us high-capacity lithium-ion batteries, 28.8-Kbps cellular modems, a wide array of PCMCIA cards, impressive display panels (that we'll also benefit from as flat-screen TVs), Plug-and-Play cards and computers, miniature pointing devices such as the "eraser head" and the GlidePoint, portable CD-ROM drives, and tiny high-capacity backup devices, just to name a few.

Windows 95 and Portable Computing

So, as a laptop or potential laptop user, what special goodies does Windows 95 have to offer you? Recognizing that computers are leaving the desktop in droves, Windows 95 doesn't just offer a few add-ons for portable users, such as a version of LapLink or specialized LCD color schemes. Much of the overall design concept of Windows 95 was influenced by portable computing needs and the desire of portable computer owners to stretch their (considerable) investment beyond the point of the forced obsolescence that rapid technological evolution often causes.

The basic advantages of running Windows on a portable are obvious: If you have a laptop with enough disk space on it, simply being able to run Windows 95 and your favorite programs anywhere you go is quite benefit enough. Many portable users are rarely in the office or have no office at all, so simply having the use of a computer, however crippled its performance, is terrific. But beyond that, consider some additional mobile abilities of Windows 95:

▶ You can plug and unplug your PCMCIA cards, serial mice, and pointing devices without rebooting Windows. The changes are detected and the correct drivers activated. (You can't plug or unplug bus mice or PS/2 mice, however.)

▶ Have a PCMCIA fax modem? From your hotel-room phone jack you can send and receive e-mail and faxes, surf the Internet, or, using RAS, log onto the network back at your office.

▶ Got a cable to connect your cellular phone to your fax modem? Then do all the above from the beach rather than your hotel room.

▶ If your laptop has a built-in or portable CD-ROM drive, you'll really be in hog heaven. You can run Myst on the beach in Bora Bora. Windows has built-in SCSI drivers to work with most portable CD-ROM drives.

▶ Have a docking station? Windows 95 reconfigures itself appropriately the moment you insert or remove the portable from its docking station, taking best advantage of what's in it.

▶ You can use Drive Space, Stacker, and DOS 6.x-compatible disk compression to double the size of your portable's hard disk.

▶ You can use Advanced Power Management (APM) to wring the most performance out of your battery.

▶ You'll be able to keep files on your desktop and laptop computers synchronized so the most up-to-date files are on the computer you're working on.

▶ You can transfer files between computers quickly via parallel or serial cable and the *direct-cable connect* program.

▶ You can send a file to print from programs even when no printer is available or attached. When you find a printer, your print jobs are all queued up, ready to print.

Notice that all these points fall into one of three general categories: squeezing more out of your hardware, staying connected to the world, and keeping your work organized.

Several of the points listed above are discussed in these other chapters:

▶ For coverage of e-mail, faxing, and Microsoft Exchange, see Part III.

▶ For coverage of the direct-cable connection for transferring files and connecting to the network, see Part V.

▶ For coverage of remote-access services with Dial-Up Connection, see Part V.

▶ For coverage of the disk-compression program, see Chapters 23 and 33.

Power Management with APM

In Chapter 7, I referred to the Power applet in the Control Panel. This applet is for managing the way your laptop uses power. Microsoft and Intel worked together to develop something called APM (Advanced Power Management) to help stretch rundown times on laptop batteries. Windows 95 implements APM version 1.1. The extent to which APM is successful depends on the design of the computer, which CPU it's running (such as whether it's an SL chip or not), whether the hard disk and screen can power down, and so forth. Many laptops have built-in utilities that you run to set up such energy-saving features. Also, because the way energy-saving features are implemented varies from machine to machine, most portables these days come with a custom version of APM designed for them. On some machines, a line in the config.sys file such as

```
devicehigh=c:\dos\apm.sys
```

loads the APM driver so power management is activated. Only APM version 1.0 is loaded this way. If you have such a line, leave it there. It's important.

Some computers (such as many from Toshiba) have APM built into their BIOS chip. In this case, you don't have to have your config.sys load APM for you. In fact, if you try to load APM, you'll get an error message saying your computer has APM built in.

The Power applet's options will vary depending on your computer, the type of processor, and APM. Suffice it to say, however, that you'll probably have a few options to choose from. Figure 30.1 shows the applet's dialog box:

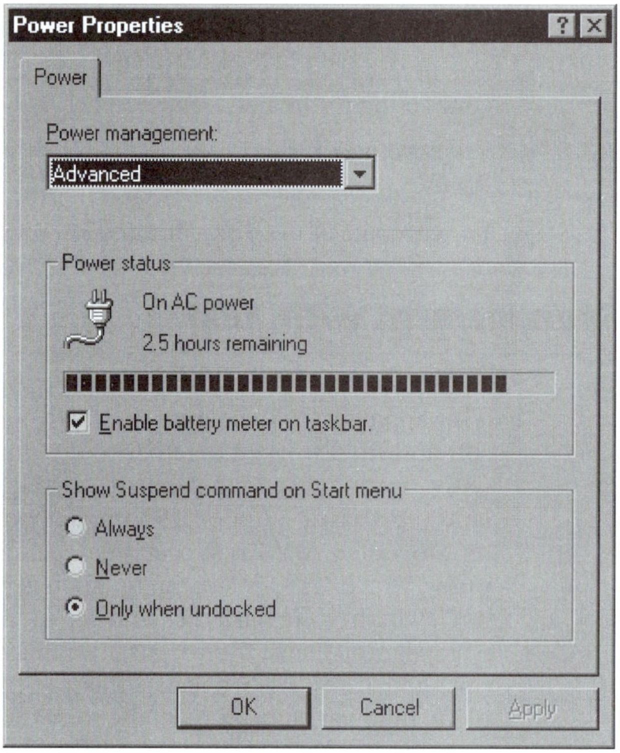

Figure 30.1   *The Power applet in the Control Panel brings up this dialog box from which you can change some settings pertaining to your laptop's power-conservation features.*

The gas gauge is particularly useful if your computer doesn't have another means of informing you of the state of the computer's battery (only laptops with voltage- and current-sensing circuitry will have such a gauge).

Tip You can also open the Power dialog box by double-clicking on the battery or AC-plug in the *system tray,* which is at the right side of the Taskbar.

Let's take the settings one at a time.

Power Management The first setting offers a drop-down list from which you choose the type of power management you want active. The options are Advanced, Standard, and Off. Choose Advanced to take advantage of special power-conservation features built into Windows 95. The Standard setting simply uses whatever conservation features you have built into your computer. The Off option deactivates any and all power-saving features of Windows 95.

> **NOTE** The settings you make in this dialog box don't affect your computer's internal hardware settings. They only affect the degree to which Windows 95 detects any power-saving features of your computer that you've activated. See your computer's manual for instructions on how to adjust such features. For example, for the greatest battery efficiency, you'll still have to use the switches or software utilities that turn on various power-down features.

Normally, you'll want to use Advanced. Windows does some spiffy power-management tricks such as putting a Suspend option on the Start button (see Chapter 3). On some computers, the Shut Down command actually powers off the computer for you without having to touch a switch (having Windows perform the shut-down procedure can prevent data loss and can correctly power down peripheral devices such as PCMCIA cards). Finally, the accuracy of the battery meter is enhanced.

When would you want to turn APM off? Well, some energy-saving features can be annoying. Particularly when you are plugged into the wall outlet, there will be times when you won't want your screen's backlight to turn off or hard disk to power down. You may always want the CPU running at full speed (another trick APM does is to power down the CPU, ports, and keyboard after a period of inactivity). Some computers sense when you're plugged into the wall and then run full bore. Others use a switch or keyboard combination that allows you to manually set conservation options on the fly. You might want to check your computer's manual on how it uses APM and what your options are.

Power Status Here's your gas gauge, showing remaining battery time. When the option box is turned on, the battery icon (AC plug icon) appears on the Taskbar. Just position the mouse pointer on the little

Part

Customizing Windows 95

Taskbar icon and wait a second. The remaining battery time will display. On some machines the setting will display a percentage instead of time.

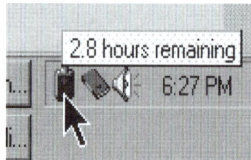

Suspend Options   If your computer supports this feature, there will be a Suspend option at the bottom of the Start Button, just above Shut Down.

As I mentioned in Chapter 3, this option lets you quickly put the computer into a hibernation state, then pick up where you left off when you power up the computer again. It's a terrific feature. However, not all computers will support it; even if yours does, make sure you save any work before you suspend just in case your laptop's battery runs down before you resume your work. If you leave the computer plugged into the AC outlet, this isn't an issue, obviously.

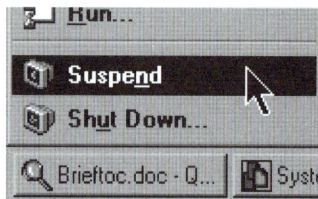

The three options in the Power dialog box pertaining to Suspend let you choose when the Suspend option will appear on the Start button's menu. Normally, this is set to *Only when undocked.* When the computer is docked, suspending it might not work because any cards and other jazz you might have hooked up to in the docking station may not come back to life when you restart the computer. When docked, just as with desktop machines, save your documents, close your applications, choose Shut Down, and then turn off your computer the normal way.

Using PCMCIA Cards

Great strides in miniaturization in the past year or two have brought us plug-in cards that are no larger than a credit card. Soon to be gone are the days when add-in cards require a toolbox and the nerve to dig inside your PC, where you wind up with little puncture wounds on your fingertips from the metal points on the back of the card. The new little cards plug in effortlessly and are standardized in size, shape, and function. They even identify themselves to your operating system.

They're called PCMCIA cards. It doesn't stand for People Can't Memorize Computer Industry Acronyms, though it should; it stands for Personal Computer Memory Card International Association, a group created in 1989 as a standards body and trade association consisting of manufacturers of semiconductors, connectors, peripherals, systems, and devices, and software developers. The end result for users is a selection of PCMCIA cards ranging from video capture cards to hard disks, network adapter cards, SCSI adapters, and, of course, modems. The cards were at first designed for portables but are now finding their way into desktop systems. Some journals and companies are beginning to call the cards simply *PC cards*.

There are three designations for the PCMCIA cards—Type I, Type II, and Type III. The only difference between the cards is their thickness: Type I devices are the thinnest (3.3 mm thick) and are primarily used for memory devices like flash RAM (cards that are like a low-capacity hard disk without moving parts). Type II cards are 5 mm thick; modems and LAN adapters are the most common of these type. Type III cards are 10.5 mm thick and are used for devices that require more space; for example, hard-disk drives and wireless communication devices. Any PCMCIA slot will accept its own size card as well as smaller cards. Thus, a Type II slot will accept a Type 1 or Type II card, but not a Type III.

There are two major versions of the PCMCIA standard. The first spec was version 1.0, released in September 1990 with only hardware addressed. The second release was version 2.0, issued September of 1991. This version added software specs for input/output cards like modems and hard drives. Release 2.01 contains typographical corrections and no new technical specs. Some of what the specs cover include the hardware configurations for pin assignments (they all have 68 pins), some electrical specifications, and the ability to detect the insertion and removal of the cards to promote *hot swapping*.

NOTE A new PCMCIA spec is under development; it will include 32-bit I/O (currently it is 16-bit) as well as add DMA support (not supported in 2.01), and it will be backward-compatible with current standards.

Part
6

Customizing
Windows 95

Adding and Removing Cards

Windows 95 is the first operating system to have Plug-and-Play support for PCMCIA cards. Just insert a card, and it will be detected. You don't have to power down before inserting. And it doesn't matter which slot you insert the card into. Once inserted, assuming Windows 95 properly recognizes the card (this doesn't *always* happen), it will load the proper software driver and activate the card. If the applicable driver isn't on your computer, you'll be prompted to insert the appropriate Windows 95 installation disk. If this is the first card you've inserted into your machine, it's possible that the PCMCIA Wizard will run. This only happens if the 32-bit PCMCIA support isn't already installed on your computer. Simply answer any questions when prompted. You may be instructed to insert disks and/or restart your machine.

Once your card commences running, you'll see a PCMCIA icon in the Taskbar's system tray.

The icon only appears if PCMCIA cards are inserted, recognized, and running. Double-click on the icon to bring up details about the status of your cards. For example, on my machine, the status is as follows:

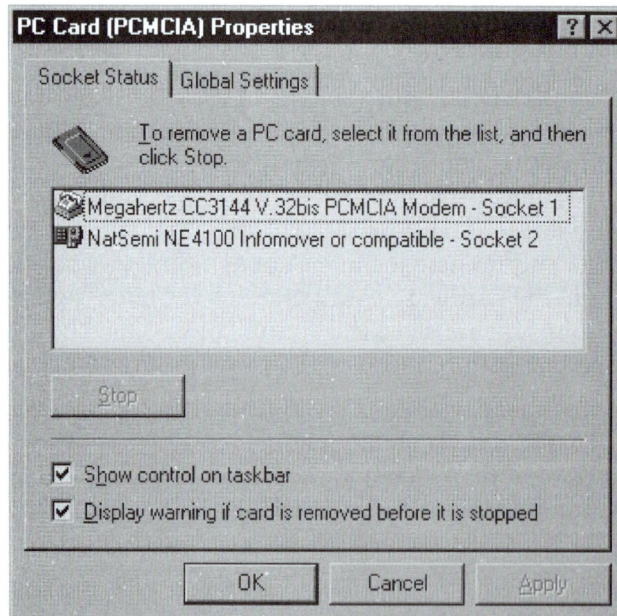

You can see here which card is in which slot. Notice the check boxes. One lets you turn off the PCMCIA icon that appears in the Taskbar. The other suppresses the warning message as explained below.

Notice that the Properties box also lets you *stop* a card by selecting it and clicking on it. What does this mean? These things are supposed to be completely Plug and Play, which means you should be able to run amuck with impunity, right? Well, not exactly. Microsoft suggests that you should stop a card before ejecting it. I've had pretty good luck simply ejecting the cards without stopping them. It won't crash your system. However, using the Stop button is a good idea because it lets Windows 95 and/or a program using the card warn you first if there is some reason you shouldn't eject it. For example, a networked user might have a file open on your machine or your modem might be in the middle of downloading your mail. If you fail to stop certain cards before ejecting, you might see this message:

Unexpected PC Card Removal   ☒

You should use the PC card icon on the taskbar to stop PC cards before removing them. Removing cards without warning the system can cause unexpected problems.

☐ Don't display this warning again.

[OK   ]

💡   **TIP**   If you are having trouble with an SRAM card (Static RAM card), check the Windows Help system under PCMCIA for some tips.

The Global Settings tab page in the Properties dialog box lets you turn off the little two-beep sounds that your computer makes when you boot up or resume from a suspended state. Each card when initialized will make such a sound. The sounds have signatures: if the second beep is higher, the card was recognized and initialized properly. If the second of the two short beeps is lower, it wasn't. I find that having the sounds on provides useful feedback, but I'm a geek. When resuming or booting up in a library, the beeps can be annoying to other people. You might want to turn off the sounds.

USING CELLULAR PHONES WITH YOUR LAPTOP FAX MODEM CARD

Getting a cell phone to work with your laptop isn't as easy as it could be. I've been trying to get mine to work for some time now and have had the runaround from more than a few companies on the issue.

There are a few things you should know. First, when shopping for both the phone and the modem, make sure they will work with each other. Call the people who make the phone and see which modems if any, support it; ditto for the modem supplier. If you already own the phone, call various modem vendors to see who supports your phone. Talk to the technical people, not the salespeople, and state the exact modem and phone make and model.

If you don't have a phone or modem yet or you're looking to upgrade, here's the scoop:

Some PCMCIA fax modems are designed for use with cell phones. They have a *direct-connect* port that lets you cable the phone and modem directly to each other without an intermediary connector module. (To connect a non–cellular-ready modem to a cell-phone, you'll need such a box; they cost about $200.) So, it makes sense to purchase a fax modem that's ready for prime time (cell-time, that is, which is always prime time when you consider the connect charges), such as the AT&T Keep in Touch PCMCIA card and the Megahertz CC, with an optional $25 to $70 cable. (The AT&T card supports a large number of phones.) There are two major functions such modems provide that non–cellular-ready cards don't: they fake the modem into thinking it's connected to a land line with dial tone; and they do compression and error detection so your cell phone can reliably cram more data across typically noisy channels.

External module boxes provide dial-tone compatibility, and some will do compression and error detection. Spectral, the most popular maker of the add-in boxes, claims the box arrangement with a non–direct-connect PCMCIA card actually works better than a fancy PCMCIA card because each box is fine-tuned for a specific brand and model of phone. I can't vouch for that, but it makes sense. Generic cellular-ready fax modems work with any number of phones, and input and output voltages and signals may vary among them. I'd say judge by the results. Try a system on spec, with return privileges, if you can. Try to get a modem with upgradable BIOS. Because the BIOS in the card stores the error-correction and compression algorithms, you'll be able to update the card as standards evolve.

Compression and error detection is another issue. As of this writing, there are two standards contending for the market: ECT and MNP-10. Both have their advantages, though neither will net you any gain unless the modem at the other end of the connection uses them. So far, most services only support the standard V.34bis that every desktop modem uses.

(continued on next page)

As for speed, getting a superfast 28.8 job isn't worth it if all your connects will be by cell phone. At this point, the highest connect speed you can expect is 9,600 bps anyway. Cell channels just won't run faster because of noise and bandwidth limitations. Don't expect that shelling out extra bucks for a digital cell phone will help either. Digital channels are quite limited and won't support data—only voice. You'll have to get a phone that is at least analog/digital with manual switching to analog when you want to transmit data.

Using a Docking Station

Laptop owners have had to make certain compromises for portability. We accept smaller, lower-resolution (albeit sharper) screens; smaller hard disks; and cramped keyboards in trade for freedom. Docking stations and port replicators are hardware solutions that provide users the best of both worlds. Whip out the computer and take it with you into the field. When you return to the office, plug your computer back into the docking station (see Figure 30.2), and you've got your favorite monitor, keyboard, pointing device, hard disks, CD-ROM, and printer at your beck and call. In some ways a docking-station

Part 6

Customizing Windows 95

Figure 30.2   *Docking stations give you the best of two worlds—lightweight portability and desktop-style peripherals.*

arrangement beats having multiple computers because you don't have the problem of maintaining duplicate hard disks and synchronizing multiple files.

A port replicator is similar to a docking station, but it doesn't provide internal slots for standard PC cards (ISA cards, not PCMCIA), hard disks, and so on, just a single quick-connect for all the junk you might want to attach to your parallel, serial, SCSI, video, sound, or other ports on the laptop.

Docking stations are great if you really need to supercharge your laptop and you don't minding sitting at a desk. Still, one of the hassles of docking stations is that you typically have to adjust a lot of settings in the operating system when you dock or undock. Like telling the computer you want to run in 800 by 600 video resolution instead of 640 by 480. Or that your CD-ROM, humongous hard drive, and Mega-Decibel sound card are now available.

Enter Windows 95. Working in conjunction with popular laptop and docking-station makers such as Toshiba and Compaq, Microsoft built in some Plug-and-Play smarts. Some computers know when you've docked or undocked. If your machine is so equipped, docking and un-docking is a no-brainer. Windows 95 applications and hardware developers are being encouraged to support the standard, so even programs in the future will know what to do when you are about to undock, such as closing certain files, issuing warnings, and so forth. Even if you're using non–Plug-and-Play equipment, there's a workaround.

With Plug-and-Play stuff, simply use your computer in each configuration as you'd expect. When docked, set up your video support and map network drives as you like. When you are about to undock, tell Windows 95 about your intentions. Your Start button will have an option called Eject PC on it. Choose it, and you'll be instructed or warned as necessary. Windows will then reconfigure itself, manage any conflicts about files in use on other drives, and load the drivers needed for going mobile. You may not even have to power down!

NOTE   Not all machines will support what's called *hot docking*, and may require that you turn off your machine and reboot before reconfiguration will occur. You should consult your computer's manual to determine the proper strategy for docking and undocking.

Non–Plug-and-Play Docking Stations

Windows 95 will detect and set up a separate hardware profile for a great majority of docking stations and port replicators. However, if yours isn't detected, or if you want to set up your machine with temporary external hardware—such as a monitor or mouse—without a port replicator or docking station, and you want to easily switch between such setups, it's possible. Just set up a *hardware profile* for each arrangement, then switch between them.

> **NOTE** Use hardware profiles for any computer where you alter the physical setup regularly in a predictable manner, such as switching between two monitors.

Tucked away within the Control Panel you'll find the hardware-profile settings option that lets you name and save hardware setups just as you can color or sound schemes. Here's how.

1. Get your system running with a superset of the hardware you're going to want to use. That is, as much external stuff—such as hard drives—as possible. This may require using the Control Panel's Add/Remove hardware applet as well (see Chapter 7).

2. Run Control Panel and choose System. Click on Hardware profiles.

3. Select the profile you want to use as a basis for your scaled-down (undocked) profile and click on Copy.

4. Name the new profile something meaningful such as *Undocked Laptop*.

5. Switch to the Device Manager tab page in the System dialog box.

6. Click on the + sign next to any piece of hardware whose inclusion/exclusion in one of your profiles you want to alter. Highlight the specific item and click on Properties.

7. At the bottom of the resulting dialog box, turn off or on the appropriate boxes.

8. Repeat this for each device whose usage will be affected by a given profile.

Part 6

Customizing Windows 95

Device usage

Place a check mark next to the configuration(s) where this device should be used.

☐ Undocked (Current)
☑ 1024 x 768 resolution with CD-ROM

[OK]   [Cancel]

If you have more than one profile set up, you'll be prompted to choose one on booting up. This isn't as neat as an automatic switchover, but it works.

> **TIP**   You might want to check the Help system under *Hardware Profiles* **for more information.**

Deferred Printing

If you regularly print out documents, working out in the field without a printer can be annoying. If you've worked on a number of projects during the course of the day, you are likely to forget what to print once you get back to the office or find a printer. Also, you have to run each application, load each document, and set up the Print dialog box before you print. This is a hassle that Windows 95 lets you circumvent by printing *offline*.

When you work offline, print jobs simply get stored up in the print queue (a disk file on your hard disk). When you find a printer, just plug it in and run the queue. If you're in the field, it's possible you won't even know what kind of printer you'll find. No problem—you can even change the driver type of the printer before printing. Here are the steps:

1. From My Computer or Explorer, right-click on the printer in question and choose Work Offline. The check mark should now be turned on.

2. Print whenever and whatever you want as though there were a printer connected. Printing to the same printer each time will help consolidate your print queue.

3. When you get to a printer, plug it into the appropriate port.

4. From My Computer or Explorer, right-click on the printer in question and choose Work Offline to turn the check mark off.

> **TIP** Actually this works with any computer in case you want to stack up a bunch of print jobs for printing later.

> **TECH TIP** If the printer you found in the Kopy Korner store in Wakeegan, Illinois, isn't the same kind you printed your queue to, open the queue window, choose Printers ➤ Properties ➤ Details, and change the driver type. Unless you've installed the new type of printer before, the print driver won't be on your hard disk and you'll be prompted to insert a disk. This is a bummer if you don't carry copies of your Windows 95 disks with you. One workaround is to create a Generic Text Only printer (see Chapter 8) and print to that when you're in the field. A generic printer driver will print to many printers one way or another, though you won't get any fancy fonts or graphics with such a driver and you might have to set the printer into a "dumb" text-only mode. Another option is to figure out which diskette(s) you're prompted for each time you create a new printer and copy the contents (it will have a single `.cab` file on it) to a dedicated folder on your hard disk. When prompted for a disk, tell Windows 95 to look in this directory.

Using the Briefcase to Synchronize Your Files

Many people have more than one computer that they use regularly. For example, you may have a laptop for use on the road or at home and a desktop machine in your office. This poses a problem: how do you keep often-used files up to date on both machines? You can manually copy files back and forth via a floppy disk, but you have to remember what file is where and which copy has the latest edits in it. The solution is Windows 95's *Briefcase*, a little utility program that provides for file synchronization between two machines.

In essence, the Briefcase is just a folder that contains copies of all the files you want to keep up to date. When you switch from your desktop computer to your laptop, you drag the briefcase to a floppy disk or to your laptop's hard disk if your laptop is networked via a network card, Remote Access Services (RAS), or Direct Cable Connect. This copies

Part 6

Customizing Windows 95

the files onto the floppy or directly onto the hard disk of the portable. If you used a floppy, you then insert the floppy into your laptop machine, hit the road, and do your work on those files. If you went direct to hard disk, you're just ready to roll. You reverse the process when you return to the office. The Briefcase program takes care of determining which copy of a given file has the latest changes in it and where they should be copied to.

Of course, the Briefcase can be used between any two computers even if they are both laptops or desktop machines. And you can have as many briefcases as you like (in case you have a number of computers or diverse tasks, each of which rely on different files).

The following steps explain how to use the Briefcase between a desktop computer and a portable computer by way of a floppy disk. The next section explains how to use a direct connection (the preferred method) rather than a floppy disk.

1. First, if you don't have a Briefcase on your Desktop, you'll have to add one. Right-click on the Desktop and choose New ➤ Briefcase. If that doesn't work, it means the program isn't installed. You'll have to install the Briefcase utility from your Windows 95 master CD or floppies using the Control Panel's Add/Remove Programs applet. Click on Start ➤ Help and search for help about installing the Briefcase.

   My Briefcase

2. Once you have a Briefcase icon on the Desktop or in a folder (you can create a Briefcase in any folder by right-clicking and choosing New ➤ Briefcase), you're ready to roll. Figure out which documents you want to keep up to date and drag them (not their shortcuts) into the Briefcase. (You can just drop them onto the Briefcase icon, or you can open its window and drag the files into that.)

3. Insert a floppy disk into your desktop machine.

4. Using My Computer or Explorer, drag the Briefcase to the floppy disk.

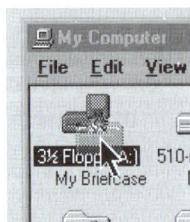

5. After some copying, all the contents of the Briefcase are now on your floppy disk. (You may be prompted to insert multiple disks if the Briefcase contains copious amounts of data.) Remove the disk and insert it into your portable.

6. Edit the document files stored in the Briefcase folder using the programs in your laptop. Editing the files from the floppy is the easiest way to manage them. You can move them off the floppy and onto the portable's hard disk, but you'll have to remember to move them back into the Briefcase before the next step.

7. When you return to your desktop computer, remove the floppy containing the Briefcase from the portable and insert it into your desktop computer.

8. Open the floppy drive's window from My Computer or Explorer. Find the Briefcase icon and double-click on it.

9. Open the Briefcase menu and click on Update All. Or select the files you want to update and choose Update Selection. In Figure 30.3 I have chosen Update All. Notice the dialog box that appears.

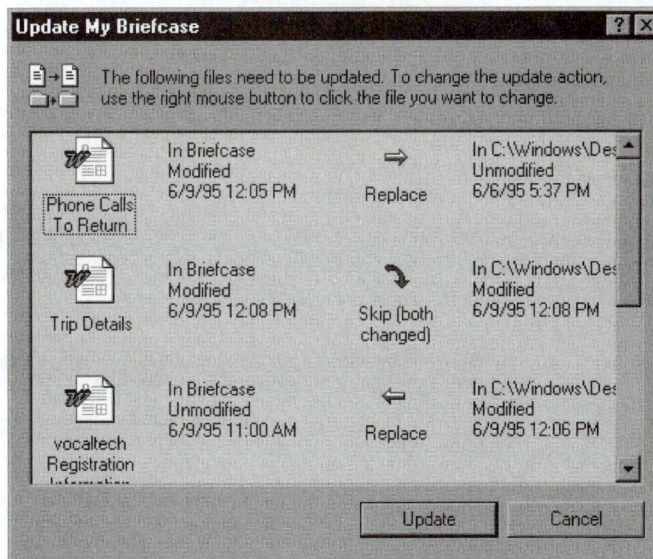

Update My Briefcase   ? ☒

📄→📄 The following files need to be updated. To change the update action,
☐→☐ use the right mouse button to click the file you want to change.

	In Briefcase Modified 6/9/95 12:05 PM	⇨ Replace	In C:\Windows\Des Unmodified 6/6/95 5:37 PM
Phone Calls To Return			
Trip Details	In Briefcase Modified 6/9/95 12:08 PM	↘ Skip (both changed)	In C:\Windows\Des Modified 6/9/95 12:08 PM
vocaltech Registration Information	In Briefcase Unmodified 6/9/95 11:00 AM	⇦ Replace	In C:\Windows\Des Modified 6/9/95 12:06 PM

Update   Cancel

Figure 30.3 When you choose Update, Briefcase reports the status of the items in the briefcase and what effect the update will have on each of them.

You can also select individual files and choose Update Selection if you want to limit the update to certain files. In either case, the matching files on both machines are compared to see which has been modified and when modifications were made. The results of the comparison appear in the box. Typically, the arrows will all point to the right, indicating that items in the Briefcase have been changed and that updates should be made to the originals in the desktop computer. Arrows will point to the left when you've made changes to the Desktop's copy of a file but not to the copy in the Briefcase. The Trip Details file in Figure 30.3 shows what happens when both files have been changed. The Update procedure will normally skip this file, letting you decide which update you want to keep. You can right-click on such a file and choose its fate from the resulting menu.

NOTE   Files that haven't been modified on either machine won't appear in the Update list.

Adjust any file's settings as you see fit and then click on the Update button. Files will be synchronized and progress reported in a box like the one shown below.

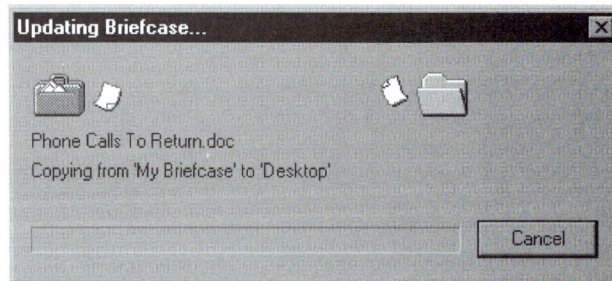

Options and Tips with Briefcase

Briefcase has some options worth noting. You can, for example, use it *without* a floppy disk if you have your computers directly connected or networked.

> **NOTE** Briefcase works best over a network, RAS, or with Direct Cable Connect (see Chapter 28). Using the floppy intermediary imposes some limitations because of the limited amount of storage space and potential for conflict between the Briefcase databases on the hard disk and on the floppy.

For directly connected machines, the procedure is slightly different from above.

1. On your desktop computer, share the folders containing the files you want to put in your Briefcase.

2. Then from your portable computer, copy those files to your laptop's Briefcase. (You can drag the files to the My Briefcase icon on your laptop's Desktop.)

3. Work on your files on your portable or laptop computer, even if it's disconnected from the desktop computer.

4. When you're finished working on the files, connect the two computers, double-click on the My Briefcase icon, choose Briefcase ➤ Update All (or click on the files you want to update and then click on Update Selection).

If at some point during the process a source file is moved or deleted, the link between the file in Briefcase and your main computer will be broken—Windows 95 won't be able to figure out what to update in this case. This creates an "orphan" file. Trying to update it will result in this message:

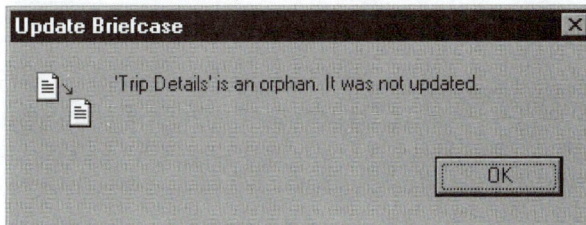

It can still be worked with directly from the briefcase, but if you want to synchronize files again, you'll have to copy the file from Briefcase to the same folder it was in when you added it to the briefcase originally. Updating should now work. Alternatively, select the orphan file, then choose File ➤ Properties. In the Update Status box, click on the Find Original button to find the original file. You can now synchronize again.

Conversely, if you want to break the link between the file in the Briefcase and its source, click on it in the briefcase and choose Briefcase ➤ Split from Original.

Portable Computing Tips

Portable computing is a black art that you only get good at with some experience. Here is just a brief smattering of my findings that you might find meaningful.

> **TIP** Steve Cummings, who authored a portion of this book, also wrote a terrific book on the subject, covering all manner of laptop know-how, including where to buy your solar battery recharger for that trip to the Andes. It's called *The Little Laptop Book* (Peachpit Press, 1993).

▶ If you use the Suspend command, you should save your work before suspending just in case your batteries die or Suspend doesn't work right.

▶ If you take your computer out of the house a lot, purchase a laptop insurance policy. Some policies will cover not only theft but any kind of damage, and compared to your laptop's price, they're a bargain.

▶ Get a decent padded bag to carry your computer in.

> **TIP** You might want to use a bag that doesn't look like a laptop computer bag. Those make an easy target for thieves.

▶ If you work outside and have trouble reading the screen, try wearing a dark shirt so your reflection on the screen is minimized. Monochrome and dual-scan screens work best in outdoor light, in that order. Active-matrix screens, though expensive and great indoors, appear black in strong sunlight.

▶ When shopping, buy a lithium-ion–batteried machine if possible. Short of that, get a nickel-metal hydride one. Nickel-cadmium (Nicad) batteries are a pain to care for because you have to regularly run them down all the way before you charge them back up to keep them healthy. Otherwise they die, and they aren't inexpensive. If you do have Nicads, make sure you cycle them regularly.

> **TECH TIP** For longest life, you should cycle all batteries once a month regardless of type, particularly if you are connected to AC most of the time. Even though nickel-metal hydride batteries are supposed to be memoryless, they do seem to be susceptible to trickle overcharges.

▶ In your laptop you can actually install drivers for several pointing devices, such as a trackball, desktop mouse, GlidePoint, and so forth. When you change pointing devices, Windows 95 will detect it.

▶ If you use a modem, carry an extra telephone cord and possibly some connectors such as a Y connector and a coupler (female-to-female) so you can reach a distant outlet and/or share a telephone on the same line.

▶ Always have a floppy disk around for transfers to other computers.

▶ If you're a hardcore road warrior and occasionally need to transfer large files between computers, don't assume the other computer has Windows 95 on it. Besides, the direct-cable-connection program is slow at transfers. Purchase the latest version of LapLink, install it, and carry a serial LapLink cable with you. Only the serial cable lets you directly install LapLink on another computer you run into even though the parallel cable in faster.

> **NOTE** For coverage of Direct Cable Connect, please refer to Chapter 26.

Part 6

Customizing
Windows 95

Chapter 31

Heavy-Duty Customizing

FEATURING

Advanced Control Panel settings

Adjusting other performance determinants

Troubleshooting

The best-laid plans of mice and men oft gang agley, as the saying goes. And so, despite the tens of thousands of work hours invested in designing and coding Windows 95 to brilliantly sleuth out your computer's hardware endowments and make the most intelligent use of them, it doesn't always pan out. True, Windows 95 beats Windows 3.x by a country mile when it comes to automated installation, hardware detection, and optimization on various counts. Still, human intervention can be advantageous at times. If you're a systems administrator, computer jock, or power user and want to tweak your computer for optimal performance, read through this chapter.

> **NOTE** Unfortunately, there isn't room in this book for all of the tricks. Check out my book *Windows 95 Secrets & Solutions* (Sybex, 1995) for more inside know-how on Windows and for tips, tricks, workarounds, and hardware-optimization angles. In that book you'll find in-depth discussions on Windows' inner workings; how to best upgrade your computer hardware for use as a desktop, workstation, or client/server-based system; how to choose monitors, hard disks, backups, UPS, RAM, CD-ROM, PCMCIA, and Plug-and-Play items; how to integrate Windows 95 into other brands of networks; how the Registry works and how to edit it; how to optimize your configuration files; and a variety of other meaty topics.

Keyboard Options

Without modifying anything via the Control Panel's Keyboard applet, your keyboard will likely work just fine. But the applet's settings determine several important behavioral characteristics of your keyboard and can be modified. Running the applet reveals what they might be (see Figure 31.1).

Most likely to be used is the character-repeat rate. Most keys repeat when you hold them down for a while. Because this setting not only controls the rate for normal keys but also affects the rate at which the Spacebar, arrow keys, and PageUp and PageDown keys work, you may have reason to make adjustments. On the first tab page, simply drag the slider to a faster or slower setting. You can test the effect of a given setting by clicking in the test text box and holding down a letter key. If it's too slow or fast, adjust and try again.

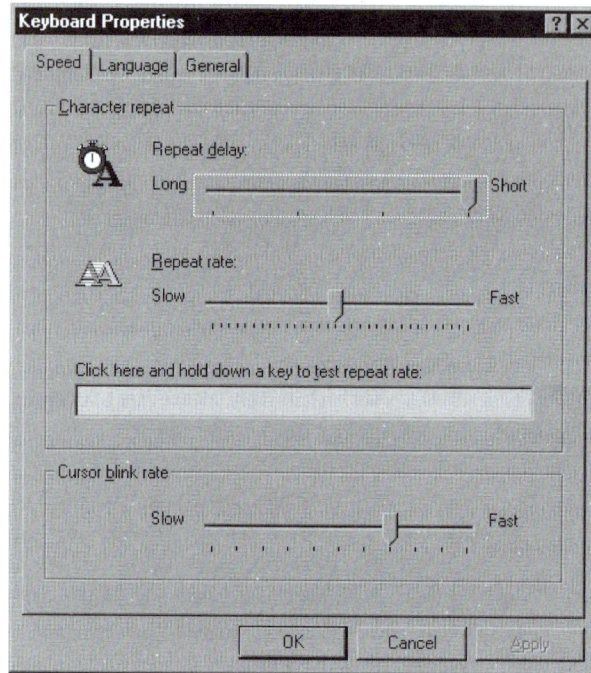

Figure 31.1 *The Control Panel's Keyboard Properties dialog box*

The *Repeat delay* setting determines how long you have to hold down a key before it starts repeating. If you tend to hesitate more than the average typist and find your screen responding with *tthhee* instead of *the*, you should lengthen the repeat delay.

At the bottom of the first tab page, you can change the cursor blink rate. This setting determines how fast the insertion point (or *I-beam*) blinks when you're editing text. Setting this too slow can cause the cursor to vanish for too long, too fast can be annoying. Drag the speed slider, then click in the test area to observe the effect.

Multiple Language Support in Windows 95

Because of differences in language and alphabet, computers marketed abroad have different key assignments than your computer. Key assignments for special characters such as accented characters, umlauts, and the like are determined in Windows 95 by choices you can make on the Keyboard applet's second tab page. During installation of

Windows 95, you're asked to confirm the language that setup has assumed is correct for your location, so typically this will be already correct. If your line of work calls for text in several languages, no problem; you can install any number of language drivers into your system, switching between them very quickly. A click on the Taskbar or a key press is all you need to switch from one driver (and thus keyboard layout) to another.

Typically you'll have only one driver showing when you open the dialog box. To add a new one, click on Add and choose a language from the resulting list. You may be prompted to insert a disk or CD-ROM so the applet can locate the proper driver. Then you'll have a second listing in the installed languages box. Here I've installed Swedish in addition to English.

Once set to another language, some keys (shifted and unshifted) will type different letters than printed on your keyboard's key caps. You'll have to experiment a bit to determine where your new keys are. Unfortunately Windows 95 doesn't include a utility that'll display a keyboard map for each language driver.

If you check Enable Indicator on the Taskbar, your Taskbar will indicate which language driver is active at any one time. Clicking on it brings up a menu that lets you easily switch between languages.

If you want to get super efficient at switching between installed languages, just activate either the Left Alt-Shift or Ctrl-Shift option. Then simply pressing that key combination toggles between languages.

If you want to remove a language driver, simply select it in the dialog box and click on Remove. Likewise, setting the default language is as easy as clicking on Set as Default. This determines which language will be used when you start up your computer.

General Keyboard Settings

Finally, on the last tab page, you'll find the General settings. Here you set the actual hardware driver that Windows 95 should use with your keyboard. I say *actual hardware driver* to distinguish from keyboard layout or language characters that will be produced when you press a key. Some keyboard brands require a special driver or have additional keys on them, such as number pads and the like. During Windows 95 setup, your keyboard was likely recognized and the correct driver installed. Should you purchase a new keyboard that is acting squirrely after you plug it in, you might want to select this tab page and click on the Change button. Your keyboard will then be checked for compatibility, and you'll have the option of installing a different type of driver. Click on Change, then Show All Devices to see a list of all the possible keyboard hardware drivers.

Working with Passwords

The Control Panel's Password applet lets you change log-on passwords, allow remote administration of the computer, and set up individual profiles that go into effect when each new user logs onto the local computer. The Passwords dialog box is shown in Figure 31.2.

Use the first page of this dialog box for typical password adjustments. More often than not you'll use the first button to change your log-on name—the password that's used when you log onto Windows. The second button lets you set other passwords—such as your password to log onto another LAN such as a Novell network. If you want, you may use the same password for each to simplify things. Passwords can be as long as 127 characters, although that's a bit more than anyone would want to bother with. You may use letters, numbers, and punctuation marks.

> **NOTE**   The maximum password length on other networks may be different. For example, NT and Novell passwords must be shorter. Check the documentation with those networks.

To change your password, click on the upper button, then in the resulting box fill in your old password, the new password, and then repeat the new password.

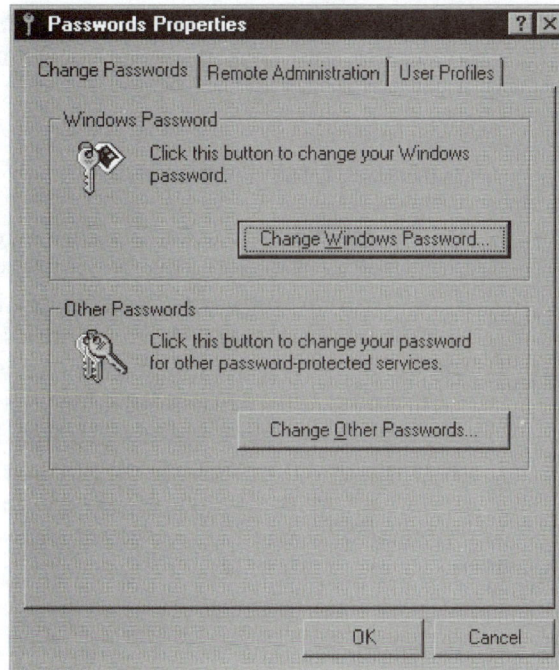

Figure 31.2 Changing passwords

CAUTION   You should not use Cut and Paste commands (Ctrl-X and Ctrl-V) to enter the passwords. Always manually enter them to prevent accidentally introducing a typo into your password and then being unable to access your hard disk or change your password.

Remote-Administration Passwords

The second tab page of the dialog box is only used for setting up passwords to allow someone at another workstation to access your computer. Recall from Part 5 that a network administrator can manage shared folders and printers on this computer and see who connects to them. Settings on this page determine which password the remote administrator has to enter remotely to create, change, or monitor shared resources on your computer. Remote administration is covered in Part 5, so I won't go into that here. However, to set up the computer for remote administration, you have to enable it first by checking the

box. Then enter the password you want to require for remote administration of your shared resources. Remember to inform your network
administrator of the password.

Multiple-User Passwords

Windows NT introduced the concept of multiple users on a given
computer workstation, (aka PC) each with his or her own settings. In
NT such an arrangement is necessary because NT's security model
necessitates that each user be given a set of security privileges controlling the use of network-shared resources. Windows 95 isn't based on
as ambitious a security model, but it still includes a decent functional
subset of NT's user-by-user customizability. By creating an entry in
the configuration Registry for each user on the system, Windows 95
can accommodate any number of different people on the same computer, each having many of their own settings. When a user signs in,
the Registry is accessed and the appropriate settings go into effect.

User Profiles

The collection of settings each user creates is called a *user profile*. A
typical user profile might include Desktop colors, screen saver, shortcuts and icons, and program groups.

As it comes from the factory, Windows 95 is set up in single-profile
mode. Each user that logs on will get the same settings regardless of the
user name and password they enter. You have to enable the multiple-user
mode before logging in as a new user; this will create a new profile in
the Registry. Here are the steps to follow to enable the multiuser
arrangement.

You should start with a pretty ordinary setup. Any settings that are
currently in effect, such as icons on the Desktop, colors, etc., will be
cloned into all subsequent profiles that get created. Then get to the
Password Properties User Profiles tab page shown in Figure 31.3.

By default the top radio button is on. Click on the second one (*Users
can…*); this activates the lower portion of the dialog box.

You have two options in the lower half of the box: You can check
either, both, or neither of these two. The options declare which settings are stored in your new profile when you make changes from the

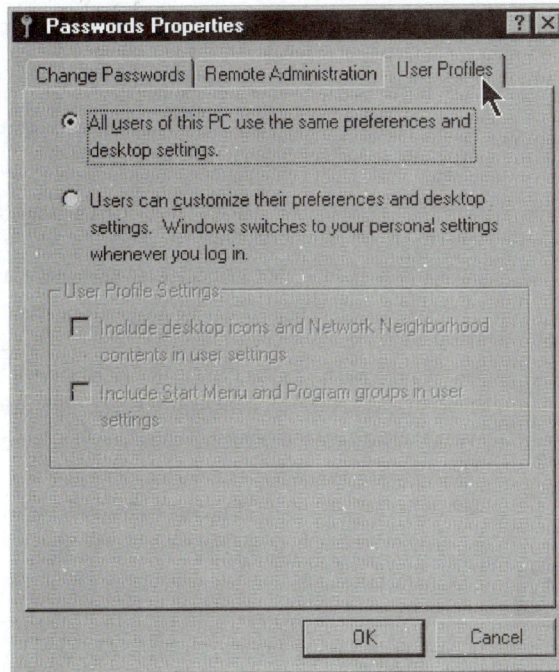

Figure 31.3 Enabling differentiated user profiles

Control Panel, property sheets, and so forth. If you elect *not* to turn on an option, you'll *share* that setting with other users. When you OK the box, you'll be told that you must restart your computer for the changes to take effect.

Once you're set up for multiple users, the machine will reboot and work just as you would expect. You have to sign in as usual. However, when someone else signs in with a name not recognized by the system, they'll see the following dialog box:

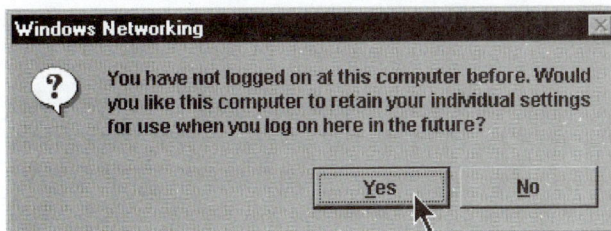

Part 6

Customizing Windows 95

Click on Yes. They will then have to verify their password. A copy of the settings currently in effect is made and assigned to the new user's environment, so the Desktop and all the other settings will come up looking like nothing new happened. But any changes the new user makes to system settings will have *no effect* on other user's settings.

There's one ramification of all this multiple customization that you might bump into. Having separate profiles on the machine might tip off certain programs that there are additional users around. Programs that previously assumed you were the only user may now ask you for some identification such as a password before performing some task that requires security of some sort. Here's an example: Microsoft Exchange, even if set to remember your password automatically, will now prompt you to re-enter the password when you attempt to log onto services such as the Microsoft Network. This prevents other users of the computer from logging on under your name, running up a bill, and reading your mail.

CAUTION   Even though certain system settings that other users make on the computer won't affect yours, this doesn't mean other users can't affect your data files, folders, hard disks, and so forth. Unlike the password protection you can assign to printers or folders that you share with users over the network, you can't password protect or specify user permissions for resources that are on your computer. Thus, once a user logs onto the system,, they are able to gain access to any files on your hard disk. If you want to more thoroughly protect individual disks, folders, and files, you'll have to use another operating system such as Windows NT.

Switching Users without Rebooting

You may have noticed when shutting down Windows that you have the option of logging on as a different user.

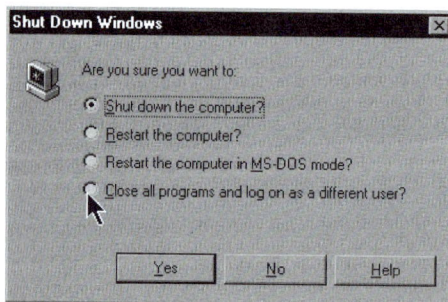

Choosing this option is an easy way to switch to another user's settings without having to wait for shutdown and reboot. It is the preferred approach, especially if resources on your machine are in use by other networked users.

Removing User Profiles

At the time of this writing, the internal procedures for adding and removing individual system settings was not always reliable nor straightforward. For example, not all of the folders on the Desktop were imported into each new user's settings. Also, a series of hard-disk subfolders are set up for each user. Turning off the multiuser settings didn't erase these folders, leaving them consuming disk space. In future releases of Windows 95, this process may be smoothed out and/or automated as it is in Windows NT.

In any case, if you decide you want to remove all but the default profile, just run the Control Panel again, choose Passwords, select the User Profiles page, and choose the first option, which will turn off the multiple-user setting. OK the box and reboot. Now, regardless of who you log in as, you'll get the same settings.

TECH TIP You can't remove just a single profile; multiuser capability is either on or off. However, even after turning off the multiuser option, all the subfolders for individual users will still be in the \Windows\Profiles folder just in case you reactivate the multiuser setting. The only way to get rid of all the potential junk in these folders is to manually delete them using Explorer or some other file-deletion program such as File Manager or XTREE. Make sure you're not deleting any important documents or programs stored in a user's subfolders.

Regional Settings

The Regional settings customize Windows for use in other countries. If you're using Windows in English in the United States, don't bother making any changes. The settings made from this box pertain exclusively to Windows and Windows applications; other programs won't take advantage of them. Even some Windows applications won't. You should do some experimenting with the settings to see if they make

Part 6

Customizing
Windows 95

any difference or read the application's manual for information about how to set the formats for it.

Choosing Regional from the Control Panel displays the dialog box you see in Figure 31.4. The settings and their explanations are shown below.

NOTE   Windows may ask you to insert one of the floppy disks when making changes.

Regional Settings selects which country you're in. All other settings change in accordance with the accepted practices in that country. Only bother changing the other options if necessary.

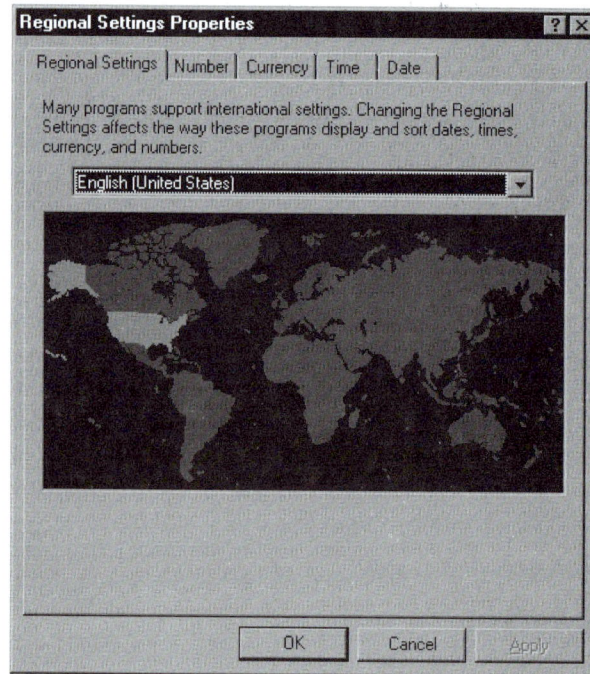

Figure 31.4   *The Regional Settings Properties dialog box. Changes you make here affect only the applications that use the internal Windows settings for such functions.*

Number displays numbers with or without decimals, commas, or leading zeroes and with different decimal separators. It also determines whether to display measurements in metric or English units and what your *list separator* should be. For example, in the now-famous sentence, "Well, it's one, two, three, what are we fighting for...," the list separator is a comma. In other languages, items listed in a sentence are separated by other punctuation marks.

Currency sets the currency indicator and the location and number of decimal digits.

Time allows for 12- or 24-hour time indication, AM or PM indicators, choice of separators, and leading zeros.

Date sets dates from a myriad of formats such as 3/6/53; 03/06/53; 3/6/1953; 06-03-1953; March 6, 1953; and others. This is useful for programs that pop the date into text at the touch of a key or translate dates from one format to another.

To change the settings, simply click on the appropriate tab page, then on the drop-down list box for the setting in question. Examples of the current settings are shown in each section, so you don't need to change them unless they look wrong.

The System

The Control Panel's System applet is quite capable. If you're a power user who digs around in the computer, goofing around with boards and various upgrades, you'll probably be using this applet a lot. It displays information about your system's internals—devices, amount of RAM, type of processor, and so on. It also lets you add, disable, and remove specific devices from your system, set up hardware profiles (for instance, to allow automatic optimization when using a docking station with a laptop), and optimize some parameters of system performance such as CD cache size and type. This applet also provides a number of system-troubleshooting tools.

Using the Device Manager

The first tab page of the System Properties dialog box simply reports the system type, registered owner, and version of Windows. The second page, Device Manager, provides a powerful overview of your entire system, displaying the classes of hardware in the computer (see Figure 31.5).

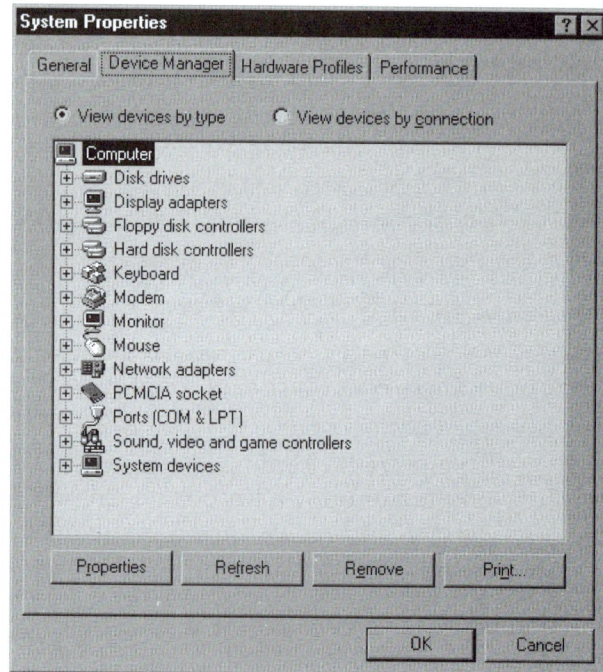

Figure 31.5   *The Device Manager displays the hierarchy of system components.*

Basic components are listed in alphabetical order by type unless you click on the *View devices by connection* radio button at the top of the window. Clicking on a plus sign displays specifics about the class of component. For example:

An X through an icon means the hardware has been disabled. A circled exclamation point through the icon means the hardware has a problem. The type of problem will be displayed in the hardware's property sheet.

You can click on a specific sub-item and learn more about it by clicking on Properties (or simply double-click on the sub-item). The resulting box will tell you whether the component is working properly, possibly who the maker of the device is, and what its version number is. Many components will have three or four property sheet pages, such as General, Settings, Driver, and Resources. The available options vary depending on the type of device. From these pages you can examine and declare a great variety of settings for your hardware devices. For example, the Settings page for your floppy drive(s) lets you reassign logical drive letters. Pages for sound cards and network cards will report DMA, IRQ, and port settings.

> **NOTE**   Many components' Properties boxes have a Device Usage section that determines which hardware configuration the components will be used in (such as when a laptop is docked or undocked; see Chapter 30 for more on multiple configurations for laptops).

You might have noticed the Remove button on the Device Manager's first page. Use this button to remove support for any device in your system that you've decided to bag and that Windows 95 didn't automatically remove for you. Windows 95 is pretty good at detecting hardware-configuration changes and will often remove unnecessary or redundant drivers when you remove a piece of hardware. But in case it doesn't, use this button.

> **CAUTION**   Many devices will have Resources and Drivers tab pages. As a rule, you'll not want to mess with the Resources and Driver settings unless you know what you're doing. Changing the address, IRQ, DAM, and other down-and-dirty system settings can lead to problems, such as a device not working or Windows not booting. If the Properties' General tab page indicates a device is working properly and doesn't report conflicts, you're probably best off leaving the component's settings alone.

> **TECH TIP**   For systems integrators who find they are altering a system's configuration regularly, are trying to get some new hardware working and having trouble with it, or want to catalog the hardware configuration of a number of systems for inventory or comparison purposes, the Print button comes in handy. In the Device Manager's dialog box, click on Print. You'll have three options determining the content of the printout, including Print to File.

Part
6

Customizing
Windows 95

Making COM Port Adjustments

If you've ever used the DOS **MODE** command to set up the communications parameters of your computer's serial COM ports, you know that it's a hassle to remember the exact syntax and *arguments* (the numbers and letters you type after the command) required for a specific setup. Because most programs that use the serial ports (such as communications programs, mouse drivers, or slow-speed networks) take care of setting the COM ports, it's rare that you need to deal with these directly anyway. But should you need to, the Device Manager lets you configure the serial (COM) ports on a machine. Under Computer, click on Ports. You'll see a dialog box for making the settings for baud rate, parity, and stop bits. The settings should match the settings of the equipment you are connecting to the port. If you're in doubt about them, consult the manual supplied with the external equipment. You may also want to refer to a book specializing in the use of asynchronous serial communications interfaces, such as *The RS-232 Solution* (2nd Edition) (Sybex, 1994).

> **TIP**   Try double-clicking on Computer at the top of the Device Manager page. This is a great troubleshooting tool to help you resolve port, IRQ, and DMA conflicts.

Optimizing Performance

The last page of the System applet is for checking and altering settings that affect the optimal performance of your system. Though Windows 95 optimizes as best it can, you may have need for or simply an interest in knowing what's going on in terms of virtual memory management, disk caching, and other performance determinants. All these settings now live in one place—on the Performance page of the System applet. Clicking on this tab brings up the screen shown in Figure 31.6.

Notice that this figure indicates my system is optimized about as much as it's going to be. I'm using 31-bit file-system, PCMCIA, and virtual-memory drivers.

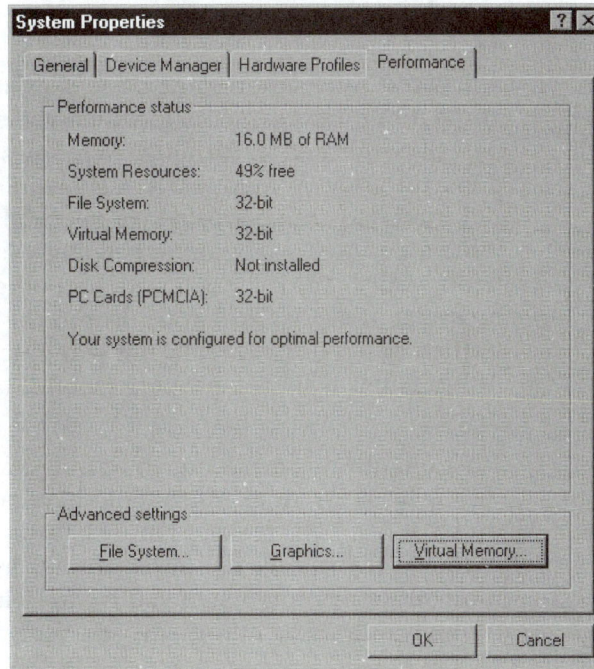

Figure 31.6 You can set and check system optimization from this page of the System applet.

There are three major performance sections you can examine using the buttons at the bottom of the dialog box:

▶ file system

▶ graphics acceleration

▶ virtual memory

I suggest you examine each dialog box carefully, read the help files, and use the ? button in the dialog boxes to get some tips about each setting before making any changes. Note that in Windows 95, the virtual memory file size is dynamically sized—and is best left that way—rather than being set to a static size. However, if you have multiple disk drives and want to ensure specific amounts of virtual memory on each or disable virtual memory swapping altogether, you can.

Other Tweaking Angles

Chapter 2 touched on some basic Windows 95 software and hardware compatibility issues, some of which will affect system throughput and overall performance. Although Windows 95 is, in many ways, a radical departure from Windows 3.x, a genie in a bottle isn't bundled in. The old tried-and-true performance essentials are still applicable. I could write a hundred pages about keeping your hardware doodads up to snuff, your hard disk organized, and other tricks for squeezing the most out of every CPU cycle. But in the end, most people don't bother, and it doesn't really net you much. In reality there are really only a few truly beneficial performance tricks worth the hassle or price.

▶ First off, always keep a bunch of free space available on your hard disk. This is essential. You should have at least 20 (some people say as much as 50) MB free on your disk for use by Windows for virtual memory. If you have too little, you'll start getting messages about running out of memory when you try to switch between programs. If you use only a few small programs at a time, this is less of an issue.

▶ Next, you should defragment your hard disk once in a while (see Chapter 23). Once a month is a good idea.

▶ If you are unhappy with the performance of your system and it's a pretty fast 486 already, increase the amount of RAM. You probably have 8 MB. 16 MB will dramatically improve things.

▶ If you don't have a local-bus hard-disk controller, switch to one. SCSI II is best, IDE on the VLB or PCI bus is good. You may be able to keep your existing drive, but make sure it's large enough and has a fast step rate (18 milliseconds or lower).

▶ Your video controller should be on the local bus too. If you're now using 256 or more colors and you can live with only 16 colors, use the Display applet in Control Panel to reduce the colors. Screen redrawing will speed up significantly.

▶ Do what you can to remove 16-bit drivers from your system. In simplest terms, this means only install and use devices that are recognized and supported by Windows 95 right off the shelf. Network cards, video controllers, CD-ROMs, PCMCIA cards, and the like should all be running with 31-bit drivers. Refer to the installation guide supplied with the product or contact the manufacturer to determine how best to do this. (It may require removing or *remming* out statements in your `autoexec.bat` and/or `config.sys` files.)

> **TECH TIP** When you install Windows 95 over an existing copy of DOS and Windows, all of the network drivers, device drivers, and utilities in your existing `config.sys`, `autoexec.bat`, and `system.ini` files are pulled into your new configuration—including files it doesn't need or can't work with. This duplication doesn't usually prevent Windows 95 from running, but it can slow it down and decrease the amount of conventional RAM available for DOS sessions.

Setting the Recycle Bin's Properties

A few final settings worth considering affect how your Recycle Bin works. Recall that when you delete files, they aren't actually erased. They get moved to the Recycle Bin, which is a directory on your hard disk. If your hard disk is modest in size or getting crammed, decreasing the size of the Recycle Bin might be in order. In some cases, you might even want to *increase* its *size*. The options in the Recycle Bin's property sheet are therefore worth a gander.

To get to the setting, right-click on the Recycle Bin icon, either on the Desktop or in Explorer, then choose Properties. The Recycle Bin settings appear as shown in Figure 31.7.

There are number of settings here to contemplate. Firstly, notice that each of your local hard disks will have a tab. If you choose *Configure drives independently*, you'll use those pages to make individual drive settings. Otherwise you'll just use the Global page.

If you don't want to be able to reclaim deleted files, check the *Do not move files...* option. This will speed up deletion. It will also free up disk space immediately on deletion of files.

As a default, 10 percent of each drive is used for the Recycle Bin. When you delete a file on drive C, it goes to drive C's Recycle Bin until you empty the bin. When you delete from drive D (if you have a second hard drive), it goes into drive D's Recycle Bin. As a Recycle Bin reaches capacity, newly deleted files will push older files off the bottom of the list, deleting them permanently. In practical terms, the

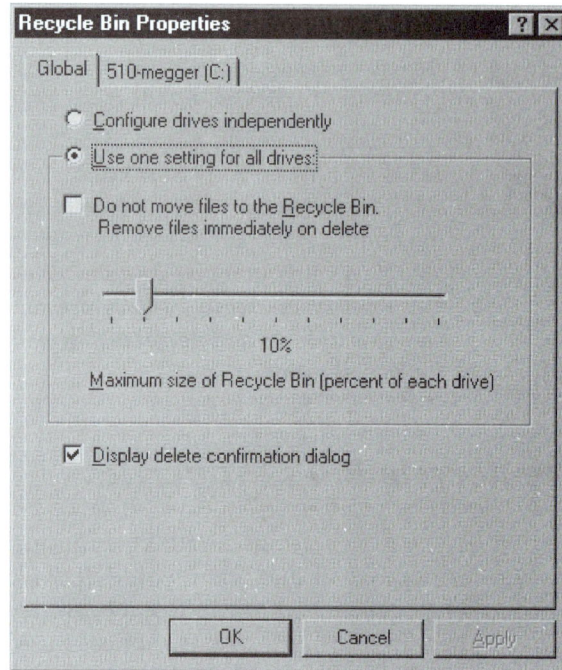

Figure 31.7   *You can set specifics of the Recycle Bin's behavior from its Properties box.*

Recycle Bin's size simply determines how long a file will be recoverable before it's pushed off the list. It also determines the maximum size file that will be recoverable after an accidental deletion. If a file is larger than the maximum size of the Recycle Bin, then it just won't be recyclable. As of this writing, you won't be warned of this, either. It will just be erased.

If you want to alter the size of your Recycle Bins, use the percentage slider. As a rule, the default of 10 percent works just fine. If you work with very large files, you may want to increase this percentage to accommodate them. If you're short on disk space and don't tend to make deletion mistakes, decrease it.

TECH TIP   When you empty the Recycle Bin, all bins are flushed. You can't empty them on a drive-by-drive basis unless you use a file-management program other than Explorer, such as File Manager (click on Start ➤ Run and enter winfile). You *can* delete specific files from the Recycle Bin using Explorer if you select and delete them individually, however.

The final check box is normally set on, requiring you to confirm before Windows 95 will empty the bin. If you find the confirmation boxes annoying, turn off this check box.

> **TIP** If you delete a folder, only the files within that folder appear in the Recycle Bin. If you restore a file that was originally located in a deleted folder, Windows recreates the folder and then restores the file to it.

Troubleshooting Windows 95

Getting help about troubleshooting: Assuming your computer boots up, there is substantial troubleshooting help in Windows 95. Choose Start ➤ Help and double-click on Troubleshooting.

Windows 95 doesn't start up when you turn your computer on: Remember, booting up can take up to a minute. Don't assume there is trouble unless there is no activity on the screen. Check that power is connected, the monitor is on, the brightness isn't turned down, the monitor cable is secure, and no floppy disk is inserted in drive A. If the problem persists, press the reset switch or turn the computer off, wait a second, and turn it on again. Still no go? Insert your start-up disk in drive A and turn the computer off and on again. If you see *Starting Windows 95...* but things get stuck after that, restart and press F8 the next time you see those words. Then choose Safe Mode from the resulting menu. Use Safe Mode to sleuth out which setting (such as screen driver) was wrong.

You are running out of memory: Try closing some programs and/or documents. Empty the Recycle Bin. Remove any unnecessary programs from the Startup folder. Use the Explorer or My Computer to delete some files. Empty the Recycle Bin again. Make sure you have at least several (preferably 10) megabytes of free space on your hard disk. Let Windows manage your *virtual memory* settings (use the Control Panel's System applet to set these). If you only have 4 MB of RAM in your computer, it's a good idea to upgrade to 8, 12, or 16.

You are running out of disk space: Empty the Recycle Bin. Delete files you don't need. Remove whole components of Windows that you never use, such as wallpaper, Exchange, sound schemes, or accessories (some of these consume large amounts of space—see Chapter 7). Remember to empty the Recycle Bin again. Use a compression program such as PKZIP to compress directories you don't use often. Use DriveSpace to compress your drive and double your available disk space (Chapter 23). Upgrade a compressed drive to DriveSpace 3 format (Chapter 32). Use ExtraPack to further compress a compressed drive (Chapter 32).

Increase the DriveSpace compression settings on your drive if the drive is already compressed. Purchase a higher-capacity hard disk.

Printing doesn't work at all: Check that the printer is on, online, filled with paper, and wired securely. Try printing a test page by running Help's printer trouble-shooter (click on Start ➤ Help ➤ Troublehsooting) or by opening the Printers folder (Start ➤ Settings ➤ Printers), right-clicking on the printer, choosing Properties, and clicking on Print Test Page. If the page prints, the problem is with your document or application program, not the printer or Windows 95. If the page doesn't print, make sure Properties ➤ Details shows the correct port for the printer (typically LPT1).

Printing looks wrong: If a partial page printed, check the page orientation. It may be set to Landscape. Check the page-layout command in the program you are printing from *and* in the Properties box for your printer (click on the Details tab, then on Settings). If just the edges of the printout are missing, decrease the margins for your document and try again. Make sure the paper size you are using matches the document size you are printing. If you get PostScript error codes instead of normal text and graphics, either you are trying to use a PostScript printer driver with a non-PostScript printer or the printer needs to be set to PostScript mode. Add the printer to your computer again using the Add Printer Wizard; choose Start ➤ Settings ➤ Printers ➤ Add Printer (Chapter 8).

Fonts don't print correctly: Use TrueType or printer fonts whenever possible. Screen fonts—such as MS-Sans Serif or System—aren't good choices. Change the font in the document and try printing again. If your printer has plug-in font cartridges, you may have the wrong one installed. In the printer's Properties box, click on the Fonts tab and ensure the correct Fonts cartridge is selected. You may have to Install Printer Fonts if the cartridge isn't listed. If TrueType fonts still aren't printing right, as a final resort you can try printing them as bitmaps instead of outlines (select this option from the Fonts tab of the Properties box).

Color printing comes out black and white: Check that you have installed the right print cartridge by looking inside the printer. In the printer's Properties box, choose Details ➤ Setup to check for a possible cartridge-selection option (it might also be available for the program you're using; select File ➤ Printer Setup).

Printing is slow: Open the Properties box for the printer, click on the Details tab, and check the spool settings (spooling should be turned on). If you're waiting a long time for a printout to appear, open the printer's Properties box, click on the Details tab, and click on Spool Settings. Try changing the spool setting from EMF to RAW.

The computer seems "stuck": First, press Esc once or twice. If it's still stuck, try Ctrl-Alt or use the Taskbar to switch to another program to see if Windows 95 is really dead. If the Taskbar is in Auto-Hide mode and doesn't appear, try Ctrl-Esc to bring up the Start list. Use these techniques to get to and save any documents you are working on, then close all programs if possible. If you suspect only one program is having trouble (such as being stuck), press Ctrl-Alt-Del *once*, then wait. In a few seconds a list of programs should come up. Select the program listed as not responding and click on the End Task button; repeat for each stuck program. Save your work and reset the computer as soon as possible.

Chapter 32
About Microsoft Plus

FEATURING

Also known as Plus Pack, Microsoft Plus is a collection of add-on programs, utilities, and other useful doodads for Windows 95. Microsoft Plus isn't supplied with Windows 95—you'll have to buy it separately. At this writing, the exact contents of the Microsoft Plus package were not finalized because the product was still in testing.

The current beta product at the time included the following options.

Option	Description	Hard-Disk Space Required
DriveSpace 3	Enhanced version of the disk-compression software supplied with Windows 95, giving you additional compression	2,649K
System Agent	For setting up automated system maintenance—such as defragmenting and file backup—during periods of system inactivity	1,509K
Internet Plus	Add-ons for Microsoft Exchange, giving you an Explorer interface and mail services for the Internet	1,429K
Master Themes	Collections of flashy sound schemes, color schemes, and cursors	18,193K
Dial-Up Network Server	Lets you set up your office computer so you can call it from home	32K

Option	Description	Hard-Disk Space Required
3-D Pinball	A pinball game with fancy graphics and sound, an example of the kind of flashy Windows 95 games we'll be seeing more of	2,288K
Visual Enhancements	Full-window drag, font smoothing, wallpaper stretching, fancy animated cursors, and additional TrueType fonts for DOS boxes	417K

If you choose to install all the options, you'll need approximately 26 MB of hard-disk space, so make sure you have enough before beginning. If you choose to install fewer options, the Setup program will tell you the amount of disk space needed for them. Master Themes takes up a whopping 14 MB, so if you are short on space, this might be the option to pare down or eliminate (especially if you only work with a 256-color video adaptor); approximately half the themes require a high-color (64-thousand-color) adaptor and look terrible on anything less.

You should read any supplied notes that came with the product, especially any Readme files on Disk 1 of the disk set. As of this writing, the primary warning in the Readme file was:

> *Plus requires a 486 or higher processor, 8 MB of memory, and a display that's capable of displaying at least 256 colors. A high-color (16-bit) display and sound card are recommended.*

Installing Microsoft Plus

Installation is similar to other Microsoft Windows products. Simply do the following:

1. Insert the first floppy disk in drive A.

2. Click on Start and choose Run.

3. Type in **A:setup** (replace A: with B: if that's the disk drive you inserted the diskette into. If you have purchased the CD-ROM version, use that drive's letter instead). The Setup screen appears (see Figure 32.1).

4. Follow the instructions. Choose Custom setup if you want to install all possible goodies, or select specific ones. Feed in the disks as necessary.

5. Depending on which options you choose to install, you may see additional instructions.

CAUTION   Do not install Plus disk compression if you are using third-party disk-compression software, such as Stacker. Use Custom mode to disable installation of Plus compression.

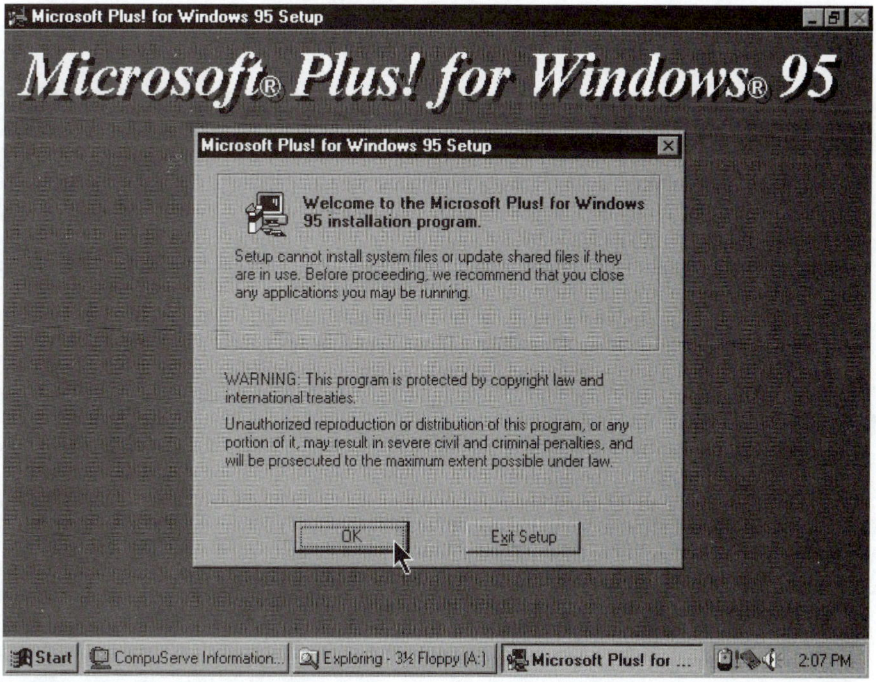

Figure 32.1   *Installing Microsoft Plus*

Running Microsoft Plus

Microsoft Plus isn't a single program; thus, after installation, you won't have a single new program icon in one specific place. Instead, your new goodies will be scattered about in their appropriate locations. Full-window drag and font smoothing will simply be built into your graphical user interface. The Pinball game will be found via Start ➤ Programs ➤ Accessories ➤ Games. DriveSpace 3 is reachable by choosing Start ➤ Programs ➤ Accessories ➤ System Tools, and so on.

The following sections will cover each of the Microsoft Plus add-ons. Remember that because the product is in flux, there may have been changes to some of the commands or features since this was written.

> **NOTE**   Dial-Up Networking is covered in Chapter 28.

DriveSpace 3

DriveSpace 3 is an enhancement to the DriveSpace program that was supplied with Windows 95. The major advantage of the updated version is that it uses more-advanced compression algorithms for providing even more space on your hard disk. On installing this part of Microsoft Plus, DriveSpace will be updated to DriveSpace 3. Open its program folder with Start ➤ Programs ➤ Accessories ➤ System Tools, and you'll see the DriveSpace 3 icon.

The new enhancements of DriveSpace 3 let you:

▶ Customize the type of compression used to save files to a compressed drive. You can save files uncompressed, in the Standard compression format, in the new HiPack format, or double-compressed in the new UltraPack format.

▶ Create compressed drives that are up to 2 gigabytes in size.

> **NOTE**   To create a 2-gigabyte compressed drive, you need an uncompressed drive that is at least 900 MB in size.

▶ Recompress a currently compressed drive using a single compression method or compress each individual file and folder using a separate method for each with ExtraPack.

▶ Uncompress an entire disk or only specific files and folders.

▶ Specify highest compression for files you seldom use, medium compression for files you use more frequently (access will be quicker).

TIP   Likely candidates for highest compression are all Help files (HLP) and setup-information (INF) files. These files are not often used; the Help files are particularly large, sometimes as much as 2 MB.

Compressing an Uncompressed Drive

To run DriveSpace 3, open its program folder as described above and choose DriveSpace 3. See Chapter 23 for a discussion of creating, sizing, removing, and uncompressing hard-disk volumes with Drive-Space. Once you have those instructions under your belt, return to this section and read on.

To gain access to the additional compression options, click on the Advanced menu and then click on Settings. A slider lets you choose various amounts of compression:

No Compression: Files will not be compressed.

Depends on Free Space: When available disk space drops below a certain amount, compression will begin. Standard compression is used.

Standard Compression: The normal method of compression used by Windows 95. Files are typically compressed to a little more than 50 percent of original size. After installing Microsoft Plus, Standard compression is improved a bit, providing even more compression while maintaining good performance when opening and saving files.

HiPack Compression: This option searches your disk for repetitive data and provides better compression than Standard while still giving you minimal slowdowns when opening files. However, because a larger portion of your disk is searched for repetitive data, compressing your drive may take longer. HiPack files are, on average, compressed to one-half their original size—a little smaller than Standard.

Part 6

Customizing Windows 95

A utility called ExtraPack provides an additional compression type:

UltraPack Compression: This option uses optimal compression technology to provide the most space savings on your hard disk. To use this feature, first upgrade your compressed drives to the DriveSpace 3 format by running DriveSpace 3 and choosing the Drive ➤ Upgrade command. You can then use UltraPack by running ExtraPack, which recompresses drives compressed in the DriveSpace 3 format to about one-third their original size. However, accessing UltraPacked files may be slow if you are using a 486-based computer because the file crunching takes advantage of certain Pentium-processor abilities.

Further Compressing Previously Compressed Drives

Unless you specify otherwise, on installing Microsoft Plus, the System Agent program (explained below) is automatically activated to run ExtraPack on any preexisting compressed drives, giving you additional space without your intervention. This process will normally kick in after the computer has been on and left idle for twenty minutes. You can change this time setting, turn off the automatic conversion altogether, or run the ExtraPack program manually if you want.

To upgrade a compressed drive, suppose you have a compressed drive such as the one in Figure 32.2.

To further compress the drive:

1. First, you have to upgrade the drive from the DriveSpace format to DriveSpace 3. Select the drive in the DriveSpace program and choose Drive ➤ Upgrade.

Now you can do a couple of things:

▶ If the System Agent is set to do extra compression automatically, just turn on your computer and let it sit idle. Recompression with ExtraPack should start after twenty minutes.

▶ You can run ExtraPack manually by choosing Start ➤ Programs ➤ Accessories ➤ System Tools ➤ ExtraPack. You'll see a box such as the one shown on the next page.

Choose the drive you want to further compress and click on OK.

NOTE   Only drives already compressed will be selectable from the drop-down list. If you want to compress an uncompressed drive, use DriveSpace 3 instead of ExtraPack.

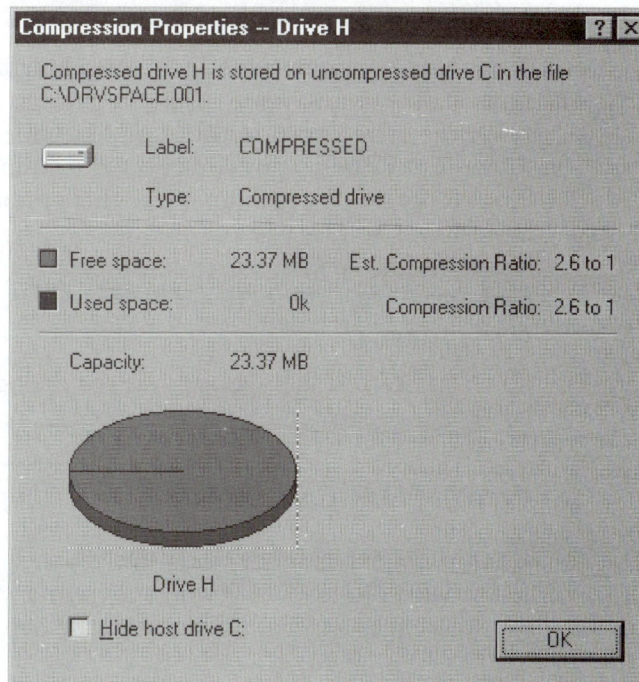

Figure 32.2   *A standard compressed drive that could be further compressed with ExtraPack*

2. You can change a number of defaults that affect ExtraPack's choices about compression. Click on the Settings button in the ExtraPack dialog box, and you'll see:

ExtraPack Settings

Compression methods

UltraPack compression provides maximum disk-space savings, but your system may seem slower when accessing UltraPacked files.

Which files do you want to UltraPack?

○ No files

○ All files (not recommended for 486-based or slower computers)

⊙ Only files not used within the last 30 days

Which compression method do you want to use for other files?

⊙ HiPack

○ None   Advanced...

☑ Save these settings as the new default settings

OK   Cancel   Exceptions...   Overview

Study these options carefully before changing them; the default settings work for most users. You can click on the Advanced button for a few more. The Exceptions button lets you specify files (or complete folders) you don't want compressed or want compressed using a specific compression technique. Use this option when you want to accelerate access to files you use frequently, particularly if you have noticed a performance penalty after compression. (You can revisit this dialog box later if you find there are files whose compression properties you need to alter.)

3. Click on Start in the main ExtraPack dialog box. A progress gauge will keep you posted on the recompression.

Creating New Compressed Drives Using DriveSpace 3

Chapter 23 explains the use of DriveSpace to compress your drives. Essentially, DriveSpace 3 works the same way as DriveSpace. The major differences are that HiPack and the Settings button shown above have been added, allowing Exceptions and the other advanced settings discussed above. When you are about to create a new compressed drive, check the Advanced menu's Settings options and set the compression method. Then go ahead and create the compressed drive.

The System Agent

The System Agent is a program that runs programs automatically! It's designed with automatic execution of system-maintenance pro- grams—such as defragmenters, compressors, and backup programs— in mind. However, it could be used for any program you want to run at a predefined time or after a predetermined period of inactivity.

Using the utility is a two-step process: first you decide which pro- gram(s) you want to run and when, then you run System Agent and leave it running in the background. The rest is automatic. Each pro- gram you add to the System Agent's list of tasks can be set to run at a different time or under different conditions.

After installing Microsoft Plus, the System Agent will already be in- stalled and activated. You'll know it's running because you'll see a lit- tle icon in the Taskbar:

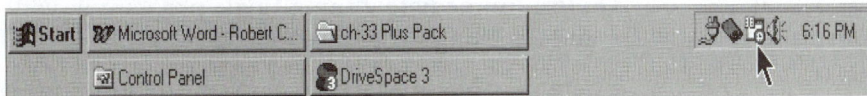

Start	Microsoft Word - Robert C...	ch-33 Plus Pack		6:16 PM
	Control Panel	DriveSpace 3		

Point to it to find out whether the System Agent is awake or asleep. Double-click on it to see what programs are currently in the list of tasks and to make adjustments.

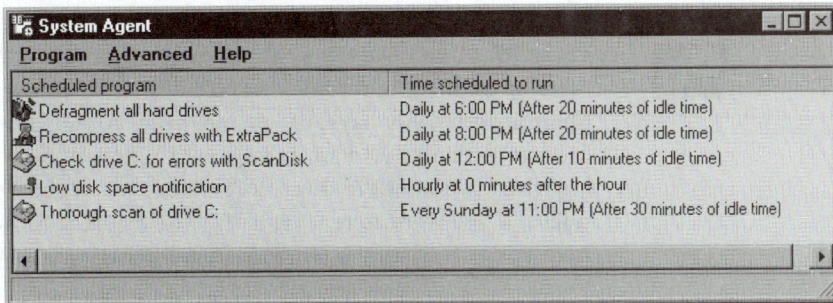

System Agent

Program   Advanced   Help

Scheduled program	Time scheduled to run
Defragment all hard drives	Daily at 6:00 PM (After 20 minutes of idle time)
Recompress all drives with ExtraPack	Daily at 8:00 PM (After 20 minutes of idle time)
Check drive C: for errors with ScanDisk	Daily at 12:00 PM (After 10 minutes of idle time)
Low disk space notification	Hourly at 0 minutes after the hour
Thorough scan of drive C:	Every Sunday at 11:00 PM (After 30 minutes of idle time)

Part
6

Customizing
Windows 95

The list on the previous page should look like yours. These are the programs that Microsoft Plus added by default to the Agent's tasks. They all pertain to hard-disk maintenance; primarily to tasks we all should do anyway but usually don't bother about until it's too late. Keep in mind that ExtraPack only works if you have compressed drives.

Most of the options you'll be concerned with are on the Programs menu. From there you add or remove programs, change the schedule for a program, change settings that apply to a program, or change the properties for that program. Settings and properties will be different for each program, but they typically allow you to change the description that appears in the System Agent's window, determine things such as which drive(s) will be affected, whether the program runs in a window or minimized as an icon, and whether the time of running and possible results of a given program are stored in a log file. You can view the log with the Advanced ➤ View Log command.

TIP   You can disable any program from running by clicking on it and choosing Programs ➤ Disable. *Disabled* then appears next to the program. To reactivate the program, toggle the command off.

You can immediately run a single program in your list by clicking on it and choosing Programs ➤ Run Now.

There may be times when you want to temporarily stop the System Agent (you may be working late and not want ScanDisk to kick in while you're out getting that midnight pizza). Just choose Advanced ➤ Suspend System Agent. Toggle the command to reactivate the System Agent.

TECH TIP   Don't like the System Agent concept at all? Well, it's possible: It takes up memory and some computing power, it might interfere with some other program you have, or you may want to run all of these system utility programs manually. In any case, you can prevent System Agent from loading when you boot Windows. Just choose Advanced ➤ Stop Using System Agent. If you want to reactivate it in the future, choose Start ➤ Programs ➤ Accessories ➤ System Tools ➤ System Agent.

Internet Plus

This option gives you an Explorer-like interface for the Internet and provides an Internet mail service. When installing this function, you'll be asked whether you want to connect to the Internet via the Microsoft Network or via your own service provider:

▶ If you choose the Microsoft Network option, you'll be asked if you want to sign up or if you already have an account.

▶ If you indicate that you have an account with another service provider, you'll be asked to provide information relevant to your account such as area code, phone number, user name, password, IP address of your DNS server (e.g., 128.8.5.1), e-mail address, Internet server, and so forth. Research this information before attempting to set up your connection.

After installing Internet Plus (even if you don't know your Internet-provider information), you'll have a new folder under Accessories called `Internet Tools`.

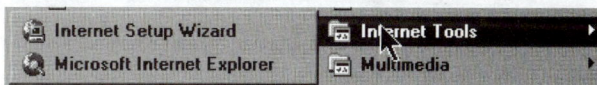

If you bail out of the Internet install, you can always run the Wizard again to set up your account.

Once installation is complete, you can get onto the Internet by choosing the Internet Explorer option. This launches what is essentially a World Wide Web browser, much like the popular program Mosaic. In fact, it's called Microsoft Mosaic and looks like Explorer crossed with Mosaic (see Figure 32.3).

The upshot here is that you have a version of Mosaic that is licensed by Spyglass Inc. to Microsoft.

What About My Internet Mail?

Internet Explorer doesn't do mail; the Web doesn't, so the Web browser can't. So, the other half of Internet Tools is an extension to Microsoft Exchange. This extension lets you send and receive mail over the Internet by adding a few features to Microsoft Exchange that

Part
6

Customizing
Windows 95

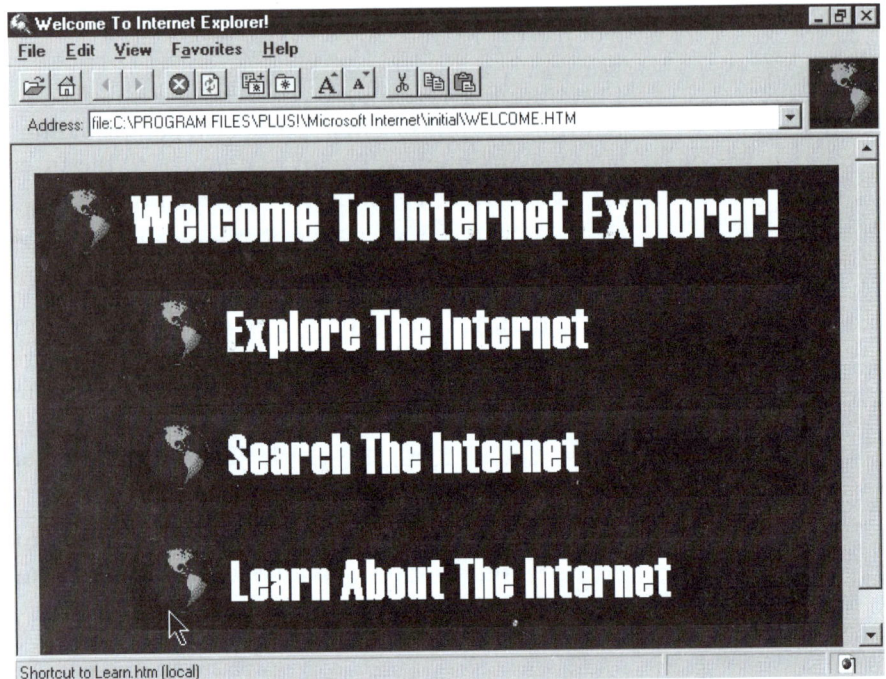

Figure 32.3   *The Internet Explorer is a Web browser. Though only representing a portion of what the Internet has to offer, the Web is quickly becoming the most traveled lane of the information superhighway. However, this Internet tool doesn't support some Internet services (such as FTP, Finger, IRC, telnet, Gopher, or newsgroups).*

tell it how to call up your Internet provider (IP). Your IP may be a separate company such as Netcom or it might be Microsoft (via the Microsoft Network). After setting up your Internet connection, you'll be prompted to choose which Microsoft Exchange profile your connection will be added to. You'll then have a few additional items in your Microsoft Exchange setup; for example, the Tools ➤ Deliver Mail Now menu will have a new option:

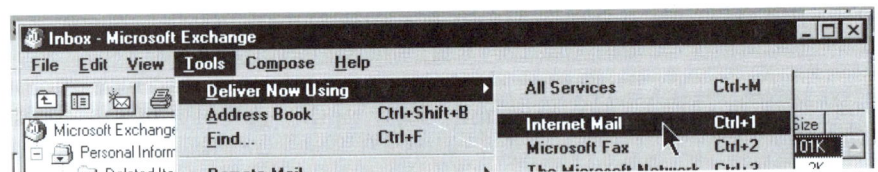

Please refer to Chapter 15 for details about Microsoft Exchange mail services and to Chapter 18 for related details about FTP and other Internet tools.

TECH TIP Unless you're dead set against using Microsoft as your Internet provider, you can eliminate some hassles by simply using the Microsoft Network as your provider. If you use another provider, be sure to purchase an account that works with Microsoft Exchange for Windows 95. Providers will begin to understand what this means in the months after the release of Windows 95. If you want to use the Web browser, you will have to have a SLIP or PPP account; if you want mail, your IP will have to provide a mailbox with a standard Internet mail address.

Master Themes

Master Themes combines sound schemes, color schemes, screen savers, and cursors for your Windows 95 system. It isn't much different from what you can achieve using the Sounds, Display, and Mouse applets from the Control Panel. The advantage of Master Themes is that settings from these three areas are pulled into one applet called Desktop Themes, making it easy to recall many settings at once. You'll find Master Themes in the Control Panel.

Master Themes isn't just a tool for organizing your own settings into groups. You also get some great sounds; Desktop backgrounds; and cute new icons for My Computer, the Recycle Bin, and Network Neighborhood.

Running the applet brings up the dialog box shown in Figure 32.4.

You can create your own schemes by setting up the screen saver, sounds, cursor, and Desktop the way you like and then saving them using the Save As button at the top of the box. However, you might find that the supplied themes give you all the variation you need. Choose a theme from the drop-down list box to see what it looks like. You can preview the screen saver, pointers, and sounds using the two Preview buttons in the upper-right corner.

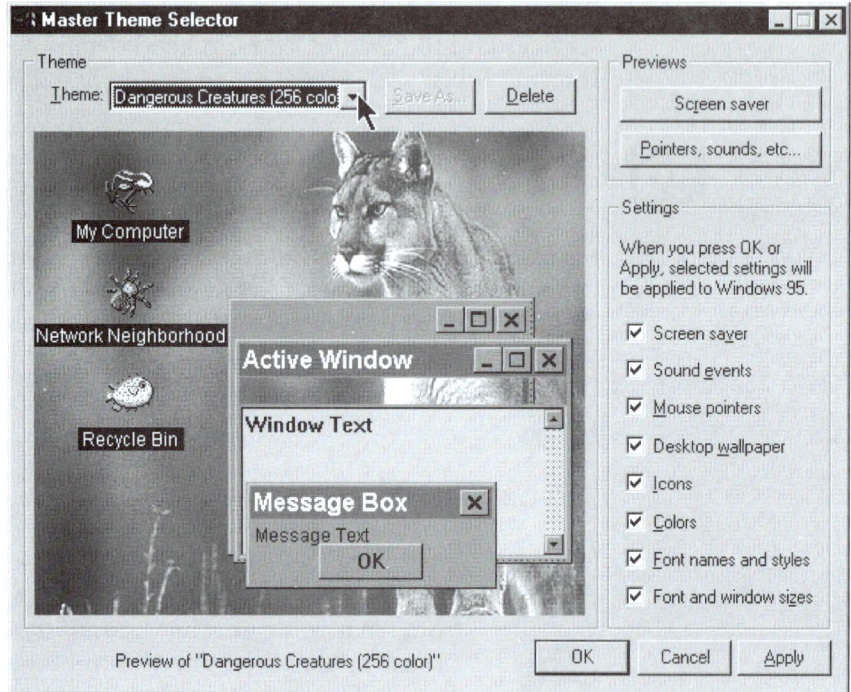

Figure 32.4   *Desktop Themes provides a means for coordinating various elements of the Windows 95 environment and saving them under a single name. An interesting variety of master themes is supplied with Microsoft Plus.*

TIP   Some of the schemes look pretty bad even in 256 colors. Because some of the visuals are actually photo-realistic, switching to a high-color or true-color setting will give you more impressive results. High-color themes are marked as such. If you *don't* have a high-color video driver, you might as well remove these schemes; it will save a significant amount of disk space.

In the Settings portion of the box, you'll see eight check boxes for things like Screen Saver, Sound Events, and so on. Each scheme includes settings for all these options. However, you might not want to load all these features when you change schemes; for example, you might like the sounds you already have but want everything else from one of the master themes. To do this, turn off the Sound Events option before clicking on Apply or OK.

To switch back to the ordinary Windows 95 settings, choose the Windows Default master theme at the bottom of the list of themes.

3-D Pinball

This is an entertainment program based on the classic time waster—the pinball machine. But it looks great. You'll find it in the Games folder (choose Start ➤ Programs ➤ Accessories ➤ Games). Once you run it, press F8 for a listing of keys that control the flippers, bump the table in different directions, and so forth. You can press F4 to switch between windowed and full-screen display. The game's physics and sound effects are realistic. It beats Solitaire and Minesweeper by a country mile!

> **TIP** The longer you hold down the spacebar, the farther back the plunger is pulled, which affects the force applied to the ball as you launch it. I also suggest setting the flippers to the F and J keys as that's where index fingers usually feel at home.

> **CAUTION** Be careful who you show the game to. Little did I know that my friend Niel is a pinball wizard. The game sucked him in so much, he kept slapping my laptop around, instinctively trying to tilt it.

Visual Enhancements

In addition to master schemes, a couple of visual enhancements are added to your system when you install Microsoft Plus:

▶ sliding Taskbar

▶ full-window drag

▶ font smoothing

▶ wallpaper stretching

▶ fancy animated cursors

▶ additional TrueType fonts for DOS boxes

Sliding Taskbar

If you have the Taskbar set to Auto Hide (from Start ➤ Settings ➤ Taskbar), it now slides away smoothly rather than just disappearing. A subtle touch.

Full-Window Drag and Resize

Next, there's the full-window drag option. If Microsoft Plus senses that your system can take it, it installs a driver that keeps the insides of your windows alive while you move them around the screen. Recall that in Windows 3.x and in the stock version of Windows 95, when dragging or resizing a window you see a little empty frame moving around. After installing Microsoft Plus, contents of the window move along with its border, even if the contents of the window are being modified at the time (such as when a chart is being redrawn or numbers are recalculating in a spreadsheet).

Font Smoothing

TrueType fonts in Windows actually comprise two font files on the hard disk: the screen fonts and the printer fonts. The screen fonts are responsible for showing you how the printed font will look and are actually only a close facsimile of the final printed font, close enough to give you a sense of the font's appearance and display accurate line breaks, pagination, and so forth.

Screen font files don't actually have all the possible sizes (2 to 127 points in Windows 3.x and to 999 points in Windows 95) built in. Instead, they are rendered via a formulaic description of the font. With smaller point sizes, this works fine. With larger sizes, the extrapolated display looks edgy, and fonts get the *jaggies* (meaning rough around the edges). A new Windows 95 feature called *font smoothing* or *anti-aliasing* mitigates this problem, in effect smoothing off the rounded edges on large fonts.

On installation of Microsoft Plus, a 32-bit font rasterizer is loaded into your system. It's optimized to *antialias* by filling in the rough spots with softer colors than the one the font is displayed in; for example, shades of gray are used for black letters. Font smoothing is compatible with any TrueType fonts, including the ones you may already have from Windows 3.x. Notice the difference between the two letters below; the one on the left uses smoothing.

> **NOTE** For support of TrueType font smoothing, you need a video setup that supports 256 colors or greater. Also, smoothing has no effect on characters larger than 190 points.

> **NOTE** Font smoothing is nothing new. Adobe's Display PostScript technology, implemented on the NeXT computer (among others) has had it for some time. But Microsoft opted not to support PostScript, developing its own TrueType instead.

Wallpaper Stretching and Animated Cursors

Stretching attractively increases the size of wallpaper images intended for standard VGA monitors (640 by 480) so they display on higher-resolution monitors such as 800 by 600 or 1,024 by 768.

Animated cursors are pointers (such as the frustrating hourglass) that put on a little show rather than just sitting there. Windows NT has animated cursors, and now Windows 95 does, too. Actually, you can use the cursors from NT or ones you download from a BBS even if you don't have Microsoft Plus. Animated cursors have an .ani extension. Microsoft Plus installs a small collection of new ANI files for you to choose from when customizing your system from the Mouse applet in the Control Panel (see Chapter 7).

New TrueType Fonts for DOS Boxes

Before installing Microsoft Plus, a DOS box in Windows 95 will have six possible TrueType font sizes for displaying DOS programs in a window: 6×12, 7×14, 7×15, 8×16, 10×20, and 12×22.

After installing Microsoft Plus, you'll have fourteen TrueType font options for displaying character-based DOS applications in a window: 2×4, 3×5, 4×7, 5×8, 5×9, 6×10, 7×11, 8×13, 8×14, 9×15, 10×16, 11×18, 12×20, and 13×22.

See Chapter 4 for a discussion of adjusting fonts in a DOS box.

Appendix

Installing Windows 95 on Your Computer

FEATURING

Running the Setup program

8. Now the Wizard begins Phase I of three phases. The first phase checks out what hardware is in your computer. Click on Next.

9. You're now asked where you want to install Windows.

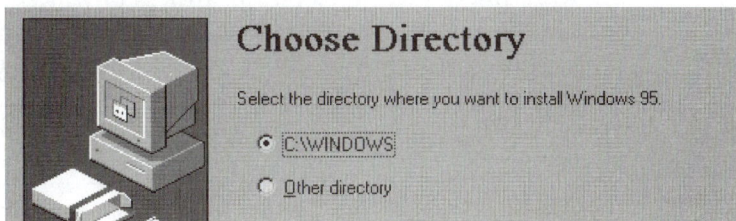

10. Your current Windows directory (if you have one) is shown as the default choice. This is the best bet. Click on Next.

11. Now Setup sleuths around for quite a while, checking out what operating system is currently in your computer. After awhile you'll see this box asking which type of installation you want to perform:

There are four basic types of installation: Typical, Portable, Compact, and Custom. The option you choose determines which accessory programs and utilities get installed. If you want full control over what gets loaded onto your machine, choose Custom. The Typical option will work fine for most users. Regardless of which you choose, the basics of Windows 95 will be identical, and you can add or delete any accessories later. If you're short on disk space, use Compact. If you choose an option for which you don't have enough disk space, don't worry. You'll be alerted and allowed to change choices.

TECH TIP   If you choose Custom, you'll be shown a screen that lets you choose which options to install. A grayed check mark next to a component means that only some of its suboptions are selected. Double-click on a component to see a list of its subcomponents or uncheck the gray check, then wait a second and click again to get a black check mark. The black check mark means all subcomponents are selected and will be installed. To ensure you install every possible component, just make sure all the check marks are black.

---

12. Click on the radio button next to the type of installation you want and then click on Next.

13. When asked to enter your user information, enter your name and company (if there is no company, leave it blank). After entering your name, click on the company line to skip down to it, then click on Next. (These lines may already be filled in for you if you're upgrading from an older version of Windows, in which case just click on Next.)

14. Now Setup sleuths around again, this time looking for hardware. It does a pretty exhaustive search, scouting for almost every known brand of add-on card, hard disk, SCSI controller, and so on. This can take some time; a little gas gauge keeps you informed of the progress. You *must* wait until the search is through. Don't cancel the search unless your computer sits idle for a good long time, like about five minutes, with no hard-disk activity (this means Setup has crashed). If that happens, reboot the machine by turning it off (*not* by pressing Ctrl-Alt-Del) and then on again. Then choose Safe Recovery when prompted. The Setup program will then pick up where it left off.

15. Now you'll be asked about setting up communications:

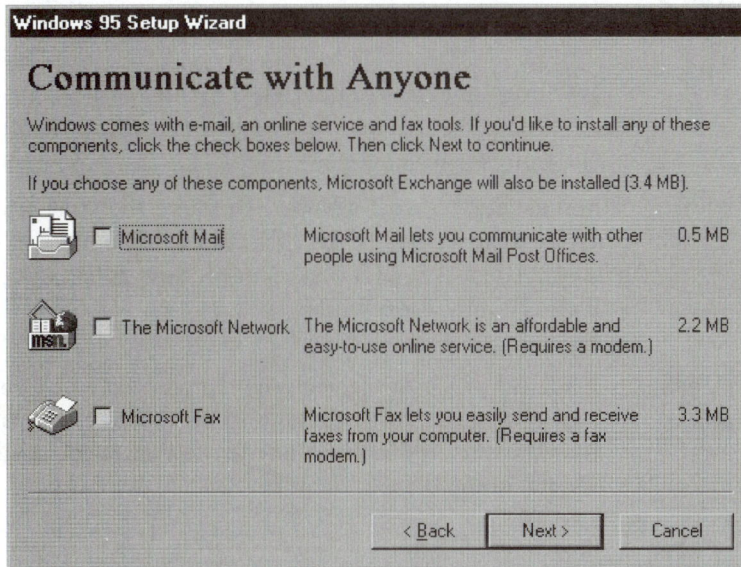

> **Windows 95 Setup Wizard**
>
> # Communicate with Anyone
>
> Windows comes with e-mail, an online service and fax tools. If you'd like to install any of these components, click the check boxes below. Then click Next to continue.
>
> If you choose any of these components, Microsoft Exchange will also be installed (3.4 MB).
>
> ☐ Microsoft Mail   Microsoft Mail lets you communicate with other people using Microsoft Mail Post Offices.   0.5 MB
>
> ☐ The Microsoft Network   The Microsoft Network is an affordable and easy-to-use online service. (Requires a modem.)   2.2 MB
>
> ☐ Microsoft Fax   Microsoft Fax lets you easily send and receive faxes from your computer. (Requires a fax modem.)   3.3 MB
>
> [< Back] [Next >] [Cancel]

Choose which if any of these options you want to install. If you don't install them now, you can later. If you have a fax modem, you'll at least want Fax so you can send and receive faxes from your computer.

16. Depending on the type of install you're doing, you may now see a box asking if you want to install the most common components automatically or choose from a list. It's up to you. The first choice is faster because you don't have to think about it. The second choice shows you the whole shooting match, and you make choices from there. If you choose the latter, see the Tech Tip above. Click on Next.

17. Next you may be asked about your network ID, including your computer's name as it will appear to others on the network, which Workgroup you're in, and a description of the computer. Fill it in as you like. It may be already filled in if you're upgrading. Ensure the Workgroup name is accurate, or you won't be let into your own Workgroup. Click on Next.

18. When asked about creating a start-up disk, choose Yes (unless you don't have a spare disk around). A start-up disk can come in handy in case your operating system gets messed up in the future somehow. Click on Next.

Appendix

> **NOTE** You can create a start-up disk later using the Add/Remove Programs applet on the Control Panel.

19. Now Setup goes into Phase II, copying a zillion files onto your hard disk. This is where the floppy-disk swapping, or simply waiting, comes in. Just click on Next.

20. When asked to insert a floppy to make the start-up disk, do so. It must be at least a 1.2-MB disk and must be in drive A (it can also be a 1.44-MB or 2.8-MB disk). Just follow the instructions; the floppy will chug along for a while.

> **TECH TIP** It's possible you will be prompted with a version-conflict message about a DLL or other support file that Setup is installing being older than the one on your hard disk. In most cases you should keep the newer version of the DLL.

21. When all the copying is over, you'll be prompted to begin Phase III, in which your computer is restarted. Just click on Finish.

22. Now your computer will seem to sit there forever with the little flashing Windows logo doing its thing. Finally, the Welcome to Windows log-on box will appear. Enter a password (you may have the option of not entering a password) and click on OK.

23. Windows 95 now sets up Plug and Play, installs Help, and does some housekeeping. Then you'll be asked to set the home time zone. Use the ← and → keys to move to your time zone. Then click on Date and Time and check for accuracy (see Chapter 7 for more about the Date and Time box).

24. Finally, you'll be prompted to restart your computer. You're done! Windows reboots, and you're up and running. Turn to Chapter 1 and begin reading *Mastering Windows 95*. We hope you enjoy the book!

Index

Note to the Reader:

Main entries are in **bold**. **Boldface** numbers indicate pages where you will find the principal discussion of a topic or the definition of a term. *Italic* numbers indicate pages where topics are illustrated in figures.

N

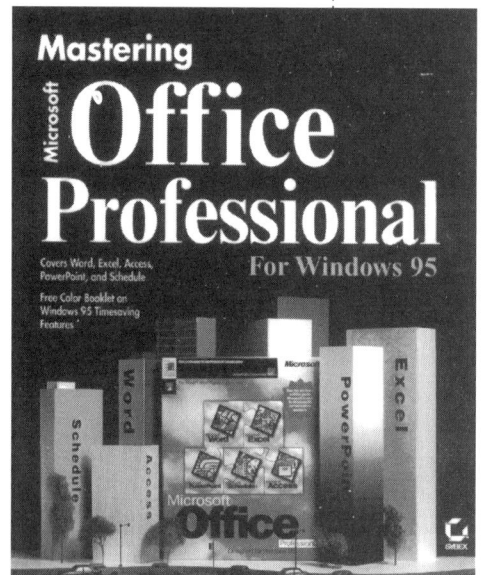

YOUR KEY
TO ACCESS DATABASES

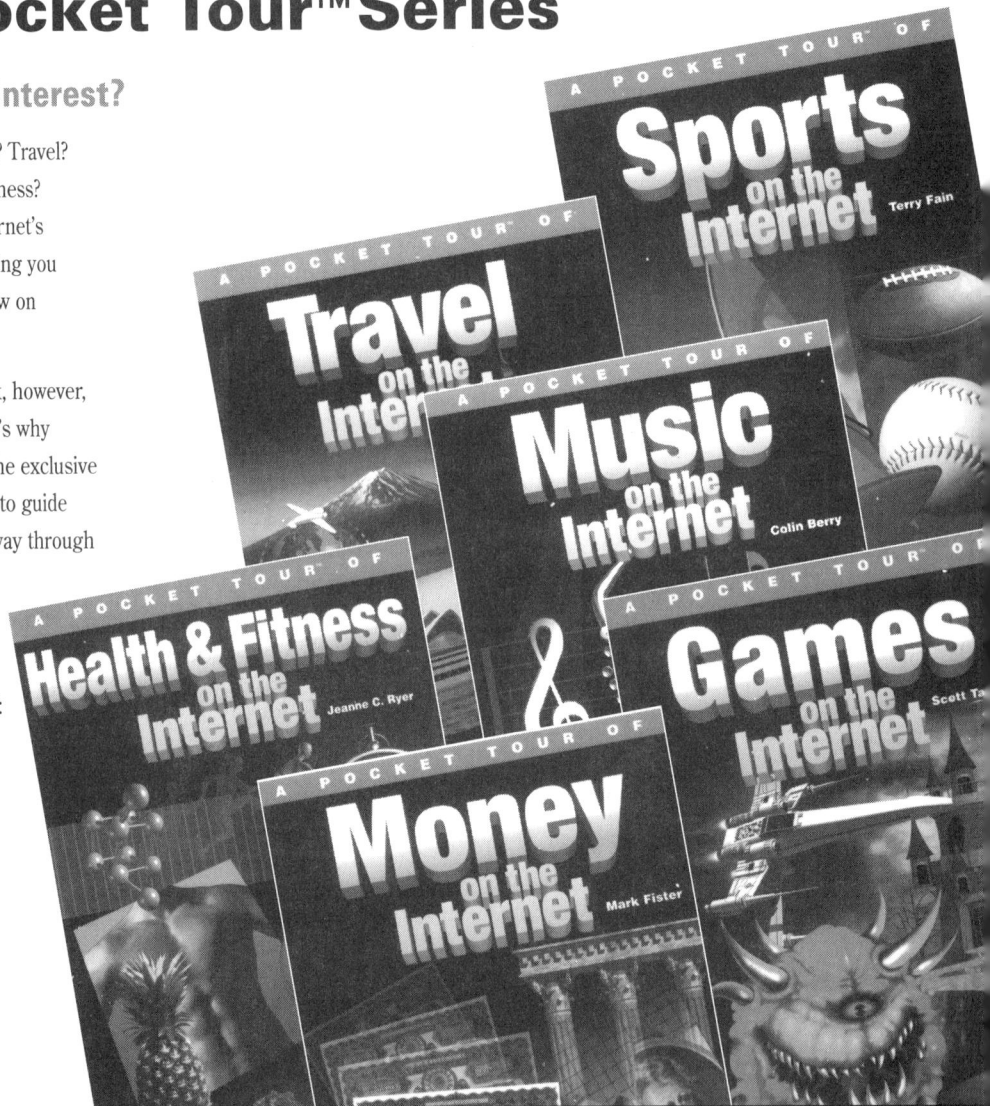

FOR EVERY COMPUTER QUESTION,
THERE IS A SYBEX BOOK THAT HAS THE ANSWER

Each computer user learns in a different way. Some need thorough, methodical explanations, while others are too busy for details. At Sybex we bring nearly 20 years of experience to developing the book that's right for you. Whatever your needs, we can help you get the most from your software and hardware, at a pace that's comfortable for you.

We start beginners out right. You will learn by seeing and doing with our **Quick & Easy** series: friendly, colorful guidebooks with screen-by-screen illustrations. For hardware novices, the **Your First** series offers valuable purchasing advice and installation support.

Often recognized for excellence in national book reviews, our **Mastering** titles are designed for the intermediate to advanced user, without leaving the beginner behind. A **Mastering** book provides the most detailed reference available. Add our pocket-sized **Instant Reference** titles for a complete guidance system. Programmers will find that the new **Developer's Handbook** series provides a more advanced perspective on developing innovative and original code.

With the breathtaking advances common in computing today comes an ever increasing demand to remain technologically up-to-date. In many of our books, we provide the added value of software, on disks or CDs. Sybex remains your source for information on software development, operating systems, networking, and every kind of desktop application. We even have books for kids. Sybex can help smooth your travels on the **Internet** and provide **Strategies and Secrets** to your favorite computer games.

As you read this book, take note of its quality. Sybex publishes books written by experts—authors chosen for their extensive topical knowledge. In fact, many are professionals working in the computer soft-ware field. In addition, each manuscript is thoroughly reviewed by our technical, editorial, and production personnel for accuracy and ease-of-use before you ever see it—our guarantee that you'll buy a quality Sybex book every time.

To manage your hardware headaches and optimize your software potential, ask for a Sybex book.

FOR MORE INFORMATION, PLEASE CONTACT:

Sybex Inc.
2021 Challenger Drive
Alameda, CA 94501
Tel: (510) 523-8233 • (800) 227-2346
Fax: (510) 523-2373

SYBEX

Sybex is committed to using natural resources wisely to preserve and improve our environment. As a leader in the computer books publishing industry, we are aware that over 40% of America's solid waste is paper. This is why we have been printing our books on recycled paper since 1982.

This year our use of recycled paper will result in the saving of more than 153,000 trees. We will lower air pollution effluents by 54,000 pounds, save 6,300,000 gallons of water, and reduce landfill by 27,000 cubic yards.

In choosing a Sybex book you are not only making a choice for the best in skills and information, you are also choosing to enhance the quality of life for all of us.

Pa-58
Dos-Promp 1 (C:>)

GET A FREE CATALOG JUST FOR EXPRESSING YOUR OPINION.

Help us improve our books and get a *FREE* full-color catalog in the bargain. Please complete this form, pull out this page and send it in today. The address is on the reverse side.

Name _____ Company _____

Address _____ City _____ State ____ Zip _____

Phone ( ) _____

1. How would you rate the overall quality of this book?

❑ Excellent
❑ Very Good
❑ Good
❑ Fair
❑ Below Average
❑ Poor

2. What were the things you liked most about the book? (Check all that apply)

❑ Pace
❑ Format
❑ Writing Style
❑ Examples
❑ Table of Contents
❑ Index
❑ Price
❑ Illustrations
❑ Type Style
❑ Cover
❑ Depth of Coverage
❑ Fast Track Notes

3. What were the things you liked *least* about the book? (Check all that apply)

❑ Pace
❑ Format
❑ Writing Style
❑ Examples
❑ Table of Contents
❑ Index
❑ Price
❑ Illustrations
❑ Type Style
❑ Cover
❑ Depth of Coverage
❑ Fast Track Notes

4. Where did you buy this book?

❑ Bookstore chain
❑ Small independent bookstore
❑ Computer store
❑ Wholesale club
❑ College bookstore
❑ Technical bookstore
❑ Other _____

5. How did you decide to buy this particular book?

❑ Recommended by friend
❑ Recommended by store personnel
❑ Author's reputation
❑ Sybex's reputation
❑ Read book review in _____
❑ Other _____

6. How did you pay for this book?

❑ Used own funds
❑ Reimbursed by company
❑ Received book as a gift

7. What is your level of experience with the subject covered in this book?

❑ Beginner
❑ Intermediate
❑ Advanced

8. How long have you been using a computer?

years _____
months _____

9. Where do you most often use your computer?

❑ Home
❑ Work

❑ Both
❑ Other _____

10. What kind of computer equipment do you have? (Check all that apply)

❑ PC Compatible Desktop Computer
❑ PC Compatible Laptop Computer
❑ Apple/Mac Computer
❑ Apple/Mac Laptop Computer
❑ CD ROM
❑ Fax Modem
❑ Data Modem
❑ Scanner
❑ Sound Card
❑ Other _____

11. What other kinds of software packages do you ordinarily use?

❑ Accounting
❑ Databases
❑ Networks
❑ Apple/Mac
❑ Desktop Publishing
❑ Spreadsheets
❑ CAD
❑ Games
❑ Word Processing
❑ Communications
❑ Money Management
❑ Other _____

12. What operating systems do you ordinarily use?

❑ DOS
❑ OS/2
❑ Windows
❑ Apple/Mac
❑ Windows NT
❑ Other _____

13. On what computer-related subject(s) would you like to see more books?

_____

_____

_____

_____

14. Do you have any other comments about this book? (Please feel free to use a separate piece of paper if you need more room)

_____

_____

_____

_____

PLEASE FOLD, SEAL, AND MAIL TO SYBEX

Started w/ Dubour — 9-92

SYBEX INC.
Department M
2021 Challenger Drive
Alameda, CA
94501

SYBEX®

Let us hear from you.

Talk to SYBEX authors, editors and fellow forum members.

Get tips, hints and advice online.

Download magazine articles, book art, and shareware.

Join the SYBEX Forum on CompuServe®

you're already a CompuServe user, just type **GO SYBEX** to join the
YBEX Forum. If not, try CompuServe for free by calling 1-800-848-8199
d ask for Representative 560. You'll get one free month of basic
rvice and a $15 credit for CompuServe extended services—a $23.95
lue. Your personal ID number and password will be activated when
u sign up.

Join us online today. Type **GO SYBEX** on CompuServe.

If you're not a CompuServe member, call Representative 560

at **1-800-848-8199**.

YBEX

(outside U.S./Canada call 614-457-0802)

SYBEX FORUM

TIPS AND SHORTCUTS

Disks

3½ Floppy (A:)

▶ To format a disk, open My Computer, right-click on the drive, and choose Format.

▶ To copy a disk, open My Computer, right-click on the drive, and choose Copy Disk.

▶ To scan, compress, or defragment a disk, click on Start ➤ Programs ➤Accessories ➤ System Tools. Then choose ScanDisk, DriveSpace, or Disk Defragmenter.

Mail

Inbox

▶ To e-mail a document you have open, choose File ➤ Send (if the program has this function), and respond to the prompts.

▶ To e-mail a document from a folder, right-click on the document and choose Send To ➤ Mail Recipient.

▶ To send a fax from within a program, choose File ➤ Print, choose Microsoft Fax as the printer, and begin printing.

Printing

HP DeskJet 540 Printer

▶ To print a document you have open, turn on the printer and choose File ➤ Print.

▶ To check the print queue for a printer, click on Start ➤ Settings ➤ Printers. Double-click on the printer.

▶ To pause, rearrange, or cancel a print job, click on Start ➤ Settings ➤ Printers, click on the job, and choose Document ➤ Pause or Document ➤ Cancel.

their own separate wallpaper, colors, and program settings. As long as you're on the network, your user profiles will be available, so you can have your own familiar desktop greet you no matter what machine you log onto. The default behavior of Windows 95, however, does not use profiles. In this video, you'll learn how to tell Windows 95 to use them.

• System Resources Monitoring— `Sysres.avi`

System resources have been a problem since Windows 3.0. They're *less* of a problem under Windows 95, but they can still cause you troubles. System resources are a small area of memory that Windows uses to keep track of all of the programs and program components currently running on your system. In this video, you'll see how to monitor system resources and you'll gain some insight into how you can run out of resources even when you're not running any programs.

• Network Neighborhood Secrets— `Netnav.avi`

If you're connected to a network, Windows 95 makes viewing and using network resources simpler than ever. This video shows you how to use the Network Neighborhood to browse a workgroup, and then go on to browse your entire enterprise network. You also learn how to designate which workgroup and domain your system is a part of.

• A Guided Tour of the Network Applet— `Netctrl.avi`

If you've viewed the previous videos on networking, then you have noticed how important the Network applet in the Control Panel is to defining and controlling networking under Windows 95. In this video, you'll take a guided tour of this applet, showing you every aspect of this extremely important—and often confusing— part of Windows 95.

• The Registry Editor Revealed!— `Regedtex.avi`

You're not a true Windows 95 expert until you're comfortable with the Registry Editor. This video provides an example of using the Registry Editor by demonstrating the *undocumented* way to change the name of the Recycle Bin.

Utilities from AllMicro on the Enclosed CD

The enclosed CD also contains special tryout versions of two useful utility programs from AllMicro:

• Skylight™

Skylight is a troubleshooting utility that allows you to uncover the mystery of how Windows is using your computer's resources. Skylight runs transparently as a Windows 3.1 application, and displays accurate real-time information about your system's memory usage. The program's built-in editor lets you easily edit WIN.INI, SYSTEM.INI, CONFIG.SYS, and AUTOEXEC.BAT.

• AllMicro AntiVirus™

AllMicro AntiVirus offers the most complete solution for the detection and elimination of thousands of computer viruses. Provides vital security by protecting your computer from all known viruses and alerting you to any new viruses entering the system. AllMicro AntiVirus verifies the security of your boot sector, partition table, LAN drives, and files—even if compressed. As an added protection, this program provides a heuristic program that, when activated, searches for behavior patterns that indicate the presence of potential viruses that might otherwise be undetectable.

The Expert Guide™
to Windows® 95

MARK MINASI

with Patrick Campbell and Christa Anderson

SYBEX • *San Francisco* • *Paris* • *Düsseldorf* • *Soest*

ACQUISITIONS MANAGER: Kristine Plachy
DEVELOPMENTAL EDITOR: John Read
EDITOR: Doug Robert
TECHNICAL EDITORS: Denise Martineau, Jon Gourdine
BOOK DESIGNER: Suzanne Albertson
TECHNICAL ARTISTS: Elizabeth Creegan, Catalin Dulfu
DESKTOP PUBLISHER: Dave Bryant at London Road Design
PRODUCTION COORDINATOR: Kimberley Askew-Qasem
INDEXER: Ted Laux
COVER DESIGNER: Ingalls + Associates
COVER PHOTOGRAPHER: Mark Johann
CD: Dan Tauber

SYBEX is a registered trademark of SYBEX Inc.

TRADEMARKS: SYBEX has attempted throughout this book to distinguish proprietary trademarks from descriptive terms by following the capitalization style used by the manufacturer.

Every effort has been made to supply complete and accurate information. However, SYBEX assumes no responsibility for its use, nor for any infringement of the intellectual property rights of third parties which would result from such use.

Library of Congress Card Number: 95-72703

ISBN: 0-7821-1519-5

Manufactured in the United States of America

10 9

*This is dedicated to my wife, Darcee.
Usually authors dedicate books to their
wives "for all the patience she's shown
while I wrote this," but I'm dedicating
this to her because I'm crazy about her.*

ACKNOWLEDGMENTS

As with most of my books, this Sybex book grew out of one of my company's technical seminars. As with so many of our successful seminars, much of the credit must be given to our sponsor, Jess Sieple, owner of Alexander Hamilton Institute, the marketing firm that handles many of our seminars.

The pace of software change—notice I didn't say "innovation"—has made it harder to turn out books like this one in a timely fashion. Once, I could do it myself, but *this* book couldn't have been done in the time that it was without my co-authors, Patrick Campbell and Christa Anderson. You see Patrick's work in the chapters on Novell and Remote Access; Christa wrote the Registry, Failure Recovery, and DOS Programs chapters. Having said that, however, I of course assume responsibility for any errors in the book. The MMCO research assistants Holliday Ridge and Leslie McMurrer provided invaluable assistance in editing and proofreading—very little gets past them! I thank them both for their essential role in creating this book and in helping to make it as error-free as possible. Thanks also to my management team of Donna Cook, Ceen Dowell, and Patrick Campbell, for shielding me from the outside baloney while I wrote this.

I would be amiss if I were to forget to mention IBM for their VoiceType Dictation Adapter for Windows. I was afflicted with carpal tunnel syndrome (the "black lung" of writers, I suppose!) while putting this together under tight deadlines. Though the version I have was not designed for Windows 95, it worked fine under Windows for Workgroups, and allowed me to write chapters 1, 2, 3, and 5 while my wrists were healing. Get those 95 drivers written, guys—my wrists are getting sore again!

Sybex's Master of the Written Word, the one and only Gary Masters, was the man who commissioned this book, and without his leadership this and many other useful tomes might never have seen the light of day. Our editor Doug Robert brought keen insights to the process, and clarity to the most confusing topics, and for that I give my thanks. If it weren't for Kristine Plachy, we'd still be waiting for the betas; thanks, Kristine. And darn, but do I miss Rudolph Langer! This was one of the last books that Dr. Langer approved before leukemia stole him from us. Wherever you are, Rudy, I'm sure you're getting some great books ready for the rest of us when we join you, if we're that lucky. There are no doubt other people who were part of putting this book together, and to those whom I have left out here, I apologize.

CONTENTS AT A GLANCE

TABLE OF CONTENTS

INTRODUCTION

WELCOME to *The Expert Guide to Windows 95*! Before we start discussing VxD's, Plug and Play, the Registry, and whether to use the Microsoft NetWare Client or the Novell NetWare Client, let me take a couple of pages and explain how this book is different from other Windows 95 books, and what's in it.

The massive pre-marketing of Windows 95 led book publishers to stoke the literary engines and churn out Windows 95 books by the dumpster-full, even before the product was available. What's this book got that others don't?

Well, most Windows books fall into one of two categories. The first kind, of which this book is most certainly not a member, are the "click and drag" books, the books that teach you how to use Windows 95; they introduce you to the GUI, discuss whether to use My Computer or Explorer, mention that there's a thing called the Registry, and offer a cook's tour of the Control Panel. The second kind is the "tips and tricks," "power user," or "secrets" kind of Windows 95 book. These books tell you that right-clicking the Inbox in 4/4 time while holding down the Alt key and whistling "The Bridge Over the River Kwai" will present a hidden 10-minute video of Bill Gates expounding on the virtues of good dental health.

Secrets are terrific things; it's fun to know them (particularly when your friends and coworkers don't), but, to me, a "secret" is just an example of incomplete documentation on Microsoft's part. I've spent 13 years as a PC support person and technical teacher, and as far as I'm concerned, the greatest secrets are the answers to the questions, "How does Windows 95 *really* work, and how can I *keep* it working?"

That's what this book is all about. Over the past six years, Sybex and other computer publishers have been kind enough to publish ten of my books,

books which are usually modifications of the course books that I use for my technical seminars. If you've ever picked up *The Complete PC Upgrade and Maintenance Guide, Mastering Windows NT Server,* or *Troubleshooting Windows,* for example, then you know what to expect: I'll explain how something works, and how sometimes it *doesn't,* and from there it's usually simple to see how to fix it. That's the basic approach of *this* book as well, with one more part added: *examples.* Nothing frustrates me more than reading something technical that lacks examples. Sadly, that describes most of the technical Windows 95 literature, so I've tried to include as many examples as possible.

Basically two kinds of people will find this book useful: PC support people and power users. When I say "PC support people," I mean anyone who has to solve a Windows problem—like "my PCMCIA card isn't recognized," "the Network Neighborhood folder is empty," or "I need to disable a system policy." It could be a person at home using Windows 95 to keep his checkbook, or it could be someone working on her company's Help Desk. As to power users, well, you know who you are.

Overview of the Contents

The book starts with a technical overview of Windows 95. In Chapter 1 you'll learn a bit about how the GUI works, discover that Windows 95 is not all that terribly great a leap from Windows for Workgroups 3.11, and find out if Windows 95 or Windows NT is the right 32-bit operating system platform for you.

Chapter 2 discusses the structure of Windows 95 with a look "under the hood" to find components with names like GDI, VMM32, and Configuration Manager. You'll need this understanding of the parts of Windows so you'll know where to go to fix problems. After all, if you didn't understand the parts of your car, you might pop the hood when trying to fix a flat tire.

Chapter 3 looks at setting up Windows 95. Sure, it's a simple matter to shove the CD into the drive and type *setup,* but this chapter looks beyond that, and provides some help for those who must install and reinstall Windows 95 on a number of machines. The secret to simplifying Windows installations is to write a Windows "installation batch file," which you'll learn to do in this chapter.

One of the newest and most important concepts for PC support people is the Registry. In Chapter 4, my co-author Christa Anderson adapted a chapter from our NT book (NT has a Registry as well) to explain what the Windows 95 Registry is, how you'd work with it, what you can do with it, and when *not* to do anything with it.

Chapter 5 begins a string of chapters about networking with Windows 95. This large chapter is an introduction to networking under Windows 95. You'll learn about protocols, network binding interfaces, client software, browsers, and the like here. It's the starting point for Chapters 6 through 8.

Chapter 6 is for the folks out there trying to make Microsoft's desktop operating system (Windows 95) work with Novell's network operating system (NetWare). You have a choice under Windows 95 about how to access a Novell server. You can either use programs written by Novell or some written by Microsoft. Choosing which to use isn't simple, and my co-author Patrick Campbell leads you through the pieces of NetWare connectivity in this chapter.

Patrick then returns in Chapter 7 with lots of information about Dial-Up Networking, the essential part of Windows 95 that makes remote networking possible. Dial-Up Networking has a bunch of nice features that aren't documented very well by Microsoft, and Patrick attempts to fill in the gaps.

Chapter 8 shows you how to leverage your network in order to use it as a PC support tool. You'll learn how to simplify Windows 95 installations by using your network, for starters. Then you'll see how to use User Profiles to allow your favorite desktop settings to follow you around the network. Profiles are even useful if you *don't* have a network, as they make it possible for you to share a computer with other users while keeping your desktop settings separate from theirs.

In Chapter 9, Christa discusses how to handle Windows 95 crashes. As Windows 95 is almost an "all-in-one" operating system, some kinds of failures are simple PC boot failures. The causes of boot failures are the same no matter what operating system you're running, so she's taken a discussion of disk failure recovery from one of my previous books and expanded it to include specifics of Windows 95, then added new sections on the Windows debugging switches and BOOTLOG.TXT, an invaluable diagnostic tool.

Now that DOS is dead, you'll have to install all of your new hardware under Windows 95. Even though Windows 95 is meant to relieve you of ever needing to deal with the arcane details, it can't do it for every piece of hardware out there, so chances are that someone you work for is going to ask you for the details anyway. It can get a little tricky; not only must you know the Control Panel, you have to understand IRQs, DMAs, I/O addresses, and so on. Chapter 10 takes you through the process, including a discussion of Plug and Play, the centerpiece of Windows 95's hardware support. What's that, you say? You don't have a Plug and Play computer? Well, if you have Windows 95, then think again—you *do* have a Plug and Play computer. It's all in Chapter 10.

Chapters 11 and 12 look at those two most important peripherals, disks and printers. You'll learn how to install new ones, diagnose problems on existing ones, and how to rev up their performance a bit.

Finally, in Chapter 13, Christa shows you how to run existing DOS programs on Windows 95. Wondering what all those settings are in the property sheets for your DOS programs? You can find out here.

That's what you'll find in this book. If you found something that you liked, or something that you didn't like, or if you think that we should have covered something in more detail, then drop me a line. You can find me at mark@www.mmco.com. Thanks for reading, and I hope this book makes your life as a Windows "techie" easier!

Typesetting Conventions

When you're talking about a new operating system, with new ways of naming files and new ways of envisioning user input and command prompts, you have to keep clear when you're talking about the new way and not the old way. In this book my editors have tried to enforce some consistency on these things to help reduce the confusion inherent in the process.

Here are a few of the conventions used to differentiate between the types of elements you'll run into in this book:

- DOS-style filenames (which follow an eight-dot-three convention) are usually shown in a special filename typeface, all uppercase.

  Example: `SYSTEM.DAT`

- Long filenames, now available with Windows 95 and any 32-bit application, are shown in the same special filename typeface, with upper/lowercase distinctions as maintained by the program or author.

  Example: `Steering Committee's version of 96 facilities budget.DOC`

- Directory and folder names are also shown in the filename typeface (and usually lowercase).

  Example: `C:\windows\mmco\windows95 book\ch01`

- File contents (for example, entries in the `WIN.INI` file), are shown in regular text, not in a special font.

  Example: "In the [UserInfo] section, the device= and timercount= lines are optimized for a single-server configuration."

- Resources that you have *named* (for purposes of sharing them over a network or making them available to other users) are usually shown in regular text, though in certain situations they're styled as italic to avoid ambiguity.

  Example: "Make your printer available over the network as *HP2 next to watercooler*."

- Menu commands and options, and options in dialog boxes, are usually regular text, but have been styled as italic whenever it might not be clear that the words you're seeing are part of the option, not part of my instruction to you.

  Example: "Double-click on the Print option on the File menu, or the Properties setting in the Display dialog box" shows option names that are perfectly clear, but "Click on *Update user data while polling*" makes it obvious that I'm not expecting you to wait until *you're* polling to click on the option.

- Text or values you are expected to type into a dialog box or file are shown as boldface.

  Examples: "Enter **2** for the number of copies"; "Change f:\123R3 to **\\server\ted\123R3**"

CHAPTER

1

Windows 95 Overview

WHAT can Windows 95 do for you and your company? Is it worth upgrading? If you've already bought 95, what benefits does it offer over competing operating systems?

In this chapter, I'll touch on many things you'll learn about later in the book. It's not my intention in this chapter to explain any of these concepts in great detail; rather, this is something of a teaser showing you some of what you'll see later.

GUI Improvements

The most visible part of 95 is its *GUI*, its Graphical User Interface. It is an improvement over the older Windows GUI in a number of ways:

- The desktop paradigm is greatly improved over previous versions of Windows.

- Folders that hold things, including other folders, allow a deeply nested storage and management structure.

- Shortcuts make getting to things easier (although they *are* somewhat inferior to the object-oriented shadows found in OS/2).

- The Taskbar makes everything just a few clicks away, and this makes it harder to get confused about what's loaded and what isn't.

- There are many more places to hide things in 95, so the Find option is useful.

- The autorun option on CD-ROMs makes software installation from a CD-ROM easier.

I know that you're probably somewhat familiar with these things, so I'll only examine them briefly.

The Desktop

Like many GUIs, Windows uses a desktop metaphor—your monitor's screen represents an imaginary desktop cluttered with folders, items, and objects like printers or modems. Personally, I've always found the whole desktop idea kind of silly, inasmuch as I can't imagine working in an office with a 14-inch desktop. I spend a lot more time shuffling things around on my tiny computer desktop than I ever did on my real-world desktop. That said, however, the desktop metaphor works in many ways, perhaps most important of which is that you can customize your desktop's colors, fonts, and the things sitting on the desktop. What I'd really like is a six foot by three foot backlit LCD panel about 7000 pixels × 2500 pixels—you know, a *real* desktop. One of these days, I guess...

It's undeniable that the 95 desktop makes a lot more sense than the 3.x desktop did. It's easier to keep things in order and there are more places to put things. Where Windows 3.x required that you fiddle with the Control Panel and the Print Manager to control your printers, for example, 95 only requires that you open the Printers folder and open whichever printer you wish to control.

Multiple Nested Folders

The Windows 3.x and OS/2 1.x user interfaces relied upon a Program Manager to let people choose applications. You could place related applications into *groups*, which were represented as folders in a file cabinet. Unlike folders in a file cabinet, however, you couldn't put a group inside a group.

Windows 95's user interface does away with the Program Manager Instead, Windows creates a directory called `C:\windows\desktop` to which the GUI programs on the screen link. Anything copied t `C:\windows\desktop` shows up on the user's screen and is represente as a small picture called an *icon*. Double-clicking on an icon *opens* that icon. To open an icon means:

- If it refers to a program—that is, if the icon represents a binary program file like the familiar .EXE files—then Windows starts the program.

- If the icon refers to a data file, then Windows looks to see which program is associated with that kind of data file. Then it launches the program and feeds it the data file. (Unfortunately, this association is still only built upon extensions, a pretty simple and dumb way of telling the operating system, or OS, what program to use to start up a file. Perhaps when Cairo arrives, they'll fix that.)

- If the icon refers to a directory on a storage device, then Windows opens up a window displaying the contents of the directory.

Even the disk drive itself is represented (in My Computer) as a series of folders. For those who are interested, the apps you can start straight from the Taskbar are located in C:\windows\start menu. There is a folder called \windows\start menu\programs, which holds folders corresponding to the old Windows 3.x groups. For example, if you upgraded your old Windows implementation or you installed old Windows 3.x applications on a 95 desktop, then you'll have groups. Suppose you've got a group called Lotus Applications, which contains an icon to start up Ami Pro 3.0, and one to start up Freelance for Windows; suppose also you've got a folder called Microsoft Apps, which contains an icon to start up Microsoft Excel 5.0. You'd then have a \windows\start menu\programs directory containing:

- A directory called Lotus Applications, containing a file called Ami Pro 3.0.lnk (note that files can have names longer than eight characters under Windows 95!) and another file called Freelance for Windows.lnk, where the .lnk files are *shortcuts*, something we'll get to in a minute.

- Another directory called Microsoft Apps, containing Microsoft Excel 5.0.lnk.

This is a terrific strength, but it's got a weakness, which you'll see in the next point.

Shortcuts

Suppose you've got (as I do) a directory that you use frequently, but it's four levels down in the directory structure. Whenever you want to get to it, you've got to open My Computer, open up the C: drive, open the first level of the directory structure, …and so on. What I'd really like is for the directory to be right on my desktop where I can get to it with a click or two, but I don't want to actually move the whole directory.

Similarly, consider commonly used programs. If my word processor sits in `C:\amipro`, then I don't want to have to open up the C: drive every time I want to start Ami. I *would*, however, like to have Ami on my desktop without moving all of the program there.

In both cases, I'm looking for a Windows *shortcut*. They've had them in the Macintosh world for years and called them *aliases*; OS/2 users have had them for years and called them *shadows*. Basically, a shortcut is just an icon that's a direct path to some other location on disk (even on some other disk, as you'll learn in the "Wired 95" chapter).

NOTE The failure of shortcuts is that opening up their properties gives you the properties of the *shortcut*, not the properties of the original object. The object-oriented version of Windows, which will appear in 1997 or 1998, may remove that limitation.

The Taskbar

Previously, Windows always had a Task List, a simple text list of which programs were active. Now there's the *Taskbar*, which not only lets you see what programs are running, but allows you to launch new ones.

The value of the Taskbar is that it gives you an at-a-glance look at all the loaded programs. Now, when one window obscures another, you don't have to wonder whether it's loaded; instead, just look at the Taskbar. You can not only see what's loaded, you can go to that program with just a click.

Powerful Search Engine Built In

The Windows desktop paradigm essentially takes your disk structure and makes it into your desktop. It's not a *terrible* paradigm (you know what they say about paradigms: "shift happens"), but it *does* imply that there are now many more places to lose a program or a data file. This is why the Find option is nice. You just specify what you're looking for and where to look for it, and the search goes on in the background while you continue to work. You can even tell it to look for particular strings of text. I *do* wish that the Find option were attached to every window instead of just the Taskbar, but it's still a nice feature.

Autorun CD-ROMs

Software vendors can now design an *autorun* CD-ROM, a CD that starts up a program as soon as you insert the disc in the CD-ROM. For example, the Windows 95 disc that I'm working with now has this file called AUTORUN.INF in its root directory:

```
[autorun]
OPEN=AUTORUN\AUTORUN.EXE
ICON=AUTORUN\WIN95CD.ICO
```

Those two lines tell 95 to run AUTORUN.EXE whenever the disc is inserted in the CD-ROM drive. The ICON= line just specifies the icon to use when displaying the CD in the Explorer view.

By the way, if you want to *disable* this feature, all you need to do is open the Control Panel, double-click on System, and choose the Device Manager tab. Then examine the properties of the CD-ROM object and uncheck *Auto-insert notification*.

Document-centric Model

One of the basic parts of Windows 95's design is the notion that users should work with documents, not applications. Each program registers with Windows in the Windows *Registry* what kinds of files the program can create or work with. This is part of how Windows knows how to open a document when you double-click it.

For example, I use Lotus Ami Pro. Prior to Windows 95, I'd create a new Ami document by starting up Ami, then clicking on File ➤ New. Under Windows 95, I just click the File and New menu items from any folder, and I get the option to create many different types of new documents, with Ami Pro as one possible type.

Of course, the basic effect of clicking the document is that Windows starts up Ami Pro; this makes me wonder what the difference is between this new document-centric and the old application-centric model. In any case, document-centricity means that Windows programs are moving away from the MDI approach, where a single Windows program might have one main (or *parent*) window and a bunch of smaller *child* windows within it (a notion Microsoft pushed hard in 3.x), to a program model where you would edit four different documents with four different copies of the word processor. This is something that Microsoft said was a really bad idea in 3.x, but now thinks is a really good idea in Windows 95. *Plus ça change* and all that.... (Actually, yet another example of how things don't change is the fact that it's *still* a pain to use characters outside of the American English set; for the life of me, I couldn't get the previous French fragment to print the lowercase cedilla on my printer. But explaining that would bring up Unicode, a discussion for another day.)

New Support Tools

Windows 95 wasn't just built with ease of use for users in mind. It's also got some good news for PC support people: new support tools. (There's also some bad news, of course: in particular, 95's greater complexity.) Some of those tools include:

- The Network Monitor Agent
- The emergency restore utility
- The configuration backup utility
- The System Policy Editor
- The network batch setup utility

- Remote registry support
- BOOTLOG.TXT

The Network Monitor Agent

With the Network Monitor Agent, you can take the Windows 95 System Monitor and the Network Watcher and extend them across the network to look at other people's workstations. It's also the client part of the Server Management System (SMS), if you use that.

Network Batch Setup Utility

Setting up Windows 3.x over a network required some real rocket science. Windows 95 has programs that will automate two very important parts of network setup: creating the shared directory on the server (NET-SETUP.EXE) and creating the batch files to simplify setup (BATCH.EXE).

Why would anyone care about these two features? Well, Windows 95 is big—it's easy for your Windows directories to reach 60MB. That may be too great a hard disk burden for many companies to inflict on a user's workstation, so some firms prefer to put most of the Windows files on a shared directory on the server. Then they do a network setup on Windows 95, and 95's setup program puts a small subset of its files on each user's workstation. That way, users aren't losing tens of megabytes by installing Windows. NETSETUP.EXE does the groundwork to make network setups possible.

Once it's time to install Windows 95, you have lots and lots of questions to answer. Walking around to dozens of machines clicking the same buttons over and over again gets old fast; this is why you'll like BATCH.EXE. There has always been a way to set up Windows with a response file, a file that pre-answers all the setup questions. It's just been a pain in the neck to actually sit down and figure out how to write one. BATCH.EXE solves that problem by supplying a bunch of dialog boxes and fill-in-the-blanks forms; these in turn generate the .INF files necessary for an unattended installation of Windows 95.

The Emergency Restore Utility (ERU)

Unlike older, simpler operating systems, Windows 95 doesn't all live in one place, and neither does one of your configurations. Backing up a Windows 95 configuration is a bit more complex than backing up CON-FIG.SYS and AUTOEXEC.BAT. That's why Windows 95 comes with the Emergency Restore Utility, or ERU. The ERU is a simple little program that just backs up all the important parts of your Windows configuration. On a smaller scale, there is a program called CFGBACK.EXE that allows you to retain up to eight Registries in backup sets.

The System Policy Editor

Through the years, support folks have wished to place bounds on the things that users can do to their individual systems. These desires didn't come out of any fascist need for control, but rather the need to provide a set of safeguards allowing users to work productively in an environment without having to worry about accidentally doing something dangerous that might cost them time or perhaps their work.

With the System Policy Editor, you can restrict the features that can be installed on a Windows 95 workstation and what kinds of changes users can make to big things (like redirectors) and small things (like wallpaper). The System Policy Editor is an extremely important tool for user support, and you'll learn how to use it in greater detail in Chapter 7.

Remote Registry Support

Most of Windows 95's configuration information no longer lives in .INI files, although those .INI files still exist (mainly for compatibility with older Windows apps). I'll discuss the Registry in a few pages, but for now just understand that it contains most of 95's setup and runtime configuration information. What's really interesting about 95's Registry is that, with the addition of a simple service, an administrator can remotely modify the Registries of other machines *over the network*. What that means is that you can examine, diagnose, and repair many network problems without ever leaving your chair.

BOOTLOG.TXT

What a difference a file makes; while earlier versions of Windows would create a BOOTLOG.TXT, it was a poorly organized file of only marginal use. Windows 95's BOOTLOG, in contrast, is better-organized and more likely to be a source of useful information to the Windows troubleshooter.

Improved Networking

A lot of what you just read concerned 95's ability to let you control things over the network. That brings up an important point: 95 and networks are much better friends than were 3.x and networks.

If you were a support person for an operating system before 1995, there was the chance that you might have lived your life and done your job without knowing anything about networks—but if you're a Windows 95 support person, then that's not even remotely possible.

32-Bit Redirector and Drivers

One of the biggest pains about networking in the DOS/Windows days was dealing with huge network drivers and protocol stacks. But under Windows 95, the network drivers, the transport stacks, and the redirectors are all native-mode 32-bit code, meaning that they *don't* live in your machine's bottom 640K. That means that networking capabilities are available to any DOS programs that you run, but those DOS programs don't pay the memory price for network capabilities.

NOTE Windows 95's network drivers are even *hot swappable*. This means that if you start up your computer without a network card in place but insert one while you're working in 95, then the network drivers and other software all load *without requiring a reboot.*

The 32-bit drivers should also be faster than the drivers you've seen in previous versions of Windows or DOS, unless you've been working with Windows for Workgroups. In that case, you won't see much of a difference, as Workgroups always used 32-bit drivers.

Simpler Redirector Interface

Windows 95 now makes it easier to understand what network programs you're loading and what programs you need.

Previous versions of Windows made adjusting your network rather difficult. The Control Panel handled some networking functions, but others were in the Windows Setup program. Under Windows 95, all of networking sits in the Control Panel.

If you imagine networking from a layered perspective, then Windows 95's networking system will make a lot of sense. Windows separates networking into three parts: the board driver, the transport protocol, and the redirector (or, as it is more and more commonly said, the client software).

Novell Redirector Built In

Many of us—67 percent of us, in fact—use Novell software. However, until Windows 95, making Windows and Novell work together has been as much fun as pulling teeth without Novocain. Microsoft has made this integration much easier because Windows 95 includes a complete Novell redirector. Although Microsoft and Novell are not the best of friends, the built-in network support in Windows 95 is far superior to what we *haven't* seen in previous versions of Windows. Windows 95 even gives you the option to use either the Novell-written redirector or a Novell-compatible redirector written by Microsoft.

The version of the NetWare client from Microsoft that ships in the Windows 95 box does not support NetWare 4.x's Novell Directory Services (NDS), but Microsoft has released a revised version of the client software which *is* NDS-aware. You can find it on Microsoft's Web site, www .microsoft.com.

Remote Registry Control and Network-Based Boots

You have probably read of the importance of the Registry in Windows 95. Even more important, in many ways, is the fact that you can store a user's Registry on a network server rather than on the user's workstation computer. This means that centrally controlling registration from a network under Windows 95 will be much simpler than it ever was with Windows 3.1. Additionally, Windows 95 offers a way to install itself on a user's workstation so that most of Windows 95 will live on the server, rather than the user's workstation; this means a tremendous savings in disk space. Of course, this was possible under earlier versions of Windows, but the fact that Windows 95 is an all-in-one operating system makes the network note auction somewhat more impressive.

These features are actually not connected; it is possible to install Windows 95 so it sits mainly on a server, but it is also possible to install 95 on a workstation but edit that workstation's Registry via the network anyway.

Better Kernel

Besides the new GUI, perhaps the most important driving force behind the creation of Windows 95 was the pressing need for a new system architecture. The Windows 3.x architecture was designed to run on 286-based computers. It probably seemed like a good idea at the time, but the corporate world's quick acceptance of 386-based computers soon shone a bright and unattractive light on Microsoft's architecture decisions.

With Windows 95, Microsoft was able to wipe the slate clean and redress many of the shortcomings of the earlier Windows merchants. Windows 95 makes full use of the 386, 486, and Pentium processors in a way that older Windows never could; that's what people mean when they say that Windows 95 is 32-bit.

Superior Multitasking

Most modern operating systems support some kind of multitasking, and Windows 3.x was no exception. Windows 3.x used a form of multitasking, also found in the Macintosh computers, called *cooperative* multitasking. This kind of multitasking is called cooperative because in order for multitasking to work at all, it relies upon the computer's applications to behave cooperatively with each other. If just one application chooses to not cooperate, then the other applications and the operating system can't do anything about it; the system is entirely at the mercy of the uncooperative application.

In contrast, Windows 95 uses a more powerful multitasking method, commonly known as *preemptive multitasking*. With preemptive multitasking, Windows 95 can force an application that is using a lot of CPU time to wait for a brief period and yield CPU time to another CPU-starved application. Related to that feature is the *asynchronous input queue* feature, which was how Windows 3.x handles queued-up mouse clicks. At some point, you have probably seen the hourglass and have waited for it to disappear before Windows would accept your mouse clicks. That was an example of the cooperative nature of Windows 3.x; until one application yielded the mouse, no other applications could receive mouse clicks. Under Windows 95, it is possible for one application to be busy, and yet you can enter mouse clicks to other applications. In fact, there is a new cursor that sometimes appears instead of the hourglass: the launch pointer. The launch pointer indicates that even though Windows 95 is busy with one application, Windows 95 can still pass mouse clicks and keystrokes to other applications.

Now, to hear Microsoft tell the story, Windows 95 will solve all the input queue problems; they say you'll never have to wait again. Unfortunately, that isn't true. It is still possible for an old Windows 3.x program to stop the entire system. For example, my electronic mail program sometimes decides to slap the hourglass up on the screen; when it does that, nothing else happens under Windows 95. When I asked a Microsoft employee about this, he agreed that, yes, it still was possible for an old Windows 3.x program to lock up Windows 95. When I indicated that I had thought that Windows 95 would help this problem, he responded that it was "just a temporary problem, until you upgrade to a Windows 95 version of your electronic mail program."

NOTE   As a matter of fact, the preceding is an observation that can be made in general about Windows 95: To get the most out of Windows 95—and for that matter in order to get many of the features of Windows 95—you must be operating only with applications designed for Windows 95. Just one non-Windows 95 application is sufficient to mess up the entire operating system on your PC.

Access to More Memory

As I mentioned before, one of Windows 3.x's big problems was that it was built for the 286 processor; the 286 processor can only access 16MB of memory, and so Windows 3.x had a problem even trying to use memory above 16MB. In contrast, Windows 95 is built around the 32-bit 386 architecture; that architecture includes a 32-bit memory model, and, as two to the thirty-second power is slightly over 4 billion, Windows 95 can access up to 4GB of memory. (Now, once the 1GB SIMMs become available, we will finally have an operating system that can use them....)

Actually, every Windows 95 program works with a mythical 2GB workspace. That may sound like a lot, but it really isn't. For those of you who are wondering, that doesn't mean that Windows 95 needs 2GB to get started. One of the interesting things about Windows 95 (to me, at least) is that it really only needs as much memory as earlier versions of Windows did; for example, if you work with Windows 3.x now, and you like the way it runs on 4MB, then you will be perfectly happy with Windows 95's performance on that same 4MB system. (That happy person, however, would not be me; I recommend an absolute minimum of 8MB RAM.)

Of course, like Windows 3.x, Windows 95 includes a virtual memory system which allows you to promise more memory than you actually have. For example, if you had an 8MB machine and wanted to run 12MB of programs, then you most likely would not receive an Out of memory error message. Instead, your system would use some of your unused disk space to fill in as memory, making up the difference between your true 8MB and the 12MB that your programs need. In that sense, Windows 95 is similar to the older version of Windows—but that is also where the two differ. As you will see in Chapter 11, Windows 95 uses a completely different approach to allocating and maintaining virtual memory.

More Resources

And speaking of memory, one of the oldest Windows problems has been that of resources. It was not uncommon to find that you had plenty of free memory under Windows 3.x but were unable to run any more programs. What kept you from running those programs? Simple: something called *system resources*. You see, Windows needs small scratchpad spaces to keep track of what is on your Windows screen and of what Windows is managing. Those scratchpad areas are called system resources. There's nothing wrong with the idea of resources, but under earlier versions of Windows, the total amount of space set aside for resources was far too small. The result? You might have plenty of RAM, but not enough resources, and so you'd often see Out of Memory errors, despite having plenty of memory.

Why were resources so very scarce under Windows 3.x? Well, remember that Windows 3.x was based on the 286 technology, which was a 16-bit technology. Two raised to the sixteenth power is 64K, so system resources were held to 64K. Given this explanation of the limits based on 286 technology, you would assume that system resources under Windows 95 would be 32-bit, or 4GB in size.

Well, that's almost true, but for purposes of backward compatibility, Windows 95 continues to retain some 64K-sized resource areas. As a result, it is still *possible* to run out of resources under Windows 95—it's just a little harder than before. Nevertheless, the frustrating fact is that resources are still a way of life under Windows 95; that is why you may find that using some of Windows 95's more advanced features, such as OLE 2.0, may be only a pipe dream. It's hard to say whether this will really be the case;

presently, there aren't enough 32-bit applications around to allow for real, honest-to-God testing.

No Speed Loss

I mentioned this a page or two ago, but it's worth re-emphasizing: Windows 95 really does get as much done in 4MB of RAM as Windows or Windows for Workgroups did. As a matter of fact, in some specialized instances, it can do a better job. That's not to say, however, that you shouldn't be looking to buy more RAM when you upgrade to Windows 95. While I recommend 8MB minimum, 16MB is much more useful, and even then, if you're buying a new machine, make sure that it lets you upgrade your RAM to 64MB or more—you may want it soon enough.

Better Protection Model

All Intel processors since the 286 have supported a memory protection model. This model makes it possible for two programs to run in the same computer without stepping on each other. This protection system is built upon a four-level privilege model; the purpose of those four privilege levels was to simplify the assignment of memory control to different programs in the computer. For example, we obviously want the kernel to know more about the system than an application does.

Windows 3.x, however, was not built with the protection model in mind—in fact, Windows 3.x ignored the protection model altogether. That led to a host of problems, including the infamous and dreaded GP fault.

Windows 95 is much better suited to the Intel protection model and exploits this feature much better than did Windows 3.x. This means that you can more easily ferret out troublesome programs under Windows 95 than under Windows 3.x.

New File System

One of the most frustrating things about designing the new version of Windows probably wasn't the problem of how to build a brand new operating system—more likely, it was the need to preserve backward compatibility with the *features*, or as we better know them, the *weaknesses* of old versions of Windows. Perhaps one of the most frustrating weaknesses was the file system. Known as the File Allocation Table, or FAT system, it was originally defined as a means of keeping track of data on floppy diskettes. Among other things, the FAT file system had the requirement that no file name could be more than eight characters long, with the option of a 3-character file extension.

Windows 95's design team must have wanted very badly to throw away the FAT altogether and build a new file system. But eliminating the FAT would also have eliminated any hope that Windows 95 would have for winning over the marketplace, inasmuch as the FAT file system is integral to many existing DOS and Windows 3.x applications.

Windows 95 solves the problem of backward compatibility in an ingenious way: The designers of Windows 95 managed to retain compatibility with eight-dot-three while at the same time allowing for filenames under Windows 95 to be up to 256 characters long. This is managed, without loss of backward compatibility, with a neat trick. When Windows 95 saves a file name whose length is greater than eight characters, Windows 95 simply stores two separate directory entries. One of these directory entries is the long filename, encoded in a way that DOS or old Windows would never see it or look for it; thus, this kept any problems from arising in the first place. Then Windows 95 creates a special filename that fits within the DOS eight-dot-three filename constraint, truncating the name using a simple algorithm. For example, a file named `Letter to my boss.doc` would be saved as `LETTER~1.DOC`. These short filenames are unique, but, unfortunately they are not very clear. This implies that using files with long names under an old DOS or Windows program will take a little getting used to; however, the compromise seems to be a good one.

Compatibility with NT Applications

Perhaps Windows 95's best feature is what I think of as its "self-destruct" feature. Windows 95 has some basic architectural flaws that probably cannot be designed away. That will be true no matter whether it's Windows 96, 97, 98, or 2099. The only way to build a robust, reliable, powerful operating system is to cut the cord with some of the older DOS and Windows applications and build a whole new operating system from the ground up. Now, that isn't practical today; there are too many of those old DOS and Windows applications on the market. Introducing an operating system that did not support these apps would be, as I mentioned about the file system, simply suicidal. But in just five short years, from 1989 to 1994, people put aside DOS programs and adopted Windows programs. Over the next few years, people will similarly adopt Windows 95 programs and put aside their old Windows 3.x programs. Once the market has reached a critical level—let's say 80 percent of applications are Windows 95 applications—then an interesting thing will happen.

You see, Windows 95 programs aren't *really* Windows 95 programs—that is to say, there's no such thing as a Windows 95 development system. Rather, there is a system called Win32 which describes the Windows 95 development system. It also happens to be the Windows NT development system, so you can really say that Windows 95 programs are Windows *NT* programs, at least for business applications.

More Complete DOS Support

Now, I just got through telling you that in a few years DOS and old Windows programs will be unimportant, but we're not there yet. In fact, one of the lingering and nagging problems about Windows 3.x was that it could not run every DOS program. In particular, Windows had problems with game programs (for which, of course, we hard-working business people have no need) and memory-hungry DOS programs, ones requiring more than, say, 550K of free conventional memory (for which we hard-working business people *do* have a great need).

Windows 95 can run a much wider array of DOS programs than the older Windows ever could. The first way that it accomplishes that is in its new and improved virtual machine model. If Windows 95 deems it necessary, it can actually reboot your system to a minimal configuration, allowing the DOS program to control the system as much as it could want to. In this case, however, Windows 95 would stop running in the background. Thus, for many of us this is not a terribly useful feature, but it's better than not being able to run the DOS program at all.

Perhaps more interesting is the memory question. Under Windows—or rather, I should say, under Windows *and* DOS—there was a heavy memory hit for supporting networks, SCSI devices, and indeed Windows itself. Only by the application of some memory manager black magic could a DOS session get more than 480K of memory. If you've never done it, try this out: open up a DOS session under Windows 95 and type **mem**. Without doing any memory management at all, I'd be surprised if you didn't end up with at least 550K of free memory—and there are still tricks that you can do to squeeze out even more RAM!

That's not to say, however, that Windows 95 will run all DOS programs and provide one hundred percent backward compatibility. In particular, you may find that Windows 95 will not support device drivers for some older hardware. It might not be a bad idea to contact your hardware vendors (assuming, of course, that they still exist) and find out whether or not their hardware is Windows 95-compatible. (Unfortunately, some vendors will simply use that as an excuse to sell you some new hardware.)

What's NOT New: VxD's, VFAT, VCACHE

Microsoft would have you believe that Windows 95 is all-new and completely different from previous versions of Windows. Certainly, much of Windows 95 *is* different, but more of Windows 95 is older stuff.

Virtual Machine Managers Aren't New

Windows 386, announced in 1988, introduced a virtual machine manager—and a look at Microsoft's device driver development kit for Windows 95 shows that *some of the original Windows 386 code is still there!*

Windows 3.0 introduced the idea of the 386 enhanced mode. This mode replaced the old system BIOS and device drivers with 32-bit protected-mode device drivers. If you still have Windows 3 around, just look in the SYSTEM.INI file under the [386enh] section and you'll see remains of device drivers like device = vmd. In this case, VmD means virtual mouse driver; there is also a VkD, a virtual keyboard driver. Look further, and you will see many of these virtual drivers. There are so many of them with similar names—virtual "something" driver—that they were given a generic name: VxD's. Those VxD's have not disappeared in Windows 95; in fact, they are a basic architectural element.

You can think of VxD's in this way. You know how much trouble TSR's or device drivers have given you under DOS? Well, VxD's will be as much trouble under Windows 95. They'll be a blessing and a curse. If someone says that something is impossible under Windows 95, then some clever programmer may think, "But not if I wrote the right VxD..."

The 32-Bit File System Isn't New

As I have mentioned before, one of the best features of Windows 95 is its "32-bitness"; part of that feature is a set of 32-bit drivers for accessing the hard disk. Of course, DOS used a 16-bit disk driver, but what did Windows 3.x use? Well, it depended on which version you used. Windows for Workgroups had a neat 32-bit file system which is basically the one included in Windows 95. (During the beta test process of Windows 95, the program was called *Chicago*; since I live in Washington, D.C., I called Windows for Workgroups *Cincinnati* as it's halfway to Chicago.)

There are two parts to the 32-bit file system: the virtual FAT (VFAT) and the virtual cache (VCACHE). Those two parts of Windows 95 are lifted almost entirely from Windows for Workgroups.

Now, you may be recalling a different 32-bit part of Windows, and recalling it with chagrin—32-bit *disk access*. That was a feature of Windows 3.x, and it was one that I never recommended that people use, as it just wasn't reliable. But the years have gone by, and Microsoft seems to have worked out the bugs from the 32-bit disk system, so I can now recommend it in good faith.

Lots of 32-Bit Is Really 16-Bit

And the ubiquitous 32-bitness of 95 isn't really accurate. Many of the 32-bit calls to Kernel, GDI, or User just get 16 zeros subtracted from the front of them and then get passed on to the 16-bit Kernel, GDI, or User; this process is called *thunking*. There are lots of thunks in Windows 95.

There's a good reason for that. First of all, the 16-bit code is already working and well-understood. Second, 32-bit code will be larger than 16-bit code, meaning Windows 95 would require more RAM to run if it truly was 32-bit. And, finally, there are a *lot* of function calls that don't benefit from 32-bitness: the time of day can fit very nicely into 16 bits, for example.

And incidentally, even 32-bit code isn't new; it was possible to run many Win32 programs under Windows for Workgroups with a tool called Win32S.

But DOS Is Gone, Right?

And if you still doubt whether there's old code remaining in Windows 95, try pressing Shift+F5 when booting; the resulting C:\> will no doubt look somewhat familiar.

You may recall that DOS 6 introduced a disk compression utility called DoubleSpace. Other (and better) disk compression utilities existed at the time, but one interesting thing about DoubleSpace was that DOS loaded it without requiring a device= statement in CONFIG.SYS; this is called the *preload* feature. It just means that certain device drivers are implicit.

Windows 95 boots just like that. Where MS-DOS was based on two programs named IO.SYS and MSDOS.SYS, Windows 95 uses a single program called IO.SYS, and that program preloads not only the disk compression routines, but also HIMEM.SYS (the memory manager), IFSHLP.SYS (the redirector), SETVER.EXE, and WIN.COM. So DOS is still there, all right.

Is This Bad?

Does this deceit spell bad news for 95? No, not really. It's just sad that Microsoft has spent so much ink and air time explaining that 95 contains all new, rewritten-from-the-ground-up code when it's not true. Windows 95 is 95 percent marketing, and 5 percent new technology. But, you know, there's another word for new code—*untested* code. Personally, I don't mind that much of 95 has been around since '88. But, as they say, the acorn doesn't fall far from the tree, meaning that there are things that 95 will probably never do as well as a freshly built system would. Hey, did somebody mention NT?

Basically, Windows 95 is just Windows for Workgroups with a new user interface and a centralized device manager with Plug and Play support.

Which Is Better for You, NT or Windows 95?

It can be confusing when you consider that Microsoft offers two PC-based, 32-bit operating systems: Windows 95 and Windows NT. Which one will work best for you?

Well, in the long run, Windows NT is more powerful. It has a rock-solid memory protection system, a no-nonsense multitasking system that even my electronic mail program can't lock up, a C2-compliant security system, and all in all, it's an industrial-strength operating system. Of course, there are some down-sides to Windows NT; that's why Microsoft sells Windows 95. Windows 95 is superior to Windows NT insofar as:

- 95 requires less memory.
- 95 runs faster on a given machine.

- 95 supports a wider array of drivers.

- 95 runs more applications than Windows NT.

- 95 costs less than NT.

The major argument against NT and in favor of 95 is the fact that NT really requires 16MB of RAM to operate minimally well, and Windows 95 can provide the same level of usefulness with just 8MB of RAM. Someday the price of RAM will fall—that day has certainly been long enough in coming—but for now the difference in price between an 8MB workstation and a 16MB workstation is significant. In a practical sense, then, the price of NT is hundreds of dollars higher than it would be if memory were cheaper. Additionally, the software price of NT is higher; where 95 costs around one hundred dollars, NT workstation costs over three hundred dollars. I hope Microsoft changes that pricing policy, but that's up to them.

Memory is not the only difference between 95 and NT on any given machine. Speed is also important. For example, I am writing this on a 75 MHz laptop computer that sometimes runs Windows 95 and sometimes runs Windows NT. When running 95, the laptop usually seems faster than when running NT. However, one reason 95 seems faster than NT is that 95 takes less time to load a program than NT does. When you're actually *running* the program, however, 95 may not be that much faster than NT. The fact that 95 starts programs faster certainly makes it *seem* faster, however.

Although 32-bit apps will often run faster under NT than under 95, 16-bit applications will run more slowly, because NT must monitor 16-bit applications closely. Existing Windows 3.x apps will run much more quickly under Windows 95. Of course, when they crash under 95, they can crash the whole system, something they would *not* do under NT. That's part of the NT/95 tradeoff.

Another important difference between Windows 95 and NT is the availability of device drivers for each. When I teach NT classes or work in NT, I am sometimes frustrated by the fact that there are many pieces of hardware for which I simply cannot get an NT device driver. This has not been a problem for Windows 95—it seems that most hardware out there has 95 drivers either in the box or coming really soon. In contrast, when I ask hardware vendors when they will have the NT drivers done, they tend to hesitate, not wanting *exactly* to tell me to take a long walk off a short pier, but you can tell they are *thinking* about it. However, it's getting better in one major area: network drivers. Windows 95 uses the NDIS 3.1 network driver specification, which, thankfully, is also the network driver specification for NT Version 3.51. That means that any time a vendor creates a network driver for Windows 95, the vendor automatically has a network driver for Windows NT Version 3.51. Now, you might think that the next step would be to unify *all* of the drivers—like hard disk adapters, video boards, etc.—but, unfortunately, that won't be so easy. The built-in secure nature of Windows NT means that merging the NT and 95 driver specification may happen one day, but not this year.

The very same Windows NT security model that makes it hard to unify device drivers is also the reason that Windows 95 runs more old applications than does Windows NT. Any DOS or Windows application that attempts to directly access hardware is rebuffed by NT.

In fact, *no* application under NT—whether it be a DOS application, an old Windows application, or even an NT application—can directly access the hardware, and that's all there is to it. Now, usually this is not a problem, as NT uses the now familiar virtual device drivers to act as stand-ins for the actual hardware. Whenever a device or Windows program requires access to a piece of hardware, NT just lets the virtual device driver fool the DOS application into thinking that it's accessing the actual hardware, and the DOS application is happy.

Unfortunately, that means that the NT designers have to create a virtual device driver for each and every possible piece of hardware. Of course, that's not too terribly hard when you're talking about common hardware: mice, keyboards, displays, and so on. But there is a class of important-but-unusual hardware that isn't prevalent enough to warrant writing a virtual device driver: take fax boards as an example.

Fax applications are perhaps NT's biggest pain. There is no problem with running a fax application designed for NT, but unfortunately there aren't too many available. There *are*, however, lots of them for Windows 3.x, and people want to run those applications under NT. However, NT doesn't like those applications to directly access the hardware, and so it does not allow them to run—thus providing a major incompatibility problem for NT and old Windows applications.

In contrast, Windows 95 has no such qualms. As it's not built with security in mind, it can run just about anything you throw at it. And, at the moment, there are so many DOS and Windows applications around that NT's inability to run a few DOS and Windows applications will hamper its acceptance in the marketplace—at least until a full suite of Win32 applications appears and renders this spotty backward compatibility less important.

Right now, there aren't as many Windows NT applications, mainly because Windows NT has largely assumed a position in the marketplace of a server operating system in a client-server world. Therefore, the most common kinds of applications for NT are big server applications, like database engines; people aren't stumbling all over themselves to write word processors for Windows NT. That *isn't* true for Windows 95; you can be sure that by the time this book is available that there will be bushels of word processors, spreadsheets, electronic mail programs, and the like for Windows 95. And, as I mentioned earlier, since any Windows 95 program is also a Windows NT program, this means that Windows NT will simultaneously find itself with a rich array of compatible applications.

Once people learn how powerful and robust Windows NT is, I think that down the road they will not choose Windows 96, 97, or 98, etc., but instead choose NT 96, 97, or 98, etc.—but that's in the future.

So, in sum, is NT better for you than 95? I think the answer is probably, "Yes, but not yet." NT will beat 95 when:

- Memory prices drop.
- Lots of 95 apps appear (which are NT apps).
- NT gets 95's GUI.
- NT's price drops.
- More NT device drivers appear.

My call on a time for that? Sometime in 1997.

CHAPTER

2

Under the Hood—
An Overview of
Windows 95 Architecture

IN some ways, Windows 95 is an improvement upon old Windows 3.x. But you'd be surprised how much of the creaky old Windows 3.x is in 95—and that will make your support and use of Windows 95 harder.

Much of Windows 95, however is an improvement over previous Windows. In this chapter, you'll learn about the good, the bad, and the ugly in Windows 95.

The Parts of an Operating System

Like all operating systems, Windows 95 has one, and only one, major job: to make your applications and hardware work together. You have purchased applications and hardware, and you want the applications to be able to use that hardware to get your job done. Simply put, all operating systems look something like Figure 2.1.

Let's zoom in on those pieces of a generic operating system before looking specifically at Windows 95.

Applications

As I said before, the main reason for having an operating system—or, for that matter, having any computer at all—is to run the applications that let you get your job done. But applications do not and *cannot* directly access hardware in the computer. (Well, actually, in many systems, the applications *do* access the hardware—but it causes a host of problems, and,

FIGURE 2.1

Pieces of an operating system

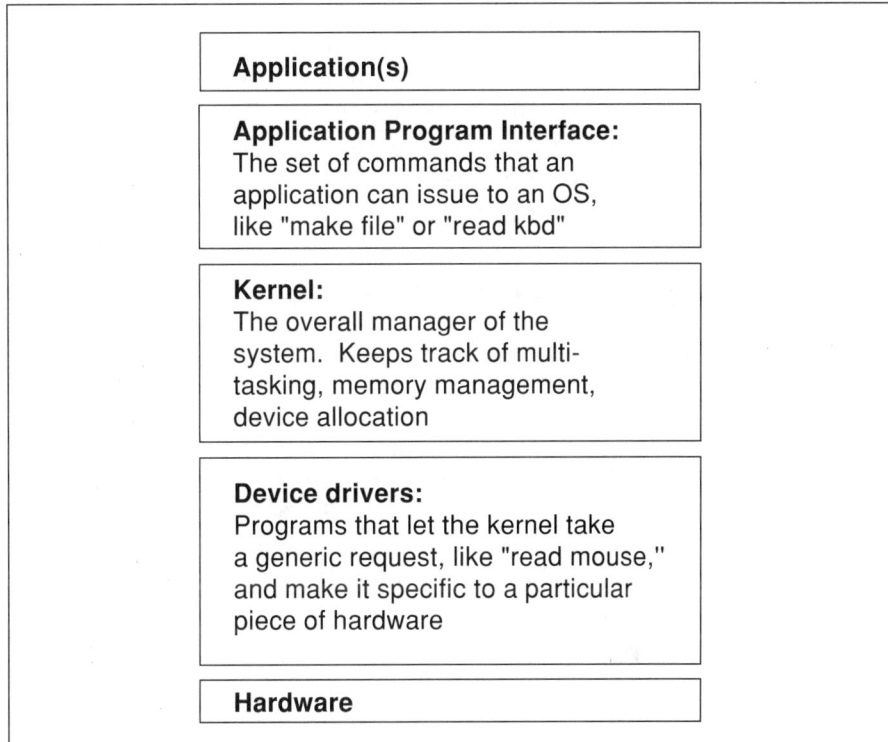

Application(s)

Application Program Interface:
The set of commands that an application can issue to an OS, like "make file" or "read kbd"

Kernel:
The overall manager of the system. Keeps track of multi-tasking, memory management, device allocation

Device drivers:
Programs that let the kernel take a generic request, like "read mouse," and make it specific to a particular piece of hardware

Hardware

truthfully, that's why we're working with Windows 95 to begin with.) If an application wants to do something like open a file, read a keystroke typed on the keyboard, or put a dialog box up on the screen, then the application does not actually do those things itself; instead, it passes that work to the operating system.

Why doesn't the application do these things? It's really a matter of control, convenience, and division of work.

Control

Control is a concern because most pieces of hardware can only accommodate the request of one piece of software at a time. For example, if three programs all simultaneously say to the disk, "What is the next free disk cluster?" then the disk subsystem could potentially give the same cluster number to all three programs; the result is that all three programs try to write their data to that same cluster. Control is also a concern with modern multitasking operating systems, because as multiple programs run, they all wish to put data on the screen, and to read mouse positions, button clicks, and keystrokes. That's not the problem. The problem lies in how to route the input to the appropriate application. After all, some applications are in the foreground and some are in the background, and no input is intended for every open program.

Convenience

Convenience is of importance because Microsoft, and for that matter *all* operating system designers, want to make writing programs for Windows 95 simple and fast for applications designers. One of the benefits of an operating system should be that it can avoid reinventing the wheel. For example, consider common dialog boxes. Prior to Windows 3.0, designers had to build their own File ➤ Open dialog boxes. You can see this in any older (pre-1992) Windows app; just click File, click Open, and look at the dialog box that results. Try it with six programs and you'll get six different dialog boxes. This is bad for two reasons. First, it makes life difficult for users trying to learn a number of new Windows programs—the things that they learn from the first Windows program do not help them in understanding subsequent Windows programs. And, second, it means that every Windows application designer must waste time reinventing the same old dialog boxes that every other Windows application designer must also reinvent. With Windows 3.1, Microsoft included a set of common dialog boxes, thereby turning a little Microsoft time into a lot of saved developer time. That's an example of the convenience part of an operating system.

Go back far enough in computer history, and you can see that more and more of the problems over which application programmers worried have been subsumed into the operating system. Back in the first days that I programmed a computer, I couldn't just say to the operating system, "get me the next keystroke." Instead, I had to write a routine in my application program that knew how to interrogate the keyboard for keystrokes. Thankfully, that's all over now—that kind of operation is generally considered to be the responsibility of the operating system rather than the application.

Division of Work

The third reason, division of work, is related to the convenience issue. Software nowadays can be so complex (using mice, high resolution graphics screens, huge mass storage devices, and networks, to name a few things) that if every applications designer had to master network programming, diskette driver programming, mouse interface, etc., then only a few very well-funded applications would ever get to market. By dividing an operating system into several pieces, it becomes possible to build and maintain a reasonably priced system.

API's

Anyway, once we believe that an operating system will be of value, the next question is, "How can an application use this operating system?" The operating system lives in one part of the computer's memory and applications live in another part, just as management in a large company works in a different part of the building from the factory workers. It is possible for a factory worker to communicate with a member of management, but usually not by just walking up to the executive suite and banging on the boss's door. Instead, there is usually some kind of well-defined interface— perhaps, in this case, a receptionist.

In the same way, an application that calls upon the operating system by simply emerging into the middle of the operating system can cause problems and the system can crash. That's why applications must access the operating system through well-defined interfaces, called *Application Program Interfaces*, or API's. An API is the published set of legal things that an operating system can do for an application—again, examples would include opening a file, reading a keystroke, or ending a program. Of course, as these are computers, there are i's to be dotted and t's to be crossed; for example, one operating system might open a file with the command DOSOPENFILE and another might open a file with the MAKEFILE command. Those two commands do the same thing, but they do it in different operating systems, in much the same way that you express the idea "hello" in so many different ways in every language. Windows NT, OS/2, and basic Windows 3.x all used different API's, and so developers have always had to decide on which API to focus their efforts. Because of the size of the Windows market, most vendors work first in the Windows market, then move from there, porting their applications from Windows to some other operating system.

This proliferation of API's, which, as you'd expect, has caused some operating systems to be application-rich while others are application-poor, has merged in Windows 95 and Windows NT into an API called the *Win32 API*. This is extremely important because it means that, as I mentioned in the last chapter, every time someone writes a Windows 95 application, Windows NT will automatically have a new application available for it.

NOTE In addition to the Win32 API, Windows 95 includes older API's of earlier operating systems. As you'd expect, that includes DOS and Windows 3.x.

The Kernel

The heart of the operating system is generally called the *kernel*, a term borrowed from the UNIX world. The kernel is the manager of the entire system. The kernel knows which program is using what memory, which program is currently in the foreground and which programs are in the background, which threads have higher priority than other threads, which programs are printing at the moment, and so on. Here, I am using the term kernel loosely; a little later, you will see that in the Windows world the kernel has several pieces—or, perhaps, I should say lieutenants.

Device Drivers

The kernel doesn't actually *control* anything, except in an indirect way. For example, the kernel never actually asks keyboard hardware whether it has a keystroke ready to be received. The reason why the kernel doesn't do that is that the software to access a keyboard can vary from one type of keyboard to another. Actually, keyboards aren't such a good example, as they are *all* pretty much compatible with one another; video boards or LAN boards are another story.

Once upon a time, operating systems were pretty much built to support only the two or three most popular pieces of hardware in any given hardware category; that wasn't much of a problem, as there often weren't more than two or three brands of a given hardware to begin with. But, as the variety and number of LAN boards, printers, and the like multiplied, it became impossible to include support for every possible piece of hardware in an operating systems kernel—at least, to do that *and* keep the kernel size under .5GB.

So, about twenty years ago, programmers began designing operating systems that had the programs which controlled hardware segregated out into separate smaller pieces of software called *device drivers*. The benefit of device drivers is obvious; for one thing, they can be updated to increase features and remove bugs without having to change the entire operating system. For another, when a new piece of hardware appears, then supporting that hardware is quite easy. All the hardware vendor must do is write a device driver for this new piece of hardware and include it with the hardware; when the user installs the device driver on the operating system, then the operating system immediately recognizes the new hardware.

Of course, that's the *good* side of the story; sadly, there is also a bad side. Suppose you were the hardware vendor creating some new printer, LAN board, or whatever; where would you place your programmer's time? You know that it takes time to write a device driver, and time is money. Will it necessarily pay you to create that Windows NT driver when you could be spending that programmer's time working on an OS/2 driver—an operating system with more users at the moment? As you'd expect, the bottom line is that vendors write the DOS and Windows 95 drivers first, as those are the largest market. OS/2 or Windows NT drivers are the poor stepchildren, and as a result they may not get support quickly—or ever.

Parts of Windows 95

Windows 95's structure parallels the structure of a generic operating system, but with pieces added on. You can see this in Figure 2.2.

FIGURE 2.2

Windows 95's structure

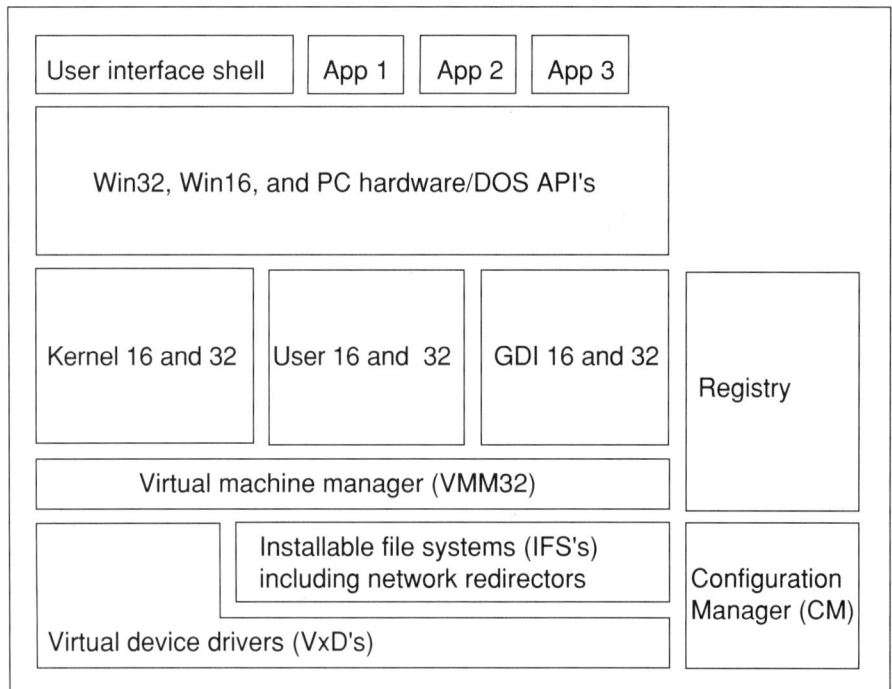

User interface shell	App 1	App 2	App 3

Win32, Win16, and PC hardware/DOS API's

Kernel 16 and 32	User 16 and 32	GDI 16 and 32	Registry

Virtual machine manager (VMM32)

Installable file systems (IFS's) including network redirectors

Virtual device drivers (VxD's)

Configuration Manager (CM)

The rest of this chapter explains these pieces and how they fit together.

API's under Windows 95

Okay, that's the overview of how operating systems are put together; now let's look at the specifics of Windows 95. Since API's were at the top of the list, let's look there first.

When Windows was first introduced in 1984, it had a wide variety of possible API calls. When Windows 3.0 appeared, Microsoft added even more calls and adapted Windows to the 286 processor architecture. As the 286 processor was 16-bit, so were the commands that a program could issue to the old Windows operating system; that set of possible commands was called the Win16 API. As you read earlier, Windows 95 has a newer API called Win32. Now, for a developer building a completely new application, Win32 is a good choice; it's more powerful, and in many ways it's easier to code for than was Win16. But there are thousands of older, yet perfectly good, Windows programs around, and if Windows 95 didn't support them then people wouldn't buy Windows 95. That's why Windows 95 includes both the new Win32 API *and* the older Win16 API. That way, it can support older and newer programs simultaneously. And that's not all; don't forget the importance of DOS programs—Windows 95 hasn't. Windows 95 includes a DOS-compatible API, and in fact it appears in some ways better than the API that ships with regular old DOS, as it supports multitasking (and the DOS API does not).

Of all of the operating systems out there, DOS is clearly the hardest one to support, paradoxically because it isn't really an operating system. Although DOS does the things that operating systems are supposed to do—provide low-level services and make the division of labor possible—for historical reasons, programmers do not use the DOS API. Instead, they write their programs to go directly to DOS's device drivers or even to the hardware itself. We'll talk more about this in a later discussion of VxD's, virtual device drivers. (And, by the way, if you're thinking that it's impressive that Windows 95 includes API's for older versions of Windows and DOS, as well as for Windows 95 itself, then take a look at OS/2; it contains API's for older Windows, DOS, older OS/2 versions, *and* modern OS/2 versions. It's kind of the Swiss Army knife of operating systems.) You might say that the true DOS API is a multitasking emulator for the original DOS API, the BIOS, and typical PC hardware.

Kernel Modules

Much of Windows is the "back office" of Windows, so to speak; the job of many parts of Windows is to support drivers and not, directly, applications. Windows programs themselves interact with six main modules I call the kernel modules:

- Kernel16
- Kernel32
- GDI16
- GDI32
- User16
- User32

Kernel16 and 32

As you read a few pages back, the kernel's job is to manage the system and to keep track of who is using what memory, who's using the printer, who has priority, and so on.

The kernel did not make its debut with Windows 95; it has, in fact, existed in Windows for the last few versions. However, as the previous version of Windows was defined for 286 processors, it would only support 16-bit instructions; that's why we refer to the older version of Windows as being 16-bit. One of the big selling features of Windows 95 is the fact that it is built for the 386 and later processors and so it can be 32-bit. For that reason, the kernel was redesigned to use the full power of 32 bits. In order to support older Windows programs, Windows 95 contains both the older kernel (which is referred to as Kernel16), as well as the new kernel, which, as you have probably guessed, is called Kernel32. This will be a pattern that you will see in many Windows components, as Microsoft was forced to retain many 16-bit pieces in Windows 95 in order to assure good backward compatibility.

GDI (Graphical Device Interface)

Like all good managers, the kernel doesn't do all of its work; it farms some of the work out to one of its helper programs called the Graphical Device Interface, or GDI. Like the kernel, GDI existed back in earlier versions of Windows, and so there is a GDI16 and a GDI32.

As you'd imagine from its name, GDI specializes in graphical things. Whenever you put a bitmap on the screen, your request is funneled through GDI. GDI has areas of control that include:

- Bitmaps
- Color
- Cursors
- Icons
- Fonts
- Graphical objects (lines, rectangles, curves, and the like)

GDI is the part of Windows that is activated whenever you try to change the color of a Windows component: a window, a button, or whatever. GDI also worries about fonts; if you have many fonts, then you stress GDI. The more advanced nature of the Windows 95 GUI (as compared to the older Windows GUI) means that GDI has a lot more to do than in previous versions of Windows; that's one reason why it's a good thing that GDI is now 32-bit. You'll see in a later section that GDI must keep track of every color, cursor, icon, etc., and so it needs a place to store information about all of these things. Those storage places are called system resources. They will turn out to be a problem area—but we'll talk about them later.

User16 and 32

Much of the business of running Windows lies in the user interaction with those windows—clicking buttons, selecting menu items, dragging icons, choosing from list boxes, and so on. Those things are all handled by a module called User. As before, older Windows used a 16-bit version of User and more recent Windows uses a 32-bit version.

Now and then, you will see an error message which indicates that the module User32 or User16 has failed; when that happens, you often get a choice to cancel, continue, or perhaps close a window. If you stop and think about it, this is kind of a contradiction in terms—here, Windows has told you that User (the part of Windows that handles button clicks) has failed, and would you please push a button to choose what to do next? I think of this as a kind of remote-control time bomb with the buttons representing the activation switches. You will not see *many* User failures, but they do occur sometimes. When they do, the best thing is to just shut down the PC and restart it.

Virtual Machine Manager (VMM32) and VxD's

While it's not considered part of the Windows kernel, there is a very important part of Windows that helps perform the functions of the kernel (as I defined it in my generic description of an operating system). This part is called the virtual machine manager, or VMM32.

The Virtual Machine Manager

As I've already told you, one of the tasks for the people designing Windows 95 was to design an operating system that could support DOS programs, particularly since they are badly behaved programs. Each DOS program is something of a spoiled child, meaning that it wants every piece of hardware for itself—DOS programs just plain don't know how to share. If a DOS program sees COM1, a serial port, then there's a good chance that it will claim that serial port for its own, even if it doesn't need it. The same thing holds true for memory—most DOS programs start out by swallowing up every byte of memory on a system. DOS programs sit on the keyboard, watching it every instant to see if you've pressed a key—and then they assume that the keystroke is for them. Obviously, DOS programs weren't born to multitask.

To get around this problem, most operating systems that multitask DOS programs—a list that includes OS/2, NT, and 95—take your PC and break it up into multiple virtual PCs, or, to use the correct term, *virtual machines*. Logically enough, the program that manages all of these virtual machines is called the *virtual machine manager*. Virtual machine managers all exploit a terrific feature of the 386 processor (and of all the processors that came to market after it in the Intel family) called *page mapping*.

The trick works something like this. Suppose you have a computer with 16MB of memory: DOS only sees 1MB of memory. That 1MB of memory, however, must be the *first* megabyte of memory—and this is where page mapping gets interesting. With page mapping, a processor can take a hunk of memory—say, the memory from the 3MB address to the 4MB address—and sort of "carve it out" of the rest of the processor's memory. Then the processor takes this 1MB of memory and says to the DOS program, "Here is your PC; it only has 1MB of memory. Trust me." Then, when the DOS program tries to access an address in this 1MB—for example, address 7000—then the page mapping feature of the processor just says, "Oh, when that program says seven thousand, I should add 3MB to that." Thus, the memory request is transparently converted into its actual physical memory address.

Managing Virtual Memory

The program that manages all of this memory juggling is, as you've probably figured out by now, the VMM32. It not only manages virtual machines, it also keeps track of virtual memory. Virtual memory gives an operating system the ability to promise more memory to its applications than it actually has; in operating system lingo, that's called *overcommitting* memory. So, for example, if your computer has 16MB of RAM, but you want to run 40MB of programs, you can—for a price.

The virtual machine manager lets you overcommit memory because it uses disk space on your computer as if it were memory. When you try to load programs beyond the actual RAM of your system, the virtual machine manager takes a look around and says, "Let's see... Which memory has programs in it, but hasn't been used in a while?"

Memory on a 386 or later computer is partitioned into 4K-sized pieces called *pages*. The part of the virtual machine manager that worries about memory—it's called (no big surprise) the *virtual memory manager*—has no real concept of programs and memory, but rather of *pages* and memory. It knows both how many pages it has committed to the various programs in the system and which ones are actually sitting in RAM and which are, well, merely promises.

For example, you might have loaded Excel a few hours ago, but haven't done anything with it for a while. The memory manager would know that nothing's touched a whole pile of pages in memory (the Excel pages) for a while, so the virtual memory manager would then take those pages and move them from RAM to disk, in a kind of staging area for virtual memory called the *paging file*. That, in turn, would free up some physical RAM, allowing you to load a new program; except for a bit of excessive disk activity, there's a good chance that you'd never even know what's going on.

If you later decide to come back to Excel, then Windows would try to access Excel's memory space. When the processor tries to execute some code in a page of memory owned by Excel, it finds that the page is not actually in RAM; this generates an hardware error condition called a *page fault*. (Just in case it wasn't clear, programs can't execute from disk—they have to be in memory to run.) The page fault wakes up the virtual memory manager, which then must make room to reload the Excel memory image. Now, it's probably still the case that there isn't enough room for all of your programs in memory, so the virtual memory manager must again figure out which programs are monopolizing memory that they're not using.

N O T E Virtual memory and virtual machine management was once a feature only found in expensive operating systems; it's a measure of how much times have changed that you see it in as basic an OS as Windows.

Virtual Device Drivers (VxD's)

While the ability to map and page memory quickly, easily, and efficiently is one of the important foundation pieces in providing a multitasking DOS environment, it's not the whole story. Not only do DOS programs steal memory at will, they also grab whatever other hardware they see, to the detriment of other programs. To explain that, I'm going to have to get a little technical here, but bear with me for just a moment. The key to understanding what stealing hardware means is something called *input/output addresses*.

Input/output addresses, or I/O addresses, are the way that a program communicates with a piece of hardware, like a keyboard, video board, LAN board, or whatever. They're similar to memory addresses, except that memory addresses only access memory and I/O addresses access all kinds of hardware. For example, an application that wishes to communicate with the keyboard does it by listening at I/O address 60; that's the standard I/O address for the keyboard. You can read further on I/O addresses in Chapter 10.

Now, as I've already said, DOS programs are a real pain in that they like to cling to the keyboard (I/O address 60) and snatch any activity before any other application (you know, like the operating system) gets it. So any virtual machine manager worth its salt will need some kind of way to keep all of those DOS applications from taking over the hardware. Fortunately, there is such a way: a virtual device driver or, in the Windows 95 world, a *VxD*.

A virtual device driver is a program that the processor kind of thumbtacks to an I/O address. To continue the keyboard example, a keyboard virtual driver would be nailed to I/O address 60. Then when a program attempted to directly access I/O address 60, the virtual keyboard driver would spring into action, behaving very much like the original piece of hardware.

A virtual keyboard driver is fairly easy to imagine: when a DOS program addresses it, saying "Hey, keyboard, are there any keystrokes for me?" then the virtual keyboard driver looks around and says, "Hmmm… is this DOS program in the foreground?" If the DOS program *is* in the foreground, then the virtual keyboard driver just passes along whatever's in the keyboard to the DOS program. If, on the other hand, the virtual keyboard driver sees that the DOS program is in the background, then, by definition, there are no keystrokes for the DOS program. (After all, how do you type into a program in the background—by walking behind the computer and typing?) In that case, the virtual keyboard driver, still masquerading as the keyboard, simply tells the DOS program, "No, there's nothing for you right now."

You can see the VxD that controls each piece of hardware by looking at the Device Manager in the Control Panel. For example, my System device manager tells me that my mouse is using two drivers, one named lmouse.vxd, and another named lmouse.drv. You can also see which drivers load and in what order by examining a file called BOOTLOG.TXT, but you must start up Windows differently than usual to see it. When you see the "Starting Windows 95..." message, press F8. You will then be given a menu of boot options, one of which is to boot and create a BOOTLOG.TXT.

Registry

If you worked with previous versions of Windows, then you are no doubt familiar with the .INI files. These files contain basic setup information and configuration data for Windows 95. They are in some ways an improvement over the old Windows 3.x approach, but they have their own problems, as you'll find when you read the next chapter. Additionally, there are pieces of information that are generated internally or *dynamically* by Windows 95; for example, every time your system starts up, it creates a map of what hardware is inside it. That is, of course, a dynamic piece of data in that it can change from usage to usage. You can't modify this; however, you might find great use for this information in troubleshooting a nasty Windows problem. You will learn more about this in the upcoming chapter on Windows hardware troubleshooting (Chapter 10). In any case, the Registry is as fundamental a part of Windows as the kernel, GDI, or the user interface manager.

IFS

There must be a way for an operating system to access storage devices. For example, in the DOS operating system, all storage devices have a similar name: a letter of the alphabet followed by a colon. Additionally, data must be organized on a storage device in a particular way. Since the days of DOS, data has been organized in a way originally designed for maintaining files on a floppy diskette (this is the famous, or perhaps infamous, FAT file system). However, if I were to ask you, "Where is the program that controls the FAT file system under DOS?" you wouldn't be able to tell me—that's because there *isn't* such a place in DOS. The FAT file system is so basic and so integral to DOS that there isn't any one place in DOS that implements the FAT.

However, with new operating systems, there is a need for more powerful and more flexible file systems. For example, the FAT file system doesn't work well on networks or on CD-ROMs; as a result, it has been difficult to implement CD-ROMs and LANs under DOS. The answer is *not*, however, to try to build a single file system that can be all things to all applications. Instead, it makes better sense to try to build an open architecture for file systems, a sort of plug-and-play capability that would allow the user to easily install CD-ROMs, LANs, optical drives, large hard drives, or whatever. After all, the lesson of the last ten years must certainly be that there is no way to design an architecture that will work as well now as in the future, since the future just isn't easy to predict.

For example, consider a case of well-executed forward thinking—the DOS device driver. The first modern version of DOS first appeared in 1983 with the introduction of DOS version 2. At the time, the designers of DOS knew well that they could not look into the future and know what hardware would be common, so they decided to leave a back door in DOS—device drivers. At the time, no machine had a CD-ROM, a local area network, or even a mouse—things that virtually every PC has these days. Without the device driver, none of those things could have been supported by DOS, and, as a result, they probably never would have taken hold in the marketplace. Device drivers made it possible for the vendors of these new pieces of hardware to introduce this hardware to DOS. Once a device driver was written for DOS, then DOS could, in many cases, simply treat the new device as just another disk with a name composed of a letter and a colon; of course, that wasn't true for everything—the mouse is an obvious example—but it was a very good model for more than ten years. My point is that we need something like this for file systems. Something like that *has* appeared, in the form of the *Installable File System* (IFS).

Actually, the IFS isn't new. It first appeared in 1989 with OS/2 version 1.2, an operating system that offered an alternative to the FAT file system in its HPFS, the High Performance File System. As implemented in Windows 95, the IFS is a sort of software socket into which can be plugged file systems like the familiar old FAT file system, network file redirectors, and CD-ROM file systems. The best news to most of us will be that file names can now be hundreds of characters long. What other benefits will IFS bring? At this writing, I cannot imagine all of the uses to which the IFS will be put; but I *can* guarantee somebody will figure out a clever use of IFS that I can't predict.

Configuration Manager

The emergence of Plug and Play technology as part of Windows 95 means that Windows 95 will treat your computer differently than have other operating systems. You see, in order for an operating system to work, it obviously must know what kind of hardware you have in your computer— and there's the rub.

How do we tell an operating system what hardware is sitting in its PC? Well, there's the obvious approach (and the one that has been used most often): Introduce a static list of hardware and drivers and require the user to reconfigure the operating system every time a new piece of hardware is added to the system. This is familiar to any veteran of operating system support. It's something that you've had to do to support DOS, Windows in its earlier incarnations, OS/2, and NT. Plug and Play, however changes that story in a number of ways.

Think about what you have to do when you add a new board to a typical computer. I can't speak for *your* experience, but mine works something like this: First, I remove the board from its box, then I root around looking for its documentation. On those occasions when the documentation is actually present, and on those rarer occasions when the documentation is accurate, I settle down to flipping DIP switches and moving jumpers to fit my new board into my PC without causing any interrupt conflicts or the like. Then, once I've run a test on the board to make sure that the board is working properly, I fire up the Setup program on my operating system; here I tell it that my new hardware—video display, SCSI adapter, or whatever—is now present, and, perhaps, also to tell it that an old piece of hardware is no longer present. And I'd *better* do this or I typically find that my operating system won't work anymore.

With Windows 95 and Plug and Play, things work very differently. First of all, there are no jumpers or switches. Plug and Play compatible hardware is completely software-configurable. Now, this may not sound very exciting in the late '90s because software-configurable boards appeared years ago in the PS/2 days. Since then, we've seen software-configurable EISA boards and even ISA boards. So what's the big deal with Plug and Play?

Well, the big deal is that Plug and Play does both the hardware installation and the software installation, and it does it automatically—or, at least as automatically as is possible. With Plug and Play computers, every board gets configured every single time you turn your computer on, believe it or not. Every time you start up your machine, new interrupts are assigned to all of your adapter cards so that they don't conflict with each other. Then, the configuration information that results is passed to Windows, which, in turn, passes that information to your hardware drivers—the VxD's.

The mastermind behind this whole operation is a new piece of software called the *Configuration Manager*. It is not only an integral part of Windows, it is also part of the system BIOS of a Plug and Play-compatible system. There's a catch, though: for full Plug and Play compatibility you'll need to buy new PCs, expansion boards, and a whole new operating system. Well, at least you have the new operating system...

What about those of us without Plug and Play hardware? Is the Configuration Manager still useful? The answer is yes, definitely. The Configuration Manager is quite useful in that it is incredibly smart about detecting hardware settings on a variety of boards—so good, in fact that there's a rumor around that the Microsoft NT developers first install Windows 95 on a machine to find out what's in the machine, and then use that information when configuring Windows NT. (Of course, this *could* just be apocryphal...) Seriously, while it is impossible for a piece of software to completely detect hardware in a non-Plug and Play system, the Windows Configuration Manager does the best job of it that I've ever seen; this will no doubt raise the minimum standard of excellence for hardware detection software in the diagnostic and operating system software business.

N O T E You will interact with the Configuration Manager mainly through the Control Panel, in the Device Manager. You'll learn more about Configuration Manager and Device Manager in Chapter 10.

System Resources under Windows 95

Starting to learn to work with Windows—either an older version or the most recent—can actually be a bit of fun. Of course, learning anything new can be frustrating and time-consuming; but, once you get it—that is, once you really understand the working-with-Windows paradigm—then you start to actually feel like there is something new and better that you can get done with this new operating system. So you start putting it through its paces, loading a bunch of programs, doing OLE... And that's when you start to find the limitations.

That's the frustrating part.

For example, anyone who has worked with Windows 3.x has come across an Out of Memory error. It displays a strange error message, saying something like "You do not have enough free memory. Close a few applications and try again." So you close a whole bunch of applications, but you *still* can't run your program. You take a quick look at the amount of free memory and see that there are perhaps tens of megabytes of memory free, yet you keep getting this annoying Out of Memory error message.

Well, Windows experts will by now know what caused this problem: system resources. Remember the Windows components named GDI and User? They have many things to keep track of. GDI must remember the name and location of every bitmap on the screen, as well as any colors of any objects on the screen, usage of cursors, icons, fonts, etc. User must keep track of every possible menu selection on each active program, as well as the location of every window on the screen, the location and state of every button on the screen, and so on. These two Windows subsystems must have a place to set aside that information, a sort of scratchpad location for keeping this information. Those scratchpad locations are called *system resources*.

Under Windows 3.x, the basic architecture was, as you know, 16-bit. That led to some important limitations, and one of the most important was in system resources. The number 2 raised to the 16th power is 64K, and that's where the trouble began. You see, GDI only had one of these 64K memory areas for recording all of its information, and, unfortunately, it was fairly easy for a heavy-duty Windows user to exceed that 64K. This led to the odd situation whereby it was possible that a user could have megabytes of free memory space—yet the user would be unable to run a program because GDI didn't have enough space to keep track of that program's cursors, colors, bitmaps, etc. (the program's system resources).

Now, when Microsoft announced Windows 95, many of us were quite happy to hear that it would be 32-bit in nature. As 2 raised to the 32nd power is over 4 billion, that would imply that system resources would no longer be a constraint. That's only partially true, unfortunately: old 16-bit programs and 32-bit OLE programs can still chew up resources.

As old programs (the 16-bit ones) aren't trained to go look for the new, bigger 32-bit heap, they keep going to the 16-bit areas. Now some of the heap space that they used to burn up they burned up indirectly: by asking GDI to do something, they caused GDI to put some data in its heap. Now, when that happens under Windows 95, GDI will usually put the data in the larger 32-bit heap. *The result:* There's more space left for the legacy apps. But it is a finite space, and so it's still possible to fill up the heaps with 16-bit applications. (When in doubt, it's always easiest to blame those legacy application developers.)

Even 32-bit applications end up putting a little information in the heap. 32-bit apps are built up out of sub-applications called *threads*, which are built either with or without message queues. The threads that need message queues are the ones that do OLE. According to Matt Pietrek in an article in *PC Magazine* ("Stability and Capacity," September 26, 1995), every eight threads with message queues used up one percent of User's heap. Depending on how OLE is implemented in your application, you may need one thread for each linkage. That means that you couldn't run more than a few hundred linkages without running out of resources, even if you're running 32-bit applications. Again, the bottom line is that it's still possible to run out of resources under Windows 95.

It may be cold comfort, but it's easier to monitor system resources under Windows 95 than it was with Windows 3.x. One of the optional applications that you can load with Windows 95 is the Resource Meter, your system resource monitor, which you see in Figure 2.3.

FIGURE 2.3

System resource
monitor

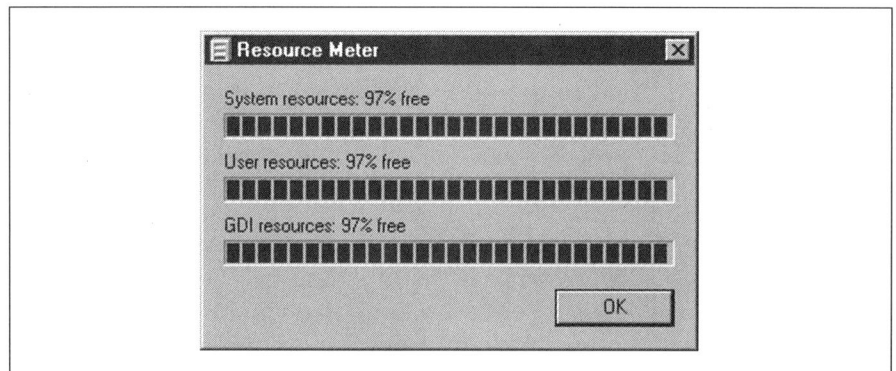

Since I've beaten up on Microsoft for keeping the 16-bit stuff around, it's only fair that I point out that the sample Resource Meter that you see in the previous figure shows a reading for my system after I opened several important applications. Under Windows 3.x, opening Ami Pro was enough to drive the resources down to 80 percent, but under Windows 95, Ami only brings resources down to 94 percent; this is quite an improvement, and not merely a cosmetic one. I have several very large documents that simply could not be worked on using Windows 3.x; I would invariably run out of resource space when trying to edit those documents. So far, that has not been the case with Windows 95.

That said, I should point out that it is still possible to run out of resources with Windows 95—it's just a bit harder. It *is* a bit frustrating, however, to see Microsoft demonstrate Windows 95 and show off how wonderful it is on resources by opening up 25 copies of their Excel spreadsheets. Understand that this is a somewhat bogus demonstration, as Excel is a so-called multiply instanced application. What that means is that when you load your first copy of Excel, then it takes up memory, resources, etc. When you start a second copy of Excel, however, it does not load a completely new copy of Excel; instead, the first copy of Excel is just augmented with a few new data areas. As a result, it is quite easy to load many copies of a single application (this multiply instanced type of application is quite common) and not see a great resource hit. To see how impressive Windows 95 can potentially be, try opening 25 *different* applications rather than 25 copies of the same application. (Of course, Microsoft doesn't do that in public demonstrations…)

What should you do about potential resource bottlenecks? Well, I'll offer the same advice to you that I offered under Windows 3.x: Use the Resource Meter to keep track of which programs are the real resource hounds. Then you can opt to avoid those applications, to contact the program authors, and to tell them to trim their applications a bit. And *please* be sure to keep an eye on the Resource Meter before you start doing any fancy OLE stuff. (If you're *really* stuck, then go to Windows NT.)

System Vulnerabilities

In a perfect world, an operating system would be no more than a toolbox of prebuilt software routines, routines to do the donkey work of programming: "put the word Hello on the screen," "draw a circle," "get the employee ID numbers of every employee born between 1965 and 1975," and so on. Applications programs would be aware of each other and could transfer data among themselves in an orderly, well-organized fashion. Unfortunately, the real world doesn't work that way. The frenetic pace of software technology advances has shortened software development cycles, making it just about impossible to ship a useful piece of software that's both *on time* and *bug free*.

So most vendors opt for on time.

That means that nobody trusts the operating system code, nobody trusts the device drivers, and nobody trusts the apps. When a piece of code crashes, we want to know which piece of code it was and who's to blame. Ideally, we'd also like to restrict the damage—a flakey application shouldn't be able to crash the whole operating system.

Memory Management under Windows 95

That's where protection models and memory management come in. You've already read a bit about memory management when you read about system resources; let's look further into how Windows 95 manages its memory.

It's possible on an x86 processor to designate privilege levels for computer code. Some programs can be designated ring 0, and that's the highest privilege level. Others are rings 1, 2, or 3, in decreasing importance. Ring 0 programs can protect memory in that they can allocate spaces of memory to particular programs and detect when another program tries to invade that space; such an invasion is called a General Protection Fault, or GPF. Ring 1 programs can also allocate memory, but only so long as they don't override a command of ring 0 programs; ring 2's can't override ring 1's, and so on.

Windows 95 uses only two rings: The virtual machine manager and its VxD's are ring 0, and everything else is ring 3, including Kernel, GDI, and User. The salient points of how Windows 95 manages and protects memory are as follows:

- The VMM32 and VxD's are protected in ring 0. (If they're buggy, however, nothing can stand against them, as they can write to any piece of memory, anywhere. And don't forget that some of your VxD's are just pieces of software that came with one of your pieces of hardware, which means that software written by some third-party hardware vendor becomes part of the central operating system— Where's your guarantee that they were all well-written?)

- The Kernel, GDI, User, and other system DLLs have their own memory space; they're ring 3, which means (read on) they're usually safe from Win32 apps.

- The Win32 programs—the Windows 95 applications—all have their own separate address spaces, and can't see out of it. Buggy Win32 programs will usually crash only themselves.

- On the other hand, Win16 programs must live in the same memory space as the Kernel, GDI, and the like, making the operating system vulnerable to bugs in Windows 3.x applications. Once again, the dirty little secret of Windows 95 is that you need Windows 95 applications to get the benefits of Windows 95.

While on the subject of Windows architecture, it is important to point out a very important weakness in the architecture of Windows 95, especially as concerns DOS programs. As you recall, each DOS program gets its own virtual machine, which is essentially a PC. As I said before, this whole idea of virtual machines is essential to the success of Windows (or, for that matter, any operating system), mostly because DOS programs are all hogs in the way they use memory and hardware on the computer.

Although I did not mention it, there is another very good reason for virtual machines: They protect one program from the bugs of another program. Here's what I mean. Suppose you are running two DOS programs, perhaps WordPerfect version 5.1 and some free DOS-based game. If the DOS-based game does something stupid and decides to crash, what happens to your Windows programs and the DOS WordPerfect program?

In a well-designed operating system, like Windows NT or OS/2, any program that dies just dies, and the operating system cleans up after it; that's all there is to it. The creators of Windows 95 decided to make a design decision that, on the one hand, reduced the amount of memory required to run Windows 95, but on the other hand weakened the walls between the virtual machines.

Under Windows 95, the first physical megabyte of RAM is directly mapped, or in other words copied, into all virtual machines. Now, that's not so bad, as there's nothing wrong with the idea of copying the first megabyte of the basic system software into every virtual machine. The problem is that the relationship between virtual machines and the physical machine is a *two-way* relationship. That means that it is possible to do something stupid on one virtual machine and cause a ripple effect on the other virtual machines.

I guess the easiest way to describe this is simply with an example. Check out the boxed instructions nearby for creatively crashing your machine.

How to Crash Your Machine

Try these steps on a Windows 95 machine—but be darn sure that you're not running anything you care about, because you are going to crash the machine!

1. Open a DOS prompt. (Just click Taskbar, then Programs, then the MS-DOS prompt.)
2. At the prompt, type **debug** and press Enter.
3. Debug's prompt, which is a dash, will show up. At that prompt, type **F 0:0 L ffff 0** and press Enter.
4. The system will stop working.

Is using Debug to crash your Windows 95 machine an unfair test of Windows 95? I don't think so. Try the exact same test on OS/2 or Windows NT and nothing bad will happen. Why couldn't this robustness have been built into Windows 95? The story I have heard is that isolating the bottom 1MB of physical memory would have required that Windows 95's minimum memory requirements go from 4MB, the official amount of memory required for a minimum Windows 95 installation, all the way up to 5MB. The story goes that the Microsoft public relations machine felt that saying that Windows 95 ran on 4MB would help its sales; I've had this story confirmed by a couple of Microsoft employees. It all makes sense, particularly when you consider that IBM was touting their upcoming version of OS/2 that ran well in just 4MB of RAM, but I wish it hadn't worked out this way.

The Hourglass Lives

Before leaving the subject of system vulnerabilities, I should mention the hourglass.

When the hourglass is displayed, that means that the part of Windows that responds to user inputs—mouse clicks and keystrokes—is busy at the moment, and can't handle anything more. This is called having a single input queue, and it's what Windows 3.x had.

The problem with this is that Windows 95 was supposed to have multiple input queues. When the pointer turns into a smaller hourglass with a pointer atop it, you can then start another program while the first program is busy. 32-bit programs can share the input queue. Badly written 16-bit applications don't.

As the Kernel, User, and GDI all have 16-bit as well as 32-bit pieces, there wasn't a way to disconnect the 32-bit subsystem from the occasional piggy 16-bit app. The result is that when a Windows 3.x program puts up the hourglass, you can't talk to *any* application—including the 32-bit ones.

And Speaking of Under the Hood...

Let's leave this chapter with a Stupid Windows 95 Pet Trick. Try this.

1. Right-click the Desktop, and choose New Folder.
2. Name it with the following "title" (don't forget the comma):
   and now, the moment you've all been waiting for
3. Right-click on the folder, choose Rename, and rename it with the following:
   we proudly present for your viewing pleasure
4. Then rename it once more, to **The Microsoft Windows 95 Product Team!**
5. Then open the folder, and you'll see an animated credits screen, complete with music.

Hey, no *wonder* the thing is tens of megabytes in size!

Controlling 95—
.INI Files and the Registry

IF you've ever used DOS or Windows, you're familiar with the array of system and hardware configuration files that accompany DOS-based operating systems: AUTOEXEC.BAT, WIN.INI, CONFIG.SYS, and SYSTEM.INI. NT users know that these files were replaced in Windows NT with a centralized configuration database called the *Registry*. Just to make life complicated, however, Windows 95 uses both kinds of configuration files: the DOS ones *and* an NT-like Registry. (Actually, there's more to it than just perversity on Microsoft's part, but we'll talk about the roles of the legacy configuration files in Windows 95 later in this chapter.)

Basically, the Registry holds all configuration information for Windows 95 and Windows 95-ready applications. Older 16-bit apps do not know to use the Registry, unfortunately, so you'll still have .INI files scattered all over your system if you use Windows 3.x programs.

Although both the DOS configuration files and the Registry have a role to play in configuring your Windows 95 environment, they look and work a little differently in Windows 95 than they do in DOS/Windows and NT. In this chapter, we'll talk about what these configuration files look like, how you can use them to tune your system, and how to avoid bollixing up your system while trying to tune it.

The Limited New Roles of AUTOEXEC.BAT and CONFIG.SYS

You probably know that, unlike previous versions of Windows, Windows 95 is an operating *system*, not an operating environment. It's not a

GUI front end to the DOS operating system (as were previous versions of Windows), but complete unto itself.

Most DOS machines use CONFIG.SYS and AUTOEXEC.BAT to set up the system hardware and operating environment. Although these files can be pretty vanilla if all you want to do is just boot the machine, the more stuff you add to the machine, the more complicated and system-specific they get. Windows 95, in contrast, does not rely on CONFIG.SYS and AUTOEXEC .BAT for system information; a file named IO.SYS and another called the Registry take care of configuring the system as the former pair of files once did.

But if you look at the root directory of your boot drive, you'll notice that you've still got a CONFIG.SYS and AUTOEXEC.BAT. If Windows 95 doesn't need these files to set up your system, then why are these files still there? Two reasons:

- To load any real-mode drivers and TSRs that your computer requires.
- To allow you to tailor DOS sessions for specific DOS programs.

Loading Real-Mode Drivers and TSRs

A few computers, but not all, need to run some real-mode (i.e., DOS) programs that aren't part of Windows 95. The statements corresponding to these programs appear in CONFIG.SYS and AUTOEXEC.BAT, and even if your particular computer requires no such programs, their configuration files will remain on your system, for the unlikely event the need arises in the future.

Creating "Roll-Your-Own" DOS Environments

You can run most DOS programs from Windows 95 and, if necessary, set up an individual AUTOEXEC.BAT and CONFIG.SYS for each one. Thus, if you've got an application that can't run if DOS is loaded high or has some other special requirements, you can set up a custom operating environment for that application.

Although we'll get into the nitty-gritty of running DOS programs under Windows 95 later in this book, for now let's talk a little about how to use `CONFIG.SYS` and `AUTOEXEC.BAT` to give a DOS application a custom-made environment.

Open My Computer and find the icon for a DOS program on your system. Right-click it, and choose Properties from the pop-up menu. A dialog box like the one in Figure 3.1 will appear.

(SNAP, if you're wondering, is a useful screen-capture program for DOS.) Click on the Program tab, and then click the Advanced button at the bottom of the Program screen. You'll see a dialog box that looks like the one in Figure 3.2.

FIGURE 3.1

Properties dialog box for SNAP.EXE

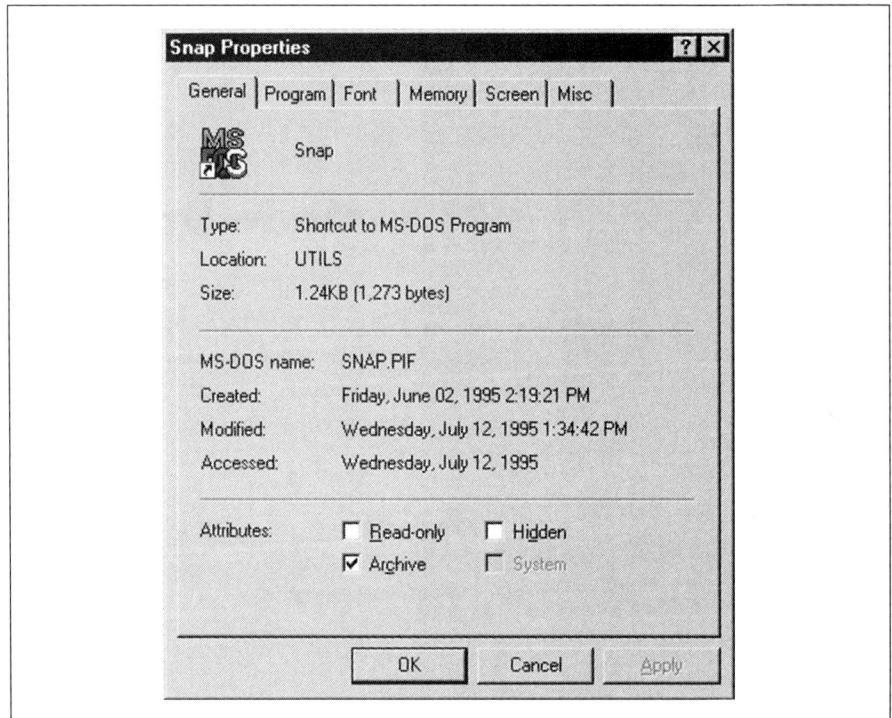

FIGURE 3.2

Advanced screen of
SNAP Properties
dialog box

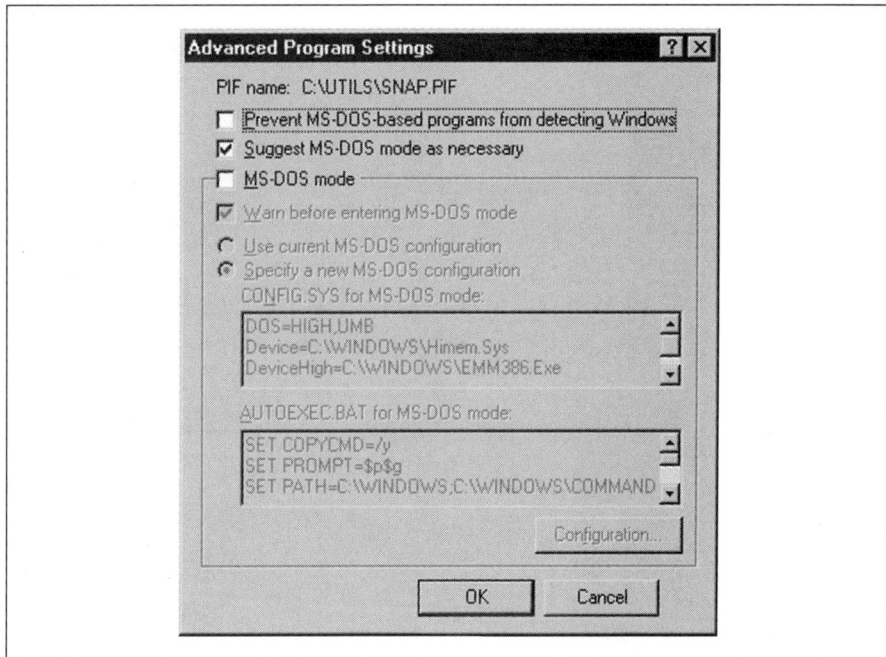

TIP Don't panic if you turn to the Advanced screen of the Properties tab for a particular DOS app and there's nothing in the CONFIG .SYS or AUTOEXEC.BAT files. You can't see their contents until you've selected MS-DOS mode at least once.

Notice the CONFIG.SYS and AUTOEXEC.BAT files that are listed. Notice also that, by default, *Suggest MS-DOS mode as necessary* is selected, and you must use the vanilla configuration files provided. By default, these files won't do much more than define an operating environment, enable EMM386, define the temporary file directory, and provide mouse support. To change them, you'll need to set the operating environment to MS-DOS mode so that they're no longer grayed out, as you see in Figure 3.3.

FIGURE 3.3

SNAP set to MS-DOS mode

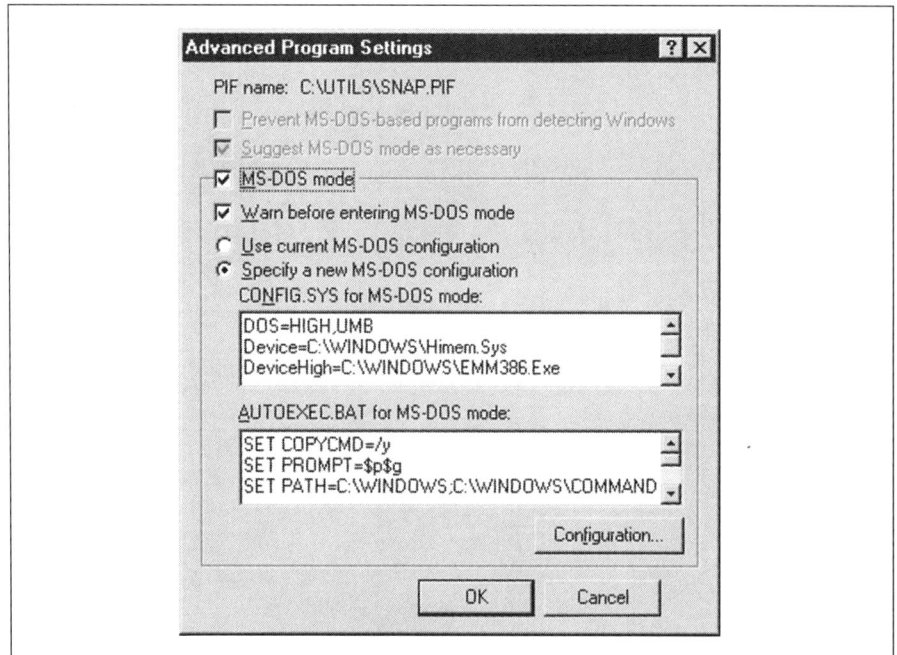

Now, you're ready to customize the configuration files for this program's DOS session. You can type in the commands you want to load, or you can select canned configuration information from the screen available after clicking the Configuration button, as you see in Figure 3.4.

I like the way that this dialog box was set up: Rather than providing you with a list of statements to add to or delete from CONFIG.SYS or AUTO-EXEC.BAT, Windows 95 lists the options to activate or deactivate and then adjusts the configuration files to correspond to your choices. By default, EMM386 (the memory manager) and mouse support are activated. If you're not sure of an option's function, right-click on it and its description will appear in the text box below the list.

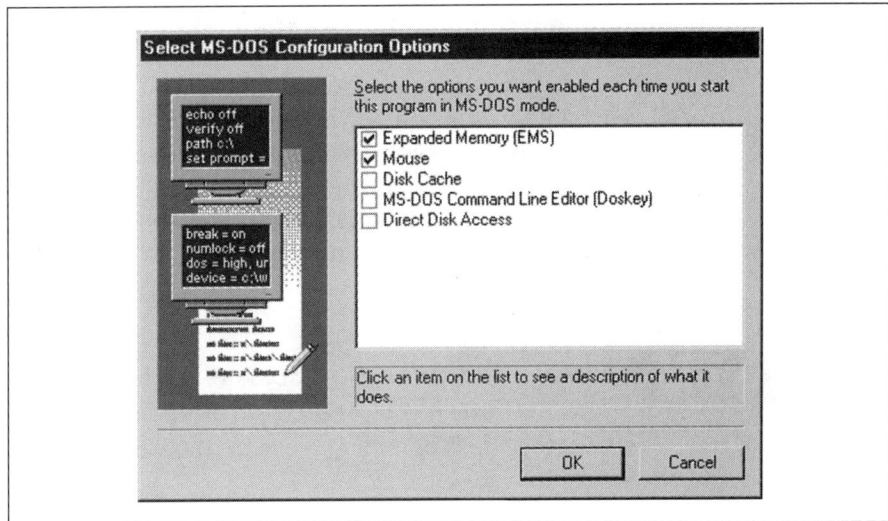

Select MS-DOS Configuration Options

echo off
verify off
path c:\
set prompt =

break = on
numlock = off
dos = high, ur
device = c:\w

Select the options you want enabled each time you start
this program in MS-DOS mode.

☑ Expanded Memory (EMS)
☑ Mouse
☐ Disk Cache
☐ MS-DOS Command Line Editor (Doskey)
☐ Direct Disk Access

Click an item on the list to see a description of what it
does.

OK   Cancel

WARNING   When editing the CONFIG.SYS and AUTOEXEC.BAT files for a
DOS session, watch what you're doing, and make sure you
make backups before you get started. There's no Restore
Defaults button.

Select the options that you want for the MS-DOS mode of the DOS session and click OK. When you return to the Advanced dialog box, you'll
notice that the changes you made are reflected in the configuration files.
Notice also that there is no Restore Defaults button, so be careful what
you do here. The only way that you can undo changes to a DOS session's
configuration files is by canceling out of the application's Properties dialog box altogether. Once you click OK to close Properties you're stuck
with the changes that you've made.

Once you've set up the CONFIG.SYS and AUTOEXEC.BAT for that DOS
session, return the program's running mode to *Suggest MS-DOS mode as
necessary*, the default. If DOS mode is necessary for the program to run
well, the configuration files that you set up will run.

Where ARE Configuration Settings Kept?

As you can set up an individual CONFIG.SYS and AUTOEXEC.BAT file for each DOS program on your system, clearly this information isn't centrally located, but is somewhere specific to each DOS program. That "somewhere specific" is the program's PIF (Program Information File), normally stored in the same directory as the program file itself. For example, SNAP's configuration information is stored in SNAP.PIF.

NOTE A DOS program does not need a PIF file to run—it only needs one if you customize its setup in some way, like changing the icon or adding a line to its CONFIG.SYS.

If Windows 95 can't find a PIF for a DOS program, it will look in APPS.INF for configuration for that file and create a new PIF from that information. APPS.INF holds default information for many DOS programs, although it doesn't update itself for new applications that you add to the system. The information in APPS.INF may not be exactly to your liking (for example, if I erase 1-2-3 version 3.1's PIF, the version stored in APPS.INF defines MS-DOS mode for the program), but once Windows 95 has recreated the PIF you can edit it via the Properties dialog, as discussed briefly in this chapter and in detail in Chapter 13.

Using DEBUG to Look at a DOS Program's PIF

PIF files are not readable in a text editor like Notepad, but you can use a DOS program called DEBUG to check out the contents of a DOS program's PIF, if you care to go through the trouble. Before starting up, however, let me issue this warning:

WARNING: *It's very easy to render your machine unbootable with DEBUG. Do* not *experiment with commands other than those listed here unless you know exactly what you're doing.*

I hate to sound grouchy, but I don't want my e-mail flooded with messages from people who've blown away their MBR and can't boot. Please keep your Startup Disk on hand at all times when working with DEBUG.

Enough lecturing—let's check out the contents of SNAP.PIF. First, I'll need to add something distinctive to its configuration so that I can find it easily. Therefore, I'll go into SNAP's Properties dialog, as we just discussed, and manually add the statement

rem elephant=pink

at the end of its CONFIG.SYS. The rem is so I don't mess up the configuration with junk lines.

Now, I'm ready to use DEBUG. I open the DOS prompt and type

DEBUG_C:\UTILS\SNAP.PIF

(All underscores indicate spaces—DEBUG is very picky about syntax.) The cursor changes to a dash, indicating that DEBUG is running.

Next, I need to find out how long SNAP is. I know that the length of a file is stored in register CX, so I'll type **r** to display the contents of all of the PIF's registers. The result looks like this:

```
AX=0000 BX=0000 CX=04F9 DX=0000 SP=FFEE BP=0000 SI=0000 DI=0000

DS=1B6C ES=1B6C SS=1B6C CS=1BPC IP=0100  NV UP EI PL NZ NA PO NC

1B6C:0100 007853   ADD [BX+SI+53],BH        DS:0053=00
```

As you can see, SNAP's PIF is 04F9 bytes long (that's hex, translating to 1273 bytes in decimal). That means that I need to search memory, starting from DS 100, for a file 04F9 bytes long that contains the string "elephant." I'll do that with this command:

s_100_1_04f9_"elephant"

That nets me the following:

```
1B6C:05E8
```

This is the segment and offset for part of SNAP.PIF. Armed with this information, I can dump the contents of this part of the PIF onto the screen with **d_1b6c:05e8**. The results are as follows:

```
1B6C:05E0                   64 6C 65 70 68 61 6E 74        elephant
1B6C:05F0 10 2D 20 70 69 6E 6B 0D-0A 91 C3 19 36 30 32 34   = pink....6024
1B6C:0600 36 30 36 20 1a 06 39 35-35 31 19 2E 19 03 03 00   606 ..9551....
1B6C:0610 13 0F 08 0E F5 0F 0F 1B-26 09 D4 D7 AA AD 00 00   .......&......
1B6C:0620 01 1F 01 03 01 07 0B 47-10 17 28 03 0C 53 54 27   .....G..(..ST'
1B6C:0630 00 00 58 3F 12 16 16 12-12 1E 1E 12 12 16 16 35   ..X?.........5
1B6C:0640 35 65 00 00 75 67 69 07-05 03 0D 0F 0D CB CB D7   5e..ugi.......
1B6C:0650 D7 D7 D7 D7 00 AA C7 D7-D7 D7 D7 93 93 93 93 1C   ..............
1B6C:0660 39 00 25 42 02 00 0B 0B                           9.%B.........
```

When you're done looking at SNAP.PIF, type **q** to quit DEBUG and exit the DOS prompt.

To view other information in the PIF, I'd use a smaller number to describe the segment, perhaps substituting **16c0:05e8** in the dump statement. The result would be earlier lines in the configuration files, as they're stored in the PIF in the order in which they appear in the Properties dialog box.

What Is the Registry?

You may still have an AUTOEXEC.BAT and CONFIG.SYS, for odd drivers and configuring DOS programs, but the meat and potatoes of your Windows 95 configuration resides in the Registry. You control the Registry with C:\windows\regedit.exe. Let's take a look; you can see the opening screen of the Registry in Figure 3.5.

This, by the way, is not the way your Registry will look when you first open it. I've expanded some parts of it to illustrate what you may see when working with it. Normally, when you start up REGEDIT, all that you'll see are the icons labeled HKEY-something. HKEY is Microsoft-ese for "*handle* (that is, pointer) to a *key*." Keys are the folders you see.

FIGURE 3.5

Registry branches,
keys, and subkeys

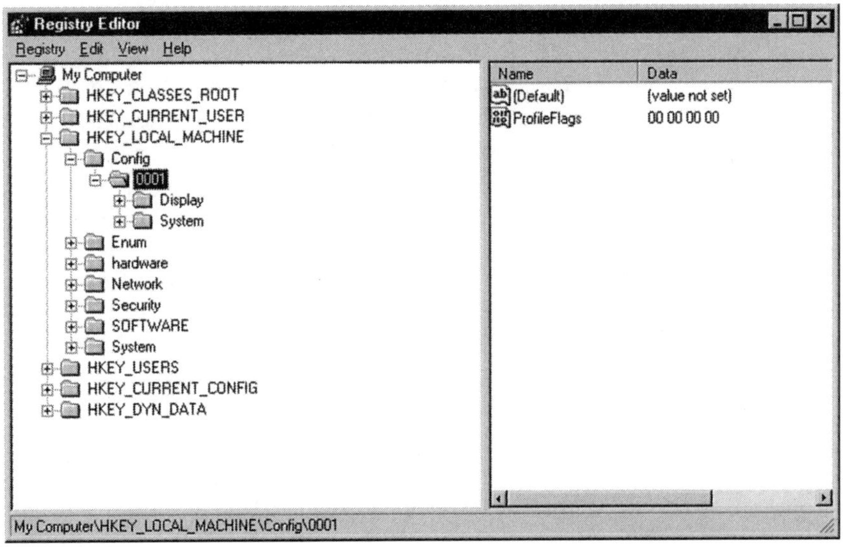

```
Registry Editor
Registry  Edit  View  Help
⊟ 🖳 My Computer                              Name              Data
  ⊞ 📁 HKEY_CLASSES_ROOT                       ab (Default)      (value not set)
  ⊞ 📁 HKEY_CURRENT_USER                       ProfileFlags      00 00 00 00
  ⊟ 📁 HKEY_LOCAL_MACHINE
     ⊟ 📁 Config
        ⊟ 📂 0001
           ⊞ 📁 Display
           ⊞ 📁 System
     ⊞ 📁 Enum
     ⊞ 📁 hardware
     ⊞ 📁 Network
     ⊞ 📁 Security
     ⊞ 📁 SOFTWARE
     ⊞ 📁 System
  ⊞ 📁 HKEY_USERS
  ⊞ 📁 HKEY_CURRENT_CONFIG
  ⊞ 📁 HKEY_DYN_DATA

My Computer\HKEY_LOCAL_MACHINE\Config\0001
```

This scary-looking database contains all of the configuration information for your computer and its network connections, your session on the computer, and the sessions of any user that logs into that computer. It's a lot of information, cryptically organized, but understanding how it works and how to get around in it is essential for working with Windows 95.

The Registry is the front end for all Windows 95 configuration data: the system configuration, the hardware configuration, the setup information for Win32-based applications, and user preferences. The actual files where this information is stored are called USER.DAT, SYSTEM.DAT, and (if you're using the Policy Editor, discussed in Chapter 8) CONFIG.POL, but they are not in human-readable form. To see your current user and system configurations all in one place, you'll need to run REGEDIT.

Some of the information in the Registry is always stored on disk, while other information is stored initially in RAM, and thus dynamically reflects changes. For example, if you adjust the configuration of a Plug and Play optical drive, that change appears immediately in the Registry.

Why Have a Registry?

Before you tune out in preparation for a discussion of esoteric techie stuff, know that there is at least one characteristic of the Registry that makes understanding it worthwhile: its compactness. You know how, before installing new software, you had to back up a whole slew of files to make sure that you could restart the computer and/or fix Windows after the changes the new software made to the system rendered it unbootable?

As the Registry contains all Windows 95 system and user information, you only need to back up USER.DAT and SYSTEM.DAT. With the Windows 95 Registry, all you have to do is export these files to another directory or to disk, name them something in English if you like, and then restore them when things go wrong. The only caveat I might make is this: Name the exported versions something that is easily identifiable when they are condensed to the eight-dot-three format that real-mode sessions demand.

What's in the Registry?

The Registry is an ASCII database pulling information from SYSTEM .DAT, USER.DAT, and (if set up) CONFIG.POL. These files are not in a form that is humanly readable, so you can only see their contents or manipulate them via the Registry (or, more usually, the Control Panel or, for CONFIG .POL, the System Policies Editor).

- SYSTEM.DAT contains hardware-related and computer-specific settings.

- USER.DAT contains user-specific information found in user profiles, such as user rights, desktop settings, and so forth.

- CONFIG.POL contains policy information relating to the system and user settings. For example, you can create a system policy controlling how users may configure their displays or the devices that they can share. Any information in the system policies file overrides the information in USER.DAT and SYSTEM.DAT. (CONFIG.POL is not mandatory to a Windows installation.)

The Registry itself contains nothing—as you can see in Figure 3.6, it's just the front end to the database of your system's configuration, a way of seeing the information in a way that makes sense to humans.

If you export the Registry, you'll create a text file with a .REG extension, but this file is only a *link* to the configuration information, not the configuration itself. You can blow away all files with the .REG extension on your machine and nothing bad will happen; your system will just recreate another Registry from the information in the .DAT files. (If you do this, then it won't create another .REG file until you export the Registry.)

NOTE The Registry itself contains no system information—it's just the human-readable representation of the information in the .DAT files, which contain information that your system requires to boot, start Windows, and keep it running.

Conversely, if you erase or rename SYSTEM.DAT and USER.DAT, then your system will not be able to load the Registry on bootup and it'll have to

FIGURE 3.6

How the Registry allows users to access Windows 95 configuration files

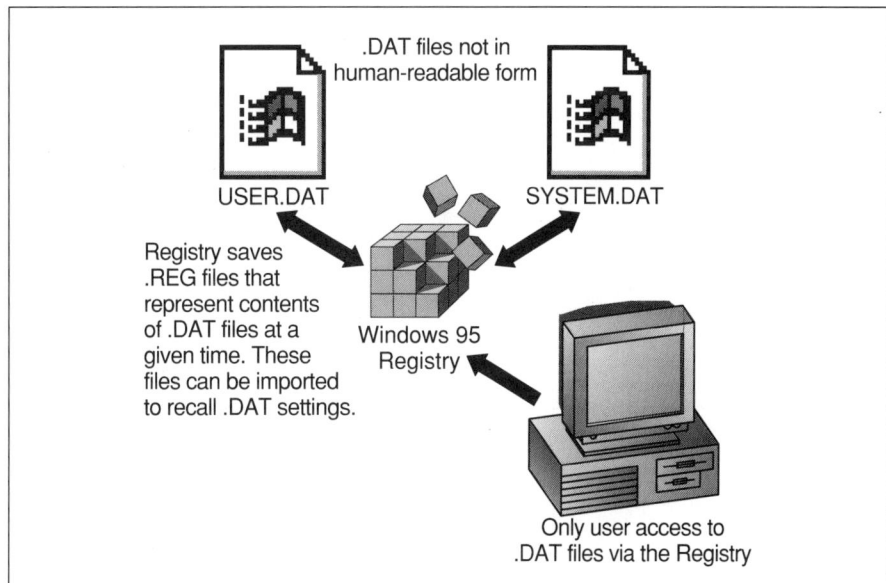

.DAT files not in human-readable form

USER.DAT

SYSTEM.DAT

Registry saves .REG files that represent contents of .DAT files at a given time. These files can be imported to recall .DAT settings.

Windows 95 Registry

Only user access to .DAT files via the Registry

rebuild the files from the backups it makes each time the machine boots successfully. (We'll discuss how that works in the Recovery chapter.)

The contents of the Registry are described in Table 3.1.

What's Not in the Registry?

The Registry does *not* contain setup information for Windows 3.x applications. This is because apps designed for previous versions of Windows don't know how to access the Registry; Win16 applications were designed to work with WIN.INI and SYSTEM.INI and to maintain their own .INI files. So long as you've still got 16-bit applications on your machine, you'll use the .INI files.

Nor does the Registry contain program-specific setup information for DOS programs. If you edit a DOS application's PIF, that information is not reflected in the Registry.

TABLE 3.1 Overview of Registry Contents

FILE NAME	DIRECTORY LOCATION (LOCAL INSTALL)	DIRECTORY LOCATION (NETWORK INSTALL)	CONTENTS	REQUIRED FOR INSTALLATION?
SYSTEM.DAT	C:\windows	C:\windows	Machine-specific information	Yes
USER.DAT	C:\windows	User's home directory	User-specific information	Yes
CONFIG.POL	Logon directory of network server	Logon directory of network server	Hardware and user information determined by policy	No

The Windows 95 Registry is NOT the Same as the Windows NT Registry

Before we go any further with this discussion, NT users should know that Windows 95's Registry is *not* the same as the NT Registry that they've come to know and love. When Microsoft was tailoring the Win32 API for Windows 95, it had to cripple its implementation slightly to permit the operating system to run on 4MB of RAM, as promised. Some Registry functions were among the casualties of this crippling.

The Windows 95 Registry isn't bad, it's just different. It works a little differently, it contains different information, the data is arranged differently, and the syntax is different. That said, your experience working with NT's Registry isn't wasted—you just can't use quite the same skills to work with Windows 95's Registry that you developed for NT's. For example:

- You cannot set Windows 95's Registry to read-only from within the Windows 95 Registry Editor. To make it read-only, you must change the access settings from the Properties dialog box.

- You cannot set group permissions to the Windows 95 Registry from within the application. By default, *anyone* can edit the Registry on the local machine. (This is not a particularly smart way to leave things, as you'll see in this chapter.)

- Windows 95's Registry does not keep *.LOG versions of important files to record changes.

Cautions about Working with the Registry

For those who haven't worked with Windows NT and so skipped the previous section, here are a few things to think about before leaping into editing the Registry:

- **In general, the Registry is *not* where you should be making changes.** Most of the configurations that you can adjust in the Registry have a GUI front end somewhere else, with a Cancel button attached. If you can make the adjustments you want from another dialog box, it's a good idea to do so, for two reasons: (1) you can cancel changes before they take effect, and (2) it's harder to screw up.

- **Know what you're editing.** Before you change any values, make sure that you know what making the change will do to your system. *If you don't know, then don't change it.* The Registry *cannot* distinguish between valid and invalid entries, so, for example, you *could* change the value of the primary network provider from "Microsoft" to "goldfish" and receive no complaints from Windows 95—at least not immediately.

- **Back up before editing.** Using the Export Registry File option in the File menu, you can save your system configuration to disk or to another drive or directory before editing it. This is a very good idea, in case you make a mistake while editing.

'Nuff said. You know that reckless meddling with your system's configuration is dangerous. Keeping that in mind, let's discuss the anatomy of your Registry and how you can safely make changes to it.

The Registry: Pieces of the Puzzle

Like the File Manager, the Registry is organized in a treelike structure. It consists of trees, subtrees, keys, and values, as you can see in Figure 3.7.

- The *tree* is the entire Registry, called My Computer. It consists of six subtrees:
  - Hkey_Classes_Root
  - Hkey_Current_User
  - Hkey_Local_Machine
  - Hkey_Users
  - Hkey_Current_Config
  - Hkey_Dyn_Data

FIGURE 3.7

Anatomy of the
Registry

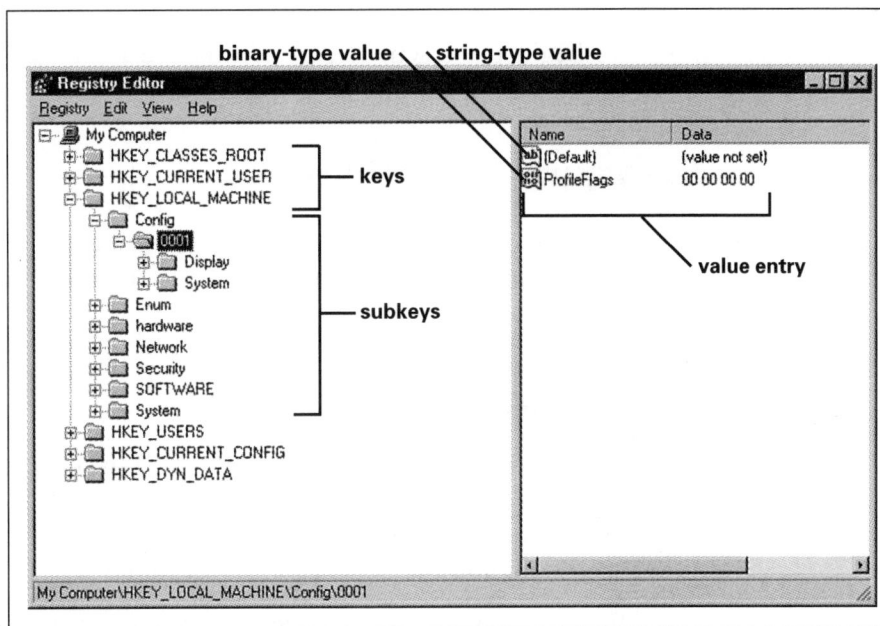

- Each of the *subtrees* controls a different part of your system. For example, Hkey_Local_Machine controls the hardware setup for your machine. (A complete list of the subtrees and their functions appears below.)

- Each of the folders within a subtree is called a *key*. (As you'll notice, keys can contain subkeys and sub-subkeys.) The keys (and subkeys) control the configuration to a specific part of the subtree's function. For example, the key called *Mouse* within the subtree Hkey_Local _Machine contains all the mouse settings.

- The actual settings within the Registry are called *values*, or *value entries*. Each value has two parts: the value name, which identifies it, and the value data, which contains the configuration information. The values may be in either of two formats:

  - Binary (or hex representations of binary numbers), used for most hardware information.

  - String (human-readable text, like "AmiProDocument") used for most software-related information.

It's very easy to make a mistake when editing binary or hex code, so, once we begin the discussion of editing the Registry, stick to editing string values.

Subtree Functions

As mentioned above, the six branches of the Registry divide up the configuration for your computer and where it fits into the network. Table 3.2 illustrates those divisions.

Opening the Registry

If you're like me, you like to play with something when learning how to use it. At the very least, it's nice to have it in front of you. Therefore, at this point you may be saying to yourself, "This talk of the Registry is all very well, but how do I *start* the silly thing?"

First of all, unless you installed Windows 95 from the CD, you *can't*—the Registry Editor is not available with the floppy disk version. Second, by default the Registry Editor is not included on any menus, perhaps so idle curiosity doesn't blow away the system configuration.

If you installed Windows 95 from the CD, you can open the Registry in a few different ways:

- Choose Run from the Start menu and type **Regedit** in the space provided.

- *Or,* open the Windows folder and double-click the icon labeled REGEDIT.

- *Or,* add the Registry Editor to the Start menu. The process is just like adding any other icon—click the Start menu, then choose Settings, then Taskbar. Click the Add button, and type **C:\windows\regedit .exe** in the text box provided. When prompted, indicate the folder in which you want to place the icon, and choose a name for the icon. The Registry Editor will now be available from whichever folder you put it in.

SUBTREE	DESCRIPTION
HKEY_Classes_Root	Contains the file associations and OLE links, the information that tells your system, "When the user double-clicks on a file with the extension .BMP, start up PBRUSH.EXE to display the file." Much of this information is duplicated in the Local_Machine subtree, as Root is a duplicate of Hkey_Local _Machine\Software\Classes.
HKEY_Current_User	Contains the user profile (colors, sounds, applications, etc.) for the person currently logged in to the machine. This subtree is a subset of Hkey_Users (described below).
HKEY_Local_Machine	Contains information about the hardware installed on the machine and the file associations and port assignments. You'll do most of your work in this subtree.
HKEY_Users	Contains both the default user profile for someone who hasn't logged in before and the profile for the current user.
HKEY_Current_Config	Points to Hkey_Local_Machine\Config, the subtree that records the current configuration of the hardware attached to the computer.
HKEY_Dyn_Data	Contains dynamic information about Plug and Play hardware attached to the computer. The information contained in this subtree is stored in RAM, so you don't have to reboot to update it.

Navigating in the Registry

Navigating in the Registry is pretty simple. When you open the Registry Editor, the six branches are visible. Click on the one you want, and it opens into its keys. Click on the key you want, and you'll see *its* keys (if the key icon has the plus sign in a box that indicates that it has subkeys) and values. Double-click on the entry in the data column of a value to edit it.

The big trick in the Registry lies not in moving around, but in finding where you want to be. When you're looking for something, how do you know where to find it?

Finding things in the Registry is partially a function of logic and experience, and partially a function of the available tools. So far as the logic part goes, where would you look for configuration information about your mouse? `Hkey_Current_User` doesn't sound very likely, as the mouse drivers for a machine won't change from user to user. `Hkey_Local_Machine` is a much more likely starter, as the mouse is part of the machine *any* user will use.

Using the Find Tool

When logic won't help you, there's always the Find tool. Think of a word that relates to the configuration information you're looking for (keep it short, as the Registry Editor's style is telegraphic, to say the least) and choose Find from the Edit menu. If the first Find that you come up with doesn't work, press F3 or choose Find Next from the Edit menu, and the Registry Editor will look for the next incidence of that word for you.

Notice that the Find tool is more useful in Windows 95 than in Windows NT, as the Registry is organized differently. Rather than devoting a separate window to each subtree, as Windows NT does, Windows 95 includes every subtree in the same window so you can extend searches from subtree to subtree.

> **TIP**
>
> When searching for a word, start as close to the top of the Registry as possible if you're not certain which subtree you should be looking in. If the word doesn't appear in the subtree in which you started, the Registry Editor will begin searching in the subtree next on the list. If you begin the search in one of the lower subtrees and the word does not appear in that subtree or any of the ones listed after it, the Registry Editor does not go to the top of the list and begin again.

Editing the Local Registry

Editing the Registry is mostly a matter of finding what you want—once you get that far, the rest is easy. The simplest way to explain how to make changes to the Registry is to do it. In this section, we'll go through the process of changing the color of the buttons from the gray of the default Windows color scheme to blue. The process includes three main steps:

- Backing up the Registry
- Editing the configuration
- Restoring the Registry (if necessary)

One problem with the Find tool: It won't search for text in Registry entries. (It *will* search for text in Registry *keys*, however.) You can get around the problem by exporting the Registry to ASCII and then searching the ASCII file.

Backing Up the Registry

Before making any changes directly to the Registry, export it to a safe place (either your local drive or, for extra security, to your computer's Startup disk). If you have this backup copy, you can restore your Registry very easily if you mess up your system. (If you don't, and the corruption is bad enough, you might have to reinstall the operating system. So don't skip this step.)

The easiest way to back up your system's configuration is to export the Registry to disk or to another directory. When Regedit exports a Registry, it is dumping out the entire Registry in a simple ASCII format. Essentially, exporting the Registry converts USER.DAT and SYSTEM.DAT to something you can view, search, and save. Once exported, those versions of the system configuration are not available to the system until you import them. In the meantime, you're able to make all the changes that you like to the Registry information. Take a look at Figure 3.8 to see how this works.

FIGURE 3.8

Exporting a Registry

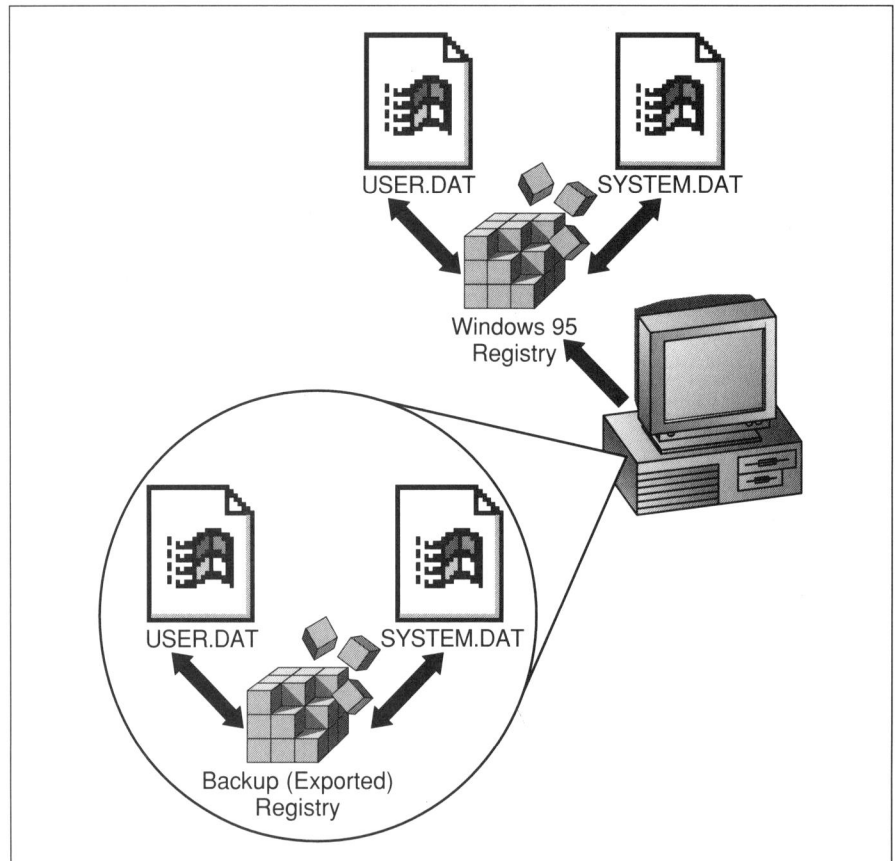

When you export a Registry it maintains a copy of the system configuration files with it. This copy, however, is isolated from the operating system (as represented by the ring around the exported files). Changes made to the current Registry do not affect the exported copies. Therefore, when you replace the current Registry with an exported one, you'll restore the operating system to the way it was when you exported the Registry.

To export the configuration information's front end, open the Registry Editor (choose Run from the Start button on the Toolbar, and type **Regedit .exe**). You should see a screen that looks like the one in Figure 3.9.

Choose Export Registry File from the Registry menu. A dialog box like the one in Figure 3.10 will appear.

FIGURE 3.9

Opening screen of the Registry Editor

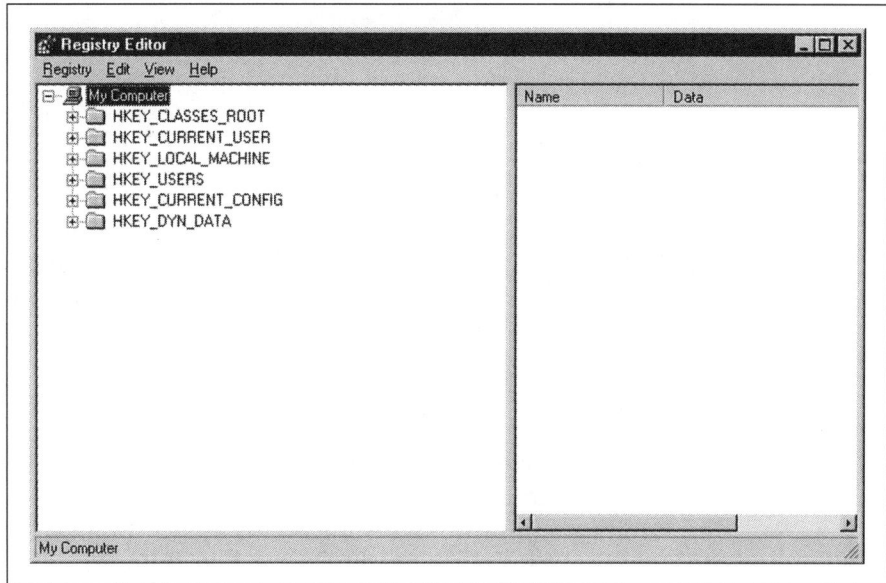

FIGURE 3.10

Export Registry File
dialog box

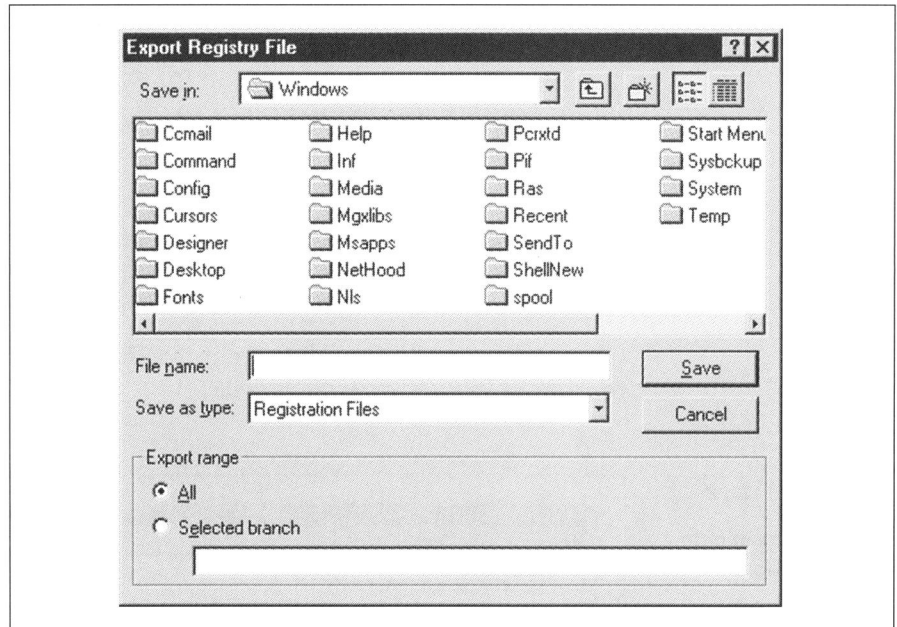

TIP

For best disaster planning when exporting your Registry, export it locally so you can import it without having to connect to network drives.

Select the disk or directory to which you want to copy your Registry and type a name for the file in the text box provided. Windows 95 supports long file names when running in protected mode, so this name can be longer than the eight-dot-three pattern you may be used to as a Windows user. As you can see in Figure 3.11, I named my backup copy **Working Registry for TSC on 6-5-95** and copied it to my \backup directory.

Click Save, and the backup copy is saved to that folder. If you open the folder, you'll see the Registry icon labeled with the name you specified.

Export Registry File
dialog box with
export information

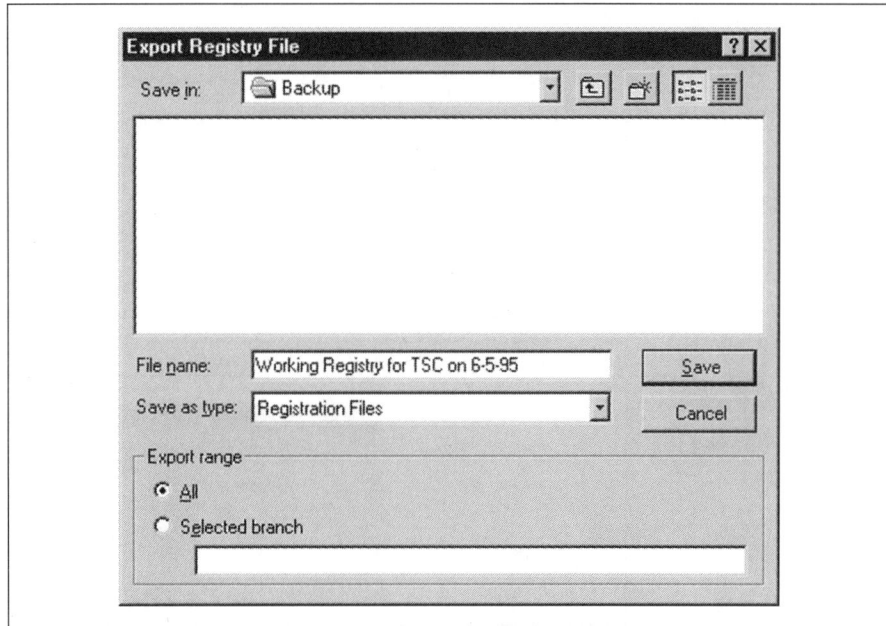

Editing the Registry's Contents

Now that we've saved the current configuration, we can mess around with it. Run Regedit to start up the Registry Editor.

As I said earlier, in this experiment we're going to edit the display to change the color of the buttons in the dialog boxes. Off the top of my head, I don't know which key the values that relate to this information are in, so I've got two options: I can guess (the subtree that relates to the current user and the display key within it seem likely contenders) or I can do a search for instances of the word "color" throughout the Registry. The second method seems like less work, so I'll use it.

Position the cursor in My Computer so that the search will extend through every subtree. From the Edit menu, choose Find. You'll see a dialog box that looks the one in Figure 3.12.

Type **color** in the Find What text box and click Find Next. While it's searching, a dialog box like the one in Figure 3.13 will appear.

FIGURE 3.12

Find dialog box

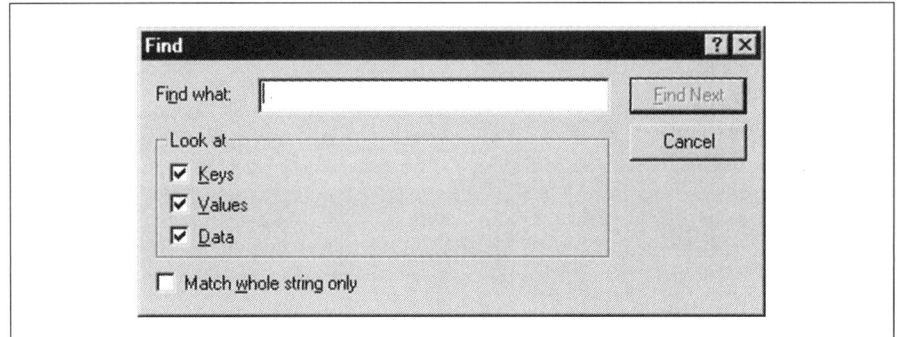

FIGURE 3.13

Searching for "color"

To keep the search as broad as possible, I've instructed the Editor to look at keys, values, *and* data for the keyword, as it does by default. If I checked *Match whole string only*, Regedit would only find "color", but this way matches like "ButtonColor" or "Colors" will count as hits as well. I'll keep it unchecked, as I'm not sure exactly how the word will appear.

The first hit, as you see in Figure 3.14, doesn't look like what I need (I can't manipulate the hex accurately), so I'll click F3 to find the next "Color."

And so it goes, until I find the one I want as in Figure 3.15.

Aha! "ButtonFace" looks like the value name I need. If you've messed around with changing color values numerically, you'll know that the value 192 192 192 indicates a nice medium gray made of middling amounts of red, green, and blue.

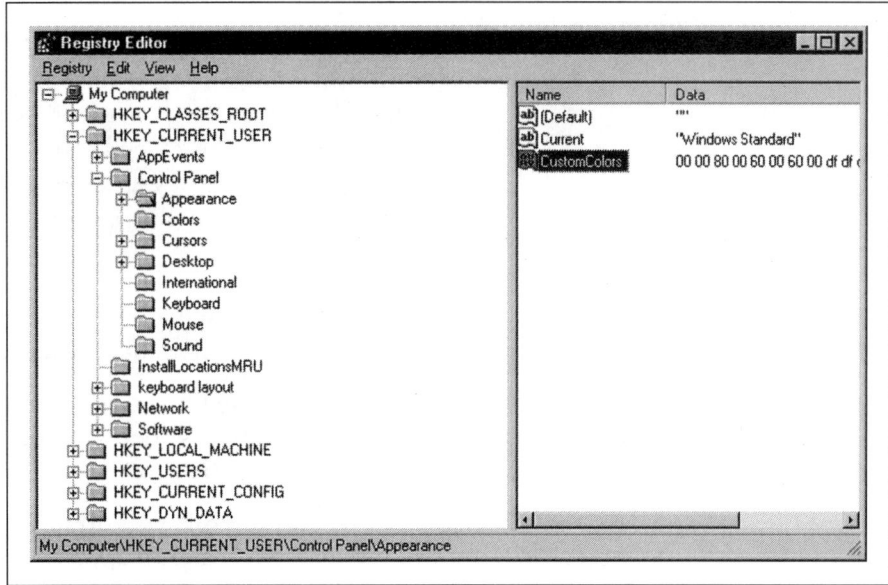

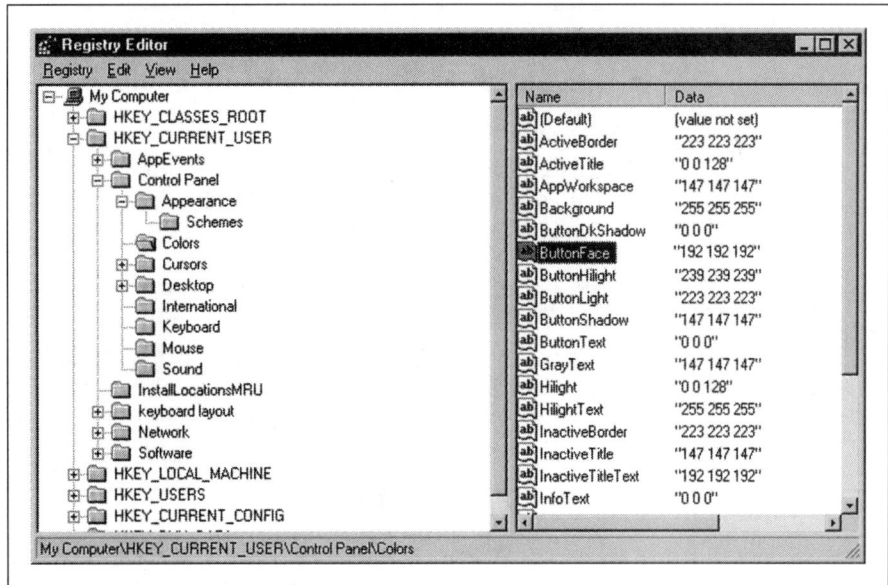

NOTE Brief digression—0 is least, 255 is most; three 0s would be black and three 255s would be white. You can get a feel for this in Paint. Open the program from the Start menu, and double-click one of the colored squares at the bottom of the screen. That will put you in a dialog in which you can edit the numeric values of the colors and see the results immediately.

To make the tops of the buttons blue, double-click on the word "Button-Face." You'll see a dialog box like the one in Figure 3.16.

Type **0 0 255** in the Value data text box to show no red and no green but full-intensity blue, and click OK. Notice that the button faces are still gray—the change has not taken effect yet.

Exit the Registry Editor and log off (you don't have to restart the computer). When the login dialog box shows up, it will be an obnoxious shade of blue.

Restoring the Registry

As the change you made is pretty easy to remember, you could restore the Registry (and get rid of that obnoxious blue) by searching for "Button-Face" and changing its value data back to 192 192 192. Once you logged off and back on again, the change would take effect.

FIGURE 3.16

Editing a Registry value

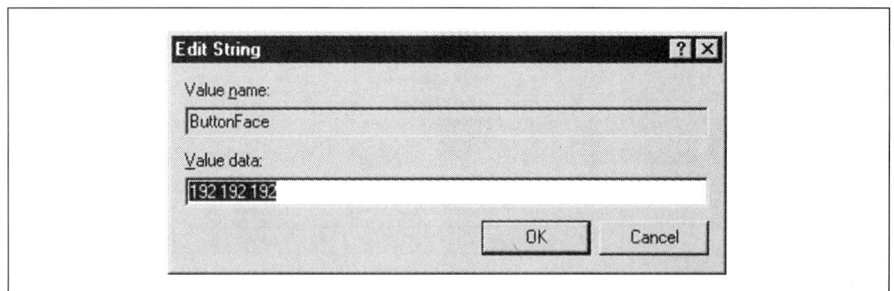

WARNING You can't reverse an importing action: once you've imported a Registry or a subtree thereof, it replaces whatever was there before. If you want to save a copy of the configuration, export it before you import the old one.

Since we're practicing for real-world changes that may not be quite so easy to reverse, however, let's do a real trial. There are two ways in which you can restore your Registry to the way it was before:

- Import the Registry from the Registry Editor.
- *Or,* activate the icon of the backup in its folder.

In either case, what you're doing is replacing the current configuration with the one you exported. As you recall from earlier in this chapter, when you export the Registry it maintains a copy of what the .DAT files looked like at the time you exported. When you import that saved file, you replace the current configuration with that saved one.

To import a saved Registry, select Import Registry File from the Registry menu and move to the directory where you stored the backup (in my case, C:\backup). You'll see the name of the backup copy as you do in Figure 3.17.

FIGURE 3.17

Importing a Registry

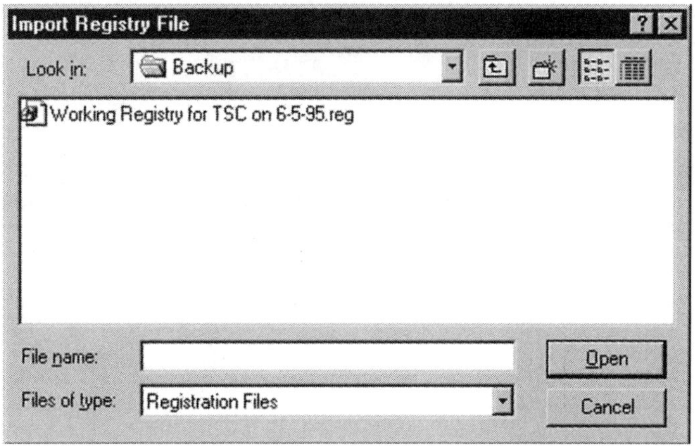

Click Open, and the Registry Editor will replace the current copy of the Registry with the one you just imported. A status box like the one in Figure 3.18 will show the progress of the importing process.

When the file is fully imported, a dialog box like the one in Figure 3.19 will announce the fact.

Importing a saved Registry from its folder is even easier. Open the folder to which you exported the file (as in Figure 3.20) and double-click it.

When you activate the saved file, it imports itself into the Registry, showing the same dialog boxes that you saw with the previous approach.

Whichever method you choose, the system configuration will revert to the one in the restored Registry as soon as you log off and log back on.

What about Duplicate Entries?

The Registry sometimes repeats itself. For example, as we noted earlier, some of the information found in Hkey_Classes_Root also appears in Hkey_Local_Machine. If the same values appear in two different subtrees, which subtree controls?

FIGURE 3.18

Importing Registry status dialog box

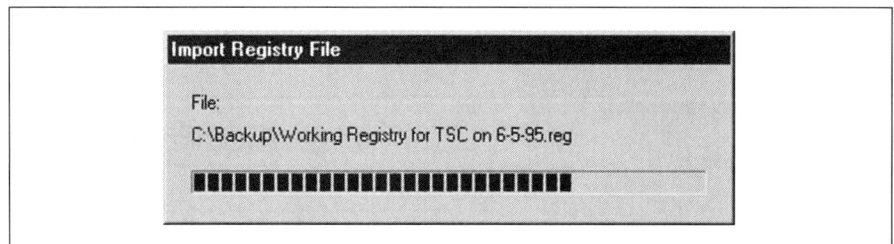

FIGURE 3.19

Import confirmed

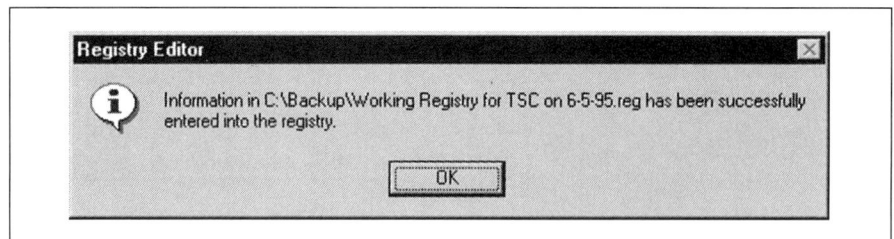

Backup

File Edit View Help

Working
Registry for
TSC on
6-5-95.reg

1 object(s) 722 bytes

The subtrees of the Registry are arranged in a hierarchy. If the same information appears in more than one subtree of the Registry and you manually change it in only one subtree, then the effect of the change upon the system depends on where that subtree falls in the hierarchy. Generally speaking, system-specific information outranks user-specific information. For example, a setting that appears in both the Local_Machine and Users subtrees will be controlled by what's in Local_Machine. Please note that this only applies to those times when you've edited the Registry directly; if you edit the system configuration from the Control Panel the settings will be updated in every subtree in which they appear.

For example, you can set file associations through the Registry to link files with a particular extension to an application. Four subtrees of the Registry contain value data for file associations: Hkey_Classes_Root, Hkey_Current_User, Hkey_Local_Machine, and Hkey_Users. By default, all files with the extension .1ST (as in README.1ST) are linked with Notepad, so if you activate a file with that extension you'll also open Notepad. If you change the file association from Notepad to Ami Pro (a Lotus word processor), you'll open up Ami Pro when you activate any file with the .1ST extension. But if you edit the file association in one subtree of the Registry at a time, here's what will happen:

- If only Hkey_Classes_Root is set to AmiPro, then .1ST files will open Ami Pro when activated.

- If only Hkey_Current_User is set to Ami Pro, then .1ST files will open Notepad when activated.

- If only `Hkey_Local_Machine` is set to AmiPro, then `.1ST` files will open Ami Pro when activated.

- If only `Hkey_Users` is set to Ami Pro, then `.1ST` files will open Notepad when activated.

NOTE

By the way, this is an excellent example of how you can make an invalid entry into the Registry without it telling you that the change won't work—you just find out when you attempt to use the system with the changes that you've wrought. Ami Pro cannot open any file that is not a valid Ami Pro document with a `.SAM` extension unless you import the file into Ami Pro using a listed filter. If you edit the Registry to open Ami Pro when you activate any file with a `.1ST` suffix, Ami Pro will start up all right when you double-click a `README.1ST` object, but it will not open the file—because it is not an Ami Pro document.

Although there appears to be a contradiction in that the Root subtree and the Local Machine subtree appear to control file associations independently of each other, remember that the Root subtree is really `Hkey_Local_Machine\Software\Classes`, so changes made to Root are changes made to that key and subkey within Local Machine.

Editing a Remote Registry

Why would you need to edit the Registry of a remote machine? It's handy for any of the following situations, where it's easier to fix the problem from your desk than it is to go to the ailing workstation or you *can't* fix the problem from the local machine.

- The person using that machine played with the display settings and turned their screen entirely black.

- You want to copy the same user configuration to several machines.

- A user has connected to the wrong network drives and can't find their files.

Editing the Registry of a remote computer works pretty much the same way as editing a local one: the main difference lies in the process of connecting to the remote Registry in the first place. In this section, we'll talk about how to connect to the remote machine (and some of the potential connection glitches you may encounter) and what you can expect to see when you've connected.

Preparing to Administer a Remote Computer

Before you can edit another computer's Registry, both you and the other computer must have at least one network protocol (like NetBEUI or IPX/SPX) in common and the Remote Registry service set up.

To install the Remote Registry (or any other) service on a computer, insert the Windows 95 CD-ROM in the drive and follow these steps:

1. Open the Control Panel and choose Networks.

2. Click on the Add button, and, in the Select Network Component Type dialog box that appears, double-click Services.

3. From the Select Network Service dialog box, click the Have Disk button. When prompted, specify the path to \Admin\Nettools \Remotreg on the CD. You'll see a file called REGSERV.INF in the menu. Select it, and click OK.

4. Select Microsoft Remote Registry from the Models list and click OK, then click OK to get out of the dialog box altogether. Windows 95 will search the CD for all the files that it needs to set up the service.

After you exit from the Network dialog, Windows 95 will tell you that you must restart for the change to take effect, but you don't have to reboot then unless you want to be able to use the Remote Registry service right away.

You'll need to install the Remote Registry Service on both the administering machine and any Windows 95 machine to be administered.

Connecting to the Remote Computer

You must initiate a specific connection to a remote machine's Registry in order to edit it. To do so, open the Registry Editor and choose Connect to Remote Registry from the Registry menu. A dialog box like the one in Figure 3.21 will appear.

Type in the name of the computer you want to administer, or, to make sure that you type it correctly and choose from the right domain, click Browse and choose it from the dialog box like the one in Figure 3.22. All machines connected to the network will be displayed, whether or not they're Windows 95 machines or have the Remote Registry service running.

Choose the machine to connect to (in this case, I'll choose AMS) and click OK. Click OK again at the next dialog box to connect to the Registry.

Troubleshooting a Remote Registry Connection

At this point, you should be successfully connected. If you are not, you may see a dialog box like the one in Figure 3.23. If you see this dialog box, make sure of the following things:

- You've connected to a machine running Windows 95.
- The Remote Registry service is running on both machines.

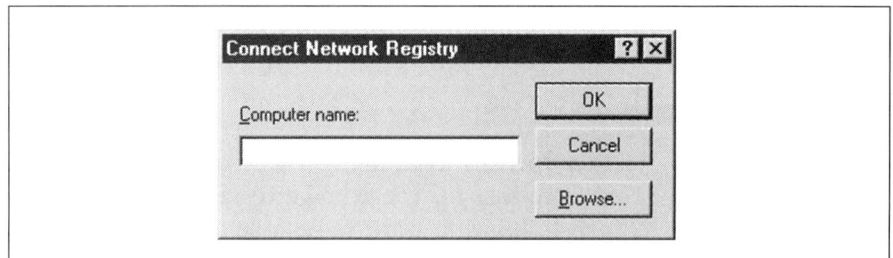

FIGURE 3.21

Connect Network Registry dialog box

FIGURE 3.22

Browse list for Remote
Registry administration

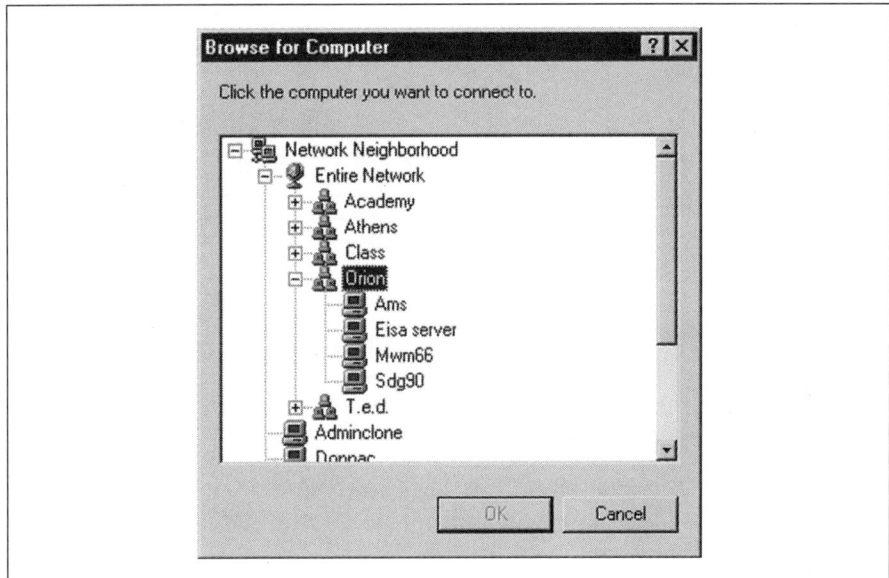

You might see a message telling you that you don't have permission to edit
the remote Registry, as in Figure 3.24. You'll see this message if:

- You've logged onto a domain that doesn't have permission to administer the machine's Registry.

- Your account is a member of a group not permitted to administer
  the remote computer (by default, only Domain Administrators have
  this permission).

If you're running NT on your network and have more than one domain,
you may wonder if establishing a *trust relationship* between two domains

FIGURE 3.23

Unsuccessful attempt
to connect to remote
Registry

FIGURE 3.24

No permission to edit
remote Registry

Error Connecting Network Registry ☒

Unable to connect to Ams. Make sure you have permission to administer this computer.

OK

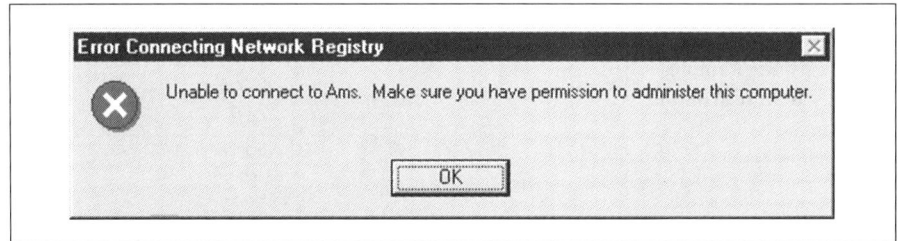

means that the trusted domain can administer machines who have permitted members of the other domain to administer them.

Nope.

No matter what the trust relationships between the two domains are, if you don't log on to the domain with explicit permission to administer the remote machine, you'll see a message like the previous one.

Permitting Other Groups to Administer Remote Registries

The previous section described how to set up a computer for remote administration of its Registry by members of the Domain Administrators group. If, for some reason, members of other groups require this ability, the setup process is a little more involved.

Open Control Panel and click on the Passwords icon. You'll see three tabs: Change Passwords, Remote Administration, and User Profiles. Click on the Remote Administration tab. You should see a dialog box that looks like the one in Figure 3.25.

In this screen, you can see the users and/or groups (by default, only the group Domain Administrators) that currently have permission to remotely administer this machine. Click the Add button to select other remote administrators. You'll see a screen that looks like Figure 3.26, with a list that includes a globe icon and various head icons.

Single heads are individuals; double heads are groups. The globe signifies everyone on the network. Notice that a list box in the upper right corner lets you specify the domain to draw administrators from. It's perfectly

FIGURE 3.25

Setting Remote
Administration options

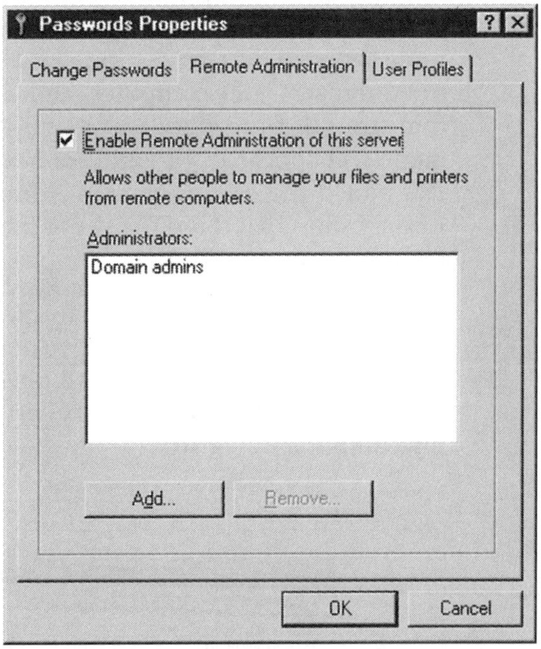

FIGURE 3.26

Adding Remote
Administrators

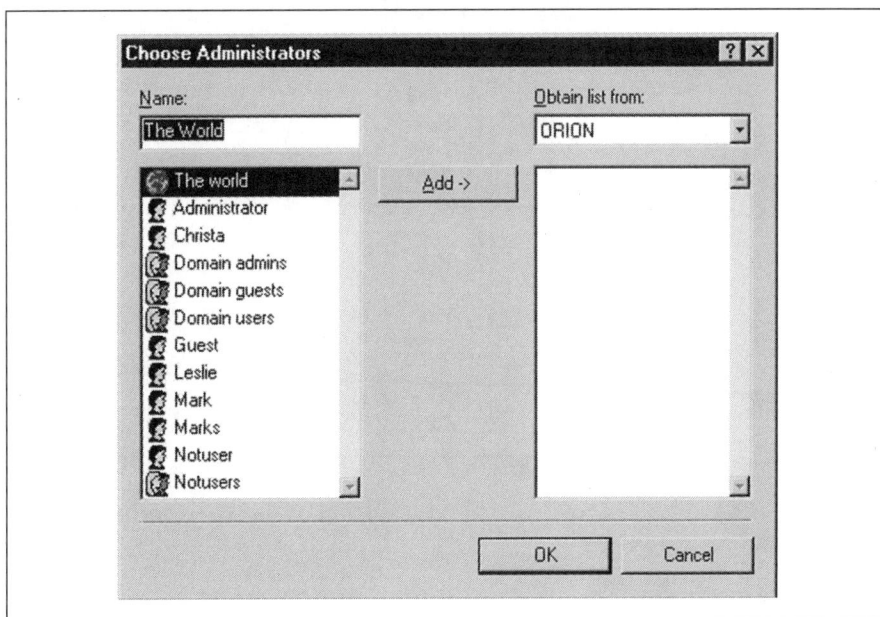

okay to have some administrators from one domain and some from another, thus eliminating the need to set up double accounts for remote administrators. Click on the individuals or groups who you want to be able to administer your computer, and then click Add. If you chose your administrators from more than one domain, the administrator's domain name will appear in parentheses next to his or her name. In Figure 3.27, I've added the group Domain Administrators from T.E.D. and the user Leslie from ORION to the list of those permitted to remotely administer my computer.

Click OK and, as you can see in Figure 3.28, you'll be back at the initial screen, where you can see the two new members added to the list. If Leslie or any member of T.E.D.'s Domain Administrator group log on to a machine with the Remote Registry service running, they will be able to edit my computer's Registry.

FIGURE 3.27

Administrators from two workgroups added to list

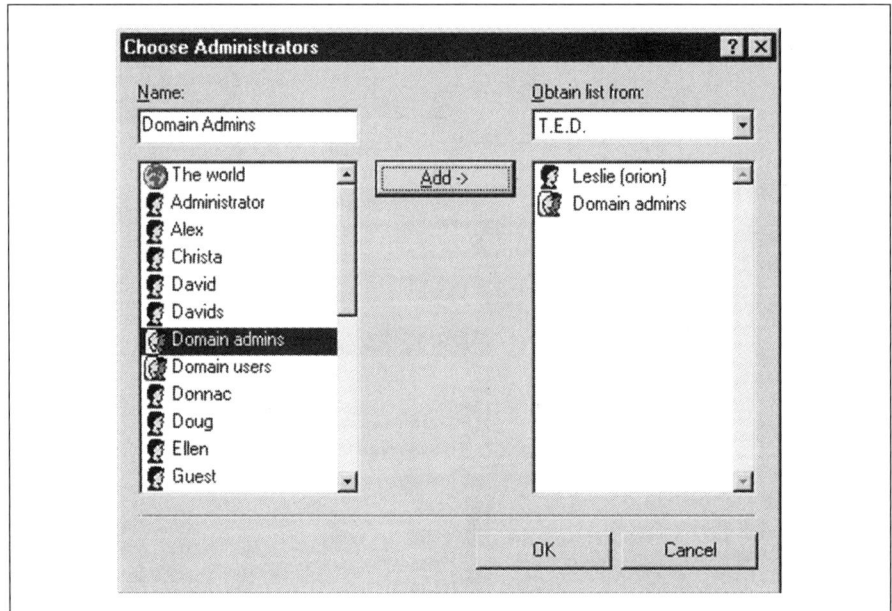

FIGURE 3.28

FIGURE 3.28

New list of remote
administrators

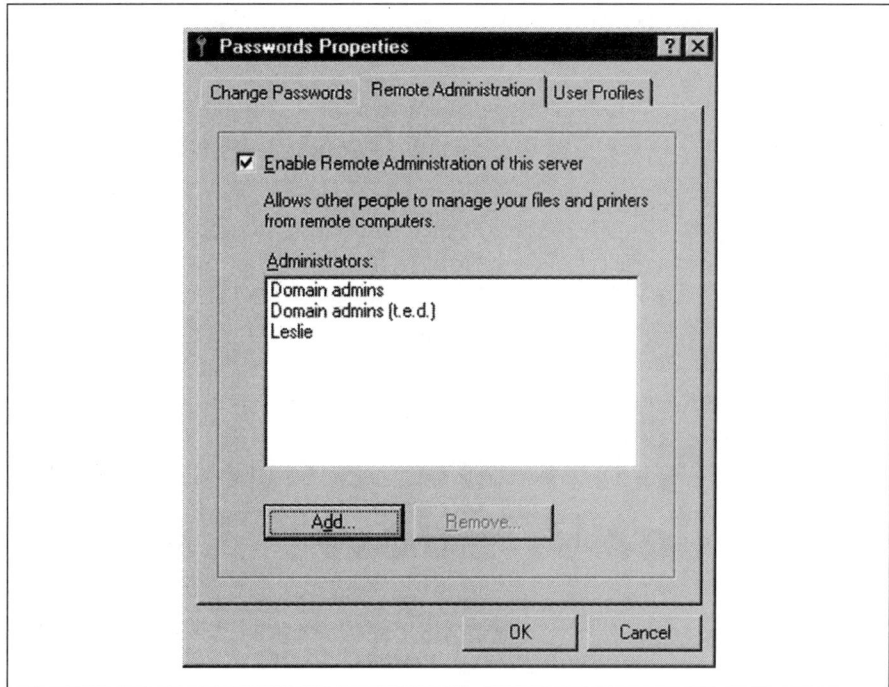

> **WARNING** When choosing the accounts that have access to your Registry,
> don't forget that you're giving people the power to destroy your
> system's configuration and require you to reinstall. Don't give
> this capability to just anyone.

To remove users or groups from the list of a machine's remote administrators, click on the name and click the Remove button. A message box will appear, asking if you're sure that you want to remove that administrator; click OK to confirm the removal. Even if you have only one administrator in the list, you can still remove it—there's no minimum.

Editing the Remote Registry

If everything went well and you saw no error messages, you're now ready to edit the remote Registry. Your screen should look like the one in Figure 3.29.

From here on out, the editing process is the same as it is for the local Registry. When you've finished making changes, exit the Registry Editor or choose Disconnect Remote Registry from the Registry menu.

WIN.INI and SYSTEM.INI under Windows 95

There are lots of files in the Windows world with the extension .INI, for *initialization*. Excel, for example, automatically creates and maintains a

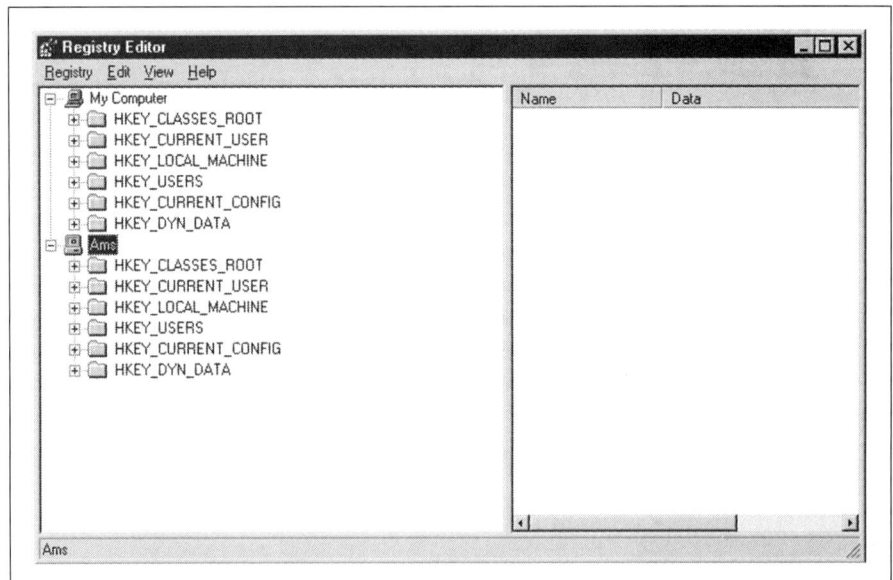

file called EXCEL.INI which tells Excel things like whether to start up in a maximized condition, what the previous few files accessed were, and what user options should be set. Most other applications create their own .INI files—Ami Pro uses AMIPRO.INI, Word For Windows creates WINWORD.INI, and so on.

If a program creates an initialization file for itself, however, that file is for its personal use *only*—other programs don't access it. For general configuration information, Win16 applications access two more general initialization files: WIN.INI and SYSTEM.INI.

Contents of .INI files

It's hard to draw a clear and distinct line between what SYSTEM.INI and WIN.INI do, as WIN.INI has existed since the Windows 1.0 days, and SYSTEM.INI has only been around since version 3.0. Although it's tempting to say that SYSTEM.INI controls the hardware configuration of Windows, and WIN.INI contains user preferences and software configuration, that's not 100 percent accurate. It *is* a decent approximation, however, so use it if you like, just to get a grasp on what these two files do.

The .INI files are all divided up into *sections*. Sections are demarcated by section names, which are surrounded by square brackets. One section, for example, is called [boot]; the [boot] section not only contains references to drivers, it also contains information about some Windows fonts, screen savers, language to use for messages, and which program shell to use.

The New Look of .INI Files

If you installed Windows 95 on top of your previous Windows directory, the installation procedure saved your Windows 3.x SYSTEM.INI and WIN.INI under the names SYSINI.W31 and WININI.W31. The contents of the old and the new files do not match—although they're similar, the entries in the new .INI files reflect the differences between a Windows overlay on DOS and the Windows 95 operating system. The old configuration information was set aside in the .W31 files, and new .INI files created from the information in the Registry.

What's different? The exact entries will vary from PC to PC, depending on your hardware and how you set up Windows, but here's some of the more important differences in each initialization file.

SYSTEM.INI versus SYSINI.W31

SYSTEM.INI, recall, is more or less responsible for recording hardware information. It contains configuration information for drivers, network setup, the display, the process of starting Windows, and so forth.

Thus, when you change the operating system, the display modes it supports, and the way that it does networking, it's not surprising that entries corresponding to those qualities should change also. Many of the important differences occur in the [boot] and [386Enh] sections of SYSTEM.INI. For example:

- The default shell in SHELL= (the program that, among other things, provides the background to Windows) differs from Windows 3.x; in Windows 95 it provides access to user programs with EXPLORER.EXE rather than to PROGMAN.EXE.

- The protected-mode screen grabber (the program that saves the information in your DOS screens when you flip from DOS programs to Windows) is now called VGAFULL.3GR instead of VGADIB.3GR. There *is* no real-mode screen grabber (indicated in SYSINI.W31 as 286Grabber) in the Windows 95 SYSTEM.INI.

- Windows 3.x defined the display font for non-Windows applications displaying either 40 or 80 columns and 25 or fewer lines (EGA80WOA.FON, for example). Windows 95 skips these entries entirely—the display settings for DOS programs are set in their Properties dialog boxes, as discussed in Chapter 13.

- The line allowing Windows to bypass DOS and BIOS to access a Western-Digital hard disk (device=*wdctrl) is now gone, as Windows 95 is its own operating system and doesn't need special statements to permit 32-bit disk access.

- Many Windows 3.x virtual device drivers are rolled into VMM.VXD, so individual statements referring to those drivers are missing from Windows 95.

- The [mci] section, which describes how Windows handles multimedia applications that use the media control interface, has some new entries for video handling.

- SYSTEM.INI under Windows 95 contains an entirely new section devoted to networking, including entries to define how TCP/IP works.

Please note that this list doesn't include *every* difference between a Windows 3.x SYSTEM.INI and a Windows 95 SYSTEM.INI, but these are some of the more important variances. There are some other differences, in that the names of some programs have changed so the entries look different (such as the mouse.drv=Logitech Mouse entry changing to mouse.drv=Logitech), but variations like that aren't really substantial. Of course, if you change your system configuration after installing Windows 95, the contents of the .INI file will change as well.

WIN.INI versus WININI.W31

WIN.INI more or less keeps track of the user setup and application software for Windows. It also keeps configuration information for Windows programs that don't have a .INI file (like Micrografx Designer). It's a much larger file than SYSTEM.INI, containing information about all of your software's fonts and OLE links.

The WIN.INI files for Windows 3.x and Windows 95 are more similar than their respective SYSTEM.INI files. The major changes are as follows:

- Some new entries relating to Windows 95's video capabilities are added to the [mci extensions] section.

- Several entirely new sections have been added, relating to:
  - the Registry
  - the ATM (Adobe Type Manager, not Asynchronous Transfer Mode) workaround for printing
  - new Microsoft applications

In general, however, you don't need to worry about these settings. They're not anything that you should need to change from inside the .INI file—path settings and other like information are more easily edited from the Control Panel or the Taskbar item on the Startup Menu.

Why Do I Have .INI Files?

.INI files have some built-in failings. They can only be nested in two layers (the [section] name and the entries included in the section). They can only be up to 64K in size. If you're using .INI files, backing up your system's configuration requires copying four files (both .INI files, CONFIG.SYS, and AUTOEXEC.BAT). If you've got this wonderful Registry that keeps all of your configuration files in one manageable database (and, even if the entries are cryptic, they're certainly no more cryptic than the entries in a CONFIG.SYS or SYSTEM.INI file), then why do you still *have* WIN.INI and SYSTEM.INI files?

The answer is: for backward compatibility.

Previous versions of Windows relied on SYSTEM.INI and WIN.INI. These two ASCII text files control roughly the same things as SYSTEM.DAT and USER.DAT respectively, so retaining the .INI files might seem to be a waste of time. But applications written for previous versions of Windows don't know how to look in the Registry for the information that they need.

Windows 95 is a 32-bit operating system, but Microsoft realized that it couldn't possibly make Windows 95 incompatible with the 16-bit applications that Windows users have been buying for years. In the interests of avoiding a riot on the front steps of the Redmond compound, Windows 95 was designed to accommodate both 32-bit applications written for 95, which can access the Registry, and 16-bit applications, which *cannot*. Hence, you've still got WIN.INI and SYSTEM.INI files floating around in your system.

If you install Windows 95 on top of Windows 3.x, then the information in WIN.INI and SYSTEM.INI is copied into the Registry during Setup. When you make changes to the Registry, either directly or via one of the graphical tools like the Control Panel, they're updated in WIN.INI and SYSTEM.INI for the use of applications not designed to work with the Registry. Note that your Windows 3.x .INI files (now with .W31 extensions) are not affected by changes to the system Registry.

Generally speaking, you shouldn't need to edit either WIN.INI or SYSTEM.INI directly—most of the settings that they control are accessible via the Control Panel. If you need to fine-tune an application (for example, to change the default source directory to import pictures from), then you'll need to make those changes to that specific application's .INI file. You can edit or view any .INI file in Notepad.

For more information on configuring old DOS and Win16 applications to work with Windows 95, turn to Chapter 13.

CHAPTER

4

Setting up 95—
Strategies and Tactics

EVER been through a major software upgrade? If you're like most PC support people, then you probably have—and I'm sure the memories aren't too positive. Now I can't say that a mass migration to Windows 95 will be easy, or even *can* be easy, but there are some right ways and some wrong ways to go about it. In this chapter, I intend to push you in the direction of some of the right ways.

I think the most important part of a successful Windows installation—or, for that matter, *any* new software installation—lies in understanding your options, the pitfalls, and ways to make the transition as automated and smooth as possible.

One thing I should mention about this chapter: As this concerns setting up Windows 95, you'll see references to things that we haven't covered yet; for example, you'll see a number of references to networking concepts, even though we haven't discussed networking yet. I must apologize for that, but there's a kind of "chicken and egg" nature to discussing setup, so I'll ask your forbearance in advance.

Getting Ready for a Windows 95 Installation

Once upon a time, in order to install a piece of software on my system, all I needed to do was create a new directory, copy the files to that directory, add the new directory to the path, and I was done. Well, those days are long gone, and modern installations require more preparation and better documentation. As I see it, the main steps in preparing for a Windows 95 installation are:

- Inventory your hardware.
- Test the hardware.
- Document the hardware.
- Inventory your current software.
- Test Windows 95 compatibility with that software.
- Prepare any PIFs for DOS software.

We'll examine some of those steps in this chapter, and some in later chapters. First, let's look at the hardware.

Inventory Your Hardware

Modern organizations using PC's often do not use a standard suite of hardware, mainly due to the commodity nature of PC hardware. (No one would have guessed this a few years ago, but in most companies it is more common to find standardized software than it is to find any kind of hardware standards.) This means that it is quite likely you will have to install Windows 95 on a wide variety of hardware, and that can pose a problem. You see, Windows 95 is very good about detecting the hardware that you have in a system, but, like any software, it cannot detect *all* hardware. So, to be prepared for the inevitable, you still have the important job of figuring out what hardware you have on your system before you embark on a Windows 95 installation.

Now, when I say that you should inventory your hardware, I don't really mean that you have to know "Compaq model Deskpro M/50, 486 processor"; actually, that kind of information is easy for the installation software to figure out. Here's what you need for your inventory:

- The type of monitor on your system.
- What expansion boards are in your system; in particular, any LAN adapters, proprietary CD-ROM interfaces, SCSI host adapters, video adapters, other unusual hard disk controllers, nonstandard parallel or serial ports, and any internal or external modems.

- What system resources the boards require—I/O addresses, IRQ levels, DMA channels, RAM addresses, and ROM addresses.

- Any network-specific information, like network names, IP addresses, DNS servers, gateways, subnet masks, and the like.

I know that gathering this information isn't fun; believe me, I know, as I've done it many times. But if you don't have the information at your fingertips when you are installing Windows 95, then there is a decent chance that you may be stopped with a difficult question right in the middle of the installation. The result would be a half-installed copy of Windows 95—not a very pretty prospect. Of course, if there is absolutely no way for you to get this information, then go ahead and install Windows 95; as I've said before, its detection software is really quite good. But gathering this information—in particular, gathering the system resource information—is absolutely essential to supporting PCs in the '90s. Even if you aren't going to install Windows 95, the utility of this information should pay for at least some of your time.

What Kind of Hardware Should You Have for 95?

While I'm on the topic of hardware, let's take a minute and talk about what sort of hardware will work with Windows 95, and especially what hardware will work best.

CPU Types

Windows 95 will run on any 386 or later processor. This is not a bogus claim, despite what some people have said about 95 requiring a 486 processor. In my experience, Windows 95 runs as well and as fast on a given piece of hardware as Windows 3.x did. If you liked the way that Windows ran on your old Windows 3.x system, then you'll like Windows 95 on that same system. Does that mean that there *isn't* any reason to upgrade your processor with Windows 95? Well, there *is* one reason: Windows 95 multitasks better than Windows 3.x, which means that you'll be more likely to attempt to multitask in the first place—and once you start multitasking, you'll develop a real need for speed. You can certainly multitask with a 16-MHz 386 processor; but, then, even though the rear bumper on my

In general, however, I often recommend SCSI hardware, largely because of its flexibility. Whereas IDE can only support hard drives and the occasional tape drive or CD-ROM, SCSI supports more devices; it is common to see scanners, tape drives, optical storage devices, CD-ROMs, and, of course, hard drives with a SCSI interface. The benefit, then, of SCSI is that you simply place one board in your system and that one board drives a variety of peripherals.

The fact of the matter, however, is that you probably have IDE hardware on your system, and that's okay—okay, that is, as long as we're talking about Windows 95. If we were discussing a less popular operating system, like NT or OS/2, then it would be a far smarter move to buy SCSI rather than IDE. There is one reason for this: software support. It is much easier to find software support for a CD-ROM attached to a SCSI host adapter than for one attached to an IDE adapter.

N O T E   The way I wrote that looks as though I am saying that you can take a CD-ROM and either attach it to an IDE or SCSI host adapter at your option—but that's not true. When you purchase a CD-ROM, one of the features that you must choose is the CD-ROM's interface type—SCSI, IDE, or proprietary.

Plug and Play

I've mentioned Plug and Play (PnP) before, but as long as I'm talking about hardware that works particularly well on Windows 95, it's worth mentioning that Windows 95 and Plug and Play are a terrific match. On the one hand I don't want to leave you with the impression that you must have Plug and Play-compatible hardware in order to run Windows 95, because you don't, but on the other hand it is certainly true that Windows 95 is enhanced by Plug and Play hardware. While Plug and Play-compatible systems are somewhat unusual at this writing, there is actually a huge number of computers out there that do Plug and Play sort of through the back door, and these are laptop computers. Many modern laptops have PC Card slots, and every PC Card laptop that I have ever seen can function as a Plug and Play computer for Windows 95.

NOTE   There is an exception to that, however; if you have a laptop with a PC Card bus system, but a docking station with normal ISA bus slots, then the Plug and Play part of Windows 95 is stymied a bit by the old ISA slots, as they do not yield to Plug and Play-type system control.

Testing Hardware

Windows 95 is like all advanced operating systems in that it requires a lot of *reliable* RAM. Also, as Windows 95 is a virtual-memory operating system, it requires that the hard disk be as dependable as the RAM; so the secret of getting a machine ready for Windows 95 is to *test your hardware*.

Testing RAM

It's very common for people to tell me that they have tested their hardware thoroughly because they have done one of the following things:

- Ran the memory test that is part of the BIOS.
- Allowed the HIMEM.SYS device driver to test memory.
- Ran the IBM PS/2 advanced diagnostics.
- Ran any basic suite of diagnostics.

And it always surprises people when I tell them this, but most memory diagnostics are of no value. You see, at one time, it was common to buy a bunch of RAM that wasn't reliable, as building RAM on a large scale was new for hardware vendors. There was a general perception in the industry that it was our job as buyers to watch out for ourselves. In the past ten years, however, memory production has become more reliable and so has memory testing by memory sales companies. You can be pretty sure when you buy a memory module today that it has been tested before it was sent to you (probably with better tools than the ones above), which is why the memory tests in the previous list are really pretty pointless.

Modern memory problems are a bit more subtle—but no less frequent. Memory chips tend not to fail by themselves; modern memory areas tend to be interactive in nature (like a memory location that tests fine all by itself, but when you put a particular bit pattern into another memory location, an unwanted bit pattern appears in the first memory location). Now, these areas are understood by memory vendors (just ask one what a walking bit error is and they'll know what you're talking about) but they are difficult to detect. Because these errors are interactive errors, vendors often cannot test for them or may lack the time to test for them; that's why *you* have to do it.

I have found only two diagnostic programs over the years that can help find these kinds of memory errors: QAPlus from DiagSoft and CheckIt from Touchstone Software. Both packages are fairly inexpensive and I recommend that you have at least one of them in your software library.

When you run these packages, you must run them from a clean-booted command prompt; that could either be just straight DOS from a boot floppy or a safe-mode command prompt from Windows 95. In any case, you must boot with no device drivers and no memory-resident programs. Additionally, these memory tests have a fast test mode and a slow test mode; run the slow test mode. And don't be surprised if you occasionally come across a system that fails the slow test mode no matter what memory you put in it; the failure can be caused by one of two things. First, and most likely, the memory address support circuitry on the motherboard could be faulty, or, more simply, you might just have a dirty memory socket—try cleaning that socket and re-inserting the memory. Alternatively, you will occasionally see a system with faulty static cache RAM. That can be very difficult to test, as I know of only one diagnostic that checks that: AMIDiag from American Megatrends Incorporated; it's another piece of software worth having around.

The reason why it's so important to test memory with Windows 95 is that, unlike DOS, Windows 95 uses all of your memory. You can think of it this way: Imagine you are walking on the second floor of an old house and you are not so certain that the floor is steady, because some of the floorboards may have rotted away. You wouldn't run the hundred-yard dash across such a floor. Instead, you'd gingerly test each board before putting your full weight on it.

It would be nice if Windows tested a floorboard before putting its weight on it—but it doesn't. If your RAM is faulty, then Windows will just crash right through the floor, taking your applications with it. That's why you must provide Windows with a completely sturdy floor in the form of thoroughly tested RAM.

Testing Disks

Now, as Windows doesn't really know the difference between RAM memory and disk memory, your disk must be every bit as reliable as your RAM—which means you need a good disk tester. The only ones that I have come across that I really trust are Steve Gibson's SpinRite program or Prime Solutions' Disk Technician Gold product. Again, you must run these on a clean PC that is only running a command prompt and nothing else.

One more thing to be aware of—these tests take *time*. Testing 16MB of RAM can take three or four hours, and testing 1GB of disk can take *days*. I know it doesn't sound like fun, but unfortunately it's necessary.

Check for Interrupt Conflicts

I may simply be beating a dead horse, but let me reiterate that it's absolutely essential that your system not have interrupt conflicts when installing any modern operating system. Now is the time to go back and make sure that there are no interrupt conflicts. The particular trouble spots to look at include:

- Sound cards set to IRQ 7, which conflicts with the parallel port.
- Ethernet cards set to IRQ 3, conflicting with a serial port.
- A third or fourth serial port added to the system, which shares an interrupt with an existing serial port.
- LAN boards set to IRQ 2 may cause problems; the answer may be to call the interrupt IRQ 9 instead of IRQ 2.

If you do not resolve interrupt conflicts with your PC before installing Windows 95, then you may get some post-installation help from the Device Manager in the Control Panel; you'll learn more about that coming up later in this chapter.

Document Your Hardware

Now that all the hardware works and you have all its resource information in one place, write it all down. After all, you'll need that information again. Since you've done all that work, don't let the effort go to waste.

If you're a small to medium-size shop, you can do what I do in my company. We tape large envelopes on the sides of our computers, and put cards inside the envelopes with information about boards. For example, suppose I installed an Ethernet card on my system. I would then get an index card and write "SMC 8216C Ethernet card installed by Minasi on 10 September 1995; uses IRQ 5, I/O address 300–30F, RAM C0000–C3FFF, no DMA or ROMs." When I need that information in a hurry, it's at my fingertips.

But wait, those of you who have already played with the Device Manager may be thinking, "Can't I get that information from Device Manager?" The answer is maybe yes and maybe no. If everything is working fine, then the answer is probably yes. But if you're mucking around with the system because something doesn't work, then the probable answer is that the Device Manager is confused, and that's why you're doing maintenance on the system in the first place.

Inventory Your Software and Test for Compatibility

Once the hardware is in place, then you'll have to worry about the part of a computer that supplies the most problems—the software. You will need a test computer loaded with both the Windows 95 software and all of the software that you use in your company.

Find Out What Software You Have

This task is simple to explain, but it will take some time to accomplish. The first thing that you need to do is make sure that you will have no 95-related software problems; do this by taking a census of all the software that everyone uses in your company. Now don't just count the big ones, like the word processor, the spreadsheet, the e-mail package, and so on; make sure you also include in your count the little programs like Calendar

Creator or those older clipper programs that have been around for the last eight years. After all, *someone* in your company uses these tools and they'll need to continue to use them once Windows 95 has been implemented in your firm. Another reason why it's important to find the little apps is that they are the programs that probably have not been tested thoroughly under 95; which means they have the greatest probability of not working under this version of Windows.

It is particularly important not to make this into a software licensing witch hunt—you don't want people hiding their applications when they see you coming. Once you have a complete list of all the software that people use in your company, then assemble all of that software on the test machine that I mentioned earlier.

Try Your Software and 95 on a Test Machine

That test machine should be connected to the network, and should be set up so that it mirrors as closely as possible a normal workstation in your company. Then sit down and put each application through its paces under Windows 95, taking notes about things that don't work properly.

Once you have the list of things that don't work properly, go back and try to find fixes. In many cases, all you'll have to do is to tweak the application a bit to solve the problem. When you find that answer, then you should put that into a file with Windows 95 upgrade notes and distribute it via the network; this way, other people don't waste time trying to make something work.

In some cases, you will find that the answer to making the application work under Windows 95 may be a simple patch that you can get from the application manufacturer, perhaps by downloading it from their bulletin board. Again, if that fixes the problem, then you should distribute the patch over your network or whatever other software distribution system you have.

You *may* find that there are some things that simply will not work under Windows 95. Now you have a hard choice: should you implement 95 or not? That will depend on how many applications do not work under 95, how many people depend on them (always remember that people are the most expensive part of a computer system and anything that keeps people from working is probably not worth the upgrade), and whether you can simply make a clean break and stop using the application.

Create PIFs for Your DOS Applications

DOS programs are different from Windows 3.x programs under Windows 95 because DOS programs require PIFs (program information files) to work properly. Building these PIFs isn't hard, but they take a little getting used to. You will learn more about that in Chapter 13.

Doing a Windows 95 Installation

Most of what's involved with a Windows 95 setup is just sticking the CD-ROM disc into its drive, logging on to it, and typing **Setup**. (I *do* hope you're installing from CD-ROM; having to install Windows 95 from floppies is the penalty for adultery in seventeen states, and fidelity rates have greatly improved since the floppy penalty was enacted.)

Once you've done one or two setups, you have probably noticed that running the Setup program is pretty labor-intensive; it insists that you click OK for little things and you have to answer a lot of specific questions about a Windows installation. You can get around that by building an *installation script* or *batch script file*. Having a batch script means that you can just say to the Setup program, "Do it," walk away, then come back a half hour later and find that the installation is mostly done, your system has rebooted, and you're back on-line. (Alternatively, you'll find that you didn't write the script correctly...)

An installation script can be a real timeserver, once you get it written. Unfortunately, many people think that they can learn to write such a file by looking in the Windows Resource Kit. There's nice information in the Resource Kit, and much of it is even accurate; but you'll find there's some information that is also *in*accurate.

There are several ways (according to Microsoft) to build a batch script:

- By hand with Microsoft documentation. This works *if* you know what you're doing.

- Automatically with SETUPLOG.TXT. Every time you install Windows 95, it actually takes the choices that you made and puts them together into a setup batch file. Kind of a neat idea, but it doesn't work without some doctoring.

- With a program called BATCH.EXE located in the admin directory of the CD-ROM. Again, a good idea, and probably the recommended path.

- By modifying the sample batch scripts in the admin\reskit\ samples directory of the CD-ROM. I've had good luck with these, as they are well-documented.

All of these options can be made to work. To my mind, it's essential to put together a batch script or two. The sad fact of the matter is that as your office's troubleshooter you *will* at some point end up reinstalling Windows a few times, just as you would have to do with any other operating system.

N O T E   Not every Windows setup option has a corresponding command in batch setup scripts, but many do.

Structure of an Installation Batch Script

Batch scripts are ASCII files, so you can create and modify them with a text editor. They look a lot like the old Windows 3.x .INI files, with sections separated by section names enclosed in square brackets. A typical batch script includes the following sections:

- **[BatchSetup]**   This is created by the BATCH.EXE program, and it's just version information. Actually, it can be deleted with no resulting problems.

- **[Setup]**   This contains overall instructions on how Setup should proceed, such as an express or a custom setup, prompt before over-writing files, and the like. Most are yes/no kinds of questions, and they're answered 1, which means yes, or 0, which means no.

- **[NameAndOrg]**   Here you fill in the user name and organization information. A related piece of information—product ID number—that you might expect would go into this section goes in [Setup] instead.

- **[Network]**   This handles the network-specific part of the installation, questions such as, "What kind of LAN adapter do you have?" or "Should we use user-level or share-level security on shared directories?"

- **[OptionalComponents]**   This is the list of parts to install, just like the Optional Components dialog box that you see when you run Setup.

There may be others, but these are the basic sections. Now let's take a look inside the sections.

The [Setup] Section

A typical [Setup] section will look like this one:

```
[Setup]
Express=1
EBD=0
ChangeDir=0
OptionalComponents=1
Network=1
System=0
CCP=0
CleanBoot=0
Display=0
PenWinWarning=0
InstallType=1
DevicePath=0
TimeZone="Pacific"
VRC=0
Uninstall=0
ProductID="9999999999"
```

The Express setting is just the Install, Express, or Custom question and, in this case, a 1 means Express (and a 0 means Custom). It's an odd kind of Express setup, however, as the batch script allows you to modify a number of things—which is what *Custom* is supposed to be, right? Display is a related setting; it answers the question "Should I display dialog boxes, or just take defaults?" You'll see Display in all the other sections as well. It seems irrelevant that it's in the [Setup] section, as it doesn't seem to do anything except quickly flash the dialog boxes if you set Display=1. Even though it shows you the dialog boxes, however, you don't get a chance to respond to them, as the Express=1 setting keeps that from happening.

EBD determines whether or not to create an Emergency Boot Disk. ChangeDir says where Setup installs Windows; 0 means to install it into the default directory. Answering 1 requires an extra line, InstallDir=, which points to wherever you want to install Windows. As you probably guessed, OptionalComponents asks whether to install optional components, PenWinWarning asks whether to display a warning about version numbers on a computer with a pen-based interface, and ProductID is the serial number of your particular copy of Windows. For large installations, you probably won't bother putting the specific serial number on each computer.

TimeZone takes a string value like "Pacific"; either look in the Resource Kit for sample values or look in the file named AUTOMATE.INF (it's on the floppies distributed with the Resource Kit). VRC=0 says that when Setup comes across a driver that has a newer date than the one it plans to install, then Setup will just install the newer driver without displaying the prompt. Uninstall says whether or not to save information needed to un-install Windows 95; a value of 0 is most common, as it means "Don't set up an uninstall option." Alternatively, a value of 5 would set up uninstall, *as long as you install to a directory other than the previous version of the Windows directory*. If you choose 5, then you have to add a BackupDir= command to this section, and you must then specify what directory to save the uninstall information to.

As is too often the case with Microsoft products, the Resource Kit doesn't document all the lines in the .INF setup files. CleanBoot, CCP, and Network aren't explained anywhere, and it's not clear what they do. For example, no matter what you set Network to, it still installs your network drivers if they are available.

The [Network] Section

A typical [Network] section looks like the following:

```
[Network]
ComputerName="aero"
Workgroup="orion"
Description="Compaq Aero laptop"
Display=0
Clients=VREDIR
Protocols=NETBEUI
Services=VSERVER
IgnoreDetectedNetCards=0
Security=domain
PassThroughAgent="orion"
```

Most of this is pretty obvious. Clients, Protocols, and Services are the names of modules to load into Windows 95. Security tells whether to use user-level security or share-level security, and PassThroughAgent tells where to find the user lists for user-level security.

For some reason, following the [Network] section, you get an [NWLINK] and a [NWREDIR] section even if you don't specify that you want a Novell client.

The [VREDIR] Section

If you've chosen the Microsoft network client, then you'll get a section called [VREDIR] that looks like this:

```
[VREDIR]
LogonDomain="orion"
ValidatedLogon=0
```

This just tells the system which NT domain to log on to and whether to log on to the domain as soon as the network logon starts.

Creating Batch Scripts with BATCH.EXE

In most cases, you will be able to get a good batch script assembled by the Batch Script INF Editor, BATCH.EXE, shipped with the Windows Resource Kit.

Start it up, and you'll see a screen as in Figure 4.1.

FIGURE 4.1

Windows 95 batch
setup dialog box

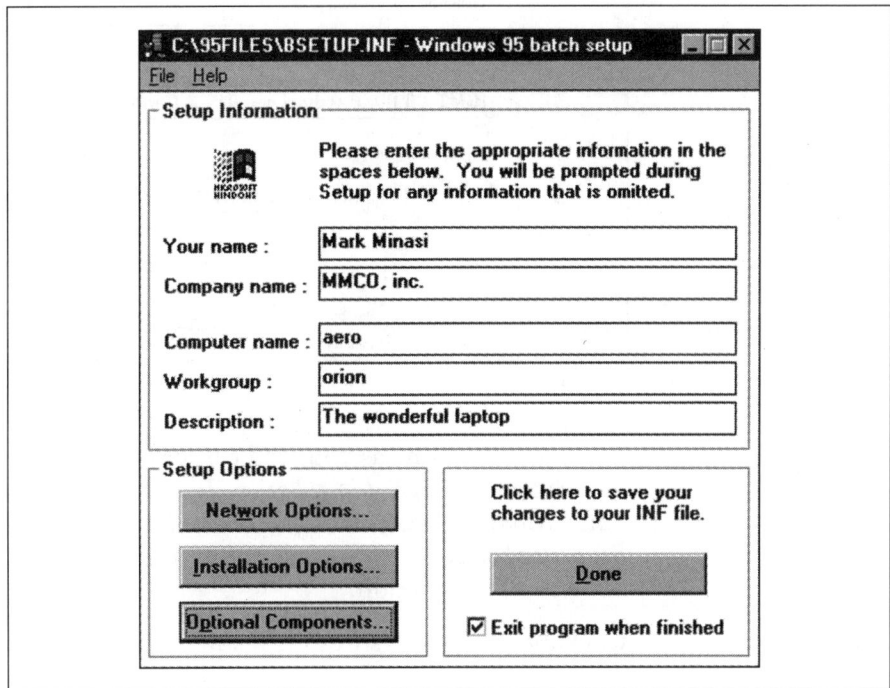

Here I've filled in a few basic pieces of information. From there, click the Installation Options, Optional Components, and Network Options buttons to specify how to install Windows 95.

When you click Installation Options, you'll see a dialog box like the one in Figure 4.2.

I'll talk about *Search source folder* in Chapter 8. *Prompt for startup disk* controls whether to create an Emergency Boot Disk, and the *PenWindows*

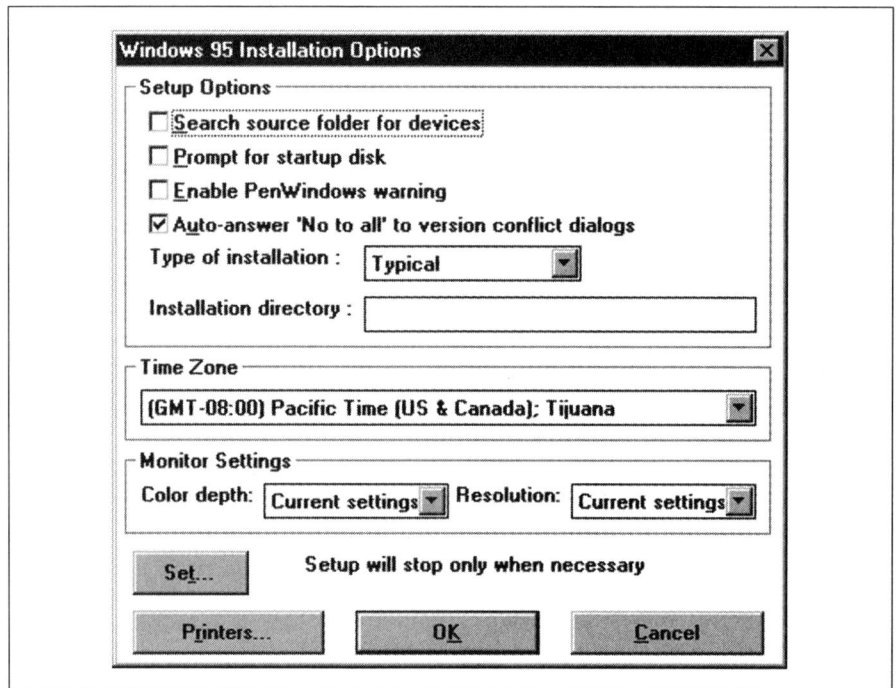

warning is the same as you read earlier in this chapter. Ditto for the *Auto-answer* option, *Type of installation*, *Installation directory*, and *Time Zone* options. *Monitor settings* lets you control how the display will look, and the *Set dialog box* controls at what points, if any, the Setup process should stop and prompt for action.

Clicking the Printers button results in a dialog box like the one in Figure 4.3.

This little stink bomb is located a few dialog boxes down into BATCH.EXE, and it's a lulu. It answers the question, "What kind of printer do you have?" Of course, you can tell Setup to stop and to prompt you while you set up Windows 95, but that's what you're trying to avoid in the first place. What you want to be able to do is to say in this dialog box, "I've got an HP series 4 on LPT1," but it's not that easy.

Printer Name is easy; it is that printer's name, which can be whatever you set it to (like "Printer next to Lunchroom"). If you share that printer, then

FIGURE 4.3

Windows 95 batch
setup—Printers

FIGURE 4.3

Windows 95 batch
setup—Printers

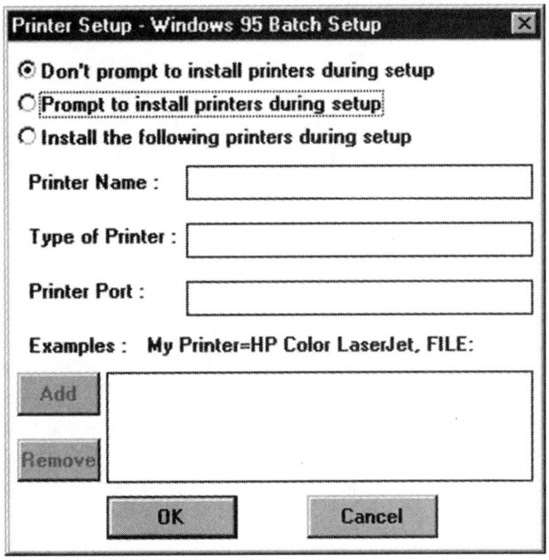

it's the name that the printer will use to advertise itself on the network. Printer Port is a port name like LPT1: that tells where the printer is attached. If the printer is a network printer, then you must construct a Universal Naming Convention (UNC) name. I'll explain UNC names in the next chapter, but briefly, they look like this:

*servername**printername*

So, for example, if you wanted to use a printer named LASERJET on a server named BIGSERVER, then you'd specify a printer port of \\\\BIG-SERVER\\LASERJET.

The annoying part of all this is the Type of Printer field. You must fill that with the *exact* name of the printer, using the same name that you'd see in Setup's Add Printer Wizard.

For example, suppose I'm setting up an HP series 4 on a server named MWM66, and say its network name is laser16. (I'd find that stuff out from a network administrator. If yours aren't helpful, find out what kind of beer they drink and get them a six-pack.) Basically I'm just attaching to a shared printer, and I'll call it netprint4. In the Printer Name field, I type **netprint4**. In the Printer Port field, I assemble the server and printer name into its UNC name, **\\mwm66\laser16**. Then I have to find the proper type of printer. The easiest way goes like so:

1. On a Windows 95 workstation, click the Start button, then Settings, and Printers. The Printers window will appear.

2. Click on Add Printer to start up the Add Printer Wizard.

3. Click on Next to see the dialog box like the one in Figure 4.4.

FIGURE 4.4

Add Printer Wizard

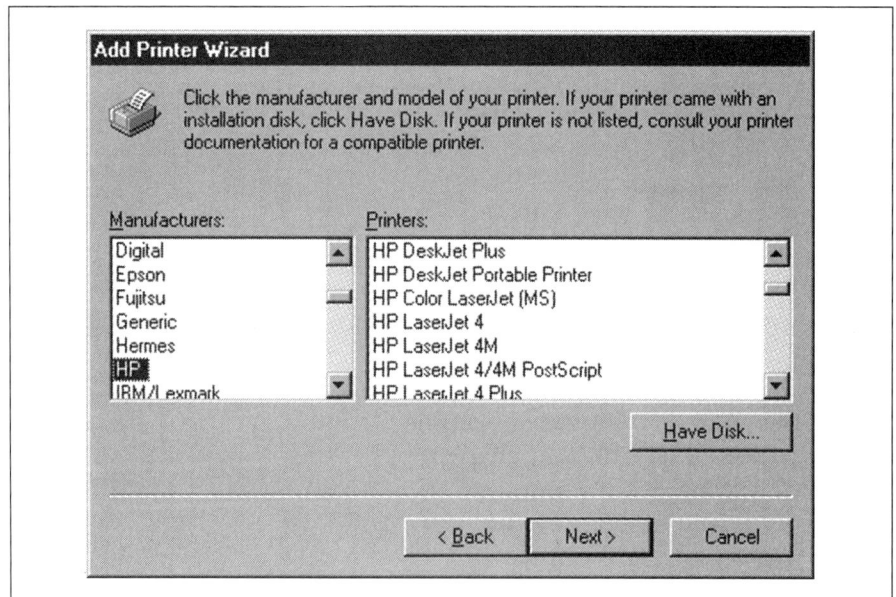

4. Browse around and find the exact printer name, like HP LaserJet 4 or HP Color LaserJet (MS).

5. Click Cancel and then close up the Printers window.

6. Now I know that the printer's true name is HP LaserJet 4, so I type that into the Type of Printer field.

7. Finally, click Add, or your work won't be saved. You'll see the line "netprint4=HP LaserJet 4,\\mwm66\laser16" in the multiline field in the Printer Setup dialog box. Yeah, it's sort of cumbersome for an easier operating system.

Back in the Batch Setup dialog box (Figure 4.1), the Optional Components button is pretty self-explanatory. For now, click the Network Options button and you'll see a dialog box like the one in Figure 4.5.

FIGURE 4.5

Windows 95 batch setup—network options

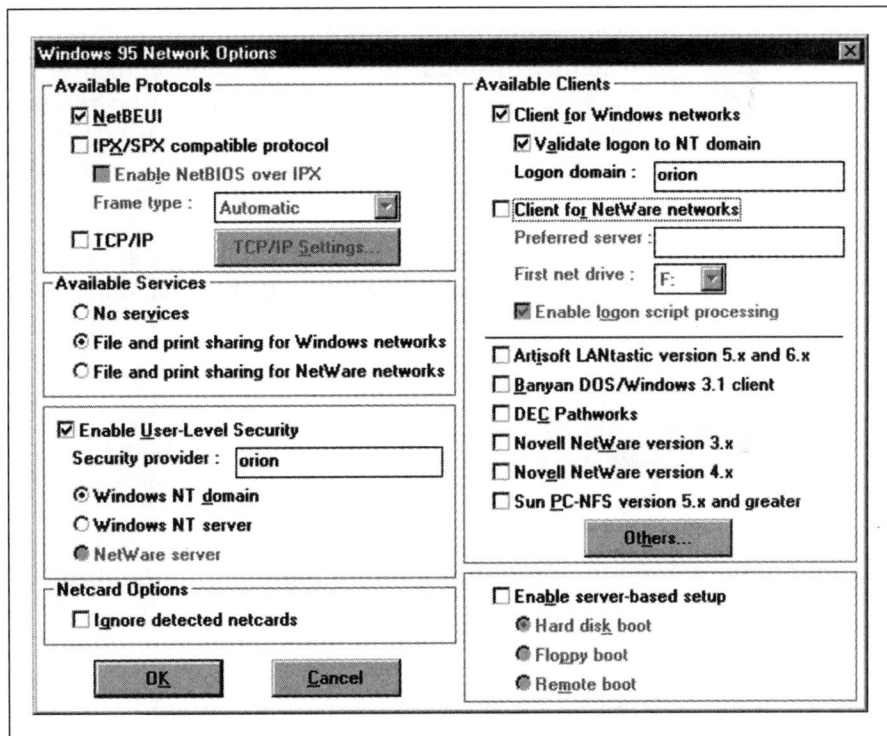

I realize that some of these options may be a bit techie for some readers, but they'll make sense after you've read the upcoming chapters on networking.

First, select a network protocol. The three mainstream protocols around which Windows 95 users will build their networks are NetBEUI,

IPX/SPX, and TCP/IP. In my example, I've built a small network, so I can use NetBEUI, the simplest of the three protocols.

Next, a Windows 95 workstation can also act as a low-powered server visible in either a Microsoft enterprise network or a Novell network. You can choose to act as a workgroup server in a Microsoft network, a NetWare 3.x file server, or not to share resources on the network at all. In many cases, the latter option is the right one, as it simplifies the network (there's less traffic from workstation-based servers advertising their wares) and saves memory on your workstation.

The panel below the Available Services panel allows you to choose whether to share with either share-level or user-level security (discussed in Chapter 5); oddly enough, this option remains enabled even if you choose not to share at all. If you select user-level security, this allows you to choose which particular users can use your shared disks, printers, or whatever.

If you choose to limit sharing to particular people, then you have to know who those people are in the first place. Windows 95 knows how to read user lists from a NetWare 3.x server or a Microsoft network server.

N O T E
Actually, Setup can read a user list from a NetWare 4.x server if that server has bindery emulation enabled.

Netcard Options are self-explanatory; Available Clients allows you to install the software necessary to use the network services offered by NetWare and/or Microsoft network servers. This is also where you specify which server to log on to (in the case of a NetWare network) or which domain to log on to (in the case of a Microsoft NT network). The next panel loads support for less-popular network systems. In Chapter 8, I'll discuss in some detail the last check box, *Enable server-based setup*, when I show you how to set up Windows 95 off a server.

Then, once you've filled in all the dialog boxes, save your work. From the main window, click File, then Save As, and save the file with a .INF extension.

Building Batch Files for Many Machines

BATCH.EXE is a nice system, but it sounds like it's almost as much work as running Setup. How can it be leveraged? With Batch-Mode Save.

BATCH.EXE has an option that will mass-produce .INF files, creating .INF files that are identical to one another in all ways save that they specify different machine names and, optionally, IP addresses. (IP addresses are used on TCP/IP networks.)

It's unfortunate that you can only modify machine names and IP addresses, as it would be nice to customize user names and other things, but it's better than nothing. Here's how you get it to work.

First, build an ASCII file with all the machine names, one name to a line. If you want to add an IP address, then put it after the machine name, separated by a comma. The file might look like this:

```
mach001
mach002,199.3.2.4
markspc
```

Notice that you needn't put IP addresses on every line. Now save the file, calling it anything with the .TXT extension. From BATCH.EXE, click File, then Batch-Mode Save, and you'll be prompted to enter a file name for the machines; tell it the name of the ASCII file. BATCH.EXE then automatically writes a sequence of .INF files that are numbered numerically—names like A0001.inf, A0002.inf, A0003.inf, and so on.

Here's the problem part: When you need to find the .INF file for a particular machine, you must remember that the 14th script is file A0014.INF and that the 14th machine is Joe Smith's.

Things You Can't Control with an Installation Batch Script

Installation batch scripts have existed since Windows 3.0, but to tell you the truth, I never used them because writing them was just about impossible due to lack of documentation. In contrast, I find that I like Windows 95 batch scripts quite a bit. In fact, I like them so much that I find the things that you *can't* do with them frustrating. One of the most important things that you can't set with an installation batch script is *ghosted connections*.

Under Windows for Workgroups, you could create persistent network connections, which are network drive mappings that would come up automatically every time you logged on to the network. It simplified logon scripts, as you didn't have to worry about setting up everyone's logical drives every time they logged on to the network. They had the down side, however, of making logons a bit slow, as the workstation had to go out and find every server and re-establish connections as soon as you logged on.

With ghosted connections, Workgroups would put off re-establishing connections until you actually tried to do something with the mapped drive. It not only sped up logons, but it was convenient for workstations that only attached to networks now and then, via Remote Access Services (now known as *Dial-Up Networking*).

Under Windows 95, it's still possible to use ghosted connections: just go to Control Panel, Networks, then select Client for Microsoft Networks, and Properties. Under Network logon options, you'll see an option labeled Quick Logon, which essentially gives you ghosted connections. Click OK, back out of the windows you've opened, and, the next time you log on, the system won't complain about all the connections it can't find, as you have not yet activated Dial-Up Networking. This option cannot be enabled with a batch logon script, nor is it the default, requiring some adjustment by hand if you want it on your workstations.

Preserving DOS with Windows 95

Windows 95 offers you a dual boot option whereby you can continue to run your older DOS. All you need to do to preserve the dual boot option is to install Windows 95 into a directory other than the original Windows directory.

Once you've done that, just press F8 when you see the "Starting Windows 95" message, and you'll see the option *Start previous operating system*. Choose that and DOS returns.

If you didn't choose dual boot to begin with, then here's all that Windows 95 needs in order to be able to boot back to DOS:

- The original IO.SYS must be in the root, and must be named IO.DOS.
- The original MSDOS.SYS must be in the root, and must be named MSDOS.DOS.
- CONFIG.SYS and AUTOEXEC.BAT from DOS should be renamed to CONFIG.DOS and AUTOEXEC.DOS.
- The file MSDOS.SYS (which is ASCII) should include, in the [options] section, the line BootMulti=1.

If all that's in place, then you'll see the option to boot another operating system when you press F8.

By the way, if you install NT, then it has an operating system picker that works with 95. OS/2's Boot Manager also works fine, but a word to the wise: Do not install Windows 95 and OS/2 on the same logical drive—they can damage each other.

Ensuring That Your System Uses 32-Bit Drivers

Recall from Chapter 2 the discussion of virtual device drivers, or VxD's. I mentioned there that Windows 95 will also use older 16-bit drivers if necessary. One of the neat things about 32-bit drivers is that they can usually emulate 16-bit driver functionality. This means that your DOS sessions get access to your network cards, CD-ROMs, or whatever, *without* losing free memory space to drivers, save for a 3K-sized driver called IFSHLP.SYS which extends IFS functionality to DOS sessions. (Recall that the IFS controls both disk-based and network-based file systems.)

Ordinarily, those 32-bit drivers get loaded automatically when you install Windows 95. But Windows 95's Setup program is a mite conservative, and so sometimes it may elect to continue to use the old 16-bit drivers. This costs you performance, sometimes stability, and less memory for DOS sessions.

You can combat that with this tip: Once you have Windows 95 installed, rename your old AUTOEXEC.BAT and CONFIG.SYS. Then reboot. Once it no longer gets instructions to load 16-bit drivers, then it'll fill in with whatever 32-bit drivers it has.

So with all this in mind, setting up batch installations should be a snap. Wait—you're still unsure about some of those network options? Turn to the next chapter, on networking 95, to fill in your network information gaps.

CHAPTER

5

Essentials of Networking 95

UNLIKE many earlier versions of Windows, 95 includes an entire network operating system built right into it. You can build a network with nothing more complicated than a bunch of Windows 95 machines.

However, that's probably not a good idea for many organizations, and instead many of us use servers running software made by Novell (NetWare), Microsoft (NT Server), IBM (OS/2 LAN Server), Banyan (VINES), or DEC (PathWorks). The presence of those servers means, first of all, that you'd like Windows 95 to be a *client* of those networks, and, secondly, that you'd like 95 to perhaps act only as a *supplementary* server.

All networks have their own paradigm, and the argot that goes with that. For example, Novell's networks have always been strongly oriented toward workstation/server architecture. Microsoft's networks grew out of a peer-to-peer network approach, and show the earmarks of that today, even though they have evolved to a workstation/server model as good as Novell's.

In this chapter, you'll learn the basic concepts that you'll need in order to introduce your 95 workstations to a Microsoft network or even to *create* a network with 95 workstations.

Microsoft Networking Overview

In a network, machines all have different kinds of roles. One of the most important distinctions is whether a machine is a workstation, a server, or both.

- A *server* is a computer on a network that runs software that makes it possible for that computer to offer *resources* on the network. Resource refers to space on a disk or use of a printer, but can also refer to the use of a modem or a program on the computer.

- A *workstation* is a computer that can use the resources made available by a server.

We usually tend to think of servers as powerful computers stuck off in a room someplace, tended to by systems administrators, but that's not necessarily the case, for better or for worse. Windows 95 computers can actually respond to many of the same commands that a larger server like a LAN Manager, NT, OS/2 LAN Server, or even a NetWare machine would respond to.

Common Server Software Types

In modern networks, you see servers of the following kinds:

- Peer-to-peer servers

- NetWare servers

- UNIX-derivative servers

- SMB-type (Server Message Block) servers

Peer-to-Peer Servers

Peer-to-peer networks are systems that allow you to share data from your workstation to other machines on the network. The main value of peer-to-peer networking is that it seems cheap; you don't have to buy a separate machine to act as a server and you don't have to buy the $1000+ software to make that PC a server.

In my opinion, it's always penny-wise and pound-foolish to do peer-to-peer. Servers are important machines, as many people depend on them to get their work done. Using a workstation as a server means that you have someone pounding away at that important shared machine. If that someone happens to discover some new and interesting bug in Word for Windows, then they may end up crashing their PC—and everybody else's network sessions, too. Additionally, if the person working at the server does something computer-intensive on their workstation, like rendering some complex graphic or recalculating a big spreadsheet, then, again, everybody is slowed down—and some people may end up thinking that the network has frozen altogether.

> **NOTE** My objections to peer-to-peer networks don't mean that it isn't a good idea now and then to transport data from one workstation to another on the network, and the peer-to-peer capabilities of Windows 95 will be useful there.

NetWare Servers

Among file servers, Novell NetWare 3.11 and 3.12 are the most popular server types; Novell software is said to run on about two-thirds of the corporate servers. Novell also sells NetWare 2.2, built for 286-based servers, and NetWare 4.10, for larger networks.

Novell's NetWare is a proprietary operating system that was mainly intended to respond quickly to network requests. Its head-down, eyes-forward approach to networking has made for servers offering the high performance to which they owe their large market share. Windows 95 machines can act as clients to a NetWare network and can also mimic a NetWare 3.x server. NetWare servers communicate with their clients and with other servers using messages formulated in a language known as NetWare Core Protocols (NCP).

UNIX-Based Servers

The multitasking nature of UNIX makes it an ideal platform upon which to build a server. UNIX-based servers fall into two categories: Banyan VINES and NFS servers.

Banyan is a company based in Massachusetts that builds a product called the Virtual Networking System, or VINES. For years, VINES was the only real alternative if you wanted to build a large enterprise network. Built atop UNIX, VINES uses networking software that is a variation on a popular set of programs collectively called the TCP/IP suite; Banyan calls theirs the VINES Internet Protocol (VIP). VINES has about five percent of the server market.

People who just want to take a garden-variety UNIX machine and make it appear as a file server to other PCs can run a program called the Network File System, or NFS, first developed by Sun Microsystems. You just put NFS server software on a UNIX machine, install compatible NFS client software on the PC, and the PC can use files on the UNIX machine as if it were a local drive.

SMB-Based Servers

Since 1985, Microsoft has sold and licensed server software built around a different language than NCP. Microsoft's server language is called Server Message Block, or SMB. SMB networks will be of main interest to us in this chapter.

Let's look at a simple Microsoft peer-to-peer network and, at the same time, introduce some concepts upon which we'll build.

As you've already read, the whole idea of a network is to share things: share space on a large disk drive, share a particular file on that disk drive, share a printer. Suppose we have a small office that needs to do some sharing, as you see in Figure 5.1.

FIGURE 5.1

Simple sharing setup

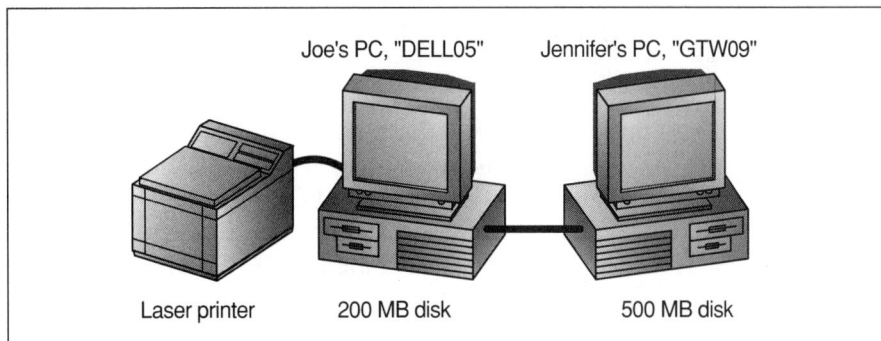

Joe's PC, "DELL05"   Jennifer's PC, "GTW09"

Laser printer   200 MB disk   500 MB disk

Now, in our simple office, Jennifer has more storage capacity on her machine than Joe does on his, but Joe has the office laser printer attached to *his* PC. Each PC has an inventory control number, like DELL05 or GTW09.

Both Jennifer and Joe work on the office accounting system, so they need to share the accounting files—either that or they'll have to pass floppies around. Since Jennifer has more disk space, they put the accounting files on her machine. So, the network problems that we need to solve are:

- Sharing Joe's printer with Jennifer.
- Sharing Jennifer's disk with Joe.

Let's solve their problem with a basic Microsoft (SMB) network. With this type of network, Jennifer just puts her hard disk on the network and Joe puts his printer on the network. Assume both of them are running Windows 95 on their systems.

Here's an important concept in Microsoft networking: You must name each machine in the network, whether it is a server or a workstation. You also must name each user (let's use Joe and Jennifer). Since the PCs need names, we may as well name the PCs with their inventory numbers.

TIP It's a bad idea to name machines after their users, as PCs may get re-assigned.

Basically, we get Joe onto Jennifer's disk and Jennifer onto Joe's printer like so:

1. Jennifer tells the Windows 95 networking software, "Take the \acctng subdirectory on my C: drive and offer it to anyone who wants it. Call it ACCTNG." ACCTNG is then called, in Microsoft enterprise networking terminology, the *share name* of that drive on Jennifer's machine (GTW09), and it's the name that others will use to access the drive over the network. I'll show you exactly how to do that in a few pages, but for now remember the important things: a machine named GTW09 is sharing a resource called ACCTNG.

2. Joe then tells the networking software on his PC, "Attach me to the ACCTNG resource on Jennifer's machine." For years, PC workstation operating systems haven't understood networking, so we've had to introduce network resources in the back door by showing these resources as *logical drives* or, in the terminology of some networks, *mapped drives*; we might say that the ACCTNG resource is *mapped* to local drive D: for Joe. Joe doesn't know whether ACCTNG is all of Jennifer's drive or just part of it. Joe's networking software then says something like, "You're now attached to ACCTNG on Jennifer's machine. It will appear to you as local drive D:."

Actually, I should mention that Windows 95 doesn't require drive letter mapping. I mention it because virtually every previous PC operating system required it, and because most applications to this day can still only address network resources by letter names. Again, Joe doesn't *have* a D: on his machine; he only has network software that takes read and write requests for a mythical drive D: and reformulates those requests into network communication to Jennifer's machine.

And, while I'm on the subject, the actual name of this network resource is \\GTW09\ACCTNG. Notice the format of this term; it's called a *Universal Naming Convention* name, or a UNC name. The two backslashes are a warning that the name following is a *machine* name; the backslash after that refers to the *share name* ACCTNG, rather than the directory name.

3. Joe, meanwhile, runs his network software and tells it to share the printer on his LPT1: port, giving it a name—again, a share name of JOLASER. Joe's machine is called DELL05, so the UNC name of that printer will be \\DELL05\JOLASER.

4. Jennifer then tells her networking software to attach JOLASER, on Joe's machine, to her LPT1: port.

From now on, whenever Jennifer tells an application program to print to a LaserJet on LPT1:, the network software will intercept the printed output and will direct it over the network to Joe's machine. The networking software on Joe's machine will then print the information on Joe's printer.

I know I left out some of the "how do we do this?" information; it's coming later, I promise. I just wanted to illustrate with that example that:

- Machines and people in a Microsoft network have names.

- Shared resources in those networks also have names.

- You specify network resource names with UNC names, in the UNC format *servername**sharename*.

- One way (and the most common way) to share network resources is to give them bogus local names, like D: or LPT1:.

I started this section by discussing what kinds of machines can be servers in the Microsoft world. Let's name them now:

- Windows 95 workstations

- Windows for Workgroups workstations

- NT workstations

- NT Servers

- A LAN Manager server

- OS/2 LAN Server

- DOS-based machines running LANtastic

- OS/2 Warp Connect machines

All of these servers use SMB type communications.

Network Workstation Types

A networked machine running any of the following cannot act as a server; it can only function as a workstation:

- Windows 3.x

- DOS

- OS/2 1.x and 2.x

You can see that pretty much all modern PC operating systems allow for workstation functionality. Unfortunately, that can make for headaches for support people. It's possible to restrict people from sharing, but we'll take that up in Chapter 8.

Lengths of Different Network Names

For bizarre historical reasons, machine names, people names, and passwords are each established according to different rules in a Microsoft network.

Machine names can be up to 20 characters long. You can include spaces, but I recommend against it; I've run into some bugs in 95 software (and NT, for that matter) when handling machines with blanks in their names.

Passwords can be 14 characters long. You can use nonletter characters, so you can have a password like "eyes.blue" with a period in the middle of it. Microsoft does not offer a means of forcing a user to use a nonletter value in their password—at least not that I know of. Uppercase and lowercase count: password and PASSWORD are two different passwords, and they couldn't substitute for each other.

Sharing Files and Printers under 95

95's GUI makes it simple either to share directories or to use shared directories.

Offering Resources on the Network

For example, suppose I want to share the Windows directory on my computer. I just open up My Computer, open up the C: drive, and right-click on the Windows folder (directory). If you've enabled sharing, one of the options you'll see on the menu is Sharing; choose it, and you'll see a dialog box like Figure 5.2.

FIGURE 5.2

Sharing dialog box

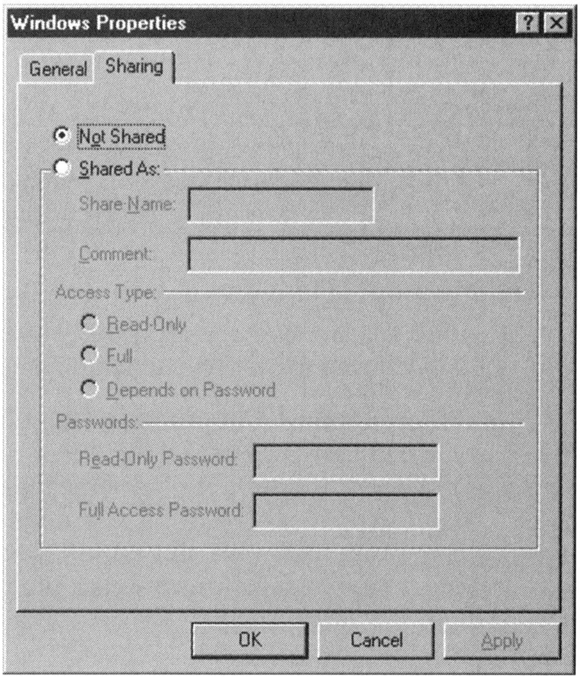

Share it by clicking the radio button labeled *Shared As:* and the dialog box like the one in Figure 5.3 will appear.

Now, this is what you see if you've selected share-level access control. It allows you to do three things: you can give the directory a share name (remember those from a few pages back, like ACCTNG?), you can determine whether people who attach to this directory can only read it or read it and write to it, and, optionally, you can set a password.

This is a nice, simple sharing approach which is virtually identical to the sharing options under Windows for Workgroups. But there's a major lack of control here, as the password option doesn't really have a lot of power to keep the wrong people from using your shared resources. Sure, you can set a password, but it's the same password that *everybody* uses, and it's easy for that kind of password to get out and around to people you might not even know.

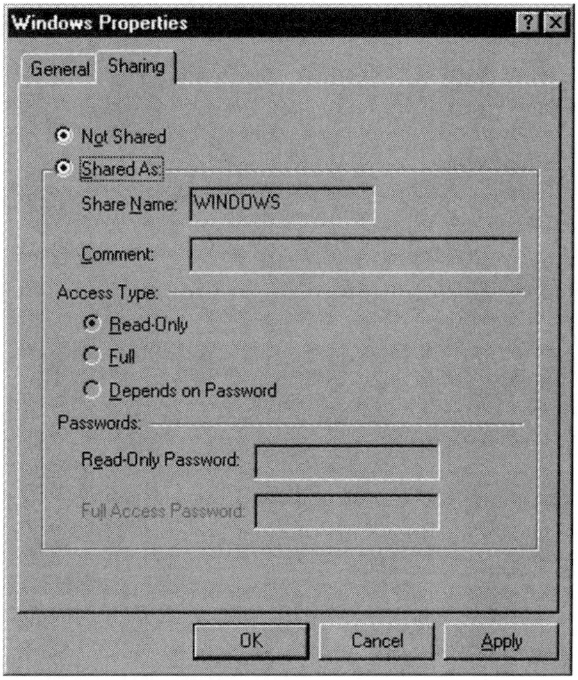

FIGURE 5.3

Sharing dialog box:
Shared As

With Windows 95 it's possible to control access in such a way that only a user named Janet or Paul, for example, may access one of your *shares* (i.e., one of your shared resources). You can restrict access to one of your shares in this way:

1. Open the Control Panel.

2. Open the Network applet.

3. You'll see three tab sheets: Configuration, Identification, and Access Control. Choose Access Control.

4. On the Access Control sheet, click *User-level access control*.

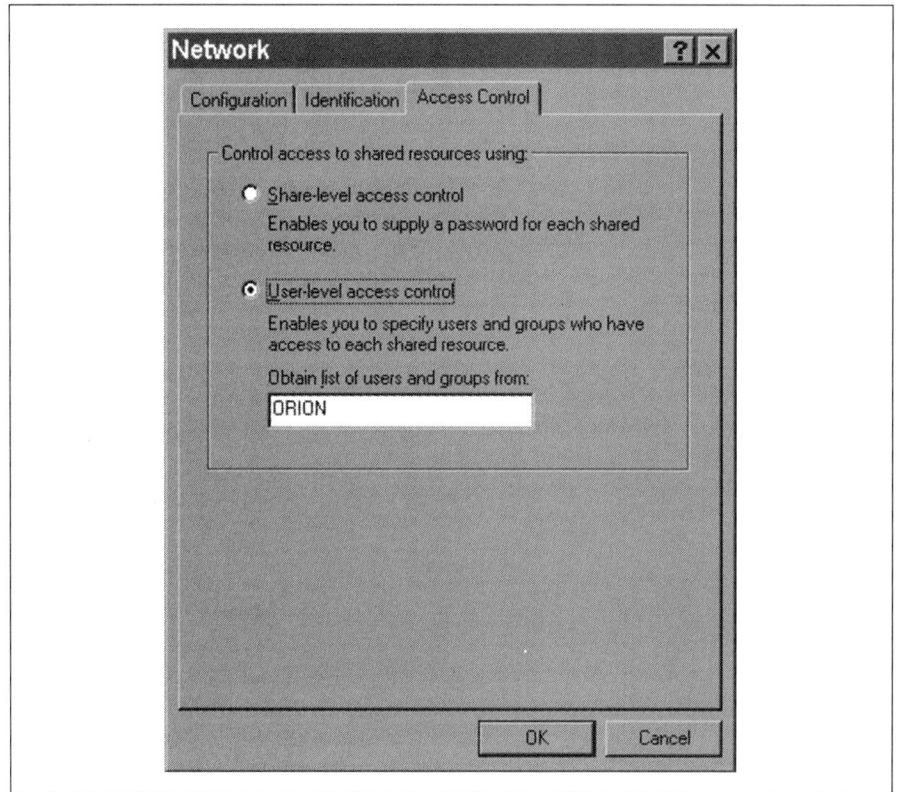

5. In the field *Obtain list of users and groups from:*, fill in the name of your NetWare server (version 3.x or 4.x), your NT Server, or your NT domain controller that contains the network names of the users to whom you are granting access. (In the case of my example, I filled in the name of my NT domain, ORION.)

NOTE   If 95 can't immediately find the server or domain you've specified, it'll prompt you for more details, so that it knows which of the three types (NetWare server, NT Server, or domain) to expect.

Now with user-level access control enabled, you'll see a different Sharing page in the Windows Properties dialog, like the one in Figure 5.4.

FIGURE 5.4

The Sharing page in the Windows Properties dialog box has changed

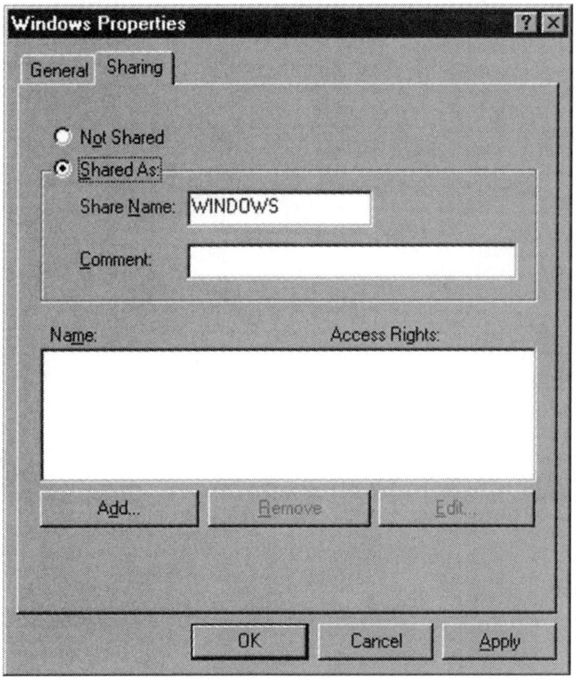

Compare this to the tab page you saw in Figure 5.3, and now you see that there's a place to specify names rather than a general-use password. You can add a name to the list by clicking the Add button, which shows a dialog box like the one in Figure 5.5.

FIGURE 5.5

Giving access to your
shares by adding users

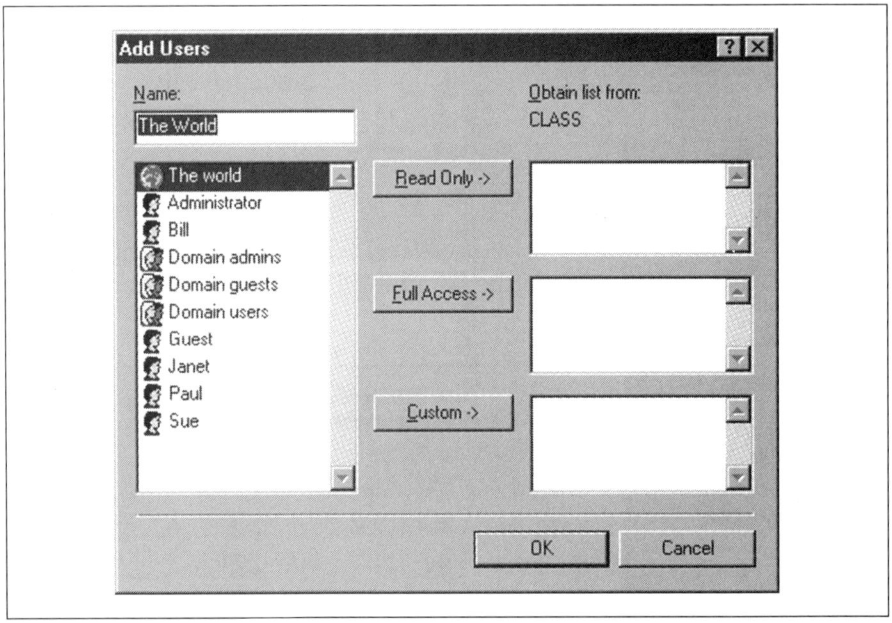

In this example, I've taken a list of users from an NT domain. The NT domain has groups of users, called *local groups*, which do not appear on this list. The list of people you see here are members of a *global group*.

As you see, you can give either read-only, full, or custom access for any particular person; just highlight the person and click the appropriate button. If you click Custom, then you see a dialog box like one in Figure 5.6.

With this dialog, you can fine-tune a user's access to your shares.

Using Network Resources with 95

Now, that was how you share something under 95, but how do you use a share that someone else is offering? Well, 95 makes using network resources simple, as you access all shared resources with the same interface, whether it's a Novell, NT, or 95-shared resource.

First, open up Network Neighborhood. It will show you the computers that it's heard from recently, as you see in Figure 5.7.

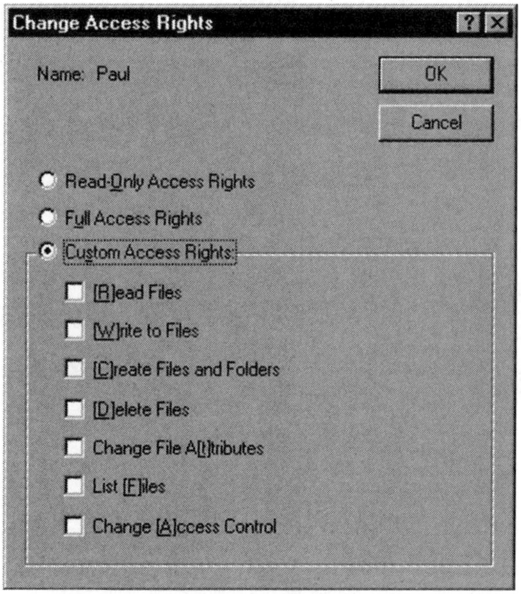

FIGURE 5.6

Granting particular
rights to a user

FIGURE 5.7

Network
Neighborhood

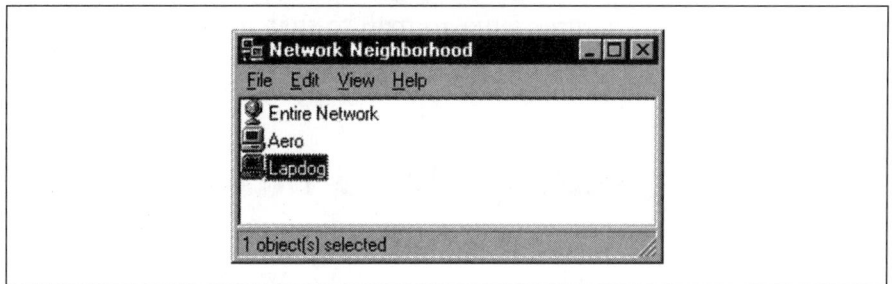

I want a directory on the server named Lapdog, so I open that up and I
see a window like in Figure 5.8.

So I see that there's a resource (a directory) called 95class available on
that server. I could actually see that resource by opening that folder (I'll
get to that later), but for now let's just map it to a drive letter, since many
programs won't know how to look for a resource named with the UNC
convention. I map the resource to a drive letter by right-clicking on the
folder and choosing Map Network Drive, which brings up a dialog box
like the one in Figure 5.9.

FIGURE 5.8

Network
Neighborhood:
Lapdog

FIGURE 5.9

Map network drive

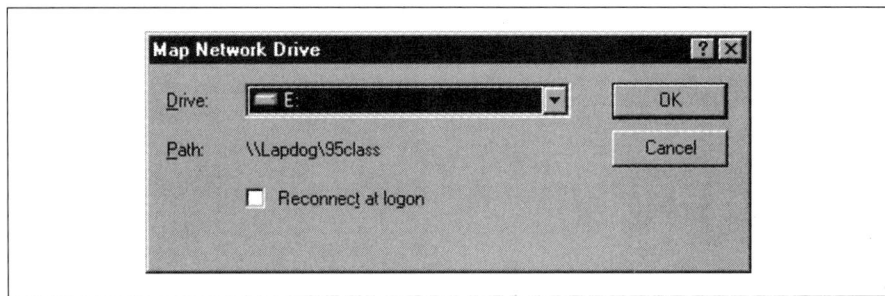

Notice the UNC name in the dialog, \\Lapdog\95class. Here, I can choose a drive letter to map to that share and decide whether I want this to be reconnected every time I log on. Click OK, and from that moment it seems as if I have a local drive named E:.

Avoiding Drive Mappings

As I've said before, you map drives to make older programs happy. But if you're just getting used to Windows 95's network options, then you may be missing some possibilities. Here are a few other approaches.

Use Shortcuts

If you have a network resource that you use frequently, create a shortcut to it. Drag it to your Desktop, and when you click on it you'll do an implicit login.

Replace Drive Letters with UNC Names

Whenever the only programs that will be using the shared resource don't have a problem with UNC names, enter that rather than a drive letter in dialog boxes. For example, my word processor looks for its style sheets on drive H:, which is really \\OURSERVER\BIGDRIVE. Having to remember that H:, not F: or G: or some other letter, is the drive my computer uses for word-processing resources makes remembering to map every new machine to that drive a bit of a pain; plugging in the UNC can be easier, because it's more clear what that drive comprises. You also may find that you're running out of drive letters; with UNCs, that's not a problem.

Use UNC Names in Batch Files

I use a personal information manager called Lotus Organizer and keep all my information in a file called BASE.OR2. But, as I travel, I want to keep my Organizer files with me. I have a machine on my desk called DESKTOP, and my laptop is called LAPTOP. My problem, of course, is that often I must shuttle the BASE.OR2 file between my desktop and my laptop. They're networked, so I share the ORGFILES directory on DESKTOP and copy the files to and fro that way.

Prior to Windows 95, I moved the file from my desktop to my laptop with the following batch file:

```
net use e: \\desktop\orgfiles
copy e:base2.org c:\orgfiles
net use e: /delete
```

The two net use commands are used to establish and to destroy the connection between the laptop and the desktop. I only have to create the bogus E: drive to make the copy command happy.

Under Windows 95, it's one line:

```
copy \\desktop\orgfiles\base.or2 c:\orgfiles
```

TIP

Get in the habit of *not* thinking in terms of mapped drive letters. Use shortcuts and UNC names to get the job done where possible.

Network Software: Drivers, Protocols, and Redirectors

Making networking work in anything but the simplest network environment means understanding the real meaning of an overused word: *compatibility*. Compatibility—or the search for it—is the source of words such as TCP/IP, NetBEUI, ODI, NDIS, redirector, and the like.

Now, you've probably been introduced to something called the OSI seven-layer model. I have something simpler—my three-layer model.

A Network Software Overview

Looking at networks from a high-level point of view, you see that LANs have the basic job of letting the applications programs (WordPerfect, Lotus 1-2-3, Quicken, or whatever) utilize the network hardware to get at data on the network; you see that in Figure 5.10.

In order for the application to use data, messages must go across network boards and through the network software that runs both in the client and the server machines. The network software can be explained in many ways, but I find it easiest to imagine it in a three-part fashion. The first, and easiest, piece of software to understand is the network board driver, as you see in Figure 5.11.

Network Board Drivers

Drivers decouple the network board from the network operating system. For example, suppose you have a Token Ring-based network. When you

FIGURE 5.10

Network overview

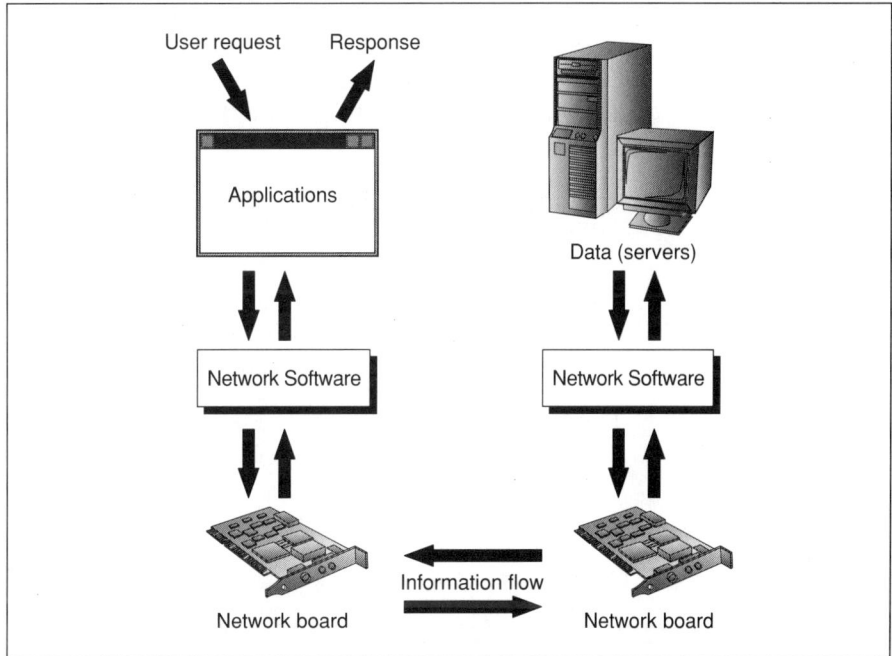

FIGURE 5.11

Network overview
with software

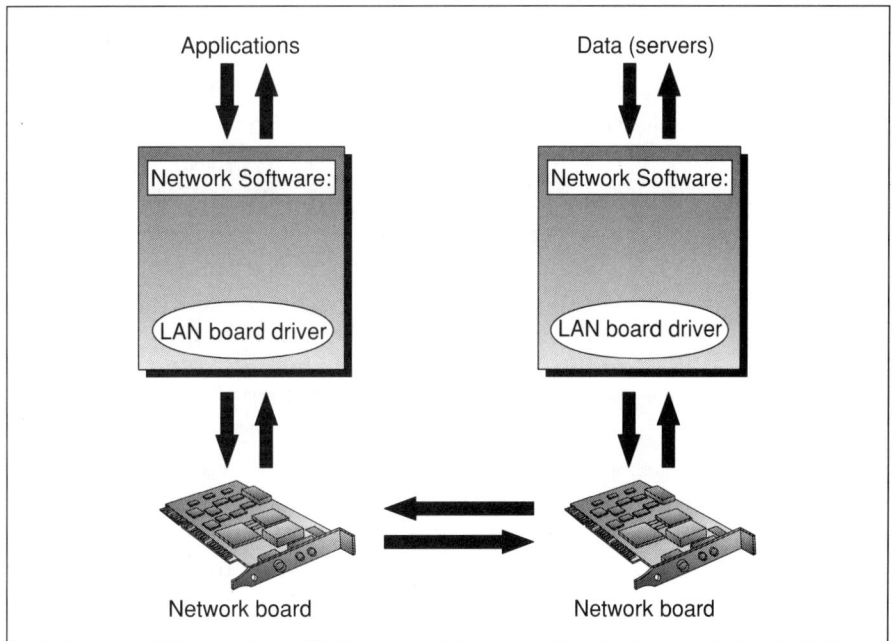

first create your network, you may start off buying boards from IBM, but you don't want to be locked into them—or into any other vendor, for that matter. But you wonder whether a competitor's token ring boards, like the Madge or 3Com token ring boards, will continue to work with your network.

The first place that 95 needs compatibility, then, is in the network boards, or "cards." A person responsible for troubleshooting networked machines needs the ability to incorporate any kind of network card into their network system, whether that card is an Ethernet, Token Ring, ARCnet, FDDI (Fiber Digital Distributed Interface), or any other board; your system must be able to incorporate boards from virtually *any* vendor.

The board driver must know such things as which IRQ a LAN board is set to, which I/O address the LAN card uses, and how to interface with the higher-layer network software.

Network Services: Redirectors and File System Mounters

Above the board driver, up at the top of the network software, is the *redirector*. It's just one of a family of network-aware applications called *network services*. A redirector fools applications into thinking that the application is getting data from a local drive rather than from the network.

For example, consider the case of WordPerfect 5.1 reading a document from a network drive. From WordPerfect's point of view, there is no network. Instead, it knows that there are one or more disk drives available, with names consisting of a letter and a colon, as in A:, B:, C:, and so on. WordPerfect was not designed to accommodate storage devices that don't have names like A: or D:. So there must be a layer of software placed between WordPerfect and the network; this software's job is to present a letter-and-colon face to WordPerfect when supplying data stored on the network. WordPerfect thinks that it is addressing local drives, but its requests for information from drives with names like D: are *redirected* to network requests, as in, "Get the data from the share named WPFILES on the server named SEYMOUR" (or \\seymour\wpfiles in UNC terminology); the redirector software does that, as you see in Figure 5.12.

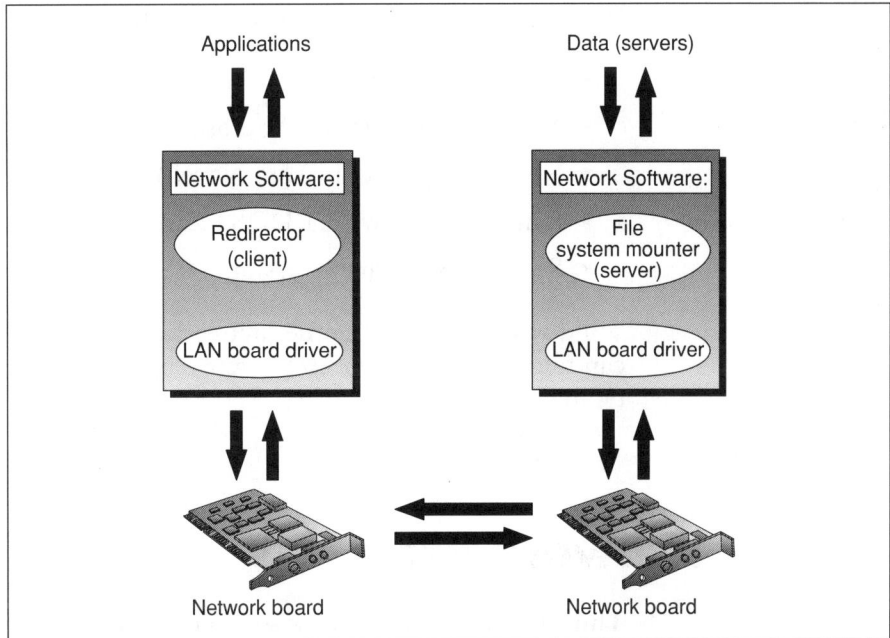

The redirector is only half of a client-server team of software. The redirector is the piece that goes on the client or workstation, and the *file system mounter* is the piece that goes on the server. There are several file system mounters in the network world. The best-known are Novell's NetWare File System, UNIX's Network File System (NFS), and Microsoft's file system mounter, which they usually just call the server. The redirector on the client and the file system mounter on the server must match, or the client can't use the server's resources. Those are the components that speak SMB, NCP, or other server command languages.

In the Internet world, you may have servers running an NFS server, in which case any workstation that wants to access it must run NFS client software. In the Novell world, the servers run a program called NFS.NLM to support the Novell File System mounter, and the workstations run a client program called NET3, NET4, NETX, or the like in order to communicate with the Novell server.

Windows 95 ships with these redirectors:

- Microsoft client
- NetWare client (from Microsoft)
- NetWare 3.x client (from Novell)
- Banyan Windows 3.1/DOS redirector
- SunSoft NFS client version 5.0

Windows 95 ships with other network services, like the SNMP agent. You can find out what services are active by opening up a command line and typing

net service /list

Network Protocols

Third in the trio of network software components is the network *protocol*. In general, a protocol is just a standardized set of rules, which are standardized for the sake of compatibility. For example, when I call you on the phone, there is a protocol that says, "When you hear the phone ring and you pick it up, then *you* should talk first, not me." It's just the common agreement in our culture as to how to communicate by phone.

In fact, this is the middle piece of the network software setup. I left this middle piece for last, as it's the most abstract of the three. You might think of the setup this way: The board driver keeps the LAN board happy, the redirector keeps the applications happy, and the *transport protocol* glues the two of them together by establishing the rules of the road for network communications. The transport protocol's position in our network software system is illustrated in Figure 5.13.

Just as we couldn't use the phone without some agreements about how to use it, NT needs a common communications language, so that all of the machines on an NT network can talk to one another without confusion. Also, because it aims to work with different types of networks, NT needs to be able to speak the networking languages used by those other kinds of networks, so it needs to be something of a polyglot. Those networking *protocols*—protocol is a somewhat more accurate term than

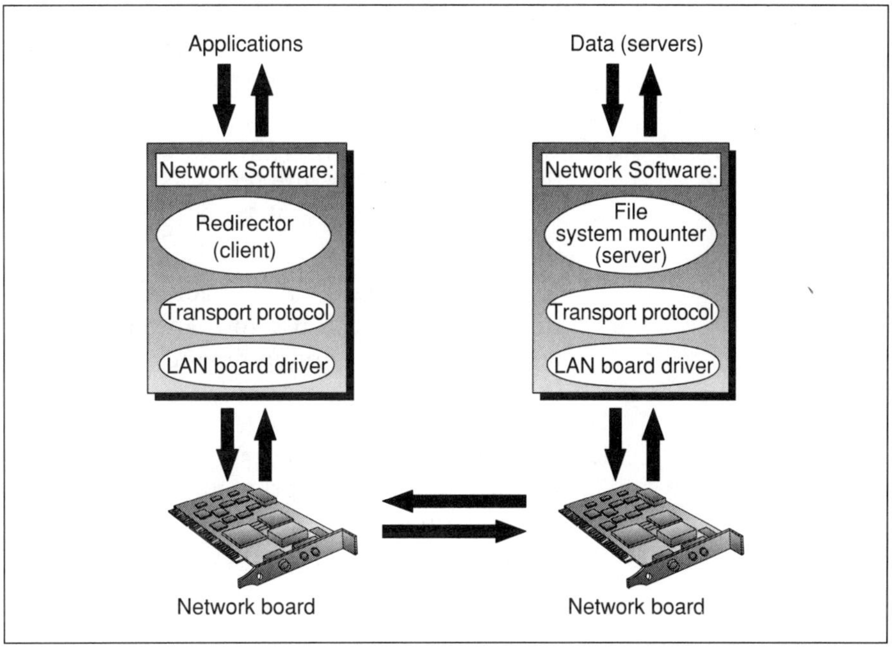

FIGURE 5.13

Network overview
with transport protocol

Figure 5.13 Network overview with transport protocol

language here—differ widely because they were each originally designed to do different things; also, most of these network protocols were never designed with compatibility with other kinds of networks in mind.

There are a number of transport protocols, and unfortunately every vendor has its own favorite protocol. Here's a quick overview of the ones you'll run across.

NetBIOS and NetBEUI

Back when IBM first started marketing their PC Network, they needed a basic network protocol *stack*, which is an implementation of a board driver, transport protocol, and redirector. They had no intention of building large networks, just small workgroups of a few dozen computers or fewer.

Out of that need grew the Network Basic Input/Output System, or Net-BIOS. NetBIOS is just 18 commands that can create, maintain, and use connections between PCs on a network. IBM soon extended NetBIOS with the NetBIOS Extended User Interface (NetBEUI), which basically is a refined set of NetBIOS commands. However, over time the names NetBEUI and NetBIOS have taken on new meanings.

- NetBEUI now refers to the actual transport protocol. It has been implemented in many different ways by different vendors, to the point where, in some ways, it is the fastest transport protocol for small networks.

- NetBIOS now refers to the actual set of programming commands that the system can use to manipulate the network—the technical term for such a set of commands is an Application Program Interface, or API.

NetBEUI is the closest thing to a native protocol for NT. Unless you tell your system to use another protocol, NetBEUI is one of the protocols that the NT Setup program installs by default; IPX/SPX, discussed next, is the other. But as I said above, NetBEUI should be your protocol of choice for small networks: it's the fastest one around.

IPX/SPX

The most popular local-area network type in the world is Novell NetWare. When the Novell folks were building NetWare, they decided to build their own protocol rather than use an existing protocol. The Novell protocol is named IPX/SPX, for Internetwork Packet Exchange/Sequenced Packet Exchange. Since it is the protocol used most often on NetWare networks, and since Microsoft wanted their software to be somewhat compatible with NetWare networks, Microsoft designed Windows 95 to include an IPX/SPX implementation.

N O T E NetWare is actually based on a Xerox protocol called Xerox Networking Services, or XNS.

IPX/SPX wasn't originally a Microsoft-supported network, but it's now one of the default protocols under 95; NetBEUI is the other.

TCP/IP (Transmission Control Protocol/Internet Protocol)

The famous "infobahn," the information superhighway, is built atop a protocol created over many years by the U.S. government. The protocol is actually a protocol stack, called the *TCP suite*. The TCP suite is a very efficient, easy-to-extend protocol whose main strength has been in *wide-area* networking; it glues together dissimilar networks and brings together similar networks that are separated by distance and low-speed connections. It's one of the best-supported, well-designed internetworking protocols around.

Traditionally, however, microcomputer networks haven't used TCP/IP as a *local-area* network protocol. But that's changing, particularly with the release of the TCP/IP suite in NT Server version 3.5, what I call "turbo TCP/IP."

Multiple Transport Stacks

Two things should be obvious by now. First of all, there is no single best network protocol. Second, you may want to run all four of the protocols described above.

You can.

One of the values of the Microsoft networking model is that it supports *multiple* transport protocols, as you see in Figure 5.14.

In Figure 5.14, you see that the client machine has four transport protocols loaded and the server has one protocol loaded. This could happen if the client machine connected to more than one server—the IPX stack might talk to a Novell server, the NetBEUI stack might allow the workstation to talk to an NT Server, and the TCP/IP stack might talk to an Internet mail router.

Network Binding Interfaces

To make all of this work, we need a way to attach the network boards to the transport stacks—to *bind* the network transport layer to the LAN

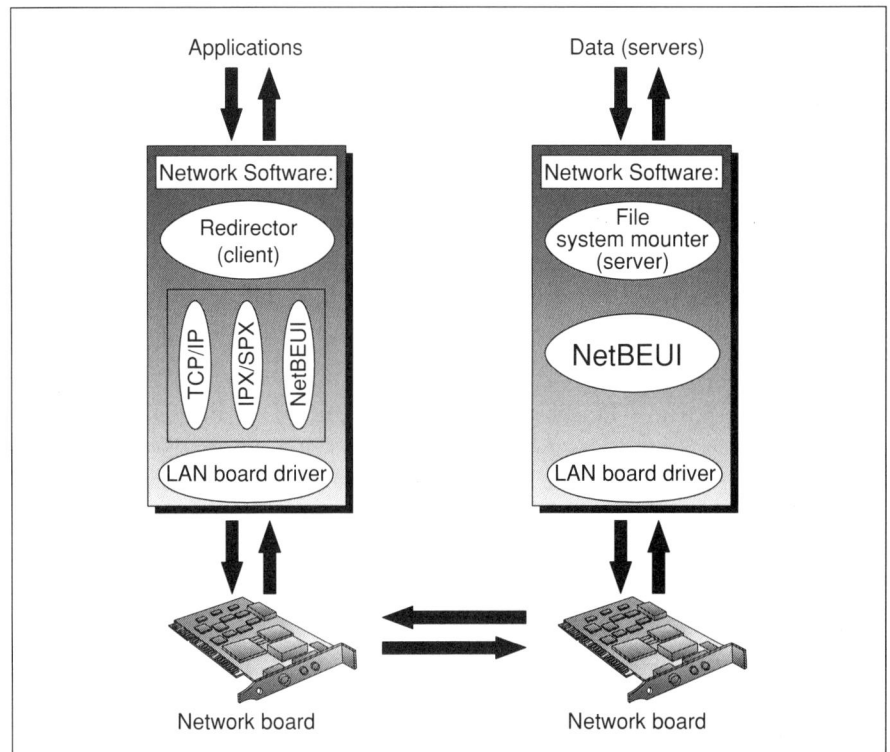

board's driver. (That's the definition of binding: to create a software connection between, essentially to marry, a network card driver and a network transport protocol. I'll talk more about binding a few paragraphs down.) That leads to the need for a very important, standard, interface—the interface between a LAN board driver and a transport stack. There are two competitors for the title of world-standard binding interface: Microsoft's NDIS and Novell's ODI.

Network Driver Interface Specification (NDIS) Version 3.1

Microsoft's standard defines the interface between a network card driver and a protocol stack with an interface called the Network Driver Interface Specification, or NDIS. NDIS-compliant drivers are easy to find for most network boards, so availability is a strong plus for NDIS. Furthermore, there are NDIS-compatible versions of the NetBEUI, TCP/IP, and SPX/IPX protocol stacks.

NDIS 3.0 drivers are particularly attractive in the DOS/Windows world because they load in extended memory, away from your precious lower 640K.

NDIS 3.1 drivers added two important features. First, they are hot-swappable, which means that they work with PC Card network boards: you can install a PC Card board after bootup and Windows 95 will load its driver, protocol, and redirector on the fly. Second, they are used for both NT 3.51 and Windows 95.

Open Data-link Interface (ODI)

Novell's answer to the binding problem is a different standard, one named the Open Data-link Interface, or ODI. At the moment, I haven't seen Windows 95-compliant ODI drivers, save for the old 16-bit ones.

Binding in General

What, exactly, does the word *binding* mean in a network context? Consider this: it's possible to have multiple boards, protocols, and clients. It wouldn't be impossible to have a computer arranged like so:

- An Ethernet board and a modem (a so-called dial-up adapter)
- NetBEUI, IPX/SPX, and TCP/IP protocols
- Microsoft network software and Novell network client software

Look at the possible flows of information: data can arrive to a PC from either the Ethernet card or the serial port/modem, it can then flow through one or all of three protocols, and then it can funnel through one of two clients. Do the math and you'll see that there are 12 different ways for data to flow through a PC.

Not all of those ways make sense, however: it would be silly to place the NetWare client atop NetBEUI, as NetWare uses IPX/SPX the majority of the time, and TCP/IP in a much smaller percentage of cases, but never, to my knowledge, NetBEUI. Similarly, if I only use the modem to connect to the Internet, then there's no point in sending data that arrives via the modem through the NetBEUI and IPX/SPX protocols.

Network binding is the term for defining which connections between board drivers, protocols, and clients make sense. You control binding via the Network applet of the Control Panel. Open the Control Panel, double-click on Network, and examine the Configuration dialog box, as you see in Figure 5.15.

FIGURE 5.15

Network Configuration dialog box

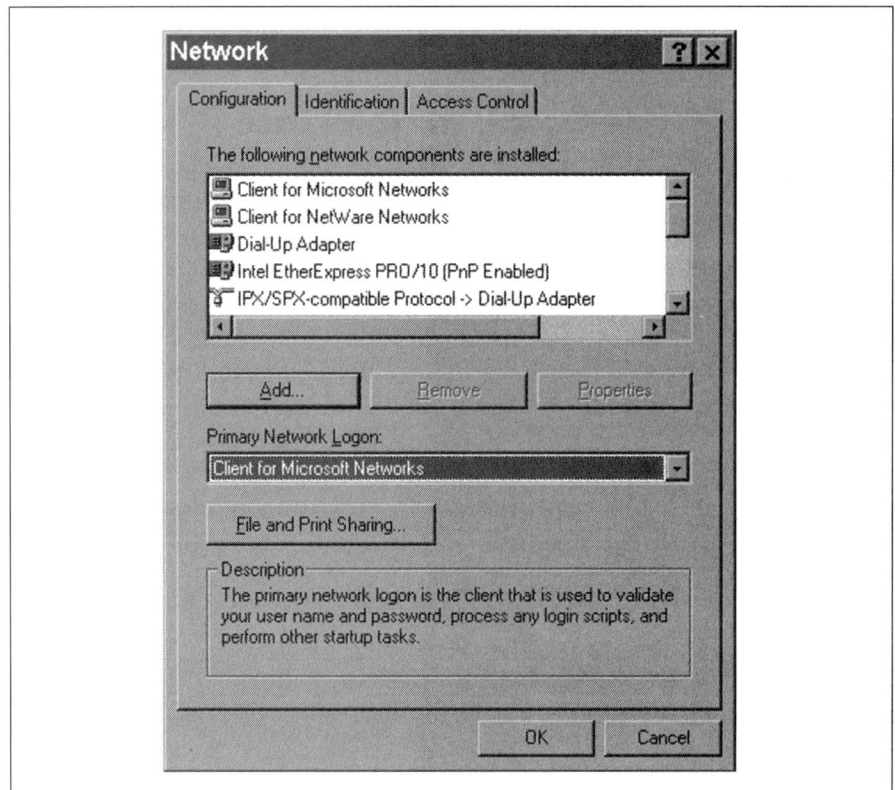

You control which board drivers are bound to which protocols by clicking on the adapter, then clicking Properties. You'll see a dialog box that includes a tab labeled Bindings, as you see in Figure 5.16.

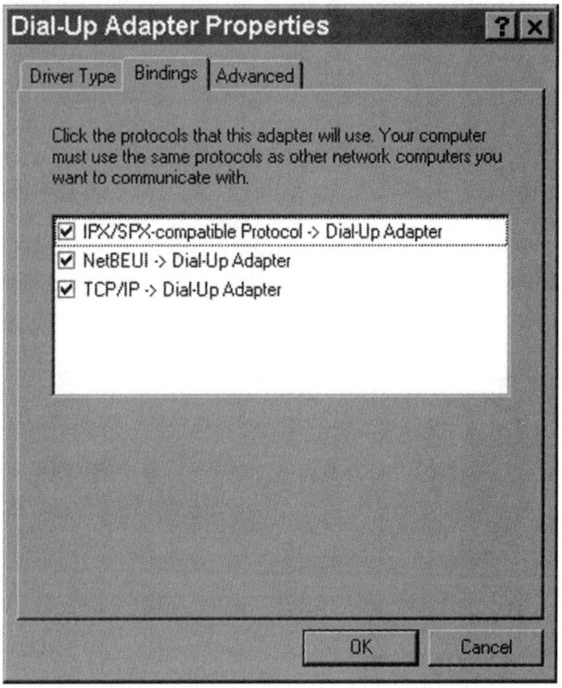

FIGURE 5.16

Dial-up Adapter
properties

Notice that this is the dialog box for the dial-up adapter, and that it's bound to each of the three protocols. To unbind, just uncheck the boxes.

What if you find that a protocol wasn't bound to an adapter to begin with? Then just click the adapter, then Add, and then Protocol. Add a protocol (even if you're already using it), and it'll be bound to the adapter.

You control which protocols bind to particular clients by clicking on a protocol and Properties. Most of the common-sense bindings are already in place—for example, the Microsoft client for NetWare networks only binds to IPX/SPX—but you can disconnect unnecessary ones and speed up your networking; after all, there's no reason to be bound by the defaults.

Network Applications Interfaces (API's)

As you've already read, most applications are unaware of the network or networks that they use. But some, like e-mail or groupware programs, *must* be cognizant of the network, and exist only *because* of the network. They need to be able to plug in and communicate with other programs running on other machines in the network.

Programmers build network-aware programs so they can be tailored to sets of commands that a network offers to applications programs; those sets of commands are called API's.

Let's use driving a car as a metaphor for using an API. When you're driving a car, you may actually have no idea what occurs under your car's hood—you just push down the accelerator and the car goes faster. Driving consists of just a few basic commands: brake the car, accelerate the car, shift the car's transmission, and so on. There is no basic command built in to a car that lets you "back the car out of the driveway," and yet you can still back a car out of a driveway; you just assemble a number of the basic commands into the actual action of backing a car out of a driveway. You have, in a sense, built a program with your car's API.

There are three API's that you'll probably come across in the 95 networking world:

- NetBIOS: A simple set of 18 commands implemented on an NT network. It is Microsoft's native network API.
- TCP/IP Sockets: The preferred API for working over an internet.
- Novell Sockets: Novell's API.

API's are important to network-aware programs. Microsoft's redirector ("Client for Microsoft networks") is a program that won't function in a PC unless there is a copy of NetBIOS running in that PC. Originally, only NetBEUI included NetBIOS, but now Microsoft has implemented an IPX/SPX that includes NetBIOS, and a TCP/IP that includes NetBIOS, so now you can run the Microsoft redirector whether your network runs the IPX/SPX, NetBEUI, or TCP/IP protocols.

Now that I've explained networking as a three-part suite of software, you might be able to make more sense of what Windows 95 provides in the way of info about your network configuration. Open up the Control Panel and click the Network icon, and choose the Configuration tab if it isn't already displayed. You'll see a dialog box like the one in Figure 5.17.

FIGURE 5.17

Network configuration dialog box

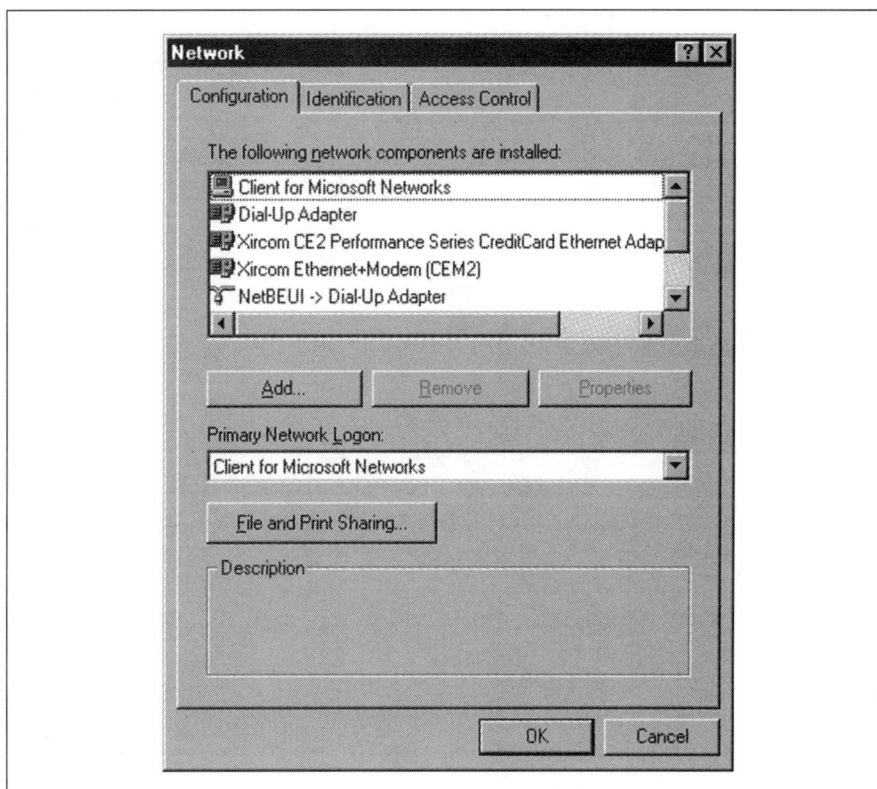

You may have to scroll to see all your components. On my computer, the following components are listed:

- Client for Microsoft Networks (redirector)
- File and printer sharing for Microsoft Networks (file system mounter, server end)
- NetBEUI Dial-up adapter (protocol binding)
- NetBEUI Xircom Ethernet+Modem (protocol binding)

- NetBEUI Xircom CE2 Performance Series CreditCard Ethernet (protocol binding)
- Xircom Ethernet+Modem (board driver)
- Dial-up adapter (board driver)
- Xircom CE2 Performance Series CreditCard Ethernet (board driver)

This is how a Windows 95 system can interact with so many networks: modular protocols, board support, and redirectors.

Browsing

Years ago, I used the IBM PC LAN program, which is the first version of what eventually became the NT Server and Windows 95 networking code. It was a nice, primitive network operating system. If you wanted to access a drive shared by a server, you said to the PC LAN program, for example, "Attach me to drive E: on the machine named AVOCADO." Nice and simple, but it had a major flaw: how did you find out in the first place that the server was named AVOCADO and that the drive that it was offering was called E:? The answer is, *you just had to know the name of the resource before you could use that resource;* there was no "scan the network to find out what's available" feature to the network. (An IBM guy once explained to me that this was "a security feature." Now, why didn't *I* think of that?)

I wanted a kind of net scan command, something that would shout to the other systems, "Hey! Whaddya got?" As it turns out, that's not very simple. The whole process of offering services on a network is part of what's known as *name services*, and they're not easy to offer.

Solving the Browse Problem

How would you make a workstation know about every service on the network? There are several approaches.

Static Service Lists

The simplest approach to letting workstations know what's available to it over the network would be to put a file with some kind of services database on every workstation, a kind of yellow pages of system capabilities. For example, you might have an ASCII file on every PC that says, in effect, "There is a file server on machine BIGPC with a shared disk called BIGDISK, and the computer named PSRV has a shared printer called HP4SI."

This has the advantage of being very simple to understand. To add a new resource, just modify the service list file.

It has the *disadvantage*, however, of being static. When any changes are made to the system, some poor fool (that would be *you*, the network administrator) has to go around to all the workstations and update the file. If there were two hundred workstations on your network, then you'd have to actually travel to each workstation and copy the static service list file to that workstation's hard disk.

This method sounds too primitive to use, but it's not completely useless. In NetWare 3.x, you identify yourself to your desired server via information in NET.CFG. That's a hard-wired server name, and would require a fair amount of editing on every workstation if you wanted to rename an important server; this is why, I suppose, you don't rename servers often in a NetWare world.

Periodic Advertising

Another approach is an occasional broadcast. Every 60 seconds, each resource on NetWare 3.11 tells the rest of the network about itself by shouting, "I'm here!" Novell calls this the Service Advertising Protocol (SAP). This is a very good idea and it works great in many cases.

It's not a perfect answer, however. Its problem is that its broadcasts take a long time to get around in an enterprise network, and can clog up the network if that network has a large number of services that are advertising. (Imagine if every store in the U.S. were to remind you that they exist *every minute* or so—you'd spend so much time responding to advertising that you'd get nothing else done, and your mailbox would be full.) That means that periodic advertising might work okay on small to medium-size

LANs, but on larger networks it would be unworkable. Adding to the problem is the fact that many router systems don't pass broadcast messages, so advertisements may not get from segment to segment.

> **NOTE**   Windows 95 supports SAP; it can advertise its shared services if you tell it to act as a NetWare server.

Name Servers

Yet another approach, and the one used by most enterprise network products, is to assign the task of keeping track of network services to one or more computers, called *browse servers* or *browse masters*. With this system, different parts (usually different geographical parts) of the network each have these browse servers, and the browse servers update each other's service information periodically. It requires a bit of setting up, but it's one of the most logical ways to keep track of network services.

Microsoft's Answer: Browse Services

Microsoft decided (perhaps rightly) that name servers were hard to set up, particularly in a peer-to-peer network environment where services would be up and down as the day went on (like on a Windows 95-based network when users periodically reboot their workstations), so they developed a different approach, called *browse services*.

In Microsoft browse services, there are computers called *browse masters* that perform functions like those of name servers. What's different about the Microsoft browse master concept (by the way, there are also browse backups, machines that back up the browse master) is that there's no one computer fixed as the browse master; it changes according to certain conditions, in a manner that I'll soon describe.

NOTE In some Microsoft literature, browse masters are called *master browsers*, so you may see either term.

You can see the information provided by a browse master—a *browse list*—when you're in the Network Neighborhood. Open up the Network Neighborhood folder, and it will look something like Figure 5.18.

Network
Neighborhood

This browse list shows you what machines are nearby (I'll tell you in a minute what I mean by "nearby") as well as offering you access to the entire network. The machines Ams, Donnac, Eisa server, Mwm66, Sdg90, and Tsc are all servers in the sense that they offer resources—shared printers or directories.

How Browsing Works

Chances are that you've used Network Neighborhood dozens of times and never wondered how it worked; most likely, it just *worked*.

But if you ever saw the flashlight shine back and forth for a few minutes, followed by a blank folder or a "Network is not available" message, then you probably wondered just how the thing works—or *doesn't* work.

First of all, browsing is an example of a *client/server* software system. Your Windows 95 workstation runs the client software, which interrogates the browse master.

The browse master runs the other half of the operation, the browse server software. As I've already told you, you needn't anoint one PC as the browse master. Actually, the PCs all get together and jointly determine which of their number should be the browse master. It could be yours!

Electing a Master Browser

If there is no master browser, then there is an *election* to determine which computer would best be master browser. Elections are held when the master browser is powered down gracefully. Consequently, if the master browser is simply turned off, then it may take a good while (almost an hour in some cases) before another one becomes active.

If you're not a master browser, then you're a backup browser (browser backups in some documents), a potential browser, or you've opted out of the whole election process. (I'll show you how to do that in a minute.) Backup browse servers also help remove some of the load from the master browser, as they can respond to browse requests.

When an election occurs, the master browser is chosen with a scoring system that works like this:

- NT Servers beat NT workstations, which beat everything else (i.e., Windows for Workgroups clients or LAN Manager servers).

- If there is a tie, then it goes to the *primary domain controller*, which is an NT server that acts as the overall security monitor for an NT network. The primary domain controller holds all the user accounts.

- If there still is a tie, then the election goes to a Preferred Master (a setting that you can make on a computer running NT). And, while Microsoft isn't too clear about it, machine type plays a role—Pentiums are preferred over 486s.

- If there are no NT machines responding, then the election takes place among the Windows 95 workstations that have their Maintain-ServerList setting set to either auto or yes.

It's that last part you should be worried about.

"If Nominated, I Will Not Run": Avoiding Browse Mastering

Windows 95 workstations should *not* be browse masters. The reason why is simple: If they become a backup browser and announce that they are available as a backup browser, then workstations can become dependent on them for browsing capabilities. Once a workstation has chosen a browser, it doesn't know enough to get a second opinion from another browser if the browse list that it receives looks screwy. Furthermore, if the master browser is an NT server and a 95 machine is acting as a backup browser but isn't logged on to the NT machine, the 95 backup browser can't obtain browse lists from the NT master browser. The result: empty browse lists.

Another potential problem: On my network, I have a 95 workstation running on a Pentium and a master browser running on an NT Server, which is running on a 486. While I'm not certain that the processor type is the root of the problem, I found my 95 workstation claiming that it was the master browser when my NT Server machine had already won the election. The existence of two machines claiming to be master browsers confused the network considerably. The answer was to tell my 95 workstation to just stay out of browse master elections.

Elections can take a lot of time on your network. You can simplify the election process and cut down on the number of elections by forcing a Windows 95 computer to never be the master browser.

Forcing a Machine to NOT Be the Master Browser

On a Windows 95 machine, go to the Control Panel, click on Network, then on File and Printer Sharing, then Properties. On the Advanced tab, you'll see Browse Master, which offers Auto, Enable, or Disable; go for Disable.

On a Windows for Workgroups machine, add this line to the [network] section of `SYSTEM.INI`:

```
MaintainServerList=No
```

The default value of MaintainServerList is auto, which means "make me a master browser if you need me to be one." A value of yes means "if there's a tie when electing browse masters, make me the master browser."

For NT workstations, there is a corresponding Registry entry,

```
MaintainServerList
```

which goes in

```
HKEY_LOCAL_MACHINE\System\CurrentControlSet\Services\
Browser\Parameters
```

It is of type REG_SZ, and its value can be true or false.

Understanding the Neighborhood: Workgroups

What is a network neighborhood? It's just a way of keeping the size of the browse list manageable.

You've learned that every Windows 95 workstation can be a server in the sense that it can share resources. That means that every 95 workstation in your company would show up—perhaps thousands of machines—whenever you requested a browse list! As servers re-announce themselves to the browse master every 12 minutes, you could have a very busy browse master.

Worse yet, there's no *point* in making everyone aware of everyone else. After all, we tend to work in *workgroups*, smaller groups of people who share data. Any organization is composed of many of these workgroups, whether formally or not. From a management point of view, I think of workgroups as being characterized by this notion: 95 percent of the data generated in a workgroup is distributed to (and is, in the main, only interesting to) the rest of the workgroup. Only about five percent of the data generated by a workgroup is shared with other workgroups.

The result: a monstrous, slow browse list that is mainly useless dross to people who want only to see the other computers in their workgroup, not every computer in the company. So what's the answer?

Simple: Create a computer analog to the workgroup. What the heck—let's even *call* it a workgroup. It's just a group of people who want to see each other's resources, but don't care much about resources outside of the workgroup.

When I was getting started in Microsoft enterprise networking, I had a good bit of trouble understanding the difference between a *workgroup* and a *domain*. Part of my confusion about workgroups, as it turns out, came from the fact that there isn't much to a workgroup. Here's my definition of a workgroup:

> **A workgroup is a collection of computers that share resources (printers, disk space, and files) and that share the same *browse list*.**

A workgroup is a *logical* notion, not a physical notion. You could, for example, have any number of workgroups on a single network segment. Conversely, you can sometimes spread a workgroup across several network segments.

When you open up Network Neighborhood, you see the browse list for your workgroup. If you open up Entire Network, then you get a list of workgroups in your network, as you see in Figure 5.19.

FIGURE 5.19

Network Neighborhood's browse list for your workgroup

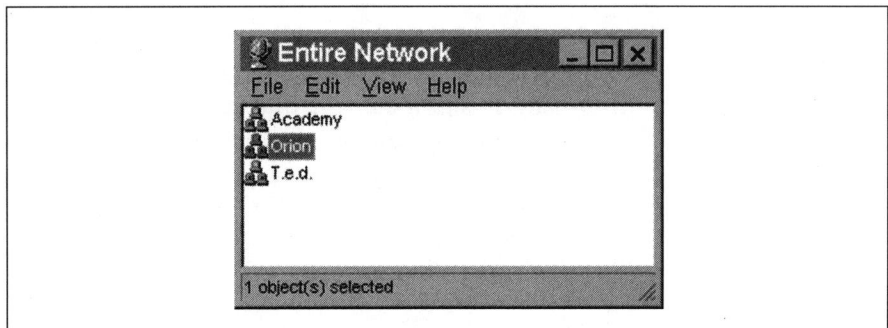

In my network, I have three workgroups: Academy, Orion, and T.e.d. If I double-click on one of those, then the browse list for that workgroup will come to my workstation.

Keeping the Browse List Short

Dividing the company's resources into workgroups helps to keep the browse lists small, but they're still cluttered with machines that aren't really servers (for example, Windows 95 machines or Windows for Workgroups workstations). Of the machines on the browse list you saw a few figures ago, only Eisa server and Mwm66 were servers. The rest were workstations, and in the main they were just cluttering up the browse list.

TIP

To save about 300K of RAM, think about disabling file and print sharing on your Windows 95 workstations. (You can also keep your users from sharing files and printers via the System Policy Editor, which we'll meet in a later chapter.) You disable the function by opening up the Control Panel and choosing Network. Pick *File and printer sharing for Microsoft networks* and click the button labeled Remove. Then reboot the system. You're no longer on the browse list, and you've saved yourself all that RAM.

Understanding and Troubleshooting Browser Issues

Browsing is significant in that it can slow down your workstation's response time and clog your network with unnecessary traffic. It can also frustrate your users if it doesn't respond quickly enough. The following paragraphs offer some browser troubleshooting information.

Browsing in General

The browsing service in Microsoft enterprise networks makes it possible for a workstation to see what the network has to offer. A few specifics about browsing:

- The master browser designates one backup browser for about every 15 computers.

- If you run multiple transport protocols, then each transport protocol needs its own set of browsers.

- Backup browsers verify their database with the master browser every 15 minutes.

- Servers first announce their existence to the master browser, then they re-announce their existence at short intervals. Eventually they settle down to announcing themselves only once every 12 minutes.

Refreshing a Browse List

In general, browse requests are resolved by either the master browser or a backup browser, so you never know who's provided your browse list. But you can force the system to browse you via the browse master with the command-line command net view.

Why Isn't My Resource on the Browse List?

You can experience browsing trouble (i.e., no browse list available or incorrect list) if computers do not exit Windows gracefully—that is, if they just get shut off without first exiting Windows. That computer may appear on the master browser's list for up to 45 minutes, even though it's not literally available as a resource. Even worse, if a *browser* terminates unexpectedly, then it may become impossible to browse for over an hour.

TIP

Remember that if you can't see something on the browser, it's not a big deal. If you know the UNC name for the resource—the name like \\markspc\c—then you can always just punch in that value and if it's available you'll get connected with no trouble, even if the browsers are all confused.

Let's look at how the browse service works in a bit more detail. It may take up to 51 minutes for the browser to notice that a resource has disappeared. This means that the browser may erroneously report that something is available when it is not. Why does that happen?

When a server (the computer offering the shared resource) is running, it announces itself to the master browser every 12 minutes. When the server stops, the master browser won't assume it has gone away for 3 announce periods, or 36 minutes. This would make it sound like the longest that you could ever wait for the browse list to work properly and eradicate a no-longer-available resource would be 36 minutes. But what if your browser is a *backup browser*? The backup browser polls the master every 15 minutes. The longest possible time for a backup browser to query the master is 15 minutes later, thus the worst case time for a server to disappear from the browse list is 51 minutes.

New services, in contrast, are announced to the master browser immediately, but, again, the backup browsers may hear of them as much as 15 minutes later, so the longest that it should take for a new service to appear on the browse list is 15 minutes.

By the way, when I said above that servers re-announced themselves to the master browser every 12 minutes, I simplified the truth a bit. The whole truth is that when a service first starts up, it announces itself more frequently. The service announces itself at intervals of 1, 4, 8, and 12 minutes after it is started, and after it reaches 12 minutes, it announces every 12 minutes afterwards.

Another reason why you might not see a resource is that its server may be using a different protocol from your workstation. You see, the services offered by the NetBEUI-using machines are maintained on a different browse list than the services offered by the TCP/IP-using machines. There is a different master browser for each transport protocol.

If you are running TCP/IP and resources do not appear on the TCP/IP browse list, it may be because the IPX and/or NetBEUI protocols are hogging the network's attention. If you can, remove the other protocols and the TCP/IP browser will work more smoothly.

NOTE

By the way, how does the network know to hold an election if someone just pulls the plug on the master browser, and the master browser doesn't get a chance to force an election? The answer is, the next time another computer asks for browse information and doesn't get a response, that computer forces an election.

TIP

If you take the other protocols off the PC, then be sure to re-enable MaintainServerList on some other machine, or NetBEUI and IPX will be without browsers.

Integrating 95 Workstations into an NT Domain

If you have an NT-based network, then you'll find accessing NT resources to be fairly easy. There are a few things to know, however, to simplify accessing resources or to save you time trying to do something that you can't do.

If you're going to log on to an NT domain, then you should tell your workstation to log right on to the domain. You know that password that you created to log on to your workstation? That's not necessarily your domain logon password. Now, if you chose a user name and a password for your 95 workstation that are the same as your domain name and password, then you're okay.

When you first log on to your 95 workstation, 95 doesn't log on to the domain. You don't log on to the domain until you try to "access a resource controlled by the domain," according to the manuals. Resources controlled by the domain are shares offered by *NT machines*—NT Server or NT workstations—where the machines have been explicitly added to the domain when installed. If Windows for Workgroups or Windows 95 machines offer resources, then those are *not* controlled by the domain.

If this still isn't clear, let's ask the question, "Why would you want a resource controlled by the domain?" The answer to that is simple: it makes it easier to administer the network. If you have 20 NT Servers scattered around your building, then you can control shares on any one of them by just sitting down at one of those servers and running a program called the Server Manager. From Server Manager, you can remotely force another NT machine to stop sharing something, to start sharing something, or to change the rules on who gets access to the share. *That's* convenience.

So the practical reason for a machine to join a domain is that the machine becomes capable of remote administration. This sounds like a good thing, and it is—so good, in fact, that you may want to be able to do this with your 95 workstations.

Unfortunately, you can't.

One of the major differences between 95 and NT is security. 95 machines cannot join a domain. 95 *users* can *log on* to a domain—but their *machines* cannot *join* a domain.

I've already said that you don't actually log on to a domain until you try to access a share controlled by the domain. This probably happens when you start up and reconnect to your permanent shares. You can, however, alternatively choose to use Quick logon, where you don't connect to a share until you actually try to use it. If there was a problem with the domain login, then you wouldn't find out about it until then.

For that reason, it may make sense for you to log directly on to the domain when you start up your system. You can do that like this:

1. Open the Control Panel. Double-click on the Network applet.
2. Choose *Client for Microsoft Networks* and click the Properties button.

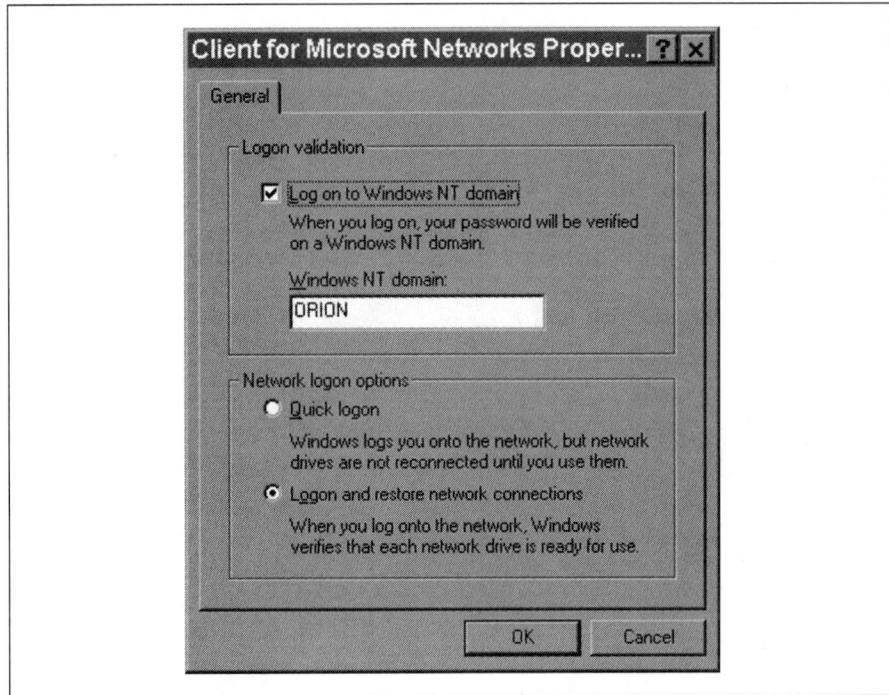

3. Click the *Log on to Windows NT domain* box and fill in the name of the domain, then click OK.

This may not make a great difference, but it may sometimes simplify figuring out why you can't get to your shares, as you'll get a message that the domain refused you a login. One bonus of doing the domain logon is that your login screen not only offers you the chance to fill in the name and password; it also lets you choose which domain to log in to.

CHAPTER

6

Windows 95 and Novell NetWare

WITH Windows 95, Microsoft has included various ways to connect to the Novell NetWare environment. Microsoft has provided a true 32-bit client that is big on performance and light on memory, but if you need closer compatibility with NetWare, or if your mainframe-connectivity VLMs or application-specific VLMs need full support, you can load your current network client software, and it will interact directly with Windows 95.

Microsoft Connections versus Novell Connections

To make Windows 95 coexist with NetWare, you have three options: You can use *Microsoft Client for NetWare Networks* (which I'll call MS Client for short), *Microsoft Service for NDS*, or *Novell NetWare Client*. Your primary decision is, do you want to use a Microsoft solution or a Novell solution? The following sections will help you to decide.

MS Client

Microsoft Client for NetWare Networks provides a complete 32-bit driver for connectivity to the NetWare world. This 32-bit driver can run completely in Windows protected mode. In addition, the driver requires only minimal overhead for conventional memory, which is important because conventional memory is still sacred under Windows 95. Finally, the complete set of software needed to make MS Client for NetWare Networks do what it does is provided with Windows 95.

Those are the hot reasons why the MS Client for NetWare Networks method makes sense; here are some others:

- **Novell script processing** Client for NetWare Networks will process the system login scripts and individual login scripts created by the network administrator of the Novell network. (Please note that MS Client for NetWare Networks does not support NetWare Directory Services (NDS) in the current iteration of Windows 95. Therefore, on 4.x servers the script processing will only take place if bindery emulation has been enabled on the server. Microsoft is promising to add this feature at a later date. I would look for it on the quarterly Tune-up packs that will be released by Microsoft.)

- **Long filename support** If you enable OS/2 naming support on your Novell server, you can save files with names up to 254 characters in length. With the OS/2 naming support enabled, your NetWare server will appear as a High Performance File System (HPFS) volume to the Windows 95 clients.

- **Storage of user profiles** You can save your user profile information on the Novell server.

- **Single peripheral systems** Because you are using the 32-bit drivers for connectivity, you can use the dial-up services that are part of the Microsoft enterprise network. On most of Microsoft's products this is referred to as remote-access service, but in Windows 95 it is known as dial-up networking. If you use MS Client for NetWare Networks, dial-up networking will allow you to attach directly to the Novell servers and process NetWare login scripts remotely. More on this in Chapter 7.

In order for MS Client for NetWare Networks to interact with Windows 95, you will need a set of DLLs and virtual device drivers (VxD's), all of which are provided with Windows 95 or can be downloaded from Microsoft.

MS Service for NDS

Another Microsoft solution is the *MS Service for NDS* (NetWare Directory Services), which you can download from Microsoft. If you are looking at the list above and are thinking that the Microsoft solution will give you the memory benefits that you need, but you also need the NDS support that is essential for a NetWare 4.x environment, then you should consider MS Service for NDS. It provides all of the functions listed above for MS Client, as well as support for your VLMs, and network administration capability with NetWare 4.x.

Novell NetWare Client

Although it's true that MS Client for NetWare Networks may talk directly to Novell servers with few problems, if you need to talk to many different *types* of servers that are using IPX as their primary protocol, you really should use *Novell NetWare Client*. MS Client is a viable option for client connectivity in terms of attaching to NetWare for file and print services, but it does not support the specialized VLMs needed to run the network administration utilities.

If you choose to connect to NetWare via Novell NetWare Client, you ensure driver compatibility with NetWare. To install Novell NetWare client, you can use the ODI driver provided on the disk that came with your network interface card. Novell NetWare Client is also preferable if you attach to different *types* of servers.

As you evaluate ways to integrate with NetWare, you will find that there are two approaches to using the Novell NetWare Client option. Keeping in mind that Novell no longer provides direct support for IPX-NETX, but that IPX-NETX is still a large percentage of the current Novell installed user base, one approach is to support the IPX-NETX drivers that are prevalent with NetWare 3.x. Or you can load IPXODI-VLM combinations, an approach that provides direct support for NDS. You can't take both approaches, however.

> **NOTE** Not all the software needed to install IPXODI-VLM combinations is provided with Windows 95; some of the drivers must be installed from the NetWare disks.

> **NOTE** As this book is being written, Novell has its own 32-bit driver solution in beta testing. By the time you read this, there may be yet another integration solution from Novell incorporating the full range of 32-bit driver support.

Setting Up MS Client for NetWare Networks

All of the MS Client for NetWare Networks drivers are included with Windows 95. The installation process assumes that you are using MS Client for NetWare Networks as the only method of communicating to a Novell server. If you choose to run MS Client for NetWare Networks in conjunction with the Novell NetWare Client software, look for the discussion later in this chapter. Now let's take a look at how to install MS Client for NetWare Networks.

Installing MS Client for NetWare Networks

Actually, this installation is really straightforward.

1. Remove the NetWare drivers from the AUTOEXEC.BAT file.
2. Choose the Network option in the Control Panel.
3. Select Add...

4. Select Client from the list in the *Select Network Client Component* area.

5. Select Microsoft as the Manufacturer.

6. Select Client for NetWare Networks, the second option on the list shown in the Figure 6.1.

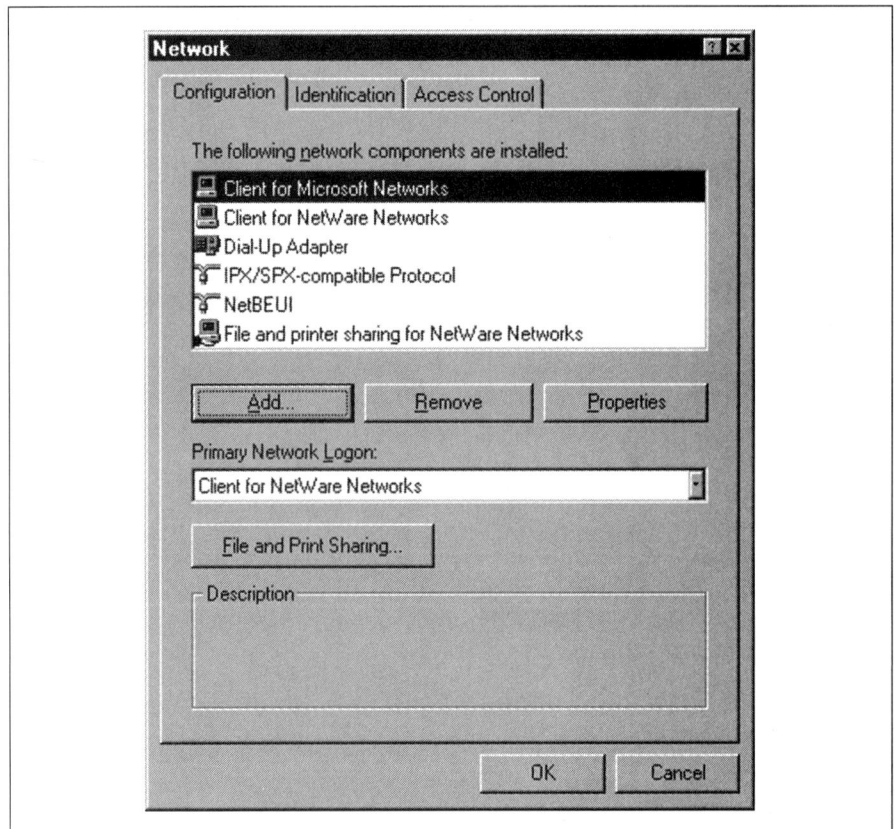

To enable printer and file sharing, click the *File and Print Sharing...* button and select your preferences, as seen in Figure 6.2.

This will install the appropriate drivers on your system and also will make the appropriate changes in the Registry. As you learned earlier, changes

FIGURE 6.2

File and Print Sharing

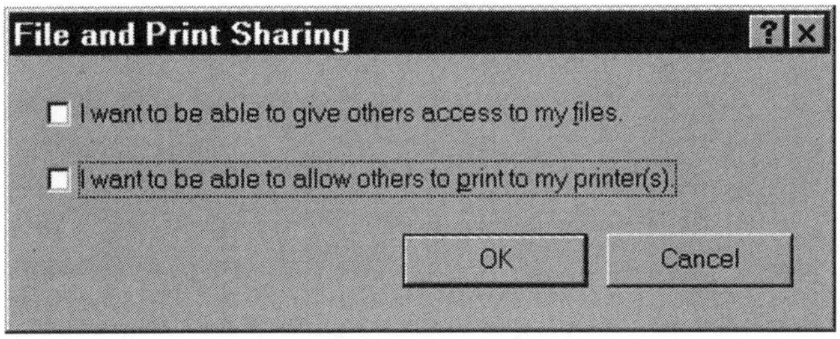

to the Registry require you to restart the computer; once you shut down and restart, the changes will take effect.

You have now completed the easier part of setting up MS Client for Net-Ware Networks. The harder part is configuring the client software to work properly with your system. Your next big hurdle will be choosing the *network binding interface* (NBI) that you want to use with Windows 95 and NetWare.

Choosing a Network Binding Interface

As discussed in Chapter 5, the network binding interface is the glue that enables your network interface card's device drivers to handle multiple protocol stacks. The NBI that Microsoft prefers is the *Network Driver Interface Specification*, or NDIS. The binding favored by Novell is called the *Open Datalink Interface* (ODI). Unfortunately, you can only load one. So which one should you choose? The choice can be difficult, but it is not fatal, as you can switch back and forth between the two relatively easily (please note the weasel word "relatively").

NDIS drivers *should* be your choice if you need to ensure that your computer system stays in protected mode for all of its communication needs. However, if you are using a program or TSR that requires the actual IPX/SPX protocol stack, and not the Microsoft emulated version, then you may need to use ODI. (An example of programs that fall into this category would be most DOS terminal emulation programs.) Keep in mind that choosing the ODI option will take up more conventional memory than NDIS, as NDIS drivers can load in extended memory. (ODI drivers cannot.) In addition, there are no Plug and Play drivers for ODI. Let's take a look at how to set up these drivers.

1. Select the Network icon in the Control Panel.

2. Choose Network Adapter from the list.

3. Select the Driver Type tab.

4. You will see the dialog box shown in Figure 6.3, with three options: Enhanced mode (32-bit and 16-bit) NDIS driver, Real mode (16-bit) NDIS driver, and Real mode (16-bit) ODI driver. Select the appropriate binding interface and click OK to continue.

FIGURE 6.3

Dial-Up Adapter Properties—choosing NDIS or ODI drivers

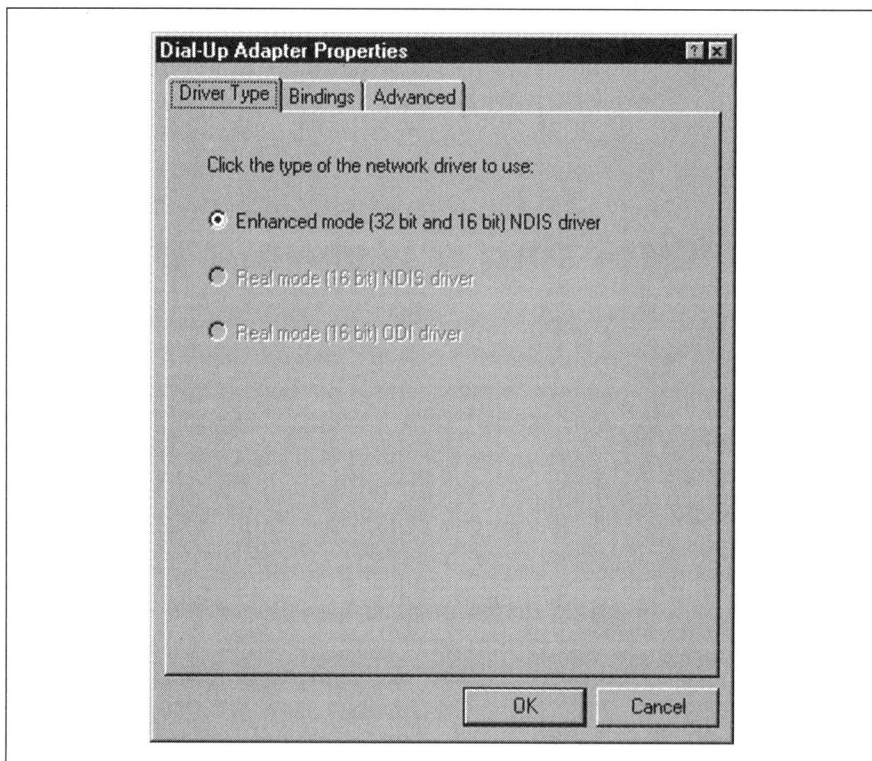

This updates your system software and requires you to shut down and then restart your system for the changes to take effect.

Using MS Client for NetWare Networks

Here are a few additional things to know about MS Client.

- Loading MS Client for NetWare Networks will only allow you to communicate via IPX/SPX. If you are looking for support for other protocols besides IPX/SPX, you will need to load a different client. For example, if you want to communicate via TCP/IP, you might load MS Client for *Microsoft* Networks instead, which includes support for the TCP/IP protocol.

- When using *File and Printer sharing for NetWare Networks*, please remove the Lastdrive= statement from CONFIG.SYS. If you put the Lastdrive= statement in CONFIG.SYS, the highest value that you can use is Z. This means you can only have 26 connections.

NOTE
MS Client for NetWare Networks has support for 32 connections, and functionality for 32 drive mappings is already enabled when you load it.

- Unfortunately, if you are a fan of the NWPOPUP, you will need to get rid of it. However, the Microsoft utility WINPOPUP will now serve this function and will display both NetWare and Microsoft broadcast messages.

- Due to the architectural design of Windows 95, whenever you create a NetWare network map (using the Map command), these mappings will apply to all virtual machines, even if you created the map in a virtual machine.

As we leave this discussion of troubleshooting MS Client for NetWare Networks, let's discuss which Novell functions you can and cannot perform.

If you are a NetWare 3.x administrator, there is good news for you. All of the NetWare utilities to which you are accustomed are still supported in the MS Client software. Even SYSCON (the network administration utility) works just fine; simply go to the DOS prompt, map a drive to the \public directory, and use the NetWare command as always.

If you are a NetWare 4.x administrator, we have some good news and some bad news. Most of the reporting commands, like Slist and Userlist, will work just fine under MS Client; however, the administrative functions of a 4.x server require NDS compliance, which MS Client does not support. If you need to remotely administrate a NetWare 4.x server under Windows 95, your only viable connectivity option is to run Novell NetWare Client.

Setting Up Novell NetWare Client

When installing Novell NetWare Client you first need to decide whether to support IPX-NETX (also referred to as *monolithic IPX*) or IPXODI-NETX or IPXODI-VLM. In either case, you need the latest drivers from Novell. The following are lists of all the files needed.

Novell files needed for a monolithic IPX install:

- IPX.COM
- NETWARE.HLP
- VNETWARE.386
- NETWARE.DRV
- NETX.EXE
- VIPX.386

Novell files needed for an IPXODI-NETX (NetWare 3.12) install:

- ODI driver from NIC manufacturer
- NETWARE.DRV

- VNETWARE.386
- LSL.COM
- NETX.EXE
- IPXODI.COM
- NETWARE.HLP
- VIPX.386
- NWPOPUP.EXE

Novell files needed for an IPXODI-VLM (NetWare 4.x) install:

- ODI driver from NIC manufacturer
- VLM files for the various services that the client will be running
- NETX.VLM

Now here are the steps to installing the Novell NetWare Client software.

1. Install the Novell drivers as usual.

   For ODI, the following lines should be in your AUTOEXEC.BAT or STARTNET.BAT file:

   ```
   |s|
   [NIC ODI Driver]
   ipxodi
   NETX
   ```

   (In the last line above, substitute VLM as needed instead of NETX.)

2. Choose the Network option in the Control Panel.

3. Select Add.

4. Select Client from the list in the Select Network Client Component area.

5. Select Novell as the Manufacturer, as shown in the Figure 6.4.

6. Select NETX or VLM as the workstation shell.

As usual, you will need to shut down the system and restart for the changes to take effect.

FIGURE 6.4

Select Novell under
Manufacturers.

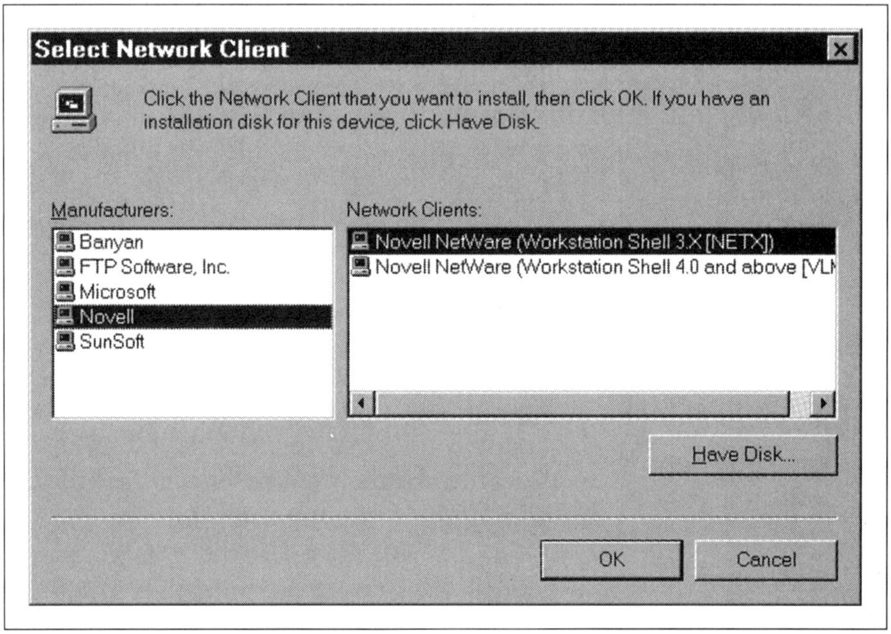

If you are working with a legacy system, and, therefore, ODI is not an option, here are the steps to enable monolithic IPX-NETX support in Windows 95:

1. Inherent in the nature of monolithic IPX is that it must be the only network option installed. Go to the Control Panel, click the Network icon, and remove all installed networking components.

2. Click Add.

3. Click Select Network Component.

4. Select Novell as the Manufacturer.

5. Select Novell IPX Monolithic Driver.

You will need to shut down and restart to have the changes take effect.

Enabling Long Filename Support on the Novell Server

As discussed earlier in this chapter, in order to enable long filename support on the NetWare server, you need to load the OS/2 name space support. Here's how you do it:

1. At the NetWare server prompt, type

   Load os2

   add name space os2 to volume sys

2. Add the following to the STARTUP.NCF file:

   load os2

3. Down the server, and at the C: prompt, copy the OS2.NAM file from the NetWare disks or CD-ROM. Place this file in the same directory as SERVER.EXE.

4. Type **SERVER** to restart the NetWare server.

Making Windows 95 Appear as a Novell Server

You may find yourself in a position where not everyone in your office uses Windows 95, but everyone does use NetWare. If you use a Windows 95 machine, you may want to share information from your machine with the rest of the network. The conventional way of doing this is to simply share the information through the Windows Explorer; this way people can access the data if they use WfW, Windows NT, or a machine running MS DOS Client. But what if the person accessing your machine only has Novell drivers loaded? You can make your Windows 95 machine and share appear as a Novell server and volume on the network.

Let's take a look at this process.

1. Ensure that you have loaded the IPX/SPX-compatible protocol.

2. In the Control Panel click on Network.

3. Select Add, then choose Service.

4. Select Microsoft as the manufacturer (as in Figure 6.5), choose the service *File and Printer Sharing for NetWare Networks*, then click OK.

FIGURE 6.5

Choosing File and
printer sharing for
NetWare Networks

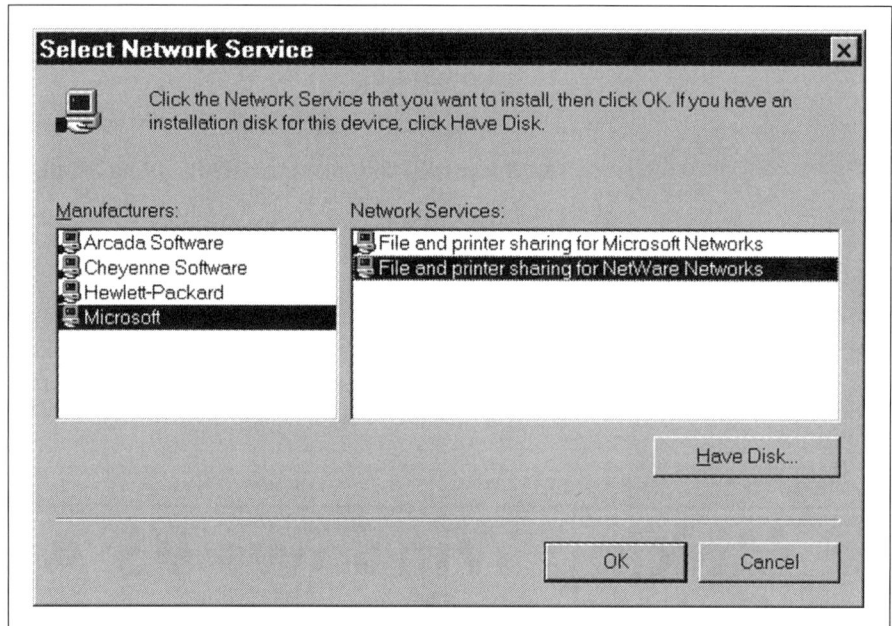

FIGURE 6.5

Choosing File and printer sharing for NetWare Networks

Please note: You cannot load the *File and Printer sharing* for both Microsoft Networks *and* for NetWare Networks.

5. Now, click on *File and Printer Sharing for NetWare Networks* in the components lists, select Properties, and enable SAP Advertising. Click OK. This will broadcast the Windows 95 machine as a Net-Ware server to the Novell network.

6. Your Windows 95 machine does not have its own security database for validating user access to itself as a NetWare server, so it must share a user list with a known NetWare server. Click on the Access Control tab and select User-level access. Provide the name of the Novell server that will be used to validate users' access to this Windows 95 "NetWare" server.

7. The final step is to restart Windows 95. (As usual, the system will prompt you to reboot.)

Now, to share resources with the NetWare world, you simply go to the Windows Explorer and share resources as you normally would. Since you have selected User-level access, you will now see the option *Add users to a share*. When you click on the Add button, a list of NetWare users and groups will appear in the pick list. At this point, you can give the users read-only, full, or custom access to this share.

If you are a NetWare client, accessing this share is as easy as mapping a drive. Keep in mind that the Windows 95 machine is the server name and the share is the volume name. So, if you have a Windows 95 machine called GTW09 and shared directory called WIN95SHR, at the NetWare client you would type the following:

map x:=GTW09\WIN95SHR:

At that point, if your system prompts you for a login name and password, provide them as they appear on the NetWare server list.

Wired 95— Remote Access with Windows 95

ONE of the biggest features Microsoft introduced as an integral part of Windows 95 is *dial-up networking*, which is the ability to remotely attach to a major network via a telephone or leased connection. This ability has many advantages.

One advantage is that it is convenient. If you leave the office and decide to continue working on a project at home, often you discover that files that you need were not saved to the floppy disk that you brought home with you. One option is to get back in your car, drive back to work, and retrieve the files from the network. But wouldn't it be so much easier and convenient to dial up your network from home and download the files? That's what's known as telecommuting.

Another advantage is remote administration. If you are a network administrator with a pager (and there are very few of you without pagers), you often get that dreaded page at 2:00 a.m. If a user locked himself out of the network (for example, he was having a bad typing day and mistyped his password three times), it becomes your job to either unlock his account or give him a new password. (Please note: If someone is actively working at 2:00 a.m., this must be a *very* important project.) Without dial-up networking, you must drive to the office and fix his user account. With dial-up networking, all you have to do is drag yourself to your computer at home, dial up the network, and perform the administrative task from home. Then, and most importantly, you get to go back to bed.

Now all of this probably sounds terrific, but you must be wondering, "How difficult is this to set up?" If you have ever worked with modems and telecommunications, you're probably fearing the adventure ahead of you. Good news! Once you get the terminology down, installing dial-up networking is not that difficult.

Let's begin with one of the largest issues—using remote-access software versus using remote-control software to communicate with your remote network.

What Is the Difference between Remote Control and Remote Access?

Once you've made the decision to let your users telecommute, you need to decide between the telecommuting methods of *remote control* and *remote access*. Both methods have similar hardware requirements: a modem, a telephone line, and a PC at the home office. The difference lies in the way in which the telecommuters access the office network. The method you choose depends on the kind of work that the telecommuters will be doing and the software that they use to do it.

Remote Control

Remote-control computing is a method of telecommuting in which the remote users actually *use* a network computer, controlling it via modem from their homes or outside offices. Thus, this kind of telecommuting requires a modem, a phone line, remote-control software, a remote PC, and a *host PC*, which is an office workstation specifically designated for dial-in use.

The Puppet Master

Remote control allows the remote user to take control of the host PC in the office via modem. The remote PC works as a front end for the remote user, letting him or her key in data and see the results on their monitor, while the only things traveling between the central office and the remote office are the input and the output. All the work is being done by the host PC in the central office—it has the applications, its processor is performing the calculations, and so forth. The remote PC does not need to have any of the necessary applications on it, it just uses the host machine's.

Remote control is best for non-GUI applications that mainly involve keyboard data entry. It becomes much slower when using mouse-intensive or graphics-intensive programs, such as Windows itself or any Windows application. To alleviate this problem, some remote-control software (such as ReachOut from Ocean Isle Software) only transmit GUI screen *changes* to the remote PC. This cuts down on traffic, at least in theory.

Disadvantages

In addition to its slowness with Windows, remote control has a few other disadvantages:

- The need for more than one PC for telecommuters—the remote PC and the host PC.

- The need for extra cabling (each machine needs its own connecting cable), power, cooling, and space.

- If the host machine locks up, then the remote user can't reset it.

- People using the host machine as a workstation tie up its use as a host.

- Security concerns. (Remember, remote control means that an office machine is logged on to the network.)

Remote Access

Remote access (also known as remote-node access) makes the remote PC a node on the network, rather than the controller of a network PC. The remote PC does all the processing necessary. The remote PC should have on its hard drive all the applications that it will need, so as to keep the data transfer to a minimum.

So Near, and Yet So Far

Remote access to a network requires a modem, a phone line, a remote PC, and remote-access software on both ends of the connection. In effect, remote access makes the remote PC a node on the office LAN. The phone line acts as a cable which connects the remote PC to the network interface card at the office. To log on to the network, the remote user dials up the remote access server (which, depending on the type of network your company is running and how the server(s) are configured, may or may not be the same computer as the file server). Once connected, the remote users must log on to the network just as they would if using one of the office PCs. (The security measures involved vary from product to product.)

Once logged on to the network, remote users can use the network just like any other user can, according to their user rights. When the remote users access files, they work on them at the remote computer, only accessing the file server to save the file or get a new one. Therefore, if the user is running Windows or other graphical user interface (GUI) applications, remote access is a faster option than remote control. Of course, it will still take remote users longer to access files on the server than it will take local users, as remote users must use telephone lines for transmission instead of fast network cable. This is obviously more of a problem with bigger files. When accessing an 11K memo, it's no big deal. Accessing a 1MB *book*, however, will take significantly longer. Since the user is running the application on the remote PC, however, at least the GUI application screen needn't travel through the phone lines; only the data needs to make the trip.

Which Is Better?

When the time comes for you to decide between remote control and remote access, consider the following points:

- What are the user's requirements? Which applications is the user running and what work does the user do?

- What hardware is compatible, and what is your computer's memory capacity?

- How will each option work with your LAN?

Essentially, when choosing between remote control and remote access, you're stuck with a choice between downloading screens (no big deal for DOS applications, but worth noting for Windows) and downloading files. No matter how you slice it, telecommuting is not, at this point, as fast as working in the office.

One option is not to limit yourself to one choice—many companies use remote control in some situations and remote access in other situations.

What Are the Setup Options for Dial-Up Networking?

The most common method of implementing dial-up networking will be via a modem. I strongly recommend that you use a modem that is following a useful standard, for example Hayes compatibility. You definitely want to avoid modems that only talk to their evil twins, like the High Speed Transmission (HST) modems which only talk to other HST modems.

Dial-up networking (DUN) does not limit you to connecting via modem. You can use DUN to attach a cable between two machines, which turns them into a small network. DUN supports a direct connection via parallel cable or null modem cable.

Dial-up networking also supports *Integrated Services Digital Network (ISDN)* connections. In order to use ISDN for dial-up connection, you must make sure that ISDN is supported in all the locations that you will be calling to and from.

NOTE   Dial-up networking is the same as *Remote Access Service* (RAS), with which you are familiar if you have used Windows for Workgroups 3.1x or Windows NT. Dial-up networking in Windows 95 is more powerful and flexible than WfW's RAS but not as complete as Windows NT's RAS.

What Connection Protocols Are Supported by Dial-Up Networking?

PPP   The protocol of choice for connecting with dial-up networking is the Point-to-Point Protocol (PPP). Microsoft has designed most of its remote access and dial-up connectivity around this protocol. At the speeds most of us will conduct our dial-up networking

(128Kbps or less), the primary advantage of PPP is that the connection does error checking of data and data compression during the transmission process. This makes for faster and more secure data transfer. Another reason to consider using PPP is that it is quickly becoming an industry-wide standard.

If you are using PPP you can connect to a network using IPX/SPX, TCP/IP, NetBEUI, or any combination of the three. Because of its power and flexibility, PPP is the default protocol when installing dial-up networking.

NetWare Connect   Novell uses software known as NetWare Connect to allow remote clients to dial up to the network. Windows 95 comes with a NetWare Connect client which allows your Windows 95 machine to attach to a NetWare Connect server directly, without going through a Microsoft gateway of any type. Even though Windows 95 machines can connect to a NetWare Connect server, it is not a reciprocal relationship; NetWare Connect clients cannot dial in to a Windows 95 server.

RAS   Dial-up networking supports RAS as implemented by Windows for Workgroups 3.11 and Windows NT 3.1. (Windows NT 3.5x now defaults to using PPP.) You may see this RAS option referred to as *asynchronous NetBEUI* in some systems' help files or in network documentation.

SLIP   An older protocol standard is the Serial Line Interface Protocol (SLIP). Unlike its PPP counterpart, SLIP does not perform error checking or data compression while transmitting data; the responsibility is placed on your hardware to perform these functions. This is not a bad thing, since most 14.4Kbps and 28.8Kbps modems *do* perform these functions.

N O T E Microsoft recommends against using SLIP except when dialing up a UNIX network that is using a dial-up server with TCP/IP.

What Are the Different Combinations for Connection Protocols and Network Protocols?

There are two parts to dial-up networking: the dial-up *server* and the dial-up *client* (the remote user's machine). Let's take a look at the various combinations from that perspective. The information is summarized in Table 7.1.

TABLE 7.1

Various Combinations of Connection and Network Protocols

CLIENTS	SERVER
TCP/IP over SLIP	UNIX remote server, Internet (SLIP Router)
IPX over NetWare Connect	NetWare Connect Server
IPX, NetBEUI, and/or TCP/IP over PPP	Internet (PPP Router), Windows 95, Windows NT RAS Server, and NetWare
NetBEUI over RAS (Asynchronous NetBEUI)	Windows 95, Windows NT, Windows for Workgroups 3.11, and LAN Manager Servers

How Do I Install Dial-Up Networking?

Installing dial-up networking is a two-step process:

1. First, you must install the dial-up networking software onto your client machine and onto your host PC or server.

2. Then you must configure the dial-up networking software as either client or server.

Installing Dial-Up Networking on the Network

Let's look at how to install the dial-up networking software on your company's host PC or server:

1. Click on Control Panel.

2. Select Add/Remove Programs.

3. Select the Setup tab.

4. Click the Communications option and then select Details.

5. Select *Dial-up networking* from the list.

You will be returned to the main window to continue with the setup— select the Next button, then.

Configuring the DUN Network Connection

Good news! You do not have to restart your system in order to configure dial-up networking.

Installing Dial-Up Networking on the Client Machine

The first step to installing dial-up networking software on a remote machine is to install all the *protocols* the remote user might need and bind them to the *dial-up adapter*. On the remote machine, go to Control Panel, choose Network, and select the dial-up adapter your remote machine will be using.

The next step is to create a new Dial-Up Networking (DUN) *connection*. Instruct your remote user to go to the DUN folder in My Computer and, within the folder, choose the Make New Connection option. The user should supply any information needed and click OK. This creates a Connection icon in the Dial-Up Networking folder.

Once the user has created the DUN connection, he or she can double-click the Connection icon at any time to dial up to the network. It may ask for the name of the server or domain they want to log on to, as well as a password. DUN will then dial the location, verify the user name and the password, and if everything checks out, allow access to the server. At this point, the user can now do anything they normally could if they were local to the network (only more slowly).

At the risk of repeating myself, I strongly recommend that remote users do not attempt to run applications across the DUN connection; they should only go DUN to get data files and information. For example, if you choose to start a network copy of Word for Windows from your remote DUN location, it could easily take over 45 minutes for the application to begin, because the entire program would have to be transported via modem to the memory of your remote DUN machine.

TIP Dial-Up Networking is designed with data in mind. The best implementation of DUN would be a remote DUN machine that has the applications loaded locally.

The recommendation also applies to remote administration. Load a copy of your network administration utilities locally on each remote DUN machine you expect to administer the network from. Of course, if you choose to follow this advice, be aware that the network vendor may require you to buy additional licenses of the network administration utilities. Many network vendors sell the utilities in sets.

Configuring a DUN Client Connection

To configure a DUN client connection, simply right-click the Connection icon that was created in the preceding section and select Properties.

Your first major decision here concerns the type of server you will be dialing up via this connection. If you typically dial to the same site, but you know that sometimes you'll want to connect via RAS (asynchronous NetBEUI) and other times you'll want to connect via NetWare Connect, use Make New Connection and create two separate connections. Then whenever you go to make your connection, you can choose from a pair of Connection icons.

You can see your choices for Type of Dial-Up Server in Figure 7.1.

Let's take a look at the different options available on this screen:

- **PPP** Used for dialing to RAS servers that are using TCP/IP, IPX, NetBEUI, or any combination of the three. DUN will automatically detect which of the three to use based on the protocols you select at the bottom of the screen.

- **NRN** Used for connecting to a NetWare Connect Server.

- **WFW/WIN NT** Used when dialing into a Windows 95 dial-up server, NT RAS Server, or WfW RAS server.

- **SLIP** Used for any implementation of SLIP of the TCP/IP protocol.

FIGURE 7.1

Type of Dial-Up Server
dialog box

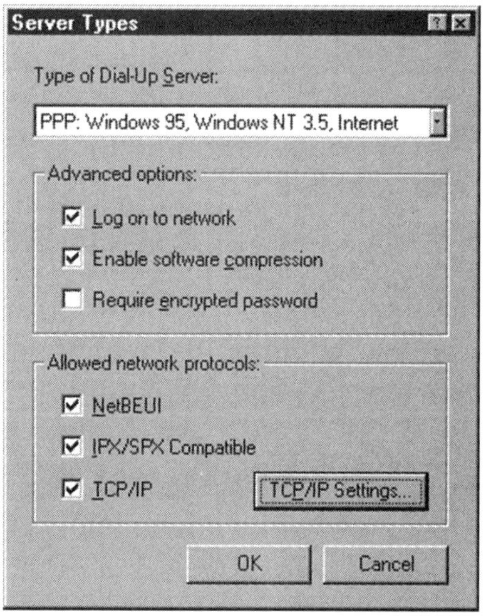

- **CSLIP** Used for any implementation of compressed SLIP connections. (Your network administrator should specify whether or not you need to use SLIP or CSLIP. The protocol must match what the dial-up server is using.)

- **Log on to network** This option, which is enabled by default, will dial up and log you into the network using the username and password you typed in when you logged into Windows 95. If this option is deselected, it will ask you for a logon name and password every time you attempt a new connection.

- **Enable software compression** This option will compress the data before it is sent to the modem (or the like) for transmission.

- **Require Encrypted Passwords** This option enables a feature known as the Challenge Handshake Authentication protocol (CHAP). CHAP will be discussed in greater detail later in this chapter.

This screen is also where you specify the protocols that you want the DUN connection to support. If you want to configure a connection to the Internet, click on the TCP/IP settings. This option will ask for information that you may need to get from your network administrator or your Internet service provider.

How Do I Test the DUN Connection?

Once you have configured your DUN connection, just double-click and the connection will be made immediately. You should see the lights of your modem flashing, and, if you have enabled the modem speaker, you should hear that distinctive squelching noise which indicates that Windows 95 is negotiating a connection.

Using Microsoft's Universal Naming Conventions (UNCs), you should now be able to access any network resource for which you have permission.

TIP

When you are connected to a network, you can go to the *Connected To* window and see the number packets sent, number of packets received, and the overall status of your connection.

Once you have established a connection for the first time, dial-up networking will be activated in any of the following circumstances:

- When you select a network resource that is not part of your network
- When a UNC directs you toward a network resource (for example, \\server\public_)
- When an application calls for a network resource

Shortcuts to Popular Network Information

If you need to dial up to many different networks, shortcuts are a great way to organize all of your frequently visited sites. It also gets you quickly to the information on those networks that you use most frequently.

Without shortcuts, I have to take the following steps every time I want to connect to my home directory at work:

1. Open the My Computer folder.
2. Open the Dial-Up Networking folder.
3. Select my connection. (In my case, it's MMCO Office.)
4. Provide a password.

At this point the system starts to negotiate the connection and to authenticate me to the network. After validation, I map a network drive to my home directory on the network (as discussed in Chapter 5) and then I can access my files.

All this gets a little tiresome quickly, and this is where shortcuts come to the rescue. To create a shortcut to my home directory, I still follow the above steps the very first time I connect, but I let Windows 95 automatically create a shortcut to the directory by clicking and dragging my network home directory folder to the desktop.

From that point on, if I want to get to my home directory then I just double-click on its shortcut. Windows 95 will now automatically call the network, validate me to the network (assuming my Windows 95 logon and network logon are identical), and take me to my home directory. If I am already connected to the network, the shortcut is still a useful way to fly directly to my home directory.

Installing the Windows 95 Server

Many users familiar with Windows NT Remote Access Server may be wondering, "What's the difference between NT's RAS and Windows 95's Server?" There are two differences:

- Whereas the Windows NT RAS is included when you purchase Windows NT, the Windows 95 Server is not included with Windows 95. If you want to install the Windows 95 Server, you need to purchase an add-on package known as Microsoft Plus!, which retails for $50.

- Connections: Windows NT can support up to 256 simultaneous connections; a Windows 95 Server can only support one connection at a time.

The first step to enabling Windows 95 Server is to install the Microsoft Plus! software. With Microsoft Plus! installed, do the following:

1. In the Connections menu, a new option, Dial-Up Server, will appear.

2. In the Dial-Up Server configuration window, click *Allow caller access*.

3. Set the Security option. You can define a password that anyone calling to this Windows 95 machine must provide in order to access the shared resources of the DUN server system. Alternatively, if you are implementing user-level security, you can specify the users that can access this machine.

4. Select *Server Type*. This option defaults to PPP, which supports TCP/IP, IPX, and NetBEUI. By selecting this option, a determination is made during the negotiation of callers to this DUN server machine. If PPP cannot negotiate a viable connection, the DUN server will automatically switch to RAS for NT and Windows for Workgroup clients.

Once you click OK, your system is now waiting to receive calls.

What about Security?

We have discussed some of the things to be considered in order for a DUN to work and to interact properly. But once you have DUN up and running, there are a few security concerns you might want to deal with.

For example, Jennifer, dialing up from home, can locate another user, say Joe, who is currently logged into the DUN server, and kick him off. All she has to do is take these four simple steps:

1. Go to My Computer.
2. Select Dial-Up Networking.
3. Select Dial-Up Server.
4. Click the Disconnect User button.

In the same vein, if Joe hasn't been kicked off yet, he can take a preemptive strike against everybody, by remotely turning off the server! All he has to do is follow the first three of the steps above and then click No Caller Access.

Fortunately, once you have DUN up and running, there are a few security features you can enable.

Password Authentication Protocol (PAP)

The first level of security is established during the connection. If you have selected PPP as your server type on both the client and the server, then you can utilize a technology known as the Password Authentication Protocol (PAP). Before the invention of PAP, the server, client, and user held the following conversation:

Server (to client): *Do you use PAP?*

Client (to Server): *No.*

Server (to Client): *What is the user's name?*

Client (to User): *What is your logon name?*

User (to Client): *Frank.*

Client (to Server): *The user says his name is Frank.*

Server (to Client): *Great, what is the user's password?*

Client (to User): *What is your logon password?*

User (to Client): *Doghouse.*

Client (to Server): *The client says his password is Doghouse.*

Server (to Client): *Thank you.*

This conversation would take place every single time the user wanted to log in to the network remotely. There is no encryption of information being sent back and forth. With some network servers, you may actually have to create a script file so this conversation can be automated. In either case, it still requires that the network administrator understand how to create the script file. Scripts in theory are very straightforward, but in practice the syntax can vary from hardware device to hardware device and from network operating system to network operating system.

If both your server and the client are using PAP, then the conversation goes something like this:

Server: *Do you use PAP?*

Client: *Yes.*

Server: *Great, then please send over the username.*

Client: *Frank.*

Server: *Great, please send over the password.*

Client: *Doghouse.*

Server: *Thank you.*

This entire conversation took place without any interaction on the part of the user. If it took any time at all, all the user saw was the hourglass while this conversation took place in the background. Unfortunately, just as you saw the password *Doghouse* in the conversation presented above, the password was sent as a simple text string across the communication line. When I last looked in Webster's dictionary under the word *security*, this wasn't part of the definition. If you are looking for a secure validation, you want to use CHAP.

> **N O T E**
>
> Now before we discuss CHAP, I would like to mention SPAP in passing. The makers of the Shiva Modem have their own Authentication protocol known as Shiva Password Authentication Protocol (SPAP). Windows 95 supports SPAP for dialing into a Shiva Server.

Challenge-Handshake Authentication Protocol (CHAP)

As said previously, CHAP allows for secure validation. If the server and client have CHAP enabled, the following conversation takes place:

Server: *Do you do CHAP?*

Client: *Yes.*

Server: *47*

Client (to itself): *Let me factor the password by 47 and send the encrypted version across the line.*

Client (to Server): *Kjsyao7r* (representing the password doghouse).

Server: *Thank You.*

Now, since the server sent a *challenge code* (47 in the example above), it knows that it will use the same number as the challenge factor to decrypt the password and then validate it. The power of CHAP is that when the first client logs in the challenge code may be 47, but when the next client logs in the challenge code dynamically changes. Since the challenge code is constantly changing, the passwords are encrypted using a different key every time.

To enable CHAP, just select Require Encrypted Password when configuring the client *and* when configuring the server. If Server Type is PPP, DUN will attempt a PAP conversation by default, unless Require Encrypted Passwords is selected.

Access to Resources with DUN

DUN allows you to specify how people may gain access to the DUN server.

- The first option is share-level security. This permits you to assign passwords to each resource that you share. You can set a password for read-only access and a different password for full-control access. The downside of this configuration is that a user may have to memorize many passwords. If you are looking for centralized control, you will want to set user-level permissions instead.

- When you set user-level permissions, Windows 95 will look for a Windows NT or NetWare server to validate a user. The user has to be a valid user of Novell network or a NT domain in order to gain access to your machine. Windows 95 still controls read-only or full-control access to the resource, but enforces these security parameters by users, not by resource.

How Do I Create a Direct Serial Connection?

Users aren't limited to actually dialing in via a phone line to set up a network connection; they can connect their remote computer directly via a serial cable. To create a direct serial connection, the first thing that you need is an acceptable cable. Any of the following will do:

- Serial null modem cable
- LapLink cable
- InterLink cable
- 25-pin parallel cable (all wires must be present)

Of the four types of cables, the parallel cable will provide the fastest throughput between machines.

Once you have made a physical connection between the machines, take the following steps:

1. Choose *Add/Remove programs* in Control Panel.

2. Select Communications in the Components list.

3. Select Direct Cable Connection.

A new icon, titled Direct Cable Connection, will appear in the My Computer window. Please make sure this icon appears on both machines before attempting to establish a connection.

The first time you click on Direct Cable Connection, the Direct Connect Wizard will appear and allow you to designate one machine as the host machine and the other machine as the guest machine.

CHAPTER

8

Supporting Windows 95 Clients on a Network

YEARS ago, people looked to PCs as an alternative to mainframe computing. When justifying the purchase of a PC, they often cited cost. "PCs are cheaper than mainframes," they said, and they were right—as long as they were only talking about the cost of the hardware.

The last twenty years of desktop computing have taught us that the real cost of owning PCs lies in supporting them. So anything that makes supporting PCs easier is a real plus.

Windows 95 doesn't solve all of a support person's remote support headaches, but it's an improvement over Windows for Workgroups or (ugh!) regular old Windows 3.1 with network drivers added. In this chapter, you'll see how you can leverage your network investment to simplify support in the following ways:

- You can simplify Windows 95 installation over a network.

- You can set up your 95 workstations to boot from shared directories on the network.

- You can use system policies to restrict user access to Windows 95 features.

- You can use user profiles so that your desktop follows you wherever you go on the network.

- You can use Net Watcher, Network Monitor, and System Monitor to watch network activity and remotely administer resource sharing over a 95 network.

Setting Up 95 for Network Installs

The prospect of walking around your company with a CD-ROM disc, or, more likely, a knapsack full of floppies to install 95 probably doesn't sound like much fun (and, coincidentally, it's *not*). You can use your *network* to make installing 95 easier in three ways:

- You can install the entire 95 system on your user's local hard disks from a network.

- You can set up 95 so that *most* of it sits on a shared directory on the server and only about three to four megabytes sits on the user's local hard disk.

- You can even set up a workstation so that it needs only a floppy to start from, and the Windows 95 installation doesn't touch the workstation's hard disk. The process *is* buggy, but you can get it to work with persistence.

In this section, you'll see how to do those things.

There are basically three groups of files that you need in order to get Windows working over a network:

- The very large shared directory (about 75MB) of Windows files. You'll usually run them from the server, but if you want you can install them entirely onto a local hard disk when doing a network installation.

- A directory containing the user's personal Windows-specific files, including the SYSTEM.DAT part of the Registry, your temporary files, and the like. This is called the *machine directory*. It ranges from 1.5MB to about 4MB in size, and each machine that can boot Windows 95 has a machine directory. The machine directory can sit on either the PC's local hard disk or the server.

- Files required to boot the user's computer up to the point where it can access the server. I call these the *boot files*; there's no official

Windows name for them. Every computer must have these boot files on either the local hard disk or a floppy disk, or, in the case of machines with remote-boot LAN adapters, on the server. These files are about 1.5 MB.

Installing 95 onto a Local Hard Disk from a Server

Installing 95 from a server is simple. Just copy all the contents of the CD-ROM's win95 folder to a directory, set the directory to read-only (just in case…), and then go to each user's workstation and connect to the shared directory. Run Setup as usual and you're done.

Installing 95 to Share a Directory on the Server

Suppose I want to install my workstations so that they boot 95 mainly from the server? Setting up 95 on a workstation entails three (or, optionally, four) steps:

1. Set up a shared directory that contains the Windows files, which will be used both for workstation setup and for people to start up Windows 95 every day.

2. Optionally, create a separate share which will hold a machine directory (a kind of home directory for each machine) on your network.

3. Create standard setup scripts.

4. Optionally, on each workstation, take the following steps:
   - Set up simple DOS-based or Windows 3.x-based network client software.
   - Log on to the shared directory.
   - Run Setup.

Those few steps have a variety of options within them; let's take a look at what those options are and how to use them.

Getting Ready: Build a Share and Then Run NETSETUP

In order to *run* Windows 95 from a network, you must first create a shared directory with the decompressed 95 files. First, go to your server and create a share in which you can store the shared files. In my examples, I'll use a share called W95SHR on my primary domain controller, named EISA Server. (Yes, there's a blank in the name. I wish I'd never done *that*, believe me, but you'll see more about that later...)

Then tell Windows to copy and decompress itself from the shipped file cabinets. You do that with NETSETUP.EXE, which you'll find on the CD in the \admin\nettools\netsetup directory. Don't try to install it with the Control Panel—it won't work. Instead, just open up the admin \nettools\netsetup folder on the CD-ROM and double-click on the NETSETUP.EXE file. Start it up and you'll see a screen, as in Figure 8.1.

FIGURE 8.1

Setting up 95 installation paths

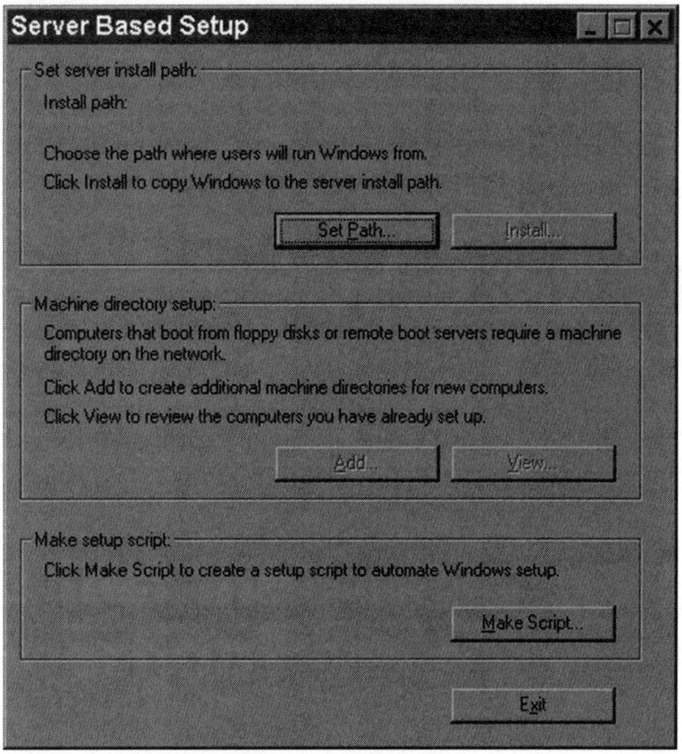

Server Based Setup

Set server install path:

Install path:

Choose the path where users will run Windows from.
Click Install to copy Windows to the server install path.

[Set Path...]   [Install...]

Machine directory setup:

Computers that boot from floppy disks or remote boot servers require a machine directory on the network.

Click Add to create additional machine directories for new computers.
Click View to review the computers you have already set up.

[Add...]   [View...]

Make setup script:

Click Make Script to create a setup script to automate Windows setup.

[Make Script...]

[Exit]

Click Set Path, and you'll be prompted for the name of the shared Windows directory to create. This name must be a UNC name, like `\\myserver\w95shr`. It would be nice to call it a name like `\\myserver \Windows 95 shared directory`, but that would make your life tougher when it comes time to access the directory when upgrading from DOS or Windows 3.x. If the share doesn't yet exist, then you'll get an error message; Netsetup cannot create an entirely new share. If, on the other hand, the share exists but the directory doesn't, then you'll be prompted as to whether or not to create it. When you have that taken care of, click Install and you'll see a dialog box like Figure 8.2.

FIGURE 8.2

Installing the shared 95 program directory

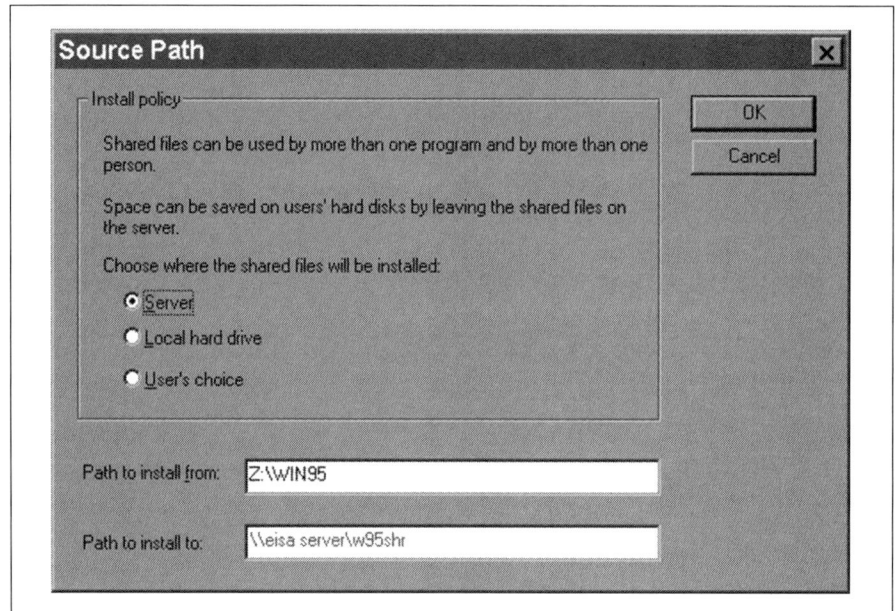

You're running Netsetup now, and you (or others) will run regular old Setup for each workstation to put Windows 95 on a workstation, or on a workstation and server working together. In the Group Install policy, you control whether Setup will allow someone to copy the files onto their local hard disk. I'd pick *User's choice*, as it doesn't affect your site license whether people run 95 from the server or if they copy it to their workstations. (You see *Server* chosen in the Figure 8.2 because it is the default, before I changed it.)

The options *Path to install from:* and *Path to install to:* should be self-explanatory. (In case you're wondering, Z: is the CD-ROM on my system.

As you can see in Figure 8.3, once you click OK, you'll see the next important dialog box, which concerns default batch files.

This creates a setup batch script with more details than you saw in the Batch Script Editor you met in Chapter 4. You do *not* have to do this now. If you do *not* create the default script the first time, you can do it later by reinvoking Netsetup, specifying the path name of the shared Windows installation you previously created, and then clicking that Make Script button at the bottom of the dialog box. Read ahead a few paragraphs before you decide to click Create Default; my recommendation is that you click Don't Create Default.

The dialog box that you see is more akin to the System Policy Editor, about which you will learn more later in this chapter, than it is to BATCH.EXE. It looks like the one in Figure 8.4.

While this is supposed to be doing a job like BATCH.EXE's, it doesn't do the same kind of job that BATCH.EXE does (and not nearly as well). I'll explain how to use this Server Based Setup Default Properties dialog, but my recommendation is that you just skip this step and choose Don't Create Default in the previous dialog box.

FIGURE 8.3

Choosing batch file scripts

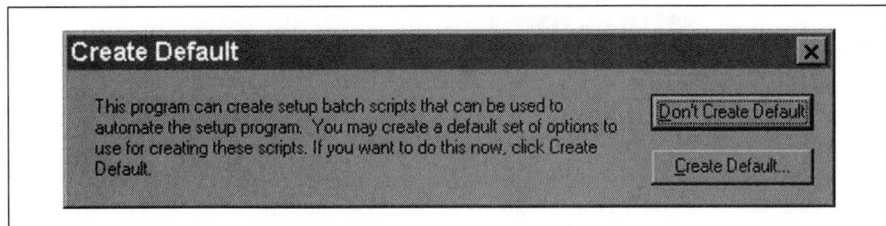

Create Default

This program can create setup batch scripts that can be used to automate the setup program. You may create a default set of options to use for creating these scripts. If you want to do this now, click Create Default.

Don't Create Default

Create Default...

FIGURE 8.4

Choices for batch
script setup

Server Based Setup Default Properties

Policies

Server Based Setup Default
  ⊞ Setup options
  ⊞ Install location
  ⊞ Name And Organization
  ⊞ Network Options
  ⊞ System Components
  ⊞ Most recently used paths (MRU)

OK   Cancel

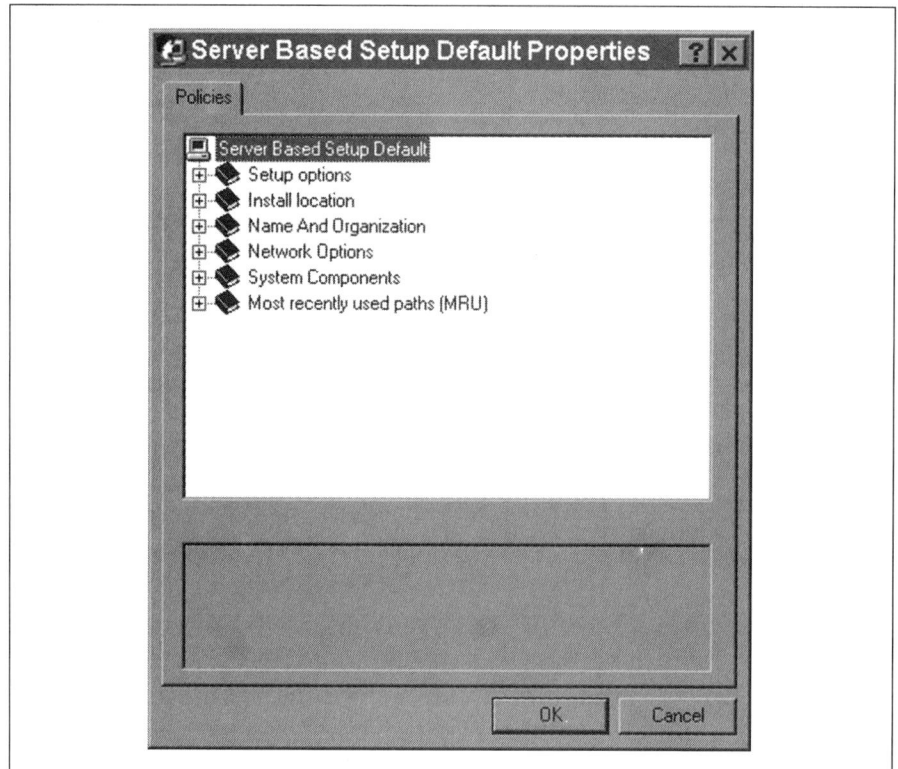

Setup Options

In the Choices for Batch Script dialog box (Figure 8.4), click the Setup
Options volume and you'll see controls relevant to the overall setup. Most
of them are either self-explanatory or similar to the BATCH.EXE dialogs,
but there are a few pitfalls. With Automated Install, you can set up the
installation to be free of user input; that's an option that you can set inside
Setup Options. With Setup Mode, you choose whether the setup is Custom, Typical, or whatever.

Install Location

Here is where you specify that Windows should be set up so that it runs
from the server, rather than the workstation's local hard disk, and whether
or not it boots from a floppy.

Name and Organization

This lets you pre-enter information, such as the name of your organization. You can fix it so that the user never sees the information upon Setup or you can just provide defaults.

You then enter the product identification number and Netsetup starts copying information to the shared directory. (Again, in my example, I've put that directory on a server called EISA Server, on a share called W95SHR.)

Network

In this section, you can ensure that people log on to the domain, specify the workgroup to join, and other similar things. There's useful stuff here, but the interface is terrible, so you'll end up fixing it by hand, as I'll next explain.

Adjust the Script

Click OK, and Netsetup will copy and expand over 75MB of files to your shared directory. You can exit Netsetup at this point and examine the script that it wrote if you allowed it to; if not, then now's a good time to run BATCH.EXE.

You'll find a file called MSBATCH.INF in the shared Windows directory. It's set to read-only, so you'll need to reset that bit before editing it. And you'll want to edit it. As I've said, Netsetup just falls down a bit on getting the .INF file correct, requiring you to look back to Chapter 4 and tweak the commands to get them right. For example, it lets you specify protocols and client software, but you're supposed to fill in the names, rather than choose them from a list. Protocol names are NETBEUI, NWLINK (the 95 name for IPX), and MSTCP. Redirector names are VREDIR (the client for Microsoft networks) and NWREDIR (the Microsoft client for NetWare networks). If you were to load all three protocols and both clients, then the line in the .INF file should end up looking like the following two lines.

```
Clients=VREDIR, NWREDIR
Protocols=NETBEUI, NWLINK, MSTCP
```

Other important settings include HDBOOT, which should be set to 1 if you're going to start your Windows machine from the hard disk or 0 if you're going to boot either from a floppy or directly off the server with a remote-booting LAN board. ReplSetup should equal 1 if you're starting from a remote-booting LAN board, and 0 if you're booting from a floppy; the whole setting is only relevant if HDBOOT=0.

Just by way of example, here's an MSBATCH.INF that I use for my network, with comments:

```
[Setup]
Express=1
InstallDir=" g:\mwm66"
EBD=0
ChangeDir=0
OptionalComponents=1
Network=1
System=0
CCP=0
CleanBoot=0
Display=0
PenWinWarning=0
InstallType=1
DevicePath=1
TimeZone=" Eastern"
Uninstall=0
VRC=0
NoPrompt2Boot=1

[NameAndOrg]
Name=" Mark Minasi"
Org=" MMCO, inc."
Display=0

[Network]
ComputerName=" MWM66"
Workgroup=" orion"
Description=" 95 workstation"
Display=0
Clients=VREDIR
Protocols=NETBEUI
IgnoreDetectedNetCards=0
HDBoot=1
RPLSetup=0
WorkstationSetup=1
```

```
DisplayWorkstationSetup=0
Security=domain
PassThroughAgent=" orion"

[VREDIR]
LogonDomain=" orion"
ValidatedLogon=1

[OptionalComponents]
" Accessibility Options" =0
" Briefcase" =0
" Calculator" =1
" Character Map" =0
" Clipboard Viewer" =0
" Desktop Wallpaper" =0
" Document Templates" =1
" Games" =0
" Mouse Pointers" =0
" Net Watcher" =0
" Object Packager" =1
" Online User's Guide" =0
" Paint" =1
" Quick View" =1
" System Monitor" =1
" System Resource Meter" =1
" Windows 95 Tour" =0
" WordPad" =1
" Dial-Up Networking" =1
" Direct Cable Connection" =1
" HyperTerminal" =1
" Phone Dialer" =1
" Backup" =0
" Defrag" =1
" Disk compression tools" =1
" Microsoft Exchange" =0
" Microsoft Mail Services" =0
" Microsoft Fax Services" =0
" Microsoft Fax Viewer" =0
" Central European language support" =0
" Cyrillic language support" =0
" Greek Language support" =0
" Audio Compression" =1
" CD Player" =1
" Jungle Sound Scheme" =0
" Media Player" =1
```

```
"Musica Sound Scheme"=0
"Robotz Sound Scheme"=0
"Sample Sounds"=0
"Sound Recorder"=1
"Utopia Sound Scheme"=0
"Video Compression"=1
"Volume Control"=1
"Additional Screen Savers"=0
"Flying Windows"=1
"The Microsoft Network"=0
```

Express=1, display=0, and NoPrompt2Boot=0 all minimize the number of mouse clicks you must do to get through the installation. Verify=0 keeps Setup from complaining if you are *re*installing Windows 95 on a machine. I still haven't figured out CCP, and ProductID is obvious. InstallType=1 is Typical, ebd=0 says to skip making an emergency boot disk, and Uninstall=0 says it's not necessary to keep the uninstall information—it usually isn't meaningful for network setups, and certainly not for floppy-based boots. Installdir tells where to install the Windows files to; this will turn out to be important for network installations.

In [network], the two references to WorkstationSetup tell Setup to do a network install using the shared binaries on w95shr, rather than to copy all of the Windows files to the local hard disk. HDBOOT=1 and RPL-Setup=0 say that you should set up to boot from the hard disk. That's not necessary; it's just how I have it set up. I'm loading the Microsoft network client (VREDIR) and the NetBEUI protocol.

I built this file with BATCH.EXE. The built-in batch file creator in Netsetup produced a file that required a pile of work to make it look like this (which is, again, why I recommend using BATCH.EXE).

Restart NETSETUP and Create Machine Directories

It's nice that you can take all of those Windows 95 files and put them in a single shared directory, rather than having to burn up tens of megabytes on the C: drive of every hard disk in your organization. But not everything can be shared. Registries, program groups, desktops, .INI files from legacy apps, and temporary and swap files are some examples of things that are specific to a particular person or workstation.

You're probably familiar with the idea that users on a network have home directories, which are directories on the server that no one can access except for its owner. As users move around, user-specific information can live in the user's home directory. But where does the machine-specific stuff, like swap files, temp files, and SYSTEM.DAT, live? It is in a kind of home directory for a particular workstation, called a *machine directory*. Each machine needs a place to put this information. On a stand-alone installation, it's mixed in with the other Windows files. On a networked installation, it can sit on a small directory called windows on the workstation's C: drive or it can be on a directory on the server. Obviously, floppy-based systems must put their machine directories on a server.

Another way of understanding machine directories is to keep in mind that they are also the *installation directory* of Windows 95. When Setup asks where to install Windows 95 to, you should point Setup to the machine directory—but I hope to have you avoid that manual labor; we'll make installing 95 over the network as automatic as is possible.

Go to your network and create a directory which will hold all of the machine directories; I called mine, uncreatively, Machine. Share that directory so that it's visible on the network.

Now return to Netsetup and click the Path button. Fill in the UNC name of the shared Windows directory that you created before. (It's w95shr in this example, not machine, remember—you now want the shared Windows directory, not the machine directory.)

In the machine directory setup part of Netsetup, click Add, and you'll see a dialog box like Figure 8.5.

I'll set up just one machine for now, but notice that there's a procedure here for setting up multiple PCs in one pass—I'll get to that later. I've created a share on EISA Server called Machine which will contain these machine directories.

I want to set up a machine called MWM66, so I fill in the name of the machine and the name of the directory where it'll keep its information, as you see in Figure 8.6.

I've said this before, but it's important to create the machine directory before running this, as I've had Netsetup give me a GPF a few times when I asked it to create the machine directory. Unfortunately, if you GPF out

FIGURE 8.5

Adding a machine
directory

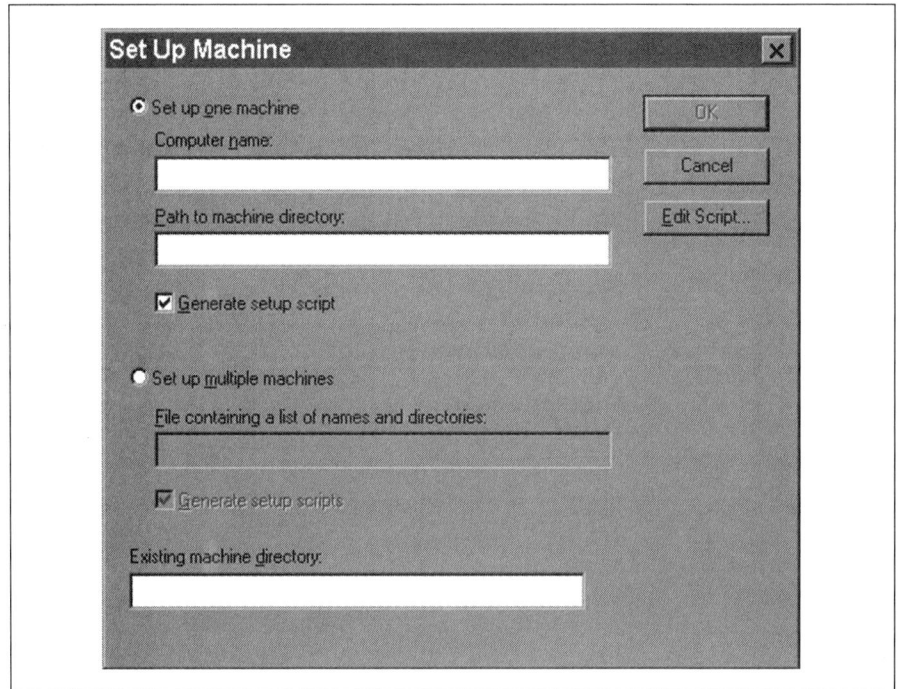

of Netsetup the first time you run it—when it creates the shared directory—then you have to zap the directory and start all over again or it won't let you create new machine directories.

And here's a bug alert: the *Path to machine directory:* field must contain a UNC name, as that's all this dialog box will accept. Unfortunately, that puts a UNC name into a script file that Netsetup creates, and running that causes an error. More on this in the next section called "Fix the Script File."

If you click the Edit Script button (*don't!*) then Netsetup brings you back to the script-builder dialog that you saw several figures back, allowing you to fine-tune a script for a particular machine. *Do not* click this button, as it will make you build a script from nothing; it won't carry over any of the settings that you specified earlier in the *default* script. If you just click OK, then it'll take your default MSBATCH.INF (the one you spent all that time fixing) and shove in the machine directory and machine name.

FIGURE 8.6

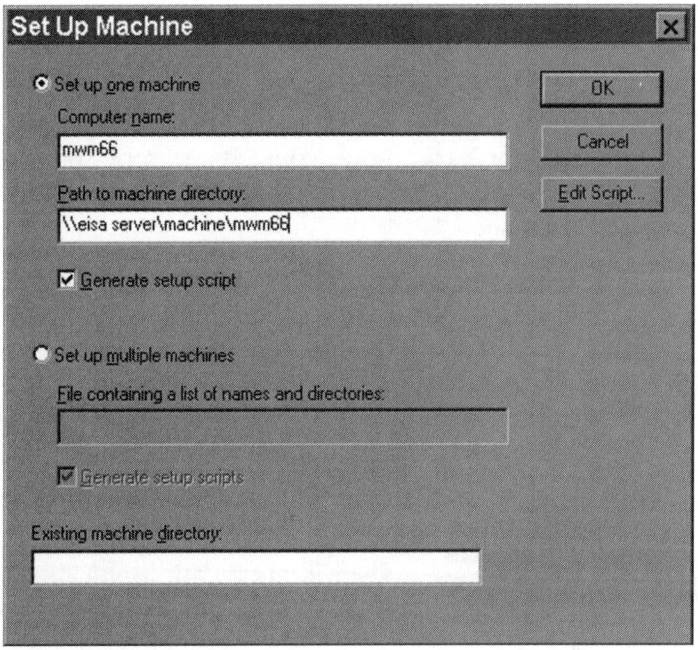

Setting the path
information for a new
machine directory

Once you've clicked OK to end Netsetup, you'll find that the machine directory has been created and the directory contains only an MSBATCH .INF file.

Fix the Script File

Once again, don't trust the network setup program. It tells your system to install Windows 95 to a machine directory named \\eisa server \machine\mwm66. The actual line in the .INF file is InstallDir= "\\eisa server\machine\mwm66"

This seems like it should be correct, but it isn't, invariably leading to a Setup error about being unable to create \\eisa server\machine \mwm66. Instead, go back and change the script file to say:

InstallDir="g:\mwm66"

or something like that, and just remember to map the \\eisa server \machine share to G: before commencing the Setup process. Yes, it's dumb, but I've tried doing setups from inside Windows 3.11, DOS with the MS Workgroup Connection, and DOS with the MS Network Client for DOS version 3.0, all with the same error message. And, by the way, don't try to save yourself a step by specifying "g:\mwm66" while still in Netsetup—it won't take direct drive-letter entries.

Setting Up the Workstation

Once you have the shared directory and any machine directories set up, you'll need to go to the workstation to do a *pull* installation. It's called a pull installation because you run a program on the workstation to pull the files from the server onto your workstation.

N O T E There is, in contrast, a *push* installation which you can accomplish without leaving your desk—but that requires that your firm use Server Management System (SMS) or a similar tool.

Running Windows 95 off the server seems a bit of a chicken-and-egg problem: how do I load an operating system off the server when I have to load software to see the server in the first place? The answer is that your workstation must run a kind of mini operating system, basically DOS, with a small real-mode redirector, to get started. There's an AUTO-EXEC.BAT and a CONFIG.SYS just like in basic MS-DOS, and it includes the Net Start and Net Use commands you need to attach to the shared Windows 95 directories.

So, that means that step one in getting your workstation to run the Windows 95 Setup program is to load some network client software under your old operating system (unless you're just upgrading or reinstalling Windows 95).

> **TIP**
>
> I have encountered a fair number of network-related Setup crashes, most often when I get to the Copying files stage of an installation for floppy disks. (You know, the bang the drum *slooooowly* part of Setup.) They're often trap "D"s on the DOS extender. The DOS extender that's blowing up is in EMM386.EXE, so it might seem like a good idea to just not load EMM386—but then you often don't have enough RAM to run Setup. I don't seem to get this problem when my redirector is the MS Network Client for DOS version 3.0, so I strongly recommend that you run that. These problems seem most prevalent when I'm making a system that can boot entirely from a floppy, so if you're doing workstation installs that will boot from the local hard disk, then you probably don't have as much to worry about.

Once you're connected to the network, map to the shared Windows directory and to the machines directory. In my example (this is easiest to understand with an example), I mapped F: to the shared Windows share and G: to the machine share. Move to the shared Windows directory and run Setup, specifying the machine directory and the MSBATCH.INF file that was created there. For example, I've mapped the network volume that contains my shared Windows files to F: and my machine directory share to G:, so I go to my shared directory and type **f:setup g:\mwm66 \msbatch.inf**

Now, even though we're going to use a setup batch script, let me describe what you'd see if you *didn't* prepare a batch script. The setup looks like a normal Windows setup, except for a few important dialog boxes.

The first new dialog box is labeled Server-based Setup. Choose *Set up Windows to run from a network server* in order to use the shared files. If you don't check that, then Setup will just create a stand-alone installation on your hard disk by copying files from the shared Windows directory. If you choose *Set up Windows to run from a network server*, then you'll get another dialog box, labeled Startup Method. It offers three options:

- Start Windows from my hard disk
- Start Windows from a floppy disk.
- Start Windows from the network (remote boot server).

In most cases, you'll choose the *from my hard disk* option.

Then Setup asks for Machine directory, prompting "Type the name of the directory where you want to put files and settings for this computer. Then click Next to continue." Again, this dialog box will not accept a UNC name; it must be a drive letter and directory name. I specify G:\mwm66, as that's the machine directory that I've created for this computer.

Setup finishes the first part of the Setup Wizard, copies some files, and reboots. Unfortunately, in the case of *my* network, the reboot failed; you may come across this as well. If you're like me and put a space in the name of your server, then Windows 95 Setup isn't too bright. It puts Net Use statements into your AUTOEXEC.BAT, without quotes:

```
net use f: \\eisa server\w95shr
net use g: \\eisa server\machine
```

This doesn't work. I just edited the AUTOEXEC.BAT file (yes, there's still one of those, and it's essential to booting Windows 95 from the network) to put quotes around the UNCs, so the commands look like this:

```
net use f: "\\eisa server\w95shr"
net use g: "\\eisa server\machine"
```

I rebooted, and Setup could finish up its work. The result: a windows directory on my C: drive with 1.4MB of files on it, and mwm66, in the Machine share, has 1.3MB in it.

Now let's get back to the setup script. Despite the notion that this has to be a hands-free installation, there are a few places where you'll have to press a key or respond to Setup:

- You get an initial "Press Enter to run Setup" message, which requires you to hit Enter.

- After Setup runs ScanDisk, you have to press X to exit ScanDisk.

- The license agreement requires an Alt+Y acknowledgment.

- Setup may complain about the presence of OS/2 or NT on the system; you must respond to those dialogs.

- When the pre-GUI part of Windows 95 loads and initially logs you on to the network, you have to enter your name and password.

- You must again log in from the GUI once 95 is up. As a matter of fact, that's a down side of running Windows off a shared directory: You have to log in twice every time you start up Windows.

Review: .INF Settings for Network Setups

Before moving on to floppy setup options, let's take a minute and focus on the particular special settings you'll need in order to direct your system to do a network setup. The commands you have to know are:

- **Installdir** This goes in the [setup] section; all of the other commands go into the [network] section. This points to the machine directory, and it should be a drive-letter name, not a UNC name.
- **WorkstationSetup** When set to 1, this tells Setup that you'll run Windows from the shared Windows directory every time that you start Windows.
- **DisplayWorkstationSetup** When set to 0, this suppresses dialog boxes, assisting in building a hands-free setup.
- **Clients and Protocols** This names the network redirectors and transport protocols.
- **HDBoot** When set to 1, this instructs Setup to put the boot files on the PC's local hard disk. If set to 0, it tells Setup either to prepare a boot floppy or to set up an area for a network boot via a LAN card with a boot ROM.
- **RPLSetup** If you've set HDBoot to 0, this tells whether to boot from floppy (set the value to 0) or LAN card (set the value to 1).

By starting from a working script and changing these values as appropriate, you can modify scripts to do any kind of installation that you like.

Setting Up 95 for Floppy-Based Boots

You can take these installations a step further and tell Windows 95 to put *all* of your files in the machine directory, and just build a floppy disk that you can use to start 95. Just go to the MSBATCH.INF file that you're using to drive Setup and change HDBOOT=1 to HDBOOT=0, and be sure that there's also a RPLSetup=0 line in the same section. You'll be prompted to create a floppy disk even if you put EBD=0 in the file, as this is a bootable floppy with a small network redirector on it.

That process generally works well, but I've found a few problems with it. As my problems may simply be due to my not having done something right, you might not experience these troubles; if so, all the better. But if you *do* run into trouble creating a floppy-based boot, take a look at this section.

Check AUTOEXEC.BAT

As I've said a number of times before, when the Setup program writes out AUTOEXEC.BAT files, it doesn't construct proper Net Use statements for servers that have spaces in their names.

Ignore the DBLSPACE Error Message

When I boot from the floppy that Windows Setup built, I get the following message:

> You are loading the incorrect version of DBLSPACE.BIN for this version of MS-DOS. Since this configuration is untested, you should correct this problem as soon as possible. Press ENTER to continue starting MS-DOS.

For the life of me, I have no idea what this is all about. But I don't use DBLSPACE (and in fact I'd imagine that nobody with a hard-diskless workstation would either), so it seems not to be a problem.

Be Careful Editing MACHINES.INI

Before your PC can start floppy-booting 95 from your network, the PC must be able to find its Registry.

Unfortunately, however, the Registry is too big to fit on a floppy, so 95 does a little kludge called Setmdir upon bootup. Setmdir assists in the process of loading 95 from the network by pointing your PC at the network location where it can find the Registry. The AUTOEXEC.BAT that my system automatically generated looked like this:

```
snapshot /s
net start
net logon /savepw:no /y
net use f: \\eisa server\c
path=f:\w95shr\;f:\w95shr\command
setmdir
```

Snapshot helps Windows 95 change your system over to protected mode, but don't worry about it; it has nothing to do with fixing your MACHINES .INI file. The Net commands start up the network and map the F: drive to my server so that the Path commands can help my bootup disk find the bulk of the Windows 95 files.

The problem comes with Setmdir.

Its name is short for *set machine directory*. Suppose you put all your machine directories on a server called Wally, on a share named Macshare, in directories named machine\pc1, machine\dellpc, machine\billspc, and so on—Setmdir is the program that lets the 95 startup routine find it.

The trick to how it does that is that all Ethernet and Token Ring boards have unique 48-bit ID numbers (which become 12-digit hexadecimal numbers), and a program called Setmdir looks up a computer's machine directory via that ID number. For example, the hexadecimal representation of the Ethernet ID on the machine I'm currently working on is 00608CDE8F48, and its machine directory is \\eisa server\c \machine\mwm66—*that's* the connection that Setmdir must make.

You could have hundreds of machines booting from floppies, so you'd have to somehow keep track of which machine used what machine directory. Windows 95 organizes all of this data by keeping it in a file called MACHINES.INI on the shared Windows 95 directory.

Let's see how I told 95 where to find the machine directory. I create an entry in MACHINES.INI with the name **[00608CDE8F48]**. It contains one parameter called **sysdatpath**. (Don't type sysdat*a*path—leave that last *a* off of *data*.) I added a Net Use command to my AUTOEXEC.BAT just so I have G: mapped to the machine share. The entire MACHINES.INI entry looks like this:

```
[00608CDE8F48]
sysdatpath=f:\machine\mwm66
```

But what if I didn't want to do the extra Net Use? You can add a mapping line after the sysdatpath line. If the machine directories were on the share named Macdata on server Wally, in a directory named machine\mwm66, then I'd add a line to map \\wally\macdata and use that map to refer to machine\mwm66, like so:

```
[00608CDE8F48]
sysdatpath=x:\machine\mwm66
x=\\wally\macdata
```

So, remember: You only need to do the extra mapping lines if your machine directories aren't already on the same share as your shared Windows files.

Just to be sure that this is clear, suppose I were going to install a second PC. First, I have to find out what its Ethernet ID is. If the machine is already running a Microsoft network client, then I probably can just go to the command line and type **net diag /s**. I'll be prompted for a network name, but I just press Enter. I see a screen like the one in Figure 8.7.

All you care about here is the *Permanent node name*, 0000C0573E82; that's the Ethernet ID. Suppose this machine's name is SDG90 and it has a machine directory in machine called sdg90. As that, too, is on my \\wally\macdata share, my MACHINES.INI now looks like this:

```
[00608CDE8F48]
sysdatpath=x:\machine\mwm66
x=\\wally\macdata
[0000C0573E82]
sysdatpath=x:\machine\sdg90
x=\\wally\macdata
```

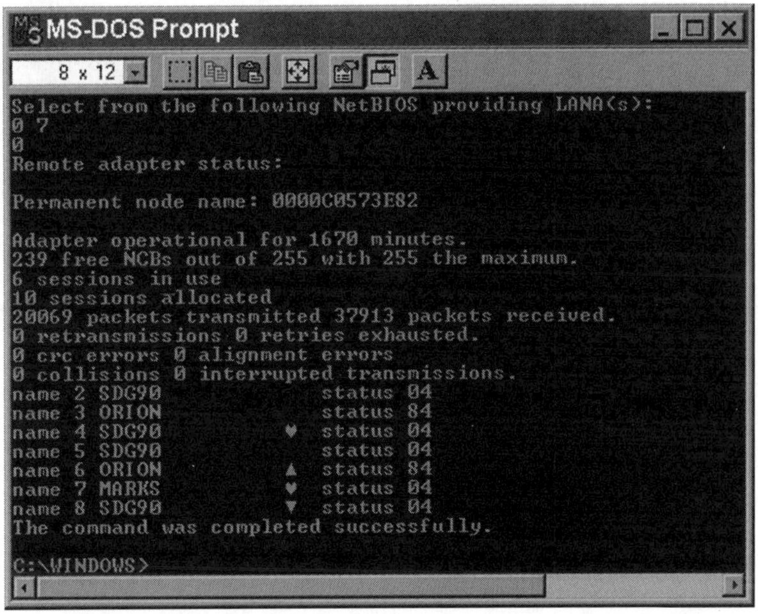

FIGURE 8.7

Finding a machine's
Ethernet ID

```
MS-DOS Prompt                                    _ □ X

 8 x 12 ▼    ▢ 🗎 🖺 ⊠  🖳🗗  A

Select from the following NetBIOS providing LANA(s):
0 7
0
Remote adapter status:

Permanent node name: 0000C0573E82

Adapter operational for 1670 minutes.
239 free NCBs out of 255 with 255 the maximum.
6 sessions in use
10 sessions allocated
20069 packets transmitted 37913 packets received.
0 retransmissions 0 retries exhausted.
0 crc errors 0 alignment errors
0 collisions 0 interrupted transmissions.
name 2 SDG90                    status 04
name 3 ORION                    status 84
name 4 SDG90           ♥        status 04
name 5 SDG90                    status 04
name 6 ORION           ▲        status 84
name 7 MARKS           ♥        status 04
name 8 SDG90           ▼        status 04
The command was completed successfully.

C:\WINDOWS>
◄                                                      ►
```

NOTE Remember, the only reason that I did the x=\\wally\macdata
lines was because the machine directories were on different
shares from the shared Windows ones.

Don't Log On as the Machine

For some reason, the simple network redirector wants to log you on with
a user name that's the same as the machine ID. That's not going to work,
because (at least on my NT-based network—you know, my *Microsoft* NT
Server-based network?) there's no automatic process for creating a user
named 00608CDE8F48. So, if you log in as that person, your bootup will
bomb, as the attempts to network shares will fail.

Now, I could imagine situations where this would be a *good* thing—perhaps you want to create machine accounts with different rights than the
users who will log on to them—but the Microsoft documentation is silent
on these matters.

N O T E   If you've been skipping past this discussion because you boot from your hard disk with help from the network, then think again: it's really convenient to be able to create a floppy that will boot a machine entirely off the network without needing any help from the hard disk.

Using User Profiles

One major way to make your Windows 95 installation more network-enabled is with *user profiles*. They're a trifle complex, so I want to introduce them in three steps:

- First, you have to understand what a user profile is and what it includes.

- Next, I'll show you how to enable your system to use user profiles—Windows 95 installations don't use them by default.

- Finally, you'll see how to keep user profiles on the network, so that they can follow users wherever they go.

Introduction to User Profiles

You may have noticed that Windows 95 asks you to log on to your machine, sometimes even if you don't have a network. The reason for that is so Windows can keep track of who's on the computer at the moment. Ordinarily, that's not information of any value. But with user profiles, it can be quite useful.

Suppose, for example, that you are a person who shares a PC with other people; perhaps you only use the PC a few hours a day, as do the two or three other people who use that PC. It can be frustrating to spend time getting your desktop set up just the way you like it, only to find that the next time you attempt to use the PC the last person who used it rearranged everything.

You may recall that the Registry is stored in two files, named USER.DAT and SYSTEM.DAT. The USER.DAT information is where the user profile information is stored, and, normally, there's only one USER.DAT on a machine, sitting in the windows directory. But, if you tell your system to allow multiple profiles (I'll show you how in a minute), then Windows will create a new directory, called \windows\profiles, which will then contain folders for each person. In Figure 8.8, you can see that on my system, I have a profiles directory with folders for a user called Mark and another called MarkS (my supervisor account). Inside each directory is a USER.DAT file; there's a USER.DA0 file in MarkS because I've used that account more than once, and so the normal backup file got created.

What's kept in a profile?

- Desktop settings, including colors, background, and any shortcuts *on the desktop*; shortcuts that aren't on the desktop won't be saved as user-specific shortcuts.

- Program groups, both names and contents.

- Virtually anything set with the Control Panel.

- Persistent network connections.

- Applications settings for apps that are 95-aware and write information to the Registry.

FIGURE 8.8

Contents of \Profiles directories

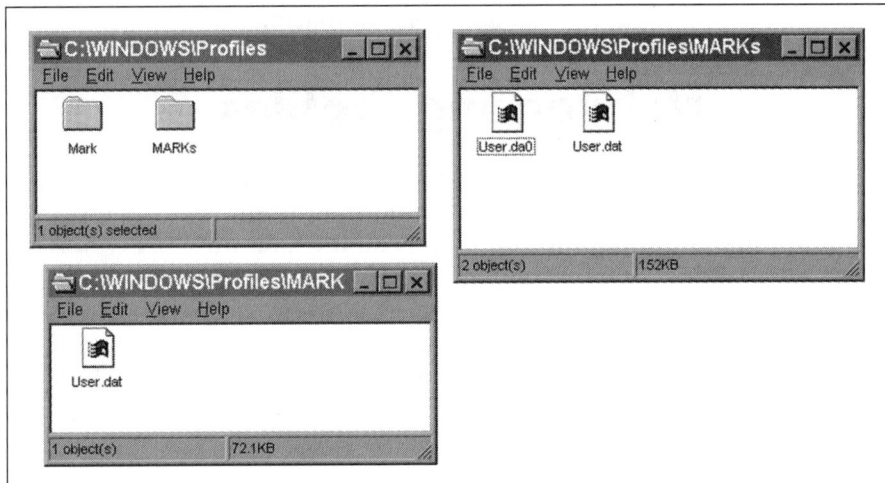

Pre-Windows 95 apps don't use the Registry, so any settings made to them are global across all users on a machine. For example, say that I log on to my computer as Mark, change the default document directory for Ami Pro, and then log off. If I log back on as MarkS, then Ami Pro will still be using the default directory that I set it to when logged on as Mark; this is because Ami uses one of the old-style .INI files to keep its settings and there's no user-specific setting capability. In contrast, if I were running the Windows 95 version of WordPro, and Mark changed WordPro's default directory, then that wouldn't affect MarkS's use of WordPro. This is because WordPro would store its configuration information in the Registry and Mark would have a different Registry from MarkS. (I suppose you could call this multiple profile disorder.)

Using Profiles

To enable Windows 95 to use profiles, start the Control Panel and open up the Passwords applet. Choose the User Profiles tab, and you'll see a dialog box like Figure 8.9.

Click the *Users can customize...* radio button. You may also want to select *Include desktop icons...* and *Include Start menu...* to complete the separation between users. I usually check *Include desktop icons* and not *Include Start Menu* because that selection means that when I install a new program as one user, then I don't see it as the second user. Keep the second one unchecked, and any new programs installed by any user will be available to all users of that machine.

Networking Profiles

This works very nicely, as I can create two personas for myself—the Mark account is my mild-mannered author/lecturer self, equipped with a crowded desktop of all the tools I use in my normal work, but none of the powers and abilities of a network administrator. The MarkS account has a simpler desktop, as it's only used when there's a network problem, and I must step into the computer's telephone booth, emerging in my uniform with the big red S (for Supervisor) on the chest.

FIGURE 8.9

Enabling user profiles

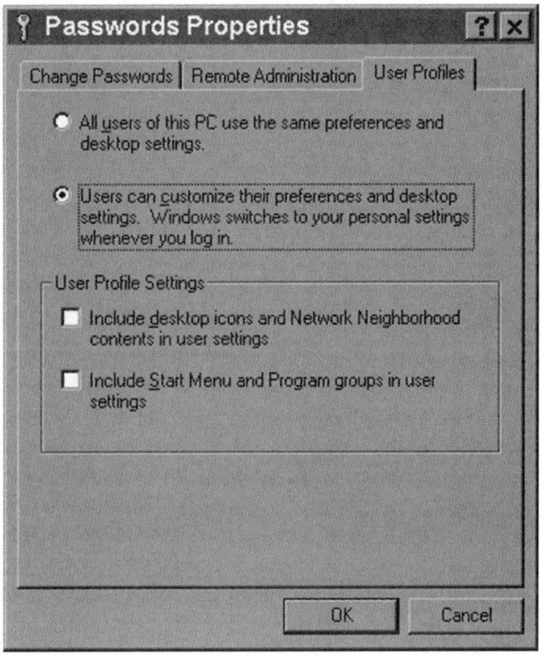

But when I go to a computer other than my own, I'm back to Square One. That computer has no knowledge of my profiles. Obviously, what I need is to network those little suckers. But how?

Quite easily, actually. It's one of those things that they engineered into Windows 95 for minimum pain and suffering. Basically, if you have a network and a home directory, then 95 automatically keeps the profiles in your home directory and looks for them when you log on. There are a few considerations you should be aware of, however:

- If the program groups rove with you on the network, then you may find yourself with a lot of pointers to programs that don't exist.

- You must have a network that you explicitly log on to; in particular, an NT or Novell network will work best.

- This will slow down your logins somewhat; I find that I usually have to wait about an extra 15 seconds to suck up the profile from the network.

All you have to do to make this work is to establish a home directory on your primary logon network. In the Novell world, it's in the MAIL directory; on an NT network, it's the USERS directory. You as administrator needn't do anything to start the system using networked profiles—95 detects the presence of a home directory and uses it, even if there are profiles on the local hard disk. The profiles on the network take precedence.

If you have an NT network, then this won't work unless you log explicitly on to the domain; if you've forgotten how to do that, here's how: You open the Control Panel, then Network, and click Client for Microsoft Networks, then Properties. You'll see a check box labeled Logon validation, which instructs Windows to log you on to an NT domain. Fill in the name of the domain, restart the computer, and you're in business.

Forcing People to Use a Particular Profile

Look in a user's home directory (if they're using profiles) and you'll find the file USER.DAT, the user-specific part of the Registry. You can forever freeze a user's profile settings by renaming USER.DAT to USER.MAN. The extension denotes a *mandatory* profile. The existence of a mandatory profile overrides other profiles, and when users log in, they'll get the settings in their USER.MAN file. If they make any changes to their 95 desktop, then the changes will remain in effect until they log out—but the changes won't be saved and aren't used the next time they log in.

To build a profile from scratch, you'll have to log on as a user, set up the desktop as you like it, and then save it so you get the USER.DAT to work from. It's a bit cumbersome, and it's probably why you'll opt for the System Policy Editor rather than mandatory profiles as a control mechanism.

By the way, user profiles exist under Windows NT as well, but they are different things altogether; there's no relationship between a 95 profile and an NT profile, unfortunately.

Controlling Desktops from the Network

Mandatory profiles are one way to exercise control over user's desktops, but they're not a really easy-to-work-with method. Windows 95 provides some other ways to control desktops. Before going on, however, I should warn you: we're about to embark on a controversial subject. But it's one that deserves a bit of discussion, if only because it seems that no one else talks about it when discussing a tool in Windows called the *System Policy Editor.*

The System Policy Editor allows a network administrator to exert a tremendous amount of control over what users can and can't do with their workstations. The big questions are: Is that right? and Should people be able to control the things on their desktops?

I'm not one hundred percent certain how I feel about this. If I were a parent of a small child, then I might like to be able to control what my child could or couldn't do with the computer, simply to protect the child from themself. But as a "power user," I would bridle at the idea of some network administrator telling me what I could and couldn't do with my computer.

On the other hand, I have *also* been a network administrator, and there are a lotta people out there who just plain don't *want* to become computer experts—they find the monstrous array of options that they're given from simply clicking the Start button to be annoying. They'll *welcome* you simplifying their user interface.

And, finally, let's face it: there are definitely some people in the workforce who waste their own time and their employer's time by playing games or tweaking their systems. We all know the guy who has a different silly bitmap every day or the woman who delights in showing you her latest set of bizarre system sounds. The computers with which we work on our jobs *aren't* our computers. They're bought and paid for by our employers, and those employers have a right to tell us that we can't play Solitaire when we're supposed to be on duty. The System Policy Editor isn't one of those tools that watch you on a minute-by-minute basis to see how many keystrokes or mouse clicks you produce—that would be, in my opinion, an invasion beyond the standard employer/employee relationship—but, in the end analysis, the decision is one that must be made by each company on its own.

How Desktop Control Works

There are several avenues for remote control.

- You can remotely view and modify Registries, provided that you have loaded support for remote Registry control on each workstation that you want to remotely control. (It's a service in the `\admin \nettools\remotreg` folder on the CD-ROM.)

- You can use mandatory user profiles to define how a workstation operates when a particular user logs on to the workstation. As you've seen, these profiles do not keep users from changing the Windows desktop while using the computer; they just keep the users from *saving* any changes. So, there's some control here, but not a lot. You must set up each desired user workstation to use these profiles.

- You can make certain profiles mandatory and unchangeable with the System Policy Editor, which creates a file called `CONFIG.POL`.

In the following sections, you'll learn more about these options (other than mandatory profiles, which we've already covered).

The System Policy Editor

As you know, Windows 95 builds a new Registry every time you start up your system, constructing it out of `USER.DAT` and `SYSTEM.DAT` for most users. Now, if you *also* have a `CONFIG.POL` file in the right place (I'll define the right place in a minute, I promise), then Windows will use restrictions in `CONFIG.POL` to modify how it builds the resulting Registry.

Using system policies requires that you have a network, and that people log on to the network; a loose association of Windows machines doing peer-to-peer networking can't use system policies. The overview on creating and using system policies is the following:

1. Install the System Policy Editor off your Windows 95 CD-ROM; it's in the `\admin\apptools\poledit` directory.
2. Create a policy file with the Policy Editor.
3. Save it as `CONFIG.POL` into your `netlogon` directory on an NT system or into the `\sys\public` directory on the user's preferred NetWare server.
4. Ensure that all your workstations log on to an NT domain or a NetWare preferred server.

And that's it. Now let's take a closer look.

Installing the System Policy Editor

First, you have to install the editor and some support files. Just open up the Control Panel, choose Add/Remove Programs, and click the Windows Setup tab. Click the Have Disk button, and then direct it to the directory that contains the Policy Editor, most likely `\admin\apptools\poledit`. You'll get the option to install both the Policy Editor and something called Group Policies; take them both. The Policy Editor will now be in `programs\accessories\system tools`.

Building a Policy

Let's see how to use this tool to start to control how people work with Windows 95. My example assumes that you have an NT-based network, but it'll work on Novell in just about the same way.

Start up the Policy Editor. Click File, and New File. You'll see a screen like Figure 8.10.

The Policy Editor lets you make either policies that are specific to particular people or blanket policies with the Default User or the Default Computer.

FIGURE 8.10

Blank user profile file

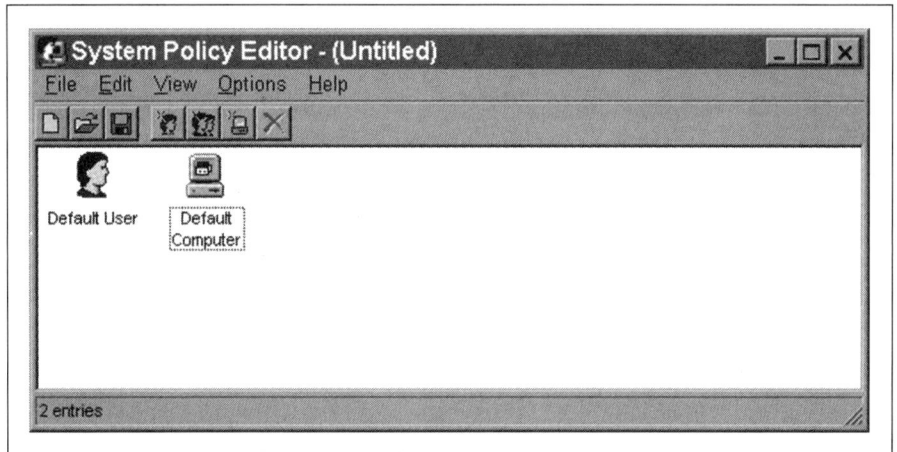

FIGURE 8.11

Preliminary user
properties dialog box

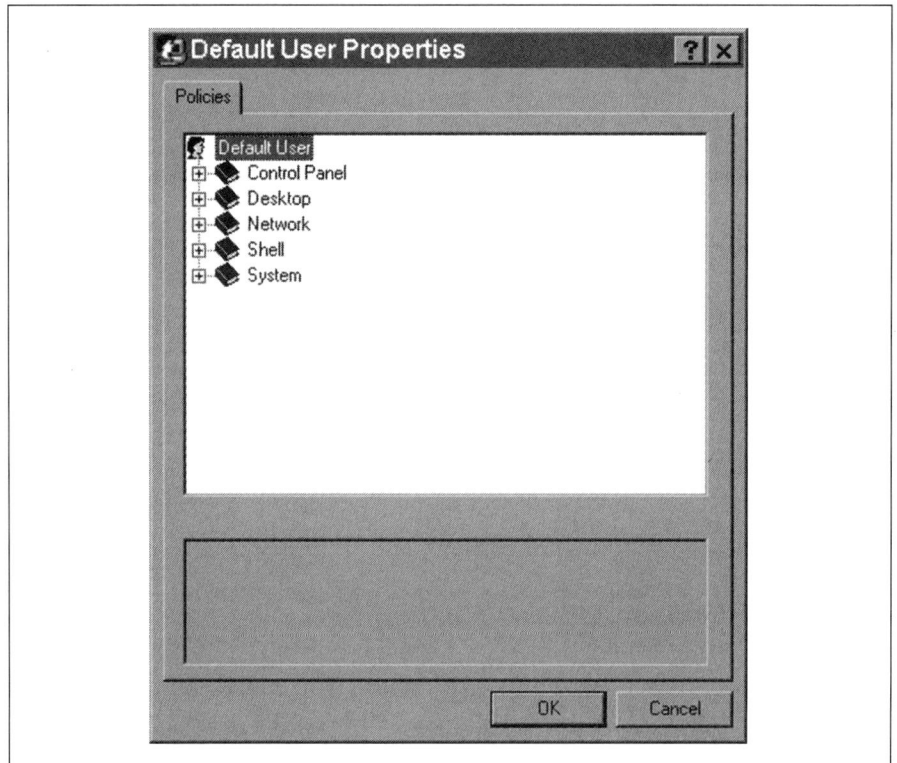

Let's set everyone's wallpaper to Rivets and take away their ability to change it (heh, heh). Wallpaper is a user-specific item, so we'll find it by double-clicking on Default user. You'll see a screen like the one in Figure 8.11.

The wallpaper is a Control Panel item, so open it up and you'll see Display as an option. Choose that, and you'll see a dialog box like Figure 8.12.

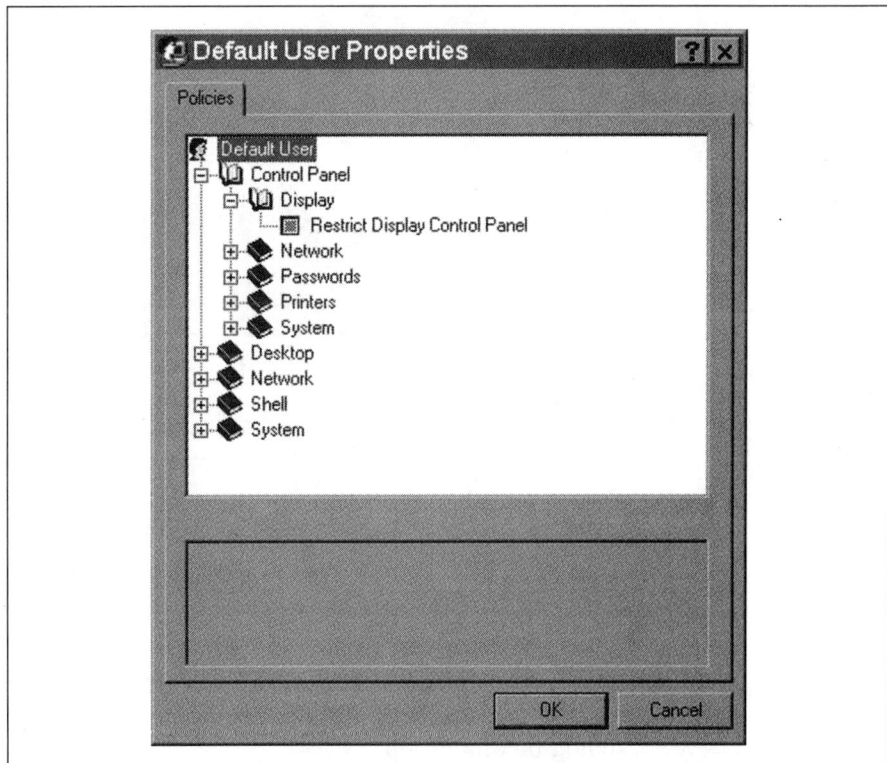

We're going to remove the user's ability to change their backgrounds, so we're restricting the Display part of the Control Panel. Notice that the check box is gray; that means that this option is neither enabled nor disabled—gray means there is no policy about this. Check the box, and you'll see a dialog box like the one in Figure 8.13.

FIGURE 8.13

Display policy in effect

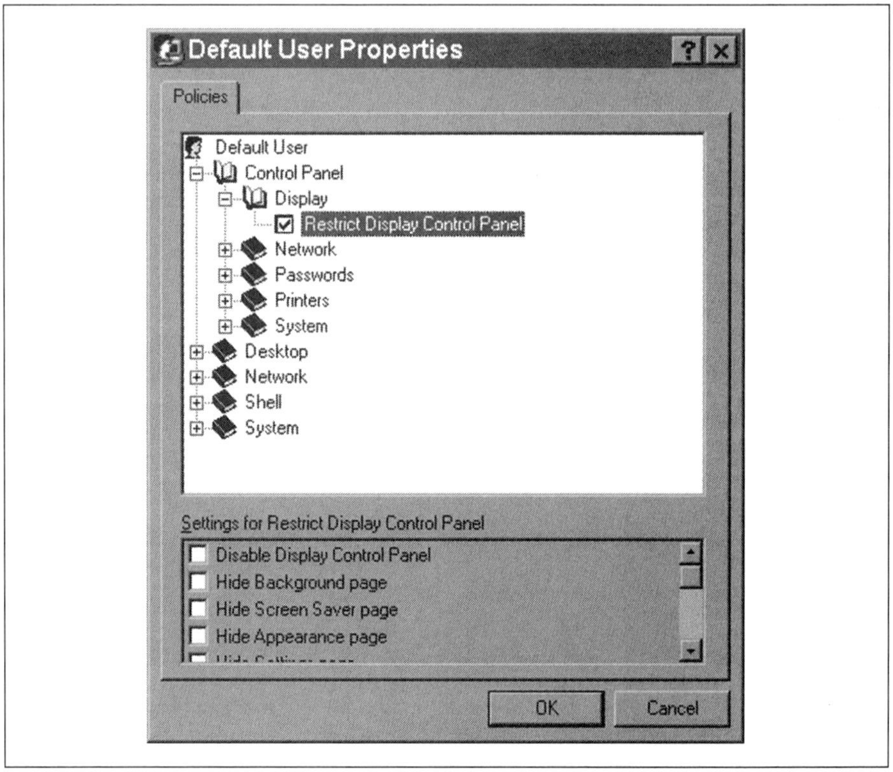

Once the box is checked, you get a panel on the lower part of the dialog box that enumerates the things that you can control. One of them is Hide Background page; check it.

Now you've removed all users' abilities to modify their wallpaper. Next, let's set the actual wallpaper. The wallpaper itself is part of the Desktop, so open up the Desktop branch and check the Wallpaper box. You'll see a dialog box like Figure 8.14.

The lower pane now lets you select a wallpaper—the drop-down list box will show you which files are available. Now you're done, so click OK.

Now all you need to do is to save this to the proper place. Its name should be CONFIG.POL. As I'm running an NT network, I save the file in the NETLOGON share on my primary domain controller, in a directory called c:\winnt35\system32\repl\import\scripts. On a NetWare

FIGURE 8.14

Setting a mandatory
wallpaper

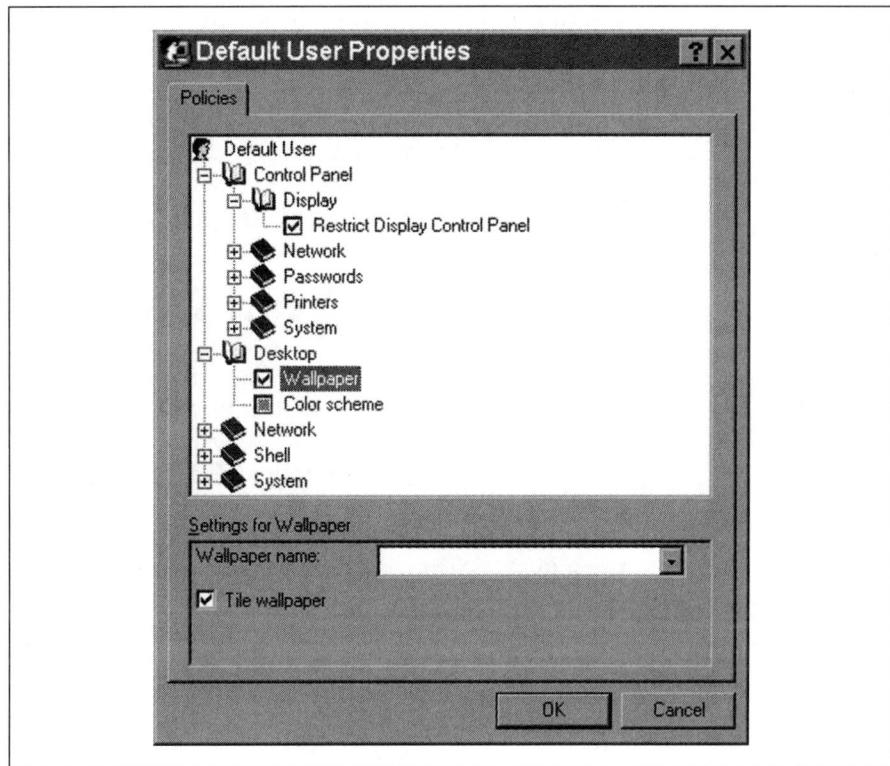

server, I'd just put it on my users' preferred server's `sys\public`
directory.

Exit the System Policy Editor and exit Windows. When you return to Windows and log on to the network, you'll see that you have the Rivets wallpaper and no way to change it.

Note that I did *not* have to have user profiles enabled in order to do this; all I had to do was to ensure that I logged on to the domain.

Defeating a Policy

Hmmm… now suppose I'm a smart, but evil, user. I want to *change* my wallpaper, dammit! Let my pixels go!

There is a way around it, also with the help of the System Policy Editor. I (the evil user) start up the System Policy Editor. This time, however, I click File/Open Registry. I see a user and a machine, just as before—except *this* time what I'm seeing refers to my machine. I double-click on the User, and I see the same categories as before: Control Panel, Desktop, Network, Shell, and System. I click on Desktop and there's the wallpaper. I change it, and the change takes place immediately; no more rivets!

Keeping Users from Defeating Policies

Okay, you're now thinking, "Gee, thanks, Mark; I was getting all excited about these system policies, but now you tell me that any user can defeat them with their own copy of the System Policy Editor. *Now* what do I do?" If you're in the System Policy Editor at the moment, take a look at `default user\system\restrictions`. One of the things that you can restrict is called *Disable Registry editing tools*. Click that one, and neither Regedit nor the System Policy Editor works.

Your next question will no doubt be, "ummm …what happens when I— I mean, a *friend* of mine—disables the Registry editing tools just for fun, but now can't do anything about it, because it's no longer possible to run Regedit or System Policy Editor?"

First, if you put the restriction in `CONFIG.POL`, rather than in the Registry of a particular machine, and if you applied it to a particular user, rather than all users, then you can just log on as someone else, run the System Policy Editor, and then change the setting.

Alternatively, you could set the policy named *Only Run Allowed Windows Applications*, and leave out Regedit and Poledit.

If you did it for *everyone*, then just log on to the network as a supervisor and take it out of the `Netlogon` or `\sys\public` directory. Use the backups from the day before as a starting point for rebuilding where you were. (`CONFIG.POL` is not an ASCII file, so it wouldn't be very easy to splice out *just* the no-edit rule.)

If you did it in the local Registry, then you might try booting up from the Windows 95 startup disk and running the simple Registry editor that comes on that disk. Delete the RestrictRun entry from the following key:

```
hkey_current_user\software\microsoft\windows
\currentversion\policies\explore
```

What If You Want CONFIG.POL Somewhere Else?

You've already seen where the policies file CONFIG.POL should go. But what if you want to put it somewhere else? You can do that, by telling your Registry to find CONFIG.POL in another location.

The System Policy Editor is also a Registry editor. From the File menu, choose Open Registry, and you see a subset of Registry entries. Change where your computer gets its CONFIG.POL from with the following changes:

1. Open up Default Computer.

2. Open up Network, then Update.

3. You'll see an option called Remote Update; choose it (as shown in Figure 8.15).

4. Where you see Update Mode, select Manual. Then, in the field labeled Path for manual update, put the path—the manual says a UNC name is required, but a drive designation seems to work sometimes—and there you should enter the location and name of the policy file. Include the name of the file; it shouldn't be \\server \share; it should be \\server\share\config.pol.

This can be useful for network systems that aren't NetWare or NT-based.

Things That Go Wrong: Troubleshooting Policies

In the process of learning about how system policies work, I managed to do a few dumb things that kept my experiments from working. Here are

FIGURE 8.15

Choose Remote Update

a few suggestions on things to look for if you're having trouble getting a policy to work.

You Get No Policy Effect at All

It's like you didn't do anything. You can cause this in a number of ways.

- Most likely is that you have a Novell network, and you've put the .POL file in the correct \sys\public directory, but you're using the *Novell* client/redirector software, not the Microsoft NetWare Client software. You must be using the Microsoft NetWare client to automatically download policies. If you're *not* using the Microsoft client, then you'll have to use manual downloading and point to the server in question *using UNC names*. For example, if your NetWare server's name is Master, and you've put the CONFIG.POL file in a directory named `policy` on the `sys` volume, then the path to the file is `\\master\sys\policy`.

- If you're running NT servers, then it is likely that your network client isn't logging on to the NT domain.

- With any other kind of network (that is, with anything other than a Novell network or NT servers), you have to enable manual downloading.

- One possible problem is a failure to read the policies correctly, whether through a network error or via a file corruption. In the very same screen where you select manual or automatic downloading, there is a check box which will instruct 95 to display error messages if there's a problem reading `CONFIG.POL`.

- While messing around in the Policy Editor, you may have edited your own Registry and disabled policies altogether. In the Settings for Remote Update screen, the one that, again, selects manual or automatic download of policies, the *default* is to *automatically* download policies. If, when playing around with the Editor, you disabled the Remote Settings box altogether, then your system will not get or obey system policies.

You Change a Policy, but the Old One Remains in Effect

Remember that the System Policy Editor can directly edit a Registry as well as the policy file. You can go directly to a workstation and make a policy that is local to that machine only. For example, suppose you impose some ugly wallpaper, but then go back in the System Policy Editor and remove the wallpaper, as well as restore the user's ability to change the wallpaper.

So the user reboots, finds that he or she is still stuck with the dumb wallpaper, and can't change it. To make things more confusing, *other* users are now freed from the wallpaper, and are using their newfound powers to set their wallpaper to all kinds of bitmaps.

Go to the user's machine and pull up their Registry with the System Policy Editor, or just access it over the network if you have remote administration enabled. Look at the Registry entries to see if you've disabled something. For example, in the Wallpaper case, look in the Local User definition under Desktop and Control Panel. Locally set Registry restrictions seem to take precedence over any found on the network CONFIG.POL.

There's Something in the Registry That You Want to Control, but There Are No Settings for It in the System Policy Editor

All the CONFIG.POL file does is to provide a kind of a mask that your Windows 95 workstation uses when building its Registry (an operation that it does every time you log on). There are dozens of entries in the Registry, but not all of them are in the System Policy Editor.

Or, at least, none of them are in the System Policy Editor *by default.* You see, the System Policy Editor works off a *template*, a file that tells it which Registry entries to play with. You can modify that by building your own templates; see the section "Using Templates" later in this chapter for more information.

You've Locked Yourself Out of the Computer with Policies

If the computer won't let you do much of anything, try this.

First, boot in Safe Mode Command Prompt. Export the Registry to a file using Regedit (yes, it works in text mode). Just type

Regedit /e tempreg.txt

Then, edit TEMPREG.TXT. Look in hkey_local_machine\system\currentcontrolset\control\update; you'll see a value entry that looks like the following:

```
"UpdateMode"=dword:00000001
"NetworkPath"=""
```

Just change 00000001 to 00000000.

Rebuild the Registry with this file, erasing any current Registry entries like so:

regedit /c tempreg.txt

Then just reboot. You're fixed.

Group Policies

It would obviously be too cumbersome to create specific policies for every user. As both NT and Novell support the notion of groups of users, Windows can leverage those groups by allowing you to set policies for entire groups.

Someone can even be a member of more than one group, with different policies. You just rank the groups in terms of their importance, and whenever there's a conflict then the policy of the more important group prevails.

There's only one trick to this: In order for this to work, you must install the file GROUPPOL.DLL on each of the network's workstations. The Policy Editor then lets you rank the relative importance of the various groups.

Custom Folders

Your control of a desktop doesn't stop there. You can customize five special folders:

- The Programs folder
- The Network Neighborhood
- Desktop icons/shortcuts
- The Start menu
- The Startup folder

You can control all of these through settings in the System Policy Editor. Look at the power of this: You can control exactly what items appear on your users' menus, and, via the Startup folder, control what programs run on your users' machines. Additionally, you can remove the MS-DOS prompt, the Run option from the Start button, and drives from My Computer, leaving no backdoor way to start other programs. Again, this may be good or bad, depending on your corporate culture.

Using Templates

Think of the System Policy Editor in this way: Insofar as it modifies Registries, it's kind of an alternative Registry Editor. But it's more than that, as you know if you've ever *used* Regedit—Regedit is about as user-unfriendly as programs get. In contrast, the System Policy Editor presents a subset of the Registry in an easier-to-read fashion.

In a sense, that's also what the Control Panel does. So how are the Control Panel and the System Policy Editor different? Well, first of all, the Control Panel only works with Registry settings; it doesn't create constraints (policies). Second, the Control Panel isn't really configurable, save for the fact that you can remove things from it—you can't add things.

Add things? Yes. Open up the System Policy Editor and you see a number of settings—all controls for parts of the Registry. But *which* parts of the Registry? Ones specified by a file called `ADMIN.ADM`.

`ADMIN.ADM` is a *template*, an ASCII file written in a programming language defined in the Resource Kit. Summarized, there are several parts to a template:

- A *class* is the subtree, like Local User or Machine.

- A *category* is just a name used to group a number of Registry items. For example, if you wanted to organize your policies so that there was a small book icon for "color," which controlled the colors of a number of disparate keys, then you'd end up taking keys from different parts of the tree. Each category entry creates one of the book icons. You can nest categories.

- *Policy* is the description for the particular value entry that you're going to modify.

- *Keyname* is, as you'd imagine, a Registry key name like `software \microsoft\windows\currentversion\policies\explorer \restrictrun`. It specifies the target of the editor item.

- Valuename is the actual name of the value within the specified key.
- *Part* tells the System Policy Editor what kind of interface item to use—a check box, list box, or whatever.

This is perhaps understood best with an example. Here, I've opened the System Policy Editor, double-clicked on User, opened Control Panel, and within that found Restrict Display Control Panel. The dialog box appears as in Figure 8.16.

FIGURE 8.16

Options for restricting display

Here's the fragment of code that handles this.

```
CLASS USER

CATEGORY !!ControlPanel
  CATEGORY !!CPL_Display
    POLICY !!CPL_Display_Restrict
    KEYNAME Software\Microsoft\Windows\CurrentVersion \Policies\System
      PART !!CPL_Display_Disable CHECKBOX
      VALUENAME NoDispCPL
      END PART

      PART !!CPL_Display_HideBkgnd CHECKBOX
      VALUENAME NoDispBackgroundPage
      END PART

      PART !!CPL_Display_HideScrsav CHECKBOX
      VALUENAME NoDispScrSavPage
      END PART

      PART !!CPL_Display_HideAppearance CHECKBOX
      VALUENAME NoDispAppearancePage
      END PART

      PART !!CPL_Display_HideSettings CHECKBOX
      VALUENAME NoDispSettingsPage
      END PART
    END POLICY
  END CATEGORY     ; Display
```

CLASS USER defines the part of this file that describes the User icon. Category !!ControlPanel says, first, create a book icon, and second, name it something defined by !!ControlPanel. !!ControlPanel is a string variable defined later in the file as:

```
ControlPanel="Control Panel"
```

The characters "Control Panel" are then displayed next to the book icon.

POLICY !!CPL_DISPLAY_RESTRICT says to display CPL_DIS-PLAY_RESTRICT, which I found later in the program to equal Restrict Display Control Panel. You see that is displayed in the top pane, but there are several potential ways to restrict the Display Control Panel. As it turns out, they are all values within the `software\microsoft\windows\currentversion\policies\system` key.

The triples that appear next look like

```
PART !!CPL_Display_Disable CHECKBOX
VALUENAME NoDispCPL
END PART
```

Each one of these triples describes a value that can live within the key. The string variable is just the label to put in the dialog box, and CHECKBOX says to just put a check box in place, rather than an edit field or list box or whatever. VALUENAME says, "Once you have the value checked or not checked by the user, then this is the name of the actual value to stuff in the Registry."

Templates make the System Policies Editor an incredibly flexible tool; you can even use it to control Registry entries created by third-party vendors. The main problem with it is that Microsoft hasn't documented all of *their* Registry entries. (Grumble, grumble; they did it for NT, though, and that's been tremendously helpful.)

Let's build a sample template for an imaginary Registry entry. Suppose I have a software company named MarkSoft, and all of my programs open up with a welcome banner. You can modify that welcome banner by adding a value called WText to `system\marksoft\currentversion\settings`; you put text in there to control the welcome banner. A template file might look like this in its entirety:

```
CLASS USER
CATEGORY !!GenlSettings
    POLICY !!WelcomeBanner
    KEYNAME Software\Marksoft\CurrentVersion\Settings
        PART !!WelcomeText EDITTEXT
        VALUENAME WText
        END PART
    END POLICY
END CATEGORY
[strings]
```

```
GenlSettings="General settings"
WelcomeBanner="Welcome banner"
WelcomeText="Text to display in welcome banner"
```

Now open the System Policy Editor and click Options ➤ Template, and tell it to read your file—save it with the extension .ADM so it's easier for the Editor to find it. Click File ➤ Open Registry, then open the User class, and you'll see a screen like Figure 8.17.

Fill in the text and save it. Restart, and start up the Registry Editor, and you see an entry for MarkSoft, as you see in Figure 8.18.

I won't deny that building your own templates won't be something that you'll do every day. But what's truly exciting (to me, anyway) is that this is a powerful support tool that I can shape to my own needs. Other utility vendors could learn from this.

FIGURE 8.17

Adding an entry
to a template

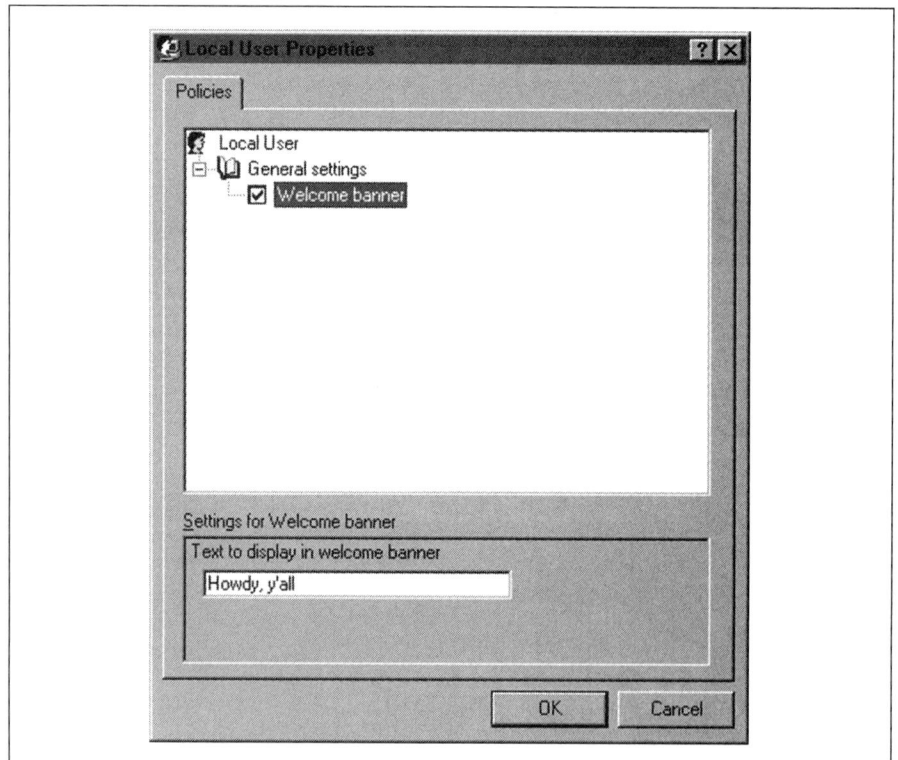

FIGURE 8.18

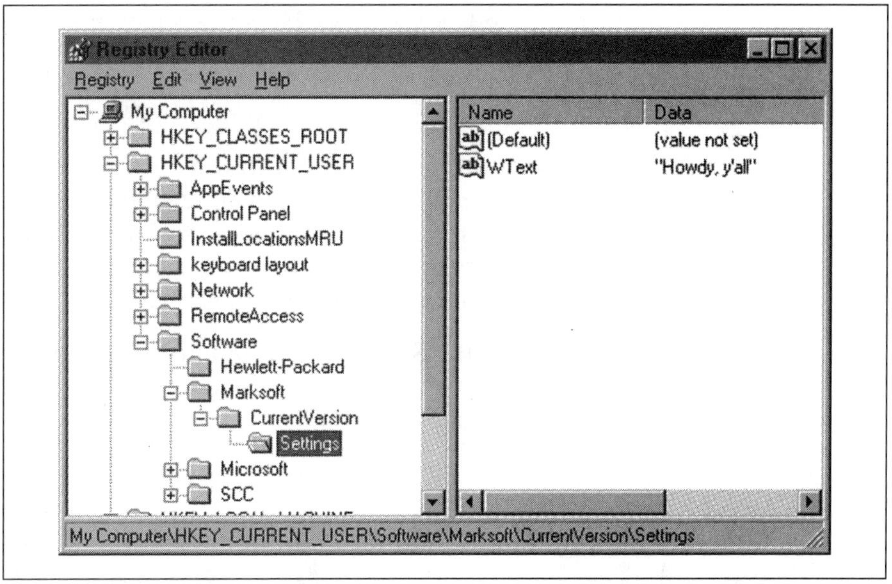

New entry displayed
in Registry

Remote Registry Modification

Both Regedit and the System Policy Editor offer the ability to modify remote Registries from the one they're running on. That's a great support tool, but there's a catch: The remote computer has to *allow* you to modify its Registry across the network before you can do it.

You allow that by installing a kind of tiny server program on each workstation, a program that allows a workstation to share its Registry over the network—even if the workstation hasn't enabled file and print sharing. In addition, you must install the same service on the machine you'll use to administer the Registries, if it's not one of the workstations.

The tiny server program is one of many network service programs that you can load in Windows. You have to do a little hunting for this one, however; it's on the CD-ROM in the \admin\nettools\remotereg directory. Just start up the Control Panel, then Network, then Add, then Service, then point the dialog box at the above directory.

By the way, it should be obvious that you must be running at least one of the same protocols on the workstations as on the support person's machine, as all of the network layers must match for the communication to work.

To access a remote Registry in the System Policy Editor, click File and Connect, then point to the machine whose Registry you want to modify. In the Registry editor, click Registry, then Connect Network Registry. The Registry editor even lets you view and modify multiple Registries from different machines simultaneously.

You can use the System Monitor across the network to monitor PCs other than the one you're working on, so long as the machines have the Remote Registry service activated.

Peeking over the Net: Net Watcher, System Monitor, and Network Monitor

Microsoft includes some network-based monitoring tools that, although they are not a complete suite of tools, are nonetheless a nice set of "free" network applications.

The System Monitor

The System Monitor allows you to log activity on your system. You can keep track of kernel activity (percent utilization of the CPU, number of virtual machines active, number of threads running), the file system, network client, network server software (number of bytes read, written, data rates per second), and the system's memory manager (amount of free memory, disk cache statistics, virtual memory statistics). While none of these are amazingly important, the fact that you can monitor them at a distance may be of value. For example, if a user complains that their machine is running too slowly, then a quick look at memory might reveal that their computer is extremely low on memory and is paging like crazy.

You can monitor a remote computer in a few ways, but the easiest is just to open up the Network Neighborhood folder, find the computer that you want to monitor, and right-click it. Choose Properties from the menu that results, and you'll be offered the option to run either Net Watcher or System Monitor, or to remotely control sharing on the remote computer's hard disk. Not just anyone can do this, however—you must have administrative rights to that machine and be running the Remote Registry service to access this information on another machine.

Using Network Monitor

Network Monitor lets you keep an eye on the flow of data on the network. It's a neat tool for keeping track of how busy the network is.

Well, that's the *good* part about it. The mildly evil part of Network Monitor is that, to really work as fully intended, it requires the System Management Server (SMS) on your system. As SMS requires NT Server, SQL Server, and a machine with a minimum of 64MB to run, it's a *whole* 'nother story...

The Network Monitor is on the CD-ROM in admin\nettools\netmon. In the Network applet of the Control Panel, click Add, then Service, then click the Add button, and choose Microsoft. Click Have Disk and fill in the directory for the Network Monitor (someone *did* claim that Windows 95 made things easier, right?). You'll see Microsoft Network Monitor Agent, so click OK until the Control Panel shuts up; your system will then reboot.

What you will see when you reboot (well, actually, you won't see it unless you look for it) is a new set of objects to monitor in the System Monitor. You'll have a new set of items under the heading Network Monitor Performance, and you'll be able to monitor the following:

- Ethernet broadcasts per second
- Ethernet multicasts per second
- Ethernet frames transmitted per second
- Ethernet bytes transmitted per second

In much the same way that you might listen to a traffic report to find out how busy a highway is, these new objects in System Monitor can allow you to see how congested your network is—an essential tool for answering the question, "Why is the network slow?"

Net Watcher

Every Windows 95 workstation is potentially a server. Not a very *powerful* server, but a server nonetheless. And if people are using your shared resources, then it might be nice to know who those people *are*.

You can do that with Net Watcher. It allows you to:

- Display who is using your shares
- Create new shares or delete existing shares
- Control sharing on remote computers

If you're used to NT Server networks, then think of this as an extremely lame version of the Server Manager program.

Windows 95 not only provides built-in networking—a somewhat *de rigueur* feature of operating systems these days—but also includes a number of network support and management tools gratis. They probably won't end up being the tools of choice for big networks, but they're a start for those who can't afford expensive third-party tools.

CHAPTER

9

Fixing Windows 95 Crashes— Failure Recovery

THE new generation of Windows is not rock-solid, although it handles crashed applications and resources better than its predecessors did. As you can't just boot the computer to DOS when Windows is misbehaving anymore (well, normally—turn to the end of the chapter for more information), this chapter will discuss how you *should* proceed when Windows falls down and can't get up. We'll talk about what's happening during the nearly invisible boot process, what components are loaded during the process, how you can track the loading, and methods to boot your PC that allow you to circumvent Windows when it's having a bad day.

Windows 95 Boot Sequence

When Windows 95 doesn't boot, it's easier to figure out why if you know what's *supposed* to happen during the boot process. This is somewhat new territory to former DOS and Windows users, so hang on.

Once you've got power to the system, the boot process takes place in four stages:

1. Loading the BIOS

2. Loading DOS drivers and TSRs (for backward compatibility only)

3. Initializing static VxD's in real mode

4. Starting up the protected-mode operating system and loading any remaining VxD's

BIOS? VxD's? Let's look at each of these in turn and figure out exactly what's going on at each stage.

Boot Step 1: BIOS Initialization

Once your system is getting power, there has to be some functioning computing hardware to use that power. As you know, at the heart of most PCs is a single circuit board called the *motherboard*. The motherboard contains the CPU, some memory, and the circuitry required to transfer data from one point on the board to another—you can recognize this circuitry by its pieces, which include the bus, the direct memory access hardware, and the interrupt controller. Most of these pieces must be functioning properly for anything at all to work on the motherboard.

Part of the memory included on the motherboard is in the form of *ROM* chips—*Read Only Memory*. ROM contains an important set of software called the *BIOS* (*Basic Input Output System*).

ROM and Bootstrapping

Why do we need the BIOS? It has to do with how CPUs work. When a CPU powers up, it doesn't know how to communicate with anything— the keyboard, display, disk drives, you name it. Before it can communicate with, say, a hard disk, a CPU needs a program in memory that tells it *how* to communicate with a hard disk. Virtually all PC programs must be read from disk before the PC can run them. This leads to a chicken-and-egg problem: The CPU needs disk-reading instructions before it can read anything from the disk, but the disk is where it loads its programs from. Where, then, does the CPU find that first disk-reading program when you first turn on the computer? That's where ROM comes in. The first disk-reading program is contained in the ROM's BIOS, the instructions that tell the CPU how to communicate with its parts.

What's a Plug and Play BIOS?

If you read the Windows 95 Resource Kit, you'll see that Windows 95 is designed for Plug and Play BIOSes, which can automatically detect Plug and Play boards in the system and configure them to use the appropriate DMA channels, interrupts, and I/O channels. Even if your PC's BIOS does not support Plug and Play, it will work with Windows 95: you'll just have to configure any add-in boards by hand using the methods discussed in Chapter 10.

N O T E In product literature, Microsoft rather endearingly calls BIOSes that do not support Plug and Play "legacy BIOSes." The fact is, *most* current BIOSes do not support Plug and Play.

How the BIOS Works

Regardless of whether your PC's BIOS supports Plug and Play, BIOS instructions are hard-wired into the ROM chips. Although RAM chips lose their contents when you shut down power on a PC, *ROMs* do *not* forget. That means that the BIOS is always available, even if some of the hardware it controls is inaccessible.

A part of the BIOS that is used only when you first power up the computer is responsible for inventorying and initializing the parts of your PC: figuring out what's there, testing the parts to make sure that they work, and preparing them to do their jobs. Now, this gets a little involved, so let's take the process one step at a time.

There are five steps to the BIOS initialization process:

1. Test some low memory.
2. Scan for other BIOSes.
3. Yield to other BIOSes.
4. Inventory the system.
5. Test the system.

Test Low Memory

In order for the BIOS to function, it needs to work with some RAM. Therefore, the first thing that most BIOSes do is test the bottom part of the system's RAM. If that test crashes, then most BIOSes can't recover. Therefore, if your PC won't boot, one troubleshooting step is to replace the lowest bank of RAM to see whether the problem is that the BIOS has no RAM to use. Unfortunately, this is not an option if the lowest bank of RAM is *soldered* on the motherboard (as is the case with some PCs).

Scan for Other BIOSes

The BIOS in your PC can't support every possible piece of hardware—LAN boards, unusual video boards, you name it—so the important functions of inventory and initialization have to go somewhere else. That is why many add-on boards have some ROM on them; you may have noticed this when installing them.

The main system BIOS allows the add-on boards to do *their* inventory and initialization first. But before that can happen, the main system BIOS must *find* those BIOSes. It does that by examining memory for BIOS *signatures* in the ROM area of memory, i.e., the addresses between 768K and 960K. Once it finds a BIOS, it can go to the next step.

Yield to Other BIOSes

Once it's found a BIOS on the add-on board, the main system BIOS passes control to the BIOS on the add-on board so that it can do whatever inventory and initialization it requires. Add-on BIOSes get to do their job before the main system BIOS.

Notice what that means: The ROM instructions on an add-in board get to run before either the system BIOS *or* the operating system. *This means that a malfunctioning board can keep your PC from booting.*

For example, consider a VGA board. It has a BIOS chip on it that contains a setup routine. That setup routine announces that the board is up and ready by putting a copyright notice on the screen. When your PC is booting, the VGA message appears *before* the memory test occurs and before the PC checks for the drives. Again, the point here is that this VGA ROM assumed total control of the system fairly early in the boot process, as will each ROM on add-in boards.

Inventory and Test the System

Once all of the add-in ROMs have gotten their time, *and assuming that their programs ran properly and returned control to the main system BIOS,* then the main system BIOS will inventory the items that it controls; these items will vary from system to system. At a minimum, the system BIOS must inventory and initialize the system memory. What does "inventory and initialize" mean here? You've seen at least one example of it a million times: the memory test. For another, ever notice the quick flash of the drive lights on the floppy and hard-disk drives? That's the BIOS doing an inventory of the storage devices.

CMOS Setup Information Read

Before we go on to the next step, where the system actually loads CONFIG .SYS and AUTOEXEC.BAT, I shouldn't neglect to at least mention the final part of the BIOS initialization, the reading of the setup information. If you've set up new computers, or added equipment to existing computers, you're aware that most computers built with 80286-or-later CPUs store a partial inventory of the computer's hardware in a chip called the *setup chip* or *CMOS chip*. Part of the BIOS's inventory process, then, involves reading that setup chip. Not *all* of the PC hardware inventory is in that chip, only the total amount of memory, the types of disk drives on the system, the type of video adapter, and whether or not the computer is equipped with a coprocessor. The chip also contains the battery-backed clock/calendar that initializes the system clock.

The CMOS is worth mentioning because this setup chip causes a *lot* of PC trouble calls. If the battery is dead, the setup information gets lost. The computer can't access the hard disk if doesn't know the hard disk's type, and consequently cannot boot if the setup chip is bad or has a dead battery. Now, while the lack of setup information *sounds* like something that's pretty obvious, it's often not obvious to the person who's reporting the trouble; so keep an eye out for it when you're on the site trying to fix the computer.

People are sometimes confused when their hard disk drive type has disappeared from the CMOS but the clock still keeps good time. How can it be that *some* of the CMOS is damaged while some is still good? It's actually quite simple. The clock is kept by a clock circuit, and the other information is kept by a memory. Memories need more power than clock circuits do. As a result, there may be a long period where your system's battery has enough power for the clock but not for the memory.

Boot Step 2: Loading Real-Mode Drivers

Once the BIOS is loaded, your PC can "see" its hardware. Now it's time to load the drivers that allow the PC to *use* the hardware. Under DOS, CONFIG.SYS contained the hardware profile. Windows 95 handles the process a little differently. When your system boots, Windows 95 polls the devices in the system to detect their hardware configuration, including the following things:

- interrupt usage
- port usage (as in COM1 or LPT2)
- computer identification
- docking-station data (if applicable and available)

Windows 95 compiles the current configuration information it accumulates into a 2-byte *hardware profile* for each device. A hardware profile is a pointer to the configuration information for that device.

NOTE In the interests of backward compatibility with 16-bit applications, Windows 95 loads the CONFIG.SYS and AUTOEXEC.BAT files at this stage of the boot process, even though it does not need these files to operate (the information in them is contained in the Registry).

Boot Step 3: Initializing Static VxD's

The third stage of the boot process loads Windows-specific device drivers (static VxD's) and WIN.COM, which supervises the loading process.

What are VxD's?

What *is* a static VxD, and why would I want to initialize one? Well, a VxD is a Windows device driver. Since the early days of operating systems, it's been clear to the designers of those systems that the part of the operating system that directly controls and manipulates the peripherals—printers, video, disk drive, etc.—should not be embedded in the operating system itself, but rather should reside in separate programs. These programs are called *drivers*. By separating the driver functions into separate programs, operating systems designers make it easier to add support for a new peripheral at a later date. Otherwise, every time that HP (for example) offered an improved driver for one of its printers, you'd have to buy—and install—an entirely new operating system.

Windows 95 is no different from older operating systems in this respect. You cannot assemble a bare-minimum Windows configuration without including drivers for the video display, the mouse, the keyboard, and, if present, a network. Windows 95 distinguishes between *real-mode drivers*, which set up some system-critical functions like the ability to boot from a SCSI drive or see upper memory, and those that Windows uses to control devices when it's in *protected mode*.

In order for Windows to control devices while in 386-Enhanced mode, it must have programs that allow Windows to treat those devices as virtual devices. Let's take the display screen as an example. Virtualizing the screen means that fifteen DOS programs can all simultaneously modify what *they* think is on the display screen, while in reality none of them is getting to the actual display screen. To work this display magic, Windows has a *Virtual Display Driver* (or VdD) that permits applications to modify the *virtual* display. There's a Virtual Mouse Driver (VmD), a Virtual Keyboard Driver (VkD), and so on. As all of these drivers have names that start with a V and end with a D, but contain something that varies in the middle, they have the generic name VxD's.

Windows 95 subdivides VxD's into two classes: *static* and *dynamic*.

- *Static VxD's* are those that Windows loads on bootup—the ones that control things like the memory manager, the configuration manager, other device loaders, and so forth. In older versions of Windows, VxD's were loaded in the [386enh] section of the SYSTEM.INI file on a device= line. In Windows 95, most of the common VxD's are rolled together into one file called VMM32.VXD. You can add additional VxD's to the system by adding them to the system\vmm32 directory. Windows 95 will load any virtual device drivers found in that directory in place of those in VMM32.

- *Dynamic VxD's* (protected mode device drivers) are for devices like disks and network cards that must be loaded at a certain time and in a certain order. Unlike static VxD's, which are loaded by VMM32, each type of dynamic VxD is loaded by a device loader designed for that type of device. For example, the device loader for disk drivers is called IOS. You can identify dynamic VxD's in the Registry by their value names: They all begin with DevLoader. Dynamic VxD's are not loaded until the final stage of the boot process.

Loading Static VxD's

VMM32.VXD loads static VxD's in three steps. The process looks like this:

1. VMM32 loads all the drivers specified in the Registry, including all drivers not directly linked to any specific piece of hardware.

2. If VMM32 finds a Registry entry with the value name StaticVxD, then it loads that device driver and initializes it. By default, all of these entries are included in hkey_local_machine\system\current-controlset\services, but VMM32 would also load any others that it found elsewhere.

3. Finally, VMM32 scans the [386enh] section of SYSTEM.INI for device= lines and loads any drivers that it finds there. Entries in SYSTEM.INI take precedence over those in the Registry.

> **NOTE**   Since entries in SYSTEM.INI take precedence over equivalent entries in the Registry, be cautious about editing SYSTEM.INI— if you specify a device= statement for which no device exists, you'll cause an error.

Boot Step 4: Loading the Operating System

After all the static VxD's are loaded, VMM32 switches the processor to run in protected mode, rather than real mode. At this stage of the game, the Configuration Manager figures out what devices are loaded. If your PC has a Plug and Play (PnP) BIOS, the Configuration Manager loads the information from it; otherwise, it looks to see what's already loaded and then loads the dynamic VxD's described in the previous section. If your PC has a Plug and Play BIOS and you're using PnP cards, the Configuration Manager then makes sure that none of the devices are conflicting with each other. If your PC does not have Plug and Play BIOS, then Configuration Manager can't prevent device conflicts: if you assign the same interrupt to two add-in cards, you'll run into device conflicts like those you'd expect.

After the Configuration Manager has established what devices are on the system, you'll see the login dialog box. Enter your name and password, and the final components of Windows will then load in the following order:

1. KRNL386.EXE loads the underlying operating system.

2. GDI.EXE and GDI32 load the graphic interface for the operating system.

3. USER.EXE and USER32 load the user interface, including such items as Network Neighborhood and Explorer.

4. Resources used by Windows 95, such as fonts, are loaded.

5. The entries in WIN.INI are checked.

6. The Desktop configuration, including colors and dialog fonts, is loaded.

Once you've logged on, the items in the Startup folder are processed, and your system is now up and running. And if it's not? Well, that's what the rest of this chapter is for.

Dissecting BOOTLOG.TXT

When you installed Windows 95, a file called BOOTLOG.TXT was created in the root directory of your boot drive. In part, it looked a bit like this:

```
[0008199D] INITCOMPLETESUCCESS = VCOMM
[0008199E] Dynamic load device C:\WINDOWS\system
\serial.vxd
[000819A0] Dynamic init device SERIAL
[000819A2] Dynamic init success SERIAL
[000819A3] Dynamic load success C:\WINDOWS\system
\serial.vxd
[000819A9] INITCOMPLETE = VCOND
[000819AA] INITCOMPLETESUCCESS = VCOND
[000819AB] INITCOMPLETE = VTDAPI
[000819AC] INITCOMPLETESUCCESS = VTDAPI
[000819AD] INITCOMPLETE = VFLATD
[000819AE] INITCOMPLETESUCCESS = VFLATD
[000819AF] INITCOMPLETE = VPMTD
[000819B0] INITCOMPLETESUCCESS = VPMTD
[000819B1] INITCOMPLETE = DiskTSD
[000819B2] INITCOMPLETESUCCESS = DiskTSD
[000819B3] INITCOMPLETE = voltrack
[000819B4] INITCOMPLETESUCCESS = voltrack
[000819B5] INITCOMPLETE = HSFLOP
[000819B6] INITCOMPLETESUCCESS = HSFLOP
[000819B7] INITCOMPLETE = ESDI_506
[000819B8] INITCOMPLETESUCCESS = ESDI_506
[000819B9] INITCOMPLETE = SERENUM
[000819BA] INITCOMPLETESUCCESS = SERENUM
[000819BB] INITCOMPLETE = LPTENUM
[000819BC] INITCOMPLETESUCCESS = LPTENUM
```

Although this doesn't look very useful, if you can decipher the information herein it can give you a clue as to what's going on with your system.

When Is Bootlog Created?

You don't get a new BOOTLOG.TXT every time you restart your system. Instead, one is created when you *first* install Windows 95; unless you install something new or are trying to isolate a boot problem as described in the following section, you don't need to create another one. When you do need one, you can create one by choosing the interactive system startup (by pressing F8) and selecting the *Create boot log* option from the menu, or by typing **win /b** from the command line to start up Windows. Essentially, you should probably keep a printout of your BOOTLOG file around for reference (you can't diagnose sick if you don't know what healthy looks like), but you don't need a new one every day.

What Can You Learn from Bootlog?

Since BOOTLOG is created only if your system boots successfully, you can use your handy printed copy of a successful boot's BOOTLOG to narrow the field of possible suspects when your system doesn't boot. For example, if you read a BOOTLOG created when your system booted successfully and notice that some of your VxD's did not load during that bootup, you can probably assume that those VxD's are not suddenly responsible for your system not being able to boot properly at a later date. The system worked before without 'em; it's not likely that it's suddenly going to freeze up now unless something *else* has changed.

You can also use BOOTLOG for troubleshooting if your system boots successfully but not all of its components start up. Reboot, create a new version of the file, and scan it for errors, as described below.

Reading BOOTLOG

BOOTLOG is divided into five parts that correspond roughly to the stages of the boot process:

- Records of loading real-mode drivers
- Records of loading VxD's (Windows device drivers, remember)
- Records of initializing system-critical VxD's

- Records of initializing devices dependent on VxD's

- Records of successful initializations

Let's look at each of these sections in turn.

Section 1: Loading Real-Mode Drivers

As you'll remember from the description of the boot process earlier in this chapter, before Windows 95 starts up it loads the DOS drivers that you used in earlier versions of Windows, so as to ensure that all of your old applications can use them. Below is a short list of some possible failures and the entries that you should look for in this short section of BOOTLOG if you encounter these failures. If the entry is missing, make sure that you have the corresponding statement in your CONFIG.SYS—for example, if you don't have access to memory beyond 640K, check for a HIMEM.SYS entry in CONFIG.SYS.

Problem: No extended (XMS) memory in which to run Windows.

BOOTLOG Entry: loadfailed=c:\windows\himem.SYS

Implication: Only the lower 640K of memory is available to your programs—you can't run Windows without extended memory.

Problem: Incorrect DOS version. (Message appears when you try to run programs or drivers that worked before.)

BOOTLOG Entry: loadfailed=c:\windows\setver.EXE

Implication: You can't run some DOS programs because they're not included in the version of DOS that the system thinks you have.

Problem: Windows 95 won't boot from a bus-mastered hard drive.

BOOTLOG Entry: loadfailed=c:\windows\dblbuff.SYS

Implication: If your boot hard-disk controller uses bus mastering, you can't boot from C:.

Problem: IFSHLP.SYS message appears briefly at command prompt; Windows won't run; and system locks up.

BOOTLOG Entry: loadfailed=c:\windows\ifshlp.SYS

Implication: The Installable File System Helper (which loads device drivers for Windows 95) did not load. Only the minimal file system in IO.SYS is available. You can't run Windows in this case either, as VFAT won't run.

Section 2: Loading VxD's

This section of BOOTLOG logs the results of every attempt to load VxD's. Note that these drivers are not *initialized* until the next section; these entries only record whether or not the drivers were even loaded into memory.

If you run into problems, make sure first of all that each Loading statement has a corresponding LoadSuccess= statement, like the sample lines below.

```
[000815B3] Loading Vxd = VMM
[000815B9] LoadSuccess = VMM
[000815C3] Loading Vxd = vnetsup.vxd
[000815C6] LoadSuccess = vnetsup.vxd
[000815C7] Loading Vxd = CONFIGMG
[000815CA] LoadSuccess = CONFIGMG
```

As we discussed earlier, remember that your system can successfully boot and work fine even if you see some Fail entries in BOOTLOG, so record the boot process while it's still working so you have some basis of comparison.

Table 9.1 lists a couple of specific VxD Load statements that you'll want to watch for if you run into problems.

Please note that, if VSHARE does not load successfully, do *not* add it to your CONFIG.SYS. Instead, since VSHARE is one of the VxD's rolled into VMM32, simply ensure that it's included in the section of the Registry labeled Hkey_Local_Machine\CurrentControlSet\Control\VMM32Files.

TABLE 9.1	IF YOU HAVE THIS PROBLEM...	...LOOK FOR THIS MESSAGE IN BOOTLOG
Loading VxD's	Cannot access DoubleSpaced or DriveSpaced (compressed) drives.	loadsuccess=c:\dblspace.bin
	Sharing violations occur.	loadsuccess=vshare

NOTE Even if VSHARE loads successfully, sharing violations can still occur. A successful load, however, at least narrows the field.

Section 3: Initializing System-Critical VxD's

The next section of BOOTLOG records the system's attempts to initialize vital VxD's, those that it requires to run at all. This longish section begins where the entries begin to look like this:

```
[0008168D] SYSCRITINIT = VMM
[0008168E] SYSCRITINITSUCCESS = VMM
[0008168F] SYSCRITINIT = VCACHE
[00081690] SYSCRITINITSUCCESS = VCACHE
```

Unlike the previous section, which only recorded the loading process, your system will not start up if there are any Fail entries in this section. Only those VxD's that loaded successfully will be initialized.

Section 4: Initializing Device VxD's

The fourth section of BOOTLOG records the system's attempt to initialize VxD's that relate to devices. The entries herein look something like this:

```
[00081714] DEVICEINIT = VMM
[00081715] DEVICEINITSUCCESS = VMM
[00081717] DEVICEINIT = VCACHE
[00081718] DEVICEINITSUCCESS = VCACHE
```

Some device VxD's are composed of a bunch of smaller drivers. The entries for these devices will look something like this:

```
[0008175B] DEVICEINIT = IOS
[00081776] Dynamic load device C:\WINDOWS\system
\IOSUBSYS\apix.vxd
[0008177E] Dynamic load success C:\WINDOWS\system
\IOSUBSYS\apix.vxd
[0008177F] Dynamic load device C:\WINDOWS\system
\IOSUBSYS\cdfs.vxd
[00081786] Dynamic load success C:\WINDOWS\system
\IOSUBSYS\cdfs.vxd
[00081788] Dynamic load device C:\WINDOWS\system
\IOSUBSYS\cdtsd.vxd
[0008178E] Dynamic load success C:\WINDOWS\system
\IOSUBSYS\cdtsd.vxd
[00081790] Dynamic load device C:\WINDOWS\system
\IOSUBSYS\cdvsd.vxd
[00081796] Dynamic load success C:\WINDOWS\system
\IOSUBSYS\cdvsd.vxd
[00081798] Dynamic load device C:\WINDOWS\system
\IOSUBSYS\disktsd.vxd
[0008179E] Dynamic load success C:\WINDOWS\system
\IOSUBSYS\disktsd.vxd
[000817A0] Dynamic load device C:\WINDOWS\system
\IOSUBSYS\diskvsd.vxd
[000817A6] Dynamic load success C:\WINDOWS\system
\IOSUBSYS\diskvsd.vxd
[000817A8] Dynamic load device C:\WINDOWS\system
\IOSUBSYS\voltrack.vxd
[000817AE] Dynamic load success C:\WINDOWS\system
\IOSUBSYS\voltrack.vxd
[000817AF] Dynamic load device C:\WINDOWS\system
\IOSUBSYS\necatapi.vxd
[000817B6] Dynamic load success C:\WINDOWS\system
\IOSUBSYS\necatapi.vxd
[000817B8] Dynamic load device C:\WINDOWS\system
\IOSUBSYS\scsi1hlp.vxd
[000817BE] Dynamic load success C:\WINDOWS\system
\IOSUBSYS\scsi1hlp.vxd
[000817C0] Dynamic load device C:\WINDOWS\system
\IOSUBSYS\rmm.pdr
[000817C5] Dynamic load success C:\WINDOWS\system
\IOSUBSYS\rmm.pdr
[000817C7] DEVICEINITSUCCESS = IOS
```

This series of entries records the initialization of the device loader, which then loads a slew of internal files. The bottom entry shown here (device-initsuccess = ios) tells you that the IOS device loader successfully loaded all of its files.

The Windows Startup Menu

If Windows doesn't boot properly when you start up the machine, and re-booting once doesn't work, you can manage the boot process with the Startup menu. Using the seven selections available, you can boot your PC in almost any way that your heart desires. (Quiet, you in the back who are claiming that there are really eight selections—we'll get to that later in this chapter.)

Contents of the Startup Menu

You can switch to the Startup menu while your computer is booting, after the system identifies the drives and you see the message "Starting Windows 95...." Press F8 when you see that message, before the logo appears. You'll see a menu like DOS 6's MultiConfig menu. If the last time you successfully booted your machine it was set up to access a network, it will include networking options, as follows:

1. Normal
2. Logged (\BOOTLOG.TXT)
3. Safe mode
4. Safe mode with network support
5. Step-by-step confirmation
6. Command prompt only
7. Safe mode command prompt only

If the system boots up too fast for you to hit F8 before the logo screen comes up, you can increase the interval during which you can access this menu by adding the line **Boot Delay=** to the [options] section of MSDOS.SYS and providing as a value the number of seconds to wait. For example, BootDelay=5 gives you five seconds to press F8 and get the Startup menu before Windows starts up. When you've edited the file, that section should look something like the following:

```
[Options]
BootGUI=1
Network=1
BootDelay=5
```

So far, so good. Now let's find out what each Startup option does, what happens when you choose them, and why you should prefer one over another.

Normal

Choose the default option, Normal, and normal is what you'll get: the system will continue booting as though you hadn't interrupted it with the F8 keystroke. This is useful if you pressed F8 by mistake, so you don't have to reboot again.

Logged (\BOOTLOG.TXT)

As with Normal, the second option directs the system to boot normally. In the background, however, Windows 95 will create a record of the boot process (as discussed earlier in this chapter) so you can watch for failed processes. Select this menu item if something isn't working right in Windows and you can't track down the problem child, but the problem isn't serious enough to warrant a more restricted system startup. You can also use this option to review the boot process when things are going well.

Safe Mode

If you choose option 3 from the Startup menu (or press F5 at the "Starting Windows 95…" message), then your PC will bypass CONFIG.SYS and AUTOEXEC.BAT; it *will* load the Registry and HIMEM.SYS so that Windows can start up in a vanilla configuration: VGA mode, no network drivers, and only the drivers needed to get Windows going. When Windows has started up, your display will appear as you left it (that is, the color scheme and fonts will not revert to Windows Default), except that it will appear in VGA mode and the words *Safe Mode* will be written in the four corners of the screen.

During the startup process, 95 will alert you to the limitations of safe mode with a dialog box like the one in Figure 9.1.

Click OK, and you'll log in to the machine. Note that you won't log into your domain or workgroup, because safe mode does not support networking.

Safe mode is for those times when you suspect that your system's configuration is messed up, but perhaps not enough to entirely prevent you from using Windows. It's good for any of the following situations:

- Windows 95 hangs after the "Starting Windows 95..." message appears.

- Windows 95 stalls for an extended period at startup.

- Something isn't working properly or works differently than you expected.

- The video does not display correctly (resolution, not color scheme).

- Your PC suddenly slows down or begins stalling repeatedly.

For example, if you accidentally changed your display to a configuration that your monitor can't handle (difficult to do, given the way that you change video resolutions in 95, but possible if you really try) or if you've added a new driver to your startup files that's playing havoc with your

FIGURE 9.1

Warning notice for
running Windows
in safe mode

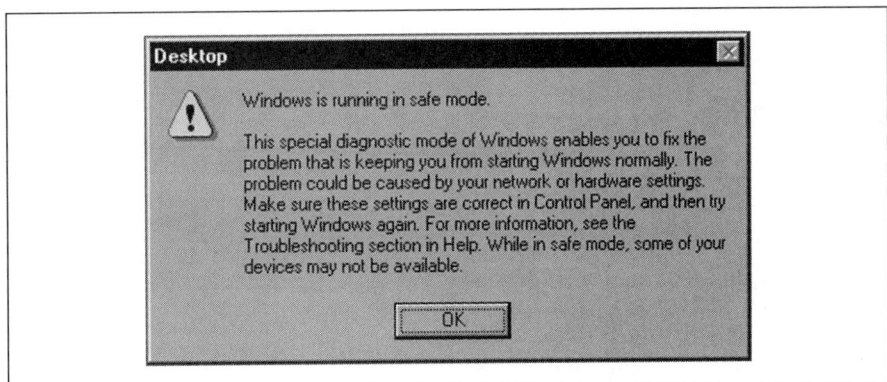

system, then safe mode can get you far enough to correct the problem. Remove the errant driver or restore the resolution to a configuration that works, and then restart your computer.

One really annoying thing about working in safe mode (or safe mode with networking, for that matter) is that 95 doesn't deal well with persistent connections that aren't currently working. It continually polls, looking for the mapped drives, and if it doesn't find them it alerts you to the fact— over and over. It's highly irritating when you're trying to fix the problem, whatever it is, and Windows insists on tugging on your hem and complaining, "Hey, I *still* can't find drive D: mapped to serverted\public." In the interests of your own sanity, make disconnecting from all persistent connections one of your first priorities when you're working in safe mode. Open the My Computer folder and right-click any drives with a red × on them, and choose Disconnect from the pop-up menu that appears. You'll have to remap those connections once you get the system started normally, but that's better than living with Windows nagging you about the connections that it can't find.

When you exit a safe mode session of Windows, your options are a bit more limited than you're used to. When shutting down, you must either shut down entirely or restart the computer in Windows 95. Although restarting the computer in DOS mode is listed as an option, you can't do it, and if you try you'll see an error message like the one in Figure 9.2.

Remember, choosing *Restart the computer in MS-DOS mode* from the Shut Down menu doesn't restart the machine, it exits the graphical user interface and leaves the basic operating system in place—there's no VMM32 running, just DOS.

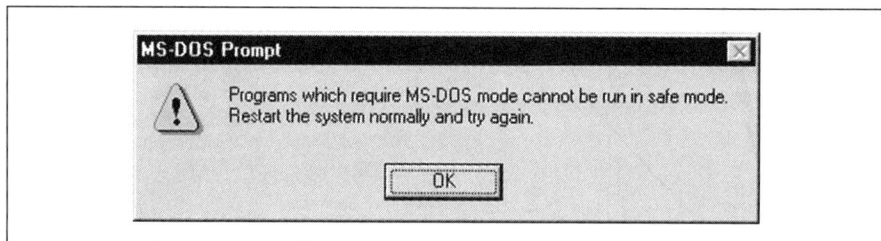

Similarly, you cannot log off a network and then back on again from regular safe mode. For that you need the second safe mode option, *Safe mode with network support.*

Safe Mode with Network Support

Choosing menu item 4 from the Startup menu (or pressing F6 at the "Starting Windows 95..." message) starts Windows 95 in safe mode, but also loads NETSTART.BAT to enable networking. This is essentially the same as running Windows in safe mode except that you have (as the logon text puts it) "limited network functionality."

It's pretty limited. Your persistent connections won't load at startup, and you can't connect to the network drives from the Network Neighborhood object either. If you log off and log back on again, you log on only to the machine, not to the network. Don't try to run Net Start from the command line, as you'll be told that you can't start or stop the network from a DOS prompt. And, as we discussed just a minute ago, you can't choose MS-DOS mode from the Shut Down menu, as programs that require DOS mode cannot run in safe mode.

Essentially, *Safe mode with network support* from the Windows Startup menu is for the same kinds of situations as *Safe mode.* If something goes fairly wrong with your system setup, but not so wrong that you can't fix it if you can get into Windows, this is a good option to choose.

Step-by-Step Confirmation

Choosing menu item 5 (or pressing Shift+F8 at the Startup menu) allows you to review each of the startup files and choose whether to implement them when starting up the computer. This enables you to review the following processes:

- Loading the Registry
- Creating BOOTLOG.TXT
- Running the files in CONFIG.SYS (confirming each separate entry in the file)
- Running AUTOEXEC.BAT (confirming each separate entry)

Choose whether or not to activate each process by pressing Enter for Yes or Esc for No. If you activate all the options, Windows will start up normally, except that you won't see the initial logo.

You should use this step-by-step confirmation option to start up Windows if you think that a particular driver or configuration setting might be causing your bootup problems. As this is a line-by-line process, it's best if you use this when you already have a pretty good idea what the problem is.

Command Prompt Only

Choosing this option allows you to start up Windows from the command prompt, and so lets you add switches to WIN.COM. The following can be useful when you need to isolate an incorrectly configured setting. The syntax is as follows (the brackets, of course, merely indicate options):

```
win [/B] [/D:[F] [M] [N] [S] [V] [X]]
```

- **/B** creates a BOOTLOG.TXT file that records operating system messages generated during system startup.

- **/D:** is used for troubleshooting when Windows 95 does not start correctly. The following switches may be used with /D:

  - **F** turns off 32-bit disk access. This is equivalent to 32Bit-DiskAccess=FALSE in SYSTEM.INI.

  Briefly, 32-bit disk access increases throughput on Western Digital-compatible disks by bypassing the BIOS. It may cause bus-mastered disks to be unstable, so try disabling it if you're having trouble with hard disk crashes. 32-bit disk access is less problematic than it was under Windows 3.x, however.

  - **M** starts Windows in safe mode. It's equivalent to choosing item 3 from the main Startup menu.
  - **N** enables safe mode with networking. It's equivalent to choosing item 4 from the main Startup menu.
  - **S** specifies that Windows 95 should not use the ROM address space between F000:0000 and 1MB to break out of a virtual machine mode. This is equivalent to SystemROMBreak-Point=FALSE in SYSTEM.INI. Use this switch if Windows 95 stalls during system startup.

Sometimes, third-party memory managers scramble ROM so that it makes a less predictable jumping point to move between real mode and protected mode, and this can cause Windows problems. If you have this problem and want to keep using the memory manager, add the line to your SYSTEM.INI.

- **V** specifies that the ROM routine will handle interrupts from the hard disk controller. This is equivalent to Virtual-HDIRQ=FALSE in SYSTEM.INI. Use this switch if Windows 95 stalls during system startup.

We'll talk more about the **V** setting elsewhere in this book, but, in brief, it causes Windows to switch to real mode whenever it needs to access the disk. It's not the best solution, but if you want to keep using that ultra-fast disk controller and its manufacturer (like most of them) has not created a VdD for it, you may discover that you don't have a choice.

- **X** excludes all of the adapter area from the range of memory that Windows 95 scans in looking for unused space. This is equivalent to EMMExclude=A000_FFFF (memory addresses 640 through 1024) in SYSTEM.INI.

Using the **X** switch keeps Windows from using *any* upper memory, so, if you're having problems with memory conflicts, think of this less as a cure than as a diagnostic tool. If this switch keeps Windows from crashing, check your documentation or start excluding ranges of memory addresses to identify the reserved memory that Windows is stomping on.

Once you've started Windows from the command line, it will start up as usual, except that you won't see the beginning logo and it seems to take a little longer than a normal startup.

Safe Mode Command Prompt Only

Select item seven from the Windows Startup menu or press Shift+F5 at the "Starting Windows 95..." message, and you'll load safe mode from the command prompt. At first, it may look as though you've booted to DOS. Don't be fooled, however: type **Ver** and the system will assure you that you're running Windows 95. Your capabilities here are pretty much those of a DOS session, however: you can start up the network, map your drives to other machines, and so forth. Getting anything done here requires a certain level of proficiency with the command line, but if you're able to get around the keyboard it's a useful mode if something's gone so badly with your system that even your VGA drivers no longer work.

From here, you can:

- Copy the .DAT files of the Registry or other system files from disk or a network directory, if your local ones are corrupted or missing
- Pull drivers from other machines to replace missing ones
- Copy or move files between drives and directories just as you would from the File Manager or the My Computer object

Generally speaking, anything that you can do from a DOS command prompt you can do from the Windows 95 prompt.

Restoring a Registry

As we've discussed elsewhere, Windows 95 keeps its system information in a file called the Registry (SYSTEM.DAT and USER.DAT). If there's no system information, then there's no Windows. Therefore, it's important to back up a working copy of your system's Registry and to know how to restore it when something happens to the original. In the best case, Windows 95 will automatically restore your Registry on bootup (we'll discuss *how* in just a minute), but you can also restore it by hand if necessary in one of the following ways:

- Run Setup and verify system files.
- Run Regedit from the command prompt in real mode and import a saved copy of the Registry.
- Run the Registry Editor from Windows and import a backed-up Registry from another location.

First, we'll discuss why you shouldn't need to use any of these options, and then how to make them work if you *do*.

Gone, but Not Forgotten: How Automatic Restore Works

Every time that Windows 95 boots successfully, it backs up SYSTEM.DAT and USER.DAT to SYSTEM.DA0 and USER.DA0, respectively. If the Registry is missing on bootup, Windows 95 will restore the Registry files from the backups. Any unsaved changes that you made to the Registry during your last session will be lost, but at least you'll have a recent copy of the configuration files.

NOTE This is similar to the Last Known Good configuration that NT users are accustomed to.

If you'd like to see how this works before you have to do it under pressure, move SYSTEM.DAT and USER.DAT from the \windows directory to a floppy disk, write-protect the disk, and set it safely aside. (Technically, you don't need to do this, but *I'm* not blowing away my Registry information on purpose without backing it up.) Then restart the machine.

When the machine starts up, it'll first flip to the familiar logo screen, but then it rethinks the situation and sends you to the Windows Startup menu. You'll see the message "Windows has detected a registry/configuration error." Selection 3 from the menu, *Safe mode*, will be highlighted, and you have 30 seconds if you want to choose another mode in which to start up Windows. ***Don't.*** Instead, press Enter so that you can restore the Registry. The logo screen and then the Windows Startup menu will appear again, but just wait patiently through it.

Windows will start up in safe mode, using the default color scheme since there's no configuration information to tell it otherwise. The Registry Problem dialog box will appear, as you can see in Figure 9.3, warning that Windows can't access the system directory and telling you that you should restore the Registry and restart.

Helpfully, the dialog box also informs you that you shouldn't just shut down (if you did, then you'd blow away the .DA0 files that contain the way

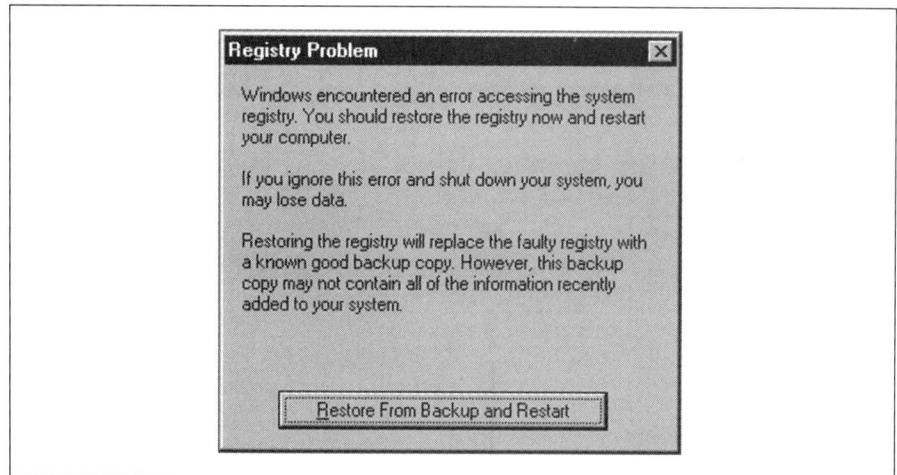

Registry Problem ✕

Windows encountered an error accessing the system
registry. You should restore the registry now and restart
your computer.

If you ignore this error and shut down your system, you
may lose data.

Restoring the registry will replace the faulty registry with
a known good backup copy. However, this backup
copy may not contain all of the information recently
added to your system.

[<u>R</u>estore From Backup and Restart]

you'd last left your configuration and you'd be stuck with the current vanilla configuration). Finally (this is a big dialog box), it tells you what
you'll get when you restore the Registry files.

Click the button on the bottom that says Restore from Backup and Restart. A dialog box like the one in Figure 9.4 will appear, asking if you
want to restart the computer now (as is required to completely restore the
Registry files).

Unless you have some pressing reason to not reboot at this time, choose
to restart. The computer will shut down and then restart as normal, having replaced the missing .DAT files with the .DA0 backups.

Of course, both of these methods require working .DA0 files. If you have
neither SYSTEM.DAT nor SYSTEM.DA0, you'll see a message informing you

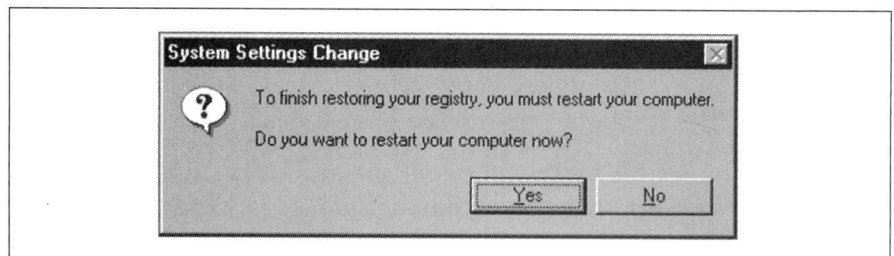

System Settings Change ✕

? To finish restoring your registry, you must restart your computer.

Do you want to restart your computer now?

[<u>Y</u>es] [<u>N</u>o]

that the Registry services are not available for this session. This innocuous-sounding statement means that most Windows operations will fail, as the Registry contains the brunt of your system's configuration. If you see this message, you'll need to rebuild the Registry, using one of the methods described below.

Restoring the Registry by Hand

If you corrupt or destroy your system's Registry, then you have a few different options depending on what the problem is and how you prepared for the eventuality. Here are some common situations:

- You accidentally imported an incorrect Registry to replace your good one, but you have a backup.

- You accidentally erased your .DAT and .DA0 files, but you backed up the Registry to the local disk or a floppy.

- You erased your .DAT and .DA0 files, and you *don't* have backups.

Replacing the Current Registry

If Windows boots normally and the problem is merely that you don't like the last change you made, you may be able to get away with simply importing the Registry and having done with it—*if* you exported a working configuration before you made the change. The following steps show you how to do this.

1. Once Windows has started up, run REGEDIT.EXE to start up the Registry editor.

2. Choose Import Registry File from the Registry menu.

3. Move to the directory where you exported the working Registry, and select the proper one. (This is where those long file names that Windows 95 supports come in handy. You can give exported copies good, descriptive names like *Configuration before installing new TCP/IP drivers* or whatnot.)

4. Click OK, and you'll import that Registry over the old one. Note that any changes that you'd made to the system configuration since exporting the Registry will be lost.

If you hadn't exported the Registry but include it as part of your backup routine, you can restore SYSTEM.DAT and/or USER.DAT from the backups. Just copy them over the existing files (or insert them into C:\windows) and reboot. Once again, any changes that you made to the system since backing up will be lost.

Please note that, if Windows 95 booted successfully then there's no point in renaming the .DAO files to .DAT files in an effort to restore the configuration. Remember, Windows 95 re-creates the .DAO versions every time that it boots successfully. If the new Registry booted, that's what's in the .DAO files, even if something's wrong with it.

Rebuilding the Registry with SETUP.EXE

All right, Windows 3.x users: what happens if you accidentally delete or corrupt a system file? If you're lucky and you know what you did, you can copy the file from your backups, but sometimes nothing will do but to re-install the entire operating system. Although it's not that tricky a job if you've done it a few times, it's certainly time-consuming, and you can probably think of better ways to spend those precious work hours.

If your system configuration is corrupted and you can't restore it from the .DAO files, you may be able to restore the corrupted or missing files from the installation CD or diskettes. You can run Setup from safe mode or protected mode; the only catch is that, to run it from safe mode, your CD must be locally available—no network support, remember.

If you run Setup after you've already installed the operating system, it will ask if it should reinstall Windows 95 or just verify installed components. If you want to verify installed components, Setup examines the setup log and reruns the installation process without completely copying all system components. During this process, Windows 95 checks the already in-stalled files against the files on the installation disks. If the file on the computer is missing or has metamorphosed into its evil twin, Setup will reinstall that file. Since only corrupted or missing files are reinstalled, this speeds up the process immeasurably.

TIP   Just to run Setup, you'll need at least 10MB of free space on your hard disk—even if you don't restore any files.

Please note that running Setup to restore the Registry will restore the files to their original configuration from when you first installed Windows 95. Most of the time, this will be okay, but it's worth keeping in mind.

Living Dangerously: Using the Command Prompt

If you have to, you can run Regedit from the command prompt and import or export Registries or edit the Registry (.REG files, not .DAT files) with a text editor.

This is potentially really, *really* dangerous, because:

- The command line is neither intuitive nor forgiving—that is, if you do something you didn't intend, you can't undo it easily.

- The Registry looks different in EDIT.COM than in its natural habitat so it's easy to get disoriented.

- Not only can the Registry still not tell a valid entry from your grocery list, it lets you wantonly edit and delete trees, keys and subkeys, not just values.

Reserve using the command prompt for those times when you're (a) really sure of what you're doing, and (b) have no other choice. No other choice in this context means that you can't run Windows at all.

You can do pretty much anything from the command prompt that you can using the GUI Registry Editor. Table 9.2 shows some actions and syntax examples.

Be *very* careful about replacing the Registry with another file (the **/c** switch). If you import a Registry file that is a branch of the entire Registry, it will only replace the branch to which it corresponds. On the other hand, if you *replace* the Registry with a file that contains only a branch of the entire file, then your system's Registry will consist only of that branch. For example, if you export hkey_current_user as newuser.reg and then

TABLE 9.2

Command line syntax
of Regedit

ACTION	EXAMPLE
Export the entire Registry to a file (NEWREG.REG).	Regedit /e newreg.reg
Export one branch (hkey_local_machine) of the Registry to a file (NEWBRNCH.REG).	Regedit /e hkey_local_machine newbrnch.reg
Import a Registry file (NEWREG.REG).	Regedit newreg.reg
Import the Registry file NEWREG.REG, made from a specific SYSTEM.DAT and/or USER.DAT, located (respectively) at *systempath* and *userpath*.	Regedit /L: *systempath* /R: *userpath* newreg.reg
Replace the current Registry with a previously exported one (NEWREG.REG).	Regedit /c newreg.reg

replace the registry with newuser.reg, you will blow away all of your hardware configuration information and default user setups. It's probably safer to stick with importing and exporting Registry files, and relegate the Replace function to the "interesting but overkill" closet.

To replace a missing Registry, type the following:

Regedit *backup registry path and filename*

where *backup registry path and filename* is where you previously exported the Registry to. Don't forget that, if you used a long file name for the exported Registry it will be listed in its shortened form when you're in real mode. For example, Backup Registry made on 8/31/95.reg will become Backup~1.reg when it's abbreviated to the eight-dot-three format.

If you can't avoid it, you can edit the Registry with EDIT.COM. Type

Edit c:\windows\testconf.reg (or whatever the name of your Registry is)

and you'll see output that looks like the following:

```
[HKEY_LOCAL_MACHINE\SOFTWARE\Classes\.ME]
@="txtfile"

[HKEY_LOCAL_MACHINE\SOFTWARE\Classes\123Worksheet]
@="1-2-3 Worksheet"

[HKEY_LOCAL_MACHINE\SOFTWARE\Classes\123Worksheet
\protocol]

[HKEY_LOCAL_MACHINE\SOFTWARE\Classes\123Worksheet
\protocol\
StdFileEditing]

[HKEY_LOCAL_MACHINE\SOFTWARE\Classes\123Worksheet
\protocol\
StdFileEditing\SetData
Formats]
@="NotesDocInfo"

[HKEY_LOCAL_MACHINE\SOFTWARE\Classes\123Worksheet
\protocol\
StdFileEditing\verb]

[HKEY_LOCAL_MACHINE\SOFTWARE\Classes\123Worksheet
\protocol\
StdFileEditing\verb\0]
@="Edit"

[HKEY_LOCAL_MACHINE\SOFTWARE\Classes\123Worksheet
\protocol\
StdFileEditing\server]
@="c:\\123r4w\\programs\\123w.EXE"
```

Reading these entries is similar to reading command-line file and directory information—the name of the branch is on the far left, and the keys and subkeys progress downward from left to right, like this:

branch\key\subkey\subkey\subkey

The part of the entry that reads @="Edit" or the like is the value name.

When using a text editor, do *not* edit any part of the Registry other than the value data. It's even easier to mess up your system's configuration here than it is in the GUI Registry Editor, as that application will not permit you to edit anything other than value data in the first place. Using a text editor, you could destructively edit the names of keys and subkeys, or delete them altogether, and you'd never get any warning that you might've just trashed your system—until it's too late.

Creating and Using a Startup Floppy

Like DOS, Windows 95 permits you to boot from a floppy in case of emergency. The only catch is that your computer's A: drive must be the 3½-inch drive, as the startup files take up more than 1.2MB, and a 5¼-inch floppy can't hold that much data. The emergency floppy contains files for booting up and (hopefully) fixing your computer, as you can see in Table 9.3.

You can create the startup floppy either while installing Windows 95 or, if you delete or lose the floppy, afterwards.

- To create the floppy *during* installation, have a junk floppy (i.e., one not containing anything you want to keep) on hand and insert it as directed.

	FILE NAME	FUNCTION
TABLE 9.3 Contents of Startup Floppy	ATTRIB.EXE	Assigns attributes (such as archived, read-only, hidden, or system file) to files.
	COMMAND.COM	Provides an operating environment. Executes AUTOEXEC.BAT and NETSTART.BAT.
	DRVSPACE.BIN	Permits the boot disk to recognize a drive compressed with Drvspace.
	EBD.SYS	Utility for the startup disk.
	EDIT.COM	Text editor for editing startup files (including the Registry, but only as a last resort—see precautions in this chapter).
	FDISK.EXE	Configures the partitions on a hard disk. With the /MBR switch, can also rebuild (but not *fix*) the MBR without destroying the data on the disk.
	FORMAT.COM	Formats the partitions on a disk.
	IO.SYS	The real-mode operating system that replaces DOS. Reads the small portion of SYSTEM.DAT on the startup disk. (Note: This is not the same IO.SYS used with DOS—that file is now called IO.DOS.)
	MSDOS.SYS	Contains information for backward compatibility between Windows 95 and MS-DOS applications. (Note: This is not the same MSDOS.SYS used with DOS—that file is now called MSDOS.DOS.)
	REGEDIT.EXE	Used to import, export, or replace all or part of the Registry.
	SCANDISK.EXE	Disk analysis and repair utility for common disk and file errors such as lost clusters, bad clusters, and cross-linked files.
	SCANDISK.INI	Initialization file for Scandisk.
	SYS.COM	Copies IO.SYS, MSDOS.SYS, and COMMAND.COM to the drive you specify.

- To create a startup floppy *after* installation, open the Control Panel, choose Add/Remove Programs, and select the Startup Disk tab.

    1. Click on the Create Disk button, and the system will begin to set up the startup files. When it's ready to write the startup disk, you'll see a dialog box like the one shown here.

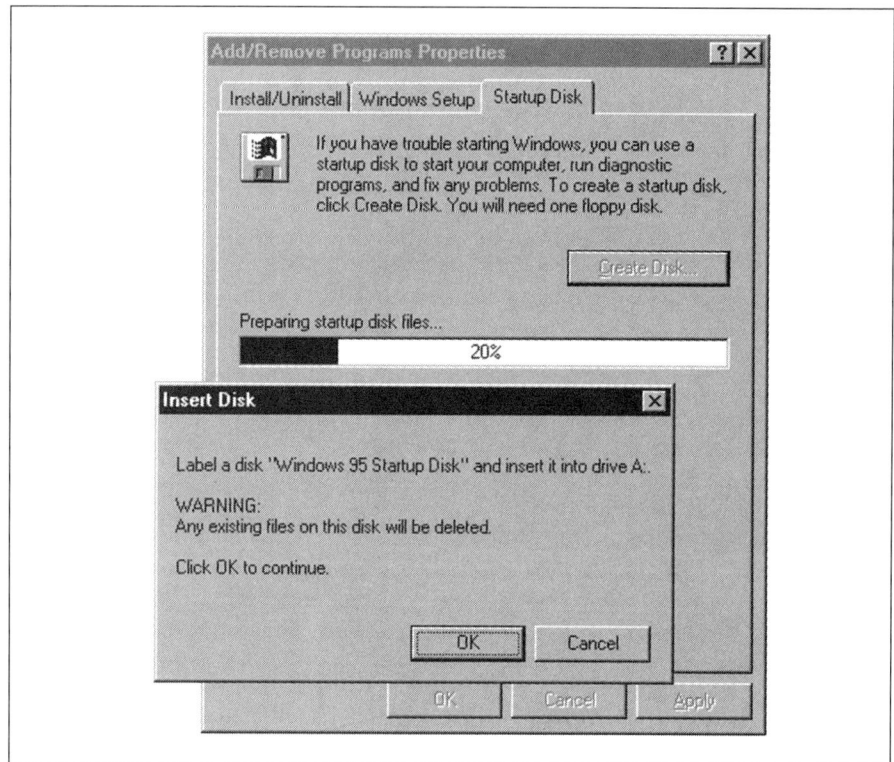

    2. Insert a disk as prompted (I recommend writing the date on the disk label as well as naming it with the Label option), and the system will create the disk. To make troubleshooting easier, it's a good idea to copy `CONFIG.SYS`, `AUTOEXEC.BAT`, `WIN.INI`, `SYSTEM.INI`, and a copy of your system's Registry onto this disk. Do that, and your startup disk will contain all the files that you need to fix your hard disk and replace your configuration.

Keep the startup floppy write-protected and labeled, so you don't delete it accidentally. If your computer will not boot normally, you'll need this disk around just to get the system going.

Booting to DOS

Okay, I lied earlier: if you really want to, it's possible to make your computer capable of booting to DOS. It just requires either some previous planning (and a lot of empty space on your hard disk to contain 40MB of operating system files) or some post-installation tweaking.

Installing Windows 95 for Dual Boot

When installing Windows 95, you have the choice of either installing the operating system to a new directory or installing it into your old Windows directory over the previous installation (as Microsoft recommends). If you go with the default, then Windows 95 overwrites Windows 3.x and absorbs any previous system settings that apply to it. This is convenient, but (as noted at the beginning of this chapter) it limits your options if something goes wrong with Windows 95.

If you decide to install to a new directory instead of going with the default, specify the new directory during installation. This will preserve your old Windows installation. Other than that, the installation process will proceed normally.

When you've finished installing Windows 95, remove the read-only attribute for MSDOS.SYS and open the file in Notepad. In the [Options] section, add the line **BootMulti=1**. When you've finished, the active portion of MSDOS.SYS should look something like the following:

```
[Paths]
WinDir=C:\WINDOWS
WinBootDir=C:\WINDOWS
HostWinBootDrv=C

[Options]
BootGUI=1
Network=1
BootMulti=1
```

Reboot and press F8 when you see the "Starting Windows 95…" message. You'll now see an eighth option in the Windows Startup menu: *Previous version of MS-DOS*. Choose that item, and DOS will boot.

Booting to DOS

Although the Windows 95 Resource Kit describes an elaborate process for setting up dual DOS/95 booting after installation, the sad fact is that it doesn't work—renaming the command interpreter with a DOS extension seems to make it unreadable, and loading COMMAND.COM doesn't work either.

However, you can still boot to DOS if necessary, using the old-fashioned method of creating a DOS bootable floppy. Go to a *DOS*-based machine and create a system disk (this *must* be a DOS machine, not a Windows 95 machine). Insert the disk in drive A: and reboot, and your system will boot to DOS, and you'll have access to any DOS programs on your system. Kludgy, but it works.

CHAPTER

10

Installing and Supporting
New Hardware

ONE of the major pluses of an advanced operating system like Windows is its ability to centralize device control. Under DOS, a high-performance video board required a number of separate video drivers—one for 1-2-3, one for WordStar, one for Harvard Graphics, and so on. With Windows 3.x, in contrast, one Windows driver served all of the Windows applications. DOS was still important under Windows 3.x, however, because most hardware installation programs were DOS-based, and nearly all of the diagnostic programs that you found for new hardware were DOS programs.

Windows 95 changes the story on device support, as it does away with DOS, requiring that you find some other way to install and test the new hardware. Ultimately, even that won't be necessary, as the world will move more and more to Plug and Play, or something like it.

Until the promises of Plug and Play start coming to fruition, most of our existing systems require that we install boards the old-fashioned way, flipping DIP switches, moving jumpers, or running proprietary software programs.

Even on those antediluvian boards, however, Windows 95 offers a plus: the *Device Manager*, a central repository of information about your system's hardware configuration. In this chapter, you'll learn how to make the Device Manager understand what kind of hardware is in your system, how to configure boards in a 95-based system, and how to best keep track of your system's hardware information under 95.

Elements of Hardware Installation

No matter what operating system you're working in, the boards you install in your system must be compatible with other boards. *Compatible* in this sense means that they don't step on each other's toes. And that's where IRQs, DMAs, and the like come into the story.

When I was a kid, there was a kind of standing joke about Christmas Eve. Parents would buy their kids all kinds of stuff, and the stuff would come in boxes, arranged in a way that no one could ever duplicate: once you took the pieces of the toy out of the box, you'd never be able to repack it the way it came. The really fun part, however, was the incredibly bad documentation that came with the toys; I think a couple of comedians in the early 60s made their entire living parodying these "assembly instructions."

The folks that made all that toy documentation needed somewhere to go as the years wore on, and it appears they moved to circuit board documentation. These documentation writers all assume that you already understand five pretty important things. Those five things are:

I/O addresses These tell you which address the circuit board uses to communicate with the CPU.

DMA channels These are used to speed up I/O to and from the system's memory. (Note that your system is severely limited in how many boards can be hooked up to use DMA.)

IRQ levels Hardware devices must use these to interrupt the CPU to force it to service them in some time-critical fashion.

ROM addresses Many boards include some of their low-level control software in ROM. The ROM requires a memory address, which must not conflict with other ROMs or any RAM in the system.

RAM buffers   Some add-in cards maintain a little RAM (8K to 64K) on board to hold data temporarily. That RAM should not conflict with any other RAM or ROM in your system.

In the first half of this chapter I'll give you the scoop on these obscure-sounding resources.

I/O Addresses

Stop and think for a minute about how the CPU talks to some other piece of hardware, like a serial port, a disk controller, or a keyboard controller. You already know how the CPU talks to one kind of hardware—the memory. You know that the CPU can know which part of what memory chip it's talking to, because each location in memory has its own unique *memory address*.

Other hardware has addresses as well, but they're not memory addresses; they're a completely different set of addresses called input/output addresses, or *I/O addresses*. Some people call them port addresses or hardware addresses. Think of the CPU as having two windows on the outside world: the memory addresses and the I/O addresses.

Much as the CPU can read and write memory addresses, it can read and write I/O addresses. There are fewer I/O addresses than there are memory addresses, a lot fewer: Any computer built with a 386 or later processor can address 4096MB of RAM, but only 64K of I/O addresses. That's not all that limiting, really; most of us won't be attaching a thousand keyboards to a single PC.

I/O addresses allow a CPU to tell its peripherals apart, as you can see in Figure 10.1.

In this example, the CPU communicates with the RAM on its left via memory addresses. It communicates with other peripherals—a keyboard controller, a serial port with a mouse on it, and an Ethernet LAN card, in this simplified example—via their I/O addresses. The keyboard controller sits at address 64, the serial port at 3F8—there's an F in the number because it's a *hex* number, which I'll get to in a minute—and the Ethernet card is at address 300.

FIGURE 10.1

Distinguishing
peripherals with
I/O addresses

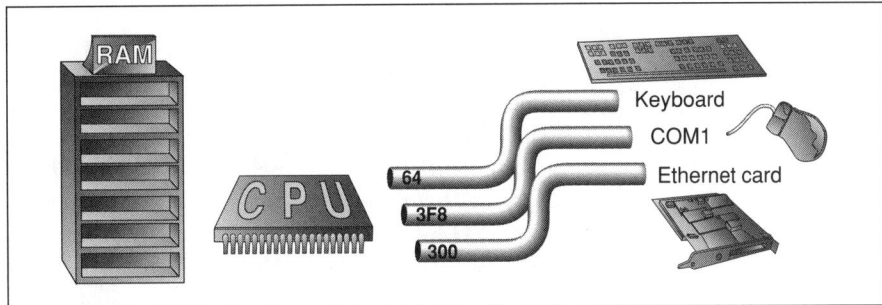

What this means is that when the CPU wants to send some data to the
Ethernet card, then it drops it down the tube labeled 300, rather than the
one labeled 3F8 or 64. (There aren't really tubes in a computer, of course;
I just like the imagery of the CPU communicating with its minions via
old-fashioned pneumatic tubes.)

It's Hex, But There Are No Spells

A quick word on the hex notation: you'll see that both memory addresses
and I/O addresses tend to be reported in *hexadecimal*, or *hex*, an alternative
way of writing numbers, preferred by techies because it lends itself to working with bytes.

Briefly, hex is just another way to represent numbers. We're all comfortable
with counting in the *decimal system*—the normal way of numbering: **0, 1, 2,
3, 4, 5, 6, 7, 8, 9**... that does it for the single digits; what comes next? Well,
we're used to the next number being a ten (**10**), which is the first number—
0—with a **1** stuck on the front of it. The number following that (eleven) is
the number that usually follows **0** (**1**, in case you've forgotten), except again
with a **1** stuck on the front of it to produce the familiar **11**, and so on.

Decimal has 10 single-character number symbols, which is why it's also
called *base 10*. Hexadecimal is based not on 10, but on *16*, and so hex needs
16 single-character number symbols. It starts off with the familiar **0**
through **9**, so it's got the first ten numbers. But after **9** comes **A**—hex uses
the letter A to represent its eleventh digit. As you'd imagine, **B** comes next,
and so on to **F** as the sixteenth digit. Therefore, the way you count in hex

is like so: **0, 1, 2, 3, 4, 5, 6, 7, 8, 9, A, B, C, D, E, F**... and then **10**. See, hex has a 10 just like the decimal system; it just arrives later.

For example, suppose I were to tell you that the COM1 serial port uses an address range from 3F8 through 3FF. (I can hear Ford Prefect of *The Hitchhiker's Guide to the Galaxy* answer, "Why? Do you think you're *likely* to tell me that?") How many addresses does COM1 then take up? Well, you know that 3F8 is the first address. After 3F*8* comes 3F*9*. Just like all the numbers you've ever known, the rightmost digit is the one that changes as the number gets bigger; 9 comes after 8, so 3F9 is the next value. Just a minute ago you learned that 9 is followed by A, so the next address would be 3FA, then 3FB, 3FC, 3FD, 3FE, and finally 3FF. (Why *finally*? Because the range is from 3F8 through 3FF, so when you get to the 3FF, you stop.) Go back and count them up, and you'll see that a serial port uses eight I/O addresses.

What does it do with all of those addresses? Several things. First of all, a serial port can both transmit and receive bytes at the same time. One address holds received data and one holds outgoing data. Of the other addresses, some will be used for status information, such as, "Does the modem have a connection to another modem?" Some will be wasted—wasted because it's easiest for a circuit designer to take either eight or sixteen addresses, due to a peculiarity in the PC hardware. If you designed a board that only required seven I/O addresses, you'd still take eight of them.

Common I/O Address Uses

That's probably a bit more than you actually wanted to know. What you really need to know about addresses is "How do you know which ones are currently taken?" Well, you can start off with Table 10.1.

Many devices have only one I/O address that they can use. Using the example of COM1 again, part of the very definition of COM1 is that it uses I/O addresses 3F8 through 3FF. Other devices may allow you to use any of a range of addresses; for example, most sound cards default to address 220, but will allow you to reconfigure them to use some other address if 220 is not available. Reconfigure a COM1 serial port, in contrast, and it's no longer a COM1 serial port.

TABLE 10.1

Common I/O Address Uses in PCs

HEX ADDRESS RANGE	USER
00–0F	DMA Controller 8237 #1
20–21	Programmable Interrupt Controller 8259A #1
40–43	Timer 8253
60–63	8255 Peripheral Controller
60–64	Keyboard Controller (AT only) 8742
70–71	Setup RAM access address (AT only)
80–8F	DMA page registers
A0–A1	Programmable Interrupt Controller #2 (8259 AT only)
A0–AF	NMI Mask Register
C0–DF	8237 DMA Controller #2 (AT only)
F0–FF	Math Coprocessor (AT only)
1F0–1F8	Hard disk controller
200–20F	Joystick controller
210–217	Expansion chassis
220–22F	FM Synthesis Interface (WAV device), Sound Blaster default
238–23B	Bus mouse
23C–23F	Alt. bus mouse
278–27F	LPT2
2B0–2DF	EGA
2E0–2E7	GPIB (AT only)
2E8–2EF	COM4 serial port
2F8–2FF	COM2 serial port

TABLE 10.1

Common I/O Address
Uses in PCs (continued)

HEX ADDRESS RANGE	USER
300–30F	Ethernet card
300–31F	Prototype card
320–32F	Hard disk controller (XT only)
330–33F	MIDI port (common location)
378–37F	LPT1 printer port
380–38F	SDLC card
3A0–3AF	BSC card
3B0–3BF	Monochrome adapter
3BC–3BF	LPT3
3D0–3DF	Color/Graphics adapter
3E8–3EF	COM3 serial port
3F0–3F7	Floppy disk controller
3F8–3FF	Com1 serial port

NOTE The key to understanding why this information is important is to know that this address cannot be used by any other device: the rule is, only one device to an I/O address. To understand why this is so, I'll steal an old analogy.

I/O Address Conflicts

Think of I/O addresses as being like post office boxes. Say the keyboard has P.O. box 64. When the keyboard has data for the system, it puts the data in box 64. When the CPU wants to read the keyboard, it looks in box 64. Box 64 is, in a very real sense, a better definition of the keyboard from the CPU's point of view than the keyboard itself is. If you plug a new board into your system, and that board uses I/O address 64, then the new board won't work, and, in addition, the keyboard will cease to work as well—you can't run two devices off the same I/O address.

Now, in reality, no one's going to design a board that uses address 64, because everybody knows that's the keyboard's. Not only that, but everybody knows you have to have a keyboard. But what about a case where you have a conflict in *optional* boards?

For example, I recently installed a Sound Blaster 16 on a PC that was already equipped with an Ethernet card and a SCSI host adapter. The Sound Blaster 16 includes a circuit called a MIDI interface, and it happened to be set at I/O address 330. Unfortunately, 330 is the I/O address used by the SCSI host adapter, so I got a disk boot failure when I turned my system on. There actually was nothing wrong with the *disk*; it was the disk's host adapter *board* that couldn't work due to the conflict with the Sound Blaster 16. Checking the documentation, I found that the sound card's MIDI circuit offered either address 330, which it was currently using, or 300. I set the address to 300 (by using a *jumper*, which is what the Sound Blaster 16 uses to set its MIDI address), reinstalled the board, and had the situation as shown in Figure 10.2.

Now my CPU's I/O address 300—that particular post office box—is shared by the MIDI circuit on the sound card and the Ethernet card. The system didn't complain when I booted up, because my system doesn't need either the sound card or the Ethernet card in order to boot. But when I tried to configure the sound card, it failed. You can see why in Figure 10.3.

FIGURE 10.2

Sharing I/O addresses between an Ethernet card and a sound card

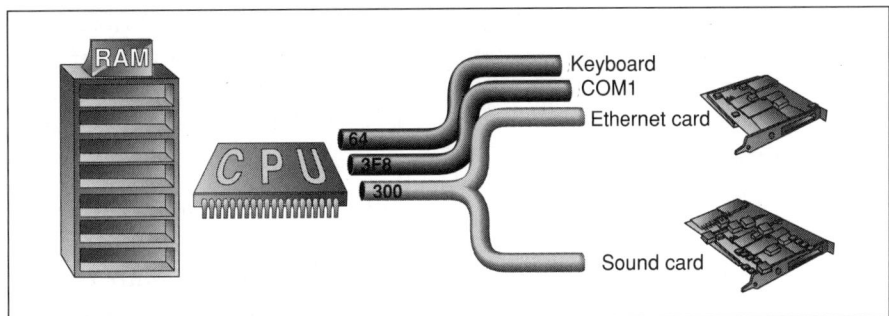

FIGURE 10.3

I/O conflict between
an Ethernet card and
a sound card

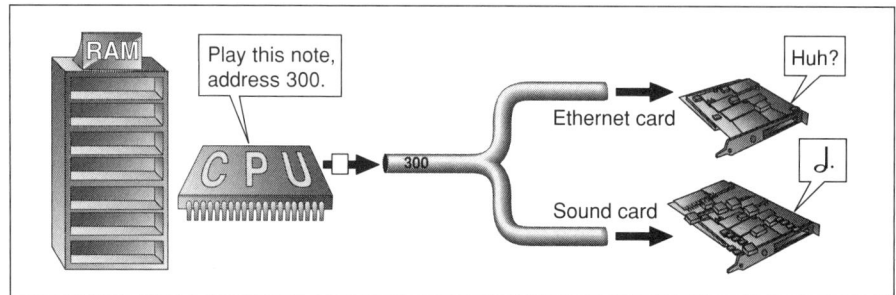

A "play this note" message went into I/O address 300. The Ethernet card has no idea how to respond to this request, and indeed may not be prepared for any requests at all. Worse yet, the electrical signal from the CPU gets split up two ways, so it may not be strong enough to actually get to *either* board.

Why did Creative Labs, the creator of the Sound Blaster 16, build a deliberate conflict into its card? The answer is, they didn't. There is no official standard for SCSI host adapter I/O addresses; Adaptec uses 330 for some of their boards, Trantor uses 350, Iomega offers a range from 320 through 350, and I'm sure other SCSI vendors have other options. Ethernet cards *tend* to sit at address 300, but that's not set in stone. What I'm saying is that the most common conflicts will be between the types of boards that appeared after the mid-80s, because, since then, there has been no central coordinating force in the PC hardware industry.

How did I solve my conflict, by the way? Well, the Adaptec board offered me 330 or 300 as my only choices, as did the sound board. The Ethernet board offered 300, 310, 320, 330, or 340. I didn't want to mess with the Adaptec board, because it was the hard disk interface, and if *it* became conflicted then I'd lose access to the vitally important hard disk—so I left the SCSI board at 330. That meant that the Sound Blaster 16 had to go to 300. The Ethernet board then played the peacemaker, as I set it to address 310.

More and more, I find that board manufacturers are moving from jumper settings to software settings, but in this case, the SCSI board and the sound board set their addresses with jumpers, and the Ethernet card set its I/O address with software. Which do I prefer? Well, software is, of course, nice. But suppose the sound board came preset to 330, as it did, and required that I run some software in order to get it to switch addresses? That would be a real pain. Think about it: I'd install the sound board at 330 initially, as I had no choice. That would disable my hard disk, requiring that I juggle floppies in order to run the program that would set a different address for the sound board. To add insult to injury, the setup program for the sound board only works once it's installed on the *hard* disk. I just might decide that getting past *that* gauntlet wouldn't be worth it, and scrap the board altogether. In contrast, all I *actually* had to do was to move a jumper. So there are pros and cons to both sides.

> **NOTE**   I've already said this, but let me repeat: You probably won't have a clue which DIP switches do what unless you have the documentation, so be sure to latch onto any switch-setting documentation you've got.

What would I have done, by the way, if the Ethernet card was set at 300 and wouldn't accept any other addresses? How would you resolve that problem? *You may not be able to resolve all I/O address conflicts,* as not all boards even give you the chance to change I/O addresses. It's hard to believe, but some boards are hard wired to use only one I/O address range. I had a LIM board that conflicted with a clock/calendar, but unfortunately neither board gave me a chance to change the I/O address. One board had to be removed—the conflict couldn't be resolved.

1K Addresses versus 64K Addresses

I mentioned that there are 64K I/O addresses. The ISA bus, however, only implements 1,024 addresses. The bottom 256 (hex locations 000 through 0FF) are only available to components on the system board. Plug-in expansion boards must use the top 768 locations (hex 100 through 3FF). Therefore, expansion boards will only allow you (if they are designed properly) to set your I/O addresses somewhere between 100 hex and 3FF hex.

MCA, EISA, PCI, and VESA slots support all 64K I/O addresses. But if you're installing a board in a system that contains a hybrid of EISA, PCI, or VESA slots as well as *ISA* slots, then you may run into a conflict. These non-ISA slots don't just support up to address 3FF hex (1K); they support up to address FFFF (64K). Note that extra digit—it's important.

There aren't many that do this currently, but some boards use I/O addresses above 3FF, and some ISA buses get confused about this. Suppose, for example, that you have some garden-variety ISA board in a hybrid ISA/VESA system at address 2D8, and a VESA local-bus video accelerator board at address E2D8. 2D8 and E2D8 look like different addresses, and they *are* different addresses—but *not* to some *ISA*-based machines. Because it's a hybrid PC, the commands to read or write data over address 2D8 might be destined for a VESA slot, or they might be intended for an ISA slot. In contrast, commands dealing with address E2D8 *must* be intended for a VESA slot, as it's impossible for address E2D8 to be relevant to an ISA slot. Unfortunately, there are hybrid motherboards that repeat *all* I/O address communications over *all* bus slots. As ISA only understands three address digits, sending a request referring to E2D8 to an ISA bus slot gets "heard" by the ISA slot as a request for address *2D8*. The result? Now you have an I/O address conflict with the ISA board at 2D8.

The bottom line is that when you're installing a board in a hybrid system, take a minute and make sure that there aren't conflicts between the four-digit I/O addresses and the three-digit I/O addresses.

I hope it's obvious by now that you can make your life a whole lot easier if you write down the I/O addresses used by your devices. Otherwise, installing a new board can be a real nightmare.

DMA Channels

Once a hard disk controller gets some data from the hard disk, that data's got to be stored in RAM. The same thing gets done when new data comes in on a local area network card. Big blocks of sound information must be zapped out to a sound card in a smooth, reliable fashion in order for that card to produce pleasant-sounding voice or music sounds. The data originates in the system's memory, and it has to get to the sound board.

A fundamental problem in computer design is getting data from memory (RAM) to or from a hard disk controller, LAN board, video capture card, sound board, video card—in short, to transfer data between memory and a *peripheral*. ("Peripheral" is easier to write than "LAN card, disk interface, etc.," so I'll stick to that from here on in.)

Programmed Input/Output (PIO)

The simplest way to move data between a peripheral and memory is via *programmed input/output*, or *PIO*. With PIO, the CPU sends commands to the peripheral through an I/O address or addresses. Let's see how that gets done with a simple example.

Suppose the CPU wants some data from a part of one of the disk drives. Data on disks, as you'll learn in the disk section, is organized into *sectors*, blocks of data that are 512 bytes long. When a PC accesses data from a disk, it can't take it in 1- or 2-byte chunks; the smallest amount of data that the CPU can ask for is a 512-byte sector. Suppose the goal for the moment is to get sector 10 from the disk and to put it into RAM. The first step is for the CPU to tell the disk interface to get the data; on many disk interfaces it does that on I/O address 1F0, as you see in Figure 10.4.

The disk interface then responds to the request, pulling the 512 bytes off the disk drive. The interface then tells the CPU that it's ready, and the CPU now has the task of getting the data from the disk interface to the RAM. Assuming that the disk interface works with the CPU via a 16-bit bus instead of a 32-bit bus (which is still, unfortunately, true in 90 percent of the PCs), the CPU requests the first two of those bytes, as you see in Figure 10.5.

The CPU then stuffs that data somewhere in RAM, as you see in Figure 10.6.

Moving those two bytes takes time, as does figuring out where to put the *next* two bytes. The CPU then requests two more bytes, puts them in RAM, figures out where the next bytes will go, and so on. Will this work?

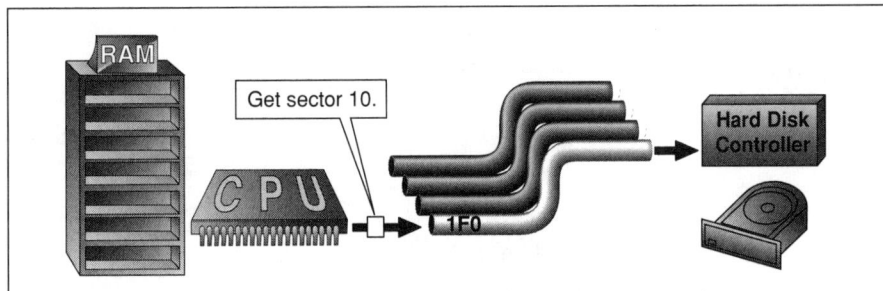

FIGURE 10.4

PIO part 1: Requesting data from the disk interface using I/O addresses

FIGURE 10.5

FIGURE 10.5

PIO part 2:
Requesting first part
of data from the disk
controller

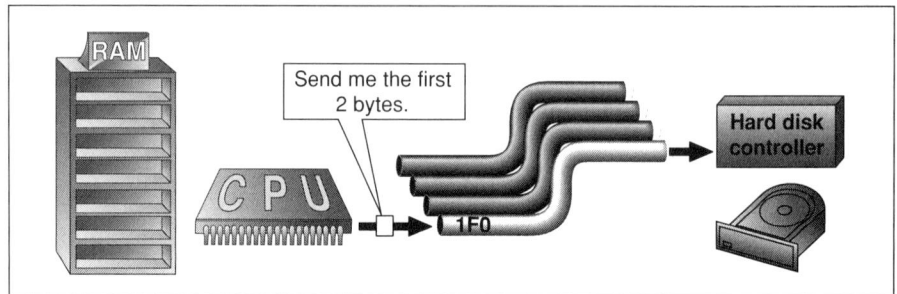

FIGURE 10.6

PIO part 3: Putting
data into RAM

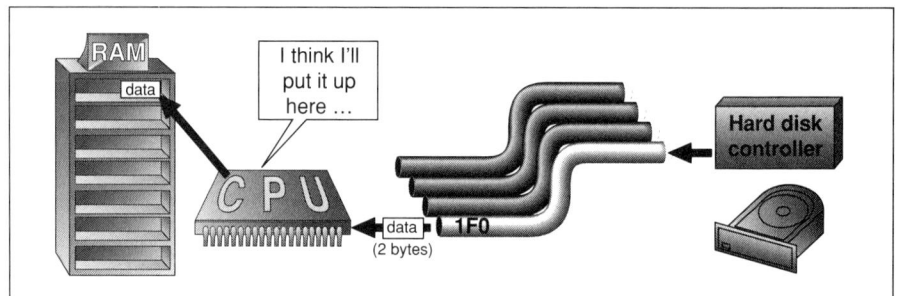

Yes, undoubtedly. Is it fast? Well, not always. Can we make this faster?
Certainly. Read on.

DMA (Direct Memory Access)

Now let's take a look at how PC CPUs access floppy disk drives. Suppose
I want to read sector 20 off of a floppy disk. Things start out very much
the same as before, as you see in Figure 10.7.

FIGURE 10.7

DMA part 1:
Requesting data from
disk controller

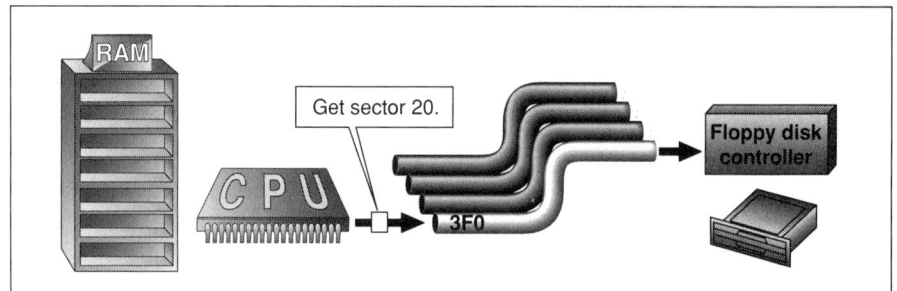

The floppy disk controller is at address 3F0, so the CPU sends the initial command out over that address. Ah, but when the floppy disk controller has the data ready, then it knows that having the CPU pick up two bytes and put them down and then pick up two *more* bytes and put *them* down, and so on, takes time. If the idea is to get the data into the RAM, why not cut out the middleman? The process is depicted in Figure 10.8.

First, there's a diversionary tactic, allowing something other than the CPU to control the bus; then, as you see in Figure 10.9, the data gets delivered to the RAM directly.

Okay, I admit that the floppy disk controller doesn't really distract the CPU; actually, it says to the CPU, "May I have direct access to the memory?" Some of the wires on the bus are DMA Request (DREQ) lines and some are DMA Acknowledge (DACK) lines. A board requests direct access to the memory bus with a DREQ line, and the CPU responds with a DACK. The idea here is to keep more than one peripheral from seizing the bus; there are multiple DMA request/acknowledge lines, more commonly called *DMA channels*.

FIGURE 10.8

DMA part 2: Diversion of the CPU by the disk controller

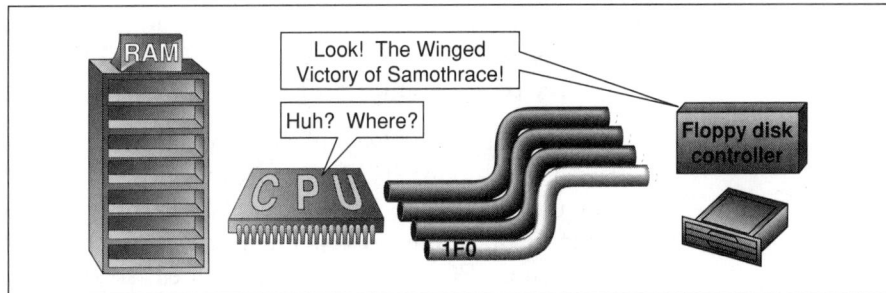

FIGURE 10.9

DMA part 3: Using the DMA channel to put data directly into RAM

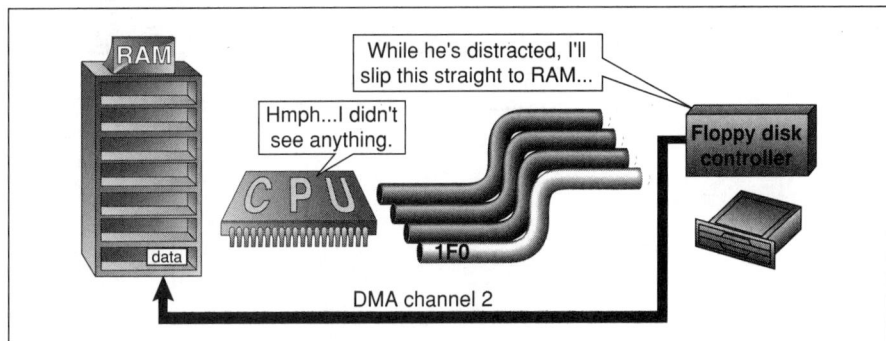

The original PC had a single DMA controller chip, the 8237. It allowed up to four DMA channels, and to this day 8-bit ISA slots only have four DMA channels available, numbered from 0 to 3.

The original PC used channel 0 for *dynamic memory refresh*. Briefly, here's how it works. There are two kinds of memory: dynamic and static. Dynamic sounds better than static, but it isn't. When you tell a static RAM (SRAM) something, it remembers it until you turn off the power or change it. Think of memory as a container of liquid, and static RAMs are ceramic mugs. You put water in them, it stays there. Dynamic RAMs (DRAMs), on the other hand, are like water cups made out of thin sheets of paper; they leak. Put data into a DRAM and it will forget whatever you tell it within 4 milliseconds (ms).

As a result, old PCs had to drop everything and do a RAM refresh every 3.86 ms. This took 5 ticks of the clock out of every 72, or about 7 percent of the PC's time. Of course, if the CPU were doing a lot of INs, OUTs, internal calculations, or the like, then you wouldn't notice the slowdown, as the whole idea of DMA is to work in parallel with the CPU. (Wouldn't static RAMs make a slightly faster computer? Yes, ...but they're more costly, lots more costly.) In more modern PCs, the RAM refresh is handled by a separate circuit. DRAMs still need to be refreshed in modern systems, but the CPU isn't involved, so no DMA is required, and channel 0 is free on most modern PCs.

On the older PCs I was referring to a minute ago, the hard disk controller used DMA channel 1, but most modern disk interfaces don't use DMA, they use PIO for reasons I'll explain in a minute; as a result, channel 1 is available on modern PCs. The floppy disk controller has employed channel 2 since PC days, and it still does; so don't assign anything else to channel 2. In general, channel 3 is unused.

Modern machines with 16-bit ISA, MCA, EISA, PC Card, PCI, or VESA slots have two DMA controllers, and thus eight DMA channels to the XT's four.

NOTE

Notice that the above implies that you only have *one* free DMA channel on an old XT-type machine, but seven available DMA channels on most modern PCs—just leave channel 2 for the floppy controller, and you're in good shape.

To DMA or Not to DMA?

You're probably wondering by now what I left out of the story. I just got finished explaining that DMA allows for faster transfers of data between peripherals and memory, and modern machines basically don't use DMA. (You're supposed to go "*huh?*" at this point.)

DMA is pretty nifty, except for one thing. In order to assure backward compatibility, the AT's designers held DMA operations to 4.77 MHz— the original PC's clock speed. Lest you skim over this because it sounds like a history lesson, *ISA bus machines still do DMA at 4.77 MHz.* Honest. If you have a shiny new 200 MHz Pentium Pro-based system on your desk and you do a DMA operation on it, the whole shootin' match slows down to just under *three percent* of that 200 MHz clock speed. The best the other buses do when DMA-ing is 8 MHz on DMA. What's the answer? Bus mastering; but I'll get to that in a minute.

Anyway, that's why you'll see that some boards give you a choice as to whether to DMA or not.

So, in summary, if you have an expansion board that needs a DMA channel,

- The only one available is generally DMA channel 3 on the old PCs.
- If you're installing a 16-bit board, try whenever possible to use the extra 16-bit-only DMAs—channels 4 through 7—to leave room for the 8-bit boards in your system.
- If you're out of DMAs, see if the board offers the option to disable DMA. Disabling them might be slower, but it might be faster. On most modern computers (above 25 MHz), PIO will probably be faster than DMA. Try it both ways to see.

You can see common DMA uses in Table 10.2.

CHANNEL	USE
0	Dynamic RAM Refresh (XT—free on AT)
1	Hard Disk Controller (XT only—free on AT), or commonly used by sound boards in AT architecture
2	Floppy Controller
3	Unused, but also used on many 16-bit sound boards (they use two DMA channels)
4–7	Available on modern PCs

Bus Mastering

This is a slight digression, but it's important, it fits in here, and I'll keep it short.

You just learned that DMA is a neat idea that is hampered by an historical error—4.77 MHz. DMA actually has another problem, although it's not one that would be immediately apparent.

DMA can transfer data from a peripheral to RAM, or RAM to a peripheral, with neither transfer requiring the CPU's intervention. But DMA can't transfer data from a *peripheral* to a *peripheral* because such an operation would be two DMA operations: peripheral to RAM, followed by RAM to peripheral.

Many boards built for the EISA, MCA, or PCI buses can do *bus master transfers*, allowing them to bypass not only the CPU, but RAM as well, transferring data between peripherals at the maximum speed that the bus supports. Bus mastering, then, can speed up a system in two ways. You see this diagrammed in Figure 10.10.

ISA supports bus mastering, but only allows one bus master board in an ISA system. EISA, MCA, and PCI systems allow multiple bus masters. It's a feature worth exploiting.

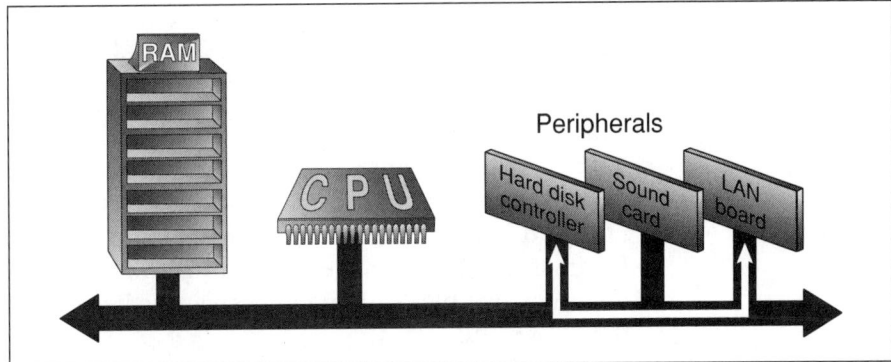

IRQ (Interrupt Request) Levels

In the DMA section, I was describing PIO. After the CPU made the request of the disk controller for the data, I then said "the disk interface then tells the CPU that it's ready..."—which was a trifle sneaky on my part. As far as the CPU is concerned, it initiates all conversations with peripherals; they "speak when they're spoken to." A peripheral gets the CPU's attention in one of two ways: *polling* or *interrupts*.

Polling

To illustrate polling, let's look at how DOS controls a parallel port in order to print data. The printer is massively slower than the CPU, so there has got to be some way to handshake the two. Things start off as you see in Figure 10.11.

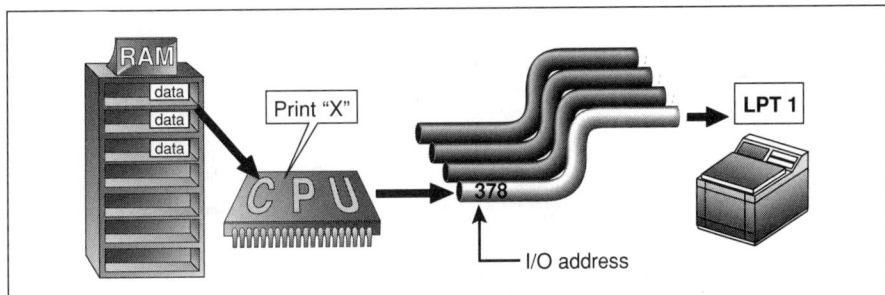

Data travels through I/O address 378, the address of LPT1, and is deposited from there into the printer. The CPU then keeps an eye on the printer, as you see in Figure 10.12.

The CPU just sits there at the pneumatic tube (forgive me) numbered 378, repeatedly checking for an indication from the printer, much as someone expecting a letter might run out to the mailbox every ten minutes. (I'd include the lyrics for that song that goes, "Wait a minute, Mr. Postman...," but then we'd have to get the copyright permission, and it's too much trouble. You might just want to hum along to get into the polling frame of mind.)

The CPU essentially sits on address 378, asking, "Are you ready now? How about *now*? How about NOW?..." It's a big waste of the CPU's time, but this polling method of waiting for an I/O device to finish its work is simple to design. Besides, in a single-tasking world like you see in DOS, the CPU doesn't have anything else to do anyway; it is singly focused on servicing the parallel port. Eventually, as you see in Figure 10.13, the port responds.

FIGURE 10.12

Polling of the printer by the CPU

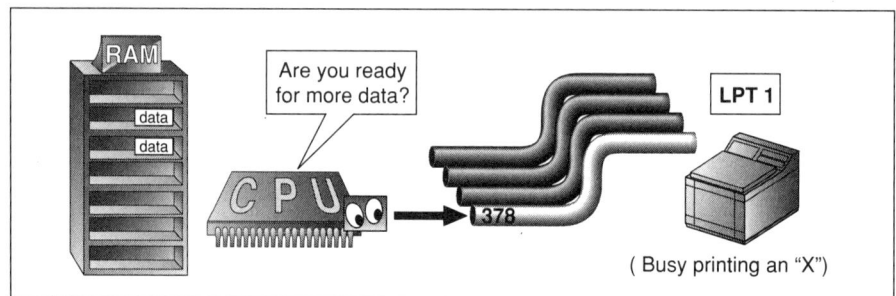

FIGURE 10.13

Response of parallel port to polling

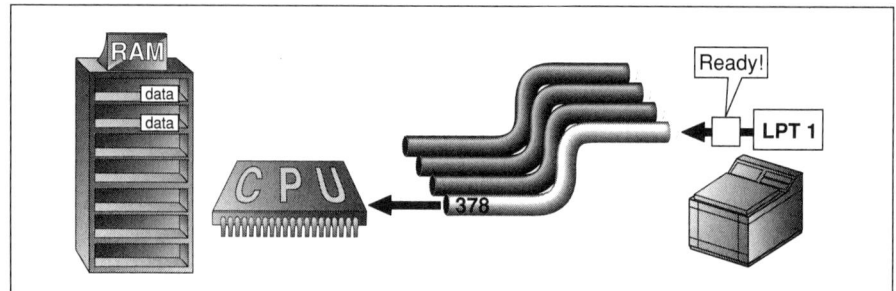

The CPU now sends another byte to the printer, and it begins all over again. As I've said, the process is wasteful but simple, and it works fine in the single-tasking DOS world.

Hardware Interrupts

But what about a multi-tasking world, such as most of us live in today? And even if you work single-tasking, there are many peripherals on your PC, and the PC can't poll them all. That's why hardware interrupts are built into the PC.

You can see how interrupts work if we look back to the discussion of how the CPU gets data from the disk interface. Recall that the CPU stuffed a "get some data" request down I/O address 1F0. Now, it takes time for the disk to return the desired data. Why not let the CPU use that time to do other things, as in Figure 10.14?

The disk interface is in its "own private Idaho," as the CPU is likewise off in its own world. But most modern disk controllers have a circuit running between themselves and the CPU, a circuit called an interrupt request level, or IRQ level. (Actually, some really high-performance SCSI host adapters don't do this.) The disk interface wakes up the CPU, as you see in Figure 10.15.

Once the CPU has been interrupted, it knows to start getting the information from the disk controller, as I described in the discussion of PIO a few pages back.

FIGURE 10.14

CPU works on other things while waiting for disk controller

FIGURE 10.15

Using IRQ levels
to get the attention
of the CPU

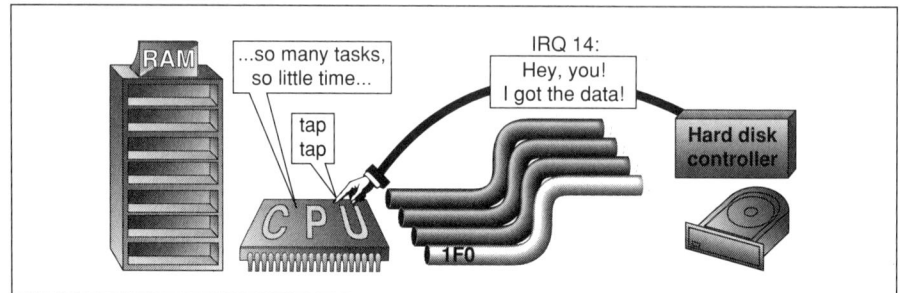

How Interrupts Work

PC interrupts were originally handled by an Intel 8259 *prioritized interrupt controller* (*PIC*); nowadays, there's no discrete 8259 on your system, it's just built into the motherboard's chipset. The 8259 is prioritized in that it has eight interrupt levels numbered from 0 to 7, and lower numbers get higher priority. That means that if interrupt 3 and interrupt 7 both ring at the same time, it's interrupt 3 that gets handled (serviced in PC hardware lingo).

When an interrupt occurs, the 8259 forces the CPU to put its current work on hold and immediately execute a program that allows it to handle the interrupt. Such a program is called, appropriately, an interrupt handler or an interrupt service routine. For example, in the disk drive example, when IRQ14 occurs, then the CPU jumps to a small program that tells it how to grab the data from the disk controller (via PIO, in the case of most PC disk interfaces), stuff it into some RAM, and return to whatever it was doing before it was interrupted.

The original PC had only one 8259, with eight interrupt lines, and that PC's bus implemented lines 2 through 7; interrupts 0 and 1 weren't on the bus because they were pre-assigned. IRQ0 is attached to a timer circuit that creates an interrupt about 18 times per second. IRQ1 is attached to the 8042 keyboard controller. Driving the keyboard interface via interrupts is a good idea, because the keyboard controller is pretty dumb. It has no memory to speak of, and so every time a keystroke arrives at the controller, it must hand off this keystroke to the CPU (who then puts it in the keyboard buffer) before another keystroke comes in. Essentially, once the keyboard controller gets a keystroke, it wants to say to the CPU, "HEY! STOP EVERYTHING! COME SERVICE ME **NOW** BEFORE

THE USER PRESSES ANOTHER KEY!!!!" And so it "rings the bell"—
it activates its interrupt line, and the CPU stops doing whatever it's doing and executes the program that moves the keystroke to the keyboard
buffer.

PCs since the AT have all been equipped with a second 8259, bringing
the total of interrupts on most PCs up to 16. You can see the common
uses for that in Table 10.3.

If you're installing a board, and it needs an IRQ, look first to IRQ2 on a
PC or IRQ5 on an AT. If those aren't available, try 3—if you don't have
a COM2, there's no conflict.

Conflicts on COM Ports: "Sharing Interrupts" Examined

I've already said a couple of times in this book that you can have COM1
or COM3, but not both, and that you can have COM2 or COM4, but not
both. *Now* I can explain it.

As you saw in the preceding interrupt table, IRQ3 is assigned both to
COM2 and to COM4. So if you had both COM2 and COM4, they'd
have to share IRQ3.

The problem with that scenario is that sharing interrupts isn't possible on
many PC add-in cards. Blame it on the ISA bus; it does not support sharing IRQs. In fact, it's unlikely but possible that inserting two boards using
the same IRQ level into the same ISA-based system could permanently
damage both boards.

Newer buses allow for IRQ sharing: MCA, EISA, PC Card, and PCI bus
slots all allow interrupt sharing, if the boards going into those slots are designed to accommodate shared interrupts—but not all are, unfortunately.
VESA doesn't support it. The preponderance of ISA and VESA systems
out there means that for most of us, IRQ sharing is out. So where did
COM3 and COM4 come from? The original PS/2 machines were designed with, of course, an MCA bus, and so IBM saw that a third party
could design an add-in card that offered a third and perhaps fourth serial
port. They wanted software support for it, so DOS 3.3—the version of
DOS released with the PS/2 in April 1987—included support for COM3
and COM4. People started asking for it, and so vendors built COM3/

TABLE 10.3

Common IRQ Uses in the PC Family

INTERRUPT LINE	DEVICE	COMMENTS
0	Timer	
1	Keyboard	
2	Cascade to IRQ9	On some systems, IRQ2 is the gateway to IRQs 9–15; avoid it if possible.
3	COM2	Can also be COM4, but only one of the two.
4	COM1	Can also be COM3, but only one of the two.
5	XT hard disk controller, LPT2	Hard disk interface used only on XTs, or alternatively for LPT2 on the unusual machine with LPT2. This is free on most modern PCs, and is the "catch-all" IRQ for bus mice, sound cards, LAN boards, etc.
6	Floppy disk controller	
7	LPT1	
8	Clock	
9	Possible cascade to IRQ2	May not be available; see text.
10		Generally available.
11		Generally available.
12	Motherboard InPort	If your PC/laptop has a built-in mouse port, it probably sits here.
13	Coprocessor	This interrupt is required even if your CPU has a numeric coprocessor built in.
14	Hard Disk	
15	Unused	Generally available.

COM4 support into their machines, even though it was a silly idea on an ISA board.

> **NOTE**
>
> If you have a mixed-bus system, like PCI and ISA, or EISA and ISA, then if ISA uses an interrupt, you can't share it through the advanced bus. For example, if an ISA board uses IRQ3, then none of the EISA boards can use IRQ3. On the other hand, if in that case no ISA board used IRQ4, then any number of EISA boards could use IRQ4—they could, that is, if the boards were designed to share IRQs, *and* if the *drivers* for the boards supported interrupt sharing. (How can you find out? It'll be in the documentation. Unfortunately, there are very few add-in cards that support IRQ sharing.)

IRQ 2 and IRQs 9 through 15

A lot of people buy themselves grief by putting their network cards on IRQ2. Don't do it. IRQ2 was available back on the 8-bit PC/XT type designs, but it serves a valuable role in modern PCs.

The PC/XT systems had a single interrupt controller, an Intel 8259 chip. The 8259 could support up to eight interrupt channels, and the original PC/XT systems hard-wired channels 0 and 1 to the system timer (a clock circuit that goes tick every 15 ms) and the 8042 keyboard controller.

The system was wired with those interrupts because IBM wanted to make sure that the keyboard and the timer had high priorities; you recall that on an 8259, when two interrupts occur at the same time, the one with the lower number gets priority.

In 1984, the first 16-bit PC compatible system was released—the IBM AT. The proliferation of add-in devices on the market made it clear that eight interrupt levels just wasn't enough. So, as I've mentioned before, IBM decided to add another 8259. The problem was that just slapping the extra 8259 onto the motherboard might present some backward-compatibility problems, so IBM decided to kind of slip in the extra 8259 via the back door, as you can see in Figure 10.16.

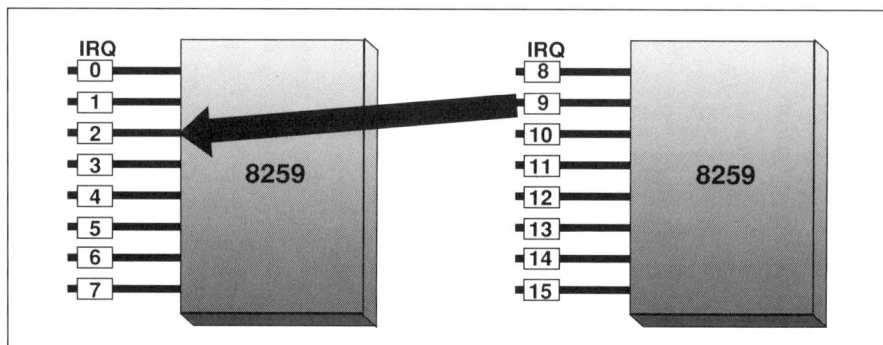

The way they did it was to take the new IRQs 8 through 15 and route them through IRQ9, then connect IRQ9 to IRQ2. Result: Whenever IRQ8 through 15 is triggered, IRQ9 goes off, which makes IRQ2 look like *it* went off. The PC's BIOS then knows that whenever IRQ2 appears, that *really* means to check the second 8259 to find out which IRQ *really* rang the bell. By the way, they also freed up IRQ5; it's no longer needed by your AT-or-later hard disk controller.

Some Advice on Choosing IRQs

This implies a few things. First, don't use IRQ2, as it already has a job: it's the gateway to IRQs 8-15. Many people set their network cards to IRQ2 and then wonder why their system randomly hangs. If you *do* use IRQ2 for some circuit board, then you may have some driver software set to IRQ9. IRQ9 and IRQ2 are electrically equal under this system, as they're tied together.

It also means that it's a good idea to avoid IRQ9, if you can.

Other things to consider when choosing interrupts:

- Because interrupts 8 through 15 slide into the architecture via IRQ2, they essentially inherit IRQ2's priority level. That means that IRQs 8 through 15 are of higher priority than IRQs 3 through 7.

- Safe IRQs are 5, 10, 11, and 15; avoid the others. You'll probably need to use these for your:

  - Sound card. If it's an 8-bit card, then your only option is IRQ5.
  - A LAN board.
  - SCSI host adapter, although some bus mastering SCSI host adapters (like the Adaptec 2742) can actually forgo interrupts, needing only a DMA channel.

NOTE Whatever you set your boards to, *write it down!* You'll need the information later.

Earlier, I suggested taping an envelope to the side of a PC and keeping important floppies there. Here are some other things to put in there. Each time I install a board (or modify an existing board), I get a new piece of paper and write down all the configuration information on the board; for example, I might note "Intel EtherExpress 16 card installed 10 July 1994 by Mark Minasi; no EPROM on board, shared memory disabled, IRQ10 used, I/O address 310 set." The Device Manager can help here, as it will print out a report of the hardware in your system; I'll discuss that later in this chapter.

I've mentioned this earlier, in the I/0 address discussion, but let me repeat: some boards don't have jumpers and DIP switches. This means that *there is no way to get them to work with conflicting boards.* For example, a client that I regularly visited had installed an IBM 5251 (System 36 terminal emulator) board and an old Quadram Quadboard in a PC. The printer port on the Quadboard and the terminal emulator wanted the same resource—which one, I'm not sure. In any case, neither had jumpers. One had to be thrown away. Moral: Find out if the expansion boards that you buy have adjustable DMA, IRQ, and I/O addresses.

I hesitate to mention this, but sometimes device conflicts can be solved by doing surgery on the boards. Just lobotomize the chips that are performing the function you wish to defeat. An example I have seen a couple of times is in serial ports. A client wanted me to set up a multifunction board in a PC with clock, memory, printer, and serial ports. He already had a board installed which provided both serial ports COM1 and COM2. The jumpers on the multifunction board allowed me to set the multifunction board's serial port to either COM1 or COM2, but not disable it altogether. What to do? A chip called the 8250 UART (Universal Asynchronous Receiver/Transmitter) is the heart of most serial ports. I found the 8250 on the multifunction board and removed it. The problem was eliminated. *Please don't try this unless you understand what you are doing.*

ROM Addresses and RAM Buffers

In addition to I/O addresses, DMA channels, and IRQ lines, there is a fourth source of conflict: ROM addresses. Some controller cards (like EGAs and hard disk controllers) require some ROM onboard to hold some low-level code. The XT controller board's ROM started at C800:0000. As before, a possibility exists that two different boards may require some software on board, and if the two boards *both* try to locate their ROM at the same location in the PC's memory address space, neither one will work.

Fortunately, some boards include jumpers to allow you to move the start address of the ROM. Most of the major boards that include ROM, like the EGA, VGA, XT-type hard disk controller, and the like, should *not* have (if it's even possible) their ROM addresses changed. Too many pieces of software rely on their standard addresses. The boards you'll see that typically include ROM are:

- Video boards, which have ROMs addressed at either address C0000 or E0000. It's usually not a good idea to move these addresses around.

- High-performance disk interfaces, which, like 32-bit IDE host adapters or SCSI host adapters, have ROMs on them; these ROMs can be moved if the board permits.

- Token Ring network adapters, which have some ROM on them; it is moveable.

- Any kind of LAN board can have ROM on it, if the PC boots from the network and not from its local hard disk. It's unusual, but some companies use this "diskless workstation" approach.

- Some high-end sound boards may have ROM on them; the ROMs contain prerecorded sounds, like samples of pianos, violins, or flutes.

- All PCs have some ROM at the top 64K of the first megabyte, the memory range from F0000 through FFFFF.

There are two things to be concerned about when configuring memory on add-in cards. First is the obvious one: Make sure that two different boards don't have memory configured to the same address.

The second thing you have to be concerned about is the effect of adapter memory on your *DOS memory manager*. Memory managers must know exactly which areas of memory are already filled up with adapter RAM or ROM, or the memory manager will overwrite the RAM or ROM, causing lots of potential system failures.

Most adapter RAM and ROM ranges vary, so I can't document them for you here, but you can see the unchanging ranges in Table 10.4.

Note the PCMCIA reference: PC Cards can take up to 64K of memory, and if you have two PC Card slots, that can mean that the entire C0000 through DFFFF range is taken.

TABLE 10.4 **Common ROM and RAM Buffer Addresses**	**FUNCTION**	**ADDRESS RANGE (HEX)**	**ADDRESS LENGTH**
	XT Hard Disk Controller	C8000–CBFFF	16K
	EGA	C0000–C3FFF	16K
	VGA	C0000–C7FFF or E0000–E7FFF	32K
	LIM Boards (may vary)	D0000–DFFFF	64K

Resolving Installation Conflicts: An Example

I'll provide you with as many installation examples as I can. Later, we'll look at the installation documentation for a few boards. But before we go on, I'd like to relate a few brief examples of installation problems and solutions that I encountered while putting a half-dozen Ethernet LAN boards into some computers. These things happened to me under DOS and older Windows, but the moral of the stories remain the same: Be careful when installing hardware.

The first LAN card I installed was an Ethernet board that used everything we've discussed—an I/O address range, a DMA channel, an IRQ channel, and some shared RAM. I left the I/O address at 300 hex, as that wouldn't conflict with the computer into which I was installing the board. The IRQ I chose was IRQ5, avoiding the more commonly used IRQ2. I avoid IRQ2 because it *can* be used in some systems, but the fact that it cascades to IRQs 8 through 15 makes me a bit nervous; in the past, using IRQ2 has caused conflicts with Windows. I set the DMA to channel 1, and put the shared RAM between CC000 through CFFFF, as I knew that it would not then conflict with the hard disk controller ROM between C8000 and CBFFF.

When I plugged the board in, however, it refused to function. A little fiddling around made me realize that the DOS memory manager that I was using was placing its memory at the same addresses as the shared memory on my LAN board, which in turn was clobbering the LAN board. I told the memory manager to exclude the range of addresses from CC000-CFFFF; the board worked fine after that. In Windows, you'd do that with the Device Manager, which I'll show you shortly.

I set the second board identically, and it refused to work. A quick check of my notebook reminded me that a sound board was using IRQ5, causing a conflict. The LAN board offered only IRQs 2 through 7, and I didn't want to use any of them, as I'd like to avoid 2 if I can, and 3 through 7 were busy, so I needed an alternative approach. A quick look at the sound board showed that it could support any IRQ up to IRQ10, so I reset the sound board to IRQ10, leaving IRQ5 free for the LAN board. Problem solved.

Trouble appeared on the next machine as well. After inserting the LAN board, not only did the LAN board not work, the video screen showed some odd colors upon bootup. It was a special Windows accelerator board, so I checked its documentation. The accelerator, as it turned out, employed the I/O address range 300 through 30F, causing a conflict with the Ethernet card. I reset the I/O address on the Ethernet card, and all was well with *that* machine.

The next computer booted up okay, but I got strange flickers on the video screen whenever I tried to test the Ethernet card with the test program supplied with the Ethernet board. The Ethernet card was failing its tests, also, so I looked more closely, and realized that I'd never opened this particular computer before.

This computer was equipped with a super VGA board. Almost all super VGA boards have an autoswitching feature that they'll optionally support, a feature whereby they automatically detect what video mode the currently running software needs, and then switch to that mode. This feature should be disabled, for two reasons. First, it causes OS/2 and Windows NT to fail, as well as a number of other programs. Second, the autoswitch mode requires that the video board use a combination of interrupts 2 and 9, which is less than desirable because it steals a much needed interrupt; in some cases, it causes a system to falsely report memory error. This super VGA card, as you can imagine by now, had the interrupt enabled, allowing for super VGA. I removed the interrupt jumper from the board—its location varies, and you must consult the documentation for your board before trying to remove the interrupt jumper. The Ethernet board ran without a hitch afterward. By the way, if you *are* planning to check your super VGA documentation to find out whether the interrupt is enabled, be aware that some manuals refer only to the interrupt and some refer only to autoswitching. If you can't find one, look for the other.

By now, as I approached the final machine, I was trying to *anticipate* problems. The LAN board placed in this last machine, like its comrades, refused to work at first. I struggled with this for a while, idly running diagnostic programs on the entire system. As I've explained before, I reasoned that if I could figure out what *didn't* work on this system that had worked *yesterday*, that would give me a clue about what the board was conflicting with. (Of course, there was the possibility that the board just plain didn't work, but the earlier experiences of the day seemed to render that doubtful.) Then I noticed that the diagnostic programs failed to notice that the PC had a mouse. Eureka! I recalled at that moment that this particular machine didn't have a serial mouse, unlike most machines in my office—it had a *bus* mouse. A bus mouse requires an interrupt-using circuit board of its own, and I was fairly sure that I'd set the interrupt on the bus mouse interface board to IRQ5. Not wanting to remove the cover from the PC unless necessary, I tried loading the mouse driver, and got the error message "interrupt jumper missing." I opened up the PC, checked the mouse board, and sure enough, it was using IRQ5. With its interrupt changed, I replaced the mouse board, and the last of the LAN boards was fired up and ready to go.

I don't want to discourage you with this story. I just want to underscore how important it is to keep documentation of what's installed in your current machines, and to share a war story with you that may give you an idea or two the next time you're having trouble making a new board behave.

Soft Setup versus Hard Setup Boards

How do you select one interrupt over another? On older boards, you flip DIP switches or move jumpers. On more and more boards, however, you run a program to control these settings.

If you get a board that has no switches, that is only set up with a diskette, then is that a Plug and Play (PnP) board? No, not necessarily. Plug and Play refers to a particular method of building a board, a way that does, indeed, use software configuration—but not every board that uses software configuration is a Plug and Play board.

Installing and Configuring New Boards with 95

Let's get down to the brass tacks of putting a board into 95 and making it work. The three parts of doing that are:

- Installing the board and physically placing it inside the machine.
- Configuring the board's resources.
- Finding, loading, and configuring a driver for the board.

In the ideal world, you just install a board, Windows detects it, and all is well. Sometimes that even *happens*, but usually there are complications. Answer these questions before installing a board:

- Does Windows have a driver for the board right there on its CD? Check the WinNews area of CompuServe or the Microsoft Network for a listing of the supported hardware. Whether your copy of Windows will support a particular board is determined partially by which Tune-up Packs you have installed in Windows, if any.

- Is the board Plug and Play? If not, make sure you know how to set its resources. If the board is Plug and Play, but your system isn't, *then enable Plug and Play anyway.* Windows 95 can often take control of the configuration of a Plug and Play board even if the BIOS doesn't support Plug and Play. (One example of this is the Intel Ethernet Pro cards. Even though they're ISA Plug and Play cards, you can stick them into any machine and Windows 95 will set the board's IRQ and I/O addresses. That's because the Ether Pro card isn't a *boot* device, at least not for most people. You get much of the power of Plug and Play on a non-PnP system for cards that aren't boot devices.)

- If there isn't a driver right on the CD, is there a Windows 95-compatible driver? If not, you can try a real-mode driver, but I don't recommend it.

The 95 Hardware Installation Roadmap

The most important question about hardware installation under Windows is, "Does the board support Plug and Play?"

Handling Plug and Play Hardware

If the board is Plug and Play, then there's usually not much to do—just plug it in and Windows will detect it. The worst thing that may happen is that Windows won't have the driver for it, so you'll have to supply a disk. In some cases, the system is complex enough that Windows can't make the board work on the first boot. If that's the case, try booting Windows two or three more times, giving the Windows Configuration Manager a chance to shuffle resources around. If things *still* don't work, then treat the Plug and Play board like a legacy board, as covered below.

Slight digression here: Not everything that claims to be Plug and Play *is*. For example, all PCI boards are *supposed* to be Plug and Play, but I've run into some troubles with PCI boards, particularly since they often do not ship with a configuration disk. These boards seem to *assume* that you'll be running them in a PnP system with a PnP operating system like Windows 95. Boards that have been tested to work in a Windows 95 environment and are Plug and Play are often indicated by a *Windows 95 Ready* sticker on their boxes.

> **NOTE**
>
> And one other thing about Plug and Play boards: Don't forget that a certain percentage of new circuit boards are just plain no good. I've never seen a figure on it, but twenty years of experience with microcomputers has led me to expect that about ten percent of the add-in cards are dead right out of the box.

What that means is that you're going to need some kind of test program, and, at least at the moment, the majority of board-level diagnostic programs are DOS-based. While most DOS-based diagnostics will work fine under Windows 95 in command-line safe mode, a few will not—for example, 3Com advises that the diagnostic program they have available as of this writing is not designed for use in this mode in Windows 95 and will not work. So keep a bootable DOS floppy around, just in case.

Handling Non-Plug and Play Boards

Installing a non-PnP board may pose some more trouble.

First of all, typically you have to set its resources so that it doesn't interfere with an existing board—no IRQ, DMA, I/O, or memory address conflicts. *Do that before you run Windows.*

For example, suppose you're installing a sound card. Sound cards often require a few I/O ranges, an IRQ level, and a DMA channel or two. Once you install the card, you have to make sure that the card doesn't step on the resources of any existing boards. If you just shove the board into the system, turn it on, and boot Windows, then you may get some nasty error messages (for example, if the built-in factory settings on the board conflict with your network board), and the conflict that you've just created will keep you from getting onto the network. Instead, try booting Windows to Safe Mode Command Prompt and set the resources from there.

Again, just a reminder: How you set resources for a board depends on the board. Some use jumpers and DIP switches, and others use software setup—you'd only use Safe Mode Command Prompt if you needed to run a software setup routine. And when you're finished setting resources on a board, *write them down.*

Next, you must first get Windows to recognize that the hardware is installed, and second, tell the Windows drivers what resources the board is using. Windows will often be able to figure out the resources, but you can hand-enter them with the Device Manager, as I'll describe in a few pages; for now, let's see how to get Windows to recognize the new board.

Windows has a set of excellent hardware detection routines, and it can detect about 80 percent (my figure, not Microsoft's) of the non-Plug and Play boards around. That's a staggering piece of work, and my hat's off to whoever wrote the code. In some cases, the hardware detection code is assisted by Windows 3.x, which means that if you were running Windows 3.x when you installed Windows 95, the 95 setup program just queried any existing 3.x drivers about the existence of add-in cards.

You may find, however, that you have to *tell* Windows that you have a new piece of hardware, and exactly what kind of hardware it is. You do that with the Hardware Installation Wizard, in the Control Panel. Open the Control Panel, and then double-click on Add New Hardware. You'll see a dialog box like in Figure 10.17.

Click Next, and you'll see the next screen, as in Figure 10.18.

Again, Windows has some nifty detection hardware, and it wants to show it off here—but *don't*. The detection software must, by its very nature, do some mildly risky things, things that *could* lock up your system or, in the worst case, damage data on your hard disk. Detection's fine for the wholesale hardware driver installation that occurs upon the initial Windows setup—and you, of course, backed up your data prior to installing Windows, so data loss isn't an issue. But if all you're doing is installing a mouse or a sound board, then you *know* what kind of hardware it is; after all, you just installed it. Click No, then Next, and you'll see a dialog box like in Figure 10.19.

FIGURE 10.17

Add New Hardware
Wizard

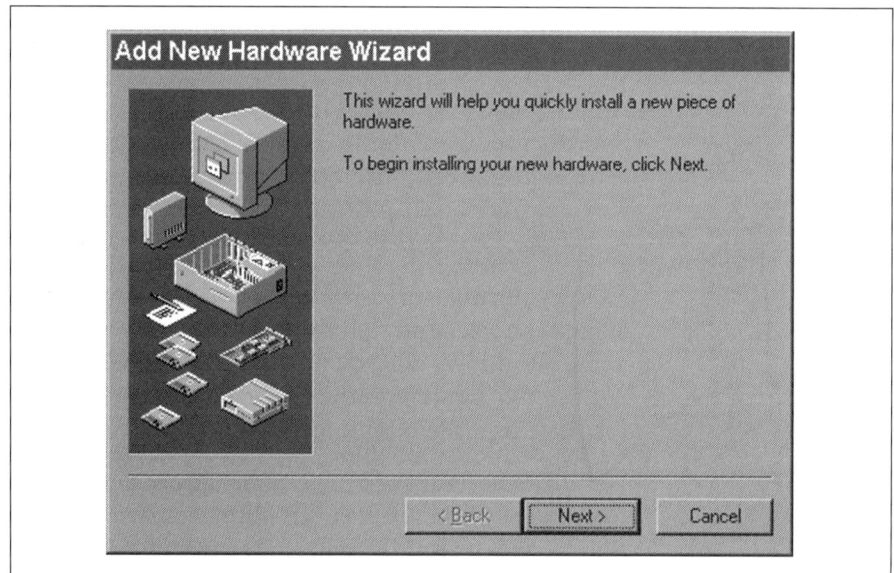

FIGURE 10.18

Add New Hardware
Wizard, detecting
the hardware

FIGURE 10.19

Manually selecting
the hardware

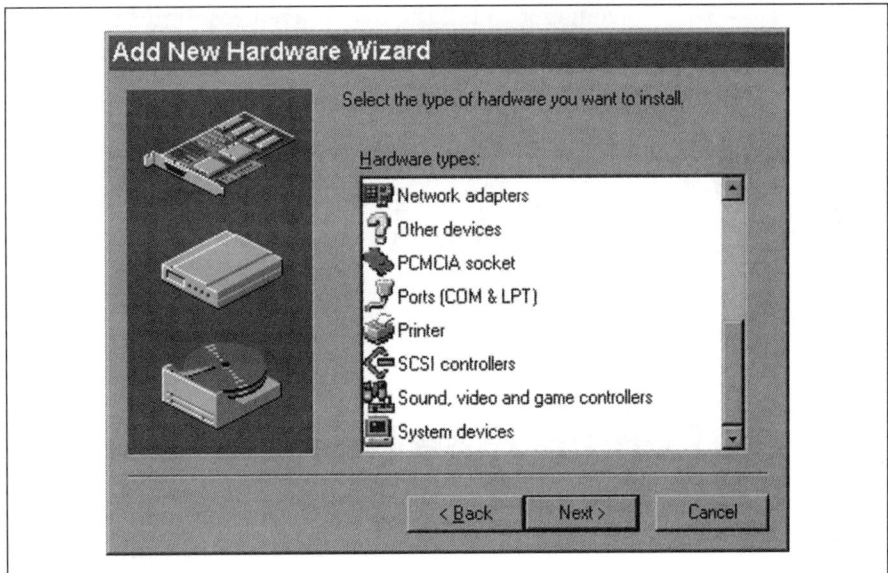

NOTE

I guess I haven't underscored this point before, but you'd go through this process for virtually *any* new hardware, not just a board; for example, you'd use this to add a new mouse, printer, or modem. If you know the name of the hardware manufacturer but aren't sure how to classify the board, then choose *Other devices*; it's a listing of all of the drivers, but is organized by manufacturer.

Once you click Next, you'll enter an installation module that's specific to the particular piece of hardware that you're installing. You may have to fill in device names, as is the case with network cards or printers, and you may have to fill in resource information, perhaps IRQs, I/O addresses, or memory addresses. Then the system will reboot, and the board will usually work. The only other possibility is that Windows may not have the driver for the board, in which case you'll have to supply the diskette with the board driver. Once you've done that, don't forget to use the Device Manager to tell the driver what resources the new board uses; see the upcoming section "Modifying Hardware Resources" to see how.

Speaking of drivers, however, it wouldn't hurt to check to see if there are more up-to-date drivers available for your new add-in board. Most vendors have a bulletin board, or, for those who are connected to the Internet, an ftp site. In the majority of the cases where I've installed a new board, I've found that the vendor has newer drivers available than the ones that came in the box.

To update a driver for an already installed device, use the Device Manager.

Running the Device Manager

Once you have your hardware configuration set up, you'll sometimes need to examine it or modify it. You can do that, with the Device Manager (DM). You get to the Device Manager by opening up the Control Panel, double-clicking on the System icon, and then choosing the Device Manager tab. You'll see a dialog box that looks like Figure 10.20.

FIGURE 10.20

Control Panel's
Device Manager

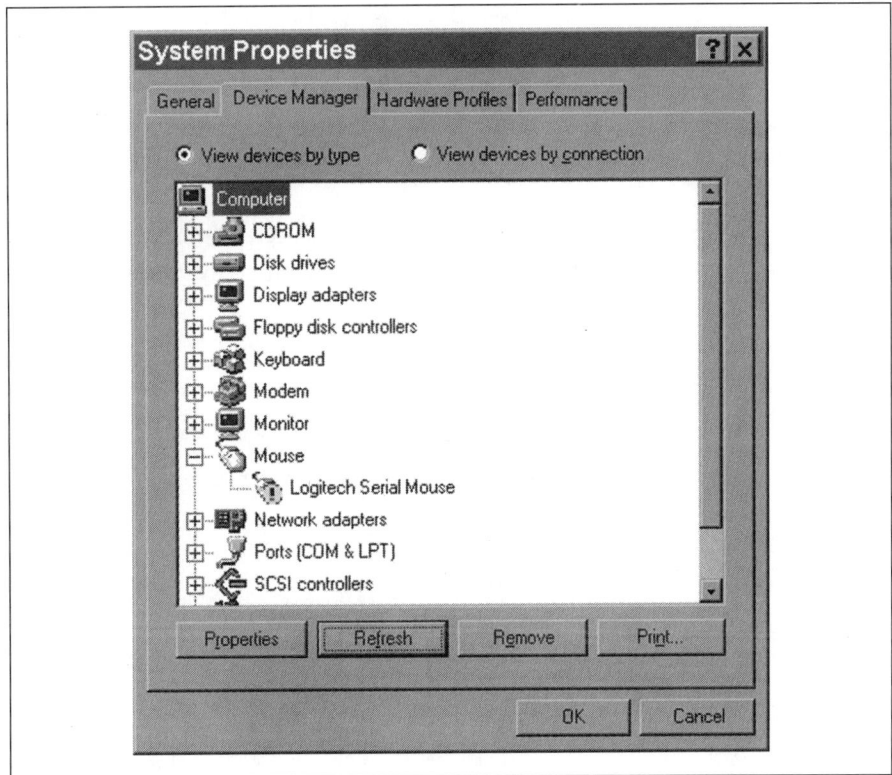

The Computer icon branches off into the different kinds of devices on your system. Any malfunctioning devices are expanded and highlighted with a yellow or red exclamation point icon to indicate some kind of failure. In the example above, you see that in the Mouse devices category, my Logitech Serial Mouse is failing in some way. (In this case, it's nothing to worry about. The problem is that I'm using the Logitech Sensa mouse; it works fine, but there's no driver for it, so I'm using the old Windows 3.x drivers, and Windows 95 is complaining about it.)

You'll use the Device Manager to do a number of things:

- The DM will let you remove a device from your Windows configuration.

- The DM spotlights troublesome hardware, as you saw in the previous example.

- You use the DM to tell Windows what resources (I/O addresses, DMA channels, IRQ levels, RAM addresses, and ROM addresses) a board uses, if the board isn't Plug and Play.

- You use the DM to install an updated device driver.

- The DM will print out a summary of your system's hardware.

Removing a device is easy; just click the device then click Remove. Ask the Device Manager to print out a system summary with Print, and you'll see a report like the one in Figure 10.21.

FIGURE 10.21

A system summary provided by Device Manager

```
Resource Summary Report
******************* SYSTEM SUMMARY *******************
Windows version: 4.00.950
Computer Name: Poorly designed clone
Processor Type: Pentium
System BUS Type: ISA
BIOS Name: American Megatrends
BIOS Date: 12/15/93
BIOS Version: Unknown
Machine Type: IBM PC/AT
Math Co-processor: Present
Registered Owner: Mark Minasi
Registered Company: Mark Minasi and Company
******************* IRQ SUMMARY *******************
IRQ Usage Summary:
    00 - System timer
    01 - Standard 101/102-Key or Microsoft Natural Keyboard
    02 - Programmable interrupt controller
    03 - Communications Port (COM2)
    04 - Communications Port (COM1)
    05 - Creative Labs Sound Blaster 16 or AWE-32
    06 - Standard Floppy Disk Controller
    08 - System CMOS/real time clock
    09 - Adaptec AHA-294X/AIC-78XX PCI SCSI Controller
    11 - Intel EtherExpress PRO/10 (PnP Enabled)
    13 - Numeric data processor
******************* IO PORT SUMMARY *******************
I/O Port Usage Summary:
    0000h-n-000Fh - Direct memory access controller
    0020h-n-0021h - Programmable interrupt controller
    0040h-n-0043h - System timer
    0060h-n-0060h - Standard 101/102-Key or Microsoft Natural Keyboard
    0061h-n-0061h - System speaker
    0064h-n-0064h - Standard 101/102-Key or Microsoft Natural Keyboard
    0070h-n-0071h - System CMOS/real time clock
    0081h-n-0083h - Direct memory access controller
    0087h-n-0087h - Direct memory access controller
    0089h-n-008Bh - Direct memory access controller
    008Fh-n-008Fh - Direct memory access controller
    00A0h-n-00A1h - Programmable interrupt controller
    00C0h-n-00DFh - Direct memory access controller
    00F0h-n-00FFh - Numeric data processor
    0201h-n-0201h - Gameport Joystick
    0210h-n-021Fh - Intel EtherExpress PRO/10 (PnP Enabled)
```

FIGURE 10.21

A system summary
provided by Device
Manager (continued)

```
    0220h-n-022Fh - Creative Labs Sound Blaster 16 or AWE-32
    0270h-n-0273h - IO read data port for ISA Plug and Play enumerator
    02F8h-n-02FFh - Communications Port (COM2)
    0300h-n-0301h - Creative Labs Sound Blaster 16 or AWE-32
    0378h-n-037Ah - Printer Port (LPT1)
    0388h-n-038Bh - Creative Labs Sound Blaster 16 or AWE-32
    03B0h-n-03BBh - ATI Graphics Pro Turbo PCI (mach64)
    03C0h-n-03DFh - ATI Graphics Pro Turbo PCI (mach64)
    03F2h-n-03F5h - Standard Floppy Disk Controller
    03F8h-n-03FFh - Communications Port (COM1)
    FF00h-n-FFFFh - Adaptec AHA-294X/AIC-78XX PCI SCSI Controller
******************** UPPER MEMORY USAGE SUMMARY********************
Memory Usage Summary:
    000A0000h-n-000AFFFFh - ATI Graphics Pro Turbo PCI (mach64)
    000B0000h-n-000BFFFFh - ATI Graphics Pro Turbo PCI (mach64)
    000C0000h-n-000C7FFFh - ATI Graphics Pro Turbo PCI (mach64)
    000C8000h-n-000CA7FFh - Adaptec AHA-294X/AIC-78XX PCI SCSI Controller
    A0000000h-n-A07FFFFFh - ATI Graphics Pro Turbo PCI (mach64)
    FFBFF000h-n-FFBFFFFFh - Adaptec AHA-294X/AIC-78XX PCI SCSI Controller
******************** DMA USAGE SUMMARY ********************
DMA Channel Usage Summary:
    01 - Creative Labs Sound Blaster 16 or AWE-32
    02 - Standard Floppy Disk Controller
    04 - Direct memory access controller
    05 - Creative Labs Sound Blaster 16 or AWE-32
```

NOTE

By the way, I often get asked, "How did you get that printout into your document?" Simple: I installed a printer called Generic TTY and printed to a file. The result was an ASCII file that I could easily incorporate into a word processing document.

Now, for years, I've been teaching classes in DOS memory management, and I've been telling people *not* to believe printouts like the one above. The reason for that is that software can't be trusted to completely detect hardware, as I suggested when I advised you to not let Windows detect your new hardware. However, I'm going to modify my "don't let software tell you about hardware" advice here: You *can* trust the Device Manager's reports for hardware you're *using*. As I've said before, the nice thing about hardware support for Windows 95 is that all the drivers are in one place, and that place—the Registry—is where the Device Manager goes to extract its information. If the hardware is working, then you can trust the Device Manager. In my case, since my sound board is making noise and recording things correctly, then I trust the reported information about the sound card. As the video board is working, I trust the video board information, and so on.

But I still don't trust the DM completely. If I had installed a LAN card and the card wasn't working, then I wouldn't trust anything the DM was telling me about the LAN card. Also, my computer has an Intel Smart Video Recorder Pro in it, complete with functioning drivers. The Pro is set at I/O address 350, IRQ15, and even *works*—albeit with old Windows 3.x drivers—but nary a word of it in the Device Manager report.

Modifying Hardware Resources

Once you've installed a non-Plug and Play card, you have to set its resources, both on the board and in the drivers.

Updating Device Drivers

Device drivers are an ever-changing thing. LAN board drivers, printer drivers, video drivers, and mouse drivers are four pieces of software that seem to change a few times a year. One of the things that you can do to make your system more reliable is to check with your hardware's vendors periodically to see if they've updated their drivers. Then you should get the new drivers, either by ordering them directly from the manufacturer or by downloading them from a manufacturer bulletin board, a communications service like CompuServe, or off an Internet ftp site.

Once you have an updated driver, you can tell Windows 95 to use it in this way:

1. Open up the Device Manager.

2. Click on the particular device whose driver you want to update.

3. Click on Properties. You'll see a dialog box like the following one.

For this example, I've chosen my display adapter. Be aware that, for some reason, you won't see a Driver tab for every piece of hardware. On my computer, I found a Driver tab for my sound card, SCSI adapter, display card, joystick, mouse, parallel and serial ports, and keyboard. In contrast, there wasn't a driver tab for the floppy drives, network card, CD-ROM, modem, or monitor. In most cases, that isn't a problem—I'm not aware of alternative floppy or monitor drivers—but for the modem and network cards, that implies that you refresh the drivers by deleting the modem or

ATI Graphics Pro Turbo PCI (mach64) ...

General | Driver | Resources

ATI Graphics Pro Turbo PCI (mach64)

Device type: Display adapters
Manufacturer: ATI Technologies
Hardware version: 001

Device status
This device is working properly.

Device usage
Place a check mark next to the configuration(s) where this device should be used.

☑ Original Configuration (Current)

OK   Cancel

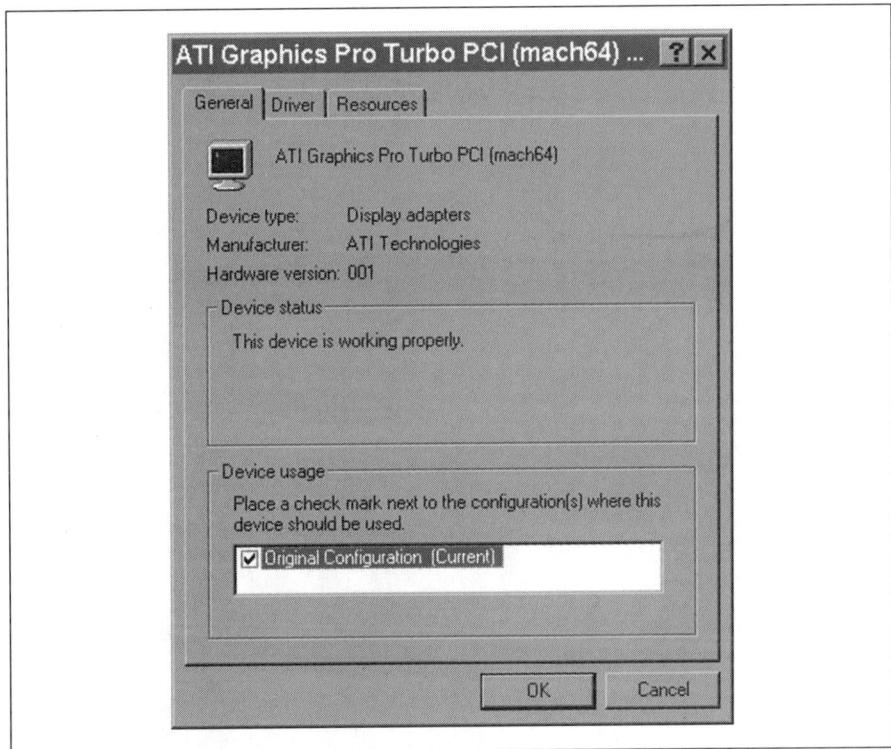

the card and then reinstalling it with the new driver; this is a somewhat cumbersome process.

By the way, since I've mentioned updating network drivers, here's an important tip: For some reason, when you delete a board and then reinstall it, the protocols get reinstalled but the client software doesn't. As a result, all of your persistent connections don't work, which leads to panic, unhappiness, and the like. Just take steps to make sure the client software is reinstalled, and all will be well.

Now, to continue:

4. Click on the Driver tab, and you'll see a dialog box like the following:

5. Now all you have to do is to click Change Driver, and yet another dialog will appear. Click *Have disk...*, insert the diskette with the new driver (or direct the dialog box to the directory with the new driver), and you will update the driver.

Working with Plug and Play Systems

One of the two or three most important things about Windows 95 is its support of the Plug and Play architecture. The idea with Plug and Play is that when you install a board into a Plug and Play-compliant system, the system would:

1. Recognize the board. ("This is an Adaptec 2942W SCSI host adapter.")

2. Ask the board what IRQs, DMAs, I/O addresses, RAM addresses, and ROM addresses it needs. ("It requires an interrupt, a 256-byte block of I/O addresses, and a 16K ROM range.")

3. Ask the board what range of IRQs, DMAs, I/O addresses, RAM addresses, and ROM addresses it can *use*. ("It can use IRQ 5, 7, 9, 10, 11, or 14, any 256-byte block from address 60K to 64K, and any ROM address from C0000 to E0000.")

4. Set those things (IRQ, etc.) so that they don't conflict with anything already in the system.

5. Ask the board for identification information, which the system can then use to tell the operating system to search for and configure the necessary drivers.

This is a step better than the basic software setup boards, because with them you have to run the setup program. With Plug and Play, in contrast, you don't do anything (in theory, anyway); you just insert the board.

In 1993, Microsoft, Intel, and Compaq proposed the standard called Plug and Play. The idea behind PnP is that board manufacturers would add circuitry to their add-in boards so that the automatic setup and the resource query (resource here means IRQ, DMA, I/O address, ROM address, or RAM buffer address) capabilities of EISA and Micro Channel would become available to machines with ISA buses. The PC's operating system could then configure and query boards directly, eliminating the need to pop the top of the PC except when actually removing or inserting a board.

The *catch* about Plug and Play is that you can't retrofit it on an existing system; it has to be built into a computer when you buy it. Furthermore, you must have an operating system, as I mentioned a page or two back, that *understands* Plug and Play, or you won't get most of Plug and Play's benefits. Of course, if you're this far along in the book, though, you know you're okay, as Windows 95 is a Plug and Play operating system.

To "do" Plug and Play, you must have:

- A system with a Plug and Play BIOS. This must be a *flash memory* because that's where the system configuration information is kept.

- A system with a Plug and Play motherboard. (Plug and Play supports the old ISA bus and the PCI bus mainly; running full Plug and Play compliancy on an EISA or Micro Channel machine may require an extra piece of software called an *EISA configuration manager* or a *Micro Channel configuration manager*. So far as I know, however, there is no EISA, MCA, or VESA Plug and Play specification; any cards in those buses will fall into the legacy category.)

- An operating system with Plug and Play support.

- Add-in cards that are Plug and Play-compliant.

So if you have an older computer that isn't Plug and Play compatible, then you can't, well, *play*. You'll need a new computer. Even if you *do* have a Plug and Play system, then you must also buy Plug and Play compatible add-in cards, and they're a mite scarce at this time.

Let's first define the parameters of Plug and Play. What is it, and what *isn't* it?

First of all, it does not unify existing software setup programs. If you have ISA boards in a Plug and Play system that have their own software setup routines (for example, most LAN or sound boards), then you'll still have to keep track of the disks containing those programs. Plug and Play can't help you there. It controls Plug and Play compatible boards only; the other guys are left out in the cold.

Why is this? I don't know. I once argued to a Plug and Play designer that Plug and Play should unify software setup, providing some way for all boards that are set up with programs to come under one roof. "It's a good idea," he conceded, "but it's not in the spec." Maybe next version.

Booting on Plug and Play Systems

What do you need to make a system Plug and Play *compatible*? First of all, a Plug and Play-compatible motherboard. These are motherboards with a BIOS that understands Plug and Play, and that also contain about 16K of *nonvolatile storage* (*NVS*). One easy way to implement this is by putting the NVS in amongst the BIOS code, which means using a *flash BIOS*; more and more systems do that these days.

You also must have add-in cards that are Plug and Play compatible. These cards are configured *every time you boot*, and that configuration is done by a routine called the *Configuration Manager* (*CM*). The CM can either be part of the BIOS, or a program loaded off disk. In order for maximum compatibility, however, the CM should be part of the BIOS.

In the ideal world (that is, everything is Plug and Play), the system powers up and the CM assumes control. It asks each board what resources it needs, and what is the range of resources that it will accept. (For example, a board might say, "I need an IRQ, and I'll take either 2, 3, 4, or 5," in the same way that the Microsoft ISA bus mouse interface does; even though there are other interrupts, its circuitry for some reason will only accept an IRQ in the range of 2 to 5.) The CM then assigns resources to cards, avoiding conflicts.

NOTE   This means that potentially installing one new Plug and Play card to a Plug and Play system could cause all of the other cards to move their resources around. What does that mean for the network, SCSI, sound, and other board drivers, which must know which resources those boards use? Well, it implies that device drivers have to be a bit smarter than they are now.

For example, any client on a Windows NT network has a file called PRO-TOCOL.INI on its hard disk. In that file are often references like IRQ=10, IOBASE=300, and so on. On a Plug and Play system, the network software must take its cues from the CM.

Once all boards are taken care of, then the system boots in the usual way. The main difference of Plug and Play is that the whole process of hardware shuffling of resources (I/O addresses, DMA channels, RAM windows, and the like) happens every time you boot the system, and (one hopes) quickly and invisibly.

Oh, by the way, can you force a particular board to a particular resource? Yes—that's called *locking* the resource. The CM on your system should allow that, or your operating system might; Windows 95 lets you do it with the Device Manager, which is in the Control Panel.

How Plug and Play Handles Older Boards

This sounds good, but suppose there are non-Plug and Play boards in the system. (The term in the business is *legacy boards,* as if they were some kind of evil inheritance.) How does the CM know to avoid the resources that those boards have already taken up?

Well, the CM needs some help finding this out. For an ISA system, it gets help when you punch in the values into a program called the *ISA Configuration Utility,* or *ICU.*

More and more ISA boards ship with a helper file for EISA systems in the form of a .CFG file. Recall that .CFG files ship with EISA boards so that the EISA configuration program can set up the EISA board, but that it's a good idea to create .CFGs for ISA boards as well; some ISA boards ship with the files.

You'd think that Plug and Play would read EISA and Micro Channel configurations, but it doesn't. For an EISA system, you'll need a modified version of your EISA setup routine, an *EISA Configuration Utility (ECU).* Plug and Play even uses a superset of the EISA configuration storage format. Micro Channel machines, correspondingly, will have an *MCU.*

Plug and Play on Non-PCI Machines

All of this Plug and Play magic relies a lot on the PCI bus and the fact that PCI cards are extremely self-aware, knowing right in their hardware what resources they need. Does that mean that it's impossible to do Plug and Play on an ISA machine? No.

There is an ISA Plug and Play specification which provides for ISA-based motherboards that, again, only require a bit more hardware: a smarter BIOS and some NVS.

The way that Plug and Play ISA works is a kind of sneaky trick. The CM needs a way to get the Plug and Play ISA-aware cards to identify themselves. It does this by sending out a query on I/O address 279, which is normally part of LPT2. Now, address 279 is a printer status port address for LPT2, and is read-only within the LPT2 specification. The CM writes data to that location and waits for a response. If they're present, the Plug and Play ISA cards respond.

How Does a System Know If It Is Plug and Play Compatible?

I recently went a few rounds with a vendor who'd sold me a supposedly Plug and Play compatible system. The vendor claimed that its system was Plug and Play compatible. Windows 95 disagreed, as did Intel's Configuration Manager software. The vendor had inserted a line in the BIOS startup that said "Intel Plug and Play Extensions version 2.2," however, and felt that ended the argument. So I checked the specification. There are several things that identify a Plug and Play system:

- The string $PnP should appear somewhere between 960K and 1024K, F0000–FFFF.

- The string ACFG should appear somewhere in the 896–960K range, E0000–EFFFF.

- The NVS (non-volatile storage) is typically somewhere around the ED000 range. The NVS is preceded by the standard 55AA signature so memory managers will skip it.

The system had none of those, so I won the argument. Again, be careful when buying Plug and Play systems, at least for a few years.

Solving Hardware Installation Problems

What do you do if you've loaded some driver that the system absolutely relies upon—a video driver is an excellent example—and you loaded it wrong, or it's faulty? And you can't even get the system to boot?

In that case, remember safe mode. Just start up Windows 95, wait for the "Starting Windows 95…" message, and press F8. You'll see a menu with several options, including Safe Mode. Boot to that, access the Device Manager, and change back to the driver that you trust. Or boot to Safe Mode Command Prompt, and run the DOS-based diagnostic to be sure that the board works properly. Those are the keys to solving hardware problems under 95: Isolate the hardware, test it, try a more vanilla driver, and double-check that the resources are entered correctly.

Well, one day, you'll just buy a board, plug it into a system, and you *will* be able to play with it instantly. But that day's not here yet, at least not for most of us. For now, if you master the concepts in this chapter, then you'll be an expert Windows 95 hardware installer.

Controlling Disks with Windows 95

FOR those of you who have pre-Windows 95 experience with utilities such as partitioning, formatting, and defragging, this chapter will not reveal any startling new concepts. Basically, Windows 95 uses the same types of programs as under DOS. (But let me make clear that you cannot use the old DOS versions of these programs on Windows 95; only use the Windows 95 versions.) The only thing which has changed in terms of these programs is their interfaces: FDISK and FORMAT can be run from within Windows 95 and the other programs have a new look. But essentially, if you previously understood the concepts behind FDISK, FORMAT, defragmentation, and DriveSpace, this chapter will not throw you any curveballs.

That said, this chapter is not without new information. Under Windows 95, the disk cache and swap file are now dynamically managed. Those of you who enjoyed tweaking and fiddling with those settings may be disappointed with these changes. Also, there are two other new concepts: the Recycle Bin and long filename support. All of these features will be discussed in this chapter.

Before You Start

Before you jump into this chapter, keep a few things in mind. First, remember to use only Windows 95 compatible products (look for an explicit reference to Windows 95 compatibility). There are programs, for example some compression software, which, if not made specifically for Windows 95, can destroy all your long filenames. If this happens you'll have to repair all your shortcuts manually. I don't know about you, but I can think of better ways to spend hours and hours of my life...

Also, it is important to perform regular backups of your system. When playing with disk utilities, you could potentially damage your hard drive, so if you don't regularly back up your hard drive, at least do it before running any type of disk utility. If something goes drastically wrong on your system and you didn't back up your drive beforehand, ...well, let's just say that you will be regretting the lack of a backup.

One last thing to keep in mind is that you should always have a Windows 95 startup disk nearby when performing invasive disk techniques on your drive. In an emergency, this disk will allow you to jump-start your computer and get to potentially vital programs. Making a startup disk is easy: Click on Add/Remove Programs within the Control Panel, choose the Startup Disk tab, then follow the directions from there.

Now, let's begin this chapter by taking a look at partitioning and formatting drives.

Disk Setup and Maintenance

In this section we'll take a look at several disk setup and maintenance issues: partitioning and formatting hard drives, undeleting files, and defragmenting your drive.

How to Partition and Format Hard Disks

You know the old saying, "The more things change the more they stay the same?" Well, this is an apt way to describe partitioning and formatting under Windows 95. Since Windows 95 still uses a FAT-based system, it relies on the old DOS programs FDISK and FORMAT to do its dirty work. So, if you understood how to partition and format drives under DOS, you'll have no problem doing it under Windows 95. However, one feature which sets Windows 95's partitioning and formatting apart from DOS is that you now can partition and format drives while still running Windows 95, as long as those drives are *non-boot drives*.

Information to Remember When Using FDISK and FORMAT

Before getting into the processes, here's some important information to keep in mind. First, you can only partition and format a drive within Windows 95 if there are no open files on the target hard drive; basically this eliminates boot drives. In the case where the drive you want to format *is* a boot drive, you must use the Windows 95 startup disk to partition and format; more on this coming up. Second, you can not repartition a disk with FDISK if the original partitions were created by Disk Manager, Storage Dimensions SpeedStor, Priam, or Everex partitioning programs. You must repartition the drive using the utility with which you originally partitioned it. Third, if you have compression software loaded on your drive, FDISK will show its *un*compressed size. In other cases, FDISK might not show information on drives compressed with other third-party software. Lastly, if you compressed your hard drive with DriveSpace, you must format the drive using DriveSpace.

That last point leads me to an example of what *not* to do when repartitioning your hard drive. Not too long ago I was experimenting with the DriveSpace compression software, and I had compressed my boot drive. I had finished for the day and decided to repartition, reformat, and restore my original data to the hard drive. I ran FDISK to repartition my drive, and was then ready to format when I saw a message which made my blood run cold. The message said that I had a compressed drive (I had forgotten to uncompress it before repartitioning) and that I needed to format it with DriveSpace. I started to panic when I thought, "Hey, DriveSpace *must* be on the Windows 95 startup disk." I looked, and there was only a file named drvspace.bin. Unfortunately, this file was no help at all. Luckily, I had a DOS 6.22 bootable floppy on hand, and I formatted the drive using the /u (unconditional) switch. Disaster averted. Morals of story:

- Don't forget to uncompress hard drives *before* repartitioning.
- Having a DOS bootable floppy on hand is a *good* thing.

Okay, end of digression. Before showing you how to partition and format, I will chance sounding repetitive and say: **Before running any disk utilities, *especially* fdisk and format, back up your hard drive! Fdisk and Format will destroy *all* the data on your hard drive. Period. If you do not back up your data, you will lose it *all*.**

In this section, we'll take a look at three possible scenarios for partitioning and formatting a hard drive:

- You want to partition and format free space on a drive.
- You just bought a new boot drive.
- You just bought an additional, non-boot hard drive.

So enough talking about it; let's go do it.

Partitioning and Formatting Extra Space on a Hard Drive

Partitioning and formatting a drive really isn't a painful process. When I originally partitioned and formatted my drive for this experiment, I left 118MB free. You may be asking yourself, "But didn't you do it while partitioning and formatting the rest of the drive?" The answer: I did it this way so I could show you how to do it from within Windows 95.

What I'll do here is show you how to create a logical drive in an extended DOS partition, then how to format the logical drive—all from within Windows 95.

Start off by opening the MS-DOS prompt and type **fdisk**. You'll see this in a screen like Figure 11.1.

Choose 1. Create DOS partition or Logical DOS drive and you'll see a screen like Figure 11.2.

Here, you want to choose 2. Create Extended DOS Partition, as you must first create an extended DOS partition before creating logical DOS drives. After typing 2, you will see a screen like Figure 11.3.

In addition to creating an extended DOS partition at this screen, you can see other partitions you have on your system. This screen shows that I have a primary DOS partition (401MB) with a volume label of LESLIE. Now to create an extended DOS partition, type in the size in megabytes (or percent of disk space, but be sure to type the number and a % sign) you wish to allocate to it. I typed in **118** and pressed Enter. This will bring you to a screen like Figure 11.4.

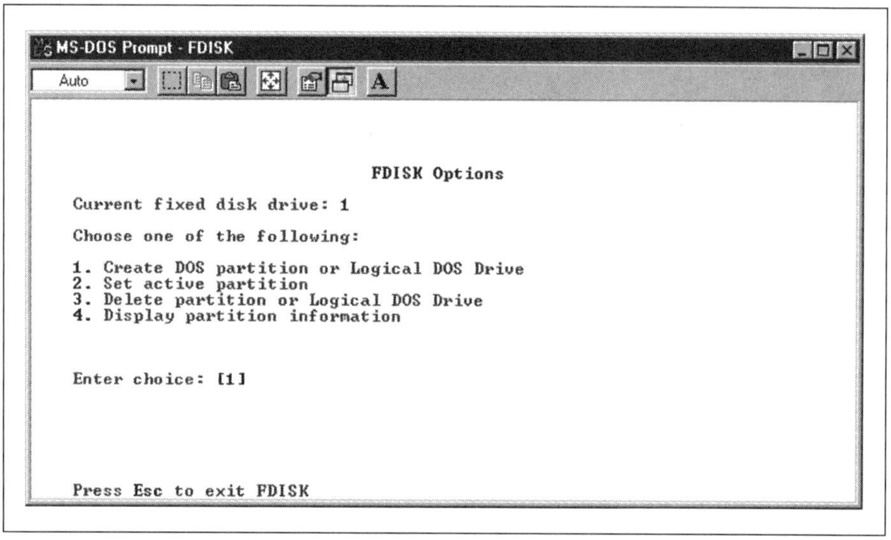

FIGURE 11.1

FIGURE 11.1

FDISK opening screen

FIGURE 11.2

Create extended DOS partition in FDISK

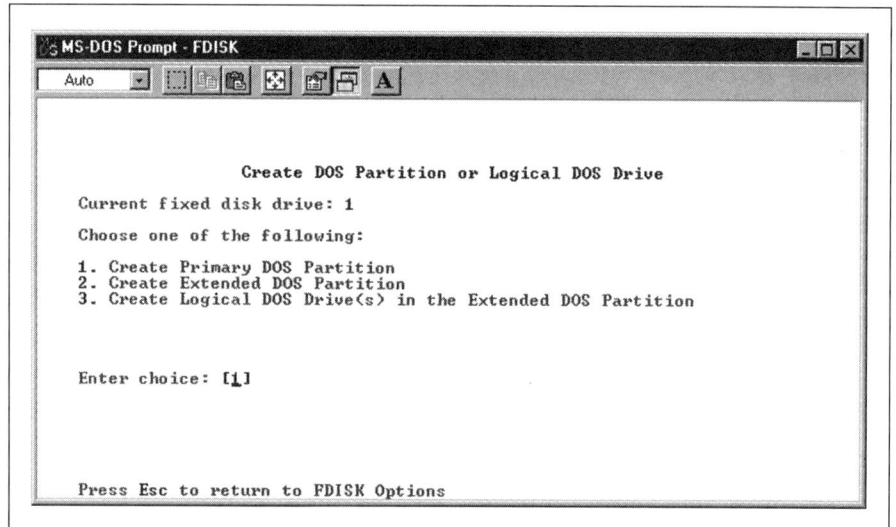

This is a sort of status screen. This informs you that FDISK created the extended DOS partition, then gives you its statistics so far. You can see that I now have a Drive C: with two partitions. The first partition is an Active (thus the A under Status) primary DOS partition 401MB in size with a volume label of LESLIE. (By the way, the Active status means that

FIGURE 11.3

FDISK Create
Extended DOS
Partition screen

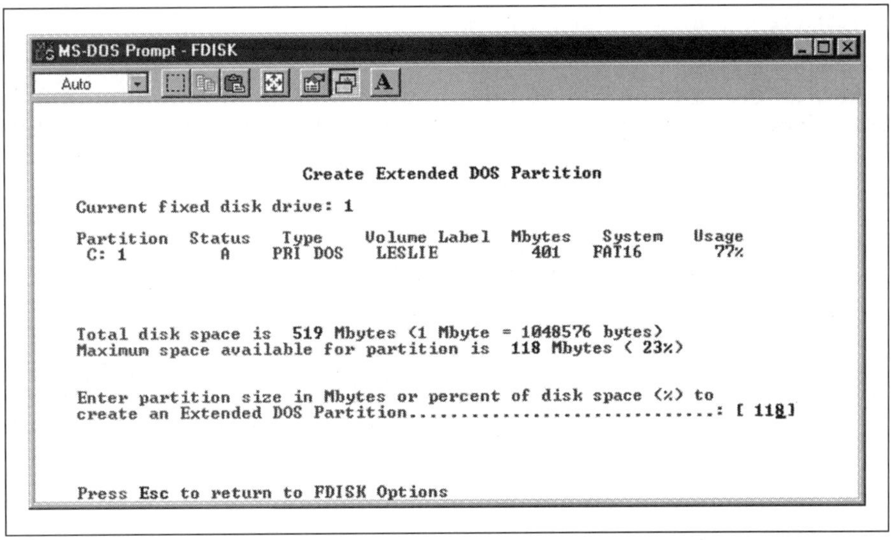

FIGURE 11.4

Extended DOS
partition created

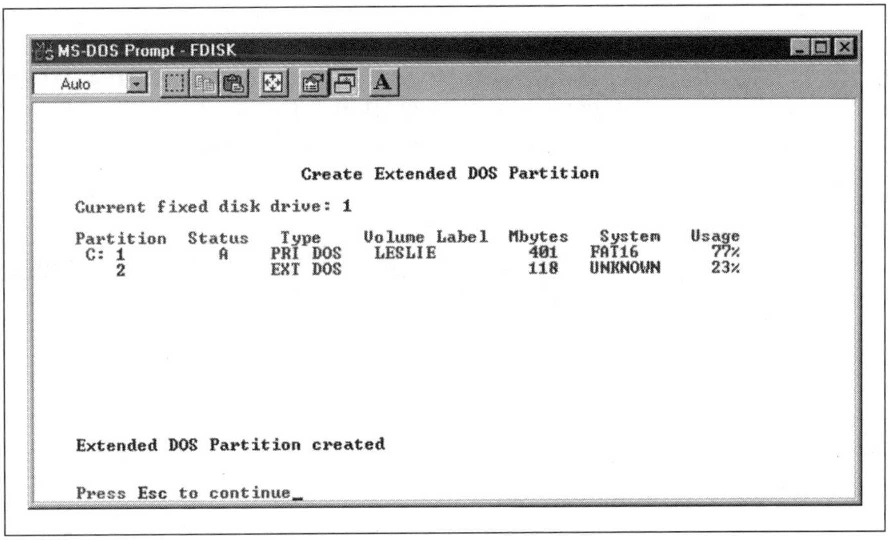

the C: drive is my boot drive.) I also have an extended DOS partition of
118MB, which is still without a volume label. Press Esc to continue and
you'll get a screen like Figure 11.5.

This screen prompts you to create logical drives. Here you need to decide how large of a logical drive you wish to create. I chose to create only one logical drive 118MB in size, so I typed **118** and pressed Enter. That brought me to a screen like Figure 11.6.

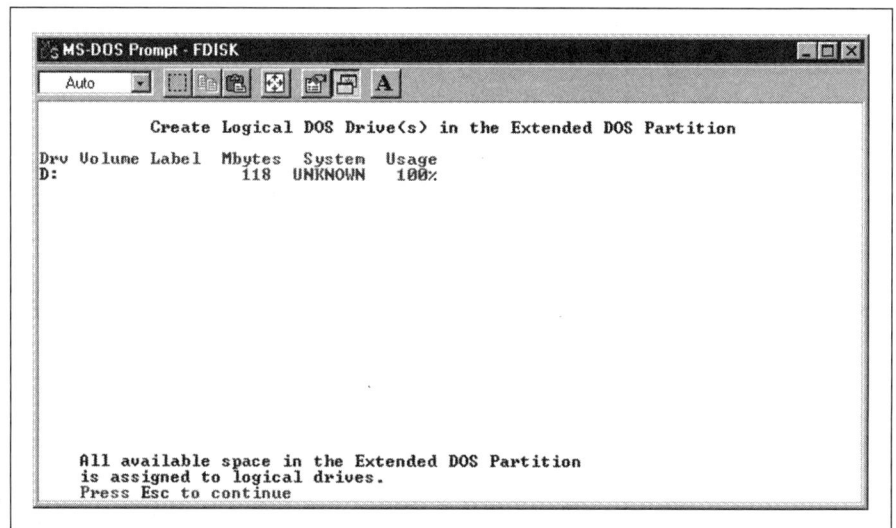

This screen tells me that I cannot create any more logical drives, as all the space in the extended DOS partition is allocated to one logical drive. Also notice that once I created a logical drive in the extended DOS partition, the logical drive received its own drive letter. Press Esc to get to the original opening FDISK screen, hit Esc again to exit FDISK, and type **exit** to end the MS-DOS prompt session. So far we're halfway done—now for formatting your drive.

You can format your disk from either the MS-DOS prompt or the Windows Explorer. Here we'll take a look at the Windows Explorer version of formatting your drive. If, however, you prefer the command prompt interface, you can format your disk from the MS-DOS prompt within Windows 95. The FORMAT command works the same as described in the section "Adding a New Boot Drive."

To format your drive, open up the Windows Explorer and right-click on the icon for your unformatted drive. You'll see the option Format; select this option and you'll see Figure 11.7.

FIGURE 11.7

Formatting a drive with the Windows Explorer

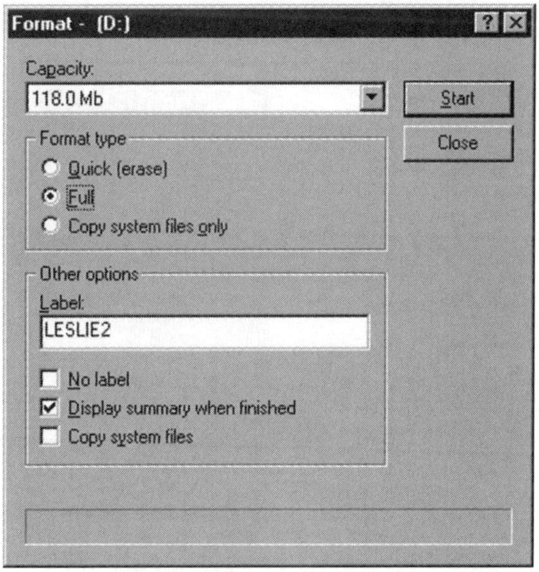

As you can see I've already typed in my desired options. Under Format type, I've chosen Full. If your drive has been formatted previously, you can choose Quick (erase). In Other options, I chose to label my drive LESLIE2 (creative, huh?) and also chose to see a summary at the end of the format. When you click on Start, you'll receive a little warning, as in Figure 11.8.

Click OK and the formatting begins. During the format, you have a gauge at the bottom of the screen to see how far the format has progressed as in Figure 11.9.

When the format is finished, a summary dialog box pops up as in Figure 11.10.

FIGURE 11.8

Warning about formatting your drive

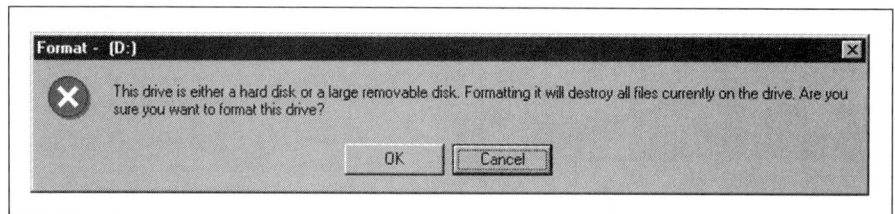

Format - (D:)

This drive is either a hard disk or a large removable disk. Formatting it will destroy all files currently on the drive. Are you sure you want to format this drive?

OK   Cancel

FIGURE 11.9

Meter: Format in process

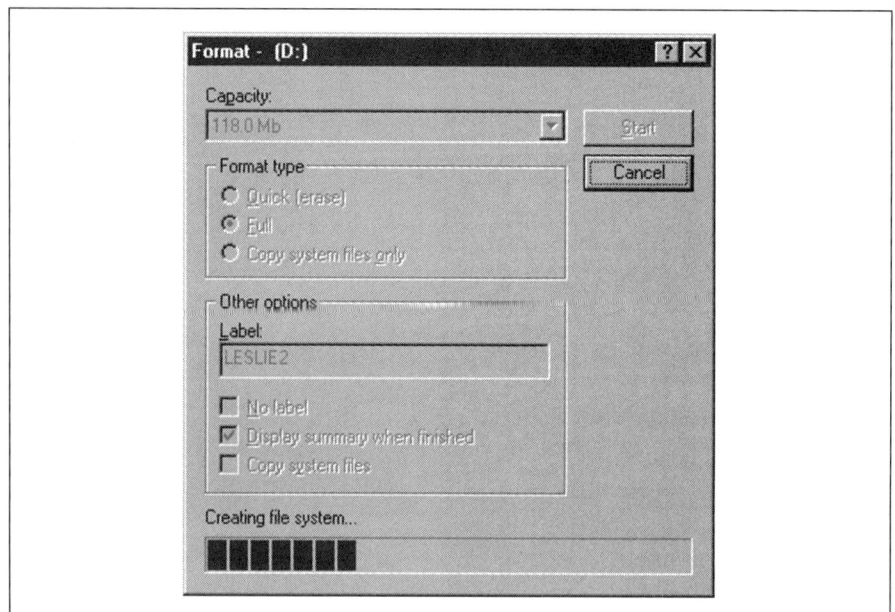

Format - (D:)

Capacity:

118.0 Mb   Start

Format type   Cancel
C Quick (erase)
C Full
C Copy system files only

Other options
Label:
LESLIE2

☐ No label
☑ Display summary when finished
☐ Copy system files

Creating file system...

FIGURE 11.10

Summary of format

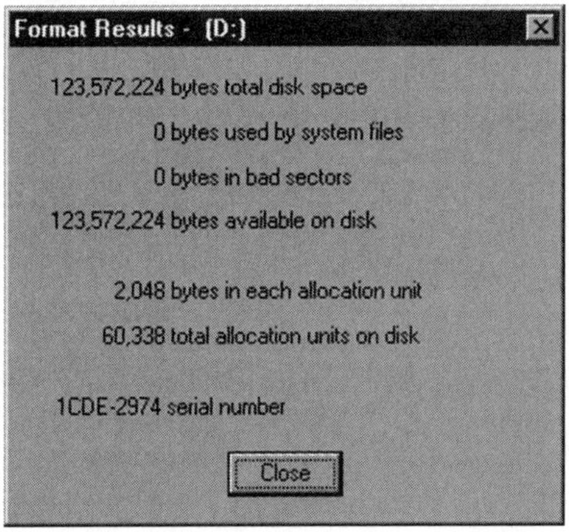

Format Results - (D:)

123,572,224 bytes total disk space

0 bytes used by system files

0 bytes in bad sectors

123,572,224 bytes available on disk

2,048 bytes in each allocation unit

60,338 total allocation units on disk

1CDE-2974 serial number

Close

Windows 95 now takes this opportunity to advise me to run ScanDisk on my newly formatted hard drive. You can see how to run ScanDisk later in this chapter.

That wasn't too bad, was it? Now let's look at a slightly trickier situation—adding a new boot drive to your system.

Adding a New Boot Drive

Imagine this: you have Windows 95 on your system and then you decide to get a new hard drive. Before you can use this drive, you need to partition and format it. You will use the same programs as in the previous section, but you will be running FDISK and FORMAT from the Windows 95 startup disk rather than from the MS-DOS prompt.

Now, before we go on, a repeat of the warning: **Back up your files from your old hard drive!** Since you will be replacing the disk where the system files reside, you will need to reinstall Windows 95. If you have a CD-ROM copy of Windows 95, make sure you have some means of getting to your CD-ROM in order to reinstall Windows 95. In addition to backing up your data files, another good idea is to back up your Windows 95 configuration files. After you partition and format, you can perform a basic install of Windows 95, then you can restore all your Windows 95 files to recover your original settings.

Insert your Windows 95 startup disk in your floppy drive and type **fdisk**. You will go through the same type of process as described in the previous section, except you will be creating a primary DOS partition instead of an extended DOS partition. You will be asked the same type of questions; however, one thing which is different, and very important, is to set the primary DOS partition as active. (FDISK will remind you to do this.) Setting the primary DOS partition active allows the computer to boot from that hard drive.

After partitioning, you'll need to format your hard drive. With your Windows 95 startup disk in the A: drive, type **format /?** to see a list of the available FORMAT switches. (As you can see in Figure 11.11, I captured this screen from within Windows 95; however, the FORMAT switches will not change.)

The only switch necessary for our purposes here is /V. The /V switch allows you to name your hard drive. At this point, type **format c:**, add any switches you desire, then press Enter. At this point the formatting begins; typically this doesn't take very long (usually no longer than 15 minutes).

There you have it. Now your hard drive is ready for the Windows 95 installation process. For more on that, consult Chapter 4.

FIGURE 11.11

FORMAT options

```
Microsoft(R) Windows 95
    (C)Copyright Microsoft Corp 1981-1995.

C:\WINDOWS>format /?
Formats a disk for use with MS-DOS.

FORMAT drive: [/V[:label]] [/Q] [/F:size] [/B ¦ /S] [/C]
FORMAT drive: [/V[:label]] [/Q] [/T:tracks /N:sectors] [/B ¦ /S] [/C]
FORMAT drive: [/V[:label]] [/Q] [/1] [/4] [/B ¦ /S] [/C]
FORMAT drive: [/Q] [/1] [/4] [/8] [/B ¦ /S] [/C]

  /V[:label]   Specifies the volume label.
  /Q           Performs a quick format.
  /F:size      Specifies the size of the floppy disk to format (such
               as 160, 180, 320, 360, 720, 1.2, 1.44, 2.88).
  /B           Allocates space on the formatted disk for system files.
  /S           Copies system files to the formatted disk.
  /T:tracks    Specifies the number of tracks per disk side.
  /N:sectors   Specifies the number of sectors per track.
  /1           Formats a single side of a floppy disk.
  /4           Formats a 5.25-inch 360K floppy disk in a high-density drive.
  /8           Formats eight sectors per track.
  /C           Tests clusters that are currently marked "bad."

C:\WINDOWS>_
```

Adding an Additional Hard Drive

Let's now look at one last scenario: You just went out and bought an additional hard drive for your system (or maybe you were lucky enough to have a friend give you one) and you need to get the drive ready for Windows 95. To get the drive operational, you'll use the exact same programs described previously in the section "Partitioning and Formatting Extra Space on a Hard Drive." But keep in mind that you must be careful about two things: (a) which drive you are going to partition and format, and (b) exactly how you will go about deciding to partition this new drive. Read on for more details.

First, you must be sure to partition and format the correct drive. It would be a Very Bad Thing to accidentally partition and format the wrong drive. Open the MS-DOS prompt and type **fdisk**. You'll see a screen like Figure 11.12.

This screen is identical to the FDISK procedure described in the first section, except for one detail. You can see there is a new fifth option called Change current fixed disk drive. This is the option which allows you to select which drive to partition—and keeps you from partitioning the wrong drive. Choose 5 and you will see Figure 11.13.

FIGURE 11.12

Opening screen of FDISK when adding another drive

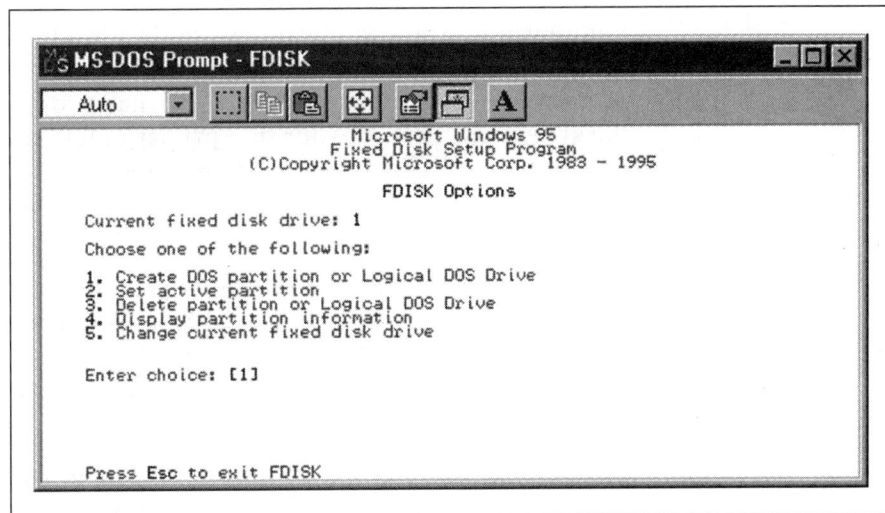

```
MS-DOS Prompt - FDISK

Auto

                    Microsoft Windows 95
                  Fixed Disk Setup Program
             (C)Copyright Microsoft Corp. 1983 - 1995

                        FDISK Options

Current fixed disk drive: 1

Choose one of the following:

1. Create DOS partition or Logical DOS Drive
2. Set active partition
3. Delete partition or Logical DOS Drive
4. Display partition information
5. Change current fixed disk drive

Enter choice: [1]


Press Esc to exit FDISK
```

FIGURE 11.13

Change current fixed
disk drive screen in
FDISK

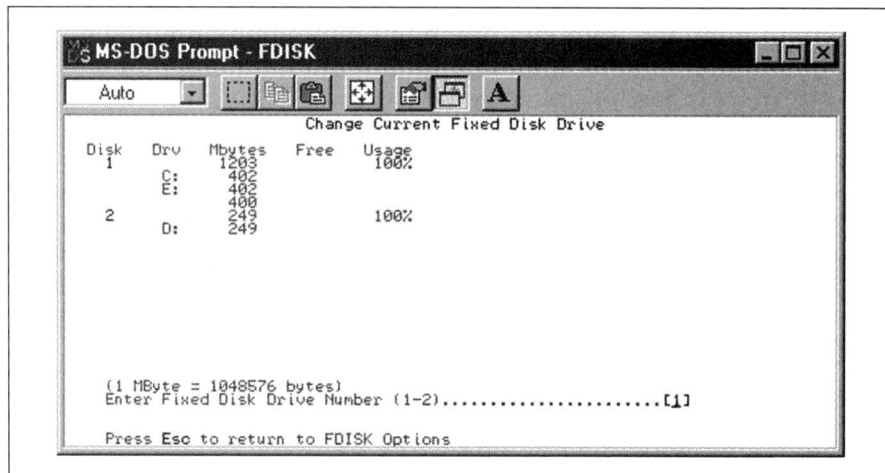

As you can see, this computer already has two physical drives which have been partitioned. To partition your newly added drive, press the appropriate disk drive number then press Enter. At this point, you would be back at the original FDISK screen, but with one difference—look at Current Fixed Disk Drive (top of the screen) and you'll see that you have changed drive numbers. Now you're ready to start, right? Well, there's one more thing.

Before you can proceed, you need to decide whether to create a *primary* DOS partition or an *extended* DOS partition. Choosing to add another primary DOS partition will affect the names of all your other drives on the system. By default, your first primary DOS partition is named drive C:. When another primary DOS partition is added to the system, its default name is drive D:. Why might this be a problem? Take a look at Figure 11.14.

As you can imagine, having your drives renamed could lead to some headaches. How can you avoid this problem? Simply partition your new drive as an extended DOS partition, not as a primary DOS partition. Figure 11.15 shows how your drive letters would be affected.

The rest is simple—just create an extended DOS partition with logical DOS drives, then format. To refresh your memory on how to do this, just turn back to the first section "Partitioning and Formatting Extra Space on a Hard Drive."

FIGURE 11.14

Adding another
primary DOS partition
to the system

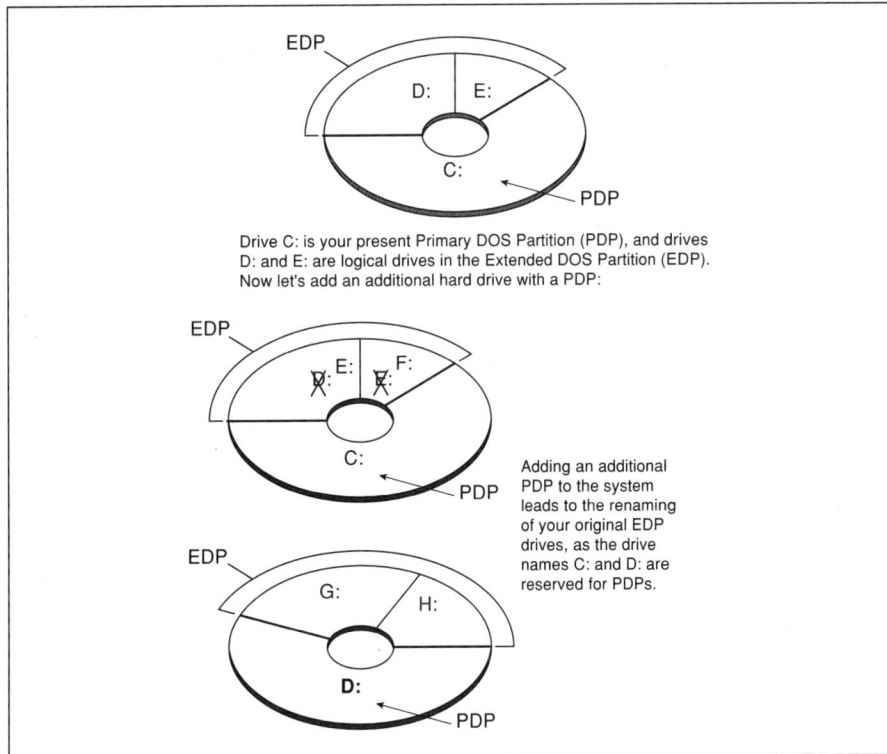

EDP

D: E:

C:

PDP

Drive C: is your present Primary DOS Partition (PDP), and drives
D: and E: are logical drives in the Extended DOS Partition (EDP).
Now let's add an additional hard drive with a PDP:

EDP

E: F:

C:

PDP

Adding an additional
PDP to the system
leads to the renaming
of your original EDP
drives, as the drive
names C: and D: are
reserved for PDPs.

EDP

G: H:

D:

PDP

Undeleting Files Under Windows 95

A handy feature which comes with Windows 95 is called the Recycle Bin.
Yes, now it seems that even computer software is politically correct and
environmentally conscious. How does the Recycle Bin work? Well, when
you delete a file from the Windows Explorer, the file isn't automatically
deleted. (This actually depends on your Recycle Bin settings, which we'll
discuss below.) In actuality, Windows 95 moves your deleted file to a
holding-space-type of directory on your hard drive.

Once a file is in the Recycle Bin, the user can undelete it by simply opening the Recycle Bin, clicking on the file, and choosing Restore from the
File menu. This restores the file to its directory at the time of its deletion.
Understand, though, that once a file is deleted from the Recycle Bin, it is
really deleted. How are files deleted from the Recycle Bin? This can occur

FIGURE 11.15

Adding an extended DOS partition to the system

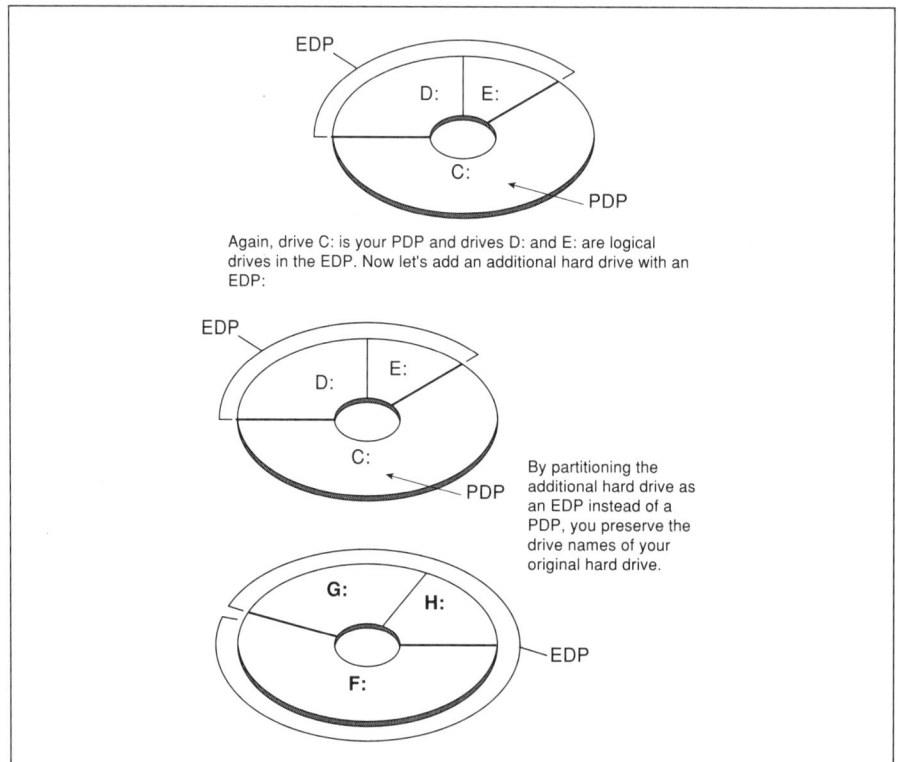

Again, drive C: is your PDP and drives D: and E: are logical drives in the EDP. Now let's add an additional hard drive with an EDP:

By partitioning the additional hard drive as an EDP instead of a PDP, you preserve the drive names of your original hard drive.

in two ways. Approach 1 is that the user can manually empty the Recycle Bin by right-clicking on the Recycle Bin icon and then selecting Empty Recycle Bin. Approach 2 is, when the Recycle Bin exceeds a certain size (set by you, but the default is 10 percent of your hard drive), the oldest files are deleted until the Recycle Bin comes under the maximum limit.

WARNING If you choose to run the Windows 3.x File Manager instead of the Windows Explorer (to run the File Manager, click Run on the Start menu and type winfile), your deleted files are really deleted and *not* sent to the Recycle Bin.

To see how to configure the Recycle Bin, right-click on the Recycle Bin and select Properties. This will lead you to Figure 11.16.

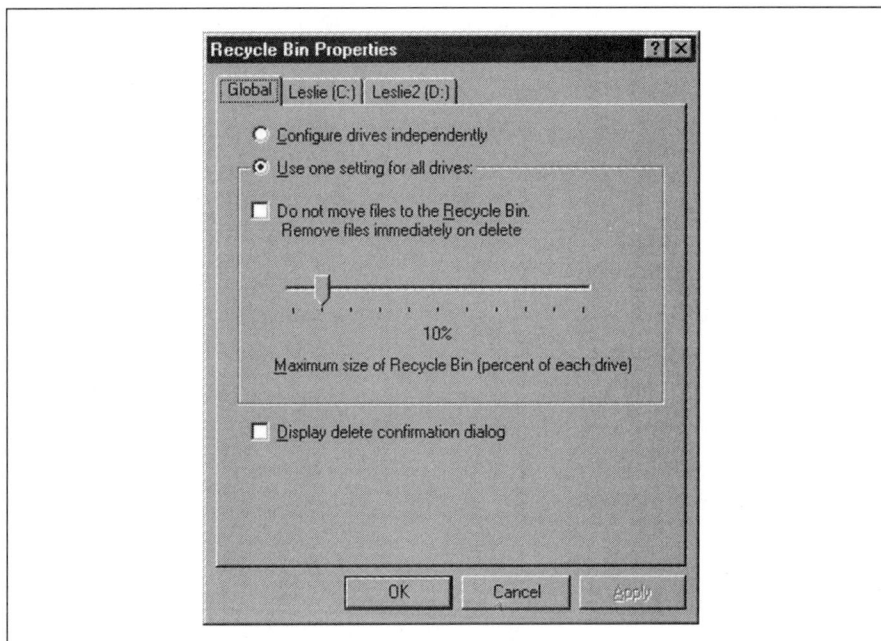

This screen shows the settings I've chosen, and all are the default values
(except *Display delete confirmation dialog*—its default is that it is checked).
Here you must make a choice concerning the configuration of your
Recycle Bin: Use one setting for all drives or Configure drives
independently.

- Use one setting for all drives: Just as it sounds, this allows you to have
  universal Recycle Bin settings for all drives on the system. If you
  choose this option, the options on other tabs, for example LESLIE2
  (D:), will be grayed out.

- Configure drives independently: When you choose this option, you
  must determine settings for each drive on your system separately. If
  you select this, there will be a \recycled directory on each hard
  drive.

Whether you choose to use one setting or to configure each drive, both
have three options in common: Do not move files to the Recycle Bin,
Maximum size of the Recycle Bin, and Display delete confirmation
dialog.

- If you choose *Do not move files to the Recycle Bin*, files will be automatically deleted and the Recycle Bin settings will be grayed out.

- If you choose to use the Recycle Bin, you can set its maximum size simply by moving the slider to the desired percentage of your disk space. (The default is 10 percent.) When the Recycle Bin exceeds its maximum size, the oldest files are deleted until the size of the Recycle Bin is less than the allotted space.

- The last option, *Display delete confirmation dialog*, lets you decide whether you want a warning when files are sent to the Recycle Bin.

That's really all there is to the Recycle Bin. Set the Recycle Bin options to suit your individual needs. If you feel you'll forget to clean out your Recycle Bin, allocate a smaller percentage of disk space. If you have a tendency to accidentally delete important files, perhaps setting a larger Recycle Bin would better fit your needs.

Optimizing Disk Speed with Defrag

Defragging your disk has traditionally been an important step in optimizing your disk speed. However, since installing Windows 95 on my system, my hard drive has been considerably less fragmented than it was with previous versions of Windows. (Why? It's discussed in an upcoming section.) That said, however, it is still important to defrag your disk on a regular basis.

Disk Defragmentation

In case you are wondering, defragmentation of drives places individual files contiguously at the beginning and free space at the end of the hard drive. As the hard drive doesn't have to access many different parts of the disk for one file, reads from and writes to the hard drive are faster and more efficient.

How often should you defragment your drive? I can say that just the other day I realized I hadn't defragmented my disk in 52 days. No, I don't have a notepad full of little tick-marks for each day that goes by without defragmenting—Windows 95 told me!

Open the My Computer group, right-click on your drive's icon, select Properties, then select the Tools tab. You'll see a screen like Figure 11.17.

This dialog box lets you see how long it has been since you last performed what typically should be routine disk maintenance procedures. Error-checking status shows how long it has been since I last checked my drive for errors with ScanDisk. Backup status tells us that Windows 95 does not know when I last backed up this drive. (This is because Windows 95's backup program is not installed, and, therefore, has not been run.) Finally, Defragmentation status shows how long it has been since I've run the Defrag on this disk.

Assuming that nearly two months worth of disk usage would result in quite a bit of file fragmentation, I clicked on the Defragment Now button to launch DEFRAG.EXE.

FIGURE 11.17

My Computer Tools tab

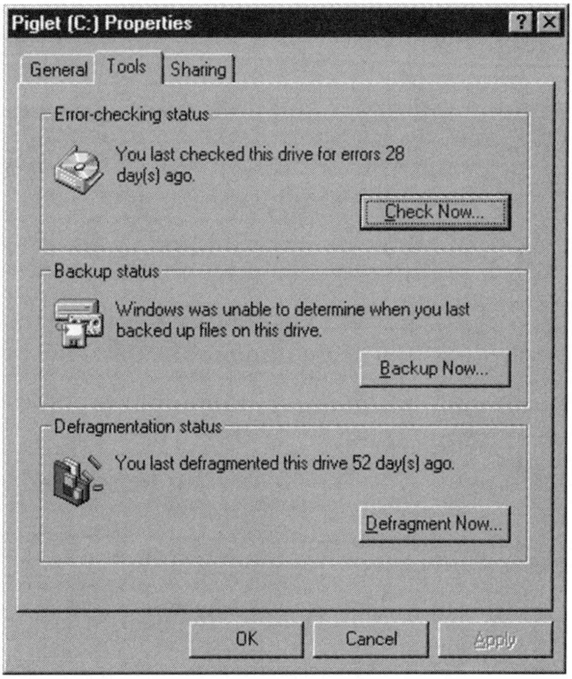

NOTE

You can also launch the defragmenter two other ways: one is by clicking the Run button from the Start menu and typing `defrag`. Another is by clicking the Start button, selecting Accessories, next choosing System Tools, and then (finally!) Disk Defragmenter. If you start defragmentation these ways, you will be prompted to specify which drive to defrag. Then the Defragmenter will proceed as described below.

Defragment Now presented me with some interesting information (see Figure 11.18).

Can this be right? Only 2% fragmented? I don't need to defragment the disk now? It is, believe it or not, true. After 52 days of daily usage there is almost no file fragmentation. This is due to new logic that Microsoft built into VFAT, Windows 95's file system.

Prior to Windows 95, saving a file was one of the worst things you could do to your disk. Over a period of time, this would cause your disk performance to degrade, sometimes noticeably (doesn't that sound like one of those motor oil ads on starting your car engine?). Under MS-DOS and Windows for Workgroups v3.11's VFAT, a great deal of file fragmentation occurred because the file system allocated the first available space found on the disk. The result was that most of your files were chopped up into tiny pieces and randomly spread across your disk.

Under Windows 95, VFAT uses a more intelligent method of allocating space when writing to the disk. By default, VFAT searches your disk for

FIGURE 11.18

Disk Defragmenter
advice dialog box

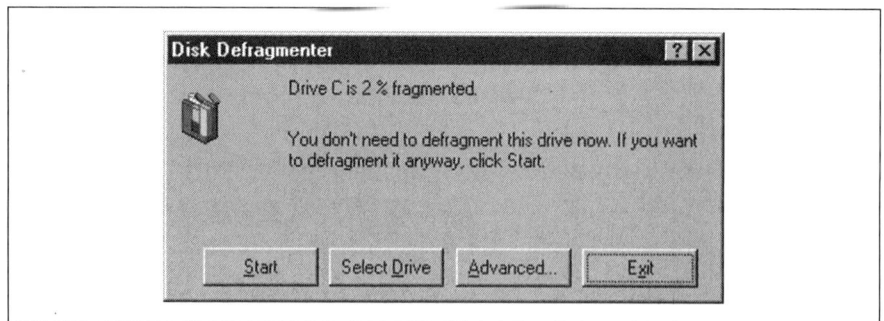

the first contiguous 0.5MB of free disk space before writing the file. This ensures that most, if not all, of your files can be written to the disk contiguously, which results in optimized performance. Unfortunately, VFAT will resort to the MS-DOS method if it cannot find at least that much free contiguous space.

Think of it this way: most of the wear on your car's engine comes from starting it. Upon startup, all of the protective oil is sitting in the oil pan; it is not coating and protecting any of the metal parts that will soon begin to rub against one another. Now imagine that you had a system in your engine that circulated the oil around all the necessary parts *before* you started it. The reduction in engine wear would be dramatic! Just as prelubricating your car's engine would dramatically reduce engine wear, prelocating a large area of free space on your disk before writing the file dramatically reduces file fragmentation.

Now back to defragging my C: drive. Even though I don't need to defragment the disk I'll do it anyway. Before defragging, let's first take a look at what options are available to us, by clicking the Advanced button.

Advanced Options under Defragmentation

While our options are somewhat limited, we do have basic control over the defragmentation process. You can see the Advanced Options screen in Figure 11.19.

The first thing to do is choose the defragmentation method:

- **Full defragmentation (both files and free space).** Choosing this option causes DEFRAG.EXE to completely rearrange your disk—all of your files are placed at the beginning of the disk and the rest is left as a big chunk of free space. Any fragmented files will be written to their new location contiguously. This is the preferred method for defragmentation, but it also takes the longest to complete.

- **Defragment files only.** If you choose this option, DEFRAG.EXE will make sure that all the files on your disk are stored contiguously by rewriting any fragmented files to a location on the disk that is large enough to hold them contiguously. This method is faster than a full defragmentation, but it has a drawback: it does not consolidate the

FIGURE 11.19

Defragging Advanced
Options screen

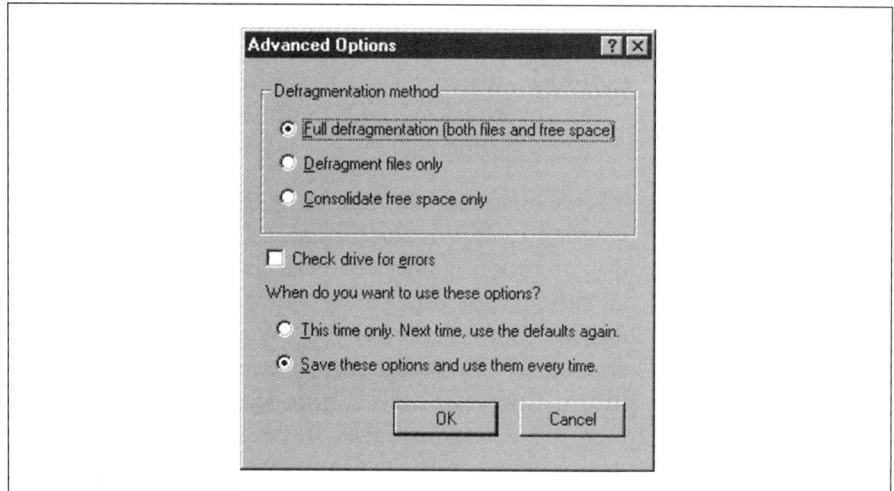

free space. The result: future files have a greater chance of becoming fragmented.

- **Consolidate free space only.** This option will cause DEFRAG.EXE to rearrange your disk so that all of the free space is in one large chunk. This option is interesting: Although it ensures that any files written to the disk in the future will not be fragmented, there is a high possibility that files already on the disk will become *more* fragmented! This happens because DEFRAG.EXE will find the largest area of free space, then move the smaller blocks of free spaces so they are contiguous with the largest one. This results in fragmentation because parts of existing files that border the large free block of space are moved into the smaller areas of free space. This may result in some non-fragmented files becoming fragmented.

The other two options are pretty simple. *Check drive for errors* simply says that the Defragmenter will check the drive for errors by running ScanDisk before performing defragmentation. The setting *When do you want to use these options* allows you to specify whether the settings you choose at this session are to be the default settings or a one-time deal.

Once you have chosen the desired options, click OK to return to the main defragging screen. Here you have the chance to change the target drive, if so desired. Click Start to begin defragmenting.

At this point, according to Microsoft, you should be able to go back to work on your computer while the Defragger runs in the background. However, the Defragger will reset itself every time there is a change in the target drive. Depending on your workload, you may wait quite some time for the Defragger to finish. So, if you work excessively from your local drive, you may want to start the defragger when you won't be using the computer very much—for example, run the program as you are leaving for lunch.

While the Defragmenter is working, you will see a defragging status bar on the screen. If you want to see each cluster during defragmentation, click on Show Details and you'll see something like Figure 11.20.

Clicking on Legend will explain the significance of the different colors on your screen while the Defragmenter is doing its job. This view of the

FIGURE 11.20

Show Details
dialog box during
defragmentation

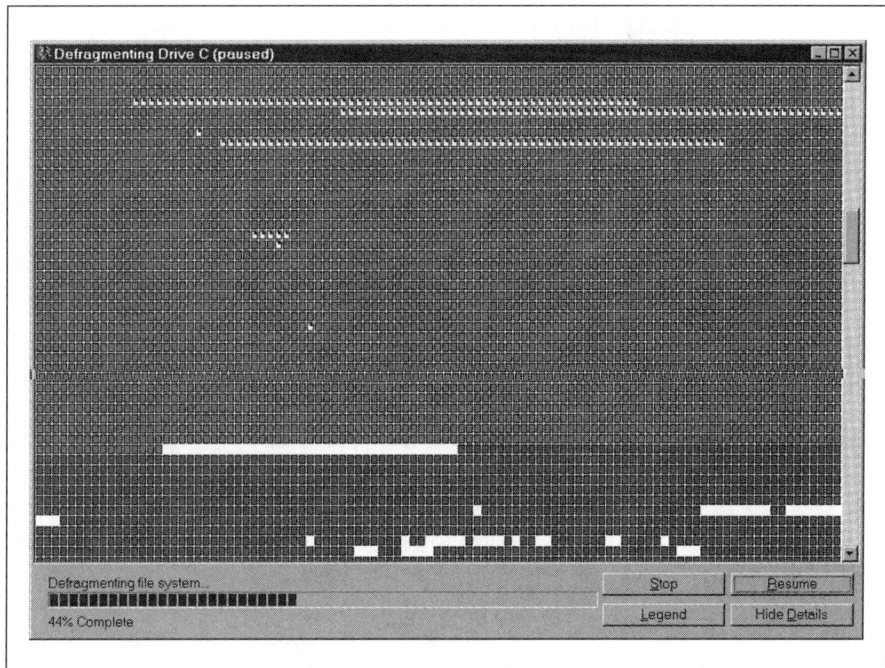

Defragmenter tends to slow it down, so when you're finished looking at this screen, select Hide Details to return to the small status screen. When the Defragmenter is finished, a dialog box will advise you to run ScanDisk to ensure the integrity of the disk. Keep on reading to learn more about ScanDisk.

Checking Disk Integrity with ScanDisk

ScanDisk is another disk utility included with Windows 95 that helps you to keep your disk in proper health. Depending on the options you choose, ScanDisk can search for and repair errors in your files, or physically on your hard drive. ScanDisk also checks for errors in the FAT, in long file-names, and with cross-linked or lost clusters.

You should run ScanDisk regularly to maintain your hard drive. In this section, we'll run ScanDisk on both an uncompressed and a compressed drive. (Information on how to compress drives is coming up in the next section.)

Running ScanDisk

To begin, click on My Computer and right-click on the appropriate drive. Next, click on Properties, then select the Tools tab. At the top of this screen you will see Error-checking status. Here you can see how long it has been since you last ran ScanDisk. Is it about time to run ScanDisk? If so, click Check Now, and you will see the screen shown in Figure 11.21.

This screen lets you choose which drive to test and gives you other options: Type of test, Automatically fix errors, and the Advanced button.

- **Type of test:** Here you can perform either a Standard or Thorough test.
  - **Standard:** As it says beneath its name, this test checks files and folders for errors. This is the faster test of the two, but it does not check the surface of the disk for errors. As seen in the previous figure, when this option is selected, the Options button is grayed out.
  - **Thorough:** This test checks everything that the Standard test checks; in addition it scans the surface of the hard drive for

errors. When you choose a Thorough test, the Options button
can be selected. More on this screen coming up.

- **Automatically fix errors:** Do you want to be prompted to fix all
  errors which ScanDisk finds or would you rather let ScanDisk go
  and fix them itself? Your selection just depends on your personal
  preference.

If you decide that a Thorough test is the way to go, select it, then click on
Options; you'll see Figure 11.22.

Let's take a look at the options on this screen.

- **System and data areas:** This instructs ScanDisk to scan for errors
  in both the system and data areas of your drive. This type of test will
  usually take longer than the following two options.

- **System areas only:** With this option selected, ScanDisk will search
  for errors in the system area only, leaving the data area unscanned.
  Unfortunately, ScanDisk cannot repair errors in the system part of

FIGURE 11.22

ScanDisk's Thorough
Options screen

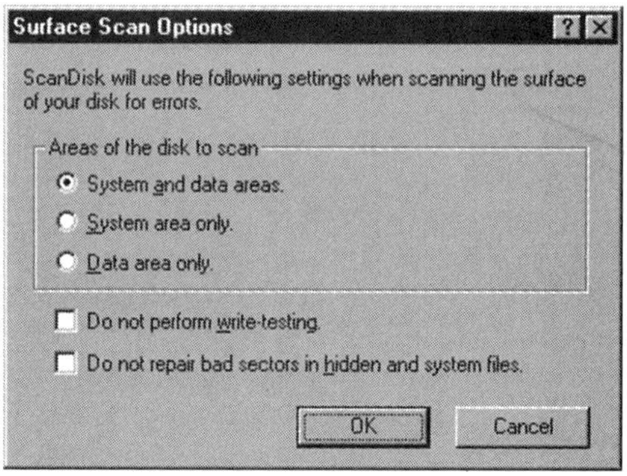

your drive. If errors are found, ScanDisk will alert you (depending on your Log settings, which is coming up).

- **Data areas only:** With this option, only the data areas, and not the system areas of the disk, are checked. Typically ScanDisk can repair errors in the data areas, and it does so by moving the data to another part of the disk. The bad area is then marked as unusable on the disk.

- **Do not perform write-testing:** Normally ScanDisk will check your disk by reading the data from your disk and then attempting to write the data back. If this box is checked, ScanDisk will read data but *not* attempt to write it back. This option is not necessary to perform on an IDE drive, because it does this kind of testing automatically.

- **Do not repair bad sectors in hidden and system files:** If this is *not* checked, ScanDisk will move any hidden or system files found to have bad sectors to other parts of the disk. This could cause programs that require system or hidden files to be in a specific place to work incorrectly. If this option is checked, ScanDisk will leave these files alone.

After selecting the desired options, click OK. This brings you back to the original screen of ScanDisk. But don't click Start just yet! There is still one other screen in which you must choose options: the Advanced Options screen. Click the Advanced button and you'll see Figure 11.23.

FIGURE 11.23

Advanced screen
in ScanDisk

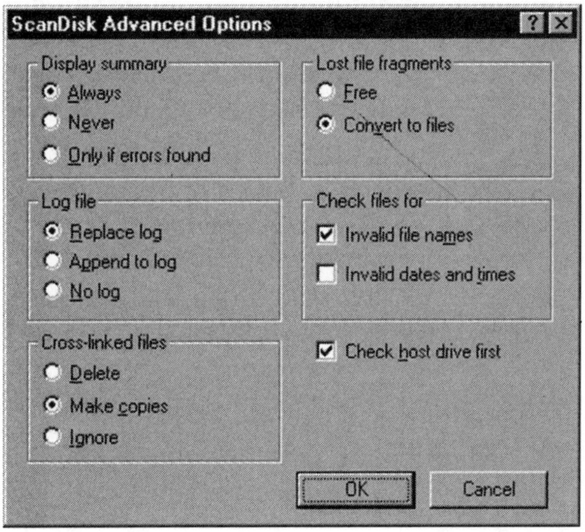

The first two options are fairly self-explanatory and how you select these options, *Display summary* and *Log* file, depends entirely on your personal preferences. Do you want to see the summaries, including information on total and free disk space, bad sectors, folders, hidden, and user files? If so, click on *Always* or *Only if errors found*. Do you want to keep a log of every run of ScanDisk? If so, click on *Append to log*. The other options, however, could use a little bit of explaining.

- **Cross-linked files:** Cross-linked files are two files which both believe they have data written to a common cluster; actually, one file is mistaken. If your primary concern is to save data, *Make copies* would be the best option to choose. This copies both files elsewhere with their own copy of the cross-linked cluster. Unfortunately, there is no way to be sure that this will save the data; there is no guarantee that one or even both of the files will have all their data intact. However, choosing *Delete* will obviously not save the data.

- **Lost file fragments:** These are clusters which are marked as being used, but have no filename associated with them (kind of a file with no name). Choosing *Convert to files* will place all of the lost file fragments in your root directory into one file. At this point you can look through the files to see if there is any data you want to save. Choosing *Free* automatically deletes the lost file fragments.

- **Check files for:** This will check for corrupted long filenames and extended attributes such as creation date and time.

- **Check host drive first:** This is an option that should remain checked, but this will only show up if you have used disk compression. When ScanDisk checks a compressed drive, this option tells ScanDisk to check the host drive before the compressed drive. (If there is a problem with the host drive, it could affect the compressed drive, which is a very good reason to check the host first.)

That pretty much wraps up ScanDisk. When you've selected all the options, click on Start. ScanDisk will give you a status bar to let you know how far the program has gone, and, depending on your Summary selection, you may get a summary report when it is finished.

Advanced File System Settings

In addition to optimizing your system with the Recycle Bin, Defrag, and ScanDisk, you can also adjust your File System settings in the Control Panel to best suit your system's needs. To review these settings, click on the System icon in the Control Panel, and select the Performance tab. You'll see a screen like the one in Figure 11.24.

This screen gives you general information concerning your system, including memory, resources, and type of file system in use. Now click File System under the Advanced settings heading, and you will see a dialog box like the one in Figure 11.25.

The three tabs available from this screen allow you to adjust the proper ties of your hard disk and CD-ROM and let you try different settings to pinpoint bottlenecks and problems on your system. Let's first take a look at the Hard Disk tab.

Hard Disk Performance

The Hard Disk tab allows you to configure two settings: the role of your machine and its read-ahead optimization. You can choose one of three role settings: Desktop computer, Mobile or docking system, or Network

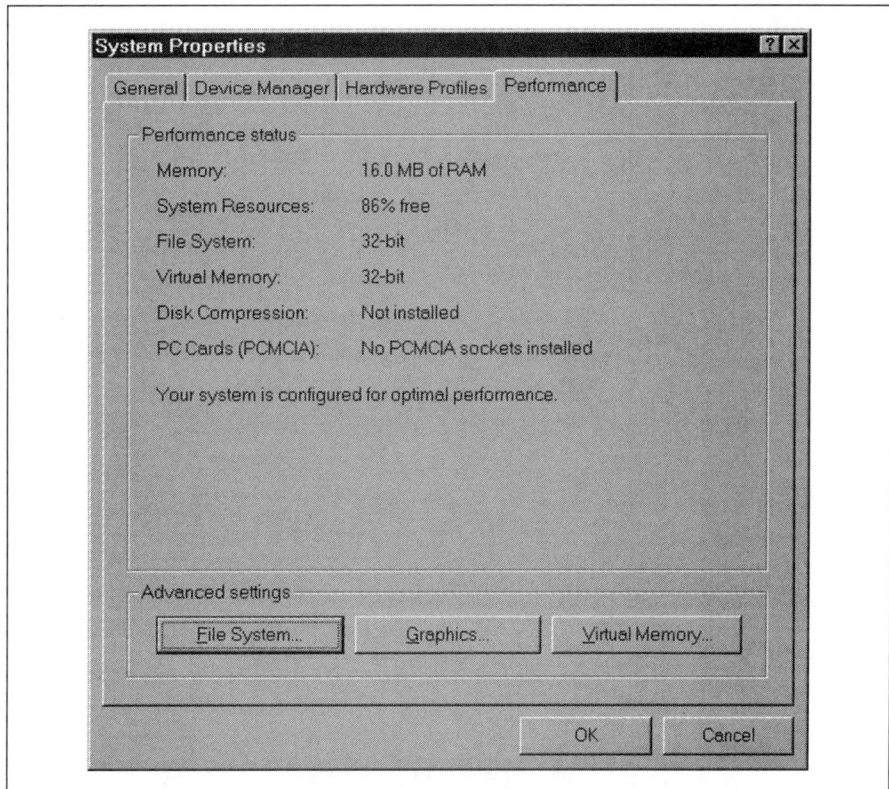

System Properties

General | Device Manager | Hardware Profiles | Performance |

┌─ Performance status ─────────────────────────────────┐
│ Memory: 16.0 MB of RAM   │
│ System Resources: 86% free   │
│ File System: 32-bit   │
│ Virtual Memory: 32-bit   │
│ Disk Compression: Not installed   │
│ PC Cards (PCMCIA):   No PCMCIA sockets installed   │
│   │
│ Your system is configured for optimal performance.   │
└──┘

┌─ Advanced settings ──────────────────────────────────┐
│   [File System...]   [Graphics...]   [Virtual Memory...] │
└──┘

[OK]   [Cancel]

server. Although these settings are fairly cut and dried, here are a few guidelines on how to determine which is best for you:

- **Desktop computer:** This setting assumes that you are using a computer in the role of a network client (or even stand-alone) with more than the minimum amount of RAM, and not running on battery power.

- **Mobile or docking system:** This is the setting for laptop computers typically running on battery power which have a minimum amount of RAM. This setting will flush out the disk cache frequently.

- **Network server:** This is the setting for network servers which have enough RAM; this setting also assumes frequent disk activity and will optimize itself for that setting.

FIGURE 11.25

Optimizing your
hard disk

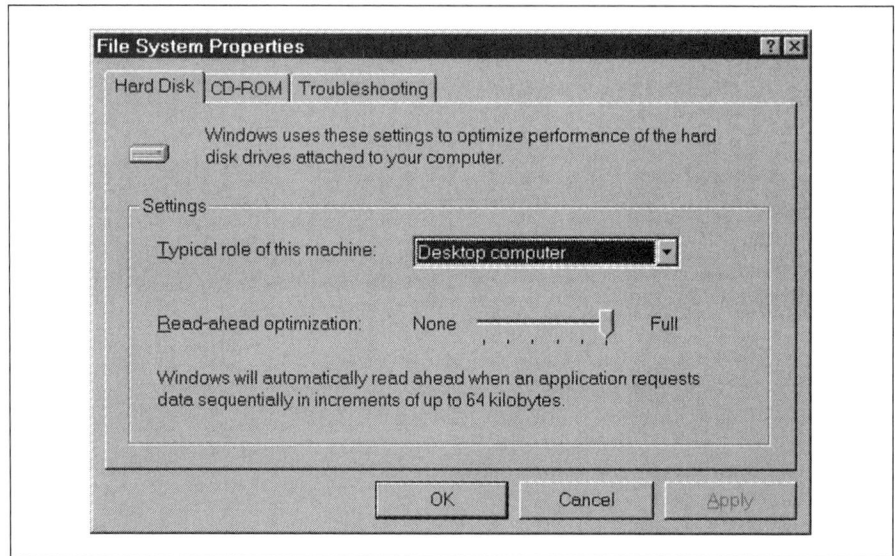

The second setting, Read-ahead optimization, lets you determine whether you want the hard drive to read ahead. Move the slider to the desired position.

CD-ROM Performance

Windows 95's new *CDFS*, or *CD File System*, offers 32-bit, protected-mode drivers, rather than Windows 3.x's real-mode MSCDEX drivers. CDFS does not use conventional memory. It allows for improved multitasking, and has a dynamically configured cache. However, you may configure a supplemental cache for improved CD-ROM performance. When you click on the CD-ROM tab, you will see the screen shown in Figure 11.26.

First, you can set *Supplemental cache size:* by moving its slider to the desired position. Keep in mind, though, that a large cache is only helpful if the cache is large enough to hold entire streams of multimedia; if not, sometimes a small to medium cache is sufficient.

Next, you must set the *Optimize access pattern for:* setting. Under CDFS, the CD-ROM reads ahead at the same rate as the application so that playback runs more smoothly. Therefore, you must base your determination

FIGURE 11.26

Optimizing CD-ROM
performance

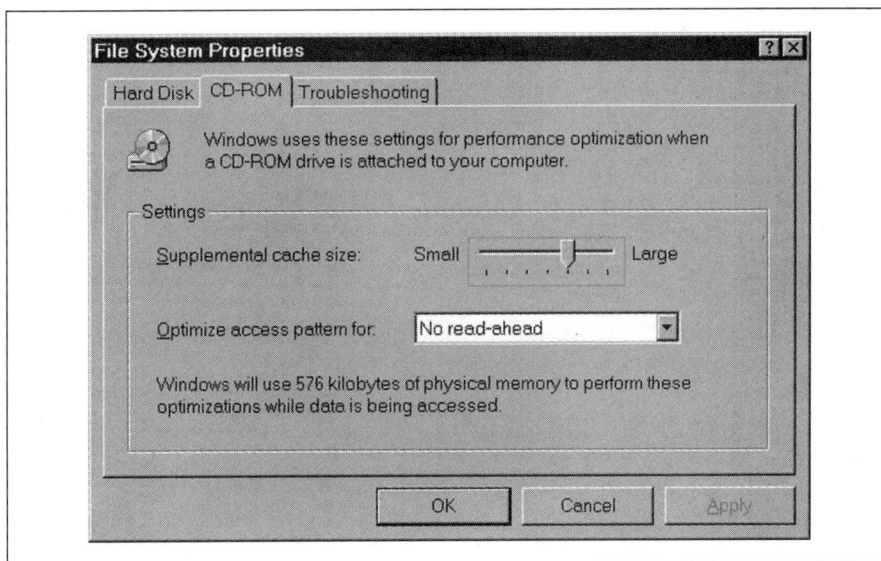

of this option on the amount of RAM on your system and the access speed of your CD-ROM.:

- With 8MB or less of RAM and a single-speed CD-ROM, a 64K cache is created.
- With 8MB to 12MB of RAM and a double-speed drive, a 626K cache is created.
- With more than 12MB of RAM and a quad-speed (or higher) drive, a 1238K cache is created.

Keep in mind that, based on your choices, different size caches will be created.

Troubleshooting Your System

The final tab in this section is the Troubleshooting tab; you can see it in Figure 11.27.

FIGURE 11.27

Troubleshooting tab in
Advanced File System
settings

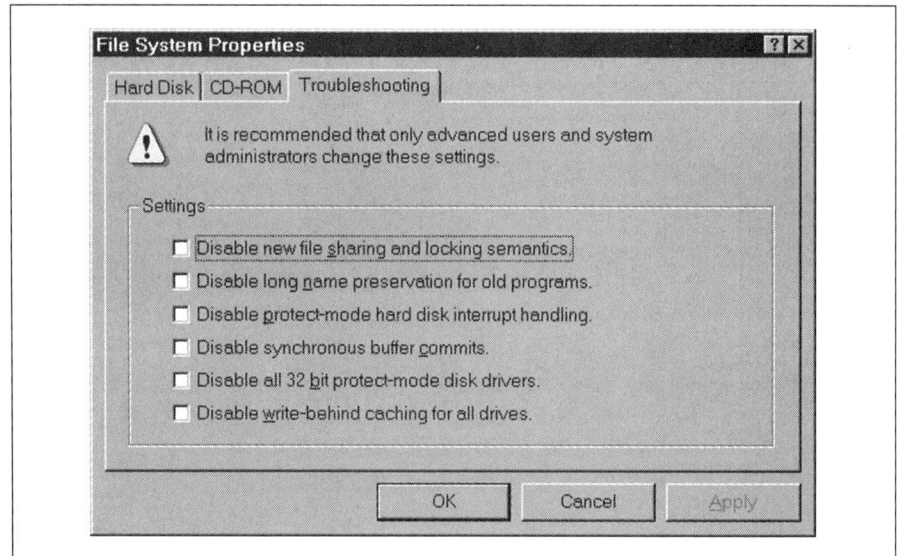

> **WARNING**
>
> Changing the settings in the Troubleshooting tab is not
> recommended, as it can lead to performance degradation.
> Change them only for the purposes of troubleshooting problems.

In this screen, you can disable many different features of the operating system in order to pinpoint problems on your system. Here's an explanation of these features:

- **Disable new file sharing and locking semantics**: You can disable this option when a DOS-based program is having trouble sharing under Windows 95. This changes the code which keeps open files from being shared and modified by other programs.

- **Disable long name preservation for old programs**: Choose this option when a legacy program cannot accept long filenames. This turns off tunneling, which preserves long filenames when used by programs which do not accept these filenames. (For more on long filenames, turn to the upcoming section, "Using Long Filename Support.")

- **Disable protect-mode hard disk interrupt handling**: When this is checked, it allows the ROM (instead of Windows 95) to handle hard disk interrupts; however, this can lead to a slowdown of your system. You may need to select this if your hard drive needs this type of interrupt handling. (By default, this is not selected; under Windows 3.x, however, the reverse was true.)

- **Disable all 32-bit protect-mode disk drivers**: As it says, this option disables all 32-bit, protected-mode drivers (except for the floppy drive); real-mode drivers are used instead.

- **Disable write-behind caching for all drives**: This entry basically disables write-caching for all drives.

That's all there is to these three Advanced File System settings. Adjusting these will help optimize performance on your system, as well as help you to troubleshoot problems when they arise.

Understanding the Disk Cache

Under Windows 3.x, if you were dissatisfied with the speed with which your hard drive accessed files, you could enable *disk caching*. You enabled software, in this case SMARTDrive, to set aside a certain amount of RAM to use as the disk cache. This allowed frequently accessed files to reside in RAM, and therefore they could be accessed faster when in RAM than when on the hard drive.

How Disk Cache Works

When you access a file from disk, the caching software makes a copy of this file and stores it in cache. The next time the user accesses the file, the software first looks for this file in the cache. If the file is in the cache, then the software does not need to look to the slow hard drive for the file, and accesses the file faster for the user. If the file is not in cache, however, it is necessary to go to the hard drive and retrieve the file. At this point, the caching software makes a copy of the file and stores it in cache again.

Disk Caching under Windows 95

The disk cache has undergone some changes from its Windows 3.x incarnation. First, Windows 95 uses a 32-bit protected-mode driver, VCACHE, instead of the 16-bit real-mode disk cache software, SMARTDrive, used with Windows 3.x. Second, an improved algorithm used in VCACHE allows for greater speed and performance than was possible under SMARTDrive. Now here's what I consider to be the best new feature of the disk cache under Windows 95: The user no longer needs to specify settings for the disk cache, as it is dynamically configured. The system determines the size of the disk cache, as determined by the need of the system.

This means the Windows 95 user is not able to control any of the disk caching settings, which you might see as a mixed blessing. However, you can do one thing to see the best disk caching performance under Windows 95: Remove any SHARE or SMARTDRV settings from either your `autoexec.bat` or `config.sys` files. Also, if you notice that your system is paging a lot, don't fear, as the disk cache will automatically shrink to free up more memory for the system.

Should You Manage the Swap File or Allow Windows to Control It?

Under Windows 3.x, managing the swap file was an important part of performance tuning. You had to decide whether to have a temporary swap file (which did not require a contiguous block of disk space) or a permanent swap file (which did require a contiguous block of disk space, but in return gave improved system performance); you had to decide how much memory the swap file should have; and you had to decide whether or not to implement 32-bit disk access. Under Windows 95, these decisions and tweaking are really not necessary. First, though, let's look at how the swap file works.

How the Swap File Works

The swap file helps resolve out-of-memory problems. If your system needs another megabyte of RAM, but you are already using all your RAM, the system will just grab a megabyte of unused disk space and use it like RAM. There is a catch, though; since disks are slower than RAM, the swap file may have a tendency to slow your machine down a bit. But if the alternative is not running the program at all because you don't have the memory, it's not such a bad thing. Basically, the swap file allows you to run programs which require more from the system than the system could handle without the swap file.

Windows 95 and the Swap File

Under Windows 95, the virtual memory swap file can be dynamically managed by Windows 95 to best meet your system's changing needs. Unlike the disk cache, however, the user may choose to control the swap file settings. Windows 95's swap file can also take up fragmented parts of the drive with little performance degradation. Although this is true, it is still a good idea to defrag your drive before you set up a new swap file. If you are running a shared version of Windows 95 from a remote machine, your swap file resides on the remote machine's directory.

Now, should you control the swap file or allow Windows 95 to control it? Personally, I would recommend to allow Windows 95 to control it. Typically, dynamic control of the swap file will result in the most efficient use of your system resources.

Managing Your Swap File

If you decide that a dynamically controlled swap file is not for you, then here's how to change and control its size. In the Control Panel, click on System, then choose the Performance tab, and then click on Virtual Memory. You'll see a screen like in Figure 11.28.

Click on the radio button next to *Let me specify my own virtual memory settings*. This will highlight the three sections underneath. *Hard disk* tells you on which hard drive the swap file presently resides and how much free space is on that drive. Here you can change the swap file's location. Typically, to see the best swap file performance, place it on a fast hard drive,

FIGURE 11.28

Virtual Memory
screen in the
Control Panel

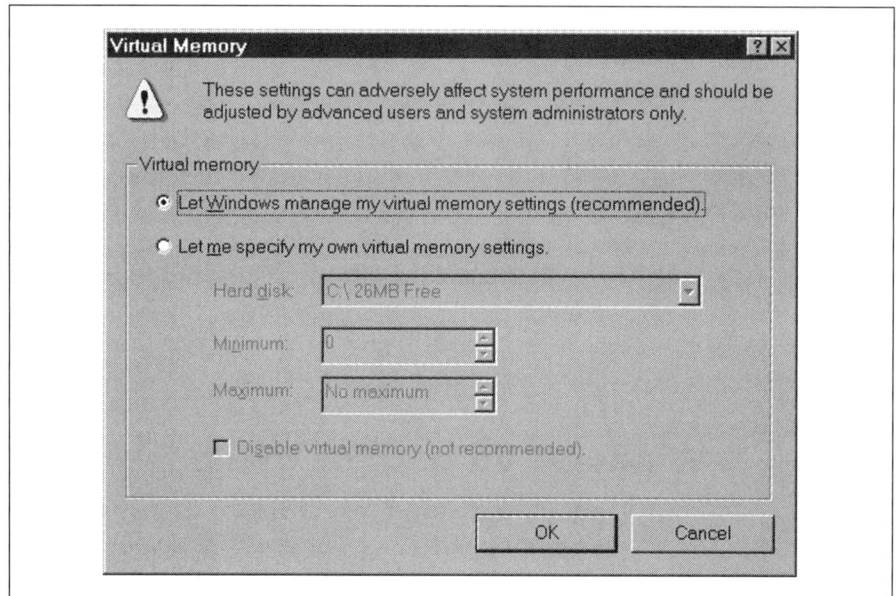

one with less user traffic, and/or one with adequate free space so it can shrink and grow as needed. Then, with *Minimum* and *Maximum*, you can specify the largest and smallest size of your swap file. If you set the value of Maximum to equal the amount of free space on a hard drive, then additional free space becomes available on the drive, and the system will assume that it can increase the size of swap file by the amount of *new* free space on the drive. The last option, *Disable virtual memory* is not recommended, as this can lead to system performance problems.

Using Long Filename Support

For years the DOS-based world has been constrained by the eight-dot-three filename, which refers to the filenames with no more than 8 characters and file extensions no longer than 3 characters. Now with the advent of long filename support, Windows 95 users are freed from these constraints. Well, kind of.

How Windows 95 Implements Long Filenames

When a user creates a new long filename, Windows 95 automatically generates a second filename (known as an *alias*) conforming to the eight-dot-three standard, for the sake of backwards compatibility. The long filename is used in applications accepting long filenames, and the alias name is the filename Windows 95 uses to work with older programs.

The newly generated alias is composed of four different parts, in the following order: the first six letters in the long filename, a tilde (~), a unique number, and then an extension. The extension is created by taking the first three letters after the last period in the long filename. If there are no periods in the long filename, Windows 95 uses the default extension of the appropriate application. You may be thinking, "But what happens if two files have the same first six letters?" That's what the number after the tilde is for: Windows 95 generates different numbers so that the two filenames are unique. Another quality of the alias names is that they are all capital letters.

N O T E   Keep in mind that many non-Windows 95 programs will not accept long filenames, even though Windows 95 will.

Let's take a look at an example. I just created three documents in Windows 95's WordPad: the first document saved is named My project for September, the second file saved is named Another project for September.doc, and the third saved is My project for October. A unique alias is created for each long filename: the first file is now MYPROJ~1.DOC, the second is ANOTHE~1.DOC, and the third is MYPROJ~2.DOC. As you can see, these filenames conform to the eight-dot-three standard for compatibility. Also of note are the two MYPROJ~ files: Windows 95 simply generated a new unique number for the second filename in order to avoid having two files with the same name.

Tunneling and Network Support for Long Filenames

Tunneling is a process which allows applications not supporting long file-names to open and save these files (whether the files are local or on the network) without destroying the long filenames. Tunneling is supported with the VFAT, NTFS, and HPFS file systems.

> **N O T E**
> Windows NT 3.1 does not accept long filenames on FAT volumes and will eliminate them. Windows NT 3.5 does not have a problem with them.

So What's the Catch?

All of this doesn't sound too bad, right? Well, before you jump in and begin to create long filenames, read the following list for the bad news.

- Unless you have applications written especially for Windows 95, you will not be able to have full support for long filenames. In the previous example, I created files with long filenames in Windows 95's WordPad; the version of Ami Pro that I use was written for Windows 3.x, and does not support long filenames. One possible way to get around this, though, is through some new products which claim to change your old apps to accept long filenames. (I haven't used any, so I can't say how they work.)

- Storing files with long filenames in the root directory can take up more than one entry; as the root directory can only store 512 entries, you must be careful with how many long filename files you store there.

- Many disk utilities not written specifically for Windows 95 will destroy long filenames. Take caution when choosing disk utilities not included with Windows 95. (This is not to say you shouldn't use non-Windows 95 disk utilities; just be careful!)

- A caution concerning alias names: Do not use the long filename of a file when issuing low-level commands (such as Copy or Rename) from a command line; use the alias. Otherwise, the operation will change the name to a different alias. For example, say you have a file with the name `Letter to mom today.txt` (alias `LETTER~1.DOC`). If you use the Copy command at the command prompt to copy it to another directory, your file `Letter to mom today.txt` will become `LETTER~2.DOC`. This changing of filenames could become extremely confusing.

DriveSpace under Windows 95

Included with Windows 95 is DriveSpace, a compression program which supports the VFAT file system and includes long filename support. Obviously, this disk compression routine is safe to use with Windows 95, but don't count on it being safe with other such programs. Be sure to check for the Windows 95 compatible sticker (or the like) on any new program you purchase. If the program isn't Windows 95 compatible, you will trash your long filenames. Two such programs are Stacker 4.0 and DriveSpace 6.x for MS-DOS; these programs will destroy long filenames on your disk.

How does compression work? Well, under Windows 95 a compressed drive really isn't a compressed drive—it's actually a *compressed volume file* (*CVF*). DriveSpace stores the new compressed drive as a CVF in the root directory of an uncompressed hard disk, which is known as the host drive. Even though the compressed drive is really only a compressed file residing on another hard disk, the compressed drive is assigned a letter and is accessed as if it is a separate hard drive. The CVF has read-only, hidden, and system attributes, and typically has a name such as `DRVSPACE.000`.

WARNING Don't mess with these files on your system. You could potentially lose the data on your compressed hard disk!

In the next few pages, we'll see:

- How to compress a new empty drive.
- How to compress a boot drive.
- How to uncompress a drive.

But first, let's take a look at the various options available within DriveSpace.

DriveSpace Options and What They Mean

Under the two main menu options in DriveSpace, Drive and Advanced, there are many different options which allow you to tailor your drives to suit your personal needs. Here we'll take a look at some of these options.

Under the Drive menu, users can choose from five options:

- The Compress and Uncompress options. I describe these in detail later in this section.
- The Properties option simply gives the user general information on the selected drive, such as whether the drive is compressed and a reading of free space versus used space on the drive.
- Format allows the user to format a compressed drive.
- The Adjust Free Space option allows the user to change the amount of free space between a compressed drive and its host drive. Take a look at Figure 11.29 to see the Adjust Free Space screen.

This screen would allow me to add more free space to Drive D: by taking space from Drive H:.

FIGURE 11.29

DriveSpace's Adjust
Free Space screen

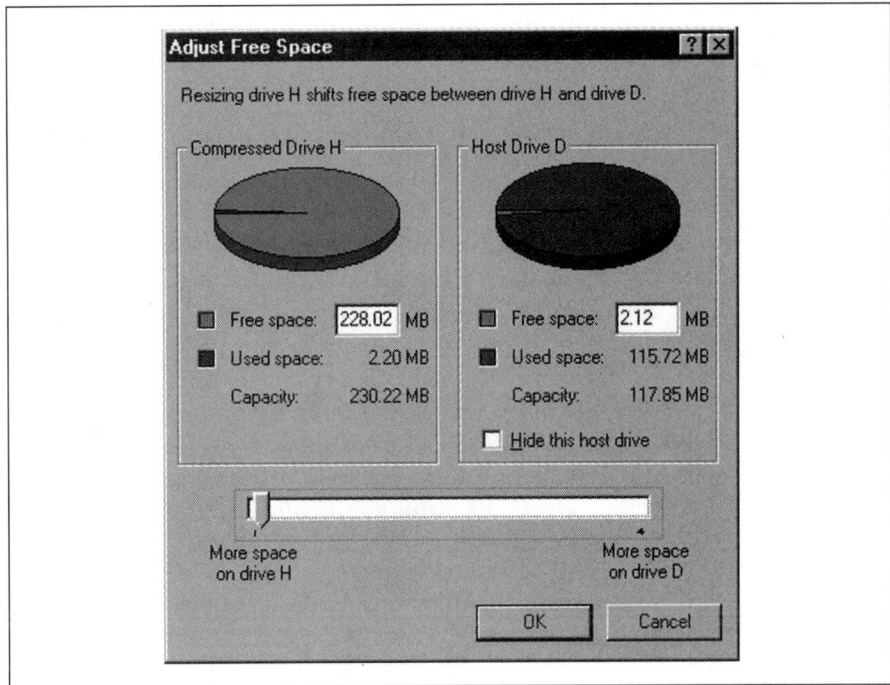

Under the Advanced menu there are eight possible options.

- The Mount and Unmount options only apply to compressed drives. To mount a compressed drive essentially means to assign it a drive letter. Unmounting, then, takes the drive letter away from a compressed drive. So for example, you could unmount a compressed drive from its host, perform Defragmentation or ScanDisk, then mount the compressed drive. This also allows a user to mount and unmount a compressed floppy disk.

- Create Empty is discussed in the following section.

- Delete deletes the selected compressed drive.

- Change Ratio allows the user to change the estimated compression ratio of future files. If you have an uncompressed drive, you know exactly how much free space you have on the drive. But when using a compressed drive, Windows 95 must estimate how much free space is available, as the amount of free space depends on the compressibility of files you will store on a drive in the future. Say that a drive is using a 2:1 ratio to estimate free space on a drive. If you store certain types of files which compress easily (bitmaps), the drive would be able to compress the bitmaps at a higher compression rate than other types of files which don't compress easily. Take a look at Figure 11.30 to see how to use this option.

What is the best ratio for you? Typically, a safe bet is to set the Estimated compression ratio at the same rate as the Actual ratio. If you know that you will be storing highly compressible files, you are safe setting the ratio higher. Remember that this doesn't change the compression rate of the files presently on your drive; this only affects how DriveSpace estimates the amount of free space on a compressed drive.

- Change Letter allows you to change the drive letter of the selected drive. Use this with caution, as changing the drive letter can affect other programs using the drive.

- Settings allows you to change the *automount* setting. The Windows 95 default is to have automount enabled. Automount means that upon startup, Windows 95 automatically mounts any unmounted compressed drive (for example, floppy drives).

- Refresh simply updates the window to reflect any recent changes to the drives.

FIGURE 11.30

Changing the compression ratio of future files

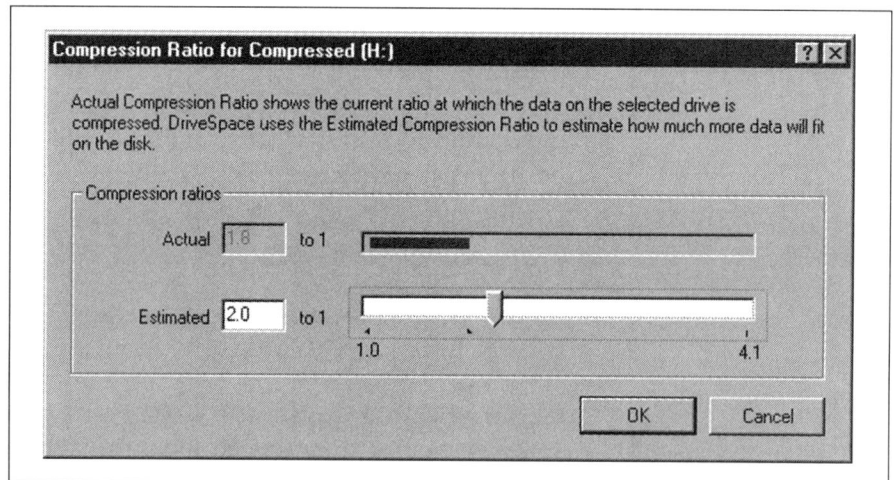

Compression Ratio for Compressed (H:)

Actual Compression Ratio shows the current ratio at which the data on the selected drive is compressed. DriveSpace uses the Estimated Compression Ratio to estimate how much more data will fit on the disk.

Compression ratios

Actual [1.8] to 1

Estimated [2.0] to 1

1.0   4.1

OK   Cancel

Up to this point, we've taken a look at the different options in the DriveSpace dialog box; now let's take a look at how to compress different types of drives.

Compressing a New Empty Drive

If you think back to the partitioning and formatting section, you'll remember that I had a 118MB logical DOS drive. Well, I decided to compress that whole 118MB drive to get more megabytes for my buck. Compressing this brand new empty drive was a snap; here's what you'd do.

First, click on the Start button and choose Run. Type **drvspace** and press Enter. Then you'll see a screen like the one in Figure 11.31.

As there is no data presently on Drive D:, I will be compressing an empty drive. Under Advanced, choose Create Empty and you'll see a screen like the one in Figure 11.32.

This screen lets you change two things: the default name of the new compressed drive and which drive will be the host. Here, you can also adjust the amount of free space between the two drives by simply typing in a

FIGURE 11.31

DriveSpace opening screen

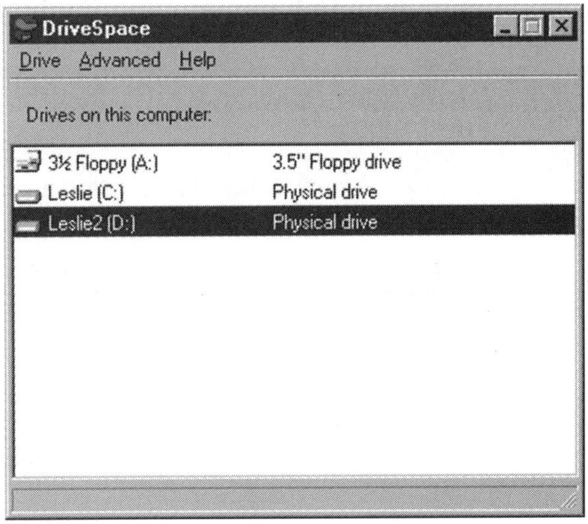

FIGURE 11.32

Creating a new empty
compressed drive

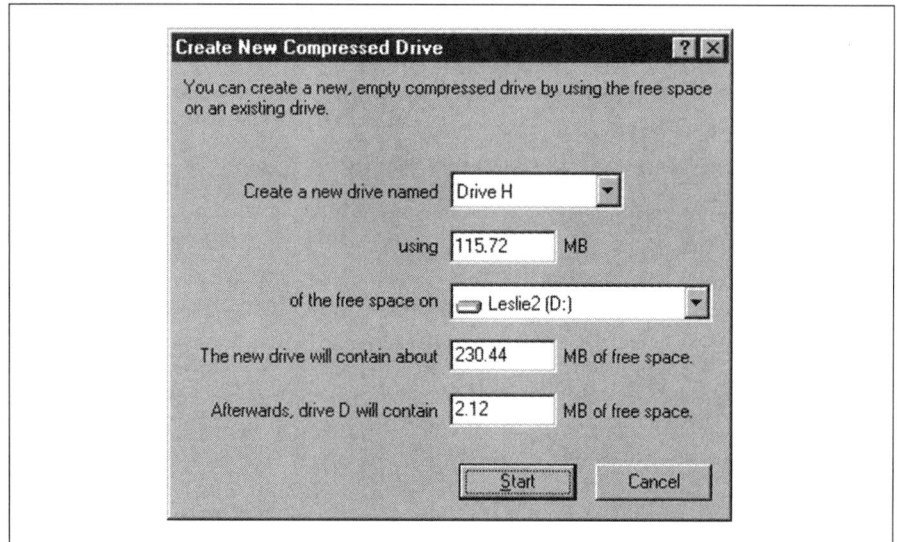

different value; the other value will automatically adjust to reflect the changes. I decided not to change anything, so I just clicked Start. A dialog box will appear on the screen and update you on the status of the compression. When completed, you'll see a screen like that in Figure 11.33.

This screen is simply a repeat of your original screen and doesn't really give any new information. It serves to let you know that the new compressed drive was created. After clicking Close, you will be prompted to restart the computer. Once you have rebooted the system, start DriveSpace again and you'll see the new compressed drive, as in Figure 11.34.

Now your new compressed drive is ready to be used.

Compressing a Boot Drive

Compressing a boot drive involves a slightly different process than compressing an empty drive, as you are compressing a drive with open files. Basically, the process is the same up to a certain point, when Windows 95 reboots in a special operating mode; this allows it to work with open files.

FIGURE 11.33

New Compressed
Drive statistics

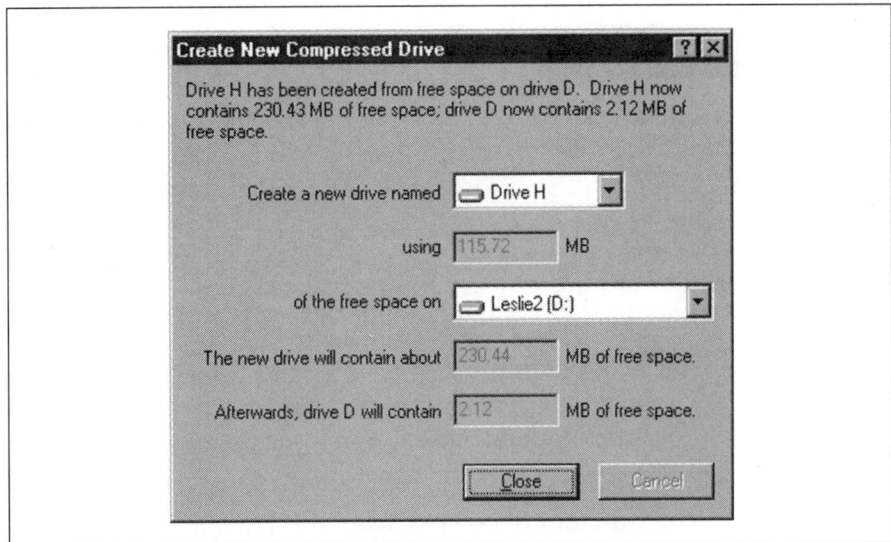

Create New Compressed Drive   ? ✕

Drive H has been created from free space on drive D. Drive H now
contains 230.43 MB of free space; drive D now contains 2.12 MB of
free space.

Create a new drive named   [💾 Drive H   ▼]

using   [115.72]   MB

of the free space on   [💾 Leslie2 (D:)   ▼]

The new drive will contain about   [230.44]   MB of free space.

Afterwards, drive D will contain   [2.12]   MB of free space.

[Close]   [Cancel]

FIGURE 11.34

DriveSpace screen
with compressed drive

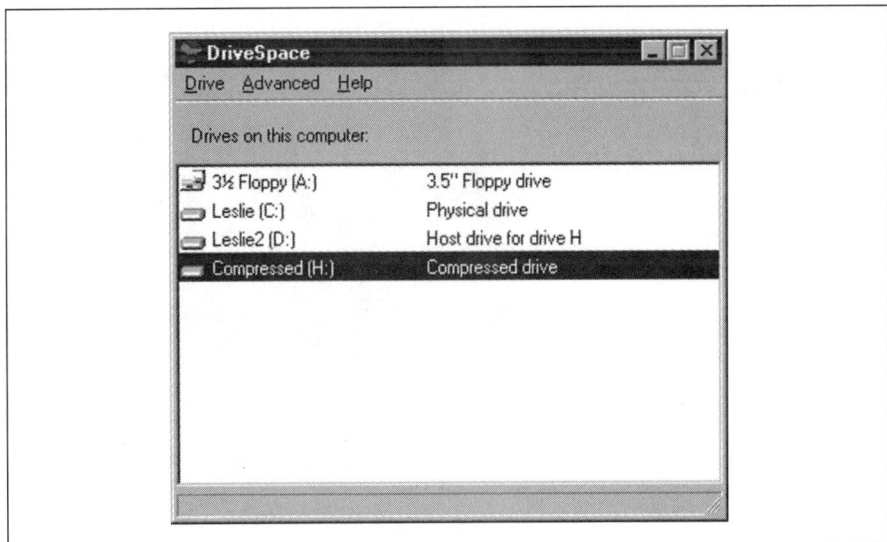

DriveSpace   _ ☐ ✕

Drive   Advanced   Help

Drives on this computer:

💾 3½ Floppy (A:)	3.5" Floppy drive
💾 Leslie (C:)	Physical drive
💾 Leslie2 (D:)	Host drive for drive H
💾 Compressed (H:)	Compressed drive

> **NOTE**
>
> Just in case you're wondering, the swap file can exist on a compressed boot drive if a protected mode driver (DRVSPACE .VXD) controls the drive. The swap file is marked as noncompressible and placed at the end of the drive, so that it can shrink and grow as needed.

To begin, run DriveSpace and select the boot drive. Next, under Drive, choose Compress. You will see Figure 11.35.

This screen tells me the statistics for Drive C: before and after compression, in terms of free and used space. Before you begin to compress, click the Options button. You'll see a screen like the screen in Figure 11.36.

This screen allows you to change the drive letter of the host drive and the amount of free space on it. If Hide host drive is checked, the host will not

FIGURE 11.35

Compress a Drive
dialog box

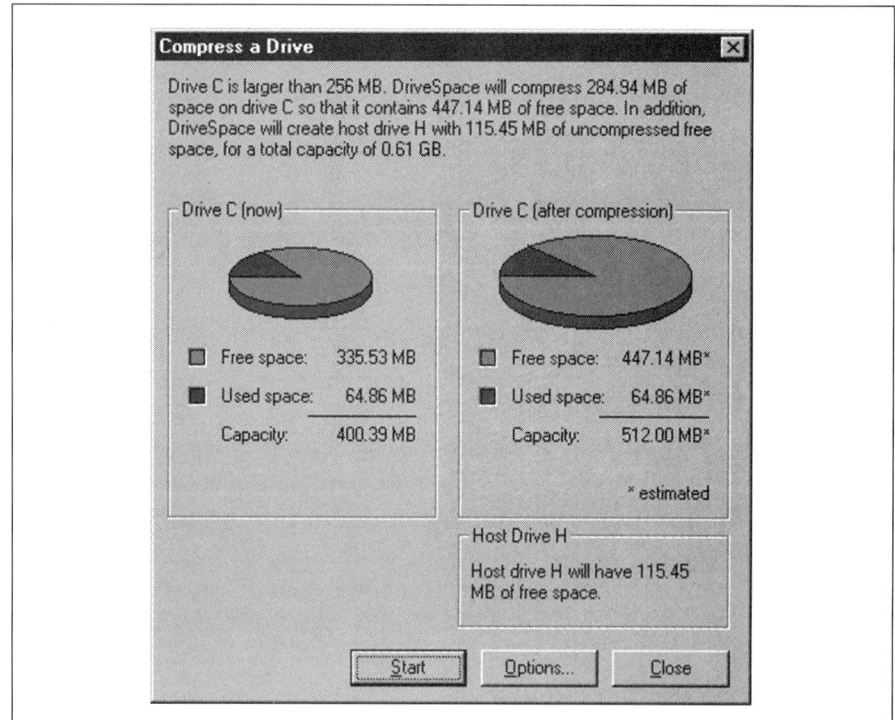

Compress a Drive

Drive C is larger than 256 MB. DriveSpace will compress 284.94 MB of space on drive C so that it contains 447.14 MB of free space. In addition, DriveSpace will create host drive H with 115.45 MB of uncompressed free space, for a total capacity of 0.61 GB.

Drive C (now)

◻ Free space:	335.53 MB
◼ Used space:	64.86 MB
Capacity:	400.39 MB

Drive C (after compression)

◻ Free space:	447.14 MB*
◼ Used space:	64.86 MB*
Capacity:	512.00 MB*

* estimated

Host Drive H

Host drive H will have 115.45 MB of free space.

Start   Options...   Close

FIGURE 11.36

Compress a drive
Options screen

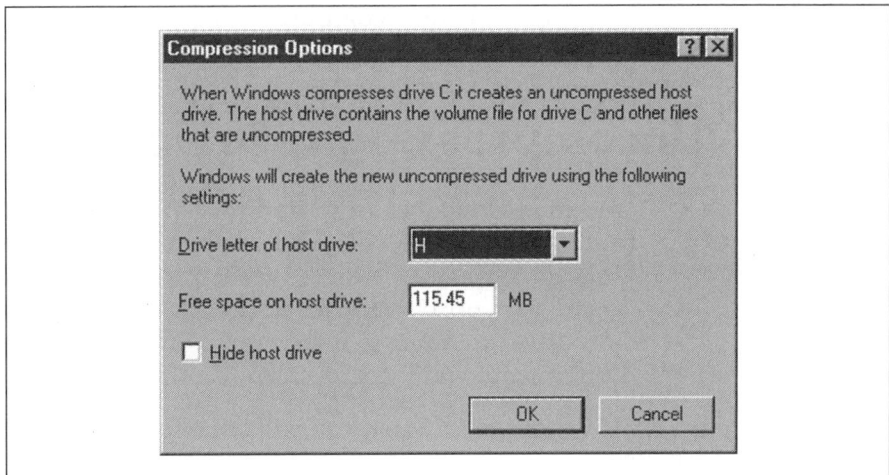

appear in My Computer, the Windows Explorer, and other browse lists. After setting the correct options, click Start, which will prompt you as in Figure 11.37.

If you haven't backed up your files at this point, do it before compressing the drive! Once your files are backed up, select Compress Now and the process begins. First, Windows 95 checks the drive for errors, then boots in a limited version of Windows. While in the limited version of Windows, you can watch the progress of the compression: Windows defrags and then compresses the drive. When finished, you will see a dialog box giving you statistics on the drive before and after compression. Upon clicking the

FIGURE 11.37

Are you sure?

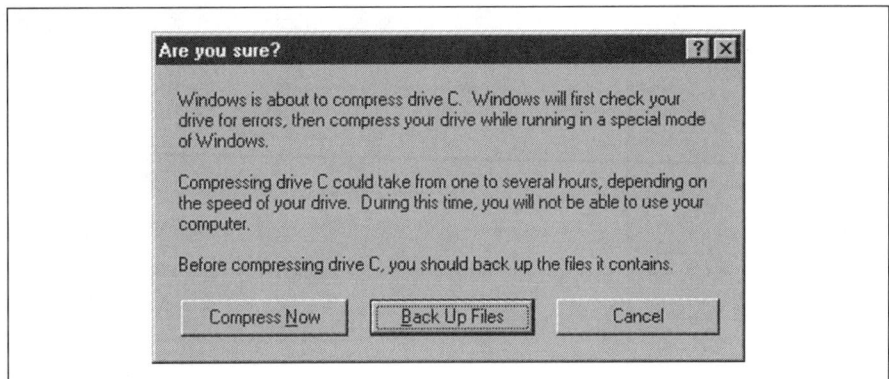

Close button, your computer will restart in Windows 95, and the compression of the boot drive is complete.

Uncompressing a Drive

You may remember from my story at the beginning of the chapter that you must uncompress a drive *before* you repartition and reformat it. Here, we'll go through the steps needed to uncompress a hard drive. Once again, start up DriveSpace and click on the compressed drive (not the host drive) you wish to uncompress. After selecting Uncompress from the Drive menu, you'll get a screen like the one in Figure 11.38.

After you select Start, you will see a series of dialog boxes:

- The first is an "Are you sure?" box, which confirms whether you really want to uncompress the drive.

- The next dialog box informs you that DriveSpace is checking for errors.

- A third asks you whether you want to remove the Recycle Bin on the host drive.

FIGURE 11.38

Uncompress a compressed drive

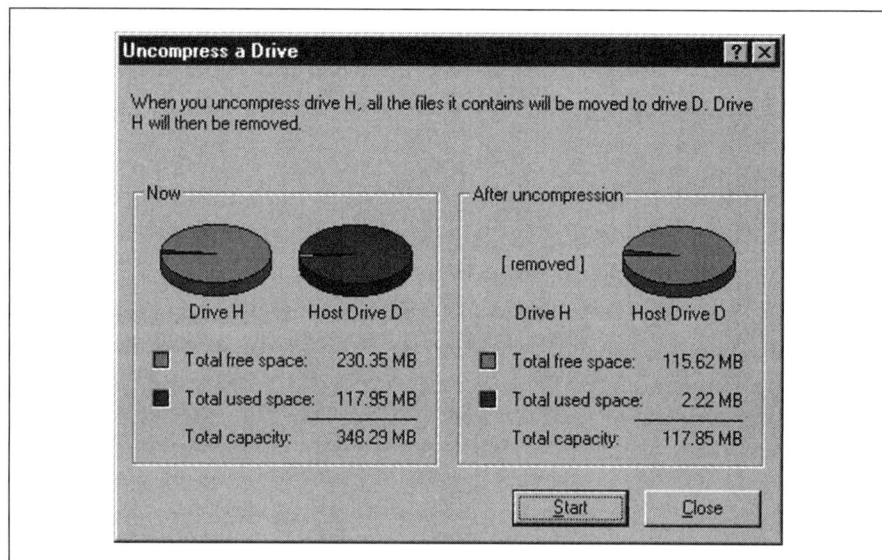

- The fourth dialog box asks you if you want to remove the compression driver from memory.

- Finally, Windows 95 gives you a status box, which tells you that uncompression is in progress.

Once DriveSpace is finished, you will see a dialog box like in Figure 11.39:

And there you have it. The decompression is complete, and, if you wish, you can safely repartition the hard drive!

FIGURE 11.39

Uncompress a Drive
final status

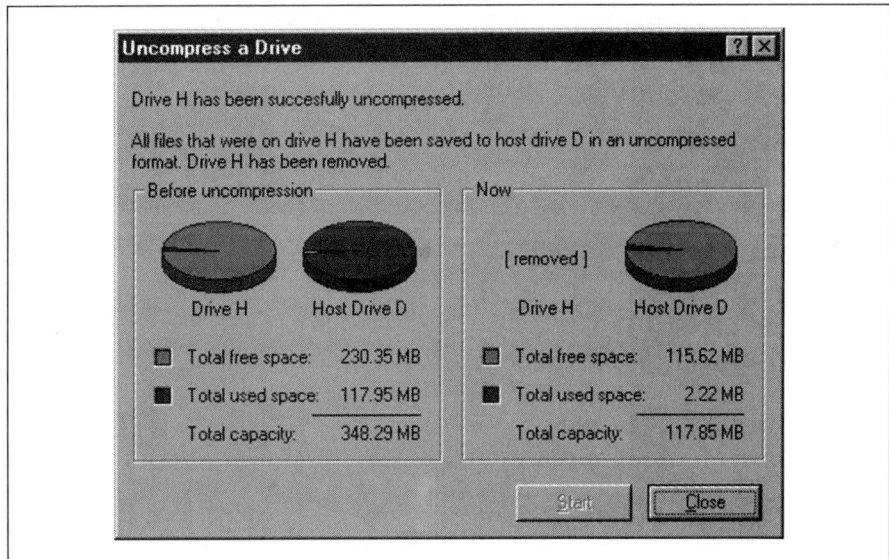

Uncompress a Drive

Drive H has been succesfully uncompressed.

All files that were on drive H have been saved to host drive D in an uncompressed format. Drive H has been removed.

Before uncompression

Drive H   Host Drive D

☐ Total free space: 230.35 MB
■ Total used space: 117.95 MB
Total capacity: 348.29 MB

Now

[removed]

Drive H   Host Drive D

☐ Total free space: 115.62 MB
■ Total used space: 2.22 MB
Total capacity: 117.85 MB

Start   Close

CHAPTER

12

Printing under 95

JUST how much better is printing under Windows 95 than printing under Windows 3.x? Well, I'd have to say that overall, it's not too bad. Printing under 95 has a few whistles and bells not previously found under older versions of Windows. You can see the differences between 95 printing and 3.x printing more clearly when you understand the details behind the printing process. Let's first take a look at Windows 3.x printing, then examine Windows 95 printing.

Here's how the process went under Windows 3.x:

1. First, the user began the print job from his or her Windows application.

2. Then, the print job was sent to the GDI (Graphical Device Interface).

3. Next, GDI sent the print job to the printer driver, as the printer couldn't understand the data in GDI's format. The printer driver was responsible for converting the print job into a language the printer could understand (typically, HPPCL).

4. When the driver finished converting, it sent the print job to the spool file.

5. At this point, the user regained control of his or her Windows application, and the following two steps were performed in the background.

6. The print job was spooled to the printer.

7. The printer then printed the document.

As you can see, the user had to wait through three stages: for the print job to pass through the GDI, then for the printer driver, then for the print job to be sent to the spool file. Once the print job was running in the background, typically the printing was slow and jerky. If you ever used

Windows 3.x, you know about all this. Under Windows 95, this process looks pretty similar, but has changes which improve the printing process, as illustrated in the following steps:

1. As above, the user initiates a print job.

2. Next, the GDI creates an EMF (Emergency Metafile). These files are typically smaller than HPPCL files, and they use less hard drive space.

3. At this point, the user regains control of the application, and the following steps occur in the background.

4. Then the GDI sends the print job to the spool file.

5. From the spool file, the job is sent to the printer.

6. The printer prints the file and the process is complete.

These improvements in printing are due to the new features under Windows 95. First, printing is controlled by a set of 32-bit virtual device drivers, as opposed to the Print Manager, which controlled Windows 3.x printing. This allows printing to run more smoothly. Also, EMF (Enhanced Metafile) spooling allows for a much faster return to application time for the user. Other improvements to Windows 95 printing include better support for DOS-based applications, built-in support for printers with bi-directional communications support, and deferred printing. This last feature allows people whose computers are not physically attached to printers to build a print queue by printing to a file.

Now that you have a feel for the improvements to the printing process, let's take a look at Windows 95's improvements to the process of adding a printer to your system.

Adding a New Printer

Under Windows 3.x and Windows NT Server 3.x, adding a printer was not completely straightforward. Users sometimes weren't sure whether to go to the Control Panel or the Print Manager... and once they did that, did they *create* a printer or *connect to* a printer? Under Windows 95, the user can always use the Add Printer Wizard to add and to connect to local and network printers. Having one central location where you can add a printer, local or network, to your system really cuts down on the confusion.

Another nice thing about the Add Printer Wizard is that if you incorrectly configure information on one screen, you can simply click the Back button and correct any errors. Just remember that you may need to re-enter some of the information on the following screens, as some settings will revert back to the defaults.

Adding a Local Printer to Your System

For this example, I'll add an HP DeskJet 550C printer to my local computer. To begin this process, go into your Printers folder and double-click on Add Printer. This will bring you to Figure 12.1.

Clicking on Next will bring you to Figure 12.2.

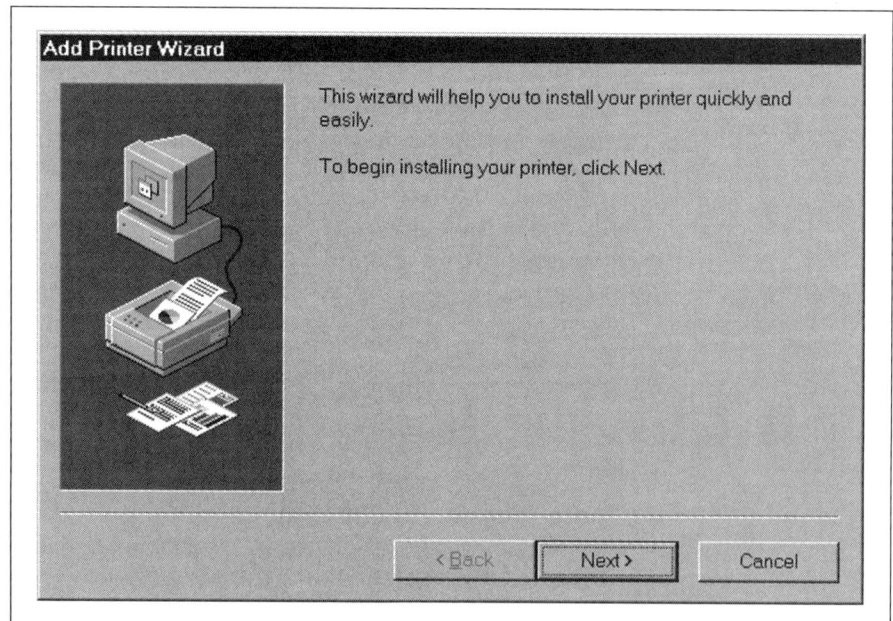

FIGURE 12.2

Add printer Wizard,
local or network
printer

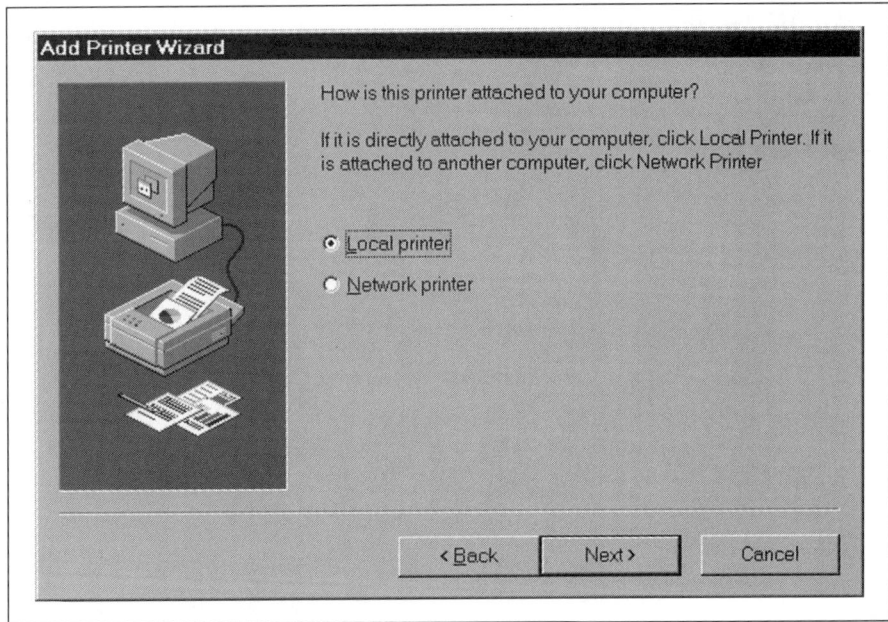

Here, you must choose whether to install a local or network printer. For this example, I will install a local printer, so I select Local printer and then click Next. This leads you to Figure 12.3.

On the left side of the screen, scroll down until you find the manufacturer of your printer, then scroll down on the right side to select the exact model of your printer. By clicking the Have Disk... button, you may choose to use the printer manufacturer's drivers.

This screen brings up the issue of whether you should use Windows 95 drivers or the manufacturer's drivers with your newly installed printer. I experimented with installing both drivers for an HP DeskJet 550C, and I found that both sets of drivers produce nearly the same print quality. (The Windows 95 drivers produced quality that was a tiny bit better than the manufacturer's drivers, but I had to look pretty hard to notice the difference.)

There is one deciding factor, however, with the printer driver issue: Just how old are your manufacturer's printer drivers? The drivers which came with the HP DeskJet 550C have dates of 1992 and 1993. Due to the fact

FIGURE 12.3

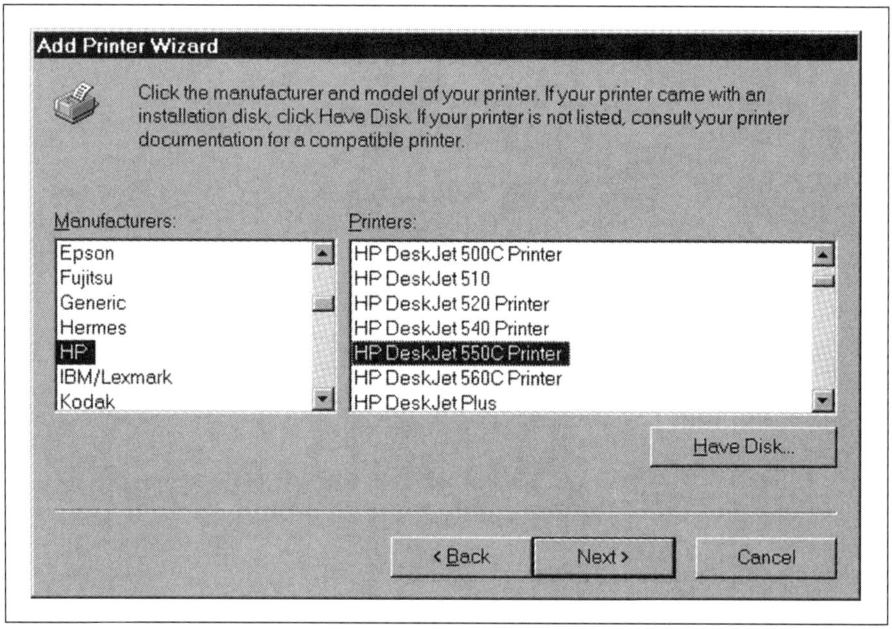

Add Printer Wizard, choose the manufacturer and model of your printer

that these drivers are at a minimum 2 years old, they do not support EMF spooling for this printer. (As you learned earlier, EMF spooling can significantly decrease the time a user must wait to regain control of his or her program.) Before deciding whether to use Windows 95's or the manufacturer's drivers, think about the age of your printer's drivers. If you have a brand new printer, it is possible that the drivers were written for Windows 95. However, if you are like many other people and own an older printer, I would recommend using the Windows 95 printers.

Now, if you decide to use Windows 95 drivers, simply click Next. (You will not see the next two screens.) However, if you decide to go with your manufacturer's drivers, click on Have Disk... and you'll see a screen like Figure 12.4.

Pop your disk in Drive A: or browse as necessary, click OK, and you'll see Figure 12.5.

This screen can be a bit confusing. Once again select your printer, then click Next. You don't need to click Have Disk..., as it will simply ask you again for the disk. After clicking Next, you'll come to Figure 12.6.

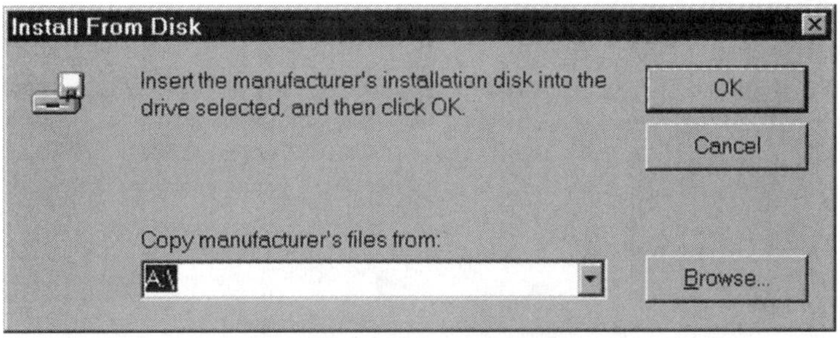

FIGURE 12.4

Add Printer Wizard, using the manufacturer's drivers

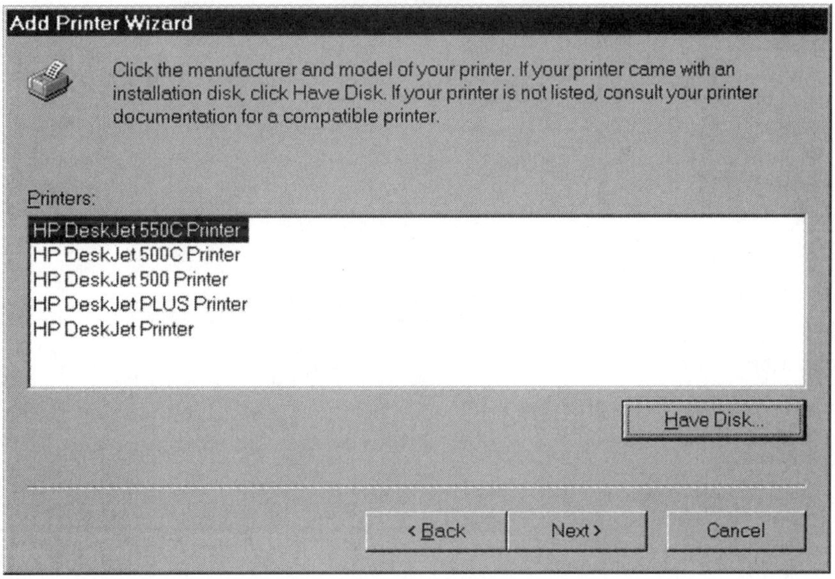

FIGURE 12.5

Add Printer Wizard, using the manufacturer's drivers (part 2)

Here, you need to decide whether to use LPT1: or LPT2:. In my case, my printer is hooked up to LPT1:, so I highlighted LPT1:. Clicking on Configure Port... gives you Figure 12.7.

At this screen, decide whether you want to spool MS-DOS print jobs and whether you want to check the port state before printing. Click OK, then click Next to leave the port-choosing screen. The next screen asks you two

FIGURE 12.6

Add Printer Wizard,
choose printer port

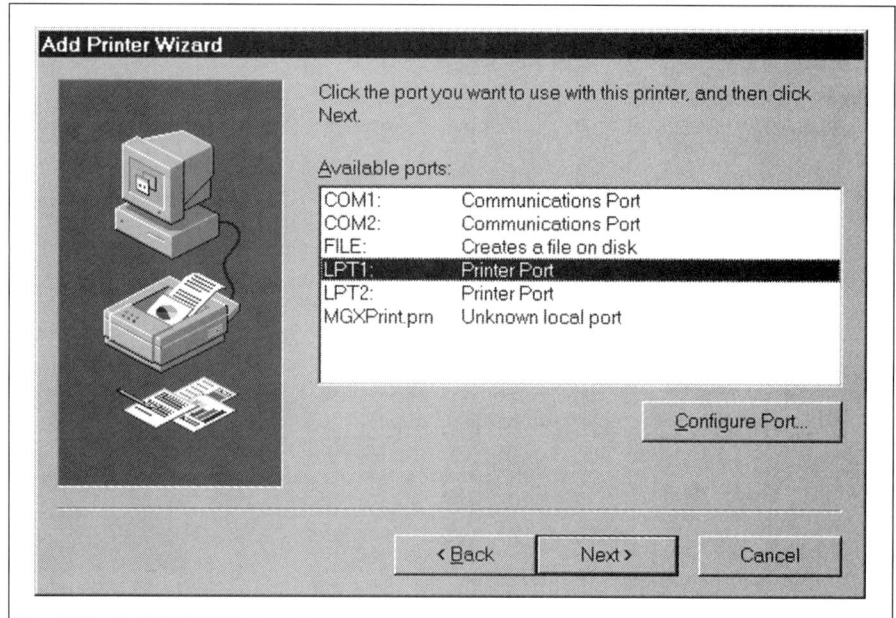

FIGURE 12.7

Add Printer Wizard,
configuring your port

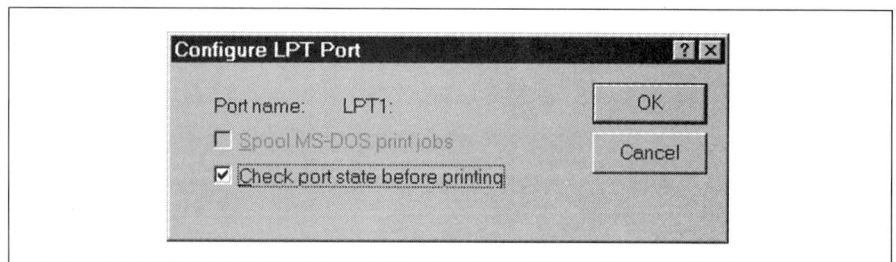

things: the printer's name and its status as the default printer. This screen
looks like Figure 12.8.

I accepted the default name of the printer, then selected the radio button
next to Yes to indicate that I wanted this printer to be the default printer.
(No is the default.) Clicking Next will bring you to Figure 12.9.

It's not a bad idea to print out a test page—if nothing prints, you definitely
know you have a problem. Another good reason to print a test page is because of the information it lists. The test page will give you statistics about

FIGURE 12.8

Add Printer Wizard, naming the printer

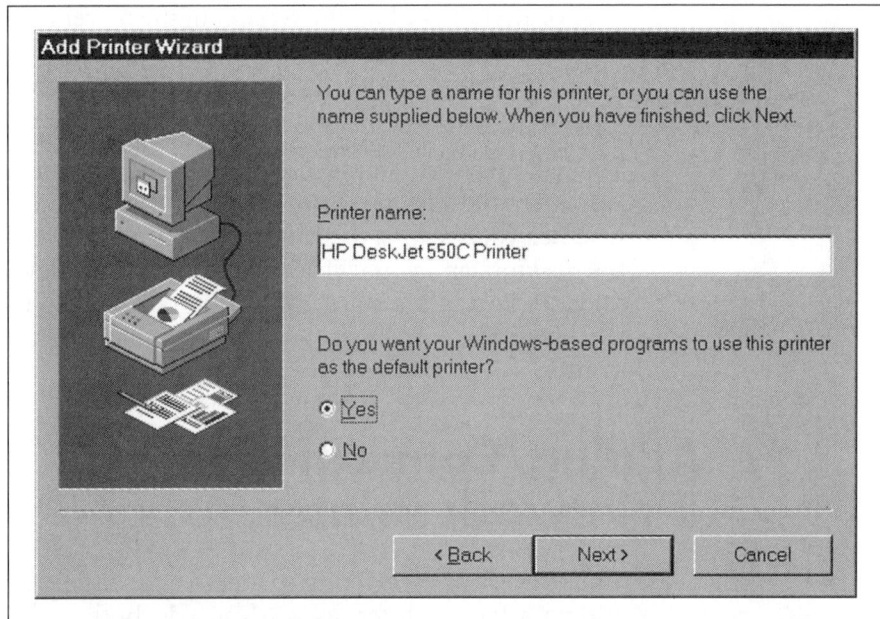

Add Printer Wizard

You can type a name for this printer, or you can use the name supplied below. When you have finished, click Next.

Printer name:

HP DeskJet 550C Printer

Do you want your Windows-based programs to use this printer as the default printer?

⦿ Yes

○ No

< Back | Next > | Cancel

FIGURE 12.9

Add Printer Wizard, printing a test page

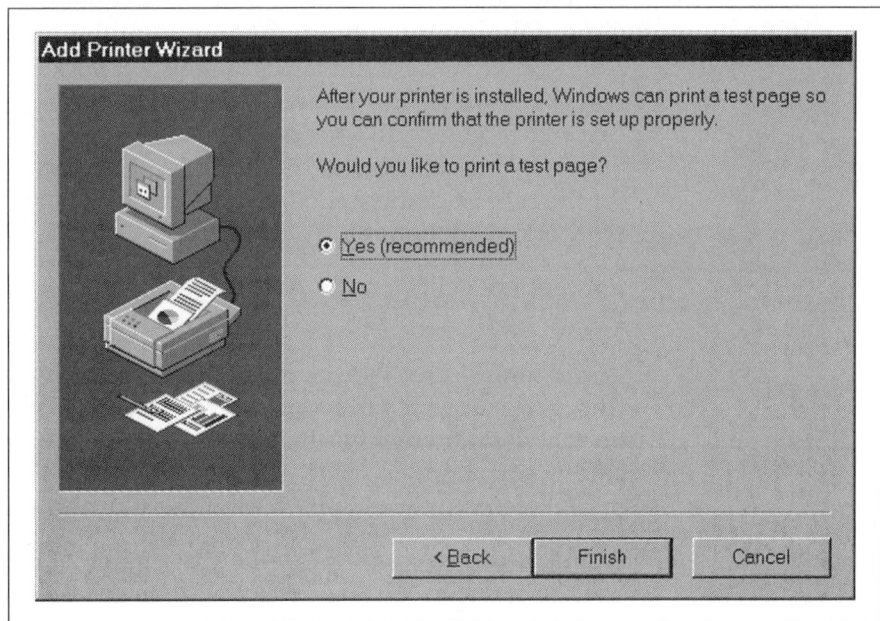

Add Printer Wizard

After your printer is installed, Windows can print a test page so you can confirm that the printer is set up properly.

Would you like to print a test page?

⦿ Yes (recommended)

○ No

< Back | Finish | Cancel

your printer, including the version of the drivers used, the port name, and the various files used by the printer. Make your selection, then click Finish. At this point, make sure you have the Windows 95 CD-ROM or disks on hand so the Add Printer Wizard can complete the process.

You will then see a status screen, which tells you which files are being copied. After the files are transferred, you will see a dialog box asking you whether your test page printed correctly. Clicking Yes brings you out to the desktop, and you will see the icon for your new printer in the Printers folder. Clicking No starts up Windows 95's help file for printing. It gives you examples of things to check to discover the problem with your printer.

Adding/Connecting to a Network Printer

The process of connecting to a network printer is fairly similar to that of adding a local printer, as you can add both local and network printers from the Add Printer Wizard. But when connecting to/adding a network printer, you have the option of beginning the process not only from the Add Printer Wizard, but also from the Network Neighborhood. Whether you begin in the Add Printer Wizard or the Network Neighborhood, the first step in getting to your printer will be browsing. Once you have found your network printer, both processes have identical screen prompts. So for the sake of doing something different, I'll begin this process from the Network Neighborhood.

First, double-click on the Network Neighborhood icon. In our network, Figure 12.10 is the screen you see.

Listed in this screen are all the available resources on our network. Select the computer which is connected to the desired printer and double-click on that computer's icon. If a printer does not show up on this list, make sure the machine is set to share its printers. (There's more on sharing printers later in the chapter.) You'll see a screen similar to Figure 12.11.

At this point you must know the share name of the printer to which you want to connect. (If you don't know, then go track down your network administrator.) In this case, I know that the printer's share name is hp550c, so I clicked once on its icon, then pulled down the File menu. From this

FIGURE 12.10

Network
Neighborhood,
connecting to a printer

FIGURE 12.10

Network
Neighborhood,
connecting to a printer

FIGURE 12.11

Network
Neighborhood,
connecting to a printer

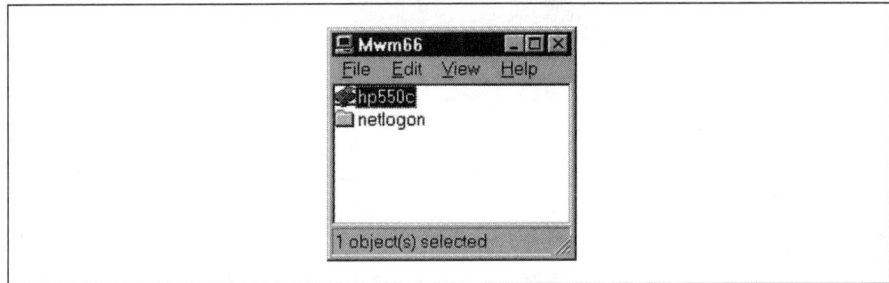

point, you can do two different things: You can choose Create a shortcut or Install the printer. What's the difference? Creating a shortcut places the printer's icon on your desktop; installing the printer places the printer's icon in your Printer folder. In both cases, you still must go through the following processes—you cannot place the icon on the desktop or in a folder without going through the installation process. For this example I've chosen Install; when you click it you'll see Figure 12.12.

The default here is No. If you will be printing from MS-DOS based programs, click the radio button for Yes and then click Next. If you chose No, then you will not see Figures 12.13 and 12.14.

As the dialog box says, in order to print from an MS-DOS-based program, the network printer must be associated with an LPT port. To do this, click on Capture Printer Port... and you'll see Figure 12.14.

FIGURE 12.12

Network
Neighborhood,
printing from DOS

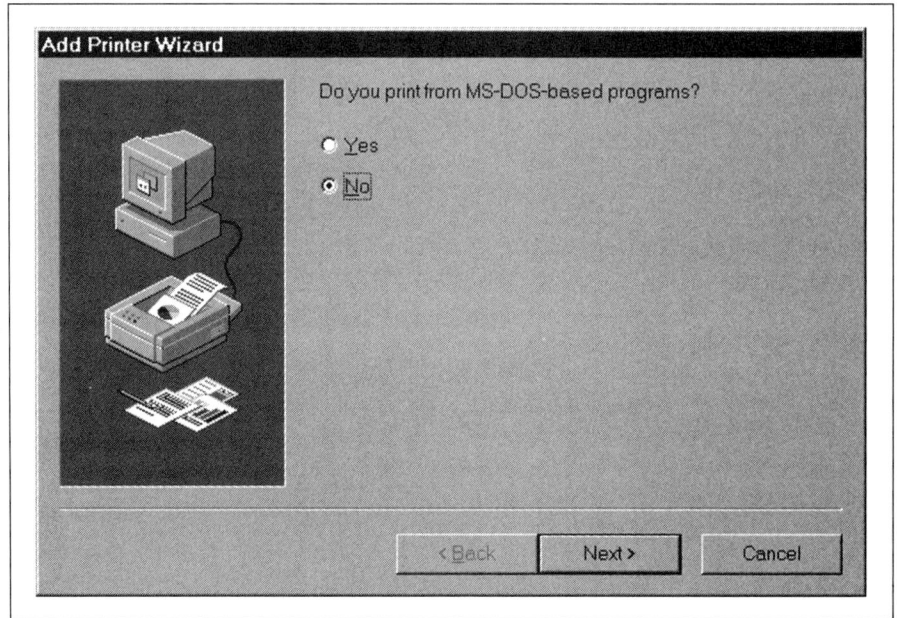

FIGURE 12.13

Network
Neighborhood,
capturing a
printer port

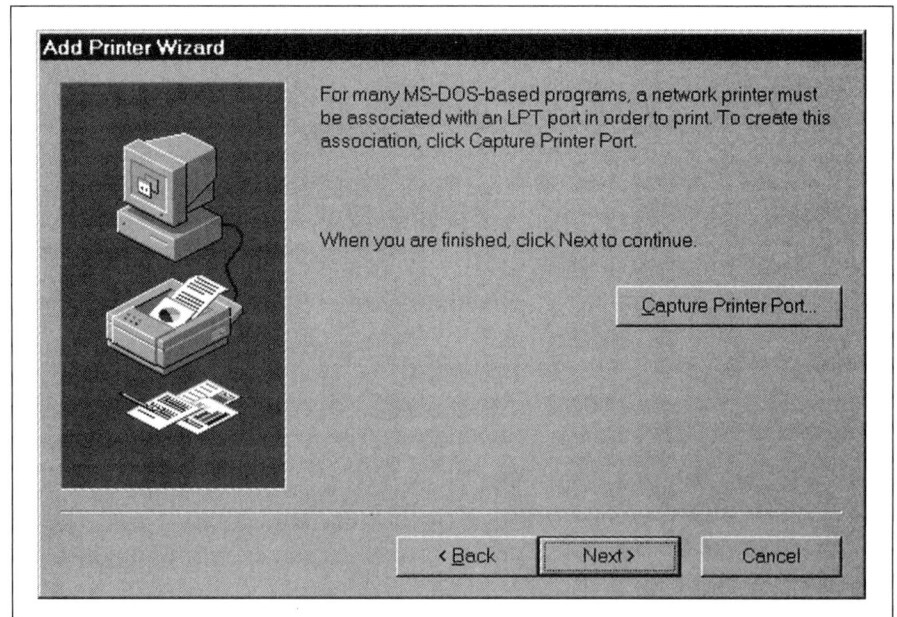

FIGURE 12.14

Network
Neighborhood,
capturing a printer
port (part 2)

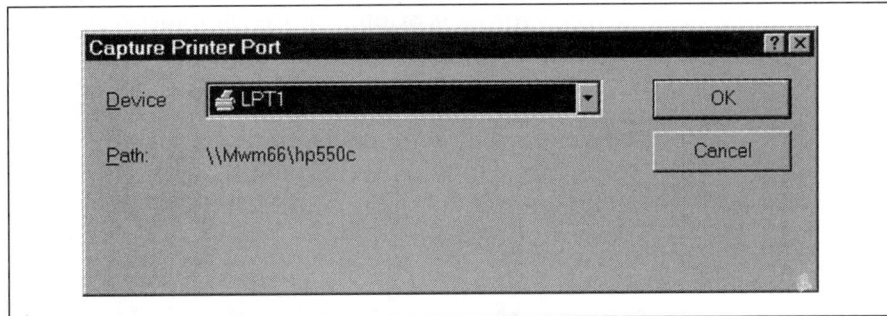

Why do this? So you can have a local printer on LPT2: and use LPT1: for a network printer. Keep in mind that LPT ports aren't important for Windows programs over a network, as everything is sent directly to the shared resource. Make sure the correct port is listed, then click OK. Now after this point, you will see the exact same screens as when you installed a local printer. You will be asked to:

- Choose the manufacturer and model of the printer (and at this point you need to decide whose drivers to use).

- Give a name to the printer and decide whether it will be the default printer.

- Decide whether to print a test page.

If you need to review these topics, consult with the previous section on adding a local printer. After you perform these steps, your network printer is ready for use.

Understanding the Printer Settings

Once you've installed your printer, there's still more to do in terms of printer setup. In the Printers folder, right-click on the newly installed printer and select Properties. This is the place where you select different settings for your printer's ports, graphics, fonts, and memory; this is what we'll discuss for the next few pages.

However, keep in mind that all printers have different capabilities, and therefore may require different settings. A setting that is best for one printer may not be the best for another. See these as suggestions and not concrete rules. Play around with the settings and find the ones that suit your printer the best.

Setting the Printer Details

Click on the second tab, Details, and you'll see a screen like Figure 12.15.

FIGURE 12.15

A network printer's
Details tab

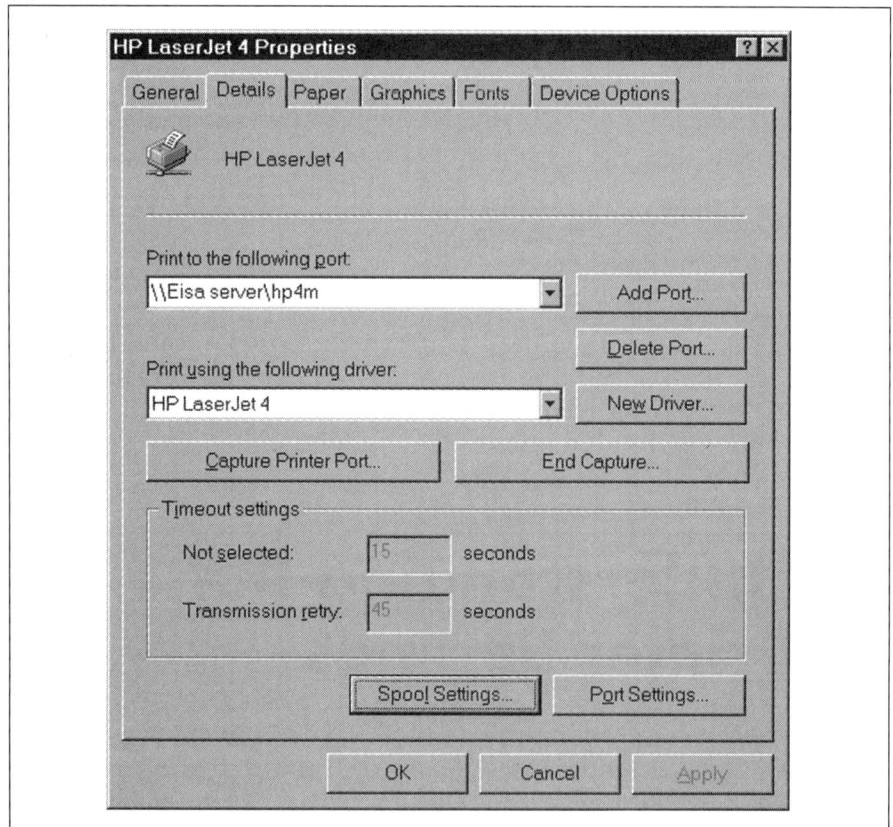

There are a few settings on this screen which require some clarification.

- **Print to the following port:** shows the port you chose during installation. It will show up as LPT*x* for a local printer and as *server* *printername* for a network printer. *Print using the following driver:* shows the driver you chose during installation.

- The **Add Port**... and **Delete Port**... buttons allow you to change the port settings for the printer. For example, if your network printer was moved to a different machine, you can click on Delete Port... and delete the present printer path. Then, you can select Add Port... and browse for the path on the network to which you want to print.

- You can select a new driver for your printer by clicking *New Driver...*. A screen will warn you that changing a printer driver may affect the appearance of your documents. Click Yes and you'll see a screen nearly identical to the one you saw when originally selecting your driver in the Add Printer Wizard.

- The **Capture Printer Port**... button allows DOS programs to print to a network printer. DOS does not understand the network path to a printer and must print to a parallel port. Whereas the DOS app prints to LPT*x*, Windows 95's print system captures everything sent to the port and then redirects it to the share. This fools the DOS program into thinking it is printing to LPT*x* when, in actuality, the DOS program is printing to a network printer. By associating a parallel port with a network printer, DOS programs can print over the network.

- **End Capture**... simply disassociates a network port from a parallel port.

- **Timeout settings:** are the default for Windows. Basically, these settings specify that Windows 95 will wait for 45 seconds for the printer to come on line before reporting an error during printing.

- **Spool Settings**... lets you choose the method by which data is spooled to the printer; you can see this in Figure 12.16.

    For faster printing, choose *Spool print jobs so program finishes printing faster.* Under this, you may choose one of the two following options: *Start printing after last page is spooled* or *Start*

FIGURE 12.16

A network printer's Details tab, spool settings

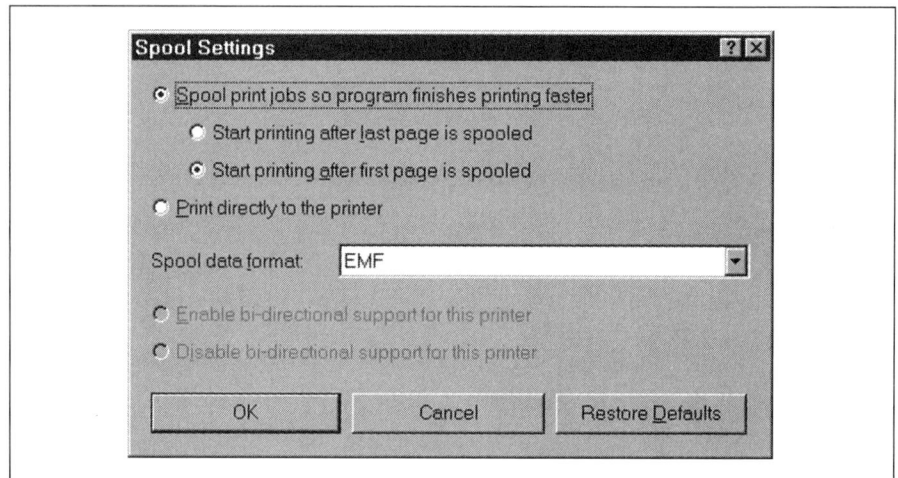

printing after first page is spooled. Your choice between the two is purely your own personal preference, but the second option typically will finish the print job faster than the first. If *Print directly to the printer* is chosen, the program cannot return control of the application until the entire document has been printed.

Spool data format: is an option available only when you choose to spool print jobs, so this is not available when you choose to print directly to the printer. This allows you to decide how the data is spooled to the printer: as raw data or as an *EMF* (*Enhanced Metafile*). When data is spooled as raw data, the printer drivers must interpret that raw data on the fly, and this results in the user waiting longer to regain control of the application. When data is spooled as an EMF, the printer does not have to interpret raw data; instead it interprets a file (EMF) created by the GDI. Interpreting the EMF is less taxing work, and can be done in the background by the printer driver, which allows the user to regain control of the application much faster.

- The two settings to Enable or Disable *bi-directional support* will only be highlighted if your printer has bi-directional support. If this is an option which your printer supports, you should take advantage of it. This enables the printer to let you know, for example, when there is a paper jam or when toner is low.

- **Port Settings**... allows you to configure the printer port; if this is not grayed out, you can decide whether to spool MS-DOS print jobs and whether to have the port checked.

Setting the Graphics Tab

This tab is quite important for the individual who needs to print high-quality graphics, as incorrect settings can lower the quality of the printed graphics. Let's take a look at the settings on this tab; you can see them in Figure 12.17.

FIGURE 12.17

A network printer's
Graphics tab

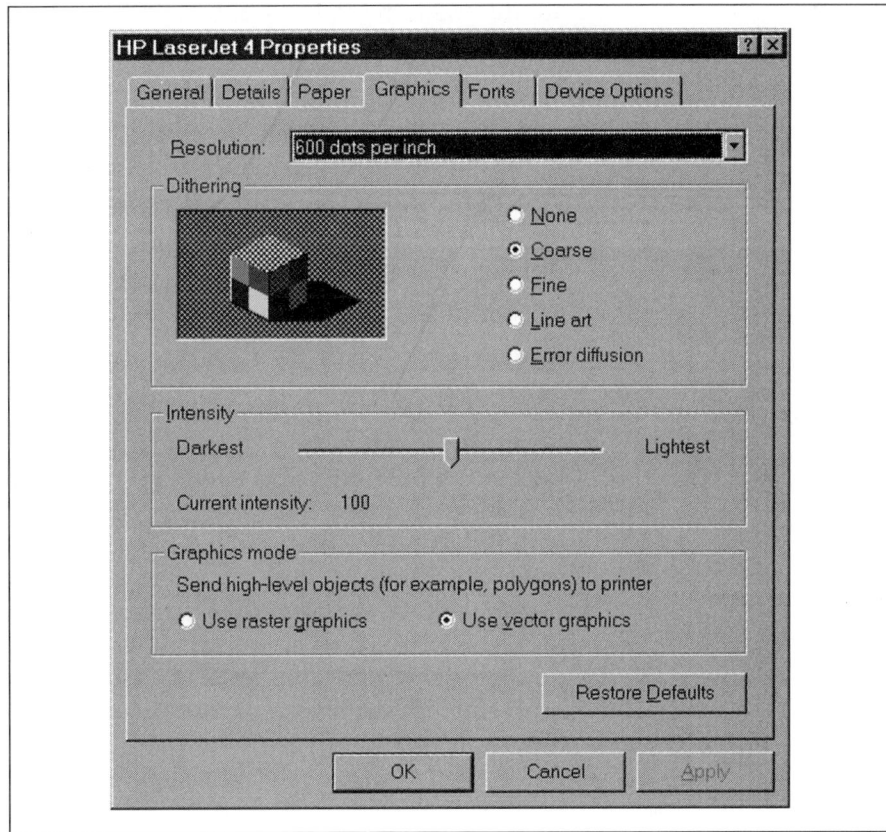

- **Resolution:** This allows you to control how finely detailed your printed graphic will appear. Resolution is the number of dots printed in one inch (measured in dots per inch, or dpi); obviously, the more dots in one inch, the more defined the picture will be. Check with your printer manual to find its highest resolution. Printing in a higher resolution can take more memory—so if you're simply printing a draft, you can change the resolution to a lower setting.

- **Dithering** is a process which produces shading in non-color printers and more realistic colors in color printers. This helps the printer know how to define a dark dot (black), a light dot (white), and all the settings in between (different shades of gray). The following are the guidelines recommended by Microsoft; however, all printers are different and you should test to see which setting gives you the best result.

  - **Fine** is typically the setting for printers capable of 200 dpi or less.
  - **Coarse** is the setting for printers capable of 300 dpi or higher.
  - **Line art** should be chosen if your graphics have sharp, well-defined borders between black, white, and gray.
  - **Error diffusion** is for printing graphics with ill-defined borders.

- **Intensity** tells you how dark your graphics will be printed. The default is 100; just move the slider to adjust this setting.

- **Graphics mode** tells the printer how to render the print jobs. Let's look at the differences between the two with an example of printing a circle. Under *Vector graphics*, the instructions, "Draw a circle" (with additional details about size, etc.) are sent to the printer. This is easier for the printer to render, but it is a greater stress on memory. With *Raster graphics*, the printer is instructed where to place every dot to form the circle. This is slower and creates more work for the CPU. So typically, vector graphics can speed up printing, but if you have problems, try switching to raster graphics.

Deciphering the Fonts and Device Options

These two tabs seem to have some of the most cryptic settings in all of the Printer Properties screens. Let's first take a look at the Fonts tab, as in Figure 12.18.

This screen is not very detailed, but is not immediately understandable. Cartridges shows you which cartridges are installed in your printer. Clicking Install Printer Fonts... allows you to install new cartridges.

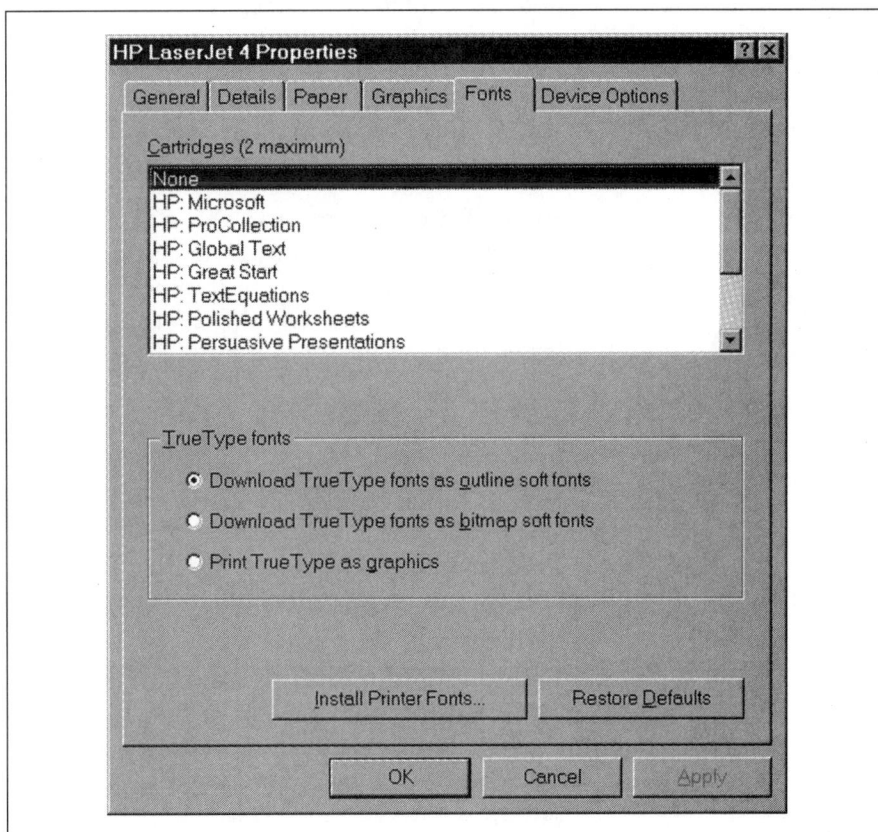

HP LaserJet 4 Properties

General | Details | Paper | Graphics | Fonts | Device Options

Cartridges (2 maximum)

None
HP: Microsoft
HP: ProCollection
HP: Global Text
HP: Great Start
HP: TextEquations
HP: Polished Worksheets
HP: Persuasive Presentations

TrueType fonts

○ Download TrueType fonts as outline soft fonts

○ Download TrueType fonts as bitmap soft fonts

○ Print TrueType as graphics

Install Printer Fonts... | Restore Defaults

OK | Cancel | Apply

The True Type fonts section can lead to a little confusion. Let's take a look at each one of these options:

- **Download True Type fonts as bitmap soft fonts:** With this option, every different character is first downloaded to the printer's memory as a bitmap. This means that for each different type of font (different point sizes, bold, italic, etc.) there will be an individual bitmap sent to the printer. After these are downloaded, the application sends only text and not bitmaps. Generally printing with this option is faster than True Type as Graphics, especially when the same type of text is used on the majority of the page.

- **Download True Type fonts as outline soft fonts:** With this option, characters are seen as a collection of lines. These outlines are downloaded to the printer's memory with instructions on how to form them. Then the application will send the outline fonts to the printer; at this point the printer interprets the instructions and creates the different fonts. Just as above, this printing can be faster than True Type as Graphics.

- **Print True Type as graphics:** In essence, each page from the application is sent to the printer as one large bitmap and printed this way. Printing True Type as graphics uses more memory, but in cases where graphics or many different types of fonts are used, it can be faster than the two above options.

Now let's discuss the Device Options tab under printer Properties. Take a look at Figure 12.19.

The settings on this screen are actually pretty straightforward.

- **Print quality:** This allows you to choose which type of text quality you want for your documents. These settings will differ from printer to printer.

- **Printer memory:** This is the amount of memory in your printer. The default is the amount of memory that the printer has at purchase. If you have increased your printer's memory, you must manually select the correct amount of memory. It is important that this setting is correct, as overestimating or underestimating the amount of memory may result in an Out of memory error.

FIGURE 12.19

A network printer's
Device Options tab

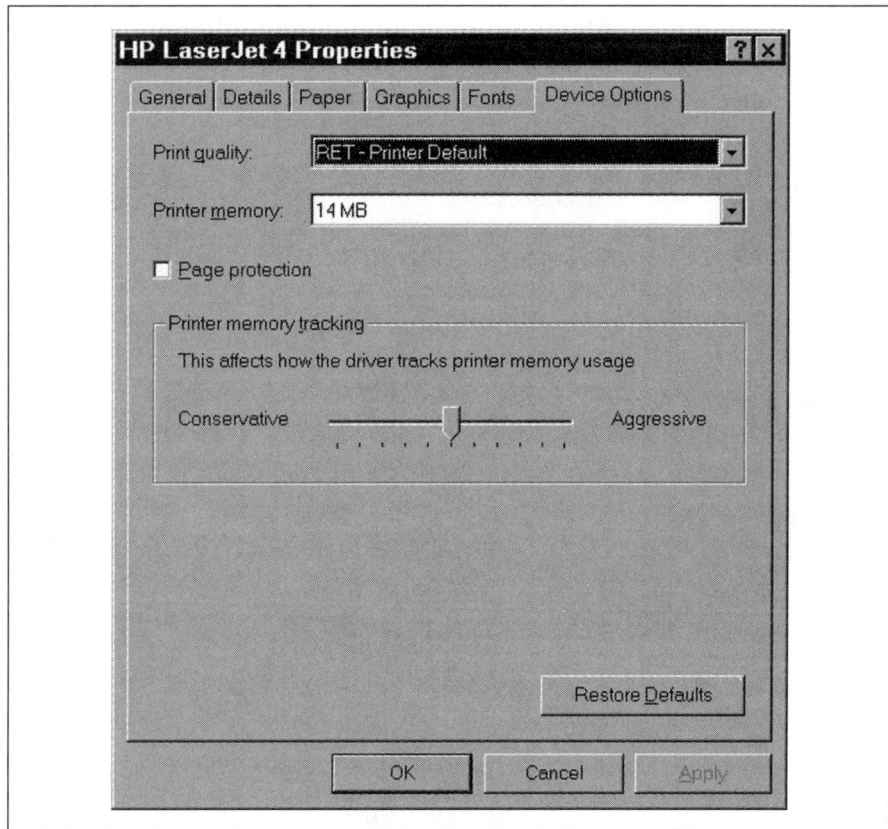

- **Printer memory tracking:** This controls how the printer driver estimates the amount of memory needed to print a page and compares it to the available memory. If this is set at Conservative, the printer driver will not try to overextend its memory capabilities, but at some points it may not print a document for which there is sufficient memory. If this is set at Aggressive, the printer driver may overestimate its memory and attempt to print documents for which there is insufficient memory.

Configuring the Sharing Tab of a Local Printer

When you install a local printer, you will see a tab that does not appear with a network printer: the Sharing tab. The reason for this is that when you install a local printer, it is directly attached to your machine; therefore you have control over which individuals can access the printer. (Sharing for network printers is performed at the server by the administrator.) So how do you share a printer attached to your own machine? Take a look at the Sharing tab for an HP DeskJet 550C printer as seen in Figure 12.20.

FIGURE 12.20

A local printer's Sharing tab

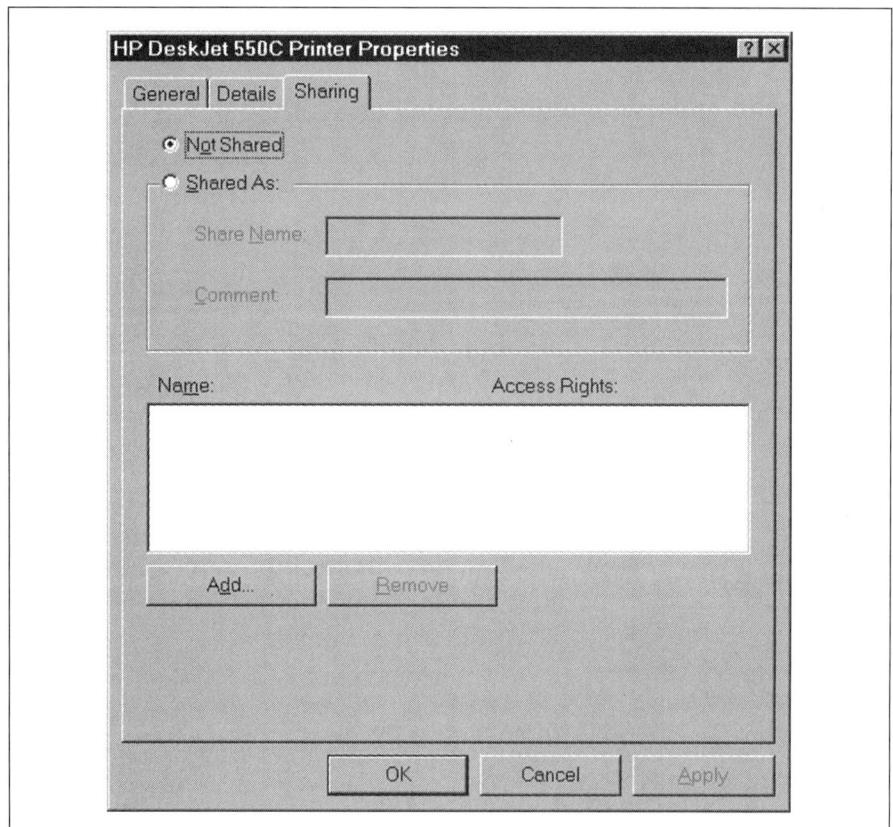

By default, the printer is not shared; it is up to you to decide if you want others to use it. Click on the radio button next to Shared As:, and the two boxes beneath will be accessible. In these two boxes, give the printer a Share Name and a Comment. Share Name is where you give the printer its name as you want it to appear on the network. (Typically, names which detail the type of printer are quite helpful.) If you add a $ to the end of the share name, it won't show up in browse lists; however, it will be available to those who know about it. Under Comment, you can type any other helpful information to help identify the printer. One useful comment would detail the location of the printer (especially if you have a large network). Figure 12.21 shows how I filled out these two boxes.

FIGURE 12.21

Sharing your
local printer

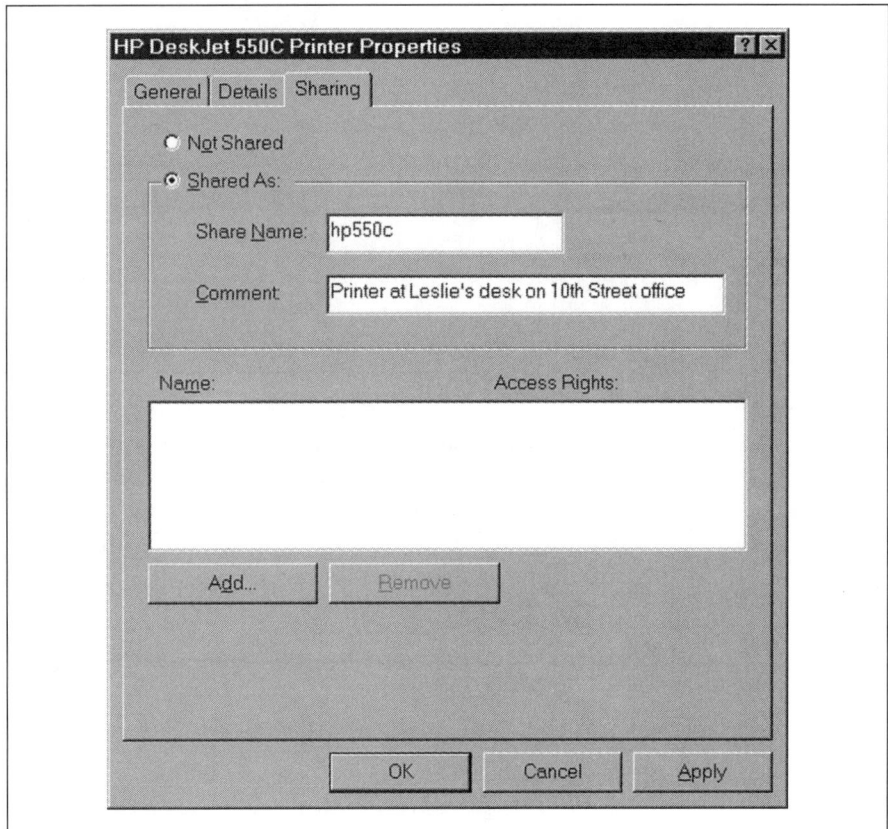

| HP DeskJet 550C Printer Properties | ? X |
| General | Details | Sharing |

○ Not Shared
⊙ Shared As:

Share Name: hp550c

Comment: Printer at Leslie's desk on 10th Street office

Name: Access Rights:

[Add...]   [Remove]

[OK]   [Cancel]   [Apply]

The next step in sharing is deciding which individuals have what type of access on your printer. Click Add... and you'll see Figure 12.22.

FIGURE 12.22

Adding users to
a local printer

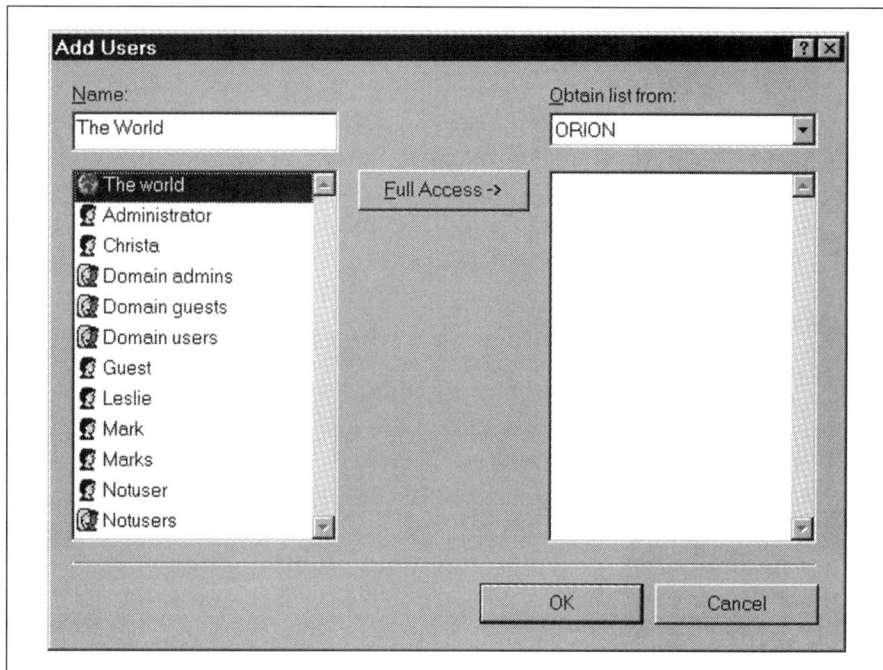

To add users, simply click on their name then click on Full Access. Under Obtain list from:, you can choose to add users from another domain if you wish. (By the way, your list of users won't appear like this unless you're connected to a Windows NT domain.) After you have added users, you should have a screen similar to Figure 12.23.

FIGURE 12.23

Completed list
of added users

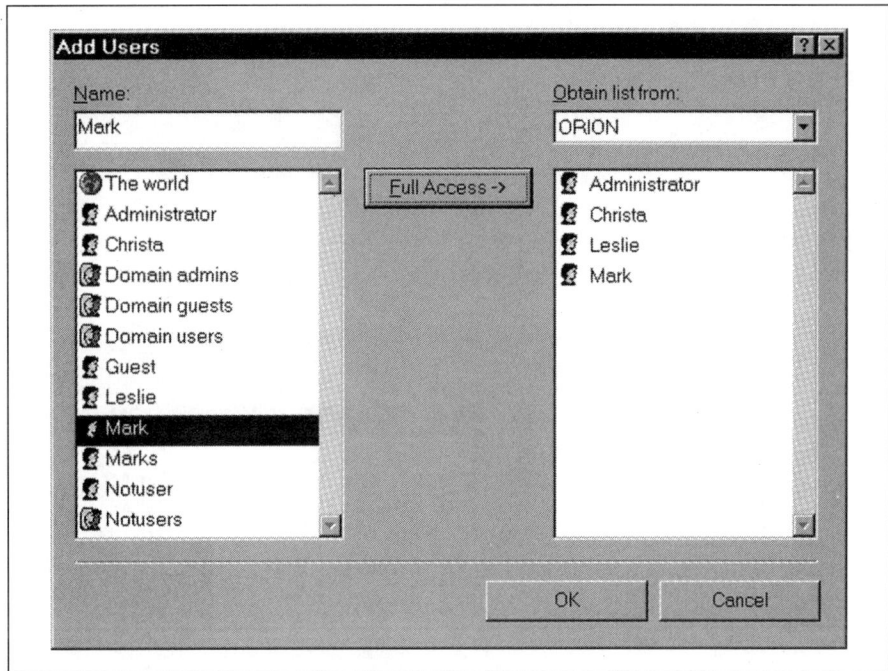

Click OK and you will return to Figure 12.24, the original sharing screen, now with the list of users.

FIGURE 12.24

Original sharing
screen with users

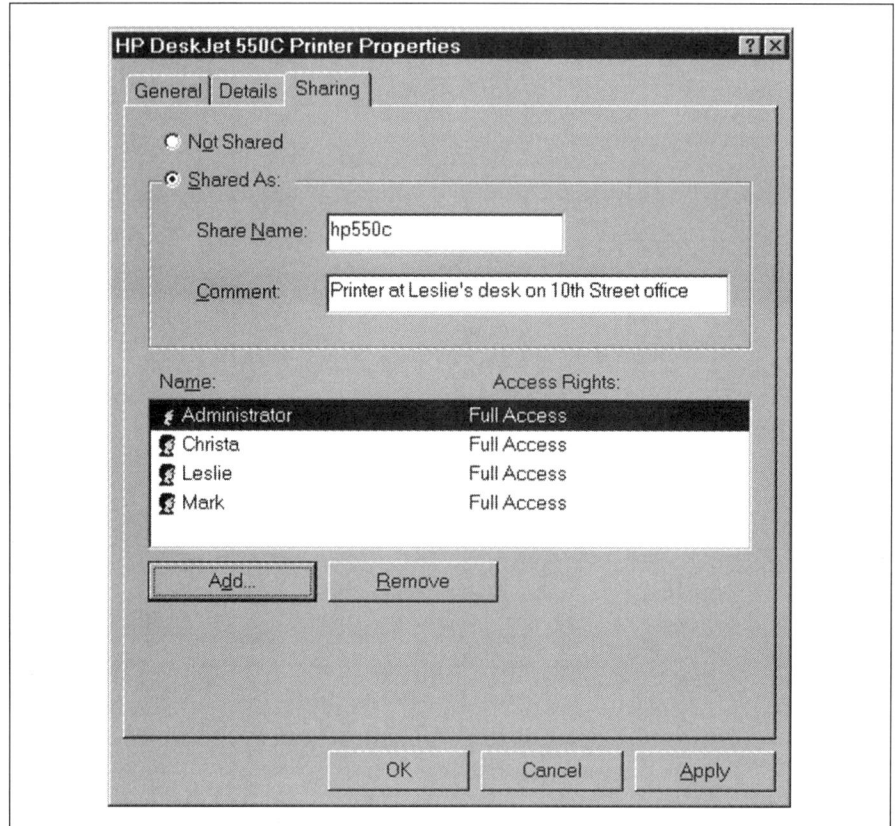

What do you do when you need to delete a user from your shared list? It's simple; just click on the individual's name and then click Remove. This gives you a screen like Figure 12.25.

Once you are finished, click OK. The red × will remain on the screen until you exit out of the printer's Properties box. When you re-enter the Properties box, the user will be deleted from the box.

FIGURE 12.25

Sharing tab after
removing a user

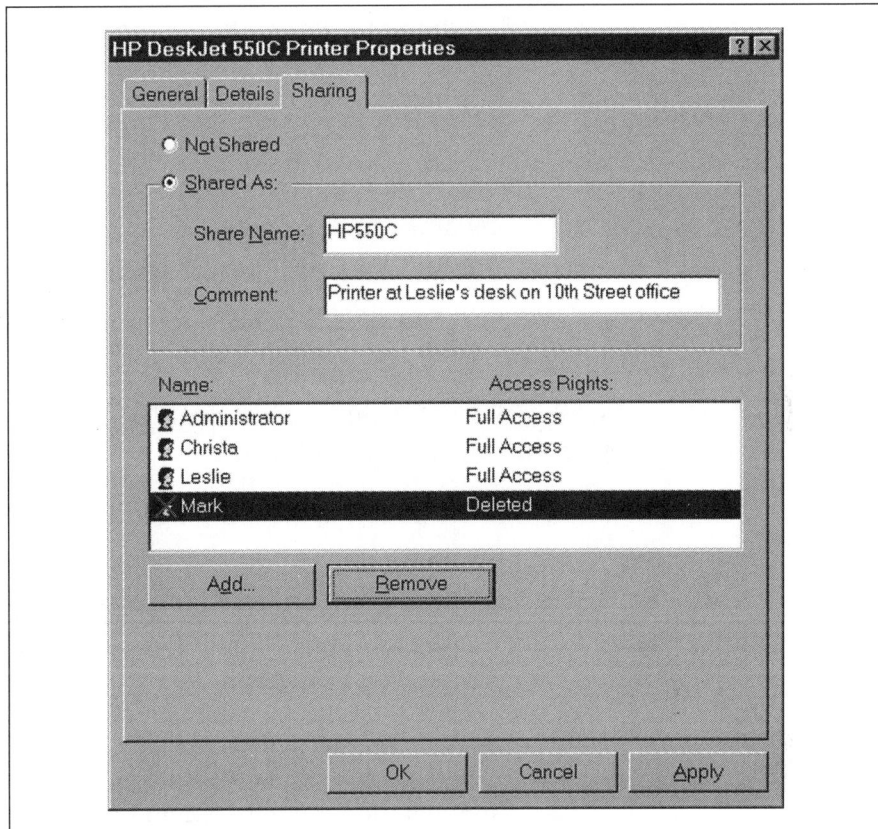

Troubleshooting Common Printer Problems

After a printer is installed, there are a myriad of things which can go wrong. In the following sections, we'll discuss how to tackle various printing problems. But before going into specific problems relating to either a local or network printer, let's simply review a few questions you can ask yourself to eliminate potential problems.

- Is the printer plugged in? If it is plugged into a strip outlet, do the other appliances plugged in work?

- Is the printer turned on? Is it on line?

- Is there paper in the printer? Is the paper jammed? Has the printer run out of toner?

- Are any of the cables loose?

- Do you have share permissions to use the printer?

- Are you connected to the correct printer?

It is usually best to make sure that all the little things are in place before looking for a high-level solution. Now let's go over some of your printer's symptoms and possible solutions.

- Symptom: Your graphics print lighter or darker than they should.

   I experienced this problem after installing Windows 95. I first thought that perhaps Windows 95 had problems with my graphics program, but I found the problem existed when I printed from several other programs. When I originally set up my Graphics tab in the printer Properties, I had set my Dithering to Fine. By playing around with the Dithering option, I found that the setting Coarse printed my graphics correctly. The reason that the Fine setting didn't fare well for me was that I typically use an HP LaserJet 4 with a resolution of 600 dpi—and the Fine setting is for printers with resolutions of 200 dpi or less. One other possible solution is to check that the Intensity setting on the Graphics page is not pointing too far towards either the right or left.

- Symptom: Printing is slow.

   First check your Spool Settings on the Details tab. Do you have it set to print directly to the printer? The fastest setting on the Details tab is *Spool jobs so program finishes printing faster*, with a sub-setting of *Start printing after first page is spooled*. Another possibility to consider is this: Are you printing documents laden with graphics? If you have your Fonts tab configured to *Download True Type fonts as bitmap or outline soft fonts*, consider changing to *Print True Type as graphics*. The latter setting uses more memory but handles graphics better than the previous two.

- Symptom: It takes too long to regain control of the application after starting a print job.

  Try setting your Spool data format box in the Details tab to EMF, rather than RAW. The EMF spooling cuts down on the return-to-application time.

- Symptom: The printer prints text or graphics which is unreadable.

  Check to make sure you have the correct driver installed for your printer.

- Symptom: You keep seeing the error "Print Overrun."

  First, check on the Device Options tab that you have the correct amount of memory installed for your printer. Remember that you must manually change the settings to reflect any memory added past the default. If you don't know how much memory your printer has, consult the printer's manual for help. You can also enable *Page protection*, which creates an output buffer.

- Symptom: Pages are only partially printed.

  Your printer may not have sufficient memory; see the previous solution.

Now that you're well-versed with Windows 95 printing, look to the next chapter to learn about DOS apps and Windows 95.

CHAPTER

13

Running Legacy Applications under Win95

WINDOWS 95 applications began hitting the shelves not long after the release of the operating system itself. The problem is, if you're a a typical user, you already have a massive investment in existing DOS and Windows apps. Unless you're prepared to replace all of your applications, you'll need to know how to keep those legacy applications up and running on Windows 95.

Windows applications under 95 require about the same fine-tuning that they did under Windows 3.x: not much. DOS applications, on the other hand, have special needs arising from their position in an alien environment. Therefore, in this chapter we'll talk about getting both DOS and Windows apps to work under Win95, focusing more on DOS applications.

How Win95 Supports Older Applications

As you read in Chapter 2, the Windows 95 kernel is 32-bit, rather than 16-bit—although 386+ computers have been around for years, only now does Windows fully support the 32-bit architecture of the 386+ family of machines. (For backward compatibility with the 286, previous versions of Windows are 16-bit. Windows 95 won't run on a 286.) Being a 32-bit operating system means that everything should happen twice as fast as it did with 16-bit Windows.

Except for one problem.

DOS and Windows 3.x applications aren't 32-bit programs. How are they supposed to use Windows 95's 32-bit API for communicating with the system hardware?

The answer, as you may remember from Chapter 2, is that they don't. Instead, Windows 95 has a 16-bit API that DOS and Windows applications can use for an operating system. That's important: The Windows 95 that, say, Excel 5.0 sees is *not* the same Windows 95 that Excel 7.0 (the 95 version) sees.

The importance of this goes beyond the fact that Windows 3.x applications and Windows 95 applications see different coding. Since all Windows applications use the same virtual machine (that is, they're not isolated from each other), that means that one Win16 application drags down the entire operating system to being 16-bit, rather than 32-bit. Through no fault of their own, applications designed for Windows 95 are reduced to a 16-bit operating system, kind of like members of a platoon who have to do pushups when one person screws up. The bottom line is that you won't get full 32-bit performance from Windows 95 unless you're only running Windows 95-optimized applications. The good news is that, once you close the last 16-bit program (*close*, not minimize), the operating system reverts to 32-bit. ("Awright, you, g'wan out—you're slowing up the rest of us.")

That's the bottom line on how Windows 95 supports Win16 applications. Running DOS applications affects Windows 95 applications less because each DOS app runs in its own virtual machine (thinking that it's the only program running on the machine).

Setting the Properties of DOS Apps

Win95 can run your DOS applications, and in many cases can run them better than DOS can. You can multitask, context-switch, and (sometimes) run them in windows. Additionally, you can load and unload TSRs without having to reboot—just close the window, and the TSR leaves memory.

A nice feature for those terribly useful DOS TSRs that you've been using forever and don't want to give up, but don't want hanging around in memory either.

Windows 3.x required a certain amount of hand-tuning to get these DOS applications to work, using a tool called the *PIF Editor*. The PIF Editor, or Program Information File Editor, is where you'd set environment variables like the amount and kind of memory the application received, whether it ran in a window or full-screen, and what fonts it used.

Windows 95 does not have a PIF editor. Instead, the job of the PIF editor is handled by the Properties dialog boxes associated with every DOS application. Properties is a little simpler to use than the PIF editor because it's broken down into smaller chunks and doesn't provide some of the options that the PIF editor does. Generally speaking, however, the two programs have the same function: fine-tuning DOS applications.

To open the Properties dialog box, right-click on an application's object (in the figure below, I've chosen Lotus 1-2-3 version 3.1), and choose Properties from the pop-up menu. You'll see a screen like the one in Figure 13.1.

Please note that only DOS applications will have such detailed Properties dialog boxes; Windows applications will only have the General tab and, if you've created a shortcut, a Shortcut tab.

WARNING Be careful when editing the contents of a program's Properties dialog. There's no Restore Defaults button.

To illustrate the function of each of these tabs, let's go through them one by one with a sample program—Lotus 1-2-3 version 3.1.

FIGURE 13.1

Opening screen of
Properties dialog

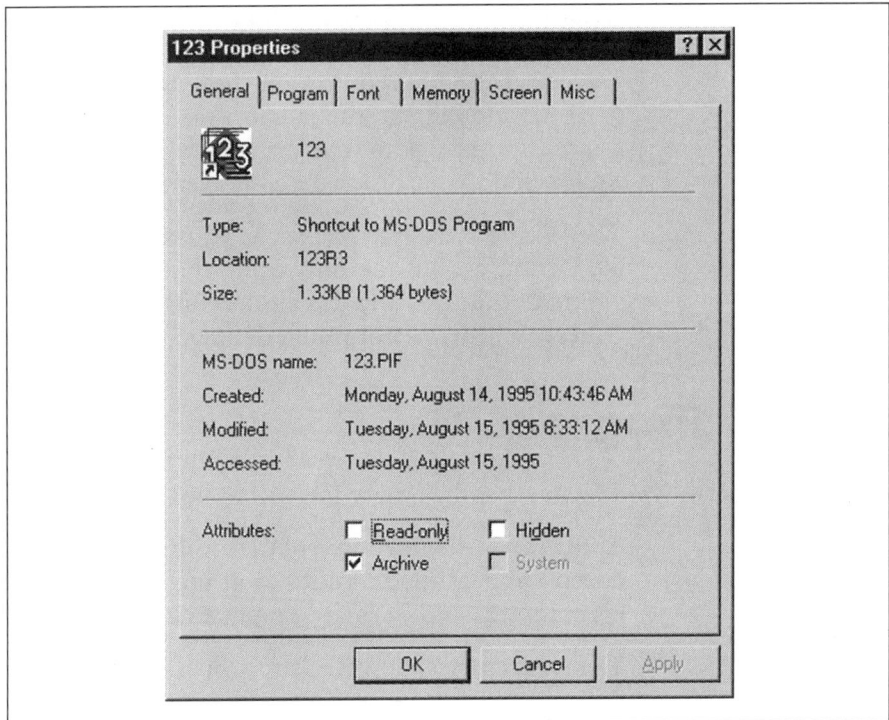

123 Properties

General | Program | Font | Memory | Screen | Misc

123

Type:	Shortcut to MS-DOS Program
Location:	123R3
Size:	1.33KB (1,364 bytes)

MS-DOS name:	123.PIF
Created:	Monday, August 14, 1995 10:43:46 AM
Modified:	Tuesday, August 15, 1995 8:33:12 AM
Accessed:	Tuesday, August 15, 1995

Attributes: ☐ Read-only   ☐ Hidden
              ☑ Archive   ☐ System

OK   Cancel   Apply

General

The opening screen in the Properties dialog (shown in Figure 13.1) gives
you some general information about the application, including:

- The file name and type
- Which folder the file is located in
- The size of the file on the hard disk
- The dates and times the file was created (if you installed the program
  after installing Windows 95), last modified, and last accessed
- The attributes associated with the file

When you install a DOS application, Win95 does a lot of the preliminary
work, so when you open this screen the file and folder information will

already be in place and uneditable. There's not much for you to do here except perhaps note the file size (remembering that this number is the space that the file requires on disk, not the amount of memory it needs to run) and adjust the attributes as necessary. For example, if you wanted to make sure that the program file gets backed up the next time you back up your disk, you could set the archive bit.

The Win95 Resource Kit warns you in rather dire terms not to adjust the file attributes, but the only thing that you really need to worry about is hiding the file (setting the hidden bit) and then not being able to find it. Otherwise, there's not much damage to be done here.

Program

The next tab has more for you to do, as you can see in Figure 13.2.

At the top is the full name of the application and its version number. This doesn't appear in the folder or at the top of the application screen when it's running, so there's little point in adjusting it.

The next entries, however, are worth exploring.

- **Cmd line** is the name of the executable file for the program. Don't change this entry, or else you won't be able to run the program. Win95 will automatically update this entry if you move a file, but be aware that not all programs will run from just any folder—homebodies, like 1-2-3, insist on their program directory.

- **Working** is the place that the application will go first to load and save data files. If you don't enter anything here, the application will look first in its program directory. You can enter any drive or directory here, so if you store all of your files in your home directory on the server, you can enter the directory information here.

  When specifying a working directory, make sure that that directory will be available. If you specify a network directory (for example) and the network is not active, you'll slow up your application as it tries to connect to the unavailable directory.

- **Batch File** allows you to specify a batch file to be run each time you start up the application. For example, there is a shareware program called Dcopy that won't work unless you specify a source drive in the

FIGURE 13.2

Program tab of
Properties dialog box

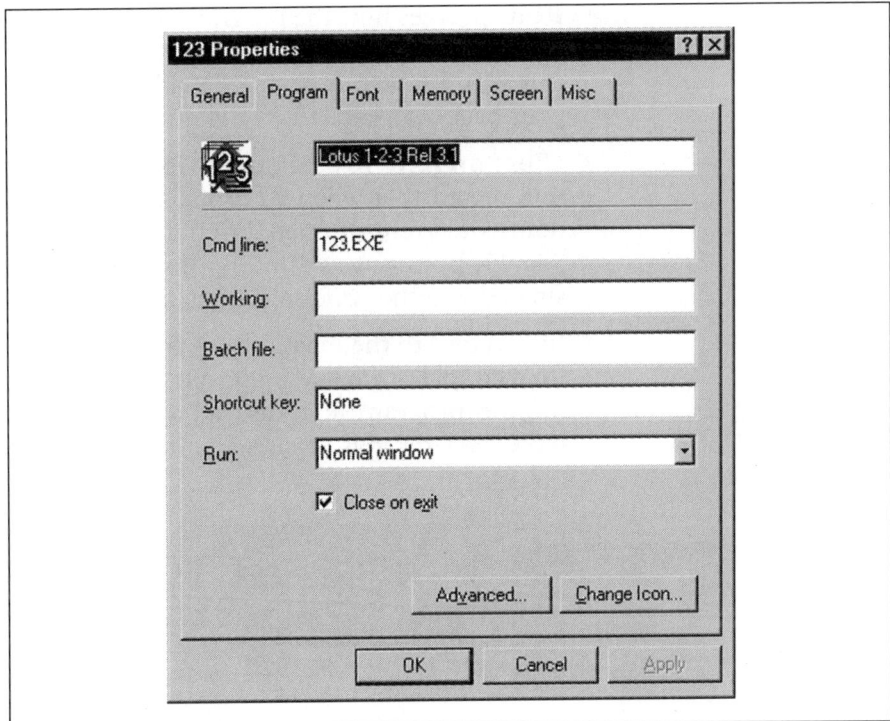

startup command. Double-click the icon, and all you'll get is instructions telling you how to start the program, and the help file. Therefore, to make this program work in Windows 95, I must type **DCOPY A** in the Batch File box. Then the program works as though I'd typed DCOPY A from the command line.

Make sure that you include the full path information if the batch file is not in the same directory as the program file.

• The **Shortcut Key** is a hotkey combination that allows you to start up an application without having to pull it from its folder or the Toolbar. Shortcut keys must include Ctrl or Alt (like Ctrl+J) and cannot conflict with any other shortcut keys, including Win95 combinations, or they won't work.

You cannot use the Tab, Escape, Enter, Spacebar, Backspace, or the Print Screen key in a shortcut key.

- **Run** specifies how the program should run: as a window, full-screen (maximized), or minimized on the desktop. Not all programs can run as a full screen, so the default Normal Window option may be your best bet.

- **Close on Exit**. In previous versions of Windows, deselecting this option meant that when you shut down an application, its DOS window would remain open. I'm not sure why this remains an option in Win95, however, as shutting down a program (windowed or not) shuts down the window with it, whether or not this box is checked.

- In addition to the main screen, the Program tab is the starting point for a couple of what Win95 calls advanced program settings: changing the program icon and adjusting the CONFIG.SYS and AUTO-EXEC.BAT settings discussed in the Registry chapter.

N O T E   The CONFIG.SYS and AUTOEXEC.BAT files in the Advanced Program Settings only apply to the program when it's running in MS-DOS mode.

Advanced Program Settings

Clicking on the Advanced button allows you to adjust the CONFIG.SYS and AUTOEXEC.BAT which that particular DOS program uses *when it's running in MS-DOS mode*. The mechanics and effects of changing these files is covered in the Registry chapter, so we don't need to go into much more detail. Just remember that there's no Restore Defaults button to revert back to the original configuration files, so be careful about what you change here. Also, you can't edit either file until you select MS-DOS mode—until then, the file information is grayed out.

Running Programs in MS-DOS Mode

In the Advanced Program Settings dialog, notice the check box that lets you prevent DOS programs from detecting Windows 95. Some DOS applications just don't like multitasking operating systems, so they'll balk if you try to run them under Win95. To get around this, try checking this option and seeing if the program will run. If it still won't, you may have to switch the computer to DOS mode. To do so, click Shut Down on the Start menu. You'll see a dialog box that looks like Figure 13.3.

Choose *Restart the computer in MS-DOS mode*, and see if the program will run like that.

> **WARNING**
>
> **Make sure that you save files in all active programs before attempting to restart the computer in MS-DOS mode.**

Please note that you shouldn't run programs in MS-DOS mode unless they won't run any other way. If you can run a program in a DOS session within Windows, then your application can still use the protected mode drivers and other advantages of the Windows 95 architecture. Run an application in MS-DOS mode, though, and not only will you have to use real-mode (slower) drivers, but you'll have to load them into memory, which takes up part of that precious 640K.

Changing the Icon

When you first install any DOS application, it gets the default MS-DOS icon, even if an icon file is included in the program directory. Boring, right? (Not to mention confusing, if all your DOS apps look alike.) To

FIGURE 13.3

Shut Down menu

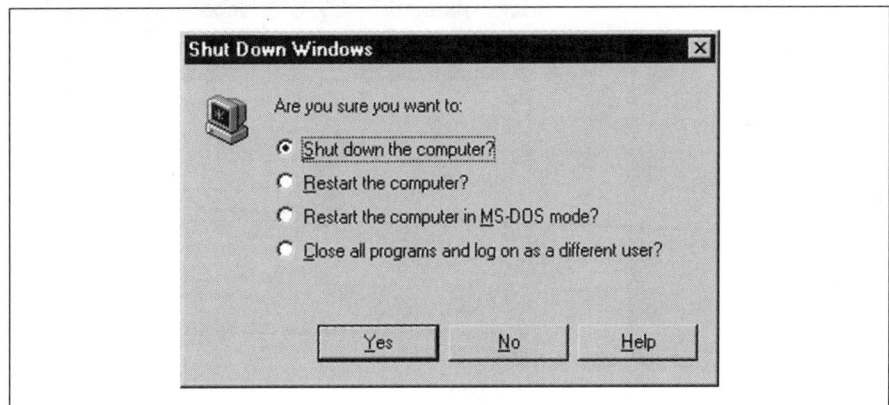

Shut Down Windows

Are you sure you want to:

- Shut down the computer?
- Restart the computer?
- Restart the computer in MS-DOS mode?
- Close all programs and log on as a different user?

Yes   No   Help

change the icon, click on the Change Icon button in the Program tab, and you'll see a dialog box that looks like Figure 13.4.

A veritable cornucopia of icons! As it happens, I know that 1-2-3 version 3.1 comes with its own icon (I can see the 123.ICO object in the 123R3 folder) so I'll browse for it instead of using one of the generic Win95 icons. I click on the Browse button, and see a dialog box like the one in Figure 13.5.

FIGURE 13.4

Change icon
dialog box

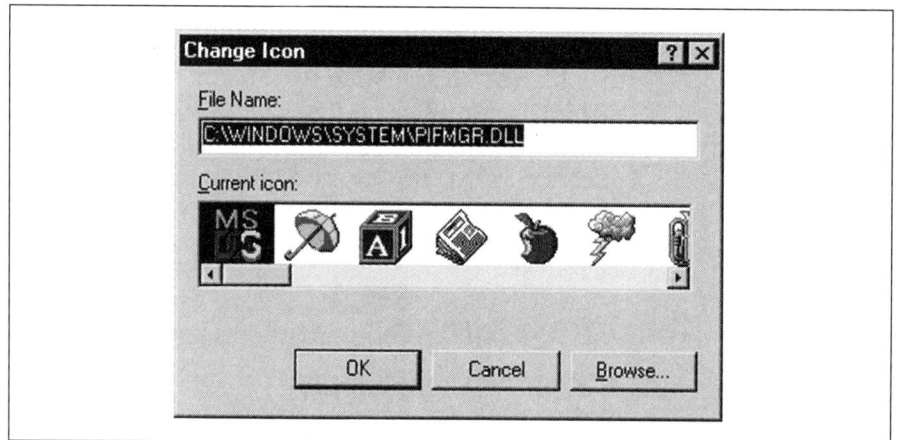

FIGURE 13.5

Browsing for the
1-2-3 icon

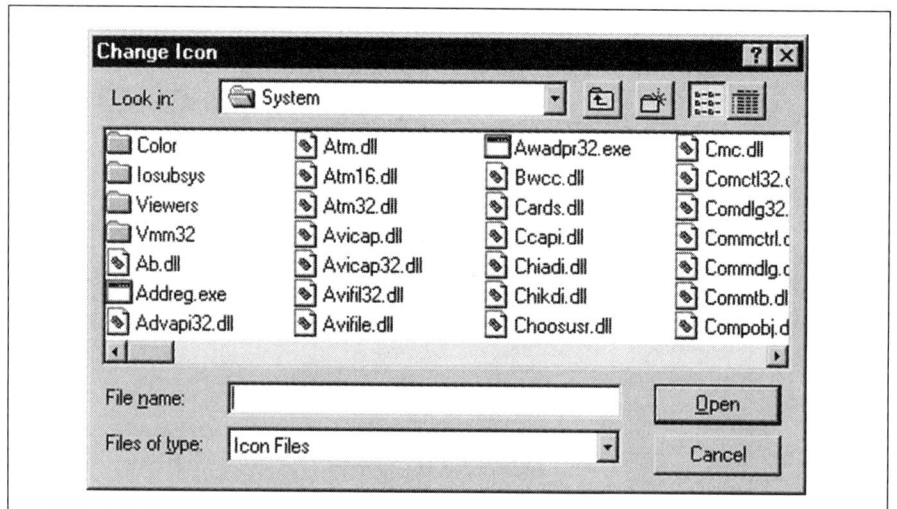

From here, I move to the 123R3 directory and choose the 1-2-3 icon (123.ICO). When I click OK, I'm back in the previous screen, as you can see in Figure 13.6.

There's only one icon in this directory, so it's selected. I choose OK to associate this icon with 123.exe, and I'm done. Now, when I open the 123R3 folder, I'll see this icon rather than the MS-DOS one.

Fonts

Click on the next tab. You'll see a screen like the one in Figure 13.7.

From this screen, you can select the font that the DOS *window* will use, choosing from either bitmapped fonts or True Type. I personally don't like the True Type fonts for DOS windows, as they're very finely drawn and thus difficult to read, but you can see how a given font will look in the Font Preview window and decide for yourself. Choosing Auto will make the font size correspond to the size of the window—if you make the window bigger or smaller, the font size will adjust accordingly. If you select a specific font size, you won't be able to resize the window. Notice how, as you select different fonts, the image in the Window Preview box changes.

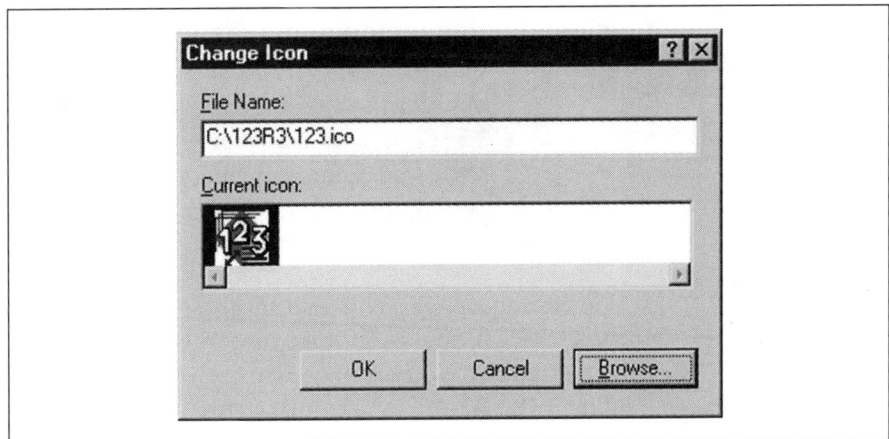

FIGURE 13.6

Choose Icon dialog box with 1-2-3 icon loaded

FIGURE 13.7

Font tab in the
Properties dialog box

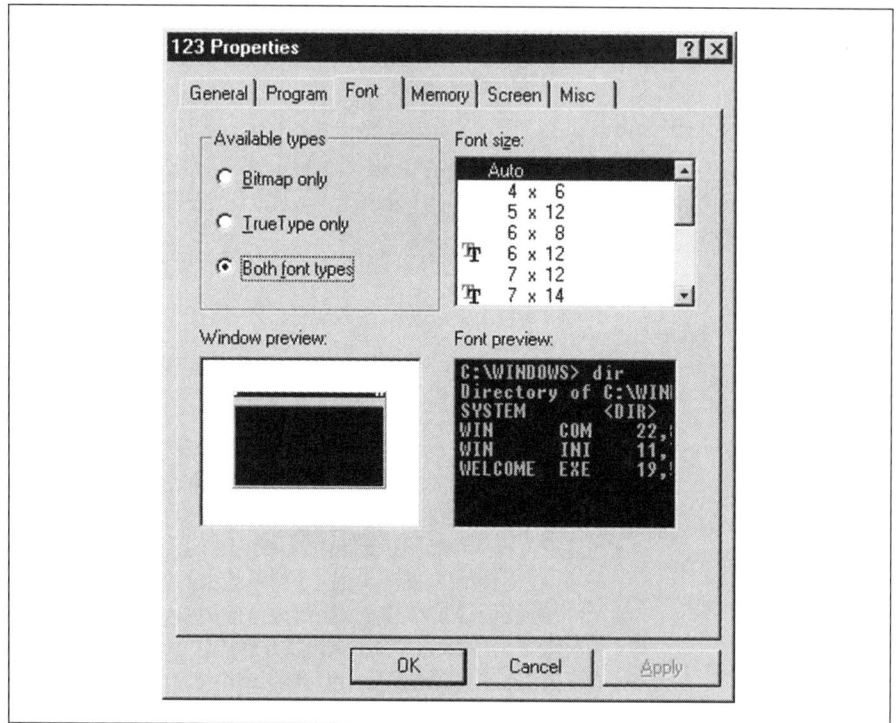

NOTE

Changing the font size here doesn't affect the font that the
application uses, if there is one—whether you choose Auto or
16×12, a Lotus 1-2-3 spreadsheet (for example) will use the
same font. Changing the font only makes a difference if the
application uses the DOS command line.

For the record, you can also set the font used by the command line from
the DOS window itself. On the toolbar (shown in Figure 13.8) either select a new font size from the drop-down list on the left end of the tool bar
or click the A button to return to the Font tab of the Properties dialog box.
Any changes to the font settings will take place immediately.

FIGURE 13.8

Toolbar for a DOS
window

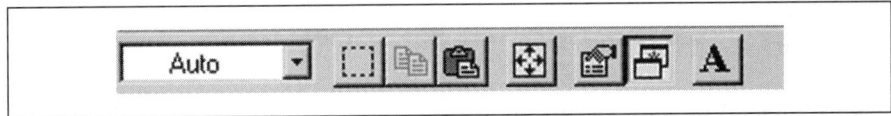

Memory

The Memory tab and Program tab contain the most important settings
for making sure that your DOS application is working properly. The Program tab controls how your application runs, while the Memory tab determines the amount and kind of memory that your application gets. You
can see 1-2-3's Memory tab in Figure 13.9.

This is a fairly complex dialog box, so let's look at each entry in turn.

FIGURE 13.9

Memory tab in 1-2-3's
Properties dialog box

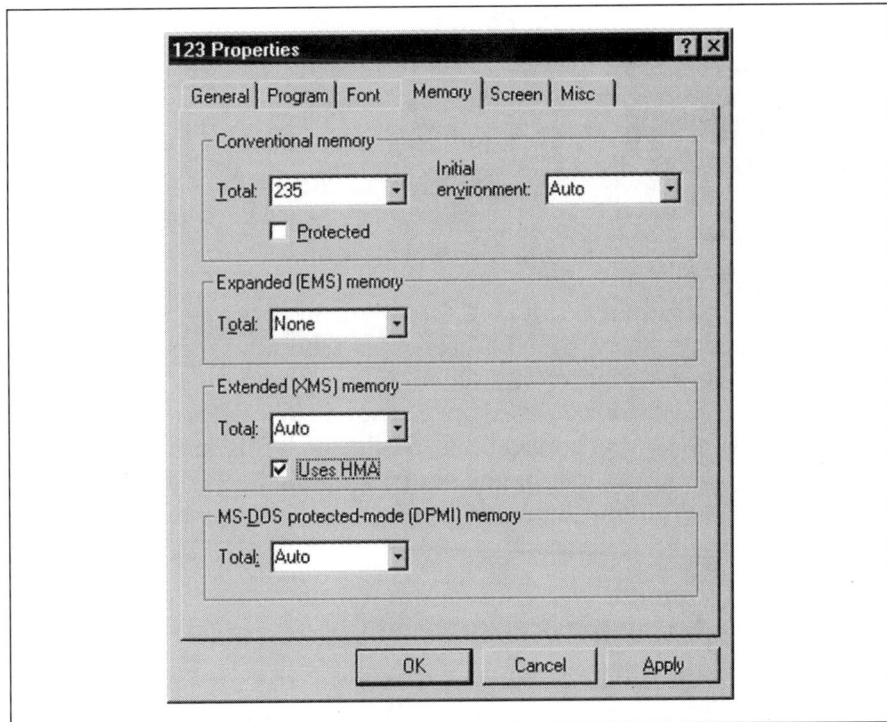

Conventional Memory

The Conventional Memory setting contains two parts: Total Memory and Initial Environment.

- **Total Memory** is the amount (in kilobytes) that 1-2-3 needs to work at all. Win95 allocated 235 bytes without me having to do anything about it, and that amount seems to work pretty well. If you're trying to reduce the amount of memory that a program uses, you can tweak this amount to see the point at which the application no longer runs. To let the application take as much conventional memory as it needs, select Auto from the drop-down list.

- **Initial Environment** sets the number of bytes (not kilobytes) reserved for COMMAND.COM, the part of DOS that understands what to do when you type a command. Win95's Help says that if this amount is set to Auto, then this parameter is set by your SHELL= statement, but *I* don't have one in my CONFIG.SYS and 1-2-3 still works fine.

WARNING Be careful when adjusting the Initial Environment setting! Sometimes, if you set this amount too low, all of Windows will crash and you'll have to reboot to get the system back.

In addition to the two drop-down list boxes, there's a small check box below the Total text box. Checking this box (Protected) keeps the application from affecting other programs if it crashes. As you probably know, one downed application in Windows often starts a domino effect of crashing applications, so although this setting may slow down your program a little it might not be a bad idea if you *know* that an application is buggy and liable to go down in flames. The difference in speed is not always noticeable.

Expanded Memory

The Expanded Memory setting specifies the amount of paged memory available to 1-2-3. Win95 set this number to Auto, but since Lotus 1-2-3 versions 3.x and later use extended memory, rather than expanded, this setting doesn't mean much for this particular application. Check your application's documentation to see if it can use expanded memory—if not, then you can select None from the list box.

In previous versions of Windows, the expanded memory manager included the bottom 640K in the expanded memory pool, so if I allocated, say, 1024K to Lotus 1-2-3 v2.2, the program would only see about 350K. That seems to be fixed in Win95—if you allocate 1024K of expanded memory to a DOS application, it gets the full amount.

Extended Memory

The Extended Memory setting determines how much memory above 1024K is available to the application. Many recent applications (including 1-2-3 version 3.1) support extended memory, but check the documentation to be sure. Do *not* set the amount of XMS memory to an amount greater than the memory physically *in* the machine, or the program won't run.

Although there's a check box in this section permitting a program to use the High Memory Area (HMA), most of the time there's no point in enabling this option. The default CONFIG.SYS specifies that DOS is loaded high, and there's only room for one program in the HMA. Unless you remove the DOS=HIGH line from CONFIG.SYS, then nothing else can use the HMA, even if you give the program permission.

DPMI Memory

The DPMI Memory setting describes the amount of *managed* extended memory that you allocate to the application. The difference between normal extended memory and DPMI memory is this: In normal extended memory, there's nothing preventing one application from attempting to access the extended memory that another application is using—with predictable results. Unless you know the specific amount of extended memory that the application will need, just leave this set at Auto, and the application will take what it needs.

Interestingly, although allocating more extended memory than physically exists on the machine will prevent the application from running, allocating more *DPMI* memory than exists on the machine doesn't seem to affect the application.

Troubleshooting Memory Settings

To a significant extent, memory settings determine how a DOS app will run or whether it will run at all. Generally speaking, 95 handles your program's memory requirements without requiring too much guidance. If your programs aren't working right, however, here are some things to check.

- **Is enough conventional memory allocated to the application?** If you play around with the conventional memory settings and set them lower than the amount of memory required, the program won't run. There's no warning system in place, so if you change the settings in the Properties box, you won't know that anything's wrong until you try to start up the application and you see an error message like the one in Figure 13.10. If the program settings allocate enough memory (or are set on Auto) but you're still getting this message, see if the program will run if you unload some programs from memory.

- **Is more expanded memory allocated than exists on the computer?** Expanded memory won't hurt programs not equipped to use it (although it wastes memory). However, if you allocate more memory than exists on the machine (for example, telling an 8MB machine that Lotus gets 16MB of expanded memory) then the program won't run. Unless you watch *very* carefully, it's not easy to tell what's going on, but in between the "welcome" screen for your application and being ignominiously dumped back in Windows 95, a brief message flashes that not enough memory is available.

  If your DOS program seems to start up and then fail, check the settings for expanded memory. Set them to None if the program can't use the memory (check the documentation), or Auto if it can.

FIGURE 13.10

Insufficient
conventional memory
warning message

Lotus 1-2-3 Rel 3.1

This program requires more conventional memory.
Unload drivers or memory-resident programs that use conventional memory, or increase the value for Minimum Conventional Memory in the program's Memory properties sheet.

OK

- **Have you allocated more extended memory than exists on the computer?** The Extended Memory setting on the dialog box determines the maximum amount of memory above 1024K that the program can use. If you specify a number greater than the amount in your PC, then your program will start up and then fail, with the message "Cannot initialize memory manager." If you see this, press Esc to clear the screen and then adjust the extended memory settings to Auto or a lower number.

  Some programs don't cope well with having an unlimited amount of memory available, so if your programs don't work, try designating a specific extended memory quota.

- **Is there sufficient memory for the operating environment?** I recommend that you leave the settings for the initial environment alone. Auto, the default setting, ensures that the application can take up as many bytes in memory as it needs for its operating environment (COMMAND.COM). COMMAND.COM doesn't require a whole lot of memory; however, if you set this value too low, the application may run normally but crash when you attempt to exit. When I set the initial environment to 0, for example, Lotus 1-2-3 started fine and worked normally, but when I exited the program the display became unreadable and I had to reboot to restore my system.

Screen

The application's screen settings determine how it will look while running and how memory is allocated to drawing the screens used. Look at Figure 13.11 to see how Windows 95 set up Lotus 1-2-3's appearance on one machine.

Full-Screen or Window?

First, there's the decision of whether to run the application as a full screen or a window. Depending on the application, you may not have a choice about this, as some applications, especially very graphically oriented ones using EGA or VGA, insist on their full screen. 1-2-3, for example, will let you *set* it to run in a window, but as soon as the program begins it will revert to a full screen.

FIGURE 13.11

Screen settings for
Lotus 1-2-3

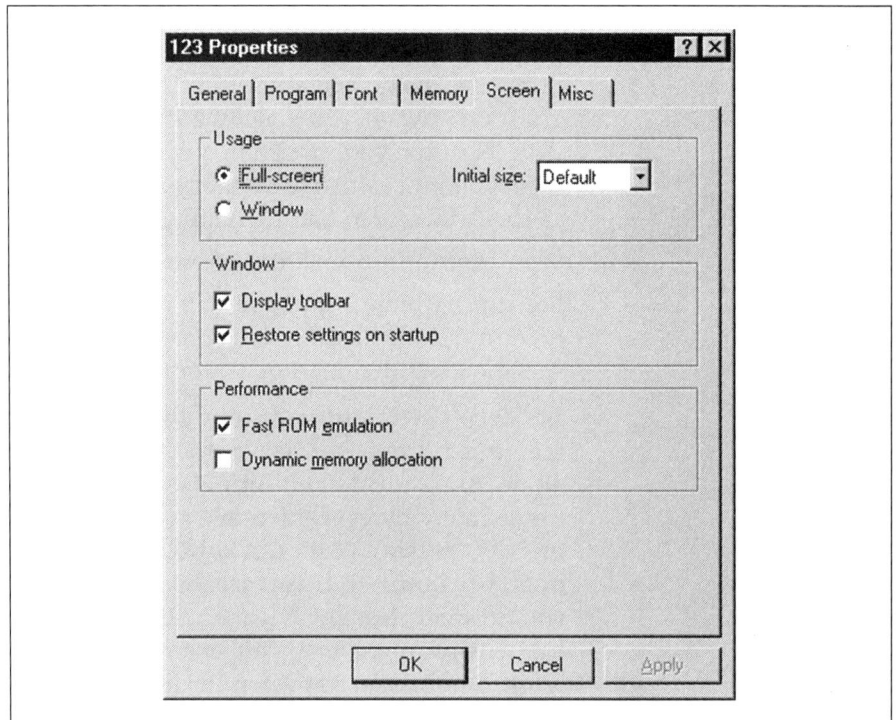

If you run the program in a window, you can set its size beforehand. If
you preset the window size, you can't resize it while the DOS session is
running.

Window Appearance

If the program will run in a window, you can specify whether to show the
DOS toolbar at the top of the window or leave it blank. Unless you prefer
the streamlined look of no toolbar, there's really no reason to remove it,
as it doesn't seem to affect program performance. By default, it's displayed. In this same section, you can use the Restore Settings parameter
to determine whether all the appearance parameters that you've set—the
font, window size, and window position—will be used the next time that
you start up the program.

Oddly enough, although these two settings only apply if you're running the program in a window, they're not grayed out even if Full Screen is selected.

Performance

There are two options that you can set to fine-tune the performance of your application: ROM emulation and Dynamic Memory Allocation.

Windows 95 contains some programs that perform the function of some of the BIOS routines found in your system ROM (like display or keyboard controls). These programs often work better than the hardwired BIOS, but unless you tell DOS programs to use them they'll consult the instructions found in the BIOS. Enabling ROM emulation causes the program to write to the screen faster, since the system will use the more efficient video-display routines in Windows 95 rather than the ones in your system's BIOS. For most applications, you won't see a noticeable difference between enabling and disabling this option, but Win95 does suggest that you leave it enabled unless your application uses nonstandard ROM functions or you're having problems getting the application to write to the screen. For most applications, however, ROM emulation should present no problems.

Some DOS applications have both text and graphic modes; one example is WordPerfect 5.0, which runs in text mode until you preview a print job, and then it switches to graphic mode. Graphic mode requires more video memory than text mode. To allocate video memory to an application only as it's needed, click Dynamic Memory Allocation, and Windows 95 will supply the program with only as much video memory as it needs, leaving the extra left over for other programs. If you select this option, then when an application switches from text mode to graphic mode Win95 will attempt to allocate more video memory to the application. If not enough video memory is available, then Win95 won't be able to run the program in graphic mode, and you may not be able to see your print preview (for example). Therefore, if you want to be sure that your program will work no matter what mode it's in, make sure that this box is *not* checked.

NOTE Unchecking Dynamic Memory Allocation does the same thing as *checking* Retain Video Memory under Windows 3.x.

Miscellaneous Settings

To finish, click on the Misc tab. It will look something like the dialog box shown in Figure 13.12.

Foreground

If you enable Allow Screen Saver (active by default), then the screen saver you chose in the Display section of the Control Panel will come up if you

FIGURE 13.12

Miscellaneous tab in the Properties dialog box

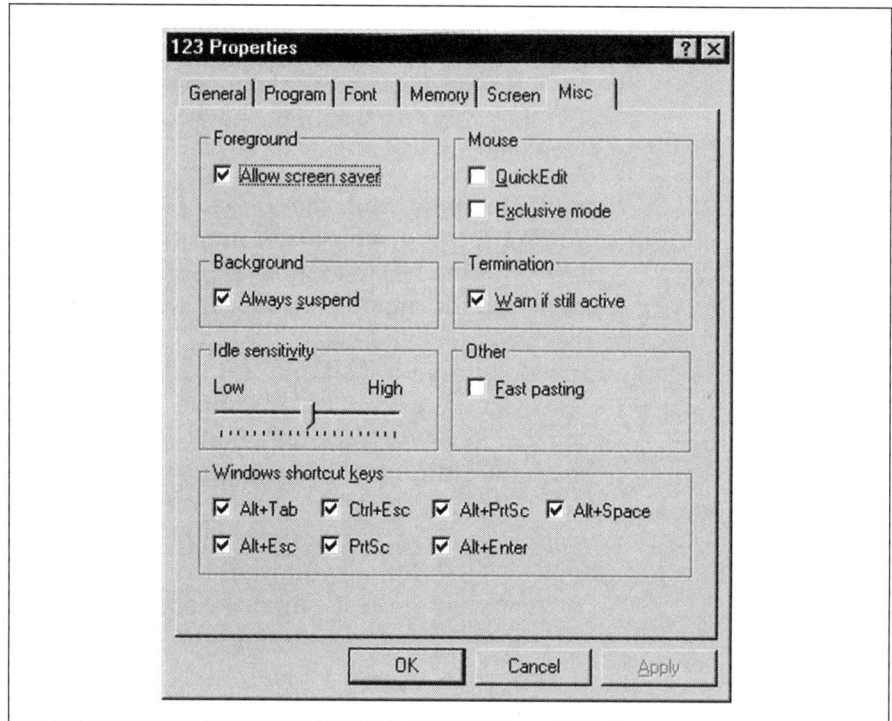

haven't input anything to the system for the predetermined amount of time.

Windowed and full-screen DOS applications recover from the screen saver somewhat differently. When you return to the screen by moving the mouse, a windowed application will be in the place you left it. If a full-screen application was active when the screen saver came up, however, then when you move the mouse to retire the screen saver you'll be back at the Win95 desktop, with the application minimized in the Toolbar. Click it to return to the application.

Background

If you click Always Suspend, Win95 will cease the operation of the DOS application when it's in the background. For example, if you're calculating a spreadsheet in 1-2-3 and then fire up a DOS game like Warlords to while away the weary hours while the spreadsheet's assembling, then the spreadsheet will stop while you're playing Warlords.

This may seem like a bad thing, but the fact of the matter is that an awful lot of programs don't do anything when they're in the background anyway; they sit, waiting for some input from you. For example, if you're working in a word processor, most of the time the system's waiting for you, even if you're a fast typist. (The only computer that I've ever seen that couldn't keep up with a fairly speedy typist was an old computerized engraver that was something of a relic even in 1988, and comparing it to modern computers is like comparing a moped to the Concorde.) Even if a program isn't doing anything except waiting, however, it's still using up CPU cycles.

To get the most out of your CPU's time, therefore, Win95 can keep them in a state of suspended animation until you express an interest in seeing them again. If you don't want Win95 to do this with one of your programs (such as that spreadsheet), then make sure that Always Suspend is not selected. This setting will only affect the program whose Properties you are adjusting.

Note that the Exclusive setting included in the Windows 3.x PIF Editor is not part of Windows 95. If you want a DOS program to get all the resources allocated to DOS programs when it's in the foreground, you'll have to check the Always Suspend option for every other windowed program at the same time.

WARNING If you're accustomed to working with 3.x's PIF Editor, be careful with this setting. Under previous versions of Windows, selecting Background meant that the program *would* run in the background; under 95, it means that it *won't*.

Idle Sensitivity

This setting affects the amount of time that a DOS application must be idle before some of its CPU cycles are allocated elsewhere. The higher the setting, the sooner an application will lose CPU cycles, although it will not lose all of them unless Always Suspend is checked.

Adjusting this setting can make DOS multitasking smoother. A simple multitasking system would perform basic *time slicing*, a process whereby X percent of the time goes to program 1, Y percent to program 2, and so on. But we can do better than that. It turns out that DOS programs tend to have one thing in common: they're interactive. As I said just a minute ago, an application spends a lot of time waiting for input.

So if there are three programs running, and two are basically waiting for input, then Win95 should give all of the CPU time to the one program that *isn't* waiting for input. The only problem is figuring out which programs are waiting for keyboard input. It's not an exact science, so Win95 has some rules of thumb that it uses to guess which programs are waiting for input and which aren't. Try fiddling with these settings to help Win95 use those rules of thumb. Depending on where you set the slider, Win95 will temporarily shut down any program needing input, automatically reactivating that program when you next give it a keystroke.

The down side (you knew there'd be one) is that it takes some time for Win95 to monitor a program for inactivity, and that time may really slow down a program. So adjust each program's PIF to the amount of idle time that you're willing to allow, but if the system seems slow, move the slider down so that more idle time is permitted. (This seems counterintuitive, to move a slider *down* to get *more* of something, but then I've always been unsure whether you turn air conditioning up or down to get colder air.) It's just one of a number of PIF options that really require some experimentation to get just right.

Here are some programs that you should probably set the idle sensitivity as low as possible for:

- Background communications
- Background printing
- 3270 emulation

Once again, if you find that an application is not getting enough resources to work in the background, adjust the setting downward.

Mouse

You can adjust how the mouse works with DOS applications in two ways:

- Permitting the user to select text for copying and cutting without using the Mark tool in the DOS toolbar.
- Restricting the mouse to just the active DOS application.

Activating QuickEdit means that you can select data within the DOS window without needing to mark it. From there, you can copy the data to another application or to Notepad. You can still copy data from an application without QuickEdit activated, but to do so, you must first click the Mark button (a rectangle with a dotted border) so you can select the data to be copied. QuickEdit just saves you a step.

If you set the mouse to Exclusive Mode, you can get the mouse back for Win95 use by pressing Alt+Tab or Alt+Esc to cycle to another application. For as long as that application is active, however, you can only use the mouse while in that application. Move the mouse from the window, and the cursor will disappear.

Termination

Warn if Still Active alerts you that a DOS program is still running if you attempt to close a DOS window without first exiting the program running in that window. Try it, and you'll see a warning like the one in Figure 13.13.

FIGURE 13.13

DOS application
still active

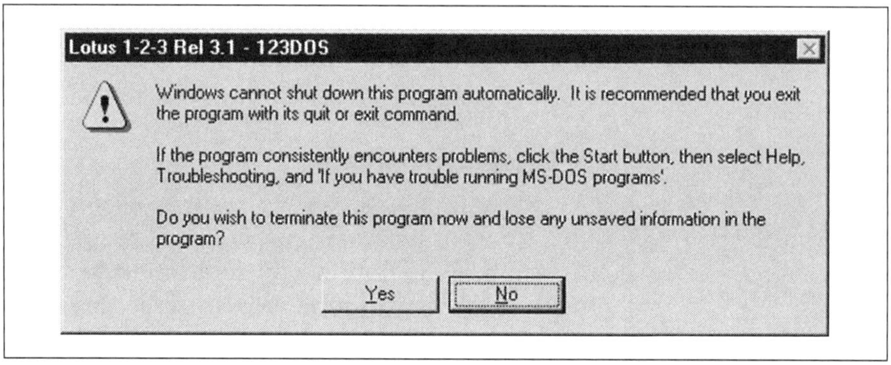

You might as well keep this option enabled (it is by default) as Win95 won't prevent you from closing the window without exiting first, but only warns you that doing so could cause problems.

Other

You know that Microsoft didn't know how to categorize something when you see it in the Other box in the Miscellaneous tab. Fast Pasting refers to how data can be pasted from the Clipboard. With this option enabled, if you have data in the Clipboard, you can actually paste it into your application just as if it were a Windows app—maybe.

If you select this check box, the application will paste information as quickly as Win95 can transfer the data. Because some applications cannot paste properly using this method, test it before relying on it—try to paste information from the Clipboard back to the application. If the paste is successful, you can use the option.

Windows Shortcut Keys

If you uncheck any of these key combinations, then you're telling Win95 to ignore them and reserve them for the use of that particular DOS application. You can't use this setting to assign shortcut keys to an application that it didn't already have—this is just for letting you get full functionality from applications designed before Windows took over some key combinations.

Defining Multitasking

Now that you're familiar with the DOS Properties dialog box, we can talk about how to optimize DOS multitasking under Win95. For this discussion to make sense, however, there's some terminology that you must know. Many of the concepts of multitasking are familiar to those who've worked with previous versions of Windows. Since, however, multitasking is one of those words that means different things to different people, let's take a minute to define a few terms you'll see in this chapter.

Multitasking, at least as I'll use it here, means being able to load more than one program into a computer. The programs may or may not all run—i.e., receive CPU time—at the same time. There are two kinds of multitasking: *context switching* and *concurrency* (also known as *concurrent multitasking*). We'll discuss the differences a little later in this chapter.

Focus refers to the particular window which is currently positioned to receive any user keystrokes or mouse clicks. The window with the focus is also known as the *active* window. If you press a key, the kernel delivers that key to that window, even if there are other windows on the screen. You can identify the focus window because it sits in front of other windows, and its title bar is a different color from the non-active windows (unless your color settings don't distinguish between active and inactive windows, of course). In Figure 13.14, Lotus has the focus; Word for Windows does not.

Note that the focus window is *not* the same as the *foreground program*, a term that you may have heard. Foreground is not meaningful when discussing Windows programs running under Win95, but it *is* meaningful when discussing Win95 while it multitasks DOS programs, as you'll see in the following two definitions.

Session refers to a group of programs that share the video screen. When you start Win95, you start a series of programs that control the Win95 screen, or desktop. Together, these programs are called the *Windows session*. Any Windows program that's running is part of the Windows session.

FIGURE 13.14

Active and inactive
windows

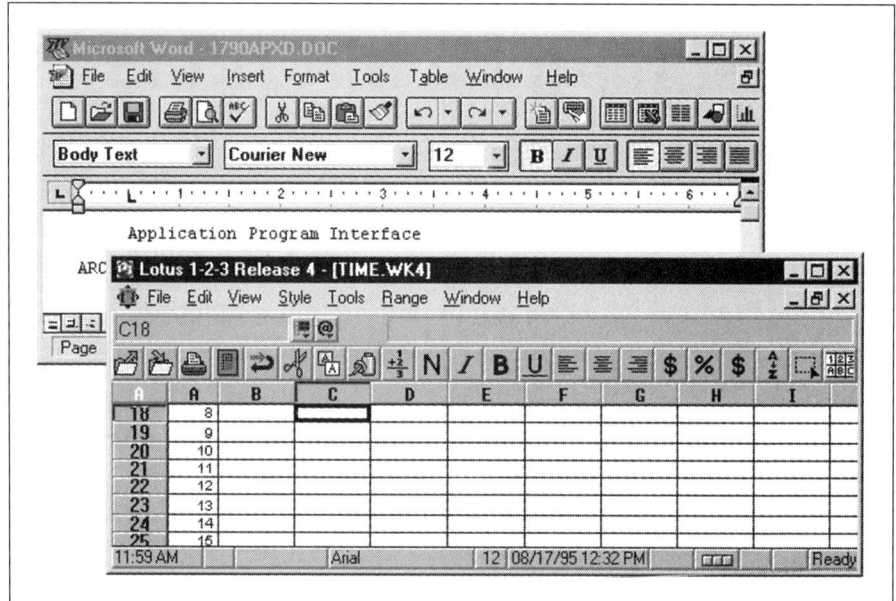

NOTE

Regardless of whether a DOS program runs in a window or
a full screen, it's running in a separate DOS session, not the
Windows session that all Windows apps share.

If, however, you're running a DOS program, the story's a little different.
Since the inception of Windows, all DOS programs running in Windows
have run in their own session, unable to see the Windows session or other
DOS sessions. DOS programs get their own sessions whether they're windowed or full-screen. These DOS sessions are called *virtual machines*, or
VMs. A session is called a virtual machine because as far as the programs
running in that session are concerned, there are no other sessions. A good
DOS multitasker must provide the illusion that each session has an entire
computer all to itself, hence the name virtual machine. We'll look at
virtual machines a little later in this chapter, in the section on DOS
multitasking.

Foreground refers to the session that is currently on-screen. If you see the
Win95 desktop at the moment, then the Win95 session is the foreground

session. If, on the other hand, you're running Lotus 1-2-3 3.1 in a DOS session, and that session is visible on-screen, then that session is the foreground session. Note that when Win95 is the foreground session, then a particular Windows program has the focus within that foreground session.

Context switching or *task switching* refers to loading two or more applications programs into a PC's memory, then switching from one to the other with some series of keystrokes. Context switching is relevant to how Win95 processes share time among themselves and also to how the 386-enhanced mode shares time between Windows programs as a whole and whatever DOS programs are running. Note that in context switching, only the active or foreground program is getting CPU time. A communications program that was downloading data would stop when shifted to the background; a word processor printing a document would suspend printing when put in the background.

That doesn't sound good, but context switching has two main benefits. First, if you spend much of your day shifting from one program to another, perhaps a word processor to a personal organizer to an electronic mail program, then context switching removes the need to constantly exit one program, load another, and then soon exit *that* program and reload the first program. Second, context switchers usually include some kind of cut-and-paste capability, providing an easy method of data integration. Context switching is simple, but it's quite enough for most of us, most of the time. One example of a pure context switcher is the DOS shell that comes with MS-DOS 5 and PC-DOS 5; it allows you to load multiple DOS programs into memory, then switch from one to the other by pressing Alt+Esc.

Concurrent multitasking is like context switching, but with the addition that the background programs continue to receive CPU time and run, even when not visible.

While concurrency sounds more complete and powerful than context switching, it's not always the preferable alternative of the two. Giving CPU time to a background process denies that CPU time to the foreground process, slowing it down—and remember, the foreground process is the one that you're directly interacting with, the one that you want to be quick and snappy in responding to your commands.

Suppose you had a spreadsheet, word processor, and graphics program loaded into Windows. You probably *wouldn't* want concurrency there, as all three are interactive programs—they basically don't do anything unless you're typing or clicking-and-dragging at them. There's no point in wasting CPU time letting the spreadsheet check the keyboard over and over again in anticipation of your next keystroke when the spreadsheet's in the background, and so couldn't *possibly* receive a keystroke.

When, then, does full multitasking make sense? Here are a few examples.

- Communications: When transferring data in the background, or even just to keep a connection open in the background, a communications program must continue to get CPU time when not in the foreground. (Again, for the purposes of these examples, "background" refers to a Windows program that does not have the focus.)

- Along the same lines, some communications programs must "wake up" periodically to poll your electronic mail, or might have to monitor the serial port so as to be able to answer the phone in the background, as is the case when you're using your PC as a fax machine.

- Printing, saving and reading files, or recalculating very large spreadsheets—all are improved by being able to do them in the background.

- Timer and alarm programs must be able to run in the background.

While the uses for concurrency aren't nearly as numerous as they are for context switching, concurrency has enough uses to make it *de rigueur* for any modern PC environment.

Background refers to any program that is not the one that the user is currently interacting with. A background window is an inactive window, and a background session is any session not currently being used. (Remembering how DOS windows get their own session, sometimes a background window and a background session can be the same thing.)

Multitasking DOS Programs Under Win95

The whole point of running DOS programs in a multitasking operating system is to let you use more than one application at a time. Here, we'll talk about how to juggle your DOS apps without dropping them.

Who Handles Multitasking?

There are actually two levels of multitasking in Win95: the Windows Kernel and the Virtual Machine Manager (VMM32.VXD). The kernel handles Windows applications. The VMM has two functions: providing a step-ladder that allows DOS programs to use XMS memory and managing the DOS sessions, or virtual machines, that you run.

> **NOTE**   VMM32 replaces WIN.386 that appeared in previous versions of Windows.

VMM32.VXD multitasks by dividing the computer into *virtual machines*. The idea with a virtual machine is that the operating system takes the computer's time and memory and divides them up, treating the system as not one computer but several computers, each a virtual machine (VM). The virtual machines are all largely unaware of one another, a very positive feature for any program that's trying to multitask DOS programs; DOS programs don't know how to share a 386, so the virtual machine manager (VMM) just carves up the PC into multiple virtual machines, and drops a copy of DOS into each machine. Each machine thinks that it has its own video board, floppy and hard disks, keyboard, and so on.

All Windows programs live in a single VM, but each DOS program is its own virtual machine. That's worth stressing—to VMM32.VXD, there *is* no such thing as a Windows program, just a big system called Windows. If you're running the Windows programs Excel, Designer, and Ami Pro, and the DOS programs 1-2-3 v3.1, dBase III+, and WordPerfect 5.1, then the VMM only sees four VMs—the Windows VM (which, unknown to the VMM, contains Excel, Designer, and Ami Pro), the 1-2-3 VM, the dBase III+ VM, and the WordPerfect VM. Remember that, as the upcoming discussion on virtual machines and priorities will seem to contradict what I said in the previous section. *The VMM can only assign a priority and control multitasking to the entire Windows VM*; it cannot reach inside and control how the kernel gives CPU time to Windows apps.

This two-layered approach to multitasking was made necessary by the nature of DOS, as I mentioned before.

Activating DOS Multitasking

In previous versions of Windows, the Windows VM was by default the only one that ran in the background. DOS VMs simply froze in place, receiving no CPU time and performing no tasks. In Win95, however, it's the other way around: By default, DOS VMs run in the background. You can demonstrate this with a simple DOS batch file. Open a DOS session and type the following at the DOS prompt:

```
copy con annoy.bat
:top
echo ^G
goto top
^Z
```

Note that you don't type the **^** symbol and a **G** in the second line of the batch file; you press Ctrl+G to make the **^G** appear on the screen. The same for the **^Z**—it appears when you press Ctrl+Z. You will then see a message like "1 file(s) copied," followed by the DOS prompt. Now type **annoy**.

This will cause the PC to beep repeatedly. Now try to switch away from the DOS session with the Alt+Esc or Ctrl+Esc key—it will keep beeping, as the program is still receiving CPU time. The only way that you can get it to quit is to either close the window or press Ctrl+C to interrupt the batch file. (Do it now, before the person in the next cubicle clubs you.)

NOTE When you're pressing Ctrl+C to stop the ANNOY batch file, make sure that the DOS window has the focus!

To keep a DOS session from operating in the background, open its Properties dialog box and turn to the Misc tab. Check the box that says Always Suspend, and that program will no longer run in the background.

Inside 386 Multitasking

As I've said, DOS programs don't share the CPU and are designed to assume that they pretty much own the CPU and anything attached to it. How, then, does the 386 mode make all of these spoiled children live together?

Well, as was suggested before, the Virtual Machine Manager first creates a virtual machine for each DOS program—an imaginary PC with a specified set of memory, I/O devices, and so on. The programs that enable the VMM to present this panoply of imaginary I/O devices are the virtual device drivers, introduced earlier in this guide as VxD's, for Virtual your device here Drivers.

Once the virtual machines are in place, the VMM must give all of them some CPU time so that they can get their programs executed. The VMM uses a *timeslicing* system whereby each program gets a certain amount of CPU time. At regular intervals, the virtual machine is interrupted by the VMM, which then hands control of the CPU over to the next program for a time, and then on to the next VM, and so on, 'round and 'round. The basic unit of measure is called a *timeslice*. Some VMs may get more timeslices than others, but they all use the same unit.

Under timeslicing, the VM Manager sets a timer programmed to "tick" every, say, 1/20th of a second. Once the timer is programmed, the VM Manager hands control of the CPU over to one of the VMs; then, 1/20th of a second later, the timer ticks—and here's the interesting part. The timer is actually able to interrupt the VM that is currently active and give control back to the VM Manager! That means there's no need for cooperative multitasking. That's why this is sometimes called *preemptive multitasking*.

So you see that the VM Manager divides up CPU time into timeslices. Each non-Windows application gets its own timeslice, and Windows gets a timeslice. That's important: all Windows apps share a single timeslice. Open up a bunch of DOS applications, and Windows will slow to a crawl. (A particularly good example is the Print Manager—slow at best, but crippled when a DOS app or two are loaded.)

NOTE Every DOS program gets its own timeslice, but all Windows apps share a single timeslice.

You can control how DOS programs (but not Windows programs) run from their Properties dialog boxes. As we discussed earlier in this chapter, turn to the Misc tab and establish whether programs should run in the background and how sensitive to idle time Win95 should be.

Tuning Tips for Better DOS Multitasking

Now that you understand how Windows doles out the CPU's attention between the programs that you run, you can tune your system for better overall multitasking. Here are some other specific suggestions.

Microsoft built into WIN386.EXE a lot of adjustment features: knobs, levers, and gears that you can often use to solve a multitasking problem. Most of these tips involve changing or adding a line in the [386enh] section of SYSTEM.INI. Why SYSTEM.INI rather than the Registry? Because DOS programs can't access the Registry, so they're dependent on old Windows settings.

Change the Order in Which You Load Programs

One tip doesn't involve SYSTEM.INI: Load your DOS applications before the Windows applications. The Windows apps will hog memory and other system resources if you load them first. Load the DOS machines first, or you may not have any memory left over.

Tweak the Minimum Timeslice

Open SYSTEM.INI and adjust the setting for MinTimeSlice (in the [386Enh] section). A smaller timeslice will make the system less efficient, because it will have to spend more time flipping between VMs, but it will ensure that your application gets the CPU's attention more often. Try 5 milliseconds (the default is 20). On a 486, you can even set it to 1. Test it out by running a DOS program in the background. For example, communications is the most demanding user of background CPU time, so if you have a DOS communications program, then try downloading a large file in the background several times, each time with a different minimum timeslice. You may find significant differences between the amount of time needed to do a large download.

Some authors recommend very simple programs that just count to themselves in the background; these are usually QBASIC programs that just count to themselves until stopped. The idea is that the multitasking setting that allows more counts while the program is in the background is the right one. The problem with this approach is that it's not realistic; it does not model the very real problem of servicing input/output devices like the serial ports. Use the download benchmark from the precedign paragraph, therefore, to find your best minimum timeslice.

Why does a smaller timeslice make the system less efficient if it means that programs get the CPU more often? The answer is *switching time*. Just as you can't switch from one work task to another without a little setup time (opening a file, or pulling out some paperwork, for example), there's some prep time involved with switching between VMs.

Let Your Programs Access Your PC's Timer Ports Directly

There's a SYSTEM.INI command called TrapTimerPorts; in a word, it can be used to make some timer-dependent programs work more smoothly and reliably. Timer-dependent programs (mainly communications programs, games, and screen blankers) need to directly reprogram the PC's timer, something that they can do without trouble under DOS. A program would use a timer to allow it to track the passage of external time. For example, if your program receives data at 9600 bps, it must know how long 1/9600 of a second is.

With this option enabled, Windows intercepts attempts to reprogram the timer, and instead simulates a timer for the application. That's a nice capability, but it just isn't as consistent as letting the program do the timing itself, and the result can be that you have programs that are too slow, too fast (in the case of games), or jerky. Set this parameter to OFF, and Windows will allow direct access to the timer hardware. For example, you'd add this line to your [386enh] section of SYSTEM.INI:

TrapTimerPorts=OFF

You'll have to add this line, as currently there is no TrapTimerPorts=ON setting—the ON condition is the default. Whichever way it's set, this is a system-wide parameter, so you can't choose which programs get the real timer and which don't—either they all do or they all don't. As there are only two settings for TrapTimerPorts—ON or OFF—it's simple to experiment to find out which setting is right for your problem software.

Turning off this option may cause the side effect that the system time maintained by Windows gets behind the time of day in the real world. If that happens, you can tell Windows to periodically resynchronize its time with the time in your CMOS (setup) clock/calendar by adding the line **SyncTime=True** just below the TrapTimerPorts line in SYSTEM.INI.

Raise Your Program's Priority When It Does I/O

There's plenty of CPU horsepower to hand around in most PCs, even in comparatively slower systems. Most of it's wasted, unfortunately, and that hurts when you're trying to get your computer to respond quickly to communication information and/or keystrokes. That's why there are two SYSTEM.INI commands, ComBoostTime and KeyBoostTime, that allow you to momentarily increase the percentage of CPU time that a program gets after it's received some communications or keyboard input. Both commands are in the [386enh] section. If you enter either one, you'll probably have to add a whole new line to SYSTEM.INI—neither appear in SYSTEM.INI by default, even though they both have default values.

- **ComBoostTime=(milliseconds):** ComBoostTime=n tells Windows to temporarily increase the priority of any program for n milliseconds after each byte was received from the communications port. The default is 2 milliseconds, a pitifully small value. I've been able to improve background downloading times by 30 percent by increasing it to 150. Just as I suggested earlier in the minimum timeslice discussion, use a DOS communications program running in the background to find the best value for ComBoostTime. Do several downloads with values of 2, 20, 200, and 2000, and see how long a download takes in each case. This will be particularly helpful for slower machines.

- **KeyBoostTime=(seconds):** similar to ComBoostTime, KeyBoostTime increases a program's priority for a short time after it receives each keystroke. *Unlike* ComBoostTime, the value is specified in seconds, so a one-millisecond boost is not specified as 1, it's specified as 0.001. Set it higher for slower machines. When running other applications in the background, increase the key boost time.

By default, Windows gives extra priority to an app for only 0.001 seconds (a millisecond) after each keystroke. Increase that value to 0.01, ten times longer. Use the download-in-the-background test with a word processor in the foreground, and try out values of 0.001, 0.01, 0.1, and 1.0. As you raise the values, the foreground program will get smoother in feel—but the download in the background will take longer. Raise the number until you can't detect the difference between its effect and that of the next *largest* number, then stick with that next-to-last number.

Make Video Faster

Here are a couple of tips for getting faster video response on your system:

1. Include the line **local=EGA$** in SYSTEM.INI. This command forces Windows to treat the video board as a local resource for each DOS machine. It costs a little memory, but it'll speed up video on some applications. Try it. It goes in the [386enh] section of your SYSTEM.INI file. You will already have a local=CON$ line in SYSTEM.INI— *do not erase it*! These lines can coexist without trouble.

2. Change the WindowUpdateTime=(milliseconds) setting. When Windows runs a DOS application in full-screen mode, it must *virtualize* the display. That means that it must take the graphical or textual output of the program and put it in a window. That's not

straightforward, because the window may not be full-screen, meaning that Windows must clip the output of the DOS program that doesn't fit in the screen. Windows does this by basically "sweeping" across the screen, scanning to see what data sits where on the display.

Once a DOS screen has been placed in a window, Windows doesn't want to have to rebuild the screen over and over again, as that takes time. Ideally, Windows would only redisplay the DOS screen when the screen changed or when the user resized the window. Unfortunately, there's no way for Windows to know when the DOS screen has been modified. So Windows just sweeps the screen every so often. Exactly *how* often is determined by the WindowUpdateTime parameter. Furthermore, DOS programs don't inform Windows of when they've modified the screen, so Windows doesn't know how often it needs to update that screen. By default, Windows updates every 200 milliseconds, whether a DOS application needs it or not. (This applies more to graphical screens than textual screens, by the way.) You can change that value with this SYSTEM.INI parameter, again in the [386enh] section.

The bigger this number is, the choppier the video seems, but then Windows doesn't waste a pile of time modifying DOS screens. Reduce the number, and screen scrolling and updates will be smoother, but at the cost of slower Windows overall. Try out different numbers and find the one that suits you best. On faster PCs, you can get away with using smaller numbers without a speed penalty; on slower PCs, it may be best to settle for some choppiness and get some more CPU speed in return.

Switching Windows

Moving from application to application is easy if you're running them in windowed sessions: just click the icon on the Taskbar that corresponds to the program you want, or click on its window. If one or more of your apps operate only in full-screen mode, however, that won't work—'cause there's no Taskbar visible. To remove the focus from a full-screen DOS application while keeping it open, you must press either Alt+Tab or Alt+Esc to return to the GUI. Your application will appear as an icon on the Taskbar.

If you've used Windows NT, you may wonder if pressing Ctrl+Alt+Del will get you a Task List from which you can select the application that you want. Nope. In Win95, if you press Ctrl+Alt+Del, the system assumes that you want to shut down a program, and it doesn't offer any mechanism for just moving to another one. You can shut down an erring application, but you can't change the focus from one open program to another.

DOS Memory Management under Windows 95

DOS memory management under Windows 95 isn't all that different from DOS memory management under DOS. Keep the number of programs loaded in conventional memory to a minimum, load DOS high, and that should prevent many memory problems.

Maximizing Conventional Memory

DOS can only see the lowest 640 kilobytes of memory, so if you're running a DOS program you're going to want to squeeze all the good from that 640K that you can. And that means that you want as much of that memory free as possible.

Load Fewer Programs (TSRs and Device Drivers)

The first step to maximizing conventional memory has already been taken for you in Windows 95. Rather than relying on external device drivers (like the one controlling your mouse) that must use part of the lowest 640K, Windows 95 includes 32-bit device drivers in the operating system that can reside in memory above 640K, thus freeing up conventional memory. You can follow in that tradition by not loading TSRs unless you really need them.

Load DOS High

By default, this step has been done for you as well. If you turn to the Program tab in a DOS program's Properties dialog, you'll notice that, by default, DOS is loaded high so that most of it isn't cluttering up conventional memory.

32-Bit Device Drivers and DOS Programs

Windows 95 is composed mostly of 32-bit (read: "faster than 16-bit") code. Part of that code includes its device drivers, which control how applications access the PC's hardware by way of the operating system. The fact that Windows 95 is its own operating system, independent of DOS, means that it doesn't have to switch back to real mode to access hardware devices—a good thing. Even better is that your DOS sessions within Windows can use these 32-bit drivers as well, since they're not running DOS as such, but emulating DOS.

If, however, you run a DOS program in exclusive MS-DOS mode, the application can't use any of the Windows 32-bit protected-mode drivers. That presents two consequences: First, the drivers are slower because they're 16-bit instead of 32-bit. Second, drivers must be loaded in memory for the application to use them. The bottom line here is that, if you can run a DOS program in Windows 95, do so—you'll probably get better performance.

Expanded Memory

Expanded memory is a classic example of how something originally intended to be a short-term solution can outlast its supposed lifespan. It came to be like this: After Lotus Corporation had captured a lot of market share and spreadsheets with 1-2-3 version 1A, it released version 2.0 with much fanfare. Unfortunately, there was a teensy problem with version 2.0: it used more conventional memory (the bottom 640K in your machine) than version 1A did. Any spreadsheets written under version 1A that used up all available conventional memory—and there were plenty—would not run under version 2.0. So Lotus, in conjunction with Intel and

Microsoft, designed a kind of workaround memory that would permit the spreadsheets to load even without sufficient conventional memory. That workaround, which still haunts us today in a few programs, is called *expanded memory*.

That's where expanded memory came from, but what is it? In a nutshell, it's non-conventional memory (either add-in boards, or in 386 machines and later, *extended* memory) that an expanded memory manager divides up into *pages* which the application can use like conventional memory. Early expanded memory required add-in expanded memory boards, but today programs that require expanded memory can use the *extended* memory (memory above the first 1024K) that's on your motherboard.

Windows 95 will automatically supply extended memory to DOS programs that can use it (unless you deselect that option from the Advanced screen of the Program tab). If you edit the expanded memory statement, do *not* use the **noems** parameter, or else Win95 won't be able to provide the memory. If you exclude any memory from potential expanded memory, use the x=*mmmm-nnnn* syntax to do so.

DPMI Support under Windows 95

Extended memory, as you probably know, is memory above the top 1024K. Under normal circumstances, DOS apps can't use extended memory—they require some special software called a *DOS extender* to boost them up to where they can see and access memory above 1024K.

Windows contains a DOS extender that allows DOS programs to use memory beyond 1024K, so long as they don't know that they're doing it. Windows maps conventional memory to one megabyte of extended memory, and then tells the DOS session, "Look! I found you this lovely computer memory that you can have for your *very own*." DOS takes the bait and accepts the extended memory as conventional memory. Any time that the application tries to access memory, it looks for an address in conventional memory, but Windows intercepts the memory access and forwards it to the address in the extended memory which that DOS application has been allotted. A nice system, as it allows DOS programs to run with what they think is conventional memory, when in reality the conventional memory is shared among a number of virtual machines.

Some DOS programs have their own DOS extenders built into them. If you need to make them work with Windows, you'll find that some do... but some don't. Is there some kind of overall rule?

Back in the days when OS/2 was still under development, and Windows was just a curiosity that no one used for anything serious, a number of companies started writing DOS programs that could access extended memory on 286 and later computers. Accessing extended memory requires installing a *supervisor* program, a program that makes sure that no program treads upon another program's territory. OS/2, Windows, and Windows NT are all examples of supervisor programs. Given that these DOS programs didn't want to multitask, however—they only wanted to support themselves in extended memory, and no other programs—they didn't need a very big supervisor program. Examples of early programs that used extended memory were Oracle, Informix, and `VDISK.SYS`, the "RAM disk" program that came with DOS 3.0 and later versions of DOS up to DOS 5.0, and the `IBMCACHE.SYS` disk cache program that IBM shipped with the PS/2. These simple supervisors were called *DOS extenders*.

All went well until someone tried to run a DOS extender program in a computer at the same time another supervisor was running—for example, running a DOS extender program in a DOS box under Windows 3.0. That led to Windows and the DOS extender fighting over who got to be the supervisor, as there's only supposed to be one supervisor program active in a PC at a time. The two supervisors slugged it out, and the PC lost. To make matters worse, memory managers must *all* be supervisors, so the simple act of running, say, the 1988 vintage of Oracle (a database) on a system that uses 386 To The Max (a memory manager) would result in a lockup.

As a result, the makers of DOS extender products got together and developed a method whereby DOS extenders could peacefully coexist. The Virtual Control Program Interface, or VCPI to us acronym-lovers, provided an agreement whereby two or more DOS extenders could coexist by defining an organized, agreed-upon method whereby one DOS extender would make a note about how it had memory organized, save that note somewhere, and then hand control over to the second DOS extender, which would then reorganize memory the way it wanted it. When it was time for DOS extender number two to hand control back to DOS extender number one, it did so by restoring things the way it had found it, and then passing the baton back to DOS extender number one.

A lot of a DOS extender's job involves keeping track of which section of memory is being used by each part of the program that it is extending. That's kept with some data structure in memory called *page tables*. Pretty much every DOS extender uses page tables (they *must*, for reasons relating to how the 286 and later chips dole out extended memory; the technical terms for these tables are the LDT, or Local Descriptor Table, and the GDT, or Global Descriptor Table), but they all organize them differently. And that's the big problem: Two programs keeping GDTs that are organized differently are bound to step on one another at some point. But that doesn't happen if we only run one program at a time, and switch the entire memory image when moving from one program to another. This is pretty much what happens with VCPI-compliant programs. They can't multitask with each other, as they each see the GDT in different ways. But they *can* share the GDT in the sense that they can unload their own GDT, and reload another VCPI program's GDT before passing control to that program.

If that isn't clear, consider the following analogy. An assembly plant runs 24 hours/day in three shifts. There's a day manager, an evening manager, and a night manager. Each are totally different in the way that they do their jobs, but they must each use the desk that sits at a good observation point above the assembly line floor. So they've made an agreement: No matter what happens on any manager's shift, that manager's got to leave their desktop clean when he leaves, the way he found it. There's no way that two of these managers could work at the desk at the same time, but they can share it in an eight-hours-at-a-time way. So it is with VCPI-compliant programs: they *context-switch* well, but do not multitask well.

For that reason, VCPI applications cannot work reliably in the multitasking framework of Windows 95. They will probably work in MS-DOS mode, however, for the simple reason that standard mode uses context-switching rather than multitasking—when you activate a DOS program under standard mode, the memory image of standard mode gets swapped out to disk, clearing the desk for the next VCPI program. Examples of programs that follow the VCPI standard are 1-2-3 version 3.0, Paradox 3.5, AutoCAD, FoxPro, and Interleaf Publisher.

One problem you may find with VCPI programs is that there are two ways for VCPI programs to access extended memory. A few use an old method of extended memory access called INT 15 access. Most, however, use a newer method whereby memory is allocated via XMS, the extended memory specification. XMS-type VCPI programs will probably run fine as DOS applications under standard mode. INT 15-type VCPI programs require that you preallocate memory for them with a parameter on your HIMEM.SYS invocation, using the /INT15=*nnnn* switch. For example, if you were planning on running a INT 15-type VCPI app that needed a megabyte of extended memory, then your HIMEM.SYS invocation in the DOS program's CONFIG.SYS would look like this:

```
device=c:\windows\himem.sys /int15=1024
```

But, to continue with the VCPI-versus-DPMI explanation: As you'd expect, the next step was to teach all of these managers how to share a desk—that is, to get all DOS extender programs to agree on how to address the GDT and LDT page tables, so that they could all have page tables in memory at the same time, allowing smooth multitasking of DOS extender applications and Windows. That standard is called the DOS Protected Mode Interface, or DPMI. That's basically the difference between Lotus 1-2-3 version 3.0 and 3.1—3.1 is DPMI compliant, 3.0 is VCPI compliant. DPMI applications should run without trouble in a DOS box under Windows, just so long as you give them XMS memory in the PIF for the DPMI-compliant application, and the vendor has implemented DPMI correctly. Not all software vendors implement DPMI completely correctly, and Lotus is one example. Although 1-2-3 version 3.1 is DPMI compliant, and as such uses extended memory, it still requires that you create an expanded memory page frame in order to run properly. Look for DOS extender applications to be DPMI compliant.

As time progresses, more and more DOS programs that use memory managers will switch to DPMI compliance, and so will run much more easily under Windows. One example is Paradox; version 3.5 was VCPI, and version 4.0 is DPMI.

Multitasking Windows 3.x Applications

Multitasking Windows 3.x programs under Windows 95 shouldn't pose any problems to experienced users of Windows 3.x once you've figured out how to use the different interface. Actually, multitasking Windows 3.x applications carries some pleasant surprises compared to using the same applications under previous versions of Windows:

- Better resource sharing, so that more programs can be open at once without hurting system performance

- Preemptive multitasking with Windows 95 actions, like printing (although not with other Win16 applications)

- Improved resource tracking, so that when you close an application its resources return to the system for use by another application

Better Resource Sharing

The biggest problem with the way that Windows 95 multitasks Win16 programs comes when you move from a machine running Windows 95 to one running Windows 3.x. Since Win95 handles resource sharing so well, you get accustomed to loading cc:Mail, loading the word processor, the spreadsheet, the other word processor, Solitaire, etc., and minimizing them on the desktop rather than closing them.

Now, if you've been using Windows 3.x, you know that loading a bunch of programs and minimizing them on the desktop is one of the fastest and most efficient ways in which you can crash your system. As a matter of fact, you don't even have to load a whole bunch of programs; just load a couple of exceptionally huge spreadsheets or documents, and your system resources will drop dramatically. I found this out the hard way some years ago as a new Windows user. As I watched the words in my document turn to gray blocks, the person looking over my shoulder commented, "Well, I'll be. I didn't know that Windows would *run* with only 3 percent resources." As a matter of fact, it wouldn't—the system crashed shortly after.

In Windows 95, you can load more programs simultaneously than will fit on the Taskbar and the system will keep running. Admittedly, it runs *better* with fewer programs open (you'll get faster response and screen redraws), but you can keep the spreadsheet, document, graphics program, e-mail program, and Solitaire minimized on your desktop and the system should function without any problems—even with only 8MB of RAM.

> **NOTE** Windows 95 does better resource handling with 8MB of RAM than Windows 3.x does with 16MB.

Some Preemptive Multitasking

Recall from earlier in this chapter that when the Virtual Machine Manager interrupts a process when its timeslice is up to pass control to the next process, that's called *preemptive multitasking*. The idea is that, even if a program is in the middle of something, once its timeslice is up, it's *up*—the VMM wrests control of the system from that program and passes it to the next one. Thus, an operating system that supports preemptive multitasking won't make you wait while a multitasking program does any of the following:

- Saves a file
- Prints a document
- Renders a drawing
- Calculates a spreadsheet

The only catch is that Win16 applications don't support preemptive multitasking with each other. Therefore, if you're running Excel 5.0 under Windows 95 and the hourglass comes up, you're stuck until it's done. On the other hand, if you were running Excel for Windows 95 (7.0), then you could do other things while the spreadsheet was calculating, because it would only have control of the system during its timeslice.

Although you don't get full preemptive multitasking until you get Win32 applications, Windows 95 allows for preemptive multitasking between Win16 applications and Windows 95 functions like printing. Therefore, although Win16 applications won't share with each other, they'll share with Windows 95.

Improved Resource Tracking

Every time that you open an application, you use Windows resources—that's the way Windows works. Unfortunately, all too often with previous versions of Windows it *also* worked that the applications wouldn't relinquish their share of the resources once they were done with them; use Designer once in a Windows 3.x session, for example, and your resources are depleted until you restart Windows.

Windows 95 not only makes applications, including Win16 applications, use resources better, it makes the applications return most of the resources when they're through. Thus, if you open all your applications, enough to slow down the system from depleted resources, once you close the applications you get almost all the resources *back* without having to reboot or restart Windows.

On my system, for example, there's 98 percent free resources when I first log on to the system. I open AmiPro and the count goes to 93 percent. Logging onto cc:Mail doesn't take much out of the system; the count remains at 93 percent. Opening Lotus 1-2-3 v. 4 demands more—the count drops to 85 percent. Loading Designer 3.11 drops the count to 81 percent. From there, I load Word 6.0 for Windows (75 percent), an undemanding PaintShop Pro (75 percent), another copy of Designer so I can compare pictures easily (one of the few drawbacks of that version is that it doesn't have a Window feature to let you flip between files) that puts me down to 70 percent, and so on. The system, by the way, is working just fine—not even slow screens.

The good part is what happens when I start *closing* all these applications. Close the second copy of Designer—back to 74 percent. Closing PaintShop Pro doesn't increase the count, but then it didn't decrease it either in the first place. When I shut down Word 6.0, the count's up to 79 percent. When I close the first copy of Designer, the count goes back to 83 percent, and after closing Lotus we're back to 88 percent... After closing everything down I can get system resources back to 93 percent. I've lost 5 percent from when I started, but that's better than older versions of Windows can do.

Why Do I Still Have .INI Files?

The Registry (discussed earlier in this book) takes over the job of containing the user and system configuration information from the `.INI` files that you came to know and love in previous versions of Windows. The only trouble is, those `.INI` files are still there—as are all the `.INI` files belonging to each Win16 program (`AMIPRO.INI`, `PSP.INI`, etc.). If Windows 95 has the Registry, why do you still have `.INI` files?

The answer is backward compatibility. Win16 programs don't know how to access the Registry, so they must get their system and user information from `WIN.INI` and `SYSTEM.INI`, as well as their specific program information from their own `.INI` file. Win16 applications don't know or care that the Registry exists, except as something that gives them an operating system to work in.

Editing a Program .INI File

Since Win16 files can't see the Registry, to configure a Win16 application, you'll need to edit its `.INI` file in Notepad (if the configuration you want is not available from the application itself). For example, I use a graphics program called PaintShop Pro to edit screen captures. PSP remembers where you pulled your last file from and returns to that directory to open files. Most of the time, this is a convenience, but when at one point our ISDN connection was having a bad hair day and the last drive I'd accessed was across the connection, it meant that, for all practical purposes, the program was unusable. I could start it up, but when I tried to open a file it went looking for the inaccessible networked drive, and looking, and looking... the program never admitted that it couldn't find the drive but kept searching until I shut the program down.

To get around this, I needed to change the default open drive, but there was no way to do this from within the program without opening a file— which I couldn't do. So, I opened up the Notepad (type **notepad** in the Run... dialog box accessible from the Start menu) to edit the file.

Now, .INI files are usually in the program directory (or, if not there, the Windows directory). I found it where I expected, and when I opened PSP.INI I saw the following:

```
[Paint Shop Pro]
OpenDir=H:\WINDOW~1\PICS
FileData=0,17
Gamma=1.25
Undo=1
SaveDir=H:\WINDOW~1\PICS
```

Many program's .INI files are pretty straightforward, as you can see here, and it was pretty easy to see where the change should be made. I edited the OpenDir entry so that it read from the local C: drive, and saved the file. The next time I opened the application, it was able to open files without any problem because it was no longer looking for an inaccessible drive.

Running DOS Diagnostic Programs

Thus far in this chapter, we've talked about memory management and how to set up DOS and Windows 3.x programs for best use under Windows 95. To finish, we'll discuss how to use an unusual class of DOS programs—diagnostics—under Windows 95.

Why Use DOS Diagnostics?

Windows 95 comes with some disk maintenance software. Why use anything else? The best reason is that diagnostics may be more accurate (not necessarily, but it's possible) when they're written by someone other than the company who designed the operating system. Just as the person proofing text shouldn't be the person who wrote it, machine diagnostics may perform a harder test when written by a third-party vendor than one written by the author of the operating system.

In addition, the maintenance tools that come with 95 are limited. You have a defragger, a disk scanner, and compression software, and, so far as hard disk maintenance goes, that's it. There's no memory testing, and no slow disk testing. Therefore, to do serious testing of your hardware, you need third-party diagnostics.

Tips for Running Diagnostics

The first consideration about running diagnostic software—programs that are intended to isolate hardware problems on your PC—is to make sure that there's as little going on in the PC as possible. To that end, don't try to run diagnostics from a DOS prompt in Windows, because at the very least you have all the graphical software loaded, probably network drivers, and so forth. Instead, before running diagnostics, I'd recommend booting the disk to Safe Mode command prompt only (press F8 when you see the "Starting Windows 95..." message during the boot process, and choose that option from the startup menu). That way, you'll have about as vanilla a configuration as you can get: no network, no GUI, no other programs running in the background.

Second, as always, if you're going to run diagnostics, make them a serious test. Most diagnostic tests of disks or memory have a slow mode and a fast mode. To do a real exhaustive test of your PC's hardware, choose the slow mode and be prepared for it to take a while. ("A while" can mean all night for a good memory test to see if your SIMMs are working properly, or even a couple of days to test a 1GB+ hard disk.)

That's about it for running legacy applications under Windows 95. Now go grab that software and get to it!

INDEX

Note to the Reader: Throughout this index **boldfaced** page numbers indicate the primary discussion of a topic. *Italicized* page numbers indicate illustrations.

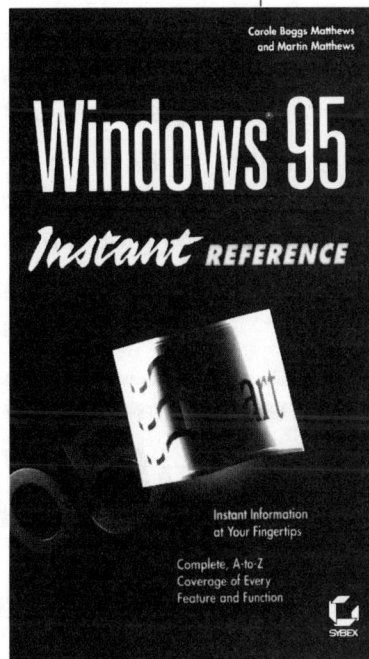

To Use This CD

The enclosed CD works best from within Windows 95. To see and hear the author's video instruction files (the .AVI files), we recommend that you have at least a double-speed CD-ROM player and a 486 66-MHz machine with a sound card.

Load the CD into your computer's CD player, go to My Computer on your Windows 95 desktop, and click on your CD drive (drive D in most cases). To use the utility programs from AllMicro, go to the AV folder (for the AntiVirus program) or the Skylight folder (for the Skylight diagnostic program) and double-click on Setup to install the program. Refer to the program's help files or documentation files for instructions on using the program. To view one of the author's .AVI files (instructional videos), go to the Videos folder and double-click on the filename you want. You must be running Windows 95 or Video for Windows to view the .AVI files.

Descriptions of the videos and programs can be found on the inside front cover of this book.

Warranty

SYBEX warrants the enclosed CD-ROM to be free of physical defects for a period of ninety (90) days after purchase. If you discover a defect in the CD during this warranty period, you can obtain a replacement CD at no charge by sending the defective CD, postage prepaid, with proof of purchase to:

SYBEX Inc.
Customer Service Department
2021 Challenger Drive
Alameda, CA 94501
phone: (800)227-2346
fax: (510) 523-2373

After the 90-day period, you can obtain a replacement CD by sending us the defective CD, proof of purchase, and a check or money order for $10, payable to SYBEX.

Disclaimer

SYBEX makes no warranty or representation, either express or implied, with respect to this medium or its contents, its quality, performance, merchantability, or fitness for a particular purpose. In no event will SYBEX, its distributors, or dealers be liable for direct, indirect, special, incidental, or consequential damages arising out of the use of or inability to use the software even if advised of the possibility of such damage.

The exclusion of implied warranties is not permitted by some states. Therefore, the above exclusion may not apply to you. This warranty provides you with specific legal rights; there may be other rights that you may have that vary from state to state.